121925

S0-BLT-769

AN

AMERICAN COMMENTARY

ON THE

NEW TESTAMENT.

EDITED BY

ALVAH HOVEY, D.D., LL.D.

———————

JUDSON PRESS
VALLEY FORGE

A

COMMENTARY

ON THE

ACTS OF THE APOSTLES.

BY

HORATIO B. HACKETT, D.D.,

PROFESSOR OF BIBLICAL LITERATURE IN NEWTON THEOLOGICAL INSTITUTION.

A NEW EDITION,

REVISED AND GREATLY ENLARGED BY THE AUTHOR.

EDITED BY

ALVAH HOVEY, D.D., LL.D.,

IN CONSULTATION WITH

EZRA ABBOT, LL.D.

JUDSON PRESS
VALLEY FORGE

Entered, according to Act of Congress, in the year 1882, by the

AMERICAN BAPTIST PUBLICATION SOCIETY,

In the Office of the Librarian of Congress, at Washington.

International Standard Book No. 0-8170-0005-4

Printed in U. S. A.

THE AUTHOR

is Permitted to Inscribe this Volume

TO

AUGUSTUS THOLUCK, D. D.,

WHOSE WRITINGS IN ILLUSTRATION OF THE SACRED WORD, AND WHOSE
PERSONAL INSTRUCTIONS, HAVE CAUSED HIS INFLUENCE TO BE
FELT AND HIS NAME TO BE HONORED IN FOREIGN
COUNTRIES AS WELL AS IN HIS OWN.

PREFACE TO THE FIRST EDITION.

It has been the writer's endeavor to present to the reader in this volume the results of the present state of biblical study as applied to the illustration of the Acts of the Apostles. Although our language contains already some valuable works devoted to the same general object, it is hoped that the dependence of the work here offered to the public on the original text, and the advantage taken of the latest investigations in this department of criticism, will render it not superfluous.

Of the importance of an acquaintance with the contents of the Acts it must be unnecessary to speak. A single reflection will render this sufficiently obvious. No person can be prepared to read the Epistles of the New Testament with the greatest advantage until he has made himself familiar with the external history of the apostle Paul and with his character and spirit, as Luke has portrayed them in his narrative. Those portions of the Acts, constituting the greater part of the whole, which relate to the great apostle must be thoroughly mastered before any proper foundation is laid for the exegetical study of the Epistles. It is the object of these Notes to assist the reader in the acquisition of this knowledge and discipline; to enable him to form his own independent view of the meaning of the sacred writer in this particular portion of the New Testament, and, at the same time, furnish himself to some extent with those principles and materials of criticism which are common to all parts of the Bible. If the plan of the work and the mode in which it is executed are such as to impart a just idea of the process of biblical interpretation, and to promote a habit of careful study and of self-reliance on the part of those who may use the book, it will be a result much more important than that all the opinions advanced in it should be approved; it is a result beyond any other which the writer has been anxious to accomplish. The grammatical references and explanations will enable the student to judge of the consistency of the interpretations given with the laws of the Greek language. The authorities cited will show the state of critical opinion on all passages that are supposed to be uncertain or obscure. The geographical, archæological, and other information collected from many different sources will unfold the relations of the book to the contemporary history of the age in which it was written, and

7

serve to present to the mind a more vivid conception of the reality of the scenes
and the events which the narrative describes.

No single commentary can be expected to answer all the purposes for which a
commentary is needed. The writer has aimed at a predominant object, and that
has been to determine by the rules of a just philology the meaning of the sacred
writer, and not to develop the practical applications or, to any great extent, the
doctrinal implications of this meaning. With such a design, no one will object to
the use which has been made of the labors of foreign scholars; it would have
been a matter of just complaint not to have used them, although with a different
aim it would be equally inexcusable not to have brought into view more frequently
the connections which exist between the Acts and the practical religious literature
contained in our own language.

I am indebted to various friends for advice and co-operation in the performance
of this labor. Among these, it becomes me to mention in particular the Rev. B. B.
Edwards, D. D., professor at Andover. It is doubtful whether I should have undertaken the work, or persevered in it, had it not been for his generous sympathy
and encouragement.

The author can recall no happier hours than those which he has spent in giving instruction on this book of the New Testament to successive classes of theological students. May the fruits of this mutual study be useful to them in the
active labors of the sacred work to which they are devoted! They are now sent
forth into a wider sphere; and here, also, may God be pleased to own them as a
means of contributing to a more diligent study and a more perfect knowledge of
his Holy Word!

NEWTON THEOLOGICAL INSTITUTION
October 31, 1851.

PREFACE TO THE REVISED EDITION.

THE present edition, as compared with the former, has been in parts rewritten, and also enlarged by the addition of about a hundred pages. In the interval since the work was first published the writer has continued to study the Acts both in a private way and occasionally as the teacher of theological classes. As the result of this further labor, the view on some passages has been modified; expressions that were found to be obscure have been made plainer; new points in the text have been elucidated; former explanations of a debatable character, according to the apparent evidence in the case, have been placed in a stronger light or advanced with less confidence; and, in general, pains have been taken in this revised form to render the notes not less critical than before, and yet freer and more varied in their contents. The last six years, too, have been signally fruitful in the appearance of valuable works relating to the Acts, either directly exegetical or subsidiary to that end. The reader will find ample proof in the following pages of the extent of my indebtedness to these contributions to biblical literature, and, at the same time, will appreciate the difficulty of using the abundant material with independence and judgment.

It has been of some service to me that since the publication of the first edition I have been enabled to visit the countries in which the Saviour and the apostles lived and the cross gained its earliest victories. The journey has made it tenfold more a labor of love to trace again the footsteps of Paul and his associates, and should add something to the interpreter's power to unfold the history of their sufferings and their triumphs.

Not to render the COMMENTARY too heterogeneous, it has seemed best to discard the idea of a supplement for the discussion of certain miscellaneous topics, as was proposed at first. As a substitute for such an appendage, the points which it was designed to embrace have been enlarged upon more fully in the present notes, and references have been given to appropriate works in which the student who desires will find more complete information. I will only add that the Greek text has been reviewed more carefully in this edition, and, unless I have erred through some inadvertence, all the variations which affect the sense materially have been brought to the reader's notice. At the suggestion of various friends, the Greek words in the notes have been translated in all cases where the remarks might otherwise be obscure to the English reader, and thus the explanations will be readily understood by all into whose hands the work may fall.

May the divine blessing rest upon this renewed endeavor to illustrate this portion of the Holy Scriptures!

NEWTON CENTRE, March 1, 1858.

EDITOR'S PREFACE.

THE Editor has the very great pleasure of presenting to the public a new edition of Dr. Hackett's Commentary, a *standard work on the Acts of the Apostles*—a work which has merited and received the highest commendation from biblical scholars in Europe and America, and which for thoroughness of investigation, critical acumen, and beauty of diction is unsurpassed by any commentary on the same book with which the Editor is acquainted.

In preparing this Commentary for the use of persons who are not familiar with the original text on which it is founded, the Editor, in consultation with Prof. Ezra Abbot, LL.D., has made it his aim—(1) to preserve in its integrity everything written by Dr. Hackett: to do this has been a pleasure as well as a duty, and great care has been taken in this respect; (2) to omit such Greek words or sentences as could be spared without diminishing the clearness or value of the Author's notes, or to substitute for them the words of the Common Version whenever this would be a help to the reader; (3) to insert in brackets, generally over his own initials, A. H., a few brief notes relating to the text or to its meaning. The Editor is responsible for everything in brackets, and Dr. Hackett for the rest. Since the second edition of this Commentary was published, the critical editions of the New Testament by Tregelles, Tischendorf (VIII.), Westcott and Hort, and the text adopted by the Anglo-American Revisers, have been issued, and it has seemed advisable to make reference on many doubtful passages to the readings found in these works, as well as to the principal manuscripts on which they are based. And (4) to notice instances in which the fourth edition of Meyer's commentary on the Acts (now translated) differs from the earlier editions used by Dr. Hackett in this Commentary. The changes made by Meyer in his fourth and last edition are somewhat numerous, and are for the most part favorable to the views of Dr. Hackett.

To have examined in detail the later objections to the authenticity or trustworthiness of The Acts would have increased the size of the Commentary beyond the prescribed limits, without adding greatly to its value. But it may be proper to refer the reader to *The Beginnings of Christianity*, by Dr. Fisher, as containing, especially in chapters xv. and xvi., important replies to these objections, and to express the belief that nothing has been discovered by the most recent scholarship which ought to weaken in the least our confidence in this part of the New Testament as being fully entitled to its ancient place in the canon of Holy Scripture.

Although Dr. Abbot has been consulted in respect to the kind of notes which might be wisely inserted in this volume, he is in no degree responsible for the views expressed in any of them; but the work has had the benefit of his accurate and practised eye in reading the proofs—a service which he was induced to render by his high regard for the Author of the Commentary, with whom he was formerly associated in the great work of preparing the American edition of Smith's *Dictionary of the Bible*.

ALVAH HOVEY.

NEWTON CENTRE MASS., March 5, 1882.

INTRODUCTION.

¿ 1. THE WRITER OF THE ACTS.

THE evidence that the book of Acts was written by Luke, to whom the Christian world are accustomed to ascribe it, is of a threefold character. It will be sufficient for the object here in view merely to indicate the line of argument which establishes the correctness of that opinion. A more complete and systematic view of the evidence must be sought in works which treat professedly of the formation and transmission of the Canon of the Scriptures.

In the first place, we have the explicit testimony of the early Christian writers that Luke wrote the Acts of the Apostles. Irenæus, who became Bishop of Lyons in A. D. 178, and who was born so early that he was intimate with those who had seen the apostles, says expressly that Luke was the author of the Acts; he quotes from him various single passages, and in one place gives a distinct summary of the last twelve chapters of the book (*Adv. Hæres.*, 3. 14. 1). He treats this authorship of the work as a matter which he had no occasion to defend, because no one of his contemporaries had called it in question. From the generation which separated Irenæus from the age of Luke we have only a few scanty remains; but these, although they contain expressions[1] which, according to the admission of nearly all critics, presuppose an acquaintance with the Acts, are silent respecting the writer. To have mentioned him by name would have been at variance with the informal mode of citing the Christian Scriptures which distinguishes the writings of that early period. The next witness is Clemens of Alexandria, who flourished about A. D. 190. This Father not only speaks of Luke as having composed the Acts in his *Stromata* (lib. 5), but is known to have written a commentary on it, which has not been preserved. Tertullian, who lived about A. D. 200, offers the same testimony. He has not only quoted the Acts repeatedly, but named Luke as the author in such a way as makes it evident that he merely followed in this the universal opinion of his age (*De Jejun.*, c. 10; *De Præscript. Hæret.*, c. 22; *De Bapt.*, c. 10, etc.). Eusebius wrote about A. D. 325. He has recorded both his own belief and that of his time in the following important statement: "Luke, a native of Antioch, by profession a physician, was mostly Paul's companion, though he associated not a little with the other apostles. He has left us examples of the art of healing souls, which he acquired from the apostles, in two divinely-inspired books; first, in the Gospel which he testifies to have written according to what eye-witnesses and ministers of the word delivered to him from the beginning, all which, also, he says that he investigated from the first;[2]

---

[1] See the passages, in Kirchhofer's *Sammlung zur Geschichte des N. T. Canons*, p. 161, *sq.*, in Lardner's *Credibility*, and in similar works.

[2] As the relative may be neuter or masculine, many take the sense of the Greek to be, *all whom he accompanied;* but the manifest allusion to Luke 1 : 2, 3 renders the other the more obvious translation.

and, secondly, in the Acts of the Apostles, which he composed, not from report, as in the other case, but according to his own personal observation " (*Hist. Eccl.*, 3. 4). It would be superfluous to pursue this testimony farther. It may be proper to add that no trace of any opposition to it or dissent from it has come down to us from the first ages of the church. Some of the early heretical sects, it is true, as the Marcionites, Manicheans, Severians, rejected the religious authority of the Acts ; but as they did this because it contradicted their peculiar views, and as they admitted without question the source from which their opponents claimed to receive it, their rejection of the book, under such circumstances, becomes a conclusive testimony to its genuineness.

In the second place, the relation in which the Acts of the Apostles stands to the Gospel which is ascribed to Luke proves that the author of the two productions must be the same individual. The writer introduces his work as a continuation or second part of a previous history, and dedicates it to a certain Theophilus, who can be no other than the person for whose special information the Gospel was written. As to the identity of the writer of the Acts with the writer of the Gospel attributed to Luke, no well-founded question has been, or can be, raised. Consequently, the entire mass of testimony which proves that Luke the Evangelist wrote the Gospel which bears his name proves with equal force that he wrote also the Acts of the Apostles. Thus the Acts may be traced up to Luke through two independent series of witnesses. And it may be confidently asserted that, unless the combined historical evidence from this twofold source be admitted as conclusive in support of Luke's claim to the authorship of the Acts, there is then no ancient book in the world the author of which can ever be ascertained by us.

In the third place, the literary peculiarities which distinguish the Gospel of Luke mark also the composition of the Acts and show that it must have come from the same hand. The argument here is founded on a different relation of the Gospel to the Acts from that to which we have just adverted. Luke being acknowledged as the author of the Gospel, we know from that source what the characteristics of his style are ; and it is maintained that these re-appear in the Acts to such an extent that we can account for the agreement only by referring the two productions to the same writer. The reality of the resemblance here asserted is conceded by critics of every name. It will be necessary to restrict the illustration of it to a few examples.[1] In Luke's Gospel, verbs compounded with prepositions are more numerous than in the other Evangelists ; they are found in the same proportion in the Acts. Matthew has $\sigma\acute{\nu}\nu$ three times ; Mark, five times ; John, three times, or, according to another reading, but twice ; while Luke employs it in his Gospel twenty-four times, and in the Acts fifty-one times. Luke has used $\ddot{a}\pi a\varsigma$ in his two books thirty-five times ; whereas it occurs in all the others but nine times. $\pi o\rho\epsilon\acute{\nu}\epsilon\sigma\vartheta a\iota$ is found in the Gospel forty-nine times and in the Acts thirty-eight times, but is rarely found in other parts of the New Testament. The construction of $\epsilon\grave{\iota}\pi\epsilon\~\iota\nu$ and $\lambda a\lambda\epsilon\~\iota\nu$ with $\pi\rho\acute{o}\varsigma$, instead of the dative of the person addressed, is confined almost exclusively to Luke. No other writer, except John in a few instances, ever says $\epsilon\grave{\iota}\pi\epsilon\~\iota\nu$ $\pi\rho\acute{o}\varsigma$, and $\lambda a\lambda\epsilon\~\iota\nu$ $\pi\rho\acute{o}\varsigma$ occurs out of Luke's writings only in 1 Cor. 14 : 6 ; Heb. 5 : 5 and 11 : 18. As in Luke's Gospel, so in the Acts, we have a characteristic use of $\delta\grave{\epsilon}$ $\kappa a\acute{\iota}$ to express emphasis or gradation ; a similar use of $\kappa a\grave{\iota}$ $a\dot{\nu}\tau\acute{o}\varsigma$ or $a\dot{\nu}\tau o\acute{\iota}$; the insertion of the neuter article before interrogative sentences ; the omission of $\delta\acute{\epsilon}$ after $\mu\grave{\epsilon}\nu$ $o\mathring{\nu}\nu$; the uniform preference of ʹ$I\epsilon\rho o\nu\sigma a\lambda\acute{\eta}\mu$ to ʹ$I\epsilon\rho o\sigma\acute{o}\lambda\nu\mu a$; and still others. Credner, in his *Intro-*

---

[1] They are drawn out more or less fully in Gersdorf's *Beitraege*, p. 160, *sq.* ; Credner's *Einleitung in das neue Testament*, p. 130, *sq.* ; Ebrard's *Kritik der evangelischen Geschichte*, p. 671, ed. 1850 ; Guericke's *Gesammtgeschichte des N. T.*, p. 166, *sq.* ; Lekebusch's *Composition und Entstehung der Apostelgeschichte*, p. 37, *sq.* ; and Dr. Davidson's *Introduction to the New Testament*, vol. i. p. 190, and vol. ii. p. 8.

duction to the New Testament, has enumerated not fewer than sixty-five distinct idioms which he considers as peculiar to Luke's diction as compared with that of the other New-Testament writers; and nearly all these he points out as occurring at the same time in both the Gospel and the Acts. It is impossible, then, to doubt, unless we deny that any confidence can be placed in this species of criticism, that if Luke wrote the Gospel which we accredit to him, he must also have written the Acts.

§ 2. BIOGRAPHICAL SKETCH OF LUKE.

According to Eusebius, as already quoted, and Jerome, who may be supposed to represent the opinion of their times, Luke was a native of Antioch. As he appears in the Acts to have spent so much time at Philippi, some modern writers have conjectured that he may have been a native or an inhabitant of that city. The historical testimony deserves more regard than an inference of that nature. That he was a Gentile by birth appears to be certain from Col. 4 : 11, 14, where Paul distinguishes him from those whom he denominates *those who are of the circumcision* (οἱ ὄντες ἐκ περιτομῆς). His foreign extraction is confirmed also by the character of his style, which approaches nearer to the standard of classical Greek than that of any other writer of the New Testament, with the exception of the apostle Paul. This feature of his language renders it probable that he was of Greek origin. Some have inferred this also from his Greek name; but it was not uncommon for Jews, as well as Romans and other foreigners, to assume such names at this period. Whether he was a proselyte to Judaism before his conversion to Christianity, or not, is a question on which critics differ. The supposition that he adopted first the Jewish religion, and had done so perhaps in early life, accounts best for his intimate acquaintance with the opinions and customs of the Jews, his knowledge of the Septuagint, and the degree of Hebraistic tendency which shows itself in his style. It appears from Col. 4 : 14 that Luke was a physician; and the general voice of antiquity, in accordance with that passage, represents him as having belonged to the medical profession. The effect of his following such an employment can be traced, as many critics think, in various passages of Luke's writings. (Comp. the note on 28 : 8.) The fact that he was trained to such a pursuit—that he was a man, therefore, of culture and observing habits of mind—is an important circumstance. It has been justly remarked that, as many of the miracles which the first promulgators of the gospel wrought in confirmation of its truth were cases of the healing of maladies, Luke, by virtue of his medical skill and experience, was rendered peculiarly competent to judge of the reality of such miracles.[1]

Of the manner in which the writer of the Acts was brought to a knowledge of the gospel we have no information. The suggestion of some of the later Fathers, that he was one of the seventy disciples, is not only without ground, but opposed to his own statement in the introduction of his Gospel, where he distinguishes himself from those who had been personal attendants on the ministry of Christ. It is evident that after his conversion he devoted himself to public Christian labors, for the most part in connection with the apostle Paul, whom he accompanied from place to place and aided in his efforts for the extension of the gospel. The first explicit allusion which he makes to himself occurs in 16 : 10, *sq.*, where he gives an account of the apostle's departure from Troas to Macedonia. In that passage Luke employs the first person plural, and thus shows that he was one of the companions of Paul on that occasion. He goes with the apostle from Troas to Philippi, and speaks of himself again in 20 : 6 as one of the

---

[1] I have made no allusion in the text to 2 Cor. 8 : 18; for it is barely possible that the author of our narrative can be meant there as "the brother whose praise is in all the churches." See De Wette's note on that passage in his *Exegetisches Handbuch zum N. Testament.*

several individuals who sailed with Paul from the same city on his last journey to Jerusalem. Whether Luke had been separated from Paul during the interval, or remained with him, cannot be certainly known. It is eminently characteristic of the sacred writers that they keep themselves out of view in their narratives. Hence some have argued that we are not to infer that Luke was necessarily absent when he employs the third person, but rather that it was a sort of inadvertence, as it were, against his design that he has now and then disclosed his personal connection with the history. The other opinion is the surer one. We cannot be certain that Luke was in the company of Paul, except at the times when his language shows that he was personally concerned in what he relates. It is clear, even according to this view, that Luke, in addition to his accompanying Paul on his first journey from Troas to Philippi, remained with him, without any known interruption, from the period of his leaving Philippi the second time to the end of his career. He goes with the apostle to Jerusalem, where the latter was apprehended and given up to the custody of the Romans (20 : 6, *sq.* ; 21 : 1, *sq.*); he speaks of himself as still with him at the close of his imprisonment at Cæsarea (27 : 1); proceeds with him on his voyage to Rome (27 : 1, *sq.*) ; and, as we see from the Epistles which Paul wrote while in that city, continued to be associated with him down to the latest period of his life of which any record remains. The apostle mentions Luke as residing with him at Rome in Col. 4 : 14; Phil. 24; and 2 Tim. 4 : 11. Of his subsequent history nothing authentic has been preserved. The traditions which relate to this period are uncertain and contradictory. According to Gregory Nazianzen, whom several later writers follow, he suffered martyrdom; according to others, and those whose testimony has greater weight, he died a natural death.

⸹ 3. AUTHENTICITY OF THE ACTS.

The foregoing sketch shows us how ample were Luke's means of information in regard to the subjects of which his history treats. Of most of the events which he has recorded he was an eye-witness. The materials which compose the body of the work lay within the compass of his own personal knowledge. The particulars which he communicates respecting Paul's life and labors before his own acquaintance with him he could have learned at a subsequent period in his intercourse with that apostle. His extensive journeyings could hardly fail to have brought him into connection with most of the other persons who appear as actors in the history. Some of his information he derived, no doubt, from written sources. The official documents which he has inserted (15 : 23, *sq.* ; 23 : 26, *sq.*) were public, and could have been copied. We assume nothing at variance with the habits of antiquity in supposing that the more extended discourses and speeches, which Luke himself did not hear, may have been noted down by others at the time of their delivery, or soon afterward, while the impression made by them was still vivid. If the writer of the Acts had any occasion for the use of such reports, his travels from one country to another must have given him access to the persons who could furnish them.[1]

We are to recollect, further, that the declaration which Luke makes at the commencement of his Gospel applies equally to the Acts. It was his habit, as we learn there, to avail himself of every possible source of inquiry, in order to ascertain the certainty of what he wrote. With such opportunities at his command, and with such a

---

[1] Some critics, as Schleiermacher, Bleek, De Wette, have thrown out the idea that Luke may have derived those parts of the Acts in which the narrator employs the first person plural from a history of Paul's missionary labors written by Timothy. (See the note on 20 : 6.) Among the writers who have shown the untenableness of that hypothesis are Ebrard, *Kritik*, u. s. w., p. 732, *sq.* ; Lekebusch, *Composition*, u. s. w., p. 131, *sq.* ; and Davidson, *Introduction*, vol. ii. p 9, *sq.*

character for diligence in the use of them, the writer of the Acts, considered simply in the light of an ordinary historian, comes before us with every title to confidence which can be asserted in behalf of the best-accredited human testimony.

But this is not all. We have not only every reason to regard the history of Luke as authentic, because he wrote it with such facilities for knowing the truth, but because we find it sustaining its credit under the severest scrutiny to which it is possible that an ancient work should be subjected.

First. This history has been confronted with the Epistles of the New Testament, and it has been shown as the result that the incidental correspondences between them and the Acts are numerous and of the most striking kind. They are such as preclude the supposition of their being the result of either accident or design. It is impossible to account for them, unless we admit that the transactions which Luke records really took place in the manner that he has related. It is the object of Paley's *Horæ Paulinæ* to develop this argument; and the demonstration of the truth of the Acts, and of the New Testament in general, which he has furnished in that work, no objector has ever attempted to refute.

Secondly. The speeches in the Acts which purport to have been delivered by Peter, Paul, and James have been compared with the known productions of these men; and it is found that they exhibit an agreement with them, in point of thought and expression, which the supposition of their common origin would lead us to expect. The speeches attributed to Peter contain peculiar phrases and ideas which impart a characteristic similarity to them as compared with the other speeches, and which appear again in his Epistles, but in no other portion of the New Testament. In like manner, the speeches of Paul evince an affinity both to each other and to his Epistles, in the recurrence of favorite words, modes of construction, and turns of thought, such as belong to no other writer. We have but one address from James, but even here we discover striking points of connection with the Epistle which bears his name. Occasion will be taken in the course of the COMMENTARY to illustrate this peculiar feature of the history.

Thirdly. We have a decisive test of the trustworthiness of Luke in the consistency of his statements and allusions with the information which contemporary writers have given us respecting the age in which he lived and wrote. The history which we read in the Acts connects itself at numerous points with the social customs of different and distant nations; with the fluctuating civil affairs of the Jews, Greeks, and Romans; and with geographical or political divisions and arrangements, which were constantly undergoing some change or modification. Through all these circumstances, which underlie Luke's narrative from commencement to end, he pursues his way without a single instance of contradiction or collision. Examples of the most unstudied harmony with the complicated relations of the times present themselves at every step. No writer who was conscious of fabricating his story would have hazarded such a number of minute allusions, since they increase so immensely the risk of detection; and still less, if he had ventured upon it, could he have introduced them so skilfully as to baffle every attempt to discover a single well-founded instance of ignorance or oversight. It adds to the force of the argument to remark that in the pages of Luke every such allusion falls from him entirely without effort or parade. It never strikes the reader as farfetched or contrived. Every incident, every observation, flows naturally out of the progress of the narrative. It is no exaggeration to say that the well-informed reader who will study carefully the book of the Acts, and compare the incidental notices to be found on almost every page with the geography and the political history of the times, and with the customs of the different countries in which the scene of the transactions is laid, will receive an impression of the writer's fidelity and accuracy equal to that of the most forcible treatises on the truth of Christianity.

The objections which sceptical writers have urged against the authenticity of the Acts relate chiefly to the supernatural character of its narrations. It does not belong to the province of biblical criticism to reply to such objections. They have adduced also a few instances of alleged offence against history or chronology or archæology, but these result from an unnecessary interpretation. We may understand the passages which are said to contain the inconsistency in a different manner, and thus remove entirely the occasion for it.

₹ 4. OBJECT AND PLAN OF THE BOOK.

The common title of the Acts—πράξεις τῶν ἀποστόλων—is ancient, but is supposed generally to have been prefixed, not by the author, but by some later hand. It is read differently in different manuscripts. It is too comprehensive to describe accurately the contents of the book. The writer's object, if we are to judge of it from what he has performed, must have been to furnish a summary history of the origin, gradual increase, and extension of the Christian Church, through the instrumentality, chiefly, of the apostles Peter and Paul. In fact, we have not a complete history, but a compendium merely, of the labors of these two apostles, who were most active in their efforts to advance the gospel, while the other apostles are only referred to or named incidentally in connection with some particular occurrence. It is not to be supposed that Luke has recorded all the facts which were known to him respecting the early spread of Christianity. On what principle he proceeded in making his selection from the mass of materials before him we cannot decide with certainty. He may have been influenced in part by the personal relation which he sustained to the individuals introduced and the events described by him. It is still more probable that the wants of the particular class of readers whom he had in view may have shaped, more or less consciously, the course of his narrative; and these readers, in the absence of any surer indication, we may consider as represented by Theophilus, who was in all probability a convert from heathenism. (See note on 1 : 1.)

In writing for such readers, we should expect that Luke would lean toward those aspects of the history which illustrated the design of God in reference to the heathen ; their right to participate in the blessings of the gospel without submitting to the forms of Judaism ; the conflict of opinion which preceded the full recognition of this right ; and the success more particularly of those apostolic labors which were performed in behalf of heathen countries. It cannot be denied that the contents of the Acts exhibit a predilection for this class of topics ; and to that extent the book may be said to have been written, in order to illustrate the unrestricted nature of the blessings of the gospel. On the other hand, it should be observed that this predilection is merely such as would spring naturally from the writer's almost unconscious sympathy with his Gentile readers, and is by no means so marked as to authorize us, according to the view of some writers, to impute to him anything like a formal purpose to trace the relation of Judaism to Christianity.

In accordance with this trait of the Acts here alluded to, we have a very particular account of the manner in which Peter was freed from his Jewish scruples. The reception of the first heathen converts into the church is related at great length. The proceedings of the Council at Jerusalem with reference to the question whether circumcision should be permanent occupy one of the leading chapters of the book. And the individual of the apostles who preached chiefly to the Gentiles, and introduced the gospel most extensively into heathen countries, is the one whom the writer has made the central object of his history, and whose course of labor he has described in the fullest manner.

Luke has pursued no formal plan in the arrangement of the Acts. The subject of his history, however, divides itself naturally into two principal parts. The first part treats of the apostolic labors of Peter, and hence particularly of the spread of Christianity among the Jews, occupying the first twelve chapters; the second, of the labors of Paul, and hence the promulgation of the gospel in Syria, Asia Minor, Greece, and Rome, occupying the remaining chapters. But the book contains other topics which are related to these only in a general way. The following division marks out to view the different sections more distinctly: 1. Outpouring of the Spirit on the day of Pentecost, and the antecedent circumstances; 2. Events relating to the progress of the gospel in Judea and Samaria; 3. The transition of the gospel to the heathen, in the conversion of Cornelius and others; 4. The call of the apostle Paul, and his first missionary tour; 5. The Apostolic Council at Jerusalem; 6. The second missionary tour of Paul; 7. His third missionary tour, and his apprehension at Jerusalem; 8. His imprisonment at Cæsarea, and voyage to Rome.

₰ 5. TIME AND PLACE OF WRITING THE ACTS.

The time when the Acts was written could not have been far distant from that of the termination of Paul's imprisonment at Rome, mentioned at the close of the history. The manner in which Luke speaks of that imprisonment implies clearly that at the time when he wrote the apostle's condition had changed; that he was no longer a prisoner, either because he had been liberated or because he had been put to death.

It does not affect the present question whether we suppose that he was imprisoned twice or only once. (See note on 28 : 31.) If we suppose that he was set at liberty, we have then a most natural explanation of the abrupt close of the book in the fact that Luke published it just at the time of the apostle's release, or so soon after that event that the interval furnished nothing new which he deemed it important to add to the history. On the other hand, if we suppose that Paul's captivity terminated in his martyrdom, it is not easy to account for the writer's silence respecting his death, except on the ground that it was so recent and so well known in the circle of his readers that they did not need the information. Thus, in both cases, the time of writing the Acts would coincide very nearly with the end of the Roman captivity of which Luke has spoken.

The question arises now, Do we know the time when that captivity ended, whether it may have been by acquittal or by death? Here we must depend upon the surest chronological data which exist, though it is not pretended that they are certain. According to a computation which has received the assent of most critics, Paul was brought as a prisoner to Rome in the year A. D. 61 or 62. In the year 64 followed the conflagration in that city, which was kindled by the agency of Nero, but which, for the sake of averting the odium of the act from himself, he charged on the Christians. This led to the first Christian persecution, so called, which is mentioned by Tacitus (*Annal.*, 15. 44), Suetonius (*Ner.*, 16), and possibly Juvenal (*Serm.*, 1. 146, *sq.*). If now Paul was set at liberty after his confinement of two years, it must have been just before the commencement of Nero's persecution—that is, in the year A. D. 63, or near the beginning of 64. But if, according to the other supposition, the two years were not completed until the persecution commenced, he must, in all probability, as the leader of the Christian sect, have soon shared the common fate, and so have been put to death about the year 64. Hence we may consider this date, or the close of A. D. 63, as not improbably the time when Luke wrote, or at least published, the Acts of the Apostles.

But if Luke wrote the book thus near the expiration of the two years that Paul was a prisoner at Rome, it is most natural to conclude that he wrote it in that city. This was also the opinion of many of the early Christian Fathers. The probability of this conclusion is greatly strengthened by the fact that Luke makes no mention of Paul's liberation or martyrdom, as the case may have been. At Rome every reader of the apostle's history knew, of course, what the result of his captivity there was; and if Luke wrote it at that place, the absence of any allusion to his fate would not seem to be so very surprising. On the contrary, if Luke wrote it at a distance from the scene of the apostle's captivity, the omission would be much more extraordinary.

§ 6. CHRONOLOGY OF THE ACTS.

The subject of the chronology of the Acts is still attended with uncertainties which no efforts of critical labor have been able wholly to remove. "After all the combinations," says Schott,[1] "which the ingenuity of scholars has enabled them to devise, and all the fulness of historical learning which they have applied to the subject, it has been impossible to arrive at results which are satisfactory in all respects." The source of the difficulty is that the notations of time are for the most part entirely omitted, or, if they occur here and there, are contained in general and indefinite expressions. We must content ourselves, therefore, with endeavoring to fix the dates of a few leading events which may be ascertained with most certainty, and must then distribute the other contents of the book with reference to these, on the basis of such incidental intimations as may be found to exist, or of such probable calculations as we may be able to form.

1. THE YEAR OF PAUL'S CONVERSION.

The date of this event is very uncertain, but an attempt has been made to approximate to it by means of the following combination. In Gal. 1 : 15–18, it is stated that Paul went up to Jerusalem from Damascus three years from the time of his conversion, and we learn from 2 Cor. 11 : 32 that Damascus, when Paul made his escape from it on that occasion, was in the hands of Aretas, King of Arabia. As this city belonged to the Romans, it is remarkable that it should have been just at that time wrested from them, and the circumstances under which such an event took place must have been peculiar. It is conjectured that a juncture like this may have led to that occurrence. Josephus relates that an army of Herod Antipas had been defeated about this time by Aretas, King of Arabia. Upon this, the Emperor Tiberius, who was a friend and ally of Herod, directed Vitellius, Roman Governor of Syria, to collect an adequate force, and to take Aretas prisoner or slay him in the attempt. Before Vitellius could execute this order news came that the emperor was dead, and, as a consequence of this, the military preparations on foot were suspended. This sudden respite afforded Aretas an opportunity to march upon Damascus and reduce it to his possession. The city, however, supposing him to have become master of it, could not have remained long in his power. We find that the difficulties with Arabia were all adjusted in the first years of the reign of Caligula, the successor of Tiberius—i. e. within A. D. 37–39; and the policy of the Romans would lead them, of course, to insist on the restoration of so important a place as Damascus. If, now, we place the escape of Paul in the *last* of these years (so as to afford time for the incidental delays), and deduct the three years during which he had been absent from Jerusalem, we obtain A. D. 36 as the probable epoch of the apostle's conversion. It is in favor of this conclusion, says Neander, that it gives us an interval neither too long nor too short for the events which took place in the church between the ascension of Christ and the conversion of Paul. Among others who fix upon the same year, or vary from it but one or two years, may be mentioned Eichhorn,

---

[1] *Erörterung einiger chronologischen Punkte in der Lebensgeschichte des Apostel Paul*, § 1.

Hug, Hemsen, Schott, Guericke, Meyer, De Wette, Anger,[1] Ebrard, Alford, Howson.[2] This date determines that of Stephen's martyrdom, which took place, apparently, no, long before Paul's conversion, and also that of Paul's first journey to Jerusalem and his subsequent departure to Tarsus.

2. The Death of Herod Agrippa.

This occurred at Cæsarea in the year A. D. 44. The statements of Josephus are de. cisive on this point. He says that Agrippa, who, under Caligula, had reigned over only a part of Palestine, received the entire sovereignty of his grandfather, Herod the Great, on the accession of Claudius—viz. in the year A. D. 41 (*Antt.*, 19. 5. 1), and, further, that at the time of his death he had completed the third year after this extension of his power (*Antt.*, 19. 8. 2). This date fixes the position of several other important events; such as the execution of James the elder, the arrest and deliverance of Peter, the return of Paul to Antioch from his second visit to Jerusalem, and his departure on his first missionary excursion.

3. The Third Journey of Paul to Jerusalem.

In Gal. 2 : 1 the apostle speaks of going up to Jerusalem *after fourteen years*, which are to be computed, in all probability, from the time of his conversion. It has been made a question whether this journey is to be understood as the second or third of the several journeys which Paul is mentioned in the Acts as having made to Jerusalem. The general opinion is that it should be understood of the third—first, because the object of that journey, as stated in 15 : 1, *sq.*, coincides exactly with that which occasioned the one mentioned in the Epistle to the Galatians; and secondly, because the circumstances which are described as having taken place in connection with the journey in 15 : 1, *sq.*, agree so entirely with those related in the Epistle.[3] Supposing, then, the identity of the two journeys to be established, we add the fourteen years already men. tioned to the date of Paul's conversion—viz. 36—and we have A. D. 50 as the year when he went up to Jerusalem the third time after he had become a Christian.[4] With this year coincides that of holding the Council at Jerusalem. Paul departed on his second missionary tour soon after his return to Antioch from this third visit to Jerusalem, and hence we are enabled to assign that second tour to the year A. D. 51.

4. The Procuratorship of Felix.

The time of this officer's recall, on being superseded by Festus (see 24 : 27), is as, signed by most critics to the year A. D. 60 or 61. The names of both these men are well known in secular history, but it so happens that we meet with only indirect state-

---

[1] *De temporum in Actis Apostolorum ratione*, p. 121, *sq.*

[2] Wieseler (*Chronologie des Apostolischen Zeitalters*, pp. 175–213) assigns Paul's conversion to A. D. 40. It was gratifying to me to find that, with this exception, all his other dates agree with those which I had been led to adopt before consulting his able treatise.

[3] The reasons for this conclusion are well stated by Hemsen, in his *Der Apostel Paulus*, u. s. w., p. 52, *sq.*, translated by the writer in the *Christian Review*, 1841, p. 66. *sq.* Dr. Davidson has discussed the question with the same result in his *Introduction*, vol. ii. pp. 112–122. See, also, Conybeare and Howson, *Life and Epistles of St Paul*, vol. i. p. 539, *sq.* (2d ed.), and Jowett *On Galatians*, p. 252.

[4] It is proper to apprise the reader that some reckon the fourteen years in Gal. 2 : 1 from the apostle's first return to Jerusalem (Gal. 1 : 18); and in that case his third journey to that city would be dated three years later. But few, comparatively, adopt this view. The apostle's conversion is the governing epoch, to which the mind of the reader naturally turns back from Gal. 2 : 1, as well as from Gal. 1 : 18.

ments relating to the point which concerns us here. It is generally agreed that these statements justify the following opinion. It is certain that Felix could not have been recalled later than the year 62. Josephus states (*Antt.*, 20. 8. 9) that Felix, soon after his return to Rome, was accused before the emperor, by a deputation from the Jews in Palestine, of maladministration while in office, and that he would have been condemned had it not been for the influence of his brother Pallas, who stood high at that time in the favor of Nero. This Pallas now, according to Tacitus (*Ann.*, 14. 65), was poisoned by Nero in the year 62. The only circumstance which impairs the certainty of this conclusion is that Tacitus states (*Ann.*, 13. 14) that Pallas had lost the favor of Nero some time before this, and had been entirely removed from public business. Hence some have placed the appointment of Festus as successor of Felix several years earlier than A. D. 61. But there is reason to believe that the disgrace of which Tacitus speaks may have been only temporary, and that Pallas may afterward have recovered his influence with the emperor. Since it is certain, according to Tacitus himself, that the death of this favorite did not occur till A. D. 62, it can be more easily supposed that Nero was again reconciled to him than that this revengeful tyrant should have suffered him to live several years after he had become odious to him. De Wette, Anger, Meyer, Wieseler, and others, admit this supposition, under the circumstances of the case, to be entirely natural.

It is less easy to fix the limit on the other side. The general belief is that Festus could not have succeeded Felix earlier than A. D. 60 or 61. Josephus relates (*Antt.*, 20. 8. 11) that Festus, after having entered on his office, permitted a deputation of the Jews to repair to Rome, in order to obtain the decision of Nero in a controversy between himself and them, and that Poppæa, the wife of Nero, interceded for them, and enabled them to gain their object. But this woman did not become the wife[1] of Nero until the year 62 (Tac., *Ann.*, 14. 49; Suet., *Ner.*, 35); and hence, as Festus must have been in Judea some time before this difficulty with the Jews arose, and as, after that, some time must have elapsed before the case could be decided at Rome, Festus may have received his appointment in the year 60 or 61. The best recent authorities, as Winer, De Wette, Anger, Meyer, Wieseler, adopt one or the other of these years.

We reach very nearly the same result from what Josephus says of his journey to Rome in behalf of the Jewish priests whom Felix had sent thither for trial before his removal from office. He informs us in his *Life* (§ 3) that he made his journey in the twenty-sixth year of his age, and, as he was born in the first year of the reign of Caligula—i. e. A. D. 37 (*Life*, § 1)—he visited Rome on this occasion about 63. His narrative, without being definite, implies that Felix at this time had not only been recalled, but must have left Palestine two or three years earlier than this. Festus was the immediate successor of Felix.

It is the more important to settle as nearly as possible some epoch in this portion of

---

[1] Some, as Neander, Wieseler, object to the stricter sense of γυνή in the passage of Josephus, but it is defended by Schrader, Meyer, and others, as the more obvious sense, whether we consider the historical facts or the usage of the word. Neander (*Pflanzung*, u. s. w., vol. i. p. 493) expresses himself with much hesitation respecting this date of the succession of Felix and Festus. It is important, for the purpose of laying up in the mind a connected view of the history, to settle upon the precise years as nearly as possible; and we ought not to deprive ourselves of this advantage merely because some of the conclusions, or the grounds of them, cannot be placed entirely beyond doubt. It is admitted that, of the dates proposed in the above scheme of chronology, the second (that of Herod's death) and the last in a lower degree (that of Paul's arrival at Rome) are the only ones that can be brought to a state of comparative certainty. In regard to the others I have not meant to claim for them anything more than the character of an approximation to the truth.

the apostle's history, since there would be otherwise so much uncertainty as to the mode of arranging the events in the long interval between this and Paul's third journey to Jerusalem. Upon this date depends the year of the apostle's arrest in that city on his fifth and last visit thither, before he was sent to Rome. His captivity at Cæsarea, which followed that arrest, continued two years, and must have commenced in the spring of A. D. 58 or 59.

5. THE ARRIVAL OF PAUL IN ROME.

The extreme limit beyond which we cannot place this event may be regarded as certain. It could not have been later than the year 62; for after 64, when the Christians at Rome began to be persecuted by the Roman Government, their situation was such that the apostle could not have remained there and preached the gospel for two years without molestation, as stated by Luke at the end of the Acts. It is impossible to obtain a more definite result than this from secular history.[1] But the date in question follows as a deduction from the one considered in the last paragraph. It is evident from the Acts that Paul proceeded to Rome almost immediately after the entrance of Festus on his office; and if this took place in A. D. 60 or 61, he must have arrived in Rome early in the spring of 61 or 62. Hence, if he arrived even in A. D. 62, he could have remained two years in captivity and then have regained his freedom (if we adopt that opinion), since Nero's persecution of the Christians did not commence till the summer of A. D. 64.

§ 7. THE CONTENTS IN CHRONOLOGICAL ORDER.

A. D.

33.—Ascension of Christ. Appointment of Matthias as an apostle. Outpouring of the Spirit at Pentecost. The gift of tongues conferred. Discourse of Peter. Three thousand are converted.—Pilate, under whom the Saviour was crucified, is still procurator of Judea. Tiberius continues emperor till A. D. 37.

33–35.—Peter and John heal the lame man. They are arraigned before the Sanhedrim and forbidden to preach. Death of Ananias and Sapphira. The apostles are scourged. Deacons appointed. Apprehension and martyrdom of Stephen. Saul makes havoc of the church.

36.—Persecution scatters the believers at Jerusalem. Philip preaches the gospel in Samaria. Hypocrisy of Simon the Magian. Baptism of the eunuch. The word is made known in Phœnicia, Cyprus, and at Antioch in Syria. Christ appears to Saul on the way to Damascus. Conversion of Paul.

37–39.—Paul spends these three years at Damascus and in Arabia. During the same time other laborers spread the gospel in Judea, Galilee, and along the coast of the Mediterranean.—Caligula becomes emperor in A. D. 37.

39.—Paul escapes from Damascus, and goes to Jerusalem for the first time since his conversion. Barnabas introduces him to the disciples. He remains there fifteen days, but is persecuted, and departs thence to Tarsus.

40–43.—During this period Paul preaches in Syria and Cilicia. Churches are gathered there. Barnabas is sent to search for him, and conducts him to Antioch. In the meantime Peter visits Joppa, Lydda, and Cæsarea. Dorcas is restored to life. Cornelius is baptized. Peter defends himself for visiting the heathen.— Claudius becomes emperor in the beginning of A. D. 41. On his accession he makes Herod Agrippa I. king over all Palestine.

---

[1] Whether this result is confirmed by τῷ στρατοπεδάρχῃ in 28 : 16 depends on the explanation of the article. (See the note on that passage.)

A. D.

44.—Paul labors "a whole year" with Barnabas at Antioch. Agabus predicts a famine in Judea. James the elder is beheaded at Jerusalem. Peter is cast into prison; his liberation and flight.—Herod Agrippa dies at Cæsarea in the summer of this year. Judea is again governed by procurators.

45.—Paul goes to Jerusalem the second time, on the alms-errand, accompanied by Barnabas. He returns to Antioch, and under the direction of the Spirit is set apart by the church to the missionary work. In the same year, probably, he goes forth with Barnabas and Mark on his first mission to the heathen.

46, 47.—He was absent on this tour about two years. He proceeds by the way of Seleucia to Salamis and Paphos in Cyprus; at the latter place Sergius Paulus believes, and Elymas is struck blind. Crossing the sea, he lands at Perga, where John Mark abruptly leaves him. He preaches in the synagogue at Antioch. Labors with success at Iconium. At Lystra he is about to be worshipped as a god, and afterward is stoned. Escapes to Derbe. Retraces his way to Perga. Sails from Attaleia, and comes again to Antioch in Syria.

48, 49.—Here he abode, it is said, "a long time." We may assign these two years to that residence. He extended his labors, no doubt, to the neighboring regions.

50.—Apostolic Council at Jerusalem. Paul makes his third journey to that city, in company with Barnabas and others, as delegates from the church at Antioch. Returns to Antioch with the decrees. Paul and Barnabas separate.

51–54.—The apostle's second missionary tour. Silas, Timothy, and Luke are associated with him. Paul revisits the churches in Syria and Cilicia. Plants the churches in Galatia. At Troas he embarks for Europe, and, among other places, visits Philippi, Thessalonica, Berea, Athens, Corinth. In this last city he remained at least a year and a half. Labored with Aquila at tent-making. Left the synagogue and preached to Greeks. He is arraigned before Gallio. In this city Paul wrote the First and Second Epistles to the Thessalonians.[1] In the spring, probably, of A. D. 54 he leaves Corinth, embarks at Cenchreæ, touches at Ephesus, lands at Cæsarea, and from there goes for the fourth time to Jerusalem, and thence to Antioch. We may allot three years, or three and a half, to this journey.—Felix became procurator of Judea in A. D. 52. In A. D. 53, Claudius bestowed on Herod Agrippa II. the former tetrarchy of Philip and Lysanias, with the title of king. In A. D. 54, Nero succeeded Claudius as emperor.

54–57.—In the autumn of A. D. 54 according to some, or early in A. D. 55 according to others, Paul entered on his third missionary tour. He goes through Galatia and Phrygia to Ephesus, where he spends the greater part of the next three years. Just before his arrival Apollos left Ephesus for Corinth. Certain disciples of John are baptized. Nearly all Asia hears the gospel. The exorcists defeated. An uproar at Ephesus. The Asiarchs befriend Paul. During this sojourn here Paul wrote the Epistle to the Galatians and the First Epistle to the Corinthians. Within the same time he made, probably, a short journey to Corinth, either directly across the Ægean or through Macedonia. While on this excursion, some suppose that he wrote the First Epistle to Timothy, and after his return to Ephesus that to Titus.

---

[1] The reasons for assigning the different Epistles to the times and places mentioned are stated in the body of the COMMENTARY.

A. D.

58, 59.—In the spring of A. D. 58, or perhaps A. D. 57 (if this tour began in 54), the apostle leaves Ephesus and proceeds to Macedonia, where he writes his Second Epistle to the Corinthians. He spent the summer in that region, and travelled probably as far west as Illyricum. In the autumn or early winter of this year he arrives at Corinth, and remains there three months. The Jews plot his destruction. At this time he wrote the Epistle to the Romans. In the ensuing spring he returns through Macedonia to Troas, where he preached and "broke bread." Miraculous recovery of Eutychus. At Miletus he addressed the Ephesian elders. Landing at Ptolemais, he proceeded to Cæsarea, and thence to Jerusalem, which is his fifth and last visit to that city. This journey occupied about four years.

58 or 59.—At Jerusalem, Paul assumes a vow, to conciliate the Jewish believers. He is seized by the Jews in the temple, but is rescued by Lysias the chiliarch. Speech to the mob from the stairs of the castle. His Roman citizenship saves him from the torture. He stands before the Sanhedrim, and narrowly escapes with his life. Forty Jews conspire against him. Lysias sends him as a state prisoner to Felix at Cæsarea.

59–61.—His captivity here continues two years. He pleads his cause before Felix, who detains him in the hope of a bribe. The Jews renew their charge against him before Festus. Paul is compelled to appeal to Cæsar. He speaks in the presence of King Agrippa, and is pronounced innocent.—Felix was superseded by Festus in A. D. 60 or 61.

62–64.—In the autumn of A. D. 60 or 61, Paul embarked at Cæsarea for Rome, and arrived there early in the following spring. He remains in custody two years. During this period he wrote the Epistles to the Ephesians, Colossians, Philippians, Philemon, and, if he suffered martyrdom at this time, the Second Epistle to Timothy, just before his death. The Epistle to the Hebrews was written, probably, in this latter part of the apostle's life. Most of those who maintain that Paul was imprisoned twice at Rome suppose (the correct opinion, as it seems to me) that he wrote the First Epistle to Timothy and that to Titus in the interval between his first and second captivity, and his Second Epistle to Timothy in the near prospect of his execution, after his second arrest.

COMMENTARY

FOR THE READER.

THE works on the Greek language to which most frequent reference has been made are the following:

W., WINER's *Grammatik des neutestamentlichen Sprachidioms*, sixth edition, 1855 (the divisions in the English translation, fourth edition, sometimes differ).

S., PROF. STUART's *Grammar of the New Testament Dialect*, second edition.

K., KUEHNER's *Greek Grammar*, translated by Edwards and Taylor.

C., CROSBY's *Greek Grammar*.

B., BUTTMANN's, Robinson's translation.

Mt., MATTHIÆ's, third edition of the original, or Blomfield's translation.

Dnld., *Gr.*, DONALDSON's *Complete Greek Grammar* (London, 1848).

Bernh., *Synt.*, BERNHARDY's *Wissenschaftliche Syntax*.

Hart., *Partkl.*, HARTUNG's *Lehre von den Partikeln, u. s. w.*

Kl., *Devr.*, *Devarius, De Gr. Ling. Particulis*, edidit KLOTZ.

Lob., *Phryn.*, *Phrynichi Eclogæ Nominum*, edidit LOBECK.

Tittm., *Synm.*, TITTMANN, *De Synonymis* in *N. Testamento*.

Pape, *Lex.*, *Handwörterbuch der Griechischen Sprache*, von DR. W. PAPE (Braunsschweig, 1842).

R. and P., *Lex.*, *Passow, Handwörterbuch der Gr. Sprache*, neu bearbeitet, u. s. w., von DR. ROST und DR. PALM (Leipzig, 1841–56).

Some other names, especially those of commentators or critics, mentioned often, as well as titles of books quoted often, have been abbreviated. A list of such contractions will be found at the end of the volume.

28

THE ACTS OF THE APOSTLES.

CHAPTER I.

THE former treatise have I made, O ^aTheophilus, of all that Jesus began both to do and teach.	1 THE [1]former treatise I made, O Theophilus, concerning all that Jesus began both to do and to teach,

a Luke 1 : 3.——1 Gr. *first.*

Ch. 1 : 1–3. RELATION OF THE ACTS TO THE GOSPEL OF LUKE.

1. μέν, *solitarium—i. e.* without any following δέ. This omission, which occurs in the best writers, is very common in this book. (See v. 18; 3 : 13; 19 : 4; 26 : 4, etc. K. § 322. R. 4; W. § 63. I. 2. e.) The writer frames the clause in which he refers to his first history (μέν) as if he had intended to add here (δέ) that he would now relate how extensively the name of Jesus had been made known, and by what means. Being led, by the allusion to the ascension of Christ, to state the circumstances of that event, he drops the proposed antithesis and leaves the subject of the book to unfold itself from the course of the narrative.—πρῶτον (*first*) stands for the stricter πρότερον (*former*), like the interchange of *first* and *former* in English. (Comp. John 1 : 15, 30; 15 : 18; and perhaps Luke 2 : 2.)—**Treat:se,** "history," as in Herod. (6. 19), and thence onward.—**Theophilus.** He appears from Luke 1 : 3 to have been a man of rank, since **most excellent,** when prefixed in the Acts to the name of a person, refers, not to character, but to station. (See 23 : 26; 24 : 3; 26 : 25.) From the fact that Luke wrote his Gospel confessedly for Gentile readers, and that both there and here he has uniformly supplied such information respecting Jewish customs and places as they would need, we may conclude that Theophilus belonged to that class of readers, and that he was not, therefore, a Jew or a resident in Palestine. The manner in which the book terminates (see Introduct., p. 21) favors the supposition that he may have lived at Rome or in Italy. Some have urged it as an argument for that opinion that Luke has merely enumerated the names of places in Italy as if his readers were familiar with them; but the proof is not conclusive. He takes for granted a similar knowledge of the geography of Asia

Minor and Greece. He inserts no explanatory notices in this part of the history, unless we are to except 16 : 12; 27 : 12.—**Which Jesus both did and taught from the beginning** —viz. of his career. ὧν (*of which*) stands by attraction for ἅ (*which*). **Began** carries back the mind to the commencement of the Saviour's history, and is equivalent in sense to **from the beginning.** Hence this verb marks the limit of the narrative in one direction, as **until what day** does in the other. This adverbial sense belongs usually to the participle (Mt. § 558), but may be admitted also in the verb. (Hmph.[1] adopts this analysis in his second edition.) It gives the same result, though less directly, if we consider the expression as elliptical : **which he began** and proceeded **both to do,** etc. (Comp. v. 22; Matt. 20 : 8; Luke 23 : 5. See W. § 66. 1. c.) Other explanations have been proposed. Meyer finds in it an implied contrast between the labors of Christ and those of the apostles. He laid the foundation ; they were to build upon it and finish what he began. This seems to me farfetched. (But in his last edition Meyer retracts this opinion, and says justly that Ἰησοῦς (**Jesus**) with that contrastive force would naturally precede the verb.) Olshausen thinks that Luke intended to suggest by **began** (ἤρξατο) that Christ only commenced his work on earth ; that he still continues, and will complete, it in heaven. Baumgarten[2] (p. 3, *sq.*) contends for the same view, and deduces from it what he supposes to be Luke's special design in writing the Acts—viz. to represent the Saviour after his ascension as still acting through the apostles, and thus carrying forward by their agency the merely incipient labors of his life on earth. Of course, this activity of Christ, who is ever present with his people (Matt. 28 : 20), could not fail to be recognized in the history (as in 3 : 26; 4 : 30; 19 : 13, etc.) ; but it is impos-

---

[1] *A Commentary on the Acts of the Apostles,* by W. G. Humphry, B. D., late Fellow of Trinity College, Cambridge, etc. (London, 1854).

[2] *Die Apostelgeschichte oder der Entwickelungsgang der Kirche von Jerusalem bis Rom,* von M. Baumgarten (1852).

2 ^aUntil the day in which he was taken up, after that he through the Holy Ghost ^bhad given commandments unto the apostles whom he had chosen:
3 ^cTo whom also he shewed himself alive after his passion by many infallible proofs, being seen of them

2 until the day in which he was received up, after that he had given commandment through the Holy 3 Spirit unto the apostles whom he had chosen: to whom he also ^lshewed himself alive after his passion by many proofs, appearing unto them by the

a Mark 16 : 19 ; Luke 9 : 51 ; 24 : 51 ; ver. 9; 1 Tim. 3 : 16....*b* Matt. 28 : 19 ; Mark 16 : 15 ; John 25 : 21 ; ch. 10 : 41, 42....*c* Mark 16 : 14 ; Luke 24 : 36 ; John 20 : 19, 26 ; 21 : 1, 14 ; 1 Cor. 15 : 5.——l Gr. *presented.*

sible that the writer, with that object in view, should have left it to be so obscurely intimated. This alleged contrast between Luke's Gospel as simply a beginning and the Acts as a continuation of Christ's personal work, so far from being put forward with prominence, as we should expect, is not distinctly drawn out in a single passage. The truth is, as Lekebusch remarks (*Composition*, u. s. w., p. 203), the narrative contains no hint of any such relation of the two histories to each other, unless this be found in **began ;** and even this word, as we have seen, admits much more naturally of a different explanation. A caution against re-garding this verb as superfluous here, or in any passage, can hardly be needed. (See W. § 65. 7. d.)

2. What day (ἧς ἡμέρας) = **the day in which** (τῆς ἡμέρας ᾗ), as in Matt. 24 : 38 ; Luke 1 : 20.— **Had given command,** I understand, with Meyer and others, as referring to Christ's command to preach the gospel to all the world, as recorded in Matt. 28 : 19, and which, from its memorable character, Luke could assume as well known to his readers. De Wette supposes it to be the command in v. 4 ; but we have then an unnecessary repetition of the same thing, and, contrary to the natural order, the allusion first and the fuller notice last. Some have proposed to extend the meaning of the word so as to embrace all the instructions which Christ gave to the apostles in relation to their future work, but the term is too specific for so general an idea ; and, besides, the obvious implication is that the giving of the command was something almost immediately antecedent to the ascension.—**Through the Holy Spirit,** his influence, guidance. This noun, as so used, may omit the article or receive it, at the option of the writer, since it has the force of a proper name. (W. § 19. 1. See also Ellicott's note on Gal. 4 : 6.) [Besides the careful statement of Winer as to the New Testament use of the article (§ 19), see Buttmann's *Gram. of the N. T. Greek* (Thayer's translation), pp. 85–90; Green's *Gram. of the New Test.*, ch. ii. p. 28, f. ; and *Bib. Sac. 1882*, pp. 159–190 : "The Article in the Revised Version," by Prof. W. S. Tyler. The rule given by Winer for the present case is that " appellatives, which, as expressing definite objects,

should have the article, are . . . employed in certain cases without it. This omission, however, only takes place when it . . . leaves no doubt in the mind of the reader whether the object is to be understood as definite or indefinite." Among the words that may thus take or omit the article are " sun," " earth," " heaven," " God," " Lord," " Holy Spirit ;" and their meaning is essentially the same whether used with or without the article. It has indeed been said that the designation " Holy Spirit," without the article, refers to the operations of the Spirit, and with the article to the Spirit as a person ; but this distinction is precarious. In English the appellative " Holy Scripture " may be used either with or without the article, after the analogy of the Greek words that are virtually proper names.—A.H.] These words attach themselves naturally to the participle(E.V., **had given command**) which they accompany, and it is forced, as well as unnecessary, to connect them with the verb in the next clause. This passage, in accordance with other passages, represents the Saviour as having been endued abundantly with the influences of the Spirit, and as having acted always in conformity with its [his] dictates. (See 10 : 38 ; Luke 4 : 1 ; John 3 : 34, etc.) That subjection was one of the laws of his dependent nature. That he revealed the command **through the Holy Spirit** cannot be meant, for the history shows that he gave this direction to them in person.—**Whom he had chosen.** The aorist stands often for our pluperfect after a relative or a relative expression. (W. § 40. 5.) —**Was taken up**—*i. e. into heaven.* (Comp. Mark 16 : 19 and Luke 24 : 51.) The abbreviation shows how accustomed the early disciples were to recur to this event.

3. To whom also. Also joins **showed himself** to **whom he had chosen.** The persons whom Christ had selected as his apostles were the same **to whom also he shewed himself,** etc. Thus they not only received their office directly from Christ, but were able to testify from their own personal knowledge to the reality of his resurrection. (Comp. 2 : 32 and 3 : 15. See note on v. 22.)—**After he had suffered**—viz. the death of the cross. (See Heb. 13 : 12 and 1 Pet. 3 : 18.) The term occurs thus absolutely in 3 : 18 and 17 : 3 (comp.

forty days, and speaking of the things pertaining to the kingdom of God:

4 [a]And, being assembled together with *them*, commanded them that they should not depart from Jerusalem, but wait for the promise of the Father, [b]which, *saith he*, ye have heard of me.

5 [c]For John truly baptized with water; [d]but ye

space of forty days, and speaking the things con-4 cerning the kingdom of God: and, [l]being assembled together with them, he charged them not to depart from Jerusalem, but to wait for the promise of the 5 Father, which, *said he*, ye heard from me: for John

a Luke 24 : 43, 49....b Luke 24 : 49; John 14 : 16, 26, 27; 15 : 26; 16 : 7; ch. 2 : 33....c Matt. 3 : 11; ch. 11 : 16; 19 : 4....d Joel 3 : 18; ch. 2 : 4; 11 : 15.——1 Or, *eating with them*

also 26, 23), and is a striking usage. It arose probably out of the impression which the painful nature of Christ's sufferings had made on the first disciples.—**In many proofs,** or if, as De Wette suggests, the idea of the verb mingles with that of the noun, **in many convincing manifestations.** τεκμήριον (*proof*) does not occur elsewhere in the New Testament, and is a very expressive term. Plato uses it to denote the strongest possible logical proof, as opposed to that which is weaker, and Aristotle employs it to signify demonstrative evidence. The language seems to show that the first Christians had distinctly revolved the question whether the Saviour's resurrection was real or not, and had assured themselves of its reality by evidence which did not admit in their minds of the shadow of a doubt. Our infallible proofs" {E. V.; Gen. V: *infallible tokens*—both founded on Beza's *certissimis signis*) does not express the sense too strongly. (Compare the idea with 1 John 1 : 1.)—**During forty days appearing to them** (as in all the earlier E. Vv.)—*i. e.* from time to time, as related by the Evangelists; not pass. *seen by them* (E. V.). ὀπτανόμενος (not elsewhere in N. T.) agrees best as middle with the active sense of the other verbs, and with 1 Kings 8 : 8 (Sept.). (See Tromm's *Concord.*, s. v.) Wahl (*Clav. Apocr.*, s. ὁράω) should not have put down the use in Tob. 12 : 9 as certainly passive. Some have argued too positively from this word that Christ rose from the grave with a glorified body. It represents his appearing to the disciples, perhaps, as occasional and sudden (comp. ὤφθη in 7 : 26), but does not decide whether the state out of which he appeared was a spiritual and invisible one, or merely some place of retirement after a temporary absence. The Saviour had accomplished the great end of his earthly work when he rose from the dead, and after that, until his ascension, appears to have mingled only at times with his followers. Some mystery rests, no doubt, on the last days of his life; but the idea that he possessed a spiritual body before he returned to heaven appears to me irreconcilable with Luke 24 : 39 and John 20 : 27. (See the article on our Lord's resurrection body in *Bibl. Sac.*, vol. ii. p. 405, *sq.*) [There are four views as to the body of Jesus during

the forty days between his resurrection and his ascension: (1) That it was his natural body, unchanged in its relations to his spiritual being, but simply reanimated, as were those of the widow's son and Jairus's daughter, the change to a spiritual body being effected afterward at his ascension. This view Dr. Hackett evidently favors. It supposes that Jesus spent a very large part of the forty days in some unknown place or places of retirement; from which coming forth occasionally and presenting himself to his disciples, he is said to have appeared to them. (2) That it was his "natural body," unchanged at the moment of reanimation, but undergoing through the forty days a gradual process of transformation into the spiritual body with which he ascended into heaven. (3) That it was the same body which was laid in the tomb, "but endued with new powers, properties, and attributes." (See Ellicott, *The Life of our Lord*, Lec. VIII., note 3.) This view appears to afford the most natural explanation of the language of the sacred writers. (4) That it was an ethereal body, something between matter and spirit. This appears to be inconsistent with the passages referred to above by Dr. Hackett.—A. H.]

4, 5. THE PROMISE OF THE SAVIOUR TO SEND THE SPIRIT.

4. Being assembled (E. V.)—*i. e.* **with them,** as mentioned in Luke 24 : 49; not **assembling them** (Kuin., Olsh., and earlier E. Vv.). Nearly all the later critics reject the middle sense as unproved.—**To await the promise,** its fulfilment, realization. (Comp. Gal. 3 : 14.) Not **promise** = *that promised*—*i. e.* the promised Holy Spirit (Rob., *N. T. Lex.*), which is less congruous with the following verb. (See W. ? 34. 3.) It is said to be the promise of the Father, because it was foretold in the Old Testament that he would bestow it. (See 2 : 16; Joel 3 : 1, 2.)—**Which you heard from me,** as recorded in Luke 24 : 49. (See also John 15 : 26; 16 : 13.) For the verb with the accusative and genitive, see K. ? 273. R. 18; W. ? 30. 7. c. The style of discourse changes suddenly from the indirect to the direct, as in 17 : 3; 23 : 22, and often. (W. ? 63. II. 2.; S. ? 196. 2.)

5. With water, as the element by which.

shall be baptized with the Holy Ghost not many days hence.

6 When they therefore were come together, they asked of him, saying, ᵃLord, wilt thou at this time ᵇrestore again the kingdom to Israel?

7 And he said unto them, ᶜIt is not for you to know the times or the seasons, which the Father hath put in his own power.

indeed baptized with water; but ye shall be baptized ¹in the Holy Spirit not many days hence.

6 They therefore, when they were come together, asked him, saying, Lord, dost thou at this time re-7 store the kingdom to Israel? And he said unto them, It is not for you to know times or seasons, which the

---

a Matt. 24 : 3....*b* Isa. 1 : 26; Dan. 7 : 27; Amos 9 : 11....*c* Matt. 24 : 36; Mark 13 : 32; 1 Thess. 5 : 1.——1 Or, *with*

---

in the Holy Spirit, as the element in which, the baptism is performed. The insertion of ἐν (*in*) may be slightly localizing with reference to a copious impartation of the Spirit's gifts and influences. [The preposition ἐν is always expressed when baptism in the Holy Spirit is spoken of, but often omitted when baptism in water is referred to—perhaps because the local sense is sufficiently expressed by the verb when followed by the *customary* element for immersion, while it needs to be made certain when that element is spiritual.—A. H.] **Not after these many days,** after not many, a few. This mode of inverting the signification of an adjective is frequent in Luke's style. If this assurance was given on the day of the ascension, only ten days were now to pass before the promised effusion of the Spirit. (Comp. v. 3 with 2 : 1.) But if, as maintained below, we are to distinguish the meeting in v. 4 from that in v. 6, we cannot decide exactly how long the interval was, not knowing on which of the **forty days** (v. 3) the earlier interview took place. **These,** being the pronoun which points out what is near at hand (ἐκεῖνος, what is more remote), represents the days as closely connected with the present. It is not superfluous, therefore, but strengthens the idea of the brevity of the interval.

6-11. HIS LAST INTERVIEW WITH THE DISCIPLES, AND HIS ASCENSION.

6. They therefore (the **them** in v. 4) **having come together** on a subsequent occasion (Calv., Olsh., E. V., and earlier E. Vv. except Wicl. and Rhem.), or **they who came together** at the time spoken of in v. 4 (Vulg., Mey., De Wet., Alf.). [In his last edition—the fourth—Meyer holds that this is a different interview from the one spoken of in v. 4, thus agreeing with Dr. Hackett.—A. H.] I incline to the first view, because, as Olshausen suggests, Luke in his Gospel (24 : 49 as compared with v. 50) appears to assign the direction to remain at Jerusalem to an earlier interview than the one which terminated in Christ's ascension (as even De Wette admits in his *Synop. Evang.*, p. 298), and because συνελθόντες (**having come together**), when understood of the same

assembling, becomes so nearly tautological after **assembling with them** in v. 4. οὖν (**therefore**) depends naturally on v. 3. The kingdom of God having been the subject of so much discourse between Christ and the apostles, they **therefore,** in this last interview, **asked him,** etc. Hence no necessary inference can be drawn from this particle (as Alf. urges) against supposing a separation after the coming together in v. 4.—**If in this time thou dost restore.** Their inquiry indicates an established faith in him as the Messiah, but betrays, at the same time, an expectation that his kingdom would be to some extent a temporal one—that it would free the nation from their dependence on the Romans and restore to them their ancient prosperity and power. This worldly view may have been the preponderant one in the question which they ask, though we are to suppose, of course, that, after having been so long associated with Christ, they had far more intelligent views respecting the spiritual nature of the Messiah's mission than the great mass of the Jews entertained. εἰ (*if*) introduces a direct question, which is contrary to classical usage, though not uncommon in the New Testament and the Septuagint. (K. ₰344. 5. i.; W. ₰ 57. 2.) Originally εἰ may have involved a suppressed thought in such cases: *saying*, We desire to know *if*, etc. (See Meyer on Matt. 12 : 10.)—**Dost restore** is present for an immediate future. (W. ₰ 40. 2; K. ₰ 255. R. 4.)

7. Times or occasions. (See Tittm., *De Synon. N. T.*, p. 39.) It is one thing to know the general period of an event; another, to know the precise time of its occurrence.— **Which the Father arranged,** or **fixed, in his own power**—*i. e.* in the sovereign exercise of it. (Comp. Matt. 21 : 23. De Wet., Mey., Hmph.) The implied inference is that he may be expected to reserve the knowledge of such decisions to himself. All the E. Vv. (as far as I know) render **hath put** (defended also by Alf.) as = *hath kept.* The perfect would be the more obvious form with that meaning, though the aorist, **put,** "placed," may imply the same. The question of the disciples, as Bengel observes, relates merely to the time when Christ

8 *But ye shall receive power, *after that the Holy
Ghost is come upon you: and *ye shall be witnesses
unto me both in Jerusalem, and in all Judæa, and in
Samaria, and unto the uttermost part of the earth.
9 *And when he had spoken these things, while they
beheld, *he was taken up; and a cloud received him
out of their sight.
10 And while they looked stedfastly toward heaven
as he went up, behold, two men stood by them *in
white apparel;
11 Which also said, *Ye men of Galilee, why stand
ye gazing up into heaven? this same Jesus, which is
taken up from you into heaven, *shall so come in like
manner as ye have seen him go into heaven.

8 Father hath ¹set within his own authority. But ye
shall receive power, when the Holy Spirit is come
upon you: and ye shall be my witnesses both in
Jerusalem, and in all Judæa and Samaria, and unto
9 the uttermost part of the earth. And when he had
said these things, as they were looking, he was taken
up; and a cloud received him out of their sight.
10 And while they were looking stedfastly into heaven
as he went up, behold, two men stood by them in white
11 apparel; who also said, Ye men of Galilee, why
stand ye looking into heaven? this Jesus, who was
received up from you into heaven, shall so come in
like manner as ye beheld him going into heaven.

a ch. 2 : 1, 4....b Luke 24 : 49....c Luke 24 : 48; John 15 : 27; ver. 22; ch. 2 : 32....d Luke 24 : 51; John 6 : 62....e ver. 2....f Matt.
28 : 3; Mark 16 : 5; Luke 24 : 4; John 20 : 12; ch. 10 : 3, 30....g ch. 2 : 7; 13 : 31....h Dan. 7 : 13; Matt. 24 : 30; Mark 13 : 26; Luke
21 : 27; John 14 : 3; 1 Thess. 1 : 10; 4 : 16; 2 Thess. 1 : 10; Rev. 1 : 7.——1 Or, *appointed by*

would establish his kingdom; and his answer,
as here given, he confines to the same point.
Their remaining misconceptions as to the nature of that kingdom were soon to be removed
more effectually than by any formal instruction.

8. But marks the opposition between what
was denied to the disciples on the one hand,
and what was to be granted to them on the
other.—**Power,** "efficiency "—*i. e.* every needful qualification to render them efficient in
their apostolic sphere. (See Luke 24 : 49.) The
power of working miracles is included, but
does not exhaust the idea.—**When the Holy
Spirit.** This clause designates the time when
they should receive this power, as well as the
source of it. The construction is that of the
genitive absolute. The dependence of πνεύματος
on δύναμιν (we miss the article in that case) is
less easy, but is preferred by some.—Read μου
for μοί after ἔσεσθε. [*i. e.* **ye shall be my
witnesses, not witnesses for me.**—A. H.]
Uttermost—*i. e. part.* Compare the language
here with Matt. 28 : 19; Mark 16 : 15. It is impossible that the disciples should not have understood from it that their sphere of labor was
to be coextensive with the world. (See the
remarks on 2 : 39.) The foregoing conversation may have taken place on Olivet (see v. 12)
or during the walk thither.

9. Saying these things, and still others
(Luke 24 : 51). His last accents were those of
love and benediction.—**Was taken up**—*i. e.*
into the air; not yet into heaven, on account
of the next verb; hence different, also, from
was taken up in v. 2, which represents the
act as completed.—**Received up** (lit. " under,"
with the cloud as it were beneath him), and at
the same time, by a pregnant construction, *away*,
hence followed by ἀπό (*from*). (See W. § 66. 2.)
This verb describes the close of the scene, as far
as it was visible to the spectators.

10. As they were gazing toward heav-
3

en. This compound imperfect is stronger than
the simple, both as to the duration of the act
and the prominence given to it. The student
should note this usage; though not rare in the
classics, it is still more common in the New
Testament. (See Green's *Gr.*, p. 103; K. § 238.
R. 7.) Kuinoel refers **into heaven** to **went
up,** which separates the words from their natural connection, and leaves **were gazing** without any indirect object, as in 3 : 4, 12; 14 : 9,
and elsewhere.—**Then behold** = Heb. *věhin-
neh.* (Comp. Matt. 9 : 10; Luke 2 : 15; 24 : 4.)
This Hebraistic use of καί in the apodosis of a
sentence, after an expression or idea of time,
is frequent in the New Testament. (See Brud.,
Gr. Concord., p. 456; W. § 53. 3. f.)—**Men,** in
form; really, angels. (See Mark 16 : 5; Luke
24 : 4.)—**Were standing** while the disciples
gazed; pluperf. = imperf. in this verb.

11. Who also said, as well as appeared to
them. (See on v. 3.)—**Why stand ye,** etc.
The precise import of this address of the angels
is not certain. As compared with such passages as Luke 24 : 5, 25, 26, and others, it may
suggest that the apostles should have been prepared in some measure for the event which had
filled them with such astonishment. They had
been distinctly apprised by Christ (see John 6 :
62; 20 : 17) that he must ascend again to God,
from whom he came; and the wonders which
they had seen in their intercourse with him
should have diminished their surprise at what
had taken place. The inquiry, as so understood,
leads naturally to the announcement which follows. It should abate the astonishment of the
disciples at what had taken place to know that
it was not the only event of the kind which
was to enter into the history of the Saviour;
he whom they had seen ascend into heaven was
destined to come again in like manner. According to Calvin, the disciples linger on the
spot, distressed at the Saviour's sudden departure from them, and still gazing upward, not

12 *Then returned they unto Jerusalem from the mount called Olivet, which is from Jerusalem a sabbath day's journey.

12 Then returned they unto Jerusalem from the mount called Olivet, which is nigh unto Jerusalem,

a Luke 24 : 52.

without a hope that possibly he might reappear. The address of the angels reproves them for this expectation, and at the same time consoles them with the assurance of his return at some future time. Meyer's view is nearly the same.—**In like manner,** lit. **in what manner**—*i. e.* visibly, and in the air (Bng., De Wet., Mey., Olsh.). The expression is never employed to affirm merely the certainty of one event as compared with another. The assertion that

21 : 1 we have **mount of the olives.** Josephus employs the designation which occurs here in *Antt.,* 7. 9. 2. Olive trees still grow on the mount of ascension, and thus vindicate the propriety of the ancient name. On their return to Jerusalem the disciples must have passed Gethsemane. What new thoughts would crowd upon their minds as they gazed at the spot after the scene just witnessed!—ἔχον, **having,** amounting to; not=ἀπέχον, **distant,**

MOUNT OF OLIVES.

the meaning is simply that as Christ had departed so also he would return is contradicted by every passage in which the phrase occurs. (See 7 : 28; Matt. 23 : 37; Luke 13 : 34; 2 Tim. 3 : 8.)

12-14. RETURN OF THE DISCIPLES TO JERUSALEM.

12. From the mount (definite from the annexed clause, though the article could be used; see Luke 19 : 29) **which is called Olivet.** We are indebted for this beautiful name to the Latin *Olivetum* (in Vulg.)—*i. e.* a place set with olives; hence the exact import of ἐλαιών. This word is so accentuated also by Lchm., Tsch., Mey., even in Luke 19 : 29 and 21 : 37, instead of ἐλαιῶν in the common editions. In Matt.

as often represented. A Sabbath-day's journey was the distance—about three-quarters of a mile—to which "the traditions of the elders" restricted the Jews in travelling on the Sabbath. In Luke 24 : 50, 51 it is said that our Saviour led the disciples as far as to Bethany, and that there, while in the act of blessing them, he was parted from them and carried up into heaven. It was at Bethany, therefore, or in the vicinity of Bethany, that the ascension took place. That account is entirely consistent with this. Bethany was on the eastern declivity of the Mount of Olives, and, as appears from Mark 11 : 1 and Luke 19 : 29, was reckoned as a part of it; so that the disciples, in returning from that place to the city, took their way naturally across the

13 And when they were come in, they went up *into an upper room, where abode both *Peter, and James, and John, and Andrew, Philip, and Thomas, Bartholomew, and Matthew, James *the son* of Alphæus, and *Simon Zelotes, and *Judas *the brother* of James.
14 *These all continued with one accord in prayer and supplication, with *the women, and Mary the mother of Jesus, and with *his brethren.

13 a sabbath day's journey off. And when they were come in, they went up into the upper chamber, where they were abiding; both Peter and John and James and Andrew, Philip and Thomas, Bartholomew and Matthew, James *the son* of Alphæus, and
14 Simon the Zealot, and Judas *the *son of James. These all with one accord continued stedfastly in prayer, ²with the women, and Mary the mother of Jesus, and with his brethren.

a ch. 9 : 37, 39; 20 : 8....b Matt. 10 : 2, 3, 4....c Luke 6 : 15....d Jude 1 ...e ch. 2 : 1, 46....f Luke 23 : 49, 55 ; 24 : 10....
g Matt. 13 : 55.——1 Or, brother. See Jude 1....2 Or, *with* certain *women*

mountain. (See Rob., *Bibl. Res.*, vol. ii. p. 100 ; or p. 431 in ed. of 1856.) Luke specifies here the distance of Olivet from the city, instead of that of Bethany, which was about two miles (comp. John 11 : 18), because the former was better known to most of his readers, and conveyed a sufficiently definite idea of the scene of the ascension.

13. Had entered (tense as in v. 2), into the city, probably, not the house. What precedes suggests the place, rather than what follows.— **Into the upper room,** of some private house, not of the temple. The opinion that it was the latter some have supposed to be required by Luke 24 : 53. But *continually,* as used there, need not signify anything more than a frequent resort ; they were in the temple *always* on the occasions when men in their state of mind would naturally repair thither. (See 2 : 46 ; Luke 2 : 37.) Even De Wette allows that the passages involve no discrepancy. As the disciples must have been well known as the followers of Christ, we cannot well suppose that the Jewish rulers would have allowed them to occupy an apartment in the temple. The upper room, either directly under the flat roof or upon it with a roof of its own, was retired, and hence convenient for private or social worship. The Hebrews were accustomed to use it for such purposes. (See 20 : 8, and Dan. 6 : 10, Sept.) Travellers describe such rooms at the present day as airy and spacious. (See *Bibl. Res.*, vol. ii. p. 229, ed. 1856.) On the formation of ὑπερῷον, see W. § 16. 2.—**Where were abiding.** Weakened in E. V. (**abode**), as if it were the simple imperf. (See on v. 10.) We could understand this of constant residence, but more naturally here of frequent resort for religious conference and prayer (De Wet.).—**James of Alphæus**—*i. e.* son : **James the son of Alphæus ;** but after **Judas** we supply **brother: Judas the brother of James.** (See Jude 1.) The nature of the relationship in such a case is not determined by the construction, but is left to the knowledge of the reader. (W. § 30. 3 ; C. § 389.)—**The Zealot = Kananite** in Matt. 10 : 4, from the Hebrew *kanna.* He

is supposed to have received this epithet on account of his former zeal as a supporter of Judaism. As there was another Simon among the apostles, he appears to have retained the name after he became a disciple, as a means of distinction, though it had now ceased to mark the trait of character from which it arose. It has been said that he took the appellation from his having belonged to a political sect known as the zealots, who are mentioned by Josephus ; but the party distinguished by that name in Jewish history did not appear till a later period.

14. With one mind. The term characterizes the entire harmony of their views and feelings. (Comp. Rom. 15 : 6.)—**Unto the** (work of) **prayer,** where **the** points out that as the appropriate way in which they were occupied. **And the supplication** the best editors regard as an addition to the text. It serves merely to strengthen the expression. (Comp. Phil. 4 : 6.)—**With women.** Among them may have been those who followed Christ from Galilee. (See Luke 23 : 55 ; 24 : 10.) It is incorrect to suppose that they are meant exclusively. The absence of the article forbids that restriction.—**And** (among them especially) **Mary.** καί (**and**) combines often a part with its whole for the sake of prominence. This is the last time that the mother of Jesus is named in the New Testament.—**His brethren** may mean *his brethren* in a strict sense, or more generally his *kinsmen,* relatives. The same question arises in regard to Matt. 13 : 55, though the closer relationship there, as well as here, is the more obvious one, and finds very strong support from Matt. 1 : 25. [That is, if, as Dr. Hackett appears to have been satisfied, the common text of that passage is correct. But Lach., Tsch., Treg., West. and Hort, and the Anglo-Am. Revisers omit **her first-born,** and read **till she had brought forth a son.** If their view of the text be adopted, the passage has no bearing on the point in question. The reading of Luke 2 : 7, however, is sure ; and it is said there that *she brought forth her first-born son,* etc. This, with the evidence

15 ¶ And in those days Peter stood up in the midst of the disciples, and said, (the number *of names together were about an hundred and twenty,)

16 Men *and* brethren, this scripture must needs have been fulfilled, *which the Holy Ghost by the mouth of David spake before concerning Judas, *which was guide to them that took Jesus.

17 For *he was numbered with us, and had obtained part of *this ministry.

18 *Now this man purchased a field with *the reward

15 And in these days Peter stood up in the midst of the brethren, and said (and there was a multitude of ¹persons *gathered* together, about a hundred and

16 twenty), Brethren, it was needful that the scripture should be fulfilled, which the Holy Spirit spake before by the mouth of David concerning Judas, who

17 was guide to them that took Jesus. For he was numbered among us, and received his ²portion in this

18 ministry. (Now this man obtained a field with the reward of his iniquity; and falling headlong, he

---

a Rev. 3 : 4....*b* Ps. 41 : 9 ; John 13 : 18....*c* Luke 22 : 47 : John 18 : 3....*d* Matt. 10 : 4 ; Luke 6 : 16....*e* ver. 25 ; ch. 12 : 25 ; 20 : 24 ; 21 : 19....*f* Matt. 27 : 5, 7, 8.... *g* Matt. 26 : 15 ; 2 Pet. 2 : 15.——1 Gr. *names*....2 Or, *lot*

---

from other sources, seems to be more consistent with the opinion that **his brethren** were either the sons of Joseph and Mary, or of Joseph by an earlier marriage, than with any other opinion.—A. H.] The brethren of Jesus had not believed on him at first (see John 7 : 5), but we discover here that they had now joined the circle of his followers.

15–22. THE ADDRESS OF PETER ON THE CHOICE OF A NEW APOSTLE.

15. In those days is indefinite as a notation of time. The same language in Matt. 3 : 1 marks an interval of thirty years. (Comp. also Ex. 2 : 11.) Here a short time only could have elapsed, as the ascension of Christ forms the limit on one side and the day of Pentecost on the other.—τε. It is worth remarking that this particle rarely occurs in the New Testament out of the Acts and the writings of Paul.— **Names = men,** as in Rev. 3 : 4 ; 11 : 13. The term may have acquired this sense from the practice of taking the census by registration or enrollment, inasmuch as the names on such a record are equivalent to persons.—ἐπὶ τὸ αὐτό— lit. **unto the same place,** implying an antecedent motion. It means, not that they were so many collectively, but that so many came **together** at this time. (See 2 : 1 ; 3 : 1 ; 1 Cor. 11 : 20 ; 14 : 23.)—**A hundred and twenty.** We are to understand these *hundred and twenty* as the number of the disciples at Jerusalem, not as the entire number of those who had believed. (See 1 Cor. 15 : 6.)

16. Men is not superfluous, but renders the address more respectful. It is a compliment to be recognized as men. (See 2 : 29, 37 ; 7 : 2 ; 13 : 15, and often.)—**Was necessary.** The tense is past, because the speaker has his mind on the part of the prediction already accomplished.—**This** refers to the double citation in v. 20. The parenthetic character of vs. 18, 19 accounts for the distance of the antecedent, which in this case follows the pronoun. (See K. ? 332. 8).—**Which the Holy Spirit spake beforehand,** etc. We have a similar testimony to the inspiration of the Scriptures from

the same apostle in 2 Pet. 1 : 21.—**Concerning Judas** belongs by both position and construction to **spake before,** not to **have been fulfilled.** ἐν or ἐπί would have followed the latter verb.—**Who became** (not *was*, E. V.) **guide,** who acted so base a part, though professedly a friend. (See Matt. 26 : 47 ; John 18 : 2, *sq.*)

17. Here the second passage in v. 20 was before the speaker's mind. That passage contemplates the case of an office transferred from one person to another ; and, since forfeiture implies previous possession, it is the object of **for he was,** etc. (ὅτι . . . ἐν ἡμῖν), to remind us that Judas had fulfilled that condition of the passage : **for he was numbered among us**—i. e. the apostles. (For that limitation of **us,** see the next clause, and also v. 26.) The full connection, therefore, is this : The prophecy speaks of a **ministry** which another shall take ; Judas held such an office, **for he was numbered,** etc. ; so that the words apply to him. To render ὅτι "although" (Hmph.) is not allowable.— **The lot,** or **office, of this ministry** which we possess—i. e. the apostleship. (Comp. Rom. 11 : 13.) **Lot** loses often its figurative sense, so as to denote a possession without any reference to the mode of its attainment. Our word "clergy" comes from this term, being founded on the idea of the order as one divinely appointed.

18. This verse and the next are considered by most critics as an explanatory remark of Luke (Calv., Kuin., Olsh., Hmph.), not as a part of Peter's address. The reader might need this information, but those who listened to the apostle may be supposed to have been familiar with the fate of Judas. It is evident that **insomuch that,** etc. (ὥστε κληθῆναι . . . αἵματος), though appropriate to the history, could hardly have belonged to the discourse. **For** in v. 20 appears to demand this view of the intervening verses. μὲν οὖν does not forbid this supposition (Alf.), since Luke certainly could adjust his own words to the context, as well as those of Peter, reported by him. Some such horrible

of iniquity; and falling headlong, he burst asunder in the midst, and all his bowels gushed out.

burst asunder in the midst, and all his bowels

end of the traitor was to be inferred (οὖν, *therefore*) from the phrase **this Scripture** (see on v. 20); and it was not at all unnatural that Luke should interrupt the speech at this point, and inform us how remarkably the death of Judas agreed with this prediction. Further, it is strange that the citation in v. 20 should be kept back so long after **this** in v. 16, except on the view that Luke inserted what intervenes. Bengel restricts the parenthesis to the explanation respecting Aceldama. μέν stands alone, as in v. 1.—*Purchased*, or *caused to be purchased*, gave occasion for it—*i. e.* it was in consequence of his act, and with the money gained by his treachery, that the field was purchased, as related in Matt. 27 : 6, *sq.* The great body of critics adopt this view of the meaning (Bez., Bretsch., Kuin., Frtz., Thol.,[1] Olsh., Ebr., Mey., Rob.). This briefer mode of expression is common in every language, and may be employed without obscurity where the reader is presumed to be familiar with the facts in the case, or when the nature of the act itself suggests the proper modification. The following are analogous examples in the New Testament. Matt. 27 : 60: "And Joseph laid the body of Christ in his own new tomb, which he had hewn out in a rock"—*i. e.* caused to be hewn out for him; John 4 : 1: "And when the Lord knew that the Pharisees heard that Jesus made and baptized more disciples than John"—*i. e.* through his disciples; for he himself baptized not. (See 7 : 21; 16 : 22; Matt. 2 : 16; 1 Cor. 7 : 16; 1 Tim. 4 : 16.) These cases are plain and no one refuses to admit the causative sense (not directly expressed, but implied) which belongs to the verb in such passages. The principle which this mode of speaking involves, the law recognizes even in regard to actions in its well-known maxim, *Qui facit per alium, facit per se* ("Who does a thing by another does it himself"). It is only by refusing to extend this usage to ἐκτήσατο that such writers as Strauss make out their allegation of a

want of agreement between this passage and Matt. 27 : 5. Fritzsche's suggestion[2] as to the reason why Luke expressed himself in this unusual manner deserves notice. He finds in it a studied, significant brevity, a sort of *acerba irrisio* ("bitter mockery"), bringing the motive and the result into pointed antithesis to each other: This man thought to enrich himself by his treachery, but all that he gained was that he got for himself a field where blood was paid for blood.—πρηνής (**on the face**) is strictly the opposite of ὕπτιος (*on the back*). His falling in that position may have occasioned the bursting asunder; that view agrees well with γενόμενος, though πρηνής admits also of the vaguer sense *headlong.*—ἐλάκησε is the first aorist from λάσκω. (W. § 15; K. § 230.)—In Matt. 27 : 5 it is said that Judas, after having brought his money and thrown it down in the temple, went and hanged or strangled himself. Objectors have represented that account also as inconsistent with this, but without reason. Matthew does not say that Judas, after having hanged himself, *did not* fall to the ground and burst asunder; nor, on the contrary, does Luke say that Judas *did not* hang himself before he fell to the ground; and it is obvious that the matter should have been so stated, in order to warrant the charge of inconsistency. We have no certain knowledge as to the mode in which we are to so combine the two accounts as to connect the act of suicide with what happened to the body. It has been thought not improbable that Judas may have hung himself from the limb of a tree on the edge of a precipice near the Valley of Hinnom, and that, the rope breaking by which he was suspended, he fell to the earth and was dashed to pieces.[3] It will be observed that Luke's statement is entirely abrupt and supposes some antecedent history. In this respect Matthew's account, instead of involving any contradiction, becomes, in fact, confirmatory of the other. It shows, first, that Luke was aware that something preceded

---

[1] In unpublished *Notes on the Gospels*.

[2] *Evangelium Matthæi recensuit et cum Commentariis perpetuis edidit Carol. Fr. A. Fritzsche*, p. 799.

[3] As I stood in this valley on the south of Jerusalem, and looked up to the rocky terraces which hang over it, I felt that the explanation proposed above is entirely natural. I was more than ever satisfied with it. I measured the precipitous, almost perpendicular walls in different places, and found the height to be, variously, forty, thirty-six, thirty-three, thirty, and twenty-five feet. Trees still flourish on the margin of these precipices, and in ancient times must have been still more numerous in the same place. A rocky pavement exists, also, at the bottom of the ledges; and hence on that account, too, a person falling from above would be liable to be crushed and mangled, as well as killed. The traitor may have struck, in his fall, upon some pointed rock, which entered the body and caused "his bowels to gush out."

19 And it was known unto all the dwellers at Jerusalem: insomuch as that field is called in their proper tongue, Aceldama, that is to say, The field of blood.

20 For it is written in the book of Psalms, ^aLet his habitation be desolate, and let no man dwell therein: and ^bhis bishoprick let another take.

21 Wherefore of these men which have companied with us all the time that the Lord Jesus went in and out among us,

19 gushed out. And it became known to all the dwellers at Jerusalem; insomuch that in their language that field was called Akeldama, that is, The field of 20 blood.) For it is written in the book of Psalms,

Let his habitation be made desolate,
And let no man dwell therein:

and,

His ¹office let another take.

21 Of the men therefore who have companied with us

---

a Ps. 69 : 25... *b* Ps. 109 : 8.——1 Gr. *overseership*

---

which he has omitted to mention; and secondly, it puts us in the way of so combining events as to account better for the incomplete representation in the Acts than would otherwise have been possible.

19. And it became known—viz. that he came to so miserable an end.—**Aceldama** = *chakal dēma* belongs to the Aramæan or Syro-Chaldaic spoken at that time in Palestine. (On that language, see *Bibl. Repos.*, vol. i. p. 317, *sq.*) It was for a twofold reason, therefore, says Lightfoot, that the field received this appellation: first, because, as stated in Matt. 27 : 7, it had been bought with the price of blood; and secondly, because it was sprinkled with the man's blood who took that price. This is the common view, and so in the first edition; but I incline now to doubt its correctness. First, **falling headlong,** in v. 18, does not define at all where Judas fell; secondly, **that field** here recalls naturally **field** above merely as the field purchased with "the reward of iniquity;" and thirdly, if Judas fell into the Valley of Hinnom, no spot there at the foot of the rocks could well have been converted into a place of burial. Nor does the conciliation with Matt. 27 : 7 demand this view. Luke may be understood here as saying that "the field of blood" which the priests purchased with the money paid to Judas, whether situated in one place or another, was called Aceldama, because the fact of the traitor's bloody end was so notorious. Matthew (27:6) mentions another reason for the appellation, which was that the money paid for the field was the "price of blood"—not a different, but a concurrent, reason, showing that the ill-omened name could be used with a double emphasis. Tradition has placed "the potter's field" (Matt. 27:6) on the side of the hill which overlooks the Valley of Hinnom. It may have been in that quarter, or argillaceous clay is still found there, and receptacles for the dead appear in the rocks, proving that the ancient Jews were accustomed to bury there.[1]

20. The writer returns here to the address. **For** specifies the prophecy to which **this** points in v. 16; hence **namely** (as in Matt. 1 : 18). (See B. ∮ 149; K. ∮ 324. 2.) The first passage is Ps. 69 : 25 slightly abridged from the Septuagint, with an exchange of **their** for **his.** Its import is, Let his end be disastrous, his abode be desolate, and shunned as accursed. It is impossible to understand the entire Psalm as strictly Messianic, on account of v. 5: "O God, thou knowest my foolishness, and my sins are not hid from thee." It appears to belong rather to the class of Psalms which describe general relations, which contain prophecies or inspired declarations which are verified as often as individuals are placed in the particular circumstances which lay within the view, not necessarily of the writer, but of the Holy Spirit, at whose dictation they were uttered. When Peter, therefore, declares that this prophecy which he applies to Judas was spoken with special reference to him (see v. 16), he makes the impressive announcement to those whom he addressed that the conduct of Judas had identified him fully with such persecutors of the righteous as the Psalm contemplates; and hence it was necessary that he should suffer the doom deserved by those who sin in so aggravated a manner.—The other passage is Ps. 109 : 8 in the words of the Seventy. We are to apply here the same principle of interpretation as before. That Psalm sets forth, in like manner, the wickedness and desert of those who persecute the people of God; and hence, as Judas had exemplified so fully this idea, he too must be divested of his office, and its honors be transferred to another.

21. Therefore, since, as foretold, the place of the apostate must be filled.—**Of these men,** etc., depends properly on **one,** in v. 22, where the connection, so long interrupted, is reasserted by **these. — In every time.** The conception divides the period into its successive parts.— **In which he came in unto us, and went out**—i. e. lived and associated with us. The

---

[1] I have taken the liberty to repeat a few sentences here already published in another work. (See *Illustrations of Scripture suggested by a Tour through the Holy Land*, p. 266.) I have taken a similar liberty in a few other passages.

22 [a]Beginning from the baptism of John, unto that same day that [b]he was taken up from us, must one be ordained [c]to be a witness with us of his resurrection.
23 And they appointed two, Joseph called [d]Barsabas, who was surnamed Justus, and Matthias.
24 And they prayed, and said, Thou, Lord, [e]which knowest the hearts of all men, shew whether of these two thou hast chosen.

all the time that the Lord Jesus went in and went
22 out [1]among us, beginning from the baptism of John, unto the day that he was received up from us, of these must one become a witness with us of his
23 resurrection. And they put forward two, Joseph called Barsabbas, who was surnamed Justus, and
24 Matthias. And they prayed, and said, Thou, Lord, who knowest the hearts of all men, shew of these

---

a Mark 1 : 1....*b* ver. 9....*c* John 15 : 27 ; ver. 8 ; ch. 4 : 33....*d* ch. 15 : 22....*e* 1 Sam. 16 : 7 ; 1 Chr. 28 : 9 ; 29 : 17 ; Jer. 11 : 20 ; 17 : 10 ; ch. 15 : 8 ; Rev. 2 : 23.———1 Or, *over*

---

entire life or course of life is described by one of its most frequent acts. It is a Hebrew mode of speaking (comp. Deut. 28 : 19 ; 31 : 2, etc.), and is used properly of those who sustain official relations or perform public labors. (See 9 : 28.) An exact construction of the Greek would have placed **unto us** after the first verb, and inserted *from us* after the second. (W. § 66. 3.)

22. Beginning and continuing **unto,** etc. The supplementary idea was too obvious to need to be expressed. (See W. § 66. I. c.)—**From the baptism of John**—*i. e.* from its beginning, as a well-known epoch. The history shows that he had been baptizing a few months before our Lord made his public appearance, and continued to do so for a time afterward (see John 3 : 27) ; but that difference, for the purpose of so general a designation, was unimportant. Not from the close of John's baptism (Hmph.), since Jesus called the other apostles earlier, and not from his own baptism by John (Kuin.), since the phrase does not admit of that restriction. (Comp. 18 : 25 ; Mark 11 : 30 ; Luke 7 : 29, etc.)—**To be a witness,** etc. The resurrection is singled out as the main point to which the testimony of the apostles related, because, that being established, it involves every other truth in relation to the character and work of Christ. It proves him to be the Son of God, the Justifier and Redeemer of men, their Sovereign and Judge. (See 4 : 33 ; John 5 : 22 ; Rom. 1 : 4 ; 4 : 24 ; 10 : 9 ; Gal. 1 : 1, etc.) Hence, Paul mentions it as one of the proofs of his apostleship, and of his qualifications for it, that he had seen Christ after his resurrection. (See 1 Cor. 9 : 1.)

23–26. THE APPOINTMENT OF MATTHIAS AS AN APOSTLE.

23. The act here is that of those addressed (see v. 15), not that of the apostles merely.—**They placed two**—*i. e.* before them, in their midst (see 5 : 27 ; 6 : 6) ; or, according to some, **appointed two** as candidates (De Wet.).—**Justus.** It was not uncommon for the Jews

at this period to assume foreign names. (See on 13 : 9.) Barsabas is mentioned only here. Some have conjectured, without reason, that he and Barnabas (4 : 36) were the same person. **Matthias** also appears only in this transaction. The traditional notices of him are not reliable. (See Win., *Realw.*,[1] vol. ii. p. 61.)

24. Praying they said ($\pi\rho\sigma\epsilon\upsilon\xi\acute{a}\mu\epsilon\nu\sigma\iota$ $\epsilon\acute{\iota}\pi\sigma\nu$), **they prayed, saying.** The participle contains the principal idea. It may be supposed to be Peter who uttered the prayer, since it was he who suggested the appointment of a successor to Judas.—**Thou, Lord,** etc. Whether this prayer was addressed to Christ or God has been disputed. The reasons for the former opinion are that **Lord,** when taken absolutely in the New Testament, refers generally to Christ ;[2] that Christ selected the other apostles as stated in v. 2 ; that the first Christians were in the habit of praying to him (see on 7 : 59 ; 9 : 14) ; and that Peter says to Christ, in John 21 : 17, " Lord, thou knowest all things," which is the import exactly of $\kappa\alpha\rho\delta\iota\sigma\gamma\nu\acute{\omega}\sigma\tau\alpha$ (**heart-knower**). The reasons for the other opinion do not invalidate these. That **heart-knower** is used of God in 15 : 8 shows only that it does not apply exclusively to Christ. The call of Peter in 15 : 7, which is ascribed to God, was a call, not to the apostleship, but to preach the gospel to the heathen ; and even if that case were parallel to this, it would be an instance only of the common usage of referring the same or a similar act indiscriminately to Christ or God. This latter remark applies also to such passages as 2 Cor. 1 : 1 ; Eph. 1 : 1 ; 2 Tim. 1 : 1. To deny that Peter would ascribe omniscience to Christ because in Jer. 17 : 10 it is said to be the prerogative of God to know the heart contradicts John 21 : 17. Some have supposed the apostle intended to quote that passage of the prophet, but the similarity is too slight to prove such a design ; nor, if the idea of **heart-knower** were drawn from that source, would the application of it here conform necessarily to its application there.—$\acute{\epsilon}\nu\alpha$ (omitted in E. V. after

---

[1] *Biblisches Realwörterbuch*, von Dr. Georg Benedict Winer (3d ed. 1848).
[2] See Professor Stuart's article on the meaning of this title in the New Testament, *Bibl. Repos.*, vol. i. p. 733, *sq.*

25 ^aThat he may take part of this ministry and apostleship, from which Judas by transgression fell, that he might go to his own place.
26 And they gave forth their lots; and the lot fell upon Matthias; and he was numbered with the eleven apostles.

25 two the one whom thou hast chosen, to take the place in this ministry and apostleship, from which Judas fell away, that he might go to his own place.
26 And they gave lots ¹for them; and the lot fell upon Matthias; and he was numbered with the eleven apostles.

Cranm.) belongs to ὅν, **which one,** or perhaps in apposition, **whom**—viz. **one that he,** etc. Tynd. and Gen. render **that the one may take,** etc.
25. For lot (κλῆρον), see on v. 17.—**This ministry and** (that) **an apostleship. And** (καί) adds a second term explanatory of the first—i. e. essentially an instance of hendiadys (Mey., De Wet.), **the ministry of this apostleship. From which he went aside,** as opposed to the idea of adhering faithfully to the character and service which his apostleship required of him; "ad normam Hebr. *soor* sq. *min* = deserere munus" (Wahl). **That he might go unto his own place.** The clause is telic, depending on **went aside.** So long as Judas retained his office, he was kept back, as it were, from his proper destiny. He must relinquish it, therefore, in order to suffer his just deserts. In this way the apostle would state strongly the idea that the traitor merited the doom to which he had been consigned. The following comment of Meyer presents the only view of the further meaning of the passage which has any respectable critical support: "What is meant here by **his own place** is not to be decided by the usage of **place** in itself considered (for τόπος may denote any place), but merely by the context. That requires that we understand by it "Gehenna," which is conceived of as the place to which Judas, in virtue of his character, properly belongs. Since the treachery of Judas was in itself so fearful a crime, and was still further aggravated by self-murder (which alone, according to Jewish ideas, deserved punishment in hell), the hearers of Peter could have had no doubt as to the sense to be attached to **own place.** This explanation is demanded also by the analogy of Rabbinic passages—e. g. Baal Turim on Num. 24 : 25 (see Lightfoot, *Hor. Hebr., ad loc.*): Balaam ivit in locum suum— i. e. in Gehennam." De Wette assents entirely to this interpretation. **Own place,** therefore, "is a euphemistic designation of the place of punishment, in which the sin of Judas rendered it just that he should have his abode" (Olsh.).
26. And they placed (probably = Heb. *nathan,* as often in the New Testament) their

lots in a vase or something similar, or perhaps **gave them** to those whose business it was to collect them. αὐτῶν (T. R.), *their,* or αὐτοῖς (Lch., Tsch.), *for them,* refers to the candidates, because the lots pertained to them. The two names were probably written on slips of parchment, perhaps several duplicates of them, and then shaken up; the one first drawn out decided the choice. The idea of throwing up the lots agrees better with βάλλειν κλήρους than with this expression.—**Fell,** came out, without reference to any particular process.—**The lot.** Definite, because it was the decisive one.—**Was numbered together with the eleven apostles**—i. e. was recognized as one of their order, and had the character of an apostle henceforth accorded to him. Hesychius sanctions this sense of the verb, though it means properly "to vote against," "condemn," which is out of the question here. De Wette renders "was chosen," "elected," which not only deviates from the classic usage, but ascribes the result to their own act, instead of to a divine interposition. The subsequent appointment of Paul to the apostleship did not discredit or abrogate this decision, but simply enlarged the original number of the apostles. (See Guericke's remarks on this point in his *Church History,* Prof. Shedd's translation, p. 47.) [The appointment of Matthias has sometimes been regarded as an unauthorized transaction: (1) Because the spirit of inspiration was not yet given to the apostles, or to any of the disciples; (2) Because there is no further reference to Matthias (by name) in the New Testament, or certain trace of his work in early tradition; (3) Because the full number of apostles (twelve) was completed by the Lord's choice of Paul; (4) Because the method of selection here adopted (by casting lots) was never afterward resorted to by the apostles. But to these objections to the validity of the transaction it has been answered: (1) That the resort to lots was perhaps justified by the want of inspiration, which would have rendered it unnecessary; (2) That several other apostles are not referred to by name in the later writings of the New Testament, or by any trustworthy early traditions; (3) That Paul may be regarded as an extra apostle for the Gentiles or as filling the place made vacant by the early

CHAPTER II.

A ND when *a*the day of Pentecost was fully come, *b*they were all with one accord in one place.
2 And suddenly there came a sound from heaven as of a rushing mighty wind, and *c*it filled all the house where they were sitting.
3 And there appeared unto them cloven tongues like as of fire, and it sat upon each of them.

1 AND when the day of Pentecost ¹was now come,
2 they were all together in one place. And suddenly there came from heaven a sound as of the rushing of a mighty wind, and it filled all the house where
3 they were sitting. And there appeared unto them tongues ²parting asunder, like as of fire; and it sat

---

a Lev. 23 : 15; Deut. 16 : 9; ch. 20 : 16....*b* ch. 1 : 14....*c* ch. 4 : 31.———1 Gr. *was being fulfilled*....2 Or, *parting among them*
Or, *distributing themselves*

---

martyrdom of James the Less; (4) That there was no occasion for the use of lots after the effusion of the Spirit at Pentecost. After noticing certain grounds of doubt as to the validity of this election, Dr. Ripley says : " Still, the transaction was performed in a very devout manner, with a practical referring of it to Divine Providence." And it may probably be added that the space given to this transaction in a very condensed history, the positive statement that Matthias was numbered with the apostles, and the total absence of any hint of a mistake on the part of the apostles and disciples in what they did, are valid arguments for Dr Hackett's view. —A. H.]

1–4. DESCENT OF THE HOLY SPIRIT.

1. When the day of Pentecost was fully come, arrived. (See Luke 9 : 51.) The action of the verb (lit. *to be completed*) refers not to the day itself, but to the completion of the interval which was to pass before its arrival (Olsh., Bmg.). Some translate **while it is completed**—i. e. in the course of it, on that day (Mey., De Wet.). The present infinitive is consistent with this view or that.—**The Pentecost** (lit. *the fiftieth*) the Greek Jews employed as a proper name. (See 20 : 16 ; 1 Cor. 16 : 8 ; 2 Macc. 12 : 32.) *Day* or *feast* determined the form. This festival received its name from its occurring on the fiftieth day from the second day of the passover ; so that the interval embraced a circle of seven entire weeks—i. e. a week of weeks. It is usually called in the Old Testament, with reference to this circumstance, the festival of weeks. Its observance took place at the close of the gathering of the harvest, and was no doubt mainly commemorative of that event. (See Jahn's *Archæol.*, ? 355.) According to the later Jews, Pentecost was observed also as the day on which the law was given from Sinai ; but no trace of this custom is found in the Old Testament or in the works of Philo or Josephus. It is generally supposed that this Pentecost, signalized by the outpouring of the Spirit, fell on the Jewish Sabbath, our Saturday. According to the best opinion, our Lord cele-

brated his last passover on the evening which began the fifteenth of Nisan (Num. 33 : 3) ; and hence, as he was crucified on the next day, which was our Friday, the fiftieth day, or Pentecost (beginning, of course, with the evening of Friday, the second day of the passover), would occur on the Jewish Sabbath. (See Wiesl., *Chronologie*, u. s. w., p. 19.)—**All** the believers then in Jerusalem. (See 1 : 15.)—ὁμοθυμαδόν = ὁμοψύχως, **with one accord.** Its local sense, *together*, becomes superfluous, followed by **in one place.** (See on 1 : 15.)

2. As of a mighty wind (lit. *blast*) **rushing along ;** not genit. absolute, but dependent on **sound,** ἦχος. (See v. 3.) πνοή = πνεῦμα. The more uncommon word is chosen here, perhaps on account of the different sense of πνεῦμα in this connection—e. g. v. 4. As used of the wind, φέρεσθαι denotes often rapid, violent, motion. (See the proofs in Kypke's *Obss. Sacr.*, vol. ii. p. 11, and in Kuin., *ad loc.*) **Filled**— i. e. the sound, which is the only natural subject furnished by the context.—**House** is probably the *house* referred to in 1 : 13 ; not the temple, for the reasons there stated, and because the term employed in this absolute way does not signify the temple or an apartment of it. [The note of Canon Cook on **filled all the house** reads thus : " As a bath is filled with water, that they might be baptized with the Holy Ghost, in fulfilment of 1 : 5 ; Chrysostom, Hom. iv. 2, on the Acts, and Hom. ii. 13, on the ascension and the beginning of the Acts." We are not to suppose that a sound like that which would have been made by a mighty wind rushing against the outside of the building, or rushing through the adjacent street, filled all the house, but rather that a sound which seemed like that of a rushing wind that entered and filled the whole house filled it. In other words, the Spirit's presence seems to have been signified and revealed by a sound that came with that presence into the house and filled it. The audible sign filling the room announced the Power represented by it as doing the same.—A. H.]

3. And there appeared to them tongues distributed—i. e. among them—**and one**—

4 And [a]they were all filled with the Holy Ghost, and began [b]to speak with other tongues, as the Spirit gave them utterance.

4 upon each one of them. And they were all filled with the Holy Spirit, and began to speak with other tongues, as the Spirit gave them utterance.

a ch. 1 : 5....b Mark 16 : 17; ch. 10 : 46; 19 : 6; 1 Cor. 12 : 10, 28, 30; 13 : 1; 14 ; 2, etc.

i. e. tongue—**sat upon each of them.** So Bng., Olsh., Wahl, De Wet., Bmg., Hmph., Rob., and most of the later critics, as well as some of the older. (Meyer comes over to this view in his last ed.) The distributive idea occasions the change of number in **sat.** (W. ? 58. 4.)—**To them** belongs strictly to the verb, but extends its force to the participle. According to this view, the fire-like appearance presented itself at first, as it were, in a single body, and then suddenly parted in this direction and that; so that a portion of it rested on each of those present. It could be called a tongue, in that case, from its shape, as extended, pointed, and may have assumed such an appearance as a symbol of the miraculous gift which accompanied the wonder. This secures to **distributed** its proper meaning (see v. 45; Matt. 27 : 35; Luke 23 : 34, etc.), and explains why the first verb is plural, while the second is singular. Calvin, Heinrichs (also Alf.), and many of the older commentators, render the participle *disparted, cleft* (as in the E. Vv. generally), and suppose it to describe the flame as exhibiting in each instance a tongue-like, forked appearance. The objection to this view is that it rests upon a doubtful sense of the word, and especially that it offers no explanation of the change from the plural verb to the singular. De Wette, after others, has adduced passages here from the Rabbinic writers to show that it was a common belief of the Jews that an appearance like fire often encircled the heads of distinguished teachers of the law. To this it has been added that instances of a similar phenomenon are related by the Greek and Roman writers. We are directed by such coincidences to an important fact in the history of the divine revelations, and that is that God has often been pleased to reveal himself to men in conformity with their own conceptions as to the mode in which it is natural to expect communications from him. The appearance of the star to the Magians may be regarded as another instance of such accommodation to human views.

4. Were all filled with the Holy Spirit (anarthrous, as in 1 : 2), a phrase referring usually to special gifts rather than moral qualities, and to these as transient rather than permanent. (Comp. 4 : 8, 31; 13 : 9, etc.) [It will be instructive to compare all the other passages in which this expression is found—viz. Luke 1 : 15, 41, 67; Acts 4 : 8, 31; 9 : 17; 13 : 9—or the equivalent expression "full of the Holy Spirit"—viz. Luke 4 : 1; Acts 6 : 3; 7 : 55; 11 : 24—together with those which apparently refer to the same endowment—viz. Acts 2 : 17; 6 : 8; 8 : 17, *sq.*; 10 : 44, 46; 11 : 15, 16; 19 : 6. A study of these passages leads to the conclusion that "being filled with the Holy Spirit," or "being baptized in the Holy Spirit," implies a reception from the Spirit of extraordinary powers, in addition to ordinary sanctifying grace. These extraordinary powers might be permanent, as the gift of prophecy to the apostles, or they might be, and generally were, temporary, as the gift of miracles.—A. H.]—**Began** (like our "proceeded") **to speak,** as soon as the symbol rested on them. This use of ἀρχο-μαι (*to begin*) as introducing what is next in order has not been duly recognized in the New Testament. **With other tongues**—*i. e.* than their native tongue. That Luke designed to state here that the disciples were suddenly endued with the power of speaking foreign languages, before unknown to them, would seem to be too manifest to admit of any doubt. It is surprising that such a writer as Neander should attempt to put a different construction on the text. He objects that the miracle would have been superfluous, inasmuch as the apostles are not known to have employed this gift of tongues in preaching the gospel. It may be replied, first, that we have not sufficient information concerning the labors of the apostles to affirm that they may not have employed the endowment for that purpose; and secondly, that we are not obliged to regard such a use of it as the only worthy object of the miracle. It may have been designed to serve chiefly as an attestation of the truth of the gospel, and of the character of the apostles as divine messengers. It is certain, at least, that Paul entertained that view of the **tongues** spoken of in 1 Cor. 14 : 22 : "Wherefore tongues are for a sign, not to them that believe, but to them that believe not." The effect produced on this occasion (see v. 12) shows how well suited such a miracle was to impress the minds of those who witnessed it. A miracle, too, in this form, may have had a symbolic import which added to its significance. It was necessary that even the apostles should be led to entertain more enlarged views respecting the comprehensive de-

5 And there were dwelling at Jerusalem Jews, devout men, out of every nation under heaven.
6 Now when this was noised abroad, the multitude came together, and were confounded, because that every man heard them speak in his own language.

5 Now there were dwelling at Jerusalem Jews, de-
6 vout men, from every nation under heaven. And when this sound was heard, the multitude came together, and were confounded, because that every man heard them speaking in his own language.

sign of the New Dispensation. This sudden possession of an ability to proclaim the salvation of Christ to men of all nations (even if we allow that it was not permanent) was adapted to recall their minds powerfully to the last command of the Saviour, and to make them feel that it was their mission to publish his name to the ends of the earth. Such a mode of conveying instruction to them was not more indirect than that employed in the vision of Peter (10 : 9, sq.), which was intended to teach the same truth. But we are not left to argue the question on grounds of this nature : the testimony of Luke is explicit and decisive. Even critics who would explain away the reality of the miracle admit that it was the writer's intention to record a miracle. Thus Meyer says : "The **other tongues** are to be considered, according to the text, as absolutely nothing else than languages which were different from the native language of the speakers. They were Galileans, and spoke now Parthian, Median, Persian, etc., therefore foreign languages, and those too—the point precisely wherein appeared the wonderful effect of the Spirit—*unacquired languages* (**new tongues** in Mark 16 : 17)—*i. e.* not previously learned by them. Accordingly, the text itself defines the sense of **tongues** as that of languages, and excludes as impossible the other explanations, different from this, which some have attempted to impose on the word."—**According as,** in respect to manner, since the languages were diverse.

5-13. IMPRESSION OF THE MIRACLE ON THE MULTITUDE.

5. δέ, **now,** transitive.—**Dwelling,** whether for a season or permanently ; hence more general than **sojourning** (v. 10; 17 : 21), but not excluding the sojourners there. No doubt many of the Jews in question had fixed their abode at Jerusalem, as it was always an object of desire with those of them who lived in foreign countries to return and spend the close of life in the land of their fathers. The prevalent belief that the epoch had now arrived when the promised Messiah was about to appear must have given increased activity to that desire. The writer mentions this class of Jews in distinction from the native inhabitants, because the narrative which follows represents that many were present who understood dif-

ferent languages. The number of these strangers was the greater on account of the festival which occurred at that time.—**Devout,** Godfearing. (See 8 : 2; Luke 2 : 25.) This sense is peculiar to the Hellenistic Greek. The term is applied to those only whose piety was of the Old-Testament type.—**Of those**—*i. e.* being—**under heaven.** The strong expression here is a phrase signifying *from many and distant lands.* A phrase of this kind has an aggregate sense, which is the true one, while that deduced from the import of the separate words is a false sense.

6. When this was noised abroad (γενομένης . . . ταύτης). These words are obscure. The principal interpretations are the following : (1) φωνῆς ταύτης (*this voice* or *sound*) refers to **other tongues** in v. 4, and the implication is that the voices of those who spoke were so loud as to be heard at a distance, and in this way were the occasion of drawing together the multitude. This interpretation secures to **this** a near antecedent, but has against it that **voice** is singular, and not plural, and that the participle is hardly congruous with the noun in that sense. Neander, who adopts this view, regards **voice** as a collective term. (2) φωνή has been taken as synonymous with φημή : *now when this report arose*—*i. e.* the report concerning this. The meaning is good, but opposed to the usage of the noun, while it puts **this** in effect for *concerning this*, which is a hard construction. Many of the older critics and the authors of nearly all the E. Vv. understood the expression in this way. (3) We may regard **voice** as repeating the idea of **sound** in v. 2: *now when this sound*—that of the descending Spirit—*occurred.* (For that signification of φωνή, comp. John 3 : 8; Rev. 1 : 15; 9 : 9; 14 : 2, etc.) γενομένης appears to answer to ἐγένετο in v. 2, and favors this explanation. The objection to it is that **this** forsakes the nearer for a remoter antecedent ; but that may occur if the latter be more prominent, so as to take the lead in the writer's mind. (See W. ¿ 23. 1.) This meaning agrees with the context. The participial clause here may involve the idea of cause as well as time ; and we may understand, therefore, that the sound in question was audible beyond the house where the disciples were assembled—that it arrested the attention of those abroad, and led them to seek out the

7 And they were all amazed and marvelled, saying one to another, Behold, are not all these which speak *Galilæans?

8 And how hear we every man in our own tongue, wherein we were born?

9 Parthians, and Medes, and Elamites, and the dwellers in Mesopotamia, and in Judæa, and Cappadocia, in Pontus, and Asia,

10 Phrygia, and Pamphylia, in Egypt, and in the

7 And they were all amazed and marvelled, saying, Behold, are not all these who speak Galilæans? 8 And how hear we, every man in our own language, 9 wherein we were born? Parthians and Medes and Elamites, and the dwellers in Mesopotamia, in Judæa and Cappadocia, in Pontus and Asia, in Phrygia and Pamphylia, in Egypt and the parts of Libya about Cyrene, and sojourners from Rome, both Jews

a ch. 1 : 11.

scene of the wonder. So Hess,[1] Schrader, Meyer, De Wette, Alford, and others. The house (v. 2) may have been on one of the avenues to the temple, thronged at this time by a crowd of early worshippers (v. 15).—**Were hearing.** (Imperf.)—**Every** alone (v. 8) or with **one** distributes often a plural subject. (See 14 : 29 ; Matt. 18 : 35 ; John 16 : 32. K. ̸ 266. 3.)—ἰδίᾳ, **his own,** usually emphatic. (W. ̸ 22. 7.)—**Dialect** = *tongue.* (See v. 11.) The term in its narrower sense here would be too narrow ; for, though some of the languages differed only as dialects, it was not true of all of them.—**Them speak.** We are not to understand by this that they all spoke in the languages enumerated, but that one of them employed this, and another that. In so brief a narrative the writer must have passed over various particulars of the transaction. We may suppose that at this time the apostles had left the room where they assembled at first, and had gone forth to the crowd collected in the vicinity.

7. Not, which leads the sentence, belongs properly to **are.** (Comp. 7 : 48. W. ̸ 61. 4.)— **All** (T. R.) was inserted here probably from v. 12.—**These,** emphatic.—**Galileans.** They were known as Galileans, because they were known as the disciples of Christ. Had the different speakers belonged to so many different countries, the wonder would have been diminished or removed.

8. How, since they were all Galileans. The object of **hear** follows in v. 11 ; but, the connection having been so long suspended, the verb is there repeated. **Every,** as in v. 6.— **In which we were born.** This remark excludes the possibility of Luke's meaning that the tongues were merely an ecstatic or impassioned style of discourse.

9. In the enumeration of the countries named in this verse and the next the writer proceeds from the north-east to the west and south. **Parthians.** *Parthia* was on the north-east of Media and Hyrcania and north of Aria, surrounded entirely by mountains. — **Medes.**

Media bordered north on the Caspian Sea, west on Armenia, east on Hyrcania, and south on Persia. **Elamites**—*i. e.* the inhabitants of *Elymais* or *Elam,* which was east of the Tigris, north of Susiana (annexed to it in Dan. 8 : 2), and south oᶠ Media, of which Ptolemy makes it a part.—**Judea.** It has excited the surprise of some that *Judea* should be mentioned in this catalogue, because, it is said, no part of the wonder consisted in hearing Aramæan at Jerusalem. But we need not view the writer's design in that light. It was rather to inform us in how many languages the disciples addressed the multitude on this occasion ; and as, after all, the native Jews formed the greater part of the assembly, the account would have been deficient without mentioning Judea. It has been proposed to alter the text to *Idumea,* but there is no authority for this.—The catalogue now passes from Cappadocia and Pontus, on the east and north-east, to the extreme west of Asia Minor. **Asia.** Phrygia being excluded here, Kuinoel and others have supposed *Asia* to be the same as Ionia ; but Winer says it cannot be shown that in the Roman age Ionia alone was called Asia. He thinks, with an appeal to Pliny, that we are to understand it as embracing Mysia, Lydia, and Caria, with Ephesus as the principal city. (See his *Realw.,* vol. i. p. 96.) Others, as Böttger,[2] whom De Wette follows, understand Mysia, Æolis, Ionia, Lydia, Caria. All admit that the term denoted not so much a definite region as a jurisdiction, the limits of which varied from time to time according to the plan of government which the Romans adopted for their Asiatic provinces.

10. Phrygia was separated by the Taurus from Pisidia on the south, with Bithynia on the north, Caria, Lydia, and Mysia on the west, Galatia, Cappadocia, and Lycaonia on the east. —**Pamphylia** was on the Mediterranean, adjacent on other sides to Cilicia, Caria, and Pisidia.—**The parts of Libya toward Cyrene.** Libya was an extensive region on the west of Egypt. One of the principal cities there was Cyrene (now Grenna), on the sea, origi-

---

[1] *Geschichte und Schriften der Apostel Jesu,* vol. i. p. 24 (Zurich, 1820).

[2] *Schauplatz der Wirksamkeit des Apostels Paulus, u. s. w.,* p. 23.

parts of Libya about Cyrene, and strangers of Rome, Jews and proselytes,
11 Cretes and Arabians, we do hear them speak in our tongues the wonderful works of God.
12 And they were all amazed, and were in doubt, saying one to another, What meaneth this?
13 Others mocking said, These men are full of new wine.

11 and proselytes, Cretans and Arabians, we do hear them speaking in our tongues the mighty works of
12 God. And they were all amazed, and were perplexed, saying one to another, What meaneth this?
13 But others mocking said, They are filled with new wine.

---

nally a Greek colony, but where at this time the Jews constituted a fourth part of the population. (See Jos., *Antt.*, 14. 7. 2.) It was the native place of Simon, who bore the Saviour's cross to Golgotha (Luke 23 : 26). This part of Africa comes into view in making the voyage from Malta to Alexandria.—**The Romans sojourning** at Jerusalem. (Comp. 17 : 21.)—**Both Jews and proselytes** a few critics restrict to **Romans** merely, but most (De Wet., Mey., Wiesl.) refer them to all the preceding nouns. The Jews generally adopted the languages of the countries where they resided. The **proselytes** were originally heathen who had embraced Judaism. The words sustain the same grammatical relation to **Cretans and Arabians,** or, at all events, are to be repeated after them. The last two names follow as an after-thought, in order to complete the list. [*Proselytes*, or Gentile converts to Judaism, were evidently somewhat numerous at this time. Many of them remained uncircumcised, and were called "proselytes of the gate." These, like Cornelius, were worshippers of the true God and well prepared to listen to the gospel of his grace. Others were circumcised and allowed to take part in the great religious festivals, as well as in the daily temple-service. At a later period a Gentile became a "proselyte of righteousness" by circumcision, baptism, and an offering (Corban). Only the last two ceremonies were required of women. The baptism of men is thus described: "When the wound [of circumcision] was healed, he was stripped of all his clothes, in the presence of three witnesses who had acted as his teachers, and who now acted as his sponsors, the 'fathers' of the proselyte (*Ketubh.* xi., *Erubh.* xv. 1), and led into the tank or pool. As he stood there, up to his neck in water, they repeated the great commandments of the law. These he promised and vowed to keep; and then, with an accompanying benediction, he plunged under the water. To leave one handbreadth of his body unsubmerged would have vitiated the whole rite." (Smith's *Dict. of the Bible*, "Proselytes"). This, however, appears to have been a later usage. There is no sufficient evidence that proselyte baptism was introduced as early as the time of Christ. (See *Baptist Quarterly*, 1872,

pp. 301–332, "Jewish Proselyte Baptism," by Dr. Toy.)—A. H.]

11. The declarative form which the English Version assigns to the sentence here (**we do hear**) is incorrect. The question extends to **of God.** (See on v. 8.) [Tischendorf, Tregelles, Meyer, and others agree with Dr. Hackett in making the question beginning with v. 8 include this verse; but Westcott and Hort and the Anglo-American Revisers suppose that the question embraces only v. 8, while this verse is declarative. It seems impossible to assign any conclusive reason for either view in preference to the other. The meaning is the same with the one as with the other. A nice rhetorical sense may lead to preference.—A. H.]—**The great things of God,** done by him through Christ for the salvation of men. (Comp. v. 38.)

12. Amazed describes their astonishment at the occurrence in general; **in doubt,** their perplexity at being unable to account for it.— **What may this perhaps mean?** ἄν attaches a tacit condition to the inquiry, if, as we think, it must import something. (See W. § 42. 1; K. § 260. 4.) This is the question of the more serious party. The hesitating form of it indicates the partial conviction which the miracle had wrought in their minds.

13. Others . . . said. Among those who scoffed may have been some of the native inhabitants of the city, who, not understanding the foreign languages spoken, regarded the discourse of the apostles as senseless because it was unintelligible to them.—Χλευάζοντες is not so well supported as διαχλευάζοντες, and expresses the idea less forcibly. Calvin: "Nihil tam admirabile esse potest, quod non in ludibrium vertant, qui nulla Dei curâ tanguntur."—ὅτι, **that,** declarative.—**Sweet wine** (γλεύκους), not *new,* as in the E. V. after all the earlier E. Vv. The Pentecost fell in June, and the first vintage did not occur till August. It is true *gleukos* designated properly the sweet, unfermented juice of the grape, but it was applied also to old wine preserved in its original state. The ancients had various ways of arresting fermentation. One of them, in use among the Greeks and Romans, was this: "An amphora was taken and coated with pitch within and without; it

14 ¶ But Peter, standing up with the eleven, lifted up his voice, and said unto them, Ye men of Judæa, and all *y*ᵉ that dwell at Jerusalem, be this known unto you, and hearken to my words:
15 For these are not drunken, as ye suppose, ᵃseeing it is *but* the third hour of the day.
16 But this is that which was spoken by the prophet Joel;
17 ᵇAnd it shall come to pass in the last days, saith God, ᶜI will pour out of my Spirit upon all flesh: and your sons and ᵈyour daughters shall prophesy, and your young men shall see visions, and your old men shall dream dreams:

14 But Peter, standing up with the eleven, lifted up his voice, and spake forth unto them, *saying*, Ye men of Judæa, and all ye that dwell at Jerusalem, be this
15 known unto you, and give ear unto my words. I or these are not drunken, as ye suppose; seeing it is *but*
16 the third hour of the day; but this is that which hath been spoken through the prophet Joel;
17 And it shall be in the last days, saith God,
I will pour forth of my Spirit upon all flesh:
And your sons and your daughters shall prophesy,
And your young men shall see visions,
And your old men shall dream dreams:

a 1 Thess. 5 : 7....*b* Isa. 44 : 3 ; Ezek. 11 : 19 ; 36 : 27 ; Joel 2 : 28, 29 ; Zech. 12 : 10 ; John 7 : 38....*c* ch. 10 : 45....*d* ch. 21 : 9.

was filled with *mustum lixivium*—*i. e.* the juice before the grapes had been fully trodden—and corked so as to be perfectly air-tight. It was then immersed in a tank of cold fresh water or buried in wet sand, and allowed to remain for six weeks or two months. The contents, after this process, were found to remain unchanged for a year, and hence the name ἀεὶ γλεῦκος—*i. e. semper mustum* " (*Dict. of Antt.*, art. "Vinum "¹). Jahn says that *sweet wine* was produced also from dried grapes by soaking them in old wine and then pressing them a second time. (See his *Archæol.*, ¿ 69.) This species of wine was very intoxicating.

14-36. THE DISCOURSE OF PETER.
The address embraces the following points, though interwoven somewhat in the discussion : *first*, defence of the character of the apostles (14, 15); *secondly*, the miracle explained as a fulfilment of prophecy (16-21); *thirdly*, this effusion of the Spirit an act of the crucified but now exalted Jesus (30-33); and *fourthly*, his claim to be acknowledged as the true Messiah (22-29 and 34-36).

14. With the eleven—*i. e.* in their name, and with their concurrence in what he said. As the multitude was so great, it is not improbable that some of the other apostles addressed different groups of them at the same time. (See on v. 6.) On such an occasion they would all naturally pursue a very similar train of remark.—**Men of Judea** are the Jews born in Jerusalem; **ye that dwell** are the foreign Jews and Jewish converts. (See on v. 5.)—**Hearken** = Heb. *haäzēn*, a Hellenistic word.

15. For justifies the call to attention. It brings forward a refutation of the charge which had been made against them.—**These** whom they had heard speak (see v. 4, *sq.*), and who were then present; not the eleven merely with Peter (Alf.).—**The third hour**—*i. e.* about nine o'clock A. M., according to our time. This was the first hour of public prayer, at which time the morning sacrifice was offered in the temple.

During their festivals the Jews considered it unlawful to take food earlier than this; still more, to drink wine. (See Light., *Hor. Hebr.*, *ad loc.*) The other hours of prayer were the sixth (10 : 4) and the ninth (3 : 1).

16. But this (which you witness) **is that which was said.** The Greek identifies the prophecy with its fulfilment.—**Through the prophet,** because he was the messenger, not the author of the message. The expression recognizes the divine origin of the book which bears his name. (See the note on 1 : 16.)—Tischendorf has no adequate reason for omitting **Joel** after **prophet.** [It is retained in his 8th ed. as well as by Treg., West. and Hort, Revisers' text, and fully justified by ℵ A B C E I P.—A. H.].

17. The citation which follows, from Joel 3 : 1-5 (2 : 28-32 in E. V.), runs for the most part in the words of the Seventy. The two or three verbal deviations from the Hebrew serve either to unfold more distinctly the sense of the original passage or to enforce it. It is the object of the prophecy to characterize the Messianic Dispensation under its two great aspects—that of mercy, and that of judgment. To those who believe, the gospel is "a savor of life unto life;" but to those who disbelieve, it is "a savor of death unto death." (See 2 Cor. 2 : 16.) Under its one aspect it was to be distinguished by the copious outpouring of the Divine Spirit on those who should acknowledge Christ; and under its other aspect it was to be distinguished by the signal punishment awaiting those who should disown his authority and reject him.—**And it shall come to pass,**etc.,stands for Heb. *věhayah aḥărë kēn*, rendered more closely in the Septuagint by **and it shall be after these things.** Peter's expression denotes always in the New Testament the age of the Messiah, which the Scriptures represent as the world's last great moral epoch. The prophet designates the same period under a more general phrase. Again, Peter places **saith God** at the begin-

18 And on my servants and on my handmaidens I will pour out in those days of my Spirit; *a*and they shall prophesy:
19 *b*And I will shew wonders in heaven above, and signs in the earth beneath; blood, and fire, and vapor of smoke:

18 Yea and on my [1]servants and on my [2]hand-maidens in those days
    Will I pour forth of my Spirit; and they shall prophesy.
19 And I will shew wonders in the heaven above,
    And signs on the earth beneath ;
    Blood, and fire, and vapor of smoke:

---

a ch. 21 : 4, 9, 10; 1 Cor. 12 : 10, 28; 14 : 1, etc....*b* Joel 2 : 30, 31.——1 Gr. *bondmen*....2 Gr. *bondmaidens*.

---

ning of the declaration ; the prophet, at the close of it. The position of the words here fixes attention at once upon the source of the prophecy, and prepares the mind to listen to it as God's utterance.—**Will pour out** is future, a later Greek form. (W. § 13 : 3; K. § 154. R. 1.) —**And** (consequential) **thus they shall prophesy.** This verb in the New Testament signifies not merely to foretell future events, but to communicate religious truth in general under a divine inspiration. It corresponds in this use to *nibbeoo* in the original passage. (See Gesen., *Lex.*, s. v.) The order of the next two clauses in the Hebrew and Septuagint is the reverse of that adopted here—viz. first, **your old men shall dream dreams,** then **your young men . . . see visions.** Hengstenberg[1] suggests that the change may have been intentional, in order to place the youth with the sons and daughters and to assign to the aged a place of honor.—**Shall dream with dreams.** The dative, as in 4 : 17 ; 23 : 24. (W. § 54. 3.) Some authorities have ἐνύπνια, the acc. **dreams,** which was probably substituted for the other as an easier construction.

18. καίγε = Heb. *vĕgam* annexes an emphatic addition : **and even** (Hart., *Partik.*, vol. i. p. 396).—**My,** which is wanting in the Hebrew, is retained here from the Septuagint. The prophet declares that no condition of men, however ignoble, would exclude them from the promise. The apostle cites the prophet to that effect, but takes occasion from the language—**my servants,** which describes their degradation in the eyes of men—to suggest by way of contrast their exalted relationship to God. Bengel : "Servi secundum carnem . . . iidem servi Dei " (" servants according to the flesh . . . also servants of God "). Similar to this is the language of Paul in 1 Cor. 7 : 22 : "For he that is called in the Lord, *being* a servant, is the Lord's freeman ; likewise also he that is called, *being* free, is Christ's servant." If we cast the eye back over this and the preceding verse, it will be seen that the effusion of the Spirit was to be universal as to the classes of persons that were

to participate in it ; in other words, it was to be without distinction of sex, age, or rank.—The modes of divine revelation and of the Spirit's operation which are specified in this passage were among the more extraordinary to which the Hebrews were accustomed under the ancient Economy. These, after having been suspended for so long a time, were now, at the opening of the Christian Dispensation, renewed in more than their former power. The prophecy relates chiefly, I think, to these special communications of the Spirit, which were granted to the first Christians. The terms of the prophecy direct us naturally to something out of the ordinary course ; and when we add to this that the facts recorded in the Acts and the Epistles sustain fully that view of the language, it must appear arbitrary, as well as unnecessary, to reject such an interpretation. Yet the prophecy has indirectly a wider scope. It portrays in reality the character of the entire dispensation. Those special manifestations of the Spirit at the beginning marked the Economy as one that was to be eminently distinguished by the Spirit's agency. They were a pledge that those in all ages who embrace the gospel should equal the most favored of God's ancient people ; they enjoy a clearer revelation, are enlightened, sanctified, by a Spirit more freely imparted, may rise to the same or higher religious consolations and attainments.

19. The apostle now holds up to view the other side of the subject. He adduces the part of the prophecy which foretells the doom of those who reject Christ and spurn his salvation. Having appealed to the hopes, the apostle turns here to address himself to the fears, of men , he would persuade them by every motive to escape the punishment which awaits the unbelieving and disobedient. (See vs. 40 and 43, below.) In the interpretation of the passage before us, I follow those who understand it as having primary reference to the calamities which God inflicted on the Jews in connection with the overthrow of Jerusalem and the destruction of the Jewish state and nation. The reasons for this opinion are briefly these : (1) The law of

---

[1] *Christology of the Old Testament, and a Commentary on the Predictions of the Messiah by the Prophets,* vol. iii. p. 140 (Dr. Keith's translation).

| 20 | ^{a}The sun shall be turned into darkness, and the moon into blood, before that great and notable day of the Lord come: | 20 | The sun shall be turned into darkness, And the moon into blood, Before the day of the Lord come, That great and notable *day*: |
| 21 | And it shall come to pass, *that* ^{b}whosoever shall call on the name of the Lord shall be saved. | 21 | And it shall be, that whosoever shall call on the name of the Lord shall be saved. |

a Matt. 24 : 29 ; Mark 13 : 24 ; Luke 21 : 25....*b* Rom. 10 : 13.

correspondence would lead us to apply this part of the prophecy to the same period to which the other part has been applied—*i. e.* to the early times of the gospel. (2) The expression, **the day of the Lord,** in v. 20, according to a very common use in the Hebrew prophets, denotes a day when God comes to make known his power in the punishment of his enemies— a day of the signal display of his vengeance for the rejection of long-continued mercies and the commission of aggravated sins. The subversion of the Jewish state was such an occasion. It appropriates fully every trait of that significant designation. (3) Part of the language here coincides almost verbally with that in Matt. 24 : 29 ; and if the language there, as understood by most interpreters, describes the downfall of the Jewish state,[1] we may infer from the similarity that the subject of discourse is the same in both places. (4) The entire phraseology, when construed according to the laws of prophetic language, is strikingly appropriate to represent the unsurpassed horrors and distress which attended the siege and destruction of Jerusalem, and to announce the extinction of the Jewish power and of the glory of the Jewish worship which that catastrophe involved. Yet here too (see on v. 18) we are to recognize the wider scope of the prophecy. The destruction of the Jews is held forth by the apostle as a type of the destruction which is to come upon every rejecter of the gospel. (See v. 21.) For the sake of contrast, Peter inserts the words **above, signs, below,** which are not in the Hebrew. **Wonders in heaven, signs on the earth,** means prodigies, celestial and terrestrial, such as may appear in the air or on the earth ; in other words, prodigies of every sort and of the most portentous kind. The idea is that calamities were to ensue equal in severity and magnitude to those which the most fearful portents are supposed to announce. The mode of speaking is founded on the popular idea that when great events are about to occur wonderful phenomena foretoken their approach. Hence what the prophet would affirm is that disasters and judgments were coming such as men are accustomed to associate with the most terrific auguries ; but he does not mean

necessarily that the auguries themselves were to be expected, or decide whether the popular belief on the subject was true or false.—**Blood, fire, vapor of smoke,** stand in apposition with **wonders and signs,** and show in what they consisted. **Blood,** perhaps, rained on the earth (De Wet.), or as in Egypt (Ex. 7 : 17), infecting the streams and rivers (Hng.) ; **fire**— *i. e.* appearances of it in the air—**and vapor of smoke,** dense smoke, hence = Heb. *temerôth ashan;* **pillars,** or clouds, **of smoke,** which darken the heavens and earth. Many have supposed these terms to signify directly slaughter and conflagration, but their grammatical relation to **wonders and signs** decides that they are the portents themselves, not the calamities portended. That view, too, confounds **the day of the Lord** with the precursors of the day. **20. The sun shall be turned into darkness.** Its light shall be withdrawn ; the heavens shall become black. A day is at hand which will be one of thick gloom, of sadness and woe. (For the frequency and significance of this figure in the prophets, see Ezek. 32 : 7 ; Isa. 13 : 10 ; Amos 5 : 18, 20, etc.)—**The moon.** Repeat here **shall be turned.** The moon, too, shall give forth signs of the coming distress. It shall exhibit an appearance like blood. Men shall see there an image of the carnage and misery which are to be witnessed on earth.— **Notable, illustrious,** signal in its character as an exhibition of divine justice. It conveys the idea of *nora* (Heb.), **fearful,** but is less definite.

21. Every one whosoever. (For ἄν with this expansive effect, comp. v. 39 ; 3 : 22, 23 ; 7 : 3, etc.) The mercy is free to all who fulfil the condition. (See the note on v. 39.)—**Shall have called upon.** Subj. aor. after ἄν = fut. exact. in Latin. The act in this verb must be past before the future in **shall be saved** can be present. (See W. ? 42. 1. 3. b.)—**The name of the Lord**—*i. e.* of Christ. (Comp. v. 36 ; 9 : 14 ; 22 : 16 ; Rom. 10 : 13.) Not simply upon him, but upon him as possessing the attributes and sustaining to men the relations of which his **name** is the index. (Compare the note on 22 : 16.)—**Shall be saved,** from the doom of

---

[1] This view is defended in the *Bibliotheca Sacra*, 1843, p. 531, *sq.*, and controverted in the same work, 1850, p. 452, *sq.*

22 Ye men of Israel, hear these words; Jesus of Nazareth, a man approved of God among you *a*by miracles and wonders and signs, which God did by him in the midst of you, as ye yourselves also know :
23 Him, *b*being delivered by the determinate counsel and foreknowledge of God, *c*ye have taken, and by wicked hands have crucified and slain :
24 *d*Whom God hath raised up, having loosed the

22 Ye men of Israel, hear these words: Jesus of Nazareth, a man approved of God unto you by [1]mighty works and wonders and signs, which God did by him in the midst of you, even as ye yourselves know ; 23 him, being delivered up by the determinate counsel and foreknowledge of God, ye by the hand of [2]lawless men did crucify and slay : whom God raised up, 24 having loosed the pangs of death : because it was not

---

a John 3 : 2 ; 14 : 10, 11 ; ch. 10 : 38 ; Heb. 2 : 4....*b* Matt. 26 : 24 ; Luke 22 : 22 ; 24 : 44 ; ch. 3 : 18 ; 4 : 28....*c* ch. 5 : 30....*d* ver. 32; ch. 3 : 15 ; 4 : 10; 10 : 40; 13 : 30, 34; 17 : 31; Rom. 4 : 24; 8 : 11 ; 1 Cor. 6 : 14 ; 15 : 15 ; 2 Cor. 4 : 14 ; Gal. 1 : 1 ; Eph. 1 : 20 ; Col. 2 : 12 · 1 Thess. 1 : 10; Heb. 13 : 20 ; 1 Pet. 1 : 21.·   —1 Gr. *powers*....2 Or, *men without the law*

---

those who reject Christ, and be admitted to the joys of his kingdom.

22. Israelites = Jews in N. T.; here both the native and foreign Jews.—Ναζωραῖον = Ναζαραῖος. The former was the broader Syriac pronunciation, as heard especially in Galilee. Hence Peter's rustic speech (Matt. 26 : 73) betrayed him in the very words of his denial. (See Win., *Chald. Gr.*,[1] p. 12.) The epithet is added for the sake of distinction, as "Jesus" was not an uncommon name among the Jews. —**A man from God** (as the source of the approval) **accredited unto you** (not, as in E. V., **among you**); **shown forth,** confirmed (25 : 7)—viz. in his Messianic character. The meaning is that in the miracles which Christ performed he had God's fullest sanction to all that he did and taught—that is, to his claim to be received as the Son of God, the promised Saviour of men. Some put a comma after **God** and render **a man** (sent) **from God, accredited** as such **by miracles,** etc. The ultimate idea remains the same, since to sanction his mission as from God was the same thing as to sustain his truth as to what he claimed to be. But the first is the more correct view, because it renders the ellipsis (**sent,** not apt to be omitted) unnecessary, and because (as Alf. suggests) the point to be established was that the Messiah was identical with a man whom they had seen and known. We have ἀπό after the participle, instead of ὑπό, because the approbation was indirect—*i. e.* testified through miracles. (See W. *§* 47. 4 ; Bernh., *Synt.*, p. 223.)—**Miracles and wonders and signs** form obviously an intensive expression, but they are not synonymous with each other. Miracles are called **powers,** because they are wrought by divine power ; **prodigies,** because they appear inexplicable to men ; and σημεῖα (**signs**), because they attest the character or claims of those who perform them (2 Cor. 12 : 12). (See Olsh. on Matt. 8 : 1). It cannot be said that the terms are used always with a distinct consciousness of that difference.—οἷς (**which**)

is attracted into the case of its antecedent.— **Also** after **as** good authorities omit. If retained, it must connect **know** with **did**—what **he did ye also know ;** or else strengthen **your- selves, also yourselves** as well as we.

23. Him is both resumptive and emphatic. (See Matt. 24 : 13 ; 1 Cor. 6 : 4. W. *§* 23. 4).— **According to the established** (firmly fixed, see Luke 22 : 22) **counsel,** plan ; the dative is that of rule or conformity. (W. *§* 31. 6. b. ; K. *§* 285. 3.) **Counsel** and **foreknowledge** may differ here as antecedent and consequent, since God's foreknowledge results properly from his purpose.—ἔκδοτον, **delivered up** to you—*i. e.* by Judas.—**Have taken** (λαβόντες) the best editors regard as an addition to the text.—**By the hands** (διὰ χειρῶν ἀνόμων) or **hand** (if after Grsb., Lchm., Tsch., and others, we read χειρός) **of lawless ones** (partitive, hence without the article ; see on 5 : 16)—*i. e.* of the heathen, as Pilate and the Roman soldiers. (Comp. Wisd. 17. 2 ; 1 Cor. 9 : 21.) The indignity which Christ suffered was the greater on account of his being crucified by the heathen. (See 3 : 13.) ἀνόμων (**law- less**) may agree with χειρῶν (**hands**), **lawless hands ;** but, as the adjective must refer still to the heathen, it is not so easy a combination as the other.—**Having fastened** to the cross—*i. e.* with nails driven through the hands and feet (John 20 : 25, 27). (See Bynæus, *De Morte Christi*, L. III. c. 6, and Jahn's *Archæol.*, *§* 262.) [Also Amer. addition to the art. "Crucifixion" in Smith's *Dict. of the Bible.*—A. H.] He imputes the act of crucifixion to the Jews because they were the instigators of it. (Comp. 4 : 10 ; 10 : 39.)—ἀνείλατε (**ye slew**) is first aorist, an Alexandrian form. (W. *§* 13. 1 ; S. *§* 63. 11. R.)

24. Raised up, not into existence, as in 3 : 22, but from the dead. The context demands this sense of the verb. (See v. 32.)— **The pains of death.** Quoted apparently from the Sept. for Heb. *chevlê maveth* in Ps. 18 : 5, **cords of death. Having loosed** agrees better with the Hebrew idea ; but, taken less strictly, **having ended,** it is not inappro-

---

[1] *Grammar of the Chaldee Language as contained in the Bible and the Targums,* translated from the German by the writer (Andover, 1845).

4

pains of death: because it was not possible that he should be holden of it.

25 For David speaketh concerning him, *a*I foresaw the Lord always before my face, for he is on my right hand, that I should not be moved:

26 Therefore did my heart rejoice, and my tongue was glad; moreover also my flesh shall rest in hope:

27 Because thou wilt not leave my soul in hell, neither wilt thou suffer thine Holy One to see corruption.

25 possible that he should be holden of it. For David saith concerning him,

I beheld the Lord always before my face;
For he is on my right hand, that I should not be moved:

26 Therefore my heart was glad, and my tongue rejoiced;
Moreover my flesh also shall *1*dwell in hope:

27 Because thou wilt not leave my soul in Hades,
Neither wilt thou give thy Holy One to see corruption.

---

a Ps. 16 : 8.——1 Or, *tabernacle.*

---

priate to **pangs.** We may conceive, in the latter case, of the pains of death as not ceasing altogether with the life which they destroy, but as still following their victim into the grave. Hence, though the Greek expression, as compared with the Hebrew, changes the figure, it conveys essentially the same thought, and may have been adopted because it was so familiar to the foreign Jews. Some contend that ὠδῖνας means *cords* in the Hellenistic Greek (Kuin., Olsh.); but the assertion is destitute of proof. In that case, too, Luke would have said **their** at the end of the sentence instead of **his,** out of regard to the figure. Others have found an allusion in the word to the resurrection as a birth (see Col. 1 : 18), and hence to death as enduring (so to speak) the pangs inseparable from giving back the dead to life. It is strange that Meyer should revive this almost forgotten interpretation.—**Because it was not possible,** since the divine purpose cannot fail. The confirmatory **because** shows that to be the nature of the impossibility in the writer's mind.

25. The quotation is from Ps. 16 : 8-11, in accordance with the Septuagint. It will be observed that in vs. 29-31 Peter takes pains to show that the portion of the Psalm under consideration there could not have referred to David, but had its fulfilment in Christ. In 13 : 36, Paul too denies the applicability of that passage to David, and insists on its exclusive reference to the Messiah. We may conclude, therefore, that they regarded the entire Psalm as Messianic; for we have in it but one speaker from commencement to end, and in other respects such a marked unity of thought and structure, that it would be an arbitrary procedure to assign one part of it to David and another to Christ. (See Prof. Stuart's interpretation of this Psalm in *Bibl. Repos.,* 1831, p. 51, *sq.*)—**Concerning, in reference to, him.**—**I saw the Lord before me** (where προ is intensive merely), looked unto him as my only helper and support; not *foresaw* (E. V., after the Genv. V.), or *saw beforehand* (Tynd.). The

verb answers to Heb. *shivvithē,* **I placed,** except that this marks more distinctly the effort made in order to keep the mind in that posture.—**Because** states why the eye is thus turned unto Jehovah.—ἐκ δεξιῶν (**on my right hand**) describes one's position as seen off from the right. A protector at the right hand is one who is near and can afford instantly the succor needed.—ἵνα is telic, *in order that.* [The meaning and use of ἵνα are carefully discussed by Winer (§ 53. 6. p. 457, *sq.,* Thayer's transl.) and by Buttmann (*Gram. of the N. T. Greek,* Thayer's transl., p. 235, *sq.*). The latter maintains that there are many predicates and constructions in the New Testament "in which the idea of purpose decidedly *recedes into the background,*" and "where the difference between the two relations (the telic and the ecbatic) [or that of purpose and that of result—in order that, so that] disappears, and it is *nearer to the ecbatic* sense [so that] than to its original final sense." But in the writings of Luke it almost always retains its original telic sense.—A. H.]

26. εὐφράνθη (**was glad).** (On the augment in verbs which begin with εὐ, see W. § 12. 1. 3; K. § 125. R. 1.).—**My tongue** stands for Heb. *kebhodhē,* **my glory**—*i. e.* soul—whose dignity the Hebrews recognized in that way. The Greek has substituted the instrument which the soul uses in giving expression to its joy. We may render both verbs as present if we suppose them to describe a permanent state of mind. (K. § 256. 4.)—**But further also,** climacteric, as in Luke 14 : 26.—**My flesh,** body as distinguished from the soul.—**Shall rest**—viz. in the grave, as defined by the next verse.—**In hope** = Heb. *labhētah,* **in confidence**—*i. e.* of a speedy restoration to life. The sequel exhibits the ground of this confident hope.

27. Because (not *that*) **thou wilt not abandon my soul into Hades. My soul,** according to Hebrew usage, an emphasized pronoun. **Hades** = Heb. **Sheol** denotes properly the place of the dead, but also, by a frequent personification, death itself, considered as a ra-

28 Thou hast made known to me the ways of life; thou shalt make me full of joy with thy countenance.

29 Men *and* brethren, let me freely speak unto you *a*of the patriarch David, that he is both dead and buried, and his sepulchre is with us unto this day.

30 Therefore being a prophet, *b*and knowing that God had sworn with an oath to him, that of the fruit of his loins, according to the flesh, he would raise up Christ to sit on his throne;

31 He seeing this before spake of the resurrection of Christ, *c*that his soul was not left in hell, neither his flesh did see corruption.

28 Thou madest known unto me the ways of life; Thou shalt make me full of gladness ¹with thy countenance.

29 Brethren, I may say unto you freely of the patriarch David, that he both died and was buried, and his 30 tomb is with us unto this day. Being therefore a prophet, and knowing that God had sworn with an oath to him, that of the fruit of his loins ²he would 31 set *one* upon his throne; he foreseeing *this* spake of the resurrection of the Christ, that neither was he

---

a 1 Kings 2 : 10 ; ch. 13 : 36....*b* 2 Sam. 7 : 12, 13 ; Ps. 132 : 11 ; Luke 1 : 32, 69 ; Rom. 1 : 3 ; 2 Tim. 2 : 8....*c* Ps. 16 : 10 ; ch. 13 : 35.

——1 Or, *in thy presence*....2 Or, one *should sit*

---

pacious destroyer. (See Gesen., *Heb. Lex.*, s. v.) The sense then may be expressed thus : Thou wilt not give me up as a prey to death ; he shall not have power over me, to dissolve the body and cause it to return to dust. On the elliptical ᾅδου, see K. § 263. b. Later critics (Lchm., Tsch.) read ᾅδην, after A B C D and other authorities.—**To see,** experience, as in Luke 2, 26.

28. Thou didst make known to me the ways of life—*i. e.* those which lead from death to life. The event was certain, and hence, though future, could be spoken of as past. The meaning is that God would restore him to life after having been put to death and laid in the grave. Kuinoel, De Wette, Meyer, concede that this is the sense which Peter attached to the words; and if so, it must be the true sense. The Greek here expresses the exact form of the Hebrew.— **With** (μετά, *not* = διά, *by*) **thy presence**—*i. e.* with thee where thou art; viz. in heaven. The Redeemer was assured that he would not only escape the power of death, but ascend to dwell in the immediate presence of God on high. It was for that "joy set before him, that he endured the cross, despising the shame, and is set down at the right hand of the throne of God " (Heb. 12 : 2).

29. The object of the remark here is to show that the passage cited above could not have referred to David.—ἐξόν, sc. ἐστί, not ἔστω, **it is lawful,** proper.—**With freedom,** without fear of being thought deficient in any just respect to his memory. His death was recorded in the Old Testament; no one pretended that he had risen, and the Psalm, therefore, could not apply to him.—David is called **patriarch,** as being the founder of the royal family. This title in its stricter use belonged to the founders of the nation.—**Among us,** here in the city. The sepulchre of David was on Mount Zion, where most of the kings of Judah were buried. (See on 5 : 6.) The tomb was well known in Peter's day. Josephus says that it was opened by both Hyrcanus and Herod, in order to rifle it of the treasures which it was supposed to

contain. The mosque, still shown as Neby Dauid, on the southern brow of Zion, cannot be far from the true site.

30. A prophet—*i. e.* divinely inspired (see on v. 17), and so competent to utter the prediction.—**Therefore,** since, unless David meant himself, he must have meant the Messiah.— **And knowing**—viz. that which follows. This knowledge he received from the prophet Nathan, as related in 2 Sam. 7 : 12-16. (See also Ps. 132 : 11 ; 89 : 35-37.) The resurrection of Christ in its full historical sense involved two points : first, his restoration to life ; and secondly, his elevation to permanent regal power. Peter inserts the remark made here to show that David, in predicting the main fact, had a view also of Christ's office as a Sovereign.—**To cause one to sit,** place him (comp. 1 Cor. 6 : 4. Whl., Mey., De Wet.), or (intrans. oftener in N. T.) **that one should sit** (Rob.). [Gloag (and Dickson) translate Meyer's words (4th ed.), incorrectly, *to sit on his throne;* for *zu setzen auf seinem Thron* means, not *to sit,* but *to seat* or *place on his throne.* Dr. Hackett's language therefore represents correctly Meyer's latest view.—A. H.] This descendant was to occupy the throne as ruler in Zion, as Messiah. (Comp. Ps. 2 : 6.) The Greek omits τινά (*one*) often before the infinitive. (K. § 238. R. 3. e.)—After **his loins** the received text adds **that he would raise up the Messiah after the flesh.** Scholz retains the words, but most editors omit them or mark them as unsupported.

31. Seeing this before repeats the idea both of **prophet** and of **knowing.** Having the knowledge derived from the sources which these terms specify, David could speak of the Messiah in the manner here represented. **The Christ** is the official title, not a proper name. —**Neither was left** (Tsch.) or **was not left behind** (given up) **unto Hades** (T. R.) ; aorist here (note the fut. in v. 27), because the speaker thinks of the prediction as now accomplished. **His soul** (T. R.) should probably [almost certainly, with ℵ A B C* D and all the later editors. —A. H.] be dropped after the verb.

32 ^aThis Jesus hath God raised up, ^bwhereof we all are witnesses.

33 Therefore ^cbeing by the right hand of God exalted, and ^dhaving received of the Father the promise of the Holy Ghost, he ^ehath shed forth this, which ye now see and hear.

34 For David is not ascended into the heavens: but he saith himself, ^fThe LORD said unto my Lord, Sit thou on my right hand,

32 left in Hades, nor did his flesh see corruption. This Jesus did God raise up, ¹whereof we all are witnesses.

33 Being therefore ²by the right hand of God exalted, and having received of the Father the promise of the Holy Spirit, he hath poured forth this, which 34 ye see and hear. For David ascended not into the heavens: but he saith himself,
The Lord said unto my Lord, Sit thou on my right hand,

a ver. 24....b ch. 1 : 8....c ch. 5 : 31 ; Phil. 2 : 9 ; Heb. 10 : 12....d John 14 : 26 ; 15 : 26 ; 16 : 7, 13 ; ch. 1 : 4....e ch. 10 : 45 ; Eph. 4 : 8....f Ps. 110 : 1 ; Matt. 22 : 44 ; 1 Cor. 15 : 25 ; Eph. 1 : 20 ; Heb. 1 : 13.———1 Or, of whom....2 Or, at

32. This (looking back to v. 24) **Jesus,** the subject of such a prophecy.—**Whose** (masc. as Wicl. after Vulg.; comp. 5 : 32; 13 : 31), or, as the verb suggests a natural antecedent (neut.), **of which**—viz. his resurrection—**we all are witnesses** (Mey. and E.V.). (See note on 1 : 22.)

33. The exaltation of Christ appears here (**therefore**) as a necessary consequent of the resurrection. (See on vs. 28, 30.)—**Having been exalted to the right hand of God** (Neand., De Wet., Olsh., Bmg, Whl., Rob.); not **by the right hand** (Calv., Kuin., Mey., Alf., E. Vv.). The connection (see especially vs. 34, 35, and comp. 5 : 31) directs us quite inevitably to the first sense; and, though the local dative *whither* may not occur in the New Testament out of this passage and 5 : 31, yet all admit that it is one of the uses of the later Greek generally, and was not unknown to the earlier Greek poetry. (See Bernh., *Synt.*, p. 94.) Winer says (§ 31. 5) that we may translate here *to the right hand* without any hesitation.—**Having received the promise**—i. e. its fulfilment in the bestowal—**of the Holy Spirit,** genit. of the object. (See on 1 : 4.)—**Poured out.** The effusion of the Spirit which is ascribed to God in v. 17 is ascribed here to Christ.—**See** refers to the general spectacle of so many speaking in foreign tongues, or possibly to the tongues of fire visible on the speakers.—**Hear** refers both to the languages spoken and to what was spoken in them.

34. For confirms **being exalted.** The exaltation was not only incident to the resurrection, but was the subject of an express prediction; and that prediction could not apply to David, **for he did not ascend to heaven**—i. e. to be invested with glory and power at the right hand of God. The order of thought, says De Wette, would have been plainer thus : **For David says, Sit at my right hand,** etc.; **but he himself did not ascend into heaven**—i. e. he says this, not of himself, but of the Messiah.—**Saith**—viz. in Ps. 110 : 1. In Matt. 22 : 43 and Mark 12 : 36 the Saviour recognizes David as the author of the Psalm, and attrib-

utes to him a divine inspiration in speaking thus of the Messiah. He cites the same passage as proof of David's acknowledged inferiority to himself.—κάθου (imperf.) is for the purer κάθησο. (W. § 14. 4 ; Mt. § 236.) **On my right hand** (see on v. 25)—i. e. as the partner of my throne. The following remarks of Professor Stuart[1] are pertinent here : "In the New Testament, when Christ is represented as sitting at the right hand of Divine Majesty (Heb. 1 : 3), or the right hand of God (Acts 2 : 33 and Heb. 10 : 12), or at the right of the throne of God (Heb. 12 : 2), participation in supreme dominion is most clearly meant. (Comp. 1 Pet. 3 : 22 ; Rom. 8 : 34 ; Mark 16 : 19 ; Phil. 2 : 6–11 ; Eph. 1 : 20–23.) At the same time, the comparison of these passages will show most clearly that Christ's exaltation at the right hand of God means *his being seated on the mediatorial throne* as the result and reward of his sufferings (see particularly Phil. 2 : 6–11, and comp. Heb. 12 : 2), and that the phrase in question never means the *original* dominion which Christ, as Logos, or God, possesses. The sacred writers never speak respecting the Logos, considered simply in his *divine* nature, as being seated at the right hand of God, but only of the Logos *incarnate*, or the Mediator, as being seated there. So, in Heb. 1 : 3, it is *after* the expiation made by the Son of God that he is represented as seating himself at the right hand of the Divine Majesty. And that this *mediatorial* dominion is not to be considered simply as the dominion of the *divine* nature of Christ as such is plain from the fact that when the mediatorial office is fulfilled the kingdom of the Mediator as such is to cease. Moreover, that the phrase *to sit* at the *right hand of God*, or *of the throne of God*, does not of itself mean *original divine* dominion is clear from the fact that Christ assures his faithful disciples they shall sit down with him on his throne, even as he sat down with the Father on his throne. (Rev. 3 : 21.) It is exaltation, then, in consequence of obedience and sufferings, which is designated by the phrase in question."

1 *Commentary on the Epistle to the Hebrews*, p. 559, *sq.* (1833).

35 Until I make thy foes thy footstool.
36 Therefore let all the house of Israel know assuredly, that God ^ahath made that same Jesus, whom ye have crucified, both Lord and Christ.
37 ¶Now when they heard *this*, ^bthey were pricked in their heart, and said unto Peter and to the rest of the apostles, Men *and* brethren, what shall we do?
38 Then Peter said unto them, ^cRepent, and be baptized every one of you in the name of Jesus Christ for the remission of sins, and ye shall receive the gift of the Holy Ghost.
39 For the promise is unto you, and ^dto your chil-

35 Till I make thine enemies the footstool of thy feet.
36 Let ¹all the house of Israel therefore know assuredly, that God hath made him both Lord and Christ, this Jesus whom ye crucified.
37 Now when they heard *this*, they were pricked in their heart, and said unto Peter and the rest of the
38 apostles, Brethren, what shall we do? And Peter *said* unto them, Repent ye, and be baptized every one of you in the name of Jesus Christ unto the remission of your sins; and ye shall receive the gift
39 of the Holy Spirit. For to you is the promise, and

a ch. 5 : 31....*b* Zech. 12 : 10 ; Luke 3 : 10 ; ch. 9 : 6 ; 16 : 30....*c* Luke 24 : 47 ; ch. 3 : 19....*d* Joel 2 : 28 ; ch. 3 : 25.——-1 Or, *every house*.

35. Until, etc. The dominion here which Christ received belonged to him as Mediator; and it is to cease, therefore, when the objects of his kingdom as Mediator are accomplished. (Comp. 1 Cor. 15 : 23–28.) The verse recognizes distinctly that limitation.

36. All the house (race) **of Israel.** οἶκος (**house**) appears to omit the article, as having the nature of a proper name. (W. ₰ 17. 10.)—**That God made him both Lord and Christ**—to wit, **this one, the Jesus whom,** etc. **This one, the Jesus** is in apposition with **him.**

37–42. EFFECT OF THE DISCOURSE IN THE CONVERSION OF THREE THOUSAND.

37. Not all, but many, of those addressed must be understood here. This necessary limitation could be left to suggest itself. **Were pierced in the heart,** dative of the sphere in which (Rom. 4 : 20 ; 1 Cor. 14 : 20). (W. ₰ 31, 3.) Some editions have καρδίαν (**heart**), accusative of the part affected. [This reading is adopted by Lach., Tsch., Treg., West. and Hort, Anglo-Am. Revisers, with ℵ A B C and other documents.—A. H.] The verb expresses forcibly the idea of pungent sorrow and alarm.—**What shall we do?** The answer to the question shows that it related to the way of escape from the consequences of their guilt.—**For men,** see on 1 : 16.

38. Upon the name of Jesus Christ, as the foundation of the baptism—*i. e.* with an acknowledgment of him in that act as being what his name imports (see on v. 21)—to wit, the sinner's only hope, his Redeemer, Justifier, Lord, final Judge. (For ἐπί with this force, see W. ₰ 48. c.) We see from v. 40 that Luke has given only an epitome of Peter's instructions on this occasion. The usual formula in relation to baptism is *into the name* as in 8 : 16; 19 : 5. It may have been avoided here as a matter of euphony, since εἰς follows in the

next clause (De Wet.).—**In order to the forgiveness of sins** (Matt. 26 : 28; Luke 3 : 3) we connect naturally with both the preceding verbs. This clause states the motive or object which should induce them to repent and be baptized. It enforces the entire exhortation, not one part of it to the exclusion of the other. [Observe (1) that forgiveness of sins is here conditioned on repentance. Hence the doctrine that sinners are forgiven unconditionally, in view of the Saviour's propitiatory death, is an error. Though mercy is offered, the wrath of God abideth on him that believeth not. (See John 3 : 36.) If one may be said in a certain sense to have been forgiven from eternity in consideration of the Lamb slain from the foundation of the world, it is because he was looked upon as having exercised repentance toward God and faith in the Lord Jesus Christ. Out of Christ the sinner is unforgiven. (2) That repentance and the prescribed expression of it by baptism are closely united. Peter did not feel it necessary to provide for exceptional cases in this address to the people. He saw that the inward change and the ritual confession of it were so knit together by nature that it was enough for him to state them in their proper order and sequence. Repentance and the first-fruits of repentance were generally inseparable. The former could not be genuine without manifesting itself in the latter. And in the circumstances of that day a willingness to be baptized was no slight evidence of a new heart. —A. H.]

39. To your children—unto your descendants (see 13 : 33); not *your little ones* (Alf.), with an appeal to v. 17, for the sons and daughters there are so far adult as to have visions and to prophesy.—**To all those afar off**—*i. e.* the distant nations or heathen. So, among others, Calvin, Bengel, Olshausen, Harless,[1] De Wette, Neander, Lange.[2] The expression was current among the Jews in that

[1] *Commentar über den Brief Pauli an die Ephesier*, p. 213, *sq.*
[2] *Das apostolische Zeitalter*, zweiter Band. p. 42 (1853).

dren, and [a]to all that are afar off, *even* as many as the Lord our God shall call.

40 And with many other words did he testify and exhort, saying, Save yourselves from this untoward generation.

41 ¶Then they that gladly received his word were baptized: and the same day there were added *unto them* about three thousand souls.

42 [b]And they continued stedfastly in the apostles'

to your children, and to all that are afar off, *even* as 40 many as the Lord our God shall call unto him. And with many other words he testified, and exhorted them, saying, Save yourselves from this crooked 41 generation. They then [1]that received his word were baptized: and there were added *unto them* in 42 that day about three thousand souls. And they continued stedfastly in the apostles' teaching and

---

a ch. 10 : 45; 11 : 15, 18; 14 : 27; 15 : 3, 8, 14; Eph. 2 : 13, 17....*b* ver. 46; ch. 1 : 14; Rom. 12 : 12; Eph. 6 : 18; Col. 4 : 2; Heb. 10 : 25.———1 Or, *having received*

---

sense. (Comp. Zech. 6 : 15; Isa. 49 : 1; 57 : 19; Eph. 2 : 13, 17, where see Dr. Hodge in his recent *Commentary.*) Even the Rabbinic writers employed it as synonymous with *the heathen.* (Schött., *Hor. Heb.*, vol. i. p. 761.) It has been objected that this explanation supposes Peter to have been already aware that the gospel was to be preached to the Gentiles; whereas it is said he afterward hesitated on the subject, and needed a special revelation to point out to him his duty. (See 10 : 10, *sq.*) But the objection misstates the ground of the hesitation; it related to the terms on which the Gentiles were to be acknowledged as Christians, not to the fact itself. On this point how is it possible that he should have doubted? The Jews in general who expected a Messiah at all believed in the universality of his reign. The prophets foretold distinctly that the Gentiles under him should form one people with the Jews, that they should both acknowledge the same God and be acknowledged of him. (See *e. g.* Mic. 4 : 1, *sq.*; Amos 9 : 12; Isa. 2 : 2, *sq.*; 40 : 5; 54 : 4, *sq.*, etc.) Add to this that the Saviour himself before his ascension had charged his disciples to go into all the world and preach the gospel to every creature. The relation in which the Gentile believers were to stand to Judaism—how far they were to practise its rites, and in that respect assimilate to the Jews—was not so well understood. On that question, it is true, they needed and received further instruction as to the course to be pursued. Those who reject the foregoing explanation suppose **all that are afar off** to denote the foreign Jews. But they are included already in **you,** since many of those addressed were pilgrims who had come to Jerusalem to celebrate the present feast. This sense of the phrase renders it superfluous.—**Whomsoever the Lord shall have called.** For the verbal form, see the note on v. 21. The expression imports that as many would secure a part in the promise as it should prove that the divine purpose had embraced.

40. Copies fluctuate between διεμαρτύρετο and διεμαρτύρατο. The imperfect agrees best with the next verb.—**Save yourselves.** For this

middle sense, see W. ¿ 39. 2.—**From this perverse** (Phil. 2 : 15) **generation**—*i. e.* from participation in their guilt and doom. (Comp. 1 Cor. 11 : 32; Gal. 1 : 4.)

41. Therefore — viz. in consequence of Peter's exhortation.—**They** (who were mentioned as penitent in v. 37) **having received his word**—viz. that in v. 38, *sq.* (De Wet., Mey.). Many adopt the substantive construction : **they who received** (Bng., Kuin., E. Vv.). The first view identifies those who believe here more distinctly with those in v. 37 who evince such a preparation for the exercise of faith, and may be preferable on that account; but the use of the participle in other respects (as we saw on 1 : 6) involves an ambiguity. **Gladly** elicits a correct idea, but is hardly genuine.—**Souls,** persons. (See v. 43; 3 : 23, 7 : 14; 27 : 37.) The frequency of this sense may be Hebraistic, but not the sense itself.— **Were baptized.** Not necessarily at once after the discourse, but naturally during the same day, if we unite the next clause (**the same day;** see on 8 : 1) closely with this. But the compendious form of the narrative would allow us, with some editors, to place a colon between the two clauses; and then the baptism could be regarded as subsequent to **were added to,** taking place at such time and under such circumstances as the convenience of the parties might require. It is proper to add (against Alf.) that the pools so numerous and large which encircled Jerusalem, as both those still in use and the remains of others testify at the present day, afforded ample means for the administration of the rite. The habits of the East, as every traveller knows, would present no obstacle to such a use of the public reservoirs.

42. Constantly applying themselves unto the teaching of the apostles. They sought to know more and more of the gospel which they had embraced.—καὶ τῇ κοινωνίᾳ (comp. εἶχον κοινά in v. 44), **and unto the communication,** distribution—*i. e.* of money or other supplies for the poor (Heinr., Kuin., Olsh., Bmg., Hmph.); **the fellowship** —*i. e.* the community, oneness of spirit and effort which bound the first Christians to each

doctrine and fellowship, and in breaking of bread, and in prayers.

43 And fear came upon every soul: and *a*many wonders and signs were done by the apostles.

[1]fellowship, in the breaking of bread and the prayers.

43 And fear came upon every soul: and many won-

43 And fear came upon every soul: and many won-

a Mark 16 : 17 ; ch. 4 : 33 ; 5 : 12.——1 Or, *in fellowship*

other (Bng., Mey., Rob.); **the communion,** meals in common (*agapæ*, which were followed by the Lord's Supper (Bez., Grot., De Wet.); **the sacrament** itself (Lightf., Est., Wlf.). I prefer the first sense of this doubtful word, because all the other nouns denote an act, not a state of mind or feeling; because the participle applies to an act rather than an abstract quality (which are objections to the second sense); because this use of the term is justified by Rom. 15 : 26; 2 Cor. 8 : 4, especially Heb. 13 : 16; and because, as the contributions would naturally be made at their meetings, the several nouns relate then to a common subject— viz. their religious assemblies. It may be added that their liberality toward the poor was so characteristic of the first Christians that this sketch of their religious habits might be expected to include that particular. *Koinonia* in the sense of our *communion*, the Lord's Supper, appears not to have prevailed before the fourth century (Suicer, *Thesaur.*, s. v., as cited by Hmph.), and hence the last of the meanings given above may be laid out of the account here. The meals in common, or ἀγάπαι, were known to be a part of the κλάσις τοῦ ἄρτου (see below), and consequently would not need to be specified in this connection by a separate term. The E. V. unites ἀποστόλων with both nouns: "the apostles' doctrine and fellowship" (also Tynd., Cranm., Gen.). With that combination we should have had regularly the genitive after the second noun, without a repetition of the article. (See W. ? 19. 3. c.) Some assume a hendiadys: "the communion in the breaking of bread" (Vulg., Wicl., Blmf.). The analysis is not only awkward, but opposed by **the** before **breaking. The breaking of the bread** denotes *the breaking of the bread* as performed at the Lord's Supper. (See 20 : 7, 11 ; 1 Cor. 10 : 16.) The expression itself may designate an ordinary meal, as in Luke 24 : 35; but that here would be an unmeaning notice. There can be no doubt that the Eucharist at this period was preceded uniformly by a common repast, as was the case when the ordinance was instituted. Most scholars hold that this was the prevailing usage in the first centuries after Christ. We have traces of that practice in 1 Cor. 11 : 20, *sq.*, and, in all probability, in v. 46, below. The *bread* only being mentioned here,

the Roman Catholics appeal to this passage as proving that their custom of distributing but one element (the cup they withhold from the laity) is the apostolic one. It is a case, obviously, in which the leading act of the transaction gives name to the transaction itself. ["The prayers" (Revised Version) is a manifest improvement on the Common Version, since the Greek article ought generally to be represented in translation. And Luke refers, without doubt, to the services of prayer which the disciples held, or, if not to distinct services of prayer, to the prayers which held a very important place in their social meetings. (See 6 : 4.)—A. H.]

43-47. BENEVOLENCE OF THE FIRST CHRISTIANS; THEIR JOY, THEIR INCREASE.

43. Unto every soul, of those who heard of the events just related—viz. the descent of the Spirit, the miracle of tongues, the conversion of such a multitude. (Comp. 5 : 5.)—**Fear,** religious awe. (See Luke 1 : 65.)—**Many,** in this position, belongs to both nouns. (See 17 : 12. W. ? 59. 5.) **Through the apostles,** as instruments, while the power was God's. (See v. 22 and 15 : 12.)—**Were wrought** (imperf.), during this general period. [Two or three remarks are suggested by the statement that miracles were wrought *through the apostles.* (1) We are not to suppose that the divine energy was literally transmitted through them—*i. e.* through their wills, hands, handkerchiefs—to the persons restored by it; but we must infer from the narrative that the miracles were wrought in answer to their believing word, or at least were so connected with them as to ratify their authority as ambassadors of Christ (3 : 16; 4 : 10; 9 : 34, 40). (2) Nearly all the miracles wrought at the apostles' word were gracious. Evil spirits were cast out (5 : 16; 16 : 18; 19 : 12), the lame and the sick were healed (3 : 6-10; 14 : 8-13), and the dead were raised to life (9 : 36-40; 20 : 9, 10). The only exceptions are the death of Ananias and Sapphira and the temporary blindness of Elymas. (3) The faith which led the apostles to ask for miracles must have been distinguished from that which they possessed in common with all true Christians. It was a special charism, a prophetic assurance as to the will of God.—A. H.]

44 And all that believed were together, and [a]had all things common ;
45 And sold their possessions and goods, and [b]parted them to all *men*, as every man had need.
46 [c]And they, continuing daily with one accord [d]in the temple, and [e]breaking bread from house to house, did eat their meat with gladness and singleness of heart,
47 Praising God, and [f]having favor with all the peo-

44 ders and signs were done [1]by the apostles[2]. And al that believed were together, and had all things common ; and they sold their possessions and goods, and parted them to all, according as any man had need.
46 And day by day, continuing stedfastly with one accord in the temple, and breaking bread at home, they did take their food with gladness and singleness of heart, praising God, and having favor with all the

a ch. 4 : 32, 34....*b* Isa. 58 : 7....*c* ch. 1 : 14....*d* Luke 24 : 53 ; ch. 5 : 42....*e* ch. 20 : 7....*f* Luke 2 : 52 ; ch. 4 : 33 ; Rom. 14 : 18.
————1 Or, *through*....2 Many ancient authorities add *in Jerusalem ; and great fear was upon all.*

44. ἐπὶ τὸ αὐτό, not *harmonious* (Calv., Kuin.), but **together**—*i. e.* they met daily in one place, as explained in v. 46. (See on 1 : 15.)—**And they had all things common,** looked upon their possessions not as their own, but held them as subject to the use of the church as they were needed. The next words refer to the act of disposing of their property, and hence these describe the antecedent principle or spirit which prompted the act. The remark is defined by οὐδὲ εἷς . . . ἔλεγεν . . . εἶναι in 4 : 32: **neither did any one say,** etc.

45. Their estates (lands) **and** other **possessions.—Them**—*i. e.* the proceeds of the sale. (W. § 22. 3.)—**As any one from time to time had need.** ἄν, with the indicative, in a relative sentence, denotes a recurring act. (W. § 42. 3. a.) As this clause qualifies also **sold** (imperf. as done again and again), it shows that they did not alienate their property at once, but parted with it as occasion required.

46. ὁμοθυμαδόν, as in v. 1.—**From house to house** (κατ᾽ οἶκον) (comp. κατὰ πόλιν in Tit. 1 : 5) —*i. e.* in different houses, some in one, some in another, or perhaps in different houses successively (E. V., Kuin., Neand.), or **at home,** in private. (See Phil. v. 2.) (Olsh., De Wet., Mey., Gen. V.) Even in the latter case we may suppose that they met in separate parties at different places ; not necessarily (as Mey.) all in a single place at once. Both renderings are justifiable. The latter may be more exact in form, since it brings out more strongly an apparent contrast between the public worship and their more private services. [See Jacob, *The Eccl. Polity of the N. T.*, p. 191, *sq.* He remarks on this expression that "the use of the singular number, and without the article, shows that when St. Luke wrote his narrative the custom of meeting in these worship-rooms for united devotions had become perfectly common and familiar ; otherwise, he would have written κατὰ τοὺς οἴκους. Just as we would say, "All the people in the city were *at church*," meaning in the different churches of the place ; whereas a stranger, unused to this custom, would say "they were *in the churches*."—A. H.] ἐν in

the place of κατά would have removed the ambiguity. Neander (*Pflanzung*, u. s. w., vol. i. p. 36) observes that a single room would hardly have contained the present number of converts. He supposes that, in addition to their daily resort to the temple, they met in smaller companies at different places, that they here received instruction from their teachers or one another and prayed and sang together, and as the members of a common family closed their interview with a repast, at which bread and wine were distributed in memory of the Saviour's last meal with his disciples. In conformity with this view, **breaking bread** may refer to their **breaking bread** in connection with the sacrament, and **did eat their meat** to their reception of food for ordinary purposes.—**With simplicity of heart,** with childlike affection toward God and one another.

47. Favor, approbation (Luke 2 : 52).—**Those who are saved,** or, more strictly, **are becoming saved** from day to day, since the present tense denotes a process going on. (See 1 Cor. 1 : 18 and 2 Cor. 2 : 15.) The Greek should have been the perfect participle, to signify that they had already secured their salvation ; and the future participle, to signify that they were certain of its completion. (See Green's *Gr.*, p. 28.) The expression implies a certainty resulting not so much from God's purpose as from human conduct. The doctrine is that those who embrace the gospel adopt the infallible means of being saved. [The expression here used, " *those that were being saved,*" is in perfect accord with the language of Paul in 2 Cor. 4 : 16 : " Though our outward man is decaying, yet our inward man is renewed " (or is being renewed) " day by day ;" and in Col. 3 : 10 : " And have put on the new man, who is being renewed unto knowledge after the image of him that created him." (Comp. 2 Cor. 3 : 18.) Luke's phraseology agrees with the doctrine of progressive sanctification, or of growth in grace, rather than with the theory of "the higher Christian life" as strenuously advocated by some at the present day. (See the Editor's little vol. entitled *The Doctrine of the Higher*

ple. And *the Lord added to the church daily such as should be saved.

people. And the Lord added ¹to them day by day those that were ²saved.

CHAPTER III.

NOW Peter and John went up together *into the temple at the hour of prayer, *being the ninth *hour*.
2 And *a certain man lame from his mother's womb was carried, whom they laid daily at the gate of the

1 Now Peter and John were going up into the temple at the hour of prayer, *being the ninth *hour*. And a certain man that was lame from his mother's womb was carried, whom they laid daily at the door of the

a ch. 5 : 14; 11 : 24....*b* ch. 2 : 46....*c* Ps. 55 : 17....*d* ch. 14 : 8.———1 Gr. *together*....2 Or, *being saved*

Chr. Life Compared with the Teaching of the Holy Scriptures.) — A. H.] — **Added** (imperf. with reference to **daily**) brings to view God's agency in that acceptance of the gospel which ensures salvation. [**To the church** is unnoticed by Hackett, doubtless because he considered it a gloss. It is omitted by Lach., Tsch., Treg., West. and Hort, after א A B C. When this is omitted, the phrase translated **together** stands in the Greek text at the close of this verse and just before the words **Now Peter and John** (3 : 1); so that it may be joined with either. The editors just named connect it with this verse and with the verb **was adding,** thus : **And the Lord was adding together day by day those that were being saved.** For **together** the Revised Version has **to them,** and Alf. **to their number.**—A. H.]

1–10. HEALING OF THE LAME MAN BY PETER AND JOHN.

1. Together (ἐπὶ τὸ αὐτό), in company. (See 1 : 15.) [And note in brackets at the close of Chapter II.—A. H.]—**Were going up,** because the temple was on Mount Moriah, and even from the gate where the miracle occurred (v. 3) a flight of steps led to the Court of the Israelites.—**The ninth.** This was our three o'clock P. M., at which time the evening sacrifice was offered. (See on 2 : 15.) The apostles and other believers at Jerusalem had not yet withdrawn from the Jewish worship (see also 21 : 23, *sq.*), and it is probable that most of them continued to adhere to the services of the temple until the destruction of the temple abolished them. But the spirit with which they performed these services was no longer the Jewish spirit. Instead of regarding their compliance with the ordinances of the law as an act of merit, they recognized Christ as " the end of the law for righteousness to every one that believeth." They viewed the sacrifices which continued to be offered, not as having any efficacy to procure the remission of sin, or as typical of an atonement still to be made, but as realized already in the death of Christ, and hence as mementoes, as often as they beheld them or participated in

them, of the " one sacrifice for sins " effected " through the offering of the body of Jesus Christ." As in the case of circumcision, so undoubtedly the Jewish Christians relinquished the other rites of Judaism only by degrees. They were brought fully to this in part by obtaining a clearer insight into the relation of the ancient Economy to the new, and in part by the occurrence of national circumstances which hastened the result. From the Jewish synagogues, on the contrary, they must have separated at once as soon as their distinctive views became known. It was impossible to avow the Christian faith and remain connected with those communities. (Compare the note on 9 : 2.) We have seen in the second chapter that, in connection with the worship of the temple, the believers at Jerusalem maintained separate religious worship among themselves.

2. [Lame from his mother's womb. He was now above forty years old (4 : 22). An account of this particular cure was probably inserted by Luke in his narrative, because the lameness was congenital, and was therefore deemed more incurable than any lameness occasioned by disease or by accident. Hence the miraculous character of the event was indubitable, and the people were moved by it.— A. H.]—**Was carried along** (relative imperf.), just then, as the apostles arrived.—**They laid** is imperf. with reference to the custom of placing the cripple here.—**The one called Beautiful.** Most interpreters think that this was the gate described by Josephus (*Bel. Jud.*, 5. 5. 3; *Antt.*, 15. 11. 3) as composed chiefly of Corinthian brass, and as excelling all the other gates of the temple in the splendor of its appearance, though it is not mentioned by him under this particular appellation. If this be so, the gate then was on the east side toward Olivet (*the eastern*, says Jos.), and was an inner gate leading from the Court of the Gentiles into the Court of the Israelites. It is not against this that Josephus speaks also of this gate as *the one without the temple* ; for he must mean (the term is not ἱερόν) *the one exterior to the temple* strictly so called, the sanctuary ; not (as Mey.) opening

temple which is called Beautiful, [a]to ask alms of them that entered into the temple;

3 Who seeing Peter and John about to go into the temple asked an alms.

4 And Peter, fastening his eyes upon him with John, said, Look on us.

5 And he gave heed unto them, expecting to receive something of them.

6 Then Peter said, Silver and gold have I none; but such as I have give I thee: [b]In the name of Jesus Christ of Nazareth rise up and walk.

7 And he took him by the right hand, and lifted *him* up: and immediately his feet and ankle bones received strength.

8 And he [c]leaping up stood, and walked, and entered with them into the temple, walking, and leaping, and praising God.

temple which is called Beautiful, to ask alms of them 3 that entered into the temple; who seeing Peter and John about to go into the temple, asked to receive 4 an alms. And Peter, fastening his eyes upon him, 5 with John, said, Look on us. And he gave heed unto them, expecting to receive something from 6 them. But Peter said, Silver and gold have I none; but what I have, that give I thee. In the name of 7 Jesus Christ of Nazareth, walk. And he took him by the right hand, and raised him up: and immediately his feet and his ankle-bones received strength. 8 And leaping up, he stood, and began to walk; and he entered with them into the temple, walking,

---

a John 9 : 8....*b* ch. 4 : 10....*c* Isa. 35 : 6.

---

from without into the enclosure of the sacred precincts. The folds of this brazen gate were fifty cubits high and forty broad, and were covered with plates of gold and silver. Luke's epithet **Beautiful** could not have had a more pertinent application. Some have thought that the gate to which he refers must have been one of the outer gates, because what is related in v. 11, *sq.*, took place in Solomon's porch, which was in the Court of the Gentiles. But we may suppose, as Lightfoot suggests, that the apostles, having been with the lame man into the temple —*i. e.* the Court of the Israelites (see v. 8)— were returning, and had reached the Court of the Gentiles when the concourse of the people there spoken of took place.—**In order to ask,** telic. This use of the infinitive with τοῦ to denote the object for which an act is performed (comp. 18 : 10 ; 26 : 18 ; Mark 4 : 3, etc.) results naturally from the nature of the genitive as the *whence-case*. The older writers supplied ἕνεκα or χάριν, but the construction is neither elliptical nor Hebraistic. (W. § 44. 4. b.; S. § 165. 3. 2; K. § 308. 2. b.)—**Those entering into the temple**—*i. e.* the court where the Jews worshipped, if, as suggested above, the lame man sat at the gate of that court. **The temple** here too may be the temple in its aggregate sense; not, perforce, the outer court (Mey.). If a noun follows an intransitive verb compounded with a preposition, it is common to repeat the preposition before the noun. (See vs. 3, 8; 22 : 6; Matt. 7 : 23, etc. W. § 56. 2.)

3. Who (ὅς), stands often where **this one** (οὗτος) would be the ordinary connective. (K. § 334. 3.)—**To receive** (omitted in v. 2) is not strictly pleonastic, but expands the idea of **asked.** (W. § 63. 4. d.) It is left out of some copies, but is genuine.

4. Look upon us. Their object appears to have been to gain his attention more fully to their words; so that, as they said, " In the name

of Jesus Christ," etc. (v. 6), he might understand to whom he was indebted for the benefit conferred upon him.

5. ἐπεῖχεν αὐτοῖς, sc. τὸν νοῦν, **Fixed his mind upon them.** (Comp. Luke 14 : 7.) The man's eager expectation looked through his countenance.—**Something,** in the way of alms. We have no evidence that he recognized Peter and John as the disciples of Christ and expected that they would heal his infirmity. Their address to him in the next verse precludes that supposition.

6. In the name—*i. e.* we speaking **in his name,** by virtue of his authority. (Comp. 16 : 18.) The language of Christ, on the contrary, when he performed a miracle, was **I say to thee,** or to that effect. (See Luke 5 : 24.)— **Of Nazareth** is added for the sake of distinction, as in 2 : 22.—**Walk** is imperative present, and not aorist, like **rise up,** because it denotes a continued act. (Comp. 8 : 26; 13 : 8, etc. W. § 43. 3. b.; S. § 141. 5.) [It ought perhaps to be stated that the three words **rise up and** are omitted by Tsch., West. and Hort, Revisers' text, and bracketed by Treg. They are wanting in א B D, and probably formed no part of the autograph of Luke.—A. H.]

7. Having taken him by the right hand, and thus encouraged him to obey their command. (See Mark 9 : 27.) **His** exemplifies the rule that a genitive which belongs to two or more nouns usually precedes them. (W. § 30. 3. 4.)—**Feet, ankles.** This particularity has been reckoned among the traces of a professional habit for which Luke is distinguished. (See on 28 : 8.)

8. Leaping forth, from the place where he sat, and *up* only as involved; not from his bed (Mey., but dropped in his last ed.), since **sat** (v. 10) shows that he was not reclining.—**Stood,** for the first time since he was born (v. 2).— **Walked to and fro,** as if to make trial of his

9 *And all the people saw him walking and praising God:

10 And they knew that it was he which *sat for alms at the Beautiful gate of the temple: and they were filled with wonder and amazement at that which had happened unto him.

11 And as the lame man which was healed held Peter and John, all the people ran together unto them in the porch *that is called Solomon's, greatly wondering.

12 ¶ And when Peter saw *it*, he answered unto the people, Ye men of Israel, why marvel ye at this? or why look ye so earnestly on us, as though by our own power or holiness we had made this man to walk?

13 *The God of Abraham, and of Isaac, and of Jacob, the God of our fathers, *hath glorified his son Jesus; whom ye *delivered up, and *denied him in the presence of Pilate, when he was determined to let *him* go.

9 and leaping, and praising God. And all the people

10 saw him walking and praising God: and they took knowledge of him, that it was he who sat for alms at the Beautiful Gate of the temple: and they were filled with wonder and amazement at that which had happened unto him.

11 And as he held Peter and John, all the people ran together unto them in the *porch that is called Solo-

12 mon's, greatly wondering. And when Peter saw it, he answered unto the people, Ye men of Israel, why marvel ye at this *man? or why fasten ye your eyes on us, as though by our own power or godliness we

13 had made him to walk? The God of Abraham, and of Isaac, and of Jacob, the God of our fathers, hath glorified his *Servant Jesus; whom ye delivered up, and denied before the face of Pilate, when he had

a ch. 4 : 16, 21....*b* Like John 9 : 8....*c* John 10 : 23 ; ch. 5 : 12....*d* ch. 5 : 30....*e* John 7 : 39 ; 12 : 16 ; 17 : 1....*f* Matt. 27 : 2....*g* Matt. 27 : 20 ; Mark 15 : 11 ; Luke 23 : 18, 20, 21 ; John 18 : 40 ; 19 : 15 ; ch. 13 : 28.———1 Or, *portico*....2 Or, *thing*....3 Or, *Child:* and so in ver. 26 ; *4* : 27, 30. See Matt. 12 : 18 ; Isa. 42 : 1 ; 52 : 13 ; 53 : 11.

newly-found strength.—**Into the temple,** its inner part, beyond the gate where the lame man had been healed. (See on v. 2.)—In **walking,** etc., Luke writes as if he were giving the recital of some eye-witness.

10. They recognized him (upon attentive scrutiny, hence imperf.) **that this one,** etc. The subject of the subordinate clause is attracted here into the principal clause, and then repeated in **this one.** (So in 4 : 13 ; 9 : 20 ; 13 : 32 ; 16 : 3, etc.) The subject of the second clause becomes in this way more prominent. (W. ₰ 66. 5 ; B. ₰ 151. I. 6. 7.) The ordinary construction would omit **him** after **recognized,** and make the sentence after **that** the object of the verb.—**For the alms** which he solicited.

11–26. THE TESTIMONY OF PETER AFTER THE MIRACLE.

11. While he is holding them fast, or **keeping near to them.** This latter signification, says De Wette, has not been fully proved, but arises naturally out of the other. Meyer adheres more correctly to the first meaning : the man, in the ardor of his gratitude, clung to his benefactors, and would not be separated from them. **He** is considered the correct reading, instead of **the lame man that was healed** in the common text (Grsb., Mey., Lchm.). The addition has been transferred to the English Version.—**Porch . . . Solomon's.** (See John 10 : 23.) This hall, or porch, was on the eastern side of the temple, in the Court of the Heathen. The general opinion is that it was called **the porch of Solomon** because it occupied the site of a porch which had been connected with the first temple. Lücke[1] thinks that it may have been a structure built by Solomon himself, which had

escaped the destruction of the first temple. Tholuck[2] expresses the same belief. It accords with this view that Josephus (*Antt.*, 20. 9. 7) calls the porch "Solomon's work." In popular speech, says Lightfoot, the Jews sometimes meant the entire Court of the Gentiles when they spoke of Solomon's porch.—**Greatly wondering** agrees with **people** as a collective term. (Comp. 5 : 16.)

12. Seeing their astonishment.—**Proceeded to speak** (Hebraistic; see 5 : 8), or perhaps **answered unto the people** (De Wet., Mey.). since their looks of wonder seemed to ask for some explanation of the miracle. (See v. 11.) —ἐπὶ τούτῳ may be neuter **at this thing** (see v. 10, E. Vv.), but more probably masculine, **at this one** (Mey., De Wet.), which prepares the way for **him,** like the succession of **this one** and **him** in v. 16. [In his last edition Meyer considers this pronoun *neuter* = **at this,** referring to v. 10, where the astonishment and surprise were occasioned by *what had happened* to the lame man.—A. H.]—**Upon us,** emphatic, as distinguished from Christ or God, to whom the miracle ought to have turned their thoughts. —**Look ye** takes its object in the dative (see also 10 : 4 ; 14 : 9), or in the accusative with εἰς. (Comp. v. 4 ; 1 : 10 ; 6 : 15.)—**As by our own** (inherent or self-acquired) **power, or** (since power had been exerted) **piety, as** the reason of its being conferred on them.—**Had made,** etc. ;—**having effected** (ecbatic infinitive) **that he should walk.** (W. ₰ 44. 4 ; S. ₰ 165. 3.)

13. Glorified, honored ; not by the miracle at this time (Mey.), but by all the mighty works which attested his mission. (See 2 : 22.)—παῖδα, not *son* = υἱός, but *servant* = Heb. *ĕbhedh*, which was one of the prophetic appellations of the

---

[1] *Commentar über das Evangelium des Johannes,* vol. ii. p. 361.

[2] *Commentar zum Evangelium Johannis,* p. 256 (sechste Auflage).

14 But ye denied [a]the Holy One [b]and the Just, and desired a murderer to be granted unto you;

15 And killed the Prince of life, [c]whom God hath raised from the dead; [d]whereof we are witnesses.

16 [e]And his name through faith in his name hath made this man strong, whom ye see and know: yea, the faith which is by him hath given him this perfect soundness in the presence of you all.

17 And now, brethren, I wot that [f]through ignorance ye did it, as did also your rulers.

14 determined to release him. But ye denied the Holy and Righteous One, and asked for a murderer to be

15 granted unto you, and killed the [1]Prince of life; whom God raised from the dead; [2]whereof we are

16 witnesses. And [3]by faith in his name hath his name made this man strong, whom ye behold and know: yea, the faith which is through him hath given him this perfect soundness in the presence of you all.

17 And now, brethren, I know that in ignorance ye

[a] Ps. 16 : 10; Mark 1 : 24; Luke 1 : 35; ch. 2 : 27; 4 : 27....[b] ch. 7 : 52; 22 : 14; Heb. 2 : 10; 5 : 9; 1 John 5 : 11....[c] ch. 2 : 24 ...[d] ch. 2 : 32....[e] Matt. 9 22; ch. 4 : 10; 14 : 9....[f] Luke 23 : 34; John 16 : 3; ch. 13 : 27; 1 Cor. 2 : 8; 1 Tim. 1 : 13.——[1] Or, Author....[2] Or, of whom....[3] Or, on the ground of

Messiah, especially in the second part of Isaiah. (See Matt. 12 : 18, as compared with Isa. 42 : 1, *sq.*) The term occurs again in this sense in v. 26; 4 : 27, 30.—μέν, as in 1 : 1. The antithetic idea may have been that in v. 17.—**Ye delivered up**—viz. to Pilate.—**Denied**, refused to acknowledge as Messiah.—**Him**. It will be seen that the writer drops here the relative structure of the sentence.—**When, or although, he decided**—viz. that it was just **to release him**. (See Luke 23 : 16; John 19 : 4.) ἐκεῖνον refers here to the nearer noun, and performs the proper office of τούτου. (W. § 23. 1.) It is not uncommon for Greek writers to interchange these pronouns.

14. But contrasts their conduct with that of Pilate.—**The Holy One** is a Messianic title, as in Luke 4 : 34.—τὸν δίκαιον, *the Just One.* The epithets mark the contrast between his character and that of Barabbas.—**A murderer,** not merely a *man*, but a man who was a *murderer.* (See Matt. 27 : 16, *sq.*; Mark 15 : 7, *sq.*)

15. But the Prince of life, or **the author of** life—*i. e.* as De Wette remarks, **of life** in the fullest sense in which the Scriptures ascribe that property to the Saviour; viz., spiritual or Christian life (comp. John 1 : 4; Heb. 2 : 10), and also natural or physical life. (Comp. John 5 : 26; 11 : 25.) Olshausen and Meyer suppose the main idea to be that of spiritual life; but the evident relation of **life** to **killed** shows that the other idea is certainly not to be excluded. A terrible aggravation in this murder was that he whom they deprived of life was himself the One who gives life to all.—**From the dead.** The article is usually omitted after ἐξ (*out of*), but inserted after ἀπό (*from*). (W. § 19.)—**Of whom** (13 : 31), or **of which, we are witnesses.** (See note on 2 : 32.)

16. Upon the faith in his name entertained by us—*i. e.* on account of their faith as the ground or condition, God had performed this act. Some construe ἐπί (*upon*) as telic: **upon the faith** as the object—*i. e.* in order to produce faith in the lame man and in others (Olsh., Hmph.). This latter meaning not only

strains the preposition, but overlooks the manifest parallelism in sense between this clause and the following, **and the faith.**—ὀνόματος is the genitive of the object, and the expression is like **faith in God** in Mark 11 : 22 and **faith in Jesus** in Rom. 3 : 22. (W. § 30. 1.)—**Whom you see,** entirely restored now to bodily vigor, **and know,** as a person who was formerly infirm, helpless.—**His name**—*i. e.* he invoked by an appeal to him as that which **his name** represents (see on 2 : 21)—**made strong** (a definite past). The reason for expressing the idea in this manner is evident from v. 6.—**The faith that** is wrought in us **through him** (De Wet., Mey., Win.). The apostles here, it will be observed, ascribe the origin, as well as the efficacy, of their faith to Christ. (Comp. 1 Pet. 1 : 21.) This second clause of the verse repeats essentially the idea of the first, in order to affirm more emphatically that it was not their own power, but the power of Christ, which had performed the miracle.—**In the presence of you all,** and hence they must acknowledge that no other means had been used to effect the miracle.

17. Having set before them their aggravated guilt, the apostle would now suggest to them the hope of mercy. **Brethren,** Peter says here, because he would conciliate his hearers; but in v. 12, where the object is reproof, crimination, he says more formally, though courteously, **men of Israel.** One of the marks of truth would be wanting without this accordance between the style and the changing mental moods of the speaker.—**That ye acted in ignorance**—*i. e.* of the full criminality of their conduct. They had sinned, but their sin was not of so deep a dye that it could not have been still more heinous. The language of Peter concedes to them such a palliation of the deed as consisted, at the time of their committing it, in the absence of a distinct conviction that he whom they crucified was the Lord of life and glory (see 13 : 27 and 1 Cor. 2 : 8); but it does not exonerate them from the guilt of having resisted the evidence that this was his character

18 But [a]those things, which God before had shewed [b]by the mouth of all his prophets, that Christ should suffer, he hath so fulfilled.

19 ¶ [c]Repent ye therefore, and be converted, that your sins may be blotted out, when the times of refreshing shall come from the presence of the Lord ;

18 did it, as did also your rulers. But the things which God foreshewed by the mouth of all the prophets, 19 that 'his Christ should suffer, he thus fulfilled. Repent ye therefore, and turn again, that your sins may be blotted out, that so there may come seasons

a Luke 24 : 44 ; ch. 26 : 22....*b* Ps. 22 ; Isa. 50 : 6 ; 53 : 5, etc. ; Dan. 9 . 26 ; 1 Pet. 1 : 10, 11....*c* ch. 2 : 38.

which had been furnished by his miracles, his life, doctrine, and resurrection. The Saviour himself, in his dying prayer, urged the same extenuation in behalf of his murderers : " Father, forgive them, for they know not what they do." Compare also the language of Paul in 1 Tim. 1 : 13 : " Who was before a blasphemer, and a persecutor, and injurious ; but I obtained mercy because I did it ignorantly in unbelief."—**As also your rulers,** who were not present, and hence are distinguished from those addressed.

18. But—*i. e.* while they did this they accomplished a divine purpose.—**All the prophets,** instead of being taken strictly, may be viewed as a phrase : **the prophets as a whole.** For this restricted use of **all** in such general expressions, see Matt. 3 : 5 ; Mark 1 : 37 ; John 3 : 26. Most of the books of the Old Testament foretell distinctly the sufferings and death of the Messiah. (Comp. Luke 24 : 27.) Olshausen regards the entire history of the Jews as typical, and in that view maintains that all the ancient prophets prophesied of Christ.—**That the Christ** (who was to come) **would,** or **must, suffer** (De Wet.). After verbs which signify "to declare," " believe," and the like, the infinitive implies often the idea of necessity or obligation. (W. § 45, 3. b.) [The true text, according to ℵ B C D E and Lach., Tsch., Treg., West. and Hort, Revisers' text, and others, reads **his Christ** instead of **the Christ.**—A. H.]—**So** refers to the previous verse : **thus,** in this way—viz. by their agency. (Comp. 13 : 27.) It is incorrect to understand it of the accordance between the fulfilment and the prediction.

19. Repent therefore, since your guilt is not such as to exclude you from the mercy procured by the Saviour whom you have crucified. —**Turn**—*i. e.* from your present course of character unto Christ (9 : 35 ; 11 : 21), or unto God (14 : 15 ; 15 : 19). What is required here includes faith as a constituent part of the act to be performed. [The word translated *repent* has a deep spiritual significance. It is an exhortation, not merely to sorrow for sin, but rather to a complete *change of mind,* in thought, feeling, and purpose. It is the act by which the soul, under

the regenerating influence of the Holy Spirit, renounces self and trusts in Christ, dies to sin and the law, and rises to a new life in God. The following verb (*turn again*) points to the same act of the soul, but perhaps with a more distinct reference to its manifestation in conduct ; so that the order of thought is naturally expressed by the order of words.—A. H.]—**That your sins may be blotted out,** obliterated as it were from the book or tablet where they are recorded. (Comp. Col. 2 : 14 ; Isa. 43 : 25.) —**In order that** (telic ; comp. Matt. 6 : 5) **the times of refreshing may come**—*i. e.* to you personally, that you may have part in the blessings of the Messiah's kingdom, for which men can be prepared only by repentance and the pardon of their sins. ἄν after ὅπως followed by the conjunctive represents the act of the verb as dependent—*i. e.* in this case on their compliance with the exhortation. (W. § 42. 6 ; Hart., *Partik.,* vol. ii. p. 289.) ὅπως as a particle of time, *when* (as in E. V.), is foreign to New Testament idiom. (See Green's *Gr.,* p. 77.) We must discard that translation here. Scholefield (*Hints,*[1] etc., p. 40) pleads faintly for retaining it, but admits that the weight of evidence is against it. It is not entirely certain whether **times of refreshing** refers to the present consolations of the gospel, or to the blessedness which awaits the followers of Christ at the end of the world, when he shall return and receive them to himself in heaven. The expression, in itself considered, would very aptly describe the peace of mind and joy which result from a consciousness of pardon and reconciliation to God. So one class of commentators understand it. Others think that the time here meant must coincide with that in the next verse, and hence suppose the apostle to have in view Christ's second coming, when those who have believed on him shall enter upon their eternal rest in heaven. (Comp. Heb. 4 : 9–11.) Taken thus, the image of the future state in ἀναψύξεως is that of relief or refreshment of the wearied soul after toils and sorrows, and is strikingly similar to Paul's **rest, relaxation** —rest which God allots to the afflicted in the day of final recompense. (See 2 Thess. 1 : 7.)

[1] *Hints for Improvements in the Authorized Version of the New Testament,* by the late Rev. James Scholefield, Professor of Greek in the University of Cambridge, England (4th ed., 1857).

20 And he shall send Jesus Christ, which before was preached unto you:

20 of refreshing from the presence of the Lord; and that he may send the Christ who hath been ap-

This is the interpretation of Chrysostom, Olshausen, De Wette, Meyer, and others. The order of the clauses decides nothing against the latter opinion, since it may be as natural in this instance to think first of the effect, and then to assign the cause or occasion, as the reverse. It is in favor of this opinion that it refers **may come** and **shall send** to the same period or event, as the close succession of the verbs would lead us to expect.—**From the presence of the Lord,** since the blessings in question (a Hebrew idiom) are laid up where he is (see 2 : 28), and must be received thence. **Lord,** which may refer to Christ or God (see on 1 : 24), applies to the latter here, since it prepares the way for the subject of the next verb.

20. And that (dependent still on ὅπως) **he may send forth**—viz. from heaven. (See v. 21; comp. **he shall show, who is the blessed and only Potentate,** etc., δείξει ὁ μακάριος καὶ μόνος δυνάστης, κ. τ. λ., in 1 Tim. 6 : 15.)—**Before appointed** or **prepared for you**—i. e. from eternity. (See 1 Pet. 1 : 20.) **Announced before** is a less approved reading. Nearly all critics understand this passage as referring to the return of Christ at the end of the world. The similarity of the language to that of other passages which announce that event demands this interpretation. The apostle enforces his exhortation to repent by an appeal to the final coming of Christ, not because he would represent it as near in point of time, but because that event was always *near to the feelings and consciousness* of the first believers. It was the great consummation on which the strongest desires of their soul were fixed, to which their thoughts and hopes were habitually turned. They lived with reference to this event. They labored to be prepared for it. They were constantly, in the expressive language of Peter, *looking for and* (in their impatience as it were) *hastening the arrival of the day of God* (2 Pet. 3 : 12). It is then that Christ will reveal himself in glory; will come to take "vengeance on them that obey not the gospel," "and to be admired in all them that believe" (2 Thess. 1 : 8); will raise the dead (John 5 : 28, 29), invest the redeemed with an incorruptible body (Phil. 3 : 21), and introduce them for the first time, and for ever, into the state of perfect holiness and happiness prepared for them in his kingdom. The apostles, as well as the first Christians in general, comprehended the grandeur of that occasion. It filled their circle of view; stood forth to their contemplations as the point of culminating interest in their own and the world's history; threw into comparative insignificance the present time, death, all intermediate events; and made them feel that the manifestation of Christ, with its consequences of indescribable moment to all true believers, was the grand object which they were to keep in view as the end of their toils, the commencement and perfection of their glorious immortality. In such a state of intimate sympathy with an event so habitually present to their thoughts, they derived, and must have derived, their chief incentives to action from the prospect of that future glory. As we should expect, they hold it up to the people of God to encourage them in affliction, to awaken them to fidelity, zeal, perseverance, and, on the other hand, appeal to it to warn the wicked and impress upon them the necessity of preparation for the revelations of the final day. For examples of this habit, the reader may see 17 : 30, 31; 1 Tim. 6 : 13, *sq.*; 2 Tim. 4 : 8; Tit. 2 : 11, *sq.*; 2 Pet. 3 : 11, *sq.*, etc. Some have ascribed the frequency of such passages in the New Testament to a definite expectation on the part of the apostles that the personal advent of Christ was nigh at hand; but such a view is not only unnecessary, in order to account for such references to the day of the Lord, but at variance with 2 Thess. 2 : 2. The apostle Paul declares there that the expectation in question was unfounded, and that he himself did not entertain it or teach it to others. But, while he corrects the opinion of those at Thessalonica who imagined that the return of Christ was then near, neither he nor any other inspired writer has informed us how remote that event may be or when it will take place. That is a point which has not been revealed to men; the New Testament has left it in a state of uncertainty: "The day of the Lord so cometh as a thief in the night;" and men are exhorted to be always prepared for it. It is to be acknowledged that most Christians at the present day do not give that prominence to the resurrection and the judgment, in their thoughts or discourse, which the New-Testament writers assign to them; but this fact is owing not necessarily to a difference of opinion in regard to the time when Christ will come, but to our inadequate views and impressions concerning the grandeur of that occasion and the too prevalent worldliness in the church, which

21 ^aWhom the heaven must receive until the times of ^brestitution of all things, ^cwhich God hath spoken by the mouth of all his holy prophets since the world began.
22 For Moses truly said unto the fathers, ^dA prophet shall the Lord your God raise up unto you of your brethren, like unto me; him shall ye hear in all things whatsoever he shall say unto you.
23 And it shall come to pass, *that* every soul, which will not hear that prophet, shall be destroyed from among the people.

21 pointed for you, *even* Jesus: whom the heaven must receive until the times of restoration of all things, whereof God spake by the mouth of his holy prophets
22 that have been from of old. Moses indeed said, A prophet shall the Lord God raise up unto you from among your brethren, ¹like unto me; to him shall ye hearken in all things whatsoever he shall speak
23 unto you. And it shall be, that every soul, which shall not hearken to that prophet, shall be utterly

a ch. 1 : 11....*b* Matt. 17 : 11....*c* Luke 1 : 70....*d* Deut. 18 : 15, 18, 19 ; ch. 7 : 37.——1 Or, *as* he raised up *me*

is the cause or consequence of such deficient views. If modern Christians sympathized more fully with the sacred writers on this subject, it would bring both their conduct and their style of religious instruction into nearer correspondence with the lives and teaching of the primitive examples of our faith.

21. Whom the heavens, indeed, must (according to the divine plan) **receive,** not *retain,* which the usage of the verb forbids. Though the ascension had taken place, we have **it is necessary** (δεῖ), and not **it was necessary** (ἔδει), because the necessity of the event is a permanent fact. Meyer explains δεῖ as in effect an imperfect, an instance merely of the rhetorical present for the past. [In his last ed. Meyer adopts Hackett's view, thus : " δεῖ does not stand for ἔδει, as if Peter wished *historically to narrate* the ascension ; but the present tense places before the eyes the necessity of the elevation of Christ into heaven as an *absolute* relation, which as such is constantly *present* until the *parousia.*"—A. H.] De Wette shifts the peculiarity of the expresson from **must** to **receive,** and renders **whom it is necessary the heavens should receive.** He alleges for this future sense that the ascension could be viewed as still incomplete because it was so recent. But the apostle, having just referred to Christ as already in heaven, whence he is to appear again (v. 20), would not be apt to speak in the very next words as if he thought of him as still lingering on the earth. Many of the Jews believed that when the Messiah appeared he would remain permanently among men. (See John 12 : 34.) Peter corrects here that misapprehension: the Saviour must return to heaven and reign there for a season before his final manifestation. The μέν (which no δέ follows) has this antithesis in **until the times,** etc. (De Wet.) : Christ would not be absent always, but for a certain time only ; not in the preceding **shall send,** etc. (Alf.), since that would make this the δέ clause, not the μέν, as it is now.—**Until** (*during* is incorrect) **the times of the restoration of all things**—i. e. to a state of primeval order, purity, and happiness,

such as will exist for those who have part in the kingdom of Christ at his second coming. The expression designates the same epoch as **times of refreshing** (Olsh., Mey., De Wet.).—**Which God spake of,** announced. (Comp. v. 24.) The relative refers to **times** as the principal word, and stands by attraction for οὕς or περὶ ὧν. It does not refer to **all things—the accomplishment of all things which,** etc., for the word rendered **restoration** will not bear that meaning.—**From the beginning.** From the earliest times of prophetic revelation. Such a period of restoration to holiness and happiness is the explicit or implied theme of prophecy from the beginning to the end of the Old Testament. Some omit the expression or put it in brackets, but the evidence for it preponderates.

22. For here (T. R. and E. V.) should be left out. **Unto the fathers,** also, is supposed to be a gloss.—μεν here responds to δέ in v. 24 : Moses on the one hand, as well as all the prophets on the other.—**Said**—viz. in Deut. 18 : 18, *sq.* The translation is partly that of the Seventy, partly new. In 7 : 37, Stephen cites this passage as having the same import which Peter ascribes to it here. Their mode of applying it shows that the Jews were agreed in referring it to the Messiah. That this was the current interpretation may be argued also from John 4 : 25. (See Hengstenberg's remarks in his *Christol.,* vol. i. p. 67, *sq.*)—**Will raise up,** cause to appear = Heb. *yakêm.*—**Like me.** The context of the original passage (comp. vv. 15, 16 with vv. 17, 18) indicates that the resemblance between them was to consist chiefly in their office as mediator. The meaning is : Since the Israelites had been unable to endure the terrors of the Divine Majesty, God would at some future time send to them another mediator, through whom he would communicate with them as he had done through Moses (Heng.). (See also Gal. 3 : 19 ; Heb. 9 : 15.)—**Whatsoever.** (See 2 : 21.)

23. Peter interrupts the sentence here to insert **and it shall be,** which is not in the Hebrew. It serves to call attention more strongly to what follows.—**Shall be utterly destroyed**

24 Yea, and all the prophets from Samuel and those that follow after, as many as have spoken, have likewise foretold of these days.

25 ^aYe are the children of the prophets, and of the covenant which God made with our fathers, saying unto Abraham, ^bAnd in thy seed shall all the kindreds of the earth be blessed.

26 ^cUnto you first God, having raised up his Son Jesus, ^dsent him to bless you, ^ein turning away every one of you from his iniquities.

24 destroyed from among the people. Yea and all the prophets from Samuel and them that followed after, as many as have spoken, they also told of these days.

25 Ye are the sons of the prophets, and of the covenant which God [1]made with your fathers, saying unto Abraham, And in thy seed shall all the families of

26 the earth be blessed. Unto you first God, having raised up his Servant, sent him to bless you, in turning away every one of you from your iniquities.

a ch. 2 : 39 ; Rom. 9 : 4, 8 ; 15 : 8 ; Gal. 3 : 26....b Gen. 12 : 3 ; 18 : 18 ; 22 : 18 ; 26 : 4 ; 28 : 14 ; Gal. 3 : 8....c Matt. 10 : 5 ; 15 : 24 ; Luke 24 : 47 ; ch. 13 : 32, 33, 46....d ver. 22....e Matt. 1 : 21.——1 Gr. covenanted.

from the people. This expression occurs often in the Pentateuch, where it denotes the sentence or punishment of death. The apostle uses it here evidently to denote the punishment which corresponds to that in relation to the soul—*i. e.* as De Wette explains it, exclusion from the kingdom of God. Peter has substituted this expression here for the Heb. *edhrōsh mēimmo*, as rendered in the Septuagint : **I will exact vengeance from him.** The only difference is that the Hebrew affirms the purpose of God to punish, while the Greek employed by Peter defines at the same time the nature or mode of the punishment.

24. All the prophets, etc., stands concisely for **all the prophets from Samuel, both he and they who followed.** The appositional clause is here merged in the genitive. **From Samuel** shapes the construction, instead of the remoter **prophets.** (Comp. Luke 24 : 27. W. ¿ 67. 2.) The literal translation, **from Samuel on, and those who followed,** involves a tautology, the second clause being comprehended in the first. Samuel is mentioned next after Moses, because so few prophets appeared in the interval between them, or so few whose names are recorded. They stand in the same proximity to each other in Ps. 99 : 6. We have no record of all that the prophets taught, and the apostle's assertion here that Samuel also bore testimony to Christ does not need to be confirmed by specific passages.—**As many as spake** (prophesied) shows, as related to the next clause (note **likewise**), how uniformly the theme of a coming Messiah had been held forth in the instructions of the ancient messengers of God. Yet the object may be to characterize the teaching of the prophetic order as such, and not of every single individual. (See note on v. 18.)

25. Ye are the sons of the prophets, and of the covenant—*i. e.* are those in the first case to whom the predictions respecting the Messiah especially appertain, and in the second are those to whom God would first (v. 26) offer the mercies which he covenanted to bestow on Abraham's spiritual seed—viz. such as believe, and thus " walk in the steps of his faith." (See Rom. 4 : 12.) **Sons** in this sense of participation, appurtenance, is a common Hebraism. (See Matt. 8 : 12 ; John 4 : 22 ; Rom. 9 : 4, etc.) Its ordinary significance, *sons*, descendants, would be incongruous with **covenant,** and should not be retained, therefore, in connection with **prophets.—Saying,** etc.—viz. in Gen. 12 : 3. God repeated the promise to Abraham and the other patriarchs at various times. (See Gen. 18 : 18 ; 22 : 18 ; 26 : 4, etc.)— **In thy seed**—viz. the Messiah (v. 26), as one of his posterity, agreeably to Paul's view in Gal. 3 : 16.

26. Unto you. Dependent on **sent** (see 13 : 26 ; 28 : 28) ; not *for you,* dat. comm. (Mey.). [Meyer's last ed. agrees with Dr. Hackett.—A. H.], dependent on **having raised up.**—πρῶτον, **first,** in the order of time. (Comp. 13 : 46 : Luke 24 : 47 ; Rom. 1 : 16.) Here too Peter recognizes the fact that the gospel was to be preached to the heathen. (See on 2 : 39.)— **Having raised up,** as in v. 22.—παῖδα, **servant,** as in v. 13.---The E. V. follows the common text, which inserts **Jesus** after **his servant,** but contrary to the best authorities (Grsb., Tsch., Mey.).—**Blessing** applies the idea of the preceding **be blessed** to the Jews, and requires **you** to be read with emphasis.— **In turning away,** etc., states how he blesses them : **in that he turns away each one from your sins**—to wit, by his gospel, which secures the pardon and sanctification of those who accept it. (See on 2 : 47.) This verb has elsewhere an active sense in the New Testament. Some (Kuin., De Wet.) disregard that usage and render *in that each one turns away,* etc. This is opposed also to **blessing,** which represents Christ here as the actor—men rather as recipients.

CHAPTER IV.

AND as they spake unto the people, the priests, and the captain of the temple, and the Sadducees, came upon them,

2 *Being grieved that they taught the people, and preached through Jesus the resurrection from the dead.

3 And they laid hands on them, and put *them* in hold unto the next day: for it was now eventide.

4 Howbeit many of them which heard the word be-

1 AND as they spake unto the people, ¹the priests and the captain of the temple and the Sadducees

2 came upon them, being sore troubled because they taught the people, and proclaimed in Jesus the resur-

3 rection from the dead. And they laid hands on them, and put them in ward unto the morrow: for it was

4 now eventide. But many of them that heard the

---

a Matt. 22 : 23; Acts 23 : 8.——1 Some ancient authorities read *the chief priests.*

1-4. THE IMPRISONMENT OF PETER AND JOHN.

1. ἐπέστησαν (**came upon**) implies commonly a hostile purpose. (See 6 : 12; 17 : 5; Luke 20 : 1.) The arrest appears to have taken place while the apostles were still speaking.—**The priests** who officiated in the temple at the time, or some of their number. The priests were divided into twenty-four classes, each of which had charge of the temple-service for a week at a time. (See 1 Chron. 24 : 3, *sq.*; 2 Chron. 8 : 14; and also Jos., *Antt.*, 7. 14. 7.) The particular duties from day to day were assigned to individuals by lot. (See Luke 1 : 9.) During the observance of the festivals the number of priests was increased, as the labors to be performed were greater. (Win., *Realw.*, vol. ii. p. 273.) It is possible that the feast of Pentecost (2 : 1) had not yet terminated.—**The commander of the temple** was an officer having a body of Levites under his command, who preserved order about the temple, and in that respect performed a sort of military service. (See Jahn's *Archæol.*, ? 365.) In 5 : 26 the Levites so employed are called his *servants.* Josephus speaks repeatedly of this guard (*e. g. Bell. Jud.*, 6. 5. 3), whose commander he designates in the same manner. In 2 Macc. 3 : 4 he is termed *the guardian of the temple.* We read of **commanders of the temple** in Luke 22 : 52, which is best explained by supposing that the temple-guard was divided into several companies, each of which had its *commander*, though this title belonged distinctively to the chief in command.—**The Sadducees.** The *Sadducees* as a sect, since those who acted in this instance represented the spirit of the party. (Comp. Matt. 9 : 11; 12 : 14; Mark 8 : 11; John 8 : 3.) Meyer supposes the article to point out those of them who were present at this time. It was probably at the instigation of this class of men that the apostles were now apprehended.

2. Being indignant. Restricted by some (Mey., De Wet.) to the nearest noun, since the motive assigned for the interference in **preached,** etc., applies only to the Sadducees,

who denied the doctrine of a resurrection. (See 23 : 8; Matt. 22 : 23.) But perhaps we may regard **because they taught the people** as more comprehensive than **preached . . . the resurrection,** etc., instead of being merely defined by it, and in that case may refer the participle to the priests as well as the others. The priests, though they might not share the hostility of the Sadducees to the doctrine of a future state (see on 23 : 8), would naturally be indignant that their office as teachers should be assumed by men like Peter and John (see Matt. 21 : 23), and especially that the Jesus whom they themselves had crucified should be proclaimed as the Messiah. (See 5 : 28.) **Are announcing in Jesus the resurrection**—*i. e.* in his example, in the fact of his alleged restoration to life. (Comp. ἐν ἡμῖν in 1 Cor. 4 : 6.) This is the best and the generally-approved interpretation (Bng., Kuin., De Wet., Mey.). Others render **are announcing the resurrection in virtue of Jesus,** by his power. (See 1 Cor. 15 : 22.) The E. Version, **through Jesus,** while the earlier E. Vv. have **in him,** appears to express that meaning. But it was not so much the general resurrection as that of Christ himself which the apostles proclaimed at this stage of their ministry. (See 1 : 22; 2 : 24; 3 : 15, etc.) The single concrete instance, however, as the Sadducees argued, involved the general truth, and, if substantiated, refuted their creed.

3. Into prison. (Comp. **in the common prison,** in 5 : 18.) This word denotes a place of custody (see Pape, *Lex.*, s. v.) as well as the act, though the latter is the proper force of such a termination. (K. ? 233. b. a.)—**Unto the morrow,** as the limit. (See Matt. 10 : 22; 1 Thess. 4 : 15.)—**For it was already evening,** and hence no judicial examination could take place until the next day. It was three o'clock when the apostles went to the temple. (Comp. 3 : 1.)

4. The word, the well-known message of Christ.—ἐγενήθη = ἐγένετο, **became—***i. e.* in consequence of the present addition. The use of

5

lieved; and the number of the men was about five thousand.

5 ¶ And it came to pass on the morrow, that their rulers, and elders, and scribes,

6 And *a*Annas the high priest, and Caiaphas, and John, and Alexander, and as many as were of the kindred of the high priest, were gathered together at Jerusalem.

word believed; and the number of the men came to be about five thousand.

5 And it came to pass on the morrow, that their rulers and elders and scribes were gathered together

6 in Jerusalem; and Annas the high priest *was there*, and Caiaphas, and John, and Alexander, and as many as were of the kindred of the high priest.

a Luke 3 : 2; John 11 : 49; 18 : 13.

this form is peculiar to the later Greek. (W. § 15; Lob., *Ad Phryn.*, p. 108.)—**The number of the men** who had embraced the gospel up to this time (Kuin., Mey., De Wet., Alf.). (See 1 : 15; 2 : 41.) A retrospective remark like this was entirely natural after having spoken of the many who believed at this time. Some suppose the new converts alone to have amounted to **five thousand**; but that is less probable, as the apostles could hardly have addressed so great a multitude in such a place. **Men** comprehends, probably, both men and women, like **souls** in 2 : 41. (Comp. Luke 11 : 31.) An emphasized or conscious restriction of the term to men would be at variance with that religious equality of the sexes so distinctly affirmed in the New Testament. (See Gal. 3 : 28.)

5–7. THEIR ARRAIGNMENT BEFORE THE SANHEDRIM.

5. Their before **rulers** refers to the Jews, as implied in vv. 1 and 4 (De Wet., Win.); not to the believers, as if to contrast their conduct with that of their rulers (Mey. formerly, but now as above); and certainly not to the apostles (Stier[1]).—**Their rulers**, etc. The Sanhedrim is here described by an enumeration of the three orders which composed that body—viz. **the chief priests,** who are mentioned last in this instance; **the elders,** or heads of families; and **the scribes,** or teachers of the law. (Comp. 5 : 21; Matt. 2 : 4; 26 : 59.) **Rulers** designates the Sanhedrists in general, since they were all rulers, while **and** annexes the respective classes to which they belonged : **and** (more definitely, comp. 1 : 14) **the elders,** etc. It was unnecessary to repeat the article, because the nouns have the same gender. (W. § 19. 4; S. § 89. 9.) [For an able though brief account of the Sanhedrim the reader is referred to Kitto's *Biblical Cyclopædia*, edited by W. L. Alexander, under the word "Sanhedrim," or to an article on the same topic in McClintock and Strong's *Cyclopædia*, etc., founded on the one in Kitto. Still briefer, but giving the principal facts, is the article in Smith's *Dict. of the Bible*. The origin of this Jewish court is now generally assigned to "a period subsequent to the Macedonian

supremacy in Palestine." "The earliest historical trace of its existence," though under another name, is supposed to be found in 2 Macc. 1 : 10; 4 : 44; 11 : 27. Dr. Hackett has named the classes of men which composed this great tribunal of the Jews. They were probably distributed as follows : twenty-four priests, twenty-four elders, and twenty-two scribes or lawyers. Only men who were morally and physically without fault were eligible to membership. They must be middle-aged, tall, good-looking, wealthy, and learned." They must also be fathers, and must have passed through various lower offices. The first place provided for this council appears to have been a hall named Gazith, in the centre of the south side of the temple-court; a later one was located, it is said, on the east side of the temple-mount.—A. H.]—**Unto Jerusalem,** as some of the rulers may have lived out of the city (Mey., De Wet.), especially at that season (see 2 : 1), when the heat had begun to be severe. εἰς is not put loosely for ἐν (Kuin.); for the distinctive force of the prepositions may always be traced, and the notice merely that they assembled in Jerusalem would be unnecessary. The substitution of ἐν (*in*) for εἰς (*unto*) in the text (Lchm.,Tsch.) is unwarranted. [Lach.,Treg., West. and Hort, with the Anglo-Am. Revisers, insert ἐν (*in*), and are supported by A B D E; while Tsch. (8th ed.) decides for εἰς (*into*), in agreement with ℵ P. The former seems therefore to be much better sustained than the latter; and there is nothing in the context or structure of the sentence recommending one more than the other.—A. H.]

6. Those named here are prominent individuals among the rulers (v. 5), not a separate class. **Annas the high priest.** The actual high priest at this time was Caiaphas (see John 11 : 49); but Annas, his father-in-law, had held the same office, and, according to the Jewish custom in such cases, retained still the same title. He is mentioned first perhaps out of respect to his age, or because his talents and activity conferred upon him a personal superiority. (See John 18 : 13.) It is entirely unnecessary

[1] *Die Reden der Apostel nach Ordnung und Zusammenhang ausgelegt.* von Rudolf Stier (zwei Bände).

7 And when they had set them in the midst they asked, *a*By what power, or by what name, have ye done this?

8 *b*Then Peter, filled with the Holy Ghost, said unto them, Ye rulers of the people, and elders of Israel,

9 If we this day be examined of the good deed done to the impotent man, by what means he is made whole ;

7 And when they had set them in the midst, they inquired, By what power, or in what name, have ye done this? Then Peter, filled with the Holy Spirit,

8 said unto them, Ye rulers of the people, and elders

9 if we this day are examined concerning a good deed done to an impotent man, *1*by what means this man

a Ex. 2 : 14 ; Matt. 21 : 23 ; ch. 7 : 27....*b* Luke 12 : 11, 12.——1 Or, *in whom*

to charge Luke with committing an error here, as Zeller so confidently affirms.[1] It is a familiar usage in every language to speak of " the governor," " the president," " the senator," and the like, though the person so termed is no longer in office.—**John and Alexander.** We know nothing positive of these men beyond the intimation here that they were priests and active at this time in public affairs. **Alexander** is another instance of a foreign name in use among the Jews. (See 1 : 23.) It is improbable that he was the Alexander mentioned in Josephus (*Antt.*, 18. 8. 1), who was a brother of Philo and Alabarch of the Jews at Alexandria. In that case he must have been visiting at Jerusalem, and hence was present in the council as a guest only, or else had not yet removed to Egypt. **And as many as were of the pontifical family**—*i. e.* those nearly related to the **high priests = pontifical family,** embracing, as that title was applied among the Jews, the high priest properly so called, his predecessors in office, and the heads of the twenty-four sacerdotal classes. (See on v. 1.) Many points relating to the organization of the Sanhedrim are irretrievably obscure, but it is generally agreed that the twenty-four priestly orders were represented in that body. (See Win., *Realw.*, vol. ii. p. 271.) The attendance of so many persons of rank on this occasion evinced the excited state of the public mind and gave importance to the decisions of the council. This is Meyer's view of the meaning. [In his last ed. Meyer agrees with Hackett, saying, " Besides Caiaphas, John, and Alexander, all the other relatives of the high priest were brought into the assembly."—A. H.] But a narrower sense of **high priest's kindred** may be adopted. It appears to me more simple to understand that John and Alexander were related to Annas and Caiaphas, and that the **as many,** etc., were the other influential members of the same family. That the family of Annas was one of great distinction appears in the fact that five of his sons attained the office of high

priest. (See on 9 : 1.) Some vary the meaning of γένους, and translate **as many as were of the class of the chief priests.** This sense renders the description of the different branches of the Sanhedrim more complete, but assigns a forced meaning to the noun.

7. Them—viz. the apostles, last mentioned in v. 3.—**In the midst,** before them, so as to be within the view of all. (Comp. John 8 : 3.) It is said that the Jewish Sanhedrim sat in a circle or a semicircle, but we could not urge the expression here as any certain proof of that custom.—**By what power,** efficacy; not *by what right,* authority, which would require ἐξουσία, as in Matt. 21 : 23. (See Tittm., *Synm.*, p. 158.)—**Or** (in other words) **in virtue of what** uttered **name.** This appears to be a more specific form of the same inquiry.—**This** —viz. the cure of the lame man. Olshausen understands it of their teaching, which is not only less appropriate to the accompanying words, but renders the answer of the apostles in vs. 9, 10 irrelevant.

8–12. TESTIMONY OF PETER BEFORE THE COUNCIL.

8. Filled with the Holy Spirit—*i. e.* anew. (See v. 31 ; 2 : 4.) Peter was thus elevated above all human fear, and assisted at the same time to make such a defence of the truth as the occasion required. The Saviour had authorized the disciples to expect such aid under circumstances like the present. (See Mark 13 : 11 ; Luke 21 : 14, 15. For the absence of the article, see on 1 : 2.)

9. If we are examined, as is confessedly the case. εἰ (*if*), in the protasis with the indicative, affirms the condition, and is logically equivalent to ἐπεί, *since.* (K. § 339. I. a.; W. § 41. b. 2.) The occasion for the present defence was a reproachful one to the Jews, and hence the speaker alludes to it thus dubiously, in order to state the case with as little offence as possible. The apodosis begins at **be it known.** —**In respect to a good deed,** benefit conferred **on an infirm man.** (Comp. John 10 :

---

[1] *Theologische Jahrbücher* (Jahrgang 1849), p. 60. It is due to the reader to place before him some examples of this writer's style of criticism. His articles on the composition and character of the Acts, published in different numbers of the periodical named above, are considered as remarkable for the industry and acuteness which they display in setting forth the internal difficulties that are supposed to embarrass Luke's history. The articles have been thrown into a volume, but I have not seen them in that form.

10 Be it known unto you all, and to all the people of Israel, *that by the name of Jesus Christ of Nazareth, whom ye crucified, *whom God raised from the dead, *even by him doth this man stand here before you whole.
11 *This is the stone which was set at nought of you builders, which is become the head of the corner.
12 *Neither is there salvation in any other: for there is none other name under heaven given among men, whereby we must be saved.

10 is ¹made whole; be it known unto you all, and to all the people of Israel, that in the name of Jesus Christ of Nazareth, whom ye crucified, whom God raised from the dead, *even* in ²him doth this man stand 11 here before you whole. He is the stone which was set at nought of you the builders, which was made 12 the head of the corner. And in none other is there salvation: for neither is there any other name under heaven, that is given among men, wherein we must be saved.

a ch. 3 : 6, 16....*b* ch. 2 : 24....*c* Ps. 118 : 22; Isa. 28 : 16; Matt. 21 : 42....*d* Matt. 1 : 21; ch. 10 : 43; 1 Tim. 2 : 5, 6.——¹ Or, *saved*....2 Or, *this* name

32.) Observe that neither noun has the article. ἀνθρώπου is the objective genitive. (Comp. 3 : 16; 21 : 20; Luke 6 : 7. S. § 99. 1. c.; K. § 265. 2. b.)—**Whereby, how** (De Wet., Mey.), not *by whom* (Kuin.). The first sense agrees best with the form of the question in v. 7.—**This one.** The man who had been healed was present. (See vs. 10, 14.) He may have come as a spectator, or, as De Wette thinks, may have been summoned as a witness. Neander conjectures that he too may have been taken into custody at the same time with the apostles.—**Has been made whole.** The subject of discourse determines the meaning of the verb.

10. By the name of Jesus Christ (the latter appellative here), through their invocation of his name. The question *how* (v. 9) is here answered.—**Of Nazareth** identifies the individual to whom the apostle applies so exalted a name. (See on 2 : 22.)—**Whom God raised,** etc., is an adversative clause after **whom ye crucified,** but omits the ordinary disjunctive. (For this asyndetic construction, see W. § 60. 2; K. § 325.) It promotes compression, vivacity of style. (For the anarthrous νεκρῶν, **dead,** see on 3 : 15.)—**In this** may be neuter = **in this name** (Mey.); or masculine, **in this one** (Kuin., De Wet.), which is more natural, since **whom** is a nearer antecedent, and **this one** follows in the next verse (and so also Mey. at present). **Stands** (E. V.); perf. = present. (See on 1 : 10.)

11. This one—viz. Christ, who is the principal subject, though a nearer noun intervenes. (See 7 : 19. W. § 23. 1; S. § 123. N. 1. Compare the note on 3 : 13. For the passage referred to, see Ps. 118 : 22.) The words, as Tholuck[1] remarks, appear to have been used as a proverb, and hence are susceptible of various applications. The sense for this place may be thus given: The Jewish rulers, according to the proper idea of their office, were the builders of God's spiritual house, and as such should have been the first to acknowledge the Messiah and exert themselves for the establishment and

extension of his kingdom. That which they had not done God had now accomplished, in spite of their neglect and opposition. He had raised up Jesus from the dead, and thus confirmed his claim to the Messiahship; he had shown him to be the true Author of salvation to men, the Corner-stone, the only sure Foundation on which they can rest their hopes of eternal life. (Comp. Matt. 21 : 42; Luke 20 : 17.) The later editors consider οἰκοδόμων more correct than οἰκοδομούντων.—**Which became the head of the corner.** Predicated, like that was set at nought, of the stone, as identical with **this one. Head of the corner** is the same as *chief corner stone* in 1 Pet. 2 : 6. (Comp. Isa. 28 : 16.) It refers, probably, not to the copestone, but to that which lies at the foundation of the edifice, in the angle where two of the walls come together, and which gives to the edifice its strength and support. (See Gesen., *Heb. Lex.*, s. rosh. 4.)

12. The salvation which the gospel brings, or which men need. (Comp. John 4 : 22. For the article, see W. § 18. 1.) The contents of the next clause render it impossible to understand the term of the cure of the lame man. It was not true that the apostles proclaimed the name of Christ as the one on which men should call, in order to be healed of their diseases.—**For neither is there any other name.** It has just been said that Christ is the only Saviour. It is asserted here that he is such, because no other has been provided.—**Which is given,** since the gospel is the fruit of mercy.—**Among men,** as the sphere in which the name is known; not dat. comm. **for men.** (See W. § 31. 6.) The latter is a resulting idea, but not the expressed one.—**In which we** (as men, and hence true of the human race) **must be saved. It is necessary** (δεῖ) is stronger than **it is lawful** (ἔξεστι), and means not *may*, but *must*, as the only alternative, since God has appointed no other way of salvation. The apostle would exclude the idea of any other mode of escape if this be neglected. (See Heb. 2 : 3.) [The

[1] *Uebersetzung und Auslegung der Psalmen*, p. 496.

13 ¶ Now when they saw the boldness of Peter and John, *and* perceived that they were unlearned and ignorant men, they marvelled ; and they took knowledge of them, that they had been with Jesus.
14 And beholding the man which was healed *b*standing with them, they could say nothing against it.
15 But when they had commanded them to go aside out of the council, they conferred among themselves,
16 Saying, *c*What shall we do to these men ? for that indeed a notable miracle hath been done by them *is* *d*manifest to all them that dwell in Jerusalem ; and we cannot deny *it.*
17 But that it spread no further among the people,

13   Now when they beheld the boldness of Peter and John, and had perceived that they were unlearned and ignorant men, they marvelled ; and they took knowledge of them, that they had been with Jesus.
14 And seeing the man who was healed standing with
15 them, they could say nothing against it.   But when they had commanded them to go aside out of the
16 council, they conferred among themselves, saying, What shall we do to these men ? for that indeed a notable ¹miracle hath been wrought through them, is manifest to all that dwell in Jerusalem ; and we
17 cannot deny it.   But that it spread no further among the people, let us threaten them, that they speak

a Matt. 11 : 25 ; 1 Cor. 1 : 27....b ch. 3 : 11....c John 11 : 47....d ch. 3 : 9, 10.——1 Gr. *sign.*

interpretation of this important verse by Dr. Hackett is a model of brevity and clearness. It is the only one, I think, that fully answers to the language of Peter.   And the truth which it brings to light affords a perfect explanation of the fact that the apostles made the Lord Jesus, and especially his death on the cross, the central theme of their preaching.   It also accounts for their zeal in preaching the word, and especially for the marvellous devotion of Paul to his great mission of carrying " the good news " of salvation through Christ to the heathen.—A. H.]

13–18. DECISION OF THE SANHEDRIM.

13. Beholding (θεωροῦντες) is the appropriate word here.   It denotes not **seeing** merely (like βλέποντες, v. 14), but seeing earnestly or with admiration.   (Tittm., *Synm.,* p. 121.)— **Having perceived,** from intimations at the time, such as their demeanor, language, pronunciation (Str.) (comp. Matt. 26 : 73), or **having ascertained** by previous inquiry (Mey., Alf.).   Meyer in his last edition prefers the first meaning to the second.   The tense, it will be observed, differs from that of the other participle.—**Unlearned and igno-rant, illiterate**—*i. e.* untaught in the learning of the Jewish schools (see John 7 : 15), **and obscure,** plebeian (Kuin., Olsh., De Wet.).   It is unnecessary to regard the terms as synonymous (E. V., Mey., Rob.).   Their self-possession and intelligence astonished the rulers, being so much superior to their education and rank in life.¹—**And they recognized them that they were with Jesus** during his ministry, were among his followers (Wicl., Tynd.) ; not **had been** (E. V.).   Their wonder, says Meyer, assisted their recollection ; so that, as they observed the prisoners more closely (note the imperf.), they remembered them as persons whom they had known before.   Many of the rulers had often been present when Christ taught publicly (see Matt. 21 : 23 ; Luke 18 : 18 ; John 12 : 42, etc.), and must have seen Peter

and John.   That the latter was known to the high priest is expressly said in John 18 : 15.

14. The order of the words here is admirably picturesque.—**With them**—viz. the apostles, not the rulers.   (Comp. **them,** just before.) —**Standing** there, and by his presence, since he was so generally known (see 3 : 16). uttering a testimony which they could not refute. Bengel makes the attitude significant : st**and**-ing *firmo talo,* no longer a cripple.—**Had noth-ing to object,** against the reality of the miracle or the truth of Peter's declaration.

15. Having commanded them to de-part out of the council. The deliberations of the assembly were open to others, though the apostles were excluded ; and hence it was easy for Luke to ascertain what was said and done during their absence.   Some of the many priests who afterward believed (see 6 : 7) may have belonged to the council at this time, or, at all events, may have been present as spectators.   It is not improbable that Saul of Tarsus was there, or even some of the Christian party who were not known in that character.

16. For that a notorious miracle—a deed undeniably of that character--**has been done,** γνωστόν (*notable*), in the sense of *widely known,* adds nothing to the text, since it merely repeats the subsequent *manifest.*—**Through them,** and hence accredited (see on 2 : 22) as the agents of a higher power.—**Manifest** agrees with **that** notable, etc., and is the predicate nominative after ἐστί understood.—**We are not able to deny it.**   (See 3 : 9, 11.)   They would have suppressed the evidence had it been possible.

17. That it (*i. e.* the sign) **may not spread.** With a knowledge of the miracle the people would associate inevitably the doctrine which the miracle confirmed.   The subject of the verb involves the idea of teaching, but it would be arbitrary to supply that word as the direct nominative.   Some have supposed the last clause in the verse to require it.—**Let us**

¹ Walch maintains this distinction in his *Dissertationes in Acta Apostolorum,* p. 59, *sq.* (Jena, 1766).

let us straitly threaten them, that they speak henceforth to no man in this name.

18 *And they called them, and commanded them not to speak at all nor teach in the name of Jesus.

19 But Peter and John answered and said unto them, *Whether it be right in the sight of God to hearken unto you more than unto God, judge ye.

20 *For we cannot but speak the things which *we have seen and heard.

21 So when they had further threatened them, they let them go, finding nothing how they might punish them, *because of the people: for all *men* glorified God for *that which was done.

22 For the man was above forty years old, on whom this miracle of healing was shewed.

18 hereforth to no man in this name. And they called them, and charged them not to speak at all 19 nor teach in the name of Jesus. But Peter and John answered and said unto them, Whether it be right in the sight of God to hearken unto you rather 20 than unto God, judge ye: for we cannot but speak 21 the things which we saw and heard. And they, when they had further threatened them, let them go, finding nothing how they might punish them, because of the people; for all men glorified God for 22 that which was done. For the man was more than forty years old, on whom this ¹miracle of healing was wrought.

---

a ch. 5 : 40....*b* ch. 5 : 29....*c* ch. 1 : 8 ; 2 : 32....*d* ch. 22 : 15; 1 John 1 : 1, 3....*e* Matt. 21 : 26 ; Luke 20 : 6, 19 ; 22 : 2 ; ch. 5 : 26 ....*f* ch. 3 : 7, 8.——l Gr. *sign.*

---

severely (lit. *with a threat*) **threaten them.** Winer (§ 54. 3) regards this combination of a verb and noun as an expedient for expressing the infinitive absolute with a finite verb in Hebrew. (See Gesen., *Heb. Gr.*, § 128. 3.) But we meet with the idiom in ordinary Greek. (See Thiersch, *De Pent. Vers.*, p. 169.) The frequency of the construction in the New Testament is undoubtedly Hebraistic. [*Severely*, or lit. *with a threat*, is omitted by the best editors, Lach., Treg., Anglo-Am. Revisers, in agreement with ℵ A B D. The only uncial copies that are quoted for it by Tsch. 8 ed. are E P. There is therefore very slight reason to suppose that it was written by Luke.—A. H.]—**Upon this name,** as the basis of their doctrine or authority. (Comp. v. 18 ; 5 : 28, 40. W. § 48. c.)

18. τό (**the**) before φθέγγεσθαι (**to speak**), points that out more distinctly as the object of the prohibition. It is not a mere sign of the substantive construction. (W. § 44. 3. c.)— **Nor to teach upon the name of Jesus** specifies the part of their preaching which the rulers were most anxious to suppress. The other infinitive does not render this superfluous.

19–22. THE ANSWER OF PETER AND JOHN.

19. In the sight of God (Hebraistic), whose judgment is true, and which men are bound to follow as the rule of their conduct.—**To hearken unto, to obey.** (See Luke 10 : 16; 16 : 31 ; John 8 : 47.)—μᾶλλον, not **more,** but **rather.** (See 5 : 29.) The question was whether they should obey men at all in opposition to God, not whether they should obey him more or less. (See further on 5 : 29.)

20. For we cannot, etc. confirms the answer supposed to be given to their appeal in **whether it is right,** etc. We must obey God, **for we cannot** (morally—*i. e.* in accordance with truth and duty) **not speak**—*i. e.* withhold, suppress—our message. The double

negation states the idea strongly. The impossibility which they felt was that of refraining from giving publicity to their knowledge ; it was not sufficient that they taught no error. To be silent would have been treachery.— **Which we saw and heard**—*i. e.* during the life of the Saviour, when they beheld his mighty works and listened to his instructions. The verbs are in the aorist, not perfect (as in E. V.).

21. Having threatened them further— *i. e.* than they had done already. (See v. 18.)— **Finding nothing,** no means, opportunity.— **Namely, how,** on what pretence. (Comp. 22 : 30; Luke 1 : 62; 9 : 46, etc.) This use of the article before single clauses distinguishes Luke and Paul from the other writers of the New Testament. It serves to awaken attention to the proposition introduced by it. (See W. § 20. 3.)—**Because of the people** belongs to the participle (Mey.), rather than to **let them go.** The intervening clause breaks off the words from the latter connection. The idea, too, is not that they were able to invent no charge against the apostles, but none which they felt it safe to adopt, because the people were so well disposed toward the Christians.

22. For he was of more years, etc. The cure wrought was the greater the longer the time during which the infirmity had existed. ἐτῶν (**years**) depends on **was** (ἦν) as a genitive of property. (K. § 273. 2. c. ; C. § 387.)—**Than forty years,** governed by πλειόνων (**more**) as a comparative. (Comp. 25 : 6.) De Wette assumes an ellipsis of ἥ, which puts the numeral in the genitive, because that is the case of the preceding noun. But most grammarians represent ἥ as suppressed only after πλέον, πλείω, and the like. (Comp. Matt. 26 : 53 as correctly read. K. § 748. R. 1; Mt. § 455. A. 4.)—**The healing,** the act of it which constituted the miracle; genitive of apposition. (W. § 48. 2.)

23 ¶ And being let go, *they went to their own company, and reported all that the chief priests and elders had said unto them.

24 And when they heard that, they lifted up their voice to God with one accord, and said, Lord, *thou *art God, which hast made heaven, and earth, and the sea, and all that in them is:

25 Who by the mouth of thy servant David hast said, *Why did the heathen rage, and the people imagine vain things?

26 The kings of the earth stood up, and the rulers were gathered together against the Lord, and against his Christ.

23 And being let go, they came to their own company, and reported all that the chief priests and the elders had said unto them. And they, when they heard it, lifted up their voice to God with one accord, and said, O ¹Lord, ²thou that didst make the heaven and the earth and the sea, and all that in them is: ³who by the Holy Spirit, *by* the mouth of our father David thy servant, didst say,
    Why did the Gentiles rage,
    And the peoples ⁴imagine vain things?
26 The kings of the earth set themselves in array,
    And the rulers were gathered together,
    Against the Lord, and against his ⁵Anointed:

a ch. 12 : 12....b 2 Kings 19 : 15....c Ps. 2 : 1.——1 Or, *Master*....2 Or, *thou* art *he that did make*....3 The Greek text in this clause is somewhat uncertain....4 Or, *meditate*....5 Gr. *Christ*.

23-31. THE APOSTLES RETURN TO THE DISCIPLES, AND UNITE WITH THEM IN PRAYER AND PRAISE.

23. Unto their own friends, in the faith. (Comp. 24 : 23; Tit. 3 : 14.) Nothing in the context requires us to limit the term to the apostles.—**The chief priests** (those of the first class) **and the elders.** This is another mode of designating the Sanhedrim. (See v. 5.)

24. With one accord must denote, as elsewhere (1 : 14; 2 : 46; 7 : 57, etc.), a concert of hearts, not of voices. If they all joined aloud in the prayer, the proof must not be drawn from this word or from **lifted up their voice**—which could be said though but one uttered the words while the others assented—but rather from the nature of the service. The prayer on this occasion was chiefly praise, and, as the words quoted were so familiar to all, it is quite possible that they recited them together. (See 16 : 25, and the remarks there.) Baumgarten's view (*Apostelgeschichte*, u. s. w., p. 93) may be near the truth : the whole company sung the second Psalm, and Peter then applied the contents of it to their situation in the terms recorded here.—δέσποτα (**Lord**) is applied to God as absolute in power and authority. It is one of the titles of Christ also. (See 2 Pet. 2 : 1; Jude 4.) —**Thou art the God,** or **thou the God,** nominative of address. The latter, says Meyer, accords best with the fervid state of their minds.

25. By the mouth, etc.—viz. in Ps. 2 : 1, 2. By citing this passage the disciples express their confidence in the success of the cause for which they were persecuted; for it is the object of the second Psalm to set forth the ultimate and complete triumph of the gospel, notwithstanding the opposition which the wicked may array against it. The contents of the Psalm, as well as the other quotations from it in the New Testament, confirm its Messianic character. (See 13 : 33; Heb. 1 : 5 and 5 : 5.)—ἵνα τί (**why**) is abbreviated for ἵνα τί γένηται (**why is it**). (W. § 25. 1; K. § 344. R. 6.) The question challenges a reason for conduct so wicked and futile. It expresses both astonishment and reproof.— **Raged,** or, which is nearer to the classic sense, **showed themselves restive,** refractory. The aorist may be used here to denote a recurrent fact. (K. § 256. 4. b.) The active form is used only in the Septuagint (Pape, *Lex.*, s. v.). The application to this particular instance does not exhaust the prophecy. The fulfilment runs parallel with the history of the conflicts and triumphs of the cause of truth. --**Peoples,** masses of men, whether of the same nation or of different nations. Hence this term includes the Jews, whom ἔθνη would exclude.—**Vain,** abortive, since such must be the result of all opposition to the plans of Jehovah.

26. Stood up, stood near, with a hostile design, which results, however, from the connection, not the word itself.—**Assembled.** In Hebrew, **sat together,** with the involved idea in both cases that it was for the purpose of combination and resistance.—**His Christ,** his Anointed One, answering to *Měshēho* in the Psalm. The act of anointing was performed in connection with the setting apart of a prophet, priest, or king to his office, and, according to the Hebrew symbology, denoted his receiving the spiritual gifts and endowments which he needed for the performance of his duties.[1] (Comp. the note on 6 : 6.) The act accompanied consecration to the office assumed, but was not the direct sign of it, as is often loosely asserted. It is with reference to this import of the symbol that the Saviour of men is called *The Christ*—i. e. *the Anointed*—by way of eminence, because he possessed the gifts of the Spirit without measure, was furnished in a perfect manner for the work which he came into the world to execute. (See on 1 : 2.)

[1] Bähr's *Symbolik des Mosaischen Cultus*, vol. ii. p. 171, *sq.*

27 For *a*of a truth against *b*thy holy child Jesus, *c*whom thou hast anointed, both Herod, and Pontius Pilate, with the Gentiles, and the people of Israel, were gathered together,
28 *d*For to do whatsoever thy hand and thy counsel determined before to be done.
29 And now, Lord, behold their threatenings: and grant unto thy servants, *e*that with all boldness they may speak thy word,
30 By stretching forth thine hand to heal; *f*and that signs and wonders may be done *g*by the name of *h*thy holy child Jesus.
31 ¶ And when they had prayed, *i*the place was shaken where they were assembled together; and they were all filled with the Holy Ghost, *k*and they spake the word of God with boldness.
32 And the multitude of them that believed *l*were of one heart and of one soul: *m*neither said any *of them*

27 for of a truth in this city against thy holy Servant Jesus, whom thou didst anoint, both Herod and Pontius Pilate, with the Gentiles and the peoples of Israel, were gathered together, to do whatsoever thy
28 hand and thy counsel foreordained to come to pass.
29 And now, Lord, look upon their threatenings: and grant unto thy *l*servants to speak thy word with all
30 boldness, while thou stretchest forth thy hand to heal; and that signs and wonders may be done
31 through the name of thy holy Servant Jesus. And when they had prayed, the place was shaken wherein they were gathered together; and they were all filled with the Holy Spirit, and they spake the word
32 of God with boldness. And the multitude of them that believed were of one heart and soul: and not one *of them* said that aught of the things which he possessed was his own;

a Matt. 26 : 3; Luke 22 : 2; 23 : 1, 8....*b* Luke 1 : 35....*c* Luke 4 : 18; John 10 : 36....*d* ch. 2 : 23; 3 : 18....*e* vers. 13, 31; ch. 9 : 27; 13 : 46; 14 : 3; 19 : 8; 26 : 26; 28 : 31; Eph. 6 : 19....*f* ch. 2 : 43; 5 : 12....*g* ch. 3 : 6, 16....*h* ver. 27....*i* ch. 2 : 2, 4; 16 : 26....*k* ver. 29....*l* ch. 5 : 12; Rom. 15 : 5, 6; 2 Cor. 13 : 11; Phil. 1 : 27; 2 : 2; 1 Pet. 3 : 8....*m* ch. 2 : 44.——1 Gr. *bond-servants.*

27. For illustrates the significance of the prophecy. It had been spoken, not without meaning: **for in truth,** etc.—After **of a truth** we are to read **in this city.** The words are left out of the E. V., and I believe of all the earlier translations into English, except the two made from the Vulgate. They are to be retained. They are found in A B D E, and more than twenty others, supported by the unanimous voice of ancient versions, and many ecclesiastical writers." (See Green's *Developed Criticism,*[1] etc., p. 94.)—**Against thy consecrated servant.** (See on 3 : 13.)—**Didst anoint,** with that rite inaugurate as king.—**And peoples of Israel** (see on v. 25), either because the Jews who put the Saviour to death belonged to different tribes, or because so many of them had come to Jerusalem from distant lands (comp. 2 : 5), and so represented different nationalities (Mey.). It is not at all probable that the singular and the plural are confounded here (Kuin.).

28. In order to do in reality, though not with that conscious intention on their part.— ἡ χείρ denotes **the power,** ἡ βουλή **the counsel,** purpose, of God. **Determined** adapts itself *per zeugma* to both nouns. The verbal idea required by the former would be **executed.**

29. Lord—*i. e.* God, which is required by **God** in v. 24, and **thy servant** in v. 30. (Comp. on 1 : 24.)—**Look upon their threats,** in order to see what grace his servants needed at such a crisis. They pray for courage to enable them to preach the word, not for security against danger.—**Entire,** the utmost. (See 13 : 10; 17 : 11, etc.) In that sense πᾶς (**all**) does not require the article. (W. § 18. 4; K. § 246. 5.)

30. In that thou dost stretch forth thy hand for healing, the effect of which as a public recognition of their character on the part of God would be to render them fearless; or, as some prefer, the construction may denote time, **while thou dost stretch forth,** etc.; so that in the latter case they ask that they may declare the truth with power as well as with courage.—**And that signs and wonders may be wrought** (Kuin., Mey., De Wet.). The clause is telic and related to **stretch forth,** like **for healing.** Some make it depend on **give,** which is too remote, and others repeat **in that** after **and** (καί).—**Thy child,** or **thy servant.**

31. The place was shaken. They would naturally regard such an event as a token of the acceptance of their prayer, and as a pledge that a power adequate to their protection was engaged for them.—**Were all filled with the Holy Spirit,** etc. They were thus endued both with courage to declare the word of God and with miraculous power for confirming its truth. They had just prayed for assistance in both respects.

32–37. THE BELIEVERS ARE OF ONE MIND, AND HAVE ALL THINGS COMMON.

32. δέ (**but**), slightly adversative, turns our attention from the apostles (v. 31) to the church at large.—**The multitude of those who believed,** like *the multitude of the disciples* in 6 : 2. This description of the union of heart and the liberality which distinguished the disciples applies to all of them, as the unqualified nature of the language clearly intimates. Meyer supposes those only to be meant who are mentioned as new converts in v. 4;[2] but the mind

[1] *A Course of Developed Criticism on Passages of the New Testament materially affected by various Readings,* by Rev. Thomas Sheldon Green, late Fellow of Christ's College, Cambridge, etc. (London, 1856).

[2] I am not surprised to find that Meyer has corrected this opinion in his new edition. [In his last ed. he says: "These—*i. e.* the multitude, etc.—are designated as *having become believers,* in reference to verse 4; but in

that aught of the things which he possessed was his own; but they had all things common.

33 And with *a*great power gave the apostles *b*witness of the resurrection of the Lord Jesus: and *c*great grace was upon them all.

34 Neither was there any among them that lacked: *d*for as many as were possessors of lands or houses sold them, and brought the prices of the things that were sold,

35 *e*And laid *them* down at the apostles' feet: *f*and distribution was made unto every man according as he had need.

36 And Joses, who by the apostles was surnamed

33 but they had all things common. And with great power gave the apostles their witness of the resurrection of the Lord Jesus: and great grace was upon 34 them all. For neither was there among them any that lacked: for as many as were possessors of lands or houses sold them, and brought the prices of the 35 things that were sold, and laid them at the apostles' feet: and distribution was made unto each, according as any one had need.

36 And Joseph, who by the apostles was surnamed Barnabas (which is, being interpreted, Son of *2*ex-

---

a ch. 1 : 8....*b* ch. 1 : 22....*c* ch. 2 : 47....*d* ch. 2 : 45....*e* ver. 37 ; ch. 5 : 2....*f* ch. 2 : 45 ; 6 : 1.——1 Some ancient authorities add *Christ*....2 Or, *consolation.*

---

does not recall readily so distant a remark.— οὐδὲ εἷς, **not even one.—Said that it was his own**—*i. e.* insisted on his right to it so long as others were destitute. (See v. 34.)—**Common,** in the use of their property; not necessarily in the possession of it. (Comp. the note on 2 : 44, *sq.*) "It is proper to remark," says Bishop Blomfield,[1] "that although an absolute community of goods existed, in a certain sense, amongst the first company of believers, it was not insisted upon by the apostles as a necessary feature in the constitution of the Christian Church. We find many precepts in the Epistles which distinctly recognize the difference of rich and poor and mark out the respective duties of each class, and the apostle Paul, in particular, far from enforcing a community of goods, enjoins those who were affluent to make a contribution every week for those who were poorer (1 Cor. 16 : 2, 3). Yet the *spirit* of this primitive system should pervade the church in all ages. All Christians ought to consider their worldly goods, in a certain sense, as the common property of their brethren. There is a part of it which by the laws of God and nature belongs to their brethren, who, if they cannot implead them for its wrongful detention before an earthly tribunal, have their right and title to it written by the finger of God himself in the records of the gospel, and will see it established at the judgment-day."

33. With great power, with convincing effect on the minds of men. (See Matt. 9 : 29; Luke 4 : 32.) Among the elements of this power we are to reckon, no doubt, the miracles which the disciples performed; but the singular number forbids the supposition that **power** can refer to miracles, except in this indirect manner.—**Grace** some understand of the **favor** which the Christians enjoyed with the people in consequence of their liberality (see 2 : 47)

(Grot., Kuin., Olsh.). It is better, with De Wette, Meyer, Alford, and others, to retain the ordinary sense: *divine favor,* grace, of which their liberality was an effect. (Comp. 2 Cor. 9 : 14.)

34. For (a proof of their reception of such grace) **there was no one needy,** left to suffer, **among them.—Estates,** landed possessions. (See 5 : 3–8; Matt. 26 : 36; Mark 14 : 32.)—πωλοῦντες ἐφερον, **sold and brought.** This combination illustrates the occasional use of the present participle as an imperfect. (W. ? 45. 1. a.; S. ? 173. 2.)

35. Placed them at the feet of the apostles. (See v. 37; 5 : 2.) The frequency of the act is determined by that of the previous verb. This appears to have been a figurative expression, signifying to commit entirely to their care or disposal. It may have arisen from the Oriental custom of laying gifts or tribute before the footstool of kings.—**Distribution was made.** The verb is impersonal. —**As any one had need** occurs as in 2 : 45.

36. δέ **(and)** subjoins an example in illustration of what is said in vv. 34, 35.—[**Joses.** Rather **Joseph,** according to the oldest MSS. and the critical editors. א A B D E, together with the Vulgate and Syriac versions, have **Joseph,** while there is very little early authority for **Joses.**—A. H.]—**Barnabas** is the individual of this name who became subsequently so well known as Paul's associate in missionary labors. (See 13 : 2, *sq.*) The appellation which he received from the apostles describes a particular trait in his style of preaching. Most suppose it to be derived from *Bar-nĕbhooah* (Syro-Chaldaic) —*i. e.* "son of prophecy"—but in a more restricted sense of the phrase as equivalent to **son of consolation,** since **prophecy** includes also hortatory, consolatory discourse (Comp. 1 Cor. 14 : 3. For other conjectures,

---

such a way that it is not merely those *many* (v. 4) that are meant, but *they,* and at the same time *all others who had till now become believers.* This is required by *the multitude,* which denotes the Christian people generally, as contrasted with the apostles." Hackett's interpretation is simple and sufficient.—A. H.]

[1] *Lectures on the Acts of the Apostles* (third edition), p. 28.

Barnabas, (which is, being interpreted, The son of consolation,) a Levite, *and* of the country of Cyprus, 37 *a*Having land, sold *it*, and brought the money, and laid *it* at the apostles' feet.

37 hortation], a Levite, a man of Cyprus by race, having a field, sold it, and brought the money and laid it at the apostles' feet.

CHAPTER V.

BUT a certain man named Ananias, with Sapphira his wife, sold a possession,
2 And kept back *part* of the price, his wife also being privy *to it*, *b*and brought a certain part, and laid *it* at the apostles' feet.
3 *c*But Peter said, Ananias, why hath *d*Satan filled thine heart to lie to the Holy Ghost, and to keep back *part* of the price of the land?

1 BUT a certain man named Ananias, with Sapphira
2 his wife, sold a possession, and kept back *part* of the price, his wife also being privy to it, and brought a
3 certain part, and laid it at the apostles' feet. But Peter said, Ananias, why hath Satan filled thy heart to ¹lie to the Holy Spirit, and to keep back *part* of

---

a vers. 34, 35 ; ch. 5 : 1, 2....*b* ch. 4 : 37....*c* Num. 30 : 2 ; Deut. 23 : 21 ; Eccles. 5 : 4....*d* Luke 22 : 3.——1 Or, *deceive*

---

see Kuinoel, *ad loc.*)—**A Levite.** He was probably a **Levite**, in distinction from **a priest**—*i. e.* a descendant of Levi, but not of the family of Aaron. [See also the important treatise of Samuel Ives Curtiss, Jr., on *The Levitical Priests : A Contribution to the Criticism of the Pentateuch*, which, in addition to its value as a defence of the Mosaic origin of the Pentateuch, sets forth very clearly the principal facts pertaining to the priests and the Levites.—A. H.] —**Cypriote by race** describes him as a Jew born in Cyprus. (Comp. 18 : 2, 24.)

37. He having land. It is not said that this estate was in Cyprus, but that is naturally inferred. The Levites, as a tribe, had no part in the general division of Canaan (see Num. 18 : 20) ; but that exclusion did not destroy the right of individual ownership within the forty-eight cities and the territory adjacent to them, which were assigned to the Levites (Num. 35 : 1-8). (Comp., *e. g.*, Lev. 25 : 32; Jer. 32 : 8.) After the Exile they would naturally exercise the same right even out of Palestine.—**The money,** which is the proper sense of the plural. (Comp. 8 : 18–20 ; 24 : 26.)

1–11. THE FALSEHOOD OF ANANIAS AND SAPPHIRA, AND THEIR DEATH.

1. We enter on a new chapter here in a two-fold sense of the expression. As Olshausen remarks, "the history of the infant church has presented hitherto an image of unsullied light ; it is now for the first time that a shadow falls upon it. We can imagine that a sort of holy emulation had sprung up among the first Christians ; that they vied with each other in testifying their readiness to part with everything superfluous in their possession, and to devote it to the wants of the church. This zeal now bore away some, among others, who had not yet been freed in their hearts from the predominant love of earthly things. Such a

person was Ananias, who, having sold a portion of his property, kept back a part of the money which he received for it. The root of his sin lay in his vanity, his ostentation. He coveted the reputation of appearing to be as disinterested as the others, while at heart he was still the slave of Mammon, and so must seek to gain by hypocrisy what he could not deserve by his benevolence."—**But** puts the conduct of Ananias in contrast with that of Barnabas and the other Christians.—**A possession,** of the nature defined in v. 3.

2. Kept back—reserved for himself—**from the price.** The genitive, which in classical Greek usually follows a partitive verb like this (K. § 271. 2), depends oftener in the New Testament on a preposition. (W. § 30. 7. c.)—**Being conscious of it to herself,** aware of the reservation just mentioned (comp. v. 9.) ; not *knowing it as well as he*, since it is the object of **also** to hint the collusion of the parties.—**A certain part,** which he pretended was all he had received.

3. Why demands a reason for his yielding to a temptation which he ought to have repelled. The question recognizes his freedom of action. (Comp. James 4 : 7.) The sin is charged upon him as his own act in the next verse.—**Has filled,** possessed, **thy heart.** (Comp. John 13 : 27.)—**That thou shouldst deceive the Holy Spirit**—*i. e.* the apostles, to whom God revealed himself by the Spirit. The infinitive is telic [denoting purpose, *in order that*] (Mey., De Wet.), and the purpose is predicated, not of Ananias, but of the tempter. Satan's object was to instigate to the act, and that he accomplished. Some make the infinitive ecbatic [denoting result, or *that*], and, as the intention of Ananias was frustrated, must then render **that thou shouldst attempt to deceive.** This is forced and unnecessary.—**The land, the estate,** field. (See 4 : 34.)

---

4 Whiles it remained, was it not thine own? and after it was sold, was it not in thine own power? why hast thou conceived this thing in thine heart? thou hast not lied unto men, but unto God.

5 And Ananias hearing these words [a]fell down, and gave up the ghost: and great fear came on all them that heard these things.

6 And the young men arose, [b]wound him up, and carried *him* out, and buried *him.*

4 the price of the land? While it remained, did it not remain thine own? and after it was sold, was it not in thy power? How is it that thou hast conceived this thing in thy heart? thou hast not lied unto men, 5 but unto God. And Ananias hearing these words fell down and gave up the ghost: and great fear came 6 upon all that heard it. And the [1]young men arose and wrapped him round, and they carried him out and buried him.

---

a vers. 10, 11....*b* John 19 : 40.——1 Gr. *younger.*

---

4. Did it not, while it remained unsold, **remain to you** as your own property? **and when sold was it not**—*i. e.* the money received for it—**in your own power?** This language makes it evident that the community of goods, as it existed in the church at Jerusalem, was purely a voluntary thing, and not required by the apostles. Ananias was not censured because he had not surrendered his entire property, but for falsehood in professing to have done so when he had not.—τί ὅτι stands concisely for τί ἐστιν ὅτι, as in v. 9; Mark 2 : 16; Luke 2 : 49 (Frtz., Mey., De Wet.). It is a classical idiom, but not common. — **Didst thou put in thy heart?** conceive the thing. (Comp. 19 : 21.) The expression has a Hebraistic coloring (comp. *sēm al-lēbh* in Dan. 1 : 8 and Mal. 2 : 2), though not unlike the Homeric ἐν φρεσὶ θέσθαι. The aorist (not perf., as in E. V.) represents the wicked thought as consummated.—**Thou hast not lied,** etc., is an intensive way of saying that the peculiar enormity of his sin consisted in its being committed against God. David takes the same view of his guilt in Ps. 51 : 6. Ananias had attempted to deceive men as well as God; but that aspect of his conduct was so unimportant, in comparison with the other, that it is overlooked, denied. (Comp. Matt. 10 : 20; 1 Thess. 4 : 8. See W. ? 59. 8. b.) It is logically correct to translate **not so much . . . as,** but is incorrect in form and less forcible. **Hast lied** governs the dative here, as in the Septuagint, but never in the classics. (W. ? 31. 5.)

5. Lit. **breathed out his soul,** *expired.*— **And great fear came upon all,** etc. Luke repeats this remark in v. 11. It applies here to the first death only, the report of which spread rapidly and produced everywhere the natural effect of so awful a judgment. Some editors (Lchm., Mey., Tsch.) strike out **these things** after **heard.** It is wanting in A B D, Vulg., *et al.,* and may have been inserted from v. 11. [It is also wanting in ℵ and is rejected by Lach., Tsch., Treg., Anglo-Am. Revisers, but is retained by West. and Hort.—A. H.] If it be genuine, however, it may refer to a single event, especially when that is viewed

in connection with its attendant circumstances. The plural does not show that the writer would include also the death of Sapphira—*i. e.* that he speaks here proleptically—which is De Wette's view.

6. The younger men = young men (νεανίσκοι) in v. 10. They were probably **the younger men** in the assembly, in distinction from the older (Neand., De Wet., Alf.). It devolved on them naturally to perform this service, both on account of their greater activity and out of respect to their superiors in age. So also Walch decides (*Dissertationes,* etc., p. 79, *sq.*). Some have conjectured (Kuin., Olsh., Mey.) that they were a class of regular assistants or officers in the church. That opinion has no support, unless it be favored by this passage.—συνέστειλαν (**wound . . . up**) is less certain than has been commonly supposed. The E. V. renders *wound up* shrouded or covered, which is adopted also by Kuin., De Wet., Alf., and others. Rost and Palm (*Lex.,* s. v.) recognize this as the last of their definitions, but rely for it quite entirely on this passage and Eurip., *Troad.,* 382. Walch (*Dissertationes,* etc., p. 79, *sq.*) argues in favor of this signification, and with success, if it be true, according to his assumption, that περιστέλλειν and συστέλλειν denote the same thing as used of the rites of burial. The Vulgate has *amoverunt,* which the older E. Vv. appear to have followed: thus, *moved away* (Wicl.); *put apart* (Tynd., Cranm.); *took apart* (Gen.); *removed* (Rhem.). This sense is too remote from any legitimate use of the verb to be defended. A third explanation, which keeps nearer both to the etymology and the ordinary meaning, is *placed together*—laid out or composed—his stiffened limbs, so as to enable the bearers to take up and carry the body with more convenience. Meyer insists on this view, and contends that πέπλοις συνεστάλησαν in Eurip., as referred to above, can be translated only *were laid out* (dressed at the same time) *in robes.* It is certain that no mode of preparing the body which was formal at all, requiring delay, could have been observed in an emergency like the present.—*Having carried forth,* out of the house and beyond the city. Except in the case of kings

7 And it was about the space of three hours after, when his wife, not knowing what was done, came in.
8 And Peter answered unto her, Tell me whether ye sold the land for so much? And she said, Yea, for so much.
9 Then Peter said unto her, How is it that ye have agreed together *a*to tempt the Spirit of the Lord? behold, the feet of them which have buried thy husband *are* at the door, and shall carry thee out.
10 *b*Then fell she down straightway at his feet, and yielded up the ghost: and the young men came in, and found her dead, and, carrying *her* forth, buried *her* by her husband.
11 *c*And great fear came upon all the church, and upon as many as heard these things.

7 And it was about the space of three hours after, when his wife, not knowing what was done, came 8 in. And Peter answered unto her, Tell me whether ye sold the land for so much. And she said, Yea, 9 for so much. But Peter *said* unto her, How is it that ye have agreed together to try the Spirit of the Lord? behold, the feet of them who have buried thy husband are at the door, and they shall carry thee 10 out. And she fell down immediately at his feet, and gave up the ghost: and the young men came in and found her dead, and they carried her out and buried 11 her by her husband. And great fear came upon the whole church, and upon all that heard these things.

a ver. 3 ; Matt. 4 : 7....*b* ver. 5....*c* ver. 5 ; ch. 2 : 43 ; 19 : 17.

---

or other distinguished persons, the Jews did not bury within the walls of their towns, (See Jahn's *Archæol.*, ⸹ 206.) This circumstance accounts for the time which elapsed before the return of the bearers. It was customary for the Jews to bury the dead much sooner than is common with us. The reason for this despatch is found partly in the fact that decomposition takes place very rapidly after death in warm climates (comp. John 11 : 39), and partly in the peculiar Jewish feeling respecting the defilement incurred by contact with a dead body. (See Num. 19 : 11, *sq.*) The interment in the case of Ananias may have been hastened somewhat by the extraordinary occasion of his death; but, even under ordinary circumstances, a person among the Jews was commonly buried the same day on which he died. (See Win., *Realw.*, vol. ii. p. 16.) Even among the present inhabitants of Jerusalem, says Tobler,[1] burial, as a general rule, is not deferred more than three or four hours.

7. Now it came to pass . . . an interval of about three hours . . . then, etc. **An interval,** etc., is not here the subject of **was** or **came to pass** (= ἐγένετο), but forms a parenthetic clause, and καί (see on 1 : 10) introduces the apodosis of the sentence (Frtz., De Wet., Mey.). For the same construction, comp. Matt. 15 : 32 ; Mark 8 : 2 (in the correct text); Luke 9 : 28. (See W. ⸹ 62. 2.) The minute specification of time here imparts an air of reality to the narrative.—**Came in**—*i. e.* to the place of assembly.

8. Answered her, addressed her. Hebraistic, after the manner of Heb. *anah.* (See on 3 : 12.) De Wette inclines to the ordinary Greek sense, **answered**—*i. e.* upon her salutation.—τοσούτου is the genitive of price—**for so much,** and no more—pointing, says Meyer, to the money which lay there within sight. Kuinoel's better view is that Peter named the sum ;

but, it being unknown to the writer, he substitutes for it an indefinite term like our "so much" or "so and so." This sense is appropriate to the woman's reply.

9. Why is it that it was agreed, concerted, **by you?** The dative occurs after the passive, instead of the genitive with ὑπό, when the agent is not only the author of the act, but the person for whose benefit the act is performed. (K. ⸹ 284. 11.) — **To tempt,** put to trial, **the Spirit,** as possessed by the apostles, whether he can be deceived or not. (See on v. 3.)—**Behold, the feet of those who buried thy husband. Behold** directs attention to the sound of their footsteps as they approached the door. What occurred before their entrance occupied but a moment.

10. Straightway, *immediately,* after this declaration of Peter. It is evident that the writer viewed the occurrence as supernatural. The second death was not only instantaneous, like the first, but took place precisely as Peter had foretold. The woman lay dead at the apostle's feet as the men entered who had just borne her husband to the grave.

11. (See note on v. 5.) **Great fear came,** etc. To produce this impression both in the church and out of it was doubtless one of the objects which the death of Ananias and Sapphira was intended to accomplish. The punishment inflicted on them, while it displayed the just abhorrence with which God looked upon this particular instance of prevarication, was important also as a permanent testimony against similar offences in every age of the church. "Such severity in the beginning of Christianity," says Benson,[2] "was highly proper, in order to prevent any occasion for like punishments for the time to come. Thus Cain, the first murderer, was most signally punished by the immediate hand of God ; thus, upon the erecting of God's temporal kingdom among the

---

[1] *Denkblätter aus Jerusalem,* von Dr. Titus Tobler, p. 325 (St. Gallen, 1853).
[2] *History of the First Planting of the Christian Religion,* etc., vol. i. p. 105.

12 ¶ And *a*by the hands of the apostles were many signs and wonders wrought among the people; (*b*and they were all with one accord in Solomon's porch.

13 And *c*of the rest durst no man join himself to them: *d*but the people magnified them.

14 And believers were the more added to the Lord, multitudes both of men and women.)

15 Insomuch that they brought forth the sick into the streets, and laid *them* on beds and couches, *e*that at the

12 And by the hands of the apostles were many signs and wonders wrought among the people; and they 13 were all with one accord in Solomon's porch. But of the rest durst no man join himself to them: how-14 beit the people magnified them; [1]and believers were the more added to the Lord, multitudes both of men 15 and women; insomuch that they even carried out the sick into the streets, and laid them on beds and ²couches, that, as Peter came by, at the least his

a ch. 2 : 43; 14 : 3; 19 : 11; Rom. 15 : 19; 2 Cor. 12 : 12; Heb. 2 : 4....*b* ch. 3 : 11; 4 : 32....*c* John 9 : 22; 12 : 42; 19 : 38... *d* ch. 2 : 47; 4 : 21....*e* Matt. 9 : 21; 14 : 36; ch. 19 : 12.——1 Or, *and there were the more added* to them, *believing on the Lord*....2 Or, *pallets*

Jews, Nadab and Abihu were struck dead for offering strange fire before the Lord ; and Korah and his company were swallowed up alive by the earth for opposing Moses, the faithful servant of God; and the two hundred and fifty men who offered incense upon that occasion were consumed by a fire which came out from the Lord; and, lastly, Uzzah, for touching the ark, fell by as sudden and remarkable a divine judgment when the kingdom was going to be established in the house of David, to teach Israel a reverence for God and divine things. Nay, in establishing even human laws, a severe punishment upon the first transgressors doth oft prevent the punishment of others, who are deterred from like attempts by the suffering of the first criminals."

12-16. THE APOSTLES STILL PREACH, AND CONFIRM THEIR TESTIMONY BY MIRACLES.

12. And, *now,* continuative.—**Many** in this position qualifies the two nouns more strongly than when joined with the first of them, as in 2 : 43. The first and last places in a Greek sentence may be emphatic. (K. ¾ 348. 6.) [It is doubtful whether **many** (πολλά) had the last place in Luke's autograph. The principal editors, with א A B D E, etc., put it after **signs and wonders,** but before **among the people. Were wrought,** it may be added, is according to decisive evidence in the imperfect tense = *were being wrought,* describing a succession of miraculous events. The *textus receptus* gives the verb in the aorist, but upon very insufficient manuscript authority.—A.H.] **And they were all with one mind in Solomon's porch**—*i. e.* from day to day. It was their custom to repair thither and preach to the people whom they found in this place of public resort. **All** refers to the apostles mentioned in the last clause (Kuin., Olsh., Alf.). Some understand it of all the believers (Bng., De Wet., Mey.), in disregard both of the natural antecedent and of the improbability that so many would assemble at once in such a place. The apostles or individuals of them are meant certainly in v. 42; and, from the simi-

larity of that passage to this, we naturally infer that Luke speaks of the same class of persons here as there.

13. But of the rest, who did not belong to the party of the apostles, who were not Christians; the same, evidently, who are called **the people** just below.—**No one ventured to associate with them** (see 9 : 26; 10 : 28)-- viz. the apostles; lit. **join himself to them.** So deeply had the miracles wrought by the apostles impressed the Jewish multitude that they looked upon those who performed them with a sort of religious awe and were afraid to mingle freely with them. **The rest,** taken as above, need not include any but unbelievers, even if we confine **all** to the apostles. If we extend **all** to the disciples generally, the notion that *the others* are believers as well as unbelievers (Alf.) falls away still more decisively. That the apostles should have inspired their fellow-Christians with a feeling of dread disturbs all our conceptions of their relations to each other, as described or intimated elsewhere.—A comma is the proper point after **them.**—**But,** as opposed to what they refrained from doing.— **Magnified them,** regarded them with wonder and extolled them.

14. This verse is essentially parenthetic, but contains a remark which springs from the one just made. One of the ways in which the people testified their regard for the Christians was that individuals of them were constantly passing over to the side of the latter.—**And still more.** (Comp. 9 : 22; Luke 5 : 15.)—**The Lord**—here Christ—many connect with **believers;** but a comparison with 11 : 24 shows that it depends rather on the verb.—**Multitudes both of men and women.** The additions were so great that Luke counts them no longer. (See 1 : 15; 2 : 41 ; 4 : 4.)

15. Insomuch binds this verse to v. 13. We have here an illustration of the extent to which the people carried their confidence in the apostles.—**Along the streets.** (See W. ¾ 49. d.)— **Upon beds and pallets.** The latter was a cheaper article used by the common people. (See *Dict. of Antt* , art. "Lectus;" and R. and P.,

least the shadow of Peter passing by might overshadow some of them.

16 There came also a multitude *out* of the cities round about unto Jerusalem, bringing [a]sick folks, and them which were vexed with unclean spirits: and they were healed every one.

17 ¶ [b]Then the high priest rose up, and all they that were with him, (which is the sect of the Sadducees,) and were filled with indignation,

18 [c]And laid their hands on the apostles, and put them in the common prison.

19 But [d]the angel of the Lord by night opened the prison doors, and brought them forth, and said,

16 shadow might overshadow some one of them. And there also came together the multitude from the cities round about Jerusalem, bringing sick folk, and them that were vexed with unclean spirits: and they were healed every one.

17 But the high priest rose up, and all they that were with him (who were the sect of the Sadducees), and 18 they were filled with jealousy, and laid hands on the 19 apostles, and put them in public ward. But an angel of the Lord by night opened the prison doors, and

---

a Mark 16 : 17, 18; John 14 : 12....*b* ch. 4 : 1, 2, 6....*c* Luke 21 : 12....*d* ch. 12 : 7 ; 16 : 26.

Lex. s. σκίμπους.) The rich and the poor grasped the present opportunity to be healed of their diseases. Instead of **beds** many read **little beds,** with reference to their portable size. We may adopt that reading, and yet distinguish the terms as before; for these couches need not have been larger than the others, in order to be more valuable.—**As Peter was passing.** The genitive does not depend on **shadow,** but is absolute.—κἄν = καὶ ἐάν, **at least,** so much as (*vel certe*). (Comp. Mark 6 : 56; 2 Cor. 11 : 16.) The separate parts can hardly be traced in this idiom. Some evolve them from an ellipsis : in order that, if Peter came, he might touch some of them, **even if** it were only his shadow (Mey.). (See Klotz, *Ad Devar.*, vol. ii. p. 139, *sq.*)

16. ἀσθενεῖς (**sick**) omits the article here, but has it in v. 15. It is there generic, here partitive : sick, sc. persons. (K. § 244. 8.) **Vexed,** etc., being added to **sick** persons, distinguishes the possessed or demoniacs from those affected by ordinary maladies. (Comp. 8 : 7.)—**Unclean**—*i. e.* morally corrupt, utterly wicked. (Comp. 19 : 12.)

17–25. RENEWED IMPRISONMENT OF THE APOSTLES, AND THEIR ESCAPE.

17. But (δέ) this success (v. 16) calls forth persecution.—**Rising up,** not from his seat in the council (for the council is not said to have been in session), but as it were mentally, **becoming excited,** proceeding to act. Kuinoel calls it redundant. (See further on 9 : 18.)— The **high priest** is probably Annas, who was before mentioned under that title. Some suppose Caiaphas, the actual high priest, to be intended. (See on 4 : 6.)—**Those with him** are not his associates in the Sanhedrim (for they are distinguished from these in v. 21), but, according to the more obvious relation of the words to **sect of the Sadducees, those with him** in sympathy and opinion—*i. e.* members of the religious sect to which he belonged. (Comp. 14 : 4.) [The word translated

sect (αἵρεσις) occurs more frequently in this book than in any other part of the New Testament. Here it is applied to the Sadducees as a religious party; in 15 : 5 and 26 : 5, to the Pharisees; and in 24 : 5–14 and 28 : 22, to the Christians. In Gal. 5 : 20 the same word is translated *parties*, and in 1 Cor. 11 : 19 *factions* (margin, *heresies*); while in 2 Pet. 2 : 1 it is rendered *heresies* in the text, but *sects* in the margin. It is the original of the English term "heresy." Thus, in the New Testament, it generally denotes a religious party separated from others by its creed or opinion. The distinctive belief of the party may be right or wrong, but it will naturally be stigmatized as error by those who reject it. Hence the word "sect" carries with it, even in the New Testament, an intimation of popular disapproval, though it may be applied to the followers of Christ.—A. H.] Josephus states that most of the higher class in his day were sceptics or Sadducees, though the mass of the people were Pharisees.—**Indignation** (13 : 45), not **envy.** A Hebraistic sense.

18. Upon the apostles—viz. Peter (v. 29) and others of them, but probably not the entire twelve. They were lodged **in the public prison,** so as to be kept more securely. It is far-fetched to suppose that δημοσίᾳ (*public*) was meant to suggest that they were treated as common malefactors.

19. The account of a similar escape is more fully related in 12 : 7, *sq.*—**During the night,** and not far from its close, as the two next verses seem to indicate. Fritzsche[1] concedes this sense of διά here, also in 16 : 9 and 17 : 10, but pronounces it entirely abnormal. Classic usage, it is true, would require *through the night*, its entire extent, and it would then follow, strangely enough, that the doors of the prison must have stood open for hours before the apostles went forth from their confinement. Meyer insists on that as the true meaning here. It is more reasonable to ascribe to Luke a degree of inaccuracy in the use of the preposition. (See W. § 47. i.)

---

[1] Fritzschiorum *Opuscula Academica*, p. 165

20 Go, stand and speak in the temple to the people *all the words of this life.
21 And when they heard *that*, they entered into the temple early in the morning, and taught. *b*But the high priest came, and they that were with him, and called the council together, and all the senate of the children of Israel, and sent to the prison to have them brought.
22 But when the officers came, and found them not in the prison, they returned, and told,
23 saying, The prison truly found we shut with all safety, and the keepers standing without before the doors: but when we had opened, we found no man within.
24 Now when the high priest and *c*the captain of the

20 brought them out, and said, Go ye, and stand and speak in the temple to the people all the words of
21 this Life. And when they heard *this*, they entered into the temple about daybreak, and taught. But the high priest came, and they that were with him, and called the council together, and all the senate of the children of Israel, and sent to the prison-
22 house to have them brought. But the officers that came found them not in the prison; and they re-
23 turned, and told, The prison-house we found shut in all safety, and the keepers standing at the doors: but when we had opened, we found no man
24 within. Now when the captain of the temple and

a John 6 : 68; 17 : 3; 1 John 5 : 11....*b* ch. 4 : 5, 6....*c* Luke 22 : 4; ch. 4 : 1.

An extreme purism in some cases is one of Meyer's faults as a critic. [By a mistranslation Gloag (and Dickson) represent Meyer as giving the same interpretation to this expression as Dr. Hackett, thus: " *Per noctem—i. e. during the night;* so that the opening, the bringing out of the prisoners, and the address of the angel occurred during the course of the night, and toward morning dawn the apostles repaired to the temple." But Meyer wrote, "*Per noctem—i. e. the night through* (die Nacht hindurch); so that," etc. It seems proper to mention this mistake in a translation which is generally correct and is likely to be in the hands of many persons.—A. H.]—*Opened the doors* (see 12 : 10), which were then closed again. (See v. 23.)—**Having brought them forth,** while the keepers were at their post (v. 23), but were restrained by a divine power from seeing them (see on 12 : 10), or, at all events, from interposing to arrest them.

20. **Go** and **speak** are present, because they denote acts already in progress. The prisoners were to proceed on their way to the temple, and to persist there in proclaiming the offensive message. (See on 3 : 6.)—**The words of this life,** eternal life, which you preach. (Comp. 13 : 26. W. § 34. 2. b.) Olshausen refers **this** to the angel: **this life** of which I speak to you; Lightfoot, to the Sadducees: **this life** which they deny. According to some, **this** belongs to the entire expression, **these words of life,** agreeing as a Hebraism with the dependent noun, instead of the governing one. (See Green's *Gr.*, p. 265.) An adjective may be so used, but not the pronoun.

21. **At early dawn.** The temple had already opened its gates to the worshippers and the traffickers (John 2 : 14, *sq.*) accustomed to resort thither. Hence the apostles could begin their work of instruction as soon as they arrived. The people of the East commence the day much earlier than is customary with us. The arrangements of life there adjust them-

selves to the character of the climate. During a great part of the year in Palestine the heat becomes oppressive soon after sunrise, and the inhabitants, therefore, assign their most important duties and labors to the early hours of the day. Nothing is more common at the present time than to see the villagers going forth to their employment in the fields while the night and the day are still struggling with each other. Worship is often performed in the synagogues at Jerusalem before the sun appears above Olivet.—**Having come**—*i. e.* to the place of assembly, which was probably a room in the temple (see 6 : 14; Matt. 27 : 3, *sq.*), and whence, apparently, the chief priest and his coadjutors sent out a summons (called . . . together, συνεκάλεσαν) to their colleagues to hasten together. On some occasions the Sanhedrists met at the house of the high priest. (See Matt. 26 : 57.)—**And all the eldership,** senate connected with the Sanhedrim. (Comp. 4 : 5; 22 : 5.) The prominence thus given to that branch of the council exalts our idea of its dignity. The term reminds us of men who were venerable for their years and wisdom. Kuinoel would emphasize πᾶσαν, as if the attendance of that order was full at this time, but was not always so. Some (Lightf., Olsh., Str., Mey.) think that this was not an ordinary session of the Sanhedrim, but that the elders of the nation at large were called upon to give their advice in the present emergency.

22. The servants who executed the orders of the Sanhedrim. (See v. 26.) Some of the temple-guard may have acted in this capacity. (See on 4 : 1.)

24. The priest, by way of eminence (1 Macc. 15 : 1; Jos., *Antt.*, 6. 12. 1); hence = **high priest,** as the same functionary is termed in v. 17 and 4 : 6.—On **the high priests,** see 4 : 6.—**Were perplexed concerning them**—*i. e.* the words reported, not the apostles (Mey., Alf.). **Words** is the more obvious antecedent; and, besides, nothing would embarrass the rulers so

temple and the chief priests heard these things, they doubted of them whereunto this would grow.

25 Then came one and told them, saying, Behold, the men whom ye put in prison are standing in the temple, and teaching the people.

26 Then went the captain with the officers, and brought them without violence: *for they feared the people, lest they should have been stoned.

27 And when they had brought them, they set *them* before the council: and the high priest asked them,

28 Saying, *Did not we straitly command you that ye should not teach in this name? and, behold, ye have filled Jerusalem with your doctrine, *and intend to bring this man's *blood upon us.

29 ¶ Then Peter and the *other* apostles answered and said, *We ought to obey God rather than men.

the chief priests heard these words, they were much perplexed concerning them whereunto this would 25 grow. And there came one and told them, Behold, the men whom ye put in the prison are in the tem-26 ple standing and teaching the people. Then went the captain with the officers, and brought them, *but* without violence; for they feared the people, lest 27 they should be stoned. And when they had brought them, they set them before the council. And the 28 high priest asked them, saying, We straitly charged you not to teach in this name: and behold, ye have filled Jerusalem with your teaching, and intend to 29 bring this man's blood upon us. But Peter and the apostles answered and said, We must obey God rather

---

a Matt. 21 : 26....*b* ch. 4 : 18....*c* ch. 2 : 23, 36; 3 : 15 ; 7 : 52....*d* Matt. 23 : 35; 27 : 25....*e* ch. 4 : 19.

---

much as the circulation of such reports at this precise moment.—**What this would become,** how it would affect the public mind in regard to the Christians and their doctrine. **This** refers to the miraculous liberation, and confirms what was said of **them.**

26–28. THEY ARE ARRESTED AGAIN AND BROUGHT BEFORE THE COUNCIL.

26. For **captain,** or **commander,** see on 4 : 1.—**That they might not be stoned** we are to connect probably with **without violence :** They brought them without violence that they might not be stoned. **For they feared the people** forms a parenthetic remark, the logical force of which is the same as if it had stood at the close of the sentence. The E. Versions generally (also Mey.) attach the last clause to **feared** instead of **brought,** but the proper connectives after verbs of fearing are μή, μήπως, and the like, and not ἵνα μή. (See W. § 56. 2. R.) Tischendorf puts a comma after **violence,** instead of a colon, as in some editions.

28. Straitly command. (See the note on 4 : 17.)—**Upon** (as their authority, see 4 : 18) **this name,** which they left unspoken as well known, or perhaps disdained to mention.—**To bring this man's blood**—*i. e.* fix upon us the guilt of having shed his blood as that of an innocent person. (Comp. Matt. 23 : 35.)— **This man** is not of itself contemptuous (comp. Luke 23 : 47 ; John 7 : 46), but could have that turn given to it by the voice, and was so uttered probably at this time.

29–32. THE ANSWER OF PETER, AND ITS EFFECT.

29. And the other **apostles.** Peter spoke in their name. (See 2 : 14.)—**To obey . . . men.** The Jews, though as a conquered nation they were subject to the Romans, acknowledged

the members of the Sanhedrim as their legitimate rulers; and the injunction which the Sanhedrim imposed on the apostles at this time emanated from the highest human authority to which they could have felt that they owed allegiance. The injunction which this authority laid on the apostles clashed with their religious convictions, their sense of the rights of the Infinite Ruler, and in this conflict between human law and divine they declared that the obligation to obey *God was paramount to every other. The apostles and early Christians acted on the principle that human governments forfeit their claim to obedience when they require what God has plainly forbidden or forbid what he has required. They claimed the right of judging for themselves what was right and what was wrong, in reference to their religious and their political duties, and they regulated their conduct by that decision. It is worthy of notice that in 4 : 19 they propound this principle as one which even their persecutors could not controvert—*i. e.* as one which commends itself to every man's reason and unperverted moral feelings.[1] In applying this principle, it will be found that the apostles in every instance abstained from all forcible resistance to the public authorities. They refused utterly to obey the mandates which required them to violate their consciences, but they endured quietly the penalties which the executors of the law enforced against them. They evaded the pursuit of their oppressors if they could (2 Cor. 11 : 32, 33), secreted themselves from arrest (12 : 19), left their prisons at the command of God; yet when violent hands were laid upon them, and they were dragged before magistrates, to the dungeon, or to death, they resisted not the wrong, but " followed his steps, who, when

---

[1] Socrates avowed this principle when in his defence he said to his judges, "*But I will obey God rather than you* " (Plat., *Apol.,* 29 D); and, unless the plea be valid, he died as a felon, and not as a martyr. (See other heathen testimonies to the same effect in Wetstein's *Novum Testamentum,* vol. ii. p. 478.)

30 *a*The God of our fathers raised up Jesus, whom ye slew and *b*hanged on a tree.
31 *c*Him hath God exalted with his right hand *to be* *d*a Prince and *e*a Saviour, *f* for to give repentance to Israel, and forgiveness of sins.
32 And *g*we are his witnesses of these things; and *so* *is* also the Holy Ghost, *h*whom God hath given to them that obey him.
33 ¶ *i*When they heard *that*, they were cut *to the heart*, and took counsel to slay them.
34 Then stood there up one in the council, a Pharisee, named *k*Gamaliel, a doctor of the law, had in repu-

30 than men. The God of our fathers raised up Jesus, 31 whom ye slew, hanging him on a tree. Him did God exalt [1] with his right hand *to be* a Prince and a Saviour, for to give repentance to Israel, and remis- 32 sion of sins. And we are witnesses[2] of these [3]things; 4and *so is* the Holy Spirit, whom God hath given to · them that obey him.
33 But they, when they heard this, were cut to the 34 heart, and were minded to slay them. But there stood up one in the council, a Pharisee, named Gamaliel, a doctor of the law, had in honor of all the people, and commanded to put the men forth a little

a ch. 3 : 13, 15 ; 22 : 14....b ch. 10 : 39 : 13 : 29 ; Gal. 3 : 13 ; 1 Pet. 2 : 24....c ch. 2 : 33, 36 ; Phil. 2 : 9 ; Heb. 2 : 10 ; 12 : 2....d ch. 3 : 15....
e Matt. 1 : 21....f Luke 24 : 47 ; ch. 3 : 26 ; 13 : 38 ; Eph. 1 : 7 ; Col. 1 : 14...g John 15 : 26, 27....h ch. 2 : 4 ; 10 : 44....i ch. 2 : 37 ;
7 : 54....k ch. 22 : 3.——1 Or, *at*....2 Some ancient authorities add *in him*....3 Gr. *sayings*....4 Some ancient authorities read *and God hath given the Holy Ghost to them that obey him*.

he suffered, threatened not, but committed himself to him that judgeth righteously" (1 Pet. 2 : 22, 23).

30. Our fathers recalls to mind the series of promises which God had made to provide a Saviour. (Comp. 3 : 25.) -**Raised up,** sent into the world. (Comp. 3 : 22 ; 13 : 23.) So Calvin, Bengel, De Wette, and others. Some supply **from the dead,** *raised up from the dead;* but that idea, being involved in **exalted,** below, would introduce a repetition at variance with the brevity of the discourse.— **Whom ye slew** (26 : 21) **by hanging,** not *slew and hanged* (E. V.).—**Wood, tree = cross,** a Hebraism. It occurs especially where the Jews are spoken of as having crucified the Saviour (10 : 39 ; 13 : 29).

31. Prince and Saviour belong as predicates to **this one :** *this one* (as, who is) *a prince and a Saviour;* not to the verb: *exalted to be a prince,* etc. (E. V.).—**To his right hand.** (See note on 2 : 33.)—**To give repentance**—*i. e.* the grace or disposition to exercise it. (Comp. 3 : 16 ; 18 : 27 ; John 16 : 7, 8.) Some understand it of the opportunity to repent, or the provision of mercy which renders repentance available to the sinner (De Wet.). The expression is too concise to convey naturally that idea, and *place of repentance* is employed for that purpose in Heb. 12 : 17. In both cases the exaltation of Christ is represented as securing the result in question, because it was the consummation of his work, and gave effect to all that preceded.

32. μάρτυρες (**witnesses**) governs here two genitives, one of a person, the other of a thing. (See Phil. 2 : 30 ; Heb. 13 : 7. W. § 30. 3. R. 3 ; K. § 275. R. 6.) Since their testimony was true, they must declare it ; no human authority could deter them from it. (Comp. 4 : 20.)—**And the Holy Spirit** (δέ) **too** is his witness. [The important MSS. א A B D* 33 and others omit δέ (*also*) ; so do the editors Lach., Tsch., Treg., West. and Hort, and Anglo-Am. Revisers.—

A. H.]—**To those who obey him**—*i. e.* by receiving the gospel. (Comp. 6 : 7.) Many suppose the apostle to refer chiefly to the special gifts which the Spirit conferred on so many of the first Christians, in order to confirm their faith as the truth of God. What took place on the day of Pentecost was a testimony of this nature, and that or some equivalent sign was repeated on other occasions. (Comp. 10 : 45 ; 19 : 6 ; Mark 16 : 20.) But to that outward demonstration we may add also the inward witness of the Spirit, which believers receive as evidence of their adoption. (Comp. Rom. 8 : 16 ; Gal. 4 : 6 ; 1 John 3 : 24.) Neander interprets the language entirely of this internal manifestation. Since the Holy Spirit testified to the gospel in both ways, and since the remark here is unqualified, we have no reason to consider the expression less extensive than the facts in the case.

33. Were convulsed with rage—lit. *were sawn asunder,* torn in pieces. The E. V. supplies "to the heart" after the verb (see 7 : 54), but the Greek text has no such reading. Some render *sawed their teeth,* gnashed them, which would require τοὺς ὀδόντας as the expressed object of the verb.—**Resolved,** determined (see 27 : 39 and John 12 : 10) ; but on the representation of Gamaliel they recalled their purpose. The issue was averted, and hence the tense is imperfect. [The imperfect tense would perhaps justify us in translating **were resolving,** were coming to a determination.—A. H.] Instead of passing a formal vote, it is more probable that they declared their intention by some tumultuous expression of their feelings. The verb may denote the act as well as the result of deliberation, **took counsel,** consulted : but men exasperated as they were would not be likely to pay much regard to parliamentary decorum.

34–39. THE ADVICE OF GAMALIEL.

34. τίμιος governs λαῷ as allied to words denoting judgment, estimation. (See W. § 31. 6.

6

tation among all the people, and commanded to put the apostles forth a little space ;

35 And said unto them, Ye men of Israel, take heed to yourselves what ye intend to do as touching these men.

36 For before these days rose up Theudas, boasting himself to be somebody ; to whom a number of men, about four hundred, joined themselves: who was slain ; and all, as many as obeyed him, were scattered, and brought to nought.

35 while. And he said unto them, Ye men of Israel, take heed to yourselves as touching these men, what 36 ye are about to do. For before these days rose up Theudas, giving himself out to be somebody ; to whom a number of men, about four hundred, joined themselves: who was slain ; and all, as many as obeyed him, were dispersed, and came to nought.

---

b. ; Mt. § 388.) The character which Luke ascribes to **Gamaliel** in this passage agrees with that which he bears in the Talmud. He appears there also as a zealous Pharisee, as unrivalled in that age for his knowledge of the law, as a distinguished teacher (see 22 : 3), and as possessing an enlarged, tolerant spirit, far above the mass of his countrymen. He is said to have lived still some fifteen years or more after this scene in the council. (See Herz., *Encyk.*, vol. iv. p. 656.[1])—βραχύ *(short)* refers evidently to time (in Wicl., *for a while*), not to space (E. V.).

35. Said. What follows is probably an outline of the speech.—**As touching these men** some join with **take heed—take heed unto yourselves in respect to these men** (E. V.) ; others with **what ye are about to do in respect to these men** (Kuin., De Wet., Mey.). Both constructions are admissible (W. § 55. 4) ; but, as **to do something in respect to** one is not uncommon in Greek (see examples in Wetst., *N. T.*), it is better to recognize an instance of that expression here.

36. Before these times. This is not the first time that zealots or seditionists have appeared ; they may have come forth with great pretensions, but ere long have closed their career with defeat and ignominy. For the sake of effect (observe **for**), Gamaliel puts the case as if the prisoners would turn out to be persons of this stamp ; but before closing he is careful to remind his associates that there was another possibility. (See v. 39.)—**Theudas.** Josephus mentions an insurrectionist named *Theudas* who appeared in the reign of Claudius, some ten years after the delivery of this speech. Gamaliel, therefore, must refer here to another man of this name ; and this man, since he preceded Judas the Galilean (v. 37), could not have lived much later than the reign of Herod the Great. The year of that monarch's death, as Josephus states, was remarkably turbulent ; the land was overrun with belligerent parties,

under the direction of insurrectionary chiefs, or fanatics. Josephus mentions but three of these disturbers by name ; he passes over the others with a general allusion. Among those whom the Jewish historian has omitted to name may have been the Theudas whom Gamaliel has here in view. The name was not an uncommon one (Win., *Realw.*, vol. ii. p. 609) ; and it can excite no surprise that one Theudas who was an insurgent should have appeared in the time of Augustus, and another fifty years later, in the time of Claudius. Josephus gives an account of four men named Simon who followed each other within forty years, and of three named Judas within ten years, who were all instigators of rebellion. This mode of reconciling Luke with Josephus is approved by Lardner, Bengel, Kuinoel, Olshausen, Anger, Winer, and others.[2] Another very plausible supposition is that Luke's Theudas may have been identical with one of the three insurgents whom Josephus designates by name. Sonntag, who agrees with those who adopt this view, has supported it with much learning and ability.[3] He maintains that the Theudas mentioned by Gamaliel is the individual who occurs in Josephus under the name of Simon, a slave of Herod, who attempted to make himself king in the year of that monarch's death. He urges the following reasons for that opinion : first, this Simon, as he was the most noted among those who disturbed the public peace at that time, would be apt to occur to Gamaliel as an illustration of his point ; secondly, he is described as a man of the same lofty pretensions (εἶναι ἄξιος ἐλπίσας παρ' ὁντινοῦν = λέγων εἶναί τινα ἑαυτόν) ; thirdly, he died a violent death, which Josephus does not mention as true of the other two insurgents ; fourthly, he appears to have had comparatively few adherents, in conformity with Luke's **about four hundred ;** and lastly, his having been originally a slave accounts for the twofold appellation, since it was very common among the Jews to assume a different

---

[1] Herzog's *Real-Encyklopädie für protestantische Theologie und Kirche* [1st edition].

[2] Jost, the Jewish historian (*Geschichte der Israeliten*, Band ii., Anh., p. 76), assents to this explanation, and admits the credibility of Luke as well as of Josephus.

[3] In the *Theologische Studien und Kritiken* (1837), p. 622, *sq.*, translated by the writer in the *Bibliotheca Sacra* (1848), p. 409, *sq.*

37 After this man rose up Judas of Galilee in the days of the taxing, and drew away much people after him: he also perished; and all, *even* as many as obeyed him, were dispersed.

38 And now I say unto you, Refrain from these men, and let them alone: *a*for if this counsel or this work be of men, it will come to nought:

39 *b*But if it be of God, ye cannot overthrow it; lest haply ye be found even *c*to fight against God.

37 After this man rose up Judas of Galilee in the days of the enrolment, and drew away *some of the* people after him: he also perished; and all, as many as 38 obeyed him, were scattered abroad. And now I say unto you, Refrain from these men, and let them alone: for if this counsel or this work be of men, it 39 will be overthrown: but if it is of God, ye will not be able to overthrow them; lest haply ye be found

---

a Prov. 21 : 30 ; Isa. 8 : 10 ; Matt. 15 : 13....*b* Luke 21 : 15 ; 1 Cor. 1 : 25....*c* ch. 7 : 51 ; 9 : 5 ; 23 : 9.

---

name on changing their occupation or mode of life. It is very possible, therefore, that Gamaliel speaks of him as Theudas, because, having borne that name so long at Jerusalem, he was best known by it to the members of the Sanhedrim ; and that Josephus, on the contrary, who wrote for Romans and Greeks, speaks of him as Simon, because it was under that name that he set himself up as king, and in that way acquired his foreign notoriety. (Tacit., *His.*, 5. 9.)—There can be no valid objection to either of the foregoing suppositions ; both are reasonable, and both must be disproved before Luke can be justly charged with having committed an anachronism in this passage.—**Was some one** of importance. τὶς (**some one**) has often that emphatic force. (W. ⸿ 25. 2. c.)

37. Judas the Galilean, etc. Josephus mentions this *Judas the Galilean,* and his account of him either confirms or leaves undenied every one of the particulars stated or intimated by Luke. (See *Bell. Jud.*, 2. 8. 1 ; *Antt.*, 18. 1. 6 ; 20. 5. 2.) He calls him twice **the Galilean,** though he terms him also **the Gaulonite** in *Antt.*, 18. 1. 1, from the fact that he was born at Gamala, in Lower Gaulonitis. He was known as the Galilean, because he lived subsequently in Galilee (De Wet.), or because that province may have included Gaulonitis. The epithet served to distinguish him from another Judas, a revolutionist, who appeared some ten years earlier than this.—**In the days of the registration**— *i. e.* in this instance of persons and property with a view to taxation (Jos., *Antt.*, 15. 1. 1). The ἀπογραφή in Luke 2 : 2, which is so carefully distinguished from this tumult, and which took place at the birth of Christ, is supposed generally to have been a census merely of the population. We learn from Josephus that soon after the dethronement of Archelaus, about the year A. D. 6 or 7, the Emperor Augustus ordered a tax to be levied on the Jews. The payment of that tax Judas instigated the people to resist, on the ground of its being a violation of their allegiance to Jehovah to pay tribute to a foreign power. (Comp.

Matt. 22 : 17.) He took up arms in defence of this principle, and organized a powerful opposition to the Roman Government.—**And he also,** etc. Josephus relates that this rebellion was effectually suppressed, and that many of those who had taken part in it were captured and crucified by the Romans. He says nothing of the fate of Judas himself.—**Were dispersed** describes very justly such a result of the enterprise. Coponius was then Procurator of Judea, and Quirinus [Quirinius], or Cyrenius (Luke 2 : 2), was Proconsul of Syria.

38. And now, in the light of such examples.—**Let them alone,** not *suffer them to depart.*—**From men,** in distinction from God (v. 39). (Comp. Matt. 21 : 25.)—**This counsel, this plan,** enterprise, **or** (more correctly) **work,** since it was already in progress.—**Will be frustrated**—*i. e.* without any interference on your part.

39. In if it is of God (comp. *if it be,* just before) the speaker reveals his sympathy with the prisoners. (See on 4 : 9.) Without declaring the truth to be on their side, he at least argues the question from that point of view.—**Lest haply,** etc. Critics differ as to the dependence of this clause. Some supply before it *see to it* or an equivalent word (see Luke 21 : 34): *Take heed lest ye be found* (in the end) *also fighting against God,* as well as men (Grot., Kuin., Rob.). Others find the ellipsis in *Ye cannot*[1] *destroy them* (more correct than αὐτό, **it**) and, therefore, I say, should not attempt it, *lest ye also,* etc. (Bng., Mey.). **Also** in both cases includes, naturally, the idea both of the impiety and the futility of the attempt. De Wette assents to those who connect the words with **let them alone,** in the last verse. [The true reading appears to be ἄφετε αὐτούς. So Lach., Treg., West. and Hort, after ℵ A B C. But this does not necessarily affect the interpretation. (Comp. Matt. 15 : 14.)—A. H.] This is the simplest construction, as μήποτε (**lest**) follows appropriately after such a verb, and the sense is then complete without supplying anything. In this case some editors would put what intervenes in brackets ; but that is incor-

---

[1] [The future tense, **will not be able,** etc., is the best-supported reading.—A. H.]

40 And to him they agreed: and when they had *called the apostles, *and beaten *them*, they commanded that they should not speak in the name of Jesus, and let them go.

41 ¶ And they departed from the presence of the council, *rejoicing that they were counted worthy to suffer shame for his name.

42 And daily *in the temple, and in every house, *they ceased not to teach and preach Jesus Christ.

40 even to be fighting against God. And to him they agreed: and when they had called the apostles unto them, they beat them and charged them not to speak 41 in the name of Jesus, and let them go. They therefore departed from the presence of the council, rejoicing that they were counted worthy to suffer dis-42 honor for the Name. And every day, in the temple and at home, they ceased not to teach and to preach Jesus *as* the Christ.

---

a ch. 4 : 18....b Matt. 10 : 17 ; 23 : 34 ; Mark 13 : 9....c Matt. 5 : 12 ; Rom. 5 : 3 ; 2 Cor. 12 : 10 ; Phil. 1 : 29 ; Heb. 10 : 34 ; James 1 : 2 ; 1 Pet. 4 : 13, 16....d ch. 2 : 46....e ch. 4 : 20, 29.

---

rect, inasmuch as the caution here presupposes the alternative in **but if it is of God.**—The advice of Gamaliel was certainly remarkable, and some of the early Christian Fathers went so far as to ascribe it to an unavowed attachment to the gospel. The supposition has no historical support, and there are other motives which explain his conduct. Gamaliel, as Neander remarks, was a man who had discernment enough to see that if this were a fanatical movement, it would be rendered more violent by opposition; that all attempts to suppress what is insignificant tend only to raise it into more importance. On the other hand, the manner in which the apostles spoke and acted may have produced some impression upon a mind not entirely prejudiced, and so much the more since their strict observance of the law and their hostile attitude toward Sadduceeism must have rendered him favorably disposed toward them. Hence the thought may have arisen in his mind that possibly, after all, there might be something divine in their cause.

40-42. THE APOSTLES SUFFER JOYFULLY FOR CHRIST, AND DEPART TO PREACH HIM ANEW.

40. Were persuaded by him—*i. e.* to spare the lives of the apostles, whom they had (see v. 33) resolved to put to death. They could not object to the views of Gamaliel, they were so reasonable; they were probably influenced still more by his personal authority. Still, their rage demanded some satisfaction: they must punish the heretics, if they could not slay them.—**Having scourged.** The instrument frequently used for this purpose was a whip, or scourge, consisting often of two lashes "knotted with bones, or heavy indented circles of bronze, or terminated by hooks, in which case it was aptly denominated a *scorpion*" (*Dict. of Antt.*, art. "Flagrum"). The punishment was inflicted on the naked back of the sufferer.

(Comp. 16 : 22.) A single blow would sometimes lay the flesh open to the bones. Hence, to scourge a person (δείρω) meant properly to excoriate, flay him. Paul says that he suffered this punishment five times (2 Cor. 11:24). It is affecting to remember that the Saviour was subjected to this laceration.

41. οἱ μέν. The antithesis does not follow.—οὖν, illative—*i. e.* in consequence of their release. [See the Revised Version, above, for the proper translation.—A. H.]—**That,** *because*, appends an explanation of the participle **rejoicing,** not of the verb.—**In behalf of the name**—*i. e.* of Jesus, which is omitted, either because it has occurred just before, or more properly because "the name" was a familiar expression among the disciples, and as such required no addition. (Comp. 3 John 7.) It is a loss to our religious dialect that the term in this primitive sense has fallen into disuse. The common text, indeed, reads **his** after **name** (Greek), but without sufficient authority.—**Were counted,** etc.—a bold oxymoron: **were accounted worthy to be disgraced.** For an explanation of the paradox, see Luke 16 : 15. The verbs refer to different standards of judgment.

42. From house to house, or **at home,** refers to their private assemblies in different parts of the city, as distinguished from their labors **in the temple.** Those who reject the distributive sense in 2 : 46 reject it also here. [See Jacob, *Eccl. Pol. of N. T.*, p. 191, *sq.*—A. H.] **Ceased not to teach,** in defiance of the prohibition which blows as well as words had just now enforced on them (v. 40). The Greek in such a case employs a participle, not the infinitive, as the complement of the verb. (K. § 310. 4. f.; W. § 45. 4.)—**Announcing the glad tidings of the Christ** (first as emphatic) **Jesus,** the latter the subject here, the former the predicate. (Comp. 9 : 20-22.) This clause defines the preceding one.

CHAPTER VI.

AND in those days, *a*when the number of the disciples was multiplied, there arose a murmuring of the *b*Grecians against the Hebrews, because their widows were neglected *c*in the daily ministration.

2 And the twelve called the multitude of the disciples *unto them*, and said, *d*It is not reason that we should leave the word of God, and serve tables.

3 Wherefore, brethren, *e*look ye out among you seven men of honest report, full of the Holy Ghost and wisdom, whom we may appoint over this business.

4 But we *f* will give ourselves continually to prayer, and to the ministry of the word.

1 Now in these days, when the number of the disciples was multiplying, there arose a murmuring of the [1]Grecian Jews against the Hebrews, because their widows were neglected in the daily ministration.

2 And the twelve called the multitude of the disciples unto them, and said, It is not [2]fit that we should for-3 sake the word of God, and [3]serve tables. [4]Look ye out therefore, brethren, from among you seven men of good report, full of the Spirit and of wisdom, whom 4 we may appoint over this business. But we will continue stedfastly in prayer, and in the ministry of the

---

a ch. 2 : 41 ; 4 : 4 ; 5 : 14 ; ver. 7....*b* ch. 9 : 29 ; 11 : 20....*c* ch. 4 : 35... *d* Ex. 18 : 17....*e* Deut. 1 : 13 ; ch. 1 : 21 ; 16 : 2 ; 1 Tim. 3 : 7.... *f* ch. 2 : 42.——1 Gr. *Hellenists*....2 Gr. *pleasing*....3 Or, *minister to tables*....4 Some ancient authorities read *But, brethren, look ye out from among you.*

1–7. APPOINTMENT OF ALMS-DISTRIBUTERS IN THE CHURCH AT JERUSALEM.

1. In these days. (See on 1 : 15.) We may assign the events in this chapter to the year A. D. 35. They relate more or less directly to the history of Stephen, and must have taken place shortly before his death, which was just before Paul's conversion.—**Was multiplied** = **becoming numerous.**—τῶν Ἑλληνιστῶν should be rendered, not Greeks, but **Hellenists.** They were the Jewish members of the church who spoke the Greek language. The other party, the *Hebrews*, were the Palestine Jews, who spoke the Syro-Chaldaic, or Aramæan. (See Win., *Chald. Gr.*, p. 19, *sq.*)—**Were overlooked** is imperfect, because the neglect is charged as one that was common.—**Ministration,** distribution of alms —*i. e.* either of food or the money necessary to procure it. Olshausen argues for the former from the adjective **daily.**

2. The twelve. Matthias must have been one of them, and the validity of his choice as an apostle is placed here beyond doubt. (See on 1 : 26.)—**The multitude**, mass, **of the disciples.** It has been objected that they had become too numerous at this time to assemble in one place. It is to be recollected, as De Wette suggests, that many of those who had been converted were foreign Jews, and had left the city ere this.—**That we, forsaking the word of God,** etc. It is not certain, from the narrative, to what extent this labor of providing for the poor had been performed by the apostles. The following remarks of Rothe present a reasonable view of that question : "The apostles at first appear to have applied themselves to this business, and to have expended personally the common funds of the church. Yet, occupied as they were with so many other more important objects, they could have exercised only a general oversight in the case, and must have committed the details of the matter to others.

Particular individuals may not have been appointed for this purpose at the beginning; and the business may have been conducted in an informal manner, without any strict supervision or immediate direction on the part of the apostles. Under such circumstances, especially as the number of believers was increasing every day, it could easily happen that some of the needy were overlooked ; and it is not surprising that the Hellenistic Christians had occasion to complain of the neglect of the widows and other poor among them."[1] The complaint, therefore, implied no censure of the apostles, but was brought naturally to them, both on account of their position in the church and the general relation sustained by them to the system under which the grievance had arisen.— **To serve tables,** provide for them. (Comp. Luke 4 : 39 ; 8 : 3.) Some render the noun *money-tables*, counters, as in John 2 : 15 ; but the verb connected with it here forbids that sense. The noun is plural, because several tables were supported. " Locutio indignitatem aliquam exprimit ; antitheton *ministerium verbi*" (Bng.).

3. Look ye out, etc. The selection, therefore, was made by the body of the church ; the apostles confirmed the choice, as we see from **we will appoint,** and from the consecration in v. 6. [But the selection was restricted to members of the church who were (1) of good repute (comp. 1 Tim. 3 : 2 ; Tit. 1 : 6, 7), and (2) full of the Spirit and of wisdom. The word **Holy** is omitted by Lach., Tsch., Treg., West. and Hort, Revisers' text, with ℵ B C² D, etc.— A. H.] καταστήσωμεν (T. R.), **we may appoint** (E. V.), is a spurious form.—**Testified to,** of good repute. (See 10 : 22 and 16 : 2.)—**Business**—lit. an affair which is held to be necessary.

4. Prayer, the (service of) **prayer.** The article points out the importance of the duty

---

[1] *Die Anfänge der Christlichen Kirche und ihrer Verfassung.* p. 164.

5 ¶ And the saying pleased the whole multitude: and they chose Stephen, *a* man full of faith and of the Holy Ghost, and *b*Philip, and Prochorus, and Nicanor, and Timon, and Parmenas, and *c*Nicolas a proselyte of Antioch :

6 Whom they set before the apostles : and *d*when they had prayed, *e*they laid *their* hands on them.

7 And *f* the word of God increased ; and the number of the disciples multiplied in Jerusalem greatly ; and a great company *g*of the priests were obedient to the faith.

5 word. And the saying pleased the whole multitude, and they chose Stephen, a man full of faith and of the Holy Spirit, and Philip, and Prochorus, and Nicanor, and Timon, and Parmenas, and Nicolas a

6 proselyte of Antioch : whom they set before the apostles: and when they had prayed, they laid their hands on them.

7 And the word of God increased ; and the number of the disciples multiplied in Jerusalem exceedingly ; and a great company of the priests were obedient to the faith.

a ch. 11 : 24....*b* ch. 8 : 5, 26; 21 : 8....*c* Rev. 2 : 6, 15....*d* ch. 1 : 24....*e* ch. 8 : 17 ; 9 : 17 ; 13 : 3 ; 1 Tim. 4 : 14 ; 5 : 22 ; 2 Tim. 1 : 6....*f* ch. 12 : 24 ; 19 : 20 ; Col. 1 : 6....*g* John 12 : 42.

(1 : 14). Prayer, evidently in this connection for the success of the word, is recognized as their legitimate work, as much as preaching.— **We will give ourselves.** This remark does not imply that they had been diverted already from their proper work, but that they wished to guard against that in future by committing this care to others. They now saw that it required more attention than they had bestowed upon it.

5. A man full of faith and of the Holy Spirit. We may retain ἁγίου (*Holy*), but the word is uncertain. [This remark was doubtless intended for the word **Holy** in verse 3 (see added note), for the adjective here is not questioned.—A. H.] The same terms describe the character of Barnabas in 11 : 24.—Of **Philip** we read again in 8 : 8, *sq.* ; 21 : 8. The others are not known out of this passage. That Nicolaus was the founder of the sect mentioned in Rev. 2 : 6 is a conjecture without proof. Many have supposed that the entire seven were chosen from the aggrieved party. Gieseler thinks that three of them may have been Hebrews, three Hellenists, and one a proselyte (*Ch. Hist.*, § 25). Their Greek names decide nothing. (See on 1 : 23.) The distributers would be taken naturally from both sides, but in what proportion we cannot tell. It would depend on their personal traits, after all, more than on their nationality, whether they were able to satisfy the disaffected.—Luke does not term the men **deacons,** though we have an approach to that appellation in v. 2. In 21 : 8 they are called **the Seven.** Some of the ancient writers regarded them as the first deacons; others, as entirely distinct from them. The general opinion at present is that this order arose from the institution of the Seven, but by a gradual extension of the sphere of duty at first assigned to them. [It is difficult to ascertain the precise duties of deacons in the apostolic churches. But that there were persons bearing this title and entrusted with some kind of service in the churches is evident from Phil. 1 : 1 and 1 Tim. 3 : 8–12. The view which has most in

its favor is that they were helpers of the pastors, especially in visiting the sick, providing for the poor, and entertaining strangers. Only those who were grave, sincere, benevolent, spiritual, could perform such service with the highest benefit to the cause. But they were not required to be, like the pastors of the churches, " apt to teach," though many of them doubtless possessed this gift also. Their service was therefore similar to that which the Seven were expected to render, and in principle the appointment of the Seven was the introduction of diaconal service. The latter would easily grow out of the former. But when Paul wrote to Timothy, miraculous gifts were no longer very frequent or necessary in the churches; hence, neither bishops nor deacons were required to be men " full of the Holy Spirit "— *i. e.* possessed of supernatural gifts. For the office of " deaconess," see notes on Rom. 16 : 1, 2 and 1 Tim. 3 : 11.—A. H.]

6. Laid, etc.—viz. the apostles. The nature of the act dictates this change of the subject. [So, likewise, does the expression **whom we will appoint** in verse 3, the statement **whom they** (the brethren) **set before the apostles** —evidently for some purpose wholly unsuggested, unless the apostles performed the laying on of hands—and the probability that the apostles offered prayer on the occasion.—A. H.] The imposition of hands, as practised in appointing persons to an office, was a symbol of the impartation of the gifts and graces which they needed to qualify them for the office. It was of the nature of a prayer that God would bestow the necessary gifts, rather than a pledge that they were actually conferred.

7. The prosperity related here is a proof that harmony had been restored, and that the prayers and labors of the apostles had suffered no interruption.—**The word of God grew,** spread and strengthened itself as a system of belief or doctrine. The next clause repeats the idea concretely by stating how rapidly the recipients of this faith were multiplied. (See note on 12 : 24.)—**And a great**

8 And Stephen, full of faith and power, did great wonders and miracles among the people.

9 ¶ Then there arose certain of the synagogue, which is called *the synagogue* of the Libertines, and Cyrenians, and Alexandrians, and of them of Cilicia and of Asia, disputing with Stephen.

10 And *a*they were not able to resist the wisdom and the spirit by which he spake.

8 And Stephen, full of grace and power, wrought 9 great wonders and signs among the people. But there arose certain of them that were of the synagogue called *the synagogue* of the Libertines, and of the Cyrenians, and of the Alexandrians, and of them 10 of Cilicia and Asia, disputing with Stephen. And they were not able to withstand the wisdom and

a Luke 21 : 15; ch. 5 : 39; see Ex. 4 : 12; Isa. 54 : 17.

---

multitude of priests. According to Ezra 2 : 36–39, the priests amounted to four thousand two hundred and eighty-nine at the time of the return from Babylon; they must have been still more numerous at this period. Such an accession of such converts was a signal event in the early history of the church.— **The faith,** faith system—*i. e.* the gospel. (Comp. Rom. 1 : 5; Gal. 1 : 23, etc.) This mode of epitomizing the plan of salvation confirms the Protestant view of it, in opposition to that of the Catholics. (See Rom. 11 : 6.)

8–15. THE ZEAL OF STEPHEN, AND HIS VIOLENT APPREHENSION.

8. Full of grace—*i. e.,* by metonymy, of gifts not inherent, but conferred by divine favor. (See v. 3.) This is the correct word rather than **faith,** which some copies insert from v. 5.—**Power,** efficiency (1 : 8), which was one of the gifts, and, as indicated by the next words, included an ability to work miracles.—**Did** (imperf.) shows that he repeated the miracles.

9. Certain from the synagogue so called of the Libertines—*i. e. libertini freedmen;* viz. Jews, or the sons of Jews, who, having been slaves at Rome, had acquired their freedom, and, living now at Jerusalem, maintained a separate synagogue of their own. When Pompey overran Judea, about b. c. 63, he carried a vast number of the Jews to Rome, where they were sold into slavery. Most of these, or their children, the Romans afterward liberated, as they found it inconvenient to have servants who were so tenacious of the peculiar rites of their religion. The Jews usually named their synagogues from the countries whence those who attended them had come; and hence Luke inserts here **the so called,** in order to reconcile the ear, as it were, to this almost unheard-of designation. Some contend that Λιβερτίνων is also a patrial name, *Libertinians*— *i. e.* Jews from a place named Libertum. Not only has the participle no apparent force in this case, but the existence of such a town is altogether uncertain.—**And Cyrenians,** etc. The construction here is doubtful. The simplest view is that which repeats τινὲς (**certain**) before each of the genitives with the implication

that the Cyrenians, Alexandrians, Cilicians, and Asiatics formed so many distinct synagogues—*i. e.* including the *Libertines* five different assemblies in all (De Wet., Mey.). The Rabbinic writers say—with some exaggeration, no doubt—that Jerusalem contained four hundred and eighty synagogues. **The** would be proper before **Cyrenians and Alexandrians,** but, as they refer to towns well known, could be omitted, as before **Egyptians** in 7 : 22 and **Thessalonians** in 20 : 4. —**Them of Cilicia** may be simply = **Cilicians,** and the article does not arise, necessarily, out of a different relation to **certain.** Some repeat **from the synagogue** as well as **certain** before the successive genitives, with the same result, of course, as to the number of synagogues. It is awkward to supply so many words, and also to shut up **the so called** to the first clause, as we must in that case, since it is so plainly inappropriate to the other names. According to others, we are to connect **Cyrenians and Alexandrians** with **Libertines,** understanding these three classes to constitute one synagogue, and the Cilicians and Asiatics to constitute another. (See W. ¿ 19. 5, marg.) It may be objected to this (though no interpretation is wholly unencumbered) that it unites **so called** too closely (for the reason given above) with the second and third noun, and also that so large a number of foreign Jews as the populous cities referred to would be likely to send to Jerusalem could not meet conveniently in a single place of worship. Wieseler (*Chronologie*, p. 63), in support of his opinion that Paul acquired his Roman citizenship (22 : 28) as *libertinus,* or the descendant of a *libertinus,* would take **and** before **Cyrenians** as explicative—**namely, to wit;** so that they were all *libertini,* and belonged to one synagogue. This is extremely forced and arbitrary. —Among the **Cilicians** who disputed with Stephen may have been Saul of Tarsus. (See 7 : 58.)—For the extent of **Asia,** see on 2 : 9.

10. The Spirit. (See v. 5.)—In **with which he spake** [the verb is imperf., denoting continuous action = **was speaking.**—A. H.], the relative belongs in sense to both nouns, but agrees with the nearest. (Comp. Luke 21 : 15·

11 aThen they suborned men, which said, We have heard him speak blasphemous words against Moses, and *against* God.

12 And they stirred up the people, and the elders, and the scribes, and came upon *him*, and caught him, and brought *him* to the council,

13 And set up false witnesses, which said, This man ceaseth not to speak blasphemous words against this holy place, and the law :

14 bFor we have heard him say, that this Jesus of Nazareth shall cdestroy this place, and shall change the customs which Moses delivered us.

15 And all that sat in the council, looking stedfastly on him, saw his face as it had been the face of an angel.

11 the Spirit by which he spake. Then they suborned men, who said, We have heard him speak blasphemous words against Moses, and *against* God.

12 And they stirred up the people, and the elders, and the scribes, and came upon him, and seized him,

13 and brought him into the council, and set up false witnesses, who said, This man ceaseth not *to* speak

14 words against this holy place, and the law : for we have heard him say, that this Jesus of Nazareth shall destroy this place, and shall change the cus-

15 toms which Moses delivered unto us. And all that sat in the council, fastening their eyes on him, saw his face as it had been the face of an angel.

---

a 1 Kings 21 : 10, 13 ; Matt. 26 : 59, 60....b ch. 25 : 8....c Dan. 9 : 26.

Stephen experienced the truth of the promise recorded in that passage.)

11. Secretly instructed, *suborned*. It was concerted between them what should be said, and to what point it should be directed.—**Blasphemous,** in the judicial sense, which made it a capital offence to utter such words. Contempt of Moses and his institutions was contempt of Jehovah, and came within the scope of the law against blasphemy as laid down in Deut. 13 : 6-10. It was on this charge that the Jews pronounced the Saviour worthy of death. (See Matt. 26 : 60, *sq*.)

12. The elders and the scribes—*i. e.* those of these classes who belonged to the Sanhedrim. The appeal was made more especially to them, because, in addition to their influence, they were mostly Pharisees, and the present accusation was of a nature to arouse especially the spirit of that sect. Hence they take the lead at this time, rather than the Sadducees.—**Caught.** The subject here is strictly **certain,** etc. (see v. 9), but we think of them naturally as acting in concert with those whom they had instigated to join with them.

13. Placed before them, *introduced* (see 4 : 7); others, **set up,** *procured*.—**False witnesses.** They accused Stephen of having spoken contemptuously of the law and the temple, and of having blasphemed Moses and God. Their testimony in that form was grossly false. It was opposed to everything which Stephen had said or meant. Yet, as Neander and others suggest, he had undoubtedly taught that the Christian Dispensation was superior to that of Moses ; that the gospel was designed to supersede Judaism ; that the law was unavailing as a source of justification ; that henceforth true worship would be as acceptable to God in one place as another. In the clearness with which Stephen apprehended these ideas, he has been justly called the forerunner of Paul. His

accusers distorted his language on these points, and thus gave to their charge the only semblance of justification which it possessed.—**For this man,** see 5 : 28.—**Does not cease** betrays the exaggerating tone of a "swift witness."— **The holy place** is the temple (21 : 28; Ps. 24 : 3, etc.), in some part of which they were assembled, as appears from **this** in the next verse.

14. Who said, etc. They imputed to Stephen these words, as authorizing the inference in v. 13. —**This** [in the Greek] repeats Jesus with a tone of contempt.—**Will destroy,** etc. It is not impossible that he had reminded them of the predictions of Christ respecting the destruction of the city and the temple.—**This place,** because the present session was held in some room or court of the temple.—**Customs** required to be observed, hence laws, as in 15 : 1 ; 21 : 21, etc.—**Delivered** may apply to what is written as well as what is oral (R. and P., *Lex*., s. v.).

15. Looking stedfastly, etc. They were **all gazing upon him,** as the principal object of interest in the assembly, and so much the more at that moment in expectation of his reply to so heinous a charge. The radiance, therefore, which suddenly lighted up the countenance of Stephen was remarked by every one present. That what they saw was merely a natural expression of the serenity which pervaded his mind can hardly be supposed. **As if the face of an angel** seems to overstate the idea, if it be reduced to that ; for the comparison is an unusual one, and the Jews supposed the visible appearance of angels to correspond with their superhuman rank. (Comp. 1 : 10 ; Matt. 28 : 3 ; Luke 24 : 4 ; Rev. 18 : 1, etc.) The countenance of Stephen, like that of Moses on his descent from the mount, shone, probably, with a preternatural lustre, proclaiming him a true witness, a servant of him whose glory was so fitly symbolized by such a token. The occasion was worthy of the miracle.

CHAPTER VII.

1-53. DISCOURSE OF STEPHEN BEFORE THE SANHEDRIM.

The speaker's main object may be considered as twofold : first, to show that the charge against him rested on a false view of the Ancient Dispensation—not on his part, but on that of his accusers ; and secondly, that the Jews, instead of manifesting a true zeal for the temple and the law in their opposition to the gospel, were again acting out the unbelieving, rebellious spirit which led their fathers so often to resist the will of God and reject his greatest favors. It appears to me that the latter was the uppermost idea in Stephen's mind, both because it occupies so much space in the body of the address (vv. 27, 39–44), and because, near the close of what is said (v. 51, *sq.*), it is put forward very much as if he regarded it as the conclusion at which he had been aiming. It may be objected that this view renders the discourse aggressive, criminatory, in an unusual degree ; but we are to remember that Stephen (see on v. 54) was interrupted, and but for that, in all probability, after having exposed the guilt of his hearers, he would have encouraged them to repent and believe on the Saviour whom they had crucified. (Bmg. has a remark to the same effect.) Yet both parts of the speech, as so understood, converge to one point—viz. that the speaker was not guilty of maligning the Ancient Economy : first, because even under that Dispensation the divine favor was bestowed independently of the law ; and secondly, because the teachers of that Economy held up the same view of its spiritual nature and encountered a similar opposition.

In the interpretation of the speech I proceed on the principle that most of Stephen's hearers were so well acquainted with his peculiar views, with his arguments in support of them, and his mode of illustration, that they had no occasion to be distinctly reminded of his doctrine at this time. (See the note on 6 : 13.) Hence, Stephen could assume that the bearing of the different remarks or occurrences brought forward in the address would suggest itself to the minds of his judges ; without pausing to tell them *this* means that or *that* means this, he could leave them to draw silently the conclusions which he wished to establish. Stephen illustrates his subject historically. That mode of argument was well chosen. It enabled him to show the Jews that their own history, in which they gloried so

much, condemned them ; for it taught the inefficacy of external rites, foreshadowed a more perfect spiritual system, and warned them against the example of those who resist the will of God when declared to them by his messengers. Stephen pursues the order of time in his narrative ; and it is important to remark that feature of the discourse, because it explains two peculiarities in it : first, that the ideas which fall logically under the two heads that have been mentioned are intermixed, instead of being presented separately ; and secondly, that some circumstances are introduced which we are not to regard as significant, but as serving merely to maintain the connection of the history.

But the address is so discursive and complex, and the purport of it has been so variously represented, that it is due to the subject to mention some of the other modes of analysis that have been proposed.

The following is Neander's view of it. Stephen's primary object was certainly apologetical ; but, as he forgot himself in the subject with which he was inspired, his apologetic efforts relate to the truths maintained by him, and impugned by his adversaries, rather than to himself. Hence, not satisfied with defending, he developed and enforced, the truths he had proclaimed, and at the same time reproved the Jews for their unbelief and their opposition to the gospel. Stephen first refutes the charges made against him of enmity against the people of God, of contempt of their sacred institutions, and of blaspheming Moses. He traces the procedure of the divine providence in guiding the people of God from the times of their progenitors ; he notices the promises and their progressive fulfilment to the end of all the promises—the advent of the Messiah, and the work to be accomplished by him. But with this narrative he blends his charges against the Jewish nation. He shows that their ingratitude and unbelief became more flagrant in proportion as the promises were fulfilled or given with greater fulness ; and their conduct in the various preceding periods of the development of God's kingdom was a specimen of the disposition they now evinced toward the publication of the gospel.[1]

According to Olshausen,[2] the speaker recapitulated the Jewish history at such length simply in order to testify his regard for the national in-

---

[1] Quoted from Ryland's translation of *The Planting and Training of the Christian Church.*
[2] *Commentar über das Neue Testament*, vol. ii. p. 719.

THEN said the high priest, Are these things so? 2 And he said, ^aMen, brethren, and fathers, heark-

1 AND the high priest said, Are these things so? 2 And he said,

a ch. 22 : 1.

stitutions, to conciliate his hearers, and show indirectly that he could not have uttered the *blasphemous words* imputed to him. (See 6 : 11.) That those addressed saw their own moral image reflected so distinctly from the narrative results from the subject, not from the speaker's intention.

Luger develops the course of thought in this way : Stephen is accused of blaspheming the temple and the law; he vindicates himself by exhibiting the true significance of the temple and the law. The main points are, first, that the *law* is not something complete by itself, but was added to the promise given to Abraham—yea, contains in itself a new promise, by the fulfilment of which the law is first brought to completion. Secondly, the temple cannot be exclusively the holy place; it is one in a series of places which the Lord has consecrated, and by this very act foreshadowed that future completion of the temple to which Solomon and the prophets point. Thirdly, it being a cause of special offence to the Jews that the Jesus rejected by them should be represented as the Perfecter of the law and the temple, Stephen showed that no objection against him could be derived from that fact, since the messengers of God had been treated with the like contempt at all periods. Fourthly, these three topics are presented, not *after* each other, but in each other. The history of Israel forms the thread of the discourse, but this is related in such a manner that examples of the different points come into view at every step.[1]

Baur's exposition of the plan has been highly commended. The contents of the discourse divide themselves into two parallel parts : on the one side are presented the benefits which God from the earliest times conferred on the Jewish nation ; on the other side is exhibited in contrast their conduct toward him. Hence the main thought is this : The greater and more extraordinary the favors which God from the beginning bestowed on the Jews, the more unthankful and rebellious from the beginning was the spirit which they manifested in return ; so that where a perfectly harmonious relation should have been found the greatest alienation appeared. The greater the effort which God made to elevate and draw the nation to him-

self, the more the nation turned away from him. In presenting this view of the Jewish character, the speaker defended indirectly his own cause. He was accused of having spoken reproachfully, not only against the law, but in particular against the temple. Hence, the direction which he gave to the speech enabled him to show that the idolatrous regard of the Jews for the temple exemplified in the highest degree that opposition between God and themselves which had been so characteristic of them from the first.[2]

It may be added that the peculiar character of the speech impresses upon it a seal of authenticity, for no one would think of framing a discourse of this kind for such an occasion. Had it been composed ideally or after some vague tradition, it would have been thrown into a different form; its relevancy to the charge which called it forth would have been made more obvious. As to the language in which Stephen delivered it, opinions are divided. His disputing with the foreign Jews (6:9) would indicate that he was a Hellenist (comp. 9 : 29), and in that case he spoke probably in Greek. The prevalence of that language in Palestine, and especially at Jerusalem, would have rendered it intelligible to such an audience.[3] The manner, too, in which the citations agree with the Septuagint favors this conclusion.

1–16. HISTORY OF THE PATRIARCHS, OR AGE OF THE PROMISES.

1. Then (δέ) binds this verse to 6 : 14.—*Are then these things so*, as the witnesses testify? Hence this was the question to which Stephen replied, and must furnish the key to his answer. We must construe the speech so as to find in it a refutation of the charge in 6 : 13. εἰ is direct here, as in 1 : 6. ἄρα = "rebus ita comparatis," under these circumstances. (See Klotz, *Ad Devar.*, vol. ii. p. 176.) The question is asked in view of the accusation. The particle is not to be struck out of the text, as in some editions. [It is elided by Lach., Tsch., Treg., West. and Hort, Anglo-Am. Revisers, on what appears to be satisfactory evidence—*e. g.* ℵ A B C.—A. H.]

2. Brethren are the spectators, **fathers** the members of the council, like our "civil fa-

[1] *Ueber Zweck, Inhalt, und Eigenthümlichkeit der Rede des Stephanus*, von Friedrich Luger.
[2] *Paulus, sein Leben und Wirken, seine Briefe und seine Lehre*, p. 42.
[3] In proof of this, see Hug's *Einleitung in das Neue Testament*, vol. ii. p. 27, *sq.*, fourth edition, and the *Biblical Repository* (1832), p. 530.

en; The God of glory appeared unto our father Abraham, when he was in Mesopotamia, before he dwelt in Charran,

3 And said unto him, *a*Get thee out of thy country, and from thy kindred, and come into the land which I shall shew thee.

4 Then *b*came he out of the land of the Chaldæans, and dwelt in Charran: and from thence, when his

Brethren and fathers, hearken. The God of glory appeared unto our father Abraham, when h · was in 3 Mesopotamia, before he dwelt in Haran, and said unto him, Get thee out of thy land, and from thy kindred, and come into the land which I shall shew 4 thee. Then came he out of the land of the Chaldæans, and dwelt in Haran: and from thence, when

a Gen. 12 : 1....*b* Gen. 11 : 31 ; 12 : 4, 5.

thers." (Comp. 22 : 1.) **Men** qualifies both nouns. (See on 1 : 16.) The English Version makes three distinct classes, instead of two.—**The God of the glory** (**the,** because peculiar to him) = *hakkabhōdh* in the Old Testament, or, among the later Jews, *hashshekēnah*—i. e. the light or visible splendor amid which Jehovah revealed himself; the symbol, therefore, of his presence (Mey., De Wet., Blmf.). (Comp. Ex. 25 : 22 ; 40 : 34; Lev. 9 : 6; Ezek. 1 : 28; 3 : 23; Heb. 9 : 5, etc.) **Appeared** (ὤφϑη) points to that sense here. (See also v. 55.) Paul speaks of this symbol in Rom. 9 : 4 as one of the peculiar distinctions with which God honored the Hebrew nation. Those miss the sense who resolve the genitive into an adjective, **the glorious God** (Kuin., Hmph.).—**When he was in Mesopotamia.** Imperf., as often in narration. (W. § 46. 6.) Abraham resided first in Ur of the Chaldees (Gen. 11 : 28), which lay probably in the extreme North of Mesopotamia, near the sources of the Tigris. The Chaldee branch of Peleg's family, to which Terah and his sons belonged, spread themselves originally in that region.[1] Xenophon found Chaldeans here in his retreat from Babylonia with the Ten Thousand. (See further on v. 4.)—**In Charran.** **Charran** = *Charan* (Gen. 11 : 31) was also in the north of Mesopotamia, but south of Ur. It was the later *Carræ* of the Greeks and Romans, where Crassus was defeated and slain by the Parthians. Its position tallies remarkably with the sacred narrative. The ruins have been identified a few miles south of Urfa, on a road from the north to the southern ford of the Euphrates. It is a perversion of the text to suppose Stephen so ignorant of the geography here as to place Charran on the west of the Euphrates. His meaning evidently is that Abraham's call in that city was not the first which he received during his residence in Mesopotamia. We have no account of this first communication to the patriarch in the Old Testament, but it is implied distinctly in Gen. 15 : 7 and Neh. 9 : 7. Philo and Josephus relate the history of Abraham in accordance with the statement here that he was called twice.

3. Said unto him, in Ur, before the migration to Charran.—**Go forth from thy country,** etc. This is quoted from Gen. 12 : 1, *sq.*, where it appears as the language addressed to Abraham when God appeared to him at Charran. But his earlier call had the same object precisely as the later; and hence Stephen could employ the terms of the second communication, in order to characterize the import of the first. **And hither,** with an imperative force; the term adapted to the speaker's position, like **this,** in v. 4.—**Whichever** (see on 2 : 21), since he "went forth not knowing whither he goes" (Heb. 11 : 8).

4. Then, after this command.—**Having gone forth from the land of the Chaldees,** which, therefore, did not extend so far south as to include Charran. It is barely possible that **having gone forth** may reach forward to **removed** (the change of subject there is against it), and in that case the second removal would have been a part of the journey from Chaldea. (Comp. Gen. 11 : 31.) The early history of the Chaldees is too obscure to allow us to define the limits of their territory. (See Herz., *Encyk.*, vol. ii. p. 617.)—**Land of the Chaldeans** suggests a region rather than a city, and Ur (for which the Sept. renders "country" in Gen. 11 : 28) was probably the name of a district among the steppes of Northern Mesopotamia. Some would identify Ur with the modern Urfa, the Edessa of the Greeks; but, though the name (dropping the last syllable) may seem to favor that combination, the surer etymology derives Urfa (as a corruption) from the Syriac Urhoi, and thus destroys all connection between Ur and Urfa. (See Tuch, p. 284, and Delitzsch, p. 407, *Über die Genesis.*) Had Ur, either as a city or region, been in Babylonia, as some conjecture, Charran, so far to the west, would have been out of the way in a migration to Canaan.—**After his father was dead.** According to Gen. 11 : 32, Terah died at Haran at the age of two hundred and five, and according to the usual inference drawn from Gen. 11 : 26 he was only seventy years old at the birth of Abraham ; so that, since Abraham left Charran at

[1] For the ethnography of the subject, see Knobel's *Völkertafel der Genesis*, p. 170, *sq*

father was dead, he removed him into this land, where-in ye now dwell.

5 And he gave him none inheritance in it, no, not *so much as* to set his foot on: [a]yet he promised that he would give it to him for a possession, and to his seed after him, when *as yet* he had no child.

his father was dead, *God* removed him into this land, 5 wherein ye now dwell: and he gave him none inheritance in it, no, not so much as to set his foot on: and he promised that he would give it to him in possession, and to his seed after him, when *as yet* he

---

---

seventy-five (Gen. 12 : 4), Terah, instead of being dead at that time, must have lived (205 — [70 + 75] =) sixty years after his son's departure from Charran. Here, again, some writers insist that Stephen has shown a gross ignorance of the patriarchal history. But this apparent disagreement admits of a ready solution if we suppose that Abraham was not the oldest son, but that Haran, who died before the first migration of the family (Gen. 11 : 28), was sixty years older than he, and that Terah, consequently, was one hundred and thirty years old at the birth of Abraham (130 + 75 = 205). The relation of Abraham to the Hebrew history would account for his being named first in the genealogy. We have other instances entirely parallel to this. Thus in Gen. 5 : 32 and elsewhere Japheth is mentioned last among the sons of Noah, but according to Gen. 9 : 24 and 10 : 21 he was the oldest of them. Lightfoot has shown that even some of the Jewish writers, who can be suspected of no desire to reconcile Stephen with the Old Testament, concede that Abraham was the youngest son of Terah. The learned Usher founds his system of chronology on this view. The other explanations are less probable. It appears that there was a tradition among some of the Jews that Terah relapsed into idolatry during the abode at Haran, and that Abraham left him on that account—*i. e.* as the Talmudists express it after his spiritual death. Kuinoel, Olshausen, and others, think that Stephen may have used **was dead** in that sense; so that the notice of Terah's natural death in Gen. 11 : 32 would be proleptic—*i. e.* in advance of the exact order of the history. The tradition of Terah's relapse into idolatry may have been well founded. Bengel offers this suggestion : " Abram, dum Thara vixit in Haran, domum quodammodo paternam habuit in Haran, in terra Canaan duntaxat peregrinum agens; mortuo autem patre, plane in terra Canaan domum unice habere coepit " [" While Terah lived in Haran, Abram had in a manner a paternal home in Haran, though living as a stranger in the land of Canaan ; but when his father was dead, he began manifestly to have his only home in the land of Canaan "]. The Samaritan

Codex reads one hundred and forty-five in Gen. 11 : 32, which would remove the difficulty, had it not been altered probably for that very purpose. The Samaritan text has no critical authority when opposed to the Masoretic.[1] **Caused him to remove,** to migrate, by a renewed command. (See Gen. 12 : 1, *sq.*)— **Into which,** because **ye dwell** (κατοικεῖτε), implies an antecedent motion.—**You,** instead of **we,** because, as a foreign Jew, Stephen excludes himself.

5. And he gave to him (during his life) **no inheritance in it,** no actual possession, but a promise only that his posterity should occupy it at some future period. It is not at variance with this that he subsequently purchased the field of Ephron as a burial-place (Gen. 23 : 3, *sq.*) ; for he acquired no right of settlement by that purchase, but permission merely to bury "his dead," which he sought as a favor because he was "a stranger and a sojourner" in the land. Lest the passage should seem to conflict with that transaction, some (Kuin., Olsh.) would render not (οὐκ) as **not yet** (οὔπω) and **gave** as pluperfect. De Wette agrees with Meyer in restricting the remark to the period of Abraham's first arrival in Canaan. He purchased the field of Ephron near the close of his life.— **Not even a foot-breadth,** a single foot. (Comp. Deut. 2 : 5.)—**That he would give it to him for a possession,** not necessarily in his own person, but in that of his descendants. The country might be said to be Abraham's in prospect of that reversion. So, in Gen. 46 : 4, God says to Jacob on his descent into Egypt : "I will bring thee up again "—*i. e.* him *in* his posterity. Others understand **possession** of Abraham's own residence in the Land of Promise.—**When he had no child.** This clause, as well as the general connection, recalls to mind the strength of Abraham's faith. It was in that way that he pleased God and obtained the promise, and not by legal observances; for circumcision had not yet been instituted or the law given. Paul reasons in that manner from Abraham's history, both in Rom. 4 : 9, *sq.*, and in Gal. 3 : 17, *sq.* Stephen may have expanded his speech at this point so as to have presented distinctly the same con-

---

6 And God spake on this wise, *a*That his seed should sojourn in a strange land ; and that they should bring them into bondage, and entreat *them* evil *b*four hundred years. ✔

7 And the nation to whom they shall be in bondage will I judge, said God : and after that shall they come forth, and *c*serve me in this place.

8 *d*And he gave him the covenant of circumcision : *e*and so *Abraham* begat Isaac, and circumcised him the eighth day ; *f*and Isaac *begat* Jacob ; and *g*Jacob *begat* the twelve patriarchs.

6 had no child. And God spake on this wise, that his seed should sojourn in a strange land, and that they should bring them into bondage, and entreat them

7 evil, four hundred years. And the nation to which they shall be in bondage will I judge, said God : and after that shall they come forth, and serve me in

8 this place. And he gave him the covenant of circumcision : and so *Abraham* begat Isaac, and circumcised him the eighth day ; and Isaac *begat* Jacob, and

a Gen. 15 : 13, 16....*b* Ex. 12 : 40 ; Gal. 3 : 17....*c* Ex. 3 : 12....*d* Gen. 17 : 9, 10, 11....*e* Gen. 21 : 2, 3, 4....*f* Gen. 25 : 26....
g Gen. 29 : 31, etc. ; 30 : 5, etc. ; 35 : 18, 23.

---

clusion ; or, as remarked in the first analysis, most of his hearers may have been so familiar with the Christian doctrine on the subject that they perceived at once that import of his allusions.

6. The speaker quotes here the passage to which he had merely alluded.--**Now** (δέ) subjoins this fuller account of the promise ; not *but*, although he was childless (Mey., taken back in his last ed.).—**Thus,** to this effect— viz. in Gen. 15 : 13-16.—**Shall be**, not **should** (E. V.). The citation mingles the indirect form with the direct.—Strangers **shall enslave,** strangers, as the subject, being involved in **in a strange land.** (See W. § 64. 3. b.)—**Four hundred years,** in agreement with Gen. 15 : 13 ; but both there and here a round number, since in Ex. 12 : 40 "the sojourning of Israel who dwelt in Egypt" is said to have been four hundred and thirty years. But here arises a chronological question to which it is necessary to advert. In Gal. 3 : 17, Paul speaks of the entire period from Abraham's arrival in Canaan until the giving of the law as embracing only four hundred and thirty years—a calculation which allows but two hundred and fifteen years for the sojourn in Egypt ; for Isaac was born twenty-five years after that arrival, was sixty years old at the birth of Jacob, and Jacob was one hundred and thirty years old when he went to reside in Egypt (430 − [25 + 60 + 130] = 215). The Seventy, in Ex. 12 : 40, and Josephus, in *Antt.*, 2. 15. 2, follow the same computation. There are two solutions of this difficulty. One is that the Jews had two ways of reckoning this period, which were current at the same time ; that it is uncertain which of them is the correct one, and for all practical purposes is wholly unimportant, since, when a speaker or writer, as in this case of Stephen, adopted this mode or that, he was understood, not to propound a chronological opinion, but merely to employ a familiar designation for the sake of definiteness. The other solution is that the four hundred and

thirty years in Ex. 12 : 40 embrace the period from Abraham's immigration into Canaan until the departure out of Egypt, and that the sacred writers call this the period of sojourn or servitude in Egypt *a potiori*—i. e. from its leading characteristic.[1] They could describe it in this manner with so much the more propriety, because even during the rest of the time the condition of the patriarchs was that of exiles and wanderers. The current chronology, Usher's system, adopts two hundred and fifteen as the number of years during which the Hebrews dwelt in Egypt.

7. I (emphatic, as one able to punish) **will judge** (Hebraistic), implying the execution of the sentence.—**After these things,** after both so long a time and such events. **These things** refers to **will judge,** as well as to the other verbs.—**And shall worship me in this place.** This clause is taken from a different passage—viz. Ex. 3 : 12, which records the declaration that God would bring the Israelites where Moses then was. But, as the words there also relate to the deliverance from Egypt, Stephen could use them to express more fully the idea in Gen. 15 : 16. In the communication to Moses, **place** refers to Sinai or Horeb, but is applied here very properly to Canaan, since the worship in the desert was a pledge of its performance in the Promised Land. **Shall worship** may intimate that God accepted their worship before they had any temple in which to offer it.

8. The covenant of circumcision—i. e. the one of which circumcision is the sign. (Comp. *sign of circumcision* in Rom. 4 : 11.)— **And thus** (οὕτωσι)—i. e. agreeably to the covenant, God gave the promised child, and Abraham observed the appointed rite. Such briefly were the contents of the covenant (see Gen. 17 : 2, *sq.*), and **begat** and **circumcised** very naturally recall them here. οὕτως as merely **then** (Mey.), in lieu of δέ or καί in this speech elsewhere, expresses too little in such a place. [Changed by Meyer in his last ed. : "**So**—i. e.

---

[1] Baumgarten, in common with others, inclines to this view in his *Theologischer Commentar zum Pentateuch*, vol. i. p. 190.

9 *a*And the patriarchs, moved with envy, sold Joseph into Egypt: *b*but God was with him,

10 And delivered him out of all his afflictions, *c*and gave him favor and wisdom in the sight of Pharaoh king of Egypt; and he made him governor over Egypt and all his house.

11 *d*Now there came a dearth over all the land of Egypt and Chanaan, and great affliction : and our fathers found no sustenance.

12 *e*But when Jacob heard that there was corn in Egypt, he sent out our fathers first.

13 *f*And at the second time Joseph was made known to his brethren ; and Joseph's kindred was made known unto Pharaoh.

14 *g*Then sent Joseph, and called his father Jacob to *him*, and *h*all his kindred, threescore and fifteen souls.

9 Jacob the twelve patriarchs. And the patriarchs, moved with jealousy against Joseph, sold him into

10 Egypt: and God was with him, and delivered him out of all his afflictions, and gave him favor and wisdom before Pharaoh king of Egypt; and he made

11 him governor over Egypt and all his house. Now there came a famine over all Egypt and Canaan, and great affliction : and our fathers found no sustenance.

12 But when Jacob heard that there was corn in Egypt,

13 he sent forth our fathers the first time. And at the second time Joseph was made known to his brethren ; and Joseph's race became manifest unto Pha-

14 raoh. And Joseph sent, and called to him Jacob his father, and all his kindred, threescore and fifteen

---

a Gen. 37 : 4, 11, 28 ; Ps. 105 : 17....*b* Gen. 39 : 2, 21, 23 ....*c* Gen. 41 : 37 ; 42 : 6....*d* Gen. 41 : 54....*e* Gen. 42 : 1....*f* Gen. 45 : 4, 16....*g* Gen. 45 : 9, 27....*h* Gen. 46 : 27 ; Deut. 10 : 22.

---

standing in this new relation to God . . . as the bearer of the covenant of circumcision."—A. H.]—**On the eighth day,** etc. (See Gen. 21 : 4.)

9. Sold (5 : 8) **into Egypt**—*i. e.* to be carried thither ; thus concisely in Gen. 45 : 4 (Heb. and Sept.).—**God was with him,** though he was exposed to such envy and injustice. It was a memorable instance in which the rejected of men was approved of God and made the preserver of his people. (See on v. 37.) The analogy between Joseph's history in this respect and that of Christ must have forced itself on Stephen's hearers.

10. Favor (with the king) **and wisdom,** both the gifts of God, but the latter helping in part to secure the former. Meyer, contrary to his first opinion, understands **favor** of the divine favor toward Joseph ; but the two nouns belong alike to **before Pharaoh,** and associate themselves readily as cause and effect. The **wisdom** was that which Joseph displayed as an interpreter of dreams, as the king's counsellor and minister.—**His house,** the palace of the sovereign, from which, in the East, all the acts of government emanate. In other words, Joseph was raised to the office of vizier, or prime minister.

12. For the history, see Gen. 42 : 1, *sq.*—ὄντα (**being,** translated **was**), instead of the infinitive after **heard,** represents the plenty in Egypt as indubitable, notorious. (K. ξ 311. 1.) The place of the abundance was well known, and **in Egypt** after the participle (T. R.) is a needless corruption for **into Egypt,** which belongs to the next verb.—**Sent our fathers first,** while Jacob himself remained still in Canaan. (See v. 15.)

13. Was recognized by his brethren (De Wet., Mey.), on declaring his name to them. (Comp. Gen. 45 : 1.) The reflexive sense, **made himself known** (Rob.), would be ex-

ceptional, and is not required here.—**And the race of Joseph was made known to Pharaoh**—*i. e.* the fact of their presence, their arrival. (See Gen. 45 : 16.) It does not mean that the king ascertained now Joseph's Hebrew origin, for he knew that already (Gen. 41 : 12), nor that Joseph's brethren were presented to him. The introduction took place at a later period. (See Gen. 47 : 2.)

14. In seventy-five souls—*i. e.* (consisting) **in,** etc. (For ἐν, see W. ξ 48. 3.) From so feeble a beginning the Hebrews soon grew to a mighty nation. (See v. 17.) Stephen would suggest to the mind that contrast. According to Gen. 46 : 27, Ex. 1 : 5, and Deut. 10 : 22, Jacob's family at this time contained seventy persons ; but the Septuagint has changed that number in the first two passages to seventy-five. In Gen. 46 : 26 the Hebrew says that Jacob's descendants, on his arrival in Egypt, were sixty-six, and in the next verse adds to these Jacob himself, Joseph, and his two sons, thus making the number *seventy*. On the other hand, the Septuagint interpolates, in v. 27, *And sons of Joseph were born to him in the land of Egypt, nine souls;* and adding these nine to the sixty-six in v. 26 makes the number *seventy-five*. It is evident from this interpolation that the Seventy did not obtain their number by adding the five sons of Ephraim and Manasseh (1 Chron. 7 : 14-23) to the seventy persons mentioned in the Hebrew text. That mode of accounting for their computation has frequently been assigned. If *sons* be taken in its wider sense, those sons and grandsons of Joseph may have been among the *nine* whom they added to the sixty-six, but it is not known how they reckoned the other two. They may have included some of the third generation, or have referred to other sons of Joseph, of whom we have no account. But, in whatever way the enumeration arose, its existence in the Greek version

15 *So Jacob went down into Egypt, *and died, he, and our fathers,

16 And *were carried over into Sychem, and laid in

15 souls. And Jacob went down into Egypt; and he
16 died, himself, and our fathers; and they were carried over unto Shechem, and laid in the tomb that

a Gen. 46 : 5....b Gen. 49 : 33 ; Ex. 1 : 6....c Ex. 13 : 19 ; Josh. 24 : 32.

shows that it was current among the Jews. That it was an *erroneous* one is incapable of proof, for we do not know on what data it was founded. At all events, Stephen could adapt himself to the popular way of speaking with entire truth as to the idea which he meant to convey ; for his object was to affirm, not that the family of Jacob, when he went down to Egypt, consisted of just seventy-five persons, in distinction from seventy-six or seventy, or any other precise number, but that it was a mere handful compared with the increase which made them in so short a time "as the stars of heaven for multitude." (See Deut. 10 : 22.) That among those whom Joseph is said to have called into Egypt were some who were already there, or were born at a subsequent period, agrees with Gen. 46 : 27 ; for it is said that " the sons of Joseph " were among " the souls of the house of Jacob that came into Egypt " with him. That representation springs from the Hebrew view, which regarded the descendants as existing already in their progenitor. (Comp. Gen. 46 : 15 ; Heb. 7 : 9, 10.) It is equivalent here to saying that the millions to which Israel had grown on leaving Egypt were all comprised in some seventy-five persons at the commencement of the residence there.[1]

16. It is mentioned in Gen. 50 : 13 that Jacob was buried in Abraham's sepulchre at Hebron (see Gen. 23 : 19), and in Josh. 24 : 32 that the bones of Joseph were laid in Jacob's tomb at Shechem, or Sychem ; as to the burial of Jacob's other sons, the Old Testament is silent. In this passage, therefore, **our fathers** may be taken as the subject of **were carried over** without **himself.** Such brevity was natural in so rapid a sketch, and not obscure where the hearers were so familiar with the subject in hand. That Joseph's brothers were buried with him at Sychem rests, doubtless, on a well-known tradition in Stephen's time. "According to Josephus (*Antt.*, 2. 8. 2), the sons of Jacob were buried at Hebron. According to the Rabbins (Light., Wetst.), the Israelites took the bones of their fathers with them to Palestine, but say nothing of Sychem ; since, however, they do not include the eleven patriarchs among those who were buried at Hebron, they probably regarded Sychem as the place of their burial " (De Wet.). Jerome, who lived but a

day's journey from Sychem, says that the tombs of the twelve were to be seen there in his time. **—In the tomb,** etc., presents a more serious difficulty. It is clear from Gen. 33 : 19 that Jacob purchased the family tomb at Sychem, and from Gen. 23 : 1, *sq.*, that Abraham purchased the one at Hebron. On the other hand, according to the present text, Stephen appears to have confounded the two transactions, representing, not Jacob, but Abraham, as having purchased the field at Sychem. It is difficult to resist the impression that a single word of the present text is wrong, and that we should either omit **Abraham** or exchange it for **Jacob.** **—Bought,** without a subject, could be taken as impersonal : **one purchased = was purchased.** (See W. ¿ 58. 9.) That change would free the passage from its perplexity. It is true, manuscripts concur in the present reading, but this may be an instance where the internal evidence countervails the external. The error lies in a single word ; and it is quite as likely, judging *a priori*, that the word producing the error escaped from some early copyist as that so glaring an error was committed by Stephen, for as a Jew he had been brought up to a knowledge of the Scriptures, had proved himself more than a match for the learned disputants from the synagogues (6:10), and is said to have been " full of the Holy Spirit " (6:5). Some attribute the difficulty to the concise, hurried style of the narrative. Biscoe states that opinion in the following terms : " The Hebrews, when reciting the history of their forefathers to their brethren, do it in the briefest manner, because it was a thing well known to them. For which reason they made use of frequent ellipses, and gave but hints to bring to their remembrance what they aimed at. This may be the case here ; and, as nothing is more easy than to supply the words that are wanting, so, when supplied, the narration is exactly agreeable to history delivered in the Old Testament : 'And were carried into Sychem, and were laid,' —*i. e.* some of them ; Jacob at least—' in the sepulchre that Abraham bought for a sum of money,' and others of them ' in that (bought) from the sons of Emmor, the father of Sychem.' Here we repeat merely **and in that** before **from the sons,** which words were easily understood and supplied by those to whom Ste-

[1] See Hengstenberg's *Authentie des Pentateuches.* vol. ii. p. 357, *sq.*

*the sepulchre that Abraham bought for a sum of money of the sons of Emmor *the father* of Sychem.

17 But when *the time of the promise drew nigh, which God had sworn to Abraham, *the people grew and multiplied in Egypt,

18 Till another king arose, which knew not Joseph.

19 The same dealt subtilly with our kindred, and evil entreated our fathers, *so that they cast out their young children, to the end they might not live.

Abraham bought for a price in silver of the sons of 17 ¹Hamor in Shechem. But as the time of the promise drew nigh, which God vouchsafed unto Abraham, the 18 people grew and multiplied in Egypt, till there arose 19 another king over Egypt, who knew not Joseph. The same dealt subtilly with our race, and evil entreated our fathers, that ²they should cast out their babes to

---

a Gen. 23 : 16 ; 33 : 19....*b* Gen. 15 : 13 ; ver. 6....*c* Ex. 1 : 7, 8, 9 ; Ps. 105 : 24, 25....*d* Ex. 1 : 22.——1 Gr. *Emmor*....2 Or, *he.*

---

phen addressed himself."[1] Again, some have deemed it sufficient to say that Stephen was not an *inspired* teacher in the strict sense of the expression, and that, provided we have a true record of the discourse on the part of Luke, we may admit an error in the discourse itself, without discrediting the accuracy of the sacred writers. Dr. Davidson thinks that Luke must have been aware of the discrepancy, and has exhibited his scrupulous regard for the truth by allowing it to remain, instead of correcting it. Calvin sanctions a still freer view: "In nomine Abrahæ erratum esse palam est ; quare hic locus corrigendus est" ["In the name of Abraham there is evidently an error; wherefore this passage should be corrected"].—**Emmor,** the father **of Sychem.** (See on 1 : 13, [where it is stated that the connection or known facts of the case must be considered in supplying the omitted noun, whether son, or father, or brother.—A. H.].)

17–46. THE AGE OF MOSES, OR THE JEWS UNDER THE LAW.

17. Not **when,** but **as,** in the degree that; hence, **drew near, was approaching.**— *The time of the* (fulfilment of the) *promise* (v. 7). (See on 1 : 4.)—Instead of ὤμοσεν (T. R.), sware, we are to read probably ὡμολόγησεν, **declared** (Lchm., Tsch., Mey.). [Also Treg., West. and Hort.—A. H.]—**Grew** and **multiplied** represent the growth in power as consequent on the increase of numbers; not a citation, but reminiscence, probably, of Ex. 1 : 7, 20.

18. Until, for this signal prosperity had its limit. Though baffled in his first scheme, Pharaoh tried other means more effectual. (See on v. 19.)—**Who knew not Joseph,** had no regard for his memory or services; not was ignorant that such a person had lived (Mey.). How could the author of such important reforms have been forgotten among a people addicted, like the Egyptians, to recording their national events? It has been supposed that a new dynasty may have ascended the throne at this time. According to Sir J. G. Wilkinson,[2]

this "new king" was Amosis, or Ames, first of the eighteenth dynasty, or that of the Diospolitans from Thebes. Some hold (*e. g.* Heeren, Jost)that the Hyksos, or shepherd-kings, had just been expelled from Egypt, and that the oppressor of the Hebrews was the first native prince who reigned after that event. The present knowledge of Egyptian history is too imperfect to admit of any positive conclusion on such a point. (For the later views and literature, see on "Ancient Egypt" in Herz., *Encyk.*, vol. i. p. 138, *sq.*)

19. Treating subtly our race. (See Ex. 1 : 10 ; Ps. 115 : 25. His policy is characterized in this manner, because his object, without being avowed, was to compel the Hebrews to destroy their children, that they might not grow up to experience the wretched fate of their parents.—**Oppressed our fathers, in order that they should cast out their infants, that these might not be preserved alive.** Both verbs (Gr.) are telic. The first states the king's object in the oppression ; the second, the object of the exposure on the part of the parents. It was using the parental instinct for destroying the child ; it was seething the kid in the mother's blood [milk]. For τοῦ ποιεῖν (**that they should make**—*i. e.* their children—**outcasts**), see on 3 : 2. The plan of the Egyptians failed; for "the more they afflicted the Hebrews, the more they multiplied and grew (EX. 1 : 12)—*i. e.* they spared their children, instead of putting them to death, and continued to increase. Pharaoh after this took a more direct course to accomplish his object: he issued a decree that all the male children of the Hebrews should be killed at birth or thrown into the Nile. (See Ex. 1 : 16–22.) The sense is different if we make τοῦ ποιεῖν ecbatic: **so that they cast out their infants,** etc. According to this view, the king's policy was in part successful; the Hebrews exposed their children of their own accord, that they might not see them doomed to so hopeless a bondage. But the infinitive construction with τοῦ (**the**) is rarely ecbatic; and, further, had the Hebrews

---

[1] *The Acts of the Apostles, confirmed from other Authors,* p. 395, ed. 1840.
[2] *Manners and Customs of the Ancient Egyptians,* vol. i. p. 42, *sq.* (2d ed.).

20 [a]In which time Moses was born, and [b]was exceeding fair, and nourished up in his father's house three months:
21 And [c]when he was cast out, Pharaoh's daughter took him up, and nourished him for her own son.
22 And Moses was learned in all the wisdom of the Egyptians, and was [d]mighty in words and in deeds.
23 [e]And when he was full forty years old, it came into his heart to visit his brethren the children of Israel.
24 And seeing one *of them* suffer wrong, he defended *him*, and avenged him that was oppressed, and smote the Egyptian:
25 For he supposed his brethren would have understood how that God by his hand would deliver them: but they understood not.

20 the end they might not [1]live. At which season Moses was born, and was [2]exceeding fair: and he was
21 nourished three months in his father's house: and when he was cast out, Pharaoh's daughter took him
22 up, and nourished him for her own son. And Moses was instructed in all the wisdom of the Egyptians;
23 and he was mighty in his words and works. But when he was well-nigh forty years old, it came into his heart to visit his brethren the children of Israel.
24 And seeing one *of them* suffer wrong, he defended him, and avenged him that was oppressed, smiting
25 the Egyptian: and he supposed that his brethren understood how that God by his hand was giving

---

a Ex. 2 : 2....*b* Heb. 11 : 23....*c* Ex. 2 : 3–10....*d* Luke 24 : 19....*e* Ex. 2 : 11, 12.——1 Gr. *be preserved alive*....2 Or, *fair unto God.*

---

destroyed their children as a voluntary act, a subsequent decree for murdering them would have been unnecessary (Ex. 1 : 16-22). It is harsh to make τοῦ ποιεῖν epexegetical: **oppressed them** (viz. by a decree) **that they must cast out**, It is difficult with this sense to see the force of **treating subtly** (κατασοφισάμενος). Besides, the histo.y shows that the Egyptians were to execute the inhuman order (Ex. 1 : 22), not the Hebrews. The object of putting Moses in the ark was to save, not destroy, him.

20. In which time—viz. this season of oppression.—**Fair for God**—*i. e.* in his view who judges truly. (Comp. **a city great for God** in Jon. 3 : 3, Sept.) It is a form of the Hebrew superlative. (W. § 36. 3; Green's *Gr.*, p. 277. For the dative, see on 5 : 34.) Josephus (*Antt.*, 2. 9. 7) speaks of the extreme beauty of Moses. (See also Heb. 11 : 23.)—**His father,** named Amram (Ex. 6 : 20).

21. Him (αὐτόν), with the participle, is not an accusative absolute, but depends on the verb, and is then repeated. (Comp. Mark 9 : 28.) It is changed in some of the best copies to αὐτοῦ. [The latter reading is much better supported than the former, having א A B C D. Lach., Tsch., Treg., West. and Hort, Anglo-Am. Revisers approve it. With this reading the English Version is correct.—A. H.]—**Took up,** not from the water or the ark, but like *tollere liberos,* **adopted.** This use both of the Greek and the Latin word is said to have arisen from the practice of infanticide among the ancients. After the birth of a child the father took it up to his bosom, if he meant to rear it; otherwise, it was doomed to perish.—**As a son,** appositional like ל before that which a person or thing becomes (W. § 32. 4. b.); not telic, **to be a son,** since the relation was an immediate one, and not prospective merely.

22. Was instructed in all the wisdom, made familiar with it; dative of the respect or manner. Tischendorf reads **in** before **wisdom.**

Some render **was trained by the wisdom** as the means of culture; dative of the instrument (De Wet., Mey.). This may be easier grammatically, but looks like modernizing the idea. The accusative would be the ordinary case after this passive (**was taught the wisdom**); but it could be interchanged with the dative. (See W. § 32. 4.)—**Mighty in words.** In point of mere fluency he was inferior to Aaron (Ex. 4 : 10), but excelled him in the higher mental attributes on which depends mainly the orator's power over the minds of others. His recorded speeches justify Stephen's encomium.—For **deeds,** comp. v. 36. [Probably it should read **in his words and deeds.**—A. H.]

23. By him, dative of the agent. [Lit. **But when a fortieth yearly time was fulfilled by him.**—A. H.] (See on 5 : 9.)— **A fortieth annual time**—*i. e.* when he was forty years old. (See the note on v. 30.)—**It came upon his heart** = Heb. *alah al-lēbh.* (See Jer. 3 : 16.)—**To visit his brethren,** in order to show his sympathy for them and minister to their relief. The Hebrews lived apart from the Egyptians, and Moses as a member of the royal family may have had hitherto but little intercourse with his countrymen.

24. Wronged, injured—viz. by blows, which the Hebrew was then receiving, as stated in the history. (See Ex. 2 : 11.)—**Wrought redress,** avenged. (See Luke 18 : 7.)—**The one overpowered**—lit. exhausted, worn out, implying a hard contest, and (the participle is present) a rescue just in time to ward off the fatal blow. —**By smiting the Egyptian** (who did the wrong) so as to kill him, see v. 28.

25. Was supposing in this interposition, and as the reason for it. This use of δέ, **for** (E. V.), is one of its metabatic [transition-making] offices. (Hart., *Partkl.*, vol. i. p. 167.) On what ground Moses expected to be known so readily, we are not informed. He may have thought that his history, so full of providential

26 *a*And the next day he shewed himself unto them as they strove, and would have s.t them at one again, saying, Sirs, ye are brethren; why do ye wrong one to another?

27 But he that did his neighbor wrong thrust him away, saying, *b*Who made thee a ruler and a judge over us?

28 Wilt thou kill me, as thou didst the Egyptian yesterday?

29 *c*Then fled Moses at this saying, and was a stranger in the land of Madian, where he begat two sons.

30 *d*And when forty years were expired, there appeared to him in the wilderness of mount Sina an angel of the Lord in a flame of fire in a bush.

31 When Moses saw *it*, he wondered at the sight: and as he drew near to behold *it*, the voice of the Lord came unto him,

26 them ¹deliverance; but they understood not. And the day following he appeared unto them as they strove, and would have set them at one again, saying, Sirs, ye are brethren; why do ye wrong one to

27 another? But he that did his neighbor wrong thrust him away, saying, Who made thee a ruler and a

28 judge over us? Wouldest thou kill me, as thou

29 killedst the Egyptian yesterday? And Moses fled at this saying, and became a sojourner in the land

30 of Midian, where he begat two sons. And when forty years were fulfilled, an angel appeared to him in the wilderness of mount Sinai, in a flame of fire

31 in a bush. And when Moses saw it, he wondered at the sight: and as he drew near to behold, there

---

a Ex. 2 : 13....*b* See Luke 12 : 14; ch. 4 : 7....*c* Ex. 2 : 15, 22; 4 : 20; 18 : 3, 4....*d* Ex. 3 : 2.——1 Or, *salvation.*

---

intimations, had pointed him out to the Israelites as their predestined deliverer. Stephen makes the remark evidently for the purpose of reminding the Jews of their own similar blindness in regard to the mission of Christ. (Comp. v. 35.)—Not **would deliver** (E. V.)—lit. **gives deliverance;** present either because the event was so near (see on 1 : 6), or because the deliverance begins with this act (Mey.).

26. Appeared, showed himself, with the involved idea, perhaps, that it was unexpected. —**To them**—*i. e.* two of his countrymen (Ex. 2:13). The expression is vague, because the facts are supposed to be familiar.—**Set them at one,** *urged them unto peace,* reconciliation. —ὑμεῖς after ἐστέ should be left out.—For ἱνατί, see on 4 : 25.—**Men** belongs to **brethren** —*men* related as *brethren are ye* (comp. 1 : 16; 2 : 29-37)—not = **Sirs** as the nominative of address (E. V.). The relationship aggravated the outrage. It was more unseemly than when the combatants, as on the day before, had been Hebrew and Egyptian. With the same appeal Abraham says to Lot, " Let there be no strife, I pray thee, between thee and me, and between my herdmen and thy herdmen; for we are men brethren " (Gen. 13 : 8 in Heb. and Sept.).

29. At this word, which showed that his attempt to conceal the murder had failed. (See Ex. 2 : 12.) His flight was now necessary to save his life; for "when Pharaoh heard this thing, he sought to slay Moses."—**In the land of Madiam,** or **Midian.** "This would seem," says Gesenius, " to have been a tract of country extending from the eastern shore of the Elanitic Gulf to the region of Moab on the one hand, and to the vicinity of Mount Sinai on the other. The people here were nomadic in their habits, and moved often from place to

place." It is common for γῆ (*land*) to omit the article before the name of a country. (See v. 36; 13 : 19. W. ? 19.)

30. Forty years having been completed. Stephen follows the tradition. It was said that Moses lived forty years in Pharaoh's palace, dwelt forty years in Midian, and governed Israel forty years. That he was one hundred and twenty years old at the time of his death, we read in Deut. 34 : 7.—**In the desert of the mount Sinai,** in the desert where this mount was situated. According to Ex. 3 : 1, this appearance of the angel took place at Horeb. Both names are given in the Pentateuch to the same locality. Of this usage the common explanation has been that " Sinai " designated a range of mountains, among which Horeb was the particular one from which the law was given. Dr. Robinson assigns reasons for thinking that " Horeb " was the general name and " Sinai " the specific one. (See his *Bibl. Res.*, vol. i. p. 120, ed. 1856.) Hengstenberg, Winer, Ewald, and others reject the old opinion.—**In the fiery flame of a bush.**—Fire supplies the place of an adjective. (Comp. 9 : 15; 2 Thess. 1 : 8. W. ? 34. 3. b.; S. ? 117. 6.)

31. To observe, contemplate—viz. the vision (see v. 32); not **to understand,** learn the cause, which would be unsuitable in the next verse.—**The voice of the Lord.** It will be seen that the angel of Jehovah in v. 30 (comp. Ex. 3 : 2) is here called Jehovah himself. Examples of a similar transition from the one name to the other occur often in the Old Testament. It has been argued from this usage, as well as on other grounds, that the Revealer, under the ancient dispensation, was identical with the Revealer or Logos of the New Dispensation.¹

---

¹ The subject is an interesting one, but does not fall properly within our present limits. The reader will find it discussed in Smith's *Scripture Testimony to the Messiah*, vol. i. p. 482, *sq.*, and in Hengstenberg's *Christology*, vol. i. p. 165, *sq.* Valuable supplementary matter (for the object is to deal only with the later objections) will be

32 *Saying* ᵃI am the God of thy fathers, the God of Abraham, and the God of Isaac, and the God of Jacob. Then Moses trembled, and durst not behold.

33 ᵇThen said the Lord to him, Put off thy shoes from thy feet: for the place where thou standest is holy ground.

34 ᶜI have seen, I have seen the affliction of my people which is in Egypt, and I have heard their groaning, and am come down to deliver them. And now come, I will send thee into Egypt.

35 This Moses whom they refused, saying, Who made thee a ruler and a judge? the same did God send *to be* a ruler and a deliverer ᵈby the hand of the angel which appeared to him in the bush.

36 ᵉHe brought them out, after that he had ᶠshewed wonders and signs in the land of Egypt, ᵍand in the Red sea, ʰand in the wilderness forty years.

37 ¶ This is that Moses, which said unto the chil-

32 came a voice of the Lord, I am the God of thy fathers, the God of Abraham, and of Isaac, and of Jacob. And Moses trembled, and durst not behold.

33 And the Lord said unto him, Loose the shoes from thy feet: for the place whereon thou standest is holy ground.

34 I have surely seen the affliction of my people which is in Egypt, and have heard their groaning, and I am come down to deliver them:

35 and now come, I will send thee into Egypt. This Moses whom they refused, saying, Who made thee a ruler and a judge? him hath God sent *to be* both a ruler and a ˡdeliverer with the hand of the angel

36 who appeared to him in the bush. This man led them forth, having wrought wonders and signs in Egypt, and in the Red sea, and in the wilderness

37 forty years. This is that Moses, who said unto the

---

a Matt. 22 : 32; Heb. 11 : 16....*b* Ex. 3 : 5; Josh. 5 : 15....*c* Ex. 3 : 7....*d* Ex. 14 : 19; Num. 20 : 16....*e* Ex. 12 : 41; 33 : 1....
f Ex. 7–11; 14; Ps. 105 : 27....*g* Ex. 14 : 21, 27–29....*h* Ex. 16 : 1, 35.——*l* Gr. *redeemer.*

---

32. I am the God, etc. In this way Jehovah declares himself to be the true God, in opposition to the idols of the heathen, and especially the author of those promises to the patriarchs which were now on the eve of being fulfilled.—**Durst not behold**—*i. e. the sight.* In Ex. 3 : 6 it is said further that "Moses hid his face"—an act prompted by his sense of the holiness of him in whose presence he stood. (Comp. 1 Kings 19 : 13.)

33. Loose the sandal of thy feet. Sandal is a distributive singular, for the plural. (W. ? 27. 1.) It was a mark of reverence in the East to take off the shoes or sandals in the presence of a superior, so as not to approach him with the dust which would otherwise cleave to the feet. On this principle, the Jewish priests officiated barefoot in the tabernacle and the temple. Hence, too, none enter the Turkish mosques at present except with naked feet, or, in the case of foreigners, with slippers worn for the occasion.—In **is holy ground** Luger finds a special reference to vv. 30, 32. The God of Abraham, Isaac, and Jacob was present, and where he appears the place is holy, though it be in the wilderness.

34. Truly I saw. ἰδὼν εἶδον = Heb. *raōh raēthē,* and so in the following verbs the tense is aorist: **I heard** when they groaned and **came down** (not **am come**) when I saw and heard. In Hebrew the infinitive absolute before a finite verb denotes the reality of the act, or an effect of it in the highest degree; after the verb, it denotes a continuance or repetition of the act. (See Gesen., *Heb. Gr.,* ? 128. 3; W. ? 45. 8.) The easier Greek construction of this idiom is that noticed on 4 : 17. For **I will send** (T. R.) read **I send** (Tsch.,

Mey.), but with a future sense. (See W. ? 13. 1.)

35. This (τοῦτον) is here emphatic. **This** (οὗτος) introduces the next three verses with the same effect.—**Denied.** The verb is plural, because, though the rejection was one person's act (v. 27), it revealed the spirit of the nation. —**As a ruler and redeemer.** (Comp. 5 : 31.) Stephen selects the words evidently with reference to the parallel which he would institute between Moses and Christ.—**In the hand** stands for Heb. *beyadh, by the hand,* agency (comp. Gal. 3 : 19), since it was through the angel in the bush that God called Moses to deliver his people. Tischendorf [also Lach., Treg., West. and Hort, after ℵ B C D E, correctly, without doubt.—A. H.] reads σὺν χειρί (unusual, but well supported), *with the hand*—*i. e.* attended by the angel's aid and power, an adjunct of **the same** rather than the verb.—**The bush** (τῇ βάτῳ) is feminine here and in Luke 20 : 37, but masculine in Mark 12 : 26.

36. Led them forth, out of Egypt. Hence we cannot render ποιήσας, **after he had shown,** performed (E. V.), because the miracles in the desert were not antecedent to the Exodus. The participle expresses here an accompanying act of **led forth, performing** (Vulg. *faciens*), since the leading forth formed a general epoch with which the associated events, whether historically prior or subsequent, could be viewed as coincident in point of time. On the force of the participle in such a case, see on 21 : 7.— For the difference between **wonders** and **signs,** see on 2 : 22. Lachmann inserts τῇ before γῇ, but on slight evidence.—Αἰγύπτῳ is more correct than Αἰγύπτου (T. R.).

37. A prophet, etc. For the explanation

---

found in Kurtz's article, *Der Engel des Herrn,* in Tholuck's *Litterarischer Anzeiger,* 1846, Nos. 11–14, and inserted, for substance. in the author's *Geschichte des alten Bundes,* vol. i. pp. 121–126.

dren of Israel, *a*A prophet shall the Lord your God raise up unto you of your brethren, like unto me ; *b*him shall ye hear.

38 *c*This is he, that was in the church in the wilderness with *d*the angel which spake to him in the mount Sina, and *with* our fathers: *e*who received the lively *f*oracles to give unto us:

39 To whom our fathers would not obey, but thrust *him* from them, and in their hearts turned back again into Egypt,

40 *g*saying unto Aaron, Make us gods to go before

children of Israel, A prophet shall God raise up unto you from among your brethren, [1]like unto me. 38 This is he that was in the [2]church in the wilderness with the angel who spake to him in the mount Sinai, and with our fathers: who received living oracles 39 to give unto us: to whom our fathers would not be obedient, but thrust him from them, and turned 40 back in their hearts unto Egypt, saying unto Aaron, Make us gods which shall go before us: for as for

---

a Deut. 18 : 15, 18 ; ch. 3 : 22....b Matt. 17 : 5....c Ex. 19 : 3, 17....d Isa. 63 : 9 ; Gal. 3 : 19 ; Heb. 2 : 2....e Ex. 21 : 1 ; Deut. 5 : 27, 31 ; 33 : 4 ; John 1 : 17....f Rom. 3 : 2....g Ex. 32 : 1.——1 Or, *as he raised up* me....2 Or, *congregation.*

---

of this prophecy, see on 3 : 22. No one can doubt that Stephen regarded Christ as the prophet announced by Moses; yet it will be observed he leaves that unsaid, and relies on the intelligence of his hearers to infer his meaning. Here is a clear instance in which the speech adjusts itself to those *suppressed* relations of the subject on which, as I suppose, its adaptation to the occasion so largely depended. By quoting this prediction of Moses, Stephen tells the Jews in effect that it was *they* who were treating the lawgiver with contempt; for, while they made such pretensions to respect for his authority, they refused to acknowledge the prophet whom he foretold and had commanded them to obey. **Lord** and **our** before **God** (T. R.) are doubtful. **Him shall ye hear** was inserted probably from 3 : 22 (Lchm., Tsch., Mey.).

38. Who was (lit. **became,** entered into connection) **with the angel and with our fathers.** The meaning is that he brought the parties into association with each other, acted as mediator between God and the people. (See Gal. 3 : 19.) This fact is mentioned to show how exalted a service Moses performed, in contrast with the indignity which he experienced at the hands of his countrymen. He was a type, Stephen would say, of the Jesus despised, crucified, by those whom he would reconcile unto God.—**In the congregation**—*i. e.* of the Hebrews assembled at Sinai at the time of the promulgation of the law. So all the best critics and the older E. Versions (Tynd., Cran., Gen., Rhem.) translate this word. It is evident that *ecclesia* here affords no countenance to the idea that the Hebrew nation, as such, constituted the church under the Ancient Economy. [The word rendered *church* (ἐκκλησία) signifies, in classical Greek, "an assembly of the citizens summoned by the crier," or "a legislative assembly." It is used in the Septuagint to denote the people of Israel when called together in an assembly (Deut. 31 : 30; Josh. 8 : 35; Judg. 21 : 8; Heb. 2 : 12). It is employed by the writers of the New Testament about ninety times to

denote a society of Christians who meet together for worship, who duly observe the ordinances, and who maintain discipline among themselves. But these writers furnish no evidence that the various churches, scattered through the provinces and cities of Western Asia and South-eastern Europe, were in any sense *one organized body or society.* In certain passages the word "church" may perhaps signify a regular assembly of disciples meeting for social worship, but not large enough to be organized into an independent society (*e. g.* Rom. 16 : 5; Philem. 1). In other passages it seems to be used of the whole company of believers in Christ, ideally considered as a great spiritual assembly (Eph. 5 : 23, *sq.*). In one place (Acts 9 : 31) it may represent all the Christians in certain provinces. The expression "Jewish Church" is sometimes used, even by Baptist writers as accurate as Dr. O. S. Stearns (perhaps in accommodation to the practice of others), in a sense not strictly warranted by the Scriptures.—A. H.] —**Lively** characterizes **oracles** with reference, not to their effect (comp. Rom. 8 : 3; Gal. 3 : 21), but their nature or design : **life-giving oracles,** commands. (Comp. Rom. 7 : 12.) The inadequacy of the law to impart life does not arise from any inherent defect in the law itself, but from the corruption of human nature.

39. Turned with their hearts unto Egypt—*i. e.* longed for its idolatrous worship, and for the sake of it deserted that of Jehovah (Calv., Kuin., De Wet., Mey.). The next words are epexegetical, and require this explanation. Some have understood it of their wishing to return to Egypt; but that sense, though it could be expressed by the language, not only disregards the context, but is opposed to Ex. 32 : 4 and Neh. 9 : 18. The Jews are there represented as worshipping the golden calf for having brought them out of Egypt, and not as a means of enabling them to return thither.

40. Gods who shall go before us—to wit, as guides, protectors. This is a literal translation from Ex. 32 : 1. The plural is best explained as that of the *pluralis excellentiæ.*

us: for *as for* this Moses, which brought us out of the land of Egypt, we wot not what is become of him.

41 [a]And they made a calf in those days, and offered sacrifice unto the idol, and rejoiced in the works of their own hands.

42 Then [b]God turned, and gave them up to worship [c]the host of heaven; as it is written in the book of the prophets, [d]O ye house of Israel, have ye offered to me slain beasts and sacrifices *by the space of* forty years in the wilderness?

43 Yea, ye took up the tabernacle of Moloch, and the star of your god Remphan, figures which ye made

this Moses, who led us forth out of the land of 41 Egypt, we know not what is become of him. And they made a calf in those days, and brought a sacrifice unto the idol, and rejoiced in the works of their 42 hands. But God turned, and gave them up to serve the host of heaven; as it is written in the book of the prophets,

Did ye offer unto me slain beasts and sacrifices Forty years in the wilderness, O house of Israel?

43   And ye took up the tabernacle of Moloch,

And the star of the god Rephan,

---

a Deut. 9 : 16 ; Ps. 106 : 19....b Ps. 81 : 12 ; Ezek. 20 : 25, 39 ; Rom. 1 : 24 ; 2 Thess. 2 : 11....c Deut. 4 : 19 ; 17 : 3 ; 2 Kings 17 : 16 ; 21 : 3 ; Jer. 19 : 13....d Amos 5 : 25, 26.

---

since Aaron made but one image in compliance with this demand of the people (called *gods, elohim*, in Ex. 32 : 8), and since the Hebrews would naturally enough transfer the name of the true God to the object of their idolatrous worship. De Wette hesitates between this view and that of **gods** as abstract, *deity*, divine power. The latter is better, perhaps, than Meyer's categorical plural—*gods*, such as the calf represented.—**For as to this Moses who led us forth,** etc. **This** is contemptuous, like *iste*. The nominative absolute strengthens the sarcasm. (W. § 29. 1.) **For** alleges the disappearance of Moses as a reason why they should change their worship; possibly, because it freed them from his opposition to their desires, but more probably because, whether he had deserted them or had perished, it showed that the God whom he professed to serve was unworthy of their confidence.

41. Made a calf (ἐμοσχοποίησαν) is elsewhere unknown to the extant Greek. They selected the figure of a calf, or more correctly bullock, as their idol, in imitation, no doubt, of the Egyptians, who worshipped an ox at Memphis, called Apis, and another at Heliopolis, called Mnevis. (Win., *Realw.*, i. p. 644 ; Herz., *Encyk.*, vol. vii. p. 214.) Mummies of the animals so worshipped are often found in the catacombs of Egypt. — **Rejoiced,** made merry, refers doubtless to the festive celebration mentioned in Ex. 32 : 6.—**The works** is plural, because the idol was the product of their joint labors. Meyer supposes it to include the various implements of sacrifice, in addition to the image (in his last edition, *works* such as this).

42. Turned away, withdrew his favor.— **Gave up** (Rom. 1 : 24) = **suffered** in 14 : 16 ; he laid, for the present, no check upon their inclinations. In consequence of this desertion, they sunk into still grosser idolatry. — **The**

host of heaven—*i. e.* the sun, moon, and stars. This form of worship is called Sabaism, from *tsabba* (Heb.), as applied to the heavenly bodies.—**In the book of the prophets**—*i. e.* the twelve minor prophets, whom the Jews reckoned as one collection. The passage is Amos 5 : 25-27.—**Have ye offered,** etc. This sign of a question requires a negative answer, and that answer is to be understood in a relative sense. (See W. § 57. 3.) **Did ye offer unto me sacrifices and offerings?**—*i. e.* exclusively. The reply is left to their consciences. Even during the eventful period in the wilderness, when the nation saw so much of the power and goodness of God, they deserted his worship for that of other gods, or, while they professed to serve him, united his service with that of idols. The question ends here.

43. And ye took up, etc. The tacit answer precedes : No, ye apostatized, **and took up the tabernacle of Moloch**—*i. e.* to carry it with them in their marches or in religious processions. This tabernacle was intended, no doubt, to resemble the one consecrated to Jehovah. Stephen follows the Septuagint. **Moloch** stands there for Heb. *Malkŏkem*—*i. e.* the idol worshipped as *your king,* which was the Moloch of the Amorites. The Seventy supply the name of the idol as well known from tradition. But there is almost equal authority, says Baur,[1] for reading *Milkom,* a proper name. That variation would bring the Greek into still closer conformity with the Hebrew.—**The star of the god**—*i. e.* an image resembling or representing a star worshipped by them as a god. —By **Remphan** (also written *Rephan, Rumpha, Rompha*) the Seventy express *kiyyoon* (Heb.), which, like most of the ancient translators, they took to be a proper name. Some of the ablest modern scholars[2] defend the correctness of that

---

[1] *Der Prophet Amos erklärt,* von Dr. Gustav Baur, p. 362.

[2] See especially Movers, *Ueber die Phönizier,* vol i. p. 289, *sq.* He maintains that *kiyyoon* may be traced as a proper name in various Oriental languages.

to worship them: and I will carry you away beyond Babylon.

44 Our fathers had the tabernacle of witness in the wilderness, as he had appointed, speaking unto Moses, *that he should make it according to the fashion that he had seen.

45 *Which also our fathers that came after brought in with Jesus into the possession of the Gentiles, *whom God drave out before the face of our fathers, unto the days of David;

The figures which ye made to worship them: And I will carry you away beyond Babylon.

44 Our fathers had the tabernacle of the testimony in the wilderness, even as he appointed who spake unto Moses, that he should make it according to the figure

45 that he had seen. Which also our fathers, in their turn, brought in with ¹Joshua when they entered on the possession of the nations, whom God thrust out before the face of our fathers, unto the days of

a Ex. 25 : 40 ; 26 : 30 ; Heb. 8 : 5.... b Josh. 3 : 14.... c Neh. 9 : 24 ; Ps. 44 : 2 ; 78 : 55 ; ch. 13 : 19.——1 Gr. *Jesus.*

translation. In this case the Greek name must have sprung from a corrupt pronunciation of the Hebrew name. (See Gesen., *Lex.*, p. 463.) According to others, *kiyyoon* should be rendered *statue*, or *statues*, and the idol would then be unnamed in the Hebrew. So Gesenius, Robinson (*N. T. Lex.*, s. v.), and others. Admitting that sense, it was unnecessary for Stephen to correct the current version ; for he adduced the passage merely to establish the charge of idolatry, not to decide what particular idol was worshipped. Whether the star-god to which they paid their homage was Saturn, Venus, or some other planet cannot be determined.—**The figures,** in apposition with **tabernacle** and **star.** The term was so much the more appropriate to the tabernacle, as it contained probably an image of Moloch. — μετοικιῶ (**will carry away**) is the Attic future.—**Beyond Babylon,** where the Hebrew and Septuagint have **beyond Damascus.** The idea is the same, for the prediction turned, not upon the name, but the fact—viz. that God would scatter them into distant lands. The Babylonian Captivity was the one best known, and, besides, in being exiled to the remoter place the Jews were transported beyond the nearer.

44. The tabernacle of witness = *Ohel haëdhooth* (Num. 9 : 15; 17 : 23), **the tabernacle of the testimony,** or law, so called because it contained the ark in which the tables of the Decalogue were kept. The law is termed a *testimony*, because it testifies or declares the divine will. Bähr's explanation (*Symbolik,* vol. i. p. 80) is different : the tabernacle was a testimony or witness of the covenant between God and his people.—**That he should make it according to the pattern which he had seen**—viz. on Mount Sinai. (See Ex. 25 : 9, 40.) By this reference Stephen reminds the Jews of the emblematical import, consequently the subordinate value, of the ancient worship. Moses, under the divine guidance, constructed the *earthly* tabernacle, so as to have it image forth certain *heavenly* or spiritual realities that were to be accomplished under "the better covenant of which Jesus is the Mediator." Here we have

the rudiments of the view which pervades the Epistle to the Hebrews. (See especially Heb. 8 : 5.) What was true of the tabernacle was true also of the first and the second temple : they were built after the same model, and were in like manner *antitypes,* or *shadows of the heavenly.* That application of the remark could be left to suggest itself. [Anything like a full account of the Jewish tabernacle would require more space than can be given to it in this COMMENTARY ; but the reader will do well to consult the treatise of Edw. E. Atwater on the *History and Significance of the Sacred Tabernacle,* also chap. iv. of Fergusson on *The Temple of the Jews,* and the articles on the tabernacle in Smith's *Dict. of the Bible,* Kitto's *Biblical Cyclopædia,* edited by W. L. Alexander, and McClintock and Strong's *Cyclopædia,* etc.— A. H.]

45. Also adds **brought in** to **should make.—Having received** (the tabernacle) —viz. from Moses or his contemporaries, since those who entered Canaan were a later generation ; not *inherited* (Alf.), a false meaning, and not *who came after,* successors (E. V., retained from Cranm.), since that substantive construction would require the article. (See Pape, s. v.)— **With Joshua,** as their leader, under his guidance.—**Into the possession of the heathen,** the territory inhabited by them. (Comp. **let the land be given unto us for a possession** in Num. 32 : 5.) ἐν (*in*) shows that the idea of rest predominates over that of motion. Meyer and De Wette translate **on taking possession of the heathen,** on their subjugation. The other meaning is better, because it supplies an indirect object after **brought in,** and adheres to the prevalent passive sense of **possession.** (See Rob., *Lex.,* s. v.)—**Unto the days of David** belongs to **brought in,** employed suggestively : *brought* the tabernacle into the land, and retained it until (inclusive) **the days of David.** Some join the words with **whom God drave out,** which exalts a subordinate clause above the principal one and converts the aorist into an imperfect : *was expelling* from Joshua until David.

46 *Who found favor before God, and *desired to find a tabernacle for the God of Jacob.

47 *But Solomon built him an house.

48 Howbeit *the most High dwelleth not in temples made with hands ; as saith the prophet,

49 *Heaven *is* my throne, and earth *is* my footstool: what house will ye build me? saith the Lord: or what *is* the place of my rest?

50 Hath not my hand made all these things?

51 ¶ Ye *stiffnecked and *uncircumcised in heart and ears, ye do always resist the Holy Ghost: as your fathers *did*, so *do* ye.

52 *Which of the prophets have not your fathers persecuted? and they have slain them which shewed before of the coming of *the Just One; of whom ye have been now the betrayers and murderers:

53 *Who have received the law by the disposition of angels, and have not kept *it*.

46 David; who found favor in the sight of God, and asked to find a habitation for the God of Jacob. But

47

48 Solomon built him a house. Howbeit the Most High dwelleth not in *houses* made with hands; as saith the prophet,

49 The heaven is my throne,
   And the earth the footstool of my feet:
   What manner of house will ye build me? saith the Lord:

Or what is the place of my rest?

50 Did not my hand make all these things?

51 Ye stiffnecked and uncircumcised in heart and ears, ye do always resist the Holy Spirit: as your

52 fathers did, so do ye. Which of the prophets did not your fathers persecute? and they killed them who shewed before of the coming of the Righteous One; of whom ye have now become b trayers and

53 murderers; ye who received the law ¹as it was ordained by angels, and kept it not.

a 1 Sam. 16 : 1 ; 2 Sam. 7 : 1 ; Ps. 89 : 19 ; ch. 13 : 22....*b* 1 Kings 8 : 17 ; 1 Chron. 22 : 7 ; Ps. 132 : 4, 5....*c* 1 Kings 6 : 1 ; 8 : 20 ; 1 Chron. 17 : 12 ; 2 Chron. 3 : 1....*d* 1 Kings 8 : 27 ; 2 Chron. 2 : 6 ; 6 : 18 ; ch. 17 : 24....*e* Isa. 66 : 1, 2 ; Matt. 5 : 34, 35 ; 23 : 22....*f* Ex. 32 : 9 ; 33 : 3 ; Isa. 48 : 4....*g* Lev. 26 : 41 ; Deut. 10 : 16 ; Jer. 4 : 4 ; 6 : 10 ; 9 : 26 ; Ezek. 44 : 9....*h* 2 Chron. 36 : 16 ; Matt. 21 : 35 ; 23 : 34, 37 ; 1 Thess. 2 : 15....*i* ch. 3 : 14....*k* Ex. 20 : 1 ; Gal. 3 : 19 ; Heb. 2 : 2.——1 Or, *as the ordinance of angels* Gr. *unto ordinances of angels.*

46. Who found favor, etc. (Comp. 13 : 22.) The tacit inference may be that, had the temple been so important as the Jews supposed, God would not have withheld this honor from his servant.—**Asked for himself,** as a privilege. We have no record of this prayer, though it is implied in 2 Sam. 7 : 4, *sq.*, and in 1 Chron. 22 : 7. In the latter passage David says, "As for me, it was in my mind to build an house unto the name of the Lord my God." In that frame of spirit he indited the hundred and thirty-second Psalm.—**To find . . . Jacob** coincides with Ps. 132 : 5 (Sept.). To express the object of David's request, Stephen avails himself of the language contained in that passage. Translate, **a habitation** (= οἶκον in v. 47, place of abode, temple) **for the God of Jacob;** not tabernacle (= σκηνή in v. 44), as in the E. Version. The tabernacle existed already, and it was not that structure, but a temple, which David was anxious to build. The confusion arises from rendering the different Greek terms by the same word.

47–53. Period of the Temple and the Prophets.

47. But (δέ, adversative). What was denied to David was granted to Solomon. (See 2 Chron. 6 : 7, 8.) Yet even the builder of the temple acknowledged (2 Chron. 6 : 18) that God is not confined to any single place of worship. The tenor of the speech would be apt to remind the hearers of that admission.

48. Howbeit . . . dwelleth. The temple was at length built, but was never designed to circumscribe the presence of the Infinite Architect (see v. 50) or to usurp the homage that belongs to him alone. The remark here was aimed, doubtless, at the superstitious reverence with which the Jews regarded the temple, and at their proneness in general to exalt the forms

of religion above its essence. For **not** in this position, see on 2 : 7. **Temples** is probably a gloss from 17 : 24.—**As saith,** etc. To give greater effect to his reproof, Stephen quotes the testimony of the prophet—viz. Isa. 66 : 1, 2.

51. There is no evidence that Stephen was interrupted at this point. Many critics assume that without reason. The sharper tone of reprehension to which the speaker rises here belongs to the place; it is an application in course of remark which precedes. We have no right to ascribe it to Stephen's irritation at perceiving signs of impatience or rage on the part of his hearers.—**Uncircumcised,** etc.— *i. e.* destitute of the disposition to hear and love the truth, of which their circumcision should have been the sign. (Comp. Lev. 26 : 41; Jer. 6 : 10; Rom. 2 : 29.) For **the heart,** see 2 : 37.— **Ye do always resist the Holy Spirit,** under whose influence the messengers of God —*e. g.* Christ and the apostles—spoke to them. To reject their testimony was to reject that of the Spirit himself. What follows appears to restrict the language to that meaning.—**Also you,** where **so** would state the comparison more exactly. (See W. § 53. 5.)

52. Whom of the prophets, etc. Stephen would describe the general conduct of the Jews toward their prophets; he does not affirm that there were no exceptions to it. Other passages, as 2 Chron. 36 : 15, 16, Matt. 23 : 37, and Luke 13 : 33, 34 make the same representation.— **Those who announced beforehand,** etc., designates the prophets with reference to the leading subject of their predictions. (See on 3 : 21–24.)—**The Just One** (3 : 14), slain by them as a malefactor.—**Now,** as the climax of the nation's guilt.—**Traitors.** (See 3 : 13.)

53. Those who were thus guilty (v. 52) acted in the character of **those who** (οἵτινες, **such**

54 ¶ ªWhen they heard these things, they were cut to the heart, and they gnashed on him with *their* teeth.

55 But he, ᵇbeing full of the Holy Ghost, looked up stedfastly into heaven, and saw the glory of God, and Jesus standing on the right hand of God,

56 And said, Behold, ᶜI see the heavens opened, and the ᵈSon of man standing on the right hand of God.

57 Then they cried out with a loud voice, and stopped their ears, and ran upon him with one accord, 58 And ᵉcast *him* out of the city, ᶠand stoned *him:*

54 Now when they heard these things, they were cut to the heart, and they gnashed on him with their teeth. 55 But he, being full of the Holy Spirit, looked up stedfastly into heaven, and saw the glory of God, 56 and Jesus standing on the right hand of God, and said, Behold, I see the heavens opened, and the Son 57 of man standing on the right hand of God. But they cried out with a loud voice, and stopped their ears, 58 and rushed upon him with one accord; and they cast him out of the city, and stoned him: and the wit-

---

a ch. 5 : 33....*b* ch. 6 : 5....*c* Ezek. 1 : 1; Matt. 3 : 16; ch. 10 : 11....*d* Dan. 7 : 13....*e* 1 Kings 21 : 13 ; Luke 4 : 29 ; Heb. 13 : 12 ...*f* Lev. 24 : 16.

---

as) **received,** etc.—**The law as** (ὡς predicative sign ; see on v. 21) **ordinances** (plural with reference to *law* as an aggregate of single acts) **of angels,** the latter not as the authors of them, in which sense they were God's, but as communicated through them. (Comp., in Heb. 2 : 2, *the word spoken through angels,* and especially, in Gal. 3 : 19, *ordained* on the part of God *through angels.*) The elliptical explanation, reckoned **unto ordinances,** as of that rank or class, affords the same meaning, but is not so simple. (See W. § 32. 4. b.) Some translate **upon the ministrations,** agency of; but that both strains the use of the preposition (not necessary even in Matt. 12 : 41) and employs the noun differently from Rom. 13 : 2 (not elsewhere in New Testament). The presence of angels at the giving of the law is not expressly stated in the Old Testament, but is alluded to in Gal. 3 : 19 and Heb. 2 : 2. Philo and Josephus testify to the same tradition. The Seventy translate Deut. 33 : 2 in such a manner as to assert the same fact. It is implied, perhaps, in Ps. 68 : 18. The Jews regarded this angelic mediation as both ennobling the law and as conferring special honor on themselves, to whom the law was given. (For a striking proof of this Jewish feeling, see Jos., *Antt.*, 15. 5. 3.) From another point of view—viz. that of Christ's superiority to angels—this angelic intervention showed the inferiority of the law to the gospel, which is the view taken in Heb. 2 : 2, and probably in Gal. 3 : 19.—**And yet ye kept it not. Law,** as the principal word, supplies the object, and not διαταγάς (E. V.). In this verse, therefore, we have the apostle's idea in Rom. 2 : 23, where he says that the Jews gloried in the law, while they dishonored God by their violations of it.

54–60. THE DEATH OF STEPHEN.

54. It is disputed whether Stephen finished his speech or not. The abrupt manner in which he closes, and the exasperation of the Jews at that moment, render it probable that he was interrupted. **Hearing,** as present, favors the same view, but is not decisive. (See

5 : 5; 13 : 48.)—For **were cut to the heart,** see on 5 : 33.

55. Full of the Holy Spirit. The Spirit revealed to his soul this scene in heaven. It was not a vision addressed to the senses. It is needless, therefore, to inquire, as Meyer now admits, whether our martyr could see the opened sky through the roof or a window.—For **the glory of God,** see on v. 2.—**Standing,** instead of sitting, as at other times. The Saviour had risen, in order to intimate his readiness to protect or sustain his servant (Bng., Kuin., Mey.). It appears to me doubtful whether we are to attach that or any other significance to the particular attitude in which he appeared.

56. Behold, etc. This declaration would tend to exasperate them still more. They are now told that he whom they had crucified, and whom they were ready to slay anew in the person of his followers, was exalted to supreme dominion at the right hand of God. (See remarks on 2 : 34.)

57. Crying. Among other things, perhaps, that he should be silent, or that he should be put to death. (Comp. 19 : 32; Matt. 27 : 23; John 19 : 12.)—**Stopped,** etc. They affected to regard his words as blasphemous, and **stopped their ears** as an expression of their abhorrence.—**Ran upon him,** etc. Under the Roman laws, the Jews had no power to inflict capital punishment without the sanction of the procurator or his proxy. (See John 18 : 31.) Nearly all critics at present concur in that view. Hence the stoning of Stephen was an illegal, tumultuous proceeding. The Roman governors connived often at such irregularities, provided the Roman interest or power suffered no detriment. As Pilate was deposed in A. D. 35 or 36, some have thought that his office may have been still vacant (see on 6 : 1), and that the Jews took greater liberty on that account.

58. Out of the city, because a place so holy was not to be defiled with blood. (See Lev. 24 : 14. Comp. the note on 14 : 19.) [At what place outside the city walls is not cer-

and *the witnesses laid down their clothes at a young man's feet, whose name was Saul.

nesses laid down their garments at the feet of a

---

a Deut. 13 : 9, 10 ; 17 : 7 ; ch. 8 : 1 ; 22 : 20.

---

tainly known. But in Conder's *Tent - Work in Palestine,* vol. i. pp. 371–376, important reasons are assigned for believing that it was a spot known by tradition as " The Place of Stoning." This place is situated near the main road to Shechem, on the east side, a little north of the Damascus gate. The writer says: "The stony road comes out from the Damascus gate, and runs beside the yellow cliff, in which are

Jesus was crucified, as well as the spot where Stephen was stoned.—A. H.]—**And the witnesses laid off their garments,** that they might have the free use of their arms in hurling the stones. The law of Moses required the witnesses in the case of a capital offence to begin the work of death. (See Deut. 13 : 10 ; 17 : 7.) The object of the law, it has been suggested, may have been to

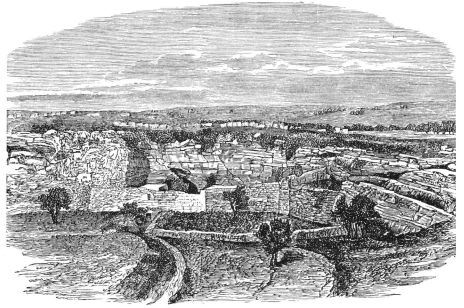

PLACE OF STONING.

excavated caverns. . . . Above the cliff, which is some thirty feet high, is the rounded knoll without any building on it, bare of trees, and in spring covered in part with scanty grass, while a great portion is occupied by a Moslem cemetery. To the north are olive-groves; to the west, beneath the knoll, is a garden. . . . The place is bare and dusty, surrounded by stony ground and by heaps of rubbish, and exposed to the full glare of the summer sun. Such is the barren hillock which, by consent of Jewish and Christian tradition, is identified with the Place of Stoning, or of execution according to the Jewish laws." Mr. Conder supposes that this knoll was the Calvary on which

prevent inconsiderate or false testimony. Many would be shocked at the idea of shedding blood who would not scruple to gain a private end or to gratify their malice by misrepresentation and falsehood.—**At his feet,** for safekeeping. (Comp. 22 : 20.) Their selecting Saul for this purpose shows that he was already known as a decided enemy of the Christians. His zeal and dialectic skill in the controversy with Stephen (see on 6 : 9) could not have failed to establish his claim to that character.—**A young man,** a designation which the Greeks could apply to a person till he was forty years old, but perhaps in common speech would rarely extend beyond the age of thirty. This term, therefore, is very

59 And they stoned Stephen, ^acalling upon *God*, and saying, Lord Jesus. ^breceive my spirit.
60 And he ^ckneeled down, and cried with a loud voice, ^dLord, lay not this sin to their charge. And when he had said this, he fell asleep.

59 young man named Saul. And they stoned Stephen, calling upon *the Lord*, and saying, Lord Jesus, re-
60 ceive my spirit. And he kneeled down, and cried with a loud voice, Lord, lay not this sin to their charge. And when he had said this, he fell asleep. And Saul was consenting unto his death.

CHAPTER VIII.

AND ^eSaul was consenting unto his death. And at that time there was a great persecution against the

1 AND there arose on that day a great persecution

a ch. 9 : 14....*b* Ps. 31 : 5; Luke 23 : 46....*c* ch. 9 : 40 ; 20 : 36 ; 21 : 5....*d* Matt. 5 : 44 ; Luke 6 : 28 ; 23 : 34....*e* ch. 7 : 58 ; 22 : 20.

indefinite as an indication of Saul's age at the time of this occurrence. In all probability, he was not far from thirty when he was converted—not much less, as the Sanhedrim would hardly have entrusted so important a commission to a mere youth (see 9 : 1, *sq.*), and not more, as his recorded life (closing about A. D. 64) would otherwise be too short for the events of his history.[1]

59. Calling upon — viz. Christ. **Lord Jesus,** just before, supplies the only natural object after this participle. "That the first Christians called on Jesus," says De Wette—*i. e.* addressed prayer to him—" is evident from 9 : 14, 21 ; 22 : 16 ; comp. 2 : 21 ; Rom. 10 : 12, *sq.*" See further on 9 : 14.—As the dying Saviour said to the Father, "Into thy hands I commend my spirit," so the dying Stephen said now to the Saviour, **receive my spirit.** [The Greek term for Lord (κύριος) signifies *one who has absolute power, authority, or control over persons or things.* It is properly translated *lord, master, owner,* etc.—*e. g.* lord of a realm, master of a slave, owner of a vineyard. It is sometimes applied, as a form of respectful Oriental address, to persons having no real claim to the title. But it is used most frequently in Scripture as a designation of God the Supreme Ruler, or of Jesus Christ his Son, who, as Mediatorial King, is Head over all things to the church. "In the Greek version of the Old Testament it represents the Hebrew *Adonai* one hundred and fourteen times ; *Adonai Elohim,* twenty-nine times ; *El,* forty-one times ; *Jah,* twenty-two times ; *Jehovah,* more than fifteen hundred times " (*Moses Stuart*). In the New Testament it is used as one of the distinctive appellations of God the Father and of Jesus Christ, being generally applied in the Gospels to God, and in the Epistles of Paul to Jesus Christ, and being used, like proper names, either with or without the article. "There are those who teach that,

with the exception of words borrowed from the Old Testament, . . . Paul never designates *God*, but always *Christ*, by the term Lord. But, omitting instances of doubtful interpretation, . . . it is at once evident that in the words ' and to each as the Lord gave' (1 Cor. 3 : 5), *the Lord* must signify *God*, because of the words that follow, especially the words ' according to the grace of God which was given to me' (v. 10). On the contrary, I hold that in the expression ' when we are judged, we are chastened by the Lord' (1 Cor. 11 : 32), the reference is to Christ, because of 10 : 22 compared with 21." (Grimm, *Lexicon of the N. T., sub voce.* See, besides Grimm, Cremer, *Biblico-Theological Lex. of the N. T.,* under κύριος, and Stuart in *Bibl. Repos.,* i. pp. 733-776.)—A. H.]

60. Establish not this sin to them, reckon or count it not to them (Rob., De Wet.). Christ had set an example of this duty, as well as enjoined it by precept. No parallel to this prayer of Stephen can be found out of Christian history. The Greeks expressed a dehortatory command or wish by μή with the subjunctive aorist when the act was one not yet commenced. (Comp. on 10 : 15.) This is Hermann's rule. (See Mt. ₴ 511. 3; K. ₴ 259. 5.) —**Fell asleep,** died. (Comp. 13 : 36 ; 1 Cor. 15 : 18, etc.) Heathen writers employed the verb occasionally in that sense ; but its derivative, *cemetery* (κοιμητήριον)—*i. e.* a place where the body sleeps in the hope of a resurrection—was first used by Christians. It marks the introduction of the more cheerful ideas which the gospel has taught men to connect with the grave.

1-3. THE BURIAL OF STEPHEN.

1. The first sentence here would have closed more properly the last chapter.—**Consenting, approving with,** them—viz. the murderers of Stephen ; so that he shared their guilt without

[1] For information in regard to the early life and training of the apostle Paul (a topic important to a just view of his character and history), the student may consult Dr. Davidson's *Introduction to the New Testament,* vol. ii. p. 122, *sq.*; Conybeare and Howson's *Life and Epistles of St. Paul,* vol. i. p. 40, *sq.* (2d ed.) ; *Selections from German Literature* (Edwards and Park), p. 31, *sq.*; Schrader's *Der Apostel Paulus,* zweiter Theil, p. 14, *sq.*; Hemsen's *Das Leben des Apostels,* u. s. w. erstes Kapitel ; and Tholuck's *Vermischte Schriften,* Band ii. p. 272, *sq.*

church which was at Jerusalem; and *they were all scattered abroad throughout the regions of Judæa and Samaria, except the apostles.

2 And devout men carried Stephen *to his burial,* and *made great lamentation over him.

3 As for Saul, *he made havock of the church, entering into every house, and haling men and women committed *them* to prison.

4 Therefore *they that were scattered abroad went everywhere preaching the word.

against the church which was in Jerusalem; and they were all scattered abroad throughout the regions of Judæa and Samaria, except the apostles.

2 And devout men buried Stephen, and made great 3 lamentation over him. But Saul laid waste the church, entering into every house, and dragging away men and women committed them to prison.

4 They therefore that were scattered abroad went

a ch. 11 : 19....*b* Gen. 23 : 2; 50 : 10; 2 Sam. 3 : 31....*c* ch. 7 : 58; 9 : 1, 13, 21; 22 : 4; 26 : 10, 11; 1 Cor. 15 : 9; Gal. 1 : 13; Phil. 3 : 6; 1 Tim. 1 : 13....*d* Matt. 10 : 23; ch. 11 : 19.

participating so directly in the act. In Rom. 1 : 32, Paul lays it down as one of the worst marks of a depraved mind that a person can bring himself to applaud thus coolly the sins of others, and in 22 : 20 he says that he himself had exhibited that mark of depravity in relation to the death of Stephen. Luke here records, probably, a confession which he had often heard from the lips of the apostle. For **was** with the participle, see on 1 : 10. — **On that day** (comp. 11 : 19); not indefinite, *at that time,* which would require the noun to be plural. The stoning of Stephen was the signal for an immediate and universal persecution.— **All** need not be pressed so as to include every individual. (See on 3 : 18.) Zeller clings to the letter, and then argues against the truth of the narrative from the improbability of such a panic. Many of those who fled returned, doubtless, after the cessation of the present danger. It is not to be supposed that the church which we find existing at Jerusalem after this was made up entirely of new members.— **Throughout the regions.** They fled at first to different places in Judea and Samaria; but some of them, probably the foreign Jews, went afterward to other countries. (See v. 4 and 11 : 19.) [**Except the apostles.** Two reasons have been assigned for their remaining in Jerusalem. Canon Cook suggests that they did so because they " were not exposed to this persecution, being Hebrews, regular attendants at the temple-service, revered and beloved for their miracles." Meyer says that they remained " because of their great steadfastness. In the absence of more special divine intimation, they resolved to remain still at the centre of the theocracy." The latter view is preferable to the former.—A. H.]

2. Bore away together—*i. e.* to the grave —joined to bury, or simply **buried,** as the force of the preposition is not always traceable in this verb. (See Pape, s. v.)—**Now** (δέ) carries back the mind to Stephen after the digression in v. 1; not *but,* in spite of, the persecution, for it was not only permitted among

the Jews, but required, that the bodies of those executed should be buried.—**Devout men** are pious Jews (see on 2 : 5) who testified in this way their commiseration for Stephen's fate and their conviction of his innocence. The Christians would not have been allowed to perform such an office; they too would have been designated as disciples or brethren.—**Lamentation,** as expressed in the Oriental way by clapping the hands or smiting on the breast.

3. Now (δέ) presents Saul again as the principal person, or possibly *but* (E. V.), contrasting his conduct with that of the **devout.—Into the houses,** one after another. The preposition marks both direction and succession.—**Dragging,** bearing off with violence. (Comp. 14 : 19; 17 : 6. See Tittm., *Synm.*, p. 57, *sq.*) We see the man's ferocious spirit in his manner. " Haling," in the English translation, is an old word for **hauling** or **hawling.—Not only men, but women.** Repeated also in 9 : 2 and 22 : 4 as a great aggravation of his cruelty.

4–8. THE GOSPEL IS PREACHED IN SAMARIA.

4. Those therefore dispersed, taken as a substantive. (Comp. 1 : 6.) The clause is illative [or inferential] as well as resumptive, since it was in consequence of the persecution (v. 1) that the disciples were led to new fields of labor.—**Went abroad**—lit. **through;** *i. e.* different places. Luke intimates the circuit of their labors more fully in 11 : 19. [**Preaching the word.** The word is the truth in respect to Christ and salvation; and preaching is announcing this word as good news. The violent dispersion of these earnest disciples resulted in a rapid diffusion of the gospel. In a simple, unofficial, but effective way the message of life was carried to multitudes who might not have heard it for a long time if the members of the church in Jerusalem had been suffered to abide peaceably in that city. Thus even persecution has been made to further the cause which it sought to destroy.— A. H.]

5 Then ^aPhilip went down to the city of Samaria, and preached Christ unto them.
6 And the people with one accord gave heed unto those things which Philip spake, hearing and seeing the miracles which he did.
7 For ^bunclean spirits, crying with loud voice, came out of many that were possess d *with them :* and many taken with palsies, and that were lame, were healed.
8 And there was great joy in that city.
9 But there was a certain man, called Simon, which

5 about preaching the word. And Philip went down to the city of Samaria, and proclaimed unto them
6 the Christ. And the multitudes gave heed with one accord unto the things that were spoken by Philip, when they heard, and saw the signs which
7 he did. ¹For *from* many of those who had unclean spirits, they came out, crying with a loud voice: and many that were palsied, and that were lame,
8 were healed. And there was much joy in that city.
9 But there was a certain man, Simon by name, who

a ch. 6 : 5....*b* Mark 16 : 17.——1 Or, *For many of those who had unclean spirits that cried with a loud voice came forth*

5. This is the **Philip** mentioned in 6 : 5 and 21 : 8 ; not the apostle of that name, for he remained still at Jerusalem. (See v. 1.) **Having come down,** because he journeyed from Jerusalem (v. 15) ; to go to that city was *to go up.* —**Unto the city of Samaria,** genitive of apposition (Grot., Kuin., Win., Rob.), or **a city** in that country (Olsh., Neand., De Wet., Mey.). That the capital was called *Samaria* at this time,

not the cause, but the time or occasion. (K. ? 289. 1. 2.)
7. For from many who had unclean spirits, they (the spirits) **went forth,** etc. **Many** (πολλῶν) depends on **from** (ἐξ) in the verb (Mey., De Wet.). (Comp. 16 : 39 ; Matt. 10 : 14.) Some (Bng., Kuin.) make **spirits** the subject of the verb, and supply **them** after **having** (Revis. **had**). The other is the more

RUINS OF COLONNADE OF SAMARIA.

as well as *Sebaste,* we see from Jos., *Antt.,* 20. 6. 2. **City** (πόλιν), with that reference, may omit the article, because **Samaria** defines it. (Comp. 2 Pet. 2 : 6. W. ? 19. 2.) It would be most natural to repair at once to the chief city, and it was there that such a man as Simon Magus (see v. 9) would be most apt to fix his abode.— **Multitudes,** in v. 6, indicates a populous city. If it was not the capital, it may have been Sychar, where the Saviour preached with so much effect (Olsh.). (See John 4 : 5, *sq.*)—**Unto them.** The antecedent lies in **city.** (Comp. 18 : 11 ; Matt. 4 : 23 ; Gal. 2 : 2. W. ? 67. 1. d.)
6. Attended, listened with eager interest; not *believed* (Kuin.), which anticipates the result in v. 12.—**When they heard, and saw,** etc. **In** (ἐν) with the infinitive denotes here,

natural order.—**Crying with a loud voice,** and testifying to the Messiahship of Jesus or the truth of the gospel. (Comp. Mark 3 : 11; Luke 4 : 41.) The expression would suppose the reader to be acquainted with the fuller account of such cases in the history of Christ. Some understand the cry here to have been an exclamation of rage or indignation on the part of the demons, because they were compelled to release their victims.—**And many,** etc. Here, too (see on 5 : 16), ordinary diseases are distinguished from demoniacal possession.
9–13. SIMON THE SORCERER, AND HIS PROFESSED BELIEF.
9. Simon. For the history of this impostor his character, and the traditions of the church respecting him, the reader is referred to Nean-

beforetime in the same city ^aused sorcery, and be-witched the people of Samaria, ^bgiving out that him-self was some great one:

10 To whom they all gave heed, from the least to the greatest, saying, This man is the great power of God.

11 And to him they had regard, because that of long time he had bewitched them with sorceries.

12 But when they believed Philip preaching the things ^cconcerning the kingdom of God, and the name of Jesus Christ, they were baptized, both men and women.

13 Then Simon himself believed also: and when he was baptized, he continued with Philip, and won-dered, beholding the miracles and signs which were done.

14 Now when the apostles which were at Jerusalem heard that Samaria had received the word of God, they sent unto them Peter and John:

---

beforetime in the city used sorcery, and amazed the ¹people of Samaria, giving out that himself was some

10 great one: to whom they all gave heed, from the least to the greatest, saying, This man is that power of God

11 which is called Great. And they gave heed to him, because that of long time he had amazed them with

12 his sorceries. But when they believed Philip preach-ing good tidings concerning the kingdom of God and the name of Jesus Christ, they were baptized, both

13 men and women. And Simon also himself believed: and being baptized, he continued with Philip; and beholding signs and great ²miracles wrought, he was amazed.

14 Now when the apostles who were at Jerusalem heard that Samaria had received the word of God,

---

a ch. 13 : 6....b ch. 5 : 36....c ch. 1 : 3.——1 Gr. nation....2 Gr. powers.

---

der's *Church History,* vol. i. p. 454, or his *Plant-ing of the Church,* p. 46, *sq.* (See note on v. 24.) —**Was there before**—*i. e.* the arrival of Philip—and had been for a long time. (See v. 11.)—**Using sorcery** states in what character and by what arts he secured so much power.— **Bewitching the nation,** either because he traversed the country or drew to himself crowds in the city where he dwelt.

10. From small unto great—*i. e.* both young and old. (See Heb. 8 : 11 ; Jon. 3 : 5, Sept.) The expression has been called a Hebra-ism, but examples of it occur in Greek writers (Mey.).—**This one is the great power of God**—*i. e.* through him is exhibited that power ; they supposed him to perform wonders which evinced his possession of superhuman gifts. The language is similar to that in Rom. 1 : 16, where the gospel is said to be **God's power unto salvation** [see *Bib. Sac.,* vol. xxxix. p. 171.—A. H.]—*i. e.* an instrumentality exhib-iting the power of God in the salvation of men. This is the more obvious view of the sense, and is the one commonly received. Neander would ascribe to the words a theosophic, concrete mean-ing. He supposes the Samaritans to have rec-ognized Simon "as more than a man : the great power which at first emanated from the invis-ible God, and through which he created every-thing else, had now appeared in a bodily form on the earth." It appears to be exacting too much from the language to understand it in that manner. **Saying that himself was some great one,** in v. 9 (comp. 5 : 36 ; Gal. 2 : 6), would not show that he himself carried his pretensions so far ; and the people are not likely to have conceded to him more than he claimed. — The variation ἡ καλουμένη μεγάλη (**which is called great**—*i. e.* is truly so, de-serves the epithet) is well supported (Grsb., Mey., Tsch.). [Also Lach., Treg., West. and

Hort, Anglo-Am. Revisers, with ℵ A B C D E, etc.—A. H.] De Wette thinks **called** a gloss, added to weaken the idea : **called great,** but not so in reality.

11. For a long time. The dative stands for the ordinary accusative, as in 13 : 20 ; John 2 : 20 ; Rom. 16 : 25. (W. § 31. 9 ; S. § 106. 4.)—**They had been bewitched by his sorceries** (lit. **put beside themselves**), not *he had bewitched them* (Vulg., E. V.). The perfect ἐξεστακέναι, says Scholefield (*Hints,* etc., p. 40), does not admit a transitive sense. (See also Brud., *Conc.,* s. v.). [The form here used is transitive. See 1 Macc. 10 : 20 ; 11 : 34.—A. H.] It was necessary that men delud-ed to such an extent should be reclaimed by ar-guments addressed to the senses. (See vv. 6, 7, 17.)

13. And Simon also himself believed— viz. the word preached ; *i. e.* professed to be a disciple, and was baptized in that character. The verb describes him with reference to his supposed or apparent state, not his actual posi-tion. He may have been not wholly insincere at first, but soon showed that he had no correct views of the gospel, that he was a stranger to its power. (See on v. 18.)—**Miracles,** or **pow-ers,** differs from **signs,** as explained on 2 : 22. Editors hesitate between **miracles and great signs** and **signs and great miracles.**

14–17. PETER AND JOHN ARE SENT TO SAMARIA.

14. There is no inadvertence here. The apostles had remained at Jerusalem (v. 1).— **Samaria** may be the name of the city or the country. (See on v. 5.) The application here would not control it there. Neander refers it to the country. In that case, as Philip had preached at one place only, we must regard the idea as generalized : his success there was hailed as the pledge of success in all Samaria.—**Unto them,** in that city or country ; the antecedent implied, as in v. 5.

15 Who, when they were come down, prayed for them, [a]that they might receive the Holy Ghost:
16 (For [b]as yet he was fallen upon none of them: only [c]they were baptized in [d]the name of the Lord Jesus.)
17 Then [e]laid they *their* hands on them, and they received the Holy Ghost.
18 And when Simon saw that through laying on of the apostles' hands the Holy Ghost was given, he offered them money,
19 Saying, Give me also this power, that on whomsoever I lay hands, he may receive the Holy Ghost.
20 But Peter said unto him, Thy money perish with thee, because [f]thou hast thought that [g]the gift of God may be purchased with money.

15 they sent unto them Peter and John: who, when they were come down, prayed for them, that they
16 might receive the Holy Spirit: for as yet it was fallen upon none of them: only they had been bap-
17 tized into the name of the Lord Jesus. Then laid they their hands on them, and they received the
18 Holy Spirit. Now when Simon saw that through the laying on of the apostles' hands the [1]Holy Spirit
19 was given, he offered them money, saying, Give me also this power, that on whomsoever I lay my hands,
20 he may receive the Holy Spirit. But Peter said unto him, Thy silver perish with thee, because thou hast

a ch. 2 : 38....b ch. 19 : 2;...c Matt. 28 : 19 ; ch. 2 : 38....d ch. 10 : 48; 19 : 5....e ch. 6 : 6; 19 : 6; Heb. 6 : 2....f Matt. 10 : 8;
see 2 Kings 5 : 16 ...g ch. 2 : 38; 10 : 45; 11 : 17.——1 Some ancient authorities omit *Holy.*

15. Having come down. Their imparting the Spirit was consequent on the journey hither (*post hoc*), but is not said to have been the object of it (*propter hoc*). That none but the apostles were empowered to bestow this gift has been affirmed by some and denied by others. (See 1 Tim. 4 : 14.) If it was a prerogative of the apostles (who had no successors in the church), the inference would be that it ceased with the extinction of that order. The Roman Catholics and those who entertain Roman Catholic views appeal to this scripture as showing the inferiority of the pastor to the bishop.—**Prayed,** etc. The Samaritans had received already the converting influences of the Spirit; and hence the object of the prayer was that their faith might be confirmed by a miraculous attestation. (See on 5 : 32.)—ὅπως (*that*), with the finite verb, circumscribes the infinitive. (Comp. 25 : 3; Matt. 8 : 34, De Wet.) Better here as telic, since prayer may be viewed as a necessary condition of the gift. (Comp. v. 24.)

17. Laid is the imperfect of a repeated act. For the import of the symbol, see on 6 : 6.—**And they received the Holy Spirit,** as the Author of the endowments conferred on them. Among these may have been the gift of tongues (see 2 : 4; 10 : 46), and also that of prophecy, as well as the power of working miracles. Middleton's rule is that the anarthrous πνεῦμα (**Spirit**) denotes only some effect or actual operation of the Spirit, while τὸ πνεῦμα (**the Spirit**) signifies the Divine Person in general, without reference to any particular instance or mode of operation. (See Green's *Gr.*, p. 229.) The distinction affects no question of a doctrinal nature; it may agree well enough with some passages, but is purely arbitrary in its application to others. The true principle is that stated on 1 : 2.

18–24. THE HYPOCRISY OF SIMON, AND ITS EXPOSURE.

18. θεασάμενος (which means **to see with interest,** or **desire**) has less external support than ἰδών (**to see**). Meyer retains the former, on the principle that the more common word would displace the less common, instead of the reverse. [In his last ed. Meyer accepts ἰδών as the original word. So Lach., Tsch., Treg., West. and Hort. The evidence in its favor is convincing.—A. H.] The ambition or cupidity of Simon had slumbered for a time, but was now aroused at the sudden prospect of obtaining a power which would enable him to gratify his selfish desires, which would place at his command unbounded wealth and influence. He had seen Philip perform miracles, but had seen no instance until now in which that power had been transferred to others. The interval between this development of his true character and his profession of the Christian faith was probably not long.—**Offered to them money.** This act has originated our word *simony,* which Webster defines as "the crime of buying or selling ecclesiastical preferment, or the corrupt presentation of any one to an ecclesiastical benefice for money or reward." It is fortunate for us that our religious institutions in this country require us to obtain our knowledge of the term from a lexicon.

19. To me also, that I may possess it like you; not **to me** as well as to others, since no example of such transfer was known to him.—**Upon whomsoever.** (See on 2 : 21.)—**This power** refers to v. 18—**this power,** authority, which he had seen them exercise—not to the clause following. Hence ἵνα is not definitive, *to wit, that,* but telic, *in order that.*

20. May thy money [lit. *thy silver*] **with thee** (= and thou) **perish**—lit. **be for destruction,** consigned thereto. This is the language of strong emotion; it expresses the intense abhorrence which the proposal excited in the mind of Peter. That it was not a deliberate wish or an imprecation is evident from v.

21 Thou hast neither part nor lot in this matter: for thy heart is not right in the sight of God.
22 Repent therefore of this thy wickedness, and pray God, *if perhaps the thought of thine heart may be forgiven thee.
23 For I perceive that thou art in *the gall of bitterness, and *in the bond of iniquity.
24 Then answered Simon, and said, *Pray ye to the Lord for me, that none of these things which ye have spoken come upon me.

21 thought to obtain the gift of God with money. Thou hast neither part nor lot in this ¹matter: for thy heart is not right before God. Repent therefore of this thy
22 wickedness, and pray the Lord, if perhaps the thought
23 of thy heart shall be forgiven thee. For I see that thou ²art in the gall of bitterness and in the bond
24 of iniquity. And Simon answered and said, Pray ye for me to the Lord, that none of the things which ye have spoken come upon me.

a Dan. 4 : 27 ; 2 Tim. 2 : 25....*b* Heb. 12 : 15....*c* Gen. 20 : 7, 17 ; Ex. 8 : 8 ; Num. 21 : 7 ; 1 Kings 13 : 6 ; Job 42 : 8 ; James 5 : 16.
——1 Gr. *word*....2 Or, *wilt become gall* (or, *a gall root*) *of bitterness and a bond of iniquity*

22, where the apostle points out to Simon the way to escape the danger announced to him. **With thee** some take to mean **with thee** who art in the way to destruction—*i. e.* may thy money share the doom to which thou art devoted. But the clause contains only one verb, and it is violent to make it thus optative and declarative at the same time.—**Because thou didst think,** deem it possible (aor., because the proposal made was the sin), **to acquire** (not passive, as in the Eng. V.) **the gift of God with money.** The gift stands opposed to **to acquire with money,** and hence means that which God bestows gratuitously on those who are qualified to receive it, not that which it is *his* prerogative to give in distinction from men. **21. Thou hast no part nor lot.** The first term is literal, the second figurative; they are conjoined, in order to affirm the exclusion spoken of with more emphasis. — **In this word,** doctrine or gospel, which we preach (Olsh., Neand.), or **in this thing**—viz. the gift of the Spirit (Bng., Mey., De Wet.). [Meyer's last ed. says "*in this word*"—*i. e.* in the power, or authority, to be a medium of the Spirit.—A. H.] The first sense accords better with the usage of the word, and is also stronger and more comprehensive; for if the state of his heart was such as to exclude him from the ordinary benefits of the gospel, much more must it render him unfit to receive the higher communications of the Spirit, or to be honored as the medium of conferring them on others. **22. Repent,** etc., occurs *in sensu prægnanti* for repent and turn **from this thy wickedness.** (Comp. *repentance from dead works,* in Heb. 6 : 1. W. ¿ 66. 2.)—For the received **God** after **pray,** most manuscripts read **the Lord.** —**If perhaps the thought of thy heart shall be forgiven thee.** Some idea like *and thus see if* appears to lie between the imperative and the indicative future. (See W. ¿ 41. p. 268.) Some attribute the problematical form of the expression to an uncertainty on the part of Peter whether the man had sincerely

repented or would repent of his sin. That view assigns the qualifying effect of ἄρα (**perhaps**) to the first clause, instead of the second, where it stands. Others, more correctly, find the ground of it in the aggravated nature of the sin, or in the apostle's strong sense of its aggravated nature, leading him to doubt whether he ought to represent the pardon as certain, even if he repented.—**The thought,** wicked purpose; a *vox media.*
23. For I see that thou art in the gall of bitterness. The gall of noxious reptiles was considered by the ancients as the source of their venom; and hence **gall,** with an allusion to that fact, becomes an expressive metaphor to denote the malice or moral corruption of the wicked. (Comp. this with Job 20 : 14; Rom. 3 : 13.) **Root of bitterness,** in Heb. 12 : 15, is a different figure. **Bitterness** describes a quality of **gall,** and is equivalent to an adjective, **bitter gall** (see on 7 : 30); so that, transferring the idea from the figure to the subject, the expression imports the same as *malignant, aggravated depravity.*—**And in the bond of iniquity**—*i. e.* not only wicked in principle, but confirmed in the habit of sin, bound to it as with a chain.—εἰς (lit. *unto*) belongs also to the second clause, and in both cases implies the idea of abandonment to the influence or condition spoken of.
24. Pray ye, etc. We may infer from Luke's silence as to the subsequent history of Simon that the rebuke of the apostles alarmed only his fears—that it produced no reformation in his character or his course of life. This conclusion would be still more certain, if it were true, as some maintain, that this Simon was the person whom Josephus mentions under the same name as the wicked accomplice of the Procurator Felix (*Antt.,* 20. 7. 2). Neander held at one time that they were the same, but afterward receded from that opinion. So common a name is no proof of their identity, and it is proof against it that this Simon, according to Justin Martyr, belonged to Samaria, while the other is said to have been a native of Cyprus.

25 And they, when they had testified and preached the word of the Lord, returned to Jerusalem, and preached the gospel in many villages of the Samaritans.

26 And the angel of the Lord spake unto Philip, saying, Arise, and go toward the south unto the way that goeth down from Jerusalem unto Gaza, which is desert.

25 They therefore, when they had testified and spoken the word of the Lord, returned to Jerusalem, and preached the gospel to many villages of the Samaritans.

26 But an angel of the Lord spake unto Philip, saying, Arise, and go [1]toward the south unto the way that goeth down from Jerusalem unto Gaza: the

1 Or, at noon

25-35. CONVERSION OF THE ETHIOPIAN.

25. And they—viz. Peter and John, probably unattended by Philip.—**Preached** (εὐηγγελίσαντο, T. R.) may state the result of their labors while they had been absent, or what took place on their return to Jerusalem. The latter view agrees best with the order of the narrative, and is required if we read **were returning** and **were preaching** (Lchm., Mey., Tsch.). [Add Treg., West. and Hort, Anglo-Am. Revisers after א A B C D E.—A. H.] This verb, according to a later Grecism (Lob., *Ad Phryn.*, p. 267), may take its object in the accusative, as well as the dative. (Comp. v. 40; 14 : 15, 21; 16 : 10; Luke 3 : 18; Gal. 1 : 9. W. ℓ 32. 1.)

26. But (δέ) answers to μέν in v. 25.—**Spake,** etc. Philip appears to have received this direction in Samaria (v. 13), and soon after the departure of the apostles. Zeller conjectures (*Theol. Jahrb.*, 1851) that he had come back to Jerusalem in the mean time; but the terms of the communication are against that view.— **Arise** involves an idiom explained in the note on 9 : 18.—**Go.** For the tense, see on 3 : 6.— **Down to the south,** because in Samaria he was so far to the north of Jerusalem. This expression points out, not the direction of the road from Jerusalem to Gaza, but that in which Philip was to travel, in order to find the road. The collocation joins the words evidently to the verb, and not, as some have represented, to the clause which follows.—**Gaza** was about sixty miles south-west from Jerusalem.—**This is desert.** Some refer the pronoun to **Gaza,** and, as that city was demolished a short time before the destruction of Jerusalem, they suppose that Luke by **desert** would describe its condition in consequence of that event. This is the opinion of Hug, Scholz, Meyer (formerly), Lekebusch, and others. But, unless Luke wrote the Acts later than A. D. 64 or 65 (see *Introduction*, ℓ 5), this explanation cannot be correct; for Gaza was not destroyed by the Romans till after the commencement of the Jewish war which resulted in the overthrow of Jerusalem. Most of the critics who contend

for a later origin of the book derive their chief argument for it from this assumed meaning of **desert.** But further, even supposing Luke to have written just after the destruction of Gaza, it appears improbable that the novelty merely of the event would lead him to mention a circumstance so entirely disconnected with his history. Others refer **this** to **way,** but differ on the question whether we are to ascribe the words to Luke or the angel. According to Bengel, Olshausen, Winer (*Realw.,* i. p. 395), De Wette, and others, they form a parenthetic remark by Luke, who would give the reader an idea of the region which was the scene of so memorable an occurrence. I prefer this opinion to any other. According to some, the words belong to the communication of the angel, and were intended to point out to the evangelist the particular road on which he would find the eunuch. In that case it seems to me that the relative pronoun would have introduced them more naturally than **this** (yet see W. ℓ 22. 4); and besides, if it were so that any one road to Gaza was known as "desert" beyond others, *Luke* may have inserted the epithet for the *reader's* information, as well as the angel for the sake of Philip. "There were several ways," says Dr. Robinson, "leading from Jerusalem to Gaza. The most frequented at the present day, although the longest, is the way by Ramleh. Anciently there appear to have been two more direct roads—one down the great Wady es-Surar by Beth-Shemesh, and then passing near Tell es-Safieh; the other through Wady el-Musurr to Betogabra or Eleutheropolis, and thence to Gaza through a more southern tract " (*Bibl. Res.,* ii. p. 640, or p. 514, ed. 1856). Another route still proceeded by the way of Bethlehem and Bethzur to Hebron, and then turned across the plain to Gaza. It passed through the southern part of Judea, and hence through a region actually called "the desert" in Luke 1 : 80. This description would apply, no doubt, to some part of any one of the roads in question. The Hebrews termed any tract "a desert" which was thinly inhabited or unfitted for tillage. (See more on v. 36.) Lange[1] spiritualizes

1 *Das apostolische Zeitalter,* zweiter Band, p. 109.

27 And he arose and went: and, behold, *a man of Ethiopia, an eunuch of great authority under Candace queen of the Ethiopians, who had the charge of all her treasure, and *had come to Jerusalem for to worship,

28 Was returning, and sitting in his chariot read Esaias the prophet.

29 Then the Spirit said unto Philip, Go near, and join thyself to this chariot.

30 And Philip ran thither to *him*, and heard him read the prophet Esaias, and said, Understandest thou what thou readest?

27 same is desert. And he arose and went: and behold, a man of Ethiopia, a eunuch of great authority under Candace, queen of the Ethiopians, who was over all her treasure, who had come to Jerusalem

28 for to worship; and he was returning and sitting in his chariot, and was reading the prophet Isaiah.

29 And the Spirit said unto Philip, Go near, and join

30 thyself to this chariot. And Philip ran to him, and heard him reading Isaiah the prophet, and said

---

a Zeph. 3 : 10....*b* John 12 : 20.

---

the expression : *this is desert* (morally), the angel's reason why the evangelist should seek to enlighten also this benighted region.

27. An Ethiopian may refer to the country where he resided (comp. 2 : 9) or to his extraction. Hence some suppose that the eunuch was a Jew who lived in Ethiopia, but most that he was a heathen convert to Judaism. Observe the meaning of **Ethiopians** in the next clause. It was customary for proselytes, as well as foreign Jews, to repair to Jerusalem for worship. (Comp. 20 : 2; John 12 : 20.)—**A eunuch,** in the proper import of the word ; not a minister of state, **courtier,** to the exclusion of that import, because it would then render **of great authority** superfluous. The latter term, *a state officer*, is a noun both in form and usage (De Wet., Rob.), and is not to be translated as an adjective with **eunuch** (Kuin., Mey.[1]).—**Candace, the queen of the Ethiopians.** Ethiopia was the name of the portion of Africa known to the ancients south of Egypt, of which Meroe, a fertile island formed by two branches of the Nile, constituted an important part. Win., *Realw.*, ii. p. 439 : "It is evident both from Strabo and Dio that there was a queen named Candace in Ethiopia who fought against the Romans about the twenty-second or twenty-third year of the reign of Augustus Cæsar. (Dio calls her queen of the *Ethiopians dwelling above Egypt.*) It is clear also from Pliny, who flourished in the reign of the Emperor Vespasian, that there was a queen of Ethiopia named Candace in his time; and he adds that this had been the name of their queens now for many years. It is beyond all doubt, therefore, that there was a queen of Ethiopia of this name at the time when Philip is said to have converted [baptized] the eunuch. Eusebius tells us that this country continued to be governed by women even to his time." (See Biscoe, p. 47.) "Candace" was the name, not of an individual, but of a dynasty, like "Pharaoh" in Egypt or "Cæsar" among the Romans.—**Over** (as in

12 : 20) **the treasure.—In order to worship** proves, not that he was a Jew, but that he was not a heathen.

28. Was reading, aloud, as we see from v. 30, and probably the Greek text, not the Hebrew, since the Septuagint was used mostly out of Palestine. It is still a custom among the Orientals, when reading privately, to read audibly, although they may have no particular intention of being heard by others.[2] It was common for the Jews to be occupied in this way, especially when they were travelling (Schöttg., *Hor. Heb.*, ii. p. 443).—It is not improbable that the eunuch had heard at Jerusalem of the death of Jesus and of the wonderful events connected with it —of his claim to be the Messiah, and the existence of a numerous party who acknowledged him in that character. Hence he may have been examining the prophecies at the time that Philip approached him, with reference to the question how far they had been accomplished in the history of the person concerning whom such reports had reached him. The extraordinary means which God employed to bring the Ethiopian to a knowledge of the gospel, and the readiness with which he embraced it, authorize the belief that in this way, or some other, his mind had been specially prepared for the reception of the truth.

29. Attach thyself to this chariot, keep near it, follow it. He heard the eunuch read for a time unobserved before he addressed him.

30. Dost thou understand then what thou readest? γε serves to render the question more definite. The answer after ἆρα is more commonly negative. (Comp. Luke 18 : 8. Klotz, *Ad Devar.*, ii. p. 180, *sq.*; W. ? 57. 2.) This is given as the rule for prose.—γινώσκεις ἃ ἀναγινώσκεις (*ginōskeis ha anaginōskeis*) is a paronomasia (comp. 2 Cor. 3 : 2), and is too striking to be accidental. Philip spoke, no doubt, in Greek, and would arouse the mind through the ear.

---

[1] [Meyer's last ed. agrees with Dr. Hackett's explanation.—A. H.]

[2] See Jowett's *Researches in Syria*, p. 443.

31 And he said, How can I, except some man should guide me? And he desired Philip that he would come up and sit with him.

32 The place of the scripture which he read was this, ^aHe was led as a sheep to the slaughter ; and like a lamb dumb before his shearer, so opened he not his mouth:

33 In his humiliation his judgment was taken away : and who shall declare his generation? for his life is taken from the earth.

34 And the eunuch answered Philip, and said, I pray thee, of whom speaketh the prophet this? of himself, or of some other man?

35 Then Philip opened his mouth, ^band began at the same scripture, and preached unto him Jesus.

31 Understandest thou what thou readest? And he said, How can I, except some one shall guide me? And he besought Philip to come up and sit with

32 him. Now the place of the scripture which he was reading was this,
He was led as a sheep to the slaughter ;
And as a lamb before his shearer is dumb,
So he openeth not his mouth:

33 In his humiliation his judgment was taken away :
His generation who shall declare?
For his life is taken from the earth.

34 And the eunuch answered Philip, and said, I pray thee, of whom speaketh the prophet this? of him-

35 self, or of some other? And Philip opened his mouth, and beginning from this scripture, preached

a Isa. 53 : 7, 8....*b* Luke 24 : 27 ; ch. 18 : 28.

31. For how could I—? The form of the reply attaches itself to the implied negative which precedes.—**Should guide,** instruct, similar to John 16 : 13.

32. Now the contents (comp. 1 Pet. 2 : 6) **of the passage** (De Wet., Mey.) ; not **of the scripture** in general, *section,* because **scripture,** being limited by the relative clause, must denote the particular place *which he was reading.* (Comp. v. 35; Luke 4 : 21.)—**Was this**—viz. Isa. 53 : 7, 8, quoted almost *verbatim* from the Septuagint.—**Was led**—*i. e.* Heb. *ëbhedh, the servant of Jehovah,* or the Messiah.— **And as a lamb,** etc. This comparison represents the uncomplaining submission with which the Saviour yielded himself to the power of his enemies. The death of Christ was so distinctly foretold in this passage that Bolingbroke was forced to assert that Jesus brought on his own crucifixion by a series of preconcerted measures, merely to give the disciples who came after him the triumph of an appeal to the old prophecies.[1]

33. In his humiliation, etc., admits most readily of this sense : **In his humiliation**— *i. e.* in the contempt, violence, outrage, which he suffered—**his judgment was taken away** —viz. the judgment due to him ; he had the rights of justice and humanity withheld from him. The Hebrew yields essentially the same meaning : **Through violence and punishment he was taken away**—*i. e.* from life (De Wet.).—**And his generation who shall fully declare?**—*i. e.* set forth the wickedness of his contemporaries in their treatment of him (Mey., De Wet., Rob.). The Hebrew sustains fully that translation. It is possible, also, to render the Greek and the original thus: **Who shall declare his posterity,** the number of his spiritual descendants or fol-

lowers? The prophet in this case points, by an incidental remark, from the humiliation of Christ to his subsequent triumph, or glorification. Hengstenberg prefers the last meaning.[2] [The same is true of Meyer in his last ed., thus: " **But his offspring who shall describe?** —*i. e.* How indescribably great is the multitude of those belonging to him, of whom he will now be the family Head (comp. Phil. 2 : 10) ! **for . . . his life is taken away from the earth ;** so that he enters upon his heavenly work relieved from the trammels of earth."—A. H.]—**For his life** conforms to the first sense of the clause which precedes better than to the second.

34. Addressing (see 3 : 12), or **answering,** in further reply to the question in v. 30 (Mey.). The passage from Isaiah is cited for the information of the reader, and this verse follows historically after v. 31.—**Of himself,** etc. The perplexity of the eunuch in regard to the application of the prophecy indicates that he was a foreigner rather than a Jew. The great body of the Jewish nation understood this portion of Isaiah to be descriptive of the character and sufferings of the Messiah.[3] "The later Jews," says Gesenius, " no doubt relinquished this interpretation, in consequence of their controversy with the Christians."

35. Opening his mouth is an imperfect Hebraism—*i. e.* was not peculiar to the Hebrew or Hellenistic writers, but most common in them. (See W. ? 3.) It arises from the Oriental fondness for the minute in description, the circumstantial. The expression occurs properly before important, weighty remarks. (Comp. 10: 34 ; Job 3 : 1 ; 32 : 20.)—**And beginning from the same scripture** is elliptical for **and beginning from this passage** and proceeding thence to others. (W. ? 66. 1. c.)

[1] Chalmers, *Evidences of Christianity,* chap. vi.

[2] For a fuller view of the original passage, the reader is referred to Hengstenberg's *Christology,* vol. i. p. 518, *sq.,* and to Professor Alexander's *Commentary on Isaiah.*

[3] See the proofs in Hengstenberg's *Christology,* vol. i. p. 484, *sq.,* and Schöttgen's *Horæ Hebraicæ,* vol. .¹. p. 647, *sq*

36 And as they went on *their* way, they came unto a certain water: and the eunuch said, See, *here is* water; *a*what doth hinder me to be baptized?

37 And Philip said, *b*If thou believest with all thine heart, thou mayest. And he answered and said, *c*I believe that Jesus Christ is the Son of God.

38 And he commanded the chariot to stand still: and

36 unto him Jesus. And as they went on the way, they came unto a certain water; and the eunuch saith, Behold, *here is* water; what doth hinder me to 38 be baptized?[1] And he commanded the chariot to

---

a ch. 10 : 47....*b* Matt. 28 : 19; Mark 16 : 16....*c* Matt. 16 : 16; John 6 : 69; 9 : 35, 38; 11 : 27; ch. 9 : 20; 1 John 4 : 15; 5 : 5, 13.——

[1] Some ancient authorities insert, wholly or in part, ver. 37 *And Philip said, If thou believest with all thy heart, thou mayest. And he answered and said, I believe that Jesus Christ is the Son of God.*

36–40. THE BAPTISM OF THE EUNUCH.

36. On their way, along (5 : 15) **the way.** —**Unto a certain water,** not **some,** as the genitive would follow that partitive sense. (C. ? 362. β.)—**What hinders** (what objection is there) **that I should be baptized?** This is the modest expression of a desire on the part of the eunuch to declare his faith in that manner, provided the evangelist was willing to administer the ordinance to him. (Comp. 10 : 47.) As De Wette remarks, the question presupposes that Philip, among other things, had instructed him in regard to the nature and necessity of baptism. As the road on which the eunuch journeyed is unknown (see on v. 26), it cannot be ascertained where he was baptized. It may interest the reader to state some of the conjectures. Eusebius and Jerome concur in saying that it took place at Bethzur (Josh. 15 : 58; Neh. 3 : 16), near Hebron, about twenty miles south of Jerusalem. The site has been identified, bearing still the ancient name. The water there at present issues from a perennial source, a part of which runs to waste in the neighboring fields, and a part is collected into a drinking-trough on one side of the road, and into two small tanks on the other side. It was formerly objected that no chariot could have passed here, on account of the broken nature of the ground; but travellers have now discovered the traces of a paved road and the marks of wheels on the stones. (See Ritter's *Erdkunde,* xvi. 1. p. 266, and Wilson's *Lands of the Bible,* i. p. 381.) The writer found himself able to ride at a rapid pace nearly all the way between Bethlehem and Hebron. The veneration of early times reared a chapel on[1] the spot, the ruins of which are still to be seen. Von Raumer defends the genuineness of this primitive tradition. In the age of the crusaders the baptism was transferred to Ain Haniyeh, about five miles south-west of Jerusalem. A fountain here on the hillside, which irrigates freely the adjacent valley, is known among the Latins as "St. Philip's Fountain." One of the ancient roads to Gaza passed here, but appears to have been less trav-

elled than the others. Dr. Robinson thinks that the parties must have been nearer to Gaza at the time of the baptism, and would refer the transaction to a wady in the plain near Tell el-Hasy. (*Bibl. Res.,* ii. p. 641; or p. 514, 1856.) [Dr. Thomson (*The Land and the Book,* new ed., 1880) supposes that Philip set out from Samaria, and on that hypothesis remarks: "He would then have met the chariot somewhere south-west of Lâtrôn. There is a fine stream of water, called Mârûbah, deep enough in some places even in June to satisfy the utmost wishes of our Baptist friends. This Mârûbah is merely a local name for the great Wady Sûrar, given to it on account of copious fountains which supply it with water during summer."—A. H.]

37. This verse is wanting in the best authorities. The most reliable manuscripts and versions testify against it. The few copies that contain the words read them variously. Meyer suggests that they may have been taken from some baptismal liturgy, and were added here that it might not appear as if the eunuch was baptized without evidence of his faith. Most of the recent editors expunge the verse. (In regard to the passage, see Green's *Developed Criticism,* p. 97, and Tregelles *On the Text of the N. T.,* p. 269.) Yet the interpolation—if it be such—is as old, certainly, as the time of Irenæus; and Augustine, in the fourth century, though he objected to a certain misuse of the text, did not pronounce it spurious. (See Humphry's note here.) Those who contend for the words remind us that the oldest manuscripts represent a later age than that of these Fathers. Bornemann puts them in brackets, as entitled still to some weight.—**The Son of God** is the predicate after **is.**

38. And he ordered (viz. the charioteer) **that the carriage should stop—lit. stand.** An instructive use of the word for 9 : 7. The eunuch's equipage corresponded with his rank. —**And both went down into the water,** not here **unto it** (which εἰς may also mean), for it stands opposed to **out of the water** (ἐκ τοῦ ὕδατος), in the next verse; besides, they

---

[1] *Palästina,* von Karl von Raumer (1850), p. 411, *sq.*

they went down both into the water, both Philip and the eunuch; and he baptized him.

39 And when they were come up out of the water, the Spirit of the Lord caught away Philip, that the eunuch saw him no more: and he went on his way rejoicing.

40 But Philip was found at Azotus: and passing

stand still: and they both went down into the water, both Philip and the eunuch; and he baptized him.

39 And when they came up out of the water, the Spirit of the Lord caught away Philip; and the eunuch saw him no more, for he went on his way rejoicing.

40 But Philip was found at Azotus: and passing through

a 1 Kings 18 : 12 ; 2 Kings 2 : 16 ; Ezek. 3 . 12, 14.

would have occasion to enter the stream, or pool, in order to be baptized into it. (Comp. **was baptized into the Jordan,** in Mark 1 : 9. See Rob., *Lex.,* p. 118.) [Dr. Plumptre, in Ellicott's *New Test. Commentary,* says : "The Greek preposition (*i. e.* εἰς) might mean simply 'unto the water,' but the universality of immersion in the practice of the early church supports the English Version."—A. H.] The preposition in κατέβησαν (**went down**) may refer to the descent from the higher ground to the water,

clause, but is put here for the sake of brevity. —Tradition says that the eunuch's name was Indich, and that it was he who first preached the gospel in Ethiopia. It is certain that Christianity existed there at an early period, but its introduction, says Neander, cannot be traced to any connection with his labors.

40. But Philip, etc., not *was* = ἦν (Kuin.), but **was found at** (lit. **unto,** from the idea of the journey thither) **Azotus**—*i. e.* was next heard of there, after the transaction in the

CÆSAREA.

or to the entrance into the water, but not to the descent from the chariot, for this verb corresponds to ἀνέβησαν in v. 39, **they went up,** whereas the eunuch only returned to the carriage.

39. Out of the water (ἐκ τοῦ ὕδατος), where some render **from,** which confounds ἐκ with ἀπό.—**The Spirit of the Lord seized** (hurried away) **Philip.** The expression asserts that he left the eunuch suddenly, under the impulse of an urgent monition from above, but not that the mode of his departure was miraculous in any other respect. This last certainly is not a necessary conclusion.—**For he went his way,** returned to his country, **rejoicing. Rejoicing** belongs logically to a separate

desert. This place was the ancient Ashdod, a city of the Philistines, near the sea-coast. The ruins consist of a mound covered with broken pottery, and of a few pieces of marble. (See Amos 1 : 8.) A little village not far off, called Esdud, perpetuates the ancient name.—**Cities** does not depend on the participle, but on the verb, as in v. 25. Among the towns through which he passed between Azotus and Cæsarea must have been Lydda and Joppa. Cæsarea was Philip's home. Here we find him again, after the lapse of more than twenty years, when the Saul who was now "breathing menace and murder against the disciples" was entertained by him as a Christian guest. (See 21 : 8.)—Luke's narrative brings us frequently to *Cæsarea.* It

through he preached in all the cities, till he came to Cæsarea.

he preached the gospel to all the cities, till he came to Cæsarea.

CHAPTER IX.

AND *a*Saul, yet breathing out threatenings and slaughter against the disciples of the Lord, went unto the high priest,

2 And desired of him letters to Damascus to the synagogues, that if he found any of this way, whether they were men or women, he might bring them bound unto Jerusalem.

1 BUT Saul, yet breathing threatening and slaughter against the disciples of the Lord, went unto the high

2 priest, and asked of him letters to Damascus unto the synagogues, that if he found any that were of the Way, whether men or women, he might bring

a ch. 8 : 3 ; Gal. 1 : 13 ; 1 Tim. 1 : 13.

---

was about sixty miles north-west from Jerusalem, on the Mediterranean, south of Carmel. It was the ancient *Tower of Strato*, which Herod the Great had rebuilt and named "Cæsarea" in honor of Augustus. It was now the residence of the Roman procurators. Its inhabitants were mostly heathen ; the Jewish population was small. (For an account of this city in its splendor and in its present state of desolation, see Conybeare and Howson's *Life and Epistles of St. Paul*, vol. ii. p. 344, *sq.*)

1-9. CHRIST APPEARS TO SAUL ON THE WAY TO DAMASCUS.

1. But turns the attention again to Saul.— **Yet** connects this verse with 8 : 3.—**Breathing menace and murder.** In 26 : 11, *being exceedingly mad.* The figure is founded apparently on the fact that a person under the excitement of strong emotion breathes harder and quicker, pants, struggles to give vent to the passion of which he is full (Wetst., Kyp., Kuin., Olsh.). *To breathe of something* (πνεῖν τινος), to be redolent, is a different expression. The genitive in this construction denotes properly that from or out of which one breathes, as the cause, source ; the accusative, that which one breathes, as the substance, element. (See W. § 30. 9. c ; Mt. § 376.) Meyer translates ἐμπνέων, *inhaling ;* but ἐν in this compound was generally lost. (See Tromm's *Concord.*, s. v.) [In his last ed. Meyer expresses a different opinion, in substantial accord with that of Dr. Hackett, thus : "In ἐμπνέων observe the *compound*, to which *against the disciples*, belonging to it, corresponds ; so that the word signifies *to breathe hard at* or *upon* an object."—A. H.]—**The high priest.** If Saul was converted in A. D. 36, **the high priest** was Jonathan, the successor of Caiaphas (deposed in A. D. 35), and a son of Ananus, or Annas ; but if he was converted in A. D. 37 or 38, the high priest was Theophilus, another son of Annas.

2. Letters, which were not merely commendatory, but armed him with full power to

execute his object. (See v. 14 ; 26 : 12.) For the apostle's age at this time, see on 7 : 58. The Jews in every country recognized the Sanhedrim as their highest ecclesiastical tribunal. In 26 : 10 (comp. v. 14, below), Paul says that he received his authority from the **high priests ;** and in 22 : 5, from the **presbytery ;** which are merely different modes of designating the Sanhedrim. (See on 4 : 5.) He says here that he had his commission from the high priest, which harmonizes entirely with the other passages, since the high priest represented the Sanhedrim in this act. On receiving Saul's application, he may have convened that body, and have been formally instructed to issue the letters. The proposal was sufficiently important to engage the attention of the entire council.—**To Damascus** states the local designation of the letters. This ancient capital of Syria was still an important city and had a large Jewish population. It lay north-east of Jerusalem, distant about one hundred and forty miles, making, for those times, a rapid journey of five or six days. The route of Saul on this expedition can only be conjectured. If the Roman roads in Syria had been opened as early as this, he went, probably for the sake of despatch, by the way of Bethel or Gophna to Neapolis, crossed the Jordan near Scythopolis, the ancient Bethshean (now Beisan), and proceeded thence to Gadara, a Roman city, and so through the modern Hauran to Damascus. By another track, which coincided in part with the preceding, he passed along the base of Tabor, crossed the Jordan a few miles above the Sea of Tiberias (where Jacob's Bridge now is), and then either ascended to Cæsarea Philippi, at the foot of Hermon, or turned more abruptly to the right, and traversed the desert, as before, on the east of Anti-Lebanon. (For the details, see Conybeare and Howson's *Life and Epistles of Paul*, vol. i. p. 83 : Scribner, 1854.) —**Unto the synagogues**—*i. e.* the officers of them, who were the **rulers of the synagogue** (Luke 8 : 49), and the **elders** associated with them (Luke 7 : 3). The former term was sometimes ap-

3 And *as he journeyed, he came near Damascus: and suddenly there shined round about him a light from heaven:
4 And he fell to the earth, and heard a voice saying unto him, Saul, Saul, *why persecutest thou me?
5 And he said, Who art thou, Lord? And the Lord said, I am Jesus whom thou persecutest: *it is hard for thee to kick against the pricks.
6 And he trembling and astonished said, Lord, *what wilt thou have me to do? And the Lord *said unto him, Arise, and go into the city, and it shall be told thee what thou must do.

3 them bound to Jerusalem. And as he journeyed, it came to pass that he drew nigh unto Damascus: and suddenly there shone round about him a light out
4 of heaven: and he fell upon the earth, and heard a voice saying unto him, Saul, Saul, why persecutest
5 thou me? And he said, Who art thou, Lord? And
6 he *said, I am Jesus whom thou persecutest: but rise, and enter into'the city, and it shall be told thee what

a ch. 22 : 6 ; 26 : 12 ; 1 Cor. 15 : 8....*b* Matt. 25 : 40, *&c.*....*c* ch. 5 : 39....*d* Luke 3 : 10 ; ch. 2 : 37 ; 16 : 30.

plied to them both. (See 13 : 15; Mark 5 : 22.) These rulers formed a college, whose province it was, among other duties, to punish those who deserted the Jewish faith. (De Wet., *Heb. Archæol.*, § 244.) Hence it belonged to them to discipline those who joined the Christian party, or, as it was proposed in this instance to carry them to Jerusalem, it was their duty to aid Saul in his efforts to apprehend the delinquents.— **The way**—*i. e.* κατ᾽ ἐξοχήν, **of the** (well-known Christian) **way,** in regard to faith, manner of life, etc. (Comp. 19 : 9, 23; 22 : 4 ; 24 : 14, 22. See the idea expressed more fully in 16 : 17; 18 : 25. W. § 18. 1.) **Way** depends on **that were** (E. V.) under the rule of appurtenance, property. (K. § 273. 2; C. § 387.)

3. Now while he journeyed, it came to pass (Hebraistic) **that he,** etc. — Damascus (Δαμασκῷ) depends on the verb (K. § 284. 3. 2), not the dative of the verb *whither*.—**A light gleamed around him.** The preposition in the verb governs **him.** In 22 : 6 it is repeated, according to the rule stated on 3 : 2. In 22 : 6, Paul says that the light which he saw was a *powerful* light, and in 26 : 13 that it exceeded the splendor of the sun at noonday. That Luke's statement is the more general one, while the intenser expressions occur in Paul's recital, is what we should expect from the truth of the history.

4. Having fallen to the earth, probably from the animal which he rode. (See 22 : 7.)— **Heard,** etc. (See also 22 : 7; 26 : 14.) The necessary inference is that Saul heard audible words, and not merely that an impression was made upon him as if he heard them. It was a part of the miracle that those who accompanied him heard the voice of the speaker, but failed to distinguish the words uttered. The communication was intended for Saul, and was understood, therefore, by him only.

5. Who art thou, Lord? He did not know yet that it was Christ who addressed him. Hence **Lord** has the significance which belongs to it as recognizing the fact that an angel, or perhaps God himself, was now speaking to him from heaven. To suppose it used

by anticipation—*i. e.* as denoting him who proved to be Christ — makes it Luke's word, and is unnatural. Yet Saul's uncertainty could have been but momentary : "Conscientia ipsa facile diceret, Jesum esse " [" His own conscience would readily suggest that it was Jesus "] (Bng.). —The remainder of the verse, as it stands in the common text—viz. **it is hard,** etc.—has been transferred to this place from 26 : 14. (See Green's *Developed Criticism,* p. 98.)

6. Most of the manuscripts begin this verse with **but.** The sentence **trembling . . . to do?** (which the English translation has copied) is wanting in the best authorities. It rests chiefly upon some of the early versions. The words **And the Lord** *said* **unto him** have been derived from 22 : 10.—**But** (ἀλλά) occurs often before a command abruptly given. (Comp. 10 : 20; 26 : 16. W. § 53. 7; K. § 322; R. 12.)— **And it shall be told thee,** etc. It would appear from the speech before Agrippa (see 26 : 16-18) that Christ may have made to Saul at this time a fuller communication than Luke has reported in this place. The verb here (**it shall be told thee,** etc.) does not exclude that supposition ; for it may import that on his arrival in the city he should be confirmed in what he had now heard, or instructed further in regard to his future labors. But some prefer to consider Paul's narrative before Agrippa as the abridged account. The message which Ananias delivered to Saul (intimated here in v. 15, but recorded more fully in 22 : 14-16) was a message from Christ ; and, as the apostle makes no mention of Ananias in 26 : 16, *sq.*, it is very possible that he has there, for the sake of brevity passed over the intermediate agency and referred the words directly to Christ which Christ communicated to him through Ananias. This would be merely applying the common maxim, *Quod quis per alium facit, id ipse fecisse putatur* [" What one does through another, that he is supposed to have done himself "].— *What thou must do* is the answer, probably, to Saul's question τί ποιήσω, *What shall I do?* recorded in 22 : 9. **Must** refers, not to duty, but the divine purpose, destination. (See 22 : 10.)

7 And *a*the men which journeyed with him stood speechless, hearing a voice, but seeing no man.

8 And Saul arose from the earth; and when his eyes were opened, he saw no man: but they led him by the hand, and brought *him* into Damascus.

7 thou must do. And the men that journeyed with him stood speechless, hearing the [1]voice, but behold-

8 ing no man. And Saul arose from the earth; and when his eyes were opened, he saw nothing; and they led him by the hand, and brought him into

---

a Dan. 10 : 7 ; see ch. 22 : 9 ; 26 : 13.——1 Or, *sound*

---

7. Were standing (see on 1 : 10) **speechless,** having stopped instantly, overcome by amazement and terror. (Comp. *were afraid,* in 22 : 9.) The adjective is more correctly written ἐνεοί. (W. § 5. 1.) This verb often means *to stand,* not as opposed to other attitudes, but to be fixed, stationary, as opposed to the idea of motion. (Comp. 8 : 38 ; Luke 5 : 2. See the *Class. Lexx.,* s. v.) In this sense the passage is entirely consistent with 26 : 14, where it is said that when they heard the voice *they all fell to the ground.* Plainly, it was not Luke's object to say that they stood erect, in distinction from kneeling, lying prostrate, and the like, but that, overpowered by what they saw and heard, they were fixed to the spot—they were unable for a time to speak or move. The conciliation which some adopt (Bng., Kuin., Bmg.) is that they fell to the ground at first, but afterward rose up and stood. It is unnecessary to urge this view ; but Zeller's objection to it — that εἱστήκεισαν, as pluperfect, excludes a previous falling—is ungrammatical.—**Hearing indeed the voice.** The genitive after this verb points out the source or cause of the hearing ; the accusative (see v. 4), that which one hears. (See the note on v. 1.) In 22 : 9, Paul says, in reference to the same occurrence, τὴν δὲ φωνὴν οὐκ ἤκουσαν τοῦ λαλοῦντός μοι, which we may render *but they understood not the voice of him speaking to me.* In adding *who spake* the writer shows that he had in mind the sense of φωνήν (*voice*), and not the mere sound. **To hear** (ἀκούω), like the corresponding word in other languages, means not only **to hear,** but to hear so as **to understand.** Of the latter usage the New Testament furnishes other clear examples. 1 Cor. 14 : 2 : "For he that speaketh in an unknown tongue, speaketh not unto men, but unto God ; for no man understands him "—lit. *no one heareth.* (Comp. v. 16, where *heareth* passes into *understandeth.*) Mark 4 : 33 : "And with many such parables spake he the word unto them, as they were able to understand it "—lit. *as they were able to hear.* Some reckon here John 6 : 60, Gal. 4 : 21, and other passages. (For instances of this sense in the classics, see Rob., *Lex.,* s. v.) The same usage exists in the Hebrew. One of the definitions of *shama* (see Gesen., *Lex.,* s. v.) is *to understand.* In Gen. 42 : 23 it is said

that Joseph's brethren "knew not that he heard them "—*i. e. understood,* in the E. V.— " for he spoke unto them by an interpreter." (See also Gen. 11 : 7.) The English language has the same idiom. We say that a person is not heard, or that we do not hear him, when, though we hear his voice, he speaks so low or indistinctly that we do not understand him. The intelligence of the writer of the Acts forbids the idea of a palpable contradiction in the two passages. Since in 22 : 9 we have φωνήν (*voice*) in the accusative case, and here in v. 7 in the genitive, φωνῆς, some would attribute to the latter a partitive sense—*i. e. something of the voice,* or indistinctly. But the difference does not hold ; for, in 22 : 7, Paul says of himself **I heard** *a voice* (φωνῆς genitive), where he cannot mean that he had only a confused perception of what was said to him. Some prefer to vary the sense of φωνή—viz. *noise* or *sound* in this place, but *voice* in 22 : 9. But, allowing the word to admit of that distinction (see on 2 : 6), it is much less common than the proposed variation in *to hear,* and much less probable here, since the use of the verb would be varied in passages so remote from each other, whereas φωνή would have different senses in almost successive verses.—**But seeing no one** who could have uttered the voice. This appears to be denied of Saul's companions, in opposition to what was true of him—viz. that simultaneously with the light he had seen a personal manifestation of Christ. (Comp. v. 17 ; 22 : 18.) That he saw the speaker as well as heard him, we may infer from the language of Barnabas in v. 27, and that of Ananias in v. 17 and 22 : 14. To the fact of his having a view of the glorified Saviour at this time Paul alludes, probably, in 1 Cor. 9 : 1, where he mentions his having seen the Lord as an evidence of his equality with the other apostles. (See the note on 1 : 3.) Neander, De Wette, Meyer, Osiander, Thiersch, and others find such an allusion in that passage.

8. And when his eyes were opened— *i. e.* his eyelids, which he had spontaneously closed when struck with the gleaming light. This expression refers usually to the recovery of one's eyesight, as in Matt. 9 : 30 ; John 9 : 10, 20, etc.—**Saw no one**—*i. e.* of his companions, because he was now blind ; or, which is a better reading, **saw nothing,** and hence

9 And he was three days without sight, and neither did eat nor drink.

10 ¶ And there was a certain disciple at Damascus, *named Ananias; and to him said the Lord in a vision, Ananias. And he said, Behold, I *am here*, Lord.

11 And the Lord *said* unto him, Arise, and go into the street which is called Straight, and inquire in the house of Judas for *one* called Saul, *b*of Tarsus: for, behold, he prayeth,

12 And hath seen in a vision a man named Ananias coming in, and putting *his* hand on him, that he might receive his sight.

9 Damascus. And he was three days without sight, and did neither eat nor drink.

10 Now there was a certain disciple at Damascus, named Ananias; and the Lord said unto him in a vision, Ananias. And he said, Behold, I *am here*,

11 Lord. And the Lord *said* unto him, Arise, and go to the street which is called Straight, and inquire in the house of Judas for one named Saul, a man of

12 Tarsus: for behold, he prayeth; and he hath seen a man named Ananias coming in, and laying his

a ch. 22 : 12....*b* ch. 21 : 39; 22 : 3.

being unable to see at all, must be led by the hand; not **no one** from whom the voice came (Bng.), since we must have here an explanation of the next clause.

9. Without sight (subjective negative), **not seeing,** as opposed to a possible idea of the reader that Saul might have regained his sight ere this; whereas οὐ (objective), in the next clause, states the historical fact. (W. § 55. 5.) Meyer, in his last edition, recalls his remark that the negatives are interchanged here.

DAMASCUS—STRAIGHT STREET.

10–18. ANANIAS IS SENT TO SAUL, AND BAPTIZES HIM.

10. That **Ananias** was one of the seventy disciples is an unsupported conjecture of some

of the older writers.—**The Lord**—*i. e.* Christ. (See v. 17.)—**Behold me** = Heb. *Hinnēnē*. This answer implies that the person hears and waits to listen further. (Comp. Gen. 22 : 1, 7 ; 27 : 1; 1 Sam. 3 : 8, etc.)

11. For **arise,** see on v. 18.—ῥύμην, **street,** or more strictly **alley,** lane (comp. Luke 14 : 21) = στενωπός (**narrow passage**) in the later Greek. (See Lob., *Ad Phryn.*, p. 40, and R. and P., *Lex.*, s. v.)—**Which is called Straight.** The principal street in Damascus at present runs through the city from east to west, and is remarkably straight in some parts, as well as narrow. The Oriental Christians say that this is the street in which Saul lodged. The traces of a triple colonnade are reported to be found in the adjacent houses on both sides of the street; and if so, they show that the present street, though not so wide, follows at least the line of an ancient street of the city. But even in that case it may be questioned whether ῥύμη would be applied to a thoroughfare adorned with works of so much splendor.—**A native of Tarsus** (22 : 3). (See on v. 30.)—**For he prays.** The act is then taking place, and is mentioned as a reason why Ananias might be sure of a favorable reception. He is informed of the vision also because that served in like manner to prepare the way for his visit.

12. And saw a man (made known to him in the vision as) **Ananias by name,** a breviloquence like that in 15 : 9.—**Placing hand upon** *him,* as a sign of the benefit which he was to be the medium of communicating. (Comp. on 6 : 6.) The expression is indefinite, like that in 12 : 1. Lachmann thinks the authority sufficient to read **his hands,** as in v. 17. [Tsch., Treg., West. and Hort, Anglo-Am. Revisers, also give the plural **hands,** either with or without the article, represented properly in English by **his.** **His hands** may therefore be accepted as the true reading.—A. H.]—**Might look up,** open his eyes and see. This sense is not common out of the New Testament. It is found (a case not usually cited) at the close of Plut., *De sera Num. vindicta.*

13 Then Ananias answered, Lord, I have heard by many of this man, *how much evil he hath done to thy saints at Jerusalem:
14 And here he hath authority from the chief priests to bind all *that call on thy name.
15 But the Lord said unto him, Go thy way: for *he is a chosen vessel unto me, to bear my name before *the Gentiles, and *kings, and the children of Israel:
16 For *I will shew him how great things he must suffer for my name's sake.
17 *And Ananias went his way, and entered into the house; and *putting his hands on him said, Brother Saul, the Lord, even Jesus, that appeared unto thee in the way as thou camest, hath sent me, that thou mightest receive thy sight, and *be filled with the Holy Ghost.

13 hands on him, that he might receive his sight. But Ananias answered, Lord, I have heard from many of this man, how much evil he did to thy saints at 14 Jerusalem: and here he hath authority from the chief priests to bind all that call upon thy name. 15 But the Lord said unto him, Go thy way: for he is a *chosen vessel unto me, to bear my name before the Gentiles and kings, and the children of Israel: 16 for I will shew him how many things he must suffer 17 for my name's sake. And Ananias departed, and entered into the house; and laying his hands on him said, Brother Saul, the Lord, even Jesus, who appeared unto thee in the way which thou camest, hath sent me, that thou mayest receive thy sight,

a ver. 1....b ver. 21; ch. 7 : 59; 22 : 16; 1 Cor. 1 : 2; 2 Tim. 2 : 22....c ch. 13 : 2; 22 : 21; 26 : 17; Rom. 1 : 1: 1 Cor. 15 : 10; Gal. 1 : 15; Eph. 3 : 7, 8; 1 Tim. 2 : 7; 2 Tim. 1 : 11....d Rom. 1 : 5; 11 : 13; Gal. 2 : 7, 8....e ch. 25 : 22, 23; 26 : 1, etc....f ch. 20 : 23; 21 : 11; 2 Cor. 11 : 23....g ch. 22 : 12, 13....h ch. 8 : 17....i ch. 2 : 4; 4 : 31; 8 : 17; 13 : 52.——1 Gr. vessel of election.

13. The reply of Ananias shows how fearful a notoriety as a persecutor Saul had acquired. (Comp. 26 : 10.)—**How great evils.—Unto thy saints**—i. e. those consecrated to him, and so his. This term as applied in the New Testament refers to the normal or prescribed standard of Christian character, rather than the actual one. (See 1 Cor. 1 : 2, as compared with 1 Cor. 3 : 2; 11 : 21, etc.) It belongs to all who profess to be disciples, and does not distinguish one class of them as superior to others in point of excellence.

14. Hath authority. Ananias may have received letters from the Christians at Jerusalem, or those who came with Saul may have divulged the object of the journey since their arrival.—**Those who call upon,** invoke in prayer, **thy name.** (Comp. 2 : 21; 7 : 59; 1 Cor. 1 : 2.) This participle is middle, not passive. The Greek for *those on whom thy name is called* would be like that in 15 : 17. The expression here is the one which the Seventy commonly use to translate *kara bhĕshĕm*, a well-known formula in the Old Testament signifying *to worship.* Gesenius (*Lex.*, p. 938) says with reference to this phrase: *To call on the name of God* is to invoke his name—i. e. to praise, celebrate, worship God. Of course, we are to attach the same meaning to the words in the New Testament. Hence this language, which states a fact so characteristic of the first Christians that it fixed upon them the name of *callers upon Christ,* shows that they were accustomed to offer to him divine honor. (See on 7 : 59.)

15. A vessel (2 Cor. 4 : 7), instrument, **of choice** —i. e. a chosen instrument. For this use of the genitive, see on 7 : 30. The similar examples in Greek belong rather to poetry. It is a common idiom in Hebrew. (Gesen. *Heb. Gr.,* § 104.)—**To bear** continues the metaphor in

vessel (Alf.).—**Kings,** rulers of the highest class. (Comp. 17 : 7; John 19 : 15.) Paul stood as a witness for Christ before the Governors of Cyprus, Achaia, and Judea, and before Herod Agrippa, and probably Nero.— **Children of Israel.** The progress of the narrative will show how faithfully he executed this part of his mission. Though he was the great apostle of the Gentiles, he never ceased to preach to his countrymen.

16. For I will show him, by experience— will cause him to learn in the course of his life (Bng., Mey.). According to De Wette, it means that God would teach him by revelation; but this verb is not employed to denote the communication of knowledge in that manner. The statement here confirms the declaration that Saul would accomplish so much for the cause of Christ, **for** (γάρ) he was to suffer much, and his labors would be efficient in proportion to his sufferings.

17. Said, etc. The address of Ananias to Saul is reported more fully in 22 : 14, *sq.* He salutes him as **brother** (ἀδελφέ)—not as of the same stock nationally (2 : 29; 21 : 1; 28 : 17), but as having now "obtained like precious faith" with himself. He could apply that title to Saul with confidence after having received such information in regard to the state of his mind and the sphere of labor to which Christ had called him.—**Jesus, who appeared, . . . camest.** Luke's account of the communication to Ananias passes over this part of it.—**Which** (ᾗ) in this clause, **in which,** omits the preposition, because the antecedent has it (a species of attraction). (Comp. *to which I have called* in 13 : 2. Mat. § 595. 4. c.)—**And mayest be filled with the Holy Spirit**—i. e. receive abundantly the extraordinary gifts and qualifications which he would need as an apostle (Comp. Gal. 2 : 7, *sq.* See the note on 1 : 8.)

18 And immediately there fell from his eyes as it had been scales: and he received sight forthwith, and arose, and was baptized.

19 And when he had received meat, he was strengthened. *Then was Saul certain days with the disciples which were at Damascus.

20 And straightway he preached Christ in the synagogues, *that he is the Son of God.

21 But all that heard *him* were amazed, and said; *Is not this he that destroyed them which called on this name in Jerusalem, and came hither for that intent, that he might bring them bound unto the chief priests?

22 But Saul increased the more in strength, *and confounded the Jews which dwelt at Damascus, proving that this is very Christ.

23 ¶ And after that many days were fulfilled, *the Jews took counsel to kill him:

18 and be filled with the Holy Spirit. And straightway there fell from his eyes as it were scales, and he received his sight; and he arose and was baptized; and he took food and was strengthened.

And he was certain days with the disciples who were at Damascus. And straightway in the synagogues he proclaimed Jesus, that he is the Son of God. And all that heard him were amazed, and said, Is not this he that in Jerusalem made havock of them who called on this name? and he had come hither for this intent, that he might bring them bound before the chief priests. But Saul increased the more in strength, and confounded the Jews who dwelt at Damascus, proving that this is the Christ.

23 And when many days were fulfilled, the Jews took

---

a ch. 26 : 20....b ch. 8 : 37....c ch. 8 : 3; ver. 1; Gal. 1 : 13, 23....d ch. 18 : 28....e ch. 23 : 12; 25 : 3; 2 Cor. 11 : 26.

---

18. There fell off from his eyes as if scales. This means that he experienced a sensation as if such had been the fact. **As if** shows that it was so in appearance, not in reality. (Comp. 2 : 3; 6 : 15, etc.) The nature of the injury which his eyes had suffered we cannot determine, but it is certain that the recovery from the injury was instantaneous and complete. We may suppose that Luke had often heard Paul relate how he felt at that moment.—**Having risen up,** and (if need be) gone forth to the place of baptism. (Comp. Luke 4 : 38. See Rob., *Lex.*, s. v. ii. 1. a), or simply **having made himself ready**—*i. e.* without delay. (Comp. Luke 15 : 18.) On this Hebraistic use of the word, see Gesen., *Lex.*, p. 919; W. § 65. 4. c. It is impossible to infer from it that he was baptized in the house of Judas, or that he was not. Damascus at the present day abounds in water, and all the better houses have a reservoir in their court or stand beside a natural or an artificial stream. (See Robinson, vol. iii. p. 400.) — **Having taken food,** after the fast of the three days. (See v. 9.)

19-23. THE LABORS OF PAUL AT DAMASCUS.

19. With the disciples, in private intercourse with them.—**Certain days** denotes too brief a period to apply to the entire residence at Damascus (Neand., De Wet., Mey.).

20. And immediately, after the days spent in the society of the Christians there.—**Preached Jesus that he is,** etc. = **preached that Jesus is,** etc. (See on 3 : 10.) **Jesus** is the individual or personal name of the Saviour; and it was the apostle's object to establish the identity of Jesus with the Son of God or the promised Messiah. (Comp. v. 22.)

21. Who destroyed, put to death. (See 22 : 3.)—**This name**—viz. that of Jesus (v. 20). The form of the remark adapts itself to the

narrative.—**Hither,** after a verb of motion; *here* in v. 14.—**For that intent** anticipates the next clause.—For **chief priests,** see on 4 : 6. —The astonishment expressed here proceeded from the Jews, whom Paul addressed in the synagogues. Most of the Christians at Damascus must have been apprised of the change in his character before he appeared in public.

22. But Saul was more strengthened— *i. e.* in his faith. (See 16 : 5; Rom. 4 : 20.) This remark describes his state after the lapse of some time subsequent to his conversion. It is made, apparently, not merely to indicate his Christian progress, but to suggest why he preached with such convincing power.—**Proving that this one is the Christ. This** recalls **Jesus,** in v. 20—the more readily because τοῦτο intervenes in v. 21.

23-25. THE FLIGHT OF PAUL FROM DAMASCUS.

23. Now when many days were accomplished. At this place, probably, we are to insert the journey into Arabia, which the apostle mentions in Gal. 1 : 17. So Neander, Hemsen, Meyer, and others. That Luke makes no allusion to this journey agrees with the summary character of his history generally, in relation to the early portion of Paul's life. It will be observed he does not say that the "many days" were all spent at Damascus, but that many had elapsed since his first arrival, before the escape which took place under the circumstances narrated. Hence the language leaves us at liberty to suppose that he passed more or less of the intermediate period elsewhere. The time that Paul was absent in Arabia belongs, probably, to the earlier part of the **many days,** rather than the latter; for in Gal. 1 : 17 he mentions Arabia before Damascus, as if the former country was the first important scene of his apostleship. The time which he spent in Arabia formed, not improb-

24 *a*But their laying await was known of Saul. And they watched the gates day and night to kill him.

25 Then the disciples took him by night, and *b*let *him* down by the wall in a basket.

26 And *c*when Saul was come to Jerusalem, he assayed to join himself to the disciples: but they were all afraid of him, and believed not that he was a disciple.

27 *d*But Barnabas took him, and brought *him* to the apostles, and declared unto them how he had seen the Lord in the way, and that he had spoken to him, *e*and

24 counsel together to kill him: but their plot became known to Saul. And they watched the gates also

25 day and night that they might kill him: but his disciples took him by night, and let him down through the wall, lowering him in a basket.

26 And when he was come to Jerusalem, he assayed to join himself to the disciples: and they were all afraid of him, not believing that he was a disciple.

27 But Barnabas took him, and brought him to the apostles, and declared unto them how he had seen

---

a 2 Cor. 11 : 32....*b* So Josh. 2 : 15 ; 1 Sam. 19 : 12....*c* ch. 22 : 17 ; Gal. 1 : 17, 18....*d* ch. 4 : 36 ; 13 : 2....*e* vers. 20, 22.

---

ably, a large part of the three years before his return to Jerusalem; for that supposition explains best the fact that he was still so unknown there as a Christian. (See v. 26.) Some critics, as Olshausen, Ebrard, Sepp,[1] would place the excursion into Arabia between v. 25 and v. 26. The objection to that view is that the apostle must then have come back to Damascus (**returned again into Damascus** in Gal. 1 : 17), in the face of the deadly hostility on the part of the Jews which had already driven him from that city.

24. Became known by Saul, to him. For the dative after the passive, see on 5 : 9. The discovery enabled the apostle to escape the danger. — **Were watching the gates**—*i. e.* with the aid of soldiers whom the governor placed at their disposal, so that the act of guarding the city could be ascribed to the Jews, as in this passage, or to the ethnarch, as in 2 Cor. 11 : 32. The Jews at this time were influential as well as numerous at Damascus, and could easily enlist the government on their side.—**Through the wall,** and at the same time *through a window through the wall,* as is stated in 2 Cor. 11 : 33—*i. e.* as commonly understood through the window of a house overhanging the wall. (Comp. Josh. 2 : 15 ; 1 Sam. 19 : 12.) Houses are built in that manner in Eastern countries at the present day. A woodcut representing such a window may be seen in Conybeare and Howson, vol. i. p. 124.[2]—**In a basket.** That those who aided Paul's escape should have used a basket for the purpose was entirely natural, according to the present customs of the country. It is the sort of vehicle which people employ there now if they would lower a man into a well or raise him into the upper story of a house. (See *Illustrations of Scripture,* p. 69.)

26–31. PAUL RETURNS TO JERUSALEM, AND FROM THERE GOES TO TARSUS.

26. This is Paul's first journey to Jerusalem since his conversion, and took place in A. D. 39. (See *Introduct.,* § 6. 1.) His motive for this step, as he states in Gal. 1 : 18, was that he might make the acquaintance of Peter.—**To join himself,** etc., *to associate* with them as one of their own faith. — **Were all afraid,** etc. If Paul had spent most of the last three years at Damascus, we should suppose that the report of his labors during that time would have reached Jerusalem and prepared the way for his more cordial reception. On the contrary, if he had been withdrawn for the most part from their knowledge, in the more retired region of Arabia, it is less surprising that they now regarded him with suspicion. [Especially if, with Davies, in Smith's *Dict. of the Bible,* Am. ed., p. 2366, we suppose that he was "seeking seclusion (there), in order that, by conferring, '*not with flesh and blood,*' but with the Lord in the Spirit, he might receive more deeply into his mind the commission given him at his conversion."—A. H.] The language, according to either view, it will be observed, does not affirm that they had never heard of his conversion, but that they could not readily persuade themselves that it was sincere. The sudden appearance of Voltaire in a circle of Christians, claiming to be one of them, would have been something like this return of Saul to Jerusalem as a professed disciple.

27. Barnabas stood high among the disciples at Jerusalem (4 : 36; 11 : 22). No one out of the circle of the apostles could have interposed a more powerful word in behalf of Saul. —**Unto the apostles**—viz. Peter and James (Gal. 1 : 19). The other apostles were probably absent from Jerusalem at this time.—**Related**

---

[1] *Das Leben Christi,* von Dr. Joh. Nep. Sep, Band iv. p. 47.

[2] Possibly another explanation may be the correct one. A few steps to the left of Bab-es-Shurkeh, the gate on the east side of Damascus, I observed two or three windows in the external face of the wall, opening into houses on the inside of the city. If Saul was let down through such a window (which belongs equally to the house and the wall), it would be still more exact to interchange the two expressions—that is, we could say, as in the Acts, that he escaped "through the wall," or, as in the Epistle to the Corinthians, that he escaped "through a window through the wall."

how he had preached boldly at Damascus in the name of Jesus.

28 And *a*he was with them coming in and going out at Jerusalem.

29 And he spake boldly in the name of the Lord Jesus, and disputed against the *b*Grecians: *c*but they went about to slay him.

30 *Which* when the brethren knew, they brought him down to Cæsarea, and sent him forth to Tarsus.

the Lord in the way, and that he had spoken to him, and how at Damascus he had preached boldly 28 in the name of Jesus. And he was with them going 29 in and going out of Jerusalem, preaching boldly in the name of the Lord: and he spake and disputed against the 1Grecian Jews; but they went about to 30 kill him. And when the brethren knew it, they brought him down to Cæsarea, and sent him forth to Tarsus.

a Gal. 1 : 18....*b* ch. 6 : 1 ; 11 : 20....*c* ver. 23 ; 2 Cor. 11 : 26.——1 Gr. *Hellenists.*

fully, since they may have heard a report of the occurrence, but had received no definite information concerning it. He could add, also, his own personal testimony to the truth of what had come to their ears.—**How he had preached boldly.** He had been himself, probably, a witness of Paul's zeal at Damascus ; and for that reason, and because his labors there were more recent, he says nothing of the residence in Arabia. —**In the name of Jesus,** as the sphere of his preaching (Mey.) ; not in virtue of authority from him.

28. Was with them, during fifteen days, as we learn from Gal. 1 : 18.—**Going in and go-**

29. To the Hellenists. (See note on 6 : 1.) He addressed himself to them because he himself was a foreign Jew and was familiar with the Greek, which they also spoke. It has been conjectured that one of the festivals may have been in progress at this time, and that these Hellenists had come to Jerusalem on that account. (Comp. John 12 : 20.)—**Went about, attempted.** Imperfect, because they were seeking the opportunity to kill him. We are not to suppose that they had ventured as yet on any open act.

30. But the brethren having ascertained—viz. their hostile design. Paul de-

TARSUS.

ing out—*i. e.* in the exercise of his ministry, as results from the next clause. For the import of this Hebraism, see on 1 : 21.

parted, in conformity with their advice. We learn from 22 : 17 that another motive concurred with this: he was informed in a vision

31 *Then had the churches rest throughout all Judæa and Galilee and Samaria, and were edified ; and walking in the fear of the Lord, and in the comfort of the Holy Ghost, were multiplied.

31 So the church throughout all Judæa and Galilee and Samaria had peace, being ¹edified ; and, walking ²in the fear of the Lord and ²in the comfort of the Holy Spirit, was multiplied.

a See ch. 8 : 1.——1 Gr. *builded up*....2 Or, *by*

that God would have him occupy a different field of labor. Without that revelation he might have thought it best to remain, in defiance of the present danger, and notwithstanding the importunity of his friends. (Comp. 21 : 13.) It is a mark of truth that we find Luke stating the outward impulse ; the apostle, the inner ground.—In **brought . . . down** the preposition marks the descent to the sea-coast. —For **Cæsarea,** see on 8 : 40. For the route hither from Jerusalem, see on 23 : 31.—**And they sent him forth to Tarsus.** This city was the capital of Cilicia, on the river Cydnus. It possessed at this time a literary reputation which rivalled that of Athens and Alexandria. It had received important political privileges both from Antony and Augustus, but did not enjoy the right of Roman citizenship. (See the note on 22 : 29.)—We might conclude from the statement here that Paul went directly to Tarsus by sea. That inference, it has been said, contradicts Gal. 1 : 21, where, speaking of his journey, Paul puts Syria before Cilicia, as if he went to the latter country through the former. It is to be noticed that these two countries are always named in that order (see 15 : 23, 41), and that order agrees with the land-route from Jerusalem to Cilicia, which was the one more commonly taken. Hence, Paul may have adhered to that order in Gal. 1 : 21 from the force of association, though in this instance he went first to Cilicia, and from there made missionary excursions into Syria. But if any one prefers, he can suppose, with De Wette, that Paul took ship at Cæsarea, and then landed again at Seleucia ; or, with Winer, Rückert, and others, that Syria, in the Epistle to the Galatians, included a part of the region between Jerusalem and Cæsarea. The term had sometimes that wider sense. Some have fixed on Cæsarea [Philippi] in the North of Palestine as the place meant here ; but in that case the epithet which distinguishes the less celebrated city from the other would have been added, as in Matt. 16 : 13 ; Mark 8 : 27. — In these regions of Syria and Cilicia, Paul remained four or five years ; for he went thither from Jerusalem in A. D. 39 (see on v. 26), and left for Antioch in A. D. 43 (see on 11 : 26). That he was occupied during this time in laboring for the spread of the gospel is not only to be inferred from the character of the man, but is expressly stated in Gal. 1 : 21-23. Further, in the sequel of the narrative (15 : 23, 41) we find churches existing here, the origin of which is unknown, unless we suppose that they were planted by Paul's instrumentality at this time. It is not an irrelevant reflection which Conybeare and Howson suggest—that during this residence of Paul in his native land "some of those Christian 'kinsmen,' whose names are handed down to us (Rom. 16 : 7, 11, 21)—possibly his sister, the playmate of his childhood, and his sister's son, who afterward saved his life (23 : 16, *sq.*) — may have been gathered by his exertions into the fold of Christ." The apostle reappears next in 11 : 25.

31-35. PETER PREACHES AT LYDDA, AND HEALS A PARALYTIC.

31. The churches now . . . had peace —*i. e.* rest from the persecution which they had suffered since the death of Stephen. It had continued for three years (see v. 26), if the subject of this paragraph be next in order after the preceding one. It is not certain that Luke mentions the cause of this respite. As Lardner, De Wette, and others suggest, it may have been owing to the troubles excited by the order of Caligula to have his image set up in the temple. (Jos., *Antt.*, 18. 8. 2-9.) The Jews may have been too much engrossed by their opposition to that measure to pursue the Christians. οὖν in that case takes up again the main thread of the history after the digression relating to Paul. Meyer makes it strictly illative from vv. 3-30, as if the peace was the result of Paul's conversion and labors. But, as he began to act on the side of the Christians so soon after the death of Stephen, we should then have too brief an interval for the persecution. Copies vary between **churches** and **church,** but favor the latter. [*E. g.* א A B C and others ; so that it is adopted by Lach., Tsch., Treg., West. and Hort, Anglo-Am. Revisers. "Observe," says Meyer, "with the correct reading, . . . the aspect of *unity*, under which Luke, *surveying the whole domain of Christendom*, comprehends the churches which had been already formed (Gal. 1 : 22) and were in course of formation. (Comp. 16 : 5.) The external bond of this unity was the apostles ; the internal, the Spirit ; Christ the one Head ; the forms of the union were not yet more fully developed than by the gradual institution of presbyters (11 : 30) **and**

32 ¶ And it came to pass, as Peter passed *through-out all *quarters*, he came down also to the saints which dwelt at Lydda.
33 And there he found a certain man named Æneas, which had kept his bed eight years, and was sick of the palsy.
34 And Peter said unto him, Æneas, *b*Jesus Christ maketh thee whole: arise, and make thy bed. And he arose immediately.
35 And all that dwelt at Lydda and *c*Saron saw him, and *d*turned to the Lord.
36 ¶ Now there was at Joppa a certain disciple named Tabitha, which by interpretation is called Dorcas: this woman was full *e*of good works and almsdeeds which she did.
37 And it came to pass in those days, that she was sick, and died: whom when they had washed, they laid *her* in *f*an upper chamber.

32 And it came to pass, as Peter went throughout all parts, he came down also to the saints who dwelt at
33 Lydda. And there he found a certain man named Æneas, who had kept his 1bed eight years; for he
34 was palsied. And Peter said unto him, Æneas, Jesus Christ healeth thee: arise, and make thy 1bed.
35 And straightway he arose. And all that dwelt at Lydda and in Sharon saw him, and they turned to the Lord.
36 Now there was at Joppa a certain disciple named Tabitha, who by interpretation is called 2Dorcas: this woman was full of good works and almsdeeds
37 which she did. And it came to pass in those days, that she fell sick, and died: and when they had washed her, they laid her in an upper chamber.

a ch. 8 : 14....*b* ch. 3 : 6, 16; 4 : 10....*c* 1 Chron. 5 : 16....*d* ch. 11 : 21....*e* 1 Tim. 2 : 10; Tit. 3 : 8....*f* ch. 1 : 13.———1 Or, pallet....2 That is, *Gazelle.*

deacons.''—A. H.]—**Galilee.** This is our only notice of the existence of churches in that native land of the apostles.—**Being built up**— *i. e.* in faith and piety. (See 1 Cor. 8 : 1 ; 14 : 4 ; 1 Thess. 5 : 11, etc.) It is contrary to usage to understand it of external organization. It does not refer to the increase of numbers, since that is the idea of the verb which follows. The E. V. makes this participle a verb, and separates it from its natural connection in the sentence.—**Walking.** A common Hebraism (see Heb. *halak*) to denote a course of conduct. —**In the fear of the Lord,** in conformity with that state of mind; dative of rule or manner. (W. ₰ 31. 6. b.)—**And in the comfort,** etc. (E. V.), belongs, not to **walking,** but to **were** (or **was**) **multiplied,** of which it assigns the cause: **and by the aid,** persuasive energy (Kuin., Mey., Rob.), **of the Holy Spirit were multiplied.** That sense of παρακλήσει (**comfort**) [from the same verb as Paraclete, *Comforter* (E. V.)—A. H.] is not certain. De Wette: The power of consolatory discourse conferred by the Spirit on those who preached. (Comp. 4 : 36.)

32. Peter may have left Jerusalem soon after the departure of Paul. (See on v. 27.)—**Passing through all** the believers in that part of the country. After **all** supply **saints** (Bng., Mey., De Wet.); not **places** (Kuin., Wiesl.). (Comp. 20 : 25 ; Rom. 15 : 28.) The narrative assumes that the gospel had been preached here already (see 8 : 44), and this was a tour of visitation.—**Also** includes the saints at Lydda among the **all.** In crossing the plain from Yafa, or Joppa, to Ramleh the traveller sees a village with a tall minaret in the south-east, and on inquiring the name is told that it is Lud or Lid. It stands on the ancient line of travel between Jerusalem and Cæsarea. It is the modern representative **of** the Lydda in our text.

33. His name may indicate that **Æneas** was

a Greek or Hellenistic Jew. He was probably a believer, as faith was usually required of those who received the benefits of the gospel.—**Since eight years,** for so long a time.—**Bed, pallet,** as in 5 : 15.

34. Spread for thyself—*i. e.* thy bed; not in future (Kuin.), but immediately (De Wet., Mey.). Others had performed that office for him hitherto. He was now to evince his restoration by an act which had been the peculiar evidence of his infirmity. The object of the verb suggests itself; it is not strictly an ellipsis.

35. Saw him, after his recovery, whom they had known before as a confirmed paralytic.—**All** may be restricted, as suggested on 3 : 18.—**The Saron** = Heb. *hashsharōn,* **the Plain.** It extended along the sea-coast from Joppa to Cæsarea, about thirty miles. Here the part nearest to Lydda appears to be meant. Some have thought (Win., *Realw.,* ii. p. 383) that Saron may designate here a village of that name.—**Who,** influenced by the miracle, **turned unto the Lord** (see v. 42) ; not **who had turned** (Kuin.). In the latter case the import of the remark would be that the miracle was a credible one, because it was so well attested. Such an apologetic interest is foreign to Luke's manner.

36–43. PETER VISITS JOPPA.

36. Joppa (Jon. 1 : 3) was north-west from Lydda (see on v. 32), the present Japha, or Yafa, on the sea-coast.—**Tabitha** = *Tĕbhēta* is Chaldee, and means a *gazelle.* We may infer from it her Jewish origin. To her Greek friends she may have been known also by the other name.—**And** (especially) **alms,** deeds of charity ; **and** explicative.

37. Having washed, they placed her in the upper chamber, of the house where they were. As the limitation suggests itself, the article is omitted. (W. ₰ 19. 1.) It is inserted in v. 39, because there it points back to

38 And forasmuch as Lydda was nigh to Joppa, and the disciples had heard that Peter was there, they sent unto him two men, desiring *him* that he would not delay to come to them.

39 Then Peter arose and went with them. When he was come, they brought him into the upper chamber: and all the widows stood by him weeping, and shewing the coats and garments which Dorcas made, while she was with them.

40 But Peter *a*put them all forth, and *b*kneeled down, and prayed; and turning *him* to the body *c*said, Tabitha, arise. And she opened her eyes: and when she saw Peter, she sat up.

41 And he gave her *his* hand, and lifted her up, and when he had called the saints and widows, presented her alive.

42 And it was known throughout all Joppa; *d*and many believed in the Lord.

43 And it came to pass, that he tarried many days in Joppa with one *e*Simon a tanner.

---

38 And as Lydda was nigh unto Joppa, the disciples, hearing that Peter was there, sent two men unto him, intreating him, Delay not to come on unto us.

39 And Peter arose and went with them. And when he was come, they brought him into the upper chamber: and all the widows stood by him weeping, and shewing the coats and garments which 40 Dorcas made, while she was with them. But Peter put them all forth, and kneeled down, and prayed; and turning to the body, he said, Tabitha, arise. And she opened her eyes; and when she saw Peter, 41 she sat up. And he gave her his hand, and raised her up; and calling the saints and widows, he pre-42 sented her alive. And it became known through-out all Joppa: and many believed on the Lord. 43 And it came to pass, that he abode many days in Joppa with one Simon a tanner.

CHAPTER X.

THERE was a certain man in Cæsarea called Cornelius, a centurion of the band called the Italian *b*and,

1 Now *there was* a certain man in Cæsarea, Cornelius by name, a centurion of the band called the Italian

---

a Matt. 9 : 25....*b* ch. 7 : 60....*c* Mark 5 : 41, 42; John 11 : 43....*d* John 11 : 45; 12 : 11....*e* ch. 10 : 6.

---

this place. It was customary among the Hebrews for women to perform this rite; but, as Luke would specify here the act rather than the agency, he employs the masculine of the participle, equivalent to the indefinite "they." (W. § 27. 6.)

38. Nigh to governs **Joppa** (dat.) as an adverb. The distance between the places is ten or twelve miles.—**Sent.** It is not said that they sent for him with any definite expectation of a miracle. It was natural that they should desire his presence and sympathy at such a time.

39. Into the upper chamber. The body was usually kept here when, for any reason, the interment was delayed. (See Jahn's *Archæol.*, § 204; Win., *Realw.*, i. p. 467.) They had been waiting in this instance for the arrival of Peter.—**The widows,** who had been the objects of her benevolence, and who now mourned the death of their benefactress. Every one must be struck at the natural manner in which this beautiful incident is introduced.—**Tunics and coats,** such as were worn by men and women. The omission of the article (suggestive of a wrong sense as inserted in E. V.) shows that they presented specimens only of her industry. Some of the garments may have been worn by those present, and others have been laid up for future distribution.—ὅσα, **which all,** which so many, not = ἁ simply, **which.**—**Made** (imperf.), **was accustomed to make.**

40. But having put all forth, caused them to retire; not with violence. (See Mark 5 : 40; John 10 : 4.) The object may have been to secure himself from observation and inter-

ruption while he prayed with fervor and agony. Elisha pursued the same course—for the same reason, probably—when he restored to life the Shunammite's son. (See 2 Kings 4 : 33; also Matt. 9 : 25.)—**Prayed.** Peter would address his prayer to Christ; for the apostles wrought their miracles in his name. (See v. 34; 3 : 6, 16; 4 : 10.)—**Arise,** stand erect. Peter speaks as one who felt assured that his prayer had prevailed. (See Matt. 17 : 20.)

42. It became draws its subject from the context—viz. the miracle.—**Upon the Lord,** Christ, whose gospel had been so signally attested as true.

43. Peter remained here **many days,** because the place was large and the people evinced a preparation for the reception of the word.—**A tanner.** The more scrupulous Jews regarded such an occupation as unclean, and avoided those who pursued it. The conduct of Peter here shows that he did not carry his prejudices to that extent.

1–8. THE VISION OF CORNELIUS THE CENTURION.

1. ἑκατοντάρχης (**centurion**) is often interchanged with ἑκατοντάρχος (21 : 32; 22 : 25, etc.). The first is the prevalent form in the later Greek. (W. § 8. 1.) The word has a uniform termination in some copies of the text.—**Italian band.** Some suppose this **cohort** to have belonged to the *legio Italica,* or *Italica prima,* of which we read in Tacitus (*Hist.,* 1. 59, 64, etc.); but the fact stated by Dio Cassius (55. 24) is overlooked —that this legion was raised by Nero, and consequently was not in existence at this period

2 ªA devout *man*, and one that ᵇfeared God with all his house, which gave much alms to the people, and prayed to God alway.

3 ᶜHe saw in a vision evidently about the ninth hour of the day an angel of God coming in to him, and saying unto him, Cornelius.

4 And when he looked on him, he was afraid, and said, What is it, Lord? And he said unto him, Thy prayers and thine alms are come up for a memorial before God.

5 And now send men to Joppa, and call for *one* Simon, whose surname is Peter:

6 He lodgeth with one ᵈSimon a tanner, whose house is by the sea side: ᵉhe shall tell thee what thou oughtest to do.

2 ¹band, a devout man, and one that feared God with all his house, who gave much alms to the people, and 3 prayed to God alway. He saw in a vision openly, as it were about the ninth hour of the day, an angel of God coming in unto him, and saying to him, Cor- 4 nelius. And he, fastening his eyes upon him, and being affrighted, said, What is it, Lord? And he said unto him, Thy prayers and thine alms are gone 5 up for a memorial before God. And now send men to Joppa, and fetch one Simon, who is surnamed 6 Peter: he lodgeth with one Simon a tanner, whose

---

a ver. 22 ; ch. 8 : 2 ; 22 : 12 ....*b* ver. 35....*c* ver. 30 ; ch. 11 : 13....*d* ch. 9 : 43....*e* ch. 11 : 14.——1 Or, *cohort.*

---

of our narrative. While no ancient writer has left any notice confirming Luke's accuracy in this passage, it so happens that an inscription in Gruter[1] informs us that volunteer *Italian* cohorts [a volunteer Italian cohort] served in Syria—*i. e.* Italian or Roman soldiers who enlisted of their own accord, instead of being obliged to perform military service. (See *Dict. of Antt.*, art. "Velones.") It is generally supposed that the Roman cohorts, instead of being incorporated always with a particular legion, existed often separately. It is probable that such an independent cohort was now stationed at Cæsarea, called the *Italian* because it consisted of native Italians, whereas the other cohorts in Palestine were levied, for the most part, from the country itself. (See Jos., *Antt.*, 14. 15. 10; *Bell. Jud.*, 1. 17. 1. Comp. the note on 27 : 1.) It is worthy of remark, as Tholuck[2] suggests, that Luke places this *Italian* cohort precisely here. Cæsarea was the residence of the Roman procurator (see on 8 : 40), and it was important that he should have there a body of troops on whose fidelity he could rely.

2. Devout and fearing God. All the centurions in the New Testament appear in a favorable light (Hmph.). (See 27 : 3; Matt. 8 : 5; Luke 7 : 2.) The one here was a worshipper of Jehovah, but had not submitted to circumcision or avowed publicly the Jewish faith. The opinion that he was a proselyte disagrees with vv. 28, 34; 11 : 1, 8; 15 : 7, for those passages show that he was regarded by the Jews at this time as belonging still to a heathen community. Cornelius was one of those men, so numerous in this effete age of idolatry, who were yearning for a better worship, and under that impulse had embraced the pure theism of the Old Testament, so much superior to every other form of religion known to them. They attended the synagogues, heard and read the Scriptures, practised some of the Jewish rites,

and were in a state of mind predisposing them to welcome the gospel of Christ when it was announced to them. This class of persons furnished the greater part of the first Gentile converts.—**The people**—viz. of the Jews. (Comp. v. 42; 26 : 17, 23; 28 : 17.) Perhaps Luke 7 : 5 brings to view one of the ways in which he applied his benefactions.

3. In a vision may be understood of an inner or of an outward *vision* (Neand.).—**Evidently, distinctly,** applies better to a perceptive act than to an act of consciousness. **Saw** is ambiguous in that respect.—**About the ninth hour,** in the course of it; accusative of time how long. (Bernh., *Synt.*, p. 116.) This hour was one of the Jewish hours of prayer (3 : 1).

4. What is it which is designed or desired? —For **Lord,** see the remark on 9 : 5.—**Prayers** and **alms,** which belong to one verb here, are assigned to two verbs in v. 31.—**For a memorial,** as such (see on 7 : 21)—*i. e.* he was now to receive evidence of his being remembered, inasmuch as God was about to open a way for his attainment of the peace of mind which he had so anxiously sought.

5. Joppa was about thirty miles south of Cæsarea.—**Send** (μετάπεμψαι) is middle, because he was to execute the act through the agency of others. (K. § 250. R. 2; B. § 135. 8.) **Simon . . . Peter.** Both names are given, so as to prevent mistake as to the individual whom the messengers were to find. This, too, is the reason for describing so minutely his place of abode.

6. By the sea-shore—viz. that of the Mediterranean. Luke states a fact here; the ground of it we learn from other sources. The sanitary laws of the ancients, it is said, required tanners to live out of the city : "Non solum ob mortua animalia, quorum usum ipsa eorum opificii ratio efflagitabat, sed etiam ob fœtidos

---

¹ Copied in Ackerman's *Numismatic Illustrations of the Narrative Portions of the New Testament*, p. 34.
² *Die Glaubwürdigkeit der Evangelischen Geschichte*, p. 174.

7 And when the angel which spake unto Cornelius was departed, he called two of his household servants, and a devout soldier of them that waited on him continually;
8 And when he had declared all *these* things unto them, he sent them to Joppa.
9 ¶ On the morrow, as they went on their journey, and drew nigh unto the city, ^aPeter went up upon the housetop to pray about the sixth hour:
10 And he became very hungry, and would have eaten: but while they made ready, he fell into a trance,

7 house is by the sea side. And when the angel that spake unto him was departed, he called two of his household-servants, and a devout soldier of them
8 that waited on him continually; and having rehearsed all things unto them, he sent them to Joppa.
9 Now on the morrow, as they were on their journey, and drew nigh unto the city, Peter went up upon the housetop to pray, about the sixth hour:
10 and he became hungry, and desired to eat: but

a ch. 11 : 5, etc.

in eorum officinis et ædibus odores et sordes" [" Not only because of the dead animals which

EXTERIOR OF SUPPOSED HOUSE OF SIMON THE TANNER.

the nature of their business called them to use, but also because of the disagreeable odor and filth of their premises "]. (Walch, *Dissertationes*, etc., vol. i. p. 125.) The convenient prosecution of their business required that they should be near the water. **He shall tell thee,** etc., at the close of this verse in the common text, was inserted in conformity with 9 : 6; 10 : 32.

7. And when the angel, etc. He despatched the messengers, therefore, on the same day, although it was so far advanced (v. 3). (Comp. **immediately** in v. 33.)— **Which spake** (ὁ λαλῶν) must be taken as imperfect. (Comp. John 9 : 8; De Wet.) —**Of those** (*i. e.* soldiers) **who waited upon him,** who stood ready to perform those personal services which he might require. Kuinoel's idea is that they acted as a house-sentry.—**Devout** accords with the description of the centurion's family in v. 2.

9–16. THE VISION OF PETER.

9. On the morrow, after their departure from Cæsarea.—**Upon the housetop,** the roof, which, according to the Oriental manner, was flat or but slightly inclined. It was the place often chosen for the performance of religious duties (Jahn's *Archæol.*, ? 24.) The

situation does not expose one necessarily to public view. A wall or balustrade three or four feet high surrounds many of the roofs in the East, where a person may sit or kneel without being observed by others. Moses required (Deut. 22 : 8) that every house should have such a protection.

10. πρόσπεινος occurs only here. The law of analogy shows it to be intensive, **very hungry. —Desired to eat,** not **would have eaten. —While they now** (not *but*) **were preparing**—*i. e.* for the evening repast. (See v. 9.) The pronoun refers to those in the family where Peter was entertained.—**Ecstasy = in Spirit** (Rev. 1 : 10)—*i. e. a trance,* or *rapture,* whereby (if we may so express it) he was transported out of himself and put into a mental state in which he could discern objects beyond the apprehension of man's natural powers. (See 11 : 5; 22 : 17.)—In the mode of instruction which

EASTERN HOUSETOP.

God employed in this instance, he adapted himself to the peculiar circumstances in which Peter was placed. "The divine light that was making its way to his spirit revealed itself in the mirror of sensible images which proceeded from the existing state of his bodily frame" (*Neand.*).

9

11 And ^asaw heaven opened, and a certain vessel descending unto him, as it had been a great sheet knit at the four corners, and let down to the earth:

12 Wherein were all manner of fourfooted beasts of the earth, and wild beasts, and creeping things, and fowls of the air.

13 And there came a voice to him, Rise, Peter; kill, and eat.

14 But Peter said, Not so, Lord; ^bfor I have never eaten any thing that is common or unclean.

15 And the voice *spake* unto him again the second time, ^cWhat God hath cleansed, *that* call not thou common.

16 This was done thrice: and the vessel was received up again into heaven.

17 Now while Peter doubted in himself what this vision which he had seen should mean, behold, the men which were sent from Cornelius had made inquiry for Simon's house, and stood before the gate,

11 while they made ready, he fell into a trance; and he beholdeth the heaven opened, and a certain vessel descending, as it were a great sheet, let down by

12 four corners upon the earth: wherein were all manner of fourfooted beasts and creeping things of the

13 earth and fowls of the heaven. And there came a

14 voice to him, Rise, Peter; kill and eat. But Peter said, Not so, Lord; for I have never eaten any thing

15 that is common and unclean. And a voice *came* unto him again the second time, What God hath

16 cleansed, make not thou common. And this was done thrice: and straightway the vessel was received up into heaven.

17 Now while Peter was much perplexed in himself what the vision which he had seen might mean, behold, the men that were sent by Cornelius, having made inquiry for Simon's house, stood before the

a ch. 7 : 56; Rev. 19 : 11....*b* Lev. 11 : 4; 20 : 25; Deut. 14 : 3, 7; Ezek. 4 : 14....*c* Matt. 15 : 11; ver. 28; Rom. 14 : 14, 17, 20; 1 Cor. 10 : 25; 1 Tim. 4 : 4; Tit. 1 : 15.

11. Beholds, with wonder. (See on 4 : 13.) —**A certain vessel,** receptacle, which is described more definitely **as a great sheet.**— **Bound by four corners,** or ends (anarthrous, since the number was not definite of itself), **and** (thus) **let down upon the earth.** The conception of the scene suggested by the text is that of the sheet upheld by cords attached to its four points, and suspended from above by an unseen power. This is the common view, and, I think, the correct one. Meyer understands **corners** of *the four corners* of heaven— *i. e.* east, west, north, and south—to which the four ends of the sheet were fastened. Neander inclines to that interpretation. **Corners** with such a reference would seem to demand the article, as much as the translation into English and German.— Lachmann expunges **bound, and,** after A B C and some other authorities [as, at present, Tsch., Treg., West. and Hort, Anglo-Am. Revisers.—A. H.]; but probably the omission of the words in 11 : 5 led to their omission here.

12. All the quadrupeds—*i. e.* as to their varieties, not individually. The text here is confused. **Of the earth** is to be retained, no doubt, but should follow **creeping things** (Lchm., Mey., Tsch.).—**And wild beasts** before **and creeping things** is not found in the controlling manuscripts. It is evident that the text in 11 : 6 has influenced the text in this passage.

13. Rise. (See on 9 : 18.) Yet Peter may have been kneeling or reclining at that moment (Mey.).—**Slay and eat**—*i. e.* any one of the creatures exhibited to him, without regard to the distinction of clean or unclean.

14. All (πᾶν), preceded by the negative, is a Hebraism for **nothing** (οὐδέν). (Comp. Matt. 24 : 22; Rom. 3 : 20; Eph. 5 : 5.) The two modes of expression present the idea from

different points of view. That of the Hebrews excepts *everything* from the action of the verb; that of the Greeks subjects *nothing* to it. (Gesen., *Heb. Gr.,* ? 149. 1; W. ? 26. 1.)—**Common** (κοινόν) is the opposite of **holy** (ἅγιον). As this sense was unusual, the more explicit **unclean** follows.

15. What God cleansed—*i. e.* declared by this symbolic act to be clean. The aorist and perfect should not be confounded here. Verbs in Hebrew have often this declarative sense. (Comp. Lev. 13 : 3, 8, 13; 16 : 30; Ezek. 43 : 3; Jer. 1 : 10, etc. See Gesen., *Heb. Lex.,* s. *tahar.*) An approximating usage exists in Greek.— **Call not thou common.** Thou is contrasted with **God.** It is not usual to insert the first or second personal pronoun as the subject of a verb, unless it be emphatic. (K. ? 302. 1; B. ? 129. 14.) The imperative is present because he was committing the prohibited act at the time. (Comp. the note on 7 : 60.)

16. This refers to the repetition of the voice, not to the vision as seen three times. Those who understand it in the latter way overlook **again a second time,** just before. The command was reiterated, in order to impress the words more deeply on the mind of Peter.

17-22. THE MESSENGERS ARRIVE AT JOPPA.

17. Doubted, was perplexed, uncertain. —**What it might be,** signify. (Comp. Luke 8 : 9; John 10 : 6.) He must have been convinced that such a revelation was not designed merely to announce the abolition of a ceremonial custom, but was not yet evident to him how much the principle comprehended, and especially in what practical manner he was to exhibit his liberation from the scruples by which he had been bound hitherto.—**Which he had seen.** (Comp. on 1 : 2.)—**Then behold,** as in 1 : 10.—διερωτήσαντες, a strengthened

18 And called, and asked whether Simon, which was surnamed Peter, were lodged there.

19 ¶ While Peter thought on the vision, ᵃthe Spirit said unto him, Behold, three men seek thee.

20 ᵇArise therefore, and get thee down, and go with them, doubting nothing: for I have sent them.

21 Then Peter went down to the men which were sent unto him from Cornelius; and said, Behold, I am he whom ye seek: what *is* the cause wherefore ye are come?

22 And they said, ᶜCornelius the centurion, a just man, and one that feareth God, and ᵈof good report among all the nation of the Jews, was warned from God by an holy angel to send for thee into his house, and to hear words of thee.

23 Then called he them in, and lodged *them*. And on the morrow Peter went away with them, ᵉand certain brethren from Joppa accompanied him.

24 And the morrow after they entered into Cæsarea. And Cornelius waited for them, and had called together his kinsmen and near friends.

25 And as Peter was coming in, Cornelius met him, and fell down at his feet, and worshipped *him*.

18 gate, and called and asked whether Simon, who was 19 surnamed Peter, were lodging there. And while Peter thought on the vision, the Spirit said unto 20 him, Behold, three men seek thee. But arise, and get thee down, and go with them, nothing doubt-21 ing: for I have sent them. And Peter went down to the men, and said, Behold, I am he whom ye seek: what is the cause wherefore ye are come? 22 And they said, Cornelius a centurion, a righteous man and one that feareth God, and well reported of by all the nation of the Jews, was warned *of God* 23 by a holy angel to send for thee into his house, and to hear words from thee. So he called them in and lodged them.

And on the morrow he arose and went forth with them, and certain of the brethren from Joppa ac-24 companied him. And on the morrow ¹they entered into Cæsarea. And Cornelius was waiting for them, having called together his kinsmen and his near 25 friends. And when it came to pass that Peter entered, Cornelius met him, and fell down at his feet,

---

a ch. 11 : 12....*b* ch. 15 : 7....*c* vers. 1, 2, etc....*d* ch. 22 : 12....*e* ver. 45; ch. 11 : 12.——1 Some ancient authorities read *he*.

---

sense, **having inquired out.** The tanner was an obscure man, and not to be found in a moment.—**Unto the gate,** which opened directly into the house or court; not **the porch,** vestibule, since the more splendid houses only had that appendage (De Wet.). (Comp. Matt. 26 : 71.)

18. And called (see v. 7), **having called,** some one, or, without any object, **having called,** announced their presence.—**If he lodges.** The present tense turns the question into a direct form. The use of the two names again (v. 5) is not unmeaning. So many persons were called "Simon" that the strangers must be minute in their inquiry.

19. διενθυμουμένου is stronger than ἐνθυμουμένου in the common text: **earnestly considering.** The first is the better-attested word.—**Three** before **men** should be omitted. It was added from v. 7; 11 : 11.

20. But turns the discourse to a new point. (Comp. 9 : 6.)—**Making no scruple**—*i. e.* to go with them, although they are heathen.—**I = Spirit** in v. 19.—**Sent them,** not perfect (E. V.).

21. Which were sent from Cornelius to him defines **men**; and since, in the public reading of the Scriptures, a new section began here, the words were necessary, in order to suggest the connection. This accounts for our finding them in a few copies. The preponderant testimony is against them.

22. Of good report occurs as in 6 : 3.—**Was divinely instructed.** (Comp. Matt. 2 : 12.) In the classics this word refers to a communication made in reply to a question, but in the New Testament and the Septuagint it drops that relative sense.—**Words,** instruction. (Comp. **shall speak to thee** in v. 32.) The first ac-

count of the vision (v. 4, *sq.*) omits this particular.

23–33. PETER PROCEEDS TO CÆSAREA.

23. On the morrow, after the arrival of the messengers.—**Certain of the brethren.** They are the six men mentioned in 11 : 12. We are not informed of their object in accompanying the apostle. They may have gone as his personal friends merely, or from a natural desire to know the result of so extraordinary a summons. In his defence before the church of Jerusalem (see 11 : 1, *sq.*), Peter appealed to these brethren to confirm his statements. Some have conjectured that he may have foreseen the necessity of that justification, and took the precaution to secure the presence of those who would be acknowledged as impartial Jewish witnesses.

24. On the morrow, after leaving Joppa. (Comp. v. 9.) Thirty miles (see on v. 5) was more than a single day's journey in the East. It must be the truth which brings out such accuracy in these details.—For εἰς in the verb repeated before the noun, see on 3 : 2.—**His near friends,** his intimate friends. The classical writers combine the words with that meaning (Kypk., Wetst.).

25. Now as it came to pass that Peter was entering, Cornelius having met him —viz. at the door or in the court of the house. The first interview appears to have taken place there, and then the centurion and the apostle proceeded to the room where the company were assembled. (See v. 27.)—**Upon the feet**—viz. of Peter, which he may have embraced at the same time. (Comp. Matt. 28 : 9.)—**Fell down, paid reverence**—viz. by prostrating himself in the Oriental manner. Since Cornelius ac-

26 But Peter took him up, saying, *a*Stand up; I myself also am a man.

27 And as he talked with him, he went in, and found many that were come together.

28 And he said unto them, Ye know how *b*that it is an unlawful thing for a man that is to keep company, or come unto one of another nation; but *c*God hath shewed me that I should not call any man common or unclean.

26 and worshipped him. But Peter raised him up, 27 saying, Stand up; I myself also am a man. And as he talked with him, he went in, and findeth many 28 come together: and he said unto them, Ye yourselves know ¹how that it is an unlawful thing for a man that is a Jew to join himself or come unto one of another nation; and *yet* unto me hath God shewed that I should not call any man common or unclean:

a ch. 14 : 14, 15 ; Rev. 19 : 10 ; 22 : 9....*b* John 4 : 9 ; 18 : 28 ; ch. 11 : 3 ; Gal. 2 : 12, 14....*c* ch. 15 : 8, 9 ; Eph. 3 : 6.——— 1 Or, *how unlawful it is for a man etc.*

knowledged Jehovah as the true God, and must have regarded him as the only proper object of worship, it is difficult to believe that he intended this as an act of religious homage. The description of his character in v. 2 and v. 22 cannot be easily reconciled with the imputation of such a design. (See more on the next verse.)

26. Raised him up, caused him to rise by the command addressed to him.—**I also myself am a man,** as well as you. Peter may have been surprised at such a mode of salutation from a Roman, whose national habits were so different; he had reason to fear that the centurion had mistaken his character—was exceeding the proper limits of the respect due from one man to another. He recoiled at the idea of the possibility of having a homage tendered to him which might partake of the reverence that belongs only to God. In other words, it is more probable that Peter, in his concern for the divine honor, warned the centurion against an act which he apprehended, than that the centurion committed an act so inconsistent with his religious faith. That inconsistency is so much the less to be admitted, because Peter had just been represented in the vision so distinctly as a man. The apostles claimed no ability to know the hearts or thoughts of men, except as their actions revealed them. Compare with this conduct of Peter that of Paul and Barnabas at Lystra (14 : 14, *sq.*). The Saviour, on the contrary, never repressed the disposition of his disciples to think highly of his rank and character. He never reminded them of the equality of his nature with their own, or intimated that the honor paid to him was excessive. He received their homage, whatever the form in which they offered it, however excited the state of mind which prompted it. This different procedure on the part of Christ we can ascribe only to his consciousness of a claim to be acknowledged as divine.

27. Conversing with him (Whl., Rob.). (Comp. **talked** in 20 : 11; 24 : 26; Luke 24 : 14, 15.) Some render **accompanying him,** which is too self-evident to be stated so formally. The first sense is peculiar to Luke.—

Went in, perhaps into an upper room. (See on 1 : 13.)

28. ὡς may qualify the adjective, **how,** in what degree (Mey.), or the verb, **how it is** (knowledge and fact accordant).—ἀθέμιτον, **unlawful.** The Jews professed to ground this view on the laws of Moses; but they could adduce no express command for it, or just construction of any command. No one of the N. T. writers employs this word, except Peter here and in 1 Pet. 4 : 3.—**To associate with** (5 : 15), **or come unto, one of another nation.** The second verb evolves the sense of the first. **Strangers** is applied to the Philistines in 1 Sam. 13 : 3–5 (Sept.), and to the Greeks in 1 Macc. 4 : 12. It has been said that Luke has betrayed here an ignorance of Jewish customs, since the Jews, though they refused to eat with the uncircumcised (Gal. 2 : 12), did not avoid *all* intercourse with them. But the objection presses the language to an extreme. We are to limit such general expressions by the occasion and the nature of the subject. The intercourse with the Gentiles, represented here as so repugnant to Jewish ideas, was such intercourse as had now taken place: it was to enter the houses of the heathen, partake freely of their hospitality, recognize their social equality. In accordance with this, we find **to associate with** exchanged for **didst eat with** in 11 : 3; the word there may be supposed to define the word here. De Wette objects that the act of eating has not been mentioned; but it is not mentioned anywhere, and yet the subsequent accusation against the apostle alleges it as the main offence. The act was, doubtless, a repeated one. (See v. 48.) An instance of it may have preceded the utterance of the words here in question. Nothing would be more natural, at the close of such a journey, than that the travellers should be supplied with the means of refreshment before entering formally on the object of the visit. Considered in this light, Peter's declaration in this verse agrees entirely with that of Josephus (*Cont. Ap.,* 2. 28): "Those foreigners (ἀλλόφυλοι) who come to us without submitting to our laws, Moses permitted not to have any intimate connections with us." (See also *Ib.,* 2. 36. Comp. John ✠

29 Therefore came I *unto you* without gainsaying, as soon as I was sent for: I ask therefore for what intent ye have sent for me?
30 And Cornelius said, Four days ago I was fasting until this hour; and at the ninth hour I prayed in my house, and, behold, *a*a man stood before me *b*in bright clothing,
31 And said, Cornelius, *c*thy prayer is heard, *d*and thine alms are had in remembrance in the sight of God.
32 Send therefore to Joppa, and call hither Simon, whose surname is Peter; he is lodged in the house of *one* Simon a tanner by the sea side: who, when he cometh, shall speak unto thee.
33 Immediately therefore I sent to thee; and thou hast well done that thou art come. Now therefore are we all here present before God, to hear all things that are commanded thee of God.

29 wherefore also I came without gainsaying, when I was sent for. I ask therefore with what intent ye 30 sent for me. And Cornelius said, Four days ago, until this hour, I was keeping the ninth hour of prayer in my house; and behold, a man stood be- 31 fore me in bright apparel, and saith, Cornelius, thy prayer is heard, and thine alms are had in remem- 32 brance in the sight of God. Send therefore to Joppa, and call unto thee Simon, who is surnamed Peter; he lodgeth in the house of Simon a tanner, by the 33 sea side. Forthwith therefore I sent to thee; and thou hast well done that thou art come. Now therefore we are all here present in the sight of God, to hear all things that have been commanded

---

a ch. 1 : 10....*b* Matt. 28 : 3 ; Mark 16 : 5 ; Luke 24 : 4....*c* ver. 4, etc. ; Dan. 10 : 12....*d* Heb. 6 : 10.

28.)—**And** (in opposition to that Jewish feeling) **God showed me**—viz. by the vision.

29. Therefore I also came—*i. e.* he was not only instructed, but obeyed the instruction **Also** connects **came** with **showed.**—**Without gainsaying** (ἀναντιρρήτως) = **without delay** (ἀναμφιβόλως) (Hesych.). It is a later Greek word.—**With what reason,** for what object; dative of the ground or motive. (W. § 31. 6. c.) Peter was already apprised that Cornelius had sent for him, in consequence of a revelation, but would desire, naturally, to hear a fuller statement of the circumstances from the centurion himself. The recital may have been necessary, also, for the information of those who had assembled.

30. Four days ago, etc., has received different explanations. (1) **From the fourth day** (prior to the vision) **was I fasting unto this hour**—*i. e.* unto an hour corresponding to that which was then passing; viz. the ninth (Hnr., Neand., De Wet.). According to this view, Cornelius had been fasting four days at the time of the angel's appearance to him. (2) **From the fourth day** (reckoned backward from the present) **unto this hour**—*i. e.* he was observing a fast which began four days before and extended up to the time then present. It was on the first of the days that he saw the angel. But **was,** as past, represents the fast as having terminated, and so would exclude **this hour.** Meyer in his second edition abandons this view for the next. (3) **From the fourth day** (reckoning backward as before) —*i. e.* four days ago **unto this hour** in which he was then speaking (Bng., Kuin., Olsh.). The fast commenced with the day and had continued unbroken until the ninth hour, when the angel appeared. This view agrees with the number of days which had elapsed since the angel's communication—viz. four—and allows time enough for the abstinence to justify the

use of **fasting.**—ἤμην (**was**) is an imperfect middle, rare out of the later Greek. (W. § 14. 2. b ; B. § 108. IV. 2.)—**And during the ninth hour** (accusative, as in v. 3), so that (**this** = ninth) it was about three o'clock in the afternoon when Peter arrived at Cæsarea.—**A man in bright clothing** = **an angel of God,** in v. 3. (See 1 : 11.)

31. Was heard (not **is** in E. V.), and so **were** (not **are**) **remembered.** (Comp. also v. 4.) He is assured now of the approval of his acts; the acts were approved when he performed them.—**Thy prayer** refers more especially to his prayer at this time. But the answer to this prayer was an answer to his other prayers, since the burden of them had doubtless been that God would lead him to a clearer knowledge of the truth and enable him to attain the repose of mind which a conscience enlightened, but not yet " purged from a sense of evil," made it impossible for him to enjoy. Hence **prayers,** in v. 4, could be exchanged here for the singular.

32. Send, therefore, because in this way he would obtain the evidence that he was approved.—μετακάλεσαι (**call for thee**) exemplifies the usage of the middle noticed on v. 5.—The verbal accuracy here, as compared with v. 5, is natural. There was but one way to report the words of such a message. The angel's voice and mien had left an impression not to be effaced.

33. Immediately agrees with the narrative in v. 7.—**Thou hast done well** (see 3 John 6), a common phrase expressive of the gratification which a person derives from the act of another (Wetst., Raph.). For the construction, comp. Phil. 4 : 14.—**In the sight of God,** with a consciousness of his presence, and hence prepared to hear and obey his message. This is a reason why Peter should speak with freedom and confidence. " Terra bona: inde fructus

34 ¶ Then Peter opened *his* mouth, and said, *a*Of a truth I perceive that God is no respecter of persons:
35 But *b*in every nation he that feareth him, and worketh righteousness, is accepted with him.
36 The word which *God* sent unto the children of Israel, *c*preaching peace by Jesus Christ: (*d*he is Lord of all:)
37 That word, *I say*, ye know, which was published

34 thee of the Lord. And Peter opened his mouth, and said,
Of a truth I perceive that God is no respecter of
35 persons: but in every nation he that feareth him, and worketh righteousness, is acceptable to him.
36 1The word which he sent unto the children of Israel, preaching 2good tidings of peace by Jesus
37 Christ (he is Lord of all,—that saying ye yourselves

---

a Deut. 10 : 17 ; 2 Chron. 19 : 7 ; Job 34 : 19 ; Rom. 2 : 11 ; Gal. 2 : 6 ; Eph. 6 : 9 ; Col. 3 : 25 ; 1 Pet. 1 : 17....*b* ch. 15 : 9 ; Rom. 2 : 13, 27 ; 3 : 22, 29 ; 10 : 12, 13 ; 1 Cor. 12 : 13 ; Gal. 3 : 28 ; Eph. 2 : 13, 18 ; 3 : 6....*c* Isa. 57 : 19 ; Eph. 2 : 14, 16, 17 ; Col. 1 : 20....*d* Matt. 28 : 18 ; Rom. 10 : 12 ; 1 Cor. 15 : 27 ; Eph. 1 : 20, 22 ; 1 Pet. 3 : 22 ; Rev 17 : 14 ; 19 : 16.——1 Many ancient authorities read *He sent the word unto....*2 Or, *the gospel.*

celerrimus" ["Good soil; thence the most speedy fruit"] (Bng.).

34–43. THE ADDRESS OF PETER.

34. See the remark on **opened his mouth** in 8 : 35.—προσωπολήπτης is a word coined to express concretely the idea of the Heb. *nasa panēm*, **respecter of persons**—*i. e.* here *partial* in the way of regarding one man as better than another, on the ground of national descent.

35. Is acceptable to him—*i. e.* his righteousness, his obedience to the divine will, as far as it extends, is as fully approved of God, though he be a Gentile, as if he were a Jew. It is evident from **I perceive,** that **he that feareth him and worketh righteousness** describes the centurion's character before his acceptance of the gospel, and, consequently, that **acceptable to him** applies to him as a person still destitute of faith in Christ. That Peter did not intend, however, to represent his righteousness, or that of any man, prior to the exercise of such faith, as sufficient to justify him in the sight of God, is self-evident; for in v. 43 he declares that it is necessary to believe on Christ, in order to obtain "the remission of sins." (Comp. also 15 : 11.) The antithetic structure of the sentence indicates the meaning. **He that feareth him,** etc., is the opposite of **respecter of persons**—*i. e.* God judges man impartially; he approves of what is excellent in those of one nation as much as in those of another; he will confer the blessings of his grace as readily upon the Gentile who desires to receive them as upon the Jew. In other words, since the apostle has reference to the state of mind which God requires as preparatory to an interest in the benefits of the gospel, the righteousness and the acceptance of which he speaks must also be preparatory—*i. e.* relative, and not absolute.[1]

36. The construction is uncertain, but the most simple is that which makes **word** (λόγον) depend on **ye know** (v. 37) in apposition with

word (ῥῆμα): **The word which he sent . . .** (I say) **ye know the thing that was done,** etc. So, essentially, Kuinoel, Meyer, Winer, and others. (See W. ≀ 62. 3.) Others refer **word** to what precedes, and supply **according to** (κατά) or take the accusative as absolute: **the word** (viz. that God is thus impartial) **which he sent,** etc. (Bng., Olsh., De Wet.). That mode of characterizing the contents or message of the gospel is unusual. The structure of the sentence is no smoother in this case than in the other. A recent writer[2] has proposed to construe **preaching** as a predicate of **he that fears God is acceptable to him, . . . having announced** (to him) **as glad tidings, peace,** etc. But the participle in this position cannot be separated without violence from the subject of **sent,** nor is the accusative in any other instance retained after this verb in the passive. (Comp. Matt. 11 : 5 ; Heb. 4 : 2.) The construction would be correct in principle, but is not exemplified.—**Sent to the sons of Israel**—*i. e.* in the first instance, as in 3 : 26 ; 13 : 26. That priority Peter concedes to the Jews.—**Peace,** reconciliation to God procured through Christ (comp. Rom. 5 : 1, 10), not **union** between the Jews and Gentiles (De Wet.)—an effect of the gospel too subordinate to be made so prominent in this connection. The apostle restates the idea in v. 43.—**This one is Lord of all.** All (πάντων) is masculine, not neuter. Peter interposes the remark as proof of the universality of this plan of reconciliation. The dominion of Christ extends over those of one nation as well as of another; they are all the creatures of his power and care, and may all avail themselves of the provisions of his grace. (Comp. Rom. 3 : 29, 30 ; 10 : 12.)

37. Ye know, etc., implies that they had already some knowledge of the life and works of Christ. The fame of his miracles may have extended to Cæsarea (see Matt. 15 : 21 ; Mark 7 : 24), or Philip, who resided there (8 : 40), may have begun to excite public attention as a

---

[1] Neander's remarks on this passage, in his *Planting of the Christian Church*, deserve attention. See the close of the second section or book.

[2] In the *Theologische Studien und Kritiken*, 1850, p. 402, *sq.*

throughout all Judæa, and *a*began from Galilee, after the baptism which John preached;

38 How *b*God anointed Jesus of Nazareth with the Holy Ghost and with power: who went about doing good, and healing all that were oppressed of the devil; *c*for God was with him.

39 And *d*we are witnesses of all things which he did both in the land of the Jews, and in Jerusalem; *e*whom they slew and hanged on a tree:

40 Him *f*God raised up the third day, and shewed him openly;

41 *g*Not to all the people, but unto witnesses chosen

know, which was published throughout all Judæa, beginning from Galilee, after the baptism which 38 John preached; *even* Jesus of Nazareth, how that God anointed him with the Holy Spirit and with power: who went about doing good, and healing all that were oppressed of the devil; for God was with 39 him. And we are witnesses of all things which he did both in the country of the Jews, and in Jerusalem; whom also they slew, hanging him on a 40 tree. Him God raised up the third day, and gave 41 him to be made manifest, not to all the people, but

a Luke 4 : 14....*b* Luke 4 : 18; ch. 2 : 22; 4 : 27; Heb. 1 : 9....*c* John 3 : 2....*d* ch. 2 : 32....*e* ch. 5 : 30....*f* ch. 2 : 24....*g* John 14 : 17, 22; ch. 13 : 31.

preacher of the gospel. Some think that Cornelius was the centurion who was present at the crucifixion of Christ (Matt. 27 : 44; Mark 15 : 39; Luke 23 : 47), since it was customary to march a portion of the troops at Cæsarea to Jerusalem for the preservation of order during the festivals. It is impossible to refute or confirm that opinion. Peter proceeds to communicate to them a fuller account of the Saviour's history, and of the nature and terms of his salvation. —**Word** (ῥῆμα) = **word** (λόγον) in v. 36 (Kuin., Mey.), or *thing* (De Wet.), which is more congruous with **happened,** and associates *the word* with the indubitable facts on which it rested.—*After the baptism*—*i. e.* the completion of John's ministry. The Saviour performed some public acts at an earlier period, but did not enter fully on his work till John had finished his preparatory mission. The difference was so slight that it was sufficiently exact to make the beginning or the close of the forerunner's career the starting-point in that of Christ. (See on 1 : 22.)

38. Jesus transfers the mind from the gospel-history to the personal subject of it. The appositional construction is kept up still. **From Nazareth,** as the place of his residence. (See Matt. 2 : 23.)—**How God anointed him with the Holy Spirit,** etc. (See note on 1 : 2 and on 4 : 26.) **Power** is defined by what follows as *power* to perform miracles. — **Went from place to place.** (Comp. 8 : 4.) —**Healing those oppressed by the devil.** His triumph over this form of Satanic agency is singled out as the highest exhibition of his wonder-working power. [Compare the briefer exposition of Canon Cook: "Three accusatives are put forward—1st, *the word,* in v. 36; 2d, *the word,* in v. 37; 3d, *Jesus of Nazareth,* in v. 38—all of them governed by *ye know.* And it is to be noted that *the word* in v. 37 is quite distinct from that in v. 36, in apposition with it, and explanatory of its meaning. Ye know . . . the teaching or message which God sent; ye know, again, . . . the matter, or the fact, the

subject or basis, of the teaching which took place throughout all Judea, the area of our Lord's teaching and miracles. Once more ye know Jesus of Nazareth."—A. H.]

39. Are (ἐσμέν) supplies the correct word after we (ἡμεῖς), but is not genuine.—**Both in the country of the Jews and in Jerusalem,** the capital of the nation and its territory here opposed to each other. The Jews inhabited not only Judea, but Galilee and a region on the east of the Jordan.—**Whom also,** an additional fact (Luke 22 : 24) in the Saviour's history (De Wet.), showing the extent of their animosity and violence. Winer (¿ 66. 3) suggests a brachylogy: **whom** (of which **also** we are witnesses) **they slew,** etc. This is too complicated.—**By hanging.** (See note on 5 : 30.) Here again the E. Version represents the Saviour as put to death before he was suspended on the cross.

41. Not unto all the people—*i. e.* of the Jews. (Comp. on v. 2.)—**But unto witnesses before appointed by God.** The choice of the apostles is ascribed indifferently to him or to Christ (1 : 2). πρό (*before*) in the participle represents the selection as made before Christ rose from the dead, not as purposed indefinitely before its execution.—The exception here made to the publicity of the Saviour's appearance accords with the narrative of the evangelists; they mention no instance in which he showed himself to any except his personal followers. Paley founds the following just remarks on that representation of the sacred writers: "The history of the resurrection would have come to us with more advantage, if they had related that Jesus had appeared to his foes as well as his friends, or even if they asserted the public appearance of Christ in general unqualified terms, without noticing, as they have done, the presence of his disciples on each occasion, and noticing it in such a manner as to lead their readers to suppose that none but disciples were present. If their point had been to have their story believed, whether true or false, or if they had

before of God, *even* to us, [a]who did eat and drink with him after he rose from the dead.

42 And [b]he commanded us to preach unto the people, and to testify [c]that it is he which was ordained of God *to be* the Judge [d]of quick and dead.

43 [e]To him give all the prophets witness, that through his name [f] whosoever believeth in him shall receive remission of sins.

44 ¶ While Peter yet spake these words, [g]the Holy Ghost fell on all them which heard the word.

45 [h]And they of the circumcision which believed were astonished, as many as came with Peter, [i]because that on the Gentiles also was poured out the gift of the Holy Ghost.

unto witnesses that were chosen before of God, *even* to us, who did eat and drink with him after he rose

42 from the dead. And he charged us to preach unto the people, and to testify that this is he who is ordained of God *to be* the Judge of quick and dead.

43 To him bear all the prophets witness, that through his name every one that believeth on him shall re- ceive remission of sins.

44 While Peter yet spake these words, the Holy

45 Spirit fell on all them who heard the word. And they of the circumcision who believed were amazed, as many as came with Peter, because that on the Gentiles also was poured out the gift of the Holy

---

a Luke 24 : 30, 43 ; John 21 : 13....*b* Matt. 28 : 19, 20 ; ch. 1 : 8....*c* John 5 : 22, 27 ; ch. 17 : 31....*d* Rom. 14 : 9, 10 ; 2 Cor. 5 : 10 ; 2 Tim. 4 : 1 ; 1 Pet. 4 : 5....*e* Isa. 53 : 11 ; Jer. 31 : 34 ; Dan. 9 : 24 ; Mic. 7 . 18 ; Zech. 13 : 1 ; Mal. 4 : 2 ; ch. 26 : 22.... *f* ch. 15 : 9 ; 26 : 18. Rom. 10 : 11 ; Gal. 3 : 22....*g* ch. 4 : 31 ; 8 : 15, 16, 17 ; 11 : 15....*h* ver. 23....*i* ch. 11 : 18 ; Gal. 3 : 14.

---

been disposed to present their testimony, either as personal witnesses or as historians, in such a manner as to render it as specious and unobjec- tionable as they could—in a word, if they had thought of anything but the truth of the case as they understood and believed it,—they would, in their account of Christ's several appearances after his resurrection, at least have omitted this restriction. At this distance of time, the ac- count, as we have it, is perhaps more credible than it would have been the other way, because this manifestation of the historian's candor is of more advantage to their testimony than the dif- ference in the circumstances of the account would have been to the nature of the evidence. But this is an effect which the evangelists could not fore- see, and is one which by no means would have fol- lowed at the time when they wrote."—**Who ate and drank with him.** (See Luke 24 : 43 ; John 21 : 13.) Hence they testified to a fact which they had been able to verify by the most pal- pable evidence. (Comp. the note on 1 : 3.) **After he rose from the dead** belongs to the clause which immediately precedes. It was after his resurrection that they had this intercourse with him. The punctuation of some editors refers the words incorrectly to v. 40.

42. To preach to the people, as above. Peter alludes to the sphere of their ministry which they were directed to occupy at first. (Comp. 1 : 8 ; 3 : 26, etc.)—**That himself,** and no other. (W. § 22. 4.)—**Judge of the living and dead**—*i. e.* of all who shall be on the earth at the time of his final appearance (1 Thess. 4 : 17), and of all who have lived previously and died. For other passages which represent Christ as sustaining this office of universal judge, see 17 : 31 ; 2 Tim. 4 : 1 ; 1 Pet. 4 : 5. Olshausen and some others understand *the living and dead* to be *the righteous* and *wicked ;* but we are to attach to the words that figurative sense only when the context (Matt. 8 : 22) or some explanatory adjunct (Eph. 2 : 1) leads the mind distinctly to it.

43. For this one (dat. comm.) **testify all the prophets.** (Comp. on 3 : 24.)—**Whoso- ever believeth,** etc., states the purport of their testimony. This clause presents two ideas— first, that the condition of pardon is faith in Christ ; and secondly, that this condition brings the attainment of pardon within the reach of all : **every one,** whether Jew or Gentile, **who believes on him shall receive remission of sins.** (See Rom. 10 : 11.) For the explana- tion of **his name,** see on 2 : 21.

44–48. CORNELIUS AND OTHERS RE- CEIVE THE SPIRIT, AND ARE BAP- TIZED.

44. Still speaking. Hence, Peter had not finished his remarks when God vouchsafed this token of his favor. (See 11 : 15.) **The Spirit** —*i. e.* as the author of the gifts mentioned in v. 46. The miracle proved that the plan of salvation which Peter announced was the di- vine plan, and that the faith which secured its blessings to the Jew was sufficient to secure them to the Gentile. A previous submission to the rites of Judaism was shown to be un- necessary. It is worthy of note, too, that those who received the Spirit in this instance had not been baptized (comp. 19 : 5), nor had the hands of an apostle been laid upon them. (Comp. 8 : 17.) This was an occasion when men were to be taught by an impressive exam- ple how little their acceptance with God de- pends on external observances.—**All** restricts itself to the Gentiles (v. 27), since they were prop- erly *the hearers* to whom Peter was speaking, and not the Jews.

45. They of the circumcision—*i. e.* the Jewish brethren mentioned in v. 23. (Comp. 11 : 2 ; Rom. 4 : 12 ; Col. 4 : 11.)—**Believed** (πιστοί = πιστεύοντες). (See 16 : 1 ; John 20 : 27.) " Verbal adjectives in τός, which have usually a passive signification, have often in poetry, and sometimes in prose, an active signification." (See K., *Ausführ. Gr.,* § 409. 3. A. 1.)—**That also**

46 For they heard them speak with tongues, and magnify God. Then answered Peter,

47 Can any man forbid water, that these should not be baptized, which have received the Holy Ghost *a*as well as we?

48 *b*And he commanded them to be baptized *c*in the name of the Lord. Then prayed they him to tarry certain days.

46 Spirit. For they heard them speak with tongues, 47 and magnify God. Then answered Peter, Can any man forbid the water, that these should not be baptized, who have received the Holy Spirit as well as 48 we? And he commanded them to be baptized in the name of Jesus Christ. Then prayed they him to tarry certain days.

CHAPTER XI.

AND the apostles and brethren that were in Judæa heard that the Gentiles had also received the word of God.

2 And when Peter was come up to Jerusalem, *d*they that were of the circumcision contended with him,

1 Now the apostles and the brethren that were in Judæa heard that the Gentiles also had received 2 the word of God. And when Peter was come up to Jerusalem, they that were of the circumcision con-

---

a ch. 11 : 17 ; 15 : 8, 9 ; Rom. 10 : 12....*b* 1 Cor. 1 : 17....*c* ch. 2 : 38 ; 8 : 16....*d* ch. 10 : 45 ; Gal. 2 : 12.

---

upon the heathen, as well as upon the Jews. The assertion is universal, because this single instance established the principle.

46. Were hearing them, while they spoke. **—With tongues,** new ; before unspoken by them. The fuller description in 2 : 4 prepares the way for the conciser statement here.

47. Can perhaps any one forbid the water that these should not be baptized? The article may contrast ὕδωρ and πνεῦμα with each other, or more naturally designate the water as wont to be so applied. The import of the question is this : Since, although uncircumcised, they have believed and received so visible a token of their acceptance with God, what should hinder their admission into the church? Who can object to their being baptized, and thus acknowledged as Christians in full connection with us? As **forbid** (κωλύω) involves a negative idea, μή (*not*) could be omitted or inserted before **should be baptized.** The distinction may be that the infinitive with μή expresses the result of the hindrance ; without μή, that which the hindrance would prevent. (See Woolsey *On the Alcestis*, v. 11.) μή after such verbs has been said to be superfluous (K. ¿ 318. 10), or simply intensive (Mt. ¿ 534. 3). Klotz (*Ad Devar.*, ii. p. 668) suggests the correct view. (See also Bernh., *Synt.*, p. 364.) [Some writers have inferred sprinkling or pouring from **forbid water:** "The water was to be brought to the converts ; and this suggests affusion, not immersion" (*Canon Cook*). Better thus : "The water is in this animated language conceived as the element offering itself for the baptism. So urgent now appeared the necessity for completing, on the human side, the divine work that had miraculously appeared" (*Meyer*).—A. H.]—**As also we** received—viz. (see 11 : 15) **in the beginning.**

48. Commanded that the rite should be performed by others ; he devolved the service on his attendants. Peter's rule in regard to the administration of baptism may have been similar to that of Paul. (See 1 Cor. 1 : 14.) [The best text reads : **And he commanded them to be baptized in the name of Jesus Christ.** Thus the name of Jesus is represented as the spiritual element in which the act of baptism takes place, just as in 2 : 38 it is spoken of as the divine basis or authority for that act, and as in 19 : 5 it is conceived of as the end to which baptism relates. But in none of these passages is the verbal formula used by administrators given.—A. H.] — **To tarry**—*i. e.* with them (Comp. 28 : 14.)

1–18. PETER JUSTIFIES HIMSELF AT JERUSALEM FOR HIS VISIT TO CORNELIUS.

1. Peter, John, and James were among the **apostles** now at Jerusalem (8 : 14; 12 : 2), and no doubt others.—**Throughout** (comp. 15 : 23) **Judea,** since **the brethren** belonged to different churches in this region. (See Gal. 1 : 22.)—**The heathen,** while still uncircumcised. (See v. 3.)

2. When he went up. There is no evidence that Peter was summoned to Jerusalem to defend his conduct. He had reason to fear that it would be censured until the particulars of the transaction were known, and he may have hastened his return, in order to furnish that information.—**They of the circumcision** are the Jewish believers, as in 10 : 45, not here a party among them more tenacious of circumcision than the others. It is implied that this tenacity was a Jewish characteristic. The narrower sense of the expression occurs in some places.

3 Saying, *a*Thou wentest in to men uncircumcised, *b*and didst eat with them.

4 But Peter rehearsed *the matter* from the beginning, and expounded *it* *c*by order unto them, saying,

5 *d*I was in the city of Joppa praying: and in a trance I saw a vision. A certain vessel descend, as it had been a great sheet, let down from heaven by four corners; and it came even to me:

6 Upon the which when I had fastened mine eyes, I considered, and saw fourfooted beasts of the earth, and wild beasts, and creeping things, and fowls of the air.

7 And I heard a voice saying unto me, Arise, Peter; slay and eat.

8 But I said, Not so, Lord: for nothing common or unclean hath at any time entered into my mouth.

9 But the voice answered me again from heaven, What God hath cleansed, *that* call not thou common.

10 And this was done three times: and all were drawn up again into heaven.

11 And, behold, immediately there were three men already come unto the house where I was, sent from Cæsarea unto me.

12 And *e*the spirit bade me go with them, nothing doubting. Moreover *f*these six brethren accompanied me, and we entered into the man's house:

13 *g*And he shewed us how he had seen an angel in his house, which stood and said unto him, Send men to Joppa, and call for Simon, whose surname is Peter;

14 Who shall tell thee words, whereby thou and all thy house shall be saved.

15 And as I began to speak, the Holy Ghost fell on them, *h*as on us at the beginning.

16 Then remembered I the word of the Lord, how that he said, *i*John indeed baptized with water; but *k*ye shall be baptized with the Holy Ghost.

3 tended with him, saying, Thou wentest in to men 4 uncircumcised, and didst eat with them. But Peter began, and expounded *the matter* unto them in order, 5 saying, I was in the city of Joppa praying: and in a trance I saw a vision, a certain vessel descending, as it were a great sheet let down from heaven by 6 four corners; and it came even unto me: upon the which when I had fastened mine eyes, I considered, and saw the four-footed beasts of the earth and wild beasts and creeping things and fowls of the heaven. 7 And I heard also a voice saying unto me, Rise, Pe-8 ter; kill and eat. But I said, Not so, Lord: for nothing common or unclean hath ever entered into 9 my mouth. But a voice answered me the second time out of heaven, What God hath cleansed, make not 10 thou common. And this was done thrice: and all 11 were drawn up again into heaven. And behold, forthwith three men stood before the house in which we were, having been sent from Cæsarea 12 unto me. And the Spirit bade me go with them, making no distinction. And these six brethren also accompanied me; and we entered into the 13 man's house: and he told us how he had seen the angel standing in his house, and saying, Send to Joppa, and fetch Simon, whose surname is Peter; 14 who shall speak unto thee words, whereby thou 15 shalt be saved, thou and all thy house. And as I began to speak, the Holy Spirit fell on them, even 16 as on us at the beginning. And I remembered the word of the Lord, how that he said, John indeed baptized with water; but ye shall be baptized *l*in

---

a ch. 10 : 28....*b* Gal. 2 : 12....*c* Luke 1 : 3....*d* ch. 10 : 9, etc....*e* John 16 : 13; ch. 10 : 19 ; 15 : 7 ... *f* ch. 10 : 23....*g* ch. 10 : 30 ....*h* ch. 2 : 4....*i* Matt. 3 : 11; John 1 : 26, 33; ch. 1 : 5; 19 : 4....*k* Isa. 44 : 3 ; Joel 2 : 28; 3 : 18.——1 Or, *with their*

---

3. (See the remarks on 10 : 28.) Notice the ground of the complaint. It was not that Peter had preached to the heathen, but that he had associated with them in such a manner as to violate his supposed obligations as a Jew. (Comp. the note on 2 : 39.) We may infer that he had avoided that degree of intimacy when he himself entertained the Gentile messengers. (10 : 23).

4. Commencing—*i. e.* proceeding to speak (see on 2 : 4), or, **beginning** with the first circumstances, **he related unto them,** etc. This repetition of the history shows the importance attached to this early conflict between the gospel and Judaism.

5. For the omission of *the* before **city,** see on 8 : 5.—**Vision** denotes here what was seen, and differs from its use in 10 : 3.—**Let down,** suspended, **by four corners**—*i. e.* by means of cords fastened to them. Luke abbreviates here the fuller expression in 10 : 11. [For Dr. Hackett's exposition of vv. 6–11, see his notes on 10 : 11–16, where the same narrative is given. —A. H.]

12. By a mixed construction, διακρινόμενον agrees with the suppressed subject of συνελθεῖν, instead of μοι. (C. § 627. β.; Mt. § 536.)—**These six brethren.** (See 10 : 23.) They had, therefore, accompanied Peter to Jerusalem, either as

witnesses for him or for his own vindication, since they had committed the same offence.

13. The angel, known to the reader from the previous narrative (10 : 3, 22). Those addressed had not heard of the vision, and must have received from Peter a fuller account of it than it was necessary to repeat here.—**Men** has been transferred to this place from 10 : 5.

14. All thy family. The assurance embraces them because they were prepared, as well as Cornelius, to welcome the apostle's message. (Comp. 10 : 2.) This part of the communication has not been mentioned before.

15. Began is not superfluous (Kuin.), but shows how soon the Spirit descended after **he began to speak.** (See on 10 : 44. W. § 67. 4.) —**In the beginning**—*i. e.* on the day of Pentecost. The order of the narrative indicates that the conversion of Cornelius took place near the time of Paul's arrival at Antioch. Some ten years, therefore (see on v. 26), had passed away since the event to which Peter alludes. (Comp. on 15 : 7.)

16. And I remembered the declaration of the Lord—*i. e.* had it brought to mind with a new sense of its meaning and application. (Comp. Matt. 26 : 75; John 12 : 16.) The Saviour had promised to bestow on his disciples a higher baptism than that of water (see 1 : 5;

17 ᵃForasmuch then as God gave them the like gift as *he did* unto us, who believed on the Lord Jesus Christ ; ᵇwhat was I, that I could withstand God?
18 When they heard these things, they held their peace, and glorified God, saying, ᶜThen hath God also to the Gentiles granted repentance unto life.
19 ¶ ᵈNow they which were scattered abroad upon the persecution that arose about Stephen travelled as far as Phenice, and Cyprus, and Antioch, preaching the word to none but unto the Jews only.
20 And some of them were men of Cyprus and

17 the Holy Spirit. If then God gave unto them the like gift as *he did* also unto us, when we believed on the Lord Jesus Christ, who was I, that I could with-
18 stand God? And when they heard these things, they held their peace, and glorified God, saying, Then to the Gentiles also hath God granted repentance unto life.
19 They therefore that were scattered abroad upon the tribulation that arose about Stephen travelled as far as Phœnicia, and Cyprus, and Antioch, speaking
20 the word to none save only to Jews. But there were

a ch. 15 : 8, 9....*b* ch. 10 : 47....*c* Rom. 10 : 12, 13 ; 15 : 9, 16....*d* ch. 8 : 1.

Luke 24 : 49) ; and the result proved that he designed to extend the benefit of that promise to the heathen who should believe on him, as well as to the Jews.—**How he said.** (See on 1 : 5.)

17. Gave, as mentioned in 10 : 44.—**Also** connects **us** with **them.**—**Having believed** refers to both pronouns (De Wet.,Mey.)—*i.e.* they all received the same gift in the same character ; viz. that of believers. Bengel (to whom Mey. assents now) limits the participle to **us.**—ἐγὼ δὲ τίς ἤμην, κ. τ. λ., combines two questions (W. § 66. 5): **Who then was I? Was I able to withstand God?**—*i. e.* to disregard so distinct an intimation of his will that the heathen should be recognized as worthy of all the privileges of the gospel, without demanding of them any other qualification than faith in Christ. **Able** suggests that such opposition would have been as presumptuous and futile as a contest between man's power and infinite power. δέ with τίς strengthens the question, as in 2 Cor. 6 : 14. It is left out of some copies, but not justly.

18. Were silent, refrained from further opposition (v. 2). (Comp. 21 : 14.)—**Glorified** (ἐδόξαζον, imp.) expresses a continued act. The sudden change of tenses led some to write the aorist (ἐδόξασαν). [The critical editors now give the aorist rather than the imperfect tense of the verb.—A. H.]—**Therefore then** (ἄραγε ; comp. Matt. 7 : 20 ; 17 : 26). More pertinent here than the interrogative **whether then** (ἄραγε, 8 : 30). The accentuation varies in different editions.—For **granted repentance** see the note on 5 : 31.—εἰς ζωήν, ecbatic, *unto life*—*i. e.* such repentance as secures it. (Comp. 2 Cor. 7 : 10.)

19–24. THE GOSPEL IS PREACHED AT ANTIOCH.

19. Those therefore dispersed recalls the reader to an earlier event in the history. (See 8 : 4.)—**From** (as an effect of) **the persecution.** (Whl., Win., Mey. Comp. 20 : 9 ; Luke 19 : 3.) This is better than to render **since the persecution.** It is more natural to be reminded here of the cause of the dispersion

than of the time when it began.—**Upon Stephen,** on his account. (Comp. 4 : 21 ; Luke 2 : 20. W. § 48. c.)—**Travelled as far as.** (See 8 : 4, 40.)—**Phœnicia,** in this age, lay chiefly between the western slope of Lebanon and the sea, a narrow plain reaching from the river Eleutherus, on the north, to Carmel, on the south. Its limits varied at different times. Among the Phœnician cities were Tyre and Sidon ; and the statement here accounts for the existence of the Christians in those places, mentioned so abruptly in 21 : 4 ; 27 : 3.—**Antioch.** Here we have the first notice of this important city. **Antioch** was the capital of Syria, and the residence of the Roman governors of that province. It was founded by Seleucus Nicator, and named after his father, Antiochus. It stood "near the abrupt angle formed by the coasts of Syria and Asia Minor, and in the opening where the Orontes passes between the ranges of Lebanon and Taurus. By its harbor of Seleucia it was in communication with all the trade of the Mediterranean, and through the open country behind Lebanon it was conveniently approached by the caravans from Mesopotamia and Arabia. It was almost an Oriental Rome, in which all the forms of the civilized life of the empire found a representative " (Conybeare and Howson, i. p. 149). (See, further, on 13 : 4.) It is memorable in the first Christian age as the seat of missionary operations for the evangelization of the heathen.

20. Whether the preachers came to Antioch before the conversion of Cornelius or afterward the narrative does not decide. Some prefer to place the arrival after his baptism, lest Peter might not seem to be the first who preached the gospel to the Gentiles. (See the note on 15 : 7.) —**But** (δέ) distinguishes the course pursued by **certain of them** from that of the other **scattered** ones. The general fact is first stated, and then the exception. — **Men of Cyprus**—*i. e.* Jews born in Cyprus. (See 2 : 5, 9.)—**Unto the Greeks,** opposed to **Jews,** in the foregoing verse. The received text has **Hellenists** (Ἑλληνιστάς) (see on 6 : 1), and the mass of external testimony favors that reading. [West-

Cyrene, which, when they were come to Antioch, spake unto [a]the Grecians, preaching the Lord Jesus.

21 And [b]the hand of the Lord was with them: and a great number believed, and [c]turned unto the Lord.

22 ¶ Then tidings of these things came unto the ears of the church which was in Jerusalem: and they sent forth [d]Barnabas, that he should go as far as Antioch.

23 Who, when he came, and had seen the grace of God, was glad, and [e]exhorted them all, that with purpose of heart they would cleave unto the Lord.

24 For he was a good man, and [f]full of the Holy Ghost and of faith: [g]and much people was added unto the Lord.

25 Then departed Barnabas to [h]Tarsus, for to seek Saul:

26 And when he had found him, he brought him

some of them, men of Cyprus and Cyrene, who, when they were come to Antioch, spake unto the [1]Greeks

21 also, preaching the Lord Jesus. And the hand of the Lord was with them: and a great number that

22 believed turned unto the Lord. And the report concerning them came to the ears of the church which was in Jerusalem: and they sent forth Bar-

23 nabas as far as Antioch: who, when he was come, and had seen the grace of God, was glad; and he exhorted them all, [2]that with purpose of heart they

24 would cleave unto the Lord: for he was a good man, and full of the Holy Spirit and of faith: and much

25 people was added unto the Lord. And he went

26 forth to Tarsus to seek for Saul: and when he had

a ch. 6 : 1; 9 : 29....b Luke 1 : 66; ch. 2 : 47....c ch. 9 : 35....d ch. 9 : 27....e ch. 13 : 43; 14 : 22....f ch. 6 : 5....g ver. 21; ch. 5 : 14.... h ch. 9 : 30.——1 Many ancient authorities read Grecian Jews....2 Some ancient authorities read that they would cleave unto the purpose of their heart in the Lord.

and Hort also adopt it.—A. H.] Wordsworth's note[1] presents the evidence on that side in a strong light. On the contrary, the internal argument appears to demand **Greeks** (Ελληνας). Some of the oldest versions and a few manuscripts support that as the original word. The majority of critics, in view of this twofold evidence, decide for **Greeks** (Grsb., Lchm., Tsch., De Wet., Mey.). It would have been nothing new to have preached at this time to the Greek-speaking Jews. (See e. g. 2 : 9; 9 : 29.) If we accept Ελληνας, the Greeks addressed at Antioch must have been still heathen in part, and not merely Jewish proselytes. No other view accounts for Luke's discrimination as to the sphere of the two classes of preachers. —**Men of Cyrene.** (See on 2 : 10.)

21. For hand of the Lord, comp. 4 : 30; Luke 1 : 66.—**With them** who preached at Antioch. The subject of discourse, both in the last verse and the next, requires this reference of the pronoun.

22. Came to the ears (lit. **was heard into the ears**) is a Hebraism, says De Wette, without any instance exactly parallel in Hebrew. — **Tidings, the report. Of these things** excludes the idea that it was a communication sent from the brethren at Antioch. —**Sent forth** derives its subject from **in Jerusalem.** (Comp. Gal. 2 : 2.) **That he should go**—i. e. with the direction **that he should go** (comp. 20 : 1); left out of some of the early versions as if unnecessary. (See W. § 65. 4. d.) [Lach., Tsch., Treg., West. and Hort, and Anglo-Am. Revisers, with ℵ A B, omit this verb.—A. H.]—**Barnabas.** (See 4 : 36; 9 : 27.)

23. The grace, or favor, of God, as manifested in the conversion of the heathen.

Exhorted all who had believed. We find

him exercising here the peculiar gift for which he was distinguished. (See on 4 : 36.) **With the purpose of the heart**—i. e. a purpose sincere, earnest.

24. Because he was a man good and full of the Holy Spirit, etc. This description states why he exerted himself so strenuously to establish the converts in their faith. Sent forth, in v. 22, is too remote to allow us to view it as the reason why they selected him for such a service.—**And much people was added,** etc. The labors of Barnabas resulted also in the accession of new believers.

25, 26. PAUL ARRIVES AT ANTIOCH, AND LABORS THERE.

25. Our last notice of Paul was in 9 : 30.— **In order to seek out,** find by inquiry or effort. It was not known at what precise point the apostle was laboring. (See Gal. 1 : 21.)— **When he had found** indicates the same uncertainty. Barnabas would naturally direct his steps first to Tarsus, whither he would proceed by sea from Seleucia (see on 13 : 4) or track his way through the defiles of the intervening mountains. Conybeare and Howson: "The last time the two friends met was in Jerusalem. In the period since that interview 'God had granted to the Gentiles repentance unto life' (v. 18). Barnabas had 'seen the grace of God' (v. 23), and under his own teaching 'a great multitude' (v. 24) had been 'added to the Lord.' But he needed assistance; he needed the presence of one whose wisdom was greater than his own, whose zeal was an example to all, and whose peculiar mission had been miraculously declared. Saul recognized the voice of God in the words of Barnabas, and the two friends travelled in all haste to the Syrian metropolis."

26. A whole year—viz. that of A. D. 44,

1 *The New Testament in the Original Greek, with Notes,* by Chr. Wordsworth, D. D., Canon of Westminster (London, 1857).

unto Antioch. And it came to pass, that a whole year they assembled themselves with the church, and taught much people. And the disciples were called Christians first in Antioch.

27 ¶ And in these days came *a*prophets from Jerusalem unto Antioch.

28 And there stood up one of them named *b*Agabus, and signified by the Spirit that there should be great dearth throughout all the world : which came to pass in the days of Claudius Cæsar.

found him, he brought him unto Antioch. And it came to pass, that even for a whole year they were gathered together ¹with the church, and taught much people; and that the disciples were called Christians first in Antioch.

27 Now in these days there came down prophets from 28 Jerusalem unto Antioch. And there stood up one of them named Agabus, and signified by the Spirit that there should be a great famine over all ²the world : which came to pass in the days of Claudius.

a ch. 2 : 17 ; 13 : 1 ; 15 : 32 ; 21 : 9 ; 1 Cor. 12 : 28 ; Eph. 4 : 11....*b* ch. 21 : 10.——1 Gr. *in*....2 Gr. *the inhabited earth.*

since it was the year which preceded Paul's second journey to Jerusalem, at the time of the famine. (See on 12 : 25.) The apostle had spent the intervening years, from A. D. 39 to 44, in Syria and Cilicia. (See on 9 : 30.) **They came together in the church,** the public assembly—*i. e.* for the purpose of worship and, as we see from the next clause, for preaching the word : **and taught a great multitude** (comp. 14 : 21), many of whom, no doubt, they won to a reception of the truth. Meyer explains **came together** of the hospitality shown to the teachers, with an appeal to Matt. 25 : 35. But the context, which should indicate that sense, is opposed to it here. [Meyer's last ed. says : *To be brought together*—*i. e.* to join themselves for common work " — an explanation almost identical with Dr. Hackett's.—A. H.]— **And the disciples were first named Christians at Antioch.** Thus ten years or more elapsed after the Saviour left the earth before the introduction of this name. Its origin is left in some uncertainty. Χριστιανοί has a Latin termination, like Ἡρωδιανοί, in Matt. 22 : 16 and Mark 3 : 6. We see the proper Greek form in Ναζωραῖος, in 2 : 22, or Ἰταλικός, in 10 : 1. Hence some infer (Olsh., Mey.) that it must have been the Roman inhabitants of the city, not the Greeks, who invented the name. The argument is not decisive, since Latinisms were not unknown to the Greek of this period. It is evident that the Jews did not apply it first to the disciples, for they would not have admitted the implication of the term—viz. that Jesus was the Messiah. It is improbable that the Christians themselves assumed it ; such an origin would be inconsistent with its infrequent use in the New Testament. It occurs only in 26 : 28 ; 1 Pet. 4 : 16, and in both places proceeds from those out of the church. The *worthy name by which ye are called,* in James 2 : 7, may be the Christian name. The believers at Antioch had become numerous ; they consisted of Gentiles and Jews ; it was evident that they were a distinct community from the latter ; and probably the heathen, whether they were Greeks or Romans or na-

tive Syrians, needing a new appellation for the new sect, called them Christians, because the name of Christ was so prominent in their doctrine, conversation, and worship. The term may not have been at first opprobrious, but distinctive merely. [The last ed. of Meyer agrees with Dr. Hackett : " The origin of the name must be derived from the *heathen* in Antioch." In a note he remarks : " Ewald (p. 441, etc.) conjectures : from the Roman magistrates ;" but evidently without approving this conjecture.—A. H.]

27–30. BARNABAS AND SAUL ARE SENT WITH ALMS TO JERUSALEM.

27. In these days—*i. e.* about the time that Paul himself came to Antioch ; for it is reasonable to suppose that an interval of some extent occurred between the prediction and the famine.—**Prophets, inspired teachers.** (See on 2 : 17.) Agabus, at least, possessed the prophetic gift, in the strict sense of that expression.

28. Having stood up, in order to declare his message more formally.—**Agabus** is known only from this passage and 21 : 10.—**Made known** (see 25 : 27), not **intimated** merely.— **Famine** (λιμόν), in the later Greek, is masculine or feminine ; hence some copies have a masculine adjective, **great ;** others, a feminine (See W. ⸹ 8. 2. 1.)—**Was about to be** contains a double future, as in 24 : 15 ; 27 : 10. The reading varies in 24 : 25. As one of its uses, the first infinitive in such a case may represent the act as fixed, certain ; the second, as future. The famine that was to take place was decreed. (See Mt. ⸹ 498. e ; C. ⸹ 583.)—**Over all the inhabited** land—*i. e.* Judea and the adjacent countries, or, according to some, the Roman Empire. The Greek and Roman writers employed the inhabited (land) (ἡ οἰκουμένη) to denote the Greek and the Roman world, and a Jewish writer would naturally employ such a term to denote the Jewish world. Josephus appears to restrict the word to Palestine in *Antt.,* 8. 13. 4. Speaking of the efforts of Ahab to find the prophet Elijah, he says that the king sent messengers in pursuit of him

29 Then the disciples, every man according to his ability, determined to send *relief unto the brethren which dwelt in Judæa:
30 *Which also they did, and sent it to the elders by the hands of Barnabas and Saul.

29 And the disciples, every man according to his ability, determined to send [1]relief unto the brethren that
30 dwelt in Judæa: which also they did, sending it to the elders by the hand of Barnabas and Saul.

CHAPTER XII.

NOW about that time Herod the king stretched forth his hands to vex certain of the church.

1 Now about that time Herod the king put forth

a Rom. 15 : 26 ; 1 Cor. 16 : 1 ; 2 Cor. 9 : 1....b ch. 12 : 25.——1 Gr. *for ministry.*

throughout all the earth, or land—*i. e.* of the Jews. Ancient writers give no account of any universal famine in the reign of Claudius, but they speak of several local famines which were severe in particular countries. Josephus (*Antt.,* 20. 2. 6 ; *Ib.,* 5. 2) mentions one which prevailed at that time in Judea and swept away many of the inhabitants. Helena, Queen of Adiabene, a Jewish proselyte, who was then at Jerusalem, imported provisions from Egypt and Cyprus, which she distributed among the people to save them from starvation. This is the famine, probably, to which Luke refers here. The chronology admits of this supposition. According to Josephus, the famine which he describes took place when Cuspius Fadus and Tiberius Alexander were procurators—*i. e.* as Lardner suggests, it may have begun about the close of A. D. 44 and lasted three or four years. Fadus was sent into Judea on the death of Agrippa, which occurred in August of the year A. D. 44. If we attach the wider sense to the word (οἰκουμένην), the prediction may import that a famine should take place throughout the Roman Empire during the reign of Claudius (the year is not specified below), and not that it should prevail in all parts at the same time. (So Wordsworth, *Notes,* p. 58.)— In (lit. upon) the reign of Claudius. On ἐπί (*upon*) in such chronological designations, see K. § 273. 4. b. The Greek idiom views the events as resting *upon* the ruler as their source or author; the English idiom, as taking place *under* his guidance or auspices.—Cæsar after Claudius (T. R.) is not warranted.

29. Of the disciples depends by attraction on every one. The ordinary construction would be (Mey., De Wet.) : The disciples in proportion as any one was prospered determined each of them, etc. The apostle Paul prescribes the same rule of contribution in 1 Cor. 16 : 2. For the augment in ηὐπορεῖτο (was prospered), see on 2 : 26. For every one after a plural verb, see on 2 : 6.— For relief—lit. ministration ; *i. e.* to their wants. The act here suggests the idea of its result or object.—To send—*i. e.* something.—

In Judea. Not the capital merely, but other parts also, since the famine was general and believers were found in different places. (See v. 1 and Gal. 1 : 22.)

30. Also connects did with determine: they executed their determination.—Unto the elders, either those at Jerusalem, who could easily forward the supplies to the destitute elsewhere, or those in Judea at large, whom the messengers visited in person. The latter idea presents itself very readily from Judea, just before, and has also this to commend it—that Paul would have had an opportunity to preach now in that province, as mentioned in 26 : 20. (See note there.) —For the office of the presbyters, see on 14 : 23.— Βαρνάβα is the Doric genitive (of Barnabas). (Comp. 19 : 14 ; Luke 13 : 29 ; John 1 : 43, etc. W. § 8. 1 ; K. § 44. R. 2.)—Meyer finds a contradiction between this passage and Gal. 2 : 1, as if Paul could not have gone to Jerusalem at this time, because he has not mentioned it in the Epistle. It is impossible to see why the reason commonly assigned for this omission does not account for it. Paul's object in writing to the Galatians does not require him to enumerate all his journeys to Jerusalem. In the first chapter there he would prove that as an apostle he was independent of all human authority ; and in the second chapter, that the other apostles had conceded to him that independence. He had no occasion, therefore, to recapitulate his entire history. Examples of the facts in his life were all that he needed to bring forward. He was not bound to show how often he had been at Jerusalem, but only that he had gone thither once and again, under circumstances which showed in what character he claimed to act and how fully the other apostles had acknowledged this claim.

1, 2. RENEWED PERSECUTION AT JERUSALEM, AND DEATH OF JAMES.

1. About that time—*i. e.* when Barnabas and Saul went to Jerusalem, as has just been related. (See on v. 25.)—Herod. This *Herod*

2 And he killed James *the brother of John with the sword.

3 And because he saw it pleased the Jews, he proceeded further to take Peter also. (Then were *the days of unleavened bread.)

4 And *when he had apprehended him, he put *him in prison, and delivered *him to four quaternions of soldiers to keep him; intending after Easter to bring him forth to the people.

5 Peter therefore was kept in prison: but prayer

2 his hands to afflict certain of the church. And he killed James the brother of John with the sword.

3 And when he saw that it pleased the Jews, he proceeded to seize Peter also. And *those* were the days

4 of unleavened bread. And when he had taken him, he put him in prison, and delivered him to four quaternions of soldiers to guard him; intending after the Passover to bring him forth to the people.

5 Peter therefore was kept in the prison: but prayer

a Matt. 4 : 21 ; 20 : 23....*b* Ex. 12 : 14, 15 ; 23 : 15....*c* John 21 : 18.

was Herod Agrippa I., son of Aristobulus, and grandson of Herod the Great. On the accession of Caligula he received, as king, the former possessions of Philip and Lysanias (see Luke 3 : 1); at a later period, the tetrarchy of Antipas; and in the year A. D. 41, Samaria and Judea, which were conferred on him by Claudius; so that, like his grandfather Herod, he swayed the sceptre at this time over all Palestine.[1]—**Stretched forth his hands** does not mean **attempted** (Kuin.), but **put forth violent hands.** (Comp. 4 : 3 ; 5 : 18 ; 21 : 27.)—**To oppress,** *maltreat.* The E. Version derives "vex" from Tyndale.—**Of the church** (lit. **from**), since the idea of origin passes readily into that of property, adherence. (W. § 47. 4.)

2. Slew him with the sword, beheaded him. The article fails, because the idea is general, abstract. (Comp. 9 : 12. W. § 19. 1.) On the mode of execution among the Jews, see Jahn's *Archæol.,* § 257. Agrippa had the power of life and death, since he administered the government in the name of the Romans. (See the note on 7 : 59.) The victim of his violence was James the Elder, a son of Zebedee and brother of John (Matt. 4 : 21 ; 10 : 2 ; Mark 1 : 19, etc.). He is to be distinguished from James the Younger, the kinsman of the Lord (Gal. 1 : 19), who is the individual meant under this name in the remainder of the history (v. 17; 15 : 13; 21 : 18). The end of James verified the prediction that he should drink of his Master's cup. (See Matt. 20 : 23.) Eusebius (2. 9) records a tradition that the apostle's accuser was converted by his testimony and beheaded at the same time with him. "The accuracy of the sacred writer," says Paley, "in the expressions which he uses here, is remarkable. There was no portion of time for thirty years before, or ever afterward, in which there was a king at Jerusalem, a person exercising that authority in Judea, or to whom that title could be applied, except the last three years of Herod's life, within which period the transaction here recorded took place." The kingdom of Agrippa

II., who is mentioned in 25 : 13, did not embrace Judea.

3–5. THE IMPRISONMENT OF PETER.

3. Seeing that it is pleasing, etc. The motive of Agrippa, therefore, was a desire to gain public favor. Josephus (*Antt.,* 19. 7. 3) attributes to this ruler the same trait of character; he describes him as eager to ingratiate himself with the Jews.—**He apprehended still further Peter also,** an imitation of the Heb. *vayyōseph* with the infinitive. (Comp. Luke 20 : 11, 12. W. § 54. 5; Gesen., *Heb. Gr.,* § 139.) —**The days of unleavened bread**—*i. e.* the festival of the passover, which continued seven days, and was so named because during that time no leaven was allowed in the houses of the Jews. The common text omits **the** before **days,** which the best editors insert as well attested. It is not grammatically necessary. (W. § 19. 2.)

4. Also carries the mind back to **to take** (συλλαβεῖν), in v. 3, the idea of which **apprehended** (πιάσας) repeats.—**To four quaternions,** four companies of four, who were to relieve each other in guarding the prison. The Jews at this time followed the Roman practice of dividing the night into four watches, consisting of three hours each. Of the four soldiers employed at the same time, two watched in the prison and two before the door, or perhaps, in this case (see on v. 10), were all stationed on the outside.—**Meaning,** but disappointed in that purpose.—**After the passover**—*i. e.* not the paschal supper, but the festival which it introduced. (Comp. Luke 21 : 1 ; John 6 : 4.) The reason for deferring the execution was that the stricter Jews regarded it as a profanation to put a person to death during a religious festival. Agrippa himself may have entertained, or affected to entertain, that scruple.—**To bring him up**—*i. e.* for trial and execution. (Comp. Luke 22 : 66.) But Herod was nearer his end than Peter.—**For the people** (dat. comm.)— *i. e.* that they might be gratified with his death.

5. Therefore, committed to such a guard. —**In the prison,** mentioned in v. 4.—**Intent,**

was made without ceasing of the church unto God for him.

6 And when Herod would have brought him forth, the same night Peter was sleeping between two soldiers, bound with two chains : and the keepers before the door kept the prison.

7 And, behold, *a*the angel of the Lord came upon *him*, and a light shined in the prison : and he smote Peter on the side, and raised him up, saying, Arise up quickly. And his chains fell off from *his* hands.

8 And the angel said unto him, Gird thyself, and bind on thy sandals. And so he did. And he saith unto him, Cast thy garment about thee, and follow me.

9 And he went out, and followed him; and *b*wist not that it was true which was done by the angel; but thought *c*he saw a vision.

10 When they were past the first and the second ward, they came unto the iron gate that leadeth unto the city; *d*which opened to them of his own accord:

was made earnestly of the church unto God for him.

6 And when Herod was about to bring him forth, the same night Peter was sleeping between two soldiers, bound with two chains: and guards before the door
7 kept the prison. And behold, an angel of the Lord stood by him, and a light shined in the cell: and he smote Peter on the side, and awoke him, saying, Rise up quickly. And his chains fell off from his
8 hands. And the angel said unto him, Gird thyself, and bind on thy sandals. And he did so. And he saith unto him, Cast thy garment about thee, and
9 follow me. And he went out, and followed; and he knew not that it was true which was done by the
10 angel, but thought he saw a vision. And when they were past the first and the second ward, they came unto the iron gate that leadeth into the city;

a ch. 5 : 19....*b* Ps. 126 : 1....*c* ch. 10 : 3, 17 ; 11 : 5....*d* ch. 16 : 26.――1 Or, *through*

earnest, not *unceasing*, constant. [Better, the adverb, **intently,** earnestly (ἐκτενῶς). So Lach., Tsch., Treg., West. and Hort, etc.—A. H.] (See Luke 22 : 44 ; 1 Pet. 4 : 8.) It is a word of the later Greek. (Lob., *Ad Phryn.*, p. 311.) All the English translators from Wiclif downward adopt the temporal sense.—**Church.** The members of the church were so numerous that they must have met in different companies. One of them is mentioned in v. 12.

6–11. THE MIRACULOUS LIBERATION OF PETER.

6. In that night, preceding the day when he was to have been executed.—**Bound with two chains.** The Roman mode of chaining prisoners was adopted in this case, and was the following : " The soldier who was appointed to guard a particular prisoner had the chain fastened to the wrist of his left hand, the right remaining at liberty. The prisoner, on the contrary, had the chain fastened to the wrist of his right hand. The prisoner and the soldier who had the care of him were said to be tied (*alligati*) to one another. Sometimes, for greater security, the prisoner was chained to two soldiers, one on each side of him " (*Dict. of Antiq.*, art. " Catena "). Paul was bound with two chains on the occasion mentioned in 21 : 33.—**And keepers before the door** (perhaps two at one station and two at another) **were guarding the prison,** not, after v. 5, *were keeping guard* (Raph., Walch).

7. In the abode = the prison. This was an Attic euphemism which passed at length into the common dialect.—**Having smitten,** in order to rouse him from sleep.—**Arise** (ἀνάστα) is a second aorist imperative. (Comp. Eph. 5 : 14.) Grammarians represent the form as poetic in the earlier Greek. (K. § 172. R. 5 ; W. § 14. 1. h.)—**His chains fell off from his hands,** or **wrists. Hand** (χείρ) the

Greeks could use of the entire fore-arm or any part of it.

8. Gird thyself. For convenience, he had unbound the girdle of his tunic while he slept. The **garment** (ἱμάτιον) which he threw around him was the outer coat, or mantle, worn over the **tunic** (χιτών). There was no occasion for a precipitate flight, and the articles which he was directed to take would be useful to him. Note the transition to the present in the last two imperatives.

9. True, actual, as distinguished from a dream or vision. Peter's uncertainty arose from the extraordinary nature of the interposition ; it was too strange to be credited. He was bewildered by the scene, unable at the moment to comprehend that what he saw and did was a reality.

10. Having passed through the first and second watch—*i. e.* as Walch (*De vinculis Petri*) suggests, first through the two soldiers stationed at Peter's door (v. 6), and then through two others near the gate which led into the city. He supposes the two soldiers to whom Peter was bound (v. 6) were not included in the sixteen (v. 4), since their office would not require them to remain awake, and consequently to be changed during the night, like the others. A more common opinion is that the **first watch** was a single soldier before the door, and the *second* another at the iron gate, and that these two soldiers, with the two by the side of Peter, made up the quaternion then on duty. But **having passed through** suggests a plural sense of **watch,** and must be said loosely, if applied to a single person. This participle after **went out,** in v. 9, indicates a different position of **the first watch** from that of the two soldiers who guarded Peter in his cell. Some have proposed that explanation. The numeral renders the article unnecessary.

and they went out, and passed on through one street; and forthwith the angel departed from him.

11 And when Peter was come to himself, he said, Now I know of a surety, that *a*the Lord hath sent his angel, and *b*hath delivered me out of the hand of Herod, and *from* all the expectation of the people of the Jews.

12 And when he had considered *the thing,* *c*he came to the house of Mary the mother of *d*John, whose surname was Mark; where many were gathered together *e*praying.

13 And as Peter knocked at the door of the gate, a damsel came to hearken, named Rhoda.

14 And when she knew Peter's voice, she opened not the gate for gladness, but ran in, and told how Peter stood before the gate.

15 And they said unto her, Thou art mad. But she constantly affirmed that it was even so. Then said they, *f*It is his angel.

which opened to them of its own accord: and they went out, and passed on through one street; and 11 straightway the angel departed from him. And when Peter was come to himself, he said, Now I know of a truth, that the Lord hath sent forth his angel and delivered me out of the hand of Herod, and from all the expectation of the people of the 12 Jews. And when he had considered *the thing,* he came to the house of Mary the mother of John whose surname was Mark; where many were gath-13 ered together and were praying. And when he knocked at the door of the gate, a maid came to 14 answer, named Rhoda. And when she knew Pe-ter's voice, she opened not the gate for joy, but ran 15 in, and told that Peter stood before the gate. And they said unto her, Thou art mad. But she con-fidently affirmed that it was even so. And they

a Ps. 34 : 7; Dan. 3 : 28 ; 6 : 22 ; Heb. 1. 14....*b* Job 5 : 19 ; Ps. 33 : 18, 19 ; 34 : 22 ; 41 : 2 ; 97 : 10 ; 2 Cor. 1 : 10 ; 2 Pet. 2 : 9..... *c* ch. 4 : 23....*d* ch. 15 : 37....*e* ver. 5....*f* Gen. 48 : 16 ; Matt. 18 : 10.

(W. § 19. 2.) That Peter passed the watch un-opposed, or perhaps unobserved (see v. 18), was a part of the miracle. (See on 5 : 19.)—**Unto the iron gate,** etc. The precise situation of the prison is unknown. The **iron gate** may have formed the termination of a court, or avenue, which connected the prison with the town. De Wette, after Lightfoot, Walch, and others, thinks that the prison was in a tower between the two walls of the city, and that this was the outer gate of the tower. Others have proposed other conjectures.—**Of itself** is equiv-alent to an adverb, **spontaneously.** (K. § 264. 3. c; B. § 123. 6.) The gate opened without any visible cause.—**Went forward one street,** or lane (9 : 11). The angel accompanied him until he was beyond the reach of pursuit.—**Immediately,** on having come thus far.

11. **Having come to himself,** recovered from the confusion of mind into which he had been thrown.—**Sent forth,** from heaven.—**From all the expectation,** of the Jews, who were so eager for his execution, and look-ing forward to it with confidence.

12–17. PETER REPAIRS TO THE HOUSE OF MARY, WHERE SOME OF THE BELIEVERS HAD ASSEMBLED FOR PRAYER.

12. **Having become aware** (14 : 6), con-scious to himself of the state of things. (Whl., Alf., Mey.) Luke reminds us of this fact again (see v. 11), as if it might appear strange that Peter acted with so much deliberation. Some render *considering*—*i. e.* either what he should do or where he should find an assembly of the disciples. Both the meaning and the tense of the participle favor this explanation less than the other.—**John . . . Mark.** This *John Mark* is called simply John in 13 : 5, 13, and Mark in 15 : 39. He is supposed to have been the

10

same Mark whom Peter terms his son in 1 Pet. 5 : 13—*i. e.* in a spiritual sense, converted by his instrumentality. There is no reason for ques-tioning his identity with the evangelist who wrote the Gospel of Mark. (See, further, on v. 25.)—**Praying.** One of the objects for which they were praying was the safety of Peter (v. 5).

13. **A maid-servant.** Her Greek name, **Rhoda,** does not disprove her Jewish origin. (See on 1 : 23.) The porter among the Jews was commonly a female. (See John 18 : 16.) That the person should be known after so long a time shows how minute was Luke's informa-tion.—**To hearken** (ὑπακοῦσαι). This was the classical term signifying to answer a knock or call at the door.

14. **And having recognized his voice** (3 : 10; 4 : 13). Peter may be supposed to have announced his name, or to have given it in reply to her inquiry.—**For gladness.** Noth-ing could be more lifelike than the description of the scene which follows. Rhoda, in the excess of her joy, forgets to open the door, runs into the house, declares the news, while Peter is left in the street still knocking and ex-posed to arrest. The passage has all the vivid-ness of the recital of an eye-witness. Mark was undoubtedly in the house at the time, and may have communicated the circumstances to Luke at Antioch, or Luke may have obtained his in-formation from Barnabas, who was a relative of the family. (See Col. 4 : 10.)

15. διϊσχυρίζετο, **affirmed confidently.—It is his angel**—*i. e.* his tutelary angel, with his form and features. It was a common belief among the Jews, says Lightfoot, that every individual has a guardian angel, and that this angel may assume a visible appearance resembling that of the person whose destiny is

16 But Peter continued knocking: and when they had opened *the door*, and saw him, they were astonished.

17 But he, [a]beckoning unto them with the hand to hold their peace, declared unto them how the Lord had brought him out of the prison. And he said, Go shew these things unto James, and to the brethren. And he departed, and went into another place.

18 Now as soon as it was day, there was no small stir among the soldiers, what was become of Peter.

19 And when Herod had sought for him, and found him not, he examined the keepers, and commanded that *they* should be put to death. And he went down from Judea to Cæsarea, and *there* abode.

16 said, It is his angel. But Peter continued knocking: and when they had opened, they saw him, and 17 were amazed. But he, beckoning unto them with the hand to hold their peace, declared unto them how the Lord had brought him forth out of the prison. And he said, Tell these things unto James, and to the brethren. And he departed, and went to an-18 other place. Now as soon as it was day, there was no small stir among the soldiers, what was become 19 of Peter. And when Herod had sought for him, and found him not, he examin-d the guards, and commanded that they should be [1]put to death. And he went down from Judæa to Cæsarea, and tarried there.

a ch. 13 : 16; 19 : 33; 21 : 40.——[1] Gr. *led away to death.*

committed to him. This idea appears here, not as a docrine of the Scriptures, but as a popular opinion which is neither affirmed nor denied.

17. Having motioned with the hand downward, as a signal that he would speak and wished them to hear. Their joy was so tumultuous that he could make them understand a gesture better than a word.—**To hold their peace.** His object was not to prevent their being overheard, and so discovered, by their enemies, but to secure to himself an opportunity to inform them how he had been liberated.—**The Lord,** as the angel had been sent by him. (See vv. 7, 11.)—**James** is distinguished from the others on account of his office as pastor of the church at Jerusalem. (See on v. 2.)—**And** (probably on the same night) **having gone forth**—*i. e.* from the house, as the context most readily suggests; hence **into another place** is indefinite, and may denote **unto another place,** in the city or out of it. It is most probable that he left the city for a time, as he must have foreseen (see v. 19) that vigorous efforts would be made to retake and destroy him. We find him at Jerusalem again a few years after this. (See 15 : 7.) He may have returned even sooner than that, as Agrippa lived but a short time after this occurrence. Catholic writers and some others hold that Peter proceeded to Rome at this time, and labored for the Jews there as the apostle of the Circumcision (Gal. 2 : 7; 1 Pet. 1 : 1). If this be true, he must have then been the founder of the church in that city, or, at all events, have established a relation to it, personal and official, stronger than that of any other teacher. It is entirely adverse to this view that Paul makes no allusion to Peter in his Epistle to the Romans, but writes with a tone of authority which his avowed policy, his spirit of independence (2 Cor. 10 : 16), would not have suffered him to employ had it belonged more properly to some other apostle to instruct and guide the Roman church. The best opinion from traditionary sources is that Peter arrived at Rome just before

the outbreak of Nero's persecution, where he soon perished as a martyr. It is related that he was placed on the cross, at his own request, with his head downward, as if unworthy to suffer in the posture of the Master whom he had denied. [Compare, on this question, *Was Peter in Rome and Bishop of the Church at Rome?* by J. Ellendorf, translated in *Bib. Sacra*, xv. pp. 569-621 and xvi. pp. 82–106; also Schaff's *Hist. of the Apostolic Church* (New York, 1854), pp. 348-374.—A. H.]

18, 19. TRIAL AND EXECUTION OF THE SOLDIERS.

18. When day had come. If the soldiers to whom Peter was bound had been changed at the expiration of each watch (see on v. 10), why did they not ascertain the escape sooner? Wieseler (*Chronologie,* u. s. w., p. 220) replies that the flight took place in the last watch, not long before break of day. This is doubtful, as it would abridge so much the time allowed for the interview at the house of Mary and for the departure from the city. The question requires no answer if Walch's opinion, as stated in v. 10, be well founded.—**Stir, commotion,** partaking of the nature both of inquiry and alarm. The former part of the idea leads the way to the question which follows. There was reason for fear, because the soldiers, in such a case, were answerable for the safety of the prisoner, and, if he escaped, were liable to suffer the punishment which would have been inflicted on him. (Comp. 16 : 27; Matt. 28 : 14.) **Soldiers** would include naturally the entire sixteen (v. 4), though the four who were on guard at the time of the escape had most reason to tremble for their lives.—**What then** (syllogistical, since he was gone) **was become of Peter?**

19. Having examined, tried, them for a breach of discipline. (See 4 : 9; Luke 23 : 14.) —We need not impute to Herod such barbarity as that of putting to death the entire detachment.—**Keepers** may be understood of those who were more immediately responsible for the prisoner's safety.—**To be led away**—*i. e*

20 ¶ And Herod was highly displeased with them of Tyre and Sidon : but they came with one accord to him, and, having made Blastus the king's chamberlain their friend, desired peace ; because *a*their country was nourished by the king's *country.*

21 And upon a set day Herod, arrayed in royal apparel, sat upon his throne, and made an oration unto them.

22 And the people gave a shout, *saying, It is* the voice of a god, and not of a man.

20 Now he was highly displeased with them of Tyr, and Sidon : and they came with one accord to him and, having made Blastus the king's chamberlain their friend, they asked for peace, because their

21 country was fed from the king's country. And upon a set day Herod arrayed himself in royal apparel, and sat on the ¹throne, and made an oration

22 unto them. And the people shouted, *saying,* The

---

a 1 Kings 5 : 9, 11 ; Ezek. 27 : 17.———1 Or, *judgment-seat*

---

to execution. The word was a *vox solennis* in this sense, as Lösner, Kypke, and others have shown. The Romans employed *ducere* in the same absolute way.—**And he went down,** etc. Herod resided usually at Jerusalem, and went now to Cæsarea, as Josephus informs us, to preside at the public games in honor of the Emperor Claudius.

20–24. DEATH OF HEROD AGRIPPA AT CÆSAREA.

20. The reader should compare the narrative of this event with that of Josephus in *Antt.*, 19. 8. 2. The Jewish historian has confirmed Luke's account in the most striking manner. He also makes Cæsarea the scene of the occurrence ; he mentions the assembly, the oration, the robe, the impious acclamations of the people, the sudden death of Herod, and adds to the rest that his terrible end was a judgment inflicted upon him for his impiety. —**Was highly displeased** may refer to an open war or violent feeling of hostility. As Josephus makes no mention of any actual outbreak between Agrippa and the Phœnicians, the latter is probably the sense of the word here. The Phœnicians may either have apprehended a war as the result of Agrippa's anger, or they may have been threatened with an interruption of the commerce carried on between them and the Jews.—**Came unto him**—i. e. in the person of their representatives ; lit. *were present*, the antecedent motion being applied. (W. § 50. 4.)—**Having persuaded,** brought to their interest.—**Blastus,** judging from his name, may have been a Greek or a Roman. His influence with the king was the reason why they were so anxious to obtain his mediation. A bribe may have quickened his sympathy with the strangers.—**Over his bedchamber,** his chamberlain. His office placed him near the king's person, and enabled him to hold the keys to his heart (Bmg.).— **Desired peace**—i. e. according to the circumstances of the case sought to avert a rupture of it, or, if it was already impaired, to effect its restoration. Their desire for this result may have been increased by the existing famine.— **Because their country was sustained,** etc.

The Tyrians and Sidonians were a commercial people, and procured their supplies of grain chiefly from Palestine in exchange for their own merchandise. This relation of the two countries to each other had existed from early times. (See 1 Kings 5 : 9 ; Ezra 3 : 7 ; Ezek. 27 : 17.)

21. On an appointed day, which, according to Josephus, was the 1st of August, and the second day of the public games.—**Arrayed,** etc. The circumstances related by Josephus may be combined (Conybeare and Howson, i. p. 158) with Luke's account, as follows: " On the second day of the festival Agrippa came into the theatre. The stone seats, rising in a great semicircle, tier above tier, were covered with an excited multitude. The king came in clothed in magnificent robes, of which silver was the costly and brilliant material. It was early in the day, and the sun's rays fell upon the king ; so that the eyes of the beholders were dazzled with the brightness which surrounded him. Voices from the crowd, here and there, exclaimed that it was the apparition of something divine. And when he spoke and made an oration to them, they gave a shout, saying, 'It is the voice of a god, and not of a man.' But in the midst of this idolatrous ostentation an angel of God suddenly smote him. He was carried out of the theatre a dying man, and on the 6th of August he was dead."—**Upon the seat,** or **throne,** provided for him in the theatre. (See on 19 : 29.) **Spoke publicly,** because, though he directed his speech to the deputies, he was heard also by the people who were present (v. 22). The Phœnicians were there as suppliants for peace, and the king's object now was to announce to them his decision. The giving audience to ambassadors and replying to them in public was not uncommon in ancient times. —**Unto them**—i. e. the Tyrians and Sidonians, as represented by their agents. The pronoun does not refer to **the common people** (δῆμος). (See W. § 22. 3. 1.) It was the messengers, not the Cæsareans, who awaited the king's answer.

22. Shouted thereupon, again and again. It enhanced the eloquence, no doubt, that what

23 And immediately the angel of the Lord *a*smote him, because *b*he gave not God the glory: and he was eaten of worms, and gave up the ghost.

24 ¶ But *c*the word of God grew and multiplied.

25 And Barnabas and Saul returned from Jerusalem, when they had fulfilled *their* ministry, and *d*took with them *e*John, whose surname was Mark.

23 voice of a god, and not of a man. And immediately an angel of the Lord smote him, because he gave not God the glory: and he was eaten of worms, and gave up the ghost.

24 But the word of God grew and multiplied.

25 And Barnabas and Saul returned [1]from Jerusalem, when they had fulfilled their ministration, taking with them John whose surname was Mark.

CHAPTER XIII.

NOW there were *f*in the church that was at Antioch certain prophets and teachers: as *g*Barnabas, and Simeon that was called Niger, and *h*Lucius of Cyrene, and Manaen, which had been brought up with Herod the tetrarch, and Saul.

1 Now there were at Antioch, in the church that was *there*, prophets and teachers, Barnabas, and Symeon that was called Niger, and Lucius of Cyrene, and Manaen the foster-brother of Herod the tetrarch, and Saul.

---

a 1 Sam. 25 : 38 ; 2 Sam. 24 : 17....*b* Ps. 115 : 1... *c* Isa. 55 : 11 ; ch. 6 : 7 ; 19 : 20 ; Col. 1 : 6....*d* ch. 13 : 5, 13 ; 15 : 37....*e* ver. 12 ....*f* ch. 11 : 27 ; 14 : 26 ; 15 : 35....*g* ch. 11 : 22–26....*h* Rom. 16 : 21.——1 Many ancient authorities read *to Jerusalem.*

---

they had heard accorded with their wishes. In such a city the bulk of the assembly would be heathen (see on 8 : 40), and **of a god** may be taken in their sense of the term.

23. Because he gave not glory to God— *i. e.* did not repel the impious flattery; was willing to receive it. Some editors insert **the** before **glory.—And having been eaten with worms, he expired.** In ascribing Agrippa's death to such a cause, Luke makes it evident that he did not mean to represent it as instantaneous. His statement, therefore, does not oppose that of Josephus, who says that Herod lingered for five days after the first attack, in the greatest agony, and then died. It is evident also, for the same reason, that Luke did not consider the angel as the author of Herod's death in any such sense as to exclude the intervention of secondary causes.

24. But contrasts slightly the fate of Herod, the persecutor of the church, with the prosperity of the church itself.—**The word of God grew,** was diffused more and more, **and increased**—*i. e.* (comp. 6 : 1) was embraced by increasing numbers. **Word** suggests the complex idea of doctrine and disciples, and the verbs which follow divide the idea into its parts.

25. BARNABAS AND SAUL RETURN TO ANTIOCH.

25. This verse appears to be introductory to the subject of the next chapter. It was proper to apprise the reader that Barnabas and Saul returned to Antioch (see 11 : 30), since the narrative of what next occurred in that city implies that they were there, and no mention has been made of their return. Paul and Barnabas made this journey to Jerusalem probably near the beginning of the year A. D. 45 ; for the famine commenced at the close of the preceding year (see on 11 : 28), and the supplies collected in anticipation of that event would naturally be forwarded before the distress began to be severe.

That the journey took place about this time results also from its being mentioned in connection with Herod's death. The two friends appear to have remained at Jerusalem but a short time, as may be inferred from the object of their mission, and still more decisively from the absence of any allusion to this journey in Gal. 2 : 1, *sq.*—**John.** John was a relative of Barnabas, as we learn from Col. 4 : 10, and this relationship may have led to the present connection. He appears next in the history as their associate in missionary labors (13 : 5).

1–3. BARNABAS AND SAUL ARE SENT TO PREACH TO THE HEATHEN.

1. The narrative mentions three different journeys of Paul among the heathen ; the account of the first of these commences here.— **Certain** (τινές ; probably not genuine) would indicate that those named were not all the teachers at Antioch.—In κατὰ τὴν ἐκκλησίαν the preposition may be directive as well as local : **in the church** and for its benefit. The office supplied a correspondent (κατά) want. Or the idea may be that of distribution : such teachers belonging to the different churches (comp. 14 : 23), the writer's mind passes along the series to those at Antioch.—**Prophets** (see on 2 : 17) is the specific term ; **teachers,** the generic. The prophets were all teachers, but the reverse was not true. (Comp. note on 14 : 23.)—**Symeon** is otherwise unknown. He was evidently a Jew, and hence in his intercourse with Gentiles (see on v. 9) was called also Niger. The latter was a familiar name among the Romans, and is a precarious reason for inferring (Alf.) that he was an African proselyte.—**Lucius** may be the *Lucius* who is mentioned in Rom. 16 : 21. Some have thought that Luke, the writer of the Acts (no doubt a native of Antioch), may be intended here ; but **Lucius** and **Lucianus,** or **Lu-**

2 As they ministered to the Lord, and fasted, the Holy Ghost said, *Separate me Barnabas and Saul for the work *whereunto I have called them.
3 And *when they had fasted and prayed, and laid *their* hands on them, they sent *them* away.

2 tetrarch, and Saul. And as they ministered to the Lord, and fasted, the Holy Spirit said, separate me Barnabas and Saul for the work whereunto I have
3 called them. Then, when they had fasted and prayed and laid their hands on them, they sent them away.

---

a Num. 8 : 14; ch. 9 : 15; 22 : 21; Rom. 1 : 1; Gal. 1 : 15; 2 : 9....*b* Matt. 9 : 38; ch. 14 : 26; Rom. 10 : 15; Eph. 3 : 7, 8; 1 Tim. 2 : 7; 2 Tim. 1 : 11; Heb. 5 : 4....*c* ch. 6 : 6.

---

cas, are different names. (See W. § 16. 4. R. 1.) —**Of Cyrene.** (See on 2 : 10.)—**Manaen** = Heb. *Menahem* (2 Kings 15 : 14) occurs only here. —**Herod the tetrarch.** This *Herod* was the one who put to death John the Baptist—a son of Herod the Great, and an uncle of Agrippa, whose death has just been related. He was now in exile on the banks of the Rhone, but, though divested of his office, is called *tetrarch*, because he was best known under that title. (See on 4 : 6.) There are two views as to the import of σύντροφος. One is that it means *comrade*—lit. *one brought up*, educated, with another. It was very common for persons of rank to associate other children with their own, for the purpose of sharing their amusements and studies, and by their example serving to excite them to greater emulation. Josephus, Plutarch, Polybius, and others speak of this ancient practice. So Calvin, Grotius, Schott, Baumgarten, and others. The more approved opinion is that it means *collactaneus*, nourished at the same breast, *foster-brother*. Kuinoel, Olshausen, Tholuck, De Wette, and others, after Walch (*De Menachemo*), adopt that meaning. The mother of Manaen, according to this view, was Herod's nurse. In either case the relation is mentioned as an honorary one.

2. Ministered refers here to the rites of Christian worship, as prayer, exhortation, fasting. (See vv. 3, 15; 14 : 23.) [The word which is here translated **ministered** (λειτουργούντων) is found in only two other passages of the New Testament—viz. in Heb. 10 : 11, where it refers to religious service in the temple and is followed by an expression which denotes the "offering of sacrifices," and in Rom. 15 : 27, where it refers to charitable service in temporal things. The corresponding noun (λειτουργία) is used in the same way—first of rendering direct service to God in the temple (Luke 1 : 23 and Heb. 9 : 6; comp. Phil. 2 : 17; Heb. 8 : 6); and secondly, of giving pecuniary help to those in need (2 Cor. 9 : 12; Phil. 2 : 30). The derived adjectives are also significant of both kinds of service. Yet the ministry of direct worship may be regarded as the leading sense of these words; so that service in worldly things is represented by them as in a true sense religious.—A. H.] — **They**—*i. e.* the prophets and teachers. The participation of others in the service is not asserted or denied. It is possible that they were observing a season of prayer with reference to this very question, What were their duties in relation to the heathen? [Meyer insists forcibly that **they** refers to the church, including the five named, and not to the latter only. Thus: "The reference of αὐτῶν (**they**), not to the collective church, but to the prophets and teachers named in v. 1, . . . is not, on account of **separate me,** and of v. 3, to be approved. The whole highly-important missionary act would, according to this view, have been performed only in the circle of five persons, of whom, moreover, two were the missionaries destined by the Spirit, and the church as such would have taken no part at all, not even being represented by its presbyters—a proceeding which neither agrees with the fellowship of the Spirit in the constitution of the apostolic church, nor corresponds with the analogous concrete cases of the choice of an apostle (ch. 1) and of the deacons (ch. 6). (Comp. also 14 : 27, where the missionaries, on their return, make their report to the church.")—A. H.]—**Separate now for me**—*i. e.* for the Holy Spirit. The Spirit makes the revelation, selects the missionaries, assigns to them their work. The personality of the agent may be inferred from such acts. The command in this form was addressed to the associates of Barnabas and Saul, but the latter would hear the same voice pointing out to them their duty and directing them to perform the service laid upon them.—**Now** (δή) strengthens the command. (See 15 : 36; Luke 2 : 15. K. § 315. 1.) The verb contains the idea both of selection and consecration.— **Unto which** (ὅ), without the preposition, because the antecedent has it. (Comp. **which thou camest** R. V., ᾗ ἤρχου, in 9 : 17.)—**I have called** has a middle sense. (W. § 39. 3.) The nature of this work—not stated here—we learn from the subsequent narrative: they were to go into foreign countries and publish the gospel to Jews and Gentiles. The great object of the mission was doubtless to open more effectually "the door of faith to the heathen."

3. Then having fasted, etc. This was a different fast from that spoken of in v. 2, and observed, probably, by the body of the church. [According to the words of Christ

4 ¶ So they, being sent forth by the Holy Ghost, departed unto Seleucia; and from thence they sailed to ^aCyprus.

4 So they, being sent forth by the Holy Spirit, went down to Seleucia; and from thence they sailed to Cyprus.

a ch. 4 : 36.

preserved in Matt. 9 : 14, 15 (also Mark 2 : 18–20; Luke 5 : 33–35), *fasting* is a natural expression, not of satisfaction, but of sorrow, of trouble. And it is never appropriate unless it is spontaneous. But even when it is spontaneous, it should not be paraded in public with outward shows of mortification (Matt. 6 : 16–18). Hence the impossibility of a genuine national fast, unless it be in time of great calamity. But Jesus does not in any of these passages condemn fasting on the part of Christians. We cannot, indeed, be certain that he anywhere enjoins it on his followers as a duty; for Matt. 17 : 21 is probably a gloss added to the true text, while the words "and fasting," in Mark 9 : 29, are at least doubtful; but the example of Christ and of apostolic Christians (Matt. 4 : 1, *sq.*; Acts 10 : 30; 13 : 2, 3; 14 : 23), together with the prediction of Jesus (Matt. 9 : 15), the implied approval of Paul (1 Cor. 7 : 5), and the Saviour's direction as to the proper manner of fasting (Matt. 6 : 16–18), prove beyond a doubt that fasting has its place at times in the best forms of Christian living.— A. H.]— On **laid their hands on them,** see 6 : 6. The act was a representative one, and, though performed by a part, involves the idea of a general participation. Paul was already a minister and an apostle (see Gal. 1 : 1, *sq.*, where he claims this character from the outset), and by this service he and Barnabas were now merely set apart for the accomplishment of a specific work. They were summoned to a renewed and more systematic prosecution of the enterprise of converting the heathen. (See on 9 : 30; 11 : 20.)— **Sent away.** That the subject of this verb includes the Antiochian Christians in general may be argued from the analogous case in 15 : 40. The brethren commended Paul to God as he departed on his second mission.

4–12. THE JOURNEY TO CYPRUS, AND ITS RESULTS.

4. Being sent forth. We may place this mission in the year A. D. 45. It does not appear that they remained long at Antioch before their departure. (See the note on 12 : 25.)— **Unto Seleucia. Seleucia** lay west of Antioch, on the sea-coast, five miles north of the mouth of the Orontes. It was situated on the rocky eminence forming the southern extremity of the hilly range called Pieria. The harbor and mercantile suburb were on level ground toward the west. A village called Antakia and interesting ruins point out the ancient site. "The inner basin, or dock (there were two ports), is now a morass; but its dimensions can be measured, and the walls that surround it can be distinctly traced. The position of the ancient floodgates, and the passage through which the vessels were moved from the inner to the outer harbor, can be accurately marked. The very piers of the outer harbor are still to be seen under the water. The stones are of great size — some of them twenty feet long, five feet deep, and six feet wide—and are fastened to each other with iron cramps. The masonry of ancient Seleucia is still so good that not long since a Turkish pacha conceived the idea of clearing out and repairing the harbor." (See authorities in Conybeare and Howson.) Those piers were still unbroken, this great seaport of the Seleucids and the Ptolemies was as magnificent as ever, under the sway of the Romans, when Paul and Barnabas passed through it on their present mission. Whether they **came down** (κατῆλθον) from the interior to the coast by land or by water is uncertain. The windings of the river make the distance about forty-one miles, but by land it is only sixteen miles and a half. At present the Orontes is not navigable, in consequence of a bar at the mouth and other obstructions; but Strabo says (16. 2) that in his time they sailed up the stream in one day. The road, though it is now mostly overgrown with shrubs, was then doubtless a well-worn track like the road from the Piræus to Athens, or from Ostia to Rome. At Seleucia the two missionaries with their companion went on board (ἀπέπλευσαν, *sailed from*) one of the numerous vessels which must have been constantly plying between that port and the fertile Cyprus. "As they cleared the port the whole sweep of the bay of Antioch opened on their left—the low ground by the mouth of the Orontes, the wild and woody country beyond it, and then the peak of Mount Casius, rising symmetrically from the very edge of the sea to a height of five thousand feet. On the right, in the south-west horizon, if the day was clear, they saw the island of Cyprus from the first. The current sets northerly and north-east between the island and the Syrian coast. But with a fair wind a few hours would enable them to run down from Seleucia to Salamis; and the

5 And when they were at Salamis, *they preached the word of God in the synagogues of the Jews: and they had also *b*John to *their* minister.

6 And when they had gone through the isle unto Paphos, they found *c*a certain sorcerer, a false prophet, a Jew, whose name was Bar-jesus:

5 Cyprus. And when they were at Salamis, they proclaimed the word of God in the synagogues of the Jews: and they had also John as their attendant.

6 And when they had gone through the whole island unto Paphos, they found a certain ¹sorcerer, a false

---

a ver. 46....*b* ch. 12 : 25; 15 : 37....*c* ch. 8 : 9.——I Gr. *Magus*: as in Matt. 2 : 1, 7, 16.

---

land would rapidly rise in forms well known and familiar to Barnabas and Mark" (Conybeare and Howson, i. p. 169). The fact that Barnabas was a native of Cyprus (4:36) may have induced them to give this direction to their journey.

5. And having arrived in Salamis. This town was on the eastern shore of Cyprus, " on a bight of the coast to the north of the river Pediæus. A large city by the sea-shore, a widespread plain with corn-fields and orchards, and the blue distance of mountains beyond, composed the view on which the eyes of Barnabas and Saul rested when they came to anchor in the bay of Salamis."—**The synagogues** indicates that the Jews here were numerous, since in other places where they were few they had only one synagogue. (Comp. 17 : 1; 18 : 4.) This intimation is confirmed by ancient testimony. In the time of Trajan (A. D. 116), the Jews in Cyprus were so powerful that they rose and massacred two hundred and forty thousand of the Greek inhabitants (Dio Cass., 68. 32). In revenge for this slaughter, Hadrian, who was afterward emperor, landed on the island and either put to death or expelled the entire Jewish population. At the time of Paul's visit many of the Cyprian Jews must have resided at Salamis, which was the seat of a lucrative commerce.—**And they had also John** (see 12 : 25) **as an assistant**—in what? **Also,** as I think, recalls most naturally **preached the word;** and the answer would be that he assisted them in the declaration of the word. (Comp. 26 : 16; Luke 1 : 2; 1 Cor. 4 : 1.) But the view of most critics is different: they suppose John to have had charge of the incidental cares of the party, so as to leave Paul and Barnabas more at liberty to preach the gospel. We are not informed how long they remained at Salamis or what success attended their labors.

6. And having passed through the whole island unto Paphos, which was at the other end of Cyprus. The city intended here was *New* Paphos, in distinction from the old city of that name, which was several miles farther south. The distance from east to west was not more than a hundred miles. The Peutingerian Table¹ (which dates probably

from the time of Alexander Severus—*i. e.* about A. D. 230) represents a public road extending from Salamis to Paphos. If that road existed at this earlier period, Paul arrived at Paphos in a short time and without difficulty. The present Baffa occupies the site of that city.
—**Found a certain Magian,** which was his professional title, since it stands for **Elymas** in v. 8; not *sorcerer* (E. V.), which would be opprobrious.—**False prophet** is the narrator's term for describing him; he was a fortuneteller, but his art was an imposition. It may appear singular that a person of his character should so mislead and captivate the prudent Sergius. But the incident presents, in fact, a true picture of the times. At that period (I abridge Conybeare and Howson's paragraph here) impostors from the East pretending to magical powers had great influence over the Roman mind. The East, but recently thrown open, was the land of mystery to the Western nations. Reports of the strange arts practised there, of the wonderful events of which it was the scene, excited almost fanatically the imagination both of the populace and the aristocracy of Rome. Syrian fortune-tellers crowded the capital and appeared in all the haunts of business and amusement. The strongest minds were not superior to their influence. Marius relied on a Jewish prophetess for regulating the progress of his campaigns. Pompey, Crassus, and Cæsar sought information from Oriental astrology. Juvenal paints to us the Emperor Tiberius "sitting on the rock of Capri with his flock of Chaldæans round him." The astrologers and sorcerers, says Tacitus, are a class of men who "will always be discarded and always cherished." [With this statement may be compared the treatise of Tholuck on the *Nature and Moral Influence of Heathenism* (translated for the *Biblical Repository*, vol. ii. p. 286), where many illustrations are given. The multitude of soothsayers at this period is said to have been enormous. "The Indians, Persians, Egyptians, Gauls, and Germans had their soothsayers; and among the Romans this art had been carried to such an extent that Fabricius enumerates toward a hundred different modes of divination." (See also Uhlhorn, *The Conflict of*

---

¹ See Forbiger's *Handbuch der Alten Geographie*, vol. i. p. 469, *sq.*

7 Which was with the deputy of the country, Sergius Paulus, a prudent man; who called for Barnabas and Saul, and desired to hear the word of God.

8 But ^aElymas the sorcerer (for so is his name by interpretation) withstood them, seeking to turn away the deputy from the faith.

9 Then Saul, (who also *is called* Paul,) ^bfilled with the Holy Ghost, set his eyes on him,

7 prophet, a Jew, whose name was Bar-Jesus; who was with the proconsul, Sergius Paulus, a man of understanding. The same called unto him Barnabas and Saul, and sought to hear the word of God. But Elymas the ¹sorcerer (for so is his name by interpretation) withstood them, seeking to turn 9 aside the proconsul from the faith. But Saul, who is also *called* Paul, filled with the Holy Spirit, fas-

---

a Ex. 7 : 11 ; 2 Tim. 3 : 8....*b* ch. 4 : 8.——1 Gr. *Magus*: as in Matt. 2 : 1, 7, 16.

Christianity with Heathenism, pp. 63, 316, etc. ; Pressensé, *Early Years of Christianity*, p. 66, etc. : C. Scribner, 1870 ; Döllinger, *The Gentile and the Jew*, vol. ii. *passim.*—A. H.]

7. Who was with the proconsul Sergius Paulus. It would not have been correct to apply this title to the governor of every Roman province, or even to the governor of the same province at different periods. It was so difficult to observe accuracy in the use of the varying titles given to Roman magistrates that several of the classic authors of this period have, beyond all question, misapplied them in various instances. Luke was exposed to error in this passage on the right hand and on the left. On the establishment of the empire, Augustus divided the provinces into two classes. Those which required a military force he retained in his own hands, and the others he committed to the care of the Senate and the Roman people. The officers or governors sent into the emperor's provinces were styled prætors or legates (*proprætores, legati*, or ἀντιστράτηγοι, πρεσβευταί) ; those sent into the people's provinces were called proconsuls (*proconsules*, ἀνθύπατοι). Cyprus, then, must have been a senatorian province at this time, and Luke has assigned to Sergius a false title. But, further, the same province was often transferred from one jurisdiction to another. Thus, in the present instance, Augustus at first reserved Cyprus to himself and committed its administration to proprætors, or legates. Strabo informs us of that circumstance, and there leaves the matter. Hence it was supposed for a long time that Luke had committed an oversight here, or had styled Sergius proconsul without knowing the exact import of the appellation. But a passage was discovered at length in Dio Cassius (53. 12) which states that Augustus subsequently relinquished Cyprus to the Senate in exchange for another province, and (54. 4) that it was governed henceforth by proconsuls : *And so proconsuls also began to be sent to those nations.* Coins, too, have been found, struck in the reign of Claudius, which confirm Luke's accuracy. Bishop Marsh mentions one on which this very title *proconsul* (ἀνθύπατος) is applied to Cominius Proclus, a governor of Cyprus. It was in the

reign of Claudius that Paul visited this island. (For similar confirmations of our history, see on 18 : 12; 19 : 38.)—**Prudent, intelligent** discerning. It may have been his possession of this quality that prompted him to seek the acquaintance of Elymas ; he may have hoped to gain from him that deeper knowledge of futurity and of the mysteries of nature which the human mind craves so instinctively. It certainly was proof of his discernment that he was not deceived by the man's pretensions— that, on hearing of the arrival of Paul and Barnabas, he sent for them, and on the strength of the evidence which confirmed their doctrine yielded his mind to it.—**Desired earnestly.** —**The word of God** designates the new doctrine from Luke's point of view (Mey.).

8. Elymas is an Arabic word which means *the wise.* It was a title of honor, like **the Magian** (ὁ μάγος), to which it is here put as equivalent. He was born, perhaps, in Arabia, or had lived there, and may have assumed this name in a boastful spirit, or may have received it from others as a compliment to his skill.— **Seeking to turn aside the proconsul from the faith**—*i. e.* from adopting it; for he was not yet a believer. (See v. 12.)

9. The also Paul (ὁ καὶ Παῦλος) = **the** (one) **also called Paul.—The** (ὁ) is the article here, not a pronoun. (W. § 18. 1.) The origin of this name is still disputed. Among the later critics, Olshausen and Meyer adhere to the older view—that Paul assumed it out of respect to Sergius Paulus, who was converted by his instrumentality. But had the writer connected the name with that event, he would have introduced it more naturally after v. 12. He makes use of it, it will be observed, before speaking of the proconsul's conversion. Neander objects, further, that it was customary among the ancients for the pupil to adopt the name of the teacher, not the teacher to adopt that of the pupil. There is force, too, in his remark that, according to this view, the apostle would seem to recognize the salvation of a distinguished person as more important than that of others ; for that Sergius was his first convert from heathenism, and received this honor on that account, assumes incorrectly that he had

10 And said, O full of all subtilty and all mischief, *thou* child of the devil, *thou* enemy of all righteousness, wilt thou not cease t᷎ pervert the right ways of the Lord?
11 And now, behold, *b*the hand of the Lord *is* upon thee, and thou shalt be blind, not seeing the sun for a season. And immediately there fell on him a mist and a darkness; and he went about seeking some to lead him by the hand.
12 Then the deputy, when he saw what was done, believed, being astonished at the doctrine of the Lord.
13 Now when Paul and his company loosed from

10 tened his eyes on him, and said, O full of all guile and all villany, thou son of the devil, thou enemy of all righteousness, wilt thou not cease to pervert
11 the right ways of the Lord? And now, behold, the hand of the Lord is upon thee, and thou shalt be blind, not seeing the sun ¹for a season. And immediately there fell on him a mist and a darkness; and he went about seeking some to lead him by the
12 hand. Then the proconsul, when he saw what was done, believed, being astonished at the teaching of the Lord.
13 Now Paul and his company set sail from Paphos,

a Matt. 13 : 38 ; John 8 : 44 : 1 John 3 : 8....b Ex. 9 : 3 ; 1 Sam. 5 : 6.——1 Or, *until*

preached hitherto to none but those of his own nation. It is more probable that Paul acquired this name like other Jews in that age, who, when they associated with foreigners, had often two names—the one Jewish, the other foreign; sometimes entirely distinct, as Onias and Menelaus, Hillel and Pollio, and sometimes similar in sound, as Tarphon and Trypho, Silas and Silvanus. In like manner, the apostle may have been known as Saul among the Jews and Paul among the heathen; and, being a native of a foreign city, as Lightfoot suggests, he may have borne the two names from early life. This explanation of the origin of the name accounts for its introduction at this stage of the history. It is here for the first time that Luke speaks directly of Paul's labors among the heathen; and it is natural that he should apply to him the name by which he was chiefly known in that sphere of his ministry. According to some, the name changes here, because Luke has followed, hitherto, written memoranda, in which the apostle was called Saul (Neand., Alf.). This hypothesis is unnecessary and improbable. Luke had no need of such memoirs, as he could learn from Paul himself all that he has related of him; and, further, the style of what precedes, instead of indicating a different hand, is homogeneous with that which follows. Zeller, though he denies that Luke wrote the Acts, maintains that a single author must have written it.—**Filled with,** etc. He was thus impelled to expose the man's wickedness and to announce his punishment.

10. Subtilty, deceit, refers to his occupation; **mischief, wickedness,** to his character. —**Son of the devil.** The kindredship is that of disposition, moral resemblance. (See John 8 : 44.) The second noun is sufficiently definite to omit the article. (W. ? 19. 1.) It has the article, however, in other passages, except 1 Pet. 5 : 8, where it stands in apposition.—**Wilt thou not cease to pervert**—*i. e.* to misrepresent, malign—**the right ways of the Lord?**—viz. those which he requires men to follow, as repentance, faith, obedience. It was Christian

truth, the gospel, which he opposed. Most critics prefer the interrogative form of the sentence as more forcible than the declarative. **Not** denies **cease** = *persist* (W. ? 57. 3), and implies the ordinary affirmative answer. **Right** suggests, possibly, a contrast with the impostor's own ways, so full of deceit and obliquity.

11. Hand of the Lord. Here God, perhaps, as the phrase is common in the Old Testament.—**Upon thee**—viz., *i. e.*, for punishment; in a good sense, in 11 : 21.—**Not seeing** states a consequence; hence μή, not οὐ.—**Until a season,** a certain time. (Comp. Luke 4 : 13.) The infliction would be temporary, either because the object (see next verse) did not require it to be permanent, or because the mildness might conduce to the man's repentance.—**A mist and darkness,** related as cause and effect, or by degrees—first one, and then the other.—**Seeking** states his habit (imperf.) during the period of his blindness.

12. Being astonished at the doctrine of the Lord—*i. e.* its confirmation by such a miracle. (Comp. Mark 1 : 27.) [Not merely, perhaps, at "its confirmation by such a miracle," but at the doctrine concerning Christ, which was so new and extraordinary in itself, as well as so wonderfully attested by the miracle. The breviloquence of Luke would be fully accounted for by this view. It would probably be incorrect to say, with Canon Cook, that "the doctrine concerning the Lord impressed the proconsul's mind more than the miraculous visitation." Teaching and miracle went together, and the wonder was due to their combined influence.—A. H.]

13–15. THEY PROCEED TO PERGA, AND THENCE TO ANTIOCH IN PISIDIA.

13. Loosed, having put to sea—lit. *having gone up* (note the etymology), because the sea appears higher than the land. Paphos was on the sea-shore, and they would embark at that place.—**Paul and his companions** (οἱ περί τὸν Παῦλον—lit. *those about Paul*). *About* (περί) presents the name after it as the central object of the group. (See John 11 : 19. W

Paphos, they came to Perga in Pamphylia: and *a*John departing from them returned to Jerusalem.

14 ¶ But when they departed from Perga, they came to Antioch in Pisidia, and *b*went into the synagogue on the sabbath day, and sat down.

15 And *c*after the reading of the law and the prophets the rulers of the synagogue sent unto them, saying, Ye men *and* brethren, if ye have *d*any word of exhortation for the people, say on.

and came to Perga in Pamphylia: and John de-
14 parted from them and returned to Jerusalem. But they, passing through from Perga, came to Antioch of Pisidia; and they went into the synagogue on
15 the sabbath day, and sat down. And after the reading of the law and the prophets the rulers of the synagogue sent unto them, saying, Brethren, if ye have any word of exhortation for the people, say

---

a ch. 15 : 38....*b* ch. 16 : 13 ; 17 : 2 ; 18 : 4....*c* Luke 4 : 16 ; ver. 27....*d* Heb. 13 : 22.

---

§ 53. i.) Hitherto the order has been Barnabas and Saul; but from this time Paul appears in the narrative as the principal person, and Barnabas as subordinate.—**Came unto Perga.** They must have "sailed past the promontories of Drepanum and Acamas, and then across the waters of the Pamphylian Sea, leaving on the right the cliffs (six hundred feet high) which form the western boundary of Cilicia to the innermost bend of the bay of Attaleia." *Perga* was the chief city of Pamphylia, situated on the Cestrus, about seven miles from its mouth. A bar obstructs the entrance of this river at the present time, but Strabo (14. 4) says expressly that it was navigable in his day as far up as Perga. The ruins of this city are to be seen still, sixteen miles north-east of the modern Adalia, or Satalia. They consist of " walls and towers, columns and cornices, a theatre and a stadium, a broken aqueduct, and tombs scattered on both sides of the site of the town. Nothing else remains of Perga but the beauty of its natural situation, between and upon the sides of two hills, with an extensive valley in front, watered by the river Cestrus, and backed by the mountains of the Taurus."[1]—**And John,** etc. Why John Mark left them so abruptly is unknown. It is certain from 15 : 38 (see the note there) that his reason for turning back was not one which Paul approved. He returned, not to Antioch, but Jerusalem, where his home was (12 : 12).

14. They—*i. e.* **they themselves,** unaccompanied by their former associate.—**From Perga.** The stay at Perga, therefore, was brief; they did not even preach there at this time. (Comp. 14 : 25.) What occasioned this singular haste? Very possibly, as Conybeare and Howson suggest, they arrived there in the spring of the year, and in order to prosecute their journey into the interior were obliged to advance without delay : " Earlier in the season the passes would have been filled with snow. In the heat of summer the weather would have been less favorable for the expedition. In the autumn the disadvantages would have been

still greater, from the approaching difficulties of winter." On the journey from the coast to the interior, Paul may have encountered some of the "perils of robbers" and " perils of rivers " to which he alludes in 2 Cor. 11 : 26. The maurauding habits of the people on the mountains which he now crossed were notorious in all ancient history. The country swarmed with banditti of the most desperate character. The physical character of the region exposed him, also, to the other class of dangers. The streams here are numerous and violent beyond those of any other tract in Asia Minor. Torrents "burst out at the base of huge cliffs or dash down wildly through narrow ravines." (See Conybeare and Howson for fuller information on these points.) —**To Antioch.** *Antioch,* which lay north from Perga, was on the central table-land of Asia Minor, on the confines of Pisidia and Phrygia. It was built by the founder of the Syrian Antioch. Under Augustus it rose to the rank of a colony. It was now an important city, inhabited by many Greeks, Romans, and Jews, in addition to its native population. The site of Antioch was first identified by Mr. Arundel in 1833.—**Day, of the Sabbath**—*i. e.* the rest-season. The plural arose, probably, from the fact that such a season included often more than one day. (See W. § 27. 3.)

15. After the reading, etc. The practice of reading the Scriptures in this manner grew up, probably, during the Exile. (Win., *Realw.,* ii. p. 548.) **Law** here designates the Pentateuch; **prophets,** the other books of the Old Testament. (See Matt. 5 : 17 ; Luke 16 : 16, etc.) The *Psalms* formed sometimes a third division. (See Luke 24 : 44.) **The rulers of the synagogue** (see on 9 : 2) **sent unto them a servant** (Luke 4 : 20). It may have been known that they were teachers, or, as Hemsen suggests, they may have occupied a seat which indicated that such was their office.—**In you,** in your minds. (Comp. Gal. 1 : 16 ; Phil. 1 : 5.)—**Exhortation.** The object was to incite them to a stricter observance of the law.

---

[1] Sir C. Fellows's *Asia Minor,* pp. 190–193.

16 Then Paul stood up, and *beckoning with *his* hand said, Men of Israel, and *ye that fear God, give audience.

17 The God of this people of Israel *chose our fathers, and exalted the people *when they dwelt as strangers in the land of Egypt, *and with an high arm brought he them out of it.

18 And *about the time of forty years suffered he their manners in the wilderness.

19 And when *he had destroyed seven nations in the land of Chanaan, *he divided their land to them by lot.

20 And after that *he gave *unto them* judges about the

16 on. And Paul stood up, and beckoning with the hand said,

Men of Israel, and ye that fear God, hearken.

17 The God of this people Israel chose our fathers, and exalted the people when they sojourned in the land of Egypt, and with a high arm led he them forth

18 out of it. And for about the time of forty years like a nursing-father bare he them in the wilderness.

19 And when he had destroyed seven nations in the land of Canaan, he gave *them* their land for an inheritance, for about four hundred and fifty years:

20 and after these things he gave *them* judges until

a ch. 12 : 17....*b* vers. 26, 42, 43 ; ch. 10 : 35....*c* Deut. 7 : 6, 7....*d* Ex. 1 : 1 ; Ps. 105 : 23, 24 ; ch. 7 : 17....*e* Ex. 6 : 6 ; 13 : 14, 16....*f* Ex. 16 : 35 ; Num. 14 : 33, 34 ; Ps. 95 : 9, 10 ; ch. 7 : 36....*g* Deut. 7 : 1....*h* Josh. 14 : 1, 2 ; Ps. 78 : 55....*i* Jud. 2 : 16.———1 Many ancient authorities read *suffered he their manners*. See Deut. 1 : 31.

16–41. THE DISCOURSE OF PAUL AT ANTIOCH.

The topics are—first, the goodness of God to Israel, especially in having promised to send to them a Saviour (16-25) ; secondly, Jesus has been proved to be this Saviour by his death and resurrection, in accordance with the prophecies of the Old Testament (26-37) ; and thirdly, it is the duty of men to receive him in this character, since they can be saved in no other way (38-41).

16. Beckoning with his hand (comp. on 12 : 16) was the customary gesture on rising to speak. It betokened respect for the audience and a request for attention.—**Who fear God,** as in 10 : 2—*i. e.* Gentiles who were friendly to Judaism, but uncircumcised. They occupied, it is said, a separate place in the synagogue. The contents of the address show that the Israelites greatly outnumbered that class of the hearers. This discourse deserves the more attention as furnishing so copious an illustration of the apostle's manner of preaching to the Jews.

17. Exalted, made them numerous and powerful.—**In the land** (ἐν γῇ). For the absence of the article, see on 7 : 29.—**With a high arm**—*i. e.* one raised on high, and so ever ready to protect and defend them. (Comp. Ex. 6 : 6.)

18. Carried them as a nurse (in the arms, as it were ; ἐτροφοφόρησεν = ὡς τροφὸς ἐβάστασεν), sustained, cared for them. The term is derived, probably, from Deut. 1 : 31. Most of the later editors prefer this to **endured their manners** (ἐτροποφόρησεν). It suits the connection better than the other word, since what the apostle would bring to view here is not so much the forbearance of God toward his people as his interposition, his direct efforts, in their behalf. It is well attested, also, though the evidence is not decisive.

19. Seven nations. (See their names in Deut. 7 : 1.) They were the principal tribes in

Palestine at that time.—**In** (the) **land**, anarthrous, as above.—**Assigned to them as a possession.** Hellenistic for the Hiphil of *nachal.*[1] **Their land,** by promise, gift ; or, better, henceforth theirs and that of their descendants.

20. After these things—viz. the conquest and occupation of the country. — **During about four hundred and fifty years he gave judges.** For the dative, see on 8 : 11. This number is the sum of the years assigned in the Old Testament to the administration of the judges, from the time of Joshua to the death of Eli, added to the sum of the years during which the nation was subject to foreign oppressors. Hence it would be very natural for the Jews to speak of four hundred and fifty years as the proximate number of years during which the judges ruled. But, whether the computation arose in that way or some other, it was certainly in use among the Jews ; for Josephus (*Antt.,* 8. 2. 1) gives the time from the departure out of Egypt till the building of the temple as five hundred and ninety-two years. If we deduct from that the forty years in the wilderness, twenty-five for the administration of Joshua (*Antt.,* 5. 1. 29 ; not stated in the Old Testament), forty for Saul's reign (see v. 21), forty for David's, and four under Solomon (1 Kings 6 : 1), we have for the period of the judges four hundred and forty-three years, which the apostle could call, in round numbers, **about four hundred and fifty years.** It is evident, therefore, that Paul has followed here a mode of reckoning which was current at that time, and which, being a well-known received chronology, whether correct or incorrect in itself considered, was entirely correct for his object, which was not to settle a question about dates, but to recall to the minds of those whom he addressed a particular portion of the Jewish history. The Hebrews had still another computation, as appears from 1 Kings 6 : 1. The time from the Exodus to the build-

[1] For the origin of such Hebraisms, see the writer's *Hebrew Exercises,* p. 96.

space of four hundred and fifty years, *until Samuel the prophet.

21 *And afterward they desired a king: and God gave unto them Saul the son of Cis, a man of the tribe of Benjamin, by the space of forty years.

22 And *when he had removed him, *he raised up unto them David to be their king; to whom also he gave testimony, and said, *I have found David the son of Jesse, *a man after mine own heart, which shall fulfil all my will.

23 *Of this man's seed hath God according *to *his* promise raised unto Israel *a Saviour, Jesus:

24 *When John had first preached before his coming the baptism of repentance to all the people of Israel.

25 And as John fulfilled his course, he said, *Whom think ye that I am? I am not *he.* But, behold, there

21 Samuel the prophet. And afterward they asked for a king: and God gave unto them Saul the son of Kish, a man of the tribe of Benjamin, for the space

22 of forty years. And when he had removed him, he raised up David to be their king; to whom also he bare witness, and said, I have found David the son of Jesse, a man after my heart, who shall do all my

23 will. Of this man's seed according to

24 promise brought unto Israel a Saviour, Jesus; when John had first preached *before his coming the bap-

25 tism of repentance to all the people of Israel. And as John was fulfilling his course, he said, What sup-

a 1 Sam. 3 : 20....b 1 Sam. 8 : 5; 10 : 1....c 1 Sam. 15 : 23, 26, 28; 16 : 1; Hos. 13 : 11....d 1 Sam. 16 : 13; 2 Sam. 2 : 4; 5 : 3....e Ps. 89 : 20....f 1 Sam. 13 : 14; ch. 7 : 46....g Isa. 11 : 1; Luke 1 : 32, 69; ch. 2 : 30; Rom. 1 : 3....h 2 Sam. 7 : 12; Ps. 132 : 11....i Matt. 1 : 21; Rom. 11 : 26....k Matt. 3 : 1; Luke 3 : 3....l Matt. 3 : 11; Mark 1 : 7; Luke 3 : 16; John 1 : 20, 27.——1 Gr. wills....2 Gr. before the face of his entering in.

ing of the temple is there given as four hundred and eighty years, which (deducting the other dates as stated above) would allow but two hundred and thirty-one years for the period of the judges. (In regard to such differences, see also on 7 : 6.) Some of the best critics read **about four hundred and fifty years, and after these things.** The four hundred and fifty years belong, then, to the preceding verse, and may be the years from the birth of Isaac, when God showed that he had chosen the fathers, to the distribution of the land of Canaan. Adding together sixty years from the birth of Isaac to that of Jacob, one hundred and thirty as the age of Jacob on going into Egypt, two hundred and fifteen as the sojourn there, and forty-seven thence to the settlement of the tribes, the sum is four hundred and fifty-two. (See again on 7 : 6.) This reading is found in the oldest manuscripts (A B C) [also ℵ B D], etc., and is approved by Griesbach (partially), Lachmann, Luthardt,[1] Green, Wordsworth, and others. The text may have been changed to relieve the difficulty (Mey.), but it is singular that the three oldest witnesses concur in that variation. A summary decision is not to be pronounced here. [It will be noticed, however, that the chief critical editors—Griesb., Lach., Tsch., Treg., West. and Hort, and Anglo-Am. Revisers—adopt the reading which removes the difficulty. Their agreement is a strong reason for believing that their judgment is sound. —A. H.]—**Unto Samuel,** who is to be included, probably, among the judges ; or ἕως may be taken as exclusive. How long he governed is not mentioned in 1 Sam. 7 : 15, nor in 28 : 3. The tradition (Jos., *Antt.,* 6. 13. 5), which is not, perhaps, of much value, makes it twelve years. ὡς would allow us to add these years to four hundred and fifty, if any one prefers that.

21. And thereafter (κἀκεῖθεν) is here an adverb of time.—**Asked for themselves,** etc. (See 1 Sam. 8 : 5 ; 10 : 1.)—**Forty years,** which agrees with Josephus (*Antt.,* 6. 14. 9). The Old Testament does not mention the length of Saul's reign.

22. Having removed him—*i. e.* from life (De Wet.) or from his office (Kuin.). The two events were coincident in point of time. Saul reigned until his death, though David was anointed as prospective king during his lifetime. **To whom** (ᾧ dat. comm.) **also he testified, saying.** The apostle quotes the substance of 1 Sam. 13 : 14 and Ps. 89 : 21. This commendation is not absolute, but describes the character of David in comparison with that of Saul. The latter was rejected for his disobedience and impiety ; David, on the contrary, was always faithful to the worship of Jehovah, and performed his commands as they were made known to him by revelation or the messengers whom God sent to him.

23. Jesus could not be the Messiah, unless he were descended from David. **This man's** stands first, in order to give prominence to his descent from that source.—**According to promise,** as made to the fathers (v. 32), not to David merely.

24. John. The Jews acknowledged John's authority as a prophet, and were bound, therefore, to admit his testimony. **Before his entrance**—*i. e.* upon his public ministry. (See Matt. 11 : 10 ; Luke 7 : 27.)—**Baptism of repentance**—*i. e.* such as required repentance on the part of those who received it. (See 19 : 4.)

25. Now as John was finishing his course, was near its close (De Wet., Mey.), not **while he was completing it** (Kuin..

cometh one after me, whose shoes of *his* feet I am not worthy to loose.

26 Men *and* brethren, children of the stock of Abraham, and whosoever among you feareth God, *a*to you is the word of this salvation sent.

27 For they that dwell at Jerusalem, and their rulers, *b*because they knew him not, nor yet the voices of the prophets *c*which are read every sabbath day, *d*they have fulfilled *them* in condemning *him*.

28 *e*And though they found no cause of death *in him*, *f*yet desired they Pilate that he should be slain.

29 *g*And when they had fulfilled all that was written of him, *h*they took *him* down from the tree, and laid *him* in a sepulchre.

pose ye that I am? I am not *he*. But behold, there cometh one after me, the shoes of whose feet I am 26 not worthy to unloose. Brethren, children of the stock of Abraham, and those among you that fear God, to us is the word of this salvation sent forth. 27 For they that dwell in Jerusalem, and their rulers, because they knew him not, nor the voices of the prophets which are read every sabbath, fulfilled 28 *them* by condemning *him*. And though they found no cause of death *in him*, yet asked they of Pilate 29 that he should be slain. And when they had fulfilled all things that were written of him, they took him down from the tree, and laid him in

a Matt. 10 : 6 ; Luke 24 : 47 ; ver. 46 ; ch. 3 : 26....*b* Luke 23 : 34 ; ch. 3 : 17 ; 1 Cor. 2 : 8....*c* vers. 14, 15 ; ch. 15 : 21....*d* Luke 24 : 20, 44 , ch. 26 : 22 ; 28 : 23....*e* Matt. 27 : 22 ; Mark 15 : 13, 14 ; Luke 23 : 21, 22 ; John 19 : 6, 15.... *f* ch. 3 : 13, 14....*g* Luke 18 : 31 ; 24 : 44 ; John 19 : 28, 30, 36, 37....*h* Matt. 27 : 59 ; Mark 15 : 46 ; Luke 23 : 53 ; John 19 : 38.

Olsh.). The forerunner was about to be imprisoned when he bore this testimony to his Successor.—**Whom do ye suppose that I am? I am not**—viz. the Messiah. The predicate is omitted as well known. (Comp. Mark 13 : 6; Luke 21 : 8; John 13 : 19.) Some critics (Calv., Raph., Kuin.) exclude the question, and render **he whom** (τίνα = ὄντινα) **ye suppose, I am not.** This punctuation does violence to the pronoun, while the sense has no advantage over the other. (See W. § 25. 1.)—**Comes after me,** etc. In this way he would express strongly his official and personal inferiority to Christ. It was an office of the lowest servants, not only among the Jews, but the Greeks and Romans, to bind and unbind the sandals of their masters. (See Jahn's *Archæol.*, § 123.)

26. Men, at the same time **brethren;** not different classes.—**You** includes both Jews and proselytes.—**Of this salvation,** which they preached (comp. 5 : 20), or procured by Jesus, named in v. 23.—**Was sent forth**—*i. e.* from God, the Author of the word.

27. For confirms the implication in **this salvation,** in v. 26 — viz. that Jesus, whom Paul preached, was the promised Saviour; **for** (γάρ) he had suffered and been put to death, and so had fulfilled what was predicted of the Messiah. De Wette, Winer (§ 57. 6), and others maintain this view of the connection. Meyer (followed by Alf.) opposes **you** in v. 26 to **they that dwell** here—*i. e.* the foreign Jews, being less guilty, had the message of salvation sent to them, which the other Jews had forfeited. This explanation arrays the passage against other passages—*e. g.* 2 : 38; 3 : 17, 26. It was not true that those who crucified the Saviour excluded themselves from the offers of the gospel.--**This one** — viz. Jesus—**not having known,** failed to recognize, **and the voices of the prophets** (not having known), **they fulfilled** them—viz. the prophecies—**by condemning** him to death. This is the simplest translation, and the one most approved (Calv.,

Grot., Kuin., Hmph.). The principal English versions agree in this sense. **Not having known** is milder than **denied,** in 3 : 13. (See note there.) In this case we must supply pronouns after **in condemning** and **fulfilled,** which refer to different antecedents. The construction may be harsh, but occasions no obscurity. Meyer renders: **Since they knew not this one . . . they also fulfilled the voices,** etc. The Jews are usually represented as rejecting Christ because they failed to discern the import of the predictions concerning him. The thought here would be inverted somewhat; the rejection appears as the reason why they misunderstand and fulfil the prophets. De Wette construes **not having known** (ἀγνοήσαντες) as a verb: **They knew him not, and the voices . . . fulfilled.** This analysis secures more uniformity in the structure of the sentence; but such a use of the participle is infrequent. Scholefield translates: **Being ignorant of this** word, and the **voices of the prophets, . . . fulfilled** it **by condemning** him. He assigns in this way a nearer antecedent to **this one** (him, E. V.), but must set aside the more obvious subject suggested to the mind by the context. It is not clear in what sense he would have us regard the rejection of Christ as fulfilling the word or gospel. — **Which are read every Sabbath,** and hence their ignorance was the more inexcusable.

28. Although they found no cause of death, none that justified it. (See 28 : 18.) They charged him with blasphemy and sedition, but could not establish the accusation. (See 3 : 13; Matt. 27 : 24; Luke 23 : 22.)

29. Laid has the same subject as the other verbs. (See v. 27.) The burial, however, was the particular act of Joseph of Arimathea and Nicodemus. (See John 19 : 38, *sq.*) What the apostle would assert is that Christ had fulfilled the prophecy which announced that he should be put to death and rise again. It was not im-

30 *But God raised him from the dead: 31 And *he was seen many days of them which came up with him *from Galilee to Jerusalem, *who are his witnesses unto the people.

32 And we declare unto you glad tidings, how that *the promise which was made unto the fathers, 33 God hath fulfilled the same unto us their children, in that he hath raised up Jesus again; as it is also written in the second psalm, *Thou art my Son, this day have I begotten thee.

30 a tomb. But God raised him from the dead: 31 and he was seen for many days of them that came up with him from Galilee to Jerusalem, who are 32 now his witnesses unto the people. And we bring you good tidings of the promise made unto the 33 fathers, how that God hath fulfilled the same unto our children, in that he raised up Jesus; as also it is written in the second psalm, Thou art my Son,

---

a Matt. 28 : 6 ; ch. 2 : 24 ; 3 : 13, 15, 26 ; 5 : 30....*b* Matt. 28 : 16 ; ch. 1 : 3 ; 1 Cor. 15 : 5, 6, 7....*c* ch. 1 : 11....*d* ch, 1 : 8 ; 2 : 32 ; 3 : 15 ; 5 : 32....*e* Gen. 3 : 15 ; 12 : 3 ; 22 : 18 ; ch. 26 : 6 ; Rom. 4 : 13 ; Gal. 3 : 16....*f* Ps. 2 : 7 ; Heb. 1 : 5 ; 5 : 5.

---

portant that he should discriminate as to the character of the agents in the transaction. Some translate **those who took him down placed him,** etc. The participle, in that relation to the verb, would require the article.

31. Those who came up with him—*i. e.* the Galilean disciples who attended him on his last journey to Jerusalem. They knew, therefore, what they testified ; their means of knowledge had been ample. This idea occurs in the Acts often.—**Now.** The resurrection rested, not on tradition, but on the testimony of living men. The English Version, after the received text, omits this particle. [But it is well supported by ℵ A C D, Vulg., Cop., Syr., and inserted by Lach., Tsch., West. and Hort, Anglo-Am. Revisers, and Treg. (in marg.). Of its importance no reader can entertain a doubt. —A. H.]—**Unto the people**—*i. e.* the Jews. (See v. 24 ; 10 : 42, etc.)

32. And so we—*i. e.* in view of these various proofs that Jesus is the Messiah. (See vv. 23, 25, 27, 31.)—**Declare** (εὐαγγελιζόμεδα) has a double accusative only here. (W. ≀ 32. 4.)— **Glad tidings** stands in the first clause with the usual effect of that attraction. (See on 3 : 10.)

33. Has completely fulfilled, stronger than **fulfilled,** in v. 27, because the resurrection, considered as involving the ascension and exaltation, was essentially the finishing act in the fulfilment of the promise relating to the Messiah.—**Having raised up Jesus** means, as Luther, Schott, Stier, De Wette, Meyer, Hengstenberg, Tholuck, and others decide, **having raised up Jesus** from the grave, not **having brought him into existence** (Calv., Bng., Kuin., Olsh.). The mind attaches that sense to the word most readily after v. 30. It was unnecessary to insert **from the dead,** because the context suggests the specific meaning. (Comp. 2 : 24, 32.) ἀναστήσας, in the sense of *having raised up* merely, expresses too little for the prophecy which that event is said to have fulfilled. The original passage refers, not to the incarnation of the Messiah, but to his inauguration or public acknowledgment on the part

of God as the rightful Sovereign of men. To no moment in the history of Christ would such a prediction apply with such significance as to that of his triumphant resurrection from the dead. The progression of the argument in the next verse demands this interpretation. To the assertion here that God had raised Jesus to life again, the apostle adds there that this life was one which death would invade no more.— **As also**—*i. e.* what took place was foretold.— **First psalm.** The second Psalm in our English Version is named here the first, because in some manuscripts the Hebrews reckoned the first Psalm merely as prefatory. **Second** has much less support. [According to the critical editors, this is not now the case. In favor of *second* (δευτέρῳ) are ℵ B C E G H L P, while Tsch. alleges for *first* (πρώτῳ) but a single uncial codex—viz. D. West. and Hort, with Anglo-Am. Revisers, retain *second.* Dr. Hackett as well as others may have been influenced by the assumed improbability that *first* would have been substituted, intentionally or unintentionally, for *second.* But may not the change have been made by a transcriber who trusted to his memory for the instant, or, better, by one who was acquainted with "some manuscripts" which treated the first psalm as *prefatory?* I perceive that Westcott and Hort urge this consideration. They say : "The authorities for πρώτῳ here and for the combination of the two Psalms are in each case Western ; so that a 'Western' scribe, being probably accustomed to read the two Psalms combined, would be under a temptation to alter *second* to *first,* and not *vice versâ.*" (Comp. Scrivener, 2d ed., p. 538.)—A. H.]—**Thou art my Son,** etc. (Ps. 2 : 7) affirms the Sonship of the Messiah, which included his divine nature. (See Rom. 1 : 4.) Hence **I have begotten thee** cannot refer to the *origin* of this relationship, but must receive a figurative interpretation ; either **I have begotten thee**—brought thee into a state of glory and power such as Christ assumed after his resurrection as Mediator at the right hand of God — or, according to a familiar Hebrew usage, **I have declared, exhibited, thee as**

34 And as concerning that he raised him up from the dead, *now no more to return to corruption,* he said on this wise, *ªI will give you the sure mercies of David.*
35 Wherefore he saith also in another *psalm,* *ᵇThou shalt not suffer thine Holy One to see corruption.*
36 For David, after he had served his own generation by the will of God, *ᶜfell on sleep,* and was laid unto his fathers, and saw corruption :

34 this day have I begotten thee. And as concerning that he raised him up from the dead, now no more to return to corruption, he hath spoken on this wise, I will give you the holy and sure *blessings* of
35 David. Because he saith also in another *psalm,* Thou wilt not give thy Holy One to see corruption.
36 For David, after he had ¹in his own generation served the counsel of God, fell on sleep, and was

---

a Isa. 55 : 3....*b* Ps. 16 : 10 ; ch. 2 : 31....*c* 1 Kings 2 : 10 ; ch. 2 : 29.——¹ Or, *served his own generation by the counsel of God, fell on sleep* Or, *served his own generation, fell on sleep by the counsel of God*

---

begotten—*i. e.* as my Son ; viz. by the resurrection from the dead. The thought here is entirely parallel to that in Rom. 1 : 4. As to the declarative sense of Hebrew verbs, see the note on 10 : 15.—**To-day** designates the precise point of time on which the prophet's eye was then fixed—viz. that of Christ's assumption of his mediatorial power, or that of his open proclamation as Messiah on the part of God when he raised him from the dead.

34. Further (as proof) **that he raised him up from the dead as one who would die no more.** δέ is progressive. **Raised up** repeats the idea of the foregoing **having raised up** (v. 33), for the purpose of describing this resurrection more fully : it would be followed by no return to death. **From the dead** does not distinguish the two words as to sense, but draws attention more strongly to the contrast between the death which he had suffered and his exemption from death in future. **No more to return,** etc., as applied to Christ, whose body underwent no change while it remained in the grave, must be equivalent to **dieth no more,** in Rom. 6 : 9. The dissolution or corruption of the body is the ordinary consequent of death ; and hence, in common speech, *to return to corruption* and *to die,* or the opposite, *not to return to corruption* and *not to die,* are interchangeable expressions. Bengel saw this import of the phrase. (See W. *§* 66. 10.) The perpetuity of Christ's existence is an important truth in the Christian system. In Rom. 5 : 10, Paul urges it as a ground of certainty that if men believe on Christ they will be finally saved, and in Rom. 6 : 9 as a pledge that, inasmuch as he "dies no more, we shall live with him." (See also John 14 : 19 ; Heb. 7 : 25, etc.) This incidental agreement of the address with Paul's circle of doctrine speaks for its genuineness.—**That** (ὅτι) is the sign of quotation [but is naturally omitted in translation.—A. H.]. **I will give,** etc., expresses the substantial sense of Isa. 55 : 3 : **I will give to you,** perform unto you, **the holy,** inviolable **promises of David** —*i. e.* made to him—**the sure.** The language is very nearly that of the Seventy. One of these promises was that David should have a

successor whose reign would be perpetual, the throne of whose kingdom God would establish for ever and ever. (See 2 Sam. 7 : 13, *sq.*) It was essential to the accomplishment of that promise that the Messiah should be exempt from death ; and hence, as Jesus had been proved to be the Messiah by his resurrection, that promise made it certain that he would live and reign henceforth, without being subject to any interruption of his existence or power.

35. Therefore also—*i. e.* because he was not mortal, in further confirmation of that fact.—**In another**—*i. e. Psalm ;* viz. 16 : 10. (See on 2 : 25, *sq.*) The inspired declaration that the Messiah should not experience the power of death had not only been verified in his resurrection, but guaranteed that he would not experience that power at any future period. —**Saith**—*i. e. God ;* viz. through David. (See v. 34 ; 1 : 16, etc.)

36. For vindicates the reference of the passage to Christ, since it could not apply to David. —μέν is antithetic to δέ in v. 37.—**His own generation,** etc., admits of a twofold translation. **Generation** may depend on **having served : having served his own generation** (been useful to it), **according to the purpose of God** (dative of norm or rule). Our English translators, Calvin, Doddridge, Robinson, and others, adopt this construction. Olshausen, Kuinoel, De Wette, Meyer, and others refer **purpose** to the participle : **having in his own generation** (dative of time), or **for it** (dat. comm.), **served the purpose,** *plan,* **of God**—*i. e.* as an instrument for the execution of his designs. (Comp. v. 22.) **Generation,** if connected with the participle, secures to it a personal object, and in that way forms a much easier expression than **purpose** with the participle. The main idea of the clause is that David, like other men, had but one generation of contemporaries—that he accomplished for that his allotted work, and then yielded to the universal law which consigns the race to death. Some join **by the purpose,** or **will,** with **fell asleep,** which renders the remark much less significant. — **And he was**

37 But he, whom God raised again, saw no corruption.
38 ¶ Be it known unto you therefore, men *and* brethren, that *a*through this man is preached unto you the forgiveness of sins:
39 And *b*by him all that believe are justified from all things, from which ye could not be justified by the law of Moses.
40 Beware therefore, lest that come upon you, which is spoken of in *c*the prophets;
41 Behold, ye despisers, and wonder, and perish: for I work a work in your days, a work which ye shall in no wise believe, though a man declare it unto you.

37 laid unto his fathers, and saw corruption: but he
38 whom God raised up saw no corruption. Be it known unto you therefore, brethren, that through this man is proclaimed unto you remission of sins:
39 and by him every one that believeth is justified from all things, from which ye could not be justified by the law of Moses. Beware therefore, lest that come upon *you*, which is spoken in the prophets;
41 Behold, ye despisers, and wonder, and [1]perish; For I work a work in your days, A work which ye shall in no wise believe, if one declare it unto you.

a Jer. 31 : 34 ; Dan. 9 : 24 ; Luke 24 : 47 ; 1 John 2 : 12....*b* Isa. 53 : 11 ; Rom. 3 : 28 ; 8 : 3 ; Heb. 7 : 19....*c* Isa. 29 : 14 ; Hab. 1 : 5.
————1 Or, *vanish away*

added unto his fathers. This expression recognizes the existence of the soul in a future state (Bng., Olsh., Doddr.). Gesenius says that it is distinguished expressly both from death and burial in Gen. 25 : 8 ; 35 : 29 ; 2 Kings 22 : 20. (See *Lex.*, s. *âsaph.*)—**Saw corruption,** as to his mortal part. (Comp. 2 : 31.)

38. Therefore (οὖν), illative. Jesus has been shown to be the Messiah, and he is, **therefore,** the Author of pardon and salvation to those who believe on him.—**Through this one** belongs to **forgiveness** rather than the verb: **through this one the forgiveness of sins** (having been procured) **is announced unto you.** (Comp. 10 : 36 ; Luke 24 : 47.) The next verse reaffirms and amplifies the proposition.

39. The sentence here depends still on **that** (ὅτι, v. 38). A comma is the proper point between this verse and the last. The apostle declares now—first, that the forgiveness which Christ has procured is not partial, but extends to all the sins of the transgressor ; secondly, that all men need it, since no other way of pardon remains for those who are condemned by the law ; and thirdly, since faith in Christ is the only condition annexed to it, this salvation is free to all.—**And that from all things—** *i. e.* sins—**from which** (= ἀφ' ὧν by attraction) **ye were not able by the law of Moses to be justified,** etc. We cannot suppose this to mean, according to a possible sense of the words, that the gospel merely completes a justification which the law has commenced or accomplished in part ; for such an admission would be at variance with the doctrine of the New Testament in regard to the utter inefficacy of all legal obedience to cancel the guilt of transgression, and the necessity of an exclusive reliance on the work of Christ for our justification. We must adopt a different view of the meaning. As Olshausen suggests, we may regard **from which,** after **from all,** not as a supplementary clause, but as explanatory of the other, or coextensive with it—viz. *from all*

sins from which (*i. e. from all* which sins) *ye were unable*, etc. In other words, the first clause affirms the sufficiency of the gospel to justify from all sins, while the second clause affirms the insufficiency of the law to the same extent —*i. e.* to justify from any sins. (Comp. Rom. 8 : 3, *sq.*) To represent this meaning to the ear, we should read **from all** with an emphasis, and **from which ye could not be justified,** etc., as parenthetic. Neander (*Pflanzung*, i. p. 195) declares himself strongly for this sense of the words. Alford's comment (similar to Meyer's) represents a different view : "Christ shall do for you all that the law could not do, leaving it for inference or for further teaching that this was absolutely *all*—that the law could do *nothing.*" According to some, the apostle concedes a certain value to the rites of Judaism : they were the appointed means of obtaining the pardon of offences which concerned the ritual merely and social or public relations. (See Lange's *Geschichte der Kirche*, ii. p. 171.) This explanation rests on a false view of the nature of the Hebrew rites. As **in,** or **by, this one** stands opposed to **in,** or **by, the law,** it belongs to **is justified,** not to **believeth.**

40. Beware, therefore, since ye are thus guilty and exposed.—**Lest that spoken,** etc., lest the declaration be fulfilled, verified in your case. The mode of citing the prophecy shows that the apostle did not regard it as spoken in view of that occasion.—**In the prophets—***i. e.* the part of the Old Testament which the Jews so named. (Comp. v. 15 ; 7 : 42 ; John 6 : 45. See W. § 27. 2.) The passage intended is Hab. 1 : 5.

41. The citation follows very nearly the Septuagint, and agrees essentially with the Hebrew. In the original passage the prophet refers to a threatened invasion of the Jewish nation by the Chaldeans, and he calls upon his countrymen to behold the judgment to which their sins had exposed them, and to be astonished, to tremble, on account of it. Of this language the apostle avails himself, in order to

42 And when the Jews were gone out of the synagogue, the Gentiles besought that these words might be preached to them the next sabbath.
43 Now when the congregation was broken up, many of the Jews and religious proselytes followed Paul and Barnabas: who, speaking to them, *persuaded them to continue in *the grace of God.
44 ¶ And the next sabbath day came almost the whole city together to hear the word of God.

42 And as they went out, they b sought that these words might be spoken to them the next sabbath.
43 Now when the synagogue broke up, many of the Jews and of the devout proselytes followed Paul and Barnabas: who, speaking to them, urged them to continue in the grace of God.
44 And the next sabbath almost the whole city was

a ch. 11 : 23 ; 14 : 22....*b* Tit. 2 : 11 ; Heb. 12 : 15 ; 1 Pet. 5 : 12.

warn the Jews whom he addressed of the punishment which awaited them if they rejected the message which they had now heard. Calvin: "Paulus fideliter accommodat in usum suum prophetæ verba, quia sicuti semel minatus fuerat Deus per prophetam suum Habacuc, ita etiam semper fuit sui similis" [" Paul accommodates legitimately to his own use the words of the prophet; for as at a former time God had threatened through his prophet, so he was always like himself"].—**Ye despisers** occurs in the Septuagint, but not in the Hebrew. The apostle could retain it in perfect consonance with the original, because it is the incredulity of the wicked, their contempt of God's threatenings, which occasions their ruin. What suggested the word to the Seventy is uncertain. It is thought that they may have read *bogĕdhēm*, **deceitful**, proudly impious, instead of *baggōyēm*, **among the heathen.**—**And wonder**, be astonished—*i. e.* at the fearful certain destruction which God prepares for his enemies. The spectacle to which the prophet directs attention here is that of the Chaldeans mustering their hosts to march against the guilty Jews.—**And perish**, unable to escape the punishment which their sins have provoked. This word elicits an idea which the Hebrew text involves, though it is not expressed here. Paul has retained it from the Septuagint.—**A work** of judgment **I work**, execute. The future act is represented as present, because it was near.—The second **work** Paul inserts for the sake of emphasis. The copies which omit it were corrected, probably, after the Septuagint.—**Which ye will not believe, though any one should fully declare it to you**—*i. e.* although apprised ever so distinctly of their danger, they would not heed it; they are infatuated, they cling to their delusive hopes of safety. The New Testament, like most of the later Greek, employs often the subjunctive aorist in the sense of the indicative future. (W. § 56. 3; Lob., *Phryn.*, p. 723, *sq.*) ὅ, at the head of the clause, is a better reading than φ. That the dative, however, is not a false construction, see Rom. 10 : 16.

42–49. THEY PREACH A SECOND TIME AT ANTIOCH.

42. The best editions insert **they** in place of **the Jews from the synagogue** in the common text, and omit **the Gentiles** before **besought. They** must refer to Paul and Barnabas. [The words are rendered by Alford, Davidson, Bible Union : **And as they** (Paul and Barnabas) **were going out, they** (the people) **besought,**etc.—A.H.] The phrase translated **the next Sabbath** (εἰς τὸ μεταξὺ σάββατον) corresponds evidently to **the next Sabbath** (τῷ ἐχομένῳ σαββάτῳ) in v. 44, and means **upon** (lit. **unto,** as the limit) **the next Sabbath** (Neand., Mey., De Wet.); not **during the intermediate week,** as explained by some of the older critics. μεταξύ has this sense in the N. T. here only, but belongs to the later Greek. That the apostles were not inactive during the interval, but labored in private circles, may be taken for granted.

43. When the synagogue was broken up seems, at first view, superfluous after **as they went out.** The procedure, says Neander, may have been this: As Paul and Barnabas were going out before the general dispersion of the assembly, the rulers of the synagogue may have requested that they would repeat their discourse on the next Sabbath. The people having then withdrawn, many of the Jews and proselytes followed the speakers, for the purpose of declaring their assent to what they had heard or of seeking further instruction.— **Worshipping**—*i. e.* God—not **devout** (E. V.) above others, but simply *worshippers* of Jehovah (see 16 : 14), and not of idols, as formerly. —**The grace of God**—*i. e.* the gospel, which is the fruit of his undeserved favor.

44. Almost the entire city assembled. Where, is not stated. Paul and Barnabas on that Sabbath may have spoken to different audiences. If they both repaired to the same synagogue, the crowd must have filled not only the synagogue itself, but every avenue to it. (Comp. Mark 2 : 2, *sq.* ; Luke 8 : 19.) The hearers on this occasion were Gentiles as well as Jews.

45 But when the Jews saw the multitudes, they were filled with envy, and *a*spake against those things which were spoken by Paul, contradicting and blaspheming.

46 Then Paul and Barnabas waxed bold, and said, *b*It was necessary that the word of God should first have been spoken to you: but *c*seeing ye put it from you, and judge yourselves unworthy of everlasting life, lo, *d*we turn to the Gentiles.

47 For so hath the Lord commanded us, *saying*, *e*I have set thee to be a light of the Gentiles, that thou shouldst be for salvation unto the ends of the earth.

48 And when the Gentiles heard this, they were glad, and glorified the word of the Lord: *f*and as many as were ordained to eternal life believed.

45 gathered together to hear the word of [1]God. But when the Jews saw the multitudes, they were filled with jealousy, and contradicted the things which 46 were spoken by Paul, and [2]blasphemed. And Paul and Barnabas spake out boldly, and said, It was necessary that the word of God should first be spoken to you. Seeing ye thrust it from you, and judge yourselves unworthy of eternal life, lo, we turn to 47 the Gentiles. For so hath the Lord commanded us, *saying*,

I have set thee for a light of the Gentiles,
That thou shouldest be for salvation unto the uttermost part of the earth.

48 And as the Gentiles heard this, they were glad, and glorified the word of [1]God: and as many as were or-

a ch. 18 : 6 ; 1 Pet. 4 : 4 ; Jude 10....*b* Matt. 10 : 6 ; ch. 3 : 26 ; ver. 26 ; Rom. 1 : 16....*c* Ex. 32 : 10 ; Deut. 32 : 21 ; Isa. 55 : 5 ; Matt. 21 : 43 ; Rom. 10 : 19....*d* ch. 18 : 6 ; 28 : 28....*e* Isa. 42 : 6 ; 49 : 6 ; Luke 2 : 32....*f* ch. 2 : 47.———1 Many ancient authorities read *the Lord*....2 Or, *railed*.

45. With indignation, as in v. 17.—**Contradicting** is neither superfluous nor Hebraistic, but, like the participle united with its finite verb in the classics, emphasizes **spake against** (Mey.) : **not only contradicting, but blaspheming.** The second participle defines the extent or criminality of the act stated by the first. (W. § 45. 8.)

46. Unto you it was necessary, because the plan of God required it. (Comp. on 3 : 26.) **First,** *first in time,* as in 3 : 26.—**And ye judge yourselves not worthy of the eternal life** —viz. which we preach. (See on 5 : 20.) This mode of speaking is not common ; it rests on the just view that a man's actions may be taken as his own self-pronounced verdict as to his character and deserts.—**Unto the heathen,** in that place. In like manner, the Jews whom they left to their doom were those at Antioch. They did not turn from the Jewish nation, as such, to labor in future for the exclusive benefit of the Gentiles. (See 18 : 5, *sq.* ; 19 : 8, *sq.*)

47. So, as they had done.—**I have set thee,** etc. See Isa. 49 : 6. The prophet announces there that the Messiah whom God promised to send would be the Saviour of the Gentiles as well as the Jews ; that all nations would be called to share in the blessings of his kingdom. The passage is quoted to show that in turning now to the heathen they were merely carrying cut the plan of God as revealed in the Old Testament (see also Isa. 11 : 1, 10 ; Rom. 9 : 25, *sq.*) ; the announcement of his purpose in regard to the unrestricted design of the gospel required them, as his messengers, to publish it to the Gentiles.

48. They glorified, extolled, **the word of the Lord.** They expressed their joy and gratitude for the mercy which had embraced them in the plan of salvation, and had given them this opportunity to secure its benefits. We see from the next clause that they received the message as well as rejoiced to hear it.—**And as many as were appointed unto eternal life believed.** This is the only translation which the philology of the passage allows. So Calvin, Kuinoel, Olshausen, Usteri,[1] De Wette, Winer, Meyer, and others. In this position the demonstrative part of ὅσοι (*those who*) must be the subject of the first verb, and the relative part the subject of the second. Hence, it is impossible to render *those who believed were appointed.* Some translate the Greek participle (τεταγμένοι) *disposed,* inclined ; but this term as passive, though it may signify *disposed* externally—as, *e. g.,* drawn up in military order—was not used to denote an act of the mind. In 20 : 13 the form is middle with an accusative virtually (see note there), and in 1 Cor. 16 : 15 the form is active with an accusative ; those cases, therefore, so unlike this, are not to be cited here. Mr. Humphry, after Whitby and others, defends still that signification, and appeals for proof of it to 2 Macc. 6 : 21. The Greek there, however, does not mean "those who were set or bent on mercy" (Hmph.), but "those appointed for the distribution of unlawful flesh." (See Wahl's *Clav. Libr. Vet. Apocrph.,* and Biell's *Lex. in LXX.,* s. σπλαγχνισμός.) The use of τεταγμένοι in that passage not only fails to support the alleged meaning, but confirms the other. **Unto eternal life** is not to be torn from its connection and joined to **believed.** In what sense men are appointed to God (comp. Rom. 13 : 1) unto eternal life is not taught very distinctly here, but must be gathered from a comparison with other passages. (For example, see Rom. 8 : 28, *sq.* ; 9 : 11 ; Eph. 1 : 4, 11 ; 2 Thess. 2 : 13 ; 2 Tim. 1 : 9 ; 1 Pet. 1 : 2.) The explanations of this text which have been opposed to the foregoing are forced and unsatisfactory. Dr. Wordsworth (to give a favorable specimen) expounds it thus : Those who had set, or marshalled, themselves to go forward in

---

[1] *Entwickelung des Paulinischen Lehrbegriffes,* p. 271 (1851).

49 And the word of the Lord was published through-out all the region.
50 But the Jews stirred up the devout and honorable women, and the chief men of the city, and *a*raised persecution against Paul and Barnabas, and expelled them out of their coasts.
51 *b*But they shook off the dust of their feet against them, and came unto Iconium.
52 And the disciples *c*were filled with joy, and with the Holy Ghost.

49 dained to eternal life believed. And the word of the Lord was spread abroad throughout all the region
50 But the Jews urged on the devout women of honorable estate, and the chief men of the city, and stirred up a persecution against Paul and Barnabas, and cast
51 them out of their borders. But they shook off the dust of their feet against them, and came unto Ico-
52 nium. And the disciples were filled with joy and with the Holy Spirit.

CHAPTER XIV.

AND it came to pass in Iconium, that they went both together into the synagogue of the Jews, and so spake, that a great multitude both of the Jews and also of the Greeks believed.
2 But the unbelieving Jews stirred up the Gentiles,

1 AND it came to pass in Iconium, that they entered together into the synagogue of the Jews, and so spake, that a great multitude both of Jews and of Greeks be-
2 lieved. But the Jews that were disobedient stirred

---

a 2 Tim. 3 : 11....*b* Matt. 10 : 14 ; Mark 6 : 11 ; Luke 9 : 5 ; ch. 18 : 6....*c* Matt. 5 : 12 ; John 16 : 22 ; ch. 2 : 46.

---

the way to eternal life professed their faith boldly in the face of every danger.

49. And the word of the Lord was conveyed through all the region—i. e. in the vicinity of Antioch. This rapid extension of the gospel we must attribute, in some measure, to the zeal of the recent converts. Paul and Barnabas also may have visited personally some of the nearest places; for Luke may have passed over an interval between this verse and the next, during which the missionaries could have made such excursions.

50-52. THEY ARE PERSECUTED, AND DEPART TO ICONIUM.

50. The devout women. They were Gentile women who had embraced Judaism (see 17 : 4), and could be easily excited against a sect represented as hostile to their faith. At Damascus, as Josephus states (*Bell. Jud.*, 2. 20. 20), a majority of the married women were proselytes. **Honorable** refers to their rank (17 : 12; Mark 15 : 43) as the wives of the *first men of the city.* It was the object of the crafty Jews to gain the men through the influence of the women, and thus effect the expulsion of the apostles from the city. Paul alludes to this persecution in 2 Tim. 3 : 11.

51. Against them = *for a testimony against them,* in Luke 9 : 5. Shaking off the dust of the feet imported disapprobation and rejection. The act derived its significancy from the idea that those renounced in this way were so unworthy that the very dust of their land was defiling. In taking this course Paul followed the direction of Christ given in Matt. 10 : 14.— **Iconium,** to which they came next, was about forty-five miles south-east from Antioch. It was the principal city of Lycaonia, situated at the foot of the Taurus. Its present name is Konieh. Leake, who approached Iconium from the mountains which separate Antioch from Philomelium, says (*Travels in Asia Minor,* p. 45):

"On the descent from a ridge branching eastward from these mountains, we came in sight of the vast plain around Konieh, and of the lake which occupies the middle of it; and we saw the city, with its mosques and ancient walls, still at the distance of twelve or fourteen miles from us." "Konieh," says another traveller, "extends to the east and south over the plain far beyond the walls, which are about two miles in circumference. Mountains covered with snow rise on every side, excepting toward the east, where a plain as flat as the Desert of Arabia extends far beyond the reach of the eye."

52. The disciples—i. e. at Antioch, where the persecution still continued. (See 14 : 22.)— **Were filled with joy and the Holy Spirit.** The relation is that of effect and author. (See Gal. 5 : 20.) The idea suggested is that, though they were called to suffer as adherents of the new faith, they had sources of consolation opened to them which more than counterbalanced their trials.

1-7. THEY PREACH AT ICONIUM, BUT ARE PERSECUTED, AND FLEE TO LYSTRA.

1. Together (κατὰ τὸ αὐτό—like ἐπὶ τὸ αὐτό in 3 : 1), not in *the same manner,* as they were wont.—*And they spake so*—viz. with this effect—*that* (ὥστε) *a great multitude,* etc. (Mey., De Wet.); not *with such power that.* **So** anticipates the next clause, and makes it more prominent. (B. § 140. 4.)—**Greeks.** As the *Greeks* here were present in the synagogue, they appear to have been proselytes (comp. 13 : 43), and hence were a different class from those in 13 : 20.

2. *But those who disbelieved* –viz. when the others believed. The present participle (ἀπει-

and made their minds evil affected against the brethren.

3 Long time therefore abode they speaking boldly in the Lord, *which gave testimony unto the word of his grace, and granted signs and wonders to be done by their hands.

4 But the multitude of the city was divided: and part held with the Jews, and part with the *apostles.

5 And when there was an assault made both of the Gentiles, and also of the Jews with their rulers, *to use *them* despitefully, and to stone them,

6 They were *ware of *it*, and *fled unto Lystra and Derbe, cities of Lycaonia, and unto the region that lieth round about:

up the souls of the Gentiles, and made them evil affected against the brethren. Long time therefore
3 they tarried *there* speaking boldly in the Lord, who bare witness unto the word of his grace, granting
4 signs and wonders to be done by their hands. But the multitude of the city was divided; and part held
5 with the Jews, and part with the apostles. And when there was made an onset both of the Gentiles and of the Jews with their rulers, to entreat them
6 shamefully, and to stone them, they became aware of it, and fled unto the cities of Lycaonia, Lystra

a Mark 16 : 20 ; Heb. 2 : 4....*b* ch. 13 : 3....*c* 2 Tim. 3 : 11....*d* Matt. 10 : 23.

ϑοῦντες, as in some editions) is less correct than the aorist.—*Rendered evil*, hostile. This sense is found in Josephus, but not elsewhere (Mey.). How the Jews produced this effect on the minds of the heathen we are not told. They sometimes alleged for that purpose that the Christians were disloyal—that they had a King of their own, and would prove dangerous to the Roman supremacy. (See 18 : 5-9.)

3. Therefore — *i. e.* because they had so much success (see v. 1), notwithstanding the opposition excited against them. Meyer regards the third and fourth verses as an inference from the first and second : "In consequence of that approbation (v. 1) and this hostility (v. 2) they preached boldly indeed for a time, but a dissension also arose among the people."—**Long time.** The entire journey was evidently a rapid one, and a stay here of a few months would be comparatively **a long time.** This is our only notice respecting the time spent at the places visited on this tour.—**Speaking boldly upon the Lord**—*i. e.* in dependence upon him. It was their reliance on Christ that inspired them with so much courage. — The best authorities omit **and** between **gave testimony** and **granted : who testifies by granting that,** etc. (Comp. 4 : 30.)

4. The multitude of the city—*i. e.* the Gentile population. Some of them may have favored the Christian party, without having attached themselves to it. (Comp. 19 : 31).— **Were with the Jews**—*i. e.* in sympathy espoused their side. (See 5 : 17.) [Here, and in v. 14, Barnabas appears to be called an apostle in the highest sense of the word as applied to men. The same title is supposed to be given to Timothy and Silvanus in 1 Thess. 2 : 6, and, possibly, to Andronicus and Junias in Rom. 16 : 7. But the words *who all are of note among the apostles*, in the last passage, probably mean who are highly esteemed in and by the apostolic circle. In the other instances it will be observed that no one of these companions of

Paul is anywhere called an apostle when spoken of alone. *Only as associated with Paul*, and possibly then for brevity's sake, is the designation given to them. Certainly they are not to be regarded as apostles in the highest official sense, as are the twelve and Paul.—A. H.]

5. Assault, rather **impulse**, as in James 3 : 4 (Mey., Alf.) ; not **onset** [though this is given in the Revised Version], because **having become aware** (v. 6) would then be superfluous, and because the object of the flight was to escape an attack. **Plot**, purpose, is too strong a sense of the word. —**With their rulers** — *i. e.* those of both nations ; viz. the heathen magistrates and the officers of the synagogue. Some restrict **their** to the Gentiles ; others, to the Jews. Here, at this distance from Jerusalem, members of the Sanhedrim could not well be meant (Rob.).

6. Having become aware—viz. of this feeling. Meyer lays no stress at present on the preposition, as if they discovered the danger as well as others. — **In order to stone them.** "Once was I stoned," says Paul in 2 Cor. 11 : 25, which was the instance mentioned in v. 19. Hence, says Paley, " had this meditated assault at Iconium been completed; had the history related that a stone was thrown, as it relates that preparations were made both by Jews and Gentiles to stone Paul and his companions; or even had the account of this transaction stopped without going on to inform us that Paul and his companions were 'aware of the danger and fled,'—a contradiction between the history and the Epistles would have ensued. Truth is necessarily consistent, but it is scarcely possible that independent accounts, not having truth to guide them, should thus advance to the very brink of contradiction without falling into it." —**Lycaonia.** The district of **Lycaonia** extends from the ridges of Mount Taurus and the borders of Cilicia, on the south, to the Cappadocian hills, on the north. " It is a bare and dreary region, unwatered by streams, though in parts liable to occasional inundations. Across

7 And there they preached the gospel.

8 ¶ [a]And there sat a certain man at Lystra, impotent in his feet, being a cripple from his mother's womb, who never had walked:

9 The same heard Paul speak: who steadfastly beholding him, and [b]perceiving that he had faith to be healed,

7 and Derbe, and the region round about: and there they preached the gospel.

8 And at Lystra there sat a certain man, impotent in his feet, a cripple from his mother's womb, who 9 never had walked. The same heard Paul speaking: who, fastening his eyes upon him, and seeing that

a ch. 3 : 2....*b* Matt. 8 : 10; 9 : 28, 29.

---

some portion of this plain Paul and Barnabas travelled both before and after their residence in Iconium. After leaving the city the two most prominent objects still in view are the snowy mountains of Mount Argæus, rising high above all the intervening hills in the direction of Armenia, and the singular mass called the 'Kara-Dagh,' or 'Black Mount,' south-east-ward, in the direction of Cilicia. This latter mountain is gradually approached, and discovered to be an isolated mass, with reaches of the plain extending round it like channels of the sea" (Conybeare and Howson, i. p. 224).—**Lystra and Derbe** were not far from the base of the Black Mountain. Their exact situation is not yet certainly known. Lystra is marked on Kiepert's map as nearly south of Iconium, about twenty miles distant; Derbe, as nearly east from Lystra, south-east from Iconium. Kiepert appears to have followed Leake's conjecture as to the site of Lystra, though no traveller speaks of any ruins at that place. Mr. Hamilton agrees with Kiepert in the position of Derbe, because it occurs on the line of a Roman road, and Divle, the modern name, resembles the ancient one. Leake, on the contrary, would place Derbe (not quite so far to the east) at Bin-bir-Kilesseh, a Turkish town, where some remarkable ruins have been found —among the rest, those of numerous churches. Others, again, think that these ruins mark the site of Lystra, since they correspond better with the early ecclesiastical reputation of this city than that of Derbe.—**The region about** designates the country in the vicinity of the places just named. A few critics have proposed to extend the term so as to include even Galatia, and would thus assign an earlier origin to the churches in that country than it is usual to assign to them. "But *the region about* (περίχωρον)," says Neander, "cannot denote an entire province; and still less the province of Galatia, on account of its geographical situation. Hence, the supposition that Paul preached the gospel to the Galatians on this first missionary-tour is certainly to be rejected." (See the note on 16 : 6.)

7. And there—viz. in those cities and the adjacent region. — **Were publishing glad**

tidings implies that they pursued their labors here for some time.

8-13. PAUL HEALS A LAME MAN AT LYSTRA.

8. At Lystra (ἐν Λύστροις), neuter plural, as in 2 Tim. 3 : 11, but feminine singular in vv. 6, 21; 16 : 1.—**Sat** (Mey., De Wet.), because he was lame and had never walked; others, **dwelt** (Kuin., Rob.), which is Hebraistic, and rare in the New Testament.—**Had walked** (περιπεπατήκει). Some editors write this pluperfect with an augment; others more correctly omit it. (W. ? 12. 9; K. ? 120. R. 2.)

9. Was hearing, while Paul preached. The Jews at this place were probably few, as no synagogue appears to have existed here. Hence the missionaries repaired to the market or some other place of public resort (comp. 17 : 17), and there entered into conversation with such as they could induce to listen to them. The scene reminds us of the manner in which those who carry the same message of salvation to the heathen at the present day collect around them groups of listeners in Burmah or Hindostan. It was on one of these occasions, as Paul was preaching in some thoroughfare of the city, that the lame man heard him; his friends, perhaps, had placed him there to solicit alms. (See 3 : 10; John 9 : 8.)—**Who looking intently upon him and seeing**—viz. from the expression of his countenance, which Paul scrutinized with such rigor. The manner in which the participles follow each other directs us to this sense. Some think that the apostle may have had at the moment a supernatural insight into the state of the man's heart. The language of the text contains no intimation of that nature.—**The faith of being healed.** The infinitive depends on the noun as a genitive construction. (Comp. Luke 1 : 57. See W. ? 44. 4.) The faith so described may be faith that the Saviour whom Paul preached was able to heal him, or, which accords better with the mode of expression, faith such as made it proper that he should receive that benefit. (See on 9 : 33.) The requisite degree of faith would include, of course, a persuasion of Christ's ability to bestow the favor in question. Paul may have been refer-

10 Said with a loud voice, *Stand upright on thy feet. And he leaped and walked.

11 And when the people saw what Paul had done, they lifted up their voices, saying in the speech of Lycaonia, *The gods are come down to us in the likeness of men.

12 And they called Barnabas, Jupiter; and Paul, Mercurius, because he was the chief speaker.

13 Then the priest of Jupiter, which was before their city, brought oxen and garlands unto the gates, *and would have done sacrifice with the people.

10 he had faith to be made whole, said with a loud voice, Stand upright on thy feet. And he leaped up 11 and walked. And when the multitudes saw what Paul had done, they lifted up their voices, saying in the speech of Lycaonia, The gods are come down to 12 us in the likeness of men. And they called Barnabas, ¹Jupiter; and Paul, ²Mercury, because he 13 was the chief speaker. And the priest of ¹Jupiter whose *temple* was before the city, brought oxen and garlands unto the gates, and would have done sacri-

---

a Isa. 35 : 6.   .*b* ch. 8 : 10 ; 28 : 6. . . .*c* Dan. 2 : 46.——1 Gr. *Zeus*. . . .2 Gr. *Hermes*.

---

ring in his remarks to the Saviour's miracles of healing, in illustration of his readiness and power to bless those who confide in him.

10. With a loud voice (μεγάλῃ τῇ φωνῇ). The article designates the voice as that of Paul (see v. 11 ; 26 . 24), while the adjective refers to the tone with which he spoke. With the idea that his voice was a powerful one, **loud** (μεγάλῃ) would have stood between the article and noun, or after the noun with the article (τῇ) repeated. [The critical editors Lach., Tsch., Treg., West. and Hort, omit the article as an addition to the true text.—A. H.]—**Stand upright,** etc. Luke makes no mention here of any direct appeal to the name of Christ before the performance of the miracle. (See on 3 :6.) That omission may be owing to the brevity of the record, or the tenor of Paul's discourse may have been so explicit in regard to the source of his authority as to render the usual invocation unnecessary. —**Leaped,** sprung up, a single act. For this aorist, see W. § 15 ; K. § 149. R. 2. The imperfect (ἤλλετο) occurs in some copies, but has no adequate support. The next verb passes to the imperfect, because it expresses a repeated act.

11. The multitudes. Their conduct shows how imperfectly they had understood the address of Paul and the object of the miracle. They saw nothing beyond what was present and palpable ; they confounded the instrument of the work with its author.—**What he had done.** (See on 1 : 2.)—**In Lycaonic**—*i. e.* the native dialect of the province. Of the nature of this dialect nothing is known with certainty. No relic of it remains, or at least has been identified ; no description of it has been handed down to us. Those who have examined the question differ in their conclusions. According to one opinion, the Lycaonic was allied to the Assyrian ; according to another, it was a corrupt species of Greek.¹ We have no reliable data for forming any opinion. Luke mentions that the Lystrians spoke in their

native tongue that we may know why the multitude proceeded so far in their design before Paul and Barnabas interposed to arrest it. In conferring with the people they had used, doubtless, the Greek, which formed at that period an extensive medium of intercourse between those of different nations.

12. Jupiter, Mercury. They fixed upon these gods because Jupiter had a temple there, and Mercury, who appeared in the pagan mythology as his attendant, excelled in eloquence. So Ovid, *Met.,* 8. 626 :

> "Jupiter huc specie mortali cumque parente
> Venit Atlantiades positis caducifer alis." ²

(See also Hor., *Od.,* 1. 10. 1-5.) Some suggest, as a further reason for such a distribution of parts, that Barnabas may have been an older man than Paul and more imposing in his personal appearance. (Comp. 2 Cor. 10 : 1, 10.)— **He who leads the discourse** is the chief speaker. (Comp. 14 : 12.)

13. The priest—*i. e.* the principal one, or the one most active, at this time. The pagan worship at Lystra must have required several priests.—**Of Jupiter who was before the city**—*i. e.* who had a statue and temple there consecrated to him. The temple of the tutelary god stood often outside of the walls.— **Garlands,** which were to adorn the victims, and perhaps the priest and the altar (De Wet.). (See Jahn's *Archæol.,* § 401. 5.) They had the garlands in readiness, but had not yet placed them on the heads of the animals. Some construe **bullocks and garlands** as = **bullocks adorned with garlands** (De Wet., Rob.). With that idea the writer would have used naturally that expression.—**Unto the gates** of the city (Neand., Rob., Alf., Mey. in his last ed.), since **city** precedes and the term is plural (as consisting of parts or being double) ; or, less probably, of the house where the apostles lodged (Olsh., De Wet.).—**Would sacri-**

---

¹ Jablonsky and Gühling, who wrote dissertations on the subject, arrived at the results stated above. (See Win., *Realw.,* ii. p. 37.)

² [" Hither Jupiter came in human form, and with his parent came the caduceus-bearing grandson of Atlas, having laid aside his wings."]

14 *Which* when the apostles, Barnabas and Paul, heard *of*, *a*they rent their clothes, and ran in among the people, crying out,

15 And saying, Sirs, *b*why do ye these things? *c*We also are men of like passions with you, and preach unto you that ye should turn from *d*these vanities *e*unto the living God, *f* which made heaven, and earth, and the sea, and all things that are therein :

16 *g*Who in times past suffered all nations to walk in their own ways.

17 *h*Nevertheless he left not himself without witness, in that he did good, and *i*gave us rain from heaven, and fruitful seasons, filling our hearts with food and gladness.

18 And with these sayings scarce restrained they

14 fice with the multitudes. But when the apostles, Barnabas and Paul, heard of it, they rent their garments, and sprang forth among the multitude, cry-

15 ing out and saying, Sirs, why do ye these things? We also are men of like ¹passions with you, and bring you good tidings, that ye should turn from these vain things unto the living God, who made

16 the heaven and the earth and the sea, and all that in them is: who in the generations gone by suffered

17 all the nations to walk in their own ways. And yet he left not himself without witness, in that he did good, and gave you from heaven rains and fruitful seasons, filling your hearts with food and gladness.

18 And with these sayings scarce restrained they the multitudes from doing sacrifice unto them.

a Matt. 26 : 65....*b* ch. 10 : 26....*c* James 5 : 17 ; Rev. 19 : 10....*d* 1 Sam. 12 : 21 ; 1 Kings 16 : 13 ; Jer. 14 : 22 ; Amos 2 : 4 ; 1 Cor. 8 : 4....
e 1 Thess. 1 : 9.... *f* Gen. 1 : 1 ; Ps. 33 : 6 ; 146 : 6 ; Rev. 14 : 7....*g* Ps. 81 : 12 ; ch. 17 : 30 ; 1 Pet. 4 : 3....*h* ch. 17 : 27 ; Rom. 1 : 20....
i Lev. 26 : 4 ; Deut. 11 : 14 ; 28 : 12 ; Job 5 : 10 ; Ps. 65 : 10 ; 68 : 9 ; 147 : 8 ; Jer. 14 : 22 ; Matt. 5 : 45.———— 1 Or, *nature.*

fice, but were disappointed (De Wet.), or **was about to sacrifice,** since the verb used (ἐθέλω) may denote an act on the point of being done. (See Mt. ? 498. e ; C. ? 583.)

14-18. THE SPEECH OF PAUL TO THE LYSTRIANS.

14. Having heard—*i. e.* a report of what was taking place ; brought to them, perhaps, by some of the converts.—**Having rent their garments**—*i. e.* according to the Jewish custom, from the neck in front down toward the girdle. (See Jahn's *Archæol.,* ? 211.) The Jews and other nations performed this act not only as an expression of sorrow, but of abhorrence on hearing or seeing anything which they regarded as impious. **Garments** may refer to the plural subject of the verb, but more probably to their outer and inner garments. (Comp. Matt. 26 : 65.) — **Sprang forth unto the crowd**—*i. e.* from the city, of which we think most readily after **city** in v. 13, or from the house, if the people had assembled in the street. The preposition (ἐξ) in the verb, therefore, does not settle the question in regard to **unto the gates.** The English translation, " ran in among them," rests upon a now rejected reading.

15. And connects what is said with what was in the mind : Ye are men, **and we are men like constituted with you.** Passing over the first clause, the speaker hastens at once to the main thought. **Of like passions** means that they had the same nature, passions, infirmities. **Declaring to you as glad tidings**—viz. **that you should turn,** etc. This requisition that they should renounce their idols is called **glad tidings,** because it was founded on the fact that God had provided a way in the gospel in which he could accept their repentance. **You** (ὑμᾶσ) answers here to the dative, as in 8 : 25.—**From these vanities,** nonentities, such as Jupiter, Mercury, and the like. **These** points back to those names. Paul and Barnabas had heard in what light

the populace looked upon them. **Vanities** (ματαίων) does not require **gods.** It is used like Heb. *hăbhalēm, ăvanēm,* which the Hebrews applied to the gods of the heathen as having no real existence. (Comp. 1 Cor. 8 : 4.) Kuinoel renders the word *vain practices,* idolatry, which destroys the evident opposition between the term and **the living God.—Who made,** etc. This relative clause unfolds the idea of **living.**

16. Left them, withdrew the restraints of his grace and providence. (Comp. on 7 : 42 and 17 : 30.) In Rom. 1 : 23 the apostle brings to view other connections of this fact. The reason why God abandoned the heathen was that they first abandoned him.—**To walk** (see on 9 : 31) **in their own ways,** dative of rule or manner. **Ways** includes belief and conduct.

17. Although indeed he left himself not without witness. The desertion on the part of God was not such as to destroy the evidence of their dependence on him, and their consequent obligation to know and acknowledge him. The apostle's object does not lead him to press them with the full consequences of this truth. It lies at the foundation of his argument for proving the accountability of the heathen, in Rom. 1 : 19, *sq.* (See also 17 : 27, *sq.*)—**Doing good, giving rain, filling,** etc., are epexegetical of **without witness,** but the second participle specifies a mode of the first, and the third a consequence of the second.— **You** before **from heaven** is the correct reading (Grsb., Lchm., Mey.), instead of the received **us. With food,** including the idea of the enjoyment afforded by such fruits of the divine bounty. With that accessory idea, **food** is not incongruous with **hearts,** and **your hearts** is not a circumlocution for **you** (Kuin.). (See W. ? 22. 7.) The common text has **our,** which appears in the English Version.

18. Did not sacrifice states the result of **restrained,** not the object : **they hardly restrained them that they did not sacrifice**

the people, that they had not done sacrifice unto them.

19 ¶ *a*And there came thither *certain* Jews from Antioch and Iconium, who persuaded the people, *b*and, having stoned Paul, drew *him* out of the city, supposing he had been dead.

20 Howbeit, as the disciples stood round about him, he rose up, and came into the city : and the next day he departed with Barnabas to Derbe.

21 And when they had preached the gospel to that city, *c*and had taught many, they returned again to Lystra, and *to* Iconium, and Antioch,

---

19 But there came Jews thither from Antioch and Iconium: and having persuaded the multitudes, they stoned Paul, and dragged him out of the city,

20 suppo-ing that he was dead. But as the disciples stood round about him, he rose up, and entered into the city : and on the morrow he went forth with

21 Barnabas to Derbe. And when they had preached the gospel to that city, and had made many disciples, they returned to Lystra, and to Iconium, and

---

a ch. 13 : 45....*b* 2 Cor. 11 : 25 ; 2 Tim. 3 : 11....*c* Matt. 28 : 19.

---

to them. (See the note on 10 : 47.)—It is interesting to compare this speech at Lystra with the train of thought which Paul has developed in Rom. 1 : 19, *sq.* It will be seen that the germ of the argument there may be traced distinctly here. The similarity is precisely such as we should expect on the supposition that he who wrote the Epistle delivered the speech. The diversity in the different prominence given to particular ideas is that which arises from applying the same system of truth to different occasions.

19–28. THEY PROCEED TO DERBE, AND THEN RETRACE THEIR WAY TO ANTIOCH IN SYRIA.

19. The Jews will be found, with two exceptions, to stir up every persecution which Paul suffers. (See on 19 : 23.)—**The crowds.** They were mostly heathen (see on v. 9), but that some Jews resided at Lystra is evident from 16 : 1.—**Having stoned Paul.** Barnabas escapes, because his associate here and in the other cities was the prominent man. The nature of the outrage indicates that the Jews not only originated this attack, but controlled the mode of it. Stoning was a Jewish punishment. In the present instance, it will be observed, they had no scruple about shedding the blood of their victim in the city. It was otherwise at Jerusalem. (See on 7 : 58.) An incidental variation like this attests the truth of the narrative.—**Supposing that he was dead** intimates a mere belief as opposed to the reality. A slight accent on the first word brings this out as the necessary meaning.

20. The disciples having surrounded him. Here we learn incidentally that their labors had not been ineffectual. Kuinoel decides too much when he says that the disciples collected around Paul in order to bury him ; it may have been to lament over him or to ascertain whether he was really dead. In that sorrowing circle stood, probably, the youthful Timothy, the apostle's destined associate in so many future labors and perils. (See 16 : 1 ; 2 Tim. 3 : 11.)—**He rose up,** etc. After the ex-

pression in v. 19, we can hardly regard this as an instance of actual restoration to life. If we recognize anything as miraculous here, it would be more justly the apostle's sudden recovery after such an outrage, enabling him to return at once to the city, and on the next day to resume his journey. Paul alludes to this stoning in 2 Cor. 11 : 25. The wounds inflicted on him at this time may have left some of those scars on his body to which he alludes in Gal. 6 : 17 as proof that he was Christ's servant.—**Unto Derbe.** (See on v. 6.) A few hours would be sufficient for the journey hither. We have now reached the eastern limit of the present expedition.

21. Having made many disciples (Matt. 28 : 19), as the result of the preaching mentioned in the other clause. One of the converts was probably Gaius, who is called a Derbean in 20 : 4. Their labors in this city appear to have been unattended by any open opposition. Hence, in 2 Tim. 3 : 11, Paul omits Derbe from the list of places associated in the mind of Timothy with the "persecutions, afflictions," which the apostle had been called to endure. Paley refers to that omission as a striking instance of conformity between the Epistle and the Acts : "In the apostolic history Lystra and Derbe are commonly mentioned together ; in 2 Tim. 3 : 11, Antioch, Iconium, Lystra, are mentioned, and not Derbe. And the distinction will appear on this occasion to be accurate ; for Paul in that passage is enumerating his persecutions, and, although he underwent grievous persecutions in each of the three cities through which he passed to Derbe, at Derbe itself he met with none. The Epistle, therefore, in the names of the cities, in the order in which they are enumerated, and in the place at which the enumeration stops, corresponds exactly with the history. Nor is there any just reason for thinking the agreement to be artificial ; for had the writer of the Epistle sought a coincidence with the history upon this head, and searched the Acts of the Apostles for the purpose, I conceive he would have sent us at once to Philippi and

22 Confirming the souls of the disciples, *and* *a*exhorting them to continue in the faith, and that *b*we must through much tribulation enter into the kingdom of God.

23 And when they had *c*ordained them elders in

22 to Antioch, confirming the souls of the disciples, exhorting them to continue in the faith, and that through many tribulations we must enter into the 23 kingdom of God. And when they had appointed

a ch. 11 : 23 ; 13 : 43....*b* Matt. 10 : 38 ; 16 : 24 ; Luke 22 : 28, 29 ; Rom. 8 : 17 ; 2 Tim. 2 : 11, 12 ; 3 : 12....*c* Tit. 1 : 5.

Thessalonica, where Paul suffered persecution, and where, from what is stated, it may easily be gathered that Timothy accompanied him, rather than have appealed to persecutions as known to Timothy, in the account of which persecutions Timothy's presence is not mentioned, it not being till after one entire chapter, and in the history of a journey three or four years subsequent to this (16 : 1), that Timothy's name occurs in the Acts of the Apostles for the first time."— **Turned back.** Advancing still eastward from this point, they would soon have reached the well-known "Cilician Gates," through which they could have descended easily to Cilicia, and then have embarked from Tarsus for Antioch. They had the choice, therefore, of a nearer way to Syria; but their solicitude for the welfare of the newly-founded churches constrains them to turn back and revisit the places where they had preached.

22. Confirming the souls of the disciples, not by any outward rite, but by instruction and encouragement, as we see in the next clause. (Comp. 15 : 32, 41 ; 18 : 23.)—**To adhere to the faith** (see 6 : 7 ; 13 : 8)—*i. e.* of Christ or the gospel. (Comp. 3 : 16 ; 20 : 21, etc.)—**That** depends on **exhorting,** which at this point of the sentence passes to the idea of affirming, teaching.—δεῖ may mean *it is necessary,* because such was the appointment of God (9 : 16; 1 Cor. 15 : 25), or because in the nature of things it was inevitable. (Comp. 2 Tim. 3 : 12.) The first is the more pertinent view, since it suggests a more persuasive motive to submission and fidelity in the endurance of trials.— **We,** who are Christians. (Comp. 1 Thess. 4 : 17.)—**The kingdom of God**—*i. e.* the state of happiness, which awaits the redeemed in heaven. The expression can have no other meaning here, for those addressed were already members of Christ's visible kingdom, and the perseverance to which the apostle would incite them has reference to a kingdom which they are yet to enter.

23. Now having appointed for them elders in every church. The verb used here, *to extend the hand* (χειροτονεῖν), signifies properly to elect or vote by extending the hand, but also, in a more general sense, to choose, appoint, without reference to that for-

mality. That formality could not have been observed in this instance, as but two individuals performed the act in question. When the verb retains the idea of stretching forth the hand, the act is predicated always of the subject of the verb, not of those for whom the act may be performed. Hence the interpretation *having appointed for them by their outstretched hands—i. e.* by taking their opinion or vote in that manner—is unwarranted; for it transfers the hands to the wrong persons. Whether Paul and Barnabas appointed the presbyters in this case by their own act solely, or ratified a previous election of the churches made at their suggestion, is disputed. If it be clear from other sources that the primitive churches elected their officers by general suffrage, the verb here may be understood to denote a concurrent appointment, in accordance with that practice; but the burden of proof lies on those who contend for such a modification of the meaning. Neander's conclusion on this subject should be stated here: "As regards the election to church offices, we are in want of sufficient information to enable us to decide how it was managed in the early apostolic times. Indeed, it is quite possible that the method of procedure differed under different circumstances. As in the institution of deacons the apostles left the choice to the communities themselves, and as the same was the case in the choice of deputies to attend the apostles in the name of the communities (2 Cor. 8 : 19), we might argue that a similar course would be pursued in filling other offices of the church. Yet it may be that in many cases the apostles themselves, where they could not as yet have sufficient confidence in the spirit of the first new communities, conferred the important office of presbyters on such as in their own judgment, under the light of the Divine Spirit, appeared to be the fittest persons. *Their* choice would, moreover, deserve in the highest degree the confidence of the communities (comp. 14 : 23; Tit. 1 : 5), although, when Paul empowers Titus to set presiding officers over the communities who possessed the requisite qualifications, this circumstance decides nothing as to the mode of choice, nor is a choice by the community itself *thereby* necessarily excluded. The

every church, and had prayed with fasting, they commended them to the Lord, on whom they believed.
24 And after they had passed throughout l'isidia,
they came to Pamphylia.

for them elders in every church, and had prayed
with fasting, they commended them to the Lord, on
24 whom they had believed. And they passed through

regular course appears to have been this: The church offices were entrusted to the first converts in preference to others, provided that in other respects they possessed the requisite qualifications. It may have been the general practice for the presbyters themselves, in case of a vacancy, to propose another to the community in place of the person deceased, and leave it to the whole body either to approve or decline their selection for reasons assigned. (Clem., cap. 44.) When asking for the assent of the community had not yet become a mere formality, this mode of filling church offices had the salutary effect of causing the votes of the majority to be guided by those capable of judging and of suppressing divisions; while, at the same time, no one was obtruded on the c(n- munity who would not be welcome to their hearts" (*Ch. Hist.*, Dr. Torrey's tr., vol. i. p. 189). —**Elders in every church.** The term is plural, because each church had its college of elders (see 20 : 17; Tit. 1 : 5), not because there was a church in each of the cities. The *elders*, or *presbyters*, in the official sense of the term, were those appointed in the first churches to watch over their general discipline and welfare. With reference to their duty, they were called, also, *overseers* (ἐπίσκοποι)—i. e. superintendents, or bishops. The first was their Jewish appellation, transferred to them, perhaps, from the similar class of officers in the synagogues; the second was their foreign appellation, since the Greeks employed it to designate such relations among themselves. In accordance with this distinction, we find the general rule to be this: Those who are called elders in speaking of Jewish communities are called bishops in speaking of Gentile communities. Hence the latter term is the prevailing one in Paul's Epistles. That the names with this difference were entirely synonymous appears from their interchange in such passages as 20 : 17, 28 and Tit. 1 : 5, 7. It may be argued, also, from the fact that in Phil. 1 : 1 and 1 Tim. 3 : 1, 8 the deacons are named immediately after the bishops, which excludes the idea of any intermediate order. Other appellations given to these officers were *pastors*, *leaders*, *presidents of the brethren*. The presbyters, or bishops, were not, by virtue of their office, teachers or preachers at the same time, nor, on the other hand, were the two spheres of labor incompatible with each other. We see from 1 Tim. 5 : 17 that some of those who

exercised the general oversight preached also the word. (Comp. also 1 Tim. 3 : 2.) The foregoing representation exhibits the view of Mosheim, Neander, Gieseler, Rothe, and others eminent in such inquiries. [From 1 Tim 3 : 2 and Tit. 1 : 9 (comp. 1 Cor. 12 : 28, 30; Eph. 4 : 11), it must be inferred that *teaching* was considered in the apostolic age a *normal* function of the church officers called elders, bishops, pastors, etc. For the first passage declares that "the bishop must be . . . apt to teach," and the second that he must " hold the faithful word, . . . that he may be able to exhort in the healthful doctrine and convict the gainsayers;" while it is pretty evident that the Christian workers classified as "teachers " in 1 Cor. 12 : 28, 30, and as "pastors and teachers " in Eph. 4 : 11, were identical in position with those frequently denominated elders or bishops. But against this view may be urged the language of 1 Tim. 5 : 17: " Let the elders that rule" (preside) "well be counted worthy of double honor, especially those who labor in the word and in teaching," which has been thought to distinguish between presiding and teaching elders. Yet the word translated "labor " means, literally, "to beat out one's self with labor;" and the apostle may intend to say that such overseers as give themselves *wholly* and *exhaustively* to their ministry should receive more honor (in the way, perhaps, of compensation) than others. The passage scarcely proves that any part of the elders did not preach at all. Nor is this proved by the circumstance that in many of the churches there were more bishops than one; for a college of bishops might easily find enough preaching to do in a pagan city. The only other church officers besides bishops recognized in the New Testament appear to be deacons, whose duties were probably of a partly secular and partly spiritual character. They often preached the gospel as evangelists.— A. H.]—**Having prayed** belongs to the following verb, not to the subordinate clause which precedes.—**Them** is defined by **on whom they had believed,** and must refer to the believers in general, not to the elders merely.

24. Having passed through Pisidia. Antioch was on the northern limit of Pisidia, and hence they traversed that district from north to south. Their journey was a descent from the mountains to the plain.

25 And when they had preached the word in Perga, they went down into Attalia: 26 And thence sailed to Antioch, *from whence they had been *recommended to the grace of God for the work which they fulfilled. 27 And when they were come, and had gathered the church together, *they rehearsed all that God had done with them, and how he had *opened the door of faith unto the Gentiles. 28 And there they abode long time with the disciples.

25 Pisidia, and came to Pamphylia. And when they had spoken the word in Perga, they went down to 26 Attalia; and thence they sailed to Antioch, from whence they had been committed to the grace of 27 God for the work which they had fulfilled. And when they were come, and had gathered the church together, they rehearsed all that God had done with them, and how that he had opened a 28 door of faith unto the Gentiles. And they tarried no little time with the disciples.

CHAPTER XV.

AND *certain men which came down from Judæa taught the brethren, *and said*, *Except ye be cir-

1 AND certain men came down from Judæa and taught the brethren, *saying*, Except ye be circum-

a ch. 13 : 1, 3....*b* ch. 15 : 40....*c* ch. 15 : 4, 12; 21 : 19....*d* 1 Cor. 16 : 9; 2 Cor. 2 : 12; Col. 4 : 3; Rev. 3 : 8....*e* Gal. 2 : 12....*f* John 7 : 22; ver. 5; Gal. 5 : 2; Phil. 3 : 2; Col. 2 : 8, 11, 16.

25. In Perga. They now preached in Perga, as they appear not to have done on their first visit. (See on 13 : 13.) Luke's silence as to the result may intimate that they were favored with no marked success. — **To Attalia.** Instead of taking ship at Perga and sailing down the Cestrus, which they had ascended on their outward journey, they travelled across the plain to Attaleia, a seaport on the Pamphylian Gulf, near the mouth of the Catarrhactes. The distance between the two places was about sixteen miles. (See on 13 : 13.) The founder of Attaleia was Attalus Philadelphus, King of Pergamus. It occupied the site of the modern Satalia, which Admiral Beaufort describes " as beautifully situated round a small harbor, the streets appearing to rise behind each other like the seats of a theatre, . . . with a double wall and a series of square towers on the level summit of the hill." (See a view of the town in Lewin's *Life and Ep. of St. Paul.*) **26. Sailed away unto Antioch,** though they may have disembarked at Seleucia, as the town and its port are one in such designations. (Comp. 20 : 6.)—**From whence,** etc. stands *in sensu prægnanti* for **whence, having been committed to the favor of God, they were sent forth.** (See 13 : 3. W. § 54. 7.)—**For the work** (telic), for its performance. **27. How great things** (on their journey) **God wrought with them**—*i. e.* in their behalf (15 : 4; Luke 1 : 72); not *by them*, which would be δι' αὐτῶν, as in 15 : 12. The phrase comes from Heb. 'asah 'im. (Comp. Josh. 2 : 12; Ps. 119 : 65, etc.) According to Meyer, **with them** is = **being with them, allied with them,** which is less simple.—**That he opened to the Gentiles a door of faith**—*i. e.* had given them access to the gospel, participation in its blessings, as well as to the Jews; not that he had opened to the apostles a door of access to the heathen. This metaphor is a favorite one with Paul (1 Cor. 16 : 9; 2 Cor. 2 : 12; Col. 4 : 3), and may

have become familiar to Luke in his intercourse with him (Alf.). **28. Abode,** etc. It is necessary to inquire here how long the apostle was probably absent on the tour followed by this residence at Antioch. We must be content with a somewhat vague answer to this question. The Apostolic Council at Jerusalem was held in A. D. 50 (*Introd.*, § 6. 3); and, as Paul departed on his first mission in A. D. 45 (see on 13 : 3), we must divide the interval from A. D. 45 to 50 between his journey among the heathen and his subsequent abode at Antioch. The best authorities, as Anger, Wieseler, Meyer, Winer, De Wette, and others, agree in this result. How we are to distribute the intermediate years is more uncertain. ˉ It will be found that the apostle travelled more extensively during his second missionary-tour than during the first; and, as the limitations of time in that part of the history allow us to assign but three years, or three and a half, to that excursion, we may consider two years, perhaps, as sufficient for this journey. This conclusion would place the return to Antioch near the close of A. D. 47, since the apostle must have set forth somewhat late in the year A. D. 45. (Comp. the note on 12 : 25 with that on 13 : 3.) Accordingly, the years A. D. 48 and 49 would be the **period not brief** (χρόνον οὐκ ὀλίγον) which Paul and Barnabas spent at Antioch between their return and the Council at Jerusalem. While they resided in that city, for the most part, they would be able, both by their own personal efforts and their supervision of the efforts of others, to extend the gospel in the regions around them.

1–5. PAUL AND BARNABAS ARE SENT AS DELEGATES TO JERUSALEM.

1. From Judea — *i. e.* from Jerusalem in Judea. (Comp. **certain from us,** in v. 24.) It is barely possible that Luke may include the

cumcised *after the manner of Moses, ye cannot be saved.

2 When therefore Paul and Barnabas had no small dissension and disputation with them, they determined that *Paul and Barnabas, and certain other of them, should go up to Jerusalem unto the apostles and elders about this question.

3 And *being brought on their way by the church, they passed through Phenice and Samaria, *declaring the conversion of the Gentiles: and they caused great joy unto all the brethren.

4 And when they were come to Jerusalem, they were received of the church, and *of* the apostles and elders, and *they declared all things that God had done with them.

cised after the custom of Moses, ye cannot be saved. 2 And when Paul and Barnabas had no small dissension and questioning with them, *the brethren* appointed that Paul and Barnabas, and certain other of them, should go up to Jerusalem unto the apos-3 tles and elders about this question. They therefore, being brought on their way by the church, passed through both Phœnicia and Samaria, declaring the conversion of the Gentiles: and they caused 4 great joy unto all the brethren. And when they were come to Jerusalem, they were received of the church and the apostles and the elders, and they rehearsed all things that God had done with them.

---

a Gen. 17 : 10; Lev. 12 : 3....*b* Gal. 2 : 1....*c* Rom. 15 : 24; 1 Cor. 16 : 6, 11....*d* ch. 14 : 27....*e* ver. 12; ch. 14 : 27; 21 : 19.

---

other churches in that country. We are not to confound this party of Judaizers with those in Gal. 2 : 12 who "came from James" (*i. e.* the church over which he presided) and caused Peter to dissemble his convictions from fear of their censure. The notice in the Epistle refers to a different and later event. (See on 18 : 23.) — **Were teaching.** They had not broached the error merely, but were inculcating it.—**That unless ye are circumcised,** etc. This transition to the direct style gives vividness to the narrative.—**According to the custom,** law (τῷ ἔθει, see 6 : 14), dative of rule or manner.—**Ye cannot be saved.** It was this enforced submission to the rite as necessary to salvation which made the error so fatally pernicious. (Comp. the note on 16 : 3.) The doctrine in this form was nothing less than an utter subversion of the scheme of Christianity. It denied the sufficiency of faith in Christ as the only condition of pardon and reconciliation. It involved the feeling that circumcision was an act of merit, and that those who submitted to it acquired a virtual right to the divine favor. In a word, it substituted the law of works for the gratuitous justification which the gospel declares to be the only way in which sinners can be saved. (See Gal. 5 : 1, *sq.*)

2. Dissension, in their views; **discussion,** on the points which that difference involved.—**Small** belongs to both nouns (De Wet.). The adjective is not repeated, because the words are of the same gender. (W. § 59. 5.) —**Them** refers to **certain men,** in v. 1. Paul and Barnabas were the disputants on one side, and the individuals from Judea on the other. It does not appear that the Christians at Antioch took any open part in the controversy. The heresy reappeared among them at a later period, and became so prevalent as to endanger the safety of the entire church. (See Gal. 2 : 11, *sq.*) Even Barnabas at that time compromised the principle for which he was now so earnest.—**They**—*i. e.* the brethren in v. 1—ap-

pointed that they should go up, etc. It appears from Gal. 2 : 2 that Paul went also, in compliance with a divine command. Whether the revelation was first and the action of the church subsequent, or the reverse, it is impossible to say. It may be that Paul was instructed to propose the mission to Jerusalem, or, if the measure originated with the church, that he was instructed to approve it and to go as one of the delegates. Either supposition harmonizes the notice in Gal. 2 : 2 with this passage.— **Certain others,** as delegates. One of them may have been Titus, since we read in Gal. 2 : 1 that he accompanied the apostle at this time. Yet perhaps **taking along also Titus,** in that place, may indicate that they travelled together as friends, and not as official associates. The fact, too, that, being uncircumcised, he was a party in some sense to this Jewish question may have disqualified him for such an appointment.

3. They having been sent forward—*i. e.* attended part of the way by some of the church as a mark of honor. (Comp. 20 : 38 ; 21 : 5 ; 3 John 6.) The word, says Meyer, does not include the *viatica,* or supplies for the journey, unless the context point that out as a part of the service rendered, as in Tit. 3 : 13.—**Passed through Phœnicia and Samaria.** (See on 11 : 19.) As Galilee is not mentioned, they travelled, probably, along the coast as far south as Ptolemais (21 : 7), and then crossed the plain of Esdraelon into Samaria.—**Unto the brethren** in the various towns on their way. We see here the fruits of the seed which had been scattered in those regions (8 : 5; 11 : 19).

4. Were cordially received. (Comp. 18 : 27.) It was not certain that, coming on such an errand, they would be greeted with entire favor. It weakens the sense to restrict it to their official recognition as messengers. [The critical editors prefer παρεδέχθησαν to ἀπεδέχθησαν, followed by Dr. Hackett, but the former may have the meaning which Dr. H. gives to the

5 But there rose up certain of the sect of the Pharisees which believed, saying, *a*That it was needful to circumcise them, and to command *them* to keep the law of Moses.
6 ¶ And the apostles and elders came together for to consider of this matter.
7 And when there had been much disputing, Peter rose up, and said unto them, *b*Men *and* brethren, ye know how that a good while ago God made choice among us, that the Gentiles by my mouth should hear the word of the gospel, and believe.
8 And God, *c*which knoweth the hearts, bare them

5 But there rose up certain of the sect of the Pharisees who believed, saying, It is needful to circumcise them, and to charge them to keep the law of Moses.
6 And the apostles and the elders were gathered to-
7 gether to consider of this matter. And when there had been much questioning, Peter rose up, and said unto them,
Brethren, ye know how that *1*a good while ago God made choice among you, that by my mouth the Gentiles should hear the word of the gospel, and be-
8 lieve. And God, who knoweth the heart, bare them

a ver. 1....*b* ch. 10 : 20; 11 : 12....*c* 1 Chron. 28 : 9 : ch. 1 : 24.——*1* Gr. *from early days.*

latter.—A. H.]. This was the apostle's third visit to Jerusalem since his conversion, and was made in the year A. D. 50. (*Introd.*, § 6. 3.) —**The church,** in general, while **and** adds the prominent parts. (See on 1 : 14.) The existence of presbyters at Jerusalem is first recognized in 11 : 30. Luke does not inform us at what time or in what manner they were appointed. It was evidently no part of his intention to unfold any particular scheme of ecclesiastical polity. The information which he gives on that subject is incidental and imperfect. —**Toward them,** in their behalf. (See on 14 : 27.)

5. But there arose (in the assembly at Jerusalem) **some of those from the sect of the Pharisees.** It is entirely natural that individuals of this class appear as the party who insist on circumcision. The attachment to forms which rendered them Pharisees out of the church rendered them legalists in it. These are the persons, evidently, of whom Paul speaks so strongly in Gal. 2 : 4.—**Them**—viz. the Gentile believers in the communication just made (v. 4).—Some regard the contents of this verse as a continuation of the report (v. 4), as if the objectors were those at Antioch, and not at Jerusalem; but in that case we should have expected and *how* or *that* as the connective between **declared** and **there** *rose up*, etc.

6-12. SPEECH OF PETER IN THE ASSEMBLY.

6. Came together, etc. This assembly is often called the first Christian Council; but we must use some license to apply the term in that way, since a Council consists properly of delegates from various churches, whereas two churches only were represented on this occasion.—**The apostles and elders** are mentioned on account of their rank, not as composing the entire assembly. It is evident from v. 23 that the other Christians at Jerusalem were also present, and gave their sanction to the decrees enacted. (See also v. 12, compared with v. 22.)—In Gal. 2 : 2, Paul states that, besides the communication which he made to the

believers in a body, he had also a private interview with the chief of the apostles. That interview, we may suppose, preceded the public discussion. The object of it appears to have been to put the other apostles in full possession of his views, and of all the facts in relation to his ministry among the heathen; so that, fortified by their previous knowledge of the case, he might have their support in the promiscuous assembly, where prejudice or misunderstanding might otherwise have placed him in a false light.—**This matter,** subject of discussion (De Wet.); not **this expression,** in v. 5 (Mey.), because the dispute had an earlier origin.

7. Since remote days, a long time ago. (Comp. **in the beginning,** in 11 : 15.) The conversion of Cornelius took place during the time that Paul was at Tarsus (see on 11 : 15); and the several years, so eventful in their character, which had elapsed since that period, would appear in the retrospect a long time.— **Made choice among us** (the apostles) **that by my mouth,** etc. (Mey., De Wet., Win.). The subsequent clause forms the proper object of **made choice.** Some supply needlessly **me** (ἐμέ) (Olsh.), and others incorrectly make **among us** a Hebraistic accusative, **selected me** or **us.** (See W. § 32. 3.) The meaning is not necessarily that no heathen had heard or embraced the gospel till Peter preached it to them, but that it was he whom God appointed to convey the gospel to them under circumstances which showed it to be manifestly his will that they should be admitted into the church without circumcision.—For the generic **nations = Gentiles,** see on 11 : 1. [This sense of the word is sometimes called Jewish, because the word was applied by the Jews to all who were not Israelites, with the understanding that they were idolaters, ignorant, for the most part, of the true God. The adjective *ethnic* is often applied to heathen religions in modern literature.—A. H.]

8. The heart-knowing God (who could judge, therefore, of the sincerity of their repentance and faith) **testified for them** (dat.

witness, ^agiving them the Holy Ghost, even as *he did* unto us;

9 ^bAnd put no difference between us and them, ^cpurifying their hearts by faith.

10 Now therefore why tempt ye God, ^dto put a yoke upon the neck of the disciples, which neither our fathers nor we were able to bear?

11 But ^ewe believe that through the grace of the Lord Jesus Christ we shall be saved, even as they.

12 ¶ Then all the multitude kept silence, and gave audience to Barnabas and Paul, declaring what miracles and wonders God had *f* wrought among the Gentiles by them.

witness, giving them the Holy Spirit, even as he did 9 unto us; and he made no distinction between us 10 and them, cleansing their hearts by faith. Now therefore why try ye God, that ye should put a yoke upon the neck of the disciples, which neither 11 our fathers nor we were able to bear? But we believe that we shall be saved through the grace of the Lord Jesus, in like manner as they.

12 And all the multitude kept silence; and they hearkened unto Barnabas and Paul rehearsing what signs and wonders God had wrought among the Gen-

---

a ch. 10 : 44....*b* Rom. 10 : 11....*c* ch. 10 : 15; 28 : 43; 1 Cor. 1 : 2; 1 Pet. 1 : 22....*d* Matt. 23 : 4; Gal. 5 : 1....*e* Rom. 3 : 24; Eph. 2 : 8; Tit. 2 : 11; 3 : 4, 5....*f* ch. 14 : 27.

---

comm.). The testimony consisted of the miraculous gifts which he imparted to them. (See 10 : 45.) He had thus shown that ceremonial obedience was not essential to his favor; for he had granted the sign of acceptance to those who were entirely destitute of that recommendation.

9. And made no distinction between us, who had practised the Jewish rites, **and them,** though they were still heathen in that respect (**without law,** 1 Cor. 9 : 21). The next clause states how he had manifested this impartiality.—**In that by faith he purified their hearts**—*i. e.* in connection with their reception of the gospel had made them partakers of the holiness which renders those who possess it acceptable in his sight. He had bestowed this blessing as fully and freely on the uncircumcised believing Gentiles as he had upon the circumcised believing Jews. Peter represents the purification as effected by faith, in order to deny the error which would ascribe that efficacy to circumcision or any other legal observance. The Jewish feeling was that the heathen were unclean so long as they were uncircumcised. The Spirit is the efficient Author of sanctification; but faith, as used here, is a belief of the truth (2 Thess. 2 : 13), especially of that which relates to the atonement of Christ (1 John 1 : 7), and the Spirit employs the truth as the means of sanctification.

10. Now therefore—*i. e.* after such evidence that God does not require the heathen to submit to Jewish rites.—**Why do ye tempt God,** make presumptuous trial of his power and patience by demanding new proofs of his will. (See 5 : 9; Matt. 4 : 7; 1 Cor. 10 : 9.) This sense is partly Hebraistic, and we must compare the verb with the Heb. *nasah*, in order to obtain the full idea.—**To put** (= putting), etc., **that you should place** (= by placing) **a yoke,** etc. This is a lax use of the epexegetical infinitive. (W. § 44. 1.)—**Which neither our fathers,** etc. " By this yoke," says Neander, " which Peter represents as having been always so irksome to the Jews. he certainly did not mean the exter-

nal observance of ceremonies simply as such, since he would by no means persuade the Jewish Christians to renounce them. But he meant the external observance of the law, in so far as this proceeded from an internal subjection of the conscience to its power, such as exists when justification and salvation are made to depend on the performance of legal requirements. Those in this state of mind must fear lest they peril their salvation by the slightest deviation from the law; they suffer the painful scrupulosity which leads to the invention of manifold checks, in order to guard themselves, by a self-imposed constraint, against every possible transgression of its commands."

11. But marks this connection : With such an experience as to the law, we no longer expect salvation from that source, **but through the grace of the Lord Jesus believe that we shall be saved.—Also they**—viz. the heathen converts. The remark suggests its own application. If the Jews had renounced their own law as unable to benefit them, and had taken the position of the Gentiles, it was inconsistent as well as useless to require the Gentiles to depend on the system of the Jews. The train of thought in Gal. 2 : 15, *sq.*, is singularly coincident with this.—The reference of **they** to **our fathers** (v. 10) introduces an idea irrelevant to the subject.

12. Became silent recalls us to the **much disputing** in v. 7. Peter's address had calmed the excitement; so that they refrained from speaking and gave Paul and Barnabas an opportunity to be heard. (Comp. **had held their peace,** in the next verse.)—**Gave audience** or **hearkened** (ἤκουον, imperf.) implies a copious narration on the part of the speakers.—**Declaring,** etc. They gave this prominence to the miracles, because these expressed so decisively God's approval of their course in receiving the heathen without circumcision. That was now the main point in question. We see from Gal. 2 : 7, *sq.*, that the narrative embraced also other topics.

13 ¶ And after they had held their peace, *a*James answered, saying, Men *and* brethren, hearken unto me:

14 *b*Simeon hath declared how God at the first did visit the Gentiles, to take out of them a people for his name.

15 And to this agree the words of the prophets; as it is written,

16 *c*After this I will return, and will build again the tabernacle of David, which is fallen down; and I will build again the ruins thereof, and I will set it up:

17 That the residue of men might seek after the Lord, and all the Gentiles, upon whom my name is called, saith the Lord, who doeth all these things.

13 tiles by them. And after they had held their peace, James answered, saying,

14 Brethren, hearken unto me: Symeon hath rehearsed how first God did visit the Gentiles, to take

15 out of them a people for his name. And to this agree the words of the prophets; as it is written,

16 After these things I will return, And I will build again the tabernacle of David, which is fallen;
And I will build again the ruins thereof, And I will set it up:

17 That the residue of men may seek after the Lord, And all the Gentiles, upon whom my name is called,

a ch. 12 : 17....*b* ver. 7....*c* Amos 9 : 11, 12.

13–21. SPEECH OF THE APOSTLE JAMES.

13. The speaker is the *James* mentioned in 12 : 17. Paul names him before Peter and John in Gal. 2 : 9, because he was pastor of the church at Jerusalem, and perhaps president of the Council.—**Proceeded to speak** (see 3 : 12), or, very properly, **answered,** since the position of the Judaistic party challenged a reply.

14. Symeon (see 13 : 1), as in 2 Pet. 1 : 1, elsewhere **Simon,** after the Heb. variation *Shēmōn* (1 Chr. 4 : 20) and *Shimŏ̆ōn* (Gen. 29 : 33). This apostle is not mentioned again in the Acts. His speech in the Council is the last act of Peter which Luke has recorded.—**At first** answers to **since remote days** in v. 7.—**Graciously visited,** like *pakadh* in its good sense.—**After his name** (Luke 1 : 59)—*i. e.* who should be called by it, known as his people (De Wet.). (Comp. v. 17; Deut. 28 : 10; Isa. 63 : 19; 2 Chr. 7 : 14, etc.) But the critical editions omit **upon = after** (ἐπί), and the dative depends then on the infinitive—*i. e.* **for thy name,** its acknowledgment, honor.

15. And with this (not masculine—viz. Peter—but neuter—viz. the fact just stated) **agree the words of the prophets.** As an example of their testimony, he adduces Amos 9 : 11, *sq.*

16. The citation conforms very nearly to the Septuagint.—**I will return and will rebuild.** The expression implies a restoration of favor after a temporary alienation. (Comp. Jer. 12 : 15.) Some recognize here the Hebraism which converts the first of two verbs into an adverb qualifying the second : **I will again rebuild.** Meyer, De Wette, Winer (§ 54. 5), reject that explanation. It is the less apposite here, as **re = again** (ἀνά) repeats the adverbial idea in the three following verbs.—**I will rebuild the tabernacle of David which has fallen**—*i. e.* will restore the decayed splendor of his family; to wit, in the person of his Son after the flesh (Rom. 1 : 3), in the Messiah.—**Tabernacle** represents the family as having fallen into

such obscurity as to occupy the humble abode of a booth or tabernacle. The next words of the text describe the same condition still more strongly.

17. That (telic, because the Saviour must be first sent) **the rest** (lit. **those left remaining) of men and all the heathen may seek out the Lord.** The Greek particle here used (ἄν) implies that it depends on them whether the purpose will be attained or defeated. (See W. § 42. 6; K. § 330. 4.) **The rest of men** are the others of them besides the Jews, and these others are **all the heathen.** The last clause is explicative, not appositional. The Hebrew has *they*—*i. e.* the people of God—*shall possess the residue of Edom*—*i. e.* those of Edom reserved for mercy—*and all the* (other) *heathen.* The Seventy may have confounded some of the original words with other similar words; but the apostle followed their translation of the passage, as it contained the essential idea for which he appealed to it. The many foreign Jews who were present were familiar with the Greek Scriptures, but not the Hebrew.—**Upon whom my name has been called**—*i. e.* given, applied to them as a sign of their relationship to God. (Comp. James 2 : 7. See the references on v. 14.) Observe that the verb is perfect. The application of the name was future when the prophecy was uttered, and was still future, to a great extent, when cited at this time; but the prediction was as good as already verified, because the purpose of God made it certain.— **Upon them** (ἐπ' αὐτούς) is a Hebraism founded on the use of *'ŏsher* as the sign of relation (Olsh., De Wet., Mey.). (Gesen., *Heb. Gr.*, § 121. 1.) The foregoing citation from Amos was pertinent in a twofold way : first, it announced that the heathen were to be admitted with the Jews into the kingdom of Christ; and secondly, it contained no recognition of circumcision or other Jewish ceremonies as prerequisite to their reception.—**All with these things** (T. R.) is not approved.

18 Known unto God are all his works from the beginning of the world.
19 Wherefore *my sentence is, that we trouble not them, which from among the Gentiles *are turned to God:
20 But that we write unto them, that they abstain *from pollutions of idols, and *from fornication, and *from things strangled, *and *from blood.
21 For Moses of old time hath in every city them that preach him, *f being read in the synagogues every sabbath day.

18 Saith the Lord, *who maketh these things known from of old.
19 Wherefore my judgment is, that we trouble not them who from among the Gentiles turn to God:
20 but that we *write unto them, that they abstain from the pollutions of idols, and from fornication,
21 and from what is strangled, and from blood. For Moses from generations of old hath in every city them that preach him, being read in the synagogues every sabbath.

a see ver. 28....b 1 Thess. 1 : 9....c Gen. 35 : 2 ; Ex. 20 : 3, 23 ; Ezek. 20 : 30 ; 1 Cor. 8 : 1 ; Rev. 2 : 14, 20 ; 9 : 20, 21....d 1 Cor. 6 : 9, 18 ; Gal. 5 : 19 ; Eph. 5 : 3 ; Col. 3 : 5 ; 1 Thess. 4 : 3 ; 1 Pet. 4 : 3....e Gen. 9 : 4 ; Lev. 3 : 17 ; Deut. 12 : 16, 23....f ch. 13 : 15, 27.——1 Or, who doeth these things which were known....2 Or, enjoin them

18. The words here are a comment of James on the prophecy.—**Known from the beginning unto God are all his works.** The present call of the Gentiles, after having been so long foretold, was an evidence and illustration of the truth here asserted. Hence, the apostle would argue, if God, in extending the gospel to the heathen without requiring them to be circumcised, was carrying into effect an eternal purpose, it became them to acquiesce in it; their opposition to his plan would be as unavailing as it was criminal.—The variations of the text in this verse are numerous, but nearly all yield the same meaning. They may be seen in Griesbach, Hahn, Tischendorf, Green, and others. Lachmann adheres to the common reading, with the exception of **Lord** for **God,** and **work** for **works.**

19. I (for my part, without dictating to others) **judge,** decide as my opinion. On **I** (ἐγώ), as thus restrictive, see W. § 22. 6. The verb affords no proof that the speaker's authority was greater than that of the other apostles. (Comp. 16 : 4.)—**That we ought not to disquiet,** molest—i. e. impose on them the yoke of Jewish ceremonies. (See v. 10.) The infinitive includes often the idea of obligation or necessity. (W. § 44. 3. b.) Meyer urges the separate force of (παρά) *further*—i. e. in addition to their faith, not justified, apparently, by usage; better, in his last edition, *thereby,* along with their conversion.

20. That we should write to them, direct by letter, **that they abstain.—Pollutions of idols** = **things sacrificed to idols,** in v. 29. The parts of the victim not used in sacrifice the heathen sold in the market as ordinary food or ate them at feasts. The Jews, in their abhorrence of idolatry, regarded the use of such flesh as allied to the guilt of participating in idol-worship itself. (See Rom. 14 : 15, *sq.* ; 1 Cor. 8 : 10, *sq.*)—**And from fornication** = licentiousness (Calv., Kuin., Olsh., Mey., De Wet.) Repeat **from** before this noun. The

other practices, it will be observed, relate to things which are not sinful *per se*, but derive their character from positive law or from circumstances. The reason, probably, for associating this immorality with such practices is that the heathen mind had become so corrupt as almost to have lost the idea of chastity as a virtue.[1] Other senses of **fornication** (πορνεία), as idolatry, incest, marriage with unbelievers, concubinage, have been proposed. It is against any such unusual signification of the word that it occurs again in the enactment (v. 29). The object of the decree would require it to be framed with as much perspicuity as possible, and would exclude the use of terms out of their ordinary acceptation.—**And from what has been strangled**—i. e. from the flesh of animals put to death in that way. The Jews were not allowed to eat such flesh, because it contained the blood. (See Lev. 17 : 13, 14 ; Deut. 12 : 16-23.)—**And from blood,** which the heathen drank often at their idolatrous feasts, and at other times and in various ways mingled with their food. [See an instructive discussion of the meaning of James, etc., in Fisher's *The Beginnings of Christianity*, p. 303.—A. H.]

21. This verse assigns a reason for the proposed restrictions, and that is that the Jewish believers, being so accustomed to hear the things in question forbidden, were naturally sensitive in regard to them ; and hence it was necessary, for the sake of peace and harmony, that the heathen converts should refrain from such practices. This view of the connection is the most natural one. Calvin, Hemsen, Olshausen, De Wette, Meyer, and others agree in it. Neander follows Chrysostom, who supposes the words to explain why it was proposed to instruct the Gentiles only : the Jews had no occasion to be informed what the law required of them, **for Moses in every city**, etc. This interpretation not only turns the mind abruptly from one train of thought to another, but appears to concede more to the advocates of cir-

---

[1] See Tholuck, *The Nature and Moral Influence of Heathenism*, in the *Biblical Repository*, vol. ii. p. 441, *sq.*

22 Then pleased it the apostles and elders, with the whole church, to send chosen men of their own company to Antioch with Paul and Barnabas; *namely,* Judas surnamed *a*Barsabas,and Silas, chief men among the brethren:

23 And they wrote *letters* by them after this manner; The apostles and elders and brethren *send* greeting unto the brethren which are of the Gentiles in Antioch and Syria and Cilicia:

24 Forasmuch as we have heard, that certain which went out from us have troubled you with words, subverting your souls, saying, Ye *must* be circumcised, and keep the law: to whom we gave no *such* commandment:

25 It seemed good unto us, being assembled with one accord, to send chosen men unto you with our beloved Barnabas and Paul

22 Then it seemed good to the apostles and the elders, with the whole church, to choose men out of their company, and send them to Antioch with Paul and Barnabas; *namely,* Judas called Barsabbas, and Silas, 23 chief men among the brethren: and they wrote *thus* by them, [1]The apostles and the elders, brethren, unto the brethren who are of the Gentiles in Antioch and 24 Syria and Cilicia, greeting: Forasmuch as we have heard that certain [2]who went out from us have troubled you with words, subverting your souls; to 25 whom we gave no commandment; it seemed good unto us, having come to one accord, to choose out men and send them unto you with our beloved Bar-

---

a ch. 1 : 23.... *b* ver. 1; Gal. 2 : 4; 5 : 12 ; Tit. 1 : 10, 11.——1 Or, *the apostles and the elder brethren*....2 Some ancient authorities omit *who went out.*

---

cumcision than the question at issue would allow. To have justified the prohibitions on such ground would be recognizing the perpetuity of the Mosaic rites, so far as the Jews were concerned; and we cannot suppose that the apostles at this time either entertained that view or would give any direct countenance to it in the minds of others.

22–29. THEY APPOINT MESSENGERS TO THE CHURCHES, AND SEND A LETTER BY THEM.

22. Then the apostles . . . resolved, having selected men from themselves, to send them, etc. The participle, **having selected** (ἐκλεξαμένους), passes into the accusative, because the object of the governing verb, **apostles** (ἀποστόλοις), serves at the same time as the subject of the infinitive. (K. § 307. R. 2.) **—Judas** is known only from this notice. His surname opposes the conjecture that he was Judas Thaddeus, the apostle. There is no proof that he was a brother of Joseph Barsabas, the candidate for the apostleship (1 : 23).—**Silas** became Paul's associate in his second missionary-tour (v. 40). For **Silas** in the Acts we have always **Silvanus** in the Epistles. The former was his Jewish name, probably; the latter, his Gentile or foreign name. (See on 13 : 9.)—**Chief men, leading,** eminent for reputation and authority (Luke 22 : 26).

23. Writing, E. V. **wrote.** The nominative of a participle refers often to a preceding substantive in a different case, when that substantive forms, in fact, the logical subject of the clause. (K. § 313. 1; W. § 64. II. 2.) The impersonal expression at the head of the sentence is equivalent to a transitive verb with the dative as nominative. (K. § 307. R. 5.)—**Throughout Antioch and Syria,** etc., since the brethren were in different places. We see here how extensively the Judaizers had attempted to spread their views. The scene at Antioch (v. 1) was only

an example of what had occurred in many other places. [The several lands are a unity with reference to the heathen converts, and hence the first only requires the article in Greek. Antioch is the capital, and is named separately on that account.—A. H.] As to the origin of the churches in Syria and Cilicia, see on v. 41.—**Greeting** (χαίρειν). It is remarkable, says Neander, that this word, as a form of epistolary salutation, occurs only here and in James 1 : 1, with the exception of 23 : 26, where it is a Roman who employs it. It would account for the coincidence, if we suppose that the apostle James drew up this document. His office as pastor of the church would very naturally devolve that service on him. The occurrence of **greeting** here and in the Epistle. Bengel, Bleek, and others point out as an indication that the two compositions are from the same hand.

24. From us, which accords with v. 1.— **Troubled, or disquieted,** perplexed. (See Gal. 1 : 7.)—**Words** may have, as Stier thinks, a disparaging force: **with words** merely, as opposed to the truth or sound doctrine.—**Subverting your souls**—*i. e.* unsettling, removing them from the pure faith of the gospel. This clause describes the effect or tendency of the views which those who received the decrees were urged by the false teachers to adopt.— **That ye must be circumcised, and keep the law.** For this power of the infinitive, see on v. 19. **Must** (δεῖν) is not to be supplied.[1]— **Whom we did not command**—*i. e.* instruct, authorize. This declaration may be aimed at a pretence on their part that they had been sent forth by the church at Jerusalem, or at least that they represented the sentiments of that church.

25. Having met together (Vulg., Neand.) but better **having become of one mind,** unanimous (Bng., Str., Mey.). Kuinoel and De Wette are undecided. According to the

---

1 [The clause may be an interpolation.—A. H.]

26 *a*Men that have hazarded their lives for the name of our Lord Jesus Christ.

27 We have sent therefore Judas and Silas, who shall also tell *you* the same things by mouth.

28 For it seemed good to the Holy Ghost, and to us, to lay upon you no greater burden than these necessary things;

29 *b*That ye abstain from meats offered to idols, and *c*from blood, and from things strangled, and from fornication: from which if ye keep yourselves, ye shall do well. Fare ye well.

30 So when they were dismissed, they came to Antioch: and when they had gathered the multitude together, they delivered the epistle:

26 nabas and Paul, men that have hazarded their lives 27 for the name of our Lord Jesus Christ. We have sent therefore Judas and Silas, who themselves also shall tell you the same things by word of mouth.

28 For it seemed good to the Holy Spirit, and to us, to lay upon you no greater burden than these neces-29 sary things; that ye abstain from things sacrificed to idols, and from blood, and from things strangled, and from fornication; from which if ye keep yourselves, it shall be well with you. Fare ye well.

30 So they, when they were dismissed, came down to Antioch; and having gathered the multitude to-

a ch. 13 : 50; 14 : 19; 1 Cor. 15 : 30; 2 Cor. 11 : 23, 26....*b* ver. 20, ch. 21 · 25; Rev 2 : 14. 20....*c* Lev. 17 : 14.

latter view, the expression represents this perfect harmony as having been attained after some diversity of opinion. (See v. 5.) **Chosen** (ἐκλεξαμένους) exemplifies again the construction in v. 22.—**Barnabas and Paul.** This deviation from the usual order of these names since 13 : 13, as De Wette remarks after Bleek, testifies to the writer's diplomatic accuracy. Paul had spent but little time at Jerusalem, and Barnabas was still a more familiar name there (comp. 9 : 27) than that of the apostle to the Gentiles.

26. Men who have given up, jeoparded, **their lives.** (Comp. 9 : 24; 13 : 50; 14 : 5, 19.) There was a special reason, no doubt, for this commendation of Paul and Barnabas. It would serve to counteract any attempts which the Jewish party might make, or had made, to discredit their religious views and impair their reputation as teachers.

27. Therefore—*i. e.* in conformity with the conclusion in v. 25.—**Also themselves by word announcing** (when they shall be present) **the same things**—*i. e.* that we now write to you (Neand., Mey., De Wet.); not *the same things* that Paul and Barnabas have taught. **By word** indicates clearly that the oral communication was to confirm the contents of the letter or the written communication. "Judas and Silas," says Stier (*Reden der Apostel,* i. p. 90), " should certify that the letter had actually proceeded from a unanimous resolve of the church at Jerusalem, and that Barnabas and Saul were thus honored and beloved there; they should give fuller information respecting the decrees, and answer every inquiry that might be proposed, as living epistles, confirmed by the letter and confirming it in return; and thus by their word they should restore again the harmony which those unsent members of their church had disturbed."

28. For it seemed good—*i. e.* and especially how it seemed good. **For** specifies the part of the letter which the writers had more par-

ticularly in view in **the same things** (v. 27). —**To the Holy Spirit and to us = to the Holy Spirit in us** (Olsh.). (See 5 : 3 and note there.) The expression represents the two agencies as distinct from each other, as well as consentaneous (De Wet.).—**Us** includes all (see v. 23) who took part in the action of the Council. They were conscious of having adopted their conclusions under the guidance of the Spirit, and claimed for them the authority of infallible decisions.—**The** (τῶν) renders **necessary** (ἐπάναγκες) an adjective. (B. ‖ 125. 6.) The things in question are said to be *necessary*—not (excepting the last of them) because they were wrong in themselves, but because the Gentile Christians were bound by the law of charity (see Rom. 14 : 15) to avoid a course which, while it involved no question of conscience on their part, would offend and grieve their Jewish brethren and lead inevitably to strife and alienation.

29. To wit, **that ye abstain.** For this definitive use of the infinitives, see W. ‖ 44. 1; C. ‖ 623.—It is not, perhaps, accidental that **fornication** has here a different position from that in v. 20. (See also 21 : 25.)—**From which if ye keep yourselves** Neander compares with **to keep himself unspotted from the world,** in James 1 : 27. The similarity is striking, and may indicate the same hand in the two passages. (See on v. 23.)— *Ye will do well,* what is right and commendable. (See 10 : 33; 3 John 6.)—**Fare ye well,** like the Latin *valete.*

30–35. PAUL AND BARNABAS RETURN TO ANTIOCH.

30. Therefore, since the foregoing decision was preliminary to their departure.—**Having been dismissed**—*i. e.* in all probability with religious services (v. 33; 13 : 3), and perhaps with an escort for some miles on the way (v. 3).—**The multitude.** (See v. 12 and 6 : 2.) They call at once an assembly of the believers to hear their report.

31 *Which* when they had read, they rejoiced for the consolation.
32 And Judas and Silas, being prophets also themselves, ^aexhorted the brethren with many words, and confirmed *them*.
33 And after they had tarried *there* a space, they were let ^bgo in peace from the brethren unto the apostles.
34 Notwithstanding it pleased Silas to abide there still.
35 ^cPaul also and Barnabas continued in Antioch, teaching and preaching the word of the Lord, with many others also.
36 ¶ And some days after Paul said unto Barnabas, Let us go again and visit our brethren ^din every city where we have preached the word of the Lord, *and see* how they do.
37 And Barnabas determined to take with them ^eJohn, whose surname was Mark.

31 gether, they delivered the epistle. And when they
32 had read it, they rejoiced for the ¹consolation. And Judas and Silas, being themselves also prophets, ²exhorted the brethren with many words, and confirmed
33 them. And after they had spent some time *there*, they were dismissed in peace from the brethren
35 unto those that had sent them forth.³ But Paul and Barnabas tarried in Antioch, teaching and preaching the word of the Lord, with many others
36 also. And after some days Paul said to Barnabas, Let us return now and visit the brethren in every city wherein we proclaimed the word of the Lord, *and*
37 *see* how they fare. And Barnabas was minded to take with them John also, who was called Mark.

a ch. 14 : 22 ; 18 : 23....*b* 1 Cor. 16 : 11 ; Heb. 11 : 31....*c* ch. 13 : 1....*d* ch. 13 : 4, 13, 14, 51; 14 : 1, 6, 24, 25....*e* ch. 12 : 12, 25 ; 13 : 5 ; Col. 4 : 10 ; 2 Tim. 4 : 11 ; Philem. 24.——1 Or, *exhortation*....2 Or, *comforted*....3 Some ancient authorities insert, with variations. ver. 34 *But it seemed good unto Silas to abide there.*

31. At the consolation (lit. **upon,** as the cause), furnished by the letter. They approve of what had been done; they rejoice at the prospect of so happy a termination of the dispute. Some understand παρακλήσει of **exhortation,** which certainly is not required by that sense of the verb in the next verse (Mey.), and does not accord well with the contents of so authoritative a letter.

32. Also themselves being prophets— *i. e.* as well as Paul and Barnabas, and so competent to give the instruction needed. — **Exhorted**—viz. in view of the present danger—that they should rely on Christ for salvation, and not cleave to the law of works. — **Confirmed** shows the happy effect of their labors.

33. With peace, the parting salutation (16 : 36; Mark 5 : 34; Luke 7 : 50). The brethren took leave of them with the best wishes for their safety and welfare. Judas and Silas both returned to Jerusalem, as their commission would require, but Silas must have soon rejoined Paul at Antioch, since we find him there in v. 40. Luke has passed over that second journey.

34. Griesbach, Lachmann, Tischendorf, and others strike out this verse. Most of the manuscripts omit it or read it variously. It is a gloss, probably, supposed to be required by v. 40. If the text be genuine, and Silas remained at Antioch, we must understand the plural in v. 33 as including one or more persons along with Judas, who had also come down from Jerusalem, though the narrative is otherwise silent concerning them.

35. Continued. This was the interval between the return to Antioch (v. 30) and the departure on the next missionary-tour (v. 40). Some propose to insert here the scene described in Gal. 2 : 11, *sq.*; but that such a reaction in favor of Judaism as appeared on that occasion should have taken place so soon after the decision at Jerusalem is altogether improbable. [On that supposition, Peter must have come to Antioch almost directly from the Council, and must at once have declared himself—by his action, at least—against the decision which he had so strenuously supported at Jerusalem. Moreover, the statement in v. 31 certainly implies that the Judaistic question was set at rest for the present. It is also clear, from 16 : 4, 5, that the churches generally were at rest after the adoption of the decrees ; and surely Antioch should not be supposed to be an exception.— A. H.]   (See note on 18 : 23.) — **And** adds **preaching**, etc., to the other participle as epexegetical : what they taught was the glad tidings or the gospel, not instructed believers and preached to those who had not believed (Alf.). (See 4 : 18 ; 5 : 42; 11 : 26 ; 28 : 31.)

36-41. PAUL AND BARNABAS RESUME THEIR WORK IN DIFFERENT FIELDS OF LABOR.

36. Now after certain days denotes, apparently, a short period. (Comp. 9 : 19 ; 16 : 12.)—δή strengthens the exhortation. (See 13 : 2.)—**Let us visit,** etc., may involve an attraction—viz. that of the subject of the last clause drawn into the first: **let us go to see . . . how the brethren are** (W. ¿ 66. 5) ; or an ellipsis: **let us visit the brethren,** and see (as in the E. V.) **how they are.—In which = where** is plural, because **every city** is collective. (W. ¿ 21. 3 ; K. ¿ 332. 5.)—**How they are,** in the mind of Paul, would have respect mainly to their spiritual welfare.

37. Determined. (See vv. 5, 33 ; 27 : 39.) The feelings of Barnabas may have influenced him in this decision more than his judgment,

38 But Paul thought not good to take him with them, *who departed from them from Pamphylia, and went not with them to the work.
39 And the contention was so sharp between them, that they departed asunder one from the other: and so Barnabas took Mark, and sailed unto Cyprus;
40 And Paul chose Silas, and departed, *being recommended by the brethren unto the grace of God.
41 And he went through Syria and Cilicia, *confirming the churches.

38 But Paul thought not good to take with them him who withdrew from them from Pamphylia, and 39 went not with them to the work. And there arose a sharp contention, so that they parted asunder one from the other, and Barnabas took Mark with him, 40 and sailed away unto Cyprus; but Paul chose Silas, and went forth, being commended by the brethren 41 to the grace of the Lord. And he went through Syria and Cilicia, confirming the churches.

*ch. 13 : 13....*b* ch. 14 : 26....*c* ch. 16 : 5.

since he and Mark were cousins (ἀνεψιοί. See Col. 4 : 10), **Wished** is an ancient reading, but on the whole less approved, in part because it softens down the altercation, and may have been added for that reason. [Yet the evidence of early MSS. (א A B C E against H L P) and versions preponderates so greatly in favor of the milder term, **wished**, that Griesb., Lach., Tsch., Treg., West. and Hort, Anglo-Am. Revisers, accept this as the word written by Luke. The narrative is clear and consistent with either word.—A. H.]
38. Deemed it just, fitting. Paul viewed the question on its ethical side, and not as a personal matter.—**Who departed from them** (13 : 13), in dereliction of his duty. (Comp. Luke 8 : 13.) — **This one** (emphatic here), who proved so fickle.—It is pleasing to know that Mark did not forfeit the apostle's esteem so as to be unable to regain it. He became subsequently Paul's companion in travel (Col. 4 : 10), and in 2 Tim. 4 : 11 elicits from him the commendation that he was "profitable to him for the ministry."
39. A severe contention arose. Barnabas insisted on his purpose; Paul, on his view of the merits of the case; and, as neither would yield, they parted. Some writers lay all the blame on Barnabas (Bmg.), in spite of the impartiality of the text. There was heat, evidently, on both sides.—**So that they departed from one another.** This separation refers, not to the rupture of their friendship, but to their proceeding in different directions, instead of laboring together as heretofore. The infinitive after **so that** (ὥστε) is said to represent the act as a necessary or logical sequence of what precedes; the indicative, as an absolute or unconditioned fact. (See Klotz, *Ad Devar.*, ii. p. 772.) It deserves to be remarked that this variance did not estrange these brethren from their work or occasion any permanent diminution of their regard for each other. In 1 Cor. 9 : 6, which was written after this occurrence, Paul alludes to Barnabas as a Christian teacher who possessed and deserved the fullest confidence of the churches. The passage

contains fairly that implication. Even the error of Barnabas in yielding to the Jewish party (Gal. 2 : 13) leads Paul to speak of him as one of the very last men (**and Barnabas**— *i. e.* **even he**) whom any one would suppose capable of swerving from the line of duty. And who can doubt that Barnabas reciprocated these sentiments toward the early, long-tried friend with whom he had acted in so many eventful scenes, and whom he saw still animated by the same affection toward himself, and the same devotion to the cause of their common Master? Luke does not mention the name of Barnabas again in the Acts. It is impossible to trace him farther with any certainty. One tradition is that he went to Milan, and died as first bishop of the church there; another is that after living some years at Rome and Athens he suffered martyrdom in his native Cyprus. The letter, still extant, which was known as that of Barnabas even in the second century, cannot be defended as genuine. (See Neander's *Church History*, vol. i. p. 657.) That such a letter, however, was ascribed to him at that early period shows how eminent a place he occupied among the Christians of his own and the succeeding age.
40. Having chosen for himself (comp. v. 22), not **thereupon**—viz. this disagreement. —**Having been committed unto the grace of God by the brethren.** Perhaps we may infer from this remark that the believers at Antioch took Paul's view of the point at issue between him and Barnabas.—**Went forth** is used of going forth as a missionary in Luke 9 : 6 and in 3 John 7.—The departure on this second tour we may place in A. D. 51; for if Paul went to Jerusalem in the year 50 (see on 15 : 4), the remainder of that year, added (if any one chooses) to the early part of the ensuing year, would suffice, probably, for the sojourn at Antioch indicated by **certain days** in v. 36. It is impossible to be more definite than this.
41. Syria and **Cilicia** lay between Antioch and the eastern limit of the apostle's first journey. We have had no account of the planting of any churches there, but they date, undoubt-

CHAPTER XVI.

THEN came he to ªDerbé and Lystra: and, behold, a certain disciple was there, ᵇnamed Timotheus, ᶜthe son of a certain woman, which was a Jewess, and believed; but his father *was* a Greek:

2 Which ᵈwas well reported of by the brethren that were at Lystra and Iconium.

3 Him would Paul have to go forth with him; and ᵉtook and circumcised him because of the Jews which were in those quarters: for they knew all that his father was a Greek.

1 AND he came also to Derbe and to Lystra: and behold, a certain disciple was there, named Timothy, the son of a Jewess who believed; but his 2 father was a Greek. The same was well reported of by the brethren that were at Lystra and Iconi- 3 um. Him would Paul have to go forth with him; and he took and circumcised him because of the Jews that were in those parts: for they all knew

---

a ch. 14 : 6....*b* ch. 19 : 22; Rom. 16 : 21; 1 Cor. 4 : 17; Phil. 2 : 19; 1 Thess. 3 : 2; 1 Tim. 1 : 2; 2 Tim. 1 : 2....*c* 2 Tim. 1 : 5.... *d* ch. 6 : 3....*e* 1 Cor. 9 : 20; Gal. 2 : 3; see Gal. 5 : 2.

---

edly, from the period of Paul's residence in that region, mentioned in Gal. 1 : 21. (See 9 : 30 and note there.) — **Confirming the churches,** not candidates for admission to them. (See 14 : 22.) One of these churches may have been at Tarsus, which Paul would naturally revisit at this time.

1–5. PAUL AND SILAS REVISIT THE CHURCHES AND DELIVER THE DECREES.

1. Derbe and Lystra are mentioned in this order (the reverse of that in 14 : 6), because the missionaries travel now from east to west.—Luke's exclamation, **and behold,** shows how much this meeting with Timothy interested his feelings.—**There**—viz. at Lystra. Some refer the adverb to Derbe; but that view, so far from being required by **of Derbe** (Δερβαῖος), in 20 : 4, is forbidden by the text there. Lystra stands nearest to **there,** and is named again in the next verse, where Luke surely would not pass over the testimony of those who had been acquainted with Timothy from early life. Wieseler combines the two opinions by supposing that Timothy may have been a native of Lystra, but was now living at Derbe.—For the family and the early education of Timothy, see 2 Tim. 1 : 5; 3 : 15. Paul terms him *my son* [lit. child] in 1 Cor. 4 : 17, probably because he had been the instrument of his conversion. (Comp. 1 Cor. 4 : 15; Gal. 4 : 19. See the note on 14 : 20.)—**Certain** is to be erased before **woman.—Believing.** (See on 10 : 45.) The mother's name was Eunice. It was an instance of the mixed marriages of which Paul writes in 1 Cor. 7 : 17, *sq.*—**A Greek,** and still a heathen, or at all events not a proselyte in full, as otherwise the son would have been circumcised.

2. Was attested, well reported of. (See 6 : 3; 10 : 22.) Supposing Timothy to have been converted during Paul's first visit to Lystra (see on 14 : 20), he had now been a dis-

ciple three or four years. During this time he had exerted himself, no doubt, for the cause of Christ both in Lystra and Iconium, and had thus given proof of the piety and talents which rendered him so useful as a herald of the cross.

3. To go forth with him, as a preacher of the word. (See 2 Tim. 4 : 5.)—**Having taken, he circumcised him,** either by his own hand (Mey., De Wet.) or procuring it to be done (Neand.). The Jews had no particular class of persons who performed this act. The Jewish custom, it is said, required merely that the administrator should not be a heathen. (See Win., *Realw.*, i. p. 157.)—**On account of the Jews,** etc. It would have repelled the Jews from his ministry to have seen him associated with a man whom they knew to be uncircumcised. Paul took this course, therefore, in order to remove that obstacle to his usefulness. The history presents Paul here as acting on the principle stated in 1 Cor. 9 : 20 : *Unto the Jews I became as a Jew, that I might gain Jews,* etc. It was under circumstances totally different that he refused to circumcise Titus, as related in Gal. 2 : 3, *sq.* He was then in the midst of those who would have regarded the act as ratifying their doctrine that circumcision was necessary to salvation. (See on 15 : 1.) In the present instance he knew (that admission is due to his character for intelligence as well as consistency) that his conduct would not be misunderstood or perverted; that the believers would view it as an accommodation merely to the prejudices of the Jews; and that the Jews themselves were in no danger of supposing him to countenance the idea that their keeping the law would entitle them to the favor of God.— Other passages extend our knowledge of this transaction. Timothy was not only circumcised, but set apart to the ministry "with the laying on of the hands of the presbytery" and of the apostle, was endued with special gifts for the office (1 Tim. 4 : 14; 2 Tim. 1 : 6), and received at the time prophetic assurances of the success which awaited him in his new career (1 Tim. 1 : 18).

4 And as they went through the cities, they delivered them the decrees for to keep, *a*that were ordained of the apostles and elders which were at Jerusalem.

5 And *b*so were the churches established in the faith, and increased in number daily.

6 Now when they had gone throughout Phrygia and the region of Galatia, and were forbidden of the Holy Ghost to preach the word in Asia,

4 that his father was a Greek. And as they went on their way through the cities, they delivered them the decrees for to keep, which had been ordained of the apostles and elders that were at Jerusalem.

5 So the churches were strengthened in the faith, and increased in number daily.

6 And they went through the region of Phrygia and Galatia, having been forbidden of the Holy

a ch. 15 : 28, 29.... *b* ch. 15 : 41.

—**For all knew his father that,** etc. The structure of the sentence is like that in 3 : 10. [That is, if the *textus receptus* is followed, but not if the text required by ℵ A B C and other documents, and approved by Griesb., Lach., Treg., West. and Hort, is correct. For with this text the construction is as follows : **for all knew that his father was a Greek,** the word Greek being emphatic by reason of its place in the clause.—It should be noticed that Paul circumcised Timothy, not on account of the Jewish believers, who might thus be led to think circumcision important, but on account of Jewish unbelievers whom he hoped to attract to his ministry.—A. H.]

4. As they journeyed through the cities, on the route pursued by them. They would visit, naturally, all the churches in Syria and Cilicia (15 : 41), and most of those on the main land, gathered during the apostle's former tour. As Antioch and Perga were so remote from their general course, it is possible that they transmitted copies of the decrees to those places. It is not certain that the word had taken root in Perga. (See on 14 : 25.)—**Delivered** (orally or in writing) **to them the decrees to keep.** The infinitive may be telic : that they should keep them ; or may involve a relative clause : which they should keep. (Comp. **which they received to hold,** in Mark 7 : 4. See W. ₰ 44. 1.) **Them** refers to the believers in these cities, not to the heathen converts merely (Mey.), since the decrees affected also the Jews.

5. Therefore—*i. e.* as the result of this visit, and of the adjustment of the controversy which had divided and enfeebled the churches. —**In the number,** of their members.

6-10. THEY PROSECUTE THEIR JOURNEY TO TROAS.

6. Phrygia. (See on 2 : 10.) To reach *Phrygia* from Iconium or Antioch, they would direct their way to the north-east.—**Region of Galatia. Galatia** was bounded on the north by Paphlagonia and Bithynia ; on the east, by Pontus and Cappadocia (separated from them by the river Halys) ; on the south, by Cappadocia and Phrygia ; and on the west, by Phrygia and Bithynia. Among the principal cities

were Ancyra, made the metropolis by Augustus, and Pessinus. Kiepert draws the line of Paul's course on his map so as to include these places, on the natural supposition that he would aim to secure first the prominent towns. (See on 18 : 1.) It is evident from the Epistle to the Galatians (see, *e. g.*, 4 : 19) that it was the apostle Paul who first preached the gospel in this country ; and, since he found disciples here on his third missionary-tour (see 18 : 23), it must have been at this time that he laid the foundation of the Galatian churches (Gal. 1 : 2). Such is the opinion of the leading critics. (See note on 14 : 6.)—**Being restrained by the Holy Spirit,** etc. The act of this participle, it will be observed, was subsequent to that of **had gone through** and prior to that of **were come** (v. 7). The course of the movement may be sketched thus : The travellers, having passed through the eastern section of Phrygia into Galatia, proposed next to preach the word in Proconsular Asia. (See on 2 : 9.) With that view, they turned their steps to the south-west, and, crossing the north part of Phrygia, came down to the frontier of Mysia, the first province in Asia which they would reach in that direction. Being informed here that they were not to execute this design, they turned again toward the north and attempted to go into Bithynia, which was adjacent to Mysia. Restrained from that purpose, they passed by Mysia—*i. e.* did not remain there to preach—and proceeded to Troas.—This portion of the apostle's travels, though they embrace so wide a circuit, admits of very little geographical illustration. Phrygia and Galatia are parts of Asia Minor of which the ancient writers have left but few notices, and which remain comparatively unknown to the present day. We must infer from 18 : 23 that Paul gained disciples in Phrygia at this time, but in what places is uncertain. Colosse was a Phrygian city, and may have received the gospel on this journey, unless it be forbidden by Col. 2 : 1. The opinion of the best critics is that the apostle includes the Colossians in that passage among those who had not "seen his face in the flesh."—**The Spirit of Jesus**—*i. e.* which he sends. There is no parallel passage, unless it be Rom. 8 : 9. **Jesus**

7 After they were come to Mysia, they assayed to go into Bithynia: but the Spirit suffered them not.
8 And they passing by Mysia *came down to Troas.
9 And a vision appeared to Paul in the night; There stood a *man of Macedonia, and prayed him, saying, Come over into Macedonia, and help us.
10 And after he had seen the vision, immediately we endeavored to go *into Macedonia, assuredly gathering that the Lord had called us for to preach the gospel unto them.
11 Therefore loosing from Troas, we came with a

7 Spirit to speak the word in Asia; and when they were come over against Mysia, they assayed to go into Bithynia; and the Spirit of Jesus suffered
8 them not; and passing by Mysia, they came down
9 to Troas. And a vision appeared to Paul in the night; There was a man of Macedonia standing, beseeching him, and saying, Come over into Mace-
10 donia, and help us. And when he had seen the vision, straightway we sought to go forth into Macedonia, concluding that God had called us for to preach the gospel unto them.
11 Setting sail therefore from Troas, we made a

has been lost from some copies, but belongs to the text. The Spirit, says Reuss, appears here in a sphere of activity made more prominent in the Acts than in all the other writings of the New Testament: "Thus, it is the Spirit who conducts Philip in the road to Gaza (8 : 29); who instructs Peter to receive the messengers of Cornelius (10 : 19 ; 11 : 12); who causes Barnabas and Paul to be sent to the heathen (13 : 2-4); who directs the missionaries in the choice of their route (16 : 6, 7); who urges Paul to Jerusalem (20 : 22); who chooses the pastors of the churches (20 : 28), etc." [1]

8. Having passed by Mysia, having left it aside without remaining to preach there. (Comp. **to sail by,** in 20 : 16, and **to pass by,** in Mark 6 : 48.) Wieseler (*Chronologie*, p. 36), Alford, Conybeare and Howson apparently, and others prefer this meaning here. Some render **having passed along Mysia**—*i. e.* the border of Mysia Minor, which belonged to Bithynia; whereas Mysia Major belonged to Proconsular Asia (De Wet.). The boundary was a political one, and no distinct frontier existed which the travellers could have had any motive for tracing so exactly.—**Came down,** from the inner highlands to the coast.—**Unto Troas,** the name of a district or a city; here the latter, called fully Alexandria Troas, on the Hellespont, about four miles from the site of the ancient Troy. It was the transit-harbor between the north-west of Asia Minor and Macedonia. Paul passed and repassed here on two other occasions (20 : 6 ; 2 Cor. 2 : 12). It is correct that Luke represents Troas here as distinct from Mysia. Under Nero, Troas and the vicinity formed a separate territory, having the rights of Roman freedom (De Wet., Böttg.).

9. A vision. Whether Paul saw this **vision** in a dream or in a state of ecstasy (see 10 : 10 ; 22 : 17) the language does not decide. **In the night** suggests one of the conditions of the first mode, but would not be inconsistent with the other.—**A man** revealed to him as a **Macedonian.** (Comp. 9 : 12.) — **Having**

crossed—*i. e.* the northern part of the Ægean. —**Help us,** because the one here represented many.

10. We sought—*i. e.* by immediate inquiry for a ship (Alf.). Paul had made known the vision to his associates. Here, for the first time, the historian speaks of himself as one of the party, and in all probability because he joined it at Troas. The introduction would be abrupt for the style of a modern work, it is true; but, on the other hand, to have had from Luke any formal account of the manner in which he became connected with the apostle would have been equally at variance with the simplicity and reserve which distinguish the sacred writers. Nor does it account at all more naturally for this sudden use of the plural to imagine (it is a figment purely) that Luke adopts here the narrative of another writer; for we may just as well suppose him to speak thus abruptly in his own name as to allow him to introduce another person as doing it without apprising us of the change. (See marginal note on p. 16.)

11-15. PAUL AND HIS ASSOCIATES ARRIVE IN EUROPE, AND PREACH AT PHILIPPI.

11. We ran by a straight course. In the nautical language of the ancients, as in that of the moderns, *to run* meant to sail before the wind. (See 27 : 16.) Luke observes almost a technical precision in the use of such terms. His account of the voyage to Rome shows a surprising familiarity with sea-life. — **Unto Samothrace,** which they reached the first day. This island, the present Samothraki, is about halfway between Troas and Neapolis, and is the highest land in this part of the Ægean, except Mount Athos. The ordinary currents here are adverse to sailing northward, but southerly winds, though they are brief, blow strongly at times, and overcome entirely that disadvantage. With such a wind, "the vessel in which Paul sailed would soon cleave her way through the strait between Tenedos

[1] *Histoire de la Theologie Chretienne*, tome second, p. 603 (Strasbourg, 1852).

straight course to Samothracia, and the next *day* to Neapolis;

12 And from thence to *a*Philippi, which is the chief city of that part of Macedonia, *and* a colony: and we were in that city abiding certain days.

straight course to Samothrace, and the day following to Neapolis; and from thence to Philippi, which is a city of Macedonia, the first of the district, a *Roman* colony: and we were in this city tarrying certain—

a Phil. 1 : 1.

and the main, past the Dardanelles, and near the eastern shore of Imbros. On rounding the northern end of this island they would open Samothrace, which had hitherto appeared as a higher and more distant summit over the lower mountains of Imbros. Leaving this island, and bearing now a little to the west, and having the wind still (as our sailors say) two or three points abaft the beam, they steered for Samothrace, and under the shelter of its high shore anchored for the night." (See the nautical proofs in Conybeare and Howson.)—**Unto Neapolis,** a Thracian city on the Strymonic gulf, the modern

Gangas, or Gangitas. It was at some distance east of the Strymon, and not on that river, as some have said. The adjacent plain is memorable in Roman history as the place where the battle was fought between the republicans, under Brutus, and the followers of Anthony and Augustus.—**Which is a chief city of the province of Macedonia,** being **a colony. First,** or **chief,** designates it as one of the first places there, and **colony** explains the ground of the epithet. Augustus had sent a colony thither (see *Dict. of Antt.,* s. *colonia*), which had conferred upon it new import-

NEAPOLIS.

Kavalla. It was north-west from Samothrace, but even with a southerly wind could be reached in seven or eight hours. As the same verb describes the remainder of the journey, it might seem as if they merely touched here, but did not land, proceeding along the coast to some harbor nearer to Philippi than this. Some writers would place the port of that city farther west than the present Kavalla. It is generally agreed, however, that Neapolis was the nearest town on the sea, and hence, though the distance was not less than ten miles, was identical with Philippi as to purposes of travel and trade. Kavalla is the nearest port at present, and the shore appears to have undergone no change, either from recession or advance.[1]

12. Philippi was on a steep acclivity of the Thracian Hermus, where this range slopes toward the sea, on the small stream called

ance. Some understand **first** geographically: *first* as they entered Macedonia, which Winer calls the simplest explanation. That Neapolis lay farther east does not clash with this view; for those who adopt it take Macedonia here in the Greek sense, which assigns Neapolis to Thrace. It is a stronger objection that Luke would then mean Greek Macedonia here, but elsewhere the Roman province so named—*i. e.* Northern Greece, in distinction from Achaia, or Southern Greece. (See on 18 : 5.) Further, **is** indicates a permanent distinction; whereas **was** would have been more natural to mark an incident of the journey (was **first** on their way). The proper capital of Macedonia (hence not **first** in that sense) was Thessalonica. If the earlier division into four parts still continued, Amphipolis was politically first in *pars prima.* "It may be added," says Akerman,

[1] My thanks are due to the Rev. Dr. Hill of Athens for inquiries in relation to this point.

13 And on the sabbath we went out of the city by a river side, where prayer was wont to be made ; and we sat down, and spake unto the women which resorted *thither.*

13 tain days. And on the sabbath day we went forth without the gate by a river side, where we supposed there was a place of prayer ; and we sat down, and spake unto the women who were come together.

"in confirmation of the words of Luke, that there are colonial coins of Philippi from the reign of Augustus to that of Caracalla." It is frequently said that this was the first place on the continent of Europe where the gospel was preached ; but we have no certain knowledge of the origin of the church of Rome, and, very possibly, it may have been founded by some of the converts on the day of Pentecost. The church at Philippi was the first church in Europe which the apostle Paul established.—**Certain days** denotes apparently the few days which they spent there before the arrival of the Sabbath.

13. Instead of the received **out of the city,** the later criticism would read **out of the gate.** This part of the narrative often shows the presence of the historian.—**Beside a river**—viz. the Gangas. The name was unimportant, but could hardly fail to be known to Luke, who was so familiar with Philippi. (See on v. 40.) [" I incline to think," writes Dr. Hackett in 1860, after visiting the site of Philippi, "that we have an intimation here that the critics are right who suppose that Luke stayed at Philippi until the apostle's second arrival here. Being an inquisitive man, as we know from the proem of his Gospel, no doubt he sought out the name of the river on his first arrival, when his curiosity was still fresh ; and, had he afterward remembered the place merely as a traveller, he would have been led quite naturally to insert the name when he wrote his history. But if, on the contrary, he was there so long that his ear became accustomed to the popular expression 'the river,' 'water,' 'stream'" (for, as the only river in the neighborhood, it would probably be thus referred to by the people.—A. H.), "it is, then, conceivable that when he came to write out his memoranda or recollections he would pass over the name, and speak unconsciously as the old habit dictated" (*Bib. Sac.,* xvii. p. 875).—A. H.] The river may possibly have been the more distant Strymon (Neand., Mey.), though, if **gate** be the correct word, the stream intended must be a nearer one. In summer the Gangas is almost dry, but in winter or after rains may be full and swollen. [In his last ed. Meyer recedes from his earlier view and adopts that of Dr. Hackett. In the month of December, 1858, soon after issuing the second edition of this COMMENTARY, Dr. Hackett had the pleasure of visiting the sites of Neapolis

and Philippi. (See *Bib. Sac.,* xvii. p. 866, etc.) He was anxious to see the Gangas full of water, and not merely the dry bed of a winter-torrent. Nor was he disappointed : "Suddenly, as we drew nearer, a roaring noise broke upon me. There was no visible cause for it ; it seemed almost as if some convulsion of nature was at hand. A few steps farther, and the mystery was cleared up : there, rushing and pouring over its rocky bed, was a wild winter-torrent, which had been formed by the recent rains. The proper bed of the stream measured, in width, sixty-six feet. One-half of this space was covered with water, varying from one and a half and two feet to four and five feet. The stones at the bottom were rounded and worn, and showed the action of a still more powerful current at times. Its course was winding as it ran past Philippi ; and it is evident that the direction of the walls had been adjusted to that of the stream. It skirts the east or south-east side, and then trends off to the south-west. . . . We crossed the stream, and at the distance of three hundred and fifty feet from its margin found a break in the line of the dilapidated walls which showed clearly where the gate had been on that side of the city. . . . Paul and his company must have entered the town here. It may be supposed to have been out of this gate that they passed when they went to preach on the river-side ; for the place on the banks, as remarked already, was near the gate, and, situated as Philippi was, no other gate would have brought them so directly to the river as this."—A. H.]—**Where** (according to an ancient usage in that city) **was wont to be a place of prayer** (Kuin., Neand., Mey., De Wet.). The Jews preferred to assemble near the water, on account of the lustrations which accompanied their worship. Neander illustrates this usage from what Tertullian says of them (*De Jejun.,* c. 16): "Per omne litus quocunque in aperto . . . precem ad cælum mittunt" ["On every shore, in whatever open place, they send prayers to heaven "]. (See also Jos., *Antt.,* 14. 10. 23.) The **place of prayer** (προσευχή) here appears to have been, not an edifice, but a space or enclosure in the open air consecrated to this use. The word was so well known as the designation of a Jewish chapel or oratory that it passed into the Latin language in that sense. The rendering **where prayer was wont to be made** (E. V.) does not agree easily with

14 ¶ And a certain woman named Lydia, a seller of purple, of the city of Thyatira, which worshipped God, heard *us:* whose *a*heart the Lord opened, that she attended unto the things which were spoken of Paul.

15 And when she was baptized, and her household, she besought *us,* saying, If ye have judged me to be

14 And a certain woman named Lydia, a seller of purple, of the city of Thyatira, one that worshipped God, heard us: whose heart the Lord opened, to give heed unto the things which were spoken by

15 Paul. And when she was baptized, and her household, she besought us, saying, If ye have judged me

a Luke 24 : 45.

---

was. Instead of the substantive verb, the predicate would be **was made** (γίνεσθαι, 12 : 5, or ποιεῖσθαι, 1 Tim. 2 : 1).—In **we . . . spake** Luke appears as one of the speakers.—**The women who came together,** for prayer. The absence of a synagogue shows that the Jews here were not numerous. Those who met for prayer were chiefly women, and even some of these were converts to Judaism.

14. **Lydia** was a very common name among the Greeks and the Romans. It is not surprising, therefore, that it coincided with the name of her country. Possibly she may have borne a different name at home, but was known among strangers as Lydia or the Lydian (Wetst.). She is said to have been **a seller of purple** (sc. cloths) **from Thyatira.** That city was on the confines of Lydia and Mysia, and the Lydians, as ancient writers testify, were *famous* for precisely such fabrics. They possessed that reputation even in Homer's time. (See *Il.,* 4. 141.) An inscription, "the dyers," has been found among the ruins of Thyatira. —**Was hearing** (ἤκουεν, relative imperf.) while he discoursed (14 : 9; 15 : 12), not when the act (**opened**) took place (Alf.).—**Whose heart the Lord opened**—*i. e.* in conformity with other passages (Matt. 11 : 25, *sq.*; Luke 24 : 45 ; 1 Cor. 3 : 6, 7), enlightened, impressed by his Spirit, and so prepared to receive the truth.—**So as to attend** (ecbatic), or, less obvious, *to attend* (telic).

15. When she was baptized. It is left indefinite whether she was baptized at once or after an interval of some days.—**And her house,** family. "Here," says De Wette, "as well as in v. 33 ; 18 : 8 ; 1 Cor. 1 : 16, some would find a proof for the apostolic baptism of children ; but there is nothing here which shows that any except adults were baptized." According to his view (in *Stud. und Krit.,* p. 669, 1830) of the meaning of 1 Cor. 7 : 14, it is impossible that baptism should have been applied to children in the primitive churches. In arguing from the case of children to that of married persons, one of whom is an unbeliever, in order to justify the continuance of the relation, "the apostle must appeal to something which lay out of the disputed case, but which had a certain similarity and admitted of an application to it. This something is nothing else than

the relation which the children of Christian parents in general sustain to the Christian Church, and the expression 'your children' refers to all the Corinthian Christians. The children of Christians were not yet received properly into a Christian community—*were not yet baptized*—and did not take part in the devotional exercises and love-feasts of the church ; accordingly, they might have been regarded as unclean (ἀκάθαρτα) with as much reason as the unbelieving converts could be so regarded. In this passage, therefore, we have a proof that children had not begun to be baptized in the time of the apostles." The **her household,** as Meyer remarks, consisted, probably, of women who assisted Lydia in her business. "When Jewish or heathen families," he says further, "became Christians. the children in them could have been baptized only in cases in which they were so far developed that they could profess their faith in Christ, and did actually profess it ; for this was the universal requisition for the reception of baptism. (See also vv. 31, 33 ; 18 : 8.) On the contrary, if the children were still unable to believe, they did not partake of the rite, since they were wanting in what the act presupposed. The baptism of children is not to be considered as an apostolic institution, but arose gradually in the post-apostolic age, after early and long-continued resistance, in connection with certain views of doctrine, and did not become general in the church til! after the time of Augustine. The defence of infant baptism transcends the domain of exegesis, and must be given up to that of dogmatics." Since a confession of faith preceded baptism, says Olshausen, "it is improbable in the highest degree that by 'her household' (οἶκος αὐτῆς) children of an immature age are to be understood : those baptized with her were relatives, servants, grown-up children. We have not, in fact, a single sure proof-text for the baptism of children in the apostolic age, and the necessity of it cannot be derived from the idea of baptism." He says on 1 Cor. 1 : 17 that "nothing can be inferred in favor of infant baptism from the word 'household' (οἶκος), because the adult members of the household (comp. 1 Cor. 16 : 15), or the servants in it, may alone be meant." Neander maintains the same

faithful to the Lord, come into my house, and abide *there*. And ⁿshe constrained us.

16 ¶ And it came to pass, as we went to prayer, a certain damsel ᵇpossessed with a spirit of divination met us, which brought her masters ᶜmuch gain by soothsaying:

to be faithful to the Lord, come into my house, and abide *there*. And she constrained us.

16 And it came to pass, as we were going to the place of prayer, that a certain maid having ¹a spirit of divination met us, who brought her masters much

---

a Gen. 19 : 3; 33 : 11 ; Judg. 19 : 21 ; Luke 24 : 29 ; Heb. 13 : 2....*b* 1 Sam. 28 : 7....*c* ch. 19 : 24.——1 Gr. *a spirit, a Python.*

---

view of this class of passages : " Since baptism marked the entrance into communion with Christ, it resulted, from the nature of the rite, that a confession of faith in Jesus as the Redeemer would be made by the person to be baptized. As baptism was closely united with a conscious entrance on Christian communion, faith and baptism were always connected with one another ; and thus it is in the highest degree probable that baptism was performed only in instances where both could meet together, and that the practice of infant baptism was unknown at this period. We cannot infer the existence of infant baptism from the instance of the baptism of whole families ; for the passage in 1 Cor. 16 : 15 shows the fallacy of such a conclusion, as from that it appears that the whole family of Stephanus, who were baptized by Paul, consisted of adults. . . . From whom (if it belonged to the first Christian age) could the institution of infant baptism have proceeded? Certainly it did not come directly from Christ himself. Was it from the primitive church in Palestine, from an injunction given by the earlier apostles? But among the Jewish Christians circumcision was held as a seal of the covenant ; and hence they had so much less occasion to make use of another dedication for their children. Could it, then, have been Paul that first introduced among heathen Christians this change in the use of baptism? But this would agree least of all with the peculiar Christian characteristics of this apostle. He who says of himself that Christ sent him, not to baptize, but to preach the gospel ; he who always kept his eye fixed on one thing, justification by faith, and so carefully avoided everything which could give a handle or a support to the notion of justification by outward things (**carnal**),--how could he have set up infant baptism against the circumcision that continued to be practised by the Jewish Christians? In this case the dispute carried on with the Judaizing party on the necessity of circumcision would easily have given an opportunity of introducing this substitute into the controversy, if it had really existed. The evidence arising from silence on this topic has, therefore, the greater weight."[1] It may

be proper to regard the decisions of such men as representing the testimony of the present biblical scholarship on this controverted subject. It is the more proper to accord to them this character, because they proceed from men whose ecclesiastical position would naturally dispose them to adopt a different view—who contend that infant baptism, having been introduced, is allowable, notwithstanding their acknowledgment that it has no scriptural warrant.—**If ye have judged**—*i. e.* by admitting her to baptism, and thus declaring their confidence in her. **If** (εἰ) is preferred to **since** (ἐπεί) out of modesty.—**Trusting to the Lord**—*i. e.* having faith in him ; a believer. (Comp. 10 : 45 ; 16 : 1.)—**Constrained us.** Not that *they* needed so much entreaty, but that *she* could not employ less, in justice to her grateful feelings. Some think that they were reluctant to accept the proffered hospitality, lest they should seem to be actuated by mercenary motives. The apostle was by no means indifferent to that imputation (20 : 34 ; 2 Cor. 12 : 17, 19), but it is incorrect to say that he never showed himself unmindful of it. He was the guest of Gaius at Corinth (Rom. 16 : 23), and was aided repeatedly by Christian friends when his circumstances made it necessary (24 : 23 ; 28 : 10 ; Phil. 4 : 15, *sq.*).

16–18. HEALING OF A DEMONIAC WOMAN.

16. Now it came to pass, on a subsequent day (Neand., De Wet.).—**Unto the place of prayer,** which may omit the article as definite, because it was the only such place there. But some editors (Grsb., Lchm.) insert *the*.—**A female slave** (Gal. 4 : 22) **having the spirit of a pythoness**—*i. e.* of a diviner who was supposed to have received her gift of prophecy from Apollo. Luke describes the woman according to her reputed character ; he does not express here his own opinion of the case. His view agreed, no doubt, with that of Paul ; and what that was we learn from the sequel. To suppose him to acknowledge Apollo as a real existence would contradict 1 Cor. 8 : 4.—**Procured.** Winer (§ 38. 5) says that the active is more appropriate here than the middle (comp. 19 : 24 ; Col. 4 : 1 ; Tit. 2 : 7), because the gain was involuntary on her part.—**Unto her masters.**

---

[1] Abridged from Ryland's translation (*Pflanzung, u. s. w.*, Band i. p. 278).

17 The same followed Paul and us, and cried, saying, These men are the servants of the most high God, which shew unto us the way of salvation.
18 And this did she many days. But Paul, *being grieved, turned and said to the spirit, I command thee in the name of Jesus Christ to come out of her. *And he came out the same hour.
19 ¶ And *when her masters saw that the hope of their gains was gone, *they caught Paul and Silas, and *drew *them into the marketplace unto the rulers,
20 And brought them to the magistrates, saying, These men, being Jews, *do exceedingly trouble our city,
21 And teach customs, which are not lawful for us to receive, neither to observe, being Romans.

17 gain by soothsaying. The same following after Paul and us cried out, saying, These men are ¹servants of the Most High God, who proclaim unto you 18 ²the way of salvation. And this she did for many days. But Paul, being sore troubled, turned and said to the spirit, I charge thee in the name of Jesus Christ to come out of her. And it came out that very hour.
19 But when her masters saw that the hope of their gain was ³gone, they laid hold on Paul and Silas, and dragged them into the marketplace before the 20 rulers, and when they had brought them unto the ⁴magistrates, they said, These men, being Jews, do 21 exceedingly trouble our city, and set forth customs which it is not lawful for us to receive, or to observe,

a See Mark 1 : 25, 34....*b* Mark 16 : 17....*c* ch. 19 : 25, 26....*d* 2 Cor. 6 : 5... *e* Matt. 10 : 18.... *f* 1 Kings 18 : 17 ; ch. 17 : 6.——
1 Gr. *bond-servants*....2 Or, *a way*....3 Gr. *come out*....4 Gr. *prætors*.

A slave among the ancients who possessed a lucrative talent was often the joint-property of two or more owners.—**By divining** (μαντευο-μένη) was the heathen term to denote the act. Luke would have said, more naturally, *by prophesying* (προφητεύουσα), had he been affirming his own belief in the reality of the pretension.—The woman was, in fact, a demoniac (see v. 18) ; and, as those subject to the power of evil spirits were often bereft of their reason, her divinations were probably the ravings of insanity. The superstitious have always been prone to attach a mysterious meaning to the utterances of the insane. We may take it for granted that the craft of the managers in this case was exerted to assist the delusion.

17. These men are servants, etc. Some have supposed that she merely repeated what she had heard them declare of themselves, or what she had heard reported of them by others. But the similarity of the entire account to that of the demoniacs mentioned in the Gospels requires us to refer this case to the same class of phenomena. (See Matt. 8 : 29; Mark 3 : 11; Luke 4 : 41 ; 8 : 28, etc.) According to those passages, we must recognize the acknowledgment here as a supernatural testimony to the mission of Paul and his associates, and to the truth of the gospel which they preached.

18. The participle here used (διαπονηθείς) Hesychius defines by **being grieved** (λυπηθείς). With that sense it would refer to Paul's commiseration of the woman's unhappy condition. Taken as in 4 : 2, **being indignant,** it would show how he felt to witness such an exhibition of the malice of a wicked spirit. (Comp. Luke 13 : 16.) The latter meaning directs the act of the participle to the same object as that of **turned and said.** It is better to preserve a unity in that respect.—**To the spirit,** who is addressed here as distinct from the woman herself. The apostle deals with the case as it actually was, and his knowledge as an inspired teacher would enable him to judge correctly of its character.

19–24. IMPRISONMENT OF PAUL AND SILAS.

19. That the hope of their gain went forth — *i. e.* with the exorcism (De Wet.).—**Having laid hold upon Paul and Silas.** Luke and Timothy may have been out of reach just at that moment (comp. 17 : 5), or may have been spared because they were Greeks.—**Into the marketplace.** In ancient cities the seats of the magistrates were erected commonly in the markets or near to them.—**Before the rulers,** called, in the next verse, **governors.** The chief magistrates in a Roman colony were the *duumviri* or *quatuorviri*, as the number was not always the same. They frequently took, however, the name of *prætors*, as one of greater honor, and that in Greek was **governors** (στρατηγοί). It appears, therefore, that the magistrates at Philippi affected this latter title. It is worthy of notice that this is the only occasion in the Acts on which Luke applies the term to the rulers of a city. Here, in a Roman colony, the government would be modelled naturally after the Roman form ; and the manner in which the narrative reveals that circumstance marks its authenticity.

20. Being Jews. They say this at the outset, in order to give more effect to the subsequent accusation. No people were regarded by the Romans with such contempt and hatred as the Jews. It is not probable that the Philippians at this time recognized any distinction between Judaism and Christianity; they arraigned Paul and Silas as Jews, or as the leaders of some particular Jewish sect.

21. Customs, religious practices.—**Which are not lawful,** etc. The Roman laws suffered foreigners to worship in their own way, but did not allow Roman citizens to forsake their religion for that of other nations. This was the general policy. But, beyond that, Judaism had been specially interdicted. "It was a *religio licita* for the Jews," says Neander, "but they were by no means allowed to propagate their

22 And the multitude rose up together against them: and the magistrates rent off their clothes, *and commanded to beat *them*.
23 And when they had laid many stripes upon them, they cast *them* into prison, charging the jailor to keep them safely:
24 Who, having received such a charge, thrust them into the inner prison, and made their feet fast in the stocks.

22 being Romans. And the multitude rose up together against them: and the ¹magistrates rent their garments off them, and commanded to beat them with
23 rods. And when they had laid many stripes upon them, they cast them into prison, charging the jailor
24 to keep them safely: who, having received such a charge, cast them into the inner prison, and made

a 2 Cor. 6 : 5 ; 11 : 23, 25 ; 1 Thess. 2 : 2.——¹ Gr. *prætors.*

religion among the *Roman* pagans; the laws expressly forbade the latter, under severe penalties, to receive circumcision. It was the case, indeed, at this time, that the number of proselytes from the pagans was greatly multiplied. This the public authorities sometimes allowed to pass unnoticed, but occasionally severe laws were passed anew to repress the evil" (*Ch. Hist.*, vol. i. p. 89). Still, the charge in this instance, though formally false, since they were not making proselytes to Judaism, was true substantially. It was impossible that the gospel should be preached without coming into collision with the Roman laws. The gospel was designed to subvert one system of false religion as well as another. It proposed to save the souls of men, without respect to the particular government or political institutions under which they lived. The apostles, in the promulgation of their message, acted under a higher authority than that of the Cæsars; and the opposition between Christianity and heathenism soon became apparent, and led to the persecutions which the Roman power inflicted on the church in the first centuries.

22. And the multitude rose up together against them. The prisoners were now in the hands of the officers; hence, we are not to think here of any actual onset upon them, but of a tumultuous outburst of rage, a cry on all sides for the punishment of the offenders. The magistrates hasten to obey the voice of the mob. —**Having torn off their garments,** not their own, but those of Paul and Silas. The rulers are said to do what they ordered to be done. (Comp. **circumcised,** in v. 3.) It was customary to inflict the blows on the naked body. Livy (2. 5): "Missique lictores ad sumendum supplicium, nudatos virgis cædunt" ["And the lictors, being sent to inflict punishment, beat the naked [youths] with rods"].—**Ordered to beat with rods.** The verb declares the mode as well as the act. Observe the official brevity of the expression. The imperfect describes the beating in its relation to **rose up against,** or as taking place under the eye of the narrator. For the latter usage, see W. § 40. 3. d.; Mt. § 505. II. 1. ¹n 2 Cor. 11 : 25, Paul

says that he was "thrice beaten with rods." This was one of the instances; the other two the history has not recorded. Such omissions prove that Luke's narrative and the Epistles of Paul have not been drawn from each other— that they are independent productions.

23. Many stripes shows that no ordinary rigor would satisfy their exasperated feelings. (See also v. 33.) The Jewish law restricted the blows to "forty save one." The severity of the punishment among the Romans depended on the equity or caprice of the judge. In regard to the silence of Paul and Silas under this outrage, see on v. 37.

24. Who having received such a command. We need not impute to the jailer any gratuitous inhumanity; he obeyed his instructions.—**Into the inner prison,** the remotest part, whence escape would be most difficult. Some confound this prison with the dungeon, which was under ground, and would be differently described. Walch's *Dissertatio de vinculis Apostoli Paulli* treats of this passage.—**And secured their feet into the block** (= *nervus*). This was an instrument for torture as well as

IN THE STOCKS.

confinement. It was a heavy piece of wood with holes into which the feet were put, so far apart as to distend the limbs in the most painful manner. Yet in this situation, with their bodies still bleeding from the effect of their recent chastisement, and looking forward to the morrow only in the expectation that it would renew their pains, they could still rejoice; their prison at midnight resounds with the voice of

25 ¶ And at midnight Paul and Silas prayed, and sang praises unto God: and the prisoners heard them.

26 ªAnd suddenly there was a great earthquake, so that the foundations of the prison were shaken: and immediately ᵇall the doors were opened, and every one's bands were loosed.

27 And the keeper of the prison awakening out of his sleep, and seeing the prison doors open, he drew out his sword, and would have killed himself, supposing that the prisoners had been fled.

28 But Paul cried with a loud voice, saying, Do thyself no harm: for we are all here.

29 Then he called for a light, and sprang in, and came trembling, and fell down before Paul and Silas,

30 And brought them out, and said, ᶜSirs, what must I do to be saved?

25 their feet fast in the stocks. But about midnight Paul and Silas were praying and singing hymns unto God, and the prisoners were listening to them;

26 and suddenly there was a great earthquake, so that the foundations of the prison-house were shaken: and immediately all the doors were opened; and

27 every one's bands were loosed. And the jailor being roused out of sleep, and seeing the prison doors open, drew his sword, and was about to kill himself,

28 supposing that the prisoners had escaped. But Paul cried with a loud voice, saying, Do thyself no harm:

29 for we are all here. And he called for lights, and sprang in, and, trembling for fear, fell down before

30 Paul and Silas, and brought them out, and said, Sirs,

---

a ch. 4 : 31....*b* ch. 5 : 19 ; 12 : 7, 10....*c* Luke 3 : 10 ; ch. 2 : 37 ; 9 : 6.

---

prayer and praise. Neander cites here Tertullian's fine remark: " Nihil crus sentit in nervo, quum animus in cælo est " ["Nothing the limb feels in the stocks when the mind is in heaven"].

25–29. AN EARTHQUAKE SHAKES THE PRISON.

25. Praying, they praised God. Their prayers and praises were not distinct acts (hence the form of the expression),but their worship consisted chiefly of thanksgiving, the language of which they would derive more or less from the Psalms. The Hebrews were so familiar with the Old Testament, especially its devotional parts, that they clothed their religious thoughts spontaneously in terms borrowed from that source. See, *e. g.*, the songs of Mary and Elizabeth (Luke 1 : 39, *sq.*), and of Zacharias (Luke 1 : 67, *sq.*) and Simeon (Luke 2 : 28, *sq.*).—**Heard, listened to them** while they sung. The imperfect describes the act; the aorist would have related it merely.

26. All the doors. Some ascribe this opening of the doors to the shock of the earthquake; others, more reasonably, to the power which caused the earthquake.—**And the chains of all**—*i. e.* the prisoners (see v. 28)—**were loosened.** (ἀνέθη, *were loosened*, is first aorist passive from ἀνίημι. B. § 108 ; S. § 81. I.) That the other prisoners were released in this manner was, no doubt, miraculous ; it was adapted to augment the impression of the occurrence, and to attest more signally the truth of the gospel. That they made no effort to escape may have been owing to the terror of the scene, or to a restraining influence which the author of the interposition exerted upon them.

27. Was about to kill himself. The jailer adopted this resolution because he knew that his life was forfeited if the prisoners had escaped. (Comp. 12 : 19 ; 27 : 42.)—**Supposing the prisoners to have fled,** and to be gone ; infin. perfect, because the act, though past, was connected with the present. (W. § 44. 7.)

28. With a voice loud. (See note on 14 : 10.)—**Do thyself no injury.** For the mode and tense, see on 7 : 60. How, it has been asked, could Paul have known the jailer's intention? The narrative leaves us in doubt on that point, but suggests various possibilities. It is not certain that the prison was entirely dark (see on v. 29), and the jailer may have stood at that moment where Paul could distinguish his form, or, as Doddridge suggests, he may have heard some exclamation from him which disclosed his purpose. The fact was revealed to the apostle, if he could not ascertain it by natural means.—**We are all here.** We do not know the structure of the prison. The part of it where the apostle was, and the position in which he sat, may have enabled him to see that no one of the prisoners had passed through the open doors, or he may have been divinely instructed to give this assurance.

29. Having called for lights, which could be carried in the hand. The noun is neuter and in the plural, not singular (E. V.). The ordinary night-lamps, if such had been kept burning, were fastened, perhaps, or furnished only a faint glimmer. **Lights** may be a generic plural, but refers, more probably, to the jailer's summoning those in his service to procure lights, to enable him to ascertain the condition of the prison. The sequel shows that the whole family were aroused.—**Fell down,** cast himself at their feet in token of reverence. (See Mark 3 : 11 ; Luke 8 : 28.) He knew that the miracle was on their account.

30–34. CONVERSION OF THE JAILER AND HIS FAMILY.

30. Having led them forth out—*i. e.* of the inner prison into another room, not into his own house. (See v. 34.)—**What must I do in order that I may be saved?** Their answer, in the next verse, shows with what meaning the jailer proposed ᵔhis question. It cannot refer to any fear of punishment from

31 And they said, aBelieve on the Lord Jesus Christ, and thou shalt be saved, and thy house.
32 And they spake unto him the word of the Lord, and to all that were in his house.
33 And he took them the same hour of the night, and washed *their* stripes; and was baptized, he and all his, straightway.

31 what must I do to be saved? And they said, Believe on the Lord Jesus, and thou shalt be saved, thou 32 and thy house. And they spake the word of [1]the Lord unto him, with all that were in his house.
33 And he took them the same hour of the night, and washed their stripes; and was baptized, he and all

a John 3 : 16, 36 ; 6 : 47 ; 1 John 5 : 10.——1 Some ancient authorities read *God.*

the magistrates; for he had now ascertained that the prisoners were all safe, and that he was in no danger from that source. Besides, had he felt exposed to any such danger, he must have known that Paul and Silas had no power to protect him; it would have been useless to come to them for assistance. The question in the other sense appears abrupt, it is true, but we are to remember that Luke has recorded only parts of the transaction. The unwritten history would perhaps justify some such view of the circumstances as this. The jailer is suddenly aroused from sleep by the noise of the earthquake; he sees the doors of the prison open; the thought instantly seizes him, "The prisoners have fled!" He knows the rigor of the Roman law, and is on the point of anticipating his doom by self-murder. But the friendly voice of Paul recalls his presence of mind. His thoughts take at once a new direction. He is aware that these men claim to be the servants of God—that they profess to teach the way of salvation. It would be nothing strange if, during the several days or weeks that Paul and Silas had been at Philippi, he had heard the gospel from their own lips, had been one among those at the river-side or in the market whom they had warned of their danger, and urged to repent and lay hold of the mercy offered to them in the name of Christ. And now suddenly an event had taken place which convinces him in a moment that the things which he has heard are realities; it was the last argument, perhaps, which he needed to give certainty to a mind already inquiring, hesitating. He comes trembling, therefore, before Paul and Silas, and asks them to tell him—again, more fully—what he must do to be saved.

31. And thou shalt be saved and thy family. They represent the salvation as ample; it was free not only to him, but to all the members of his household who accept the proffered mercy. The apostle includes them, because, as we see from the next verse, they were present and listened with the jailer to the preaching of the gospel. As Meyer remarks,

thy house belongs in effect to **believe** and **be saved,** as well as **thou.**

32. And they spake to him the word of the Lord, and to all who were in his house. This refers to the more particular instruction respecting the way of salvation, which they proceeded to give after the general direction in the preceding verse.—**Those in his family** (τοῖς ἐν τῇ οἰκίᾳ αὐτοῦ) cannot embrace infants, because they are incapable of receiving the instruction which was addressed to those whom the expression designates here.

33. Taking them along, say Conybeare and Howson correctly, implies a change of place. The jailer repaired with Paul and Silas from the outer room (see **out** (ἔξω), in v. 30) to the water, which he needed for bathing their bodies.—**Washed from their stripes** stands concisely for **washed** and cleansed them **from their stripes.** (W. § 47, 5. b.) This verb, says Dr. Robinson (*Lex. N. T.,* s. v.), signifies to wash the entire body, not merely a part of it, like *nipto* (νίπτω). Trench says: "*νίπτειν* (*niptein*) and νίψασθαι (*nipsasthai*) almost always express the washing *of a part* of the body (the hands, in Mark 7 : 3; the feet, in John 13 : 5; the face, in Matt. 6 : 17; the eyes, in John 9 : 7); while λούειν (*louein*), which is not so much 'to wash' as 'to bathe,' and λούσθαι (*lousthai*), or, in common Greek, λούεσθαι (*louesthai*), 'to bathe one's self,' imply always, not the bathing of a part of the body, but *of the whole.* (Comp. Heb. 10 : 23; Acts 9 : 37; 2 Pet. 2 : 22; Rev. 1 : 5; Plato, *Phæd.,* 115 *a.*"[1] To the same effect, see Tittm., *Synn. N. T.,* p. 175.[1])—**Was baptized.** The rite may have been performed, says De Wette, in the same fountain or tank in which the jailer had washed them. "Perhaps the water," says Meyer, "was in the court of the house; and the baptism was that of immersion, which formed an essential part of the symbolism of the act. (See Rom. 6 : 3, *sq.*)" Ancient houses, as usually built, enclosed a rectangular reservoir or basin (the *impluvium* so called) for receiving the rain which flowed from the slightly-inclined roof. Some suggest that they may have used a κολυμβήθρα (*columbethra*) or *swimming-bath,* found

[1] *Synonyms of the New Testament* (p. 216), by Richard Chenevix Trench, King's College, London (New York, 1857).

34 And when he had brought them into his house, ^ahe set meat before them, and rejoiced, believing in God with all his house.
35 And when it was day, the magistrates sent the serjeants, saying, Let those men go.
36 And the keeper of the prison told this saying to Paul, The magistrates have sent to let you go: now therefore depart, and go in peace.
37 But Paul said unto them, They have beaten us openly uncondemned, ^bbeing Romans, and have cast

34 his, immediately. And he brought them up into his house, and set ¹meat before them, and rejoiced greatly, with all his house, ²having believed in God.
35 But when it was day, the ³magistrates sent the
36 ⁴serjeants, saying, Let those men go. And the jailor reported the words to Paul, saying, The ³magistrates have sent to let you go: now therefore come forth.
37 and go in peace. But Paul said unto them, They have beaten us publicly, uncondemned, men that

---

a Luke 5 : 29 ; 19 : 6....b ch. 22 : 25.———1 Gr. a table....2 Or, having believed God....3 Gr. prætors....4 Gr. lictors.

---

within the walls of the prison (Grsb., Rosnm., Kuin.). Such a bath was a common appurtenance of houses and public edifices among the Greeks and Romans. Whether the Gangas flowed near the prison, so as to be easily accessible, cannot be decided.—And all his are evidently the all in his house to whom they had just preached the word, as stated in v. 32.

34. Having brought them up into his house, which appears to have been over the prison.—**He rejoiced with all his family—** i. e. he and all his family rejoiced. **Having believed in God** states the object or occasion of their joy. (Comp. 1 Cor. 14 : 18.) This act, like that of the verb, is predicated of the jailer's family as well as of himself.

35–40. THEY ARE SET AT LIBERTY, AND DEPART FROM PHILIPPI.

35. The sergeants = the rod-bearers (lictores), who waited upon Roman magistrates and executed their orders. In the colonies they carried staves — not fasces, as at Rome. It deserves notice that Luke introduces this term just here. Though applied occasionally to Greek magistrates as bearing the staff of authority, it was properly in this age a Roman designation, and is found here in the right place as denoting the attendants of Roman officers.—**Release them.** The rulers did not command them to leave the city, but expected them, doubtless, to use their liberty for that purpose. It is uncertain how we are to account for this sudden change of disposition toward Paul and Silas. The magistrates may have reflected in the interval on the injustice of their conduct and have relented, or possibly, as they were heathen and superstitious, they had been alarmed by the earthquake, and feared the anger of the gods on account of their inhumanity to the strangers.

36. The jailer reported these words unto Paul—i. e. from the lictors, who, therefore, did not accompany him into the prison. The same verb occurs in v. 38, of the answer

which the lictors conveyed to the magistrates. —**That they have sent**—sc. a message, or messengers.—**In peace,** unmolested. (See on 15 : 33.) The jailer anticipates their ready acceptance of the offer.

37. Said unto them, the lictors—i. e. by the mouth of the jailer.—**Having scourged us publicly uncondemned, men who are Romans.** Almost every word in this reply contains a distinct allegation. It would be difficult to find or frame a sentence superior to it in point of energetic brevity. Both the Lex Valeria and the Lex Porcia made it a crime to inflict blows or any species of torture on a Roman citizen : " Facinus est vinciri civem Romanum, scelus verberari, prope parricidium necari"[1] (Cic. in Verr., 5. 66).—**Publicly.** It would have been a crime to have struck them a single blow, even in secret ; they had been cruelly scourged in open day, and before hundreds of witnesses. — **Uncondemned.** The Roman laws held it to be one of the most sacred rights of the citizen that he should be tried in due form before he was condemned : " Causa cognita multi possunt absolvi ; incognita quidem co ndemnari nemo potest "[2] (Cic. in Verr., 1. 9). Even slaves had an admitted legal as well as natural right to be heard in their defence before they were punished.—**Romans.** In 22 : 28, Paul says that he was "free-born." In regard to the probable origin of his Roman citizenship, see the note on 22 : 25. It appears that Silas possessed the same rights, but it is not known how he obtained them. At first view it may appear surprising that Paul did not avow himself a Roman at the outset, and thus prevent the indignity to which he had been subjected. " But the infliction of it," says Biscoe, "was so hasty that he had not time to say anything that might make for his defence ; and the noise and confusion were so great that, had he cried out with ever so loud a voice that he was a Roman, he might reasonably believe

---

[1] [" It is a crime to bind a Roman citizen ; a heinous offence to scourge him ; almost a parricide to put him to death."]
[2] [" When a case has been tried many may be acquitted ; but while it is yet untried no one can be condemned."]

us into prison ; and now do they thrust us out privily ? nay verily ; but let them come themselves and fetch us out.

38 And the serjeants told these words unto the magistrates : and they feared, when they heard that they were Romans.

39 And they came and besought them, and brought *them* out, and *a*desired *them* to depart out of the city.

40 And they went out of the prison, *b*and entered into *the house of* Lydia : and when they had seen the brethren, they comforted them, and departed.

are Romans, and have cast us into prison ; and do they now cast us out privily ? nay verily ; but let 38 them come themselves and bring us out. And the [1]serjeants reported these words unto the [2]magistrates : and they feared, when they heard that they 39 were Romans ; and they came and besought them ; and when they had brought them out, they asked 40 them to go away from the city. And they went out of the prison, and entered into *the house of* Lydia : and when they had seen the brethren, they [3]comforted them, and departed.

a Matt. 8 : 34....*b* ver. 14.———1 Gr. *lictors*....2 Gr. *prœtors*....3 Or, *exhorted*

that he should not be regarded. Seeing also the fury of the multitude (v. 22), it is not improbable he might think it most advisable to submit to the sentence pronounced, however unjust, in order to quiet the people and prevent a greater evil ; for he was in danger of being forced out of the hands of the magistrates and torn in pieces. But, whatever were the true reasons which induced the apostle to be silent, the overruling hand of Providence was herein plainly visible ; for the conversion of the jailer and his household was occasioned by the execution of this hasty and unjust sentence."— **And do they now send us forth secretly ?** Some render the verb **thrust forth,** which is too strong (comp. 9 : 40) and draws away the emphasis from **secretly,** to which it belongs. —**No, certainly** (οὐ γάρ), they do not dismiss us in that manner. In this use, γέ (resolving γάρ into its parts) strengthens the denial, while ἄρα shows the dependence of the answer on what precedes : *not according to that—i. e. after such treatment.* Klotz (*Ad Devar.*, ii. p. 242), Winer (§ 53. 8. b), and others adopt this analysis.—**They themselves,** instead of sending their servants to us.—In asserting so strongly their personal rights, they may have been influenced in part by a natural sense of justice, and in part by a regard to the necessity of such a vindication of their innocence to the cause of Christ at Philippi. It was important that no stain should rest upon their reputation. It was notorious that they had been scourged and imprisoned as criminals ; and if, after their departure, any one had suspected or could have insinuated that possibly they had suffered not without cause, it would have created a prejudice against the truth. It was in their power to save the gospel from that reproach, and they used the opportunity. It may be proper at times to allow the wicked or misguided to trample upon our individual rights and interests if they choose, but those

13

who are " set for the defence of the gospel " owe their good name and their influence to Christ and the church, and have a right to invoke the protection of the laws against any invasion of their means of public usefulness.

38. Reported back. (See on v. 36.)— **Were afraid.** They had cause for apprehension. (Comp. 22 : 29.) A magistrate who punished a Roman citizen wrongfully might be indicted for treason ; he was liable to suffer death and the confiscation of all his property (Grot.).

39. Entreated, begged (3 : 3). This was not an unexampled humiliation for a Roman officer. Lucian mentions a case of false imprisonment in which the governor of a province not only acknowledged his error, but paid a large sum of money to those whom he had injured, in order to bribe them to be silent.

40. Unto Lydia, whose guests they were (v. 15), and where the disciples may have been accustomed to meet.—**The brethren,** who had been converted at Philippi, and who formed the beginning of the church afterward addressed in the Epistle to the Philippians. This church was founded, therefore, about A. D. 52. We have evidence in that letter that no one of all the churches planted by Paul possessed so entirely his confidence or exhibited the power of the gospel in greater purity.— **Exhorted**—viz. to be firm, to cleave to the gospel (comp. 11 : 23) ; not **comforted,** which would be too specific for the occasion.—**They went forth.** The narrator, it will be seen, proceeds now in the third person, and maintains that style as far as 20 : 5. Some have inferred from this that Luke remained at Philippi until Paul's last visit to Macedonia. We find Timothy with the apostle at Berea (17 : 14), but whether he accompanied him at this time or rejoined him afterward cannot be decided. (See further on 17 : 10.)

CHAPTER XVII.

NOW when they had passed through Amphipolis and Apollonia, they came to Thessalonica, where was a synagogue of the Jews:

2 And Paul, as his manner was, *a*went in unto them, and three sabbath days reasoned with them out of the scriptures,

3 Opening and alleging, *b*that Christ must needs have suffered, and risen again from the dead; and that this Jesus, whom I preach unto you, is Christ.

1 Now when they had passed through Amphipolis and Apollonia, they came to Thessalonica, where 2 was a synagogue of the Jews: and Paul, as his custom was, went in unto them, and for three ¹sabbath 3 days reasoned with them from the scriptures, opening and alleging, that it behoved the Christ to suffer, and to rise again from the dead; and that this Jesus, whom, *said he*, I proclaim unto you, is the Christ.

a Luke 4 : 16; ch. 9 : 20; 13 : 5, 14; 14 : 1; 16 : 13; 19 : 8....*b* Luke 24 : 26, 46; ch. 18 : 28; Gal. 3 : 1.———1 Or, *weeks*

1-4. THEY PROCEED TO THESSALO-NICA, AND PREACH THERE.

1. The place which invited their labors next was *Thessalonica*, about a hundred miles south-west of Philippi. They travelled thither on the great military road which led from Byzantium to Dyrrachium, or Aulona, opposite to Brundusium, in Italy. It was the Macedonian extension of the Appian Way. They could accomplish the journey in three or four days (Wiesl.).—On leaving Philippi they came first to **Amphipolis,** which was south-west, distant about thirty miles. This place was about three miles from the sea, on the eastern bank of the Strymon, which flowed almost round it and gave to it its name.—**Apollonia,** their next station, was about the same distance south-west from Amphipolis. They remained a night, perhaps, at each of these towns.—**Thessalonica** was a rich commercial city

Pind., p. 157) and read: From Philippi to Amphipolis, thirty-two miles; from Amphipolis to Apollonia, thirty-two miles; from Apollonia to Thessalonica, thirty-six miles.—**The synagogue,** definite, because the Jews in that region may have had but one such place of worship. (W. § 17. 1.)

2. Here, again, **according to his custom,** Paul betakes himself first to the Jews. (Comp. 13 : 5, 14; 14 : 1.) **Custom** (εἰωθός) has the construction of a noun, but governs the dative as a verb. (Comp. Luke 4 : 16.) The genitive would have been the ordinary case. (W. § 31. 7. N. 2.)—**From the Scriptures.** He drew the contents of his discourse from that source. (W. § 47. p. 333.)

3. Opening—*i. e.* the Scriptures—unfolding their sense. (Comp. Luke 24 : 32.)—**Propounding,** maintaining.—**That the Messiah must suffer,** in order to fulfil the

THESSALONICA.

near the mouth of the Echedorus, on the Thermaic Gulf, about twenty-eight miles nearly west of Apollonia. It is now called *Saloniki*, having a population of seventy thousand, of whom thirty thousand are Jews. Luke's record almost reminds us of a leaf from a traveller's note-book. He mentions the places in their exact order. We turn to the *Itinerarium Antonini Augusti* (ed. Parth. et

Scriptures. (Comp. 3 : 18; Matt. 26 : 54, 56; Mark 14 : 49.)—**And that this one**—viz. he who was to die and rise again—**is the Messiah Jesus**—*i. e.* the Jesus called Messiah—**whom I announce unto you.** The scope of the argument is this: The true Messiah must die and rise again; Jesus has fulfilled this condition of prophecy, and is therefore the promised Messiah. (Comp. 2 : 24, *sq.*; 13 : 27, *sq.*)

4 ^aAnd some of them believed, and consorted with Paul and ^bSilas; and of the devout Greeks a great multitude, and of the chief women not a few.

5 ¶ But the Jews which believed not, moved with envy, took unto them certain lewd fellows of the baser sort, and gathered a company, and set all the city on an uproar, and assaulted the house of ^cJason, and sought to bring them out to the people.

6 And when they found them not, they drew Jason and certain brethren unto the rulers of the city, crying, ^dThese that have turned the world upside down are come hither also;

4 And some of them were persuaded, and consorted with Paul and Silas; and of the devout Greeks a great multitude, and of the chief women not a few. 5 But the Jews, being moved with jealousy, took unto them certain vile fellows of the rabble, and gathering a crowd, set the city on an uproar; and assaulting the house of Jason, they sought to bring them 6 forth to the people. And when they found them not, they dragged Jason and certain brethren before the rulers of the city, crying, These that have turned

---

a ch. 28 : 24....*b* ch. 15 : 22, 27, 32, 40....*c* Rom. 16 : 21....*d* ch. 16 : 20.

---

4. Certain of them—*i. e.* of the Jews. (See vv. 1 and 2.)—**Attached themselves** (middle sense) **to Paul and Silas** (Olsh., Whl., Rob.). This is the easier sense, and receives support from v. 34 and 14 : 4, where we meet with the same thought in like circumstances. Others render *were allotted*, granted to them, as it were by divine favor. This may be the surer philological sense, and is adopted by Winer (¿ 39. 2), De Wette, Meyer, and Alford.—**And of the first women** (comp. 13 : 50) **not a few.** The women were evidently "devout" (σεβομένων) or proselytes (comp. 13 : 50), as well as the men; so that all those mentioned as converts in this verse were won to Christianity from the Jewish faith, not from a state of heathenism. But in 1 Thess. 1 : 9, Paul speaks as if many of the Thessalonian Christians had been idolaters (**ye turned to God from idols**). Hence it is possible, as Paley conjectures, that this verse describes the result of Paul's labors during the three weeks that he preached in the synagogue (v. 2), and that an interval which Luke passes over preceded the events related in vv. 5–10. During this interval the apostle, having been excluded from the synagogue by the bigotry of the Jews, may have preached directly to the heathen. Another opinion is that he preached to the Gentiles during the week-time, while on the Sabbath he labored for the Jews in their public assemblies (Neand.).

5–9. THE JEWS ACCUSE PAUL AND SILAS BEFORE THE MAGISTRATES.

5. Which believed not (T. R.) lacks support.—**Lewd fellows,** or **market-loungers** (*subrostrani, subbasilicani*). Had it been in the East, where such people loiter about the gates, the term would have been inappropriate. It is instructive to observe how true the narrative is to the habits of different nations, though the scene changes so rapidly from one land to another. But why should the Jews seek such coadjutors? The reason is found in their situation: the Jews out of Judea had but little

power, and must secure the aid of the native inhabitants.—**Jason** was their host (v. 7), and also a relative of Paul, if he was the one mentioned in Rom. 16 : 21. In the latter case he must have been at Corinth when Paul wrote the Epistle to the Romans. So common a name amounts to little as proof of the relationship.—**Sought to bring them unto the people,** and at the same time **to the rulers of the city** (v. 6)—*i. e.* into the forum, where the magistrates were accustomed to try causes in the presence of the people. (Comp. 16 : 19.) They raised a mob (ὀχλοποιήσαντες), in order to arrest the offenders, but **to the people** shows that they expected the trial to take place before an orderly assembly.

6. But not having found them, they dragged Jason and certain brethren before the city rulers. Instead of changing their plan on failing to apprehend the leaders, they seized upon such others as fell in their way, and treated them as they had designed to treat Paul and Silas. Lange's remark is incorrect that they would have sacrificed the strangers at once to the popular fury, but must be more cautious in dealing with citizens. The **brethren** appear to have been with Jason at the time of the assault; probably they were some of the Thessalonians who had believed. —**These** are Paul and Silas, since they are those whom Jason entertained.—**Are present also here,** as they have been in other places, and for the same purpose.—Here and in v. 8, Luke terms the magistrates of Thessalonica **politarchs;** and his accuracy in this respect is confirmed by an inscription of that place. (See Boeckh's *Corpus*, vol. ii. p. 53, No. 1967.) The inscription, which is of the Roman times, gives a list of seven magistrates bearing this title. This is the more worthy of remark because the title is a very rare one, and might easily be confounded with that of **poliarchs,** which is another appellation of magistrates in Greek cities.[1]

---

[1] This note is due to President Woolsey, in the *New Englander*, vol. x. p. 144.

7 Whom Jason hath received: and these all do contrary to the decrees of Cæsar, *a*saying that there is another king, *one* Jesus.

8 And they troubled the people and the rulers of the city, when they heard these things.

9 And when they had taken security of Jason, and of the others, they let them go.

10 ¶ And *b*the brethren immediately sent away Paul and Silas by night unto Berea: who coming *thither* went into the synagogue of the Jews.

11 These were more noble than those in Thessalonica, in that they received the word with all readiness of mind, and *c*searched the scriptures daily, whether those things were so.

7 ¹the world upside down are come hither also; whom Jason hath received: and these all act contrary to the decrees of Cæsar, saying that there is another

8 king, *one* Jesus. And they troubled the multitude and the rulers of the city, when they heard these

9 things. And when they had taken security from Jason and the rest, they let them go.

10 And the brethren immediately sent away Paul and Silas by night unto Berœa: who when they were come thither went into the synagogue of the

11 Jews. Now these were more noble than those in Thessalonica, in that they received the word with all readiness of mind, examining the scriptures

---

a Luke 23 : 2 ; John 19 : 12 ; 1 Pet. 2 : 13....*b* ch. 9 : 25 ; ver. 14....*c* Isa. 34 : 16 ; Luke 16 : 29 ; John 5 : 39.——1 Gr. *the inhabited earth.*

---

7. All these—viz. Paul, Silas, and their followers. The pronoun includes more than its grammatical antecedent. — **The decrees of Cæsar**—*i. e.* the Roman laws against rebellion or treason. They are said to be **the decrees of the emperor**—*i. e.* of each successive emperor—because they emanated from him, guarded his rights, and had the support of his authority. The reigning emperor at this time was Claudius.—**Another king,** sovereign. (Comp. John 19 : 15 ; 1 Pet. 2 : 13.) [It is noticeable also that the preaching of Paul in this city must have contained references to a future coming and reign of Christ which may have been laid hold of and perverted by enemies, especially as they seem to have been misunderstood by some who believed. (See 1 Thess. 4 : 14 ; 5 : 2, 23 ; 2 Thess. 1 : 7, 8 ; 2 : 1–12.)—A. H.] The Greeks applied this term to the emperor, though the Romans never styled him *rex.*

8. Troubled, etc. The statement alarmed them, because the existence of such a party in their midst would compromise their character for loyalty and expose them to the vengeance of their Roman masters. (See on 19 : 40.)

9. Having taken bail, or **security.** Said to be a law-phrase adopted in Greek for *satis accipere.* What they engaged would naturally be that, as far as it depended on them, the public peace should not be violated, and that the alleged authors of the disturbance should leave the city (Neand.). Instead of combining the two objects, some restrict the stipulation to the first point (Mey.), while others restrict it to the last (Kuin.).—**The others** who had been brought before the tribunal with Jason. (See v. 6.)—**Let them go, dismissed them** from custody—viz. the Thessalonians, not the missionaries who had escaped arrest.

10–13. PAUL AND SILAS PROCEED TO BERŒA.

10. Immediately, on the evening of the day of the tumult. Paul and Silas had spent three or four weeks at least in Thessalonica (see v. 2), and very possibly some time longer. (See on v. 4.) Weiseler proposes six or eight weeks as the term of their residence in that city. Being obliged to leave so hastily, Paul was anxious for the welfare and stability of the recent converts, and departed with the intention of returning as soon as the present exasperation against him should be allayed so as to justify it (1 Thess. 2 : 18). Subsequent events frustrated this purpose, and under that disappointment he sent Timothy to them to supply his place (1 Thess. 3 : 2). It may be added that while Paul was here he received supplies twice from the church at Philippi. (See Phil. 4 : 15, 16.) From this source, and from his own personal labor, he derived his support, without being dependent at all on the Thessalonians. (See 1 Thess. 2 : 9 ; 2 Thess. 3 : 8.)—**During the night.** This secrecy indicates that they were still in danger from the enmity of the Jews. (Comp. 20 : 3.)—**Unto Berea.** Berea, now *Verria*, was about forty-five miles southwest of Thessalonica, on the Astræus, a small tributary of the Haliacmon. (See Forbg., *Handb.,* iii. p. 1061.) The modern town has six thousand inhabitants, of whom two hundred are Jews, ten or fifteen hundred Turks, and the rest Greeks.

11. More noble, in their disposition.—For **all** without the article, see on 4 : 29.—**From day to day.** The (τό) particularizes the repetition or constancy of the act. (W. ? 20. 3.)—**If these things** taught by Paul **were so,** as he affirmed—*i. e.* when examined by the Scriptures. [A rare encomium! And if it was a proof of true nobleness in the Bereans to test the apostle's doctrine by comparing it with the sacred Scriptures in their possession, it must be a proof of true nobleness to do the same thing now—*to prove all things* and *hold fast that which is good* (1 Thess. 5 : 21), to subject novel opinions to a thorough comparison with the established word of God. The duty of private

12 Therefore many of them believed ; also of honorable women which were Greeks, and of men, not a few.
13 But when the Jews of Thessalonica had knowledge that the word of God was preached of Paul at Berea, they came thither also, and stirred up the people.
14 *a*And then immediately the brethren sent away Paul to go as it were to the sea: but Silas and Timotheus abode there still.
15 And they that conducted Paul brought him unto Athens: and *b*receiving a commandment unto Silas and Timotheus for to come to him with all speed, they departed.
16 ¶ Now while Paul waited for them at Athens,

12 daily, whether these things were so. Many of them therefore believed ; also of the Greek women of honorable estate, and of men, not a few. But when the
13 Jews of Thessalonica had knowledge that the word of God was proclaimed of Paul at Berœa also, they came thither likewise, stirring up and troubling the
14 multitudes. And then immediately the brethren sent forth Paul to go as far as to the sea: and Silas
15 and Timothy abode there still. But they that conducted Paul brought him as far as Athens: and receiving a commandment unto Silas and Timothy that they should come to him with all speed, they departed.
16 Now while Paul waited for them at Athens, his

a Matt. 10 : 23....*b* ch. 18 : 5.

interpretation is therefore plain. Whoever can understand the words spoken by a living teacher can, if he will, interpret the same words when written in a book, or compare them with other written words. There is also in this passage clear evidence that Luke and the Bereans, and the apostle likewise, looked upon the Old-Testament Scriptures as being a suitable standard by which to try the preaching of Paul, and therefore as possessing divine authority.—A. H.]
12. Many of them believed [*i. e.* of the Jews just described. A large part of those who resorted to the synagogue for worship were probably of Jewish derivation, though some of them may have been proselytes from heathenism. — A. H.]. **Greek** (adj.) agrees with both **women** and **men.** The men were Greeks as well as the women. (See the note on 2 : 42.)—For **honorable,** see 13 : 50.—**Few** ʹ(ὀλίγοι) may be masculine, because **men** is the nearer word, or out of regard to the leading gender.
13. Also associates Berea with Thessalonica. —**There also** belongs to the participle, not to the verb. They excited the populace **there also** as they had done in Thessalonica.— Luke's narrative implies that the Jews were somewhat numerous and influential at Berea. Coins of this city are still extant, and, unlike most other examples of ancient money, have on them no pagan figure or symbol. Akerman suggests (*Num. Illustr.*) in explanation of this singular fact that the magistrates may have rejected such devices as a concession to the feelings of the Jewish population.
14, 15. PAUL ADVANCES TO ATHENS.
14. To go as it were to the sea—lit. **to journey as upon the sea ;** *i. e.* as if with such a purpose. The Greek particle here used, (ὡς) with *upon* (ἐπί), *unto* (εἰς), or *toward* (πρός), denotes design, but leaves it uncertain whether the design be executed or professed merely. (See W. ⸹ 65. 9 ; K. ⸹ 290. R. 2 ; B. ⸹ 149.) Lachmann would substitute *unto* (ἕως) for *as* (ὡς)—as

far as **unto the sea**—but against the evidence. [With Lach. agree Tsch., Treg., West. and Hort, Anglo-Am. Revisers, after ℵ A B E, many cursives, and the Vul., Syr., and Copt. versions. The evidence *now* is therefore for rather than against **unto** (ἕως).—A. H.] Some suppose the movement here to have been a feint — that Paul's conductors, having set out ostensibly for the sea, afterward, in order to elude pursuit, changed their course and proceeded to Athens by land (Grot., Bng., Olsh.). But in that event they would have passed through various important places on the way, and Luke might be expected to name some of them, as he has done in v. 1. The journey by land would have been two hundred and fifty-one Roman miles (*Itiner. Anton.*). [Besides, if the best-supported text is followed, the basis for a conjecture that going to the sea may have been a feint is taken away.—ʹA. H.] With a fair wind Paul and his party could have sailed from Berea or the mouth of the Haliacmon to Athens in about three days (Wiesl.) ; and the probability is that they took this more expeditious course (Win., De Wet., Wiesl., Mey.). (For an interesting sketch of the places and objects which would be seen on such a voyage the reader is referred to Conybeare and Howson, i. p. 403, *sq.*)—**Timothy** was last mentioned in 16 : 1.
15. Those who conducted—lit. set him along on the journey, whether by sea or land. —**Having received** before their departure, rather than **receiving** (E. V.), which might imply that they returned in consequence of the command.—**With all speed,** or **as soon as possible** (K. ⸹ 239. R. 2. d)—*i. e.* after performing the service for which they had remained. Whether they rejoined the apostle at Athens or not is uncertain. (See on the next verse.)
16-18. HOW HE WAS AFFECTED BY THE IDOLATRY AT ATHENS.
16. While he was waiting for them— viz. Silas and Timothy. The most natural inference from 1 Thess. 3 : 1 is that Timothy, at

^ahis spirit was stirred in him, when he saw the city wholly given to idolatry.

spirit was provoked within him, as he beheld the

a 2 Pet. 2 : 8.

least, soon arrived, in accordance with Paul's expectation, but was immediately sent away by the apostle to Thessalonica. As Silas is not mentioned in that passage, it has been supposed that he may have failed for some reason to come at this time, or, if he came, that, like Timothy, he may have left again at once, but for a different destination; which last circumstance would account for the omission of his name in that passage of the Epistle. Our next notice of them occurs in 18 : 5, where they are represented as coming down from Macedonia to Corinth; and we may suppose either that they went to that city directly from Berea, without hav-

otherwise unknown to the extant Greek, but is formed after a common analogy (*e. g.* κατάμπελος, κατάδενδρος, κατάφοβος, etc.). The epithet applies to the city, not directly to the inhabitants. A person could hardly take his position at any point in ancient Athens where the eye did not range over temples, altars, and statues of the gods almost without number. Petronius says satirically that it was easier to find a god at Athens than a man. Another ancient writer says that some of the streets were so crowded with those who sold idols that it was almost impossible for one to make his way through them. Pausanias declares that Athens had more im-

ATHENS.

ing followed Paul to Athens, or that they returned from Athens to Macedonia and proceeded from there to Corinth. The latter view assumes that Luke has passed over the intermediate journey in silence. Such omissions are entirely consistent with the character of a fragmentary history like that of the Acts. Still other combinations are possible.—**His spirit was aroused in him.** (Comp. 15 : 39; 1 Cor. 13 : 5.) This verb represents the apostle as deeply moved with a feeling allied to that of indignation at beholding such a profanation of the worship due to God as forced itself upon his view on every side.—**Full of idols** (κατείδωλον), not **given to idolatry.** The word is

ages than all the rest of Greece put together. Wetstein quotes Xenophon, Isocrates, Cicero, Livy, Strabo, Lucian, and others as bearing the same testimony. Luke, therefore, has not applied this epithet at random. The Greek language offered to him a hundred other terms which would have stated what was true in relation to a heathen city, but we see that he has chosen among them all the very one which describes the precise external aspect of Athens that would be the first to strike the eye of a stranger like Paul. This mark of accuracy in the writer those obliterate, or very nearly obliterate, who make the expression refer to the devotion of the Athenians to idolatry.[1]

[1] Hermann (*Ad Vig.*, p. 638, ed. 1824) turns aside to correct this error: "Κατείδωλος πόλις, *Actor. Apost.* 17, 16, non est, uti quidam opinantur, *simulacris dedita urbs*, sed *simulacris referta.*"

17 Therefore disputed he in the synagogue with the Jews, and with the devout persons, and in the market daily with them that met with him.
18 Then certain philosophers of the Epicureans, and of the Stoics, encountered him. And some said, What will this babbler say? other some, He seemeth to be a setter forth of strange gods: because he preached unto them Jesus, and the resurrection.

17 city full of idols. So he reasoned in the synagogue with the Jews and the devout persons, and in the marketplace every day with them that met with 18 him. And certain also of the Epicurean and Stoic philosophers encountered him. And some said, What would this babbler say? other some, He seemeth to be a setter forth of strange [1]gods: be-

---

1 Gr. demons.

---

17. The apostle's ordinary course was to address himself exclusively at first to his own countrymen and the Jewish proselytes. At Athens he departed from this rule.—**Therefore**—*i. e.* being aroused by the sight of so much idolatry. The spectacle around him urges him to commence preaching simultaneously to Jews and Greeks. Some adopt a looser connection: **therefore**—*i. e.* being at Athens (De Wette). Some restrict **therefore** to the second clause: his zeal impelled him to preach in the market. It is arbitrary to divide the sentence in that manner.—**In the market** —*i. e.* of the city, not the one in which he happened to be (Mey.). It is generally admitted that the Athenians had properly but one market, although Leake has shown it to be probable that "during the many centuries of Athenian prosperity the boundaries of the Agora, or at least of its frequented part, underwent considerable variation."[1] The notices of ancient writers are somewhat vague as to its course and extent, but it is agreed that the site was never so changed as to exclude the famous *Poecilé* (στοὰ ποικίλη), which, according to Forchhammer's Plan, stood off against the Acropolis on the west. In this porch, as is well known, the philosophers, rhetoricians, and others were accustomed to meet for conversation and discussion; and hence it lay entirely in the course of things that some of these men should fall, as Luke states, in the way of the apostle.

18. The Epicureans. The *Epicureans* were the " minute philosophers," the Greek Sadducees of the age; they admitted the existence of gods, but regarded them as indolent beings who paid no attention to the actions or affairs of men; they had no faith in a providence or in accountability or in any retribution to come. Their great practical dogma was that a wise man will make the most of all the means of enjoyment within his reach. Epicurus, the founder of the sect, had taught a higher idea of happiness, but his followers in the Roman age, and earlier still, had reduced it to the grossest sensualism. The frivolous spirit of

this sect appears, perhaps, in the first of the questions addressed to Paul. — **The Stoics.** The *Stoics* were distinguished in some respects for a more reflecting turn of mind; they extolled virtue, insisted on subjecting the passions to reason, and urged the importance of becoming independent of the ordinary sources of enjoyment and suffering. Some of the most admired characters of antiquity belonged to this school. But the Stoics were essentially fatalists in their religious views; they were self-complacent, boasted of their indifference to the world, and affected a style of morals so impracticable as to render them almost necessarily insincere or hypocritical. In Epicureanism, it was man's sensual nature which arrayed itself against the claims of the gospel; in Stoicism, it was his self-righteousness and pride of intellect; and it is difficult to say which of the two systems rendered its votaries the more indisposed to embrace the truth. It might have seemed to the credit of Christianity had it been represented as gaining at least a few proselytes, in this centre of Grecian refinement, from the ranks of its scholars and philosophers; but Luke has no such triumphs to record. He relates the case as it was; the apostle was ridiculed, his message was treated with contempt. — **Encountered him, conversed** or **disputed with him** (E. V., De Wet.; comp. 4 : 15); not *met with him*, as in 20 : 14 (Bng. Mey.), since the form, as imperf., applies better to a discussion than to a single contact of the parties such as Luke mentions here. **And said** agrees with either sense. [There is but a slight difference between the view of Meyer in his last ed. and that of Dr. Hackett. For Meyer says: "That it was Epicureans and Stoics who *fell into conflict* with him, . . . and not Academics and Peripatetics, is to be explained . . . from the greater contrast of their philosophic tenets with the doctrines of Christianity. The one had their principle of pleasure, and the other their pride of virtue. And both repudiated faith in the Divine Providence." Only, the imperfect tense of the verb is favorable to the translation given by Dr. Hackett. — A. H.]—

---

1 *Athens and Demi*, p. 217.

19 And they took him, and brought him unto Areopagus, saying, May we know what this new doctrine, whereof thou speakest, is?

19 cause he preached Jesus and the resurrection. And they took hold of him, and brought him ¹unto ²the Areopagus, saying, May we know what this new

1 Or, *before....*2 Or, *the hill of Mars*

What would this babbler say? does he mean to say. The particle (ἄν) sharpens the taunt: if he has any meaning (Mey.). (See W. § 42. 1; C. § 604.) The word translated **babbler** (σπερμολόγος) denotes strictly a seed-gatherer, and then, as used here, one who picks up and retails scraps of knowledge without sense or aim, *an idle prater.*— **Strange,** or **foreign, gods,** hitherto unknown to us. As the expression is cited from the mouth of the Greeks, we are to attach to it their sense of **demon** (δαιμόνιον), which was different from that of the Jews. The noun may be plural, because it refers to Jesus as an example of the class or category (see W. § 27. 2; S. § 95. 2), or it may be founded on what Paul had said to them concerning God, especially his agency in raising up Christ from the dead. (Comp. v. 31.) The latter is the best view (De Wet.). Both Jesus and the God of whom they now heard were new to them. Many of the older critics, and some of the more recent, explain the plural as embracing **resurrection** (ἀνάστασιν), supposing the Athenians to have understood Paul to speak of some goddess when he preached to them the resurrection. But one can hardly conceive that the apostle would express himself so obscurely on this subject as to give them any occasion for falling into so gross a mistake, and we are not authorized by any intimation in the narrative to impute to them a wilful perversion of his language.

19–21. PAUL REPAIRS TO MARS' HILL TO EXPLAIN HIS DOCTRINE.

19. And taking hold upon him, not with violence, which would be at variance with the general spirit of the transaction, but rather by the hand, for the purpose of leading him onward. (Comp. 9 : 27 ; Mark 8 : 23 ; Luke 9 : 47.) —**Upon Mars' Hill**—*i. e.* the top of it. (Comp. 10 : 9 ; Matt. 4 : 5 ; 24 : 16, etc.) The Areopagus, whither Paul was now brought, was a rocky eminence a little to the west of the Acropolis. (See Leake's *Athens*, p. 165.) The object of the movement was to place the apostle in a situation where he could be heard by the multitude to greater advantage. The following is Dr. Robinson's description of this locality : " This is a narrow, naked ridge of limestone rock rising gradually from the northern end, and terminating abruptly on the south over against the west end of the

Acropolis, from which it bears about north, being separated from it by an elevated valley. This southern end is fifty or sixty feet above the said valley, though yet much lower than the Acropolis. On its top are still to be seen the seats of the judges and parties, hewn in the rock ; and toward the south-west is a descent by a flight of steps, also cut in the rock into the valley below. Standing on this elevated platform, surrounded by the learned and the wise of Athens, the multitude perhaps being on the steps and the vale below, Paul had directly before him the far-famed Acropolis, with its wonders of Grecian art ; and beneath him, on his left, the majestic Theseium, the earliest and still most perfect of Athenian structures ; while all around other temples and altars filled the whole city. On the Acropolis, too, were the three celebrated statues of Minerva—one of olive-wood ; another, of gold and ivory, in the Parthenon, the masterpiece of Phidias ; and the colossal statue in the open air, the point of whose spear was seen over the Parthenon by those sailing along the gulf" (*Bibl. Res.*, i. p. 10, *sq.*). The reader would do well to consult the admirable article on "Athens" in Smith's *Dictionary of Greek and Roman Geography*. He will find a plan of that city and a view of the Acropolis restored, as seen from the Areopagus, in Conybeare and Howson's work. To understand the peculiar boldness and power of the speech we must have distinctly before us the objects and scenes which met the apostle's view at the moment.—Some translate ἐπὶ τὸν Ἄρειον πάγον **before the Areopagus,** instead of **upon Mars' Hill** (comp. 16 : 19 ; 18 : 12 ; 24 : 8), and maintain that Paul was arraigned at this time before the celebrated court of that name, and underwent a formal trial on the charge of having attempted to change the religion of the state. But this opinion rests entirely upon two or three expressions which, like the one just noticed, are ambiguous in themselves ; while in other respects the entire narrative, as well as the improbability of such a procedure, testify against the idea. First, we find here no trace whatever of anything like the formality of a legal process ; secondly, the professed object of bringing the apostle **upon Mars' Hill** was to ascertain from him what his opinions were, not to put him on his defence for them

20 For thou bringest certain strange things to our ears: we would know therefore what these things mean.

21 (For all the Athenians and strangers which were there spent their time in nothing else, but either to tell, or to hear some new thing.)

20 teaching is, which is spoken by thee? For thou bringest certain strange things to our ears: we would know therefore what these things mean.

21 (Now all the Athenians and the strangers sojourning there ¹spent their time in nothing else, but

---

1 Or, *had leisure for nothing else.*

---

before they were known ; thirdly, the manner in which the affair terminated would have been a singular issue for a judicial investigation in the highest court of Athens ; and finally, the speech which Paul delivered on the occasion was precisely such as we should expect before a promiscuous assembly, whereas, if he had stood now as an accused person before a legal tribunal, his plea has most strangely failed to connect itself, at any single point, with that peculiarity of his situation. It proves nothing in regard to the question to show that the court of the Areopagus had powers (that is admitted) which would have given to it jurisdiction in the case of Paul, supposing that he had been charged at this time with subverting the established worship, since the narrative on which we must rely for our information as to what was done not only contains no evidence that the Athenians took this serious view of his doctrine, but ascribes their eagerness to hear him to a mere love of novelty. (See v. 21.) Calvin, Kuinoel, Neander, Winer, Olshausen, De Wette, Meyer, Baur, Doddridge, and the best critics generally, at present reject the opinion that Paul was carried before the Areopagus for a judicial examination. The authority of Chrysostom, among the ancient critics, stands in favor of it. A few among the Germans, as Hess, Hemsen, Scholz, follow on that side, except that some of them would say (this is true of Hemsen) that the Areopagus was called together, not exactly to try the apostle, but to hear from him some account of his doctrine. "The process," says Wordsworth, "may have been only a preparatory inquiry. . . . They who laid hands on him may have intended to frighten the apostle by the judicial associations of the place, and to drive him out of the city." Most of our English commentaries assume that Paul was arraigned at this time as a religious innovator. The other ambiguous expressions which have been supposed to favor this view will be noticed in their place.—**Can we know ?** Would it not have been an excess even of the Attic politeness to have interrogated a prisoner at the bar in this manner? The object, too, of the inquiry, as defined by the accompanying terms, shows clearly that they did not regard him as occupying that position.

20. Strange, surprising, since the things were foreign, unheard of before.—**Thou bringest to our ears.** This phrase, drawn from common life, has an appearance of reality in this connection.—**What these things mean** (τί ἂν θέλοι). (See on v. 18.) The singular **what** (τί), in apposition with **these things** (ταῦτα), should be noticed. It is not precisely like the plural. "The singular (τί)," says Krüger (*Gr.*, ⸙ 61. 8. 2), "may stand in such connections as *what are these* (τί ταῦτά ἐστι), when the question is, What sort of a whole—what combined result—do the particulars form?" [It may be remarked, however, that the text is doubtful. Lach., Tsch., Treg., West. and Hort, and the Anglo-Am. Revisers, in accord with ℵ A B and several cursive MSS., give τίνα θέλει, instead of τί ἂν θέλοι. It is difficult to decide between the readings, but fortunately the meaning is nearly the same with either.—A. H.]

21. The object of this verse is to explain why they addressed to him such inquiries. Their motive for proposing them was that their curiosity might be gratified.—**Now all Athenians.** The omission of the article unites the characteristic more closely with the name as its invariable attendant. (K. ⸙ 246. 5. a.)—**Strangers,** etc.—*i. e.* the foreigners permanently resident there (comp. 2 : 10), *whence the same customs,* as Bengel remarks.—**Spent their leisure for nothing else.** This sense of the verb is a later usage. (Lob., *Ad Phryn.,* p. 125.) The imperfect does not exclude the continued existence of the peculiarity, but blends the reference to it with the history. (See similar examples in 27 : 8; John 11 : 18; 18 : 1 ; 19 : 14. K. ⸙ 256. 4. a ; C. 567. γ.)—**Newer,** sc. than before. (W. ⸙ 35. 4 ; S. ⸙ 118. 4 ; K. ⸙ 323. R. 7.) The comparative or the positive form of the adjective could be used in this phrase, but the former characterizes their state of mind more forcibly than the latter. Bengel has hit the point of the idiom : "Nova statim sordebant; *noviora quærebantur*" ["New things were presently despised ;—*newer things were sought*"].—It is worth remarking that this singular scene of setting up the apostle to speak for the entertainment of the people occurs, not at Ephesus or Philippi or Corinth, but at Athens—not only the only place in all his journeying where Paul met with such a reception, but just the place where the incident arises in perfect harmony with the disposition and the tastes of the people. We know from the testimony of ancient writers that this fondness for hearing and telling some new thing, which Luke mentions, was a notorious characteristic of the Athenians. Their great orator reproaches them with the same propensity: *Tell me, do you wish, going about from marketplace to marketplace, to inquire: What new thing is said?* etc. (*Philipp.* I. 43.) The entirely incidental manner in which the exemplification of this trait comes forth in the narrative here bears witness to its authenticity.

Outline of the Course of Thought.—
The speech which Paul delivered at this time is remarkable for its adaptation, not only to the outward circumstances under which he spoke, but to the peculiar mental state of his auditors. De Wette pronounces it "a model of the apologetic style of discourse." "The address of Paul before this assembly," says Neander, "is a living proof of his apostolic wisdom and eloquence; we perceive here how the apostle, according to his own expression, could become also a heathen to the heathen that he might win the heathen to a reception of the gospel." "The skill," says Hemsen, "with which he was able to bring the truth near to the Athenians deserves admiration. We find in this discourse of Paul nothing of an ill-timed zeal, nothing like declamatory pomp; it is distinguished for clearness, brevity, coherence, and simplicity of representation." Dr. Robinson, speaking under the impression produced on his mind by a personal survey of the scene, says that, "masterly" as the address is as we read it under ordinary circumstances, "the full force and energy and boldness of the apostle's language can be duly felt only when one has stood upon the spot."[1] The writer can never forget the emotions of thrilling interest which were excited in his own mind as he read and rehearsed the discourse on that memorable rock.—We have first the introduction, which, in the technical language of rhetoric, is eminently conciliatory. The apostle begins by acknowledging and commending the respect of the Athenians for religion (vv. 22, 23). He states next, at the close of v. 23, his design, which is to guide their religious in-

stincts and aspirations to their proper object —*i. e.* to teach them what God is, his nature and attributes, in opposition to their false views and practices as idolaters. He goes on then, in pursuance of this purpose, to announce to them —first, that God is the Creator of the outward, material universe (v. 24); secondly, that he is entirely independent of his creatures, having all-sufficiency in himself (v. 25); thirdly, that he is the Creator of all mankind, notwithstanding their separation into so many nations and their wide dispersion on the earth (v. 26); and fourthly, that he has placed men, as individuals and nations, in such relations of dependence on himself as render it easy for them to see that he is their Creator and Sovereign Disposer, and that they are the creatures of his power and goodness, and that it is their duty to seek and serve him (vv. 27, 28). The ground has thus been won for the application which follows. At this point of the discourse, stretching forth his hand, as we may well suppose, toward the gorgeous images within sight, he exclaims: "We ought not, therefore, to suppose that the Deity is like unto gold, or silver, or stone, sculptured by the art and device of men" (v. 29). And that which men ought not to do they may not safely do any longer. It was owing to the forbearance of God that they had been left hitherto to pursue their idolatry without any signal manifestation of his displeasure; they were *now* required to repent of it and forsake it (v. 30), because a day of righteous judgment awaited them which had been rendered certain by the resurrection of Christ (v. 31). Here their clamors interrupted him. It is not difficult, perhaps, to conjecture what he would have added. It only remained, in order to complete his well-known circle of thought on such occasions, that he should have set forth the claims of Christ as the object of religious hope and confidence—that he should have exhorted them to call on his name and be saved.—It will be seen, therefore, by casting the eye back, that we have here all the parts of a perfect discourse—viz. the exordium, the proposition or theme, the proof or exposition, the inferences and application. It is a beautiful specimen of the manner in which a powerful and well-trained mind practised in public speaking conforms spontaneously to the rules of the severest logic. One can readily believe, looking at this feature of the discourse, that it

---

[1] Some object that the speech has been overpraised, because Paul did not succeed in bringing it to a formal close. The astonishment which one feels as he reads the address is not that the speaker was interrupted at length when he came to announce to the Athenians the peculiar doctrines of Christianity, but that he could command their attention so long while he bore down with such effect on their favorite opinions and prejudices, exposed their error, and arraigned them as guilty of the grossest inconsistency and absurdity of conduct.

22 ¶ Then Paul stood in the midst of Mars' hill, and said, Ye men of Athens, I perceive that in all things ye are too superstitious.

23 For as I passed by, and beheld your devotions, I

22 either to tell or to hear some new thing. And Paul stood in the midst of the Areopagus, and said, Ye men of Athens, in all things I perceive that

23 ye are [1]very religious. For as I passed along, and

---

1 Or, *somewhat superstitious.*

---

was pronounced by the man who wrote the Epistles to the Romans and Galatians, where we see the same mental characteristics so strongly reflected. As we must suppose, at all events, that the general scheme of thought— the *nexus* of the argument—has been preserved, it does not affect our critical judgment of the discourse whether we maintain that it has been reported in full or that a synopsis only has been given. On this point opinions differ.

22–31. THE SPEECH OF PAUL ON MARS' HILL.

22. Stood. Paul spoke, of course, in the open air. A skilful hand has pictured to us the scene : " He stood on that hill in the centre of the Athenian city, and with a full view of it. The temple of the Eumenides was immediately below him ; and if he looked to the east, he beheld the Propylæa of the Acropolis fronting him, and the Parthenon rising above him ; and on his left the bronze colossus of Minerva, the champion of Athens ; and the temple of Victory to the right ; behind him was the temple of Theseus ; and a countless multitude of smaller temples and altars in the Agora and Ceramicus below him " (Wordsworth, p. 85. See also his *Athens and Attica,* ch. xi.).—**In the midst of Mars' Hill** could be said of a place or an assembly. It is one of the ambiguous expressions advert- ed to above (p. 201), which leave it un- certain whether **Mars' Hill** is to be un- derstood of the hill or the court assem- bled there. — **Men of Athens.** The remark just made is to be repeated here. It is the style of address which Paul would necessarily use in speaking to a concourse of Athenians, and, at the same time, he might use it in speaking before judges. In the latter case, however, the Greeks oftener said *O men judges* (ὦ ἄνδρες δικασταί). (See Stalb., *Plat. Apol.,* 17. A.) —**In every respect,** as it were, in every possible mode of exhibition.—**As** (ὡς)—*i. e.* those who correspond to this character —**more religious** (sc. than others) **I see you** (De Wet., Win. See W. § 35. 4). For the suppressed term of the com- parison, see on v. 21. Josephus (*Contr. Ap.,* 2. 11) calls the Athenians *the most devout of*

the Greeks. See other testimonies in Wetstein. The word just translated **more religious** (viz. δεισιδαιμονεστέρους, a *vox media*) may sig- nify also **more superstitious.** It is improb- able, as a matter of just rhetoric, that the apostle employed it in that reproachful sense at the outset of his remarks. That he used it in a good sense is evident for another rea- son. " He proceeds," says Neander, " to de- duce their seeking after God (which he doubt- less considered as something good) from this *deisidaimonia* (comp. 25 : 19), or religious pro- pensity, so prevalent among the Athenians. He announced himself as one who would guide their *deisidaimonia*, not rightly conscious of its object and aim, to a state of clear self-conscious- ness by a revelation of the object to which it thus ignorantly tended."

23. And closely observing the objects of your religious veneration, I found also an altar. *Sebasmata* denotes, not acts of worship, devotions (E. V.), but temples, images, altars, and the like. It is a generic term, under which **also** arranges **altar** as one

AREOPAGUS, ATHENS.

of the class.—**Had been inscribed** (pluperf.) includes the present, and is to be explained like

found an altar with this inscription, TO THE UN-
KNOWN GOD. Whom therefore ye ignorantly worship, him declare I unto you.

observed the objects of your worship, I found also
an altar with this inscription, [1]TO AN UNKNOWN
GOD. What therefore ye worship in ignorance, this

[1] Or, TO THE UNKNOWN GOD.

the imperfect in v. 21.—**To an unknown God**
(ἀγνώστῳ θεῷ). "That there was at least one
altar at Athens with this inscription," says
Meyer, "would appear as historically certain
from this passage itself, even though other testimonies were wanting, since Paul appeals to a
fact of his own observation, and that, too, in
the presence of the Athenians themselves."
But the existence of such altars at Athens is
well attested by competent witnesses. Philostratus, in his *Life of Apollonius* (6. 2), says: "*It
is more discreet to speak well of all the gods, and
especially at Athens, where are erected altars also
of unknown gods.*" Pausanias (in his *Description
of Attica*, 1. 1) says that such altars (*altars of
unknown gods*) existed at Phaleron, one of the
harbors of Athens. It has been made a question how we are to understand the use of the
plural in these passages—whether as referring
to the number of the altars on which the inscription occurred, or to the number of the
gods to whom the altars were dedicated. Some
have assumed the latter as the correct view,
and have said that Paul has arbitrarily changed
the plural into the singular, in order to accommodate the fact to his purpose, or even that the
writer, by this inaccuracy, has betrayed himself as a person who had no direct knowledge
of the circumstances which he professes to relate. But even if the inscription on these altars
was in the plural, it does not follow that Paul
may not have found one having the language
which he recites. Here would be Luke's positive testimony to the fact, and that outweighs
the mere silence of other writers. Such appears
to be Bengel's view. Again, it would not follow that he has necessarily misrepresented the
sense, admitting that he may have substituted
the singular for the plural. The heathen
writers often employed *gods* to convey the general idea of divine power, providence, deity,
and the like.[1] With that meaning, the plural
could be relinquished for the singular or the
singular for the plural, just as an individual
pleased. Here the apostle might have preferred
god, merely for the sake of its stricter *formal*
accordance with the doctrine which he was
about to advance. Kuinoel appears at a loss
to decide whether the plural in the case under
remark has reference to the number of the

altars or to that of the gods. Some, as Calvin
and Olshausen, apparently concede that Paul
deviated from the strict form of the inscription,
but deny that he violated its proper import or
availed himself of any unworthy artifice.—But
even the appearance of a difficulty here vanishes entirely when we give to the language of
Philostratus and Pausanias the interpretation
which is beyond any reasonable doubt the correct one. Winer states his view of the case
thus: "It by no means follows from the passages (of the writers above named) that each
single one of the altars mentioned by them had
the inscription (*to*) *unknown gods* in the plural,
but more natural that each one separately was
dedicated (*to*) *an unknown god*, but this singular
the narrators were obliged to change into the
plural, because they spoke of all those altars in
a collective way. It appears, therefore, that
there were several altars in different places at
Athens with the inscription *to an unknown god.*"
(See his *Realw.*, i. p. 111.) Such is the decision,
also, of Eichhorn, Hess, Hemsen, Meyer, De
Wette, and others. It should be added that
several of the older commentators render *agnosto
theo, to the unknown God,* supposing the God of
the Jews—*i. e.* Jehovah—to be meant. Such a
view mistranslates the Greek and violates all
historical probability.—The precise historical
origin of the altars at Athens bearing this inscription has been disputed. The conjectures
are various. One is that they were very ancient
and that it was at length forgotten to whom
they had been originally built, and that the
words in question were placed on them at a
later period to apprise the people that it was
unknown to what gods they belonged. If that
was their character, it is not easy to see what
proper point of connection the apostle could
have found for his remark with such a relic of
sheer idolatry. Another is that in some time
or times of public calamity the Athenians, not
knowing what god they had offended—whether
Minerva or Jupiter or Mars—erected these altars
so as to be sure of propitiating the right one.
The same objection may be made as before,
since their ignorance in this case relates merely
to the identity of the god whom they should
conciliate, and involves no recognition of any
power additional to their heathen deities. The

---

[1] For examples of this interchange, see the passages collected by Pfanner in his *Systema Theologiæ Gentilis
Purioris*, p. 102, and elsewhere.

24 *a*God that made the world and all things therein, seeing that he is *b*Lord of heaven and earth, *c*dwelleth not in temples made with hands;
25 Neither is worshipped with men's hands, *d*as

24 set I forth unto you. The God that made the world and all things therein, he, being Lord of heaven and earth, dwelleth not in ¹temples made with 25 hands; neither is he served by men's hands, as

a ch. 14 : 15....*b* Matt. 11 : 25....*c* ch. 7 : 48....*d* Ps. 50 : 8. ——1 Or, *sanctuaries*

most rational explanation is unquestionably that of those who suppose these altars to have had their origin in the feeling of uncertainty, inherent, after all, in the minds of the heathen, whether their acknowledgment of the superior powers was sufficiently full and comprehensive; in their distinct consciousness of the limitation and imperfection of their religious views, and their consequent desire to avoid the anger of any still unacknowledged god who might be unknown to them. That no deity might punish them for neglecting his worship or remain uninvoked in asking for blessings, they not only erected altars to all the gods named or known among them, but, distrustful still lest they might not comprehend fully the extent of their subjection and dependence, they erected them also to any other god or power that might exist, although as yet unrevealed to them.—No one can say that this explanation ascribes too much discernment to the heathen. Not to insist on other proofs which might be adduced, such expressions as the comprehensive address, *At o deorum quicquid in cælo regit*, etc. [" But, all ye gods who rule in heaven," etc.] (Horat., *Epod.*, 5. 1); the oft-used formula in the prayers of the Greeks and Romans, *Si deo, si deæ;* and the superstitious dread which they manifested in so many ways, of omitting any deity in their invocations,—prove the existence of the feeling to which reference has been made. Out of this feeling, therefore, these altars may have sprung, because the supposition is so entirely consistent with the genius of polytheistic heathenism; because the many-sided religiousness of the Athenians would be so apt to exhibit itself in some such demonstration; and especially because Paul could then appeal with so much effect to such an avowal of the insufficiency of heathenism, and to such a testimony so borne, indirect, yet significant, to the existence of the one true God.—Under these circumstances, an allusion to one of these altars by the apostle would be equivalent to his saying to the Athenians thus: " You are correct in acknowledging a divine existence beyond any which the ordinary rites of your worship recognize; there is such an existence. You are correct in confessing that this Being is unknown to you; you have no just conceptions of his nature and perfections." He could

add then with truth, **Whom, therefore, not knowing, ye worship, this one I announce unto you.** The inverted order gives point to the declaration. **Not knowing** has the same object as the verb, and means *having no just knowledge* of him whom they worshipped; not *ignorantly*, as if they did not know whither their worship was directed. The word points back evidently to **unknown** (ἀγνώστῳ). Later editors read **what . . . this** (ὁ . . . τοῦτο) instead of **whom . . . this one** (ὃν . . . τοῦτον); in which case **god** (θεῷ) in the inscription would be taken more abstractly as a divine power. The external evidence is not decisive. Meyer defends the common reading in his first edition, and the other in his second. [Lach., Tsch., Treg., West. and Hort, and the Anglo-Am. Revisers adopt the neuter on the strong evidence of א* A* B D.—A. H.] The personal sense of **god** may have been thought to concede too much to heathenism, and so have caused the pronouns to be changed. **Worship** (εὐσεβεῖτε) has seemed to some a strong term, as the cognate words in the New Testament always express the idea of true piety; but the term occurs further only in 1 Tim. 5 : 4, and denotes there, not the exercise of piety, but of something merely kindred to it—filial reverence. It needs only a similar modification to adapt it to the use required here.

24. The God whom Paul announced is the Maker of all things, and, as such, necessarily distinct from their false gods. That is the point of connection between this verse and the preceding.—**This one** (by his right as Creator) **being the Lord,** Sovereign, **of heaven and earth.** It was self-evident, therefore, that he was not to be confounded with any of their idols, whose existence was limited by the space which they occupied.—**Made with hands** is contrasted with that made the world, etc.— **In temples.** The statues or images were kept in the recesses of the temple.—**Dwelleth.** The mass of the heathen in practice make no difference between the symbol and its object; the block was the god. (Comp. 19 : 26.)

25. The apostle illustrates the character of the true God still further by another contrast between him and the deities of the heathen. He is independent of his creatures; he needs

though he needed any thing, seeing *he giveth to all life, and breath, and all things;
26 And hath made of one blood all nations of men for to dwell on all the face of the earth, and hath de-

though he needed any thing, seeing he himself giv-
26 eth to all life, and breath, and all things; and he made of one every nation of men for to dwell on all

a Gen. 2 : 7 ; Num. 16 : 22 ; Job 12 : 10 ; 27 : 3 ; 33 : 4 ; Isa. 42 : 5 ; 57 : 16 ; Zech. 12 : 1.

nothing from them; they can earn no merit by serving him.—**And** (after a preceding negative) **he is not ministered unto by human hands,** or **hands of men. Human** is a more correct reading than **of men** (T. R.). The verb here implies more than mere worship. The heathen considered it meritorious to lavish wealth on the temples and shrines of their idols; they brought to them costly gifts, and even offerings of food and drink, as if they stood in need of such things, and could be laid under obligation to their worshippers. The prayer of Chryses, priest of Apollo (*Il.,* 1. 37, *sq.*), expresses the true spirit of heathenism in this respect:

"If e'er with wreaths I hung thy sacred fane,
Or fed the flames with fat of oxen slain,
God of the silver bow! thy shafts employ:
Avenge thy servant, and the Greeks destroy."

—**As if needing something besides**—*i. e.* (note the compound, προσδεόμενος) out of himself as necessary to his perfection.—**Since he himself gives. Himself** is emphatic as opposed to the idea that his creatures are able to give to him.—**The whole**—*i. e.* of the things which they enjoy. In such an expression, the article (τά) restricts the adjective to the class of objects intimated by the preceding words or the context. Some editors omit the article here. (Comp. Rom. 8 : 32; 1 Cor. 9 : 22; Phil. 3 : 8, etc.) But in most of these passages, too, the manuscripts fluctuate.

26. And he made of one blood every nation of men that they should dwell. This is the more obvious view of the construction, and is the one which has been generally adopted (so several of the best critics (Kuin., De Wet., Mey., Alf.) regard **made** here as an instance of its use with an accusative and infinitive, like that in Matt. 5 : 32; Mark 7 : 37, and translate: **and he caused every nation of men** (sprung) **from one blood to dwell. To dwell** (κατοικεῖν) connects itself more easily in this way, it is true, with the rest of the sentence; but the facility thus gained renders the expression hard at **of one blood;** so that we must supply a word to make the thought flow smoothly. [Lach., Tsch., Treg., West. and Hort, and Anglo-Am. Revisers omit the word *blood* (αἵματος) as an addition to the text. It is wanting in ℵ A B and other documents.—A.H.]

The main idea, beyond question, is that God has created the entire human race from a common stock; and the more prominent way, therefore, in which the translation first stated brings forward this proposition appears to me to be a reason for preferring it. It is an objection to the other mode that it assigns a too subordinate place to the principal thought. But why does the apostle single out thus the universal brotherhood of the race? Olshausen says it was intended as a reproof to the Athenians for their contempt of the Jews; Meyer, Neander, De Wette, and others consider it as directed essentially against the polytheism of the heathen. If all are the children of a common parent, then the idea of a multiplicity of gods from whom the various nations have derived their origin, or whose protection they specially enjoy, must be false. The doctrine of the unity of the race is closely interwoven with that of the unity of the divine existence. This more comprehensive view of the meaning, however, does not exclude the other, since, if all nations have the same Creator, it would at once occur that nothing can be more absurd than the feeling of superiority and contempt with which one affects to look down upon another. As the apostle had to encounter the prejudice which was entertained against him as a Jew, his course of remark was doubly pertinent, if adapted, at the same time, to remove this hindrance to a candid reception of his message.—**To dwell** (κατοικεῖν) is the infinitive of design. The various lands which the different families of mankind occupied, with all the advantages connected with their position, God had assigned to them. (Comp. Deut. 32 : 8 ; Ps. 115 : 16.) Yea, he had proceeded from the very first with a view to their welfare. He designed, in creating men, that they should inhabit and possess the earth as their own; that they should all of them enjoy the manifold blessings allotted to them in the various places of their abode. It was to him that they were indebted for what they enjoyed, and not to accident or their own enterprise or the favor of some imaginary god. The remark, made as applicable to all lands, has its justification in the fact that, notwithstanding the inequalities which diversify the condition of nations, they have severally their peculiar advantages; it is natural for every people to esteem their own

termined the times before appointed, and *a*the bounds of their habitation;
27 *b*That they should seek the Lord, if haply they might feel after him, and find him, *c*though he be not far from every one of us:

the face of the earth, having determined *their* appointed seasons, and the bounds of their habitation;
27 that they should seek God, if haply they might feel after him, and find him, though he is not far from

a Deut. 32 : 8....b Rom. 1 : 20....c ch. 14 : 17.

country—in some respects, at least—as the best.[1] But the remark was specially aimed, beyond doubt, at the feeling of self-congratulation with which the Athenians were prone to contemplate the peculiar felicity of their own position, their national renown, their past and present prosperity. This view of the meaning prepares the way for the thought which is next introduced.—**Having fixed the appointed seasons and limits of their abode.** The second participle repeats the idea of the first, not superfluously, but with the evident effect of affirming it more strongly. (The approved reading is προστεταγμένους, rather than προτεταγμέ-νους, T. R.) The apostle, by adding this, admonishes the Athenians that they, like every other people, had not only received their peculiar advantages from the common Creator, but that they could hold them only during the continuance of his good-will and favor. In assigning to the nations their respective abodes he had fixed both the *seasons* of their prosperity and the *limits* of their territory—*i. e.* it was he who decided *when* and *how long* they should flourish and *how far* their dominion should extend. We have the same idea exactly in Job 12 : 23. The remark was adapted both to rebuke their spirit of self-elation and to warn them of the danger of slighting a message from him who had their destiny so perfectly at his command. Some explain these last words as referring to the limits which God has assigned to the lives of men individually : they have their appointed seasons and bounds, beyond which they cannot pass. But that idea lies out of the present circle of view, as the subject of discourse here relates to nations, and not to individuals. It is also philologically inadmissible, since **their** can naturally refer to **men** only as connected with **every nation.**—The anti-polytheistic aim, which forms to such an extent the ground-tone of the discourse, is to be recognized, perhaps, also in this part of it. The separation of men into so many different nations might seem to oppose the idea of their common parentage; that separation itself is therefore represented by the apostle as having been contemplated in the divine plan.—It will be observed that what the apostle affirms in

this verse as true of God is also intended to be denied in regard to polytheism. The conception, therefore, thus brought before the minds of his heathen auditors was a vast one. All that power exerted in giving existence to men controlling their destiny, exalting entire nations or casting them down, which they had parcelled out among such an infinity of gods, they are now led to concentrate in a single possessor; they obtain the idea of one infinite Creator and Ruler.

27. To seek (ζητεῖν), telic, **that they should seek.** This infinitive attaches itself more particularly to the part of the sentence which commences at **should dwell,** and states the moral object which God had in view with reference to men in making such provision for their convenience and happiness. It was that they might be led by such tokens of his goodness **to seek him**—*i. e.* a more perfect knowledge of him and of their obligations to him. Some, on the contrary, make the infinitive depend almost wholly on the clause just before, and find the connection to be this—that, excited by the proofs of his power, as manifested in the varying fortunes of nations, *they should seek,* etc. But, as already explained, the controlling idea in that clause is that of the goodness of God (subject, as to its continuance, to the divine pleasure); while that of his power, as displayed in the infliction of judgments, is only incidentally involved. Again, that clause is a subordinate one, as its structure shows, and that it should break off *should seek* so much from the main part of the sentence would be violent.—**If perhaps they might feel after him and find him. Feel after** (ψηλαφήσειαν) denotes, properly, the motions of a blind man who gropes along after an object in the dark. On the peculiar Æolic termination, see W. § 13. 2. d; K. § 116. 9; B. § 103. marg. 14. This verb is chosen, as well as the problematical form of the expression (εἰ ἄραγε), because the apostle would concede the comparative indistinctness of the light which the heathen have to guide them.—**Although indeed.** This clause is added to show that the concession just made was not intended to exculpate the heathen for their estrangement from God.

[1] Tacitus has recognized this principle in his fine remark (*Germ.*, § 2) : " Informem terris, asperam cælo, *nisi si patria sit.*"

28 For [a]in him we live, and move, and have our being; [b]as certain also of your own poets have said, For we are also his offspring.

29 Forasmuch then as we are the offspring of God, [c]we ought not to think that the Godhead is like unto gold, or silver, or stone, graven by art and man's device.

30 And [d]the times of this ignorance God winked at; but [e]now commandeth all men every where to repent:

28 each one of us: for in him we live, and move, and have our being; as certain even of your own poets have said, For we are also his offspring. Eeing

29 have said, For we are also his offspring. Being then the offspring of God, we ought not to think that [1]the Godhead is like unto gold, or silver, or

30 stone, graven by art and device of man. The times of ignorance therefore God overlooked; but now he [2]commandeth men that they should all everywhere

a Col. 1 : 17; Heb. 1 : 3....*b* Tit. 1 : 12....*c* Isa. 40 : 18....*d* ch. 14 : 16; Rom. 3 : 25....*e* Luke 24 : 47; Tit. 2 : 11, 12; 1 Pet. 1 : 14; 4 : 3.——1 Or, *that which is divine*....2 Some ancient authorities read *declareth to men.*

Although so benighted as to be compelled to grope for the object of their search, it was still within reach; they had not, after all, so far to go for a knowledge of God that they might not find it if they would. (Compare the sentiment with 14 : 17, and especially with Rom. 1 : 20.)

28. We live and move and exist. The different verbs present the idea on every side. We derive our existence solely from God; we depend on him every instant for life, activity, being itself. Without him we should neither continue to live, nor be such as we are, nor have been at all. From creatures thus dependent the evidence of a creator cannot be very deeply hidden, if they have only a disposition to seek for it.—**As also**—*i. e.* the sentiment is not only true, but has been acknowledged.—**Among you**—*i. e.* Greeks, in distinction from Jews; not Athenians, in distinction from other Greeks.—**For his offspring also are we.** Derivation implies dependence. The creature cannot exist apart from the Creator. The apostle brings forward the citation correctly, therefore, as parallel in sentiment to **in him we live,** etc. He quotes it as an avowal that we owe our being and its preservation to a higher Power; the mythological idea of Jupiter does not enter into the meaning.[1] The genitive article (τοῦ) stands here for the pronoun. (W. § 17. 1; S. § 94. 1.) The words form the first half of a hexameter, and are found in Aratus, a Cilician poet, who flourished about B. c. 270. The celebrated hymn of Cleanthes to Jupiter (v. 5) contains almost the same words —viz. *for we are offspring of thee.* The same idea, variously expressed, occurs in several other Greek writers. The form of the citation the apostle took, undoubtedly, from Aratus, but says **certain have said,** because he would generalize the idea as if he had said, The truth is so plain that even your poetry recognizes it. (See on v. 18.) According to some, he uses

the plural because he had in mind other passages where the thought is found, or, according to others, because he inferred that so obvious a remark must be a common one. **For also,** as Meyer observes correctly, has no logical connection with Paul's speech, but is to be viewed merely as a part of the citation, which it was necessary to retain on account of the verse.

29. Forasmuch, then, or **since, therefore, we are the offspring of God.** The inference drawn here is that idolatry is supremely absurd, inasmuch as it makes that which is destitute of life, motion, intelligence, the source of these attributes to others. (Comp. Isa. 44 : 9, *sq.*)—In **we ought** Paul connects himself with them, and thus softens the rebuke.—**A thing graven** stands in apposition with the nouns which precede—*i. e.* the state or form of the materials just enumerated, artificially wrought.

30. The relation of this verse and the one following to the preceding verse is this: Since such is the nature of idolatry, you must **therefore** (οὖν) repent of it, because God now lays upon you his command to this effect, in view of the retributions of a judgment to come. The most important word here is **winked at** (ὑπεριδών). It does not occur further in the New Testament, but is found often in the Septuagint, where it signifies "to neglect," which is its proper classical sense, then "to despise," but especially "to suffer to pass as if unnoticed," "to withhold the proof of noticing a thing which is, at the same time, a matter of distinct knowledge"—a frequent sense of the Hebrew *'alam* in Hiphil and Hithpael. (See Deut. 22 : 3, 4, etc.) In this last signification the verb represents perfectly the apostle's meaning here. God had hitherto permitted the heathen to pursue their own way without manifesting his sense of their conduct, either by sending to them special messengers to testify

[1] No more than in the words of Milton:

"Fame is no plant that grows on mortal soil;
  *   *   *   *   *   *
But lives and spreads aloft by those pure eyes,
And perfect witness of all-judging Jove."

31 Because he hath appointed a day, in the which *he will judge the world in righteousness by *that* man whom he hath ordained; *whereof* he hath given assurance unto all *men*, in that *b*he hath raised him from the dead.

32 ¶ And when they heard of the resurrection of the dead, some mocked: and others said, We will hear thee again of this *matter*.

33 So Paul departed from among them.

34 Howbeit certain men clave unto him, and believed: among the which *was* Dionysius the Areopagite, and a woman named Damaris, and others with them.

31 repent: inasmuch as he hath appointed a day, in the which he will judge *the world in righteousness *by *the man whom he hath ordained; whereof he hath given assurance unto all men, in that he hath raised him from the dead.

32 Now when they heard of the resurrection of the dead, some mocked; but others said, We will hear thee concerning this yet again. Thus Paul went out from among them. But certain men clave unto him, and believed: among whom also was Dionysius the Areopagite, and a woman named Damaris, and others with them.

a ch. 10 : 42; Rom. 2 : 16; 14 : 10....*b* ch. 2 : 24.——1 Gr. *the inhabited earth*....2 Gr. *in*....3 Or, *a man.*

against it, as he did to the Jews, or by inflicting upon them at once the punishment deserved. The idea is virtually the same, therefore, as that of **suffered** (εἰασε), in 14 : 16, and **gave them up** (παρέδωκεν), in Rom. 1 : 24. To understand **overlooked** (ὑπεριδών) as meaning that God would not judge or punish the heathen for the sins committed in their state of idolatry would be at variance with Paul's theology on this subject as he has unfolded it in Rom. 1 : 20 ; 2 : 11, *sq.* Not only so, but the repentance which the apostle now calls upon them to exercise presupposes their guilt.

31. Because states the reason why the heathen also, as well as others, must repent: they could not, without this preparation, be safe in the day of righteous judgment which awaited them.—**In** (the person of) **the man whom he appointed. Man** omits the article, because a definite clause follows. (W. § 21. 4; S. § 89. 3.) The dative of the pronoun (ᾧ) stands, by attraction, for the accusative.—**Having afforded assurance to all,** confirmation—viz. of a judgment to come: It is impossible to say just how much the apostle intended to represent as proved by the resurrection of Christ. He himself referred to it, undoubtedly, in the first place, as establishing the possibility of such a resurrection of all men from the dead as was involved in his doctrine of a general judgment; but whether he had yet developed this doctrine so far that the Athenians perceived already this bearing of the fact is uncertain. It was enough to excite their scorn to hear of a single instance of resurrection. Again, the resurrection of Christ from the dead confirms the truth of all his claims ; and one of these was that he was to be the Judge of men. (See John 5 : 28, 29.) But whether the apostle meant to extend the argument to these and other points we cannot decide, as he was so abruptly silenced.

32-34. PAUL IS INTERRUPTED, AND LEAVES THE ASSEMBLY.

32. The apostle was heard with attention until he came to speak of the resurrection, when, at the announcement of a doctrine

which sounded so strangely to the ears of the Athenians, some of them broke forth into expressions of open contempt.—**A resurrection of the dead.** Both nouns omit the article in this frequent combination, except in 1 Cor. 15 : 42. (W. § 19.) As we do not know how much of Paul's idea the Athenians had apprehended, it is doubtful whether we are to take the plural here as generic or numerical—*i. e.* whether Christ merely be meant, or men in general.—**We will hear thee again concerning this** —viz. matter. Not so naturally masc., with reference to **him,** in v. 31. It is disputed whether we are to understand this as said seriously, or as a courteous refusal to hear anything further from him. The latter is the prevalent view : and so Kuinoel, Hemsen, De Wette, Meyer, Bloomfield, Conybeare and Howson. The manner in which Paul now left the assembly, the immediate termination of his labors at Athens, and the adversative **but** (δέ), in v. 34, favor this interpretation. Such a mode of speaking, too, was entirely consonant to the Athenian character. Calvin, Grotius, Rosenmüller, Alford, are among those who impute a serious meaning to the language.

33. So—lit. **and thus ;** *i. e.* after these events, or with such a result. (Comp. 20 : 11; 28 : 14.)—**From among them**—*i. e.* of those whom he had addressed, not from the city. (Comp. 18 : 1.)

34. Howbeit, rather **but certain** (Mey., De Wet.), appears to be contrasted in the writer's mind with what is stated in v. 32 respecting the effect of Paul's speech ; the favorable is opposed to the unfavorable. Yet the conjunctive (δέ) may be continuative.—**Clave,** etc., not adhering, but **joining,** attaching, themselves, **to him.—The Areopagite**—*i. e.* one of the judges in the court of the Areopagus. The number of these judges varied at different times. Eusebius and other ancient writers say that this Dionysius became afterward bishop of the church at Athens and ended his life as a martyr.—**And a woman,** not the wife of Dionysius, as some have said, for the article

CHAPTER XVIII.

A FTER these things Paul departed from Athens, and came to Corinth; 2 And found a certain Jew named ^aAquila, born in Pontus, lately come from Italy, with his wife Priscilla;	1 AFTER these things he departed from Athens, 2 and came to Corinth. And he found a certain Jew named Aquila, a man of Pontus by race, lately come

a Rom. 16 : 3 ; 1 Cor. 16 : 19 ; 2 Tim. 4 : 19.

and pronoun would then have been added (comp. 5 : 1), or at least the article. (Comp. 24 : 24.) It has been inferred, from her being singled out thus by name, that she was a woman of rank, but beyond this nothing is known of her.

1-11. ARRIVAL OF PAUL AT CORINTH, AND HIS LABORS THERE.
1. From Athens. Wieseler limits the apostle's stay at Athens to fourteen days. The estimate is necessarily conjectural. It is certain that, although Paul spent the most of the two next years in Corinth and the vicinity, he did not direct his steps again to that city. On his third missionary-tour he came once more into this part of Greece, but at that time passed by Athens, certainly once and again, without repeating his visit thither. [If it be asked, Why did he not return again and again to this beautiful city, "the eye of Greece," the home of art and philosophy and liberal thought? the only answer which his character allows is this : The people of other cities were more likely to welcome the gospel. "It is a serious and instructive fact that the mercantile populations of Thessalonica and Corinth received the message of God with greater readiness than the highly-educated and polished Athenians." (See Conybeare and Howson, vol. i. p. 381 : C. Scribner, 1854.)—A. H.]—**To Corinth.** The distance from Athens to Corinth by land is about forty-five miles. The summit of the Acropolis

CORINTH AND ACROCORINTHUS.

of the one city can be distinctly seen from that of the other. **Came** does not show how Paul

travelled. The voyage, says Wieseler, could be made easily in two days. A Greek seaman informed the writer that with a very fair wind he had made the passage in three hours, though on the average in five or six hours ; that in bad weather he had been five days on the way. The steamers between the Piræus and Kalimaki, the eastern port of the modern Corinth, occupy usually four hours.— *Corinth* at this period was the seat of the Roman proconsulate for Achaia, or the southern province of Greece. "In consequence of its situation," says Neander, "this city furnished a very important central point for the extension of the gospel in a great part of the Roman Empire ; and hence Paul remained here, as in other similar places, a longer time than was otherwise usual for him."

2. Aquila. The nominative is *Aquilas* ('Ακύλας, v. 26). **Aquila** and **Priscilla,** or **Prisca** (Rom. 16:3), were Roman names, and it was common for Jews to assume such names when they lived out of Palestine. (See on 13 : 9.) That Aquila was born in Pontus harmonizes with 2 : 9 and 1 Pet. 1 : 1, for we see from those passages that Jews resided in that country. As we have no account of his conversion at Corinth, the probability is that Aquila embraced the gospel at Rome. So Hemsen, Olshausen, Neander, Wieseler, and others conclude. Some allege **a certain Jew** as proof that he was still unconverted (Mey., De Wet.) ; but he is introduced in that manner on account of what follows. The notice apprises us that he was one of the **all Jews** whom the decree banished. At this early period no distinction would be made between Jews and Jewish Christians. Aquila accompanied Paul to Ephesus (vv. 18, 26), and was still there when the apostle wrote the First Epistle to the Corinthians (1 Cor. 16 : 19). We find him at Rome again when Paul wrote the Epistle to the Romans (Rom. 16 : 3, sq.), and at a still later period at Ephesus a second time (2 Tim. 4 : 19). The nature of his business (v. 3) led him frequently to change the place of his residence.—**Because Claudius had ordered,** etc. Luke refers unquestionably to the edict mentioned by Suetonius (*Claud.,* c. 25) : "Judæos, impulsore Chresto, assidue tumultu- antes Roma expulit" ["The Jews, constantly

(because that Claudius had commanded all Jews to depart from Rome:) and came unto them.

3 And because he was of the same craft, he abode with them, *and wrought: for by their occupation they were tentmakers.

4 *And he reasoned in the synagogue every sabbath, and persuaded the Jews and the Greeks.

5 And *when Silas and Timotheus were come from Macedonia, Paul was *pressed in the spirit, and testified to the Jews *that Jesus was Christ.

from Italy, with his wife Priscilla, because Claudius had commanded all the Jews to depart from Rome:

3 and he came unto them; and because he was of the same trade, he abode with them, and they wrought; 4 for by their trade they were tentmakers. And he reasoned in the synagogue every sabbath, and *persuaded Jews and Greeks.

5 But when Silas and Timothy came down from Macedonia, Paul was constrained by the word, testi-

a ch. 20 : 34; 1 Cor. 4 : 12; 1 Thess. 2 : 9; 2 Thess. 3 : 8....b ch. 17 : 2....c ch. 17 : 14, 15....d Job 32 : 18; ch. 17 : 3; ver. 28.
——1 Gr. *sought to persuade.*

making disturbance, Chrestus being the instigator, he expelled them from Rome"]. Neander remarks on that passage as follows: "We might suppose that some factious Jew then living, of this name, one of the numerous class of Jewish freedmen in Rome, was intended. But as no individual so universally known as the Chrestus of Suetonius seems to have been considered by that writer is elsewhere mentioned, and as *Christos* (Χριστος) was frequently pronounced *Chrestos* (Χρηστός) by the pagans, it is quite probable that Suetonius, who wrote half a century after the event, throwing together what he had heard about the political expectations of a Messiah among the Jews and the obscure and confused accounts which may have reached him respecting Christ, was thus led to express himself in a manner so vague and indefinite" (*Church History,* vol. i. p. 49). The Roman historian does not mention the year of that expulsion, and we may suppose it to have been about A. D. 52, in accordance with our plan of chronology. **Lately** shows that it was still a recent event when Paul arrived at Corinth. Some writers would identify this decree with that *De mathematicis Italia pellendis* which Tacitus mentions. (*Ann.,* 12. 52.) The *mathematici,* or, as they are called, *Chaldæi,* were banished on the ground of their aiding conspirators against the emperor by the use of their art as astrologers. Wieseler (*Chronologie,* p. 121, *sq.*) argues that the Jews may have been confounded with that class of men, and were consequently banished by the same decree. If that point were established, it would furnish a striking confirmation of the correctness of our chronology; for the edict to which Tacitus refers can be shown to have been published in A. D. 52. But it must remain uncertain whether the two events have any chronological connection with each other.

3. Wrought, labored for his subsistence. He reminds the Corinthians of this fact in 1 Cor. 9 : 6, *sq.,* and 2 Cor. 11 : 7, *sq.*—**For they were tentmakers as to the trade,** or (with τῇ τέχνῃ, according to Lchm., Tsch.) [also Treg., West. and Hort, Anglo-Am. Revisers.

with א A B E L P, certainly the true reading.— A. II.] **in respect to the trade** (which they had). The accusative (τὴν τέχνην) would be a limiting accusative like **in like manner** (τὸν τρόπον) in Jude, v. 7. (W. § 32. 6 ; K. § 279. 7.) The Jews, more especially after the Exile, held the mechanic arts in high estimation. It was a proverb among them that the father who neglected to bring up his son to a trade taught him to be a thief. The composition of **tentmakers** (σκηνοποιοί) indicates a definite sense. It is difficult to see why some should suppose it to mean *manufacturers of tent-cloth.* It has not been shown that the usage differed from the etymology. Tent-making was a common trade in Cilicia, the native country of the apostle. A coarse species of goat's hair, called *cilicium,* was produced there in great abundance, and was much used for that purpose. A person accustomed to work on that material could work, doubtless, on any other. Paul had acquired the trade, in all probability, during his boyhood, while he lived at Tarsus.

4. Reasoned, or **discoursed** (διελέγετο, imperf.), from week to week; whereas **discoursed** (διελέχθη, aorist), in v. 19, refers to a single occasion.—**Greeks**—*i. e.* Greek proselytes who attended the synagogue. (Comp. 13 : 43; 14 : 1.) The apostle had not yet addressed himself to the heathen. (See v. 6.)

5. In Now when [or as] they came down, when (ὡς) is not merely temporal (Alf.), but represents the **was pressed** etc. as immediately consequent on the arrival of the two friends.—**Macedonia** denotes here the Roman province of that name, comprising Northern Greece as distinguished from Achaia, or Southern Greece. (See on v. 1.) It is left uncertain, therefore, from what particular place Silas and Timothy arrived at this time. (Comp. on v. 16.)—**Was pressed, or was engrossed** (lit. **held together), with the word** (Vulg., Kuin., Olsh., De Wet., Bmg., Rob.). The arrival of his associates relieved him from anxiety which had pressed heavily upon him (comp. 1 Thess. 3 : 6, *sq.*), and he could now devote himself with unabated energy to his

6 And *a*when they opposed themselves, and blasphemed, *b*he shook *his* raiment, and said unto them, *c*your blood *be* upon your own heads; *d*I *am* clean: *e*from henceforth I will go unto the Gentiles.

7 ¶ And he departed thence, and entered into a certain *man's* house, named Justus, *one* that worshipped God, whose house joined hard to the synagogue.

8 *f* And Crispus, the chief ruler of the synagogue, believed on the Lord with all his house; and many of the Corinthians hearing believed, and were baptized.

9 Then *g*spake the Lord to Paul in the night by a vision, Be not afraid, but speak, and hold not thy peace:

10 *h*For I am with thee, and no man shall set on

6 fying to the Jews that Jesus was the Christ. And when they opposed themselves, and 1blasphemed, he shook out his raiment, and said unto them, Your blood *be* upon your own heads; I am clean: from
7 henceforth I will go unto the Gentiles. And he departed thence, and went into the house of a certain man named Titus Justus, one that worshipped God,
8 whose house joined hard to the synagogue, And Crispus, the ruler of the synagogue, 2believed in the Lord with all his house; and many of the Corinth-
9 ians hearing believed, and were baptized. And the Lord said unto Paul in the night by a vision, Be
10 not afraid, but speak, and hold not thy peace: for I

a ch. 13 : 45 ; 1 Pet. 4 : 4....*b* Neh. 5 : 13 ; Matt. 10 : 14 ; ch. 13 : 51....*c* Lev. 20 : 9, 11, 12 ; 2 Sam. 1 : 16 ; Ezek. 18 : 13 ; 33 : 4....*d* Ezek. 3 : 18, 19 ; 33 : 9 ; ch. 20 : 26....*e* ch. 13 : 46 ; 28 : 28....*f* 1 Cor. 1 : 14....*g* ch. 23 : 11....*h* Jer. 1 : 18, 19 ; Matt. 28 : 20.——1 Or, *railed* ....2 Gr. *believed the Lord.*

work. He had the support, also, of their personal co-operation. We see from 2 Cor. 1 : 19 that Silas and Timothy took an active part in the proclamation of the gospel at Corinth. We see also from 1 Cor. 2 : 3, where the apostle says that he was among the Corinthians "in weakness and in fear and much trembling," that he was in a state of mind to need urgently the presence and sympathy of such coadjutors. Some say it means simply that Silas and Timothy found Paul employed thus anxiously when they arrived (Mey., Alf.) ; but, unless they had something to do with the fact, it would be unimportant whether it occurred before or after their coming : its interest, in that case, lay wholly in its being a part of the apostle's experience. The common text has **by the Spirit** after **was engrossed : he was impelled by the Spirit,** or **by his own spirit,** his fervent zeal. (Comp. v. 25.) The evidence decides for **the word** (τῷ λόγῳ) as the original term (Grsb., Mey., Tsch.).

6. But opposing themselves is not to be taken as explanatory of **was engrossed** (against Mey.), but as describing the conduct of the Jews occasioned by the apostle's *being engrossed.*—**Blaspheming,** sc. his words, message. (Comp. 13 : 45 ; 19 : 9.)—**Shaking out his garments**—*i. e.* the dust upon them—as a witness against them. For the significancy of the act, see on 13 : 51.—**Your blood**—*i. e.* the consequences of your guilt. (Comp. 20 : 26 ; Ezek. 33 : 5.)—**Upon your head**—*i. e.* let it come. (Comp. Matt. 23 : 35.)—**I am pure,** have discharged my duty. Some point the text so as to read, **pure I henceforth will turn unto the Gentiles** (Lchm., Alf.). The two clauses utter the idea more forcibly than one, and are better suited to so grave a declaration. (Comp., also, 20 : 26 and Matt. 27 : 24.) On the nature of this desertion of the Jews, see on 13 : 46.

7. Having departed from there—*i. e.* the

synagogue (see v. 4), not from the city or from the house of Aquila.—**Went into the house of a certain Justus.** The meaning is, not that he left Aquila and went to lodge with Justus (Alf.), but that he preached in future at the house of the latter, which was so much the more convenient because it was near the synagogue where they had been accustomed to assemble. Paul pursued precisely the same course at Ephesus. (See 19 : 9.)—**Worshipping God** describes Justus as a foreigner who had embraced Judaism, but was not yet a believer. He opened his house for the use of the Christians, because he had more sympathy with them than with the Jews. His moral position was certainly unique, and it is easy to believe that he soon exchanged it for that of a believer.

8. Crispus was one of the few persons at Corinth whom Paul himself baptized. (See 1 Cor. 1 : 14.)—**Believed with all his house.** Here is another instance in which a whole family received the gospel. (Comp. 16 : 15 ; 1 Cor. 1 : 16.) The Apostolical Constitutions (VII. 46) say that Crispus became Bishop of Ægina. —**The Corinthians** who believed were native Greeks, not Jews at Corinth.—**Believed** is imperfect [denoting a continued act], from the relation of the act to **hearing.**

9. By, or **through, a vision,** as the medium of communication ; a form was seen as well as a voice heard. (Comp. 9 : 12 ; 16 : 9 ; 22 : 18.)—**Fear not.** The form of the imperative implies that he was beginning to despond. (See the note on 10 : 15.)—**Speak**—*i. e.* con- tinue to speak. Observe the use of the subjunctive aorist in the next verb.

10. And no man—lit. **and no one**—**shall attack thee** (telic) **to injure thee**—*i. e.* no one shall attempt it with success (De Wet.) ; or ecbatic, **so as to injure thee.** The infinitive with the genitive article (τοῦ) denotes more commonly a purpose. The Jews made an

thee to hurt thee: for I have much people in this city.

11 And he continued *there* a year and six months, teaching the word of God among them.

12 ¶ And when Gallio was the deputy of Achaia, the Jews made insurrection with one accord against Paul, and brought him to the judgment seat,

13 Saying, This *fellow* persuadeth men to worship God contrary to the law.

14 And when Paul was now about to open *his* mouth, Gallio said unto the Jews, *a* If it were a matter of wrong

am with thee, and no man shall set on thee to harm

11 thee: for I have much people in this city. And he dwelt *there* a year and six months, teaching the word of God among them.

12 But when Gallio was proconsul of Achaia, the Jews with one accord rose up against Paul, and

13 brought him before the judgment-seat, saying, This man persuadeth men to worship God contrary to

14 the law. But when Paul was about to open his mouth, Gallio said unto the Jews, If indeed it were

a ch. 23 : 29 ; 25 : 11, 19.

effort to destroy the apostle after this promise (**v. 12, *sq.***), but were defeated.—**Because I have much people**—*i. e.* many who are appointed to become such. (See 13 : 48 and 15 : 17.) Hence the activity of the apostle must have free scope until they were converted.

11. And he abode a year and six months. It has been questioned whether this designation of time extends merely to the arrest mentioned in v. 12 (Mey.) or embraces the entire sojourn at Corinth. " I regard the latter view," says Wieseler (*Chronologie*, p. 46), " as undoubtedly the correct one. This appears, in the first place, from the particle *and* (τε), which connects this verse in the closest manner with what precedes, and consequently with ' The Lord said, Fear not, but speak and be not silent; . . . and *so* (W. § 53. 2) he abode a year and six months, teaching among them the word of God.' [But the connective τε is not so well attested as δέ. The latter is found in ℵ A B, etc., and adopted by Lach., Tsch., Treg., West. and Hort, and Anglo-Am. Revisers.—A. H.] The main thought of the words which the Lord addresses to Paul in the vision (**vv. 9, 10**) is unquestionably ' Speak in this city, and be not silent,' and accordingly the period of time, in v. 11, during which the apostle obeys this command of Christ, must refer to the *whole* time in which he had spoken at Corinth and was not silent—*i. e.* must include the time until his departure. In the second place, this follows from the general nature of the statement : ' He abode there a year and six months.' (Comp. Luke 24 : 49.) " Anger (p. 63) adopts the same conclusion. De Wette calls it the prevalent view, but prefers the other.—**Among them**, in the city (**v. 10**). (See on 8 : 5.)

12–17. PAUL IS ARRAIGNED BEFORE GALLIO.

12. Gallio was a brother of Seneca, the celebrated moralist. His original name was Novatus. He assumed that of Gallio out of gratitude to a distinguished rhetorician of that name who adopted him as a son. Seneca dedicated his books *De Ira* and *De Vita Beata* to

this brother. In one of his Letters (104) he speaks of Gallio as having resided in Achaia, though he does not mention in what capacity he was there. Luke's narrative represents him as acting a part in striking harmony with his reputed character. He was known among his contemporaries as the "dulcis Gallio." He had the social qualities which make a man a general favorite. " Nemo mortalium," says Seneca, " uni tam dulcis est, quam hic omnibus " [" No mortal is as pleasant to one person as he was to all "] (*Quæst. Nat.*, L. 4. Præf.). Luke's **cared for none of these things**, in v. 17, indicates the easy temper which contributes so much to personal popularity. Gallio, like his brother, was put to death by the murderous Nero.—**Was the deputy**, etc.—lit. **was governing Achaia as proconsul.** This province (see on v. 1) consisted of Hellas and the Peloponnesus. Here, too, we have a striking example of Luke's accuracy. Under Tiberius (Tac., *Ann.*, 1. 76) and Caligula, the two preceding emperors, Achaia had been an imperial province, governed by proprætors. But Claudius had restored it to the Senate (Suet., *Claud.*, c. 25), and under that form of administration its governors were styled proconsuls. Paul was at Corinth in the reign of Claudius. (Comp. the note on 13 : 7.)—**Before the tribunal** (ἐπὶ τὸ βῆμα). The **tribunal** (βῆμα) was a seat or chair from which the Roman magistrates dispensed justice. It was sometimes fixed in one place and was sometimes movable, so as to accommodate the judge, wherever he might wish to hold his court.

13. Contrary to the law, not of the Romans, but of the Jews (comp. **and of your law,** in v. 15); not of both Romans and Jews (Lange), as the charge in that form demanded investigation. What Luke has stated here is a summary of the charge. That the Jews went more into detail is evident from Gallio's reply in v. 13.

14. Wrong and **wicked villany** designate the act perhaps legally and ethically—this, as an offence against morality ; that, as an offence against the state or the personal rights of

or wicked lewdness, O *ye* Jews, reason would that I should bear with you:

15 But if it be a question of words and names, and *of* your law, look ye *to it;* for I will be no judge of such *matters.*

16 And he drave them from the judgment seat.

17 Then all the Greeks took [a]Sosthenes, the chief ruler of the synagogue, and beat *him* before the judgment seat. And Gallio cared for none of those things.

a matter of wrong or of wicked villany, O ye Jews,

15 reason would that I should bear with you: but if they are questions about words and names and your own law, look to it yourselves; I am not

16 minded to be a judge of these matters. And he

17 drave them from the judgment-seat. And they all laid hold on Sosthenes, the ruler of the synagogue, and beat him before the judgment-seat. And Gallio cared for none of these things.

a 1 Cor. 1 : 1.

others.—**I would have suffered you,** would have listened patiently to your complaint; but, the condition in the protasis not being true, he could not now do it. (For ἄν with the aorist indicative in the subordinate clause, see W. ∥ 43. 2; B. ∥ 139. 3. 2; K. ∥ 327. b.) Gallio makes known his decision as a thing settled.

15. Concerning a doctrine (περὶ λόγου) and **names** (ὀνομάτων), because they had accused Paul of teaching that Jesus was the Messiah. —**For I do not wish to be judge of these things.** For (γάρ) (T. R.) is logically correct, but comes from a copyist. It was out of his province to take cognizance· of such questions. The Roman laws allowed the Jews to regulate their religious affairs in their own way. Lysias (23 : 29) and Festus (25 : 19) placed their refusal to interfere on the same ground. —The reply which Luke attributes to Gallio has been justly cited as a mark of that candor which distinguishes the truth. A panegyrist, a dishonest narrator, says Paley, would be too jealous for the honor of his cause to represent it as treated superciliously by those of eminent rank.

16. Drove them away, dispersed them. The verb shows that they left reluctantly, but not that any violence was used. A peremptory refusal, a decisive manner, would be sufficient for the purpose.

17. The interpretation of this passage has influenced the text. Some of the younger manuscripts insert **the Jews** after **all,** as if the Jews, disappointed in their design against the apostle, attempted, as their next resort, to avenge themselves on one of his principal followers. But the evidence for this reading is entirely inadequate; and it is incredible, also, that Luke should mention Sosthenes merely as a ruler of the synagogue, if he had become in fact a Christian. The best authorities have **all** without any appendage, and **the Greeks** in the common editions must be viewed as a gloss, correct as an explanation, but textually spurious. As the Jews could have had no motive for maltreating one of their own number, **all** must be the body of those present, such as the subalterns of the court and the Greeks whom the tumult had drawn together. **Sosthenes** was

probably the successor of Crispus (v. 8), or, as Biscoe conjectures, may have belonged to another synagogue in the city. He appears to have taken an active part in the prosecution; and hence the Greeks, who were always ready to manifest their hatred of the Jews, singled him out as the object of their special resentment. In winking at this, says De Wette, Gallio may have carried his impartiality too far. If he was the Sosthenes who is called "the brother" in 1 Cor. 1 : 1, he must have been converted after this, and have removed to Ephesus. The coincidence in the name is the only reason for supposing the same person to be meant in both places.—**Beat** (ἔτυπτον, imperf.) shows how thorough a beating Sosthenes received. It may not be wronging Gallio to suspect that he looked through his fingers and enjoyed the scene.— **None of these things** (οὐδὲν τούτων) includes most naturally the dispute between the Jews and Christians, as well as the abuse of Sosthenes.—**Was a care to** (ἔμελεν), when used as a personal verb, requires in prose a neuter subject. (K. ∥ 274. R. 1; Mt. ∥ 348. R. 2.) The indifference of Gallio is not mentioned in commendation of him, but as suggesting why the affair had such a termination. Owing to the proconsul's disposition, the Jews were unsuccessful; so far from inflicting any injury on the apostle, their attempt recoiled in disgrace and violence upon themselves. [The narrative of Luke bears the stamp of complete accuracy. Even his remark that **Gallio cared for none of these things** may have been made with no intention of either blaming or commending him. But, in the light of this remark, we cannot suppress the feeling that the easy-going indifference of this amiable ruler to matters of religion (as well as to the abuse of Sosthenes) was inconsistent with any deep moral earnestness. He could not have been, in any true sense, a "seeker after God." He may safely be classed with those who make this world their portion. It is not, therefore, surprising that many interpreters have fixed their minds on the bearing of this remark upon the attitude of Gallio toward religion, and have looked on

18 ¶ And Paul *after this* tarried *there* yet a good while, and then took his leave of the brethren, and sailed thence into Syria, and with him Priscilla and Aquila; having *a*shorn *his* head in *b*Cenchrea: for he had a vow.

18   And Paul, having tarried after this yet many days, took his leave of the brethren, and sailed thence for Syria, and with him Priscilla and Aquila; having shorn his head in Cenchreæ: for he had a

---

a Num. 6 : 18 ; ch. 21 : 24....b Rom. 16 : 1.

---

him as a specimen of those who are careless about God and eternal life.—A. H.]

18–22. PAUL PROCEEDS BY THE WAY OF EPHESUS AND CÆSAREA TO JERUSALEM, AND FROM THERE TO ANTIOCH.

18. Having remained yet many days, after the arrest. Whether the arrest took place at the end of the year and a half mentioned in v. 11, or in the course of that time, is subject, as we have seen, to some doubt. Even if the arrest was subsequent to the year and six months, the *many days* here need not be supposed to extend the sojourn at Corinth beyond a few additional months (Wiesl.). During this period the apostle planted churches in other parts of Achaia, either by his own personal labors or by the instrumentality of his converts. (See 2 Cor. 1 : 1.) It was during this visit at Corinth, also, that Paul wrote the First and Second Epistles to the Thessalonians. That he wrote the first of them here appears from several circumstances: first, Paul had been separated from the Thessalonians but "a short time" (1 Thess. 2 : 17); secondly, Timothy and Silas were with him (1 Thess. 1 : 1), as they were according to Luke (18 : 5); thirdly, the apostle had been lately at Athens (1 Thess. 3 : 1), and whence, also, according to our narrative (18 : 1), he came directly to Corinth; and finally, he writes to the Thessalonians as recent converts whose knowledge was very imperfect. The date of this Epistle, therefore, would be A. D. 52 or 53. (See note on 18 : 23.) If the First Epistle was written at Corinth, the Second must have been written at the same place. Timothy and Silas were still with the apostle (2 Thess. 1 : 1); and, as the object of the Second Epistle was to correct a wrong impression made by the First (comp. 2 Thess. 2 : 1, *sq.*, with 1 Thess. 4 : 16, *sq.*, and 5 : 1, *sq.*), the interval between the two must have been short. **—Having bid adieu** (ἀποταξάμενος) is an Alexandrian sense. (See Lob., *Ad Phryn.*, p. 24.) Among others, he now took leave of Silas, and perhaps of Timothy, though we find the latter with him again at Ephesus (19 : 22). **— Unto Syria,** as his remoter destination; he embarked for Ephesus in the first instance (v. 19). **Having shorn the head** most critics understand of Paul (Chryst., Calv., Neand., Olsh., Hems., De Wet., Win., Wdsth.); some of Aquila

(Grot., Kuin., Wiesl., Mey.). **Paul** (Παῦλος) is the leading subject, and the reader connects the remark spontaneously with him. It is only as an act of reflection, on perceiving that **Aquila** (Ἀκύλας) stands nearer, that the other connection occurs to the mind as a possible one. **And with him Priscilla and Aquila** may intervene between **having shorn** and **Paul,** because the clause is so evidently parenthetic, and because **sailed** has a tendency to draw its several subjects toward itself. It is urged for the other view that Luke has placed the man's name after that of the woman, contrary to the natural order; but that no stress can be laid on that circumstance is clear from Rom. 16 : 3 and 2 Tim. 4 : 19, where the names follow each other in the same manner. Some principle of association, as possibly that of the relative superiority of Priscilla, made it customary to speak of them in that order.—**In Cenchreæ,** which was the eastern port of Corinth, distant about ten miles. A church had been gathered here (Rom. 16 : 1). The modern name is Kikries, a little south of Kalamaki, and under the traveller's eye, therefore, who crosses the isthmus. **—For he had a vow**—*i. e.* one resting upon him; not assumed at this time. This clause states why he shaved his head. The cutting off of the hair was a Jewish practice, and took place at the expiration of a vow, not at the commencement of it. It is an erroneous statement, therefore, that the apostle subjected himself to the vow at this time and went to Jerusalem to obtain absolution from it. Neander would support that opinion from Josephus (*Bel. Jud.*, 2. 15), but he adopts for that purpose an interpretation of the passage which nearly all others reject. The nature of Paul's vow on this occasion is uncertain. It could not have been a strict Nazarite vow—*i. e.* such a vow observed in due form—for a person could absolve himself from such an obligation only at Jerusalem, where his hair, which had grown during the time that he had been a Nazarite, was to be cut off and burnt as an offering in the temple (Num. 6 : 2, *sq.*). (See Jahn's *Archæol.*, ∮ 395.) We have no *account* of any deviation from that rule. Yet it is not unreasonable to suppose that in later times the original institution may have been relaxed or modified—that after the Jews came to be dispersed it was held to be lawful

THE ACTS.

19 And he came to Ephesus, and left them there: but he himself entered into the synagogue, and reasoned with the Jews.

20 When they desired *him* to tarry longer time with them, he consented not;

21 But bade them farewell, saying, *a*I must by all means keep this feast that cometh in Jerusalem: but I will return again unto you, *b*if God will. And he sailed from Ephesus.

22 And when he had landed at Cæsarea, and gone up, and saluted the church, he went down to Antioch.

19 vow. And they came to Ephesus, and he left them there: but he himself entered into the synagogue.

20 and reasoned with the Jews. And when they asked

21 him to abide a longer time, he consented not; but taking his leave of them, and saying, I will return again unto you, if God will, he set sail from Eph-

22 esus. And when he had landed at Cæsarea, he went up and saluted the church, and went down to

a ch. 19 : 21 ; 20 : 16....*b* 1 Cor. 4 : 19 ; Heb. 6 : 3 ; James 4 : 15.

to terminate a Nazarite vow at other places, adhering to the prescribed usages as near as the circumstances allowed. If it was not a vow of this peculiar character, it may have been of the nature of a thank-offering, and not subject to the regulations to which the Nazarite was required to conform. It must be confessed that the present knowledge of Jewish antiquities is not sufficient to clear up fully the obscurity of the passage. It contains, says De Wette, a Gordian knot still untied.

19. Unto Ephesus, which was on the Cayster, not far from its mouth. It could be approached at that time by water, though the site of the ancient city is now two or three miles from the coast. With a favoring wind, the passage from Corinth to Ephesus could be made in two or three days. Cicero mentions that he on one occasion, and his brother Quintus on another, occupied two weeks in passing from Ephesus to Athens (*Ad Attic. Ep.*, 6, 8. 9 ; *ib.*, 3, 9) ; but the voyage in both instances was retarded by extraordinary delays. (See further on 28 : 13.)—**But he himself** (αὐτὸς δέ). This emphasis brings forward Paul again as the prominent person, after the information that his companions stayed at Ephesus. The order of statement outruns the history a little, as occurs in other cases. (Comp. v. 1.) Luke cannot well mean that the apostle separated himself from Priscilla and Aquila and went into the synagogue without them (Mey.). So unimportant a circumstance would not be made so prominent. Nor is it at all probable that **there** (αὐτοῦ) was opposed in the writer's mind to the synagogue as being out of the city (Alf.) ; for in that case some intimation like *without the city* (see 16 : 13), or at least *going out*, would hardly be withheld from the reader.

21. Some critics reject all in this verse from **must** to **Jerusalem** (Bng., Grsb., Neand., Lchm., Tsch.) ; others defend the clause (Olsh., De Wet., Wiesl., Mey., Bmg., Alf.). The words may be doubtful, but with the present evidence should not be separated from the text. As Meyer suggests, they may have been omitted

from not perceiving the reference of *gone up* (ἀναβάς), in v. 22, and consequently any occasion for such haste in prosecuting the journey. —**The coming feast.** It must have been one of the principal feasts which Paul was so anxious to keep at Jerusalem—in all probability, the passover or Pentecost. In either case, we discover here that the apostle made the journey in the spring of the year. Wieseler (p. 48) thinks that it was the later festival, Pentecost, chiefly because Paul embarked at Corinth instead of travelling through Macedonia, as the state of navigation would have rendered expedient earlier in the season.—For **keep**—lit. **do** (ποιῆσαι)—comp. **keep**—lit. **do—the passover** (ποιῶ τὸ πάσχα), in Matt. 26 : 18.—**At Jerusalem.** (See on 8 : 40.)—**But I will return again,** etc. The apostle soon fulfilled that promise (19 : 1).

22. And having landed — lit. **having come down,** from the sea to the land. (Comp. 27 : 5.) — **Cæsarea** was the most convenient seaport in the vicinity of Judea. (See further on 8 : 40.)—**Having gone up**—*i. e.* to Jerusalem (Calv., Neand., Olsh., Mey., De Wet., Wiesl.). This absolute use of the verb occasions no obscurity after the statement respecting Paul's destination in v. 21. A few have understood it as *going up* into the city above the harbor. But to mention that circumstance in addition to the arrival would give to it a singular prominence as contrasted with the general rapidity of the narrative.— **Went down** (κατέβη), at the close of the verse, would be inappropriate to the geographical relation of Cæsarea to Antioch (Neand.).—**The church**—*i. e.* at Jerusalem. It should be noticed that this is the *fourth* journey which Paul has made to that city since his conversion. No doubt he arrived in season to observe the feast, as nothing is said of any disappointment in that respect.—**Into Antioch.** How long the apostle was absent on the tour, which terminated with his return to Antioch, can only be conjectured. The year and six months at Corinth (v. 11) would be likely to constitute the greater portion of the period. Wieseler pro-

23 And after he had spent some time *there*, he departed, and went over *all* the country of ^aGalatia and Phrygia in order, ^bstrengthening all the disciples.

24 ¶ ^cAnd a certain Jew named Apollos, born at Alexandria, an eloquent man, *and* mighty in the scriptures, came to Ephesus.

25 This man was instructed in the way of the Lord; and being ^dfervent in the spirit, he spake and taught

23 Antioch. And having spent some time *there*, he departed, and went through the region of Galatia and Phrygia in order, stablishing all the disciples.

24 Now a certain Jew named Apollos, an Alexandrian by race, ¹a learned man, came to Ephesus; and he

25 was mighty in the scriptures. This man had been ²instructed in the way of the Lord; and being fer-

---

a Gal. 1 : 2; 4 : 14....*b* ch. 14 : 22; 15 : 32, 41....*c* 1 Cor. 1 : 12; 3 : 5, 6; 4 : 6; Tit. 3 : 13....*d* Rom. 12 : 11.——1 Or, *an eloquent man*....2 Gr. *taught by word of mouth.*

---

poses six months as the time occupied between leaving Antioch and the arrival at Troas (16 : 8). He would allow six months, also, for the apostle's labors in Europe before his arrival at Corinth. The time which this estimate allows for the Asiatic part of the tour may be too limited. The apostle visited extensively the churches in Syria and Cilicia, planted new churches in Phrygia and Galatia, and travelled very circuitously throughout his journey between Antioch and Troas. It may be safer to assign a year at least to such varied labors. According to this view, the apostle was absent on his second mission about three years; and if we place his departure early in A. D. 51, he reached Antioch again in the spring or summer of 54. Anger, Wieseler, Meyer, Winer, and others agree in supposing Paul to have arrived in Corinth in the autumn of A. D. 52. The admission of the date fixes the main point in this part of the chronology.

23. DEPARTURE OF PAUL ON HIS THIRD MISSIONARY-TOUR.

23. A certain time. The time now spent at Antioch was apparently short. It was during this time, as most critics suppose, that Peter arrived here and the scene took place between him and Paul, of which we have an account in Gal. 2 : 11, *sq.* (See on 15 : 35.) Neander (*Pflanzung*, i. p. 351) agrees with those who insert the occurrence here. Baumgarten (ii. p. 331) adds himself to the same class. The apostle's *when Peter came*, in Gal. 2 : 11, affords no clue to the time. We may assume that the apostle went forth again to the heathen about the beginning of the year A. D. 55.—**In successive order.** This refers, probably, not to the countries named, but to the different places in them where churches existed. In accordance with the representation on Kiepert's map, we may suppose that Paul went first to Tarsus, thence in a north-western direction through Galatia, and then, turning to the south-west, passed through Phrygia, and so on to Ephesus. That course accounts for Luke's naming Galatia before Phrygia, instead of the order in 16 : 6.

24–28. APOLLOS COMES TO EPHESUS,

AND IS MORE FULLY INSTRUCTED IN THE GOSPEL.

24. Meyer calls this section "a historical episode." Luthardt says that it is entirely germane to the narrative: while Paul labors in Asia, another builds still farther upon the foundation laid by him in Europe.—**Apollos** = Apollonius. As a native of Alexandria he had received, probably, says Neander, "the Jewish-Grecian education peculiar to the learned among the Jews of that city, and had acquired also great facility in the use of the Greek language."—**Eloquent** (λόγιος), (Olsh., De Wet., Mey.), or **learned** (Neand.). The first sense is the best, because **mighty in the scriptures** ascribes to him then a different talent, and because his superior faculty as a speaker appears to have been the reason why some of the Corinthians preferred him to Paul. (See 1 Cor. 1 : 12; 2 : 4; 2 Cor. 10 : 10.) **In the scriptures.** He was familiar with them, and could use them with power as a source of argument and appeal. (See v. 28.) This clause points out the sphere of his eloquence.

25. This one was instructed in the way of the Lord, probably by some disciple of John who had left Judea before the Saviour commenced his public course, or possibly by John himself, whose earlier ministry Apollos may have attended. Some infer from **the things concerning Jesus** that Apollos was aware that Jesus was the Messiah; but the following **knowing,** etc., limits that expression, and, if explained correctly below, excludes a knowledge of that fact. His ignorance in this respect was one of the defects in his religious belief, and at the same time his views of the deeper Christian doctrines must have been meagre in comparison with those possessed by the apostles. For the construction of **way** (ὁδόν), see W. § 32. 5; K. § 281. 2.—**Being fervent in spirit,** zealous in his disposition. It is less correct to understand **spirit** of the Holy Spirit, since that gift appears in the New Testament as the proper fruit and seal of the Christian faith, which Apollos had not yet adopted. (See Gal. 3 : 2.) For other places where *spirit* refers to the mind, comp. 19 : 21;

diligently the things of the Lord, *aknowing only the baptism of John.

26 And he began to speak boldly in the synagogue: whom when Aquila and Priscilla had heard, they took him unto *them*, and expounded unto him the way of God more perfectly.

27 And when he was disposed to pass into Achaia, the brethren wrote, exhorting the disciples to receive him: who, when he was come, *bhelped them much which had believed through grace:

28 For he mightily convinced the Jews, *and that* publicly, *cshewing by the scriptures that Jesus was Christ.

vent in spirit, he spake and taught carefully the things concerning Jesus, knowing only the baptism 26 of John: and he began to speak boldly in the synagogue. But when Priscilla and Aquila heard him, they took him unto them, and expounded unto him 27 the way of God more carefully. And when he was minded to pass over into Achaia, the brethren encouraged him, and wrote to the disciples to receive him: and when he was come, he *1helped them much 28 who had believed through grace: for he powerfully confuted the Jews, *2and that* publicly, shewing by the scriptures that Jesus was the Christ.

CHAPTER XIX.

AND it came to pass, that, while *dApollos was at Corinth, Paul having passed through the upper coasts came to Ephesus: and finding certain disciples,

1 AND it came to pass, that, while Apollos was at Corinth, Paul having passed through the upper country came to Ephesus, and found certain disci-

---

a ch. 19 : 3....b 1 Cor. 3 : 6....c ch. 9 : 22; 17 : 3; ver. 5....d 1 Cor. 1 : 12; 3 : 5, 6.——1 Or, helped much through grace them that had believed....2 Or, shewing publicly

---

John 11 : 33; 13 : 21; Rom. 12 : 11 (probably); 2 Cor. 2 : 12.—**Accurately** (v. 26)—*i. e.* his doctrine was correct as far as his knowledge extended.—**Knowing only the baptism of John,** which differed from that of the apostles mainly in these respects: first, that theirs recognized a Messiah who had come; and secondly, that it was attested by the extraordinary gifts of the Spirit (19:6). Since John, however, taught that the Saviour was about to appear, and that repentance, faith in him, and holiness were necessary to salvation, Apollos, though acquainted only with his teaching, could be said with entire truth to be **instructed in the way of the Lord.** It is not affirmed that he had submitted to John's baptism, but we suppose that from the nature of the case. That he was rebaptized, Luke does not assert; though, if we regard his moral position as analogous to that of the Johannean disciples mentioned in the next chapter, we should infer from what is related there that such was the fact. Meyer considers the cases dissimilar, and denies that Apollos was rebaptized.

26. Began, but did not preach long with such imperfect views. As soon as Aquila and Priscilla heard him they proceeded to instruct him more fully.—The verb (παρρησιάζεσθαι) means to **speak boldly.** He exposed their sins, required them to repent and be prepared for the kingdom of the Messiah. (Comp. Matt. 3 : 2, *sq.*)—**More perfectly,** *more accurately.*

27. Unto Achaia, of which Corinth was the capital. (See on v. 1.) It was that city which he proposed to visit. (Comp. 19 : 1; 1 Cor. 1 : 12; 3 : 4.) What he heard from Priscilla and Aquila may have turned his thoughts to this field of labor.—**They wrote and exhorted** (lit. *exhorting they wrote*). The participle contains the principal idea. (See 1 : 24.) Some supply **him** after **exhorted** (Calv., Kuin.); but

that assigns to the verb and participle different objects and confuses the sentence. Besides, Apollos was not averse to the journey (**was disposed,** βούλομενου), and had no need of exhortation. In 2 Cor. 3 : 1, Paul alludes to this letter of commendation, or to the practice of granting such letters, exemplified in this case of Apollos.—**Contributed** (as a helper) **much to those who have believed,** and still believe. (See W. ½ 40. 4. a.) It is not meant that he confirmed them in their faith as Christians, but that he co-operated with them in their promulgation and defence of the truth. The next verse explains the remark.—**Through grace** belongs to the participle [**had believed**] (De Wet.), not to the verb [**helped**] (Mey.). The natural sense is that which results from the order of the words. The doctrinal idea is that of **the faith which is through him,** in 3 : 16.

28. Powerfully that the Messiah was Jesus, none other than he. (Comp. v. 5.)

1-7. PAUL COMES TO EPHESUS, AND REBAPTIZES CERTAIN DISCIPLES OF JOHN.

1. While Apollos was at Corinth. This notice apprises us that Paul did not arrive at Ephesus till after the departure of Apollos. (Ἀπολλώ—the regular genitive; see 1 Cor. 3 : 4—here rejects ν in the accusative. Comp. 21 : 1. K. ½ 48. R. 1; W. ½ 8. 2.)—**The upper parts,** in the interior, as compared with the coast. The expression may be understood of the mountains on the frontier of Phrygia and Asia, which the apostle would cross on his route.—**Certain disciples.** Luke ascribes to them that character (comp. **when ye believed,** in v. 2), because, though their knowledge was so imperfect, they were sincere; they

2 He said unto them, Have ye received the Holy Ghost since ye believed? And they said unto him, *We have not so much as heard whether there be any Holy Ghost.
3 And he said unto them, Unto what then were ye baptized? And they said, *Unto John's baptism.
4 Then said Paul, *John verily baptized with the baptism of repentance, saying unto the people, that they should believe on him which should come after him, that is, on Christ Jesus.
5 When they heard *this*, they were baptized *in the name of the Lord Jesus.

2 ples: and he said unto them, Did ye receive the Holy Spirit when ye believed? And they said unto him, Nay, we did not so much as hear whether *the 3 Holy Spirit was *given*. And he said, Into what then were ye baptized? And they said, Into John's bap-4 tism. And Paul said, John baptized with the baptism of repentance, saying unto the people, that they should believe on him who should come after him, 5 that is, on Jesus. And when they heard this, they were baptized into the name of the Lord Jesus.

a ch. 8 : 16; see 1 Sam. 3 : 7....*b* ch. 18 : 25....*c* Matt. 3 : 11 ; John 1 : 15, 27. 30 ; ch. 1 : 5 ; 11 : 16 ; 13 : 24, 25....*d* ch. 8 : 16.
——1 Or, *there is a Holy Spirit*

possessed the elements of a true faith, and acknowledged the name of Christ as soon as the apostle made it known to them. It is probable that they were strangers who had just arrived at Ephesus, and when the apostle found them had not yet come in contact with any of the Christians there.

2. For if (εἰ) in a direct question, see on 1 : 6. The inquiry appears abrupt, because we have so broken an account of the circumstances of the case. Undoubtedly, something preceded which led the apostle to suspect that the men entertained inadequate or mistaken views of the gospel.—**The Holy Spirit** here means the **Spirit** as the author of miraculous gifts, as is made evident by v. 6.—**Did ye receive** (note the aorist) **when ye believed?** (ἐλάβετε πιστεύσαντες). The participle refers to the same time as the verb.—**But we did not hear** (when baptized) **even if there be a Holy Spirit.** A negative usually precedes **but not** with this force (= No—on the contrary), but could be omitted with the effect of a more earnest denial. (See W. ⸹ 53. 7.) **The Holy Spirit** must have the meaning in their reply which it had in Paul's question. Hence it is unnecessary and incorrect to supply *given* (δοθέν) or *poured out* (ἐκχυνόμενον) after **be.** (Comp. John 7 : 39.)

3. Unto what, as the object of faith and confession, **therefore, were ye baptized?** —**Unto the baptism of John** should have the sense here which it has in other passages (comp. 1 : 22; 10 : 37; Matt. 3 : 7; Luke 7 : 29, etc.)—viz. the baptism which John administered, or such as he administered. They may have received the rite from John himself, or from some one whom he had baptized, but who had not advanced beyond the point of knowledge at which John's ministry had left his disciples. That Apollos had baptized them is not at all probable; for the presumption is that he had left Ephesus before their arrival (see on v. 1), and because, if he had not, they would have received from him more correct views, after his own better acquaintance with Chris-

tianity. The answer of the men, therefore, was not that they had been baptized unto John as the Messiah, and the idea that their error was that of adhering to him as the Messiah has no support from this expression. That some, however, at a very early period entertained that opinion of John is a fact well established. The Zabians, or Nazoraeans, or Mendaeans, as they are variously called, who were discovered in the East about the middle of the seventeenth century, are supposed to be a remnant of that sect. (See Neand., *Ch. Hist.*, vol. i. p. 376, and *Christian Review*, January, 1855.)

4. Indeed (μέν) after **John,** which some editors reject, is genuine (Mey., Tsch., De Wet.). The reply of Paul is apparently this: *"John indeed preached repentance and a Saviour to come (as you know); but the Messiah whom he announced has appeared in Jesus, and you are now to believe on him as John directed."*—**That is** presents the adversative idea, instead of the ordinary **and** (δέ). (W. ⸹ 63. I. 2. e; K. ⸹ 322. R. 4.)—**Baptized** (ἐβάπτισε) governs **baptism** (βάπτισμα), on the principle of affinity in point of sense. (Comp. Luke 7 : 29. W. ⸹ 32. 2; K. ⸹ 278. 1.)—**Christ** is common before **Jesus,** but is unwarranted here.

5. Now they (whom Paul addressed) **having heard were baptized.** Whether Paul himself or some assistant performed the rite the history does not decide. Their prompt reception of the truth would tend to show that the defect in their former baptism related not so much to any positive error as to their ignorance in regard to the proper object of faith. Some of the older writers maintained that Luke records these words as a continuation of Paul's remark : *Now they* (whom John addressed) *having heard were baptized.* It was the object of such commentators to rescue the passage from those who appealed to it, in order to justify rebaptism. They maintained this exegesis not only against the Anabaptists, but, as Baumgarten mentions, against the Catholics, who disparaged John's baptism for the purpose of exalting the Christian sacraments

6 And when Paul had [a]laid *his* hands upon them, the Holy Ghost came on them; and [b]they spake with tongues, and prophesied.
7 And all the men were about twelve.
8 [c]And he went into the synagogue, and spake boldly for the space of three months, disputing and persuading the things [d]concerning the kingdom of God.
9 But [e]when divers were hardened, and believed not, but spake evil [f]of that way before the multitude, he departed from them, and separated the disciples, disputing daily in the school of one Tyrannus.
10 And [g]this continued by the space of two years;

6 And when Paul had laid his hands upon them, the Holy Spirit came on them; and they spake with tongues, and prophesied. And they were in all about twelve men.
8 And he entered into the synagogue, and spake boldly for the space of three months, reasoning and persuading *as to* the things concerning the kingdom of God. But when some were hardened and disobedient, speaking evil of the Way before the multitude, he departed from them, and separated the disciples, reasoning daily in the school of Tyrannus.
10 And this continued for the space of two years; so

a ch. 6 : 6 ; 8 : 17....*b* ch. 2 : 4 ; 10 : 46....*c* ch. 17 : 2 ; 18 : 4....*d* ch. 1 : 3 ; 28 : 23....*e* 2 Tim. 1 : 15 ; 2 Pet. 2 : 2 ; Jude 10....
f See ch. 9 : 2 ; 22 : 4 ; 24 : 14 ; ver. 23....*g* See ch. 20 : 31.

as distinguished from those of the first dispensation. The Council of Trent, for instance, asserted: "Si quis dixerit baptismum Johannis eandem vim cum baptismo Christi habuisse, Anathema esto" [*i. e.* "If any one shall say that the baptism of John had the same efficacy as the baptism of Christ, let him be anathema."—A. H.] (Sess. VII., *De Baptismo*, C. 1). This interpretation not only sets aside the more obvious meaning for a remote one, but palpably misstates the fact in regard to John's baptism : he did not administer it in the name of Jesus. This view of the passage may be said to be obsolete at present. [**In the name of the Lord Jesus.** Better *into*, or *unto*, *the name of the Lord Jesus*. Luke does not give the formula of Christian baptism, but briefly indicates that by their baptism they were consecrated to the service of the Lord Jesus. (Comp. Gal. 3 : 27 : *For as many of you as have been baptized into Christ have put on Christ*.)—A. H.]

6. Compare this verse with 10 : 44–46.—**With tongues**—*i. e. other* (2 : 4), or *new* (Mark 16 : 17).—For **prophesied,** see on 2 : 17.

7. All the men, *together.* **All** ($\pi \hat{a} s$), in this adverbial sense ($= \tau \grave{o} \ \pi \hat{a} \nu$, $\tau \grave{a} \ \pi \acute{a} \nu \tau a$), occurs especially in connection with numerals. (Comp. 27 : 35.) It is rare to find the adjective with this force before the substantive. (See K. Ausf., *Gr.*, § 489. β; Vig. ed. Herm., p. 135.)—And thus those twelve men who came forward so abruptly in our history disappear as suddenly, leaving us in doubt whence they came, where they had been, and in some respects what particular phase of religious belief they represented. The episode is one of strange interest from the very fact of its suggesting so many questions the solution of which our imperfect knowledge of the first Christian age has put beyond our reach.

8–12. PAUL PREACHES AT EPHESUS, AND CONFIRMS THE WORD BY MIRACLES.

8. For **spake boldly** = *preached boldly*, see on 18 : 26.—**Persuading**—*i. e.* them, *persuading them of the things.* (Comp. 28 : 23.) The

first accusative specifies the aim of the act. (K. § 279. 4.)

9. Divers, or *some*—*i. e.* of the Jews, as results from **synagogue,** in v. 8.—**That way** —lit. *the way; i. e.* of Christian belief and practice ; not concretely, sect, party. (Comp. v. 23; 9 : 2).—**Before**—*i. e.* **in the presence of the multitude.** This attempt to prevent others from believing showed how **hardened** ($\acute{\epsilon} \sigma \kappa \lambda \eta$-$\rho \acute{v} \nu o \nu \tau o$) they were more fully than their own rejection of the gospel.—**Separated the disciples**—*i. e.* from the Jews in the synagogue. —**In the school**—viz. the place where he taught. This **Tyrannus,** otherwise unknown, was probably a teacher of philosophy or rhetoric who occupied the apartment at other hours. Whether he rented it to the Christians or gave them the use of it is uncertain.

10. By the space of two years. These *two years* are exclusive of the three months mentioned in v. 8; for **this** opposes expressly the preaching in the school of Tyrannus to that in the synagogue. It is probable that they are exclusive, also, of the time occupied by the events which took place after v. 21 ; for in 20 : 31, Paul reminds the Ephesians that he had labored *three years* among them ; so that nine months, or six months at least (if we regard *three years* there as a general expression), must be added to the two years and three months mentioned here. The retrospective remark in v. 20 would be a very natural one for the writer to make on the completion of a distinct period.—It was during this abode of Paul at Ephesus, and probably not long after his arrival there, that he wrote the Epistle to the Galatians. In Gal. 4 : 13, Paul speaks of the *former time* ($\tau \grave{o} \ \pi \rho \acute{o} \tau \epsilon \rho o \nu$) when he preached in Galatia ; and hence (taking the expression in its strict import) he had been there twice when he wrote the Epistle. He must have written it, therefore, on his third missionary-tour (at least, not before it), since he founded the Galatian churches on his second tour (see on 16 : 6) and *confirmed* them on his present journey to Ephesus. (See 18 : 23.) Further,

so that all they which dwelt in Asia heard the word of the Lord Jesus, both Jews and Greeks.

11 And ᵃGod wrought special miracles by the hands of Paul:

12 ᵇSo that from his body were brought unto the sick handkerchiefs or aprons, and the diseases departed from them, and the evil spirits went out of them.

13 ¶ ᶜThen certain of the vagabond Jews, exorcists, ᵈtook upon them to call over them which had evil spirits the name of the Lord Jesus, saying, We adjure you by Jesus whom Paul preacheth.

that all they that dwelt in Asia heard the word of 11 the Lord, both Jews and Greeks. And God wrought 12 special ¹miracles by the hands of Paul: insomuch that unto the sick were carried away from his body handkerchiefs or aprons, and the diseases departed 13 from them, and the evil spirits went out. But certain also of the strolling Jews, exorcists, took upon them to name over those who had the evil spirits the name of the Lord Jesus, saying, I adjure you by

---

a Mark 16 : 20; ch. 14 : 3....*b* ch. 5 : 15; see 2 Kings 4 : 29....*c* Matt. 12 : 27....*d* See Mark 9 : 38; Luke 9 : 49.———1 Gr. *powers.*

---

if *so soon*, in Gal. 1 : 6, refers (as, on the whole, I think it does) to the brief interval since Paul was among the Galatians, it follows that he wrote his Epistle to them during the early part of his sojourn at Ephesus. In this city Paul could obtain easily the knowledge of the Galatian heresy which gave occasion to the letter. A partial conclusion may be drawn from another argument. If we are to place Paul's rebuke of Peter between his second and third journeys (see on 18 : 23), he could not have written to the Galatians, at all events, *before* his departure on this tour. The foregoing data are not decisive, but furnish the best-supported opinion. We may refer the Epistle to the year A. D. 56. (See note on 21 : 17.)—**So that all who inhabited Asia**—viz. the Roman province of that name (2:9). Ephesus was the capital of this province, the centre of commerce and religious worship (v. 26), to which the people resorted from all parts of the country. Hence the apostle had an opportunity to preach to a vast number, in addition to those who resided in the city; and at the same time, through the agency of those converted through his labors, he could have introduced the gospel into regions which he did not visit in person. It was but forty years after this that Pliny, in his celebrated letter to Trajan, says, even in reference to the more distant Bithynia: "Multi omnis ætatis, omnis ordinis, utriusque sexûs etiam, vocantur in periculum et vocabuntur. Neque enim civitates tantum, sed vicos etiam atque agros superstitionis istius contagio pervagata est" ["Many of every age, of every rank, and also of either sex, are brought, and will be brought, into peril. For the contagion of this superstition has not only spread through cities, but also through villages and country places."] —A. H.]

11. Special—lit. *not casual; i. e.* uncommon, extraordinary. (Comp. 28 : 2.) As the sequel shows (v. 12), the miracles were remarkable, because they were performed without the personal agency or presence of the apostle. They were not generically different from those wrought on other occasions.—**By**, or *through*, **the hands**

of **Paul,** not as laid upon the sick (some of the results being involuntary on his part), but through his instrumentality.

12. So that (because God so wrought by him) **also**—*i. e.* among other miracles.—**Were brought,** etc.—*i. e.* **were carried from his body,** to which the articles had been touched for the purpose of receiving the healing power that was supposed to reside in him. (See Luke 8 : 46.) They resorted to this course, probably, because the throng was so great that the sick could not be brought directly to the apostle, or in some instances were too infirm to be removed from their houses. [It pleased God to work the miracles through Paul in that way, because it was in that way that the Ephesians expected the miracles, and hence would receive them as a testimony for Paul and his teaching. —A. H.]—**Handkerchiefs** (Lat. *sudaria*)—lit. *sweat-cloths.* They had their name from the use to which they were principally applied.— **Aprons,** such as artisans and servants wore when engaged about their work. This too is a Latin word (*semicinctia*) which had passed into the later Greek. (See on 11 : 26.)—It is evident from **the diseases** and **the evil spirits** that the writer made a distinction between ordinary diseases and those inflicted by evil spirits. (Comp. on 5 : 16; 8 : 7.)

13-17. THE DEFEAT OF CERTAIN JEWISH EXORCISTS.

13. The common text has **certain of the vagabond,** etc. The more approved reading is **certain also of the vagabond,** etc. (Grsb., Tsch., Mey.). **Also** joins **certain** of with Paul, with reference to the act in **to call: they also attempted to call,** as he called.— Not **vagabond** opprobriously, but **wandering** from place to place in the practice of their arts.— **Exorcists.** That was their professed, reputed occupation. They appear to have regarded Paul as one of their own class, but of a higher order. They supposed he had obtained a name more potent than any employed by them, and that by means of it he could perform in reality the wonders to which they merely pretended.—**We adjure,** etc., rather **I adjure you by the Jesus.**

14 And there were seven sons of *one* Sceva, a Jew, *and* chief of the priests, which did so.
15 And the evil spirit answered and said, Jesus I know, and Paul I know; but who are ye?
16 And the man in whom the evil spirit was leaped on them, and overcame them, and prevailed against them, so that they fled out of that house naked and wounded.
17 And this was known to all the Jews and Greeks also dwelling at Ephesus; and *a*fear fell on them all, and the name of the Lord Jesus was magnified.
18 And many that believed came, and *b*confessed, and shewed their deeds.
19 Many of them also which used curious arts brought their books together, and burned them before all *men* : and they counted the price of them, and found *it* fifty thousand *pieces* of silver.

14 Jesus whom Paul preacheth. And there were seven sons of one Sceva, a Jew, a chief priest, who did this.
15 And the evil spirit answered and said unto them, Jesus I *1*know, and Paul I know; but who are ye?
16 And the man in whom the evil spirit was leaped on them, and mastered both of them, and prevailed against them, so that they fled out of that house naked and wounded. And this became known to all, both Jews and Greeks, that dwelt at Ephesus;
17 and fear fell upon them all, and the name of the
18 Lord Jesus was magnified. Many also of them that had believed came, confessing, and declaring their
19 deeds. And not a few of them that practised *2*curious arts brought their books together, and burned them in the sight of all : and they counted the price of them, and found it fifty thousand pieces of silver.

a Luke 1 : 65 ; 7 : 16 ; ch. 2 : 43 ; 5 : 5, 11....*b* Matt. 3 : 6.——1 Or, *recognize*....2 Or, *magical*

For the double accusative, compare Mark 5 : 7; 1 Thess. 5 : 27. (See W. § 32. 4 ; C. § 428.)

14. For the Doric form of the name Sceva (Σκευᾶ), see on 11 : 30.—**And chief of the priests**—lit. **a chief priest,** a priest of the higher class. (See on 4 : 6.) — **Seven.** The numeral is too remote from *certain* (τινές) to be indefinite, **several.** (See on 23 : 23.) — **Which did so.** [This, a participial expression in the Greek] denotes a habit. The next verse relates an instance of their practice.

15. The evil spirit—viz. the one whom they were attempting to exorcise on a certain occasion.—**Jesus I know**—i.e. *the Jesus* (whom you invoke) *I know; i. e.* his authority and power —**and the Paul** (whom you name) **I know** *well* as the servant-messenger of God. (Comp. 16 : 17.) The article is probably significant here, though, as the nouns are proper names, it may be a little uncertain.—**Ye** precedes **who** [in the Greek text], because it takes the emphasis.

16. And the man (impelled by the evil spirit) **leaping upon them.—Overcame,** having overpowered them, **and prevailed**— lit. **was strong**—showed himself such against them, or **both ;** viz. by tearing off their garments and beating them. *Both* is more correct than *them* (Grsb., Mey., Tsch.).—**Naked** need not be taken in its strict sense. It could be applied to those stripped partially of their raiment. (Comp. John 21 : 7.)—**Out of,** or **from out of, that house,** where the transaction took place. The pronoun reveals a more definite scene in the writer's view than he has described.—In the occurrence related here we are to recognize a special design on the part of God. It was important, says Neander, that the divine power which accompanied the gospel should in some striking manner exhibit its superiority to the magic which prevailed so extensively at Ephesus, and which by its apparently great effects deceived and captivated so many. It

would have a tendency to rescue men from those arts of imposture, and prepare their minds for the reception of the truth.

18-20. MANY ARE CONVERTED, AND CONFESS THEIR SINS.

18. And many that believed, or *and many of the believers* (convinced by such evidence)—lit. *of those who have believed,* and still believe. The language ascribes to them a definite character, but does not decide when it began. They were probably new converts (De Wet., Alf.), as the confession made by them would be inconsistent with the life required of those who had been recognized as Christians. They were a different class, also, from those spoken of in the next verse ; hence, not the jugglers themselves, but their dupes—those who had confided in them and been accessory to the wicked delusion.—**Came** (imperf.), one after another. — **Their deeds,** superstitious practices (Olsh., Mey., De Wet.), not their sins in general (Kuin.). It is better to restrict the meaning in this connection, especially as with the other sense the more obvious term would be *sins* (ἁμαρτίας), and not *deeds* (πράξεις).

19. Many of them also, better **and many of those who practised magic arts** —lit. *things overwrought,* curious, recondite.— **Their books,** or **the books** which contained their mysteries—*i. e.* magical signs, formulas of incantations, nostrums, and the like. —**Burned** (imperf.) (κατέκαιον) describes them as throwing book after book into the blazing pile.—**And found,** etc., **and they found,** the sum, **fifty thousand** (*i. e. drachmas*) **of silver money.** It was common in such designations to omit the name of the coin. (See Bernh., *Synt.,* p. 187.) The *Attic drachm* passed at this time among the Jews and Romans for a *denarius,* and was worth about fifteen cents ; so that the books amounted to seventy-five hundred dollars. Some supply *shekel* as the elliptical word, which, reckoning that coin at sixty

20 *So mightily grew the word of God and prevailed.
21 ¶ *After these things were ended, Paul ²purposed
in the spirit, when he had passed through Macedonia
and Achaia, to go to Jerusalem, saying, After I have
been there, ³I must also see Rome.
22 So he sent into Macedonia two of ⁴them that

20 So mightily grew the word of the Lord and prevailed.
21 Now after these things were ended, Paul purposed
in the spirit, when he had passed through Macedonia
and Achaia, to go to Jerusalem, saying, After I have
22 been there, I must also see Rome. And having sent

---

a ch. 6 : 7 ; 12 : 24....b Rom. 15 : 25 ; Gal. 2 : 1....c ch. 20 : 22....d ch. 18 : 21 ; 23 : 11 ; Rom. 15 : 24–28....e ch. 13 : 5.

---

cents, would make the amount four times as great. But as the occurrence took place in a Greek city, and as Luke was not writing for Jews, it is entirely improbable that he has stated the sum in their currency. All books in ancient times were expensive, and especially those which contained secrets or charms held in such estimation,

20. Grew . . . and prevailed, or **grew and was strong,** mighty. The first verb refers to the general extension of the gospel ; the second, to its influence on the conduct of those who embraced it. What precedes illustrated the remark in both respects. [Instead of **the word of God,** the better manuscripts read **the word of the Lord.**—A. H.]—This verse presents a striking coincidence as compared with 1 Cor. 16 : 9. It was here at Ephesus, and about this time, that Paul wrote the First Epistle to the Corinthians. That it was written at Ephesus is certain from 1 Cor. 16 : 8. But Paul visited this city only twice—the first time when he touched here on his way to Jerusalem (18, 19), and again at this present time of his prolonged residence here. He could not have written the Epistle on his first visit, because the church at Corinth, so recently gathered, would not answer then to the character which it bears in the Epistle, and still more decisively because Apollos, who was the head of one of the parties there (1 Cor. 1 : 12), did not proceed to Corinth (18 : 27) till shortly before Paul's second arrival at Ephesus. Again, Paul speaks in 1 Cor. 4 : 17 of having recently sent Timothy to Corinth (comp. 1 Cor. 16 : 10), and here in the Acts (19 : 22) Luke speaks evidently of the same event, which he represents as preparatory to the apostle's intended visit to the same place. As Paul now left Ephesus in the spring of A. D. 57 (see note on 20 : 1), he wrote his First Epistle to the Corinthians a few months before his departure.

21, 22. THE APOSTLE PROPOSES TO LEAVE EPHESUS.

21. A new epoch begins here—viz. that from the end of the year and three months to Paul's departure.—**These things,** up to this time since the arrival at Ephesus, not so naturally those relating merely to the exorcism and its effects.—**Purposed in the spirit,** or **placed in his mind,** purposed. (See on 5 : 4.)—

Macedonia and **Achaia** occur here also in the Roman sense. The order of the names indicates that the apostle intended at this time to have proceeded directly from Corinth to Jerusalem. An unexpected event (see 20 : 3) compelled him to change his plan.—**I must also, sq. It is necessary that I should see also Rome,** not in order to fulfil any revealed purpose of God, but to satisfy his own feelings. He was anxious to visit the believers there, and to preach the gospel in that metropolis of the world. (See Rom. 1 : 11, 14.)—Paley institutes a striking comparison between this verse and Rom. 1 : 13 and 15 : 23–28: "The conformity between the history and the Epistle is perfect. In the first passage of the Epistle we find that a design of visiting Rome had long dwelt in the apostle's mind ; here, in the Acts, we find that design expressed a considerable time before the Epistle was written. In the history we find that the plan which Paul had formed was to pass through Macedonia and Achaia ; after that, to go to Jerusalem ; and when he had finished his visit there, to sail for Rome. When the Epistle was written, he had executed so much of his plan as to have passed through Macedonia and Achaia, and was preparing to pursue the remainder of it by speedily setting out toward Jerusalem ; and in this point of his travels he tells his friends at Rome that when he had completed the business which carried him to Jerusalem he would come to them when he should make his journey into Spain." Nor is the argument to be evaded by supposing the passages to have been adjusted to each other in this manner : "If the passage in the Epistle was taken from that in the Acts, why was Spain put in? If the passage in the Acts was taken from that in the Epistle, why was Spain left out? If the two passages were unknown to each other, nothing can account for their conformity but truth."

22. Timothy was at Corinth when last mentioned (18 : 5). He would be likely to cross over to Ephesus on hearing of Paul's arrival there. But what connection is there between the apostle's sending Timothy into Macedonia and his own purpose to proceed to Achaia? We obtain an answer to that question from 1 Cor. 4 : 17–19. We learn there that Timothy was

ministered unto him, Timotheus and ªErastus; but he himself stayed in Asia for a season.
23 And ᵇthe same time there arose no small stir about ᶜthat way.
24 For a certain *man* named Demetrius, a silversmith, which made silver shrines for Diana, brought ᵈno small gain unto the craftsmen;
25 Whom he called together with the workmen of like occupation, and said, Sirs, ye know that by this craft we have our wealth.
26 Moreover ye see and hear, that not alone at Ephesus, but almost throughout all Asia, this Paul hath persuaded and turned away much people, saying that ᵉthey be no gods, which are made with hands:
27 So that not only this our craft is in danger to be

into Macedonia two of them that ministered unto him, Timothy and Erastus, he himself stayed in Asia for a while.
23 And about that time there arose no small stir con-
24 cerning the Way. For a certain man named Demetrius, a silversmith, who made silver shrines of ¹Diana, brought no little business unto the crafts-
25 men; whom he gathered together, with the work-men of like occupation, and said, Sirs, ye know that
26 by this business we have our wealth. And ye see and hear, that not alone at Ephesus, but almost throughout all Asia, this Paul hath persuaded and turned away much people, saying that they are no
27 gods, which are made with hands: and not only is

a Rom. 16 : 23 ; 2 Tim. 4 : 20....*b* 2 Cor. 1 : 8....*c* See ch. 9 : 2....*d* ch. 16 : 16, 19....*e* Ps. 115 : 4 ; Isa. 44 : 10–20 ; Jer. 10 : 3.
——1 Gr. *Artemis.*

not to stop in Macedonia, but to pass on to Corinth, the capital city of Achaia, and prepare the church for the approaching visit of the apostle. Thus "the narrative agrees with the Epistle; and the agreement is attended with very little appearance of design. One thing at least concerning it is certain—that if this passage of Paul's history had been taken from his letter, it would have sent Timothy to Corinth by name, or at all events into Achaia."—**Erastus** may be the person of that name in 2 Tim. 4 : 20, but, as he travelled with Paul, the best critics distinguish him from the Erastus in Rom. 16 : 23 (Neand., De Wet., Win.). The office of the latter as "treasurer of the city" would demand his more constant presence at Corinth.—**He himself stayed**—lit. **he himself** (while they departed) **kept back unto Asia ;** *unto* not *in* (De Wet., Rob.), and not *for* as dat. comm. (Win.), uncommon before a proper name, but *unto* as the direction toward which (Mey.).

23–27. DEMETRIUS EXCITES A TUMULT AT EPHESUS.

23. As at Philippi (16 : 19), so here, the Greeks instigated the riot ; their motive was the same —fear of losing the means of their ill-gotten wealth. (See note on 14 : 19.)—**The same time**—lit. *about that time ;* viz. that of Paul's intended departure. —**About that way,** or, *concerning the way.* (See on 9 : 2.)

24. For, etc., explains why a tumult arose. —**Silver shrines** (not *for,* in E. V., but) **of Artemis.** These were small portable images resembling the temple at Ephesus and containing a figure of the goddess. The manufacture of these shrines was a lucrative business, as they were in great request ; they were set up in houses as objects of worship, or carried about the person as having the supposed power to avert disease and other dangers. They were not only sold here in Asia, but sent as an article of traffic to distant countries. **Demetrius,** it would seem, was a wholesale dealer in such

shrines. He executed orders for them, and employed **artisans,** who received lucrative wages [see R. V.] for their labor.—(Comp. παρείχετο with the active form in 16 : 16.)

25. Whom he called together, etc., or **whom having assembled and the other workmen** in his employ. The *artisans* (τεχνί-ται) performed the more delicate processes, and the **workmen** (ἐργάτας) the rougher work. So Bengel, Kuinoel, Hemsen, and Meyer distinguish the two nouns from each other. It appears improbable that Demetrius would confine his appeal to his own men. It may be better to understand **workmen** of the laborers in general who were devoted to such trades, whether they exercised them on their own account or that of some employer.—**Of like occupation.** The Greek (τὰ τοιαῦτα) limits the reference to shrines—*i. e.* definitely, *such things* as those. (Comp. Matt. 19 : 14 ; 2 Cor. 12 : 2, 3. K. ? 246. 4.) It is incorrect to extend the pronoun so as to include statuary, pictures, coins, and the like (Blmf.).—**Ye know = ye know well.** (See v. 15.)—**This** refers to **making shrines** in Luke's narrative. It stands, therefore, for some equivalent term or idea in the speech of Demetrius.—**Wealth,** *prosperity.*

26. Of, or *from* (not *at*), **Ephesus** depends on **much people** as a genitive of possession. —**Asia** has, no doubt, its Roman sense. The effect ascribed here to Paul's labors agrees with the statement in v. 10.—**Turned away,** or **turned aside**—*i. e.* from our mode of worship.—**That they be,** etc., **that they are not gods which are made by hands.** The mode of speaking illustrates the disposition of the heathen to identify their gods with the idols or temples consecrated to them. (See on 17 : 24.) We can imagine the effect of these words on such auditors, uttered with a look or gesture toward the splendid temple within sight.

27. This our craft. Rather, *this part,* branch, *of our labor* (Kyp., Mey.). The idea

set at nought; but also that the temple of the great goddess Diana should be despised, and her magnificence should be destroyed, whom all Asia and the world worshippeth.

28 And when they heard *these sayings*, they were full of wrath, and cried out, saying, Great *is* Diana of the Ephesians.

29 And the whole city was filled with confusion: and having caught ᵃGaius and ᵇAristarchus, men of

there danger that this our trade come into disrepute; but also that the temple of the great goddess ¹Diana be made of no account, and that she should even be deposed from her magnificence, 28 whom all Asia and ²the world worshippeth. And when they heard this, they were filled with wrath, and cried out, saying, Great *is* ¹Diana of the Ephe-29 sians. And the city was filled with the confusion: and they rushed with one accord into the theatre,

a Rom. 16 : 23 ; 1 Cor. 1 : 14....*b* ch. 20 : 4 ; 27 : 2 ; Col. 4 : 10 ; Philem. 24.———1 Gr. *Artemis*....2 Gr. *the inhabited earth.*

is that their art as silversmiths, of whatever use it might be in other respects, would soon be ruined, as to this particular application of it. —**For us** (ἡμῖν, dat. incomm.), to our detriment. Their receipts had declined perceptibly already, and at this rate would soon be cut off altogether.—**But also,** etc., **but also the temple of the great goddess Artemis** is in danger, etc. **Is in danger** extends also into this clause and governs the following infinitive. **Great** was one of the special titles of the Ephesian Diana. In regard to her temple, reckoned as one of the wonders of the world, the reader will find ample details in Conybeare and Howson. The edifice in Paul's time had been built in place of the one burnt down by Herostratus on the night of Alexander's birth, and was vastly superior to it in size and grandeur. No ruins of it remain at present on the spot; but the traveller sees some of the columns in the mosque of St. Sophia, at Constantinople, originally a church, and in the naves of Italian cathedrals.—The words translated **should be despised** mean **to come into contempt** (Mey.); *in redargutionem venire* (Vulg.)—*i. e. to be confuted*, rejected (De Wet.). The noun occurs only here, and its meaning must be inferred from its relation to the cognate words. A result of *confutation* is shame, loss of character; and hence the expression could be used to signify that they feared lest their business should lose its credit in the public estimation.—**And her magnificence,** etc., *and also that her glory will be destroyed*, etc. The discourse here changes from the direct to the indirect, as if **he said** had introduced this part of the sentence. We have a similar transition in 23 : 24. (See W. ? 64. III. 2.) **And** (τε, needlessly exchanged by some for δέ) joins the clause with what precedes, while **also** [see Dr. Hackett's translation] adds another argument to enforce the speaker's object.— **The world** (ἡ οἰκουμένη). (Comp. on 11 : 28.) The temple at Ephesus had been built at the common expense of all the Greek cities of Asia. Pilgrims repaired thither from all nations and countries.—The speech of Demetrius deserves attention for its artful character. He

takes care, in the first place, to show his fellow-craftsmen how the matter affected their own personal interest; and then, having aroused their selfishness, he proceeds to appeal with so much the more effect to their zeal for religion. His main reliance, as Calvin thinks, was upon the first: "Res ipsa clamat non tam pro aris ipsos quam pro focis pugnare, ut scilicet culinam habeant bene calentem" ["The nature of the case makes it evident that they are fighting, not so much for their altars as for their household fires; that, forsooth, they may have their kitchens well warmed"].

28–34. THE MOB SEIZE TWO OF PAUL'S COMPANIONS AND RUSH TO THE THEATRE.

28. Full of wrath, against Paul and the Christians.—**Cried out, continued crying.** The Greeks lived so much in the open air Demetrius may have harangued his men in public; if in private, the rioters had now gone into the street. Perhaps they traversed the city for a time with their outcry before executing the assault spoken of in the next verse, and swelled their number with recruits on the way.

29. And the whole city was filled with confusion, or **tumult, the tumult,** if we read the article. The evidence for the article is not decisive [but it is very strong, א* A B D² H L P ; so that the critical editions now all insert it. On the other hand, the evidence for **whole** before **city** is not decisive.—A. H.]. —**And they rushed with one accord into the theatre.** The subject of the verb here includes those who excited the disturbance and those who joined in it. They rushed to the theatre, because it was the custom of the Greeks, though not of the Romans, to use their theatres for public business as well as for sports. (See on 12 : 21.) The multitude had evidently no definite plan of action, and no definite idea of the cause of the present excitement. (See v. 32.) All they knew was that some danger threatened their religion, and under that impression they hastened as with one impulse (ὁμοθυμαδόν) to the usual place of concourse for further inquiry or for consultation. Remains of the theatre at Ephesus are still visible. Its

15

Macedonia, Paul's companions in travel, they rushed with one accord into the theatre.

30 And when Paul would have entered in unto the people, the disciples suffered him not.

31 And certain of the chief of Asia, which were his friends, sent unto him, desiring *him* that he would not adventure himself into the theatre.

32 Some therefore cried one thing, and some another: for the assembly was confused; and the more part knew not wherefore they were come together.

33 And they drew Alexander out of the multitude, the Jews putting him forward. And *a*Alexander *b*beck-

having seized Gaius and Aristarchus, men of Mace-30 donia, Paul's companions in travel. And when Paul was minded to enter in unto the people, the 31 disciples suffered him not. And certain also of the *1*Asiarchs, being his friends, sent unto him, and besought him not to adventure himself into the thea-32 tre. Some therefore cried one thing, and some another: for the assembly was in confusion; and the more part knew not wherefore they were come to-33 gether. *2*And they brought Alexander out of the multitude, the Jews putting him forward. And

---

a 1 Tim. 1 : 20 ; 2 Tim. 4 : 14....*b* ch. 12 : 17.———1 i. e. officers having charge of festivals in the Roman province of Asia....2 Or, *And some of the multitude instructed Alexander.*

---

outline can be traced, showing its dimensions to have been larger than those of any other theatre known to us from ancient times. It was built on the side of a lofty hill, with the seats rising in long succession one above another, and, like similar edifices among the ancients, was entirely open to the sky. A recent traveller judges that it was large enough to contain thirty thousand persons. The temple of Diana could be seen from it, at no great distance, across the marketplace. Luke has violated no probability, therefore, in representing so many people as assembled in such a place.— **Having caught** (συναρπάσαντες), **after having seized along** (out of the house, prior to **rushed,** ὥρμησαν), or (coincident with the verb), **having seized along** when they rushed. (See note on 21 : 7.) Meyer prefers the first mode; De Wette, the second. (See W. § 45. 6. b. For a different explanation of σύν in the participle, see Rob., *Lex.*, s. v.)—**Gaius,** or **Caius,** who was a Macedonian, is not the one mentioned in 20 : 4, or in Rom. 16 : 23 and 1 Cor. 1 : 15 ; for the former belonged to Derbe ; the latter, to Corinth.—**Aristarchus** was a Thessalonian (20 : 4). (See further on 27 : 2.)

30. Paul. Paul may have been absent from his abode at the time of the assault, as was the case at Thessalonica (17 : 6). **Unto the people** in the theatre (v. 31). His idea may have been that his appearance there in person, or a declaration that he was willing to have his conduct examined, would allay the tumult. (Comp. v. 37.) His anxiety must have been the greater from his not knowing to what danger the friends who had fallen into the hands of the mob might be exposed.—**The disciples,** who were, no doubt, native Ephesians. They understood their countrymen too well to encourage the apostle's inclination.

31. The chief of Asia. The *Asiarchs* were ten men (Mey.) chosen annually from the chief towns in Proconsular Asia to superintend the games and festivals held every year in honor of the gods and the Roman emperor. They

were chosen from the wealthier class of citizens, since, like the Roman aediles, they were required to provide for these exhibitions at their own expense. Those who had filled the office once retained the title for the rest of life. One of the number acted as chief Asiarch, who resided commonly at Ephesus. The Bithyniarchs, Galatarchs, Syriarchs, were a similar class of magistrates in other provinces of Western Asia. —Akerman offers here the following just remark : "That the very maintainers and presidents of the heathen sports and festivals of a people to whom the doctrine of Christ and the resurrection was foolishness were the friends of Paul was an assertion which no fabricator of a forgery would have ventured upon. We cannot penetrate the veil which antiquity has thrown over these events, and are only left to conjecture, either that Christianity itself had supporters, though secret ones who feared the multitude, in these wealthy Asiatics, or that, careless of the truth of what the apostle preached, they admired his eloquence and wished to protect one whom they considered so highly gifted."

32. Therefore (οὖν), resumptive, as in 9 : 31; 8 : 4. It puts forward the narrative from the point reached in v. 29. The two preceding verses relate to a collateral circumstance.

33. And they drew, etc. **Now out of the crowd,** from their midst, **they**—viz. the Jews—**urged forward Alexander.** "As the Jews here lived in the midst of a numerous Greek population who viewed them with constant aversion, any special occasion roused their slumbering prejudices into open violence, and they had then much to suffer. Hence the Jews on this occasion feared that the anger of the people against the enemies of their gods—especially as many of them did not know who were really intended—would be directed against themselves, and they were anxious, therefore, that one of their number, a man by the name of Alexander, should stand forward, in order to shift the blame from themselves upon the

oned with the hand, and would have made his defence
unto the people.

34 But when they knew that he was a Jew, all with
one voice about the space of two hours cried out, Great
is Diana of the Ephesians.

35 And when the townclerk had appeased the people,
he said, Ye men of Ephesus, what man is there that
knoweth not how that the city of the Ephesians is a
worshipper of the great goddess Diana, and of the
image which fell down from Jupiter?

Alexander beckoned with the hand, and would
34 have made a defence unto the people. But when
they perceived that he was a Jew, all with one
voice about the space of two hours cried out, Great
35 *is* [1]Diana of the Ephesians. And when the town-
clerk had quieted the multitude, he saith, Ye men
of Ephesus, what man is there who knoweth not
how that the city of the Ephesians is temple-keeper
of the great [1]Diana, and of the *image* which fell

1 Gr. *Artemis.*

Christians; but the appearance of such a person, who himself belonged to the enemies of
their gods, excited in the heathen still greater
rage, and the clamor became more violent."
This is the view of Neander, and is the one
adopted by Kuinoel, Hemsen, Olshausen, Winer,
and most others. Some, on the contrary, as
Calvin, Meyer, Wieseler, understand that Alexander was a Jewish Christian, and that the
Jews, who recognized him as such, pushed him
forward, in order to expose him to the fury of
the populace. **Would have made his defence** has been said to favor this opinion; but
it may refer to a defence in behalf of the Jews
as well as of the Christians. The Alexander
in 2 Tim. 4 : 14 could hardly have been the
same person; **the coppersmith** may have
been added there to distinguish him from this
individual.—**The Jews thrusting (putting)
him forward.** The subject of this subordinate clause is the same as that of the principal
clause which precedes; whereas, according to
the ordinary rule, it is only when the subjects
are different that the genitive absolute is employed. The participle προβαλλόντων (*thrusting*)
would have been regularly in the nominative.
Exceptions like this occur in the classics. The
idea of the secondary clause acquires in this
way more prominence. (See K. § 313. R. 2, as
compared with § 312. 3.)

34. [A literal rendering would be: *And perceiving that he was a Jew there was one voice from
all for about two hours, crying, Great is Diana*,
etc. The Greek participle (ἐπιγνόντες) translated
perceiving] is nominative, as if **all cried out**
(ἐφώνησαν ἅπαντες) had followed, instead of **one
voice from all** (φωνὴ μία . . . ἐκ πάντων). (See
W. § 63. I. 1.) The expression with that change
would have been more correct, but less forcible.
(μία ἐκ πάντων is a *callida junctura* which will arrest the reader's attention.)—**About the space
of two hours.** Their unintermitted cry **for
about two hours, Great is Diana of the
Ephesians!** not only declared their attachment to her worship, but, according to the
ideas of the heathen, was itself an act of wor-

ship. (Comp. 1 Kings 18 : 26; Matt. 6 : 7.) The
Mohammedan monks in India at the present
time often practise such repetitions for entire
days together. They have been known to say
over a single syllable having a supposed religious efficacy until they exhaust their strength
and are unable to articulate any longer.[1]—It
has been remarked that the reverberation of
their voices from the steep rock which formed
one side of the theatre (see on v. 29) must have
rendered the many-mouthed, frenzied exclamation still more terrific.

35-40. SPEECH OF THE CITY RECORD-
ER, WHO QUELLS THE UPROAR AND
DISPERSES THE MULTITUDE.

35. The town-clerk = the recorder. In
the cities of Asia Minor, as appears from notices
and inscriptions, this was the title of a very
important magistrate with various functions,
though his more immediate province was to
register the public acts and laws or to preserve
the record of them. (See Win., *Realw.*, i. p. 649.)
He was authorized to preside over public assemblies, and is mentioned on marbles as acting
in that capacity. He stood next in rank to the
municipal chief, and performed his duties during the absence or on the death of that officer. A
recorder, or town-clerk, of Ephesus is often
mentioned on coins of that city. (See *New
Englander*, x. p. 144.)—**Had appeased the
people,** or **having stilled the crowd,** by
showing himself to them and making a sign
(13 : 16) that he wished to speak.—In **for what
man is there,** the conjunction refers to a suppressed thought: You have no occasion for this
excitement, **for what human being is there,**
etc. **Of men** (comp. 1 Cor. 2 : 11), and not **man**
(T. R.), is to be read here. [Literally: **Who of
men is there,** etc.—A. H.]—**That knoweth
not,** etc., or **who does not know, that the
city of the Ephesians is keeper,** guardian,
of the great Diana; and hence it was unbecoming in them to be so sensitive, as if their
reputation was at stake. **Goddess** after **great**
(T. R.) should be omitted. **Worshipper—**lit.
*temple-sweeper—*became at length an honorary

1 See Tholuck's *Auslegung der Bergpredigt* (3d ed.), p. 328, *sq.*

36 Seeing then that these things cannot be spoken against, ye ought to be quiet, and to do nothing rashly.
37 For ye have brought hither these men, which are neither robbers of churches, nor yet blasphemers of your goddess.
38 Wherefore if Demetrius, and the craftsmen which are with him, have a matter against any man, the law is open, and there are deputies: let them implead one another.
39 But if ye inquire any thing concerning other matters, it shall be determined in a lawful assembly.

36 down from [1]Jupiter? Seeing then that these things cannot be gainsaid, ye ought to be quiet, and to do
37 nothing rash. For ye have brought hither these men, who are neither robbers of temples nor blas-
38 phemers of our goddess. If therefore Demetrius, and the craftsmen that are with him, have a matter against any man, [2]the courts are open, and there
39 are proconsuls: let them accuse one another. But if ye seek any thing about other matters, it shall be

---

1 Or, heaven....2 Or, court days are kept

---

title, and as such was granted to certain Asiatic cities in recognition of the care and expense bestowed by them on the temple and worship of their favorite deities. It is found on coins of Ephesus struck about Paul's time.—**The image which fell**—lit. **the image fallen from Jupiter,** and hence so much the more sacred. There was a similar tradition in regard to a statue of Artemis in Taurus (Eurip., *Iph. T.*, 977), and also one of Pallas at Athens (Pausan., i. 26. 6).

36. These things—viz. the established reputation of the Ephesians for their attachment to the worship of Diana, and the well-known origin of her image. Hence the argument is twofold: They had no reason to fear that such a people (**temple-keeper**) could be induced to abandon a religion which so wonderful an event (**fallen from Jupiter**) had signalized. —**Ye ought**—lit. **it is necessary that you ;** *i. e.* morally, *you ought.*

37. For confirms the implication in **rashly** —*i. e.* that they had acted rashly.—**These** refers to Gaius and Aristarchus. (See v. 29.) Paul was not present.—**Robbers of temples,** not **of churches.** It is singular that the latter translation, so incorrect, should be found in all the English versions except Wiclif's and the Rheims, which, being drawn from the Vulgate, have "sacrilegious." The temples among the heathen contained votive offerings and other gifts, and were often plundered.—**Nor yet,** etc.—lit. **nor blaspheming your goddess.** It was the effect of Paul's preaching to undermine idolatry and bring the worship of Artemis into contempt; but as at Athens, so here, he had refrained from denunciation, opprobrium, ridicule, and had opposed error by contending for the truth. Hence the recorder could urge that technical view of the apostle's conduct and deny that he had committed any actionable offence. It would almost seem as if, like the Asiarchs, he was friendly at heart to the new sect.

38. Wherefore, better *therefore,* since the men are innocent in regard to such crimes as sacrilege and blasphemy.—**With him**—*i. e.,* his associates in the complaint against Paul. (Comp. 5 : 17.) The speaker knew of their connection with the case from something which they had done or said in the assembly, which Luke has not related.— **The law is open**—lit. **court-days are kept,** observed. The days are so called because the courts were held in the forum. (Comp. 16 : 19; 17 : 5.) It is contended by some that this adjective (ἀγόραιοι) should be marked as proparoxytone in this sense, but as circumflex when used as in 17 : 5. (See W. § 6. 2.) The distinction is a doubtful one.—**And there are deputies**—*i. e.* **proconsuls.** The plural is generic (comp. Matt. 2 : 20), as but one such officer presided over a province. The coins of Ephesus show that the proconsular authority was fully established there in the reign of Nero. Akerman gives the engraving of one which has the head of that emperor on the obverse, and on the reverse a representation of the temple of Diana, with the words: [Money] *of the Ephesians, Neocori, Æchmocles Aviola, Proconsul.*—**Let them implead each other** is a technical phrase.

39. They were a mob, and could transact no public business. — **Inquire,** etc. **But if ye make any demand** (stronger than the simple verb) **concerning other things** than those of a private nature.—**In the** [not **a**] **lawful assembly,** which this is not. "Legitimus cœtus est qui a magistratu civitatis convocatur et regitur"[1] (Grot.). [Canon Lightfoot says that "by a 'lawful assembly' he means one of those which were held on stated days already predetermined by the law, as opposed to those which were called together on special emergencies out of the ordinary course, though, in another sense, these latter might be equally 'lawful.' An inscription found in this very theatre in which the words were uttered illustrates this technical sense of 'lawful.' It provides that a certain silver image of Athene shall be brought and 'set at every lawful (regular) assembly above the bench where the boys sit.' " Occasional assemblies might be lawful, if prop-

---

1 "A legitimate assembly is one which is convoked by the magistrate of the city, and over which he presides."

40 For we are in danger to be called in question for this day's uproar, there being no cause whereby we may give an account of this concourse.
41 And when he had thus spoken, he dismissed the assembly.

40 settled in the regular assembly. For indeed we are in danger to be ¹accused concerning this day's riot, there being no cause *for it:* and as touching it we shall not be able to give account of this concourse.
41 And when he had thus spoken, he dismissed the assembly.

CHAPTER XX.

AND after the uproar was ceased, Paul called unto *him* the disciples, and embraced *them*, and ªdeparted for to go into Macedonia.

1 AND after the uproar was ceased, Paul having sent for the disciples and exhorted them, took leave of

---

a 1 Cor. 16 : 5 ; 1 Tim. 1 : 3.———1 Or, *accused of riot concerning this day*

---

erly conducted, without undertaking to do what belonged to those appointed beforehand.—A. H.]

40. For justifies the intimation in **lawful** as to the character of the present concourse. **—We are in danger.** They were in danger of being called to account by the proconsul. The Roman Government watched every appearance of insubordination or sedition in the provinces with a jealous eye. Thousands were often put to death in the attempt to suppress such movements. It was a capital offence to take any part in a riotous proceeding. The speaker's hint, therefore, was a significant one. **—Uproar** depends on **concerning,** not on the verb. (The accent on περί is not drawn back, though its noun precedes (B. § 117. 3), because an adjective phrase follows.)**—There being no cause** explains, not why they were liable to be arraigned, but how seriously it would terminate if the affair should take that direction.— **Whereby,** or *in virtue of which.*—This speech is the model of a popular harangue. Such excitement on the part of the Ephesians was undignified, as they stood above all suspicion in religious matters (vv. 35, 36); it was unjustifiable, as they could establish nothing against the men (v. 37); it was unnecessary, as other means of redress were open to them (vv. 38, 39); and finally, if neither pride nor justice availed anything, fear of the Roman power should restrain them (v. 40). [The publication in 1877 of *Discoveries at Ephesus, including the Site and Remains of the Great Temple of Diana,* by J. T. Wood, F. A. S., has confirmed almost every important comment of Dr. Hackett on this narrative, as well as the remarkable agreement of the narrative itself with the religious, civil, and architectural condition of Ephesus at that time. After calling attention to the discoveries of Mr. Wood, and especially to several very instructive inscriptions, Canon Lightfoot—a most competent authority — remarks : " With these facts in view, we are justified in saying that ancient literature has preserved no picture of the Ephesus of imperial times . . . comparable for its lifelike truthfulness to the narrative of St.

Paul's sojourn there in the Acts " (*Cont. Rev.*, 1878, p. 288, etc.). The inscriptions published by Mr. Wood confirm the representation that Ephesus was called " the temple-warder of Artemis " and " the nurse of its own Ephesian goddess ;" that Artemis was called " the great goddess," and even " the greatest goddess ;" that the making of gold and silver shrines of the goddess was a flourishing business in the city ; that regular and occasional assemblies were held in the theatre ; and that " the proconsul," " the recorder," and " the Asiarchs " were well-known officials, the duties of the recorder being very important and often mentioned.—A. H.]

1-6. PAUL PROCEEDS A SECOND TIME TO GREECE, AND RETURNS FROM THERE TO TROAS.

1. And after the uproar = *Now after the tumult had ceased.* This clause shows that Paul left Ephesus soon after the disturbance, but furnishes no evidence, says Neander, that his departure was hastened by it. We may conclude that Paul " tarried at Ephesus until Pentecost," pursuant to his intention expressed in 1 Cor. 16 : 8, and, consequently, that he left that city in the spring or summer of A. D. 57 or 58. (Comp. note on 18 : 23 with that on 19 : 10.)—Before taking leave of Ephesus we must notice another event which Luke has not recorded, but which belongs to this part of the history. In 2 Cor. 12 : 14 (written on the way to Greece) the apostle says : *Behold, this third time I am ready to come unto you.* The connection decides that *third time* belongs to *come.* It cannot refer to a third intention merely to visit the Corinthians ; for he is saying that, as he had " not been burdensome to them " hitherto when he was among them, so in his present visit he would adhere to the same policy. Again, in 2 Cor. 13 : 1, he says, *This third time I am coming.* Here it is expressly said that the apostle was now on the point of making his third journey to Corinth. The correct inter-

2 And when he had gone over those parts, and had given them much exhortation, he came into Greece,

2 them, and departed for to go into Macedonia. And when he had gone through those parts, and had given them much exhortation, he came into Greece.

pretation of 2 Cor. 1 : 15, 16 presents no obstacle to this construction of the passages here referred to. The sixteenth of these verses explains the fifteenth. The apostle has reference in v. 16 to a journey to Corinth which he had proposed, but had failed to execute — viz. a journey into Macedonia by the way of Corinth, and then a return to Corinth from Macedonia; and in v. 15 he says that this plan would have secured to the Corinthians "a second benefit" (δευτέραν χάριν) in connection with the tour proposed—i. e. the benefit of his presence, not once merely, but a second time. There is every reason to suppose, therefore, that Paul had been at Corinth twice when he wrote his Second Epistle to the church in that city. So conclude, among others, Michaelis, Schrader,Bleek, Lücke, Schott, Anger, Rückert, Credner, Neander, Olshausen, Meyer, Wieseler, Osiander, Cony. and Hws. But where in Luke's narrative are we to insert this second journey to Corinth? Of the different answers given to this question, I regard that as the most satisfactory which places the journey within the period of Paul's residence of three years at Ephesus. It would have been easy for him to have crossed over from the one city to the other at any time; and, considering the urgent reasons for such a visit furnished by the condition of the Corinthian church, one would think that he could hardly have refrained from availing himself of the opportunity. As his stay there was probably very brief and unattended by any important event, Luke has made no mention of it. Schrader, Rückert, Olshausen, Meyer, Wieseler, Conybeare and Howson, and others intercalate the journey at this point. Neander suggests that Paul, at the commencement of this missionary-tour, may have extended his travels before his arrival at Ephesus so far as to have included Greece. Anger, Schott, and some others think that Paul's second visit to Corinth may have been a return to that city from some excursion which he made into the neighboring regions during the year and a half of his first sojourn at Corinth (18 : 1. *sq.*).— **Embraced,** *having embraced,* them. How many tears of affection must have been shed! How many prayers must have been offered for each other and for the cause of Christ! From such hints as those in vv. 37, 38 and in 21 : 5, 6, we can call up to ourselves an image of the scene. They must have parted with a presentiment, at least, that the apostle was now taking his final leave of Ephesus.

(See vv. 25, 38.)—**Departed**—lit. **went forth to go into Macedonia.** The direction which the apostle took we learn from 2 Cor. 2 : 12, 13. He proceeded to Troas, where he had expected to meet Titus, whom he had sent to Corinth, in order to ascertain the effect of his First Epistle to the church in that city. It was his intention, apparently, to remain and labor for a time at Troas, in case the information for which he was looking should be favorable. But not finding Titus there, and being unable to endure a longer suspense, he embarked at once for Macedonia. On his arrival there he met with Titus, and was relieved of his anxiety. (See 2 Cor. 7 : 6.) **2. Those parts**—*i. e.* the region of Macedonia.—**And had given them,** etc.—lit. *having exhorted them;* viz. the believers [*with much discourse*]. (See on 16 : 40.) The expression shows that he now revisited the places where he had preached on his first visit here—viz. Philippi, Thessalonica, Berea. It was here and now that Paul wrote his Second Epistle to the Corinthians. That he wrote the letter in Macedonia is evident from 2 Cor. 9 : 2-4. He speaks there of his boasting to the churches of Macedonia of the liberality of the Corinthians, and of the possibility that some of the Macedonians would accompany him to Corinth. (See, also, 2 Cor. 7 : 5.) The apostle now, as far as we know, was in that country only three times. When he was there first, he had not yet been at Corinth at all (16 : 11); and when he passed through that province on his last return to Jerusalem (v. 3), he was going in the opposite direction, and not advancing to Corinth, as stated in the Epistle. He wrote the Second Epistle to the Corinthians, therefore, on this second journey through Macedonia, in the summer, probably, or early autumn, of A. D. 58. (See note on 21 : 17.)—In Rom. 15 : 19, Paul speaks of having published the gospel *as far as Illyricum,* which was a country on the west of Macedonia. It was at this time, probably, that he penetrated so far in that direction. It could not have been on his first visit to Macedonia (16 : 12, *sq.*) ; for the course of his journey at that time is minutely traced in the Acts, from his landing at Philippi to his leaving Corinth. He moved along the eastern side of the peninsula, and was kept at a distance from Illyricum When he passed through Macedonia next (v. 3), he had already written the Epistle to the Romans. Lardner pronounces this geographical

3 And *there* abode three months. And *a*when the Jews laid wait for him, as he was about to sail into Syria, he purposed to return through Macedonia.
4 And there accompanied him into Asia Sopater of Berea; and of the Thessalonians, *b*Aristarchus and Se-

3 And when he had spent three months *there*, and a plot was laid against him by the Jews, as he was about to set sail for Syria, he determined to return 4 through Macedonia. And there accompanied him *l*as far as Asia Sopater of Berœa, *the son of* Pyrrhus;

---

a ch. 9 : 23 ; 23 : 12 ; 25 : 3 ; 2 Cor. 11 : 26....*b* ch. 19 : 29 ; 27 : 2 ;   Col. 4 : 10.————1 Many ancient authorities omit *as far as Asia*.

---

coincidence sufficiently important to confirm the entire history of Paul's travels.—**Into Greece,** which stands here for *Achaia* (18 : 12; 19 : 21), as opposed to Macedonia. Wetstein has shown that Luke was justified in that use of the term. Paul was proceeding to Corinth, the capital of the province. (Comp. Rom. 16 : 1.)

3. The **three months** spent here preceded the summer of this year. (See v. 6.) The stay was thus brief because the apostle was anxious to return to Jerusalem (v. 16). The Jewish plot was contemporaneous with his leaving, but did not occasion it.—(ποιήσας is anacoluthic for ποιή-σαντι. See 19 : 24.)—It was just before his departure from Corinth that Paul wrote the Epistle to the Romans. That it was written at Corinth admits of being proved by several distinct arguments. One is that Paul was the guest of Gaius at the time (Rom. 16 : 23); and Gaius, as we learn from 1 Cor. 1 : 14, was one of the converts at Corinth whom Paul baptized. Again, he commends to the Roman Christians Phœbe, a deaconess of the church at Cenchreæ (see on 18 : 18), who was on the point of proceeding to Rome (Rom. 16:1), and was probably the bearer of the letter. Further, the apostle's situation, as disclosed in the Epistle, agrees with that in the Acts at this time. Thus he was on the eve of departing to Jerusalem (Rom. 15 : 25), was going thither with contributions for the Jewish believers (Rom. 15 : 25, 26), and after that was meditating a journey to Rome. The date of the Epistle, therefore, was the spring of A. D. 58 or 59.—**As he was,** etc.—lit. *as he is about to embark for Syria,* with the intention of going directly to Jerusalem. (See, also, 19 : 21.) The effect of the conspiracy was to change his route, but not to cause him to depart prematurely. He came with the design of passing only the winter there. (See 1 Cor. 16 : 6.)— He purposed, *it was thought best that he should return through Macedonia.* The infinitive depends on *purpose* (γνώμη) as a sort of appositional genitive. The expression indicates that he took this course as the result of advice or consultation. [In his explanation of this clause Dr. Hackett follows the *textus receptus,* in which *judgment,* or *purpose* (γνώμη), is the subject of *became* (ἐγένετο)—lit. *a judgment,* or *purpose,* was *formed of his returning—i. e. that he should return —through Macedonia.* And with this text there

appears to be an implication that the judgment in question was a "result of advice or consultation." But no such implication is contained in the best-supported text (reading γνώμης instead of γνώμη), which may be literally translated *he became of* (or *came to have*) a judgment (or *purpose*) *to return through Macedonia.* This reading is adopted by the recent editors and required by ℵ A B* E. It will be noticed that the Revised Version does not differ in sense from the Common Version, and that they reproduce the meaning of the best Greek text. Whether, then, the apostle's purpose was formed with or without consultation is wholly uncertain.—A. H.] How his journeying by land rather than by sea would enable him to escape the machinations of the Jews is not perfectly clear. The opinion that he was waiting to have the navigation of the season reopen, but was compelled to hasten his departure before that time, is certainly incorrect; for it is said he was on the point of embarking when the conspiracy of the Jews was formed or came to be known. It is possible that the Jews intended to assault him on his way to the ship, or else to follow and capture him after having put to sea. Hemsen's conjecture (*Der Apostel Paulus, u. s. w.,* p. 467) is that he had not yet found a vessel proceeding to Syria, and that his exposure at Corinth rendered it unsafe for him to remain, even a few days longer, until the arrival of such an opportunity.

4. Accompanied, or **followed, him,** formed his party. This could be said, though they did not travel in company all the time. The verb belongs to all the names which follow, but agrees with the nearest.—The best manuscripts read **Pyrrhus** after **Sopater,** genitive of kindredship (see on 1 : 13), *Sopater* son of *Pyrrhus.* This addition distinguishes *Sopater,* perhaps, from *Sosipater,* in Rom. 16 : 21, since they are but different forms of the same name (Win.).—**Of the Thessalonians** is a partitive genitive.—**Aristarchus** was mentioned in 19 : 29. The **Gaius** in that passage must be a different person from the one here, since they belonged to different countries. This Gaius is probably the individual of this name to whom the apostle John wrote his Third Epistle. Some critics (Kuin., Olsh., Neand.) would point the text so as to make

cundus; and *Gaius of Derbe, and *Timotheus; and of Asia, *Tychicus and *Trophimus.

5 These going before tarried for us at Troas.

6 And we sailed away from Philippi after *the days of unleavened bread, and came unto them *to Troas in five days; where we abode seven days.

7 And upon *the first *day* of the week, when the dis-

and of the Thessalonians, Aristarchus and Secundus; and Gaius of Derbe, and Timothy; and of

5 Asia, Tychicus and Trophimus. But these ¹had gone before, and were waiting for us at Troas.

6 And we sailed away from Philippi after the days of unleavened bread, and came unto them to Troas in five days; where we tarried seven days.

7 And upon the first day of the week, when we were

a ch. 19 : 29....*b* ch. 16 : 1....*c* Eph. 6 : 21 ; Col. 4 : 7; 2 Tim. 4 : 12 ; Tit. 3 : 12....*d* ch. 21 : 29; 2 Tim. 4 : 20....*e* Ex. 12 : 14, 15 ; 23 : 15 ....*f* ch. 16 : 8; 2 Cor. 2 : 12 ; 2 Tim. 4 : 13....*g* 1 Cor. 16 : 2; Rev. 1 : 10.——1 Many ancient authorities read *came, and were waiting.*

Gaius one of the Thessalonians, and join of **Derbe** with **Timothy**. But that division not only puts **and** out of its natural place, but disagrees with 16 : 1, where Timothy appears as a native of Lystra.—**Secundus** is otherwise unknown.—Luke supposes **Timothy's** origin to be familiar to the reader, and so passes it over (De Wet., Mey.).—**Tychicus** is named in Eph. 6 : 21; Col. 4 : 7; Tit. 3 : 12; and 2 Tim. 4 : 12. He was one of the most trusted of Paul's associates.—**Trophimus,** who was an Ephesian, appears again in 21 : 29 and 2 Tim. 4 : 20. He, and probably Aristarchus (27 : 2), went with the apostle to Jerusalem. The others may have stopped at Miletus, since the language in v. 13 intimates that the party kept together after leaving Troas. Consequently, **into Asia** would state the destination of the majority of the travellers and would be consistent with the fact that two of them went farther. [Many ancient authorities omit " as far as Asia" (*Revised Version*).—A. H.].

5. These—viz. the seven mentioned in v. 4, not the two named last. It is entirely arbitrary to limit the reference of the pronoun.—**Going before,** or *having gone forward*, from Corinth in advance of Paul and Luke. It is barely possible that they shipped at once for Troas, but it is more probable that they journeyed through Macedonia, both because **followed** (v. 4) suggests a common route of the parties, and because Sopater and the others may have been sent thither to finish the alms-collection which Paul had commenced.—**Us.** Luke resumes here the first person plural, which has not occurred since 16 : 17. (See the remarks on 16 : 40.)

6. We must include the writer of the narrative, Paul, and possibly others, in distinction from those who had gone forward to Troas. As Timothy was one of those who preceded the apostle, it is evident that he and the writer of the narrative were different persons. Tholuck, Lange,¹ Ebrard, and others pronounce this passage sufficient of itself to disprove the hypothesis that Timothy, not Luke, wrote the

portions of the Acts in which the historian speaks as an eye-witness.—**We sailed forth from Philippi**—*i. e.* from its harbor on the coast. (See note on 16 : 12.)—**After the days of unleavened bread,** the festival of the passover (see on 12 : 3), which no doubt they observed, not in the Jewish spirit any longer, but with a recognition of Christ as the true Paschal Lamb. (See John 1 : 36 and 1 Cor. 5 : 7.) Some think that they remained at Philippi for the sake of the celebration (Mey.); but we must view that as an inference altogether, Luke mentions the passover only in its chronological relation to the voyage. Calvin suggests as the motive for remaining that Paul would find the Jews more accessible to the truth during the season of such a solemnity.—**In five days**—lit. **unto five days,** as the limit reached; they were so long on the way. The passage on the apostle's first journey to Europe occupied two days only. (See 16 : 11.) Adverse winds or calms would be liable, at any season of the year, to occasion this variation.—**Seven days** may be indefinite, *a week's time.* (Comp. 21 : 4; 28 : 14.) They arranged it so as to bring a Sabbath within the time spent there. If the number be exact, then they arrived just at the close of the week, since they left the day after the Sabbath (v. 7).

7-12. PAUL PREACHES AT TROAS, AND ADMINISTERS THE SACRAMENT.

7. On the first day of the week, not on *one of the Sabbaths,* Jewish festivals, which overlooks the article, and not on *the one of them* next after their arrival, since that would imply that they passed more than one such festival here, contrary to Luke's statement that they left on the day following. In the New Testament *one* (εἷς) stands generally for *first* (πρῶτος) in speaking of the days of the week. (See Matt. 28 : 1; Mark 16 : 2; John 20 : 19, etc. W. § 37. 1.) It is an imitation of the ordinal sense of *'āchadh.* (See Gesen., *Heb. Gr.*, § 118. 4.) The passages just cited, and also Luke 24 : 1, John 20 : 1, and 1 Cor. 16 : 2, show that *week* is one of the senses of *sabbata.* The Jews reckoned the

---

¹ *Das Leben Jesu nach den Evangelien dargestellt,* Erstes Buch, p. 251.

ciples came together *a*to break bread, Paul preached
unto them, ready to depart on the morrow; and continued his speech until midnight.

8 And there were many lights *b*in the upper chamber,
where they were gathered together.

9 And there sat in a window a certain young man
named Eutychus, being fallen into a deep sleep: and

gathered together to break bread, Paul discoursed
with them, intending to depart on the morrow; and
8 prolonged his speech until midnight. And there
were many lights in the upper chamber, where we
9 were gathered together. And there sat in the window a certain young man named Eutychus, borne

---

a ch. 2 : 42, 46 ; 1 Cor. 10 : 16 ; 11 : 20, etc....*b* ch. 1 : 13.

---

day from evening to morning, and on that
principle the evening of *the first day of the week*
would be our Saturday evening. If Luke
reckons so here, as many commentators suppose, the apostle then waited for the expiration
of the Jewish Sabbath, and held his last religious service with the brethren at Troas at the
beginning of the Christian Sabbath—*i. e.* on
Saturday evening—and consequently resumed
his journey on Sunday morning. But, as
Luke had mingled so much with foreign
nations and was writing for Gentile readers,
he would be very apt to designate the time in
accordance with their practice; so that his
evening or night of *the first day of the week*
would be the end of the Christian Sabbath,
and the morning of his departure that of
Monday. Olshausen, Neander, De Wette,
Meyer, and most other critics recognize here
a distinct trace of the Christian Sabbath in that
early age of the church. (See also 1 Cor. 16 :
2 and Rev. 1 : 10.) It is entirely immaterial,
of course, to the objects of the day or the validity of the apostolic example, whether the first
Christians began their Sabbath in the Jewish
way. on Saturday evening, or at midnight, a
few hours later. " Since the sufferings of Christ,"
says Neander, "appeared as the central point of
all religious experience and life; since his resurrection was considered as the foundation of
all Christian joy and hope,—it was natural that
the communion of the church should have
specially distinguished the day with which the
memory of that event had connected itself."
But the introduction of the Sabbath was not
only in harmony with Christian feeling, but,
as we have good reason to believe, was sanctioned and promoted by the special authority
of the apostles. " It is in the highest degree
probable," says Meyer, "that the observance
of the Sabbath rests upon apostolic institution.
Since the gospel was extended among the
heathen, who had not been accustomed to the
Jewish Sabbath, it was natural and necessary
that the apostles should instruct them in regard to such a day, on account of the importance of the resurrection of Christ; and this
supposition is an indispensable one, in order to
account for the very early and general cele-

bration of the Christian Sabbath." In support
of the last remark, this author refers to Justin
Martyr, who, born at the beginning of the
second century, says (*Apol.* I.) that the Christians of his time, "both in the cities and the
country, were accustomed to assemble for worship on the day called Sunday" (τῇ τοῦ ἡλίου
λεγομένῃ ἡμέρᾳ).—**When the disciples came
together,** rather **we being assembled,** not
the disciples, the received reading, which our
version follows. The latter term may have
been inserted to provide an antecedent for
them. The use of the pronoun is like that
in 8 : 5.—For **to break bread,** see on 2 : 42,
46.

8. Many lights, better **now there were
many lamps;** and hence the fall of the
young man was perceived at once. So Meyer
explains the object of the remark. But that
relation of the circumstance to the rest of
the narrative is not clearly indicated. It has
much more the appearance of having proceeded
from an eye-witness, who mentions the incident, not for the purpose of obviating a difficulty which might occur to the reader, but
because the entire scene to which he refers
stood now with such minuteness and vividness
before his mind. The moon was full at the
passover (*v.* 6), and after the lapse now of somewhat less than three weeks only appeared as a
faint crescent in the early part of the night
(Conybeare and Howson).—**In the upper
room,** which, as appears from the next verse,
was on the third story. (See note on 1 : 13.)—
Not **where they were,** but **where we
were, assembled.** In the received text the
verb is **they were** (ἦσαν), which accords with
the variations in the last verse.

9. In a window—lit. **upon the window,**
the seat of it. " It will be recollected that there
were no windows of glass; and the window
here mentioned was a lattice of joinery or a
door, which on this occasion was set open on
account of the heat from the many lights and
the number of persons in the room. It should
be observed that the windows of such places in
general reached nearly to the floor; they would
correspond well to what our word ' window '
signified originally—viz. *windore. wind-door ; i. e.*.

as Paul was long preaching, he sunk down with sleep, and fell down from the third loft, and was taken up dead.

10 And Paul went down, and *fell on him, and embracing *him* said, *Trouble not yourselves; for his life is in him.

11 When he therefore was come up again, and had broken bread, and eaten, and talked a long while, even till break of day, so he departed.

12 And they brought the young man alive, and were not a little comforted.

13 ¶ And we went before to ship, and sailed unto Assos, there intending to take in Paul: for so had he appointed, minding himself to go afoot.

down with deep sleep; and as Paul discoursed yet longer, being borne down by his sleep he fell down 10 from the third story, and was taken up dead. And Paul went down, and fell on him, and embracing him said, Make ye no ado; for his life is in him.

11 And when he was gone up, and had broken the bread, and eaten, and had talked with them a long 12 while, even till break of day, so he departed. And they brought the lad alive, and were not a little comforted.

13 But we, going before to the ship, set sail for Assos, there intending to take in Paul: for so had he ap-

a 1 Kings 17 : 21 ; 2 Kings 4 : 34....*b* Matt. 9 : 24.

a door for the admission of wind or air."[1]—**Being fallen into,** or **being overcome with, deep sleep.—Sunk down**—lit. **having been borne down from** (the effect of) **the sleep** into which he had sunk. This second participial clause states a result of the condition described by the first.—**Fell down.** The window projected (according to the side of the room where it was situated) either over the street or over the interior court; so that, in either case, he fell from the third story upon the hard earth or pavement below.—**Was taken up dead,** which it is entirely foreign to any intimation of the context to qualify by adding "in appearance" or "as they supposed."

10. Fell upon him, and having embraced him, after the fashion of Elisha in 2 Kings 4 : 34. As in that instance, so in this, the act appears to have been the sign of a miracle.—**Trouble not yourselves,** or **Do not lament,** which, according to the Oriental habit and the import of the word, they were doing with loud and passionate outcry. (Comp. Matt. 9 : 23 ; Mark 5 : 39. See on 10 : 15.)—**For his life is in him,** which he could say, whether he perceived that it was not extinct or had been restored.

11. Broken bread, *the bread* already spoken of in v. 7. The article, which the T. R. omits, belongs here (Tsch., Lchm., Mey.). The fall of Eutychus had delayed the Lord's Supper, which Paul now proceeds to administer.—**And eaten,** or **having eaten,** because, probably, they connected a repast with the sacrament. (See on 2 : 42.)—**A long while** may refer to the time occupied in the entire service, or, more naturally in this connection, to the remainder of the night after the preceding interruption.—**Even till,** or **until, daybreak,** about five o'clock A. M. at that season (Alf.).—**So,** or **thus,** after these events. (Comp. 17 : 33 ; 28 : 14.)—**Departed,** *went forth*—i. e. on his journey. Yet the term may not exclude a brief interval between the religious services and

his departure, and during that time the vessel could weigh anchor and start for Assos. (See on v. 13.)

12. Brought the young man into the assembly (Hems., Mey.), not to his home. The subject of the verb is indefinite. This circumstance is supplementary to what is stated in v. 11, not subsequent to it in point of time. —**Alive,** or **living,** which suggests as its antithesis that he had been dead, or, at least, that such was their belief.—**Were comforted,** or **consoled**—viz. by his restoration to them. Some understand it of the effect of Paul's discourse, which is incorrect, as that is not here the subject of remark.—**Not a little,** very much. Observe the litotes.

13-16. THEY PROSECUTE THE JOURNEY TO MILETUS.

13. We—viz. the writer and the other companions of the apostle.—**Went before**—lit. **having gone forward,** though, from the circumstances of the case, it could not have been long first. They may have left as soon as the assembly broke up, while Paul still remained a short time (see on v. 11), or, in order to reach Assos in good season, may have left even before the conclusion of the service. **They** spent the entire week at Troas, as well as Paul (see v. 6), and hence could not have preceded him before the end of that time.—**Unto Assos,** which was a coast-town in Mysia, south of Troas.—**There**—lit. **from there,** because the writer has his mind, not on their arrival, but the subsequent departure or progress. —**For so** (that they should take him at that place) **he had arranged for himself,** the passive in the sense of the middle. (W. ¿ 39. 3.) —**Minding** (μέλλων) refers to his intention.—**To go afoot.** This foot-journey, according to the best evidence, was about twenty miles. A paved road extended from Troas to Assos; so that, starting even as late as seven or eight o'clock A. M., Paul could have reached Assos in the afternoon. A friend of the writer, a native of Greece, stated

14 And when he met with us at Assos, we took him in, and came to Mitylene.

15 And we sailed thence, and came the next *day* over against Chios; and the next *day* we arrived at Samos, and tarried at Trogyllium; and the next *day* we came to Miletus.

14 pointed, intending himself to go ¹by land. And when he met us at Assos, we took him in, and came

15 to Mitylene. And sailing from thence, we came the following day over against Chios; and the next day we touched at Samos; and ²the day after we came

1 Or, *on foot*....2 Many ancient authorities insert *having tarried at Trogyllium.*

that he himself had travelled on foot between the two places in five hours. The distance by sea is about forty miles. His object, it is conjectured, may have been to visit friends on the

day, the second from Troas.—**Over against** —*i. e.* **opposite to**—**Chios,** the modern Scio, south of Lesbos. The language intimates that, instead of putting into the harbor, they lay off

ASSOS, FROM THE SEA.

way, or to have the company of brethren from Troas whom the vessel was not large enough to accommodate.

14. And when, or **as, he met with us** seems to imply that he found them already there.— **At Assos**—lit. **unto,** because the preceding verb implies the idea of the journey thither on the part of Paul. **Mitylene,** where they appear to have stopped over-night, was on the east side of Lesbos, the capital of that island. The distance from Assos by sea was thirty miles; so that the voyage hither from Troas was an easy one for a day. Castro, the present capital, stands on the site of the ancient city. The name of the island is now Metilino or Metelin, a corruption of Mitylene.

15. The next day, or **on the following**

the coast during the night.—**And upon the next day** (the third from Troas) **we put along unto Samos.** This island is still farther down the Ægean. At one point it approaches within six miles of the mainland. It retains still the ancient name. They may have touched here, but, as appears from the next clause, did not stop long.—**And tarried**—lit. **and having remained at Trogyllium,** which was their next night-station, since **on the following day,** being the fourth, they arrived at Miletus. Trogyllium most commentators suppose to be the promontory and the town of that name in Southern Ionia, opposite Samos where it is nearest to the shore. There was also an island of the same name on the coast of this promontory (Strab., 14. 636), which, says Forbiger (*Handb.,* ii. p.

16 For Paul had determined to sail by Ephesus, because he would not spend the time in Asia: for *a*he hasted, if it were possible for him, *b*to be at Jerusalem *c*the day of Pentecost.

16 to Miletus. For Paul had determined to sail past Ephesus, that he might not have to spend time in Asia; for he was hastening, if it were possible for him, to be at Jerusalem the day of Pentecost.

a ch. 18 : 21 ; 19 : 21 ; 21 : 4, 12....*b* ch. 24 : 17....*c* ch. 2 : 1 ; 1 Cor. 16 : 8.

170), was unquestionably the Trogyllium intended in this passage. The apostle would have been nearer to Ephesus at Trogyllium on the mainland than he was at Miletus, but a better harbor or greater facility of intercourse may have led him to prefer the more distant place for his interview with the elders. [The words *tarried at Trogyllium;* and are omitted by the later editors, in agreement with ℵ A B C E and other documents.—A. H.]—**Miletus** was

friends had evidently some control of the vessel. The number being so great, they may have chartered the craft (as is very common in the Levant at present) ; at all events, they must have had sufficient influence with the captain to induce him to consult their wishes.—**Because he would not,** or, **that it might not happen to him**—*i. e.* that he might avoid inducements—**to spend time in Asia.** He might have gone to Ephesus and returned

VIEW OF MITYLENE.

on the confines of Caria, twenty-eight miles south of Ephesus, and just below the mouth of the Meander. They reached here on the fourth day from Troas, hence either on Wednesday or Thursday, some doubt existing (see on v. 7) as to the day of the week when they sailed from Troas.

16. The external testimony requires κεκρίκει instead of ἔκρινε (Grsb., Lchm., Mey.) : **For he had determined to sail past Ephesus,** which explains why they had left that city at the north ; they were opposite to it when at Samos. As it depended on his decision whether they stopped or proceeded, Paul and his

during the time that he remained at Miletus ; but he feared to trust himself there, lest the importunity of friends or the condition of the church might detain him too long, or even lead him to alter his purpose.—**For he hasted,** or *was hastening,* **if it were possible for him,** etc. More than three of the seven weeks between the passover and Pentecost had elapsed already. One had expired before they left Philippi ; they were five days on their way to Troas, remained there seven days, and were four days on the way to Miletus.—For **Pentecost,** see on 2 : 1.—**To be** (γενέσθαι)—lit. **to come to be—** implies motion, and takes after it **unto, at** (εἰς).

17 ¶ And from Miletus he sent to Ephesus, and called the elders of the church.

18 And when they were come to him, he said unto them, Ye know, *from the first day that I came into Asia, after what manner I have been with you at all seasons,

19 Serving the Lord with all humility of mind, and

17   And from Miletus he sent to Ephesus, and called
18 to him the ¹elders of the church.   And when they were come to him, he said unto them,
     Ye yourselves know, from the first day that I set foot in Asia, after what manner I was with you all
19 the time, serving the Lord with all lowliness of

a ch. 18 : 19 ; 19 : 1, 10.——1 Or, *presbyters*

17–35. THE ADDRESS OF PAUL TO THE EPHESIAN ELDERS AT MILETUS.

17. His subject is fidelity in the ministerial office—first, as illustrated in his own example; and secondly, as required of those whom the Spirit has called to this office.   In vv. 18–21 he reminds his hearers of his conduct while he lived among them; in vv. 19–25 he informs them that he is about to be separated from

ordinary English reader, which now it is not." —Luke speaks only of the Ephesian elders as summoned to meet the apostle at Miletus: but, as the report of his arrival must have spread rapidly, it could not have failed to draw together others also, not only from Ephesus, but from the neighboring towns where churches had been established. (See on v. 25.)

18. Ye is emphatic. (See on 10 : 15.)—**From**

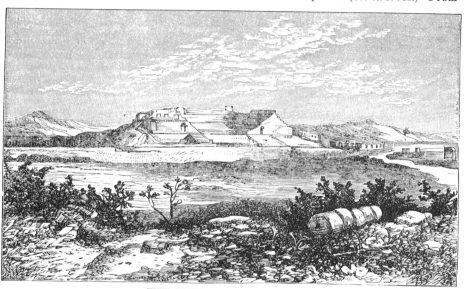

VIEW OF THEATRE, ANCIENT MILETUS.

them, to meet no more on earth; and in vv. 26–35 he charges them to be watchful for the safety of the flock which had been entrusted to them, and was to be exposed in future to so many dangers. — **Elders = overseers** (v. 28). (Comp. note on 14 : 23.)   Our English translators render the latter term " overseers " in v. 28, contrary to their usual practice.   " The E. V.," says Mr. Alford, very candidly, " has hardly dealt fairly in this case with the sacred text, since it ought there, as in all other places, to have been ' bishops,' that the fact of *elders* and *bishops* having been originally and apostolically synonymous might be apparent to the

the first day I came unto Asia we are to connect with **after what manner I have been with you,** or *how I conducted* (Kuin., De Wet.), not with **ye know** (Mey.).   As was to be foreseen, Meyer corrects himself here in his last edition.—The duration of the period (**the whole time**) is stated in v. 31. The position of *the* before *all* or *whole* is exceptional, as in Gal. 5 : 14 and 1 Tim. 1 : 16.   (See K. § 246. 5. β.)

19. With all, the utmost (see on 4 : 29). **lowliness of mind,** humility ; its opposite is *minding high things* (Rom. 12 : 16).   (Comp. Phil. 2 : 3 and 1 Pet. 5 : 5.)   This use of *all*, says Tho-

with many tears, and temptations, which befell me [a]by the lying in wait of the Jews:

20 And how [b]I kept back nothing that was profitable unto you, but have shewed you, and have taught you publicly, and from house to house.

21 [c]Testifying both to the Jews, and also to the Greeks, [d]repentance toward God, and faith toward our Lord Jesus Christ.

22 And now, behold, [e]I go bound in the spirit unto Jerusalem, not knowing the things that shall befall me there:

mind, and with tears, and with trials which befell 20 me by the plots of the Jews: how that I shrank not from declaring unto you anything that was profitable, and teaching you publicly, and from house to 21 house, testifying both to Jews and to Greeks repentance toward God, and faith toward our Lord Jesus 22 [1]Christ. And now, behold, I go bound in the spirit unto Jerusalem, not knowing the things that shall

a ver. 3....b ver. 27....c ch. 18 : 5....d Mark 1 : 15 ; Luke 24 : 47 ; ch. 2 : 38....e ch. 19 : 21.—— 1 Many ancient authorities omit Christ.

luck,[1] is eminently Pauline. (Comp. Eph. 1 : 3–8; 4 : 2; 6 : 18; 2 Cor. 12 : 12; 1 Tim. 3 : 4; 2 Tim. 4 : 2; Tit. 2 : 15; 3 : 2.)—**With tears,** of solicitude for their salvation. (See v. 31. Comp. 2 Cor. 2 : 4 and Phil. 3 : 18.) **Many** before **tears,** in the common text, should be dropped (Grsb., Mey., Tsch.).—**Temptations, trials,** persecutions which he suffered from his countrymen. Luke has not spoken distinctly of these Jewish machinations at Ephesus, but in 19 : 9 he describes a state of feeling on the part of the Jews, which must have been a prolific source of hostility both to the person of the apostle and to the objects of his ministry. That his situation there was one of constant peril we see from 1 Cor. 15 : 31, 32; 16 : 9; and 2 Cor. 1 : 8–10.

20. How I kept back nothing depends still on **ye know** (v. 18), but illustrates, at the same time, the intervening **how I was with you,** etc.: **how** (not *that*) **I kept back nothing of the things expedient**—*i. e.* out of regard to men's censure or their favor. How perfectly this remark harmonizes with Paul's character we have proof in such passages as 2 Cor. 4 : 2; Gal. 1 : 10; 1 Thess. 2 : 4.—**But have showed,** etc. [The structure of the Greek is different—viz.] **that I should,** or **might** (telic, as if in denial of the possibility that he could mean to preach less than the entire truth), **not announce unto you and teach you**—viz. the things expedient for them. But both clauses contain a negative idea, and the rule stated on 10 : 47 may apply here: he withheld nothing from them that **he should** (as the effect of such withholding) **not announce and teach.** In other words, the infinitive states, not the object of **kept back,** as before, but a consequence of the suppression if unhindered. (See W. § 44. 4. Comp. v. 27, below.) —**Publicly,** *in public,* as in the synagogue (19 : 8) or in the school of Tyrannus (19 : 9).— **From house to house,** better **in houses,** private assemblies.

21. Repentance toward God—lit. the **repentance** (which is meet) **in respect to God;** *i. e.* exercised toward him as especially wronged by transgression. (See Ps. 51 : 4.) De Wette supposes a breviloquence, as in 8 : 22: **repentance** (with a return) **unto God.** (Comp. 26 : 20.) The first sense agrees best with the use of **unto,** or **in respect to** (εἰς), in the next clause. "In God the Father," says Olshausen, "lies expressed the idea of the strict righteousness to which the repentance directs itself; in Christ, the idea of the compassion to which the faith has reference."—" It appears," says Tholuck, "to belong to the peculiarities of the apostle that he in particular appeals so often to his blameless manner of life. The occasion for this lies sometimes in the calumnies of his enemies, as when he says, in 2 Cor. 1 : 12, 'For our boasting (καύχησις) is this, the testimony of our conscience, that in simplicity and godly sincerity, not with fleshly wisdom, but by the grace of God, we have had our conversation in the world, and more especially among you.' The eleventh chapter shows what adversaries he had in view in this self-justification. But often these appeals spring only from that just confidence with which he can call upon others to imitate him, as he himself imitates the Saviour. Thus, in 1 Cor. 11 : 1, he cries, 'Be ye followers of me, even as I also am of Christ;' and in Phil. 3 : 17, 'Brethren, be followers together of me, and mark them who walk so as ye have us for an ensample.' Such personal testimonies are not found in the other Epistles of the New Testament, nor are they frequent in the writings of other pious men; on which account we are authorized to consider their occurrence in this discourse (vv. 18-21) as a mark of its historical character."

22. Bound in the spirit—*i. e.* his own, in his mind, feelings (19 : 21), constrained by an invincible impulse or sense of duty (Hnr., Kuin., De Wet., Rob.), so as to be indifferent to danger on the one hand (v. 23), and perhaps

1 Die Reden des Apostels Paulus in der Apostelgeschichte, mit seinen Briefen verglichen, in the Studien und Kritiken, 1839, p. 305, sq. I have drawn several of the notes on this address from that instructive article.

23 Save that *a*the Holy Ghost witnesseth in every **c**ity, saying that bonds and afflictions abide me.
24 But *b*none of these things move me, neither count I my life dear unto myself, *c*so that I might finish my course with joy, *d*and the ministry, *e*which I have received of the Lord Jesus, to testify the gospel of the grace of God.

23 befall me there: save that the Holy Spirit testifieth unto me in every city, saying that bonds and afflic-
24 tions abide me. But I hold not my life of any account, as dear unto myself, *l*so that I may accomplish my course, and the ministry which I received from the Lord Jesus, to testify the gospel of the

---

a ch. 21 : 4, 11 ; 1 Thess. 3 : 3....*b* ch. 21 : 13 ; Rom. 8 : 35; 2 Cor. 4 : 16....*c* 2 Tim. 4 : 7....*d* ch. 1 : 17 ; 2 Cor. 4 : 1....*e* Gal. 1 : 1 ; Tit. 1 : 3.———*l* Or, *in comparison of accomplishing my course*

---

immovable under any remonstrance or appeal on the other (21 : 13). The expression may be compared with our mode of speaking when we say "bound in good faith, in conscience," and the like. Some understand **spirit** of the Holy Spirit: urged by his influence or command (Calv., Kypk., Wdsth.). But that meaning is the more doubtful here, because *the Holy,* in the next verse, appears to be added to distinguish that *Spirit* from this. The sense **bound in the spirit**—*i. e.* viewing himself as already in chains, a prisoner in imagination, though not yet in body (Chrys., Grot., Bng., Conybeare and Howson)—anticipates the sequel of the sentence, and is too artificial where all the rest is expressed with so much simplicity. Meyer's first explanation was *bound on the Holy Spirit* (Rom. 7 : 2 ; 1 Cor. 7 : 27)—*i. e.* dependent on him; but I am pleased to see that in his last edition he defends the first of the views given above. **23. Save**—*i. e.* **but knowing.—From city to city,** as he pursued the present journey.— **Witnesseth, testifies fully to me,** not by an inward revelation (for why should he have received that *from city to city?*), but through the prophetic announcement of others. Luke has not recorded the instances ; they may have occurred at Philippi, at Troas, at Assos. He mentioned two such communications which were made to Paul after this. (See 21 : 4, 11.) The common text leaves out **to me,** which belongs after the verb.—**Await me,** not wherever he went, but at Jerusalem. **I go . . . unto Jerusalem** determines the place.—Paley compares this verse with Rom. 15 : 30, which Epistle the apostle had just written at Corinth. He there entreats the Roman Christians "to strive together with him in their prayers to God for him, that he might be delivered from them who believed not in Judea." The two passages, therefore, "without any resemblance between them that could induce us to suspect that they were borrowed from one another, represent the state of Paul's mind, with respect to the event of the journey, in terms of substantial agreement. They both express his sense of danger in the approaching visit to Jerusalem : they both express the doubt which

dwelt upon his thoughts concerning what might there befall him."
24. None of these things move me—lit. **I make account of nothing;** *i. e.* which I may be called to suffer. On the contrary, as he says in 2 Cor. 12 : 10, "I take pleasure in infirmities, in reproaches, in necessities, in persecutions, in distresses, for Christ's sake." Another reading draws the two clauses of the common text into one: *but of no account do I esteem my life worthy for myself.* The construction is less simple than the other, and may have given place to it on that account (Tsch., Mey., Alf.). [This reading is very well given in the Revised Version: **But I hold not my life of any account, as dear unto myself.** The reading is without doubt correct, being supported by א* B C D² and several of the earliest versions.— A. H.]—**So that I might,** etc.—lit. **thus** (*i. e.* with this aim, to wit) **in order to finish my course.** That he should shrink from no danger, that he should be willing to offer up his life for the sake of the gospel, he regarded as due to his office, as essential to his character as an approved minister of Christ. **So,** or *thus,* strengthens merely the telic force of the construction. It occurs with the infinitive here only (unless we add 17 : 14), and in the phrase *as I may so say* (ὡς ἔπος εἰπεῖν, Heb. 7 : 9). (W. ? 44. 1.) Alford refers **so** to **dear**—held not his life *so precious as to finish,* etc. But he must arbitrarily insert for that purpose the correlative "so," and even then translates the common reading only, and not the one received into his text.—Some critics (Lchm., Mey., Tsch.) [also Treg., West. and Hort, Anglo-Am. Revisers, with א A B D, and the Syr., Coptic, Vulg. Vss. —A. H.] omit **with joy** after **my course.** It is wanting in several important authorities.— **To testify the gospel,** etc., defines in what the **ministry** consisted. The infinitive may depend on the verbal idea involved in that noun (De Wet.): (commanding or requiring) **that I should testify fully,** etc.; or it may follow as epexegetical.—In the sublime language of this verse we hear distinctly the voice of the man who on approaching the end of his career could say, "I am now ready

25 And now, behold, *a*I know that ye all, among whom I have gone preaching the kingdom of God, shall see my face no more.
26 Wherefore I take you to record this day, that I am *b*pure from the blood of all *men.*
27 For *c*I have not shunned to declare unto you all *d*the counsel of God.
28 ¶ *e*Take heed therefore unto yourselves, and to all the flock, over the which the Holy Ghost *f*hath

25 grace of God. And now, behold, I know that ye all, among whom I went about preaching the king-
26 dom, shall see my face no more. Wherefore I tes-
tify unto you this day, that I am pure from the
27 blood of all men. For I shrank not from declaring
28 unto you the whole counsel of God. Take heed
unto yourselves, and to all the flock, in the which

a ver. 38; Rom. 15 : 23....*b* ch. 18 : 6; 2 Cor. 7 : 2....*c* ver. 20....*d* Luke 7 : 30; John 15 : 15; Eph. 1 : 11....*e* 1 Tim. 4 : 16;
1 Pet. 5 : 2....*f* 1 Cor. 12 : 28.

to be offered, and the time of my departure is at hand. I have fought a good fight, I have finished my course, I have kept the faith. Henceforth there is laid up for me a crown of righteousness, which the Lord, the right-eous judge, shall give me at that day " (2 Tim. 4 : 6-8). (Comp. also Phil. 2 : 17.)

25. And now resumes the thought in v. 22.—**Know** expresses, not an apprehension or a presentiment, but a conviction. **For I know this** (T. R.) has more against it than for it. Paul's **I know** having been fulfilled, Zeller sees evidence of the *post eventum* character of the word in that agreement.—**That ye all shall see my face no more,** etc. If Paul's Roman captivity closed with his death, he cer-tainly never saw the Ephesian elders after this interview. " Nor, if we suppose him to have been liberated, can any contradictory result be urged on that ground, since the traditions of the fathers decide nothing in regard to the journeys of the apostle between his supposed liberation and his second captivity " (*Meyer*). It has been proposed to emphasize **all,** as if some of them, at least, might hope to renew their intercourse with him; but the qualifica-tion is inconsistent with vv. 37, 38.—**Among whom I have gone,** or **among whom I went about,** may intimate a wider circuit of labor than that furnished by a single city. The apostle either addressed those who had come from different churches in the region (see on v. 17), or at this point of the discourse recognized those before him as representatives of these churches. Some understand *I went about* to describe Paul's labors in various parts of Ephe-sus, or the visit which he made to the houses of the presbyters. The expression favors the wider view, says Neander, but is not incon-sistent with the other. [**Preaching the king-dom of God,** rather the **kingdom,** for the words **of God** are probably an addition to the text. But they are unnecessary, for no other kingdom than that of God or of Christ could be called the **kingdom** by Paul in such a con-nection as this. And there is something very suggestive in these brief expressions : *the way, the word, the kingdom, the brotherhood.* They

condense a great movement into a term of childlike simplicity.—A. H.]

26. Wherefore, or **therefore,** since it was proper for him to close his ministry with such a testimony.—**I take you to record** (μαρτύρομαι = μαρτυρέω), *I testify,* declare as a witness, as in Gal. 5 : 3 and Eph. 4 : 17, and occasionally in the classics (Pape, *Lex.,* s. v.). It means prop-erly *obtest,* call to witness, with the accusative of a person.—**That I am pure,** etc. (See on 18 : 6.) The expression is peculiar to Paul's speeches. In this clause **am** may have been displaced from the text (Grsb., Lach., Mey.). [It has been restored by all the late editors, Tsch., Treg., West. and Hort, Anglo-Am. Re-visers, as well as by those named by Dr. Hack-ett, and it is justified by א B C D E, Pesh., Cop. —A. H.]

27. For I have not shunned—lit. for I **shrunk not back** (while among you) **that I should not declare unto you.** (Comp. on v. 20.)—**All the counsel**—i. e. **the whole plan**—**of God** as to the way of saving men unfolded in the gospel.

28. Take heed, therefore (since in future the responsibility will rest on you), **unto yourselves** (that ye be faithful) **and unto all the flock** (that they be kept from error). Here Paul speaks just as he writes in 1 Tim. 4 : 16.—**Over the which,** strictly **in which,** since the bishops made part of the flock, while they had the direction of it.—**The Holy Spirit hath made** may refer to their having been chosen under the direction of the Spirit (13 : 2; 14 : 23), or to their having been qualified for their office by the Spirit (1 Cor. 12 : 8).—**To feed** in-cludes the idea not only of instruction, but of government and of supervision in general. (Comp. 1 Pet. 5 : 2. See the note on 14 : 23.)—**The church,** etc. **The church of the Lord** or **God.** The reading here is disputed. The external testimony preponderates in favor of **the Lord,** and most of the recent critics ac-cept that as the original word, as Griesbach, Lachmann, Bornemann, Tischendorf, Meyer, Tregelles. Some, as Bengel, Rinck, Scholz, Mill, Alford, decide for **God.** The internal argument is claimed on both sides. It is said

made you overseers, to feed the church of God, [a]which he hath purchased [b]with his own blood.

29 For I know this, that after my departing [c]shall grievous wolves enter in among you, not sparing the flock.

30 Also [d]of your own selves shall men arise, speaking perverse things, to draw away disciples after them.

31 Therefore watch, and remember, that [e]by the space of three years I ceased not to warn every one night and day with tears.

32 And now, brethren, I commend you to God, and [f]to the word of his grace, which is able [g]to build you up, and to give you [h]an inheritance among all them which are sanctified.

the Holy Spirit hath made you [1]bishops, to feed the church of [2]the Lord, which he [3]purchased with his

29 own blood. I know that after my departing grievous wolves shall enter in among you, not sparing

30 the flock; and from among your own selves shall men arise, speaking perverse things, to draw away

31 the disciples after them. Wherefore watch ye, remembering that by the space of three years I ceased not to admonish every one night and day with tears.

32 And now I commend you to [4]God, and to the word of his grace, who is able to build *you* up, and to give *you* the inheritance among all them that are sancti-

---

a Eph. 1 : 7, 14; Col. 1 : 14, Heb. 9 : 12; 1 Pet. 1 : 19; Rev. 5 : 9....*b* See Heb. 9 : 14....*c* Matt. 7 . 15; 2 Pet. 2 : 1....*d* 1 Tim. 1 : 20; 1 John 2 : 19....*e* ch. 19 : 10.. .*f* Heb. 13 : 9....*g* ch. 9 · 31. ..*h* ch. 26 : 18; Eph. 1 : 18; Col. 1 : 12; 3 : 24; Heb. 9 : 15; 1 Pet. 1 : 4. ——1 Or, *overseers*....2 Some ancient authorities, including the two oldest MSS., read *God*....3 Gr. *acquired*....4 Some ancient authorities read *the Lord*.

---

that **God** agrees best with the usage of Paul, since in his Epistles *church of God* occurs eleven times, *church of Christ* once, but never *church of the Lord.* It is replied to this that the uncommon expression is more likely to have been exchanged for the ordinary one than the reverse.[1] Wordsworth inclines to ϑεοῦ (God), mainly for internal reasons. (See Humphry's note on the other side.) The variations *the Lord God, the God and Lord,* and *the Lord and God* are too slightly supported to require notice.—**Which he purchased,** or *which he* (redeemed and thus) *obtained for himself* (as a possession). (Comp. *that he might redeem us from all iniquity, and purify unto himself a peculiar people* (Tit. 2 · 14) and *a people for possession* (1 Pet. 2 : 9).—**With his own blood** represents the atonement as consisting pre-eminently in the sacrifice and death of Christ. (See Matt. 20 : 28; Rom. 3 : 24; Eph. 1 : 7; 1 Tim. 2 : 6; Heb. 9 : 12; 13 . 12, etc.)

29. This gives prominence to the following clause. (Comp. 9:21.)—**Shall enter in** is said of those who should come to them from other places.—**After my departing,** or **departure,** not *after my decease* (De Wet.). The same expression occurs in Herodotus (9 . 17).—**Grievous**—*i. e.* **violent,** rapacious—**wolves,** which represent here, not persecutors, but false teachers. (See v. 30 and Matt. 7 : 15.) These men would be as far from corresponding to their professed character as guardians of the flock as fierce wolves are unlike the faithful shepherd.

30. Of your own selves, or **from you yourselves**—*i. e.* from their own community, not necessarily from the number of those present.—That the danger which Paul announced

was realized we learn from the Epistles to Timothy (see especially 2 Tim. 2:17) and from Rev. 2 : 2. The latter passage shows that some of these false teachers, in order to strengthen their influence, laid claim to the authority of apostles.

31. Therefore watch, since their vigilance should be equal to the dangers which threatened them.—**And remember**—lit. **remembering,** etc. How they should **watch,** with what constancy and solicitude, they had been taught by his own example.—**The space of three years** may be a proximate expression, but must come nearer to *three* years than *two.* (See the note on 19 : 10.) In Rev. 2 : 2, 3 we have an interesting proof that the apostle's admonition was not in vain. "Thou hast tried them," it is said of the church at Ephesus, "who say that they are apostles and are not, and hast found them liars; . . . and for my name's sake hast labored and hast not fainted."

32. I commend you to God and to the word of his grace—*i. e.* in this connection to the power of this word, as the instrumentality which God employs for the religious confirmation and security of his people. [It is not, however, to be supposed that "the word of his grace" is the only instrumentality employed by God. His Spirit and providence are also directed to the same end; but the word is named because of its great importance in building up the people of God in faith and love and holy activity.—A. H.]—**Brethren** fails in so many copies as to be doubtful.—**Which** (or **who**) **is able** it is best to refer to **God** as the principal word (Calv , Bng., Mey., De Wet.), not to **word** (Hnr., Kuin.).—**To build you up.** To build up further (a compound verb,

---

[1] For a view of the testimonies in the case, see Davidson's *Lectures on Biblical Criticism,* p. 175, *sq.* He adopts *the Lord* as the probable reading. Green (p. 111) comes to the same conclusion. [See also Dr. Ezra Abbot *On the Reading "Church of God," Acts 20 : 28, Bib. Sac.,* 1876, p. 313, *sq.,* and Westcott and Hort, *The New Test. in Greek Appendix,* p. 98, *sq.*—A. H.]

16

33 *I have coveted no man's silver, or gold, or apparel.
34 Yea, ye yourselves know, *that these hands have ministered unto my necessities, and to them that were with me.
35 I have shewed you all things, *how that so laboring ye ought to support the weak, and to remember the

33 fied. I coveted no man's silver, or gold, or apparel.
34 Ye yourselves know that these hands ministered unto my necessities, and to them that were with me. In all things I gave you an example, how that
35 so laboring ye ought to help the weak, and to re-

a 1 Sam. 12 : 3 ; 1 Cor. 9 : 12 ; 2 Cor. 7 : 2 ; 11 : 9 ; 12 : 17....b ch. 18 : 3 ; 1 Cor. 4 : 12 ; 1 Thess. 2 : 9 ; 2 Thess. 3 : 8....c Rom. 15 : 1 ; 1 Cor. 9 : 12 ; 2 Cor. 11 : 9, 12 ; 12 : 13 ; Eph. 4 : 28 ; 1 Thess. 4 : 11 ; 5 : 14 ; 2 Thess. 3 : 8.

T. R.) is Pauline, but has less support here than *to build up*. "This term reminds us of Eph. 2 : 20, and can be taken only in the sense of that passage. Remarkable, also, is the expression **an inheritance among all them that are sanctified.** Here all gives prominence to the idea of a great company of the holy, and reminds us again of Eph. 3 : 18. The expression **an inheritance among the sanctified**—*i. e.* participation in the spiritual blessings which exist among them—is likewise peculiarly Pauline, and occurs further only in the words of Paul in 26 : 18 and in Eph. 1 : 18 " (*Tholuck*).

33. He warns them against avarice, against a sordid spirit.—**Have coveted**—lit. **coveted** when he was with them, not perf., as in E. V.—**Apparel, raiment.** The wealth of the Orientals consisted in part of costly garments; they trafficked in them or kept them in store for future use. (See Ezra 2 : 69 ; Neh. 7 : 70 ; Job 27 : 16 ; 2 Kings 5 : 26.) This fact accounts for the allusion to the destructive power of the moth, as well as rust, in Matt. 6 : 19 and James 5 : 2.

34. And to those that were with me is an instance of varied construction : **and to** (the wants of) **those with me.** (W. § 63. II. 1.) Those referred to here are Timothy, Erastus, Luke, and others who traversed sea and land with the apostle, attached to him as personal friends, and still more as friends of the cause which they served.— **These hands,** which we may suppose him to have held up to view as he spoke, and which may have been marked with traces of the toil to which they were inured. (See the note on 17 : 10 and 18 : 3.)—This allusion to the apostle's habit of manual labor while he was at Ephesus accords remarkably with 1 Cor. 4 : 11, 12. Luke has said nothing of it in his narrative of Paul's residence in that city (19 : 1, *sq.*). But in the above-named passage of the Epistle, which Paul wrote just before his departure from Ephesus, we find him saying, "*Unto this present hour* . . . we labor, working with our own hands." Nothing could be more undesigned than this agreement. " It is manifest that if the history in this passage had been taken

from the Epistle, this circumstance, if it appeared at all, would have appeared in its *place*—that is, in the direct account of Paul's transactions at Ephesus. The correspondence would not have been effected, as it is, by a kind of reflected stroke—that is, by a reference in a subsequent speech to what in the narrative was omitted. Nor is it likely, on the other hand, that a circumstance which is not extant in the history of Paul at Ephesus should have been made the subject of a fictitious allusion in an Epistle purporting to be written by him from that place, not to mention that the allusion itself, especially in time, is too oblique and general to answer any purpose of forgery whatever " (*Paley*).

35. All things. Not **all things** as the object of **I have shewed** (E. V., Hmph.), but adverbial, **in all ways**—*i. e.* by doctrine and by example. (Comp. 1 Cor. 10 : 33 ; Eph. 4 : 15.)—**So laboring**—viz. as I have done.—**That you ought to assist the weak,** feeble—*i. e.* the poor, whom this mode of designation contrasts with the rich, who are strong, powerful (Chrys., Kuin., Olsh., De Wet., Rob., Cony. and Hws.). The examples in Wetstein sanction this meaning of *the weak*. (See also Rob., *Lex.*, s. v.) But the stricter sense of the word (4 : 9 ; 5 : 15 ; Matt. 25 : 39, etc) is entirely appropriate : *the weak*—*i. e.* those unable, in consequence of physical infirmity, to labor for their own support. The apostle would enforce here the duty of industry and self-denial, in order to procure the means of relieving those who are disabled by any cause from taking care of themselves. He holds up to them his own example—his diligence in labor, his disinterestedness—as worthy of their imitation. (Comp. 2 Thess. 3 : 7, *sq.*)—Others understand **the weak** of the *weak* in their religious faith or principles. The apostle's object, as they argue, was to exhort the elders to maintain themselves by their own labor, out of regard to those who would not appreciate their claim to support, who would take offence at the appearance of anything like a mercenary spirit in their teachers. So Calvin, Bengel, Neander, Meyer, Tholuck, and others. It is alleged that this interpretation is necessary, in order to make the cases parallel—that, as Paul

words of the Lord Jesus, how he said, It is more blessed to give than to receive.

36 ¶ And when he had thus spoken, he *a*kneeled down, and prayed with them all.

37 And they all wept sore, and *b*fell on Paul's neck, and kissed him,

member the words of the Lord Jesus, how he himself said, It is more blessed to give than to receive.

36 And when he had thus spoken, he kneeled down, 37 and prayed with them all. And they all wept sore,

---

a ch. 7 : 60 ; 21 : 5....*b* Gen. 45 : 14 ; 46 : 29.

---

labored for his own support, so the object of their labor must be the same. But **so laboring** does not require that sort of correspondence. Instead of the same application of the fruits of his industry, the **so** may refer equally well to the *manner* and *spirit* of his labor—*i. e.* to his assiduity in it—and his benevolence, which he would have them imitate, though the class of persons to be benefited in the two cases was different. The positive objections to this exegesis are—first, that the language is too mild, as understood of such illiberality ; secondly, that some word or the context should define **weak,** qualified by *in the faith* in Rom. 14 : 1, *sq.*, and in effect by *in their conscience* in 1 Cor. 8 : 9 (compared with v. 7) ; and thirdly, that it destroys the opposition between the giving of personal favors and the reception of them, as contemplated in the words of Christ. The use of *the weak* in 1 Thess. 5 : 14 weakens, it is true, the second objection. It may be added that Paul, although he waived his own right to a maintenance from those to whom he preached, was remarkable for the decision with which he asserted that right in behalf of others. (Comp. Rom. 15 : 27 ; 1 Cor. 9 : 13, 14 ; Gal. 6 : 6 ; 1 Tim. 5 : 17, 18. See also the Saviour's rule on this subject, in Luke 10 : 7.) Hence, if the explanation under remark were correct, it would array the author of the speech against the Epistles. It would justify Zeller's objection that the true Paul, after representing his own assumption of the expenses of his support (for example, in 1 Cor. 9 : 1–27) as unprescriptive and voluntary, would not so forget himself as to impose his example in that respect upon the Ephesian teachers as one which they must follow.—**How he said,** or **that he himself said.** Our English translation overlooks the emphasis.—**It is more blessed to give than to receive.** The evangelists have not recorded this saying of Christ. It comes down to us here as an interesting specimen of the many such words that fell from his lips and were treasured up in the memory of the first disciples, but which no similar application has rescued from oblivion. It will be noticed that Paul alludes to the remark as familiar to his hearers.—The best authorities read *rather to give* (μᾶλλον διδόναι) instead of the inverse order.

—Nothing is wanting to attest the Pauline origin of this Miletian speech. It agrees with Paul's history, reflects Paul's character, bears the stamp of Paul's style. This last point deserves a fuller illustration. The following examples show the linguistic affinity between the discourse and the apostle's writings. *To serve the Lord, God,* or *Christ* (δουλεύειν τῷ κυρίῳ, θεῷ or Χριστῷ) occurs in v. 19, above, six times in Paul, elsewhere only in Matt. 6 : 24 and Luke 16 : 13 ; *lowliness of mind* (ταπεινοφροσύνη) is found only in v. 19, five times in Paul, and once in 1 Pet. 5 : 5 ; *shunned,* or *kept out* (ὑποστέλλω) in vv. 20, 27 and in Gal. 2 : 12 ; *the profitable* (τὸ συμφέρον) in v. 20, once in Heb. 12 : 20, and three times in the First Epistle to the Corinthians ; *service,* or *ministry* (διακονία), in v. 24, and twenty-two times in Paul ; *testify* (μαρτύρομαι) in v. 26 and in Gal. 5 : 3 and Eph. 4 : 17 ; *sparing* (φείδομαι) in v. 29, in 2 Pet. 2 : 4, and seven times in Paul ; *warn, admonish* (νουθετεῖν) in v. 31, and seven times in Paul, *laboring* (κοπιᾶν) in v. 35, in Paul, on the contrary, thirteen times ; and the hortatory *watch* (γρηγορεῖτε) in v. 31, elsewhere only in 1 Cor. 16 : 13. (See Lekebusch, *Composition der Apostelgeschichte,* p. 339.)

36–38. PAUL PRAYS WITH THE ELDERS, AND EMBARKS AGAIN.

36. He kneeled down, or **having kneeled** (7 : 60 ; 9 : 40). This was the attitude in prayer which prevailed among the early Christians, except on the Sabbath and during the seven weeks before Pentecost, when they generally stood. They regarded the latter posture as the more appropriate one for the expression of gratitude, and adopted it, therefore, on joyful occasions (Hmph.). It cannot be shown that the distinction was observed at this early period.

37. The scene here was a touching one ; the simplicity of Luke's description heightens the effect of it. We feel instinctively that the eye must have seen what the pen has portrayed in so natural a manner.—**And fell on Paul's neck,** or **and having fallen upon the neck of Paul.** In the same manner Joseph manifested his strong affection for Benjamin his brother (Gen. 45 : 14), and for Jacob his father (Gen. 46 : 29), after their long separation from each other. It was in accordance with Oriental manners.—**Kissed,** or **kissed tenderly** (com-

38 Sorrowing most of all for the words ^awhich he spake, that they should see his face no more. And they accompanied him unto the ship.

38 and fell on Paul's neck, and kissed him, sorrowing most of all for the word which he had spoken, that they should behold his face no more. And they brought him on his way unto the ship.

CHAPTER XXI.

AND it came to pass, that after we were gotten from them, and had launched, we came with a straight course unto Coos, and the *day* following unto Rhodes, and from thence unto Patara:

2 And finding a ship sailing over unto Phenicia, we went aboard, and set forth.

1 AND when it came to pass that we were parted from them, and had set sail, we came with a straight course unto Cos, and the next day unto Rhodes, 2 from thence unto Patara: and having found a ship crossing over unto Phœnicia, we went aboard, and

a ver. 25.

pound) and (imperf.) **again and again.** The evangelist uses this word to describe the affected earnestness of the traitor's kiss (Matt. 26 : 49).

38. Words which he spake, more accurately **the word which he had spoken** (pluperf.) ; dative by attraction.—**That** (ὅτι) is declarative.—**See** (ϑεωρεῖν = ϑεάομαι. Tittm., *De Syn.*, p. 120), **behold,** contemplate. It suggests the idea of the interest and affection with which they looked upon that countenance for the last time. The writer's tact in using this word of the Ephesians, but **shall see** (ὄψεσϑε) of Paul, in v. 25, should be noticed.—**Accompanied,** or **sent him forward,** escorted him, **unto the ship.** (See the note on 15 : 3 and the illustration on 21 : 5.) It is implied that the roadstead where the vessel lay was at some distance from the town. The site of Miletus, though originally on the coast, has gradually receded, till it is now ten miles from the sea. It must have lost its maritime position long before the apostle's time, though not so far inland then as at present.

1–6. THEY CONTINUE THE VOYAGE TO TYRE.

1. And it came to pass, etc., **when now it came to pass that we put to sea.** The construction is like that in v. 5. Luke certainly, as one of the **we,** Trophimus (21 : 29), and Aristarchus (27 : 2) accompanied Paul to Jerusalem. As the others who belonged to the company (20 : 4) are not mentioned again, the probability is (*ex silentio*) that they proceeded no farther. Some suppose that Timothy went at this time from Miletus to Ephesus, and assumed or resumed the oversight of the church there.—**After we were gotten from them** —*i. e.* **having departed from them** (De Wet., Rob.) ; less probably, *having torn ourselves away* (Chrys., Kuin., Mey.). Usage weakened the etymological sense, and in Luke 22 : 41 an

emphasis appears to me out of place.—**Having run straight** shows that the wind was in their favor. (See on 16 : 11.)—(Κῶ is for Κῶν, like Ἀπολλώ, in 19 : 1.) **Coos.** *Cos* was about forty miles from Miletus, directly south, and could have been reached in six hours. It was one of the smaller islands of the archipelago, on the Carian coast, between the promontories, on which stood Cnidus and Halicarnassus. Its present name is *Stanchio*, which has arisen from a slurred pronunciation of *es tan kōn*, like Stambul from *es tan polin*.—Having rounded Cape Crio, the ancient Triopium, they turned their prow eastward and sailed along the southern shore of Asia Minor. **Rhodes** was at the entrance of the Ægean, on the coast of Caria. The celebrated Colossus was prostrate at this time, having been overthrown by an earthquake.—**Patara** was a coast-town of Lycia, at some distance from the left bank of the Xanthus. " Now its port is an inland marsh, generating poisonous malaria, and the mariner sailing along the coast would never guess that the sand-hills before him blocked up the harbor into which St. Paul sailed of old."[1] Patara was best known for its celebrated oracle of Apollo, which in the height of its authority had almost rivalled that of Delphos. How near to it, in the person of these wayfaring men, was now brought the Power which was to subvert that great delusion of heathenism ! How soon after this could it be said, in the words of Milton's *Hymn on the Nativity of Christ,*

> " The oracles are dumb ;
>   No voice or hideous hum
> Runs through the archèd roofs in words deceiving.
>   Apollo from his shrine
>   Can no more divine,
> With hollow shriek the steep of Delphos leaving.
>   No nightly trance or breathèd spell
> Inspires the pale-eyed priest from the prophetic cell."

2. The party take now another vessel. We are not informed of the reason for this measure. The vessel which had brought them thus far

---

[1] *Travels in Lycia,* by Spratt and Forbes, vol. i. p. 31.

3 Now when we had discovered Cyprus, we left it on the left hand, and sailed into Syria, and landed at Tyre: for there the ship was to unlade her burden.

4 And finding disciples, we tarried there seven days: *who said to Paul through the Spirit, that he should not go up to Jerusalem.

3 set sail. And when we had come in sight of Cyprus, leaving it on the left hand, we sailed unto Syria, and landed at Tyre: for there the ship was to unlade her burden. And having found the disciples, 4 we tarried there seven days: and these said to Paul through the Spirit, that he should not set foot in

---

a ver. 12 ; ch. 20 : 23.

---

may have been adapted only to sailing along the shore, or they may have engaged the use of it (see on 20 : 16) only until they should find an opportunity like the present. **Sailing over, crossing over,** just as they arrived. This particularity is as graphic "as if taken from a journal written during the voyage." The present participle denotes often an appointed or approaching act. (Comp. v. 3 ; 27 : 6. W. § 45. 1. b.)

3. **And when we had discovered, or and having had a view of, Cyprus**—lit. having had it brought up to sight, made visible to us above the horizon. The language is that of an eye-witness, and of one familiar with the phraseology of seamen, who are accustomed to speak of *raising* the land when they approach it. The opposite expression is *to conceal the land.* (See Krüg., *On Thucyd.*, 5. 65 ; Stallb., *On Prot.*, 338. A.) The corresponding Latin words, says Mr. Humphry, are *aperire* and *abscondere.* (Virg., *Æn.*, 3. 275, 291.) Some render *being shown Cyprus,* having it pointed out to us in the distance (Rob.), but the composite form indicates a more specific sense. This verb, which in the active governs a dative and accusative, retains the latter in the passive. (W. § 39. 1 ; K. § 281. 3.)—**We left it,** [or in the participial form of the Greek] **having left it behind.**—**On the left** is an adjective, not an adverb. (K. § 264. 3. a.) They passed, therefore, to the south of the island. They must have had a fair wind to enable them to take that course. The view of Cyprus must have carried back the apostle's mind to the days which he and Barnabas had spent there in the missionary work.—**We sailed unto Syria** refers to the voyage to Tyre; for in the Roman age Syria included Phœnicia (Win.), of which Tyre was the commercial emporium. (For its present state, see Rob., *Bibl. Res.*, iii. 392, *sq.*) The most important ruins lie at present beneath the sea. It was with melancholy interest that I looked down upon them through the calm waters in the long twilight which closed the 10th of May, 1852.—[The next clause] is best taken as brachylogical : **for** having come **thither, the ship was unlading**—*i. e.* about to unlade—**the cargo.** (See W. § 45. 5.) This use of the participle coincides essentially with that in v. 2. (See, further, Matt. 26 : 28 ; Luke 22 : 19.) Some understand *thither* of the conveyance of the freight from the ship to the town : **for thither** (after the arrival) **was the ship unlading the cargo** (Mey., De Wet.). The writer would not be likely to specify so minute a circumstance. *Thither* (ἐκεῖσε) is not to be confounded with *there* (ἐκεῖ). The clause assigns the reason (γάρ) for their stopping at this port. The voyage from Patara to Tyre need not have exceeded two days, if the wind was fair and the vessel in a good condition. The distance is three hundred and forty geographical miles.[1]

4. **And finding**—lit. **and having found** —**out the disciples** who lived there, because, being strangers, they must make inquiry. The English Version overlooks both the preposition and the article. The gospel had been preached here at an early period. (See on 11 : 19.) The Saviour had performed some of his miracles in the vicinity of Tyre and Sidon. (See Matt. 15 : 21 ; Mark 7 : 24.)—**We tarried.** (See on 10 : 48.)—**Seven days** may be indefinite, as was remarked on 20 : 6. We cannot doubt that they occupied the time spent here in making known the word, and in consulting for the welfare of the Tyrian church.—**Who said to Paul through the Spirit that he should not go up unto Jerusalem**—*i. e.* if he had any regard to his own safety or personal welfare, or to their affectionate solicitude on his account. (Comp. *besought,* etc., in v. 12.) They were informed by the Spirit that bonds and afflictions awaited the apostle at Jerusalem ; but it was not revealed to them as the will of God that he should desist from his purpose to proceed thither.

---

[1] The writer embarked at Beirut (on the coast, to the north of Tyre) at half-past six o'clock P. M. ; the next day, at ten o'clock, we arrived off against Larnica, on the island of Cyprus, and on the following night, at two o'clock A. M., came to anchor in the harbor of Rhodes. This was very nearly the apostle's track, except in the inverse order. An ancient vessel, under circumstances entirely favorable, would almost equal the speed of a Levant steamer.

5 And when we had accomplished those days, we departed and went our way ; and they all brought us on our way, with wives and children, till *we were* out of the city : and *a*we kneeled down on the shore, and prayed.
6 And when we had taken our leave one of another, we took ship ; and they returned *b*home again.
7 And when we had finished *our* course from Tyre, we came to Ptolemais, and saluted the brethren, and abode with them one day.
8 And the next *day* we that were of Paul's company departed, and came unto Cæsarea : and we entered into the house of Philip *c*the evangelist, *d*which was *one* of the seven ; and abode with him.

5 Jerusalem. And when it came to pass that we had accomplished the days, we departed and went on our journey ; and they all, with wives and children, brought us on our way, till we were out of the city :
6 and kneeling down on the beach, we prayed, and bade each other farewell ; and we went on board the ship, but they returned home again.
7 And when we had finished the voyage from Tyre, we arrived at Ptolemais ; and we saluted the breth-
8 ren, and abode with them one day. And on the morrow we departed, and came unto Cæsarea : and entering into the house of Philip the evangelist, who was one of the seven, we abode with him.

---

a ch. 20 : 36....*b* John 1 : 11....*c* Eph. 4 : 11 ; 2 Tim. 4 : 5....*d* ch. 6 : 5 ; 8 : 26, 40.

---

5. And when we had accomplished— *i. e.* **when it came to pass that we had accomplished.** (See the first clause in v. 1.)— **Those days,** rather **the days** named in v. 1. **—All sending us forward,** etc. (See on 20 : 38.)—**Till out of the city,** quite out of it, beyond the suburbs, where they could be alone and undisturbed.—**Upon the beach.** The word denotes a smooth shore, as distinguished from one precipitous or rocky. (Comp. 27 : 39.) [See also Matt. 13 : 2. By the kindness of a friend, I am able to refer also to two passages of Herodotus which illustrate the special sense of this word—viz. vii. 59 and vii. 188.—A. H.] Luke manifests an autoptic accuracy here. A level, sandy beach extends for a considerable distance on both sides of the site of the ancient Tyre.—Modern missionary life presents its parallels to the scene so briefly sketched in this verse. The following extract occurs in the journal of a college friend, whose field of labor is in the region of Paul's birthplace. Speaking of his departure with his family from Aintab for a temporary absence, the missionary says : "More than a hundred of the converts accompanied us out of the city ; and there, near the spot where one of our number had once been stoned, we halted, and a prayer was offered amid tears. Between thirty and forty escorted us two hours farther, on horses and mules, singing hymns as we proceeded on our way. Then another prayer was offered, and with saddened countenances and with weeping they forcibly broke away from us. It really seemed as though they could not turn back."[1]

7–16. FROM TYRE THEY PROCEED TO PTOLEMAIS, AND THENCE TO CÆSAREA AND JERUSALEM.

7. And when we had finished, etc.—lit. **Now we, completing** (thereby) **the voyage, came down from Tyre to Ptolemais.** When the participle and the verb combined thus are both in the past tense, the act of the participle

may be antecedent to that of the verb or simultaneous with it. The sense must decide this ambiguity.—**From Tyre,** in this position, belongs to the verb **came down,** not to **voyage** or **course** (E. V.). Their arrival at Ptolemais terminated the sea part of their journey. The distance is a moderate day's journey by land. A vessel with a good breeze would make the run in a few hours. This city was the ancient Accho (Judg. 1 : 31), still called Akka by the Arabians, and Acre, or St. Jean d'Acre, by Europeans. It is on the Mediterranean, at the north angle of a bay which bears the same name, and sweeps in the form of a semicircle toward the south as far as Mount Carmel. The graceful curve of the bay appears to great advantage from the top of that mountain.—**The brethren** who were there. (See on v. 4.)

8. They now travelled by land. Issuing from the south-eastern gate, in ten minutes they would cross the Belus, now the Nahmen, then for three hours would proceed along the beach with the surf breaking at their feet, at the base of Carmel would ford the mouth of the Kishon (el-Mukatta), and, turning that headland, follow the line of the coast to Cæsarea. The distance hither from Akka is about forty miles.—The received **that were of Paul's company,** before **departed,** is untenable. A church reading began here, and a more definite subject than **we** was needed to suggest the connection. The gloss has passed into our English translation.—**Unto Cæsarea.** This is the third time that Paul has been at *Cæsarea.* He was here on his journey from Jerusalem to Tarsus (9 : 30), and again on his return to Antioch from his second missionary progress (18 : 22). **Philip.** (See on 8 : 40.)—**The evangelist.** This title appears to have been given to those who had no stated pastoral charge, but travelled from place to place and preached as they had opportunity. (See Eph. 4 : 11 ; 2 Tim. 4 : 5.) **Which was**—better **who was—of the**

---

[1] Rev. B. Schneider, in the *Missionary Herald,* vol. xlviii. p. 201 (1852).

9 And the same man had four daughters, virgins, ᵃwhich did prophesy.

10 And as we tarried *there* many days, there came down from Judæa a certain prophet, named ᵇAgabus.

11 And when he was come unto us, he took Paul's girdle, and bound his own hands and feet, and said, Thus saith the Holy Ghost, ᶜSo shall the Jews at Jerusalem bind the man that owneth this girdle, and shall deliver *him* into the hands of the Gentiles.

12 And when we heard these things, both we, and they of that place, besought him not to go up to Jerusalem.

13 Then Paul answered, ᵈWhat mean ye to weep and to break mine heart? for I am ready not to be bound only, but also to die at Jerusalem for the name of the Lord Jesus.

9 Now this man had four daughters, virgins, who did 10 prophesy. And as we tarried there some days, there came down from Judæa a certain prophet, named 11 Agabus. And coming to us, and taking Paul's girdle, he bound his own feet and hands, and said, Thus saith the Holy Spirit, So shall the Jews at Jerusalem bind the man that owneth this girdle, and shall deliver him into the hands of the Gen-12 tiles. And when we heard these things, both we and they of that place besought him not to go up 13 to Jerusalem. Then Paul answered, What do ye, weeping and breaking my heart? for I am ready not to be bound only, but also to die at Jerusalem

---

a Joel 2 : 28 ; ch. 2 : 17....*b* ch. 11 : 28....*c* ver. 33 ; ch. 20 : 23....*d* ch. 20 : 24.

---

seven (E. V.) recalls Philip as already known to us in another capacity. (See 6 : 5.) But the best critics reject the Greek article (τοῦ) rendered *who* or *which;* and the participle (ὄντος), translated *was*, becomes then ambiguous: either causal, **since he was of the seven** (De Wet., Alf.), or simply historical, as in the other case. (See Green's *Gr.*, p. 190.) It is improbable that the office merely influenced Paul, and so much the less since, according to this view, it would be the inferior office which Philip no longer held, and not his present one. The participle (ὄντος) follows the tense of the other verbs, and is past. (W. § 45. 1.) Philip, as an evangelist, had relinquished his service at Jerusalem; perhaps the occasion for it had been only temporary.

9. And the same man, or **now this one had four daughters**, etc. Luke mentions the fact as remarkable, and not as related in any way to the history. It is barely possible that they too (see v. 10) foretold the apostle's approaching captivity.

10. And as we tarried—lit. **remaining several days** (comp. 13 : 31; 27 : 20), a longer time than in the other places on the way. Having travelled rapidly since he left Miletus, and being now within two days of Jerusalem, the apostle had no occasion to hasten his journey. (See 20 : 16.)—**Agabus** has been mentioned in 11 : 28. He cannot well be a different person, as some have thought; for not only his name, but office (**prophet**) and residence (**from Judea**), are the same in both instances. Whether he had heard of Paul's arrival and came to Cæsarea on that account (Bmg.) must be left undecided.

11. And bound, etc. The prophet performed the act on himself, not on Paul. The pronoun should be *his own* (αὐτοῦ), not *his* (αὐτοῦ). (Many of the best manuscripts read ἑαυτοῦ.) **So shall bind**, etc., **so shall bind**

at Jerusalem the Jews. The Romans put the apostle in chains, but they did it at the instigation of the Jews.—Agabus, like the ancient prophets, accompanied his prediction with a symbolic act which served to place the event foretold more vividly before them; the scene, being thus acted out before their eyes, was rendered thus present, real, beyond what any mere verbal declaration could possibly have made it.

"Segnius irritant animos demissa per aurem
Quam quæ sunt oculis subjecta fidelibus, et quæ
Ipse sibi tradit spectator." [1]

Examples similar to this are frequent in the Old Testament. (See 1 Kings 22 : 11; Isa. 20 : 1, *sq.*; Jer. 13 : 1, *sq.*; Ezek. 4 : 1, *sq.*, etc.)

12. We—viz. the writer, Trophimus, Aristarchus (see on 20 : 4), and possibly others.—**The natives** restricts itself to the Christians of the place.

13. What mean ye is the language of remonstrance: *What are you doing that you weep*, etc. The same mode of expression occurs in Mark 11 : 5.—**For I am ready**, etc. Their opposition was not only painful to him (**to break mine heart**), but was useless, for (γάρ) he was not to be shaken in his purpose (De Wet.); or, which agrees better with **I am ready,** their distress was unnecessary, **for** he deemed it a privilege, not a hardship, to suffer in the cause of Christ. (Comp. 5 : 41.) [Was it right for Paul to persist in going up to Jerusalem? Agabus had uttered a true prediction, and we may assume that Paul believed it to be true. But Agabus brought no command from the Lord to Paul. Was, then, this prediction sent to him as an intimation that he ought to forbear rushing into such danger? This is not affirmed. Or was it made to him that he might be prepared for the result, and accept it as a part of God's plan of his life? Neither is this

---

[1] "Those things which enter through the ear affect our minds more slowly than those that are presented to the faithful eyes, and which the spectator himself delivers to himself."

14 And when he would not be persuaded, we ceased, saying, "The will of the Lord be done.
15 And after those days we took up our carriages, and went up to Jerusalem.
16 There went with us also *certain* of the disciples of Cæsarea, and brought with them one Mnason of Cyprus, an old disciple, with whom we should lodge.
17 [b]And when we were come to Jerusalem, the brethren received us gladly.

14 for the name of the Lord Jesus. And when he would not be persuaded, we ceased, saying, The will of the Lord be done.
15 And after these days we [1]took up our baggage, and
16 went up to Jerusalem. And there went with us also *certain* of the disciples from Cæsarea, bringing *with them* one Mnason of Cyprus, an early disciple, with whom we should lodge.
17 And when we were come to Jerusalem, the breth-

a Matt. 6 : 10 ; 26 : 42 ; Luke 11 : 2 ; 22 : 42....*b* ch. 15 : 4.——[1] Or, *made ready*

affirmed. But the apostle may perhaps have believed that the latter was God's design, and he may have been right in his belief. His own purpose seems not to have wavered; and it surely may have been the Spirit of Christ who gave him courage to persevere in the way he had chosen.—A. H.]

15. The text fluctuates here, but the word (ἐπισκευασάμενοι) which signifies **having packed up our baggage,** having placed it upon the beasts of burden, has decidedly the best support. (Comp. ἐπισκευασάμενοι ὑποξύγια, in Xen., *Hell.,* 7. 2. 18.) This is ever an important item in Eastern travelling; and it was natural that Luke, a companion of the journey, should mention it. If the alms which they were carrying to Jerusalem (24 : 17) consisted in part of raiment or provisions, the loading and unloading would require more than ordinary attention. Another reading (ἀποσκευασάμενοι) signifies *having packed away our baggage—i. e.* at Cæsarea, where they left it, or at least the superfluous part of it (Olsh.). The reason for such a step is not obvious. If it was their sea-luggage and unnecessary for the rest of the way, it is surprising that they did not leave it at Ptolemais, where they ended the voyage. Some insist that if we adopt this word rather than the other we may obtain from it the same meaning : *having packed our baggage away —i. e.* from the place where they had stored it —in order to carry it with them (Mey., De Wet.). That appears to me a forced interpretation. [In his last ed. Meyer agrees with this remark.—A. H.] (παρασκευασάμενοι and ἀποταξά-μενοι are explanatory variations.)—"The English Version," says Mr. Humphry, "uses the word 'carriage' in the sense of 'things carried,' baggage, as in Judg. 18 : 21 and 1 Sam. 17 : 22. Cranmer has 'took up our burdens,' and the Geneva Version 'trussed up our fardels.'"—For the route in "going up" to Jerusalem, see on 23 : 31.

16. And there went with us also of the disciples [*i. e. certain* of the disciples, τινὲς being understood]. (Comp. John 16 : 17. W. § 64. 4.)—**Bringing us to Mnason with whom we should lodge** (Olsh., Mey., De Wet. ἄγοντες . . .

Μνάσωνι stands by attraction for ἄγοντες παρὰ Μνά-σωνα παρ' ᾧ ξενισθῶμεν). His relation to them as their host was more important to them than his name, and presents itself first, therefore, in the order of statement. **Mnason** could depend possibly on **bringing—bringing us to Mnason** (W. § 31. 5); but the construction is hard. Some render *bringing Mnason—i. e.* with them from Cæsarea, which attributes to them an improbable act, while it leaves the dative equally irregular.—**An old**—*i. e. an ancient* (not an *aged*) **—disciple,** one who had long been such. He may have been converted on the day of Pentecost (comp. *in the beginning,* in 11 : 15) or have been a personal follower of Christ.

17–26. PAUL ASSUMES A VOW TO CONCILIATE THE JEWISH BELIEVERS.

17. The apostle arrives now at Jerusalem— for the *fifth* time since he left it on his persecuting errand to Damascus. It is the last recorded visit that he ever made to the Jewish capital. His present return could not have taken place later than the spring of A. D. 59, since we must reserve two years for his imprisonment at Cæsarea (24 : 27), and two for his imprisonment at Rome, before we come to A. D. 64. (See *Introduction,* § 6. 5.) If we fix upon this limitation on that side, we have then four years as the term of the apostle's third missionary excursion, which we may distribute as follows: He left Antioch about the beginning of A. D. 55 (see on 18 : 23), and reached Ephesus in the spring of that year. Here he spent about three years (20 : 31), and proceeded to Macedonia in the spring of A. D. 58. (See on 20 : 1.) He was occupied here and in other parts of Northern Greece during the summer and autumn of that year (see on 20 : 2), and arrived at Corinth early in the following winter. Having spent the next three months in that city (20 : 3), he returned to Macedonia and embarked for Syria in the spring of A. D. 59. Or our scheme of chronology admits of a slightly different combination : If we suppose two years and six months or nine months to exhaust *three years,* in 20 : 31, we may assign Paul's return to Jerusalem to the spring of the preceding year—viz. that of A. D. 58. The apostle may have left

18 And the *day* following Paul went in with us unto
*a*James; and all the elders were present.
19 And when he had saluted them, *b*he declared particularly what things God had wrought among the
Gentiles *c*by his ministry.
20 And when they heard *it*, they glorified the Lord,
and said unto him, Thou seest, brother, how many
thousands of Jews there are which believe; and they
are all *d*zealous of the law:
21 And they are informed of thee, that thou teachest all the Jews which are among the Gentiles to forsake
Moses, saying that they ought not to circumcise *their*
children, neither to walk after the customs.

18 ren received us gladly. And the day following Paul
went in with us unto James; and all the elders were
19 present. And when he had saluted them, he rehearsed
one by one the things which God had wrought among
20 the Gentiles by his ministry. And they, when they
heard it, glorified God; and they said unto him, Thou
seest, brother, how many ¹thousands there are among
the Jews of them who have believed; and they are
21 all zealous for the law: and they have been informed
concerning thee, that thou teachest all the Jews
who are among the Gentiles to forsake Moses, telling
them not to circumcise their children, neither to

---

a ch. 15 : 13; Gal. 1 : 19; 2 : 9....*b* ch. 15 : 4, 12; Rom. 15 : 18, 19....*c* ch. 1 : 17; 20 : 24....*d* ch. 22 : 3; Rom. 10 : 2; Gal. 1 : 14
——1 Gr. *myriads*.

Antioch on his third tour sufficiently early in
A. D. 54 (see on 18 : 22) to have spent several
months at Ephesus before Pentecost in A. D. 55;
and he could then have completed the two remaining years of his residence in that city at
Pentecost in A. D. 57. The advantage of this
computation would be that it frees us from the
necessity of crowding the two years of the apostle's Roman captivity so near the year A. D. 64.
—**The brethren received us gladly.** This
may refer to the more private friendly greetings which preceded the interview on the next
day. Luke may have been struck with this
cordiality the more because Paul and his friends,
as preachers to the heathen, had reason to apprehend some coldness. (See the note on 15 : 4
and Rom 15 : 31.) The interview would be
likely to take place in the house of Mnason, but
the brethren is too general to be understood merely of him and his family.
  18. The notice here relates to a more public
reception.— **On the following day,** after
their arrival.—**With us**—viz. Luke and Paul's
other companions. It was now, probably, that
the gifts of the foreign churches were delivered
up to the almoners.—**James.** This is *James*
the Younger, who presided over the church at
Jerusalem. (Comp. 12 : 17.) As no one of the
other apostles is mentioned in this part of the
narrative, it is probable that they were either
not living or were laboring in foreign lands.—
The elders. The pastor and *the presbyters* are
named as the principal persons (see 15 : 6), not
as excluding others.
  19. Had saluted them—lit. **having embraced them.** He had performed the same
act of courtesy on his preceding visit to them.
(See 18 : 22.)—**Through his ministry,** in the
course of his recent journey.
  20. How many thousands, rather **how
many myriads,** stands for a large but indefinite number: *what multitudes.* (Comp. 1 Cor.
4 : 15 and 14 : 19.)—**Zealous of the law,** or
zealots for the law, an objective or causative genitive. (Comp. Gal. 1 : 14. K. ? 265. 2. b.)

  21. That thou teachest, etc.—lit. **that
thou dost teach apostasy from Moses,**
etc. Neander presents the following just view
of the transaction related here: "This accusation
against Paul was certainly false in the form in
which it was alleged; for he opposed the external observance of Judaism only so far as the
justification and sanctification of men were made
to depend upon it. It was his principle that no
one should abandon the national and civil relations in which he stood at the time of his
conversion, except for important reasons; and,
in accordance with this principle, he allowed
the Jews to adhere to their peculiarities, among
which was the observance of the Mosaic law
(1 Cor. 7 : 18). But it could not fail to happen that
those who entered into Paul's ideas of the relations of the law to the gospel, and were thus
freed from their scrupulous regard for the
former, would be led into a freer line of conduct in this respect; and individuals might
carry this disposition farther than Paul desired.
It may be that such instances gave occasion to
the charge that he persuaded the Jewish Christians to release themselves from the law. It is
indeed true that, when it was once admitted
that circumcision avails nothing as a means of
obtaining an interest in the kingdom of God, this
rite must sooner or later fall away of itself. But
Paul would not hasten this result by any arbitrary or violent act; he would leave it to be the
work of time, and would have no one break
away capriciously from the relations in which
he has been called to be a Christian. Hence,
without deviating from the principles of strict
sincerity, he could repel that accusation of the
Jewish zealots. He was far from entertaining
the hatred against Judaism and the ancient
theocratic nation with which his violent opponents charged him. In conformity with the
principle avowed in his Epistles—viz. that he
became a Jew to the Jews, as he became a
heathen to the heathen and weak to those who
were weak—he declared himself ready to do
what James proposed to him, in order to refute

22 What is it therefore? the multitude must needs come together: for they will hear that thou art come. 23 Do therefore this that we say to thee: We have four men which have a vow on them; 24 Them take, and purify thyself with them, and be at charges with them, that they may [a]shave *their* heads: and all may know that those things, whereof they were informed concerning thee, are nothing; but *that* thou thyself also walkest orderly, and keepest the law.

22 walk after the customs. What is it therefore? they 23 will certainly hear that thou art come. Do therefore this that we say to thee: We have four men 24 who have a vow on them; these take, and purify thyself with them, and be at charges for them, that they may shave their heads: and all shall know that there is no truth in the things whereof they have been informed concerning thee; but that thou

a Num. 6 : 2, 13, 18 ; ch. 18 : 18.

that accusation. He consented to refute it by taking part in the Jewish worship in a mode which was highly esteemed by pious Jews."

22. What, therefore, is it?—viz. which the occasion requires. (Comp. 1 Cor. 14 : 15, 16.)—**The multitude,** etc.—lit. **it is entirely necessary** (inevitable) **that a multitude** (viz. of the Jewish Christians) **should come together;** *i. e.* around Paul as he appeared in their public assemblies, in the temple and elsewhere, in order to watch his conduct and see whether their suspicions of him were just. It is not meant that the church would assemble in a body for the purpose of consultation (Calv., Grot.); for with that idea we should have had *the* before **multitude.** (Comp. 4 : 32; 15 : 12, 30.) Nor does the language intimate that Paul's advisers apprehended any violent outbreak on the part of the Jewish Christians (Kuin.); the subsequent riot which led to his apprehension originated, not with them, but with the unbelieving Jews. (Comp. v. 27.) [It may also be noted that Treg., West. and Hort, and the Anglo-Am. Revisers omit the words *a multitude must come together* as an addition to the original text. Treg. adduces B C*, the Peshito and Harklean Syriac, the Memphitic, Thebaic, and Armenian versions for the omission. For the whole verse with these words omitted, see the Revised Version above.—A. H.]

23. This that, or **which, we say to thee** —viz. James and the elders; for the subject of this verb must be the same as that of **said,** in v. 20. The narrative does not allow us to separate James from the others, as if he merely acquiesced in the proposal, while the responsibility of suggesting it lay wholly with them (against Cony. and Hws.).—The **four men** were certainly Jews, and may be supposed, from the relation implied in **we have,** to have been also Jewish believers.—**Which have,** or **having, a vow upon themselves,** which, as appears from every circumstance of the description, must have been a Nazarite vow. This vow bound those who assumed it to let the hair grow, to abstain from intoxicating drink, and in other respects to maintain a life of ascetic rigor (Num. 6 : 2, *sq.*). It was left to their option

how long they continued such a vow, though it seems to have been customary among the Jews of this period to extend it at least to thirty days (Jos., *Bell. Jud.,* 2. 15. 1). "When the time specified in the vow was completed, the Nazarite offered a ram of a year old for a burnt-offering, a sheep of the same age for a sin-offering, a ram for a thank-offering, a basket of unleavened cakes, and a libation of wine. His hair was shaven off at the gate of the sanctuary, and cast into the fire where the thank-offering was burning. He offered as a wave-offering to God the shoulders of the thank-offering and two cakes, which were both given to the priest" (Jahn's *Archæol.,* ¿ 395).

24. Them take—lit. **these taking—with thyself.—Purify thyself with them,** as associates in the vow.—**Purify thyself with them,** enter upon the same course of abstinence and religious consecration. Conybeare and Howson understand **purify thyself** of the ordinary ablutions before entering the temple; but in that case **with them** loses its significance, since the apostle's purification would have no more relation to them than to any other Jews.—**And be at charges with them,** strictly *spend upon them,* incur expense on their account. "As, in some instances, the Nazarites had not sufficient property to enable them to meet the whole expense of the offerings, other persons who possessed more defrayed the expense with them or shared it with them, and in this way were made parties to the vow." The Jews looked upon it as an act of special merit to assist a Nazarite in this manner. Josephus relates (*Antt.,* 19. 6. 1) that Agrippa I., on his arrival at Jerusalem after having obtained the sovereignty of Palestine, paid the expense of numerous indigent Nazarites who were waiting to be released from their vows. He intended it as a thank-offering for his good fortune.— **And all may know.** [According to the true text, ℵ A B C D E, and other documents, it must be translated with Dr. Hackett] *and all shall know,* by this act. The readings (γνῶσι and γνώσωνται) rendered *all may know* (E. V.) are grammatical corrections, founded on the false view that this clause depends on **that,** in the previous clause. **Thyself also,** as well as other Jews.

25 As touching the Gentiles which believe, [a]we have written and concluded that they observe no such thing, save only that they keep themselves from things offered to idols, and from blood, and from strangled, and from fornication.

26 Then Paul took the men, and the next day purifying himself with them [b]entered into the temple, [c]to signify the accomplishment of the days of purification, until that an offering should be offered for every one of them.

25 thyself also walkest orderly, keeping the law. But as touching the Gentiles who have believed, we [1]wrote, giving judgment that they should keep themselves from things sacrificed to idols, and from blood, and from what is strangled, and from forni-26 cation. Then Paul [2]took the men, and the next day purifying himself with them went into the temple, declaring the fulfilment of the days of purification, until the offering was offered for every one of them.

---

a ch. 15 : 20, 29....b ch. 24 : 18....c Num. 6 : 13.——1 Or. enjoined Many ancient authorities read sent....2 Or, took the men the next day, and purifying himself, etc.

---

25. As touching, etc. **But** (as we are both aware) **in regard to the Gentiles who have believed**, etc.—**We**—i. e. the apostles and Christians at Jerusalem, for the adoption of the decree was properly their act (comp. 15 : 22), and not that of Paul and the other delegates from Antioch, who submitted to them the question which the decree settled (15 : 1). The object of the reminiscent remark in this verse was to obviate any scruple that Paul might feel lest the proposed measure should interfere with the liberty of the Gentile converts.—**Save only**, etc. (See the note on 15 : 20.)

26. Took refers to his connecting himself with the men (v. 24), while **purifying himself** defines the nature of the connection. **The next day**—i. e. on the following day after his interview with James, and the third since his arrival at Jerusalem (v. 18).—**With them** belongs certainly to **purifying himself** (see v. 24), and perhaps to **entered into**—not, in the latter case, necessarily because he now took them to the temple in order to absolve them at once from their vow (Cony. and Hws.), but because it may have been important that they should be present when he declared his intention to assume their expenses.—**To signify,** etc.—i. e. **announcing**—viz. to the priests (**into the temple** suggests the persons)—**the completion** (lit. filling out) **of the days of the purification.** In other words, making known the interval (viz. seven days) between this declaration and the end of the vow and the bringing of the necessary offerings. So essentially Stier, Kuinoel, De Wette, Meyer, Wordsworth, and others. **The,** before **purification,** defines the purification as that referred to in **purifying himself with them**; hence that of those associated in the act, not that of the men merely, and not that of Paul merely (both mistakes have been made). The convenience of the priests may have required this notification to enable them to prepare for the concluding ceremony at the temple. Others (as Wiesl.) explain **accomplishment** of the actual expiration of the days during which the men's vow was to continue. Such a view leaves no

time for the apostle's partnership with them, and thus conflicts both with **purifying him**[c]**self with them,** and with **found me purified in the temple,** in 24 : 18. The apostle's arrest (v. 27) was subsequent to his present appearance in the temple, and at the time of the arrest, as we see from the words just quoted, he was still observing his part of the vow.—**Until that an offering**—rather **until the offering** (known as necessary)—**was brought.** This clause depends naturally on announcing, etc., and, as it formed a part of the notice which Paul gave in the temple (hence oratio directa), would have naturally the subjunctive (until it should be brought, as in 23 : 12, 21; 25 : 21), instead of the indicative. It may be an instance, as Meyer suggests, in which the direct form of the announcement glides over into the past of the narrative. (See K., Ausfh. Gr., § 846.) Some carry back the clause to **entered into the temple** as elliptical: went into the temple and stayed there until the offering was brought. In that case we must pass over the nearer point of connection for a remoter one, and must even insert the word in the text which renders that connection possible. Further, it is improbable that Paul lodged two or three days in the temple; and yet, as he speaks of himself as there on the day of the riot, in order to bring the final offerings (24 : 18), it would follow, on this view of the subject, that he had remained there from his first repairing to the temple till that time. The true emphasis of **for every one** lies in the fact that Paul was to be answerable for the expenses of the offering of each one, not (as Cony. and Hws.) that he would remain in the temple until each one's offering was presented. [If the course of Paul in following the advice of James is called in question as inconsistent with his religious principles, and therefore immoral, it may be answered—(1) That he had all along conceded to Jewish Christians a right to observe the Mosaic law, and had recognized the fact that Peter, James, and John were as truly entrusted with the apostleship for the circumcision as he himself was with the apostleship for the uncircumcision (Gal. 2 : 7). (2)

27 And when the seven days were almost ended, *the Jews which were of Asia, when they saw him in the temple, stirred up all the people, and *laid hands on him,

28 Crying out, Men of Israel, help: This is the man, *that teacheth all *men* every where against the people, and the law, and this place: and further brought Greeks also into the temple, and hath polluted this holy place.

27 And when the seven days were almost completed, the Jews from Asia, when they saw him in the temple, stirred up all the multitude, and laid hands on

28 him, crying out, Men of Israel, help: This is the man, that teacheth all men everywhere against the people, and the law, and this place: and moreover he brought Greeks also into the temple, and hath

a ch. 24 : 18....*b* ch. 26 : 21....*c* ch. 24 : 5, 6.

This concession, since he was himself a Jew, might now be openly made by joining with Christian Jews in a ceremony of the law, provided his motive in so doing was not likely to be misunderstood. And we may assume that at this time any misunderstanding of it would be very improbable, since his teaching as to Gentile converts was well known. He had insisted with emphasis upon the fact that observing the law of Moses was not a means of salvation and must not be required of Gentile Christians; he might, therefore, now safely show that he did not condemn his Jewish brethren for observing the law of their fathers, though doing this was not a means of salvation. (3) This expression of fellowship with them, while they were walking by the light which they had received, would, it was hoped, win their good-will and perhaps diminish the bitter enmity which burned against him in the hearts of unbelieving Jews. Thus, without sacrificing an iota of Christian principle, he consented to live as a Jew with the Jews that he might lead them into the truth.—A. H.]

27-30. PAUL IS SEIZED BY THE JEWS AND DRAGGED FROM THE TEMPLE.

27. And when the seven days, etc., or **now as the seven days, were about to be completed**—*i. e.* in all probability the seven days announced to the priests as the limit to which the vow of the Nazarites would extend, and as the period, also, of the apostle's partnership in that consecration. This is the readiest explanation, and the one to which most critics assent (Bng., Kuin., Olsh., Mey., De Wet., Alf.). Neander's idea is that their vow embraced only seven days in all, and that Paul joined them on the last of these days. Against that construction stands the inference from *which have a vow on them*, in v. 23, that the vow had been resting on them for a considerable time before the apostle's connection with them, and also that *that they may shave their heads* (v. 24) would signify very little, if the ceremony was to take place at the expiration of a single week.—Wieseler (p. 105) has revived the opinion of some of the older interpreters—viz. that **the**

seven days were those observed as the feast of Pentecost. His arguments are mainly two —first, as obviating an objection that this meaning suggests itself readily enough after the information (20 : 16) that Paul was hastening to keep the Pentecost at Jerusalem; and secondly, that the reckoning of the twelve days between his arrival there and his subsequent trial at Cæsarea demands this explanation. Conybeare and Howson adopt the same view. But the article before **seven days** recalls quite irresistibly *the days of the purification* just spoken of, and the twelve days mentioned in 24 : 11 may be computed in different ways (see note there), and hence, though compatible with that theory, do not establish it. Above all, the assumption that the Jews observed Pentecost as a hebdomadal festival is too uncertain to be made the basis of an explanation. The law of its institution prescribed but one day, though the later Jews, it would seem, added a second. (Win., *Realw.*, i. p. 243.)—**The Jews which were of Asia**—lit. **the Jews from Asia;** *i. e.* the province of that name, where Paul had resided so long (20 : 31). Some of them may have been from Ephesus, who would recognize Trophimus (v. 29) as a fellow-townsman. The Jews here, the authors of this riot, were not believers, and hence not of the class of Jews whom the apostle expected to conciliate.

28. Help—*i. e.* to apprehend him, or to wreak vengeance on him.—**And further,** etc., *and further also.* (Comp. 2 : 26.) It is one of Luke's peculiar phrases.—**Greeks** may be the plural of the class or category, because what Paul had done in the case of one he might be said, in point of principle, to have done for many; or it may have been an exaggeration for the purpose of increasing the tumult.—**Into the temple**—*i. e.* the part of it interdicted to foreigners. The outer court or enclosure was called the Court of the Gentiles, and could be entered by them without profanation. The second court, or that of the Israelites, was surrounded with marble pillars, on which, as Philo states, was inscribed, in Latin and Greek, "On penalty of death, let no foreigner go farther."

29 (For they had seen before with him in the city ªTrophimus an Ephesian, whom they supposed that Paul had brought into the temple.)

30 And ᵇall the city was moved, and the people ran together: and they took Paul, and drew him out of the temple: and forthwith the doors were shut.

31 And as they went about to kill him, tidings came unto the chief captain of the band, that all Jerusalem was in an uproar.

32 ᶜWho immediately took soldiers and centurions, and ran down unto them: and when they saw the chief captain and the soldiers, they left beating of Paul.

33 Then the chief captain came near, and took him, and ᵈcommanded *him* to be bound with two chains; and demanded who he was, and what he had done.

29 defiled this holy place. For they had before seen with him in the city Trophimus the Ephesian, whom they supposed that Paul had brought into

30 the temple. And all the city was moved, and the people ran together: and they laid hold on Paul, and dragged him out of the temple: and straight-

31 way the doors were shut. And as they were seeking to kill him, tidings came up to the ¹chief captain of the ²band, that all Jerusalem was in

32 confusion. And forthwith he took soldiers and centurions, and ran down upon them: and they, when they saw the chief captain and the soldiers,

33 left off beating Paul. Then the chief captain came near, and laid hold on him, and commanded him to be bound with two chains; and inquired who he

---

a ch. 20 : 4....*b* ch. 26 : 21....*c* ch. 23 : 27 ; 24 : 7....*d* ver. 11 ; ch. 20 : 23.——1 Or, *military tribune* Gr. *chiliarch*: and so throughout this book....2 Or, *cohort*

---

29. Had seen before, on some previous occasion, or possibly *had seen away*, at a distance (Mey.). [In his fourth ed. Meyer adopts the temporal sense, translating thus: "*For there were people who had before* (before they saw the apostle in the temple, v. 27) *seen Trophimus with him.*" —A. H.] In this compound the preposition refers elsewhere to the future (out of question here) or to space, not to past time (R. and P., *Lex.*). The retrospective sense lies so near to the use of **before** (πρό), and occurs so readily here, that we need not scruple to admit it.—For **Trophimus,** see on 20 : 4. He was a foreigner (**Ephesian**), and not a Jew from Ephesus.— **When they supposed**—*were supposing*—etc. They had seen Trophimus in the city with him, and from that rushed to the conclusion that he had brought Greeks into the temple. "Zelotæ *putantes,*" says Bengel, "sæpe errant" ["Zealots, in supposing, often err"].

30. Drew him, etc., or *dragged him,* **out, of the temple,** so as not to pollute it with blood (Olsh., Mey., De Wet.). They had determined already to kill him. Bengel conjectures (whom Bmg. follows) that they wished to prevent him from taking refuge at the altar. But the Mosaic law restricted the right of asylum to those who had been guilty of accidental murder. (See Ex. 21 : 13, 14.)—**The doors** (of the second court) **were closed,** probably by the Levites, who had the care of the temple. (See the note on 4 : 1.) They may have feared that the crowd would return or some new disturbance arise.

31-40. THE ROMAN COMMANDER RESCUES PAUL FROM THE HANDS OF THE JEWS.

31. And as they went about, etc., or **now while they are seeking, to kill him.** They were beating him for that purpose. (See v. 32.) But, as the onset had been sudden and they were not furnished with weapons, some delay intervened. It was nothing, in all human appear-

ance, but that momentary delay that saved now the life of the apostle. The Roman officer had time to appear and snatch him from impending death.—**Tidings came,** etc., **a report went up, to the chiliarch of the cohort.** (See his name in 23 : 26.) It was but the work of a moment to convey to him the information. He had his station in the Castle of Antonia, which was on a rock or hill at the north-west angle of the temple-area. The tower at the south-east corner of the castle "was seventy cubits high, and overlooked the whole temple with its courts. The fortress communicated with the northern and western porticos of the temple-area and had flights of stairs descending into both, by which the garrison could at any time enter the court of the temple and prevent tumults" (*Bibl. Res.,* i. p. 432). During the festivals it was customary to keep the troops in readiness to suppress the riots which were so liable to occur at such times. (Comp. on 10 : 37, and see Jos., *Antt.,* 20. 5. 3 ; *Bell. Jud.,* 5. 5. 8.) —The Turkish garrison stands at present very nearly on the site of the old castle. The traveller obtains his best view of the Court of the Harem, or mosque of Omar, the ancient temple-area, from the roof of this garrison.

32. Centurions, each with his proper complement of men, The chiliarch ordered out a force sufficiently large to intimidate all opposition.—**Ran down unto**—better **upon—them.** To that despatch Paul was indebted for his escape. Note also **immediately.** This verb corresponds to *went up,* in v. 31.—**Now when they saw the chiliarch,** etc. They knew the consequences too well to run the risk of a collision with the Roman troops. (See on 19 : 24.)

33. To be bound with two chains—*i. e.* to have his arms fastened to two soldiers, one on each side of him. The mode was described in the note on 12 : 6.—**Who he was**—lit. **who he might be,** since his name and rank were

34 And some cried one thing, some another, among the multitude: and when he could not know the certainty for the tumult, he commanded him to be carried into the castle.

35 And when he came upon the stairs, so it was, that he was borne of the soldiers for the violence of the people.

36 For the multitude of the people followed after, crying, *a*Away with him.

37 And as Paul was to be led into the castle, he said unto the chief captain, May I speak unto thee? Who said, Canst thou speak Greek?

38 *b*Art not thou that Egyptian, which before these days madest an uproar, and leddest out into the wilderness four thousand men that were murderers?

34 was, and what he had done. And some shouted one thing, some another, among the crowd: and when he could not know the certainty for the uproar, he commanded him to be brought into the

35 castle. And when he came upon the stairs, so it was, that he was borne of the soldiers for the vio-

36 lence of the crowd; for the multitude of the people followed after, crying out, Away with him.

37   And as Paul was about to be brought into the castle, he saith unto the chief captain, May I say something unto thee? And he said, Dost thou know

38 Greek? Art thou not then the Egyptian, who before these days stirred up to sedition and led out into the wilderness the four thousand men of the

a Luke 23 : 18 ; John 19 : 15 ; ch. 22 : 22....*b* See ch. 5 : 36.

uncertain.—**And what he has done.** The form of the inquiry presupposes that he had committed some crime. (W. § 41. 4. c.) He put the question to the crowd, as the responsive clamor shows in the next verse.

34. Into the castle, rather *into the garrison* or *barracks;* not the *castle* as a whole (E. V.), but the part of it assigned to the soldiers.

35. Upon the stairs which led up to the castle. On arriving here the crowd pressed on Paul, so as to awaken the fear of some outrage or treachery. Some think that he was lifted off his feet by the throng, and then taken and carried up the stairs.—**So it was,** or **it happened, that he was borne** (in their arms or on their shoulders) **by the soldiers. It happened** is not superfluous. **Was borne** alone would have pointed out less distinctly the peril of his situation, as evinced by their adopting such a precaution.

36. Now was heard again the shout which thirty years before surrounded the prætorium of Pilate, "Away with him, away with him" (Cony. and Hws.). **Away with** (αἶρε) is imperative present, because **followed after** (imperf.) represents the cry as a continued one. (See 22 : 22. Comp. **away with** (ἄρον), in John 19 : 15, where the aorist precedes.)

37. Canst thou speak Greek?—lit. dost thou know Greek? The adverb stands in the place of the object (comp. οὕτω, in 20 : 13), and *to speak* is not to be supplied (Kuin.). (Comp. *those understanding Syriac,* in Xen., *Cyr.,* 7. 5. 31, and in Latin *Græce nescire.* Mey., De Wet.)

38. Art not thou, etc., more precisely, **Art thou not therefore the Egyptian?**—*i. e.* as I supposed. The negative particle here used (οὐκ) indicates an affirmative answer with reference to the speaker's former state of mind. (W. § 57. 3.) The commander, on being addressed in Greek, concludes that he is mistaken; for it was notorious (it would seem) that the Egyptian was unable to speak that language. He could not have drawn that inference solely

from his Egyptian origin, for the Greek was now spoken more or less in almost every country.—Of this Egyptian impostor Josephus has given two different accounts, which need to be reconciled with each other as well as with Luke. In his *Bell. Jud.* (2. 13. 5) he relates that a juggler (γόης), whom he also denominates **the Egyptian,** having procured for himself the reputation of a prophet, led a great multitude of about thirty thousand men out of the desert to the Mount of Olives, and promised them that the walls of Jerusalem would fall down at his command; but Felix fell upon them, the Egyptian fled with a small number—lit. *with a few.* Most of his followers were slain or taken prisoners, and the rest of the crowd (τὸ λοιπὸν πλῆθος) dispersed. In his *Antt.* (20. 7. 6; he wrote this work later than his *Jewish War)* he states that this Egyptian came to Jerusalem, that he persuaded the populace to go out with him to the Mount of Olives, where he would exhibit to them the wonder before mentioned; and then he speaks of the attack of Felix, and in that connection says merely that *four hundred* of the Egyptian's people were slain and *two hundred* were taken captive, without any further addition. "Here, now," says Tholuck (*Glaubwürdigkeit,* p. 169), "Josephus has in all appearance contradicted himself in the most glaring manner; for in one case the Egyptian brings the people from the desert to the Mount of Olives, in the other from Jerusalem; in the one case the greater part of thirty thousand people are slain or taken prisoners, in the other the number of the slain amounts to only four hundred—that of the prisoners to only two hundred. This example serves to illustrate an important rule of criticism, so often violated by sceptical writers in relation to the Bible, and that is that, if the general credibility of an historian be acknowledged, we are bound to reconcile an apparent difference by interpretation or combination. The application of this principle here enables us to view the matter

39 But Paul said, *a*I am a man *which am* a Jew of Tarsus, *a city* in Cilicia, a citizen of no mean city: and, I beseech thee, suffer me to speak unto the people.
40 And when he had given him license, Paul stood on the stairs, and *b*beckoned with the hand unto the people. And when there was made a great silence, he spake unto *them* in the Hebrew tongue, saying,

39 Assassins? But Paul said, I am a Jew, of Tarsus in Cilicia, a citizen of no mean city: and I beseech
40 thee, give me leave to speak unto the people. And when he had given him leave, Paul, standing on the stairs, beckoned with the hand unto the people; and when there was made a great silence, he spake unto them in the Hebrew language, saying,

CHAPTER XXII.

MEN, *c*brethren, and fathers, hear ye my defence *which I make* now unto you.

1 BRETHREN and fathers, hear ye the defence which, I now make unto you.

a ch. 9 : 11 ; 22 : 3....*b* ch. 12 : 17....*c* ch. 7 : 2.

thus. The man had at first a band of *sicarii*, and a rabble had also attached themselves to him; these people he leaves behind on the Mount of Olives, and leads thither out of Jerusalem an additional crowd; so that the entire multitude might amount to about thirty thousand men. As usually happens in such cases, curiosity merely had drawn together most of them. Only a smaller company belonged to the train of his followers, and among these were the *sicarii;* the attack of the Romans was directed properly against these, of whom Felix slew four hundred, and made two hundred prisoners. With a small number—*i. e. with the four thousand of whom Luke speaks*—he escaped into the desert; the remaining mass—*i. e. the multitude* of which the first passage of Josephus speaks—dispersed. In this or in a similar way the Jewish historian may be reconciled with himself and with the writer of the Acts."—**Into the desert**—viz. between Egypt and Palestine, as he came from that direction.—**The four thousand.** The event was so recent that the precise number was still known. The same Felix was Procurator of Judea at this time. (See 23 : 24.)—**Murderers,** *sicarii, assassins,* a Latinism. They received their name from the Roman *sica,* a curved dagger adapted by its form to be concealed beneath the clothes; they could use it for striking a fatal blow in a crowd without being observed.

39. I am a man, etc., as analyzed by Meyer, contains two clauses: **I am indeed** (μέν) not the Egyptian, but **a Jew from Tarsus. And** (δέ), below, can hardly be antithetic.—**Cilicia** depends on **city;** not in apposition with an implied genitive in **of Tarsus** (E. V.).—**No mean, not unnoted.** On the contrary, says Josephus (*Antt.*, 1. 6. 1), the most important city of all Cilicia. Many of the coins of Tarsus bear the title of *Autonomous* and *Metropolis.* (See on 9 : 30.)

40. Paul stood, etc. "What nobler spectacle," exclaims Chrysostom, "than that of Paul at this moment! There he stands, bound

with two chains, ready to make his defence to the people. The Roman commander sits by to enforce order by his presence. An enraged populace look up to him from below. Yet in the midst of so many dangers, how self-possessed is he, how tranquil!" **In the Hebrew tongue**—lit. **dialect;** *i. e.* in the Syro-Chaldaic or Aramæan, as in John 5 : 2; 19 : 13. (See on 6 : 1.) In that language, if he was not more intelligible to most of his hearers, he could at least "speak more directly to the hearts of the people."

1–21. PAUL'S SPEECH ON THE STAIRS OF THE CASTLE.

1. As we examined Luke's account of Paul's conversion (9 : 1-18) in connection with this address, it will be sufficient, for the most part, to refer the student to the notes there, so far as the two narratives coincide. I subjoin Mr. Humphry's introductory paragraph: "Though the subject-matter of this speech has been related before, it assumes here a fresh interest from the manner in which it is adapted to the occasion and the audience. The apostle is suspected of disaffection to the Mosaic law. In order to refute this charge, he addresses them in Hebrew; he dwells on his Jewish education and on his early zeal for the law; he shows how at his conversion he was guided by Ananias, a man devout according to the law, and of good report among the Jews at Damascus, and how he subsequently worshipped in the temple at Jerusalem. So far they listen to him; but he no sooner touches on the promulgation of the gospel among the heathen (v. 21) than he is interrupted, and his fate would probably have been the same as Stephen's, had he not been under the protection of the Roman captain."—For **brethren and fathers,** see on 7 : 2. Some of the rulers mingled with the crowd, whom Paul knew personally or recognized by some badge of office. Here too (1 : 16) **men** is complimentary and belongs with *that

2 (And when they heard that he spake in the Hebrew tongue to them, they kept the more silence: and
he saith,)
3 ᵃI am verily a man *which am* a Jew, born in Tarsus, *a city* in Cilicia, yet brought up in this city, ᵇat
the feet of ᶜGamaliel, *and* taught ᵈaccording to the perfect manner of the law of the fathers, and was ᵉzealous
toward God, ᶠas ye all are this day.
4 ᵍAnd I persecuted this way unto the death, binding and delivering unto prisons both men and women.
5 As also the high priest doth bear me witness, and
ʰall the estate of the elders: ⁱfrom whom also I received letters unto the brethren, and went to Damascus, to bring them which were there bound unto Jerusalem, for to be punished.
6 And ᵏit came to pass, that, as I made my journey,

2 And when they heard that he spake unto them in
the Hebrew language, they were the more quiet: and
he saith,
3 I am a Jew, born in Tarsus of Cilicia, but brought
up in this city, at the feet of Gamaliel, instructed
according to the strict manner of the law of our
fathers, being zealous for God, even as ye all are
4 this day: and I persecuted this way unto the death,
binding and delivering into prisons both men and
5 women. As also the high priest doth bear me witness, and all the estate of the elders: from whom
also I received letters unto the brethren, and journeyed to Damascus, to bring them also that were
there unto Jerusalem in bonds, for to be punished.
6 And it came to pass, that, as I made my journey,

ℨ ch. 21 : 39 ; 2 Cor. 11 : 22; Phil. 3 : 5....ᵇ Deut. 33 : 3 ; 2 Kings 4 : 38 ; Luke 10 : 39....ᶜ ch. 5 : 34.... ᵈ ch. 5 : 5....ᵉ ch. 21 : 20 ; Gal.
1 : 14....ᶠ Rom. 10 : 2....ᵍ ch. 8 : 3 ; 26 : 9, 10, 11 ; Phil. 3 : 6 ; 1 Tim. 1 : 13... ʰ Luke 22 : 66 ; ch. 4 : 5....ⁱ ch. 9 : 2 ; 26 : 10, 12..
ᵏ ch. 9 : 3 ; 26 : 12, 13.

orce to both nouns.—The pronoun **my** (μου)
depends, not on **hear** (ἀκούσατε ; comp. 1 : 4),
)ut on **defence** (ἀπολογίας).

3. The common rule would place **verily** (μέν)
after the participle (γεγεννημένος, **born**). [But
the best editors reject this particle (**verily**) as
an addition to the text of Luke. The sense is
perfect without it, and the MSS. א A B D E and
others do not have it.—A. H.] It stands out of
its place now and then in the best writers. (W.
ℨ 61. 5.) The opposition lies, evidently, between
Paul's foreign birth and his education at Jerusalem. — **In,** or **of, Cilicia** depends, not on
city, understood, but on **Tarsus** under the
rule of possession. (W. ℨ 30. 2.)—Critics point
this sentence differently. Many of the older
commentators, whom Meyer follows, place the
comma after **Gamaliel,** instead of **city,** so as
to bring a participle at the head of the several
clauses. This division promotes the rhythm at
the expense of the sense. The comma should
be put, undoubtedly, after **city** (Grsb., Lchm.,
De Wet.). Tischendorf follows this punctuation in his second edition [and in his eighth].
At the feet of Gamaliel is appropriate to
taught (πεπαιδευμένος), but not to **brought up**
(ἀνατεθραμμένος), the latter having respect to his
physical growth or progress to manhood ; the
former, to his professional training. **Having
been brought up in this city** forbids the
supposition that Paul was an adult when he
went to reside at Jerusalem. (Comp., also, 26 :
4.) He must have removed thither from Tarsus in his boyhood or early youth. It is surprising that Eichhorn and Hemsen should
maintain, in opposition to such evidence, that
Paul did not enter the school of Gamaliel until
the thirtieth year of his age. (See note on 7 :
58.) *To be taught at one's feet* was a proverbial
expression among the Jews, founded on the fact
that in their schools the teachers, whether they
stood or sat, occupied a higher place than the

pupils. (Schöttg., *Hor. Hebr.,* p. 477.) **According to the perfect manner** = after the
most straitest sect, in 26 : 5. Paul had beer
a Pharisee, and in his zeal for Judaism had sur
passed all the adherents of that sect who had
been students with him under Gamaliel. (See
Gal. 1 : 13.)—**The paternal law** (πατρῴου νόμου)
= **law of the fathers** (νόμου τῶν πατέρων).
(Comp. τῷ πάτρῴῳ θεῷ, in 24 : 14.) — **Toward
God**—lit. of God. The genitive (θεοῦ) is like
the genitive in 21 : 20.

4. **This way** (19 : 23) stands concisely for
those of this way. (Comp. 9 : 2.)—**Unto the
death,** rather *unto death.* Not the aim merely
(Grot., Mey.), but result, of his persecution.
The facts in the case justify the strongest
sense of the expression. (See v. 20 and 26 :
10.) — **Both men and women.** (See on
8 : 2.)

5. **As also the high priest doth bear me
witness,** or **testifies** (= is witness), **for me**
—*i. e.* the **high priest** at that time (see on 9 :
1), who was known to be still living. Some
construe the verb incorrectly as future.—**Unto
the brethren** = to the synagogues, in 9 : 2
—*i. e.* unto the Jewish rulers of the synagogue,
whom Paul recognizes as brethren (as in v. 1)
to show that he was not hostile to his countrymen or alienated from them (21 : 28). (Comp.
Rom. 9 : 1, *sq.*) **Was journeying,** not **went**
(E. V.).—**To bring,** etc.—lit. in order to
bring also those there ; lit. *thither,* because
the speaker's mind passes from where he is to
them. Not the emigrants *thither* (Mey., Alf.),
since the Jews had resided there too long to be
viewed in that light.—**For to be punished,**
or, **that they might be punished**—viz. by
imprisonment (v. 4 ; 8 : 3), by stripes (v. 19 ; 26 : 11),
or by death (v. 4 ; 8 : 1).

6. **And it came to pass,** etc., or **but it
happened to me as I journeyed** (the participle as imperfect) **that.** etc.—**To me jour-**

and was come nigh unto Damascus about noon, suddenly there shone from heaven a great light round about me.

7 And I fell unto the ground, and heard a voice saying unto me, Saul, Saul, why persecutest thou me?

8 And I answered, Who art thou, Lord? And he said unto me, I am Jesus of Nazareth, whom thou persecutest.

9 And *they that were with me saw indeed the light, and were afraid; but they heard not the voice of him that spake to me.

10 And I said, What shall I do, Lord? And the Lord said unto me, Arise, and go into Damascus; and there it shall be told thee of all things which are appointed for thee to do.

11 And when I could not see for the glory of that light, being led by the hand of them that were with me, I came into Damascus.

12 And *bone Ananias, a devout man according to the law, *having a good report of all the *Jews which dwelt there,

13 Came unto me, and stood, and said unto me, Brother Saul, receive thy sight. And the same hour I looked up upon him.

and drew nigh unto Damascus, about noon, suddenly there shone from heaven a great light round 7 about me. And I fell unto the ground, and heard a voice saying unto me, Saul, Saul, why persecutest 8 thou me? And I answered, Who art thou, Lord? And he said unto me, I am Jesus of Nazareth, whom 9 thou persecutest. And they that were with me beheld indeed the light, but they heard not the voice 10 of him that spake to me. And I said, What shall I do, Lord? And the Lord said unto me, Arise, and go into Damascus; and there it shall be told thee of 11 all things which are appointed for thee to do. And when I could not see for the glory of that light, being led by the hand of them that were with me, I 12 came into Damascus. And one Ananias, a devout man according to the law, well reported of by all 13 the Jews that dwelt there, came unto me, and standing by me said unto me, Brother Saul, receive thy sight. And in that very hour I *looked up on him.

---

a Dan. 10 : 7 ; ch. 9 : 7....*b* ch. 9 : 17....*c* ch. 10 : 22....*d* 1 Tim. 3 : 7.——1 Or, *received my sight* and looked *upon him.*

---

neying is not an instance of the dative absolute, but depends on **it happened.** (Comp. v. 17. W. ∮ 31. 2. R. 2.)—**About mid-day.** (See on 9 : 3.) That he should have had such a vision (**a great light**) at such an hour made it the more impossible that he should be deceived.— For περί, in περιαστράψαι, repeated before ἐμέ, see on 3 : 2.

7. The first aorist termination (ἔπεσα), which is changed in some copies to the second aorist (ἔπεσον), is an Alexandrian form. (Comp. Gal. 5 : 4. W. ∮ 13. 1. a.) Transcribers have probably altered this termination to the second aorist in some other passages, as John 6 : 10; Heb. 3 : 17; Rev. 7 : 11. For the same form in the classics, see K. ∮ 154. R. 2; B. ∮ 114.

9. They that were with me = the men that journeyed with him, in 9 : 7. (Comp. 26 : 14.) So those might be described who happened to be travelling with Saul in the same caravan; but the common view is more correct —that they are the men who accompanied him as his assistants. He would need the aid of others to enable him to convey his prisoners in safety to Jerusalem (v. 5).—**But they heard not,** rather **but the voice of him who spoke to me they understood not.** For this translation, see the remarks on 9 : 7.

11. And when, etc., or **as now, I saw not**—*i. e.* anything; here only without an object. —**For the glory,** etc.—lit. **from the glory,** splendor—**of that light,** which was "above the brightness of the sun." (See 26 : 13.) "The history (9 : 9) mentions simply the fact of his blindness, but the apostle states its cause, as an eye-witness would naturally do" (Birks, p. 328).[1]

12. Religious (εὐσεβής) is the authorized word, not *devout* (εὐλαβής). [According to evidence now accessible, the latter instead of the former is the authorized word. Thus *eulabēs* is given by ℵ B H L P, and is received into the text by all the late editors, while *eusebēs* is found in but one uncial codex, E, and is therefore rejected.—A. H.] "The historian (9 : 10) calls Ananias a disciple; but the apostle 'a devout man according to the law, having a good report of all the Jews who dwelt there.' Such a description was admirably suited to his immediate object—to conciliate his audience in every lawful way. How consistent it was with the other account appears from 21 : 20, in the words of James: 'Thou seest, brother, how many thousands of Jews ⁘⁘⁘ are who believe, and *they are all zealous of the law*'" (Birks, p. 329). **That dwelt**—*i. e.* in Damascus.

13. And stood, or **standing near,** in order to place his hands upon him. (Comp. 9 : 17.) — The recapitulation here omits the vision to Ananias, related so fully in the history. (Comp. 9 : 10, *sq.*) The circumstances of that event were unimportant to the apostle's defence, and would have made his commission to the Gentiles needlessly prominent at this stage of his address.—**Receive thy sight**—lit. **look up** and see; and so in the next clause, **I looked up upon him.** We are to think of Paul as sitting there blind, and Ananias as standing before him (Mey.). The verb does not vary its meaning, but suggests in the first instance what it asserts in the second. The involved idea prevails over the direct one in such a use as that in 9 : 12.

---

[1] *Horæ Apostolicæ*, by the Rev. T. R. Birks, late Fellow of Trinity College, Cambridge (London, 1850).

14 And he said, *a*The God of our fathers *b*hath chosen thee, that thou shouldest know his will, and *c*see *d*that Just One, and *e*shouldest hear the voice of his mouth.
15 *f*For thou shalt be his witness unto all men of *g*what thou hast seen and heard.
16 And now why tarriest thou? arise, and be baptized, *h*and wash away thy sins, *i*calling on the name of the Lord.

14 And he said, The God of our fathers hath appointed thee to know his will, and to see the Righteous One, 15 and to hear a voice from his mouth. For thou shalt be a witness for him unto all men of what thou hast 16 seen and heard. And now why tarriest thou? arise, and be baptized, and wash away thy sins, calling on

---

a ch. 3 : 13 ; 5 : 30....*b* ch. 9 : 15 ; 26 : 16....*c* 1 Cor. 9 : 1 ; 15 : 8....*d* ch. 3 : 14 ; 7 : 52....*e* 1 Cor. 11 : 23 ; Gal. 1 : 12....*f* ch. 23 : 11....*g* ch. 4 : 20 ; 26 : 16....*h* ch. 2 : 38 ; Heb. 10 : 22....*i* ch. 9 : 14 ; Rom. 10 : 13.

---

14. The God of our fathers is another of "those conciliatory touches which mark a real discourse."—**Hath chosen thee,** etc., or **appointed** (destined, as in 3 : 20) **thee, to know his will,** not as to the way of saving men (*i. e. counsel,* in 20 : 27), but as to what he was to do and suffer in his future sphere of labor. (Comp. 9 : 15, 16.)—**And to see.** (See the last remark on 9 : 7.)—**That Just One,** or *the Just One,* as in 3 : 14 ; 7 : 52.

15. For thou shalt be his witness, or *a witness for him,* **unto all men.** This is the reason why Christ had revealed himself to Paul. (Comp. Gal. 1 : 16.) **All men** takes the place of **Gentiles and kings and the children of Israel,** in 9 : 15. The more guarded phraseology here evinces the tact of the speaker. Paul would keep back for the present the offensive *unto Gentiles,* which, when uttered at length (v. 21), was the last word the bigoted Jews would bear from him.—The idea of our English "martyr" was not attached to *witness* (μάρτυρ or μάρτυς) till a later period. We see the word in its progress to that signification in v. 20 and Rev. 17 : 6. Toward the close of the second century it had become so honorable a title that the Christians at Lyons who had been condemned to suffer torture or death, fearful that they might waver in the moment of extremity, refused to be called "martyrs." "This name," said they, "properly belongs only to the true and faithful Witness, the Prince of life, or at least only to those whose testimony Christ has sealed by their constancy to the end. We are but poor, humble confessors—*i. e.* ὁμόλογοι." (Euseb., *Hist.,* 5. 2.)—**Of which** (ὧν) instead of **which** (ἅ), required by the verb, arises from the suppressed *those things* (ἐκείνων) after **witness.** [The full expression would therefore be *of those things which thou hast seen and heard.* The English *what* represents both the demonstrative and relative—viz. *that which* or *those things which*—and so gives the *implied* as well as the *expressed* meaning of the Greek.—A. H.]

16. Arise stands opposed to **tarriest thou** —*i. e. without delay.* (See on 9 : 18.)—**Be baptized,** or, with a stricter adherence to the

form, **have thyself baptized** (De Wet.). One of the uses of the middle is to express an act which a person procures another to perform for him. (W. § 38. 3 ; K. 250. R. 2.) This is the only instance in which the verb occurs in this voice with reference to Christian baptism. In the analogous case (1 Cor. 10 : 2) the reading is middle or passive [with a considerable predominance of authority in favor of the passive.—A. H.].—**And wash** (bathe) **away thy sins.** This clause states a result of the baptism in language derived from the nature of that ordinance. It answers to **for the remission of sins,** in 2 : 38—*i. e.* submit to the rite in order to be forgiven. In both passages baptism is represented as having this importance or efficacy, because it is the sign of the repentance and faith which are the conditions of salvation. (Comp. *ye are washed,* in 1 Cor. 6 : 11.) [Baptism *represents* the new or spiritual birth by which the subject of it enters on a life of trust in Christ and peace with God, or, more exactly, by which he *has entered* upon this new life. For this entrance upon the new life must, in the order of time, precede the ritual act by which it is voluntarily confessed. Hence, as a matter of fact, every proper subject of baptism is already a believer in Christ, regenerate, forgiven, cleansed, and baptism simply bears witness, by a solemn emblematic rite, of that which has been done for and by the candidate in his spiritual relations to God. "When any declaration or service is the appointed means of professing faith or obedience, making such profession or performing such service is said to secure the blessings which are promised to the faith thereby professed" (Hodge). The spiritual facts are *pictured,* as it were, and so acknowledged, by the significant ordinance prescribed by the Lord.—A. H.] The sort of outward washing expressed by this verb has been noticed on 16 : 33. Hence, there can be no question as to the mode of baptism in this instance; for if it be maintained that *baptisai* is uncertain in its meaning, a definition is added in *apolousai* which removes the doubt.—**Calling on the**

17 And *a*it came to pass, that, when I was come again to Jerusalem, even while I prayed in the temple, I was in a trance;
18 And *b*saw him saying unto me, *c*Make haste, and get thee quickly out of Jerusalem: for they will not receive thy testimony concerning me.
19 And I said, Lord, *d*they know that I imprisoned and *e*beat in every synagogue them that believed on thee:
20 *f*And when the blood of thy martyr Stephen was shed, I also was standing by, and *g*consenting unto his death, and kept the raiment of them that slew him.
21 And he said unto me, Depart: *h*for I will send thee far hence unto the Gentiles.
22 And they gave him audience unto this word, and *then* lifted up their voices, and said, *i*Away with such a *fellow* from the earth: for it is not fit that *k*he should live.

17 his name. And it came to pass, that, when I had returned to Jerusalem, and while I prayed in the 18 temple, I fell into a trance, and saw him saying unto me, Make haste, and get thee quickly out of Jerusalem: because they will not receive of thee 19 testimony concerning me. And I said, Lord, they themselves know that I imprisoned and beat in 20 every synagogue them that believed on thee: and when the blood of Stephen thy witness was shed, I also was standing by, and consenting, and keeping 21 the garments of them that slew him. And he said unto me, Depart: for I will send thee forth far hence unto the Gentiles.
22 And they gave him audience unto this word; and they lifted up their voice, and said, Away with such a fellow from the earth: for it is not fit that he

a ch. 9 : 26 ; 2 Cor. 12 : 2....*b* ver. 14....*c* Matt. 10 : 14....*d* ver. 4 ; ch. 8 : 3....*e* Matt. 10 : 17....*f* ch. 7 : 58....*g* Luke 11 : 48 ; ch. 8 : 1; Rom. 1 : 32....*h* ch. 9 : 15 ; 13 : 2, 46, 47 ; 18 : 6 ; 26 : 17 ; Rom. 1 : 5 ; 11 : 13 ; 15 : 16 ; Gal. 1 : 15, 16 ; 2 : 7, 8 ; Eph. 3 : 7, 8 ; 1 Tim. 2 : 7; 2 Tim. 1 : 11....*i* ch. 21 : 36....*k* ch. 25 : 24.

name of the Lord, or *on his name. His name* supplies essentially the place of **in,** or **upon, the name of Jesus Christ,** in 2 : 38. (See the note on that clause.) **The Lord** after **name** has much less support than **his.** The pronoun can refer only to Christ. (Comp. on 9 : 14.)

17. For this journey to Jerusalem, see on 9 : 10.—**It happened** (ἐγένετο) governs **to me** (μοι), as in v. 6.—In **while I prayed** the construction changes to the genitive absolute. On account of this intervening clause, the accusative (με) accompanies **was** (γενέσθαι), though **happened,** or **came to pass** (ἐγένετο), has the same logical subject. (See on 15 : 23. W. § 44. 3.)—On **trance,** or *ecstasy*, see 10 : 10. Some, as Schott, Wieseler, and others, would identify this "ecstasy" with the vision to which Paul alludes in 2 Cor. 12 : 2, and would establish by this coincidence the date of the composition of that Epistle. But as the apostle had so many similar revelations in the course of his life, and as the character of this vision is so unlike that described in 2 Cor. 12 : 2, the conjecture that they are the same must be pronounced vague and improbable.

18. Quickly accords with Gal. 1 : 18. On this first visit Paul remained at Jerusalem but fifteen days, and received this command, probably, on one of the last of them. In that passage of the Epistle the apostle says nothing respecting this vision in the temple, as it was sufficient for his object to mention the reason for this journey thither and the brevity of his stay.—**For,** or *because,* **they** (viz. his unconverted countrymen) **will not receive thy testimony**—*i. e.* although he should continue to declare it to them. (See the note on 9 : 30.)

19. I said, etc. The apostle states the reason here why he supposed Jerusalem to be his proper field of labor. His history as a con-

verted blasphemer and persecutor was notorious in that city; the testimony of such a man might be expected to have more weight among those who had witnessed the change in his character than among those to whom his previous life was unknown.

20. Of thy witness, not **martyr** (E. V.). (See on v. 15.)—**I also,** or **then** (see on 1 : 10), **I myself.**—In respect to **consenting,** see the note on 8 : 1. **Unto his death** the critical editions of the text omit or put in brackets. It is probably an addition from 8 : 1.—On **kept,** etc. (φυλάσσων, κ. τ. λ.), see 7 : 58.

21. Depart is present, because he was to obey at once. He proceeded to Syria and Cilicia (9 : 30 and Gal. 1 : 21), and remained there three or four years before his arrival at Antioch. (See on 9 : 30.) As he was ordered to leave Jerusalem because God would send him to the Gentiles, we may infer (though this is not the common opinion) that he preached to heathen as well as Jews during his sojourn in those regions. (See note on 13 : 3.)—"Paul relates this vision to show," as Alford remarks, "that his own inclination and prayer had been that *he might preach the gospel to his own people,* but that it was by the imperative command of the Lord himself that he went to the Gentiles."

22–29. PAUL PLEADS HIS ROMAN CITIZENSHIP, AND ESCAPES THE TORTURE.

22. Gave him audience, *continued to hear.* —**Unto this word**—viz. that God would send him to the heathen.—**Away with** (αἶρε) is present, because it was a repeated cry. (See on 21 : 37.)—For the article with **such a one, the one such as he,** see on 19 : 25.—**For it was not fit he should live,** imperfect, because he had forfeited life long ago. (W. § 41. 2.) Meyer refers the past tense to the chiliarch's interference: he ought not to have rescued the man, but should have left him to his fate. Some

23 And as they cried out, and cast off *their* clothes, and threw dust into the air,

24 The chief captain commanded him to be brought into the castle, and bade that he should be examined by scourging; that he might know wherefore they cried so against him.

25 And as they bound him with thongs, Paul said unto the centurion that stood by, ^aIs it lawful for you to scourge a man that is a Roman, and uncondemned?

26 When the centurion heard *that*, he went and told

23 should live. And as they cried out, and threw off their garments, and cast dust into the air, the chief captain commanded him to be brought into the castle, bidding that he should be examined by scourging, that he might know for what cause they

25 so shouted against him. And when they had tied him up ¹with the thongs, Paul said unto the centurion that stood by, Is it lawful for you to scourge

26 a man that is a Roman, and uncondemned? And

---

a ch. 16 : 37.——1 Or, *for*

---

copyists, stumbling, apparently, at the imperfect, wrote *is not fit* (καθῆκον or καθῆκει).

23. The Greek translated **cast off their clothes** means, not *throwing off their garments* as a preparation for stoning Paul (Grot., Mey.) —for he was now in the custody of the Roman captain—but *throwing them up*, tossing them about, as a manifestation and an effect of their incontrollable rage. Their **casting dust into the air** was an act of the same character. This mode of demonstrating their feelings was suited, also, to inflame the populace still more, and to impress the tribune with the necessity of conceding something to their demands. Sir John Chardin, as quoted by Harmer,¹ says that it is common for the peasants in Persia, when they have a complaint to lay before their governors, to repair to them by hundreds or a thousand at once; they place themselves near the gate of the palace, where they suppose they are most likely to be seen and heard, and there set up a horrid outcry, rend their garments, and throw dust into the air, at the same time demanding justice.

24. Commanded him, etc. It is not surprising that the chiliarch gave this order. He had been unable to follow Paul's address, on account of his ignorance of the language; and, witnessing now this renewed outburst of rage, he concludes that the prisoner must have given occasion for it by some flagrant offence, and determines, therefore, to extort a confession from him.—**And bade,** or *directing*, **that he should be examined by scourges.** The plural refers to the blows or lashes of the scourge. It was proposed to torture him into an acknowledgment of his supposed crime.—**That he might know,** *ascertain.* — **They cried so against him,** better **were so crying out against him,** not *cried* (E. V.).

25. And as they bound him with thongs has received two different explanations. Some, as De Wette, Meyer, Robinson, render *But as they* (sc. the soldiers; see on v. 29) *stretched him forth for the thongs*—i. e. for the scourge, which consisted sometimes of two or more lashes or cords.

They placed the apostle in an upright posture, so as to expose him more fully to the blows, or caused him to lean forward, in order to receive them more effectually. The stripes, it will be remembered, were inflicted on the naked back. (See 16 : 22.) Others translate *they stretched him forth with the thongs*, against a block or pillar—i. e. bound him to it with them—preparatory to his being scourged. The article in this case would designate *the thongs* as those which it was customary to use on such occasions. Böttger (*Schauplatz*, pp. 3–6), who advocates the view last stated, deduces a strong confirmation of it from v. 29. It is said that the chiliarch feared when he ascertained that Paul was a Roman citizen, because he *had bound him;* but that fear could not relate to the command in 21 : 33, for he kept Paul in chains until the next day (v. 30), and Felix left him still in that condition at the expiration of his term of office (24 : 27). It was not contrary to the Roman laws for a magistrate to bind a criminal or suspected person for safekeeping, although he was known to be a Roman citizen; and hence it is difficult to see what can be meant by *had bound*, in v. 29, unless it be the binding connected with the scourging to which the commander had ordered Paul to be subjected. That was an outrage which was not to come near the person of a Roman even after condemnation; the infliction of it, on the part of a judge or magistrate, exposed him to the severest penalty. (Wdsth. concurs in this view.) Several critics (*e. g.* Kuin., Olsh.) render the verb (προέτειναν) *delivered*, consigned—i. e. to the scourge—which is too vague for so specific a term.—**Unto the centurion standing there,** etc., having charge of the inquisition. It was the custom of the Romans to commit the execution of such punishments to that class of officers. (Comp. Mark 15 : 39.)—**And** (that too) **uncondemned,** without previous trial. (See on 16 : 37.)

26. The word rendered **take heed** in the English Version, Griesbach and others omit, after decisive authorities. It was added, ap-

---

¹ *Observations*, vol. iv. p. 203.

the chief captain, saying, Take heed what thou doest: for this man is a Roman.

27 Then the chief captain came, and said unto him, Tell me, art thou a Roman? He said, Yea.

28 And the chief captain answered, With a great sum obtained I this freedom. And Paul said, But I was *free* born.

29 Then straightway they departed from him which should have examined him: and the chief captain also was afraid, after he knew that he was a Roman, and because he had bound him.

---

when the centurion heard it, he went to the chief captain, and told him, saying, What art thou about 27 to do? for this man is a Roman. And the chief captain came, and said unto him, Tell me, art thou 28 a Roman? And he said, Yea. And the chief captain answered, With a great sum obtained I this citizenship. And Paul said, But I am *a Roman*. 29 born. They then who were about to examine him straightway departed from him: and the chief captain also was afraid, when he knew that he was a Roman, and because he had bound him.

---

parently, to give more point to the caution.— **For this man is a Roman.** It may excite surprise that the centurion believed Paul's word so readily. We have the explanation of this in the fact that a false claim of this nature was easily exposed and liable to be punished with death. (Suet., *Claud.*, c. 25.) It was almost an unprecedented thing that any one was so foolhardy as to assert the privilege without being entitled to it.

27. Tell me, etc. He asks the question, not from any doubt of Paul's veracity, but in order to have the report confirmed from his own lips, and at the same time to elicit an explanation of so unexpected a fact. The inquiry indicates his surprise that a man in Paul's situation should possess a privilege which he himself had procured at such expense.

28. With a great sum, *for a great sum.* It has been inferred from this circumstance, and from his name, that Lysias was a Greek. It was very common under the emperors to obtain the rights of citizenship in this way. Havercamp says, in a note on Josephus (*Antt.*, 1. p. 712), that a great many Jews in Asia Minor were Roman citizens at this time who had purchased that rank. It did not always require great wealth to procure it. A few years earlier than this, in the reign of Claudius, "the rights of Roman citizenship were sold by Messalina and the freedmen with shameless indifference to any purchaser, and it was currently said that the Roman *civitas* (*Dict. of Antt.*, s. v.) might be purchased for two cracked drinking-cups."—*Also* [not represented in the Eng. Ver.] connects the fact of his freedom with its origin. —**I was free-born,** or *I was born a Roman*— *i. e.* he had inherited his rights as a Roman citizen. In what way the family of Paul acquired this distinction is unknown. Many of the older commentators assert that Tarsus enjoyed the full privileges of citizenship, and that Paul possessed them as a native of Tarsus. But that opinion (advanced still in some recent works) is certainly erroneous. The passages in the ancient writers which were supposed to confirm it are found to be inconclusive; they prove

that the Romans freed the inhabitants of Tarsus from taxation, allowed them to use their own laws, and declared their city the metropolis of Cilicia, but they afford no proof that the Romans conferred on them the birthright of Roman citizenship. Indeed, the opinion to that effect, could it be established, so far from supporting Luke's credibility, would bring it into question; for it is difficult to believe that the chiliarch, after being told that Paul was a citizen of Tarsus (21:39), would have ordered him to be scourged, without any further inquiry as to his rank. It only remains, therefore, that Paul's father or some one of his ancestors must have obtained Roman citizenship in some one of the different ways in which foreigners could obtain that privilege. It was conferred often as a reward for fidelity to the Roman interest or for distinguished military services; it could be purchased, as was mentioned above; or it could be acquired by manumission, which, when executed with certain forms, secured the full immunities of freedom to the emancipated. In which of these modes the family of Paul became free can only be conjectured. Some adopt one supposition; some, another. Nothing is certain beyond the fact that Paul inherited his citizenship.

29. Which should have examined him are soldiers who aided the centurion (v. 25). Luke does not mention the command of Lysias which caused them to desist so promptly.— **After he knew,** or **having ascertained, that he is a Roman.** "Illa vox et imploratio, 'Civis Romanus sum,' quæ sæpe multis, in ultimis terris, opem inter barbaros et salutem tulit" ["That voice and outcry, 'I am a Roman citizen,' which often to many in the most distant lands among barbarians has brought help and safety"],[1] proved itself effectual also in this instance.—**Because he had bound him.** Those who understand this of his having ordered him to be chained, in 21:33, must suppose that his present fear was very transient. **Loosed,** in v. 30, shows that Paul was kept in chains during the night.

---

[1] Cic. *in Verr. Act.*, 2. 5. 57.

30 On the morrow, because he would have known the certainty wherefore he was accused of the Jews, he loosed him from *his* bands, and commanded the chief priests and all their council to appear, and brought Paul down, and set him before them.

30 But on the morrow, desiring to know the certainty, wherefore he was accused of the Jews, he loosed him, and commanded the chief priests and all the council to come together, and brought Paul down, and set him before them.

CHAPTER XXIII.

AND Paul, earnestly beholding the council, said, Men *and* brethren, *a* I have lived in all good conscience before God until this day.

2 And the high priest Ananias commanded them that stood by him *b* to smite him on the mouth.

1 AND Paul, looking stedfastly on the council, said, Brethren, I have lived before God in all good con-
2 science until this day. And the high priest Ananias commanded them that stood by him to smite him

---

a ch. 24 : 16 ; 1 Cor. 4 : 4 ; 2 Cor. 1 : 12 ; 4 : 2 ; 2 Tim. 1 : 3 ; Heb. 13 : 18....*b* 1 Kings 22 : 24 ; Jer. 20 : 2 ; John 18 : 22.

---

30. PAUL IS EXAMINED BEFORE THE SANHEDRIM.

30. For the use of the article (τό) before the interrogative clause, see on v. 21.—**Wherefore he was accused of the Jews,** or **why he is accused on the part of the Jews,** not directly or formally, but, in point of fact, by their persecution of him, their clamor for his death. *On the part of* (παρά) is a more exact preposition in this sense (W. ? 47. p. 327) than *by* (ὑπό), which has taken its place in some manuscripts. [ὑπό is sustained by superior manuscript testimony, א A B C E, and is given in all the late critical editions of the Greek Testament. The action of the Jews was *virtually* an accusation made by them against Paul. The diplomatic evidence need not be overruled.—A. H.] Some have joined **of,** or *from,* **the Jews** with **to know the certainty,** etc., as if it could not follow a passive verb.—**From his bands,** after **loosed,** expands the idea, and was added to the text probably for that purpose. It is destitute of critical support.—**Having brought down Paul,** from his prison in the castle (see on 21 : 31) to the lower place where the Sanhedrim assembled. According to Jewish tradition, that body transferred its sittings at length from Gazith, an apartment in the inner temple (see on 6 : 13), to a room on Mount Zion, near the bridge over the Tyropœon. It was here, probably, that the Council met at this time ; for Lysias and his soldiers would not have presumed to enter the sacred part of the temple. The Romans conceded to the Jews the right of putting any foreigner to death who passed the forbidden limits. (Comp. on 21 : 28. See Lewin, ii. p. 672.[1])

1-10. PAUL'S SPEECH BEFORE THE JEWISH COUNCIL.

1. In, better *with,* **all good conscience,** or, more strictly, *consciousness*—*i. e.* of integrity

and sincerity. (See on 20 : 21.)—**I have lived unto God**—*i. e.* for his service and glory ; dative of the object. (See Rom. 14 : 18 ; Gal. 2 : 19.) The verb refers to his conduct in all respects, not specially to his political or civil relations. (Comp. *let your manner of life be worthy of the gospel* (Rev. Ver.), in Phil. 1 : 27.)—**Until,** or *unto,* **this day,** from the time that he became a Christian. As his conduct before his defection from Judaism was not in question now, he had no occasion to speak of that part of his life, though he could claim in some sense to have acted conscientiously even then. (See 26 : 9.)

2. The high priest Ananias. This *Ananias* is to be distinguished from the Annas, or Ananus, of whom we read in 4 : 6, Luke 3 : 2, and John 18 : 13. He is unquestionably, says Winer (*Realw.,* i. p. 57), the son of Nebedæus, who obtained the office of high priest, under the Procurator Tiberius Alexander, in the year A. D. 48, and was the immediate successor of Camydus, or Camithus (Jos., *Antt.,* 20. 5. 2). He filled this office also under the Procurator Cumanus, but, having been implicated in a dispute between the Jews and the Samaritans, he was sent by the Syrian proprætor to Rome, in A. D. 52, in order to defend himself before the Emperor Claudius. The subsequent history of Ananias is obscure. He either lost his office in consequence of this journey, or, which is more probable (Jos., *Antt.,* 20. 6. 3), he was acquitted, and continued to officiate as high priest until he was superseded by Ismael, son of Phabi, just before the departure of Felix from Judea. In the latter case, says the same writer, he was the actual high priest at the time of the occurrence related here, and is called **high priest** on that account, and not because he had formerly held the office or because he occupied it during a vacancy.—**Those who stood near to him,** not members of the Council or spectators, but the servants in attendance. (See on 4 : 1.)—**To strike his mouth.** The mouth must be shut

---

[1] *The Life and Epistles of St. Paul,* by Thomas Lewin of Trinity College, Oxford (1851).

3 Then said Paul unto him, God shall smite thee, *thou* whited wall: for sittest thou to judge me after the law, and *ª*commandest me to be smitten contrary to the law?

4 And they that stood by said, Revilest thou God's high priest?

5 Then said Paul, *b*I wist not, brethren, that he was the high priest: for it is written,*c*Thou shalt not speak evil of the ruler of thy people.

3 on the mouth. Then said Paul unto him, God shall smite thee, thou whited wall: and sittest thou to judge me according to the law, and commandest me

4 to be smitten contrary to the law? And they that

5 stood by said, Revilest thou God's high priest? And Paul said, I knew not, brethren, that he was high priest· for it is written, Thou shalt not speak evil

---

a Lev. 19 : 35; Deut. 25 : 1, 2 ; John 7 : 51....*b* ch. 24 : 17....*c* Ex. 22 : 28 ; Eccles. 10 : 20 , 2 Pet. 2 · 10 ; Jude 8.

---

that uttered such a declaration. It was not to be endured that a man arraigned there as an apostate from the religion of his fathers should assert his innocence. This mode of enjoining silence is practised in the East at the present day. "As soon as the ambassador came," says a traveller in Persia, " he punished the principal offenders by causing them to be beaten before him ; and those who had spoken their minds too freely he smote upon the mouth with a shoe." He relates another instance: " 'Call the Ferasches,' exclaimed the king, 'let them beat the culprits until they die.' The Ferasches appeared and beat them violently, and when they attempted to say anything in their defence, they were struck on the mouth."[1]

3. God shall smite thee. The apostle declares in terms suggested by the outrage that God would punish the author of the brutal insult; he does not imprecate vengeance on him or predict that he would die by violence. As Ananias was killed by an assassin (Jos., *Bell. Jud.*, 2. 17. 9), some have supposed Paul's language to prefigure such an end.—**Thou whited wall**—*i. e.* hypocrite, because, as stated in the next clause, he did one thing while he professed another. For the origin of the expression, see Matt. 23 : 27. The Jews painted their sepulchres white, so as not to defile themselves by coming unexpectedly in contact with them ; hence they were fair to the eye, while they were full of inward corruption. (Jahn's *Archæol.*, § 207.)—**For sittest thou**, etc.—lit. **and dost thou sit?** etc. (The verb is a later form for κάθησαι. Lob., *Ad Phryn.* p. 358.) **And** conforms here to its use in questions designed to bring out the inconsistency of another's views or conduct. (Comp. Mark 4 : 13 ; Luke 10 : 29. K. § 321. R. 1.)—**To judge,** etc. **Judging me according to the law** states what was true of him in theory; **transgressing the law,** what was true in point of fact.

5. I did not know, at the moment, bear in mind (Bng., Wetst., Kuin., Olsh., Wdsth.). (Comp. the use of this verb in Eph. 6 : 8; Col. 3 : 34.) Some understand that Paul *did not know* —was ignorant—that Ananias was now the high

priest, a possible ignorance, certainly, since he had been absent from the country so long, and the high priest was changed so frequently at that period. On the contrary, if the high priest presided on such occasions or wore an official dress, Paul could tell at a glance who that dignitary was, from his position or his costume. But this view is liable to another objection : it renders the apostle's apology for his remark irrelevant, since he must have perceived, from the presence of Ananias, that he was at least one of the rulers of the people, and entitled to respect on account of his station. [A few interpreters (including Alford and Farrar) have thought it possible to account for Paul's language on this occasion by assuming that his eyesight was so imperfect as to prevent his recognizing persons at a little distance from himself. In support of this hypothesis, they refer—(1) to his total blindness, occasioned by the intense light which shone from heaven at the time of his conversion (9 : 8), and to the probability that his eyes did not fully recover from the effect of that light. But his sight was restored by miracle (9 · 18), and therefore, we naturally infer, fully restored. (2) To his noteworthy habit of looking very earnestly at the persons whom he was about to address (13 : 9; 14 : 9; 23 : 1)—a habit which may have been due to imperfect vision. Yet this habit is so natural, and so often observed in public speakers, that it cannot be trusted as a proof of impaired sight. (3) To his words in Gal. 4 : 15 : "For I bear you witness, that, if possible, ye would have plucked out your eyes and given them to me." But Alford, after examination, remarks : "The inference, then, of any ocular disease from these words themselves seems to me precarious." (4) To the possibility that *acute* ophthalmia may have been " the thorn in his flesh" from which Paul sought relief in vain (2 Cor. 12 : 7, 8) (The ablest argument for this view is in *The Life and Work of St. Paul*, by Canon Farrar, vol. i. Excursus X.) But, whatever may be thought of Paul's thorn in the flesh, the view that the apostle made no mistake in this instance, but continued to speak

---

[1] Morier's *Second Journey through Persia*, pp. 8, 94.

6 But when Paul perceived that the one part were Sadducees, and the other Pharisees, he cried out in the council, Men *and* brethren, *a*I am a Pharisee, the son of a Pharisee. *b*of the hope and resurrection of the dead I am called in question

7 And when he had so said, there arose a dissension between the Pharisees and the Sadducees: and the multitude was divided.

8 *c*For the Sadducees say that there is no resurrection, neither angel, nor spirit but the Pharisees confess both.

6 of a ruler of thy people. But when Paul perceived that the one part were Sadducees, and the other Pharisees, he cried out in the council, Brethren, I am a Pharisee, a son of Pharisees: touching the hope and resurrection of the dead I am called in 7 question. And when he had so said, there arose a dissension between the Pharisees and Sadducees: 8 and the assembly was divided. For the Sadducees say that there is no resurrection, neither angel, nor

a ch. 26 : 5 ; Phil 3 · 5 ....*b* ch. 24 . 15, 21 ; 26 : 6 ; 28 · 20....*c* Matt. 22 : 23 ; Mark 12 : 18 , Luke 20 : 27.

in a spirit and tone of holy indignation, seems to be the best clue to an interpretation of his language.—A. H.] Others think that Paul spoke ironically, meaning that he did not know or acknowledge such a man as high priest (Mey., Bmg.). The sarcasm so covertly expressed would not have been readily understood, and the appeal to Scripture in that state of mind becomes unmeaning, not to say irreverent.—**For it is written** connects itself with an implied thought *Otherwise I should not have so spoken,* **for it is written**—viz in Ex. 22: 28. The passage applies to any civil magistrate, as well as to the high priest. Paul admits that he had been thrown off his guard; the insult had touched him to the quick, and he had spoken rashly. But what can surpass the grace with which he recovered his self-possession, the frankness with which he acknowledged his error? If his conduct in yielding to the momentary impulse was not that of Christ himself under a similar provocation (John 18 : 22, 23), certainly the manner in which he atoned for his fault was *Christlike.*

6. But when Paul perceived, etc. Neander: " In order to secure the voice of the majority among his judges, Paul availed himself of a measure for promoting the triumph of the truth which has been oftener employed against it—the *divide et impera* in a good sense: in order to produce a division in the assembly, he addressed himself to the interest for the truth which a great part of his judges acknowledged, and by which they really approached nearer to him than the smaller number of those who denied it. He could say with truth that he stood there on trial because he had testified of the hope of Israel and of the resurrection of the dead; for he had preached Jesus as the One through whom this hope was to be fulfilled. This declaration had the effect of uniting the Pharisees present in his favor, and of involving them in a violent dispute with the Sadducees. The former could find no fault with him. If he said that the spirit of a deceased person or that an angel had appeared to him, no one could impute that to him as a

crime; what he meant by this, and whether what he alleged was true or not, they did not trouble themselves to decide."—**Of the hope,** etc., strictly **for hope's sake and** (that) **a resurrection of the dead** (Mey., De Wet.) —*i. e.* by hendiadys, *the hope of the resurrection* (Kuin., Olsh.). The first mode of stating it analyzes the grammatical figure.

7. There arose a dissension, difference of views respecting Paul's case. (See on 15 . 2.) —As the effect of this difference, **the multitude was divided,** took opposite sides.

8. That there is no resurrection, nor angel or spirit. (See Mark 12 : 18.) *Nor* (μηδέ) adds a second denial to the first, while *or* (μήτε) expands this denial into its parts. (See W. ½ 55. 6.) [It should, however, be remarked that Lach., Tsch., Treg., West. and Hort, and the Anglo-Am. Revisers adopt the reading μήτε—μήτε = *neither—nor* This text is supported by ℵ A B C E.—A. H.] Josephus confirms this statement as to the belief of the Sadducees. In one place (*Bell. Jud.,* 2 8. 14) he says that " the Sadducees reject the permanence or existence of the soul after death, and the rewards and punishments of an invisible world;" and in another place (*Antt.,* 18. 1. 4), that " the Sadducees hold that the souls of men perish with their bodies." The Talmudists and other Jewish writers make the same representation.—**Confess both**—*i. e.* according to the above analysis, a resurrection and the reality of spiritual existences, whether angels or the souls of the departed Josephus belonged to the sect of the Pharisees, and he represents their opinion to have been " that souls have an immortal vigor, and are destined to be rewarded or punished in another state according to the life here, as it has been one of virtue or vice, that the good will be permitted to live again (*i. e.* in another body on the earth), and that the wicked will be consigned to an eternal prison " (*Antt.,* 18. 1. 3). " There was a variety of opinions concerning the resurrection," says Biscoe, " among the Pharisees or traditionary Jews. In this account of it, which resembles the heathen idea of transmigration, Josephus

9 And there arose a great cry: and the scribes *that were* of the Pharisees' part arose, and strove, saying, *a*We find no evil in this man: but *b*if a spirit or an angel hath spoken to him, *c*let us not fight against God.

10 And when there arose a great dissension, the chief captain, fearing lest Paul should have been pulled in pieces of them, commanded the soldiers to go down, and to take him by force from among them, and to bring *him* into the castle.

11 And *d*the night following the Lord stood by him, and said, Be of good cheer, Paul: for as thou hast testified of me in Jerusalem, so must thou bear witness also at Rome.

12 And when it was day, *e*certain of the Jews banded together, and bound themselves under a curse, saying that they would neither eat nor drink till they had killed Paul.

9 spirit: but the Pharisees confess both. And there arose a great clamor: and some of the scribes of the Pharisees' part stood up, and strove, saying, We find no evil in this man: and what if a spirit hath spoken to him, or an angel?

10 And when there arose a great dissension, the chief captain, fearing lest Paul should be torn in pieces by them, commanded the soldiers to go down and take him by force from among them, and bring him into the castle.

11 And the night following the Lord stood by him, and said, Be of good cheer: for as thou hast testified concerning me at Jerusalem, so must thou bear witness also at Rome.

12 And when it was day, the Jews banded together, and bound themselves under a curse, saying that they would neither eat nor drink till they had

a ch. 25 : 25 ; 26 : 31....*b* ch. 22 : 7, 17, 18....*c* ch. 5 : 39....*d* ch. 18 : 9 ; 27 : 23, 24....*e* vers. 21, 30 ; ch. 25 : 3.

---

as I apprehend, has given us that which comes nearest to his own belief, or which he was inclined to have the Greek philosophers understand to be his own. For he is accused by learned men—and certainly not without reason—of sometimes accommodating the Jewish revelation to the sentiments of the heathen, or bringing it as near to what was taught by them as might be.''

9. The scribes, etc., **the scribes of the party of the Pharisees, contended,** disputed violently. They appear as the champions of their party, because they were the men of learning and accustomed to such debates.—**But if a spirit spoke to him, or an angel.** Undoubtedly, a designed aposiopesis. A significant gesture or look toward the Sadducees expressed what was left unsaid — that is not an impossible thing, the matter then assumes importance, or something to that effect. (See W. ℥ 64. II.) For other examples of aposiopesis, see Luke 19 : 42 and 22 : 42. Some maintain that the sentence is incomplete, because the remainder was unheard amid the tumult that now ensued. The common text supplies **let us not fight against God** as the apodosis ; but the testimonies require us to reject that addition. It was suggested, probably, by *fighting against God*, in 5 : 39.

10. Lest Paul, etc., strictly **lest Paul should be pulled in pieces by them,** as the parties struggled to obtain possession of him, their object being, on the one side, to protect him; and on the other, to maltreat or kill him.—**The soldiers,** or **the soldiery,** some of the troops stationed in the castle. (See v. 27.)—Observe the collateral **and** (τε) before **to bring** (ἄγειν), since the rescue and the conveyance to the garrison are parts of the same order. [Paul's stratagem—if it may be so called —was perfectly right; for he was in the presence of men who knew, or ought to have known,

the substance of Christian doctrine, and he simply called their attention to a fundamental part of that doctrine. He reminded the members of the Great Council that in proceeding against him they were assailing a bold defender of truth which many of them held to be of vital importance. This it was proper for the Pharisees to consider before they gave their voice against the accused. And if it was a matter which they ought to consider, it was one which he might fitly press upon their attention. If reflection led them to oppose the other members of the Sanhedrim, and thus to prevent a criminal act, so much the better for him and for them. The words of Paul in v. 6 should be compared with 1 Cor. 15 : 12-20, where the apostle assigns its place to the doctrine of the resurrection. If he could write thus to Christians, why could he not speak in a similar strain to the adversaries of Christ?—A. H.]

11–15. A CONSPIRACY OF THE JEWS TO SLAY PAUL.

11. The Lord—*i. e.* Christ.—**Be of good cheer, be courageous still.** The tense is present. Though he had not begun to despond, he was on the eve of trials which would expose him to that danger. — **Paul** is (Παῦλε), in the T. R., which the E. V. retains, to be struck out.—**Unto Jerusalem** and **unto Rome** involve an ellipsis like that noticed on 8 : 40.—**Must,** or **is necessary,** because such was the purpose of God. (Comp. 27 : 24.) Paul had long cherished a desire to see Rome (19 : 21 ; Rom. 1 : 13), but, as far as we know, he was now assured for the first time that such was to be his destiny.

12. Banded together, having formed a combination (Mey., Rob.), which **conspiracy,** in v. 13, defines more precisely.—**The Jews,** since this party of them manifested the Jewish spirit. (See the last remark on 4

13 And they were more than forty which had made this conspiracy.

14 And they came to the chief priests and elders, and said, We have bound ourselves under a great curse, that we will eat nothing until we have slain Paul.

15 Now therefore ye with the council signify to the chief captain that he bring him down unto you to-morrow, as though ye would enquire something more perfectly concerning him: and we, or ever he come near, are ready to kill him.

16 And when Paul's sister's son heard of their lying in wait, he went and entered into the castle, and told Paul.

17 Then Paul called one of the centurions unto *him*, and said, Bring this young man unto the chief captain: for he hath a certain thing to tell him.

18 So he took him, and brought *him* to the chief

---

13 killed Paul. And they were more than forty who 14 made this conspiracy. And they came to the chief priests and the elders, and said, We have bound ourselves under a great curse, to taste nothing until we 15 have killed Paul. Now therefore do ye with the council signify to the chief captain that he bring him down unto you, as though ye would judge of his case more exactly: and we, or ever he come 16 near, are ready to slay him. But Paul's sister's son heard of their lying in wait, [1]and he came and en-17 tered into the castle, and told Paul. And Paul called unto him one of the centurions, and said, Bring this young man unto the chief captain: for 18 he hath something to tell him. So he took him,

---

1 Or, *having come in* upon them, *and he entered* etc.

1.) **Certain of the Jews** is an unapproved reading.

14. The chief priests and the elders— *i. e.* those of these classes who were hostile to Paul, the Sadducee members of the Council (Mey., De Wet.). This limitation suggests itself without remark, after the occurrence which has just been related. — **We have bound our-selves,** etc.—lit. **we cursed ourselves.** The expression points to some definite ratification of the atrocious oath. The reflexive of the third person (see v. 12) may follow a subject of the first or second person. (K. ? 303. 8; B. ? 127. n. 5.)

15. With the council — namely, *the San-hedrim ; i. e.* in the name of that body, as if it was their united request.—**To-morrow** has been added to the text in some copies, because it occurs in v. 20.—**More perfectly,** or **more ex-actly,** than on the former trial.—**Or ever he come near,** or **before he has come near—** *i. e.* to the place of assembly. Their plan was to kill him on the way. (See v. 21.)—**To kill** depends on **ready** as a genitive construction. (W. ? 44. 4.)—It would be difficult to credit the account of such a proceeding, had Luke related it of any other people than the Jews. Here, as Lardner suggests (*Credibility*, i. p. 224), are more than forty men who enter into a conspiracy to take away Paul's life in a clandestine manner, and they make no scruple to declare it to the Council, relying upon their approbation. It is clearly implied that these teachers of religion, these professed guardians of the law, gave their assent to the proposal ; they had nothing to object, either to so infamous a design or to the use of such means for accomplishing it. But, out of place as such a passage would be in any other history, it relates a transaction in perfect harmony with the Jewish opinions and practices of that age. A single testimony will illustrate this. Philo, in speaking of the course to be pursued toward a Jew who forsakes the worship of the true God, lays down the following principle: " It is highly proper that all who have a zeal for virtue should have a right to punish with their own hands, without delay, those who are guilty of this crime ; not carrying them before a court of judicature or the Council, or, in short, before any magistrate, but they should indulge the abhorrence of evil, the love of God, which they entertain, by inflicting immediate punishment on such impious apostates, regarding themselves for the time as all things—senators, judges, prætors, sergeants, ac-cusers, witnesses, the laws, the people ; so that, hindered by nothing, they may without fear and with all promptitude espouse the cause of piety." Josephus mentions a similar combination against the life of Herod, into which a party of the Jews entered on account of the religious innovations which they charged him with introducing (*Antt.*, 15. 8. 1–4).

16–22. THE PLOT IS DISCLOSED TO THE ROMAN COMMANDER.

16. Paul's sister's son, better **the son of Paul's sister.** Whether the family of this sister resided at Jerusalem, or the nephew only, does not appear from the narrative. His anxiety for the safety of Paul may have arisen from a stronger interest than that prompted by their relationship to each other. (See the nota on 9 : 30.) He was not a bigoted Jew, at all events; for in that case he would have allowed no tie of blood, no natural affection, to interfere with the supposed claims of his religion.— **Having entered into the castle,** whence it appears that his friends, as afterward at Cæsarea (24 : 23), had free access to him. Lysias may have been the more indulgent, because he would atone for his fault in having bound a Roman citizen.—**Their lying in wait**—lit. **the ambush,** which the Jews were preparing.

18. The prisoner shows that Paul was still

captain, and said, Paul the prisoner called me unto *him*, and prayed me to bring this young man unto thee, who hath something to say unto thee.

19 Then the chief captain took him by the hand, and went *with him* aside privately, and asked *him*, What is that thou hast to tell me?

20 And he said, *a* The Jews have agreed to desire thee that thou wouldst bring down Paul to-morrow into the council, as though they would enquire somewhat of him more perfectly.

21 But do not thou yield unto them: for there lie in wait for him of them more than forty men, which have bound themselves with an oath, that they will neither eat nor drink till they have killed him: and now are they ready, looking for a promise from thee.

22 So the chief captain *then* let the young man depart, and charged *him*, *See thou* tell no man that thou hast shewed these things to me.

23 And he called unto *him* two centurions, saying, Make ready two hundred soldiers to go to Cæsarea, and horsemen threescore and ten, and spearmen two hundred, at the third hour of the night,

24 And provide *them* beasts, that they may set Paul on, and bring *him* safe unto Felix the governor.

25 And he wrote a letter after this manner:

and brought him to the chief captain, and saith, Paul the prisoner called me unto him, and asked me to bring this young man unto thee, who hath

19 something to say to thee. And the chief captain took him by the hand, and going aside asked him

20 privately, What is that thou hast to tell me? And he said, The Jews have agreed to ask thee to bring down Paul to-morrow unto the council, as though thou wouldest inquire somewhat more exactly con-

21 cerning him. Do not thou therefore yield unto them, for there lie in wait for him of them more than forty men, who have bound themselves under a curse, neither to eat nor to drink till they have slain him: and now are they ready, looking for the

22 promise from thee. So the chief captain let the young man go, charging him, Tell no man that

23 thou hast signified these things to me. And he called unto him two of the centurions, and said, Make ready two hundred soldiers to go as far as Cæsarea, and horsemen threescore and ten, and spearmen two hundred, at the third hour of the

24 night: and *he bade them* provide beasts, that they might set Paul thereon, and bring him safe unto

25 Felix the governor. And he wrote a letter after this form:

---

a ver. 12.

---

bound—*i. e.* by a chain to the arm of a soldier.—**Who hath**—*i. e.* since he has—**something to say to thee.** (Comp. **for he hath**, etc., in v. 17.)

21. Lie in wait, which they were doing, inasmuch as their plot was already so mature. (Comp. *making an ambush*, in 25 : 3.)—**Forty**—*i. e. men*, as in v. 13.—**Are ready**—*i. e. to kill him.* (Comp. v. 15.)—**Looking for, or awaiting, the** (expected) **promise from thee.** The word translated **promise** (ἐπαγγελία) has this constant sense in the New Testament.

22. Note the change to the direct style in **that thou hast showed these things to me.** (W. § 63. II. 1. Comp. Luke 5 : 14.) The opposite change occurs in v. 24.

23–30. THE LETTER OF LYSIAS TO FELIX.

23. Two centurions, more exactly **some two or three of the centurions ;** not *one or two* (Cony. and Hws.), from the nature of the expression, and because less than two would be an inadequate command for so large a force. Though it is not said expressly, the inference is that these officers were to take charge of the expedition, as well as prepare for it. The pronoun (τὶς, *a certain one, some one*) joined with numerals renders them indefinite. (Comp. some *two of his disciples*, in Luke 7 : 19. W. § 25. 2. b : K. § 303. 4.)—**Soldiers,** who, as they are distinguished from the other two classes named, must be the ordinary, heavy-armed legionaries.—**Spearmen** (δεξιολάβους) occurs only here and in two obscure writers of the Iron Age. "Its meaning," says De Wette, "is a riddle." The proposed explanations are these: *side-guards*, military lictors who guarded

prisoners, so called from their taking the right-hand side (Suid., Bez., Kuin.) ; *lancers* (Vulg., E. V.), a species of light-armed troops (Mey.), since they are mentioned once in connection with archers and peltasts. Codex A reads *spearmen, jaculantes dextra* (Syr.). (See De Wette's note here.)—**At the,** or *from the,* **third hour**—*i. e.* nine o'clock with us, it being implied that they were to march at that hour, as well as be ready.

24. And to provide, etc., **and that they should provide beasts of burden,** as two or more would be needed for relays or for the transportation of baggage. The discourse changes at this point from the direct to the indirect. (Comp. on 19 : 27.)—**That they may set,** or **that having mounted Paul** (on one of them) **they might convey him in safety unto Felix.** *Through* (διά) in the verb refers to the intermediate space, not to the dangers through which they were to pass. (Comp. 18 : 27 ; 27 : 44 ; 1 Pet. 3 : 20.)—**Felix** was the Procurator of Judea, having received this office from the Emperor Claudius, probably in the autumn of A. D. 52 (Win., Ang., Mey.). He was originally a slave, was a man of energy and talents, but avaricious, cruel, and licentious. Tacitus (*Hist.*, 5. 9) has drawn his character in a single line : " Per omnem sævitiam ac libidinem jus regium servili ingenio exercuit " [" With all cruelty and lust he exercised the royal power in the spirit of a slave "]. (See further on 24 : 3–24.)

25. Wrote—lit. **writing**—belongs to the subject of *said* (E. V. **saying**), in v. 23.—**After this manner,** or **containing this outline,** or **draught**—*i. e.* a letter to this effect. The Roman

26 Claudius Lysias unto the most excellent governor Felix *sendeth* greeting.

27 *ᵃ*This man was taken of the Jews, and should have been killed of them : then came I with an army, and rescued him, having understood that he was a Roman.

28 *ᵇ*And when I would have known the cause wherefore they accused him, I brought him forth into their council :

29 Whom I perceived to be accused *ᶜ*of questions of their law, *ᵈ*but to have nothing laid to his charge worthy of death or of bonds.

30 And *ᵉ*when it was told me how that the Jews laid wait for the man, I sent straightway to thee, and *ᶠ*gave commandment to his accusers also to say before thee what *they had* against him. Farewell.

31 Then the soldiers, as it was commanded them, took Paul, and brought *him* by night to Antipatris.

26   Claudius Lysias unto the most excellent governor
27 Felix, greeting. This man was seized by the Jews, and was about to be slain of them, when I came upon them with the soldiers, and rescued him, hav-
28 ing learned that he was a Roman. And desiring to know the cause wherefore they accused him, [1]I
29 brought him down unto their council : whom I found to be accused about questions of their law, but to have nothing laid to his charge worthy of
30 death or of bonds. And when it was shewn to me that there would be a plot [2]against the man, I sent him to thee forthwith, charging his accusers also to speak against him before thee.[3]
31   So the soldiers, as it was commanded them, took

---

a ch. 21 . 33 ; 24 . 7....*b* ch. 22 : 30....*c* ch. 18 . 15 ; 25 : 19....*d* ch. 26 : 31....*e* ver. 20.. .*f* ch. 24 : 8 ; 25 : 6.———1 Some ancient authorities omit *I brought him down unto their council*....2 Many ancient authorities read *against the man on their part*....3 Many ancient authorities add *Farewell.*

---

law required that a subordinate officer, in sending a prisoner to the proper magistrate for trial, should draw up a written statement of the case. The technical name of such a communication was *elogium.*

26. Most excellent is an honorary epithet. (See on 1 : 1.)—**Governor** stands in the New Testament for the more specific *procurator* (ἐπί-τροπος). (Comp. Matt. 27 : 2.)—**Greeting.** (Comp. the last remark on 15 : 23.)

27. This man is the object of **rescued,** which **him** repeats, on account of the distance of the noun from the verb. (Comp *of these,* τούτων, in 1 : 22.)—**On the point of being killed,** not **should have been** (E. V.).—**With an army,** rather **with the military.** (See v. 10.)—**Having learned that he is a Roman,** which is stated as a reason why Lysias was so prompt to rescue him. It was not until after he had taken Paul into his custody that he ascertained his rank ; but, as was not unnatural, he wished to gain as much credit as possible in the eyes of his superior. This deviation from truth, says Meyer, testifies to the genuineness of the letter. Some resolve *having learned* into *and I learned,* as if he learned the fact that Paul was a Roman citizen after his apprehension. The Greek of the New Testament affords no instance of such a use of the participle. (See W. ₰ 46. 2.) Luke with his inquisitive habits (see his Gospel, 1 : 1) would find an opportunity to copy the letter during his abode of two years at Cæsarea.

28. Would have known, rather **wishing to know,** or **ascertain** (γνῶναι and ἐπιγνῶναι are both found), **the crime** (not *charge*), of which, at this stage of the affair, Paul was supposed to be guilty. The weaker sense of this noun (Cony. and Hws.) makes **accused** repetitious.—**Wherefore**—lit. **on account of which**—**they were accusing him,** not

formally, but by their continued outcry, as Luke has related.—**I brought him down,** in person, as he must be present to gain the desired information. (See on 22 : 30.)

29. Of, or **concerning, questions of their law.** (See the note on 18 : 15.)—As **death** and **bonds** denoted the highest and lowest penalties of the law, the idea is that Paul had no crime alleged against him that required his detention or punishment (Böttg.). Every Roman magistrate before whom the apostle is brought declares him innocent.

30. The writer falls out of his construction here. He says *a plot having been told me* (μηνυθείσης) at the beginning of the sentence, as if he would have added *that was about to be* (τῆς μελλούσης), but in the progress of the thought adds the infinitive (μέλλειν), as if he had commenced with *they having told me that a plot* (μηνυσάντων . . . ἐπιβουλὴν) *was about to be.* The idea of the thing disclosed gives place to that of the persons who disclose it. (W. ₰ 63. I.) [Alexander attempts a literal translation of the Greek as follows : "*But a plot against the man having been reported to me,* (as) *about* (or *that it was about*) *to be* (attempted) *by the Jews.*" *By the Jews* is to be removed from the text (see below), and it will then in the simplest version : *But a plot . . .* (as) *about to be—i. e.* carried into effect.—A. H.] **By the Jews,** after **about to be,** the recent editors omit (Tsch., De Wet., Mey.).—**I sent,** since the future act would be past on the reception of the letter. (Comp. Phil. 2 : 28 ; Philem. 11. W. ₰ 41. 5. 2.)—**Before thee.** ["A peculiar phrase appropriated to judicial hearing, as in Matt. 28 : 14 " (*Alexander*).]

31–35. PAUL IS SENT TO FELIX AT CÆSAREA.

31. Took—lit. **having taken—up** answers to *having mounted Paul,* in v. 24.—**By night,**

32 On the morrow they left the horsemen to go with him, and returned to the castle:

33 Who, when they came to Cæsarea, and delivered the epistle to the governor, presented Paul also before him.

34 And when the governor had read *the letter*, he asked of what province he was. And when he understood that *he was* of ^aCilicia;

35 ^bI will hear thee, said he, when thine accusers

32 Paul, and brought him by night to Antipatris. But on the morrow they left the horsemen to go with him, and returned to the castle: and they, when they came to Cæsarea, and delivered the letter to

34 the governor, presented Paul also before him. And when he had read it, he asked of what province he was; and when he understood that he was of Cilicia,

35 I will hear thee fully, said he, when thine accusers

a ch. 21 : 39.....*b* ch. 24 : 1, 10 ; 25 : 16.

---

rather **during the night,** which would include the hours from nine o'clock P. M. (v. 23) to six A. M.—**Unto Antipatris,** which was about thirty-eight miles from Jerusalem, on the route to Cæsarea. It was built by Herod the Great, on the site of a place called Caphar Saba, and was named by him Antipatris, in honor of his father Antipater. (See Jos., *Antt.*, 16. 5. 2 ; *Bell. Jud.*, 1. 21. 9.) The modern Kefr Sâba, about ten miles from Lud, the ancient Lydda, stands, no doubt, on the same spot.¹ It is an instance like Ptolemais (21 : 7), in which the original name regained its sway on the decline of the power which imposed the foreign name. The Romans had two military roads from Jerusalem to Antipatris, a more southerly one by the way of Gibeon and Beth-horon, and a more northerly one by way of Gophna (*Bibl. Res.*, ii. p. 138). If Paul's escort took the latter as the more direct course, they would arrive at Gophna about midnight, and at daybreak would reach the last line of hills which overlook the plain of Sharon. Antipatris lay on a slight eminence at a little distance from the base of these hills. To perform this journey in the time allowed would require them to proceed at the rate of about four miles an hour. As those who conducted Paul had a good road (traces of the old Roman pavement are still visible), they could accomplish a forced march of that extent in nine hours. Strabo says that an army, under ordinary circumstances, could march from two hundred and fifty to three hundred stadia in a day—*i. e.* an average of about thirty miles. Forbiger (*Handb. der Geog.*, p. 551) gives a table of the various distances of a day's journey among the ancients. Some understand the words to mean that they *brought him by night*, in distinction from the day ; in which case,

they could have occupied two nights on the road. It is suggested that the escort may have proceeded to Nicopolis the first night, which was twenty-two Roman miles from Jerusalem, and, remaining there the next day, have arrived at Antipatris the night following. Biscoe, Meyer,² Kuinoel, and others adopt this opinion. In this case **on the morrow,** in v. 32, must denote *the morrow* after the arrival at Antipatris on the second night, instead of *the morrow* after leaving Jerusalem, as the text would more obviously suggest. If it be thought necessary, we may consider **during the night** as applying only to the greater part of the journey. It would be correct to speak of the journey, in general terms, as a journey by night, although it occupied two or three hours of the following day. This view, which Winer maintains (*Realw.*, i. p. 65), allows us to assign twelve hours to the march, and the rate of travelling would then be a little more than three miles the hour.

32. They left the horsemen, etc. The remaining distance to Cæsarea was not more than twenty-five miles. They were now so far from the scene of danger that they could with safety reduce the escort. Whether they had orders to do this or acted on their own discretion we are not told. They commenced their return to Jerusalem on *the morrow*, but after so hurried a march would travel leisurely, and may have occupied two days on the way.

34. The governor appears in the common text without sufficient reason.—**He asked**—lit. **having asked—from what province he is.** He makes the inquiry, perhaps, because the letter stated that Paul was a Roman citizen.

35. I will hear thee fully. Observe

---

¹ See the account of a visit to Kefr Sâba by the late Dr. Smith, in the *Bibliotheca Sacra*, 1843, p. 478, *sq.* : "It is a Muslim village, of considerable size, and wholly like the most common villages of the plain, being built entirely of mud. We saw but one stone building, which was apparently a mosque, but without a minaret. No old ruins, nor the least relic of antiquity, did we anywhere discover. A well by which we stopped, a few rods east of the houses, exhibits more signs of careful workmanship than anything else. It is walled with hewn stone, and is fifty-seven feet deep to the water. The village stands upon a slight circular eminence near the western hills, from which it is actually separated, however, by a branch of the plain." Raumer (*Palästina*, p. 132, 3d ed.) and Ritter (*Erdkunde*, xvi. p. 571) suppose Antipatris to have been at this place.

² J. A. G. Meyer, in his *Versuch einer Vertheidigung und Erläuterung der Geschichte Jesu und der Apostel aus Griechischen und Römischen Profanscribenten* (p. 461).

are also come. And he commanded him to be kept in ᵃHerod's judgment hall.

also are come: and he commanded him to be kept in Herod's ¹palace.

CHAPTER XXIV.

AND after ᵇfive days ᶜAnanias the high priest descended with the elders, and *with* a certain orator *named* Tertullus, who informed the governor against Paul.

2 And when he was called forth, Tertullus began to accuse *him*, saying, ᵈeeing that by thee we enjoy great quietness, and that very worthy deeds are done unto this nation by thy providence,

3 We accept *it* always, and in all places, most noble Felix, with all thankfulness.

1   AND after five days the high priest Ananias came down with certain elders, and *with* an orator, one Tertullus; and they informed the governor against

2 Paul.   And when he was called, Tertullus began to accuse him, saying,

Seeing that by thee we enjoy much peace, and that by thy providence evils are corrected for this

3 nation, we accept it in all ways and in all places,

a Matt. 27 : 27....*b* ch. 21 : 27....*c* ch. 23 : 2, 30, 35 ; 25 : 2.——1 Gr. *Prætorium.*

---

the compound verb (διακούσομαι). The expression exhibits a singular conformity to the processes of Roman law. The rule was, *Qui cum elogio* (see on v. 25) *mittuntur, ex integro audiendi sunt* ["Those who are sent with an elogium must be fully heard"]. The governor of a province was not to give implicit credit to the document with which a prisoner was sent to him; he must institute an independent examination of the case for himself. (See Böttger, *Beiträge, u. s. w.,* ii. p. 8.) — In **Herod's judgment hall,** *in the prætorium of Herod—i. e.* in the palace built by him at Cæsarea, and now occupied as the residence of the Roman procurators. Paul was confined in some apartment of this edifice, or within its precincts. (See Win., *Realw.,* ii. p. 324.)

1-9. TERTULLUS ACCUSES PAUL BEFORE FELIX.

1. As to **Ananias,** see on 23 : 2.—**And,** or *now,* **after five days**—*i. e.* in popular usage on the fifth since Paul's departure from Jerusalem (Kuin., Mey., De. Wet.), not since his capture there or since his arrival at Cæsarea. The escape from the Jewish conspiracy is nearest to the mind here after what has been related; and further, according to Roman usage, a case referred like this should be tried on the third day, or as soon after that as might be possible. (Comp. 25 : 17. See Böttger, ii. p. 9.) The reckoning in v. 11 admits of this decision.— **With the elders**—*i. e.* the Sanhedrists, represented by some of their number. (τινῶν, "some of," is a gloss.)—**Orator Tertullus.** As the people in the provinces were not acquainted with the forms of Roman law, they employed advocates to plead for them before the public tribunals. *Tertullus* was one of this class of men, and may have been a Roman or a Greek. It is not certain that "the proceedings before

Felix were conducted in Latin.   In ancient times the Romans had attempted to enforce the use of Latin in all law-courts, but the experiment failed.   Under the emperors trials were permitted in Greek, even in Rome itself, as well in the Senate as in the forum; and it is unlikely that greater strictness should have been observed in a distant province" (*Lewin,* ii. p. 684).—**Informed the governor against Paul,** lodged their complaint.   "The beginning of any judicial action," says Geib, "consisted in the formal declaration on the part of the accuser that he wished to prosecute a particular person on account of a certain crime."[1]

2. And when he (Paul) **was called forth** —lit. **he having been called** [there is nothing answering to **forth** in the Greek text.—A. H.], after information of the case had been given (**informed,** v. 1), but before the charges against him were produced.   The Roman law secured that privilege to the accused. (See 25 : 16.) Nothing could be more unstudied than this conformity to the judicial rule.—**Began,** or **proceeded, to accuse.**   Tertullus insisted on three charges—viz. sedition (**a mover of sedition**), heresy (**a ringleader of the sect of the Nazarenes**), and profanation of the temple (**who also hath gone about to profane the temple**). (See on vv. 5, 6.)

3. In this verse [which in the original begins with the speech of Tertullus, **Seeing,** etc., E. V.—A. H.] the participial clause forms the object of **we accept.** (Comp. *I thank God that I speak with tongues more than you all,* in 1 Cor. 14 : 18.   W. § 46. 1. a.)   Translate **that we enjoy much peace through thee, and** (the benefit of) **many** (sc. πολλῶν) **excellent deeds performed for this nation by thy prudence, we acknowledge, with all gratitude.**   Most critics transfer the idea of **much** to **worthy deeds** (De Wet., Mey., Rob.), which term refers to the general measures of his administration. [According to the

4 Notwithstanding, that I be not further tedious unto thee, I pray thee that thou wouldest hear us of thy clemency a few words.

5 ªFor we have found this man *a* pestilent *fellow*, and a mover of sedition among all the Jews throughout the world, and a ringleader of the sect of the Nazarenes:

6 ᵇWho also hath gone about to profane the temple: whom we took, and would ᶜhave judged according to our law.

7 ᵈBut the chief captain Lysias came *upon us*, and with great violence took *him* away out of our hands,

8 ᵉCommanding his accusers to come unto thee: by examining of whom thyself mayest take knowledge of all these things, whereof we accuse him.

9 And the Jews also assented, saying that these things were so.

4 most excellent Felix, with all thankfulness. But, that I be not further tedious unto thee, I intreat 5 thee to hear us of thy clemency a few words. For we have found this man a pestilent fellow, and a mover of insurrections among all the Jews throughout ¹the world, and a ringleader of the sect of the 6 Nazarenes: who moreover assayed to profane the 8 temple: on whom also we laid hold:² from whom thou wilt be able, by examining him thyself, to take knowledge of all these things, whereof we accuse 9 him. And the Jews also joined in the charge, affirming that these things were so.

---

a Luke 23 : 2 ; ch. 6 : 13 ; 16 : 20 ; 17 : 6 ; 21 : 28 ; 1 Pet. 2 : 12, 15....*b* ch. 21 : 28....*c* John 18 : 31....*d* ch. 21 : 33....*e* ch. 23 : 30.——— 1 Gr. *the inhabited earth*....2 Some ancient authorities insert *and we would have judged him according to our law.* 7 *But the chief captain Lysias came, and with great violence took him away out of our hands,* 8 *commanding his accusers to come before thee.*

---

text now generally accepted, a word meaning *reforms* should be substituted here.—A. H.] The speaker employs the first person plural, because he identifies himself with his clients.—**Always and in all places** some join with **are done:** *both in every way and everywhere* (Rob.); others with **we accept,** or *acknowledge*, and render *both always and everywhere*, not merely now and here (De Wet., Mey.). The first is the surer sense of the Greek (πάντη). The best editors write this word without iota subscript. (W. § 5. 4. e.)—The language of Tertullus is that of gross flattery. History ascribes to Felix a very different character. Both Josephus and Tacitus represent him as one of the most corrupt and oppressive rulers ever sent by the Romans into Judea. He deserved some praise for the vigor with which he suppressed the bands of robbers by which the country had been infested. The compliment had that basis, but no more.

4. Notwithstanding, etc., **but that I may not hinder,** weary, **thee too much,** I will be brief—*i. e.* in what he proposes to advance. **Further,** or *too much*, refers, not to the few words of his preamble (Mey.), as if that was beginning to be tedious, but to his subsequent plea.—**Wouldst hear,** etc.—lit. **to hear us briefly,** where the adverb qualifies the verb. It is unnecessary to supply *about to speak* after *us*.

5. The sentence is irregular. We should have expected **we took him** at the beginning of the apodosis (v. 6); but, instead of that, the writer says **whom also,** influenced, apparently, by **who also** in the clause which precedes. (W. § 46. 2.)—**For, or namely:** the case is as follows. (Comp. 1 : 20.)—**A pestilent fellow**—lit. **pest,** like our use of the word.—**A mover,** etc., **exciting disturbance unto all the Jews**—*i. e.* among them and to their detriment. The latter idea occasions the use of the dative. The charge is that he set the Jews at variance with one an-

other, not that he excited them to rebel against the Romans.—**Nazarenes** occurs here only as a term of reproach (Olsh.). (See on 2 : 22.)

6. Who also hath gone about, or attempted, etc. (See 21 : 28.)—The entire passage, **and would have judged** to **by examining,** etc. (vv. 6-8), is of doubtful authority. It is rejected by Griesbach, Bengel, Mill, Lachmann, Tischendorf, De Wette, and others. Manuscripts of the first class omit the words, and others contain them with different variations. "If they are genuine," says Meyer, "it is difficult to see why any one should have left them out; for **and would have judged according to our law** would be no more offensive in the mouth of the advocate who speaks in the name of his client than the preceding **we took.** The indirect complaint against Lysias, in v. 7, was entirely natural to the relation of the Jews to this tribune, who had twice protected Paul against them." It is urged for the words that their insertion answers no apparent object, and that they may have been dropped accidentally (Wdsth.).—**We would,** simply **we wished to, judge,** etc. We obtain a very different view of their design from 21 : 31 ; 26 : 21.

7. In the words **with much violence** Tertullus misstates the fact. The Jews released Paul without any struggle on the appearance of Lysias. (See 21 : 32.)—**Before thee.** (See on 23 : 30.)

8. Of whom would refer to Paul, if we exclude the uncertain text which precedes, but more naturally to Lysias, if we retain it. (Comp. v. 22.)—**By examining** may be used of any judicial examination. It is impossible to think here of a trial by torture, since both Paul and Lysias were exempt from it in virtue of their rank as Roman citizens. It was illegal, at all events, to have recourse to this measure. (See Conybeare and Howson's note, ii. p. 322.)

9. And the Jews also assented, or assailed him, at the same time—viz. by as-

10 Then Paul, after that the governor had beckoned unto him to speak, answered, Forasmuch as I know that thou hast been of many years a judge unto this nation, I do the more cheerfully answer for myself:
11 Because that thou mayest understand, that there are yet but twelve days since I went up to Jerusalem *for to worship.
12 *And they neither found me in the temple disputing with any man, neither raising up the people, neither in the synagogues, nor in the city:

10 And when the governor had beckoned unto him to speak, Paul answered,
Forasmuch as I know that thou hast been of many years a judge unto this nation, I do cheerfully make
11 my defence: seeing that thou canst take knowledge, that it is not more than twelve days since I went up
12 to worship at Jerusalem: and neither in the temple did they find me disputing with any man or stirring up a crowd, nor in the synagogues, nor in the city.

a ver. 17 ; ch. 21 : 26....b ch. 25 : 8 ; 28 : 17.

serting that the charges were true. This is a better reading than *assented* (συνέθεντο), agreed, though we have that word in 23 : 20.

10–23. PAUL'S DEFENCE BEFORE FELIX.

10. Of many years, or **since many years.** As Felix became procurator probably in A. D. 52 (see on v. 24), he had been in office six or seven years, which was comparatively a long time at this period, when the provincial magistrates were changed so rapidly. Some of them exceeded that term of service, but a greater number of them fell short of it. Before his own appointment as procurator he had also governed Samaria for some years, under Cumanus, his predecessor. (See Herz., *Encykl.,* iv. p. 354.) **Nation** depends on **judge** as dat. comm., **judge for this nation,** since the relation existed ideally for their benefit. (B. § 133. 2. h ; W. § 31. 2.) Paul avoids the usual *people,* and says *nation,* because he is speaking to a foreigner. (See also v. 17.)—**More cheerfully** (T. R.), or **cheerfully** (Tsch.) ; the former more correct, since the comparative, as less obvious, was liable to be displaced. [Yet, while this is true, the weight of evidence from manuscripts is so much in favor of *cheerfully*— viz. א A B E with many important *cursives,* against H L P—that all the editors, Lach., Tsch., Treg., West. and Hort, the Anglo-Am. Revisers, accept it.—A. H.]

11. Mayest understand, better **since you are able to know**—*i. e.* by inquiry, or (Tsch.) [also Lach., Treg., West. and Hort, and Revisers] *to ascertain* (ἐπιγνῶναι). Paul adds this as another reason why he was encouraged to reply. The subject lay within a narrow compass. Felix could easily ascertain how the prisoner had been employed during the time in which he was said to have committed the crimes laid to his charge.—The common text inserts *than* before *twelve* [= *not more than twelve days*], which the later editions omit. (See on 4 : 22.) The best mode of reckoning the *twelve days* is the following: First, the day of the arrival at Jerusalem (21 : 17) ; second, the interview with James (21 : 18) ; third, the assumption of the vow

(21 : 26) ; fourth, fifth, sixth, and seventh, the vow continued, which was to have been kept seven days (being interrupted on the fifth) ; eighth, Paul before the Sanhedrim (22 : 30 ; 23 : 1-10) ; ninth, the plot of the Jews and the journey by night to Antipatris (23 : 12, 31) ; tenth, eleventh, twelfth, and thirteenth, the days at Cæsarea (24 : 1), on the last of which the trial was then taking place. The number of complete days, therefore, would be twelve, the day in progress at the time of speaking not being counted. The *five days* mentioned in v. 1, above, agree with this computation, if, as suggested there, we reckon the day of leaving Jerusalem as the first of the five, and that of the arrival at Cæsarea as the last. So, essentially, Wetstein, Anger, Meyer, De Wette, and others. Some, as Kuinoel, Olshausen, would exclude the days spent at Cæsarea, and extend the time assigned to the continuation of the vow. But **there are . . . since I** (note the tense) evidently represents the days as reaching up to the present time. According to Wieseler's hypothesis, that Paul was apprehended on the second day of the vow, *the seven days* in 21 : 27, form no part of the series. He distributes the time as follows : Two days on the journey from Cæsarea to Jerusalem (21 : 15) ; third, interview with James ; fourth (*Pentecost*), seizure of Paul in the temple ; fifth, the session of the Sanhedrim ; sixth, the departure by night to Cæsarea ; seventh, the arrival at Cæsarea ; twelfth (five days after that), the journey of Ananias from Jerusalem (24 : 1) ; and thirteenth, his arrival at Cæsarea and the trial of Paul.— **From which = since** (ἀφ' ἧς) is abbreviated for *from the day which* (ἀπὸ τῆς ἡμέρας ἧς).—**For to worship,** or **in order to worship**—*i. e.* in the temple, which was an object entirely different from that imputed to him. For this use of the future participle, see B. § 144. 3.

12. The grammatical analysis here requires attention. The first **neither** extends to **people,** and **or** (not *nor*) connects merely the participial clauses (**disputing,** etc., and **raising up,** etc.), not **found** expressed with that verb repeated. Before the second and third **neither**

13 Neither can they prove the things whereof they now accuse me.

14 But this I confess unto thee, that after *the way which they call heresy, so worship I the *God of my fathers, believing all things which are written in *the law and in the prophets:

15 And *have hope toward God, which they themselves also allow, *that there shall be a resurrection of the dead, both of the just and unjust.

16 And *herein do I exercise myself, to have always a conscience void of offence toward God, and *toward* men.

17 Now after many years *I came to bring alms to my nation, and offerings.

13 Neither can they prove to thee the things whereof 14 they now accuse me. But this I confess unto thee, that after the Way which they call [1]a sect, so serve I the God of our fathers, believing all things which 15 the prophets: having hope toward God, which these also themselves [2]look for, that there shall be a resur- 16 rection both of the just and unjust. Herein do I also exercise myself to have a conscience void of 17 offence toward God and men alway. Now after some years I came to bring alms to my nation, and

---

a See Amos 8 : 14 ; ch. 9 : 2....*b* 2 Tim. 1 : 3.... *c* ch. 26 : 22 ; 28 : 23.... *d* ch. 23 : 6 ; 26 : 6, 7 ; 28 : 20.... *e* Dan. 12 : 2 ; John 5 : 28, 29.... *f* ch. 23 : 1.... *g* ch. 11 : 29, 30 ; 20 : 16 ; Rom. 15 : 25 ; 2 Cor. 8 : 4 ; Gal. 2 : 10.——1 Or, *heresy*....2 Or, *accept*

---

we are to insert again **found . . . people;** so that both acts—the having disputed and the having excited a tumult—are denied with reference to the temple, the synagogues, and the city.—The **disputing** was not in itself censurable, but in this instance he could urge that he had not even had any religious discussion during the few days in question.—**In the synagogues,** at Jerusalem, where they were numerous. (See on 6 : 9.)—**In**—*i. e.* **throughout**—**the city,** up and down the streets (Alf.), not excluding **disputing,** but referring especially to **raising up the people.**

14. Having replied to what was falsely alleged, he states now (δέ adversative) what was true in the case.—**That after,** etc., **that according to** (those of) **the way** (9 : 2 ; 19 : 9, etc.) **which** (not *in which*) **they call a sect** (αἵρεσιν, with a shade of reproach) **so** (*i. e.* after their mode) **I worship,** etc. This appears to me more simple than to make **so** prospective: *so* —viz. *by believing all things,* etc. (Mey., De Wet.). —**In the law**—*i. e.* **throughout the law,** in all the books of Moses. (See on 13 : 15.)

15. And have hope, or having a hope, **in reference to God**—*i. e.* founded on him, since his word and his promise furnish the only basis of such a hope. — **Which also,** etc., **which also these themselves entertain, that it is appointed there shall be** (see on 10 : 28) **a resurrection of the dead,** etc. *These themselves* are the Jews present, viewed as representatives of the nation. Hence most of his accusers here were Pharisees, and the breach between them and the Sadducees (23 : 7) had been speedily repaired. **The dead** (νεκρῶν), in T. R., lacks the requisite support (Lchm., Tsch.). **Both of,** etc., **not only of the just** (those accepted as such by faith), **but of the unjust.** The resurrection of the wicked, in order to be punished, is as clearly taught here as that of the righteous, to be rewarded. The apostle represents this hope as the prevalent Jewish faith. (Comp. 26 : 7.) "The Sadducees," says

18

Biscoe (p. 68), "were so few in number that they were not worthy of his notice by way of exception. Josephus expressly tells us 'that they were a few men only of the chief of the nation' (*Antt.*, 18. 1. 4); that they prevailed only with the rich to embrace their sentiments, and that the common people were all on the side of the Pharisees (*ib.*, 13. 10. 6).''

16. Herein, rather **therefore** (comp. John 16 : 30)—*i. e.* in anticipation of such a day.— **Also I myself,** as well as others who exemplify the proper effect of this doctrine. It is impossible, the apostle would argue, that he should entertain such a persuasion and yet be guilty of the crimes imputed to him.—**Exercise,** *strive,* exert myself.—**Void of offence**— that is, **blameless;** lit. not made to stumble, preserved from it, and hence unoffended. The term is passive here, as in Phil. 1 : 10, but active in 1 Cor. 10 : 32.

17. The defence here (**Now** (δέ) metabatic) goes back to the specification in v. 6.—**After several years**—*i. e.* of absence. It was now A. D. 58 or 59. He had made his last visit to Jerusalem in the year A. D. 54 or 55.—**To bring alms,** or **in order to bring alms,** which he had collected in the churches of Macedonia and Achaia for the relief of the believers at Jerusalem. (See Rom. 15 : 25, 26 ; 1 Cor. 16 : 1-4 ; 2 Cor. 8 : 1-4.) This allusion is very abrupt. It is the first and only intimation contained in the Acts that Paul had been taking up contributions on so extensive a plan. The manner in which the Epistles supply this deficiency, as Paley has shown, furnishes an incontestable proof of the credibility of the New Testament writers. — **Offerings** depends loosely on **to bring:** and while there I was making, or would have made, *offerings;* which, after the information in 21 : 26, we naturally understand of those that he engaged to bring in behalf of the Nazarites. They are not *the oblations* which were made during the feast of Pentecost, since no connection would exist then between of-

18 *a*Whereupon certain Jews from Asia found me purified in the temple, neither with multitude, nor with tumult.

19 *b*Who ought to have been here before thee, and object, if they had ought against me.

20 Or else let these same *here* say, if they have found any evil doing in me, while I stood before the council,

21 Except it be for this one voice, that I cried standing among them, *c*Touching the resurrection of the dead I am called in question by you this day.

22 And when Felix heard these things, having more perfect knowledge of *that* way, he deferred them, and said, When *d*Lysias the chief captain shall come down, I will know the uttermost of your matter.

18 offerings: ¹amidst which they found me purified in the temple, with no crowd, nor yet with tumult:

19 but *there were* certain Jews from Asia—who ought to have been here before thee, and to make accusation,

20 if they had aught against me. Or else let these men themselves say what wrongdoing they found, when

21 I stood before the council, except it be for this one voice, that I cried standing among them, Touching the resurrection of the dead I am called in question before you this day.

22 But Felix, having more exact knowledge concerning the Way, deferred them, saying, When Lysias the chief captain shall come down, I will determine

a ch. 21 : 26, 27 ; 26 : 21....*b* ch. 23 : 30 ; 25 : 16....*c* ch. 23 : 6 ; 28 : 20....*d* ver. 7.——1 Or, *in* presenting *which*

ferings and the purification spoken of in the next verse.

18. Whereupon, rather **in which,** the business of the offerings. For this use of the pronoun, comp. 26 : 12.—**They** (sc. the Jews) **found me purified as a Nazarite in the temple. Purified** must have this sense here, since it points back so evidently to 21 : 24, 26.—**Neither with,** etc., **not with, a mob,** as Tertullus had given out (v. 5), but conducting himself altogether peaceably.—He now retorts this charge of a riot upon the true authors of it.—**But certain Jews from Asia.** It is they who excited a tumult, not I. The verb could be omitted (a true picture of the speaker's earnestness), because it suggests itself so readily from **tumult,** and because the details of the affair have been related at such length (21 : 27). The common text omits **but** (δέ), and makes **certain Jews** the subject of **found.** This is incorrect, as **but** (δέ) must be retained. Our English translation is founded on the omission of this particle. [The Revised Version (see above) represents correctly the Greek text as interpreted by Dr. Hackett.—A. H.]

19. Who ought, etc., *whom it became,* **to be present,** imperfect, because they should have been there already (comp. καθῆκεν in 22 : 22). The instigators of the riot were the persons to testify how it arose.—**If they had aught,** better **if they might have anything,** a possibility purely subjective, and hence optative.

20. Or, etc. (since the proper witnesses are not here), **let these themselves** (see vv. 1, 15) **say what crime they found.** With **if** (εἰ) in the T. R. we must read *if they found any,* etc. (E. V.) ; but **if** is unauthorized.

21. Except it be, etc., *no other offence than* (that) **concerning this one expression.** The sentence is framed as if *some other offence* had preceded (Mey., De Wet.). The Sadducees might object to his avowal of a belief in the resurrection, but the rest of his countrymen would esteem that a merit, and not a crime. [The meaning of Paul's confession is: "If they

can find fault with me for any definite action that was wrong, it can be for no other than my language about the resurrection of the dead ; for that language did occasion a fierce debate and great disorder." Thus, Paul frankly admits that he had uttered a sentiment which led to strife, but he evidently believes that Felix knows how to estimate that language aright. Is it possible that he had forgotten his prediction of God's judgment on the high priest, especially if he had seen it to be an ill-advised word, and had been moved to apologize for it on the spot?—A. H.]—**That I cried,** correctly (ἧς ἔκραξα) **which I cried,** an attracted genitive, instead of the accusative, which this verb would properly take as having a kindred sense. In Matt 27 : 50 and Mark 1 : 26 *voice* (φωνῇ) after the same verb denotes the instrument of speech, not, as here, what was spoken. (See W. § 24. 1.)

22. Them—viz. both parties, like **your,** just below.—**Having more perfect knowledge,** etc., strictly **knowing the things in regard to the way** (the Christian sect) **more accurately**—*i. e.* than to give a decision against Paul (comp. 25 : 10) or than the complaint against him had taken for granted. "Since Felix," says Meyer, "had been already procurator more than six years, and Christianity had spread itself, not only in all parts of Judea, but in Cæsarea itself, it is natural that he should have had a more correct knowledge of this religion than the Sanhedrists on this occasion had sought to give him ; hence he did not condemn the accused, but left the matter in suspense." Other explanations of the comparative are the following : *knowing the case more accurately*—*i. e.* as the result of the present trial (which would have been a reason for deciding it, instead of deferring it) ; *knowing it more accurately* than to postpone it—*i. e.* (a remark of Luke) Felix should have acquitted Paul at once (which brings a severe reflection on his conduct into too close connection with the account of his lenity in the next verse) ;

23 And he commanded a centurion to keep Paul, and to let *him* have liberty, and *a*that he should forbid none of his acquaintance to minister or come unto him.

24 And after certain days, when Felix came with his wife Drusilla, which was a Jewess, he sent for Paul, and heard him concerning the faith in Christ.

25 And as he reasoned of righteousness, temperance, and judgment to come, Felix trembled, and answered, Go thy way for this time; when I have a convenient season, I will call for thee.

23 your matter. And he gave order to the centurion that he should be kept in charge, and should have indulgence; and not to forbid any of his friends to minister unto him.

24 But after certain days, Felix came with Drusilla, [1]his wife, who was a Jewess, and sent for Paul, and heard him concerning the faith in Christ Jesus.

25 And as he reasoned of righteousness, and [2]temperance, and the judgment to come, Felix was terrified, and answered, Go thy way for this time; and when I have a convenient season, I will call thee unto me.

a ch. 27 : 3 ; 28 : 16.———1 Gr. *his own wife.*....2 Or, *self-control*

and finally, *knowing the case more exactly—i. e.* (joined with what follows) when I thus know it, after hearing the testimony of Lysias, judgment shall be given. This last sense is out of the question, because it disregards utterly the order of the words, as well as the proper meaning of the following verb (διαγνώσομαι), **I will know fully,** not *will decide.*

23. The (not *a*), before **centurion,** designates *the centurion* as the one who had charge of Paul, and perhaps other prisoners (see 27 : 1 ; 28 : 16), whether he belonged to Cæsarea or had come from Jerusalem. This officer is not necessarily the one who had conducted the troops from Antipatris (23 : 32), in distinction from the one who returned, since *the* admits of the other explanation, and since *some two,* in 23 : 32, leaves the number indefinite. Hence, as the article does not identify the centurion, the inference to that effect (Blunt,[1] p. 323, and Birks, p. 344) is not to be urged as a proof of the verity of the history.—**To keep Paul** [according to the best authorities, *him*, not *Paul*], not middle, *to keep him* (E. V.), but *that he should be kept as a prisoner,* be guarded.—**And should have respite,** or **alleviation**—*i. e.* be treated with indulgence, and not subjected to a severe captivity. One of the favors which he received is mentioned in the next clause.—The grammatical subject changes before **should forbid,** of which **and** (καί; note τέ between the other verbs) admonishes the reader.—**Serve him,** minister to his wants.—**Or come unto him** is doubtful, and may be borrowed from 10 : 28.

24-27. PAUL TESTIFIES BEFORE FELIX AND DRUSILLA.

24. Came—lit. **having come,** not to Cæsarea, after a temporary absence, but to the place of audience. (Comp. 5 : 22; 25 : 23.)—**With Drusilla, his wife, being a Jewess,** which would imply that she still adhered to the Jewish religion. This Drusilla was a younger daughter of Agrippa I., who was mentioned in 12 : 1, *sq.*, and a sister of Agrippa II., who is mentioned in 25 : 13. We turn to Josephus

(*Antt.*, 20. 7. 1, *sq.*) and read the following account of her : "Agrippa gave his sister Drusilla in marriage to Azizus, King of the Emesenes, who had consented to be circumcised for the sake of the alliance. But this marriage of Drusilla with Azizus was dissolved in a short time after this manner. When *Felix was procurator for Judea* he saw her, and, being captivated by her beauty, persuaded her to desert her husband, transgress the laws of her country, and marry himself." "Here," as Paley observes, "the public station of Felix, the name of his wife, and the circumstance of her religion, all appear in perfect conformity with the sacred writer." The fate of this woman was singular. She had a son by Felix, and both the mother and the son were among those who lost their lives by the eruption of Mount Vesuvius in A. D. 79.—Luke does not inform us why Felix summoned Paul to this conference. We may infer, from the presence of Drusilla, that it was on her account. In all probability, it was to afford her an opportunity to see and hear so noted a leader of the Christian sect.

25. Of righteousness, or **concerning justice,** which the conduct of Felix had so outraged. Tacitus (*Ann.*, 12. 54) draws this picture of him as a magistrate : " Relying upon the influence of his brother at court, the infamous Pallas, this man acted as if he had a license to commit every crime with impunity."—**And temperance**—*i. e.* **self-control,** especially continence, chastity. Here we have another and double proof of the apostle's courage. At the side of Felix was sitting a victim of his libertinism, an adulteress, as Paul discoursed of immorality and a judgment to come. The woman's resentment was to be feared as well as that of the man. It was the implacable Herodias, and not Herod, who demanded the head of John the Baptist.—**Trembled**—lit. **having become alarmed.**—**For this time,** or **as to what is now,** for the present (Kyp., De Wet., Mey.). The construction is that of an adverbial accusative. (K.

[1]*Undesigned Coincidences in the Writings of the Old and New Testaments,* by Rev. J. J. Blunt, London, 1847.

26 He hoped also that *a*money should have been given him of Paul, that he might loose him: wherefore he sent for him the oftener, and communed with him.

27 But after two years Porcius Festus came into Felix' room: and Felix, *b*willing to shew the Jews a pleasure, left Paul bound.

26 He hoped withal that money would be given him of Paul: wherefore also he sent for him the oftener, 27 and communed with him. But when two years were fulfilled, Felix was succeeded by Porcius Festus; and desiring to gain favor with the Jews, Felix left Paul in bonds.

CHAPTER XXV.

NOW when Festus was come into the province, after three days he ascended from Cæsarea to Jerusalem.
2 *c*Then the high priest and the chief of the Jews informed him against Paul, and besought him,

1 FESTUS therefore, [1]having come into the province, after three days went up to Jerusalem from Cæsarea.
2 And the chief priests and the principal men of the Jews informed him against Paul; and they besought

---

a Ex. 23 : 8....*b* Ex. 23 : 2 ; ch. 12 : 3 ; 25 : 9, 14....*c* ch. 24 : 1 ; ver. 15.——1 Or, *having entered upon his province*

---

§ 279. R. 10.)—Place a comma or colon, not a period, at the end of the verse.

26. Hoped also, better **at the same time also** (that he gave this answer) **hoping.** The participle connects itself with **answered** (comp. 23 : 25), and is not to be taken as a finite verb.—**That money will be given to him by Paul**—*i. e.* as an inducement to release him.—**That he might loose him** (E. V.) suggests a correct idea, but is not genuine. Felix had conceived the hope that his prisoner would pay liberally for his freedom. He may have supposed him to have ample resources at his command. He knew that his friends were numerous, and had been informed (see v. 17) that they were not too poor or too selfish to assist one another.

27. But after two years, or **two years now having been completed**—*i. e.* since Paul's imprisonment at Cæsarea.—**Porcius Festus,** etc., rather **Felix received Porcius Festus as successor.** Luke wrote first, or we might suspect him of having copied Josephus, who says, *but Porcius Festus was sent as a successor to Felix* (*Antt.*, 20. 8. 9). As to the year in which this change in the procuratorship took place, see *Introduction*, § 6. 4.—**Willing to show,** etc., rather **and wishing to lay up favor for himself with the Jews,** to make himself popular among them, which was the more important at this time, as they had a right to follow him to Rome and complain of his administration, if they were dissatisfied with it. His policy was unsuccessful. (See *Introduction*, § 6. 4.) An act like this on leaving such an office was not uncommon. Thus, Albinus, another corrupt Procurator of Judea, having heard that Gessius Florus had been appointed to succeed him, liberated most of the state prisoners at Jerusalem, in order to conciliate the Jews.—**Left Paul bound,** or **left Paul behind chained,** still a prisoner, instead of setting him at liberty. I correct my former note here in view of Conybeare and Howson's suggestion. As we are not to infer from *respite*

(ἄνεσιν, not *liberty*), in 24 : 23, that Paul was freed from his chains, *bound* does not mean that he was rebound after a temporary release. Wieseler (p. 380) has shown that the *custodia libera* was granted only to persons of rank; and hence Paul could not have enjoyed that favor, as is proved, also, by his subjection to the surveillance of the centurion. Meyer has changed the note in his last edition to agree with this view. According to De Wette, Felix loaded Paul again with the chains which he had removed. Lange (ii. p. 326) speaks of the *custodia libera* as exchanged now for the *custodia militaris*.

1–5. FESTUS REFUSES TO BRING PAUL TO JERUSALEM.

1. Now, therefore, since he was the successor of Felix.—"The new procurator," says Mr. Lewin (ii. p. 699), "had a straightforward honesty about him which forms a strong contrast to the mean rascality of his predecessor. He certainly did not do all the justice that he might have done; but, allowing somewhat for the natural desire to ingratiate himself with the people of his government, his conduct, on the whole, was exemplary, and his firmness in resisting the unjust demands of the Jews cannot fail to elicit our admiration."—**After three days**—*i. e.* on the third, which allows him one day for rest between his arrival at Cæsarea and his departure for Jerusalem.

2. If the high priest (T. R.) be correct, this *high priest* must have been Ismael, son of Phabi, who succeeded Ananias (Jos., *Antt.*, 20. 8. 8). Two years have elapsed since the trial before Felix (24 : 1, *sq.*), at which Ananias was so active. Instead of the singular, some read *the high priests* (Lchm., Tsch.), which was introduced, probably, to agree with v. 15 (De Wet., Alf.). [The plural is now also approved by Treg., West. and Hort, Anglo-Am. Revisers, and is justified by preponderating evidence—*e. g.* א A B C E L, Syr. and Cop. Versions.—A. H.]

3 And desired favor against him, that he would send for him to Jerusalem, *laying wait in the way to kill him.

4 But Festus answered, that Paul should be kept at Cæsarea, and that he himself would depart shortly *thither.*

5 Let them therefore, said he, which among you are able, go down with *me,* and accuse this man, *bif there be any wickedness in him.

6 And when he had tarried among them more than ten days, he went down unto Cæsarea; and the next day sitting on the judgment seat commanded Paul to be brought.

7 And when he was come, the Jews which came down from Jerusalem stood round about, *c*and laid many and grievous complaints against Paul, which they could not prove.

8 While he answered for himself, *d*Neither against the law of the Jews, neither against the temple, nor yet against Cæsar, have I offended any thing at all.

9 But Festus, *e*willing to do the Jews a pleasure, answered Paul, and said, *f* Wilt thou go up to Jerusalem, and there be judged of these things before me?

3 him, asking favor against him, that he would send for him to Jerusalem; laying a plot to kill him on 4 the way. Howbeit Festus answered, that Paul was kept in charge at Cæsarea, and that he himself was 5 about to depart *thither* shortly. Let them therefore, saith he, who are of power among you, go down with me, and if there is anything amiss in the man, let them accuse him.

6 And when he had tarried among them not more than eight or ten days, he went down unto Cæsarea; and on the morrow he sat on the judgment seat, 7 and commanded Paul to be brought. And when he was come, the Jews who had come down from Jerusalem stood round about him, bringing against him many and grievous charges, which they could not 8 prove; while Paul said in his defence, Neither against the law of the Jews, nor against the tem-9 ple, nor against Cæsar, have I sinned at all. But Festus, desiring to gain favor with the Jews, answered Paul, and said, Wilt thou go up to Jerusalem, and there be judged of these things before me?

a ch. 23 : 12, 15....*b* ch. 18 : 14; ver. 18....*c* Mark 15 : 3; Luke 23 : 2, 10; ch. 24 : 5, 13....*d* ch. 6 : 13; 24 : 12; 28 : 17....*e* ch. 24 : 27....*f* ver. 20.

—**The chief,** etc., *the first men,* are the *chief priests and the elders* in v. 15, except that the **high priest** mentioned separately here would be one of the **high priests** there. [But it should be plural here as well as there.] **Besought,** as imperfect, shows their importunity.

3. And desired, etc.—lit. **asking for themselves a favor against him;** viz. **that he would send for him,** etc.—**Laying wait**—*i. e. making an ambush,* arranging for it. (See 23 : 21.) They anticipated no obstacle to their plan, and may have already hired their assassins and pointed out to them the cave or rock whence they were to rush forth upon their victim. (Comp. the note on v. 16.)

4. Answered—viz: to their second request. (See note on v. 16.)—**That Paul was kept as a prisoner at** (lit. *unto*) **Cæsarea,** as the Jews were aware; and hence, as the governor was about to proceed thither, it would be more convenient to have the trial at that place. The English Version—viz. **that Paul should be kept**—conveys the idea of a too peremptory refusal. So decided a tone would have given needless offence. *Was kept* (τηρεῖσθαι) announces a fact rather than a purpose.—*Unto* (εἰς) *Cæsarea* (more correct than *in* with the dative) opposes tacitly his being kept back *unto Cæsarea* to his removal thence; not unlike *unto Asia,* in 19 : 22.

5. Which among you are able—lit. the **powerful among you,** your chief men, not those who are able, who may find it easy or possible to perform the journey (Calv., Grot., E. V.). Their attendance at the trial was imperative, and the magistrate would not speak as if they were to consult their convenience merely in such a matter. Kuinoel has shown that *the powerful of Jews* was common among the Jews as a designation of their rulers. (See Jos., *Bell. Jud.,* 1. 12. 4; 2. 14. 8 and elsewhere. Comp. also 1 Cor. 1 : 26 and Rev. 6 : 15.) Conybeare and Howson, after Meyer, render *those who are competent,* are authorized to act as prosecutors, but without offering any proof of that absolute use of the term.—**Said** (φησί) should stand before **among you** (ἐν ὑμῖν), not after it (T. R.).

6–12. PAUL APPEALS FROM FESTUS TO CÆSAR.

6. Had tarried, etc.—lit., *having now spent*— **not more than eight or ten days**—*i. e.* having returned speedily, as he had intimated (*shortly,* in v. 4). Instead of *not more than eight or ten* (Grsb., Tsch., Mey.), as above, the received text (and so E. V.) reads **more than ten days,** as if Festus (δέ, adversative, *but*) had not fulfilled his word (v. 4).—**The next day** = *on the morrow,* in v. 17.

7. Stood round about, *stood around,* **him,** not the tribunal (Kuin.). (Comp. *against whom when the accusers stood up,* in v. 18.)—Most manuscripts omit **against Paul** after **complaints.** Tischendorf writes *laid against* (καταφέροντες); but others defend the simple participle (φέροντες).—The **heavy charges** (**complaints**), as the defence of the apostle shows (v. 8), were heresy, impiety, and treason. (Comp. 24 : 5 : 6.)

9. And there be judged—lit. **there to be judged** (viz. by the Sanhedrim)—**before me;** *i. e.* in his presence, while he should preside (Mey., De Wet., Wiesl.), and perhaps confirm or reject the decision. There are two views as to the import of this proposal. One is that Festus intended merely to transfer the trial

10 Then said Paul, I stand at Cæsar's judgment seat, where I ought to be judged : to the Jews have I done no wrong, as thou very well knowest.
11 ªFor if I be an offender, or have committed any thing worthy of death, I refuse not to die : but if there be none of these things whereof these accuse me, no man may deliver me unto them. ᵇI appeal unto Cæsar.
12 Then Festus, when he had conferred with the council, answered, Hast thou appealed unto Cæsar? unto Cæsar shalt thou go.
13 And after certain days king Agrippa and Bernice came unto Cæsarea to salute Festus.

10 But Paul said, I am standing before Cæsar's judgment-seat, where I ought to be judged : to the Jews have I done no wrong, as thou also very well know
11 est. If then I am a wrong-doer, and have committed any thing worthy of death, I refuse not to die : but if none of those things is *true*, whereof these accuse me, no man can ¹give me up unto them. I
12 appeal unto Cæsar. Then Festus, when he had conferred with the council, answered, Thou hast appealed unto Cæsar : unto Cæsar shalt thou go.
13 Now when certain days were passed, Agrippa the king and Bernice arrived at Cæsarea, ²and saluted

a ver. 25; ch. 18 : 14 ; 23 : 29 ; 26 : 31....*b* ch. 26 : 32 ; 28 : 19.———1 Gr. *grant me by favor*: and so in ver. 16....2 Or, *having saluted*

from Cæsarea to Jerusalem, and the other is that he wished to change the jurisdiction in the case—to surrender Paul to the Jews and allow them to decide whether he was innocent or guilty. The explanation last stated agrees best with the intimations of the context. The reply of the apostle (*I stand*, etc., in v. 10), and the fact that he proceeds at once to place himself beyond the power of Festus, would appear to show that he regarded the question (**Wilt thou,** etc.) as tantamount to being deprived of his rights as a Roman citizen.

10. I stand at, etc., or **before the tribunal of Cæsar am I standing,** am under Roman jurisdiction, since Festus was the representative of the emperor. The answer of Festus, *Unto Cæsar hast thou appealed, unto Cæsar shalt thou go* (v. 11), is founded on the apostle's subsequent **I appeal unto Cæsar,** and is not proof (Wdsth.) that Paul viewed himself as "already standing in his own resolve before *Cæsar's* judgment-seat." **Where I ought to be judged** (present), to be having my trial—as matter of right (δεῖ), not because it is God's will. (Comp. v. 24 and 24 : 19).—**As thou very well knowest,** or rather **as also thou perceivest better**—*i. e.* than to make such a proposal. (Comp. 24 : 22. W. ₰ 34. 4.) Such a comparative is very convenient as suggesting something which it might be less courteous to express (Wdsth.). After hearing the charges against Paul, and his reply to them, Festus knew that the prisoner was entitled to be set free, instead of giving him up to a tribunal where his accusers were to be his judges. The temporizing Roman confesses in v. 18 that Paul was right in imputing to him such a violation of his convictions.

11. If I be an offender, or **if therefore I am unjust,** guilty—*i. e.* in consequence of past wrong-doing. The verb expresses here the result of an act, instead of the act itself. (See W. ₰ 40. 2. c.) **For,** in the common text, is incorrect. The clause is illative with reference to the assumption (**v. 9**) that the Jews might find him guilty. Some combine the present

and past in ἀδικῶ (*am unjust*), and render *if I have done and am doing wrong*. (See K. ₰ 255. R. 1.)—**Worthy of death** defines the degree of guilt. If it was such that he deserved to die, he was willing to die.—**If there is nothing of what** (Gr.) = *if there is none of these things which*.

12. When he had conferred, etc., *having spoken with the council*—*i. e.* the assessors or judges (πάρεδροι, *consiliarii*), who assisted him at the trial. It was customary for the proconsul, or his substitute, to choose a number of men whose office it was to aid him in the administration of justice. The proconsul himself presided, but was bound to consult his assessors, and to decide in accordance with the views of the majority. (See Geib's *Geschichte*, p. 243, *sq.*) The subject of consultation in this instance, doubtless, was whether the appeal should be allowed or refused. Writers on Roman law inform us that the provincial magistrates had a certain discretionary power in this respect. An appeal to the emperor was not granted in every case. It was necessary to consider the nature of the accusation, and also the amount of evidence which supported it. Some offences were held to be so enormous as to exclude the exercise of this right ; and when the crime was not of this character, the evidence of guilt might be so palpable as to demand an immediate and final decision.—**Thou hast appealed unto Cæsar** is declarative (not a question, as in E. V.), and repeats Paul's last word before the consultation, for the purpose of attaching to it the verdict.—**Unto Cæsar shalt thou go,** be sent, announces the ready conclusion in regard to the present appeal. I perceive no severity in this answer (Bng.), beyond that of the abrupt official form. The prisoner is told that the government would carry out his appeal and take measures to convey him to Rome. (See on 27 : 1.)

13-22. FESTUS CONFERS WITH AGRIPPA CONCERNING PAUL.

13. And after, etc.—lit. **certain days being past,** since the appeal. **Agrippa the**

14 And when they had been there many days, Festus declared Paul's cause unto the king, saying, *There is a certain man left in bonds by Felix:
15 *About whom, when I was at Jerusalem, the chief priests and the elders of the Jews informed *me*, desiring *to have* judgment against him.
16 *To whom I answered, It is not the manner of the Romans to deliver any man to die, before that he which is accused have the accusers face to face, and have license to answer for himself concerning the crime laid against him.
17 Therefore, when they were come hither, *without any delay on the morrow I sat on the judgment seat, and commanded the man to be brought forth.

14 Festus. And as they tarried there many days, Festus laid Paul's case before the king, saying, There is
15 a certain man left a prisoner by Felix: about whom, when I was at Jerusalem, the chief priests and the elders of the Jews informed *me*, asking for sentence
16 against him. To whom I answered, that it is not the custom of the Romans to give up any man, before that the accused have the accusers face to face, and have had opportunity to make his defence con-
17 cerning the matter laid against him. When therefore they were come together here, I made no delay, but on the next day sat down on the judgment-seat,

a ch. 24 : 27....*b* vers. 2, 3....*c* vers. 4, 5....*d* ver. 6.

king. This *Agrippa* was a son of the Agrippa whose tragical end has been related in 12 : 20–24. At his father's death, as he was considered too young to succeed him on the throne, Judea was committed again to the government of procurators. He passed his early life at Rome. In A. D. 50, on the death of Herod, his uncle, he received the sovereignty of Chalcis, and in A. D. 53 the dominions of Philip and Lysanias (Luke 3 : 1), at which time he assumed the title of king. In the year A. D. 55, Nero added to his possessions a part of Galilee, and Perea. He died, after a reign of nearly fifty years, in A. D. 100. It will be observed that, although Luke in this passage styles Agrippa a king, he does not style him King of Judea; whereas, in speaking of his father (12:1, *sq.*), he not only applies to him this title, but mentions an instance of his exercise of the regal power at Jerusalem. The facts stated above show how perfectly this distinction conforms to the circumstances of the case.—**Bernice** was the eldest daughter of Agrippa I., and a sister of Drusilla (24 : 24). She was noted for her beauty and her profligacy. Luke's accuracy in introducing her at this stage of the history is worthy of remark. After a brief marriage with her first husband she became the wife of Herod, her uncle, King of Chalcis, and on his death remained for a time with Agrippa, her brother. She was suspected of living with him in a criminal manner. Her third marriage, with Polemon, King of Cilicia, soon dissolved, and returned to her brother not long before the death of the Emperor Claudius. She could have been with Agrippa, therefore, in the time of Festus, as Luke represents in our narrative. Her subsequent connection with Vespasian and Titus made her name familiar to the Roman writers. Several of them, as Tacitus, Suetonius, and Juvenal, either mention her expressly or allude to her.—**To salute** —**in order to salute**—**Festus.** It was their visit of congratulation. Agrippa, being a vas-

sal of the Romans, came to pay his respects to this new representative of the power on which he was dependent.

15. Informed—*i. e.* judicially, brought accusation. (Comp. v. 2; 24 : 1.)—**Asking for themselves justice against him.** The idea of condemnation lies in **against him,** not in *justice* or *judgment*. Tischendorf decides against *condemnation* (καταδίκην). [In his 8th ed. Tsch. gives this word, meaning *condemnation*, and Lach., Treg., West. and Hort, the Anglo-Am. Revisers, with ℵ A B C and many cursives.— A. H.]

16. In v. 3 the request of the Jews was that Paul might be brought to Jerusalem; and in that case the accusers and the accused would have met face to face. Hence the reply of Festus here, in order to warrant his objection, must relate to a different proposal—viz. that he would condemn Paul at once (see v. 24) and in his absence. On his declaring that as a Roman magistrate he could not be guilty of such injustice, the Jews, as it would seem, changed their tactics. If it was so that the parties must confront each other, they asked then that he would summon the prisoner to Jerusalem and have him tried there. But this second request was a mere pretence. They knew the weakness of their cause too well to await the result of a trial, and wanted only to secure an opportunity to waylay and kill the apostle on the road. The two proposals may have been made at different times, so that in the interval they could have begun the ambuscade (as intimated in v. 3), believing that, though baffled in the first attempt, they could not fail in the second. —**It is not the manner,** etc., better **that it is not a custom, for Romans,** if it was for Jews. The article (E. V.) obscures the opposition.—**Man** (as generic) declares the rule to be universal. The claim to this impartiality was a *human* right in the eye of the Roman law.— **To die,** after **man** (T. R., and hence E. V.), is unapproved.

18 Against whom when the accusers stood up, they brought none accusation of such things as I supposed: 19 *But had certain questions against him of their own superstition, and of one Jesus, which was dead, whom Paul affirmed to be alive. 20 And because I doubted of such manner of questions, I asked *him* whether he would go to Jerusalem, and there be judged of these matters. 21 But when Paul had appealed to be reserved unto the hearing of Augustus, I commanded him to be kept till I might send him to Cæsar. 22 Then *b*Agrippa said unto Festus, I would also hear the man myself. To-morrow, said he, thou shalt hear him. 23 And on the morrow, when Agrippa was come, and Bernice, with great pomp, and was entered into the place of hearing, with the chief captains, and principal men of the city, at Festus' commandment Paul was brought forth. 24 And Festus said, King Agrippa, and all men which are here present with us, ye see this man, about whom *c*all the multitude of the Jews have dealt with me, both

18 and commanded the man to be brought. Concerning whom, when the accusers stood up, they brought no charge of such evil things as I supposed : but had certain questions against him of their own ¹religion, and of one Jesus, who was dead, whom Paul affirmed 20 to be alive. And I, being perplexed how to inquire concerning these things, asked whether he would go to Jerusalem, and there be judged of these matters. 21 But when Paul had appealed to be kept for the decision of ²the emperor, I commanded him to be 22 kept till I should send him to Cæsar. And Agrippa *said* unto Festus, I also ³could wish to hear the man myself. To-morrow, saith he, thou shalt hear him. 23 So on the morrow, when Agrippa was come, and Bernice, with great pomp, and they were entered into the place of hearing, with the chief captains, and the principal men of the city, at the command 24 of Festus Paul was brought in. And Festus saith, King Agrippa, and all men who are here present with us, ye behold this man, about whom all the

---

a ch. 18 : 15 ; 23 : 29....*b* See ch. 9 : 15....*c* vers. 2, 3, 7.———1 Or, *superstition*....2 Gr. *the Augustus*....3 Or, *was wishing*

---

18. Against whom—lit. **around whom**—belongs to **stood up** (comp.v. 7),not to **brought.** The antecedent of **whom** (οὖ) is **man,** not the remoter **judgment-seat. Charge** (αἰτίαν—that is, τούτων, of those things).—**Which** (ὧν = ἅ by attraction) **I was suspecting**—*i. e.* some capital offence, as treason, murder, or the like.

19. Concerning their own religion, not *superstition.* (Comp. the note on *more religious,* not *too superstitious,* in 17 : 22.) Agrippa was known to be a zealous Jew, and Festus would not have been so uncourteous as to describe his faith by an offensive term. **Own** (ἰδίας) refers, not to the subordinate *whom, his own*— viz. Paul's—but to **accusers,** the leading subject. —**Concerning a certain Jesus,** etc. As to Luke's candor in recording this contemptuous remark, see note on 18 : 15.

20. Doubted, or *perplexed,* uncertain, as Festus may have said with truth, but could not honestly assign as the motive for his proposal. (See v. 9, above.)—**In regard to the dispute concerning this one**— viz. Jesus (v. 19)—not *this matter,* as if it were neuter. But the best reading is *concerning these things*—viz. in relation to their religion and the resurrection of Jesus.

21. But when Paul appealed, etc.—lit. **but Paul having appealed** (and so demanded) — **that he should be kept** in Roman custody, instead of being tried at Jerusalem.—**With a view to the examination of Augustus.** The Senate conferred this title on Octavius in the first instance, but it was given also to his successors.—**I commanded that he should still be kept** (infinitive present) at Cæsarea. In **should be kept,** just before, the time is entirely subordinate to the act.— **Until I shall send him** (T. R.), but the surer

word is *shall send up* (ἀναπέμψω. Lchm., Tsch., Mey.). (Comp. Luke 23 : 7, 11.) Festus would intimate that he was waiting only until a vessel should sail for Italy.

22. I would also, or **I myself also could wish**—*i. e.* were it possible. The Greeks employed the imperfect indicative to express a present wish which the speaker regarded, or out of courtesy affected to regard, as one that could not be realized. (Comp. Rom. 9 : 3; Gal. 4 : 20. W. ₴ 41. 2 ; S. ₴ 138. 3 ; K. ₴ 259. R. 6.) It is less correct to understand the wish as one long entertained.

23-27. PAUL IS BROUGHT BEFORE AGRIPPA.

23. With great—lit. **much—pomp,** display, which consisted partly in their personal decorations (comp. 12 : 21), and partly in the retinue which attended them.— **Unto the place of audience,** which the article represents as the customary one (Olsh.), or as the one to which they repaired on this occasion (Mey.).—**With the chief captains**—lit. **the chiliarchs,** the commanders of the cohorts stationed at Cæsarea, which were five in number (Jos., *Bell. Jud.,* 3. 4. 2). (Comp. the note on 27 : 1.)

24. The procurator could say **all the multitude of the Jews,** because he had reason to know that the Jewish rulers (vv. 2, 15) who had demanded the death of Paul represented the popular feeling. Meyer suggests that a crowd may have gone with them to the procurator and enforced their application by clamoring for the same object.—**Dealt with me,** or **interceded** (in its bad sense here) **with me,** against him. A genitive or dative may follow this verb.—(Some manuscripts read *zēn autón* (ζῆν αὐτόν), and others *autón zēn* (αὐτόν ζῆν)·

at Jerusalem, and *also* here, crying that he ought *a*not to live any longer.

25 But when I found that *b*he had committed nothing worthy of death, *c*and that he himself hath appealed to Augustus, I have determined to send him.

26 Of whom I have no certain thing to write unto my lord. Wherefore I have brought him forth before you, and specially before thee, O king Agrippa, that, after examination had, I might have somewhat to write.

27 For it seemeth to me unreasonable to send a prisoner, and not withal to signify the crimes *laid* against him.

multitude of the Jews made suit to me, both at Jerusalem and here, crying that he ought not to live 25 any longer. But I found that he had committed nothing worthy of death: and as he himself appealed to the emperor I determined to send him. 26 Of whom I have no certain thing to write unto my lord. Wherefore I have brought him forth before you, and specially before thee, king Agrippa, that, after examination had, I may have somewhat to 27 write. For it seemeth to me unreasonable, in sending a prisoner, not withal to signify the charges against him.

CHAPTER XXVI.

THEN Agrippa said unto Paul, Thou art permitted to speak for thyself. Then Paul stretched forth the hand, and answered for himself:

1 And Agrippa said unto Paul, Thou art permitted to speak for thyself. Then Paul stretched forth his hand, and made his defence:

a ch. 22 : 22....*b* ch. 23 : 9, 29 ; 26 : 31....*c* vers. 11, 12.——*l* Gr. *the Augustus.*

and so, in the next verse, some read *thanatou auton* (θανάτου αὐτόν), and others *auton thanatou* (αὐτόν θανάτου). Such transpositions, which have no effect on the sense, show how unimportant are many of the various readings of the sacred text.)—**Crying against** him, etc. (See on v. 15.)—**Not any longer** (μηκέτι). A qualification like this in a negative sentence requires a compound containing the negative (μή or οὐκ) which precedes. (K. § 318. 6 ; B. § 148. 6.)—**I have determined,** rather **I decided**—viz. at the time of the trial when he appealed. The perfect (E. V.) is less accurate than the aorist tense.

26. Of whom, etc., or **concerning whom, I have nothing sure,** definite, **to write to the sovereign.** In such cases of appeal it was necessary to transmit to the emperor a written account of the offence charged as having been committed, and also of all the judicial proceedings that may have taken place in relation to it. Documents of this description were called *apostoli,* or *literæ dimissoriæ.*—**Lord** is the Greek for *dominus.* The writer's accuracy should be remarked here. It would have been a mistake to have applied this term to the emperor a few years earlier than this. Neither Augustus nor Tiberius would allow himself to be called *dominus,* because it implied the relation of master and slave. The appellation had now come into use as one of the imperial titles. —**I may have what** (future) **I shall write,** not *what to write* (E V.). Some repeat *certain* after **somewhat** (Mey.), which is not necessary. Meyer leaves out the ellipsis in his new edition.

27. For it seemeth unreasonable, or **it appears to me absurd.** It was illegal too ; but Festus thinks of the act as being a violation, not so much of the law as of the propriety which dictated the law.—**To send,**

etc., or better **that any one** (De Wet.) **sending a prisoner should not also signify the charges** (not *crimes*) **against him.** Some would make *one sending* the subject of *should signify,* without any ellipsis. (K. § 238. R. 2. e.) Some supply *I* as the subject. It is more forcible in such a case to state the general rule or principle which controls the particular instance, Josephus (*Bell. Jud.,* 2. 14. 1) describes Festus as a reasonable man, who was not destitute of a regard for justice and the laws, and who approved himself to such of the Jews as were willing to submit to any foreign rule. What Luke relates of him shows him to be worthy of this encomium.

1–23. PAUL'S SPEECH BEFORE AGRIPPA.

1. This speech of the apostle is similar to that which he delivered on the stairs of the castle (22 : 1, *sq.*). The main topic is the same in each—viz. the wonderful circumstances of his conversion ; but in this instance he recounts them, not so much for the purpose of asserting his personal innocence as of vindicating the divine origin of his commission and the truth of the message proclaimed by him. So far from admitting that he had been unfaithful to Judaism, he claims that his Christian faith realized the true idea of the religion taught in the Old Testament. On the former occasion "he addressed the infuriated populace and made his defence against the charges with which he was hotly pressed—of profaning the temple and apostatizing from the Mosaic law. He now passes by these accusations, and, addressing himself to a more intelligent and dispassionate hearer, he takes the highest ground, and holds himself up as the apostle and messenger of God. With this view, therefore, he paints in

2 I think myself happy, king Agrippa, because I shall answer for myself this day before thee touching all the things whereof I am accused of the Jews:
3 Especially *because I know* thee to be expert in all customs and questions which are among the Jews: wherefore I beseech thee to hear me patiently.
4 My manner of life from my youth, which was at the first among mine own nation at Jerusalem, know all the Jews;
5 Which knew me from the beginning, if they would testify, that after *a*the most straitest sect of our religion I lived a Pharisee.

2 I think myself happy, king Agrippa, that I am to make my defence before thee this day touching all the things whereof I am accused by the Jews: 3 [3]especially because thou art expert in all customs and questions which are among the Jews: where-4 fore I beseech thee to hear me patiently. My manner of life then from my youth up, which was from the beginning among mine own nation, and 5 at Jerusalem, know all the Jews; having knowledge of me from the first, if they be willing to testify, how that after the straitest sect of our religion

a ch. 22 : 3 ; 23 : 6 ; 24 : 15, 21 ; Phil. 3 : 5.——1 Or, *because thou art especially expert*

more striking colors the awful scene of his conversion, and repeats more minutely that heavenly call which was impossible for him to disobey (v. 19), and in obeying which, though he incurred the displeasure of his countrymen (v. 21), he continued to receive the divine support (v. 22) " (*Humphry*, p. 192). — **Thou art permitted to speak,** etc. It is Agrippa who gives the permission to speak, because, as he **was** the guest on this occasion, and a king, he presides by right of courtesy. (Comp. 21 : 40.) —**Stretched forth** — lit. **having stretched forth—the hand** is the same as *beckoned with the hand*, in 13 : 16 (comp. 21 : 40) and in 19 : 33. The gesture was the more courteous, because the attention asked for was certain, from the known curiosity of the hearers. On the arm which Paul raised hung one of the chains to which he alludes in v. 29.

2. Of the Jews, simply **by Jews,** without the article (comp. 22 : 30), because he would represent the accusation as purely *Jewish* in its character. The best manuscripts omit **the** before the proper name.—**King.** For Agrippa's claim to the title, see on 25 : 13.—Some copies place **shall answer** after **happy ;** others, after **before thee.** The first is the best position, because it secures a stronger emphasis to the pronoun (Grsb., Tsch.).—The object of **I have thought** is the same as the subject, but the latter, which is more prominent, controls the case of **shall** ($\mu\epsilon\lambda\lambda\omega\nu$). This verb is perfect, **have thought,** not *think* (E. V.). Paul distinguishes the tenses in Phil. 3 : 7, 8.

3. Especially, rendered *namely* in the older versions (Tynd., Cran., Gen.), states why Paul was so eminently fortunate, not how much Agrippa knew.—**Since thou art expert**—lit. **a knower.** The accusative is anacoluthic, instead of the genitive (Mey., Win., Rob.). (W. § 32. 7.) Some explain it as an instance of the accusative absolute; but we have no clear example of that construction in the New Testa-

ment. *Eyes,* in Eph. 1 : 18, has been cited as an example of it, but stands really in apposition with *spirit,* or depends on *may give.* Beza's unauthorized *knowing* (whence *because I know,* in E. V.) obviates the irregularity. The Rabbinic writers[1] speak of Agrippa as having excelled in a knowledge of the law. As the tradition which they follow could not have flowed from this passage, it confirms the representation here by an unexpected agreement. — **Among Jews** (not **the Jews**), of whom we are led to think as existing in different places. (W. § 53. d.)—**Therefore** ($\delta\iota\delta$). In the presence of such a judge he proposes to speak at length, and requests a patient hearing.

4. Therefore ($o\check{v}\nu$)—*i. e.* encouraged thus, he will proceed. [This word is not represented in the Common English Version.—A. H.] The apostle enters here on his defence.—**From my youth.** (See on 22 : 3.) — **At first,** rather **from the beginning,** refers to the same period of his life, but marks it more strongly as an early period. It will be observed that, while the apostle repeats this idea in the successive clauses, he brings forward in each case a new circumstance in connection with it. He states, first, *how long* the Jews had known him ; secondly, *where* they had known him so long (**among mine own nation and in Jerusalem**) ; and thirdly, *what* (**that after the strictest sect,** etc.) they had known of him so long and in that place.

5. Which knew me from the beginning, rather **knowing me before**—*i. e.* the present time.—**If they would be willing to testify,** as he had not the confidence in their honesty to expect.—**That according to the strictest sect,** in regard both to doctrine and manner of life. (See 22 : 3.) Josephus describes this peculiarity of the Pharisees in similar language : " A sect that seem to be more religious than others, and to interpret the laws more strictly " (*Bell. Jud.,* 1. 5. 2). **That** reaches back to **know** (v. 4).

[1] Sepp gives the testimonies in his *Das Leben Christi,* vol. iv. p. 138.

6 *a*And now I stand and am judged for the hope of
*b*the promise made of God unto our fathers:
7 Unto which *promise* *c*our twelve tribes, instantly
serving God *d*day and night, *e*hope to come. For
which hope's sake, king Agrippa, I am accused of
the Jews.
8 Why should it be thought a thing incredible with
you, that God should raise the dead?
9 *f*I verily thought with myself, that I ought to do
many things contrary to the name of Jesus of Nazareth.
10 *g*Which thing I also did in Jerusalem: and many

6 I lived a Pharisee. And now I stand *here* to be
judged for the hope of the promise made of God
7 unto our fathers; unto which *promise* our twelve
tribes, earnestly serving *God* night and day, hope to
attain. And concerning this hope I am accused by
8 the Jews, O king! Why is it judged incredible with
9 you, if God doth raise the dead? I verily thought
with myself, that I ought to do many things con-
10 trary to the name of Jesus of Nazareth. And this

a ch. 23 : 6....*b* Gen. 3 : 15; 22 : 18; 26 : 4; 49 : 10; Deut. 18 : 15; 2 Sam. 7 : 12; Ps. 132 : 11; Isa. 4 : 2; 7 : 14; 9 : 6; 40 : 10; Jer. 23 : 5;
33 : 14, 15, 16; Ezek. 34 : 23; 37 : 24; Dan. 9 : 24; Mic. 7 : 20; ch. 13 : 32; Rom. 15 : 8; Tit. 3 : 13....*c* James 1 : 1....*d* Luke 2 : 37;
1 Thess. 3 : 10; 1 Tim. 5 : 5....*e* Phil. 3 : 11....*f* John 16 : 2; 1 Tim. 1 : 13....*g* ch. 8 : 3; Gal. 1 : 13.

6. And now compares his present with his former position. If his rigor as a Pharisee had been a merit in the eyes of the Jews, his hope as a Christian was merely that of the true Israel, and should as little be imputed to him as a crime.—**Of the promise**—*i. e.* of a Messiah—**made unto our fathers** (Kuin., Olsh., De Wet., Mey.). The same expression occurs in Paul's discourse at Antioch (13 :32), where it is said that God fulfilled *the promise*, or showed it to be fulfilled, by raising up Jesus from the dead. (See the note on that passage. Comp. 28 : 20.)—**Unto which**—viz. the promise, its accomplishment. This is the natural antecedent, and not the remoter **hope.** (δωδεκάφυλον) translated **twelve tribes** (= ταῖς δώδεκα φυλαῖς, in James 1 : 1) exists only here, but is formed, after the analogy of other compounds, from the Greek numeral *twelve* (δώδεκα). The Jewish nation consisted of those who were descended from the twelve tribes; which fact justifies the expression historically, though the twelve tribes had now lost their separate existence.—**Instantly**—*i. e.* (ἐν ἐκτενείᾳ) **with earnestness.** (See on **without ceasing** (ἐκτενῆς), in 12 : 5.) The noun is a later Grecism. (Lob., *Phryn.*, p. 311.) Such forms help us to fix the age of the New-Testament writings. **Worshipping night and day.** This was a phrase which denoted habitual worship, especially as connected with fasting and prayer. (See Luke 1 : 75; 2 : 37; 18 : 1; 1 Thess. 5 : 17; 1 Tim. 5 : 5.)

7. For which hope's sake, or **concerning which hope, I am accused.** The apostle means to say that he accused of maintaining that this hope of a Messiah had been accomplished in Jesus, and had been accomplished in him because God raised him from the dead. The presence of the latter idea in the mind of the apostle leads to the interrogation in the next verse.—**Agrippa,** after **king,** has decisive evidence against it.—**Of the Jews**—lit. **by Jews**—is reserved to the end of the sentence, in order to state more strongly the inconsistency of such an accusation from

such a source. Here, too, the article (E. V.) weakens the sense and is incorrect.

8. What? or **Why?** (τί) is printed in some editions as a separate question: **What? Is it judged incredible?** Other editions connect the interrogative with the verb: **Why is it judged incredible?** Griesbach, Kuinoel, De Wette, Conybeare and Howson, and others prefer the first mode; Knapp, Hahn, Meyer, Tischendorf, and others prefer the second mode. The latter appears to me more agreeable to the calm energy of the apostle's manner. ("It is decisive against the other view," says Meyer in his last edition, "that τί alone was not so used; the expression would be *For what? What then?* or *What now?*" The examples of τί as interrogative in Rom. 3 : 3, 9; 6 : 15, and Phil. 1 : 18 agree with this criticism.)—**With you** extends the inquiry to all who were present. The speaker uses the singular number when he addresses Agrippa personally. (See vv. 2, 3, 27.)—**If God raises the dead,** where *if* is not for *that*, but presents the assertion as one that the sceptic might controvert. — **Raises** (ἐγείρει) is present, because it expresses a characteristic act. The resurrection of Jesus was past, but illustrated a permanent attribute or power on the part of God.

9. This verse is illative, with reference to the preceding question.—**I verily,** rather **I indeed therefore**—*i. e.* in consequence of a spirit of incredulity, like that of others. **Seemed to myself,** *thought.* The pronoun opposes his own to another and higher judgment. This same act in which Paul gloried at the time appeared to him as the crime of his life after he became a Christian. In 1 Cor. 15 : 9 he declares that he "was the least of the apostles, that he was not meet to be called an apostle, because he persecuted the church of God."—**To the name,** or **against the name of Jesus.** (Comp. πρός, in Luke 23 : 12.)—**Many things contrary**—*i. e. many things hostile.*

10. Which thing (ὅ) refers to the collective idea—in *many things hostile*, etc.—**Also** connects

of the saints did I shut up in prison, having received
authority *from the chief priests; and when they were
put to death, I gave my voice against *them.*
11 *b*And I punished them oft in every synagogue,
and compelled *them* to blaspheme; and being exceedingly mad against them, I persecuted *them* even unto
strange cities.

I also did in Jerusalem: and I both shut up many
of the saints in prisons, having received authority
from the chief priests, and when they were put to
11 death, I gave my vote against them. And punishing them oftentimes in all the synagogues, I strove
to make them blaspheme; and being exceedingly
mad against them, I persecuted them even unto

a ch. 9 : 14, 21 ; 22 : 5....b ch. 22 : 19.

did with thought.—And many, etc., adds
the facts in illustration of what was stated in
general terms.—**The saints** is no doubt a
chosen word here. It does not occur in Luke's
account of the apostle's conversion (9:1, *sq.*).
Paul himself avoids it in his speech to the
Jews (22:4, *sq.*), who were so sensitive in regard
to any claim of merit in behalf of the Christians. "But here, before Agrippa, where there
was no such need of caution, the apostle in-
dulges his own feelings by giving them a title
of honor which aggravates his own guilt"
(*Birks*, p. 327).—**I,** emphatic. The imprisoning
was the speaker's act.—The common text omits
in before **prisons, I shut up unto prisons,**
which would be an instance of the local dative
sometimes found after verbs compounded with
κατά. (See Bernh., *Synt.*, p. 243.) But Griesbach, Tischendorf, and others allege good authority for reading *in prisons,* which would be
the ordinary construction. (Comp. Luke 3:
20.)—**From the chief priests.** (See the note
on 9:2.)—**And as they** (which refers to **saints**
as a class, not to all those imprisoned) **were
put to death, I brought,** or **cast, my vote
against them**—*i. e.* encouraged, approved, the
act (Bng., Kuin., De Wet., Mey.). (Comp. *consenting,* in 22 : 20.) Some insist on the literal
sense of the phrase, and infer from it that Paul
was a member of the Sanhedrim and voted
with the other judges to put the Christians to
death. But the Jews required, as a general
rule, that those who held this office should be
men of years; and Paul, at the time of Stephen's martyrdom, could hardly have attained
the proper age. It is said too, on the authority
of the later Jewish writers, that one of the
necessary qualifications for being chosen into
the Sanhedrim was that a man should be the
father of a family, because he who is a parent
may be expected to be merciful—a relation
which, from the absence of any allusion to it
in the apostle's writings, we have every reason
to believe that he never sustained. The expression itself affords but slight proof that Paul
was a voter in the Sanhedrim. *Psēphos* (ψῆφος),
a stone used as a ballot, like our "suffrage,"
signified also opinion, assent, and accompanied
various verbs, as *to place* and *to cast down,* as

meaning to think, judge, sanction, with a figurative allusion to the act of voting. Plato
uses the term often in that sense. (See R. and
P., *Lex.*, p. 2576.)—**Them** agrees with the intimation of other passages (8:3; 9:1; 22:4) that
Stephen was not the only victim whose blood
was shed at this time.

11. Punished them, etc., or **and punishing them often throughout all the synagogues,** in the different places where he pursued his work of persecution. (See 22 : 19.)
"The chief rulers of the synagogues," says
Biscoe (p. 81), "being also the judges of the
people in many cases, especially those which
regarded religion (comp. on 9 : 2), chose to give
sentence against offenders and see their sentence
executed in the synagogue. Persons were always scourged in the presence of the judges
(Vitr., *De Synag. Vett.*, p. 177). For, punishment being designed 'in terrorem,' what more
likely to strike the mind with awe and deter
men from falling into the like errors than to
have it executed in their religious assemblies
and in the face of the congregation? Our Lord
foretold that his disciples should be scourged in
the synagogues (Matt. 10 : 17; 23 : 34); and we learn
here that Paul was an instrument in fulfilling
this prediction, having beaten them that believed in every synagogue."—**I compelled,**
rather **I was constraining them** (*i. e.* urged
them by threats and torture) **to blaspheme**—
viz. Jesus or the gospel. (Comp. 13 : 45; James
2 : 7.) The imperfect states the object, not the
result, of the act. That, among the many who
suffered this violence, every one preserved his
fidelity, it would be unreasonable to affirm.
We learn from Pliny's letter to Trajan (Lib. X.
97) that heathen persecutors applied the same
test which Saul adopted for the purpose of as-
certaining who were truly Christians: "Pro-
positus est libellus sine auctore, multorum
nomina continens. Qui negabant esse se Chris-
tianos aut fuisse, cum praeeunte me deos appel-
larent et imagini tuae (quam propter hoc jus-
seram cum simulacris numinum adferri) ture ac
vino supplicarent, praeterea maledicerent Christo
—*quorum nihil posse cogi dicuntur qui sunt revera
Christiani*—dimittendos esse putavi" ["An
anonymous note was presented, containing the

12 *a*Whereupon as I went to Damascus with authority and commission from the chief priests,

13 At midday, O king, I saw in the way a light from heaven, above the brightness of the sun, shining round about me and them which journeyed with me.

14 And when we were all fallen to the earth, I heard a voice speaking unto me, and saying in the Hebrew tongue, Saul, Saul, why persecutest thou me? *it is* hard for thee to kick against the pricks.

15 And I said, Who art thou, Lord? And he said, I am Jesus whom thou persecutest.

16 But rise, and stand upon thy feet: for I have appeared unto thee for this purpose, *b*to make thee a minister and a witness both of these things which thou hast seen, and of those things in the which I will appear unto thee;

12 foreign cities. [1]Whereupon as I journeyed to Damascus with the authority and commission of the chief 13 priests, at midday, O king, I saw on the way a light from heaven, above the brightness of the sun, shining round about me and them that journeyed with 14 me. And when we were all fallen to the earth, I heard a voice saying unto me in the Hebrew language, Saul, Saul, why persecutest thou me? 15 is hard for thee to kick against [2]the goad. And I said, Who art thou, Lord? And the Lord said, I am 16 Jesus whom thou persecutest. But arise, and stand upon thy feet: for to this end have I appeared unto thee, to appoint thee a minister and a witness both of the things [3]wherein thou hast seen me, and of

---

a ch. 9 : 3 ; 22 : 6....*b* ch. 22 : 15.———1 Or, *On which errand*....2 Gr. *goads*....3 Many ancient authorities read *which thou hast seen.*

---

names of many. Those who denied that they were or had been Christians, when, after my example, they called on the gods and made supplication with incense and wine to thy statue (which for this cause I had commanded to be brought with the images of the gods)—*none of which things, it is said, can those who are really Christians be compelled to do*—I dismissed."—A. H.].— **Even unto**, etc., or **as far as even unto, the foreign cities,** as those would be called which were out of Judea. Among these Luke and Paul single out Damascus, because a train of such events followed the apostle's expedition to that city.

12. Whereupon—lit. **in which also,** while intent on this object. (Comp. *in which*, in 24 : 18.) *Also*, so common in Luke after the relative, some of the best copies omit here.—**Authority** and **commission** (ἐξουσίας and ἐπιτροπῆς) strengthen each other ; he had ample power to execute his commission.

13. At midday (ἡμέρας μέσης). (" μέση ἡμέρα, pro meridie communis dialecti est, at μέσον ἡμέρας, aut μεσημβρία (22:6) elegantiora." [1] See Lob., *Ad Phryn.*, p. 55.)—**In the way = along the way** (Mey., Rob.), not *on the way* (De Wet.). —For **me,** after **shining round about,** see on 9 : 3.—For **those journeying with me,** see on 22 : 9.

14. And when, etc.—lit. **and we all having fallen down upon the earth,** from the effect of terror, not as an act of reverence. (Comp. 9 : 4 ; 22 : 17.) In regard to the alleged inconsistency between this statement and *stood speechless* in 9 : 7, see the note on that passage. —**It is hard for thee to kick against the pricks,** or **goads.** [The original text has no article before *goads*.—A. H.] The meaning is that his opposition to the cause and will of Christ must be unavailing ; the continuance of it would only bring injury and ruin on himself. Wetstein has produced examples of this proverb from both Greek and Latin writers.

(Euripides (*Bacch.*, v. 791) applies it as here : θυμούμενος πρὸς κέντρα λακτίζοιμι, θνητὸς ὢν θεῷ. Terence (*Phorm.*, 1. 2. 27) employs it thus : " Nam quæ inscitia est, Advorsum simulum calces?" Plautus (*Truc.*, 4. 2. 55) has it in this form : "Si stimulos pugnis cædis, manibus plus dolet.") The Scholiast on Pind. (*Pyth.*, 2. 173) explains the origin of the expression : "The figure is from oxen. For those that are untrained in farm-work, when goaded by the ploughman, kick the goad, and are beaten the more." The same or a similar proverb must have been current among the Hebrews, though this is the only instance of it found in the Scriptures. The common plough in the East at present has but one handle. The same person, armed with a goad six or eight feet long, holds the plough and drives his team at the same time. As the driver follows the oxen, therefore, instead of being at their side as with us, and applies the goad from that position, a refractory animal of course would kick against the sharp iron when pierced with it. In early times the Greeks and Romans used a plough of the like construction.

16. For this purpose prepares the mind for what follows. (See on 9 : 21.)—**For** shows that the command to arise was equivalent to assuring him that he had no occasion for such alarm (v. 14) ; the object of the vision was to summon him to a new and exalted sphere of effort.—**To appoint thee as a minister,** call him to his destined work. The antecedent purpose must be sought in the nature of the act, rather than in the verb. (See on 3 : 20.)— Understand *of those things* (τούτων), after **witness,** as the attracting antecedent of **which** (ὧν).—ὧν τε ὀφθήσομαί σοι is an unusual construction. The best solution is that ὧν stands for ἅ as a sort of explanatory accusative (K. § 279. 7.): *as to which*, or (= δι' ἅ), *on account of which* (Mey.), *I will appear unto thee.* (See W. § 39. 3

---

[1] [The apostle uses here a more common form for *midday*, while in ch. 22 : 6 he employs one more elegant.]

17 Delivering thee from the people, and *from* the Gentiles, *a*unto whom now I send thee,
18 *b*To open their eyes, *and* *c*to turn *them* from darkness to light, and *from* the power of Satan unto God, *d*that they may receive forgiveness of sins, and *e*inheritance among them which are *f* sanctified by faith that is in me.
19 Whereupon, O king Agrippa, I was not disobedient unto the heavenly vision :
20 But *g*shewed first unto them of Damascus, and at Jerusalem, and throughout all the coasts of Judæa, and

17 the things wherein I will appear unto thee ; delivering thee from the people, and from the Gentiles,
18 unto whom I send thee, to open their eyes, ¹that they may turn from darkness to light, and from the power of Satan unto God, that they may receive remission of sins and an inheritance among them
19 that are sanctified by faith in me. Wherefore, O king Agrippa, I was not disobedient unto the heav-
20 enly vision : but declared both to them of Damascus first, and at Jerusalem, and throughout all the coun-

a ch. 22 : 21....*b* Isa. 35 : 5 ; 42 : 7 ; Luke 1 : 79 ; John 8 : 12 ; 2 Cor. 4 : 4 ; Eph. 1 : 18 ; 1 Thess. 5 : 5....*c* 2 Cor. 6 : 14 ; Eph. 4 : 18 ; 5 : 8 ; Col. 1 : 13 ; 1 Pet. 2 : 9, 25....*d* Luke 1 : 77....*e* Eph. 1 : 11 ; Col. 1 : 12....*f* ch 20 : 32....*g* ch. 9 : 20, 22, 29 ; 11 : 26 ; and chaps. 13 ; 14 ; 16 ; 17 ; 18 ; 19 ; 20 ; 21.——1 Or, *to turn them*

1.) Many commentators assign an active sense to the verb : *which I will cause thee to see* or *know*. This use of the verb has no warrant either in classic or Hellenistic Greek. [Westcott and Hort, with the Anglo-Am. Revisers, adopt a reading, supported by B C* and the Syriac Versions, which may be translated as follows : *both of the things wherein thou hast seen me* (the pronoun *με* being added to the received text), *and of the things wherein I will appear unto thee.* Rejecting the pronoun, the Bible Union revision and the translation of Davidson agree in the following version : *both of the things which thou sawest, and of the things in which I will appear to thee.* It is difficult to decide upon the text, and the meaning is not essentially changed by the reception or rejection of the pronoun.—A. H.]

17. Delivering thee from the people— *i. e.* of the Jews (see on 10 : 2)—**and the Gentiles** = *heathen.* For this sense of the participle, see 7 : 10 ; 12 : 11 ; 23 : 27. Such a promise was conditional, from the nature of the case. It pledged to him the security which he needed for the accomplishment of his work until his work was done. Some render the words (ἐξαιρούμενός σε) **selecting thee,** so as to find here the idea of *a chosen vessel,* in 9 : 15 (Kuin., Hnr., Rob., Cony. and Hws.). This interpretation would suit *from the people,* but, as De Wette and Meyer remark, it is inappropriate to *from the heathen.* Paul was not one of the heathen, and could not be said to be chosen from them.— **Unto whom** refers to both the nouns which precede.—The correct text inserts *I* (emphatic) before *thee,* and omits **now.**—**I send** is present, because his ministry is to begin at once.

18. It is important to observe the relation of the different clauses to each other. **To open their eyes** states the object of **send.**—**That they may turn** derives its subject from **their.** The verb is intransitive (see v. 20 ; 14 : 15), not active, *in order to turn them* (E. V.). This clause states the designed effect of the illumination which they should receive.—**That they may obtain forgiveness of sins** expresses the direct object of the second infinitive and the

ultimate object of the first.—For **an inheritance among the sanctified,** see the note on 20 : 32.—**By faith in me** our English translators and some others join with **sanctified ;** but the words specify, evidently, the condition by which believers obtain the pardon of sin and an interest in the heavenly inheritance. **Which are sanctified** is added merely to indicate the spiritual nature of the **inheritance.**

19. Whereupon—lit. **whence,** accordingly ; *i. e.* having been so instructed, and in such a manner.—**I was not** = **I proved not disobedient** affirms the alacrity of his response to the call more strongly than if the mode of expression had been positive, instead of negative. **Disobedient** attaches itself to the personal idea of **vision,** and demands that element in the meaning of the word. The service required of him, and so promptly rendered, evidently was that he should preach the gospel to Jews and Gentiles (v. 17). It is impossible to reconcile such intimations with the idea that the apostle after this remained for years inactive in Arabia, or spent the time there in silent meditation and the gradual enlargement of his views of the Christian system. I cannot agree with Dr. Davidson that " Paul was not a preacher of the gospel in Arabia, but went through a process of training there, for the purpose of preaching it." (See his *Introduction,* ii. p. 80.)—**The heavenly vision,** manifestation of the Saviour's person. (Comp. Luke 1 : 22 ; 24 : 23 ; 2 Cor. 12 : 1. See the note on 9 : 7.)

20. To those in Damascus first, as stated in 9 : 20 and implied in Gal. 1 : 17.—**Jerusalem** with *in* repeated, **in Jerusalem ;** hardly *unto* as a direct dative (Mey.). [The best authorized text reads *and also Jerusalem.*—A. H.] —**And unto** (*i. e.* with a union of the local idea with the personal, the inhabitants of) **all the region of Judea.** (Comp. *told it in the city,* in Luke 8 : 34.) Meyer extends **them** from the other clause into this : *and unto those throughout all the region.* But in his last edition he gives up this analysis and approves the other.

then to the Gentiles, that they should repent and turn to God, and do *a*works meet for repentance.

21 For these causes *b*the Jews caught me in the temple, and went about to kill *me*.

22 Having therefore obtained help of God, I continue unto this day, witnessing both to small and great, saying none other things than those *c*which the prophets and *d*Moses did say should come:

23 *e*That Christ should suffer, *and f* that he should be the first that should rise from the dead, and *g*should shew light unto the people, and to the Gentiles.

---

try of Judæa, and also to the Gentiles, that they should repent and turn to God, doing works worthy 21 of ¹repentance. For this cause the Jews seized me 22 in the temple, and assayed to kill me. Having therefore obtained the help that is from God, I stand unto this day testifying both to small and 23 great, saying nothing but what the prophets and Moses did say should come; ²how that the Christ ³must suffer, *and* ²how that he first by the resurrection of the dead should proclaim light both to the people and to the Gentiles.

---

a Matt. 3 : 8....*b* ch. 21 : 30, 31....*c* Luke 24 : 27, 44; ch. 24 : 14; 28 : 23; Rom. 3 : 21....*d* John 5 : 46....*e* Luke 24 : 26, 46....*f* 1 Cor. 15 : 20; Col. 1 : 18; Rev. 1 : 5....*g* Luke 2 : 32.——1 Or, *their repentance*....2 Or, *if* Or, *whether*....3 Or, *is subject to suffering*

—The apostle during his labors in Syria and Cilicia, after his first visit to Jerusalem, was as yet unknown in person to the churches of Judea. (See Gal. 1 : 22.) Hence he must have preached there, as intimated in that passage, at a later period. He could have done so when he went thither at the time of the famine (see on 11 : 30) or while he was at Jerusalem between his first and second mission to the heathen (18 : 22).—**Works meet for repentance**—*i. e.* **deeds worthy of repentance,** such as showed that they were changed in heart and life. Zeller charges that Paul would not have spoken so, because his doctrine was that of justification by faith alone. The answer is that in Paul's system good works are the necessary evidence of such faith, and, further, that **by faith that is in me,** above (v. 18), shows that he adhered fully on this occasion to his well-known doctrinal view.—**And do,** or do-**ing,** deserts the case of **Gentiles** [dat.], and agrees with *they* (αὐτούς) as the suppressed subject of the verbs.

22. Having therefore obtained assistance from God, since, exposed to such dangers in the fulfilment of his ministry (*went about to kill me*, in v. 21), he must otherwise have perished. The assistance was an inference (οὖν) from his present safety.—**Testifying to both small and great** (Rev. 11 : 18; 13 : 16; 19 : 5), not *young and old* (8 : 10). The phrase admits either sense, but the more obvious distinction here is that of rank, not of age. The grace of God is impartial; the apostle declared it without respect of persons. It is uncertain whether this (*marturomenos*) is the correct participle, or the received *marturoumenos*. The latter word would mean *attested*, approved, *both by small and great* (Bretsch., Mey.). (Comp. 6 : 3; 10 : 22; 16 : 2.) It is objected that the sense with the latter reading is impossible, because Paul was so notoriously despised and persecuted by Jews and heathen (Alf.). But the meaning might be that, though not openly approved, he had received that verdict at the bar of their con-

sciences; he had not failed to commend himself and his doctrine to every man's better judgment. The avowal would imply no more than Paul affirms to be true of all who preach faithfully the system of truth which he preached. (See 2 Cor. 4 : 2.) Some render *marturoumenos* as middle, *bearing witness*, instead of passive, but confessedly without any example of that use. Knapp, Hahn, Tischendorf, Baumgarten, and others approve of *marturomenos*. It has no less support than the other word, and affords an easier explanation. [Rather, far more support; for this participle is also accepted by Griesb., Lach., Treg., West. and Hort, and the Anglo-Am. Revisers. Moreover, it rests upon such codices as ℵ A B H L P, while the other reading (μαρτυρούμενος) has but one good uncial, E, in its favor. The case is therefore very clear. —A. H.]

23. This part of the sentence attaches itself to **saying** rather than to **which should come. If the Messiah can suffer** (*passibilis* in Vulg.), not so much as a possibility of his nature as one of the conditions of his office —*i. e.* would be appointed or allowed to suffer, and so could be subject to infirmity, pain, death. (Verbals in τός express possibility and correspond to Latin adjectives in *ilis*. B. § 102. N. 2.) The apostle, as I understand, approaches the question on the Jewish side of it, not on the Christian; and that was whether the Messiah, being such as many of the Jews expected, *could suffer*, not whether *he must suffer*, in order to fulfil the Scriptures. **If** presents the points as questions which he was wont to discuss. Many of the Jews overlooked or denied the *suffering* character of the Messiah, and stumbled fatally at the gospel because (their *stumbling-block*) it required them to accept a *crucified* Redeemer. (Some make εἰ = ὅτι, *that*—*i. e.* the sign of a moderated assertion.) — **The Christ, the Messiah** as such; not a personal name here. —**The first that should rise from the dead** = *the first-born from the dead,* in Col. 1 : 18. If Moses and the prophets foretold that

24 And as he thus spake for himself, Festus said with a loud voice, Paul, *thou art beside thyself; much learning doth make thee mad.
25 But he said, I am not mad, most noble Festus; but speak forth the words of truth and soberness.
26 For the king knoweth of these things, before whom also I speak freely: for I am persuaded that none of these things are hidden from him; for this thing was not done in a corner.
27 King Agrippa, believest thou the prophets? I know that thou believest.
28 Then Agrippa said unto Paul, Almost thou persuadest me to be a Christian.

24 And as he thus made his defence, Festus saith with a loud voice, Paul, thou art mad; thy much
25 learning doth turn thee to madness. But Paul saith, I am not mad, most excellent Festus; but
26 speak forth words of truth and soberness. For the king knoweth of these things, unto whom also I speak freely: for I am persuaded that none of these things is hidden from him; for this hath not been
27 done in a corner. King Agrippa, believest thou the
28 prophets? I know that thou believest. And Agrippa *said* unto Paul, ¹With but little persuasion thou

---

a 2 Kings 9 : 11 ; John 10 : 20 ; 1 Cor. 1 : 23 ; 2 : 13, 14 ; 4 : 10.————1 Or, *in a little time*

---

the Messiah would suffer, die, and rise from the dead, it followed that Jesus was the promised Saviour of men and the Author of eternal life to those who believe on him. The apodosis (**should show light,** etc.) depends logically on the protasis (*if the Christ can suffer,* etc.).

24–29. THE ANSWER OF PAUL TO FESTUS.

24. Thus—lit. **these things**—refers more especially to the words last spoken (Mey.), and not in the same degree to the entire speech (De Wet.). The idea of a resurrection, which excited the ridicule of the Athenians (17 : 32), appeared equally absurd to the Roman Festus, and he could listen with patience no longer. It is evident that **these things,** in v. 26, has reference to *should rise from the dead,* in v. 23 ; and the intermediate *these things* would not be likely to turn the mind to a different subject. —The participle rendered **spake for himself** may be present, because Festus interposed before Paul had finished his defence (Mey.).— **Loud voice.** (See on 14 : 10.) The "loud voice" was the effect of his surprise and astonishment.—**Thou art mad,** which he says earnestly, not in jest (Olsh.), because it really appeared to him that Paul was acting under an infatuation which could spring only from insanity (Neand., Mey., De Wet.). Bengel: "Videbat Festus, naturam non agere in Paulo; gratiam non vidit" ["Festus saw that nature was not working in Paul; grace he did not see"].—[The words translated **much learning**] (τὰ πολλὰ γράμματα) admit of two senses: *the many writings* which thou readest (Kuin., Mey., Cony. and Hws.), or *the much learning* which thou hast or art reputed to have (Neand., De Wet., Alf.). The latter is the more natural idea (as Meyer now holds), and may have been suggested to the mind of Festus from his having heard that Paul was distinguished among the Jews for his scholarship. It is less probable that he was led to make the remark because he was struck with the evidence of superior knowledge evinced in Paul's address. It was able

and eloquent, but would not be characterized as learned in any very strict sense of the term.

25. I am not mad, etc. This reply of Paul is unsurpassed as a model of Christian courtesy and self-command. Doddridge takes occasion to say here that "if great and good men who meet with rude and insolent treatment in the defence of the gospel would learn to behave with such moderation, it would be a great accession of strength to the Christian cause."— **Most noble = most excellent,** as in 23 : 26. —**Of truth,** as opposed, not to falsehood (his veracity was not impeached), but to the fancies, hallucinations, of a disordered intellect.—**Soberness** is the opposite of *mania—i. e. a sound mind.*

26. For the king knows well concerning these things—viz. the death and resurrection of Christ. The apostle is assured that Agrippa has heard of the events connected with the origin of Christianity, and could not deny that they were supported by evidence too credible to make it reproachful to a man's understanding to admit the reality of the facts.— **Before whom**—lit. **unto whom also** (*i. e.* while he has this knowledge and on that account)—**I speak boldly,** without fear of contradiction.—**In a corner,** secretly (litotes); on the contrary, at Jerusalem, the capital of the nation. The expression was current in this sense (Wetst.).—**This thing = these things,** just before. The plural views the circumstances in detail; the singular, as a whole. (See the note on 5 : 5.)

27. Believest thou, etc. As Agrippa professed to believe the Scriptures which foretold that the Messiah would rise from the dead, he was bound to admit that there was nothing irrational or improbable in the apostle's testimony concerning an event which accomplished that prophecy.

28. Almost, etc., or **in a little time** (at this rate), **you persuade me to become a Christian** (Wetst., Raph., Kuin., Neand., De

29 And Paul said, *a*I would to God, that not only thou, but also all that hear me this day, were both almost, and altogether such as I am, except these bonds.
30 And when he had thus spoken, the king rose up, and the governor, and Bernice, and they that sat with them:
31 And when they were gone aside, they talked between themselves, saying, *b*This man doeth nothing worthy of death or of bonds.

29 wouldest fain make me a Christian. And Paul *said*, I would to God, that [1]whether with little or with much, not thou only, but also all that hear me this day, might become such as I am, except these bonds.
30 And the king rose up, and the governor, and Bernice, and they that sat with them: and when they had withdrawn, they spake one to another, saying, This man doeth nothing worthy of death or

---

a 1 Cor. 7 : 7....*b* ch. 23 : 9, 29 ; 25 : 25 ——1 Or, *both in little and in great, i. e.*, in all respects.

Wet., Rob.). It was not uncommon in Greek to omit *time* (χρόνος) after this adjective. Wetstein, Raphel (*Annott.*, ii. p. 188), and others have produced decisive examples of this ellipsis. By taking *in little* (ἐν ὀλίγῳ) as quantitative, instead of temporal, Meyer brings out this sense from the expression : *With little—i. e.* trouble, effort— *you persuade me to become a Christian ;* in other words (said sarcastically), You appeal to me as if you thought me an easy convert to your faith. This would be, no doubt, the correct explanation, if, with Meyer, Tischendorf, and others, we adopt *in great* (ἐν μεγάλῳ) as the correct reading in Paul's reply, instead of *in much* (ἐν πολλῷ) ; but the testimony for the common text outweighs that against it (Neand., De Wet.). [As the evidence is now reported, this does not appear to be the case. Lach., Tsch., Treg., West. and Hort, and Anglo-Am. Revisers agree in accepting ἐν μεγάλῳ, *in great*, as the true text. In this they are supported by ℵ A B, the three most important uncials, and by the Vul., Syr., and Cop. Versions.—A. H.] It is held, at present, to be unphilological to translate *in little*, *almost* (Bez., Grot., E. V.). The Greek for that sense would have been *of little* (ὀλίγου), it needs *little* (ὀλίγου δεῖ), or *by little* (παρ, ὀλίγον). The translation of the Common Version appears first in the Geneva Version. Tyndale and Cranmer render : " Somewhat thou bringest me in mind for to become a Christian." Agrippa appears to have been moved by the apostle's earnest manner, but attempts to conceal his emotion under the form of a jest.
29. I could pray to God—*i. e.* if I obeyed the impulse of my own heart, though it may be unavailing. (For ἄν with the optative, see W. § 41. 1. b ; B. § 139. m. 15.)—**Both almost, and altogether,** rather than **both in a little and in much time.** We may paraphrase the idea thus : " I could wish that you might become a Christian *in a short time,* as you say ; and if not in a short time, *in a long time.* I should rejoice in such an event, could it ever take place, whether it were sooner or later." If we read *in great* (ἐν μεγάλῳ) [as the evidence—see above —requires.—A. H.], the words would then
19

mean *whether by little effort or by great,* whether he was to be converted with ease or difficulty.
—**Except these chains,** which were hanging upon his arms as he made his defence. (See note on 12 : 6.) Though separated from his keepers, he must wear still the badges of his condition. Hess writes (ii. p. 459) as if the soldiers were present and Paul was bound to them. Some have taken the language as figurative : *except this state of captivity.* The literal sense is not inconsistent with an occasional Roman usage. Tacitus mentions the following scene as having occurred in the Roman Senate (*Ann.*, 4. 28) : " Reus pater, accusator filius (nomen utrique Vibius Serenus), in senatum inducti sunt. Ab exilio retractus et tum *catena* vinctus, orante filio. At contra reus nihil infracto animo, obversus in filium *quatere* vincla, vocare ultores deos," etc. [" A father the accused, his son the accuser (the name of each was Vibius Serenus), were led into the Senate. He had been brought back from exile and then was bound with *a chain*, the son arguing against him. On the other hand, the accused, his spirit in no degree shaken, turned toward his son, shook his chain, and called on the gods as his avengers "].
30–32. AGRIPPA PRONOUNCES PAUL INNOCENT.
30. The best authorities read **rose up** without **and when he had thus spoken.—The** is repeated before **king** and **governor,** because they are the titles of different persons —**Those who sat with them** are the military officers and magistrates who are mentioned in 25 : 23. The parties are named as rising and leaving the hall in the order of their rank.
31. And when, etc., or **and having retired,** withdrawn from the place of audience (see 25 : 23), not apart simply in the same room.
—**Talked with one another.** The object of the conference was to ascertain Agrippa's opinion in regard to the merits of the case. For **nothing worthy of death,** etc., see on 23 : 29.
—**Does nothing,** in that he holds such opinions, pursues such a course. (See W. § 40. 2. c.)

32 Then said Agrippa unto Festus, This man might have been set at liberty, *if he had not appealed unto Cæsar.

32 of bonds. And Agrippa said unto Festus, This man might have been set at liberty, if he had not appealed unto Cæsar.

CHAPTER XXVII.

A ND when *it was determined that we should sail into Italy, they delivered Paul and certain other prisoners unto *one* named Julius, a centurion of Augustus' band.

1 AND when it was determined that we should sail for Italy, they delivered Paul and certain other prisoners to a centurion named Julius, of the

a ch. 25 : 11....*b* ch. 25 : 12, 25.

It is not an instance of the present for the perfect (Kuin.).

32. Could have been (not *could be*) **released**—*i. e.* at any previous time since his apprehension, before his appeal to Cæsar. It will be seen that both verbs are in the past tense. As the appeal has been accepted, it could not be withdrawn, even with the consent of the parties. The procurator had now lost the control of the case, and had no more power to acquit the prisoner than to condemn him (Böttg., Grot.).—One effect of Agrippa's decision may have been that Festus modified his report, and commended Paul to the clemency of the court at Rome. (See on 28 : 16.)

1-5. PAUL EMBARKS AT CÆSAREA FOR ROME, AND PROCEEDS AS FAR AS MYRA.

1. When, or **as,** presents **it was determined** as immediately antecedent to **delivered.**—**Was determined** relates to the time of departure, not to the original purpose that Paul should be sent. (See 25 . 21.)—**That we should sail** (τοῦ ἀποπλεῖν) is a lax use of the telic infinitive, the conception being that the decision took place with a view to the sailing. (W. ? 44. 4. b.)—**We** includes the historian as one of the party; last used in 21 : 18.—**Proceeded to deliver** (imperfect as related to **was determined**), or *delivered*, as a series of acts. The plural subject of the verb refers to those who acted in this case under the command of the procurator.—**Other**—*i. e.* additional—**prisoners,** not different in character from Paul (viz. heathen), as Meyer supposes. (Luke uses that term and ἄλλος indiscriminately. See 15 : 35; 17 : 34.)—The statement here that not only Paul, but certain other prisoners, were sent by the same ship into Italy, implies, as Paley remarks, after Lardner, that the sending of persons from Judea to be tried at Rome was a

common practice. Josephus confirms this intimation by a variety of instances. . Among others, he mentions the following, which is the more pertinent, as it took place about this time. "Felix," he says (*Life*, ? 3), "for some slight offence, *bound and sent to Rome* several priests of his acquaintance, honorable and good men, to answer for themselves to Cæsar."—**Of Augustus' band,** or **of the Augustan cohort.** It is well established that several legions in the Roman army, certainly the second, third, and eighth, bore the above designation. No ancient writer, however, mentions that any one of these was stationed in the East. Some critics suppose, notwithstanding the absence of any notice to this effect, that such may have been the fact, and that one of the cohorts belonging to this legion, and distinguished by the same name, had its quarters at Cæsarea. The more approved opinion is that it was an independent cohort assigned to that particular service, and known as the Augustan or imperial, because, with reference to its relation to the procurator, it corresponded in some sense to the emperor's life-guard at Rome.[1] It may have taken the place of the Italian cohort, which was mentioned in 10 : 1, or very possibly, as Meyer suggests, may have been identical with it. The two names are not inconsistent with this latter opinion. *Augustan* may have been the honorary appellation of the cohort, while it was called *Italian* by the people, because it consisted chiefly of Italians or Romans. The other four cohorts at Cæsarea, as stated by Josephus (*Antt.,* 20. 8. 7 ; 19. 9. 2.), were composed principally of Cæsareans, or Samaritans. Hence, again, some explain the words as meaning *Sebastenean* or *Samaritan cohort,* since the city of Samaria bore also the Greek name *Sebaste,* in honor of the Emperor Augustus. But in that case, as Winer (*Realw.,* ii. p. 338), De Wette. Meyer, and others decide, we should have expected *Sebastene,* instead of *Sebastēs,* or an adjective equivalent in sense,

[1] Such exceptions to the general system occur under every military establishment. Speaking of that of England at a certain period, Mr. Macaulay says that "a troop of dragoons, which did not form part of any regiment, was stationed near Berwick, for the purpose of keeping the peace among the moss-troopers of the border."

2 And entering into a ship of Adramyttium, we launched, meaning to sail by the coasts of Asia; one *Aristarchus, a Macedonian of Thessalonica, being with us.

2 Augustan [1]band. And embarking in a ship of Adramyttium, which was about to sail unto the places on the coast of Asia, we put to sea, Aristarchus, a Macedonian of Thessalonica, being with

a ch. 19 : 29. ——1 Or, *cohort*

---

formed like *Italian*, in 10 : 1. Wieseler (p. 391) has proposed another view of the expression. It appears that Nero organized a body-guard which he denominated Augustani (Suet., *Ner.,* 20. 25) or Augustiani (Tac., *Ann.,* 14. 15). The critic just named thinks that Julius may have been a centurion in that cohort, whose station of course was at Rome, and that, having been sent to the East for the execution of some public service, he was now returning to Italy with these prisoners under his charge. But that guard, as Wieseler himself mentions, was organized in the year A. D. 60; and, according to his own plan of chronology in the Acts, it was in that very year that Paul was sent from Cæsarea to Rome. This coincidence in point of time leaves room for a possibility that the centurion may have left his post of duty thus early, but it encumbers the supposition with a strong improbability. Conybeare and Howson admit the force of this objection. The Roman discipline, says Meyer, would have given the procurator no claim to the service of such an officer.

2. A ship, or *a vessel,* **of Adramyttium,** which was a seaport of Mysia, on the eastern shore of the Ægean Sea, opposite to Lesbos. It was on a bay of the same name, and was then a flourishing city. Pliny speaks of it as one of the most considerable towns in that vicinity. No antiquities have been found here except a few coins.—Some critics prefer *which* (*i. e.* the vessel) *was about to sail* to the common *meaning to sail* (Grsb., Mey., Tsch.), though it is doubtful whether the latter should be relinquished (De Wet.). [Besides the critical editors mentioned by Dr. Hackett, we must now add Treg., West. and Hort, and the Anglo-Am. Revisers, as accepting the former reading—viz. *which was about to sail,* etc. It is supported by the best MSS. —*e. g.* ℵ A B.—A. H.]—**To sail the places along** (the coast of) **Asia**—*i. e.* touch at them here and there on the way to their port. This intransitive verb may govern an accusative, after

the analogy of *to go a way* (πορεύεσθαι ὀδόν) and the like. (K. 279. R. 5. See Krüg., *Gr.,* § 46. 6. 3.) Some regard *places* as the place *whither* (Win., De Wet.), which confounds the incidental delays with the end of the voyage. A few copies [but these the oldest and best.— A. H.] have *unto* (εἰς) after *to sail* (πλεῖν), which was inserted, no doubt, to render the construction easier. As Myra was one of the places where the ship stopped, *Asia* here may denote Asia Minor. Luke's prevalent use of the term restricts it to the western countries washed by the Ægean.—It would appear that they embarked in this Adramyttian ship because they had no opportunity at this time to sail directly from Cæsarea to Italy. "The vessel was evidently bound for her own port, and her course from Cæsarea thither necessarily led her close past the principal seaports of Asia. Now, this is also the course which a ship would take in making a voyage from Syria to Italy; they would, therefore, be so far on their voyage when they reached the coast of Asia, and in the great commercial marts on that coast they could not fail to find an opportunity for proceeding to their ulterior destination."[1] The opportunity which they expected presented itself at Myra (v. 6).—**Aristarchus.** This is the *Aristarchus* named in 19 : 29; 20 : 4. Our English translators speak of him, very strangely, as "*one* Aristarchus," as if he were otherwise unknown. That he accompanied Paul to Rome appears also from Philem. 24; Col. 4 : 10, which Epistles the apostle wrote while in that city. In the latter passage he terms Aristarchus *fellow-prisoner,* which, if taken literally, would lead us to suppose that he too had been apprehended and was now sent as a prisoner to Rome. But in Philem. 24 he is called merely *fellow-laborer,* and hence it is more probable that he went with the apostle of his own accord, and that he received the other appellation merely as a commendatory one, because by such devotion to him he had thus made Paul's captivity as it

---

[1] *The Voyage and Shipwreck of St. Paul,* etc., by James Smith, Esq., of Jordanhill, F. R. S., etc. (London, 1848 and 1856.) I have availed myself freely of the illustrations of this valuable treatise in the commentary on this chapter and the next. No work has appeared for a long time that has thrown so much light upon any equal portion of the Scriptures. The author is entirely justified in expressing his belief that the searching examination to which he has subjected the narrative has furnished a new and distinct argument for establishing the authenticity of the Acts. It would occasion too much repetition to quote this work in a formal manner. I am indebted to Mr. Smith for nearly all the quotations from English travellers, and for most of the explanations which involve a knowledge of nautical matters.

3 And the next *day* we touched at Sidon. And Julius **courteously entreated Paul, and gave *him* liberty to go unto his friends to refresh himself.
4 And when we had launched from thence, we sailed under Cyprus, because the winds were contrary.

3 us. And the next day we touched at Sidon: and Julius treated Paul kindly, and gave him leave to 4 go unto his friends and ¹refresh himself. And putting to sea from thence, we sailed under the lee of

a ch. 24 : 23 ; 28 : 16.——1 Gr. *receive attention.*

were his own. This is the general opinion of critics. We have every reason to suppose that Luke also went as the voluntary companion of the apostle.

3. **We landed at Sidon,** the modern Saida. This city had anciently one of the finest harbors in the East, and was celebrated at this time for its wealth and commerce. It was the rival of Tyre. (See 21 : 3.) The vessel stopped here, perhaps, for purposes of trade. They must have sailed quite near to the shore, and the views on land which passed under their notice were—first, the mountains of Samaria in the background; then the bold front of Carmel ; the city of Ptolemais, with the adjacent plain of Esdraelon ; the hills about Nazareth ;¹ and perhaps the heads of Gilboa and Tabor, the white cliffs of Cape Blanco or Ras el-Abiad, Tyre with its crowded port, and the southern ridges of Lebanon.—Saida is now the seat of a flourishing mission from this country, with an outpost at Hasbeiya, near the foot of Mount Hermon. —The distance from Cæsarea to Sidon was sixty-seven geographical miles. As they performed the voyage in a single day, they must have had a favorable wind. The prevailing winds now in that part of the Mediterranean, at the period of the year then arrived, are the westerly ;² and such a wind would have served their purpose. The coast-line between the two places bears north-north-east. The season of the year at which Paul commenced the voyage is known from v. 9. It must have been near the close of summer or early in September.—**Courteously entreated.** It is interesting to observe that the centurion manifested the same friendly disposition toward the apostle throughout the voyage. (See v. 43 ; 28 : 16.) It is not impossible that he had been present on some of the occasions when Paul defended himself before his judges (see 24 : 1 ; 25 : 23), and that he was not only convinced of his prisoner's innocence, but

had been led to feel a personal interest in his character and fortunes.—**His friends,** or the **friends,** believers, in that place. Sidon was a Phœnician city ; and, as we learn from 11 : 19, the gospel had been preached in Phœnicia at an early period. (See on 21 : 4.) The narrative presupposes that Paul had informed the centurion that there were Christians here.—(πορευθέντα agrees with the suppressed subject of τυχεῖν. Comp. 26 : 20. K. ₴ 307. R. 2. It is corrected in some manuscripts to πορευθέντι, agreeing with αὐτῷ, implied after ἐπέτρεψε.)

4. **We sailed under Cyprus because the winds were contrary.** It is evident from the next verse that they left this island on the left hand and passed to the north of it, instead of going to the south, which would have been their direct course in proceeding from Sidon to Proconsular Asia. The reason assigned for this is that the winds were adverse to them. Such would have been the effect of the westerly winds, which, as before stated, prevail on that coast at this season, and which had favored their progress hitherto. It may be supposed, therefore, that, these winds still continuing, they kept on their northern course after leaving Sidon, instead of turning toward the west or north-west, as they would have done under favorable circumstances. It is entirely consistent with this view that they are said to have *sailed under Cyprus,* if we adopt the meaning of this expression which some of the ablest authorities attach to it. Wetstein has stated what appears to be the true explanation, as follows : "Ubi navis vento contrario cogitur a recto cursu decedere, ita ut tunc insula sit interposita inter ventum et navem, dicitur ferri *infra* insulam " [" When a ship is forced by a contrary wind to depart from its proper course, so that an island may then be interposed between the wind and the ship, it is said to be carried *under* (*infra*) the island."—A. H.]. (*Nov. Test.,* ii. p.

¹ From Neby Ismail, on the hill behind Nazareth, I could see distinctly Mount Carmel, with its foot running out into the sea, the entire sweep of the bay from Carmel to Akka, the plain of Akka and the town itself, with glimpses of the Mediterranean at other points up and down the coast between the opening hills. It is not certain that Tabor can be made out at sea, though the sea can be distinguished as a blue line along the edge of the horizon from the summit of Tabor.

² An English naval officer, at sea near Alexandria under date of July 4, 1798, writes thus: "The wind continues to the westward. I am sorry to find it almost as prevailing as the trade-winds." Again, on the 19th of the next month, he says: "We have just gained sight of Cyprus, nearly the track we followed six weeks ago, so invariably do the westerly winds prevail at this season."

5 And when we had sailed over the sea of Cilicia and Pamphylia, we came to Myra, *a city* of Lycia.
6 And there the centurion found a ship of Alexandria sailing into Italy; and he put us therein.

5 Cyprus, because the winds were contrary. And when we had sailed across the sea which is off Cilicia and Pamphylia, we came to Myra, a *city* 6 of Lycia. And there the centurion found a ship of Alexandria sailing for Italy; and he put us

637). According to this opinion, ὑπό (= *infra*) in the verb affirms merely that the ship was on that side of the island from which the wind was blowing—*i. e.* to use a sea phrase, on the leeside. It decides nothing of itself with respect to their vicinity to the island, though, from the nature of the case, it would not be natural to speak of *sailing under a land*, or being *on the lee of it*, unless the land was somewhere near, rather than remote. In this instance they passed within sight of Cyprus, since that island was visible from the Syrian coast. (See the note on 13 : 4.) Many commentators, on the other hand, rendered the expression *we sailed near Cyprus*—as it were, *under* its projecting shore. In this case they must have had a different wind from that supposed above, in order to enable them to cross from the coast of Palestine to that of Cyprus; but, having gained that position, they must then have gone around to the north of that island, in accordance precisely with the other representation.

5. The sea of, or better the sea along, Cilicia and Pamphylia—*i. e.* the coast of those countries. The Cilician Sea extended so far south as to include even Cyprus. That pass the Greeks called also *Aulon Cilicium*.[1] The Pamphylian Sea lay directly west of the Cilician. Luke says nothing of any delay in these seas, and the presumption is that the voyage here was a prosperous one. This agrees perfectly with what would be expected under that coast at that season of the year. Instead of the westerly winds which had been opposed to them since their departure from Sidon, they would be favored now by a land-breeze[2] which prevails there during the summer months, as well as by a current which con-

stantly runs to the westward along the coast of Asia Minor.[3] Their object in standing so far to the north was no doubt to take advantage of these circumstances, which were well known to ancient mariners.—**Myra . . . of Lycia.** *Myra* was in the the south Lycia, two or three miles from the coast (Forbg., *Handb.*, ii. p. 256). The vicinity abounds still in magnificent ruins, though some of them, especially the rock-tombs, denote a later age than that of the apostle.[4] The ancient port of Myra was Andriaca, which was identified by Captain Beaufort at the bay of Andraki, "where the boats trading with the district still anchor, or find shelter in a deep river opening into it."

6–12. INCIDENTS OF THE VOYAGE FROM MYRA TO CRETE.
6. An Alexandrian ship about sailing. The participle describes a proximate future, as in 21 : 2, 3, etc. This ship was bound directly for Italy, having a cargo of wheat, as we learn from v. 38. (See the note there.) Egypt at this time, it is well known, was one of the granaries of Rome, and the vessels employed for the transportation of corn from that country were equal in size to the largest merchant-vessels of modern times. Hence this ship was able to accommodate the centurion and his numerous party, in addition to its own crew and lading. Josephus states (*Life*, ? 3) that the ship in which he was wrecked in his voyage to Italy contained six hundred persons. Myra was almost due north from Alexandria, and it is not improbable that the same westerly winds which forced the Adramyttian ship to the east of Cyprus drove the Alexandrian ship to Myra. The usual course from Alexandria to Italy was by the south of Crete; but when this was impracticable, vessels sailing from that port were ac-

---

[1] Hoffmann's *Griechenland und die Griechen*, vol. ii. p. 1385.

[2] M. de Pagés, a French navigator, who was making a voyage from Syria to Marseilles, took the same course, for which he assigns also the reason which influenced, probably, the commander of Paul's ship. "The winds from the west," he says—" and consequently contrary—which prevail in these places in the summer forced us to run to the north. We made for the coast of Caramania (Cilicia), in order to meet the northerly winds, and which we found accordingly."

[3] "From Syria to the Archipelago, there is a constant current to the westward" (Beaufort's *Description of the South Coast of Asia Minor*, p. 39). Pocock found this current running so strong between Rhodes and the continent that it broke into the cabin windows even in calm weather (*Description of the East*, vol. ii. p. 236).

[4] "The village of Dembra (the Turkish name of the modern Myra) occupies a small part of the site of the ancient city of Myra. The acropolis crowns the bold precipice above. We commenced the ascent to the acropolis, at first exceedingly difficult until we found an ancient road cut out of the rock, with steps leading to the summit. The walls of the acropolis are entirely built of small stones with mortar. We saw no remains of any more substantially or solidly built structures; but it is evidently the hill alluded to by Strabo, upon which ' Myra is said to have been situated ' " (Spratt and Forbes, vol. i. p. 132).

7 And when we had sailed slowly many days, and scarce were come over against Cnidus, the wind not suffering us, we sailed under Crete, over against Salmone;

7 therein. And when we had sailed slowly many days, and were come with difficulty over against Cnidus, the wind not [1]further suffering us, we sailed

1 Or, *suffering us to get there*

---

customed to stand to the north till they reached the coast of Asia Minor, and then proceed to Italy through the southern part of the Ægean. (See the proofs of this statement in Wetstein.) The Alexandrian ship was not, therefore, out of her course at Myra, even if she had no call to touch there for the purposes of commerce. It may be added that "the land-breeze on the Cilician coast appears to be quite local, and consequently might enable Paul's ship to reach Myra, although the prevalent wind did not admit of the ships in that harbor proceeding on their voyage."—This vessel must have reached Myra in August or early in September, according to v. 9, below. That an Alexandrian wheat ship now should have been here, just at this time, suggests a coincidence which may be worth pointing out. At the present day the active shipping season at Alexandria commences about the 1st of August. The rise of the Nile is then so far advanced that the produce of the interior can be brought to that city, where it is shipped at once and sent to different parts of Europe. At the beginning of August in 1852, as I saw it stated in the circular of a commercial house at Alexandria, there were twelve vessels then taking on board grain cargoes, just received from Upper Egypt. Thus it appears that the Alexandrian ship mentioned by Luke may have left Egypt not only after the grain harvest of the year had been gathered (it is ripe at the end of March), but just at the time when cargoes, or the earliest cargoes of that kind, could be obtained there; and, further, that the ship would have had, after this, just about the time requisite for reaching Myra when Paul's ship arrived at the same place.—**He put us on board of it** (ἐνεβίβασεν, etc., a *vox nautica*). It will be noticed that Luke employs such terms with great frequency and with singular precision. He uses, for example, not less than thirteen different verbs which agree in this—that they mark in some way the progression of the ship, but which differ inasmuch as they indicate its distance from the land, rate of movement, direction of the wind, or some such circumstance. With the exception of three of them, they are all nautical expressions.

7. And when we had sailed slowly many days. The distance from Myra to Cnidus is not more than a hundred and thirty geographical miles. They occupied, therefore, "many days" in going a distance which with a decidedly fair wind they could have gone in a single day. We must conclude from this that they were retarded by an unfavorable wind. Such a wind would have been one from the north-west, and it is precisely such a wind, as we learn from the *Sailing Directions for the Mediterranean*, that prevails in that part of the Archipelago during the summer months. According to Pliny, it begins in August and blows for forty days. Sailing-vessels almost invariably experience more or less delay in proceeding to the west in this part of the Mediterranean at that season of the year. But with north-west winds, says Mr. Smith, the ship could work up from Myra to Cnidus, because, until she reached that point, she had the advantage of a weather shore, under the lee of which she would have smooth water, and, as formerly mentioned, a westerly current; but it would be slowly and with difficulty. **Scarce** = **with difficulty** refers, evidently, to this laborious progress, and not (E. V.) to the fact of their having advanced barely so far.— **Cnidus.** *Cnidus* was the name both of a peninsula on the Carian coast, between Cos on the north and Rhodes on the south, and of a town on the Triopian promontory which formed the end of this peninsula. It is the town that is intended here. It was situated partly on the mainland and partly on an island, with which it was connected by a causeway, on each side of which was an artificial harbor (Forbg., *Hand.*, ii. p. 221). "The small one," says Captain Beaufort, "has still a narrow entrance between high piers, and was evidently a closed basin for triremes. The southern and largest port is formed by two transverse moles; these noble works were carried into the sea at the depth of nearly a hundred feet. One of them is almost perfect; the other, which is more exposed to the south-west swell, can only be seen under water." [1]—**The wind not permitting us unto it**—*i. e.* to approach Cnidus,

---

[1] *Caramania; or, A Brief Description of the South Coast of Asia Minor*, p. 76: "Few places bear more incontestable proofs of former magnificence. The whole area of the city is one promiscuous mass of ruins, among which may be traced streets and gateways, porticos and theatres."

8 And, hardly passing it, came unto a place which is called The fair havens; nigh whereunto was the city of Lasea.

9 Now when much time was spent, and when sailing was now dangerous, *a*because the fast was now already past, Paul admonished *them*,

8 under the lee of Crete, over against Salmone; and with difficulty coasting along it we came unto a certain place called Fair Havens; nigh whereunto was the city of Lasea.

9 And when much time was spent, and the voyage was now dangerous, because the Fast was now al-

a Lev. 23 : 27, 29.

---

to take shelter in the harbor there, which would have been their first preference. They adopted, therefore, the only other alternative which was left to them. The word rendered **to permit** (προσεάω) does not occur in the classics. In this the preposition (πρός) cannot well mean *further*, as some allege, since they would have had no motive to continue the voyage in that direction, even if the weather had not opposed it.[1] **We sailed under** (*i. e.* to the leeward of) **Crete against Salmone,** a promontory which forms the eastern extremity of that island and bears still the same name. An inspection of the map will show that their course hither from Cnidus must have been nearly south. The wind drove them in this direction. It has been said that they avoided the northern side of Crete, because it furnished no good ports; but such is not the fact. Soudra and Longa Spina are excellent harbors on that side of the island. Having passed around Salmone, they would find a north-west wind as much opposed to them in navigating to the westward as it had been between Myra and Cnidus; but, on the other hand, they would have for a time a similar advantage: the south side of Crete is a weather shore, and with a north-west wind they could advance along the coast until they reached that part of it which turns decidedly toward the north. Here they would be obliged to seek a harbor and wait until the wind changed. The course of movement indicated by Luke tallies exactly with these conditions.

8. And with difficulty coasting along it —viz. Crete, not Salmone, since the former, though not so near, is the principal word. Besides, Salmone was not so much an extended shore as a single point, and, at all events, did not extend so far as the place where they stopped. This participle is a nautical word.— **Unto a certain place called Fair Havens.** No ancient writer mentions this harbor, but no one doubts that it is identical with

the place known still under the same name, on the south of Crete, a few miles to the east of Cape Matala. This harbor consists of an open roadstead, or rather two roadsteads contiguous to each other, which may account for the plural designation. It is adapted, also, by its situation, to afford the shelter in north-west winds which the anchorage mentioned by Luke afforded to Paul's vessel. Nautical authorities assure us that this place is the farthest point to which an ancient ship could have attained with north-westerly winds, because here the land turns suddenly to the north.—**Nigh where-unto = near to which was the city Lasea.** The vicinity of this place appears to be mentioned because it was better known than Fair Havens. In the first edition I wrote that all trace of Lasea was supposed to be lost. Since then an English traveller in Crete reports that the name is applied by the natives to the site of an ancient town on the coast, about five miles east of Fair Havens. Two white pillars, masses of masonry, and other ruins occur on the spot.[2] Here **near** (ἐγγύς) governs **which** (ᾧ) as an adverb. **Was** incorporates the notice with the history without excluding the present. (Comp. 17 : 21, 23. K. ? 256. 4. a.)

9. Now when much time, or, lit., **now a long time having elapsed**—*i. e.* since the embarkation at Cæsarea. The expression is to be taken in a relative sense. On leaving Palestine they expected to reach Italy before the arrival of the stormy season, and would have accomplished their object had it not been for unforeseen delays.—**And when the sailing,** etc., or **the navigation, being now unsafe** —*i. e.* at this particular period of the year. (πλοός is a later Greek form for πλοῦ. W. ? 8. 2. b; S. ? 22. 2.)—**Because also the fast was now past. Also** adds this clause to the one immediately preceding, in order to fix more precisely the limits of the **already** there by informing us how far the season was advanced. (See W. ? 53. 3. c.)—**The fast** denotes

---

[1] Mr. Smith supposes that the winds did not permit their proceeding on their course, and in his second edition (p. 76) urges against me the authority of Admiral Penrose as maintaining the same view. It is not claimed that the Greek word is at all decisive, but that the nautical reason demands their interpretation. It does not become me to urge my opinion on such a point in opposition to that of experienced navigators. One would say as a critic that προσεῶντος in such proximity to κατὰ τὴν Κνίδον would have naturally the same local direction.

[2] Mr. Smith inserts an interesting account of this discovery (p. 262) in his edition of 1856.

10 And said unto them, Sirs, I perceive that this voyage will be with hurt and much damage, not only of the lading and ship, but also of our lives.

11 Nevertheless the centurion believed the master and the owner of the ship, more than those things which were spoken by Paul.

12 And because the haven was not commodious to

10 ready gone by, Paul admonished them, and said unto them, Sirs, I perceive that the voyage will be with injury and much loss, not only of the 11 lading and the ship, but also of our lives. But the centurion gave more heed to the master and to the owner of the ship, than to those things which 12 were spoken by Paul. And because the haven was

---

the fast by pre-eminence (κατ᾽ ἐξοχήν), which the Jews observed on the great day of expiation, which fell on the 10th of the month Tisri, about the time of the autumnal equinox. (See Lev. 16 : 29; 23 : 27. Jahn's *Archæol.*, ₰ 357.) Philo also says that no prudent man thought of putting to sea after this season of the year. The Greeks and Romans considered the period of safe navigation as closing in October and recommencing about the middle of March. Luke's familiarity with the Jewish designations of time rendered it entirely natural for him to describe the progress of the year in this manner. It was not on account of the storms, merely, that ancient mariners dreaded so much **a** voyage in winter, but because the rains prevailed then, and the clouds obscured the sun and stars, on which they were so dependent for the direction of their course. (See the note on v. 20.)—**Admonished,** or *exhorted,* them—viz. to remain here and not continue the voyage. It is not stated in so many words that this was his object, but it may be inferred from the argument which he employs, and from the representation in the next two verses, that they renewed the voyage in opposition to his advice. (See also v. 21.)

10. I perceive, have reason to think. This verb expresses a judgment which he had formed in view of what they had already experienced, as well as the probabilities of the case, looking at the future. The revelation which he afterward received respecting their fate he announces in very different terms. (See v. 23.) He may be understood as declaring his own personal conviction that if they now ventured to sea again the ship would certainly be wrecked, and that among so many some of them at least would lose their lives. None lost their lives, in fact, and hence Paul could not speak as a prophet here. The apostles were not infallible, except in their sphere as religious teachers. —In **that with hurt,** etc., we have [in the original] a union of two different modes of expression. The sentence begins as if **this voyage will be** was to follow, but on reaching that verb the construction changes to the infinitive with its subject, as if **that** had not

preceded. (See W. ₰ 63. 2. c.) Such variations are so common, even in the best writers, that they are hardly to be reckoned as anacoluthic.— **With violence** (lit. **insolence**—*i. e.* of the winds and waves) **and much loss.** The second noun states an effect of the first, which is applied here in a sort of poetic way, like our "sport" or "riot" of the elements. Kuinoel quotes *keeping off the heat and the violence from the rains,* in Josephus (*Antt.,* 3. 6. 4), as showing this sense. Horace has the same idea in his "ventis debes ludibrium" (*Od.,* 1. 11. 14). To render the words *injury* and *loss* does violence to the first of them and makes them tautological. Some have relied for this meaning on Pindar (*Pyth.,* i. 140) ; but the poet is speaking, says Professor Vömel,[1] not of a shipwreck, but a sea-fight, and *insolence* is used there in its strictest sense. Meyer understands it of the *rashness,* the presumption, which they would evince in committing themselves again to the deep. If we assume that meaning here, we are to retain it naturally in v. 21 ; and it would not be there a term of reproach, which we should not expect the apostle to employ in such an address.

11. The centurion. In regard to the termination, see on 10 : 1.—**The master,** or **the steersman,** whose authority in ancient ships corresponded very nearly with that of the captain in our vessels.—**The owner,** to whom the ship belonged. The proprietor, instead of chartering his vessel to another, frequently went himself in her, and received as his share of the profit the money paid for carrying merchandise and passengers. The owners of the cargo hired the captain and the mariners.—**Those things spoken by Paul** changes the object of the verb (*believed*) from that of a person to a thing. (Comp. 26 : 20.)

12. Not commodious, or **not well situated,** inconvenient. The harbor deserved its name, undoubtedly (see v. 8), for many purposes, but in the judgment of those to whose opinion it was most natural that the centurion should defer it was not considered a desirable place **for wintering** (πρὸς παραχειμασίαν). The question was not whether they should attempt

---

[1] Of the Gymnasium at Frankfort-on-the-Main. In his *Programme* for 1850 he inserts a translation of this chapter of the Acts, with some critical remarks.

winter in, the more part advised to depart thence also, if by any means they might attain to Phenice, *and there* to winter; *which is* an haven of Crete, and lieth toward the south-west and north-west.

not commodious to winter in, the more part advised to put to sea from thence, if by any means they could reach Phœnix, and winter *there; which is* a haven of Crete, looking ¹north-east and south-east.

¹ Gr. *down the south-west wind and down the north-west wind.*

---

to proceed to Italy during the present season, but whether they should remain here in preference to seeking some other harbor where they might hope to be more secure. In this choice of evils, the advice of Paul was that they should remain here; and the event justified his discernment.¹—**The more part,** or **the majority.** Their situation had become so critical that a general consultation was held as to what should be done.—**Thence also,** or **also from there,** as they had sailed previously from other places. (See vv. 4, 6; ἐκεῖθεν (Lchm.) is less correct.)—**Unto Phœnix,** which must have been a town and harbor in the south of Crete, a little to the west of Fair Havens. (Comp. on v. 13.) The palm trees in that region are supposed to have given occasion to the name. Strabo mentions a harbor with this name on the south of Crete, and Ptolemy mentions a town called Phœnix, with a port which he terms Phœnicus. On the contrary, Stephanus Byzantinus calls the town Phœnicus, which Hierocles, again, calls Phœnice. (See Hoffm., *Griechenland,* ii. p. 1334.) The best way to harmonize these notices is to suppose that the different names were at times applied promiscuously to the town and the harbor. It is uncertain with what modern port we are to identify the ancient Phœnix. Anapolis, Lutro (unless the places differ merely as town and harbor), Sphakia, Franco Castello, Phineka, have each been supposed to be that port.—**If by any means they might be able,** etc. Those who advise the step consider it perilous. —**A harbor looking toward Lips and toward Corus**—*i. e.* the points from which the winds so called blew; viz. the south-west and the north-west. The intermediate point between these winds is west, so that the harbor would have faced in that direction, while the opposite shores receded from each other toward the south and north. This mode of employing the names of the winds is a constant usage in the ancient writers to designate, as we say,

the points of the compass. Such is the general view of the meaning of this expression, and there can be no doubt of its correctness.—Mr. Smith (p. 80) maintains that the Phœnix of Luke is the present Lutro. That harbor, however, opens to the east. To reconcile Luke's statement with this circumstance, he understands *toward Lips and toward Corus* to mean *according to the direction* in which those winds blew, and not, as is generally supposed, *whence* they blew. "Now this is exactly the description of Lutro, which looks or is open to the east; but, having an island in front which shelters it, it has two entrances—one looking to the north-east, which is κατὰ Λίβα, and the other to the south-east, κατὰ Χῶρον." But it is unsafe to give up the common interpretation for the sake of such a coincidence; it rests upon a usage of the Greek too well established to justify such a departure from it. This mode of explaining *toward Lips* (κατὰ Λίβα) involves, I think, two incongruities: first, it assigns opposite senses to the same term—viz. *south-west* as the name of a wind, and *north-east* as the name of a quarter of the heavens; and secondly, it destroys the force of **looking,** which implies, certainly, that the wind and the harbor confronted each other, and not that they were turned from each other. Mr. Smith adduces *according to wave and wind* from Herodotus (4. 110); but the expression is not parallel as regards either the preposition or the noun. The preposition denotes there conformity of motion, and not of situation where the objects are at rest, and *wind* does not belong to the class of proper names, like Lips and Corus, which the Greeks employed in such geographical designations. "There is a passage in Arrian," he says, "still more apposite to this point. In his Periplus of the Euxine, he tells us that, when navigating the south coast of that sea toward the east, he observed during a calm a cloud suddenly arise, which was driven before the east wind. Here there can be no mistake; the

---

¹ Paul's dissent from the general opinion has appeared to some very singular; for the bay at Fair Havens, open to nearly one-half of the compass, was ill adapted, it was thought, to furnish a permanent shelter. But recent and more exact observations establish the interesting fact that " Fair Havens is so well protected by islands and reefs that, though not equal to Lutro, it must be a very fair winter harbor; and that, considering the suddenness, the frequency, and the violence with which gales of northerly wind spring up, and the certainty that if such a gale sprung up in the passage from Fair Havens to Lutro (Phœnix), the ship must be driven off to sea, the prudence of the advice given by the master and owner was extremely questionable, and that the advice given by St. Paul may possibly be supported even on nautical grounds " (Smith, p. 88, 1856).

13 And when the south wind blew softly, supposing that they had obtained *their* purpose, loosing *thence,* they sailed close by Crete.
14 But not long after there arose against it a tempestuous wind, called Euroclydon.

13 And when the south wind blew softly, supposing that they had obtained their purpose, they weighed 14 anchor and sailed along Crete, close in shore. But after no long time there beat down from it a tem-

cloud must have been driven to the west." But to translate *toward the east* (κατ' εὖρον) in that manner assumes the point in dispute. The context presents no reason why we should not adopt the ordinary sense of such phrases—viz. *toward the east; i. e.* the cloud appeared in that quarter. In this expression, therefore, *Eurus* would denote the point from which the east wind blows, and not whither.[1] [In his last ed. Meyer refers to the discussion of Dr. Hackett and adheres to his view; but, as will be noticed, the Revisers appear to have been convinced that the view of Mr. Smith is correct.—A. H.]

13–16. A STORM RAGES, AND DRIVES THE VESSEL TO CLAUDE.

13. And when, etc., **now when a south wind blew moderately.** After passing Cape Matala, the extreme southern point of Crete, and only four or five miles to the west of Fair Havens, the coast turns suddenly to the north; and hence, for the rest of the way up to Phœnix, a south wind was as favorable a one as they could desire.—**Supposing that,** etc., or **thinking to have gained their purpose,** regarding it as already secured. It was some-

what less than forty miles from Fair Havens to Phœnix. With a southern breeze, therefore, they could expect to reach their destination in a few hours.—**Loosing thence,** more correctly *having weighed—i. e.* anchor.—**They coasted along Crete nearer**—sc. than usual; *i. e.* quite near. This clause, as we see from the next verse, describes their progress immediately after their anchorage at Fair Havens. It applies, therefore, to the first few miles of their course During this distance, as has been suggested already, the coast continues to stretch toward the west; and it was not until they had turned Cape Matala that they would have the full benefit of the southern breeze which had sprung up. With such a wind they would be able just to weather that point, provided they kept near to the shore. We have, therefore, a perfectly natural explanation of their proceeding in the manner that Luke has stated.

14. Not long after, strictly **after not long,** shortly. (Comp. 28 : 6.) The tempest, therefore, came upon them before they had advanced far from their recent anchorage. They were still much nearer to that place than they were to Phœnix. It is important to observe

[1] The writer published some remarks on Mr. Smith's explanation of κατὰ Λίβα καί κατὰ Χῶρον in the *Bibliotheca Sacra*, 1850, p. 751. Mr. Smith has had the kindness to address to me a letter, stating some additional facts ascertained since the publication of his work on *The Voyage and Shipwreck of Paul.* In this letter he reaffirms his view of the expression referred to, and calls my attention again to the passage in Arrian as conclusive in support of his position. A distinguished Hellenist (Professor Felton of the university at Cambridge) has favored me with the following remarks on that passage: " It is true that the cloud of which Arrian speaks was borne toward the west; but that is not expressed by κατ' εὖρον, but must be inferred from the circumstances of the case. The course of the voyage they were making was eastward ; after a calm, during which they used their oars alone, 'suddenly a cloud springing up broke out nearly east of us' (ἄφνω νεφέλη ἐπαναστάσα ἐξεῤῥάγη κατ' εὖρον μάλιστα), and brought upon them a violent wind. The wind, of course, was an easterly wind, because it made their further progress toward the east slow and difficult. But the navigator in the phrase κατ' εὖρον is speaking of the direction in which he saw the cloud, not in which the cloud was moving. If he had been simply describing the direction in which the cloud was moving, as Herodotus is describing the motion of the ship (and not the direction in which the ship is seen from another point), then κατ' εὖρον would mean *with the Eurus* or *before the Eurus.* . . . If a person is floating on the wind, or driven by the wind, if he is in motion according to the wind, then, of course, his direction is determined by that of the wind. But if he is at rest and looking according to the wind, he is looking where the wind is the most prominent object—that is, he is facing the wind, as Arrian's crew were facing the cloud and the wind, and not turning his back upon it." As this question has excited some interest, it may be well to mention how it is viewed in works published since the preceding note was written. Humphry (1854) says (p. 202) that Mr. Smith's passages are not quite conclusive as to βλέποντα κατὰ Λίβα. He supposes Phœnix to be the modern Phineka, which opens to the west, and thus adopts the common explanation of the phrase. Alford (1852) agrees with Smith that κατὰ Λίβα and similar combinations denote *whither,* and not *whence,* the winds blow, but intimates a purpose to fortify his ground against objections in a future edition. Conybeare and Howson (ii. p. 400) would admit an instance of that usage in Jos., *Antt.* 15. 9. 6 (*sic*), but say that the other alleged proofs are untenable or ambiguous. They mediate between the two opinions by suggesting that the point of view (βλέποντα) is from the sea, and not the land; so that κατὰ Λίβα would have its usual meaning and yet the harbor open toward the east, like Lutro. Wordsworth (p. 120) has a copious note on this question. He reviews the arguments on both sides, and sums up with the result that we should " not abandon the ancient interpretation," or, at all events should " suspend our decision till we have more complete topographical details for forming it."

15 And when the ship was caught, and could not bear up into the wind, we let *her* drive.

15 pestuous wind, which is called Euraquilo: and when the ship was caught, and could not face the

this fact, because it shows what course the ship took in going from Crete to Claude.—**There arose**, etc.—lit. **a typhonic wind struck against it ;** *i. e.* the ship.—*Struck* may imply *itself*, or be intransitive. Luke employs *it*—lit. *her*—because the mental antecedent is *ship* (fem.), which actually occurs in v. 41, though his ordinary word is *vessel* (neut.). It would be quite accidental which of the terms would shape the pronoun at this moment, as they were both so familiar. (See W. ∤ 47. 5. k.) **Against** (κατά) takes the genitive, because the wind was unfriendly, hostile, as in the Attic phrase *to smite the head* (Bernh., *Synt.*, p. 238). Some critics, as Kuinoel, De Wette, Meyer, refer *it* to *Crete*, and render *drove* us or the ship *against it*. Similar is the Geneva Version : " There arose agaynste Candie a stormye wynd out of the north-east." But how can we understand it in this way, when we are told in the next verse that they yielded to the force of the wind and were driven by it toward Claude, which is south-west from Fair Havens? We must discard that view, unless we suppose that the wind in the course of a few minutes blew from precisely opposite quarters. Luther refers *it* to *purpose* (v. 13) : *struck against it*, defeated their purpose. Tyndale lived for a time with the German Reformer at Wittenberg, and took his translation, perhaps, from that source: " Anone after ther arose agaynste their purpose a flawe of wynd out of the north-easte." The Greek expression is awkward for such an idea, and is unsupported by proper examples. Some recent commentators refer *it*, as before, to the island, but vary the preposition : *struck down from it*—viz. Crete; *i. e.* from its mountains, its lofty shores (Alf., Cony. and Hws., Hmph., Wdsth.). The preposition admits confessedly of this sense; but does the verb? Was it used of winds, unless the object *struck* was added or implied after it? And if the *striking* was in the writer's mind here and led to the choice of this particular verb, how can κατ᾽ αὐτῆς (*i. e.* the ship) fail to be this object? It is questionable whether " to strike down," as said of a wind, and " to blow, come, rush down," are convertible terms, and, unless they are so, *arose* in Matt. 8 : 24, *descended* in Matt. 7 : 25, and *ariseth* (R. V.) in Mark 4 : 37 do not bear specially on the case. In the Greek *Thesaurus*

(Paris. ed., ii. p. 90) it is said of the verb (βάλλειν) : " It is used in the sense of striking of the sun, of light, of a voice, of any sound whatsoever, approaching a body." It occurs of winds in *Il.*, 23, 217, but with the accusative of the object struck.[1] **Typhonic** describes the wind with reference to the whirling of the clouds occasioned by the meeting of opposite currents of the air. Pliny (2 : 48), in speaking of sudden blasts, says that they cause a vortex which is called " typhoon," and Aulus Gellius (19 : 1) mentions certain figures or appearances of the clouds in violent tempests which it was customary to call " typhoons." This term is intended to give us an idea of the fury of the gale ; and its name—Εὐρακύλων, as the word should most probably be written—denotes the point from which it came ; *i. e. Euroaquilo*, as in the Vulgate, *a north-east wind*. This reading occurs in A and B, which are two of the oldest manuscripts, and in some other authorities. It is approved by Grotius, Mill, Bengel, Bentley, De Wette, and others. Lachmann inserts it in his edition of the text [as also Tsch., Treg., West. and Hort, and the Anglo-Am. Revisers. Tsch. adduces for this reading ℵ A B* in his 8th ed.—A. H.]. This word, says Green (p.117), " which simply Grecizes *Euroaquilo*, demands the preference among the various shapes of the name." The internal evidence favors that form of the word. A north-east storm accounts most perfectly for the course of the ship, and for the means employed to control it, mentioned or intimated in the sequel of the narrative. (The other principal readings are Εὐροκλύδων (T. R., Tsch.2), compounded of εὖρος and κλύδων, *Eurus fluctus excitans*, or, as De Wette thinks more correct, *fluctus Euro excitatus;* and Εὐρυκλύδων, from εὐρύς and κλύδων, *broad wave*.) It appears, therefore, that the gentle southern breeze with which they started changed suddenly to a violent north or north-east wind. Such a sudden change is a very common occurrence in those seas. An English naval officer, in his *Remarks on the Archipelago*, says : " It is always safe to anchor under the lee of an island with a northern wind, as it dies away gradually ; but it would be extremely dangerous with southerly winds, as they almost invariably shift to a violent northerly wind."

15. Being seized, caught by the wind.—

---

[1] This criticism may not be useless if it should serve to elicit further inquiry before discarding the common view. My means do not allow me to treat the subject more fully at present.

[But Tsch. changed his opinion and adopted Εὐρακύλων. See statement in brackets above.—A. H.]

16 And running under a certain island which is called Clauda, we had much work to come by the boat:
17 Which when they had taken up, they used helps, undergirding the ship; and, fearing lest they should

16 wind, we gave way *to it*, and were driven. And running under the lee of a small island called [1]Cauda, we were able, with difficulty, to secure the
17 boat: and when they had hoisted it up, they used helps, under-girding the ship; and, fearing lest

1 Many ancient authorities read *Clauda.*

To look in the face, withstand. It is said that the ancients often painted an eye on each side of the prow of their ships. It may not be easy to determine whether the personification implied in this mode of speaking arose from that practice, or whether the practice arose from the personification.—**Giving up,** the vessel to the wind. Some supply *ourselves* as the object of the participle, in anticipation of the next verb. The idea is the same in both cases.—**We were borne,** not hither and thither, but at the mercy of the wind, the direction of which we know from the next verse.

16. Running under a certain small island called Claude. This island Ptolemy calls Claudos. It bears now the name of Gozzo. As the gale commenced blowing soon after the departure from Fair Havens, the ship, in order to reach Claude, must have been driven to the south-west. Their course, had they been near Phœnix at the commencement of the storm, would have been due south. The effect which the wind produced shows what the direction of the wind was; it must have been from the north or north-east, which agrees, as we have seen, with the probable import of the name which Luke has employed to designate the wind. **Running under** implies, first, that they went before the wind (see on 16 : 11); and secondly, according to the view suggested on v. 4, that they passed Claude, so as to have the wind between them and that island—that is, since the direction of the wind has been already determined, they went to the south-east of it instead of the north. That they approached near to the island at the same time may be inferred from their being able to accomplish the object mentioned in the next clause. Others infer their vicinity to the island from the preposition, which they take to mean *under* the coast; but, as in the other case, they suppose that this was the southern coast, from the direction in which such a wind must have driven the ship. —**We had much work,** or **we were able with difficulty, to secure the boat.** Luke includes himself, perhaps not from sympathy merely, but because he took part in this labor. The preservation of the boat was important, as affording the last means of escape. (See v. 30.) They may have begun already to have forebodings of the result. Those expert in maritime

affairs say that while a vessel is scudding before a strong gale her boat cannot be taken on board or lashed to the side of the vessel (see on v. 32) without extreme danger. Hence it is probable that when on the southern side of Claude they were sheltered somewhat against the storm, and were able to arrest the progress of the ship sufficiently to enable them to accomplish this object. Yet the sea even here was still apparently so tempestuous as to render this a difficult operation. It may have added to the difficulty that the boat having been towed more than twenty miles through a raging sea could hardly fail to have been filled with water. They had omitted this precaution at the outset, because the weather was mild and they had expected to be at sea but a few hours. It will be observed that Luke has not stated why they found it so difficult to secure the boat. We are left to conjecture the reasons.

17-20. THEY UNDERGIRD AND LIGHTEN THE SHIP, BUT DESPAIR OF SAFETY.

17. They used helps—*i. e.* ropes, chains, and the like—for the purpose specified in the next clause; viz. that of **undergirding the ship.** Most scholars take this view of the meaning, and it is doubtless the correct one. De Wette would extend *helps* so as to include other similar expedients : *they used helps,* of which *undergirding the ship* was an example. **Helps** cannot denote the *services* of the passengers, as some have said; for we have no such limiting term annexed as that sense of the expression would require. The "helps" here are the *hypozomata* (ὑποζώματα), which Hesychius defines as "cables binding ships round the middle." It is probable that ships were occasionally undergirded with planks; but that could only be done in the harbor, and was a different thing from performing the process at sea. But how, the question arises next, were the cables applied so as to accomplish the proposed object? Falconer, in his *Marine Dictionary,* describes the mode of undergirding ships, as practised in modern navigation, in the following terms : "To frap a ship (*ceintrer un vaisseau*) is to pass four or five turns of a large cable-laid rope round the hull or frame of a ship to support her in a great storm or otherwise, when it is apprehended that she is not strong enough to resist the violent efforts of the sea.

fall into the quicksands, strake sail, and so were driven.

they should be cast upon the Syrtis, they lowered the

This expedient, however, is rarely put in practice." In ancient times it was not uncommon to resort to this process. The larger ships or their more extended voyages carried with them *hypozomata* or ropes for undergirding, so as to be prepared for any emergency which might require them. The Attic arsenals kept a supply of them always on hand for public use. This mode of strengthening a ship at sea, although not adopted so often as it was anciently, is not unknown in the experience of modern navigators. In 1815, Mr. Henry Hartley was employed to pilot the Russian fleet from England to the Baltic. One of the ships under his escort, the Jupiter, was frapped round the middle by three or four turns of a steam-cable. Sir George Back, on his return from his Arctic voyage in 1837, was forced, in consequence of the shattered and leaking condition of his ship, to undergird her. The Albion, a British frigate, in 1846 encountered a hurricane on her voyage from India, and was under the necessity of frapping her hull together to prevent her from sinking. To these more recent instances many others of an earlier date might be added.[1] The common representation in regard to the ancient mode of applying the *hypozomata* to a ship makes it different from the modern usage. Boeckh's view is the one followed in most of the recent works. According to his investigations, the ropes, instead of being passed under the bottom and fastened on deck, "ran in a horizontal direction around the ship from the stern to the prow. They ran round the vessel in several circles, and at certain distances from one another. The length of these *tormenta*, as they are called in Latin, varied accordingly as they ran around the higher or lower part of the ship, the latter being naturally shorter than the former. Their number varied according to the size of the ship."[2] Mr. Smith, in his *Dissertation on the Ships of the Ancients* (p. 173, *sq.*), controverts the foregoing opinion, as being founded on a misapprehension of the passages in the ancient writers which have been supposed to prove it. He maintains that the

cables, instead of being applied lengthways, were drawn around the middle at right angles to the ship, and not parallel to it.[3] The other mode, he says, "must have been as impracticable as it would have been unavailing for the purpose of strengthening the ship." Luke states a fact simply in relation to this matter; he does not describe the mode. The question, therefore, is one of archæological interest merely; it does not affect the writer's accuracy. —**Lest they should fall into,** etc., **lest they should be stranded upon the Syrtis.** The verb literally means *to fall out—i. e.* from the sea or deep water upon the land or rocks. (Comp. vv. 26, 29.) Syrtis Major is here meant, which was on the coast of Africa, southwest from Crete. This gulf was an object of great dread to mariners, on account of its dangerous shoals. The other Syrtis was too far to the west to have been the one to which they would feel exposed in their present situation. Some have taken *Syrtis* to denote a *sand-bank* near Claude; but, as any such bank there must have been comparatively unknown, the writer with that allusion would more naturally have left out the article.—**Strake sail,** or **having lowered the sail.** The word rendered *sail* (σκεῦος) is indefinite, and may be applied to almost any of the ship's appurtenances, as sails, masts, anchors, and the like. Many have supposed it to refer here to the mast, or, if there was more than one in this case, to the principal mast; but it would seem to put that supposition out of the question that, according to all probability, the masts of the larger sailing-ships among the ancients were not movable, like those of the smaller vessels, but were fixed in their position, and would require to be cut away—a mode of removal which the accompanying participle shows could not have been adopted in the present instance. The surprising opinion of some, that [the part here referred to] is the anchor, is contradicted by the following **so were driven.** Of the other applications of the word, the only one which the circumstances of the

---

[1] Some suppose that Horace alludes to this practice in *Od.*, 1. 14. 6: "Sine funibus Vix durare carinæ Possint imperiosius Æquor." I was once explaining this passage to a college class according to that view, when one of the members who had been at sea stated that he himself had assisted in such an operation on board a vessel approaching our own coast.

[2] This is quoted from the *Dictionary of Greek and Roman Antiquities*, Art. "Ships." The account rests on Boeckh's authority. The writer of the article on "Navis" in Pauly's *Real-Encyclopädie der classischen Alter-thumswissenschaft* follows the same authority.

[3] The mode of executing this manœuvre, as I am informed, or at least one mode, is to sink the ropes over the prow, and then draw them toward the middle of the ship, fastening the ends on deck.

18 And we being exceedingly tossed with a tempest, the next *day* they lightened the ship;

18 gear, and so were driven. And as we labored exceedingly with the storm, the next day they

ship at this juncture naturally suggest is that it refers to the sail. It is not certain how we are to take the article here. It leads us to think most directly, perhaps, of the large, square sail which was attached to the principal mast. The ancients had vessels with one, two, and three masts.[1] **The** would then point out that sail by way of eminence. The presumption is that if the ship carried other sails, as cannot well be doubted, they had taken them down before this; and now, having lowered the only one which they had continued to use, they let the vessel "scud under bare poles." This is the general view of the meaning. It would follow from this that the wind must have changed its direction before they were wrecked on Melita; for some thirteen days elapsed before that event, during which the storm continued to rage, and within that time, had they been constantly driven before a northeast wind, they must have realized their fear of being stranded on the African coast.—But an eastern gale in the Levant, at this season of the year, is apt to be lasting; the wind maintains itself, though with unequal violence, for a considerable time in the same quarter. Professor Newman of the London University states the following fact[2] in his own experience: "We sailed from Larnica, in Cyprus, in a small Neapolitan ship with a Turkish crew on the 2d of December, 1830. We were bound for Latika, in Syria, the course almost due east, but were driven back and forced to take refuge in the port of Famagousta, the ancient Salamis. Here we remained wind-bound for days. Owing to our frequent remonstrances, the captain sailed three times, but was always driven back, and once after encountering very heavy seas and no small danger. It was finally the 1st of January, if my memory does not deceive me, when we reached the Syrian coast." It was probably such a gale which Paul's ship encountered— that is, a series of gales from the east, but not a constant hurricane; for the seamen were able to anchor and to let down their boat, and a part of the crew to attempt to escape in it to the shore. If, then, we assume that the wind blew from the same point during the continuance of the storm, we must suppose that they adopted some precaution against being driven upon the African coast, which Luke does not mention,

although his narrative may imply it. The only such precaution, according to the opinion of nautical men, which they could have adopted in their circumstances, was to *lie-to*—*i. e.* turn the head of the vessel as near to the wind as possible, and at the same time keep as much sail spread as they could carry in so severe a gale. For this purpose they would need the principal sail; and the sail lowered is most likely to have been the sail above it—*i. e.* the topsail, or *supparum*, as the Romans termed it. By the adoption of these means they would avoid the shore on which they were so fearful of being cast, and drift in the direction of the island on which they were finally wrecked. *The*, according to this supposition, would refer to the sail as definite in the conceptions of the writer, or as presumptively well known to the reader.—**So were driven, thus** (*i. e.* with the ship undergirded, and with the mainsail lowered, or, it may be, with the topsail lowered and the stormsail set) **they were borne on** at the mercy of the elements. Here closes the account of the first fearful day.

18. And we, etc., **now we being violently tempest-tossed.—On the following day**—*i. e.* after their attempt to reach the port of Phœnix. The night brought to them no relief. The return of day disclosed to them new dangers. The precaution of undergirding had accomplished less than they hoped. It was evident that the ship must be lightened or founder at sea. Their next step, therefore, was to try the effect of this measure.—**Lightened the ship, proceeded to throw overboard,** is one of the sea-phrases which Julius Pollux mentions as used by the ancients to denote the lightening of a ship at sea. The noun omits the article, because they cast out only a part of what the vessel contained. We are not told what it was that they sacrificed at this time; it may have been their supernumerary spars and rigging, and some of the heavier and more accessible articles of merchandise with which the ship was laden. It appears from v. 38 that the bulk of the cargo consisted of wheat, and they reserved that until the last. The seamen in the vessel in which Jonah embarked had recourse to the same expedient. "There was a mighty tempest in the sea, so that the ship was like to be broken. Then the mariners were

---

[1] See Pauly's *Real-Encyklopädie der classischen Alterthumswissenschaft*, vol. v. p. 463.
[2] Mentioned in Mr. Smith's letter alluded to on p. 297.

19 And the third *day* ^awe cast out with our own hands the tackling of the ship.
20 And when neither sun nor stars in many days appeared, and no small tempest lay on *us*, all hope that we should be saved was then taken away.

19 began to throw *the freight* overboard; and the third day they cast out with their own hands the ¹tack-
20 ling of the ship. And when neither sun nor stars shone upon *us* for many days, and no small tempest lay on *us*, all hope that we should be saved was now

---

a Jon. 1 : 5.——1 Or, *furniture*

---

afraid, and cried every man unto his god, and cast forth the wares that were in the ship into the sea, to lighten it of them " (Jon. 1 : 4, 5).

19. The **third day** arrives, and the storm has not abated. They are obliged to lighten the ship still more. This renewed necessity appears to indicate that the ship was in a leaking condition, and that the danger from this cause was becoming more and more imminent. It was one of the great perils to which ancient vessels were exposed. Their style of architecture was inferior to that of modern vessels; they were soon shattered in a storm, "sprang leaks" more easily, and had fewer means for repairing the injury. " In the accounts of shipwrecks that have come down to us from ancient times, the loss of the ship must in a great number of instances be ascribed to this cause. Josephus tells us that on his voyage to Italy the ship sunk in the midst of the Adriatic Sea (βαπτισθέντος γὰρ ἡμῶν τοῦ πλοίου κατὰ μέσον τὸν 'Αδρίαν). He and some of his companions saved themselves by swimming; the ship, therefore, did not go down during the gale, but in consequence of the damage she sustained during its continuance. One of St. Paul's shipwrecks must have taken place under the same circumstances; for he tells us, A day and a night I have been in the deep (2 Cor. 11 : 25), supported, no doubt, on spars or fragments of the wreck. In Virgil's description of the casualties of the ships of Æneas, some are driven on rocks; others, on quicksands ; but

'Iaxis laterum compagibus *omnes*
Accipiunt inimicum imbrem, remisque fatiscunt.'¹

The fact that the ships of the ancients were provided with *hypozomata*, or cables ready fitted for undergirding, as a necessary part of their stores, proves how liable they were to such casualties." It is easy to see, therefore, what must have been the fate of Paul's ship had they not discovered land so providentially : she must have foundered at sea and all on board have perished. — **We cast out with our hands the furniture of the ship,** such as tables, beds, chests, and the like (Mey., De Wet., Lng., Alf., Wdsth.). The self-inflicted loss in this case (αὐτόχειρες), which affected so much the

personal convenience of each one, showed how urgent was the danger. Yet **furniture,** or **tackling** (σκευήν), is a very doubtful word. Some understand it of the masts, yards, sails, and other equipments of the ship similar to these. With this interpretation, we must regard the term as applying to that class of objects in a general way ; for we see from v. 29 that they retained at least some of their anchors, and from v. 44 that at the last moment they had boards and spars at command to assist them in reaching the shore. According to some, again, as Wetstein, Kuinoel, Winer, it denotes the baggage of the passengers. **With our own hands** is more significant with that sense, but **ship,** as genitive of the container, *the baggage on board the ship,* is very harsh. The expression means, says Smith, "the mainyard, an immense spar, probably as long as the ship, and which would require the united efforts of passengers and crew to launch overboard. The relief which a ship would thus experience would be of the same kind as in a modern ship when the guns are thrown overboard."—Some read **we cast out ;** some, *they cast out.* Tischendorf retains the former, as in T. R. [Not in his 8th ed., which gives the third person plural of the verb, as do Treg., West. and Hort, the Anglo-Am. Revisers, according to preponderating evidence.—A. H.] Meyer is too positive that the first person betrays its origin in *with our own hands* (αὐτόχειρες). [The critical note in Meyer's last ed. reads : " *They cast out*, approved by Griesb., adopted by Lach. and Born., after A B C ℵ, min. vulg. The recepta is *we cast out*. As this might just as easily be inserted on account of αὐτόχειρες, as the third pl. on account of ἐποιοῦντο, the preponderance of witnesses has alone to decide, and that in favor of the third person." Yet in his note on the verse he still says : " *With our own hands* gives to the description a sad vividness," etc.—A. H.]

20. Now neither sun nor stars shining upon us for many days, and a storm not slight pressing upon us. Observe the force of the compounds. The absence of the sun and stars increased their danger, since it deprived them of their only means of observa-

---

¹ [" The joints of their sides being loosed, all the ships receive the hostile flood and gape with chinks."]

21 But after long abstinence, Paul stood forth in the midst of them, and said, Sirs, ye should have hearkened unto me, and not have loosed from Crete, and to have gained this harm and loss.

22 And now I exhort you to be of good cheer: for there shall be no loss of *any man's* life among you, but of the ship.

23 ªFor there stood by me this night the angel of God, whose I am, and ᵇwhom I serve,

24 Saying, Fear not, Paul; thou must be brought be-

21 taken away. And when they had been long without food, then Paul stood forth in the midst of them, and said, Sirs, ye should have hearkened unto me, and not have set sail from Crete, and have gotten this injury and loss. And now I exhort you

22 to be of good cheer: for there shall be no loss of

23 life among you, but *only* of the ship. For there stood by me this night an angel of the God whose

24 I am, whom also I serve, saying, Fear not, Paul;

---

a ch. 23 : 11....*b* Dan. 6 : 16 ; Rom. 1 : 9 ; 2 Tim. 1 : 3.

---

tion. The Greeks and Romans, in the most improved state of navigation among them, were reluctant to venture out to sea beyond the sight of land. During the day they kept the high lands on shore, or some island, in view, to direct them, and at night depended, for the same purpose, on the position, the rising and setting, of different stars (*Dict. of Antt.*, Art. "Ship"). The *many* or *several days* include, probably, the three days which have been mentioned, but how many of the eleven days which followed (v. 27) before the final disaster is uncertain. We do not know how long the interval was between Paul's address and that event. The expression would be inappropriate, however, unless it comprehended the greater part of them.—**Then**—*i. e. for the future*, thenceforth (λοιπόν). They relinquish now their last hope of escape; destruction seemed to be\ inevitable. In their condition they must have felt that their only resource was to run the vessel ashore. But the state of the weather rendered it impossible for them to distinguish in what direction the shore lay; and thus they were unable to make the only further effort for their preservation which was left to them. In judging of the dangers which menaced them, we must take into account the state of the vessel, as well as the violence of the storm. The verb rendered **was taken away** means was utterly taken away.—*Of being saved* depends on **hope** as a genitive construction. (Comp. 14 : 9.)

21–26. THE APOSTLE CHEERS THEM WITH THE HOPE OF DELIVERANCE.

21. Long abstinence denotes *much abstinence* as to time and degree—*i. e.* both long-continued and severe, but not entire. (See on v. 33.) This abstinence was not owing to their want of provisions (see v. 33), but was the effect—in part, at least—of their fears and dejection of mind (see vs. 22, 36); and in part, also, of the difficulty of preparing food under such circumstances, and of the constant requisition made upon them for labor. "The hardships which the crew endured during a gale of such continuance, and their exhaustion from labor

at the pumps, and hunger, may be imagined, but are not described."—**You ought** (past, as a violated duty), **having obeyed me,** because the counsel was wise, not authoritative as from an apostle.—**And not to have set sail.** The verb (ἀνάγεσθαι) is present, because they were still at sea. Note the aorist which follows.— Paul recalls to mind their former mistake in disregarding his advice, not to reproach them, but in order to show his claim to their confidence with reference to the present communication. (μέν is unattended here by any responding δέ).—**And to have escaped**—lit. **gained** —**this violence and loss.** (See on v. 10.) *Lucrari* was used in the same manner. An evil shunned is a gain as well as a good secured. As *violence* refers to something actually suffered, it cannot mean *harm* to their persons (Cony. and Hws.); for the exemption from such injury, of which Paul assures them in the next verse, and still more emphatically in v. 34, applies, undoubtedly, to the whole voyage.

22. But of the ship. There shall be no loss **except of the ship.** This limitation qualifies, not the entire clause which precedes, but only **there shall be no loss,** which we are to repeat before the words here. *Only* (μόνον) would have marked the connection more precisely. (See W. § 66. 1. e.) As to the rest, compare the remarks on *I perceive*, in v. 10.

23. Stood by me. Whether *the angel* appeared to the apostle in a vision or a dream, the mode of statement does not enable us to decide. (See on 16 : 9.)—**This night,** just passed, or that which was passing. Most think it probable that Paul did not communicate the revelation to those in the ship until the return of day.—**Whose I am,** to whom I belong as his property; in other words, whose servant I am. —**Whom also I worship,** to whom I offer religious service and homage. This verb refers to external acts of worship, and not to religious life in general, except' as the latter may be a concomitant of the former.

24. Thou must be brought, etc., or **thou must stand, before Cæsar.** (See on 23 : 11.)

bre Cæsar: and, lo, God hath given thee all them that
sail with thee.
25 Wherefore, sirs, be of good cheer: *a*for I believe
God, that it shall be even as it was told me.
26 Howbeit *b*we must be *cast* upon a certain island.
27 But when the fourteenth night was come, as we
were driven up and down in Adria, about midnight
the shipmen deemed that they drew near to some
country;

thou must stand before Cæsar: and lo, God hath
25 granted thee all them that sail with thee. Wherefore, sirs, be of good cheer: for I believe God, that
it shall be even so as it hath been spoken unto me
26 Howbeit we must be cast upon a certain island.
27 But when the fourteenth night was come, as we
were driven to and fro in the *sea of* Adria, about
midnight the sailors surmised that they were draw-

---

a Luke 1 : 45 ; Rom. 4 : 20, 21 ; 2 Tim. 1 : 12....*b* ch. 28 : 1.

To remind the apostle of this still unfulfilled
purpose of God was the same thing as to assure
him that he would escape the present danger.—
**God has given to thee all those who sail
with thee.** They should be preserved for his
sake. No one supposes the declaration here to
affirm less than this. Many think that it implies also that Paul had prayed for the safety
of those in the ship with him, and that he receives now the assurance that his prayer in
their behalf has prevailed. " For I hope," says
Paul in Philem. 22, " that through your prayers
I shall be given unto you." Such is the view of
Calv., Bng., Olsh., De Wet., Lange, and others.
Bengel remarks here : " Facilius multi mali cum
paucis piis servantur, quam unus pius cum
multis reis perit. Navi huic similis mundus "
[" More easy is it that many of the wicked are
saved with one pious man than that one pious
man perishes with many of the guilty. The
world is like this ship "].

25. I believe, etc. It is evident from v. 32
that the apostle had acquired a strong ascend-
ency over the minds of the passengers in the
ship, if not of the others. He could very properly, therefore, urge his own confidence in God
as a reason **(for)** why they should dismiss their
fears **(be of good cheer)**—so far, at least, as
the preservation of their lives was concerned.

26. Upon a certain island—*i. e.* **upon
some island.** More than this was not revealed to him. Paul was as ignorant of the
name of the place where they were wrecked
as the rest of them. (See v. 39.)—**Howbeit**
(= *but*) (δέ) opposes what they must suffer to
what they would escape. — **Must** in such a
communication may represent the event as
not merely certain, but certain because it was
fixed by the divine purpose.—**Be cast away.**
(See the remark on v. 17.)

27–32. THE DISCOVERY OF LAND, AND
THE FRUSTRATED ATTEMPT OF THE
MARINERS TO DESERT THE SHIP.

27. The fourteenth night, since their departure from Fair Havens.—**As we were borne
through** (sc. the waters; comp. v. 5) **in the
Adriatic.** They may have been driven hither
and thither or onward in one direction ; the
participle is indefinite. Mr. Smith's calculation

assumes a uniform drift toward Melita. It has
been said that the modern Malta lies too far
south to be embraced in the sea so designated.
The statement is erroneous. In its restricted
sense the Adriatic was the sea between Italy
and Greece, but in a wider sense it comprehended also the Ionian Sea around Sicily, near
which was Melita. (Forbg., *Handb.*, ii. p. 19 ;
Win., *Realw.*, i. p. 23.) The later Greek and
Roman writers, as Biscoe has shown, gave the
name to the entire sea as far south as Africa.
—**The shipmen,** etc., **the mariners suspected that some land was approaching
them.** As Mr. Smith remarks, Luke uses here
the graphic language of seamen, to whom the
ship is the principal object, whilst the land
rises and sinks, nears and recedes. The narrator does not state on what ground they suspected their vicinity to the land. It was, no
doubt, the noise of the breakers. This is usually the first notice of their danger which
mariners have in coming upon a coast in a
dark night. This circumstance furnishes rea-
sen for believing that the traditional scene of
the shipwreck is the actual one. It is impossible to enter St. Paul's Bay from the east without passing near the point of Koura ; and while
the land there, as navigators inform us, is too
low to be seen in a stormy night, the breakers
can be heard at a considerable distance, and in
a north-easterly gale are so violent as to form
on charts the distinctive feature of that headland. On the 10th of August, 1810, the British
frigate Lively fell upon these breakers in a dark
night, and was lost. The quartermaster, who
first observed them, stated in his evidence at
the court-martial that at the distance of a
quarter of a mile the land could not be seen,
but that he saw the surf on the shore.—The
distance from Claude to the point of Koura
is four hundred seventy-six and six-tenths
miles. Luke's narrative allows a fraction over
thirteen days for the performance of this voyage. It must have occupied a day, or the greater
part of a day, to have reached Claude after they
left Fair Havens. (See vv. 13–16.) According
to the judgment of experienced seamen, " the
mean rate of drift of a ship circumstanced like
that of Paul " (*i. e.* working its way in such a

28 And sounded, and found it twenty fathoms: and when they had gone a little further, they sounded again, and found it fifteen fathoms.
29 Then fearing lest we should have fallen upon rocks, they cast four anchors out of the stern, and wished for the day.

28 ing near to some country; and they sounded, and found twenty fathoms: and after a little space, they
29 sounded again, and found fifteen fathoms. And fearing lest haply we should be cast ashore on rocky ground, they let go four anchors from the stern, and

---

direction in a gale of moderate severity, against a north-east wind) would be thirty-six and a half miles in twenty-four hours. "Hence, according to these calculations," says Mr. Smith (p. 122, *sq.*), "a ship starting late in the evening from Claude would, by midnight on the fourteenth, be less than three miles from the entrance of St. Paul's Bay. I admit that a coincidence so very close as this is, is to a certain extent accidental; but it is an accident which could not have happened had there been any great inaccuracy on the part of the author of the narrative with regard to the numerous incidents upon which the calculations are founded, or had the ship been wrecked anywhere but at Malta."

28. And when they had gone a little further. There was but a short distance, it will be observed, between the two soundings; and the rate of decrease in the depth of the water—viz. first **twenty fathoms,** and then **fifteen**—is such as would not be found to exist on every coast. It is said that a vessel approaching Malta from the same direction finds the same soundings at the present day.—The Greek word meaning **fathom** (ὀργυιά, from ὀρέγω, *to stretch*) signifies "the extension of the hands with the breadth of the breast" (*Etym. Magn.*).

29. Upon rocks—lit. **upon rough**—*i. e. rocky*—**places.** Their apprehension arose, not from what they saw, but from what they had reason to fear in a dark night on an unknown coast. The alarm was well founded; for "the fifteen-fathom depth here is as nearly as possible a quarter of a mile only from the shore, which is girt with mural precipices, and upon which the sea must have been breaking with great violence."—**They cast,** etc., or **having cast, out four anchors from the stern.** "To anchor successfully in a gale of wind on a lee-shore requires holding-ground of extraordinary tenacity. In St. Paul's Bay, the traditional locality of the shipwreck, the anchorage is thus described in the *Sailing Directions:* "The harbor of St. Paul is open to easterly and north-east winds. It is, notwithstanding, safe for small ships, the ground generally being very good; and while the cables hold there is no danger, *as the anchors will never start.*'" The ancient vessels did not carry, in general, so

large anchors as those which we employ; and hence they had often a greater number. Athenæus mentions a ship which had eight iron anchors. Paul's ship, as we see from the next verse, had other anchors besides those which were dropped from the stern. One object of anchoring in that way was to arrest the progress of the ship more speedily. No time was to be lost, as they knew not that they might not founder the next moment upon the shoals where the breakers were dashing. Had they anchored by the bow, we are told, there was reason for apprehending that the vessel would swing round and strike upon the rocks. The ancient ships were so constructed that they could anchor readily by the prow or the stern, as circumstances might require. Another advantage of the course here taken was that the head of the vessel was turned toward the land, which was their best position for running her ashore. That purpose they had, no doubt, formed already. "By cutting away the anchors (τὰς ἀγκύρας περιελόντες), loosing the bands of the rudders (ἀνέντες τὰς ζευκτηρίας), and hoisting the *artemon* (ἐπάραντες τὸν ἀρτέμονα)—all of which could be done simultaneously—the ship was immediately under command, and could be directed with precision to any part of the shore which offered any prospect of safety."—The English ships-of-war were anchored by the stern in the battle of Copenhagen, and rendered very effective service in that position. Conybeare and Howson mention the singular fact that Lord Nelson stated after the battle that he was led to adopt that plan because he had just been reading this twenty-seventh chapter of the Acts.—**They wished for day,** or, lit., **desired that day might come.** The remark is full of significance. In the darkness of the night they could not tell the full extent of the dangers which surrounded them. They must have longed for returning day on that account. In the mean time it must have been difficult to preserve a vessel which had been so long tempest-tossed from sinking. Their only chance of escape was to strand the ship as soon as the light enabled them to select a place which admitted of it. It is evident that every moment's delay must have been one of fearful suspense, as well as of peril, to them.

30 And as the shipmen were about to flee out of the ship, when they had let down the boat into the sea, under color as though they would have cast anchors out of the foreship,
31 Paul said to the centurion and to the soldiers, Except these abide in the ship, ye cannot be saved.
32 Then the soldiers cut off the ropes of the boat, and let her fall off.
33 And while the day was coming on, Paul besought *them* all to take meat, saying, This day is the fourteenth day that ye have tarried and continued fasting, having taken nothing.
34 Wherefore I pray you to take *some* meat: for this is for your health: for *a* there shall not an hair fall from the head of any of you.

30 [1] wished for the day. And as the sailors were seeking to flee out of the ship, and had lowered the boat into the sea, under color as though they would lay out anchors from the foreship, Paul said to the centurion and to the soldiers, Except these abide in the ship, ye cannot be saved. Then the soldiers cut away the ropes of the boat, and let her fall off
33 And while the day was coming on, Paul besought them all to take some food, saying, This day is the fourteenth day that ye wait and continue fasting, having taken nothing. Wherefore I beseech you to take some food: for this is for your safety: for there shall not a hair perish from the head of any

30. And as the shipmen, etc. This ungenerous attempt of the seamen to escape confirms the remark before made—that the ship was probably in so shattered a state as to render it uncertain whether it could outride the storm until morning. They may have had another motive for the act. The shore might prove to be one on which they could not drive the vessel with any hope of safety, and they may have deemed it more prudent to trust themselves to the boat than to remain and await the issue of that uncertainty.—**When they had let down,** etc., **having lowered down, the boat,** which they had previously hoisted on board. (See vv. 16, 17.)--**Out of the foreship,** or **from the prow,** since it was nearer thence to the shore, and [it] was there only that they could pretend to need anchors, the stern being already secure.—**Cast anchors,** not **to cast out** (E. V.), but **stretch out, anchors.** The idea of extending the cables runs into that of carrying out and dropping the anchors. Favored by the darkness, and under color of the pretext assumed, they would have accomplished their object, had not Paul's watchful eye penetrated their design.

31. Said to the centurion, etc. Paul addressed himself to **the centurion and the soldiers,** because the officers of the ship were implicated in the plot, or, in consequence of the general desertion, had no longer any power to enforce their orders. The soldiers are those who had charge of the different prisoners (v. 1), subject, probably, to the command of the centurion who had the particular care of the apostle.—**These,** viz. the mariners.—**Ye,** or **you, cannot be saved.** The pronoun is emphatic. The soldiers were destitute of the skill which the management of the ship required. It could not be brought successfully to land without the help of the mariners. This remark of Paul proves that the plan to abandon the vessel was

not confined to a portion of the crew, but was a general one.

32. Cut off the ropes of the boat, which fastened it to the vessel; not those by which they were lowering it, as that was already done (v. 30). The short sword of the soldiers furnished a ready instrument for the summary blow.—**Let her**—*i.e.* the boat—or **let it, fall off** (*i. e.* from the side of the vessel), go adrift. The next billow may have swamped the frail craft.

33–35. PAUL ASSURES THEM AGAIN THAT THEIR LIVES WOULD BE SAVED.

33. And while the day, etc., or **now until it should be day**—*i. e.* in the interval between the midnight mentioned in v. 27 and the subsequent morning.—**This day** is appositional in sense with **day** in the first clause.—**Tarried**—lit. **waiting**—for the cessation of the storm (De Wet.).—**And continued fasting,** rather **ye continue fasting,** where the adjective supplies the place of a participle. (W. § 45. 4.)—**Having taken nothing,** adequate to their proper nourishment, no regular food, during all this time. (See v. 21.) "Appian," says Doddridge, "speaks of an army which for twenty days together had neither food nor sleep; by which he must mean that they neither made full meals nor slept whole nights together. The same interpretation must be given to this phrase." The apostle's language could not be mistaken by those to whom it was addressed. (Comp. v. 21.)

34. For this (viz. that they should partake of food) **is important for your preservation.** (For πρός (*from*) with this sense, see W. § 47. 5. f.) [" *For your deliverance,* strictly, *is on the side,* as it were, *of your deliverance.*"— A. H.] They would have to submit to much fatigue and labor before they reached the shore, and needed, therefore, to recruit their strength. —**For there shall not a hair fail,** etc. This was a proverbial expression, employed to convey an assurance of entire safety. (See 1 Kings 1 : 52; Luke 21 : 18.)

35 And when he had thus spoken, he took bread, and *gave thanks to God in presence of them all: and when he had broken *it*, he began to eat.
36 Then were they all of good cheer, and they also took *some* meat.
37 And we were in all in the ship two hundred three-score and sixteen *b*souls.
38 And when they had eaten enough, they lightened the ship, and cast out the wheat into the sea.

35 of you. And when he had said this, and had taken bread, he gave thanks to God in the presence of all:
36 and he brake it, and began to eat. Then were they all of good cheer, and themselves also took food.
37 And we were in all in the ship two hundred three-
38 score and sixteen souls. And when they had eaten enough, they lightened the ship, throwing out the

a 1 Sam. 9 : 13 ; Matt. 15 : 36 ; Mark 8 : 6 ; John 6 : 11 ; 1 Tim. 4 : 3, 4....*b* ch. 2 : 41 ; 7 : 14 ; Rom. 13 : 1 ; 1 Pet. 3 : 20.

35. Bread. This word, by a Hebraistic usage, often signifies *food* in the New Testament; but **broken,** which follows, appears to exclude that sense here. Yet the present meal had, no doubt, its other accompaniments, the bread only being mentioned because that, according to the Hebrew custom, was broken and distributed among the guests after the giving of thanks. The apostle performed on this occasion the usual office of the head of a Hebrew family. Olshausen expresses the fanciful opinion—as it seems to me—that the Christians among them regarded this act as commemorative of the Lord's Supper, though the others did not understand Paul's design. The language employed here, it is true, more frequently describes that ordinance, but it is used also of an ordinary meal. (See Luke 24 : 30.)
36-38. THEY PARTAKE OF FOOD AND AGAIN LIGHTEN THE SHIP.
36. Then, etc.—lit. **having—all now become cheerful.** It is not accidental that the writer makes this remark in connection with **they took some meat.** In their despair they had lost their inclination to eat; but the return of hope brought with it a keener sense of their wants, and they could now think of satisfying their hunger. (See on vv. 21, 33.) — **They also themselves** as well as he. The apostle had set them the example (**began to eat**), and they all followed it.
37. The emphatic **all,** in v. 36, leads the writer to specify the number.—**All the souls together.** For this adverbial use of *all* (πᾶς), see the note on 19 : 7. For this use of **souls,** see on 2 : 41.—**Two hundred and seventy-six.** The number of persons on board shows that the vessel must have been one of the larger size. In the reign of Commodus one of the Alexandrian wheat-ships was driven by stress of weather into the Piræus, and excited great curiosity on the part of the Athenians. Lucian visited this vessel, and has laid the scene of one of his Dialogues (πλοῖον ἢ εὐχαί) on board of her. From the information furnished by him it has been estimated that the keel of this ship was about one hundred feet in length, and that she would measure between eleven and twelve hundred tons. Her dimensions,

therefore, although inferior to those of many modern vessels, " were quite equal to those of the largest class of modern merchantmen." Luke's ship was engaged in the same commerce (being, to use Lucian's language, *one of the ships transporting grain from Egypt into Italy*); and we have no reason to be surprised at her containing such a number of men. (See further on v. 6.)
38. Lightened the ship. Among the nautical terms of Julius Pollux we find *to lighten the ship.* (See on v. 18.) Luke states merely the fact that *they lightened the ship* again (it is the third time), but gives no explanation of it. The object may have been to diminish the depth of water which the ship drew, so as to enable them to approach nearer to the shore before striking. It has been conjectured, also, that the vessel may have been leaking so fast that the measure was necessary, in order to keep her from sinking. — **Casting out the wheat, or grain,** corn, since the term has frequently that wider sense. As suggested on v. 18, we are to understand here that they threw into the sea the grain which constituted the cargo, or the bulk of the cargo, which the ship carried. The fact that the ship belonged to Alexandria is presumptive proof that she was loaded with grain, since that was the principal commodity exported from Egypt to Italy. The explicit notice here that they lightened the ship by throwing the grain into the sea harmonizes with that presumption and tends to confirm it. Some have thought that **wheat** may denote the ship's provisions; but these would have consisted of various different articles, and would not naturally be described by so specific a term as this. The connection, which has been said to favor the opinion last stated, agrees equally well with the other. Having their hopes revived by the spectacle of Paul's undisturbed serenity and by his animating address, and being reinvigorated after so long a fast by the food of which they had partaken, they were now in a condition both of mind and body to address themselves to the labors which their safety required. This view, therefore, places their lightening of the ship in a perfectly natural connection with the circum-

39 And when it was day, they knew not the land:
but they discovered a certain creek with a shore, into
the which they were minded, if it were possible, to
thrust in the ship.

40 And when they had taken up the anchors, they
committed *themselves* unto the sea, and loosed the rud-

39 wheat into the sea. And when it was day, they
knew not the land: but they perceived a certain
bay with a beach, and they took counsel whether
40 they could ¹drive the ship upon it. And casting off
the anchors, they left them in the sea, at the same

---

1 Some ancient authorities read *bring the ship safe to shore.*

---

stances related just before. In addition to this,
as Hemsen urges, their remaining stock of provisions, after so protracted a voyage, must have
been already so reduced that it could have had
little or no effect on the ship whether they were
thrown away or retained.—Mr. Blunt (p. 326)
has very properly called attention to the manner in which the narrative discloses to us the
nature of the ship's cargo. In the fifth verse
we are informed that the vessel "into which
the centurion removed Paul and the other
prisoners at Myra belonged to *Alexandria* and
was *sailing into Italy.* From the tenth verse we
learn that it was a merchant-vessel, for mention
is made of its *lading,* but the nature of the lading is not *directly* stated. In this verse, at a distance of some thirty verses from the last, we find,
by the merest chance, of what its cargo consisted.
The freight was naturally enough kept till it
could be kept no longer, and then we discover for
the first time that it was *wheat*—the very article
which such vessels were accustomed to carry
from Egypt to Italy. These notices, so detached
from each other, tell a continuous story, but it
is not perceived till they are brought together.
The circumstances drop out one by one in the
course of the narrative, unarranged, unpre-
meditated, thoroughly incidental; so that the
chapter might be read twenty times and their
agreement with one another and with contemporary history be still overlooked."

**39-44. THE SHIPWRECK.—THOSE ON
BOARD ESCAPE TO THE SHORE BY
SWIMMING, OR ON FRAGMENTS OF THE
VESSEL.**

39. They knew not, or **they recognized
not, the land** within view. The day has
dawned, and they could now distinguish it.
It has appeared to some surprising that none
of those on board should have known a place
with which those at least who were accustomed
to the sea might be expected to have been so
well acquainted. The answer is that the scene
of the shipwreck was remote from the principal
harbor, and, as those who have been on the
spot testify, distinguished by no marked feature
which would render it known even to a native,

if he came unexpectedly upon it. The bay so
justly known as St. Paul's Bay is at the north-
west extremity of the island, and is formed by
the main shore on the south, and the island of
Salmonetta on the north. It extends from east
to west, two miles long and one broad at the
entrance, and at the inner end is nearly land-
locked on three sides. It is several miles north
of Valetta, the famous rock-bound harbor of
Malta.¹ **They perceived a certain inlet,**
creek, *having a shore,* one open or smooth (see
on 21 : 5), on which they could run the ship
with a hope of saving their lives. "Luke uses
here the correct hydrographical term." The
remark implies that the coast generally was
unsafe for such an attempt. The present con-
formation of the coast on that side of Malta
confirms Luke's accuracy in this particular.
The shore there presents an unbroken chain
of rocks, interrupted at only two points.—
**Into which they determined, if they
could, to thrust forth** (*i. e.* from the sea),
to drive ashore, **the ship.** (For ἐξῶσαι, from
ἐξωθέω, see W. § 15 ; K. § 165. 7.) The wind must
have forced them to the west side of the bay,
which is rocky, but has two creeks. One of
these, Mestara Valley, has a shore. The other
has no longer a sandy beach, but must have
had one formerly, which has evidently been
worn away by the action of the sea. The vessel grounded (v. 41) before they reached the
point on shore at which they aimed, though
they may have entered the creek.

40. And when, etc., may be translated
**and having entirely cut away the anchors
they abandoned them unto the sea.** On
this force of the preposition in the Greek participle (περιελόντες), comp. *was taken away* (περιη-
ρεῖτο), in v. 20. It has been referred to the position of the anchors as being around the ship;
but they had all been dropped from the stern
(v. 29), and, as the strain would be mainly in one
direction, they would not be likely to be found
on different sides of the vessel. Our English
translators followed the Vulgate in their inac-
curate version of this clause.—**At the same
time having unfastened the bands of the**

---

1 Smith's chart of St. Paul's Bay is copied in Conybeare and Howson, with the necessary explanations. I had
the gratification of a hurried visit to this locality on my way to Alexandria. It appeared to me to fulfil every
condition of the narrative as the scene of the apostle's shipwreck.

der bands, and hoised up the mainsail to the wind, and made toward shore.

41 And falling into a place where two seas met, *they ran the ship aground; and the forepart stuck fast, and remained unmoveable, but the hinder part was broken with the violence of the waves.

time loosing the bands of the rudders; and hoisting up the foresail to the wind, they made for the beach.

41 But lighting upon a place where two seas met, they ran the vessel aground; and the foreship struck and remained unmoveable, but the stern began to break

a 2 Cor. 11 : 25.

rudders. Most of the ancient vessels were furnished with two rudders. No sea-going vessel had less than two, although small boats and river-craft, such as those on the Nile, were sometimes steered by one. The *rudders* (πηδάλια) were more like oars or paddles than our modern helm. They were attached to the stern, one on each quarter, distinguished as the right and the left rudder. In the larger ships the extremities of the rudders were joined by a pole, which was moved by one man and kept the rudders always parallel. (See *Dict. of Antt.,* Art. " Gubernaculum.") When a vessel was anchored by the stern, as was the case here, it would be necessary to lift the rudders out of the water and to secure them by bands. These bands it would be necessary to unfasten when the ship was again got under weigh. (ἀνέντες is the second aorist participle in the active from ἀνίημι. K. § 180. See on 16 : 26.)—**Having hoisted the foresail to the wind.** The word rendered *foresail* (ἀρτέμων) has been taken by different writers as the name of almost every sail which a vessel carries—*e. g.* mainsail, topsail, jib, etc. We have no ancient definition of the term which throws any certain light upon its meaning. It passed into some of the modern languages, where it is variously applied, but occurs in no ancient Greek author out of Luke's account of this voyage. Most commentators, without any attempt to substantiate their opinion, put it down as the " mainsail." The nautical argument is said to be in favor of the foresail—*i. e.* the sail attached to the mast nearest the prow, or, if there was but one mast, fixed to a spar or yard near the prow. "As the ancients depended for speed chiefly upon one principal sail, an appendage or additional sail at the bow of the ship was required for the purpose of directing the vessel when in the act of putting about; for, although there could be no difficulty in bringing the ship's head to the wind with the great sail alone, a small sail at the bow would be indispensable for making her 'pay off'—that is, bringing her head round; otherwise, she would acquire stern-way, and thereby endanger the rudders, if not the ship itself." The vessels on coins and in other an-

cient representations exhibit a sail of this description. With this sail raised, it is said that a ship situated like that of Paul would move toward the shore with more precision and velocity than with any other. " A sailor will at once see that the foresail was the best possible sail that could be set under the circumstances."

41. And having fallen into a place having two seas. This has been supposed by many commentators to have been a concealed shoal or sand-bank, formed by the action of two opposite currents. In the course of time such a bank, as is frequently the case at the mouth of rivers or near the shore, may have been worn away;[1] so that the absence of any such obstruction there at the present time decides nothing against that supposition. It has also been understood to have been a tongue of land or promontory, against the shores of which the sea beat strongly from opposite quarters. It is not stated that any projection exists there now to which Luke's description, if explained in that manner, would apply. Mr. Smith is of the opinion that **a place having two seas** may refer to the channel, not more than a hundred yards in breadth, which separates the small island Salmonetta from Malta, and which might very properly be called a place where "two seas meet," on account of the communication which it forms between the sea in the interior of the bay and the sea outside. He would place the scene of the shipwreck near that channel, and, according to the representation on his map, a little to the north of the place to which tradition has generally assigned it. The creek near here, at present without a beach (see v. 39), may be the one which they attempted to enter.— The final shock now ensues. **And the prow, sticking fast, remained immovable, but the stern was broken by the violence of the waves.** "This is a remarkable circumstance, which, but for the peculiar nature of the bottom of St. Paul's Bay, it would be difficult to account for. The rocks of Malta disintegrate into extremely minute particles of sand and clay, which when acted upon by the currents or surface agitation form a deposit of tenacious clay, but in still water, where these

[1] For examples of this, see Lyell's *Principles of Geology,* p. 285, *sq.* (8th ed.. 1850).

42 And the soldiers' counsel was to kill the prisoners, lest any of them should swim out, and escape. 43 But the centurion, willing to save Paul, kept them from *their* purpose; and commanded that they which could swim should cast *themselves* first *into the sea*, and get to land:

42 up by the violence *of the waves.* And the soldiers' counsel was to kill the prisoners, lest any *of them* 43 desiring to save Paul, stayed them from their purpose: and commanded that those who could swim should cast themselves overboard, and get first to

causes do not act, mud is formed; but it is only in the creeks where are no currents, and at such a depth as to be undisturbed by the waves, that the mud occurs. In Captain Smyth's chart of the bay the nearest soundings to the mud indicate a depth of about three fathoms, which is about what a large ship would draw. A ship, therefore, impelled by the force of a gale into a

infinitive. (W. § 44. 8; S. § 162. 3. 2.) Meyer, after Fritsche, never admits this use, but insists on *that* (ἵνα) as telic even here.—Of the rigor with which those were liable to be punished who were charged with the custody of prisoners, if the latter escaped from them in any way, we have had proof in 12 : 19 and 16 : 27.

43. It will be recollected that, according to

BAY OF ST. PAUL FROM THE SOUTH.

creek with a bottom such as has been described, would strike a bottom of mud, into which the fore-part would fix itself and be held fast, whilst the stern was exposed to the force of the waves. —Meyer defends **of the waves** (τῶν κυμάτων) with good reason against Tischendorf and others.

42. It is the soldiers who initiate this scheme, since they only, and not the mariners, were interested in the fate of the prisoners.—**Counsel,** better, **plan,** resolution, not *counsel* merely. (Comp. **purpose,** below.)—**To kill=that they should kill the prisoners** defines *plan,* and circumscribes the declarative or supplementary

the Roman custom, each of the prisoners was chained to a particular soldier, who was his keeper. As to the relation of these soldiers to the centurion, see on v. 31.—**Kept, or restrained, them from their purpose.** Thus it happened again (see v. 24) that Paul's companions were indebted to their connection with him for the preservation of their lives. **And** connects this clause with the next, because of their co-ordinate relation to **willing.**—The participle (ἀποῤῥίψαντας) translated **"cast themselves"** has a reciprocal sense.—**Get,** etc.— lit. **to go forth,** not from the ship, which is the force of *from* (ἀπό) in the participle just

44 And the rest, some on boards, and some on *broken pieces* of the ship. And so it came to pass, *a*that they escaped all safe to land.

44 the land: and the rest, some on planks, and some on *other* things from the ship. And so it came to pass that they all escaped safe to the land.

CHAPTER XXVIII.

AND when they were escaped, then they knew that *b*the island was called Melita.
2 And the *c*barbarous people shewed us no little kindness: for they kindled a fire, and received us

1 AND when we were escaped, then we knew that 2 the island was called ¹Melita. And the barbarians showed us no common kindness: for they kindled a

a ver. 22....*b* ch. 27 : 26....*c* Rom. 1 : 14 ; 1 Cor. 14 : 11 ; Col. 3 : 11.——1 Some ancient authorities read *Melitene.*

before, but from the sea (**upon,** or **to, the land,** ἐπὶ τὴν γῆν).

44. The rest is the subject of *to go forth* (E. V. **get**), repeated from the preceding clause. —**Upon boards,** such, probably, as were in use about the ship, but not parts of it, which would confound this clause with the next.— **Upon some of the pieces from the ship,** which they themselves tore away or which the surge had broken off. Most critics distinguish the two expressions in this manner. Kuinoel renders *boards* (σανίσιν) tables. A few understand that term of the permanent parts of the vessel, and *some of the pieces from the ship* (τινων ἀπό τοῦ πλοίου) of such things as seats, barrels, and the like, which were floating away from the wreck. But articles of this description they would be likely to have lost or to have thrown into the sea before this time.—**So, thus**—*i. e.* in the two ways that have been mentioned.—**Escaped safe**—lit. **were saved.** This was not the first peril of the kind from which the apostle had been delivered. In 2 Cor. 11 : 25 he says, "Thrice I suffered shipwreck, a night and a day have I spent in the deep;" and he recorded that statement several years before the present disaster. [Meyer says: "This shipwreck was at least the *fourth* (2 Cor. 11 . 25) which Paul suffered." He also remarks: "Hackett treats chap. xxvii. with special care, having made use of many accounts of travels and notes of navigation."—A. H.]

———

1–10. THEIR ABODE DURING THE WINTER AT MELITA.

1. They knew = they ascertained (by intercourse, probably, with the inhabitants) **that the island is called Melita.** That this was the modern Malta cannot well be doubted. An island with the same name, now Meleda, lies up the Adriatic, on the coast of Dalmatia, which some have maintained to be the one where Paul was wrecked. Bryant defended that opinion. It is advocated still in Valpy's *Notes on the New Testament.* The argu-

ment for that opinion founded on the name Adriatic has been already refuted in the remarks on 27 : 27. It has also been alleged for it that no poisonous serpents are found at present on Malta. Mr. Smith mentions Coleridge (*Table Talk,* p. 185) as urging that difficulty. The more populous and cultivated state of the island accounts for the disappearance of such reptiles. Naturalists inform us that these animals become extinct or disappear as the aboriginal forests of a country are cleared up, or as the soil is otherwise brought under cultivation. (See note on v. 3.) It would be difficult to find a surface of equal extent in so artificial a state as that of Malta at the present day. The positive reasons for the common belief as to the place of the shipwreck are—that the traditional evidence sustains it ; that Malta lies in the track of a vessel driven by a north-east wind ; that the reputed locality of the wreck agrees with Luke's account ; that the Alexandrian ship in which they re-embarked would very naturally winter there, but not at Meleda ; and that the subsequent course of the voyage to Puteoli is that which a vessel would pursue in going from Malta, but not from the other place. Malta is sixty miles from Cape Passero, the southern point of Sicily, and two hundred miles from the African coast. It is farther from the main land than any other island in the Mediterranean. It is seventeen miles in length, nine miles in its greatest breath, and sixty miles in circumference. It is nearly equidistant between the two ends of the Mediterranean. Its highest point is said to be six hundred feet above the level of the sea.

2. And the barbarous people. The inhabitants are called *barbarians* with reference to their language—which was not that either of the Greeks or Romans—not because they were rude and degraded. It is strange that Coleridge should say that the Melitæans cannot be meant here, because they were highly civilized. These islanders belonged to the Phœnician race and spoke a Semitic dialect, most probably the Punic—*i. e.* the Phœnician as spoken by the people of Carthage. "The

every one, because of the present rain, and because of the cold.

3 And when Paul had gathered a bundle of sticks, and laid *them* on the fire, there came a viper out of the heat, and fastened on his hand.

fire, and received us all, because of the present rain, 3 and because of the cold. But when Paul had gathered a bundle of sticks, and laid them on the fire, a viper came out [1]by reason of the heat, and fastened

---

1 Or, *from the heat*

Hebrew language," in its widest extent, says Hupfeld, "was the language, not merely of the Hebrews, but of the other nations that inhabited *Canaan*, or *Palæstina*, especially of the Phœnicians, so renowned as a commercial people in the ancient world, and of the Carthaginians descended from them. This is proved especially by the proper names of the Canaanites in the Bible, and of the Phœnicians and Carthaginians in the classic writers, which are all formed in the Hebrew manner, and also by the remains of the Phœnician and the Punic language on Phœnician monuments and in the classics, so far as these have been as yet deciphered."[1] The Greeks and Romans who settled on the island at different times never introduced to any great extent their language or customs.—**No little** = *no ordinary*. (See on 19 : 11.)—**Received to themselves,** or to their regard. (Comp. Rom. 14 : 1 ; De Wet.), not to their fire (Mey.). [In his last ed. Meyer agrees with Dr. Hackett.—A. H.]—**On account of the rain which came upon** us (De Wet., Rob.) ; the *present rain* (Wetst., E. V.). They would suffer the more from this inclement weather after so much exposure and fatigue. This remark in regard to the rain and cold disproves the assumption of some critics that it was a sirocco wind—*i. e.* from the south-east—which Paul's ship encountered. That wind does not continue to blow more than two or three days, and is hot and sultry even as late as the month of November.

3. And when Paul, etc.—lit. **now Paul —having collected a great number** (a heap) **of dry sticks,** such as would naturally be found among the rocks around the shore.—**A viper** (ἔχιδνα). The Greeks applied this term to that reptile in distinction from

other serpents, as is evident from Aristotle (Lib. I. c. 6) : "The other serpents produce eggs ; the echidna only is viviparous." Vipers are the only viviparous serpents in Europe. It was remarked above that the viper is unknown in Malta at the present day. "No person," says Mr. Smith, "who has studied the changes which the operations of man have produced on the fauna (animals) of any country will be surprised that a particular species of reptiles should have disappeared from that of Malta. My friend the Rev. Mr. Landsborough, in his interesting excursions in Arran, has repeatedly noticed the gradual disappearance of the viper from that island since it has become more frequented. Mr. Lyell,[2] in quoting the travels of Spix and Martius in Brazil, observes : 'They speak of the dangers to which they were exposed from the jaguar, *the poisonous serpents*, crocodiles, scorpions, centipedes, and spiders. But with the increasing population and cultivation of the country, say these naturalists, these evils will gradually diminish ; when the inhabitants have cut down the woods, drained the marshes, made roads in all directions, and founded villages and towns, man will by degrees triumph over the rank vegetation and the noxious animals.' "—**Out of,** or *from*, **the heat,** the effect of it (De Wet.), or (less appropriate to the noun, from the place of it, as explained by Winer (§ 47. 5. b.) and others. But the best manuscripts read ἀπό (Lchm., Tsch., Mey.), and the sense then is (comp. 20 : 9 ; Luke 19 : 3) *on account of the heat*. The viper had evidently been taken up among the sticks which Paul had gathered ; and, as may be inferred from **laid on the fire,** had been thrown with them into the fire. This latter supposition is required by the local sense of *out of the heat*, and is entirely consistent with

---

[1] It has been frequently asserted that the ancient Punic is the basis of the language spoken by the native Maltese of the present day. That opinion is incorrect. Malta, at the time of the Saracen irruption, was overrun by Arabs, from whom the common people of the island derive their origin. The dialect spoken by them is a corrupt Arabic, agreeing essentially with that of the Moors, but intermixed to a greater extent with words from the Italian, Spanish, and other European languages. The Maltese language approaches so nearly to the Arabic that the islanders are readily understood in all the ports of Africa and Syria. Gesenius first investigated thoroughly this dialect in his *Versuch über die maltesische Sprache*, etc. (Leipzig, 1810). He has given the results of this investigation in his article on "Arabien" in *Ersch and Gruber's Encyklopädie*. In his *History of the Hebrew Language* he remarks that, although the ancestral pride of the Maltese themselves may dispose them to trace back their language to the old Punic, yet it contains nothing which is not explained far more naturally out of the modern Arabic than as the product of so ancient a tongue.

[2] *Principles of Geology* (7th ed.), p. 655.

4 And when the barbarians saw the *venomous* beast hang on his hand, they said among themselves, No doubt this man is a murderer, whom, though he hath escaped the sea, yet vengeance suffereth not to live.

5 And he shook off the beast into the fire, and *a*felt no harm.

6 Howbeit they looked when he should have swollen, or fallen down dead suddenly: but after they had looked a great while, and saw no harm come to him, they changed their minds, and *b*said that he was a god.

7 In the same quarters were possessions of the

4 on his hand. And when the barbarians saw the beast hanging from his hand, they said one to another, No doubt this man is a murderer, whom, though he hath escaped from the sea, yet Justice

5 hath not suffered to live. Howbeit he shook off the beast into the fire, and took no harm. But they

6 expected that he would have swollen, or fallen down dead suddenly: but when they were long in expectation, and beheld nothing amiss come to him, they changed their minds, and said that he was a god.

7 Now in the neighborhood of that place were lands

a Mark 16 : 18 ; Luke 10 : 19....*b* ch. 14 : 11.

the causal sense. The viper was probably in a torpid state, and was suddenly restored to activity by the heat. It was now cold, in consequence both of the storm and the lateness of the season (v. 2) ; and such reptiles become torpid as soon as the temperature falls sensibly below the mean temperature of the place which they inhabit. Vipers, too, lurk in rocky places, and that is the character of the region where the incident occurred. They are accustomed, also, to dart at their enemies, sometimes several feet at a bound ; and hence the one mentioned here could have reached the hand of Paul as he stood in the vicinity of the fire.[1] Instead of **having come forth** (ἐξελθοῦσα, T. R.), the more descriptive διεξελθοῦσα (Tsch, Mey.) represents the viper as *having come forth* (from the fire) *through* the sticks among which it was taken up.—**Fastened itself,** in the sense of the middle. This reflexive use of the active occurs only here, which accounts for the middle form, as read in some copies.

4. Now as the barbarians saw the animal hanging from his hand, to which it clung by the mouth. Aristotle also uses *animal* (θηρίον) of the viper. That it was "venomous" (E. V.) results, not from this mode of designation, but from *echidna*. Luke does not say expressly that Paul was bitten, but the nature of the reptile, the leap, the clinging to his hand, leave us to infer that with almost entire certainty. Those who stood near and witnessed the occurrence supposed, evidently, that such was the fact. That he should have escaped being bitten under such circumstances would have been hardly less miraculous than that the ordinary effect of the poison should have been counteracted. We seem to be justified, according to either view, in regarding his preservation as a fulfilment of the promise of Christ in Mark 16 : 17, 18. On the form of the participle (κρεμάμενον), see K. ₰ 179. 5.—**This man is a murderer.** They perceived from his chain,

perhaps, or some other indication, that Paul was a prisoner. The attack of the viper proved to them that he must have committed some atrocious crime. **Murderer** points, not to a specific offence, but to the class of offenders to which they supposed he might belong.—**Justice suffered not to live.** Observe the past tense. They considered his doom as sealed. Vengeance, in their view, had already smitten his victim.

5. Suffered no evil. This statement agrees with the supposition either that he had not been bitten or that the poison had produced no effect upon him.

6. When he should have swollen, or **that he would be inflamed** (lit. **burn**), since inflammation is attended with heat.— **Or that he would suddenly fall down dead.** Sudden collapse and death ensue often from the bite of serpents. Shakespeare speaks as a naturalist when he says of the asp-bitten Cleopatra,

"Trembling she stood, and on the sudden dropped."

—**No harm**—lit. **nothing bad,** *injurious;* in a moral sense in Luke 23 : 41.—**Changed** may take after it **their mind** or omit it.—**That he was a god.** Bengel: "Aut latro, inquiunt, aut deus; sic modo tauri, modo lapides (14 : 13, 19). Datur tertium: *homo* Dei " [" Either a robber, or a god; thus now bullocks, now stones (14 : 13, 19). There is a third: *man of* God."—A. H.].

7. Around that place, the one where they were wrecked. Tradition places the residence of Publius at Citta Vecchia, the Medina of the Saracens, which, though in the centre of Malta, is but a few miles from the coast. (See on v. 1.) —There can be no doubt that **Publius** is called **the first** (or *chief*) **of the island** because he was the Roman governor. Melita was first conquered by the Romans during the Punic wars, and in the time of Cicero (4 Ver. c. 18) was annexed to the prætorship of Sicily. The prætor of that island would naturally have

[1] For the information in this note concerning the habits of the viper, I am indebted chiefly to Professor Agassiz of Cambridge.

chief man of the island, whose name was Publius; who received us, and lodged us three days courteously.

8 And it came to pass, that the father of Publius lay sick of a fever and of a bloody flux: to whom Paul entered in, and ^aprayed, and ^blaid his hands upon him, and healed him.

9 So when this was done, others also, which had diseases in the island, came, and were healed:

10 Who also honored us with many ^chonors; and when we departed, they laded us with such things as were necessary.

belonging to the chief man of the island, named Publius; who received us, and entertained us three days 8 courteously. And it was so, that the father of Publius lay sick of fever and dysentery: unto whom Paul entered in, and prayed, and laying his hands 9 on him healed him. And when this was done, the rest also who had diseases in the island came, and 10 were cured: who also honored us with many honors; and when we sailed, they put on board such things as we needed.

---

a James 5 : 14, 15....*b* Mark 6 : 5 ; 7 : 32 ; 16 : 18 ; Luke 4 : 40 ; *ch.* 19 : 11, 12 ; 1 Cor. 12 : 9, 28....*c* Matt. 15 : 6 ; 1 Tim. 5 : 17.

---

a legate or deputy at this place. The title **first** (πρῶτος), under which he is mentioned here, has been justly cited by apologetic writers, as Tholuck, Ebrard, Krabbe, Baumgarten, Lardner, Paley, Conybeare and Howson, as a striking proof of Luke's accuracy. No other ancient writer happens to have given his official designation ; but two inscriptions, one in Greek and the other in Latin, have been discovered in Malta, in which we meet with the same title employed by Luke in this passage.[1] It is impossible to believe that Publius or any other single individual would be called the *first man* in the island, except by way of official eminence. It will be observed that the father of Publius was still living, and during his lifetime he would naturally have taken precedence of the son, had the distinction in this case been one which belonged to the family.[2]—**Lodged,** or better **entertained, us**—viz. Luke, Paul, Aristarchus (27 : 2), and no doubt the noblehearted Julius ; not the entire two hundred and seventy-six (Bmg.), as so indiscriminate a hospitality would be uncalled for and without any sufficient motive.

8. Sick of a fever—lit. **of fevers.** The plural has been supposed to describe the fever with reference to its recurrent attacks or paroxysms. This is one of those expressions in Luke's writings that have been supposed to indicate his professional training as a physician. (See also 12 : 23 ; 13 : 11 ; and especially the comparison (*His sweat was as it were great drops of blood falling down,* etc.) in his Gospel (22 : 44).) It is correct to attach to them that significancy. No other writer of the New Testament exhibits this sort of technical precision in speaking of diseases. The disorder with which the father of Publius was affected was dysentery combined with fever. It was formerly asserted that a dry climate like that of Malta would not produce such a disorder, but we have now the testimony of physicians resident in that island that it is by no means uncommon there at the present day.

10. Who also, on their part—*i. e.* while they came and were healed of their maladies. —**Honored us** (viz. Paul and his companions) **with many honors,** courtesies. They were entertained with a generous hospitality, and

---

[1] " The one in Greek is supposed to form a votive inscription by a Roman knight, named Aulus Castricius, ' first of the Melitans' (πρῶτος Μελιταίων), to the emperor. The Latin inscription on the pedestal of a column was discovered at Citta Vecchia, in excavating the foundation of the Casa del Magistrato, in 1747."

[2] I have allowed this note to remain as it stood in the other edition, as it represents the general opinion of scholars respecting the official rank of Publius. Yet it is possible that they have erred in assigning its precise import to the title. I insert, with thanks for the suggestion, the following criticism of President Woolsey on this point: " The best information which we can obtain respecting the situation of Malta at the time of Paul's visit renders it doubtful, to say the least, whether the interpreters are in the right as it regards the station of Publius. In a Greek inscription of an earlier date we find mention made of two persons holding the office of *archon* or magistrate in the island. A later inscription of the times of the emperors may be translated as follows : ' Lucius Pudens, son of Claudius, of the tribe Quirina, a Roman eques, first [πρῶτος, as in Acts] and patron of the Meliteans, after being magistrate and having held the post of flamen to Augustus, erected this.' Here it appears that the person named was still chief man of the island, although his magistracy had expired. From this inscription and others in Latin found at Gozzo, it is probable that the inhabitants of both islands had received the privilege of Roman citizenship and were enrolled in the tribe Quirina. The magistracy was, no doubt, that of the Duumvirs, the usual municipal chief officers. The other titles correspond with titles to be met with on marbles relating to towns in Italy. Thus the title of *chief* corresponds to that of *princeps* in the colony of Pisa, and is probably no more a name of office than the title of *patron.* For no such officer is known to have existed in the colonies or in the *municipia,* and the *princeps coloniæ* of Pisa are mentioned at a time when it is said that, owing to a contention between candidates, there were no magistrates."

The difference does not affect the value of the alleged proof of the narrator's accuracy ; for in either case the term is a Roman title, and is applied by Luke to a person who bears it at the right time and in the right place. Indeed, the appellation of *prince* or *patron* would be more striking than that of *magistrate,* inasmuch as the range of its application is narrower, and a writer who was not stating the truth would be more liable to introduce it under circumstances that would render it inadmissible.

11 And after three months we departed in a ship of Alexandria, which had wintered in the isle, whose sign was Castor and Pollux.
12 And landing at Syracuse, we tarried *there* three days.
13 And from thence we fetched a compass, and came to Rhegium: and after one day the south wind blew, and we came the next day to Puteoli:

11 And after three months we set sail in a ship of Alexandria, which had wintered in the island, 12 whose sign was ¹The Twin Brothers. And touch-13 ing at Syracuse, we tarried there three days. And from thence we ²made a circuit, and arrived at Rhegium: and after one day a south wind sprang up,

---

1 Gr. *Dioscuri*....2 Some ancient authorities read *cast loose*.

---

distinguished by marks of special regard and kindness. Some render the Greek word (τιμαῖς) *rewards* or *presents;* but the next clause appears to limit their reception of the favors in question to the time of their departure and to the relief of their necessary wants. It is certain that they did not even then accept the gifts which were proffered to them as a reward for their services; for that would have been at variance with the command of Christ in Matt. 10 : 8.

11–16. PROSECUTION OF THE JOURNEY TO ROME.

11. After three months. The *three months* are the time that they remained on the island. They were probably the months of November, December, and January. The season may have admitted of their putting to sea earlier than usual. The arrival at Melita could not have been later than October, for a brief interval only lay between the fast (27:9) and the beginning of the storm (27:27).—**In a ship which had wintered there.** Luke does not state why this vessel had wintered here. It is a circumstance which shows the consistency of the narrative. The storm which occasioned the wreck of Paul's vessel had delayed this one so long that it was necessary, on reaching Melita, to suspend the voyage until spring. This vessel had been during the winter at Valetta, which must always have been the principal harbor of Malta.—**With the sign Dioscuri,** or **distinguished by Dioscuri**—*i. e.* having images of Castor and Pollux painted or carved on the prow, from which images the vessel may have been named. This use of figure-heads on ancient ships was very common. (See *Dict. of Antt.*, Art. "Insigne.") Castor and Pollux were the favorite gods of seamen, the winds and waves being supposed to be specially subject to their control. It is of them that Horace says (*Od.*, 1. 12. 27–32; see, also, *Od.*, 1. 3. 2) :

"Quorum simul alba nautis
    Stella refulsit,
Defluit saxis agitatus humor;
Concidunt venti, fugiuntque nubes,
Et minax (quod sic voluere) ponto
    Unda recumbit." ¹

The sign (παρασήμῳ) may be a noun or an adjective. The former appears to have been most common in this application. . The other construction is easier as regards the dative, and is preferred by De Wette.

12. At Syracuse. This city, the capital of Sicily, on the south-eastern coast of that island, was about eighty miles north from Melita. It was built partly on the adjacent island of Ortygia, and from that circumstance, or, as others say, because it included at length several villages, may have received its plural name. The modern Siracusa, or Siragossa, occupies only a part of the ancient city—viz. Ortygia (Forbg.). —**We tarried.** They may have stopped here for trade, or in the hope of a better wind.

13. Fetched a compass — lit. **having come around,** or **about.** The sense of the preposition it is impossible to determine with certainty. One supposition is that it refers to their frequent alteration of the ship's course; in other words, to their tacking, because the wind was unfavorable. So Smith, Conybeare and Howson, and others explain the word. Mr. Lewin thinks that "as the wind was westerly, and they were under the shelter of the high mountainous range of Etna, they were obliged to stand out to sea, in order to fill their sails, and so come to Rhegium by a circuitous sweep." ² Another view is that they were compelled by the wind to follow closely the sinuosities of the coast, to proceed circuitously. De Wette says—which is much less probable— that they may have gone *around* Sicily, or the southern extremity of Italy.—**Unto Rhegium,** now Reggio, which was an Italian seaport opposite to the north-eastern point of Sicily. Here

---

¹ [" As soon as their propitious star has shone out upon the mariners, the heaving water flows down from the rocks, the winds fall, the clouds flee away, and the threatening wave (for so have they willed) sinks down upon the sea."]

² " I was informed by a friend many years ago that when he made the voyage himself from Syracuse to Rhegium, the vessel in which he sailed took a similar circuit, for a similar reason." *Lewin*, ii. p 736).

they remained a day, when the wind, which had been adverse since their leaving Syracuse, became fair, and they resumed the voyage. The steamers between Naples and Malta touch at Messina, and Reggio appears in full view on the Italian side. If Paul passed here in Feb-

nals is classical. (K. § 264. 3. b.)—**To Puteoli. Puteoli,** now Pozzuoli, was eight miles northwest from Neapolis, the modern Naples. It derived its name from the springs (*putei*) which abound there, or from the odor of the waters (*a putendo*).[1] Its earlier Greek name was *Di*

THE MOLE OF PUTEOLI.

ruary (v. 11, above), the mountains on the island and on the main land were still covered with snow, and presented to the eye a dreary aspect.—**A south wind having arisen on** them. (Comp. the compound participle in v. 2 and in 27 : 20. The dative of the person is often expressed after ἐπί with this force. See Herod., 8. 13.)—**On the second day.** (Comp. John 11 : 39.) This adverbial use of the ordi-

kairarcheia. It was the principal port south of Rome. Nearly all the Alexandrian and a great part of the Spanish trade with Italy was brought hither. The seventy-seventh Letter of Seneca gives a lively description of the interest which the arrival of the corn-ships from Egypt was accustomed to excite among the inhabitants of that time. A mole with twenty-five arches stretched itself into the sea at the

---

[1] As examples, travellers will recollect the Grotto del Cane near Cumæ, and the Baths of Nero at Baia.

entrance of this bay, alongside of which the vessels as they arrived cast anchor for the delivery of their freight and passengers. Thirteen of the piers which upheld this immense structure show their forms still above the water, and point out to us as it were the very footsteps of the apostle as he passed from the ship to the land.—The voyage from Rhegium to Puteoli, which the Castor and Pollux accomplished in less than two days, was about one hundred mentions several voyages which would be considered very good in modern times. He says that the prefects Galerius and Babilius arrived at Alexandria, the former on the seveuth, the latter on the sixth, day after leaving the Straits of Messina. He states, also, that passages were made, under favorable circumstances, from the Straits of Hercules to Ostia, in seven days; from the nearest port of Spain, in four; from the province of Narbonne, in three; and from

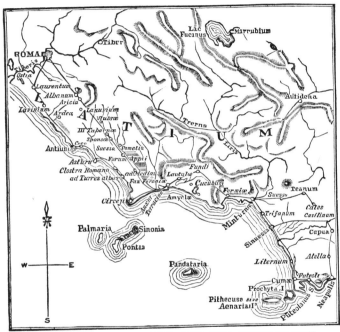

ROUTE OF PAUL ALONG THE VIA APPIA FROM PUTEOLI TO ROME.

and eighty miles. The passage, therefore, was a rapid one, but, as examples of the ancient rate of sailing show, not unprecedented. Herodotus states that a ship could sail seven hundred stadia in a day and six hundred in a night —*i. e.* thirteen hundred in twenty-four hours— which would be at the rate of about one hundred and fifty English miles a day. Strabo says that a voyage could be made from Sammonium to Egypt in four days, reckoning the distance at five thousand stadia, or about five hundred and seventy-three miles. This would be sailing one hundred and forty-three miles in twenty-four hours, or six miles an hour. Pliny

Africa, in two. Probably the most rapid run mentioned by any ancient writer is that of Arrian, in his Periplus of the Euxine, who says that "they got under way about daybreak," and that by midday they had come more than five hundred stadia—that is, more than fifty geographical miles, which is at least eight miles an hour.[1] The mean of the foregoing examples is seven miles an hour; and if we suppose that the Castor and Pollux sailed at that rate, the passage would have required only about twenty-six hours. This result agrees perfectly with Luke's account; for he states that they left Rhegium on one day and arrived at Puteoli

---

[1] I have relied for these statements partly on Forbiger, and partly on Biscoe and Smith.

14 Where we found brethren, and were desired to tarry with them seven days: and so we went toward Rome.
15 And from thence, when the brethren heard of us, they came to meet us as far as Appii forum, and The three taverns: whom when Paul saw, he thanked God, and took courage.
16 And when we came to Rome, the centurion delivered the prisoners to the captain of the guard: but

14 and on the second day we came to Puteoli: where we found brethren, and were intreated to tarry with them seven days: and so we came to Rome.
15 And from thence the brethren, when they heard of us, came to meet us as far as The Market of Appius, and The Three Taverns: whom when Paul saw, he thanked God, and took courage.
16 And when we entered into Rome, [1]Paul was suf

---

1 Some ancient authorities insert *the centurion delivered the prisoners to the captain of the prætorian guard: but.*

---

on the next. Their course, it will be observed, was nearly due north, and they were favored with a south wind.

14. With (lit. **upon**) **them.** (Comp. 21 : 4.) The local idea blends itself with the personal. (See W. ? 48. c.)—**Seven days, or a week.** (See on 20 : 6.) They had an opportunity to spend a Sabbath with the Christians there. The centurion granted this delay, not improbably, in order to gratify the wishes of Paul. After such events the prisoner would have a power over his keeper well nigh unbounded. In the mean time, the news of the apostle's arrival would travel to Rome, and thus prepare the way for what we read in the next verse.—**And so,** after the interval thus spent, **we went unto Rome,** not *came,* unless the remark be proleptic. The incidents in v. 15 occur on the way thither. On leaving Puteoli, Julius and his party would proceed naturally to Capua, about twelve miles, the nearest point for intersecting the Appian Way. The distance from Capua to Rome by this road was about one hundred and twenty-five miles.[1]

15. Two companies of the Christians at Rome went forth to meet the apostle, but separately and at different times. Hence the advanced party reached **Appii Forum,** about forty miles from Rome, before Paul appeared; the later party met him at *Tres Tabernæ* (E. V. **Three Taverns**), which was thirty miles from Rome (*Itiner. Antonin.*). Other estimates (*Itiner. Hieros.*) place *Appii Forum* a few miles nearer to Rome. This town was named from Appius Claudius Cæcus, who built the Appian Way. It lay on the northern border of the Pontine Marshes, at the end of the canal which extended thither from a point a few miles above Anxur or Terracina. Horace (*Sat.,* 1. 5. 4) speaks of Appii Forum as "full of boatmen," who were engaged in forwarding passengers over this canal, a distance of twenty miles. The Appian Way ran near the canal, and it would depend on circumstances unknown to

us whether the centurion travelled in one mode or the other. Strabo mentions that night-travellers (as in the case of Horace) usually preferred the boat. The present Locanda di Foro Appio, a wretched inn, marks, probably, the site of Appii Forum. It is almost the only human shelter in the midst of a solitude enlivened once by incessant commerce and travel. —**Three Taverns,** as appears from one of Cicero's letters to Atticus (2 : 12), must have been near where the cross-road from Antium fell into the Appian Way. It is thought to have been not far from the modern Cisterna, the bulk of which lies on the traveller's left in going from Rome to Naples, under the shadow of the Volscian hills.—**Whom Paul seeing gave thanks to God and took courage.** He may have met a few of the Roman Christians in foreign lands, but was a stranger to nearly all of them except in name, and would approach the city with the natural anxiety of one who had yet to learn what feelings they entertained toward him. Such a cordial reception, such impatience to see him and welcome him to their hearts, would scatter all his doubts and thrill his bosom with gratitude and joy. The church at Rome contained heathen converts as well as Jewish. The apostle of the Gentiles would have a special cause for encouragement and thanksgiving in the presence of such witnesses of the success of the gospel in the great metropolis.

16. As Paul travelled on the Appian Way, he must have entered Rome through the Capenian Gate, not far from the modern Porta San Sebastiano. — **The centurion delivered the prisoners to the commander of the camp** —*i. e.* the prætorian camp, where the emperor's body-guard was quartered. (See Phil. 1 : 13.) This camp, or garrison, had been built by Sejanus, the favorite of Tiberius, in the vicinity of the *Porta Nomentana* (Win.). The exact spot is known to be that within the projection at the north-east corner of the present city wall.

---

[1] Conybeare and Howson's map of this journey to the city will enable the reader to follow the apostle's course very distinctly. [It gives the Campanian or Consular road from Puteoli to Capua. Lewin (*Life and Epistles of Paul,* whose map is given) thinks he went by the coast road from Cumæ to Sinuessa, and there struck the Appian Way.]

*Paul was suffered to dwell by himself with a soldier that kept him.

fered to abide by himself with the soldier that guarded him.

a ch. 24 : 25 ; 27 : 3.

Nearly all critics at present, as Olshausen, Anger, De Wette, Meyer, Wieseler, suppose this officer—*i. e.* the *præfectus prætorio*—to be meant here. The prisoners who were sent to Rome from the provinces were committed to his custody. There is a difference of opinion in regard to the article. The command of the prætorian guard was originally divided between sole prefect at that time, and he urges the expression as a reason for assigning the apostle's arrival to A. D. 62, or the year preceding. It is very possible that this view is the correct one. It would furnish a striking coincidence between Luke's narrative and the history of the times. Yet, in speaking of *the prefect*, the writer may have meant the one who acted in this particular

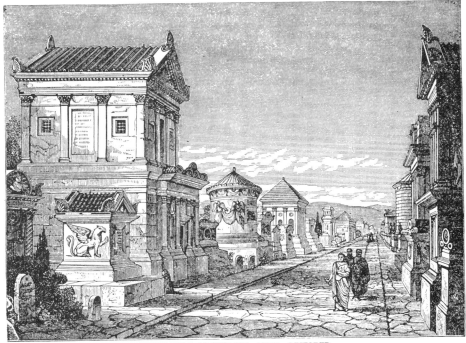

FIFTH MILE OF THE VIA APPIA, RESTORED.

two prefects; but during the reign of Claudius, Burrus Afranius, a distinguished Roman general, was appointed sole *præfectus prætorio*, and retained this office as late, certainly, as the beginning of A. D. 62. On his death the command was committed again to two prefects, as it had been at first ; and this continued to be the arrangement until a late period of the empire. The time of Paul's arrival at Rome could not have been far from A. D. 62, as admits of being shown by an independent calculation. (See *Introd.*, ₰ 6. 5.) Wieseler (p. 86) supposes *the commander of the camp* to refer to Burrus, as case, the one who took into his charge the prisoners whom the centurion transferred to him, whether he was sole prefect or had a colleague with him. (Comp. 24 : 23.) De Wette assents to Meyer in this explanation of the article. The expression, as so understood, does not affirm that there was but one prefect, or deny it.[1] —**But Paul was suffered**—lit. **but it was permitted to Paul** (*i. e.* by the prefect to whom he had been consigned)—**to dwell by himself,** instead of being confined with the other prisoners. This was a favor which the Roman laws often granted to those who were

[1] [This clause is now omitted by the best editors. – A. H.]

17 And it came to pass, that after three days Paul called the chief of the Jews together: and when they were come together, he said unto them, Men *and* brethren, *a*though I have committed nothing against the people, or customs of our fathers, yet *b*was I delivered prisoner from Jerusalem into the hands of the Romans.

18 Who, *c*when they had examined me, would have let *me* go, because there was no cause of death in me.

19 But when the Jews spake against *it*, *d*I was constrained to appeal unto Cæsar; not that I had ought to accuse my nation of.

20 For this cause therefore have I called for you, to see *you*, and to speak with *you*: because that *e*for the hope of Israel I am bound with *f* this chain.

17 And it came to pass, that after three days he called together [1]those that were the chief of the Jews: and when they were come together, he said unto them, I, brethren, though I had done nothing against the people, or the customs of our fathers, yet was delivered prisoner from Jerusalem into the [18] hands of the Romans: who, when they had examined me, desired to set me at liberty, because there [19] was no cause of death in me. But when the Jews spake against it, I was constrained to appeal unto Cæsar; not that I had aught to accuse my nation of.

20 For this cause therefore did I [2]intreat you to see and to speak with me: for because of the hope of

a ch. 24 : 12, 13 ; 25 : 8....b ch. 21 : 33....c ch. 22 : 24; 24 : 10 ; 25 : 8 ; 26 : 31....d ch. 25 : 11....e ch. 26 : 6, 7....f ch. 26 : 29 ; Eph. 3 : 1 ; 4 : 1 ; 6 : 20 ; 2 Tim. 1 : 16 ; 2 : 9 ; Philem. 10, 13.——1 Or, those that were of the Jews first....2 Or, call for you, to see and to speak with you

not suspected of any very serious offence. The centurion, who had already shown himself so friendly to the apostle, may have interceded for him, or the terms in which Festus had reported the case (see on 26 : 32) may have conciliated the prefect. In the use of this liberty, Paul repaired first to the house of some friend (v. 23), and afterward rented an apartment for his own use (v. 30).—**With the soldier who guarded him,** and to whom he was fastened by a chain. Different soldiers relieved each other in the performance of this office. Hence, as Paul states in Phil. 1 : 13, he became in the course of time personally known to a great number of the prætorian soldiers, and through them to their comrades. The notoriety which he thus acquired served to make his character as a prisoner for the sake of the gospel more widely known, and thus to aid him in his efforts to extend the knowledge of Christ. To this result the apostle refers in Phil. 1 : 12, *sq.*

17–22. PAUL HAS AN INTERVIEW WITH THE CHIEF MEN OF THE JEWS AT ROME.

17. After three days, on the third from his arrival. (Comp. 25 : 1.) The apostle's untiring activity is manifest to the last.—**The Jews** are the unbelieving *Jews,* not the Jewish Christians. Their **first** men would be the rulers of the synagogue, or would include them.—**Against** (ἐναντίον) governs the dative here, as in 1 Thess. 2 : 15. (Comp. 26 : 9.)—**Though I have committed,** better **though I had done.—From Jerusalem,** whence he had been sent to Cæsarea.—**Into the hands of the Romans**—viz. Felix and Festus, who represented their countrymen. The remark applies to them, as is evident from *examined,* in the next verse.

19. Spake against, or *objecting,* describes very mildly the opposition of the Jews to the apostle's acquittal. **Brethren, the people,**
21

our fathers, Israel, which follow so rapidly breathe the same conciliatory spirit. Such expressions show how self-forgetting Paul was, how ready to acknowledge what was common to his opponents and himself.—**I was compelled to appeal unto Cæsar,** as his only resort, in order to save himself from assassination or judicial murder. (Comp. 25 : 9, *sq.*)—**Not that I had,** or **not as having** (*i. e.* because I had) **anything** (as the motive for this appeal) **to charge against my nation**—viz. before the emperor. The apostle would repel a suspicion which he supposed it not unnatural for the Roman Jews to entertain, or possibly would deny an imputation with which the Jews in Palestine had actually aspersed him (Wiesl.). Paul says **my nation** (ἔθνους μου), and not *people* (see λαῷ above), because the word **Cæsar,** just before, distinguishes the Romans and the Jews from each other.

20. On this account therefore—viz. that his feelings toward the Jews were so friendly.—**I called,** invited, **you that I might see** you. Some supply *me* as the object of *to see* [*i. e. called you to see me*], which destroys the unity of the sentence.—**For on account of the hope of Israel**—*i. e.* the hope of a Messiah which the nation entertained. (Comp. 26 : 6.) This clause is co-ordinate with the one which precedes. It states an additional reason why he had sought the present interview.—**I am compassed with this chain,** have my arm bound with it. So, also, when the apostle wrote in Phil. 4 : 4, "Rejoice in the Lord always; and, again, I say, Rejoice," he was manacled as a felon, and was liable at any moment to be condemned to the wild beasts or the block. The construction is similar to that of the accusative after passive verbs. (Comp. *is compassed with infirmity*—περίκειται ἀσθένειαν—in Heb. 5 : 2.)

21 And they said unto him, We neither received letters out of Judæa concerning thee, neither any of the brethren that came shewed or spake any harm of thee.
22 But we desire to hear of thee what thou thinkest: for as concerning this sect, we know that everywhere *it is spoken against.

21 Israel I am bound with this chain. And they said unto him, We neither received letters from Judæa concerning thee, nor did any of the brethren come
22 hither and report or speak any harm of thee. But we desire to hear of thee what thou thinkest: for as concerning this sect, it is known to us that everywhere it is spoken against.

a Luke 2 : 34; ch. 24 : 5, 14; 1 Pet. 2 : 12; 4 : 14.

21. We received neither letters, etc. This statement refers to their having received no official information, either written or oral, in regard to the circumstances under which Paul had been sent to Rome. Some have supposed the Jews to be insincere in this declaration, as if it was improbable that they should have been uninformed in regard to so important an event. But we have no sufficient reason for calling in question their veracity. The Palestine Jews could hardly have foreseen the issue to which the case was so suddenly brought, and hence, before the apostle's appeal, would have deemed it unnecessary to apprise the Jews at Rome of the progress of the trial. It is barely possible that they could have forwarded intelligence since the appeal had taken place. Paul departed for Italy evidently soon after he had appealed, and must have availed himself of one of the last opportunities for such a voyage which the season of the year allowed. Having spent the winter at Melita, he had proceeded to Rome at the earliest moment in the spring; so that in the ordinary course of things he must have arrived there in advance of any ship that might have left Palestine after the reopening of navigation.—Repeat **from Judea** after **that came.**—**Any one of the brethren,** of our countrymen—*i. e.* as a special messenger, as a complainant.

22. But (though in the absence of such information we offer no complaint) **we deem it proper** (Mey., Rob.) **to hear from thee.** (Comp. 15 : 38.) The verb may also mean *we desire* (De Wet., E. V.), but is less common in that sense.—**For concerning this sect,** of which Paul was known to be an adherent; and, as that circumstance (**for**) was not in his favor, they intimate that he was bound to vindicate himself from the reproach of such a connection. The Jews, it will be observed, in their reply to the apostle, abstain from any allusion to the Christians at Rome; indeed, they might have expressed themselves in the same manner had no church existed there at this time, or had they been entirely ignorant of its existence. To understand them, however, as affirming that they had heard of the sect only by report, that they possessed no personal knowledge of any who were connected with it, is certainly unauthorized. Baur[1] proceeds on this false assumption, and then represents the passage as inconsistent with the Epistle to the Romans, which was written several years before this, and exhibits to us a flourishing church in the Roman metropolis. Zeller says the same thing. The peculiarity in the case is not by any means that the Jews denied that they were acquainted with those who held the Christian faith, but that they avoided so carefully any reference to the fact; what they knew was matter of general notoriety (**everywhere it is spoken against**); they decline the responsibility of asserting anything on the ground of their own personal knowledge. Various explanations have been given of this reserve on the part of the Jews. Olshausen's hypothesis is that the opposition between the Jewish Christians and the Jews had become such, before Claudius banished the latter from Rome, as to separate them entirely from each other, and consequently that the Christians there remained, in fact, unknown to the Jews who returned to Rome after the decree of banishment ceased to be in force. This view is improbable, and has found no supporters. The opinion of many of the older critics, to which Tholuck[2] also has returned, is that the **chief of the Jews** affected to be thus ignorant in regard to the Roman Christians—that they wished to deceive the apostle, and uttered a direct falsehood when they told him that they had received no information concerning him from the Palestine Jews. The best account of this peculiarity, it appears to me, is that which Philippi has suggested in his recent commentary on the Epistle to the Romans.[3] The situation of the Jews at Rome, after their recent banishment by Claudius, was still critical and insecure. It was very important for them to avoid the displeasure of the government—to abstain from any act or attitude that would

1 *Paulus, der Apostel, sein Leben und Wirken, seine Briefe und seine Lehre,* p. 368, *sq.*
2 *Commentar zum Briefe Pauli an die Römer* (1842), p. 14.
3 *Commentar über den Brief Pauli an die Römer,* von Friedrich A. Philippi (1848), p. xv.

23 And when they had appointed him a day, there came many to him into *his* lodging; *a*to whom he expounded and testified the kingdom of God, persuading them concerning Jesus, *b*both out of the law of Moses, and *out of* the prophets, from morning till evening.
24 And *c*some believed the things which were spoken, and some believed not.
25 And when they agreed not among themselves, they departed, after that Paul had spoken one word, Well spake the Holy Ghost by Esaias the prophet unto our fathers,
26 Saying, *d*Go unto this people, and say, Hearing ye shall hear, and shall not understand; and seeing ye shall see, and not perceive:
27 For the heart of this people is waxed gross, and their ears are dull of hearing, and their eyes have they closed; lest they should see with *their* eyes, and

23 And when they had appointed him a day, they came to him into his lodging in great number; to whom he expounded *the matter*, testifying the kingdom of God, and persuading them concerning Jesus, both from the law of Moses and from the prophets,
24 ets, from morning till evening. And some believed the things which were spoken, and some disbelieved.
25 And when they agreed not among themselves, they departed, after that Paul had spoken one word, Well spake the Holy Spirit through Isaiah the prophet
26 unto your fathers, saying,
Go thou unto this people, and say,
By hearing ye shall hear, and shall in no wise understand:
And seeing ye shall see, and shall in no wise perceive:
27 For this people's heart is waxed gross,
And their ears are dull of hearing,
And their eyes they have closed;
Lest haply they should perceive with their eyes,

a Luke 24 : 27; ch. 17 : 3; 19 : 8....*b* See on ch. 26 : 6, 22....*c* ch. 14 : 4; 17 : 4; 19 : 9....*d* Isa. 6 : 9; Jer. 5 : 21; Ezek. 12 : 2; Matt. 13 : 14, 15; Mark 4 : 12; Luke 8 : 10; John 12 : 40; Rom. 11 : 8.

revive the old charge against them of being quarrelsome or factious. They saw that Paul was regarded with evident favor by the Roman officers; they had heard from him that the procurator would have acquitted him, but the obstinate Jews had compelled him to appeal to Cæsar. Having had no intelligence from Judea, they might fear that their countrymen there had gone too far, and had placed it in the power of Paul to use the circumstance to the disadvantage of the Jewish cause at Rome. Hence they considered it advisable for the present to conciliate the apostle, to treat him mildly, to keep out of sight their own relations to the Christian sect. They say what was true. No special and express information had been forwarded to them respecting his person and the occurrence mentioned by him, and they knew that the sect had everywhere an evil name. But they suppress their own view in regard to the Christian faith as something they do not consider it necessary and expedient to avow, and, out of fear of the Roman magistrates, would draw as little attention as possible to their hostile position toward the Christians.

23–29. HIS SECOND INTERVIEW WITH THE JEWS.

23. And when they had appointed, etc., or **now having appointed for him a day,** at his own suggestion, perhaps, since by leaving it to them to designate the time he would be more sure of their presence.—**Unto his lodging.** The term implies (Hesych.) that it was a place where he was entertained as a guest (comp. Philem. 22); and those critics are right who distinguish it from the "hired house" mentioned in v. 30. The apostle, at first, as would be natural, was received into some one of the Christian families at Rome; but after a time, for the sake of greater convenience or inde-

pendence, he removed to apartments which would be more entirely subject to his own control. That Aquila (Rom. 16 : 3) became his host again, as he had been at Corinth (18 : 3), is not impossible.—**Many,** strictly **more** than on the former occasion.—**And persuading them of the things concerning Jesus.** For the double accusative, see on 19 : ˙8. Here too, the act of the participle refers to the speaker's aim or object, without including the result. It may be inferred from what follows that the greater part of those whom Paul addressed withstood his efforts to win them to the truth. (Comp. v. 25.)

24. Some (οἱ μέν) and **some** (οἱ δέ) distribute the Jews into opposite parties. The proportion which the convinced bore to the unbelieving we must gather from the drift of the narrative.

25. Agreed not, etc.—lit. **and being discordant among one another.** This variance they may be supposed to have evinced by an open declaration of their different views, by the expression of dissent and objection on the part of those who disbelieved.—**After that Paul,** or **Paul having said one word,** at the time of their departure (De Wet.), not as the occasion of it (Mey.). It was *one* final, significant word, as opposed to many words. (Comp. Luke 20 : 3.) — **Through Isaiah.** (See on 2 : 16.)

26. Saying—viz. Isa. 6 : 9, *sq.*, cited according to the Seventy. The passage is quoted also in Matt. 13 : 14, *sq.*, and John 12 : 40.—For the Hebraistic **hearing ye shall hear,** see the note on 4 : 17.—**And shall not understand** (οὐ μὴ συνῆτε) may express the future result with more certainty than the future indicative. (See on 13 : 41.)—For **seeing ye shall see** (βλέποντες βλέψετε), see on 7 : 34.

hear with *their* ears, and understand with *their* heart, and should be converted, and I should heal them.

28 Be it known therefore unto you, that the salvation of God is sent *a*unto the Gentiles, and *that* they will hear it.

29 And when he had said these words, the Jews departed, and had great reasoning among themselves.

30 And Paul dwelt two whole years in his own hired house, and received all that came in unto him,

31 *b*Preaching the kingdom of God, and teaching those things which concern the Lord Jesus Christ, with all confidence, no man forbidding him.

And hear with their ears,
And understand with their heart,
And should turn again,
And I should heal them.

28 Be it known therefore unto you, that this salvation of God is sent unto the Gentiles: they will also hear.[1]

30 And he abode two whole years in his own hired dwelling, and received all that went in unto him,

31 preaching the kingdom of God, and teaching the things concerning the Lord Jesus Christ with all boldness, none forbidding him.

---

a Matt. 21 : 41, 43 ; ch. 13 : 46, 47 ; 18 : 6 ; 22 : 21 ; 26 : 17, 18 ; Rom. 11 : 11....*b* ch. 4 : 31 ; Eph. 6 : 19.——1 Some ancient authorities insert ver. 29 *And when he had said these words, the Jews departed, having much disputing among themselves.*

---

28. Therefore—*i. e.* since they are so hardened and incorrigible.—**That to the Gentiles the salvation was sent**—*i. e.* by God, in the coming of the apostle to Rome.—**They** (emphatic), although they are heathen.—**Also will hear** it—viz. the message of this salvation. The object of the verb is implied in **was sent** (ἀπεστάλη).—**Also** (καί) connects the reception with the offer of the gospel.—Our eyes trace here the last words in Luke's record which fell from the lips of Paul. It is remarkable that they are precisely such words. The apostle of the Gentiles points again to his commission to preach to all nations, and declares that the heathen, to whom he was sent, shall accept the Saviour whom the Jews disowned.

29. This verse in the common text repeats what has been said in the eighteenth verse. It appears to be not genuine. Its principal witnesses are G H, the Ethiopic, and some of the later Fathers. It is wanting in A B E, the Syriac, and the best Latin authorities. Leading critics, as Mill, Lachmann, Tischendorf, Green, reject the verse. [Also West. and Hort, Treg., and the Anglo-Am. Revisers.—A. H.]

30, 31. THE CONDITION OF THE APOSTLE DURING HIS CAPTIVITY.

30. **Dwelt**—lit. **remained two whole years ;** *i. e.* in the state mentioned, with the evident implication that at the end of that time his condition changed. Some critics deny

the correctness of this inference, but the better opinion affirms it. Had the apostle been still in confinement, the writer would have employed more naturally the present tense or the perfect (*remains* or *has remained*), instead of the aorist. The reader's conclusion is that the two years completed the term of the apostle's captivity, and that when Luke penned the sentence the prisoner was either at liberty or else was no longer living. Lekebusch (p. 415) pronounces this view an inevitable one. (See on next verse.)—The **two whole years** would bring the narrative down to A. D. 64. Some months lay between the commencement of this year and the outbreak of Nero's persecution. (See *Introd.*, p. 27.)—**In his own hired house**—*i. e.* hired at his own expense. In the bosom of a Christian church, the apostle could not have been destitute of the means of providing for such an expense. We learn also, from Phil. 4 : 14, 18, that during this captivity Paul received supplies from the church at Philippi.—**Received,** in its special sense, **received gladly,** because it afforded him such joy to preach the gospel. (Comp. 15 : 4 ; 18 : 27.)

31. **Teaching**—*i. e.* them. The construction is similar to that in v. 23.—**Without molestation,** on the part of the Roman Government.[1] According to the Roman laws, a citizen under arrest, in ordinary cases, could

---

1 Agrippa I. was imprisoned in early life at Rome. The account of his captivity confirms so entirely Luke's account of the manner in which Paul was treated as a Roman prisoner (so unlike our modern usages) that it may not be amiss to mention some of the circumstances. We obtain the information from Josephus (*Ant.*, 18. 6. 5, *sq.*). Agrippa, on being arrested, was committed to Macro, the prætorian prefect, and confined in the prætorian camp. He was there kept under a guard of soldiers, to one of whom he was chained (called his συνδετός). A particular centurion had the oversight of the prisoner and the soldiers who guarded him. But the condition of those confined in this manner depended very much on the character of those who had the immediate charge of them. The soldiers who watched Agrippa treated him at first with great severity. Hence, Antonia, a sister-in-law of Tiberius and a friend of Agrippa, interceded with Macro and induced him to appoint a guard known to be of a milder disposition. The situation of Agrippa was now improved. His friends, who had been excluded from him, were permitted to visit him and to supply his necessary wants. (Comp. 24 : 23.) But during this time, about six months, he was still confined in the prætorian camp. On the death of Tiberius the mode of his captivity was changed again. Caligula ordered him to be removed from the prætorium to the house which he had occupied before he was bound. Here he was still guarded as a prisoner, but was subject to so much less restraint that his condition was one of comparative liberty. His captivity, in this last form of it, was doubtless like that of Paul during the two years that he "dwelt in his own hired house" at Rome.

give security or bail, and thus enjoy his personal liberty until he was brought to trial. The freedom granted to Paul was so ample that one might almost suppose that he was permitted to exercise that right; but it is rendered certain by Phil. 1 : 13, 16 that he continued to be guarded by a Roman soldier.—Among the friends with Paul during this confinement who have been mentioned in our narrative were Luke, Timothy, Epaphras, Mark, Aristarchus, and Tychicus. The interruption of his personal intercourse with the churches caused the apostle to address them by letter, and thus the restraint on his liberty proved the means of opening to him a sphere of activity which has given him access to all nations, which makes him the contemporary of every age. As nearly all critics allow, he wrote during this captivity his Epistles to the Ephesians, the Colossians, the Philippians, and Philemon.—It must suffice to allude merely to the subsequent history of the great apostle. I cannot hesitate to agree with those who believe that Paul, on being brought to trial under his appeal to the emperor, was acquitted, and, casting aside his chains, went forth to labor again for the spread of the gospel. We see from his letters written while he was a captive that he was expecting to regain his liberty. (See, for example, Phil. 1 : 25 ; 2 : 23, 24; Philem. 22.) Even if Paul entertained this belief as a matter of judgment merely, and not in the exercise of a faith warranted by a special revelation, we must allow, at all events, that he had good means for forming a correct opinion of his prospects, and should be supposed, therefore, to have realized his hope, and not to have been condemned contrary to such manifest intimations of a different result. The journeys and labors indicated in the Pastoral Epistles make the supposition of an interval between a first and second imprisonment important, if not indispensable, as a means of reconciling Luke's account with this part of the apostle's correspondence. The facts mentioned in the letters to Titus and Timothy have no natural place in the portion of Paul's history recorded in the Acts. The style too and the circle of ideas in these Epistles indicate a later period in the life of the writer and in the progress of the churches than that of the conclusion of Luke's narrative. Finally, the historical testimony, as derived from the earliest sources, asserts a second Roman captivity in the most explicit manner. Clemens, the disciple and companion of Paul, affirms that the apostle, before his martyrdom, travelled " to the boundary of the West "—an expression which the Roman writers in that age applied to the trans-Alpine countries; and the Canon of Muratori (A. D. 170) represents " a journey into Spain " as a well-known event in Paul's history. Eusebius states the common belief of the early churches in these words : "After defending himself successfully it is currently reported that the apostle again went forth to proclaim the gospel, and afterward came to Rome a second time and was martyred under Nero."— Hints in the Epistles and traditions supply all that is known or conjectured respecting this last stage of the apostle's ministry. It is supposed that on being liberated (writers do not agree as to the precise order) he visited again parts of Asia Minor and Greece; went to Crete and founded, or more probably strengthened, the churches there; made his long-contemplated journey to Spain; wrote his First Epistle to Timothy and his Epistle to Titus; after several years of effective labor was apprehended again as a leader of the Christian sect; was brought a second time as a prisoner of Christ to Rome; was tried there, and condemned to suffer death. His Roman citizenship exempted him from the ignominy of crucifixion, and hence, according to the universal tradition, he was beheaded by the axe of the lictor. The same testimony places his martyrdom in the year A. D. 68, the last year of Nero's reign. It was in the daily expectation of this event that he wrote the last of his Epistles, the Second to Timothy. It is in that Epistle—written as the aged servant of Christ looked back to his trials all surmounted, forward to the hour when he should soon " be for ever with the Lord," yet amid his own joy still mindful of the welfare of others—that we hear his exultant voice : " I am now ready to be offered, and the time of my departure is at hand. I have fought a good fight, I have finished my course, I have kept the faith. Henceforth there is laid up for me a crown of righteousness, which the Lord, the righteous judge, shall give me at that day ; and not to me only, but unto all them also that love his appearing."

ABBREVIATIONS.

NAMES OF WRITERS ABBREVIATED IN THE NOTES.

THE works of those referred to in the following list are mostly commentaries, and may be presumed to be well known. The titles of some of those which are less common have been given at the foot of the page where they occur for the first time.

Alf. . . . . . . Alford.
Ang. . . . . . . Anger.
Bez. . . . . . . Beza.
Blmf. . . . . Bloomfield.
Bmg. . . . . . . Baumgarten.
Bng. . . . . . . Bengel.
Böttg. . . . . Böttger.
Bretsch. . . . Bretschneider.
Brud. . . . . . Bruder.
Calv. . . . . Calvin.
Chryst. . . . . Chrysostom.
Cony. and Hws. Conybeare and Howson.
De Wet. . . . De Wette.
Doddr. . . . . Doddridge.
Ebr. . . . . . . Ebrard.
Forbg. . . . . Forbiger.
Frtz. . . . . . . Fritzsche.
Gesen. . . . . Gesenius.
Grot. . . . . . . Grotius.
Grsb. . . . . Griesbach.
Hems. . . . . Hemsen.
Heng. . . . . Hengstenberg.
Herz. . . . . Herzog.
Hesych. . . . Hesychius.
Hmph. . . . . Humphry.

Hnr. . . . . . Heinrichs.
Krüg. . . . . Krüger.
Kuin. . . . . Kuinoel.
Kyp. . . . . Kypke.
Lchm. . . . . Lachmann.
Light. . . . . Lightfoot.
Lng. . . . . . Lange.
Mey. . . . . . Meyer.
Neand. . . . . Neander.
Olsh. . . . . . Olshausen.
Raph. . . . . Raphael.
Rob. . . . . . Robinson.
Schöttg. . . . Schöttgen.
Str. . . . . . Stier.
Suid. . . . . . Suidas.
Thol. . . . . Tholuck.
Treg. . . . . Tregelles.
Tsch. . . . . Tischendorf.
Vitr. . . . . . Vitringa.
Wdsth. . . . . Wordsworth.
West. and Hort. Westcott and Hort.
Wetst. . . . . Wetstein.
Whl. . . . . . Wahl.
Wiesl. . . . . Wieseler.
Win. . . . . . Winer.

OTHER ABBREVIATIONS.

Cranm. . . . . Cranmer's Version of N. T.
E. V. . . . . Common English Version.
Genv. . . . . Geneva Version.
Tynd. . . . . Tyndale's Version.

T. R. . . . . . Received Greek Text.
Vulg. . . . . Vulgate N. Testament.
Wicl. . . . . Wiclif's Version.

LIST OF ILLUSTRATIONS.

VIEWS.

MAPS.

INDEX I.

TO THE HISTORY.

INDEX II.

TO THE NOTES.

22

THE END.

COMMENTARY

ON THE

EPISTLE TO THE ROMANS.

ALBERT N. ARNOLD, D. D.,

AND

REV. D. B. FORD.

JUDSON PRESS

VALLEY FORGE

PRINTED IN U. S. A.

PREFACE.

When Dr. Arnold's manuscript exposition of Romans—which by reason of ill health he could not amplify to the extent desired—was placed in my hands by the general editor, with the request that I would duplicate its pages, I undertook the task with very great hesitancy, yet with this encouraging thought that, however unimportant might be my contributions, I could not, with the excellent work of my now lamented friend included, make a really poor commentary. In endeavoring to fill out and complete a work so well elaborated, I have not been specially ambitious to display original authorship, but have frequently quoted from some of the ablest commentators and other writers, and I trust that not a few of my readers will unite with me in thanking the Giver of every good gift that other men, in their studies and writings, have labored on this the profoundest treatise of inspiration, and that we have entered into their labor. The additions, whether original or selected, which I have made to Dr. Arnold's commentary, are either enclosed in square brackets in the body of the text, or else are inserted as foot notes, with the initial of my name attached. And now, having finished my moiety of the work, I can only commend our united labor to the God of all power and grace, that he may make it the means of promoting his truth and glory, of establishing believers in the faith of the gospel, and even of winning some to embrace "the righteousness of God which is through faith of Jesus Christ."

Hanover, Mass.

DAVID B. FORD.

INTRODUCTION TO THE EPISTLE OF PAUL THE APOSTLE TO THE ROMANS.

I. ORIGIN OF THE CHURCH AT ROME.

WE have no certain means of knowing at what precise time Christianity first gained a footing at Rome. It would seem, however, to have been many years before the date of the apostle's letter to the disciples there. They were then a numerous body (1 : 7), too numerous, apparently, to assemble conveniently or safely in one place, and therefore distributed into several companies. (16 : 5, 14, 15.) Some of them had long been disciples of Christ (16 : 3, 4 compared with Acts 18 : 2 ; 16 : 5, 6, 7, 12), their faith was already spoken of throughout the whole world (1 : 8 ; 16 : 19), and Paul had for many years been intending to visit them. (1 : 13 ; 15 : 23.) All these indications point to a numerous church, of no recent origin. [Thus a Christian church *may* have been planted there before it was at Philippi.]

We read of visitors or sojourners from Rome, both Jews and proselytes, at Jerusalem on the day of Pentecost. (Acts 2 : 10.) It is very probable that some among these were converted at that time, and soon after returned to Rome, and thus became the nucleus around which was afterward gathered the church to which Paul wrote. [As Fritzsche says: "They left Rome as Jews and returned as Christians."]

Had any one of the apostles been the founder of the church in Rome, we should probably have had, in the Book of Acts or in the Epistle itself, some intimation of this fact. The later tradition, which attributes to Peter the planting of the Christian faith in this metropolis of the world, is not only unsupported by any historical evidence, but is burdened with very serious difficulties. Jerome says ("De viris illustribus." Ch. I.) that Peter went to Rome in the second year of Claudius, A. D. 42, to confute Simon Magus, and that he was bishop there for twenty-five years. But we know that he was imprisoned in Jerusalem by Herod Agrippa in the fourth year of Claudius ; that he was there at the Council (Acts 15 : 7, seq.), in the tenth year of Claudius—at which time, probably, the agreement mentioned in Gal. 2 : 9 was made among the apostles, that Peter, James, and John should devote their labors chiefly to the Jews, and Paul and Barnabas to the Gentiles ;—that he was at Antioch with Paul and Barnabas, between the years A. D. 50 and A. D. 55 (Gal. 2 : 11–13); that he wrote his First Epistle from Babylon (1 Peter 5 : 13) ; probably A. D. 63 or 64, possibly seven or eight years earlier. It is not likely that there would have been no mention of Peter in the salutations in Rom. 16, if he had been at that time in Rome ; nor that he would have been passed over in silence if he had been there with Paul when the latter wrote his five epistles from that city (Ephesians, Philippians, Colossians, Philemon, 2 Timothy). Thus it appears that Peter is mentioned in the New Testament on four different occasions between the years A. D. 42 and A. D. 67, each time as being far from Rome; and that no mention is made of him on six different occasions within the same period when he would naturally have been mentioned by Paul if he had been in Rome. In fact, there is scarcely any period of half a dozen years, during all these twenty-five, when he could have resided continuously at Rome, consistently with the historical notices of him in the New Testament. [Paul's invariable rule "not to build upon another man's foundation" nor to "glory in another's province in regard to things made ready to his hand," is alone sufficient to prove that Peter was not the *founder* of the church in Rome—a fact which many Roman Catholic writers freely acknowledge. Meyer remarks that "our Epistle—since Peter cannot have been there before it was written—is a *fact destructive of the historical basis of the Papacy* in so far as this is made to rest on the founding of the Roman Church and the exercise of its episcopate by that apostle." This, of course, does not disprove the possibility that Peter may in after years have come to Rome and labored there in the gospel (without, however, founding any particular church), and that he there finally suffered martyrdom. Bishop Lightfoot even conjectures that both apostles may at some time have been together in Rome, that they exchanged once more the hands of fellowship, that they gathered, or preached to, two separate, though not necessarily antagonistic communities (traces of whose origin he finds in Phil. 1 : 15–18 ; Col. 4 : 11), and that this basis of fact "possibly underlies the tradition that St. Peter and St. Paul were joint founders of the Roman Church, and may explain the discrepancies in the lists of the early bishops." (See his "St. Paul and the Three," p. 337, in his "Commentary on Galatians.") But it is marvelous that this separation, if it ever existed. was so soon composed, for Bishop Lightfoot concedes that "at the close of the first century we see no more traces of a twofold church," all the Christian communities being united under the presiding eldership of Clement, and that we never hear of it afterward. On the contrary, Ignatius of Antioch and Dionysius of Corinth, both of whom wrote letters to Rome, and Hegesippus, who visited Rome, all of whom lived in the second century, assert or imply in their writings the unity and orthodoxy of the Roman Christians. To the frequent boast of Papists that they belong to that church which was the *first* and which will be last, we may simply reply that the *Jerusalem* Church was the *first* church of Christ on earth. If priority of age is anything, we should prefer to be a Jerusalem Catholic rather than a Roman Catholic. We are aware that some adherents of this church now disclaim the term "Roman." But if Rome with its hierarchy were sunk by some earthquake's shock, as it yet may be, the high and special claim of this church would at once be rendered null and void.]

Neither is it probable that the church at Rome owed its origin to any other apostle. There is no intimation of this kind in the New Testament ; and we know that Paul made it his rule not to build on another man's foundation. (Rom. 15 : 20 ; compare 2 Cor. 10 : 14–16.) He speaks of the Romans as belonging to his field of labor (1 : 13–15), and from the salutations in chap. 16, it appears that, although he had not yet visited them, many of them had been intimately connected with him. (16 : 3–9, 11, 13.) While, therefore, there is every probability that the church at Rome was not founded by the direct labors of any apostle, it seems to have been more closely connected in its early history with the labors of Paul than with those of any of the rest. [We may therefore say of Paul, that he was, directly or indirectly, the founder of all the historic churches of Asia Minor and of Europe.]

II. COMPOSITION OF THE CHURCH IN ROME.

The view generally held is, that the Gentile element predominated in the early Roman Church. It is plain that there was a very considerable Jewish element. (2 : 17–29 ; 3 : 1–4, 9–21 ; 4 : 1 ; 7 : 1–4 ; and chapters 9–11). There was a large population of Jews in Rome. Pompey brought many captives thither from Judea ; and these had greatly multiplied in the course of a century. Josephus speaks of eight thousand as attaching themselves to an embassy which appealed to Augustus. ("Antiq.," xvii. 11, 1.) This emperor assigned to them for their residence a district beyond the Tiber. About the time when Paul wrote his epistle, Seneca complains that many Romans had embraced the Jewish religion (he uses the expression "victi victoribus leges dederunt—the conquered have given laws to the conquerors."—Augustine, "De Civitate Dei," Lib. vi., ch. 11), and Juvenal scoffs at Judaizing Romans (Sat. xiv., v. 96–104). Still, the Jews formed but a comparatively insignificant portion of the population of the great capital of the world;[1] and it seems most probable that a church which had existed so long, and become so widely known, must have been mostly made up of Gentile converts. The tenor of the Epistle confirms this. It is as the apostle of the Gentiles that Paul writes them. (1 : 5, 6, 13 ; 9 : 3, 4 ; 10 : 1 ; 11 : 13, 14, 22, 23, 25, 30, 31 ; 15 : 15, 16.) ["From the description of most of the persons named in chap. 16, from the express approval given to the doctrine in which the Romans had been instructed, (6 : 17 ; 16 : 17), and even from the fact of the composition of the letter itself, inasmuch as not one of the now extant letters of the apostle is directed to a *non-Pauline* church, we may with certainty infer that *Pauline* Christianity was preponderant in Rome ; and from this it is a further necessary inference that a very important part of the Roman Church consisted of *Gentile Christians.*" (Meyer.) These Gentile believers, however, may have been Jewish proselytes before they became Christians, and so the church of Rome may have been "primarily, at least, one of the churches of the circumcision." (Plumptre.) Similar is the view of Jowett, who describes the Roman Church as of "Gentile origin and Jewish character." And this view is not inconsistent with the *generally* Pauline character of their doctrine, since a majority of them may have come from Greece and Asia Minor, and may have been some of Paul's earliest converts in those countries.]

It seems most likely, on the whole, that the Gentile element formed the majority : but these Gentile believers were probably in large part of Greek, rather than of Roman origin. The names mentioned in the salutations are largely Greek. The earliest Latin versions of the New Testament were made for use in the provinces rather than at Rome ; the names of the early bishops are more generally Greek than Latin ; and the earliest literature of the Roman Church was in Greek. (Justin Martyr, Clement, Caius, Hippolytus, etc.).

III. AUTHENTICITY OF THE EPISTLE.

The proof that the Apostle Paul wrote this Epistle is such as to satisfy every unprejudiced inquirer. It bears his name. It has been received as his without question from the earliest times. Its language and style agree with those of his other undoubted epistles. It presents many striking coincidences, as to matters of fact, with other parts of the New Testament. Compare 15 : 25–31 with Acts 20 : 2, 3 ; 24 : 17 ; 1 Cor. 16 : 1, 4 ; 2 Cor. 8 : 1–4 ; 9 : 2. Also, 16 : 21–23 with Acts 20 : 4 ; and 16 : 3, seq. with Acts 18 : 2, 18–26 ; 1 Cor. 16 : 19, seq.

In fine, it is no exaggeration to say, that there is no ancient writing of which the authorship is more certain than that of this Epistle. Even Baur questions the last two

---

[1] Gibbon, in chapter xxxi., says: "We may fairly estimate the inhabitants of Rome at twelve hundred thousand." Conybeare and Howson and Canon Farrar put theirs at "more than two millions." According to Dr. Schaff, the Jews in Rome itself "numbered from twenty to thirty thousand souls, had seven synagogues and three cemeteries."—(F.)

chapters only. [For resemblances between this Epistle and other epistles of Paul, especially that to the Galatians, see Lightfoot's "Commentary on the Galatians," pp. 44–48; and for "Undesigned Coincidences," see Paley's "Horæ Paulinæ," chapter II.]

IV. THE PLACE FROM WHICH THE EPISTLE WAS SENT.

Three names in the salutations very distinctly point to Corinth as the place where this Epistle was written.

1. We learn from 16 : 23 that the apostle was the guest of Gaius when he wrote it; and this Gaius was one of the converts baptized by Paul at Corinth. (1 Cor. 1 : 14.) Identity of persons is not, indeed, certainly inferred from identity of names, especially when the name is a very common one. But in connection with other known circumstances, the identity of the persons is in this case a very safe inference. What more natural, than that the apostle should be entertained by one of the very few Corinthians whom he had baptized with his own hands.

2. Phebe, who is commended to the Roman disciples (16 : 1), and who seems to have been the bearer of the Epistle, was a member, very probably a deaconess, of the church at Cenchrea, the Eastern port of Corinth.

3. Erastus, designated as the chamberlain, or treasurer, of the city (16 : 23), is mentioned in 2 Tim. 4 : 20, in connection with Corinth. See also Acts 19 : 21, 22.

We may consider it settled, therefore, that the Epistle to the Romans was written from Corinth. (The confirmation furnished by the subscription is of little account, as the subscriptions were added at a later date, and some of them are unquestionably false.)

V. DATE OF THE EPISTLE.

Paul's first missionary tour was confined to Asia Minor. (Acts 13 : 4, 14.) On his second tour (Acts 15 : 36 ; 18 : 21), he visited Corinth, and remained there at least a year and a half. (Acts 18 : 11-15.) At this time he became acquainted with Aquila and Priscilla, and labored with them in their common handiwork, as well as in the work of the gospel. (Acts 18 : 2, 3.) But the Epistle to the Romans could not have been written at this time ; for, when it was written, Aquila and Priscilla were in Rome. (16 : 3-5). No subsequent visit of Paul to Corinth is expressly mentioned in Acts ; but he intimates, in 2 Cor. 13 : 1, that he had already visited them *twice ;* and we know that on his third missionary tour (Acts 18 : 23 ; 21 : 8), he spent three months in Greece. (20 : 2, 3). He would not be likely to omit visiting that city of Greece, which was, in a Christian point of view, the most important of all. At this time, Sopater, Gaius, Timothy, and probably Erastus, were with him, (Acts 20 : 4, seq. ; 19 : 21, 22.) Now all these were with him when he wrote to the Romans. (16 : 21, 23.) Paul's plans at this time, as described in the Acts and in the Epistles to the Corinthians, agree exactly with those indicated in this Epistle. He was about to go to Jerusalem (Acts 20 : 22), to carry thither the contributions which had been gathered by the Christians of Macedonia and Achaia for the relief of their brethren in Judea (Acts 24 : 17 ; 1 Cor. 16 : 2-4; 2 Cor. 8 : 6-11), intending, after he had done this, to visit Rome. (Acts 19 : 21.) All these circumstances agree with what he writes to the Romans in 15 : 23-28.[1] It is quite certain, therefore, that this

[1] The fact that no mention is made of this charitable collection in the Epistle to the Galatians, while it is mentioned in other letters of this group (1, 2, Corinthians, Romans) is urged by Bishop Wordsworth in proof that the Epistles to the Corinthians were written subsequently to that to the Galatians, especially as its mention, had it been then undertaken, would have been exceedingly appropriate to the design of this Epistle, and could hardly have failed to find place in it.—(F.)

Epistle was written during the time which Paul spent in Corinth, while engaged in his third missionary journey.

It remains to fix, as nearly as we can, the *date* of that visit. We will take, as the surest and most convenient starting point, A. D. 52, the date of the decree of Claudius, banishing the Jews from Rome. See Hackett on Acts, notes on 18 : 2. Aquila and Priscilla had already reached Corinth after that decree, and Paul dwelt there with them at least a year and a half. He could hardly have left Corinth before the spring of A. D. 54. Embarking from Cenchrea, he sailed for Syria (Acts 18 : 18), by way of Ephesus, Cesarea, and Jerusalem. At Ephesus he made but a short stay, spending probably one Sabbath with his countrymen there (Acts 18 : 9), and leaving Aquila and Priscilla there. Proceeding thence to Cesarea, and landing there, he went up to Jerusalem, and saluted the church, and probably spent the Passover with them (Acts 18 : 21, 22); after which he went down to Antioch, and "spent some time there" (Acts 18 : 23) before he set out on his third missionary tour.

It must have been as late as the autumn of A. D. 54, perhaps the spring of A. D. 55, when he started on this journey. He went through Galatia and Phrygia to Ephesus (Acts 18 : 23 ; 19: 1-4), where he spent about two and a half years. (Acts 19 : 8, three months ; ver. 10, two years ; ver. 21, 22, a season. All these periods seem to be distinct and successive.) He could not have left Ephesus earlier than the spring of A. D. 57. He spent the ensuing summer in Macedonia and Achaia (Acts 20 : 1-6), and probably at this time proceeded as far west as Illyricum (15 : 19)—for it is hardly possible to find any earlier place for that journey—before he came into Greece. (Acts 20 : 3.) His abode there of three months (Acts 20 : 3) could hardly have begun much before the close of A. D. 57, and would consequently end in the early part of A. D. 58. When he left Corinth, the winter was past, for he purposed at first to go by sea (Acts 20 : 3) ; yet the spring could not have been far advanced, for he hoped to be at Jerusalem at the Feast of Pentecost in May. (Acts 20 : 16.)

The Epistle to the Romans was therefore probably written in the early part of A. D. 58.

According to the chronology of Conybeare and Howson, Paul was taken from Cesarea to be carried as a prisoner to Rome, in August, A. D. 60. (Vol. II., p. 543 Scribner's ed.)[1] He had been a prisoner at Cesarea for two years. (Acts 24 : 27.) Allowing five or six months for the previous journey from Corinth to Jerusalem, and the occurrences at the latter place before he was removed to Cesarea (Acts 20 : 3 ; 23 : 35), we have a very satisfactory corroboration of our previous calculation. Two years and five months, reckoned backward from August, A. D. 60, would bring us to March A. D. 58.

VI. OCCASION OF WRITING THE EPISTLE.

[The Epistle to the Romans was not written, like those to the Corinthians and the Galatians, to correct local abuses and errors; but for the most part it is encyclical, or catholic, in its nature, and would be well adapted to the needs of any church existing in the apostle's time. For in the churches of that age there were, to a greater or less degree, Judaizing tendencies on the one hand, and Hellenizing or paganizing tendencies on the

[1] Paul would then arrive at Rome in the spring of A. D. 61, the seventh year of Nero's reign, and the twenty-fourth of his life. The great fire at Rome, and the consequent persecution of Christians occurred A. D. 64, and hence were probably subsequent to Paul's release from imprisonment. It is now commonly supposed that after a brief second imprisonment he was beheaded on the Ostian Way, in the year 66 or 67. Nero committed suicide A. D 68.—(F.)

other ; and we cannot suppose the Roman Church formed an exception in this respect. (14 : 12 ; 16 : 17.) During the third missionary tour of the apostle, he wrote the first four epistles of the New Testament, that to the Romans being the last written. A short time before inciting this letter, he had, with much anguish of heart, written to the paganizing Corinthians, and to the Judaizing Galatians. As some of them doubted or denied that he was an apostle, he felt obliged in these letters to assert and prove his divine call to the apostleship ; but his principal endeavor was to win back his erring brethren from their disorders and immoralities, and from their vain trusting in the ritual ceremonies of Judaism, those "weak and beggarly rudiments," to seek salvation in which was, to him, like seeking the living among the dead. And now, in a calmer frame of mind, he sits down to write out for the benefit of his brethren in the world's capital whom he intended speedily to visit, and from whom he would fain secure a favorable reception for himself, and for the gospel which he preached, the substance of that which had so recently and so intensely occupied his mind, to wit : "The position of the Christian in reference to the Law, and of the relations of Judaism to Heathenism, and of both to Christianity." (Farrar.) He had preached the gospel of grace in the principal cities of the East, and he would naturally wish to do the same in the imperial city, of whose church he may have heard much from the lips of Aquila and Priscilla,[1] among whose members he had many personal friends, and in whose welfare he felt the deepest interest. But he knew the dangers which would attend his journey to Jerusalem, as well as the common uncertainties of life, and thus he who had oftentimes been hindered hitherto (1 : 13 ; 15 : 22) might again be prevented from orally communicating the gospel to his Roman brethren. "Besides," as Godet remarks, "should he arrive at Rome safe and sound, he had too much tact to think of putting the members of such a church, as it were, on the catechumen's bench. In these circumstances how natural the idea of filling up, by means of writing, the blank which Providence had permitted, and of giving, in an *epistolary treatise* addressed to the church, the Christian instruction which it had missed, and which was indispensable to the solidity of its faith." At this time also, as Paul was about to depart for the East to carry the offerings of Gentiles to the poor saints in Jerusalem, Phebe, a deaconess in the neighboring church of Cenchrea, was, as is commonly supposed, about to sail in an opposite direction for the Empire's capital city, which Paul said he "must see." (Acts 19 : 21.) And this her journey Romeward furnished, of course, a convenient opportunity of sending the letter. In this way, apparently, originated "The Epistle of Paul to the Romans," which is characterized by Dr. Schaff as "the epistle of the epistles," by Dr. Meyer, as "the grandest and richest in contents of all the apostle's letters,"[2] and by Coleridge, as "the most profound work in existence."]

VII. LANGUAGE IN WHICH THE EPISTLE WAS WRITTEN.

[It might be supposed that Paul, when writing to the Romans, would, if he were able, use the Latin tongue, since the letter was not only addressed to Roman residents,

---

[1] De Wette and Meyer *versus* Hemsen, Hug, Olshausen, Neander, Wieseler, Farrar, and Plumptre, hold that these were Paul's converts at Corinth, and were not members of the Roman Church. It will be recollected that Paul abode with these two disciples at Corinth for the space of at least one year and six months.—(F.)

[2] The last literary work of Dr. Meyer (died June 21st, 1873) was the preface (written March, 1873) to the English edition of his "Commentary on Romans." And it is an interesting circumstance that the words inscribed on his tombstone are taken from this Epistle: 14 : 8 : "Whether we live, we live unto the Lord; and whether we die, we die unto the Lord ; whether we live therefore, or die, we are the Lord's."—(F.)

but was written by an amanuensis who bore a Latin name.¹ But it must be remembered that the Greek language had at this time become well-nigh universal. "It was," says Gibbon, "almost impossible, in any province, to find a Roman subject of a liberal education who was at once a stranger to the Greek and to the Latin language." As vouchers for this general acquaintance with Greek on the part of the Romans, Tholuck, in Chapter 3, of his "Introduction," cites Tacitus, Ovid, Martial, Juvenal, and Suetonius. It is, moreover, a singular circumstance, yet "nothing is more certain than that the Church of Rome was at this time a Greek, and not a Latin Church." See Smith's "Bible Dictionary," p. 2746, also II. of this Introduction. "The literary language at Rome," says Godet, "was Greek. This is established by the numerous Greek inscriptions in the Catacombs, by the use of the Greek language in the letter of Ignatius to the Church of Rome, in the writings of Justin Martyr composed at Rome, and in those of Irenæus composed in Gaul," as also in those of Hippolytus, Bishop of Ostia, the seaport of Rome. "The early bishops and divines of Rome were Greeks by descent or education, or both. Pope Cornelius addressed the churches in the Hellenic language in the middle of the third century. The Apostle's Creed, even in the Roman form, was originally composed in Greek. The Roman Liturgy (ascribed to Clement of Rome) was Greek. The inscriptions in the oldest catacombs, and the epitaphs of the popes down to the middle of the third century, are Greek." (Schaff.) We may add that most of the manuscripts discovered in the ruins of Herculaneum appear to have been written in Greek. Milman, in his "Latin Christianity," says: "The Church of Rome, and most, if not all, the churches of the West were, if we may so speak, Greek religious colonies." Tarsus also, where Paul was born, was of Greek origin, and was celebrated for its Greek schools and learning. The geographer Strabo (born about 60 B. C.) says that in its zeal for learning and philosophy it excelled even Athens and Alexandria. Paul "doubtless spoke Greek from childhood" (Tholuck), and we do not suppose that he utterly discarded Greek study in Jerusalem. His liberal-minded teacher, "Rabban Gamliel," favored Greek study, and, according to the Talmud, knew Greek literature better than any other doctor of the law. "A thousand students were in the academy of my grandsire," said a descendant of Gamaliel, "five hundred of whom studied the Greek"; and the Talmud maintains that Paul "had always a Grecian poem on his lips." Indeed, Dr. Isaac M. Wise, President of the Hebrew Union College, Cincinnati (from whose writings we have made these last extracts) says, in his "History of the Hebrews' Second Commonwealth," p. 307, that "in the academy at Jerusalem he (Paul) was noted as paying more attention to Greek poetry and infidel books than to his studies"! From Acts 21 : 37 we are assured that

¹That Paul must have had considerable acquaintance with the Latin language, if not at the time this Epistle was written, at least some years afterward, is most certain. The Latin dialect would, of course, naturally extend itself wherever the Roman Government was established, and this had at that time become almost universal. This language was stamped on the national coins; it was used in trade, in public edicts, in legal proceedings. Paul always was a subject of the Roman Government, was born in a Roman "free city," and passed his life in Roman colonies and provinces. In every country of his residence he could have seen Roman soldiers, centurions, chiliarchs, or military tribunes (Acts 21: 31), prætors and lictors (Acts 16: 20, 35), proconsuls and procurators, or "governors." (Acts 13: 7; 23: 24.) Latin was used to some extent in Palestine and in Jerusalem. It was one of the three languages which were inscribed, not only on the inner separating wall of the Court of the Gentiles, forbidding any foreigner to go within the sanctuary on pain of death (Josephus' "Antiquities," xv., xi., 5; "Wars," vi., ii., 4), but also on the Saviour's cross. The word Christian, though first expressed in Greek letters, was yet put in a Latinized form. And when we further consider that Paul, as is commonly believed, was chained to a Roman soldier during his two years' imprisonment in Cesarea and his two years' imprisonment at Rome, to say nothing of his long-protracted sea voyage, we must conclude that the apostle in his last years was familiarly acquainted with Latin.—(F.)

Paul could speak Greek.   He certainly quoted several times from the Greek poets (Acts 17 : 28 : 1 Cor. 15 : 33; Titus 1 : 12), and with some of them—as when he refers his Athenian audience to certain (τινες) of their own poets (to wit, Aratus and Cleanthes)—he seems to have had more than a hearsay acquaintance.   We have spoken of Greek as a current language among the ancients.[1]   The Old Testament Apocrypha was written mainly in Greek (only Ecclesiasticus and 1 Maccabees were originally written in modern Hebrew), and the Old Testament was translated, not into Aramaic, or modern Hebrew, but into Greek, and it was this version of the Seventy which the New Testament writers mainly used.   Noticeable also is the fact that the Epistle to the Hebrews and James' Epistle to the Jews of the "Dispersion" were written, not in Aramaic, but in Greek. The Greek dialect, too, seems to have been almost as common in Palestine as the vernacular Aramaic.   Indeed, Dr. Roberts, author of the "Companion to the Revised Version," endeavors to show in his "Discussions on the Gospels" that Christ and the apostles spoke mostly in Greek, and only occasionally in Aramaic.   Of course, he would decide that *all* the Gospels and other New Testament Scriptures were originally spoken or written in Greek.   Similarly, S. G. Green, in his "Grammar of the Greek Testament" : "It was the Greek of the Septuagint, in all probability, our Lord and his apostles *generally* spoke.   The dialect of Galilee was not a corrupt Hebrew, but a provincial Greek."   Josephus, a Jewish priest, who lived in the time of the apostles, wrote his "Wars" and "Antiquities" in Greek, though he states that he composed the first-named work originally in Hebrew for the benefit of the "Upper Barbarians."   That the Greek people or language had penetrated even into barbarian regions is evident from Seneca's query : "What is the meaning of Greek cities in barbarous countries, and the Macedonian language among Indians and Persians?"   For the general prevalence of the Greek language, especially in Palestine in the time of Christ, see Hug's "Introduction to the New Testament," pp. 326–340; Dr. Schaff's "Companion to the Greek Testament," p. 7; Prof. Hadley's article on the "Language of the New Testament," and B. F. Westcott's article on the New Testament, in Smith's "Bible Dictionary," pp. 1590, 2139; also articles on the "Language of Palestine in the Age of Christ and the Apostles," in the April and July numbers of the "Biblical Repository" for 1831.]

VIII.   THE OBJECT OF THE EPISTLE.

The main object which the apostle had in view in writing this Epistle is nowhere formally stated; but it may be inferred from the Introduction, and from the contents of the Epistle.   In the Introduction he expresses his earnest desire to visit the disciples at Rome, in order to contribute something to their confirmation and spiritual comfort. (1 : 11, 12.)   Doubtless he had the same end in view in writing to them; and he seeks to attain this end by unfolding the way of justification and salvation through faith in Christ.   The object of his letter, then, is to present such an exhibition of the way of justification and salvation through faith in Christ, as would be adapted to comfort and confirm the disciples at Rome.   The Epistle might well take its title from the sixteenth verse of the first chapter : "The Gospel the Power of God unto Salvation to every one that believeth"; and the manner in which the apostle treats this subject is adapted to

---

[1] Paul evidently needed not to be specially endowed with the gift of tongues, as Wordsworth supposes, in order to obey his Lord's last command, since a knowledge of Greek and Hebrew alone would enable him to preach intelligibly in almost all parts of the civilized world.—(F.)

promote the spiritual confirmation and comfort of all who devoutly study this Epistle. May the readers of the following notes find them helpful toward that happy result.

Pawtuxet, R. I.   ALBERT N. ARNOLD.

[On the 11th day of October, 1883, the writer of the above lines ceased from his earthly toils, and entered into rest. Yet his labors for Christ were not felt by him to be irksome, and those especially which were spent in the study of this noble Epistle were manifestly to him an exceeding pleasure and delight. In a letter, dated January 7, 1882, he thus writes : "I heartily wish that you may have as much enjoyment in the performance of your work as I had in the performance of mine. And may the blessing of our common Master rest upon our joint work to the glory of his name and the benefit of his people." We are glad to be assured, but are not surprised to learn, that in his last days the comfort of the Scriptures, and especially of the great doctrines of grace, did not fail him. The old theology, which was his soul's food in life, was his abundant support in his last days. On hearing, shortly before his death, of the apparently approaching end of a greatly endeared classmate and friend, Thomas D. Anderson, D. D., he said : "Mine is an abundant entrance. Tell him (speaking his friend's name) that we shall soon[1] meet above, sinners saved by sovereign grace—sovereign, redeeming grace." "And this," says the narrator, Dr. J. C. Stockbridge, "he kept repeating over and over, as if he would gather up all he wished to say, of what was profoundest and dearest in his religious faith, and concentrate it upon that which was the very heart and substance of his creed, 'sovereign, redeeming grace.'" If, since the days of the apostles, there have lived any Christian men whose kindliness and guilelessness of spirit, whose blamelessness of life, and whose diligence in Christian labor, could furnish a ground of acceptance with God, one of those men, in my opinion, was Albert Nicholas Arnold. And yet, had it been suggested to him from without, or from within, that he could properly place this reliance upon the righteousness of his character and the goodness of his varied and abundant works, laboring as he had done, so assiduously as a preacher and pastor, a missionary, a theological instructor and writer, the thought, we believe, would have been repelled by him with as emphatic a "God forbid" as was ever uttered by the Apostle Paul. Yet no one was more careful than he to maintain good works, both as a fruit and evidence of his love for Christ and of his faith in him. May the readers of these lines, by a deep consciousness of their lost condition by nature, and by a rich experience of the "sovereign, redeeming grace" of the gospel, be made to feel that we need no other or better theology than that which is so plainly set forth in the writings of this blessed apostle, and which our beloved and now lamented friend sought to embody in these pages.]

ANALYSIS OF THE EPISTLE.

PART I.—*Introduction.* (1 : 1–15.) (*a*) Salutatory. (Ver. 1–7.) (*b*) Conciliatory. (Ver. 8–15.)

PART II.—*Doctrinal.* (1 : 16–11 : 36.)

§1. ALL MANKIND IN A SINFUL AND CONDEMNED STATE, AND THEREFORE IN NEED OF THE SALVATION WHICH THE GOSPEL REVEALS. (1 : 16–3 : 20.) The subject opened. (1 : 16, 17.)

---

[1] It was "soon," the 19th of the ensuing December, that the beloved Anderson, a man of kindred spirit with Arnold, followed him to the land of rest. What a world of darkness they have left for what a world of light! Gladly would we exchange, for just their first moment's experience in bliss, all the theology of all the schools of earth.—(F.)

I. The general sinfulness of men proved. (1 : 18–2 : 29.)

    A. In the case of the Gentiles. (1 : 18–22.) God has made known his displeasure against all ungodliness and unrighteousness. (Ver. 18.) The Gentiles are both ungodly (ver. 19–23) and unrighteous. (Ver. 24–32.)

    B. In the case of the Jews. (2 : 1–29.) Those who practice the same sins which they condemn in others are equally inexcusable (2 : 1), for God's judgment will be impartial (ver. 2–5), and justly most severe against those who have the most light. (Ver. 6–16.) Neither the possession of the law (ver. 17–24), nor the covenant of circumcision (ver. 25–29), will exempt them from condemnation.

II. Objections stated and answered. (3 : 1–8.) Objection 1. The Jew has no advantage over the Gentile. (Ver. 1.) Answer : The possession of God's word is a great advantage. (Ver. 2.) Objection 2. God's faithfulness obliges him to show favor to the Jews, notwithstanding their unfaithfulness. (Ver. 3.) Answer : God's faithfulness must not be questioned, however unfaithful men may be. (Ver. 4.) Objection 3. It would be unjust in God to punish those whose sins are the occasion of displaying his righteousness. (Ver. 5, 7.) Answer : The principle which this objection assumes leads to conclusions manifestly false and impious ; as,

    (*a*) That God cannot righteously judge and punish any. (Ver. 6)

    (*b*) That it is lawful to do evil that good may come. (Ver. 8.)

III. The charge of universal sinfulness renewed, and confirmed by proofs from Scripture. (Ver. 9–20.)

§ 2. THE WAY OF JUSTIFICATION AND SALVATION THROUGH FAITH IN CHRIST. (3 : 21–5 : 21.)

I. The gospel method of justification described, as being—

    A. In its *nature,*

        (1) Conditioned not on works, but on faith. (3 : 21, 22.)

        (2) Available for all mankind. (Ver. 22.)

        (3) Needed by all. (Ver. 22, 23.)

        (4) Entirely gratuitous. (Ver. 24.)

    B. As having, for its *ground,* the propitiatory sacrifice of Christ. (Ver. 24, 25.)

    C. For its direct *object,* the reconciliation of God's righteousness with man's salvation. (Ver. 25, 26.)

    D. For its indirect *results,*

        (1) The exclusion of all boasting. (Ver. 27, 28.)

        (2) The display of God's impartial mercy to both Jews and Gentiles. (Ver. 29, 30.)

        (3) The confirmation, not the subversion, of the law. (Ver. 31.)

II. That the above method of justification is in harmony with the teachings of Scripture is shown by the examples of Abraham and David. (4 : 1–25.)

    (1) Abraham was justified, not by works, but by faith. (Ver. 1–5.)

    (2) David teaches that justification is not of merit, but of grace. (Ver. 6–8.)

    (3) Circumcision is not indispensable to justification ; for Abraham was justified before he was circumcised. (Ver. 9–12.)

    (4) The law is not the ground of justification ; for Abraham, who was justified, not by the law, but by faith, is in this respect the pattern of all who are justified, both Jews and Gentiles. (Ver. 13–17.) This illustrious pattern is more fully described and commended. (Ver. 18–25.)

III. The happy results of the gospel way of justification, both to the individual believer, and to the race at large. (5 : 1–21.)

A. As it respects the individual believer, the results are :

(1) Peace with God, including free access to him. (Ver. 1, 2.)

(2) Joyful hope of future glory. (Ver. 2.)

(3) Afflictions made subservient to the confirmation of our hope. (Ver. 3, 4.)

(4) The certainty of this hope.

(a) For God has already given us his Spirit. (Ver. 5.)

(b) He has already shown the fullness of his love to us, by giving his Son to die for us while we were yet sinners. (Ver. 6–8.)

(c) By thus beginning the work of our salvation while we were enemies, he has given the surest pledge that he will complete it now that we are reconciled to him (ver. 9, 10), so that we have a present and abounding joy. (Ver. 11.)

B. As it respects the race at large, the benefits of the gospel way of justification are illustrated by a comparison between Adam and Christ. (Ver. 12–21.)

(a) The resemblance between the two cases. (Ver. 12–14.)

(b) The differences stated under several aspects. (Ver. 15–17.)

(c) Recapitulation of the whole, showing how men are regarded and treated in consequence of their connection with Adam and Christ respectively. (Ver. 18, 19.) As the law discloses and even aggravates, the triumphs of sin, reigning in death, so the gospel displays the superior triumphs of grace, reigning unto life, through Jesus Christ. (Ver. 20, 21.)

§ 3. THIS WAY OF JUSTIFICATION FAVORABLE TO HOLINESS. (6 : 1–8 : 39.)

PROPOSITION I. Gratuitous justification does not lead to sinful living. (6 : 1–23.)

(a) The objection stated. (Ver. 1.)

(b) Its validity denied. (Ver. 2.)

(c) The grounds of that denial. (Ver. 3–23.)

I. The justified believer, agreeably to the very import of his baptism, is brought into such a connection and comformity with Christ as dying and rising to a new life, that he cannot continue in the old life of sin. (Ver. 3–6.) As Christ's death on account of sin is never to be repeated (ver. 7–10), so the believer must regard his own separation from sin as final. (Ver. 11–14.)

II. The very fact that he is not under the law, but under grace, forbids that sin should have dominion over him. (Ver. 14, 15.) For his relation to the law and to grace is like the relation of a servant to his master : Before justification, he is a servant of sin, under an influence which secures his obedience to evil ; after justification, he is a servant of righteousness, under an influence which secures his obedience to good. (Ver. 16–20.) The former service results in death, the latter in eternal life ; and the knowledge of these opposite consequences is a still farther security for his continued fidelity to his new Master. (Ver. 21–23.)

PROPOSITION II. So long as men remain under the law, they continue under the power of sin. (7 : 1–25.)

(a) The believer's relation to the law may be illustrated by the case of marriage. (Ver. 1–6.) As the wife is freed from her conjugal obligations by the death of her husband, so that she is afterward at liberty to be married to another man (ver. 1–3) ; so we are freed from our connection

B

with the law, that we may enter into a new connection with Christ. (Ver. 4.) The fruit of that first connection was sin. (Ver. 5.) The fruit of this second connection is holiness. (Ver. 6.)

(*b*) The law has no power to convert a sinner, or to make a bad man good ; this illustrated by Paul's own experience before his conversion (ver. 7-13), (the effect of the law is to make sin known (ver. 7), and also to excite it to greater activity (ver. 8-11), so that, while the law is good (ver. 12), it becomes the occasion of manifesting more fully the exceeding sinfulness of sin.) (Ver. 13.)

(*c*) The law has no power to sanctify a saint, or to make a good man better : this illustrated by Paul's own experience after his conversion. (Ver. 14-24.) (Even the renewed man, who assents to the excellence of the law, and desires and purposes to fulfill its requirements, finds that the remains of indwelling sin often prove too strong for his good resolutions (ver. 14-23); so that, as long as he looks to the law, he gets no effectual help or comfort in his strivings after holiness. (Ver. 24.) Hence the conclusion, that if we are ever to be freed from the dominion of sin, it must be by becoming connected with Christ. (Ver. 25.)

PROPOSITION III. Grace accomplishes what the law could not accomplish. (8:1-17.)

(*a*) Grace furnishes not only a justifying righteousness (ver. 1), but also a regenerating and sanctifying power. (Ver. 2.) The way in which this is done briefly explained. (Ver. 3, 4.)

(*b*) Sanctification is the indispensable evidence of justification. (Ver. 5-17.) The justified will certainly walk in newness of life, because :

(1) Their inward moral disposition is thoroughly changed. (Ver. 5-8.)

(2) The Spirit of God dwells in and actuates them. (Ver. 9-13.)

(3) They are children of God, not only by a formal adoption on his part, but also by a filial spirit on theirs. (Ver. 14-17.)

PROPOSITION IV. The sufferings which believers undergo in this life are not inconsistent with their being fully justified and accepted of God. (Ver. 17-30.)

(*a*) For they suffer with Christ, that they may be glorified with him. (Ver. 17.)

(*b*) There is an immeasurable disproportion between the present sufferings and the future glory. (Ver. 18.) The greatness of that future glory is seen :

(1) In the unconscious longing for its coming which pervades all nature. (Ver. 19-22.)

(2) In the conscious longing of believers, notwithstanding the happiness which they enjoy in the present foretaste of it. (Ver. 23-25.)

(*c*) Suitable spiritual supports are afforded them while these sufferings continue. (Ver. 26, 27.)

(*d*) They are assured that all these sufferings are working for their good. (Ver. 28-30.)

PROPOSITION V. The certainty of the salvation of believers is established. (Ver. 31-39.) They for whose salvation (ver. 31) God has given his Son, and for whom the Son (ver. 32, 33) of God has died and risen from the dead (ver. 34), can never be separated from the love of either by any vicissitudes of the present life (ver. 35–37), or by any other events or agencies whatsoever. (Ver. 38, 39.)

§ 4. THE REJECTION OF THE JEWS. (9 : 1–11 : 36.)

(a) The *fact* of their rejection, though very lamentable (ver. 1–5), is not inconsistent with God's truth and justice : not with his *truth*, because the blessings which they fail to secure were never promised indiscriminately to all the natural seed of Abraham (ver. 6–13) ; not with his *justice*, because—

(1) These blessings are God's free gifts, bestowed according to his sovereign pleasure. (Ver. 14–18.)

(2) The unbelieving Jews only receive the righteous recompense of their willful sin. (Ver. 19–24.)

(3) Indeed, their rejection is plainly foretold by their own prophets. (Ver. 25–29.) In fine, the Gentiles obtain righteousness through faith in Christ, and the Jews fail to obtain it because of unbelief. (Ver. 30–33.) Thus it appears that :

(b) The *cause* of the failure of the Jews to attain justification (for which failure the apostle again expresses his sorrow) (10 : 12) is, that they persist in seeking justification in their own false way, instead of seeking it in God's true way. (Ver. 3–11.) Justification is attainable on precisely the same terms by Jews and Gentiles. (Ver. 12–13.) Therefore the gospel ought to be preached to all nations. (Ver. 14, 15.) All this is confirmed by the testimony of the Scriptures. (Ver. 16–21.)

(c) There is a *limit* to this rejection, both as to persons, and as to time. (Chap. 11.)

I. As to *persons*, it is not *total*, for Paul himself (ver. 1), and many others among the Jews (ver. 2–5), have obtained justification through free grace (ver. 6), though the greater part of the nation has been rejected (ver. 7), as their own Scriptures had foretold. (Ver. 8–10.)

II. As to *time*, it is not *final;* but God designs, by this temporary rejection of the Jews, to facilitate the conversion of the Gentiles. (Ver. 11–16.) The Gentiles are admonished not to glory over the Jews, as if their advantage over them was due to any merit of their own. (Ver. 17–22.) So soon as the Jews turn from their unbelief, God is able and willing to save them. (Ver. 23, 24.) Nay, more; he has positively determined that they shall at last turn and be saved. (Ver. 25–32.) In all this, his unsearchable wisdom is gloriously displayed. (Ver. 33–36.)

PART III.—*Practical.* (12: 1–15 : 13.) (a) General Precepts, applicable to all. (12: 1–13 : 14.) (b) Special Directions in regard to the treatment of those who are weak and over-scrupulous. (14 : 1–15 : 13.)

(a) General Precepts.

(1) Exhortation to entire consecration to God. (12 : 1.) This results in a practical conformity to his will (ver. 2), and in humility. (Ver. 3.)

(2) Duties to the church (ver. 4–8), and to the brethren. (Ver. 9–13.)

(3) Duties to the world, and especially to enemies. (Ver. 14–21.)

(4) Duties to rulers. (13 : 1–7.)

(5) The duty of love to all men. (Ver. 8–10.)

(6) All these duties enforced by the consideration that salvation is near. (Ver. 11–14.)

(*b*) Special Directions in regard to the treatment of brethren whose consciences are weak and are over-scrupulous. (14 : 1–15 : 13.)

I. The Christian who regards the Jewish restrictions as to days and meats as still binding is to be received without disputations. (14 : 1, 2.)

(*a*) Because this weakness does not hinder his acceptance with God. (Ver. 3, 4.)

(*b*) Because he is conscientious in it. (Ver. 5–9.)

(*c*) Because all such differences should be referred to the final judgment. (Ver. 10–12.)

II. Those who, through better knowledge, are free from such scruples, must not so use their freedom as to lead their weaker brethren into sin. (Ver. 13.)

(*a*) Because, though the use of this liberty is not wrong in itself, yet it is a breach of charity to use it to the injury of a brother. (Ver. 14, 15.)

(*b*) Because such a course brings religion into reproach. (Ver. 16.)

(*c*) Because the *use* of this liberty is no essential part of Christian duty. (Ver. 17, 18.)

(*d*) Because it is inconsistent with the obligation to promote the peace of the church, and the edification of the brethren. (Ver. 19.) They therefore who know that the eating of certain meats is not sinful, must not use their liberty in such a way as to entice others who have not this knowledge to do the same thing in violation of their consciences. (Ver. 20–23.) They must rather bear the infirmities, and seek the edification of the weak. (15 : 1, 2.) Thus they must imitate the self-denying example of Christ. (Ver. 3–7.) For Christ, agreeably to the predictions of the prophets, has received both Jews and Gentiles, and united them into one body. (Ver. 8–13.)

PART IV.—*Personal.* (15 : 14–16 : 23.)

(1) As to his own relations and feelings toward them. (15 : 14–33.) The apostle declares his confidence in them. (Ver. 14.) He justifies the freedom with which he has addressed them. (Ver. 15.) This he does on the ground of his office as the apostle of the Gentiles. (Ver. 16–21.) He expresses his hope of visiting them soon. (Ver. 22–29.) He asks their prayers in his behalf. (Ver. 30–33.)

(2) After bespeaking their Christian hospitality and kind offices for Phebe, a servant of the church, at Cenchrea (and probably the bearer of the Epistle) (16 : 1, 2), he sends his salutations to various members of the church. (Ver. 3–16.)

(3) He warns them against those who cause divisions. (Ver. 17–20.)

(4) He adds salutations from Christian friends who were with him. (Ver. 21–23.)

PART V.—*Conclusion.* (16 : 24–27.)

(1) *Benediction.* (Ver. 24.) (2.) *Doxology*—embodying a brief summary of gospel doctrine. (Ver. 25–27.)

PAUL'S EPISTLE TO THE ROMANS.

CHAPTER I.

PAUL, a servant of Jesus Christ, called *to be* an apos- | 1   Paul, a [1] servant of Jesus Christ, called *to be* an
tle, separated unto the gospel of God. |

1 Gr. *bondservant.*

PART I. (Ch. 1: 1-15.) INTRODUCTION. (*a*) Salutatory. (Ver. 1-7.)

1. Paul. It was the custom of the ancients to place the name of the writer of a letter at the beginning of the letter instead of at the end. We have many examples of this in the Greek and Latin classics. [With this name, a verb "writes" (γράφει), or "greeting" (χαίρειν) or, in full, *gives greeting*, as in 2 John 10, 11) Rev. Ver. (λέγει χαίρειν), is properly understood; but in all the epistles of the New Testament, save that of James, the name of the writer, when expressed in the salutation, stands independently. "Here the substance of the verb (χαίρειν) appears in the following *grace to you*, etc., as an independent sentence, and invocation of blessing of richer fullness." (Philippi.) On the New Testament use of this verb, see ver. 7.] The writer of this Epistle is called by his Hebrew name, Saul, until after his conversion. The name Paul is found about one hundred and sixty times in the New Testament—about one hundred and thirty times in the Acts, nearly thirty times in his own epistles, including the salutation in all the thirteen, and once it is mentioned by Peter. (2 Peter 3: 15.) It is first introduced in Acts 13: 9, and the name Saul, which has been used more than twenty times before, is never used afterward, except in four or five places, where the apostle recounts the words addressed to him by Jesus, and by Ananias, at the time of his conversion. (Acts 22: 7, 13; 26: 14.) Some have supposed that the name Paul was assumed by the apostle out of respect to Sergius Paulus. But though the change from Saul to Paul is first mentioned in connection with the account of the conversion of this Roman proconsul, it is more probable that both names were borne by him from the beginning. It was no uncommon thing in that age for Jews, especially such as associated much with foreigners, to be known among their own countrymen by their Hebrew name, and among foreigners by a different name; and the fact that the apostle was born in a foreign city, and inherited the rights of a Roman citizen (Acts 22: 28), makes it probable that both names belonged to him from early life. And on this supposition, the change from the Hebrew to the Roman name is appriately made by Luke just at the point where he begins directly to speak of Paul's labors in his chosen and recognized sphere as the "apostle of the Gentiles." Compare Dr. Hackett's note on Acts 13: 19.

[In the Talmud, Paul, as certain Jewish writers affirm, is called "Acher"—that is, "Another"; and one modern rabbi supposes he was so called because he went under an assumed name, or was virtually anonymous. Perhaps the name was given to him as one belonging to another and different faith, and was thus nearly equivalent to *heterodox* or heretic. Or possibly it was applied to Paul even more contemptuously, just as the ancient rabbis, unwilling to speak the name pig, called it "the other thing." If any one wishes to see how far modern rationalistic Judaism can caricature the noblest of lives and of characters, let him look at the account given of Paul, and other apostles of Jesus Christ, in the "Origin of Christianity," and in the "History of the Hebrews' Second Commonwealth," by Dr. Isaac M. Wise. We may add that this "Acher," according to the Talmud, was a married man, and that he left daughters.]

A servant of Jesus Christ. The word here translated 'servant' is the same that is properly translated slave in classic Greek. Its use here is indicative of humility, but not of servility. The more absolutely submissive a man is to Jesus Christ, the more surely is he free from bondage to man. "To serve God is true liberty," says Augustine. So also for

21

substance says the Scripture. See Ps. 116: 16; 119: 45; John 8: 36.[1] Paul gives himself this title only here, and, in connection with Timothy, in Phil. 1: 1. Elsewhere in the beginning of his epistles he styles himself simply an apostle of Jesus Christ.

The use of the two names 'Jesus Christ' is connected with some important peculiarities in the original manuscripts of the New Testament. In the first place, one of the names is often omitted in the best manuscripts, where our English version has them both. In the second place, the order of the two names is often inverted. This inversion is often represented in the English; always, indeed, where the Greek manuscripts are uniform; but they often differ among themselves. The omissions and inversions consitute a large number of the so-called "various readings" in the New Testament manuscripts. These are obviously of very little importance. Other peculiarities in the use of the two are more important. Among these are the various proportions in which the two are used in different parts of the New Testament. In the gospels the name Jesus is used between five hundred and six hundred times. The word Christ is used in the gospels about fifty times in connection with the name Jesus, and about as many times by itself. It is usually accompanied by the article in Greek, and is manifestly used as a descriptive designation, and not as a simple proper name. Jesus, the Christ, the Anointed, the Messiah—the two latter words having the same meaning, in English and Hebrew, that the former has in Greek. In the Acts our Saviour is commonly called simply Jesus (about fifty

times), the word Christ being added about fifteen times, and this last word being found by itself scarcely more than a half a dozen times. In the epistles, the two words are found together nearly two hundred times; the name Jesus alone less than twenty times; but the word Christ, now in the lapse of time come to be used, according to a general law of language, no longer as a descriptive appellation, but simply as a proper name, is found by itself about two hundred and thirty times. Such a progress in the use of the word from a descriptive to a proper name, can only be accounted for by the fact that the epistles were written at a later date than the gospels, or, at least, as representing a later date in the use of language; for the gospels represent a use of language from thirty to fifty years earlier than their composition. On this basis —namely, that the appellation Christ, from being always a descriptive designation in the gospels, has come to be commonly a proper name in the epistles—an ingenious refutation of Dr. David F. Strauss' "Life of Christ" has been published by Dr. O. T. Dobbin. Dr. Strauss assumed that the epistles were written before the gospels assumed their present form [so Dr. Weiss in his "Biblical Theology"], and this assumption is a fundamental principle of his whole mythical theory of the origin of the gospels. Dr. Dobbin's work is entitled "Tentamen Anti-Straussiánum: the Antiquity of the Gospels asserted on Philological Grounds in Refutation of the Mythic Scheme of Dr. David Frederick Strauss: an Argument." London, 1845, 8vo, pp. 113. Of this work Allibone, in his "Dictionary of Authors,"

---

[1] Many writers designate Paul as "the *slave* of the Lord Jesus Christ," but as this term carries with it the idea of enforced and degrading bondage (similarly to the Greek, ἀνδράποδον), it is better to employ the word found in the margin of the Revised Version—namely, *bondservant*. As in the Old Testament, the title, "servant of Jehovah," is generally applied to officially distinguished personages, so it is thought by some that in the New Testament the "servant of Christ" is one who is officially appointed to some special service. It is evident, however, that in Paul's estimation all true Christians are servants of the Lord Jesus. (Rom. 14: 18; 1 Cor. 7: 22; Eph. 6: 6; Col. 3: 24.) The Christian service of Paul, faith in Christ and love for him as a Saviour, was ever accompanied with obedience to him as Lord. (See, for example, his beginning and ending of this Epistle with the words: *obedience of faith*.) And how great was the change from his

being a raving and murderous persecutor of Christians to his becoming a willing bondservant of Jesus Christ. For some twenty years the apostle had now been engaged in Christ's service—a service which had brought him much of trial and suffering. Even at the commencement of it his divine Master had to announce to him how many things he must suffer for his name's sake. (Acts 9: 16.) He had at this time undergone all those trials and afflictions which are enumerated in 2 Cor. 11: 24-33, that "Iliad of Woes." At the time of writing this Epistle he was bearing in his body the deep brand-marks of his service to Christ (Gal. 6: 17), and soon after this, and for many years, he was to be "a prisoner of Christ Jesus," bound with chains, not to a granite wall, where he might have some privacy and be alone with God, but to some, perhaps, rough and unfeeling Roman soldier—an intolerable bondage.—(F.)

vol. I, p. 507, quotes the following opinions: "A work in no common degree acute, learned, eloquent, and—what is rarer still in a region so often traversed—original." "Complete, conclusive, and unanswerable." "It leaves Dr. Strauss without a loophole whereby to escape, and establishes most unanswerably the antiquity of the gospels."

[The titles which Paul gives himself in his several salutations are quite varied. In 1 and 2 Thessalonians we have simply "Paul"; in Philemon, "a prisoner of Jesus Christ"; in Philippians, he calls himself and Timotheus "servants of Jesus Christ"; in Titus, "a servant of God and an apostle of Jesus Christ"; in 1 Corinthians, "called an apostle of Jesus Christ, through the will of God"; in 2 Corinthians, Ephesians, Colossians, 2 Timothy, "an apostle of Jesus Christ, by the will of God"; in 1 Timothy, "an apostle of Christ Jesus by the commandment of God our Saviour and Lord Jesus Christ, which is our hope"; and in Galatians, "an apostle, not of men, neither by man, but by Jesus Christ, and God the Father." An interesting paper, Bishop Ellicott says, might be written on these peculiarities of designation. In 2 Corinthians, Philippians, Colossians and Philemon, Timothy is associated with Paul in the greetings; in 1 and 2 Thessalonians, Silvanus and Timothy; in 1 Corinthians, Sosthenes; and in Galatians, "all the brethren who are with me." Though Timothy was present when Paul wrote to the Romans, yet he only sends his salutation at the end of the Epistle.] **Called to be an apostle.** The former title is more general; this more specific and official. The words 'to be,' supplied by the translators, might well be omitted, as they are in many recent versions. [There is some force, however, in what the "Five Clergymen" say, in their revised translation of the Romans, that, " 'called an apostle' is too like 'named an apostle'; a *called apostle* seems to indicate that there are some apostles not called." We think the Common Version here cannot be bettered.] Apostles are special officers in the Christian Church, whose principal functions are to be eye-witnesses of the resurrection of Christ (Luke 24 : 48; Acts 1 : 21, 22; 1 Cor. 9 : 1), authoritative teachers of his doctrines and commands (John 16 : 13; 1 Cor. 14 : 37; 2 Peter 3 : 2), founders of his churches under him the Supreme Founder

(Matt. 16 : 18; 1 Cor. 3 : 10; Eph. 2 : 20; Rev, 21 ; 14), and possessors and dispensers of miraculous gifts. (Matt. 10 : 8 ; Acts 8 : 14-17; 19 : 6.) And in order to exercise these functions legitimately, one must have a special and direct call from Christ. He must be a called apostle. "The sudden call of the persecuting Saul to the apostleship of the Gentiles corresponds to the sudden call of the Gentiles to Christianity, just as the gradual instruction of the Jewish apostles accords with the long training of the Jewish nation for the gospel." (Schaff.) [The term apostle (occurring seventy-nine times in the New Testament, chiefly in the writings of Luke and Paul) literally signifies one that is sent, and is used in its simple unofficial sense in 2 Cor. 8 : 23 ; Phil. 2 : 25 of the "messengers" of the churches. It seems to be applied in an official sense to others than the twelve (1 Cor. 15 : 7), certainly to Barnabas, though as a companion of Paul (Acts 14 : 4, 14); to James, the Lord's brother (Gal. 1 : 19), who was probably not one of the twelve (see Bishop Lightfoot's discussion of "The Name and Office of an Apostle," in his "Commentary on Galatians," pp. 92-100); perhaps to Sylvanus and Timothy, as associated with Paul (1 Thess. 2 : 6), and to Andronicus and Junias, as some think. (Rom. 16 : 7.) In 2 Cor. 11 : 5; 12 : 11, Paul speaks ironically of certain literally "supereminent apostles," and in 2 Cor. 11 : 13 of "false apostles." In the case of Paul the term is used, as Alford says, "in its higher and peculiar meaning in which the Twelve bore the title." Like them, he had seen the risen Jesus (1 Cor. 9 : 1), and had been called more directly than Matthias was by the Lord himself. The call to the apostleship, however, is generally in Paul's writings represented as proceeding from God the Father (Rom. 15 : 15; 1 Cor. 15 : 10; Eph. 3 : 2), through the Lord Jesus. (Rom. 1 : 5.) In Gal. 1 : 1 he received it "through Jesus Christ and God the Father." Our Saviour, in Matt. 22 : 14, makes a wide distinction between called (invited) and chosen (κλητοί and ἐκλεκτοί); but in Paul's case the calling was effectual, its idea being akin, as De Wette suggests, to that of election. The calling, considered as distinct from the choice, took place in time, while the choice was from eternity. Compare Gal. 1 : 15; 2 Thess. 2: 13, 14. The apostle was not called to fill the place of Judas, to which Matthias had been

2 (Which he had promised afore by his prophets in the holy Scriptures.)

2 apostle, separated unto the gospel of God, which he promised afore [1] through his prophets in the holy

1 Or, by.

mistakenly elected, nor to fill the place of James, John's brother, who had been killed with the sword. His call was a special one, and wholly independent of that of the twelve. Their apostolate had Palestine and the twelve tribes of the Dispersion mainly in view. Paul was chosen to be the apostle to the Gentiles. Our Saviour, in Acts 9: 15, calls him "a vessel of election," (Revised Version, margin), and so he speaks of himself as *called* of God to the apostleship. In thus ascribing his apostolate, not to his own choice or merits, but to the power and will of God, he, at the very outset, strikes, as it were, the keynote of the whole Epistle. Converted and called in the manner he was, he could not but ascribe all his salvation to the good pleasure and sovereign grace of God. With his experience " he knew not how," as Olshausen says, "to preach anything save the grace of God in Christ." To be an " Arminian " or to talk like an " Arminian " was for him an utter impossibility.]

Separated unto the gospel of God. Compare Acts 9: 15: Gal. 1: 15. The purpose for which Paul was thus set apart was the formal and official announcement to men of God's glad tidings. [" Set apart to preach the gospel." (Noyes.) Verbs derived from *horos* (ὅρος), a boundary or line of separation, are of frequent use in the New Testament. 'Of God' is not the genitive objective, gospel concerning God, but subjective—the gospel of which God is the author or giver. (De Wette.) Both nouns are destitute of the article. The first, or governing noun, generally accompanied with the article, is made sufficiently definite by the genitive or noun which follows —*God's* (one and only) Gospel; and grammarians tell us where one noun is without the article the other frequently is so, " on the principle of correlation." Similar examples of nouns without the article are found in ver. 16, 17, 18, and elsewhere. The above cited passages in Acts and Galatians show us that Paul was separated unto the gospel both before and after his conversion. Perhaps the setting apart of which he here speaks occurred at the time of his conversion, when the Lord virtually appointed him to be an apostle to the Gentiles in the words " Unto whom I

send thee." (Acts 26: 17; also 22: 21.) As the term Pharisee denotes one who is separated or set apart, it may be, from the mass of men to the special keeping of the law and the traditions, so some have thought that Paul would here represent himself, by way of contrast, as separated unto the *gospel;* but there is no evidence that he here alludes to this matter. This 'gospel of God' (see 15: 16; 1 Thess. 2: 2, 8, 9; 1 Peter, 4: 17) is elsewhere called "the gospel of Christ" (15: 19; Gal. 1: 7: Phil. 1: 27); "the gospel of the kingdom" (Matt. 4: 23); "the gospel of the grace of God." (Acts, 20: 24); "the gospel of peace" (Eph. 6: 15); and "the gospel of your salvation." (Eph. 1: 13.) Twice in this Epistle and once elsewhere, the apostle speaks of it as "my gospel."]

2. Which he had promised afore by his prophets. [" Not only the four great and twelve minor prophets are meant, nor the order of prophets in general, commencing with Samuel (Acts 3: 24), but all men by whom prophecies concerning Christ are found recorded in the Old Testament Scriptures. Even Moses and David belong to these prophets." (Philippi.) See Acts 28: 23; Luke 24: 27, 44. Alford thinks the expression is "used in the strictest sense. Moses gave the *law;* the prophets proclaimed the *gospel.*" The verb employed here signifies to promise aforehand rather than to preannounce, though some, as Stuart and Philippi, decide for this latter.] This is one of the many passages which show the intimate connection between the Old Testament and the New. The gospel is in the Old Testament; according to the pithy saying of Augustine, "the New Testament is veiled in the Old; the Old Testament is unveiled in the New." "*Novum Testamentum in Vetere latet; Vetus Testamentum in Novo patet.*" For specimens of passages of similar import, compare Acts 10: 43; 26: 22, 23; 1 Peter 1: 10, 11. It was especially important to keep this connection before the minds of the Jewish converts, "lest," as Chrysostom remarks, "any one should think he was introducing some novel doctrine." **In the holy Scriptures.** The epithet 'holy' is ascribed to the Scriptures only here and 2 Tim. 3: 15. [The literal

3 Concerning his Son Jesus Christ our Lord, which was made of the seed of David according to the flesh;

3 scriptures, concerning his Son, who was born of 4 the seed of David according to the flesh, who was

translation of the latter passage is *sacred writings.*] In 16: 26 and Matt. 26: 56, we have "the Scriptures of the prophets," or "*the prophetic Scriptures*," as the Greek reads, and in Matt. 26: 56, "the Scriptures of the prophets." Elsewhere the word translated Scripture is used without any qualifying adjective. It is used about fifty times in the New Testament, about thirty times in the singular, and twenty in the plural, always accompanied in the Greek text by the definite article, except in three or four places, where it is made definite by some qualifying adjective or descriptive phrase, as in John 19: 37; Rom. 16: 26; 2 Tim. 3: 16; 2 Peter 1: 20. [Here the noun has no article, but is sufficiently defined by the adjective 'holy'; hence, "the holy Scriptures." (De Wette.) By Meyer's rendering: "In holy writings" —that is, in such writings as are holy (as especially the prophetic), the *kind* of Scriptures is specially characterized. Regarded in the light of a proper name, it may either retain or dispense with the article, just as we speak of Scripture or the Scripture.] Whether in the singular or in the plural, whether with the article or without, it is never used in the New Testament of any writings but those which were recognized by the Jews as inspired. It is *directly* applied, of course, only to the Old Testament writings; but *indirectly* and *constructively* it may be applied to the New.

3. Concerning his Son. [Some commentators quite naturally join this phrase to gospel in ver. 1, making ver. 2 parenthetical. The greater number, we think, connect it with the verb 'promised.' The idea is essentially the same in either case. "The personal object of the ancient promises is the Son of God." (Hodge.) The name **Jesus Christ our Lord** which follows the word 'Son' in our Common Version, properly belongs at the end of ver. 4. We may notice here how early and how often in the apostle's letters the words 'Christ' and 'gospel' are mentioned. He could not write long, we might almost say, on any subject, without referring to that "name which is above every name." An illustration of this is found in 2 Cor. 8: 9-15, where, in inculcating the duty or "grace" of giving, he must refer to the example of him who "though

he was rich, yet for your sakes became poor," and in closing the discussion of that topic (9: 15), he is led by the thought of the preciousness of our poor earthly gifts, to lift his heart in gratitude to God for "his unspeakable gift," the gift of "his own Son." (Rom. 8: 32.) See Ellicott's "Notes on Ephesians," especially chapter 2, verse 7, in regard to Paul's frequent repetition of this "only name." In this respect Paul differs widely from James, the Lord's brother, who, though calling himself "a servant of the Lord Jesus Christ," yet mentions this name expressly but twice in his epistle, and "the gospel" not once. Both writers were inspired of God, but the men were different, or the bent of their minds was different. Paul being himself no advocate of a "dead faith," would not, we suppose, object to a single *sentiment* in James, but would heartily endorse each one. Yet Paul, if we may express our feelings in the language of hyperbole, could no more write the Epistle of James, than he could create a world.]

Which was made. The distinction between 'was' and 'was made' (γίνομαι, to become) is finely illustrated by comparing John 1: 1, 2, with John 1: 14. The expression 'was made' here implies that his human nature began to be, when he was "made of a woman." (Gal. 4: 4.) The phrase **according to the flesh** does not mean that his human nature was limited to his flesh—that is, to his body; but the expression is used here, as in John 1: 14, and often elsewhere, to signify the whole human nature, "body, soul, and spirit," of which the outward, visible tabernacle of the flesh is the concrete representation to our senses. (Alford.) [On the limiting phrase, 'according to the flesh,' Dr. Hodge thus remarks: "It obviously implies the superhuman character of Jesus. Were he a mere man, it had been enough to say that he was of the seed of David; but as he is more than man, it was necessary to limit his descent from David to his human nature." The same phrase is used in 4: 1, in reference to Abraham, where (connected with the verb *hath found*) it denotes, according to Godet, "human activity in its state of isolation from the influence of God," and is probably equivalent to "his own labor," or "from works," of ver. 2. It is used of the relation which Paul sustained to the Jews (9: 3) when he calls them his kinsmen *by race* or nationality. Again, in 8: 4 we read of those who walk according to the flesh and according to the spirit, where 'according to the flesh' (κατὰ σάρκα) seems nearly equivalent to the "law of sin in the members." But none of these senses is applicable to the phrase 'according to the flesh' when used in the case of Christ, which is to be interpreted rather in the light of such expressions as: "The word became flesh"; "was manifested in the flesh"; "has come in the flesh"; "made in the likeness of men"; "made of a woman," etc. See John 1: 14; 1 Tim. 3: 16; 1 John 4: 2; Phil. 2: 7; Gal. 4: 4.]

The seed of David, rather than of Abraham, as an intimation of his *kingly* character, and in allusion to such passages in the Old Testament as Ps. 89. Compare Matt. 1: 1; 2 Tim. 2: 8. [Meyer supposes that Jesus' descent from the seed of David must be traced through the paternal or male line, and hence, though holding that Jesus was the Son of God and that Paul's Son of God "is conceived in a *metaphysical sense*, as he who had proceeded out of the *essence* of the father, like him in substance," he at the same time denies to the Saviour a virgin birth, giving no credence to the later embellished accounts (as he would regard them) in Matthew and Luke which assert it, and affirms that Paul nowhere, not even in Rom. 8: 3; Gal. 4: 4, indicates the view of a supernatural generation of the bodily nature of Jesus. But *if* Mary sprang from the "seed of David," it is senseless to deny that Jesus was born of David's seed.[1] Besides, as Philippi says: "To concede to the apostle the conception of the metaphysical divine Sonship and to deny to him faith in the birth of God's Son of the virgin, is to impute to him a conception dogmatically inconceivable." Godet thus remarks on this subject: "But would this supposition (of an unmiraculous birth) be consistent, on the one hand, with the idea which the apostle forms of Jesus' *absolute* holiness; on the other, with his doctrine of the transmission of sin to the whole human race? He speaks of Jesus as 'sent in the *likeness* of sinful flesh,' as one 'who knew no sin,' and ascribes to him the part of an *expiatory victim*, which excludes the barest idea of a *minimum* of sin. And yet according to him all Adam's descendants participate in the heritage of sin. How reconcile these propositions, if his view is that Jesus descends from David and from Adam, absolutely in the same sense as the other descendants of Adam or David? Paul thus necessarily held the miraculous birth, and that so much the more, as the fact is conspicuously related in the Gospel of Luke, his companion in work. A contradiction between these two fellow-laborers on this is inadmissible.[2] It is therefore through the intervention of Mary alone, that Jesus, according to Paul's view, descended from David. And such also is the meaning

---

[1] Rabbi Wise (in his "History of the Hebrews' Second Commonwealth," pp. 245, 258) with great unwisdom makes Jesus deny his own Davidian descent (Luke 20: 41; compare Matt. 22: 42, 43), in the very gospels which most explicitly assert it! That Jesus was of the line of David is a fact abundantly affirmed by himself and his apostles, and this claim, if false, should have been disproved by Paul's own teacher, Gamaliel, himself, as the rabbis affirm, a descendant of David, and by other Jews of that age, all of whom, in accordance with their sacred Scriptures (Ps. 89: 36; 132: 11, 12; Jer. 23: 5), expected their promised Messiah to be of the seed of David. (Matt. 22: 42; John 7: 42.) "That Jesus," says De Wette, on Matt. 1: 17, "was actually of the race of David is plain from the account of Hegesippus in Eusebius' 'Ecclesiastiacal History,' III, 20, that the grandsons of Judas, his brother, were, as the posterity of David, summoned before the Emperor Domitian." (See further in Notes to Geikie's "Life of Christ," chapter VIII; also Farrar's "Early Days of Christianity," chapter XI. and Broadus on "Matthew," pp. 2, 6.) The

Jews have ceased looking for a Messiah, yet to come from the lineage of David and from the tribe of Judah. *Their tribal descent is now lost forever*, and thus no future (pretended) Messiah from among the Jews can prove his descent from the "house and family of David." The Jews, indeed, make one exception as to the loss of their tribal descent, and maintain that tribal distinction is still preserved by the descendants of Levi. If this be so, yet God has taken from them their especial duty, and they have now no religious rites of divine appointment to perform.—(F.)

[2] Luke was Paul's almost constant companion for some ten or twelve years (see Prof. Bliss' "Commentary on Luke," p. 10), and his sole faithful attendant during the apostle's last days; "only Luke is with me," 2 Tim· 4: 11. Must not the evangelist, who "traced the course of all things accurately from the very first," and the writer of our Epistle have often conversed on all the more important matters relating to our Lord's earthly history?—(F.)

4 And declared *to be* the Son of God with power, according to the Spirit of holiness, by the resurrection from the dead :

1 declared *to be* the Son of God 2 with power, according to the spirit of holiness, by the resurrection of the 5 dead ; *even* Jesus Christ our Lord, through whom we

1 Gr. *determined*......2 Or, *in.*

of the genealogy of Jesus in Luke's Gospel." See also Neander's "Life of Christ," p. 19, on our Lord's Davidian descent, and p. 16, on the silence of John and of Paul in regard to the miraculous conception.]

4. Declared — literally, *defined*, nearly equivalent to *demonstrated*, and contrasted with 'was made,' to show how different he really *was* from what he *seemed* to be to the superficial view of men. [This word, "declared," occurring in seven other places in the New Testament (Luke 22: 22; Acts 2: 23; 10: 42; 11: 29; 17: 26, 31; Heb. 4: 7) is here, in the view of most commentators, equivalent to designated, or instated ; Chalmers says: "determinately marked out." It must not be taken in the sense, *destined to become something* (Meyer against Hofmann) ; for Christ *was* the Son of God before the foundation of the world. The two predicates—'was made,' and 'was declared'—both refer to *his* Son, here regarded as the *entire* person of Jesus. (DeWette.)] **With** (literally, *in*) **power.** This qualifying clause may be connected directly with the immediately preceding words, and the sense will then be, defined by his resurrection to be the Son of God with power, in contrast with his seeming weakness as a mere man. So Stuart, [Schaff, Philippi, and Dorner also, who says that " previously, therefore, he was not Son of God in power, although he was Son."] Or the words may be connected with the word 'declared,' and so they would indicate the strength of the proof of his divine Sonship—"declared mightily," as the Genevan Version has it. This interpretation seems, from Acts 4: 33, to be admissible, in spite of the assertion of Stuart, that this word is used only of *actual power,* and not of *logical force.* In the passages referred to above, it seems to be used in a similar sense with our

word power, in such expressions as a powerful argument, powerful conviction, etc. So Alford, Meyer, [Olshausen, DeWette, Godet, Hodge. For the adverbial use of this word, see Col. 1: 29; 2 Thess. 1: 11.] **According to the Spirit of holiness.** The reference here is not to the Holy Spirit, as a divine person, distinct from the Son [Wordsworth and Forbes], but to Christ himself, in his spiritual, holy, divine nature, as distinguished from his lower nature, as the seed of David. "The divine side of Christ's nature, with the essential characteristic of holiness." (Lange.) See a similar use of the word 'spirit' [as contrasted with the 'flesh' of Christ] in 1 Tim. 3: 16; 1 Peter 3: 18. Compare John 4: 24. [This word 'holiness' (ἁγιωσύνη, not ἁγιασμός, sanctification) occurs also in 2 Cor. 7: 1; 1 Thess. 3: 13, and is here the "genitive of characterizing quality"—*i. e.*, it characterizes the spirit of Christ. De Wette defines this spirit of holiness as the "*spiritual* side of the life of Christ, *yet* with the attribute of holiness," etc., for which definition Dr. Schaff (in Lange, as above quoted) would substitute the *divine* side of Christ's person *with* the essential characteristic of holiness. Prof. Shedd, in his "Commentary on Romans," says: "The spirit that constituted Christ's rational soul in distinction from his animal soul was from the seed of David; but the *pneuma* (spirit) here attributed to Christ was something in respect to which he was *not* of the seed of David." Perhaps we can do no better than to adopt the interpretation of Philippi, to wit: " *The spirit of holiness* is the higher, heavenly, divine nature of Christ, according to which, or in which, he is the Son of God."1 In reference to Paul's use of these correlative terms, 'according to the flesh,' 'according to the spirit,' Prof. Jowett thus remarks: "An-

1 Godet, however, thinks that by the phrase, '*spirit of holiness,*' Paul would denote the "action displayed on Christ by the Holy Spirit during his earthly existence." And Prof. Stuart regards the expression, 'according to the Spirit,' etc., not as antithetic to the phrase, 'according to the flesh,' but as referring to his dispensing the Holy Spirit *after* his resurrection. But we must regard these parallel phrases as evidently antithetic;

and, as Dr. Gifford observes, necessarily representing constituent parts of Christ's own being. Scripture thus appears to give two principal reasons why Jesus is called the Son of God: 1, because of his miraculous conception; 2, in a higher sense, because of his holy spiritual nature in his pre-existing state.—Prof. W. S. Tyler, in " Bib. Sac.," October, 1865.—(F.)

tithesis is a favorite figure in the writings of
St. Paul, almost (may we not say?) the form
in which he conceives the gospel itself. There
are times before, and times after, a first Adam
and a second Adam, the law and faith, the
flesh and the spirit, the old man and the new
man, death, life, burial, resurrection; the
identity and difference of the believer and
his Lord. 'All things are double, one against
the other.' "]

By the resurrection from the dead.
Christ's resurrection from the dead was a
powerful demonstration of his divine Sonship. In reply to the objection that Lazarus
and several others were raised from the dead,
the peculiar circumstances of Christ's resurrection are to be noted. 1. His death and
resurrection were predicted in the Old Testament (Ps. 16: 9-11; 110: 1, 4; Isa. 53: 7-12), and repeatedly foretold by himself. (Matt. 16: 21; 17:
22, 23; John 10: 17, 18, and in more than a
dozen other places.) 2. Jesus raised himself
from the dead. (John 2: 19-22.)[1] 3. Jesus rose,
not like Lazarus, to a second term of mortal
life, but to die no more. (Rom. 6: 9.) 4. Jesus'
human nature was glorified after his resurrection. (John 12: 23, 24; Acts 17: 31.) These peculiarities separate the resurrection of Jesus widely
from all former instances of restoration to life.
[A very literal translation of this phrase,
which does not elsewhere occur, would be:
out of resurrection of (the) *dead.* In phrases
similar to this the Greek article is almost
invariably in the New Testament omitted
from the word *dead.* The preposition (ἐκ)
denotes the "source *out of* which convincing
evidence flows." (Winer, 367.) We should
have expected here, "by *his* (or the) resurrection, *from* the dead." Some supply this
preposition (ἐκ or ἀπό) as in the example
quoted by Bengel from Herodotus (ἀναστάντες
βαθρῶν); literally, *rising of seats,* meaning, of
course, rising from the seats. The article and
preposition seem to be omitted here to make
the idea of resurrection as general as possible,
embracing that of Christ and "of others as
involved in his" (R. D. C. Robbins), or "that
resurrection of which Christ is the first

fruits." (Principal Sanday.) Winer regards
the expression, *the resurrection of the dead,*
as taken "absolutely and generically, although consummated only in a single individual." Paul, in Eph. 1: 19, 20, speaks of
the resurrection of Christ as effected by the
"working of the strength of the might of
God"—that is, by the divine omnipotence.
The meaning, then, of the clause before us is,
in substance, that God, by his omnipotence,
instated in the sight of angels and men Jesus
Christ, as (in accordance with his higher
nature) the Son of God, by effecting his resurrection from the dead. What accrued to
Christ by his resurrection was, as Meyer says,
"not the full *reality* (see 8: 3; Gal. 4: 4), but
the full *efficiency* of the Son of God," since he
was now raised above the limitations of his
kenosis, or self-emptying, and was shown to
be Lord of all. Through the force of this
potent demonstration of his divine Sonship,
even a 'doubting Thomas' was led to say to
Christ and of him: 'My Lord and my God.'
Of the resurrection of our Lord from the
dead, Paul had an assured conviction, and he
makes the fact of this resurrection not only a
proof of Christ's divine Sonship, but the
ground of his own salvation. Hence, the importance which in his view the resurrection
of Christ has in our Christian faith and hope
can hardly be described in words. See 1 Cor.
15: 17. In Paul's discourse to the Athenians
(Acts 17: 31), he affirms that God hath *instated*
or designated the man Christ Jesus to be the
Judge of the world, whereof a sufficient assurance unto all men is the fact that "God
hath raised him from the dead." The full
name, **Jesus Christ our Lord,** on which the
apostle loves to dwell, is here in apposition
with the preceding 'Son of God,' and serves
to introduce the statement which follows.
The name Jesus is personal, while Christ is
official. "The Son of David and Son of God
is thus finally described by three well-known
titles: 'Jesus,' which identifies him as the
crucified *Saviour;* 'Christ,' the promised
Messiah, and ' our Lord.' the exalted King, to
whom 'all power is given in heaven and in

[1] Paul, in 1 Thess. 4: 14, speaks of Christ's dying and
rising as if both acts were of his own choice and power.
See John 2: 19; also John 10: 18, where, however,
Christ says: "This commandment I received from my
Father." The usual representation of the Scriptures is

that God raised Jesus from the dead. Acts 2: 32; 3: 15,
26; 4: 10; 5: 30; 10: 40; 13: 30, 33; 17: 31; Rom. 8: 11;
1 Cor. 15: 15; 2 Cor. 4: 14; Col. 2: 12; 1 Thess. 1: 10; 1
Peter 1: 21; Fritzsche on Rom. 1: 4; see, however, Ellicott on Col. 2: 13.—(F.)

5 By whom we have received grace and apostleship, for obedience to the faith among all nations, for his name:

received grace and apostleship, unto obedience 1 of faith among all the nations, for his name's sake:

1 Or, to the faith.

earth.' " (Dr. Gifford, in "Bible Commentary.") Here 'our Lord' (or Master) may also refer to the relation which Paul and other Christian believers sustained to him as servants. Prof. Stuart states in his "Commentary" that "Paul gives to Christ, exclusively, the title of Lord in more than two hundred and fifteen instances." See notes on 10: 12.]

5. By whom we have received. [The preposition (διά) with the genitive (*through*) denotes the instrumental or immediate agency, while a different preposition (ὑπό) would denote the primary and remote agency. In this overflowing salutation, as Meyer terms it, Paul must again recur to the grace of his high calling of God in and through Jesus Christ. Compare 15: 16, also Eph. 3: 8. "Unto me who am less than the least of all saints is this grace given, that I should preach among the Gentiles the unsearchable riches of Christ."] The indefinite past 'received' is better here than the perfect ' have received.' To whom does the plural ' we' refer? Not to those to whom he writes; for they had not received the apostleship. Not to Paul's companions, regarded as joining with him in addressing the Roman disciples; for neither had they received the apostleship, nor is there any mention of such in the beginning of this Epistle, as there is some of Paul's letters. (1 Cor. 1: 1; 2 Cor. 1: 1; Phil. 1: 1; Col. 1: 1; 1 Thess. 1: 1; 2 Thess. 1: 1.) The ' we' may refer to the apostles as a class; or it may refer to Paul alone, and the clause, **among all nations,** favors this latter view. That the apostle did not regard it as improper thus to use the plural, when referring only to himself, appears from 3: 9, "*we* have before proved, etc." (2 Cor. 1: 8-12; 7: 5-8; Gal. 1: 8, 9.) **Grace and apostleship,** [not grace of apostleship, but] the common grace of God, by which he was called, converted, sanctified, and sustained; and, in addition to this, the special grace by which he was called to be the apostle of the Gentiles. The former is referred to in 1 Cor. 15: 10, and the latter in Eph. 3: 8. **For obedience to the faith among all nations.** This may be the genitive of apposition, for the Greek reads "obe-

dience of faith" [meaning, according to Philippi, Godet, Hodge, the obedience which consists of faith]. Faith *is* obedience, because it is commanded; or it may be the genitive of subject; for faith *produces* obedience [Stuart]. Or the genitive may be taken in a broader sense [as by Meyer, DeWette], in which it is nearly equivalent to the dative, denoting that to which obedience is rendered, as in the expression, "obedience of Christ." (2 Cor. 10: 5.) Our translators have not hesitated to treat the genitive in such cases as a dative. See Acts 22: 3, Revised Version. "Zealous *for* God." [See also 1 Peter 1: 22, Revised Version, obedience to the truth, compared with Rom. 10: 16, "They obeyed not (rendered not obedience to) the gospel," and especially (Acts 6: 7) "were obedient to the faith." The preposition before obedience (εἰς) has in such connections the general meaning: *with reference to;* here it means *for the promoting of.* The word "obedience" is destitute of the article, but is made definite by the noun in the genitive which follows; and this latter noun, as belonging to the class of general abstract terms, which commonly do not take the article, is also without it. ' Faith,' the important word of this Epistle, denotes, according to DeWette, not a doctrinal system, but "the new salvation which consists in faith as opposed to works." Meyer also remarks that "faith," in the New Testament, "is always *subjective,* though often, as in the present instance, conceived of *objectively* as a power." Yet see Hodge's comments on Rom. 12: 6. 'Among all the nations,' or Gentiles, the word being used in both senses. Here the latter is preferable, as the apostolate of Paul had special reference to the Gentiles. (11: 13; 15: 16.) The word occurs fifty-five times in Paul's epistles, and is generally rendered Gentiles.] **For his name.** [DeWette and Godet refer this phrase to the whole preceding part of this verse. Others more properly connect it with the words, 'obedience of faith.' During many long years of trial and persecution Paul sought to promote this sacred obedience among the Gentile nations, not for his own glory, but for the name and sake of Christ.

6 Among whom are ye also the called of Jesus
Christ:
7 To all that be in Rome, beloved of God, called *to be*

6 among whom are ye also, called *to be* Jesus Christ's:
7 to all that are in Rome, beloved of God, called *to be*

Nothing will so help us to live and suffer for the
gospel, or to perform any unpleasant duty, as
the thought that we are doing it for that blessed
name. Compare 2 Cor. 12: 10.] All was for
glory of his name: grace comes by him;
apostles testify of him; saving faith has him
for its object. In the *name* of Christ is
summed up all that he was, did, and suffered.
Compare Acts 5: 41; 9: 16; 15: 26; 21: 13;
1 Thess. 1: 12.

6. Among whom. The relative 'whom'
refers to 'all nations' in the preceding verse,
and so appropriately introduces the direct
address to the Roman disciples in the following verse: they were a part of the 'all nations'—
that is, they were mainly Gentiles ('nations'
and 'Gentiles' being but different translations
of the same Greek word), and so belonged
properly to Paul's jurisdiction as the Apostle
of the Gentiles. (Gal. 2: 9.) [De Wette and Meyer
(versus Rückert, Fritzsche, Philippi, Lange,
Godet, and the Revised Version) reject the
comma after the 'ye' and render: *Among
whom ye also are called*, or, *the called ones.*
So also Alford, who says: "The assertion,
'among whom are ye,' is flat and unmeaning."] **The called of Jesus Christ.** Not
merely called by Jesus Christ, but "Jesus
Christ's called ones." The calling here is not
the general external call, as in Matt. 20: 1;
22: 14; but the personal, internal, effectual
call, the call that is responded to in obedience,
as always in the epistles, and Revelation.
Compare 8: 28, 30; 1 Cor. 1: 24; Jude 1; Rev.
17: 14. [The rendering, *called by Jesus Christ*,
(adopted by Alford, Godet, Shedd,) is grammatically admissible. See "beloved of (by)
God" in the next verse. But in Paul's type
of doctrine, the calling generally proceeds
from God the Father. (8: 30; 9: 24; Gal. 1: 15; 1 Cor.
1: 9; 7: 15, 17; 1 Thess. 2: 12; 2 Thess. 2: 14; 2 Tim. 1: 9.)
Hence, with DeWette, Meyer, Philippi, we
would regard the genitive as possessive, and
the called ones as *belonging to Christ*, or, as
above: "Jesus Christ's called ones." Such
are called, as below, "to be saints," called in
hope, in peace, in sanctification, for freedom,
into the fellowship of Christ, and unto life
eternal. (Eph. 4: 4; 1 Cor. 7: 15; 1 Thess. 4: 7; Gal. 5: 13;
1 Cor. 1: 9; 1 Tim. 6: 12.) See Ellicott on Eph. 4: 4.]

7. To all that be in Rome. Connect this
verse immediately with ver. 1. [As no verb
of greeting is expressed, we may make 'all
that be in Rome' denote simply the receivers
of the letter, just as the name Paul indicates
the writer. One MS. (G.) of the ninth century, omits here, and in ver. 15, the words 'in
Rome,' but "this quite isolated omission,"
says Meyer, "is of no critical weight." He
supposes that some church sought, by omitting
those words, to adapt the letter to their own
particular church use in public reading. The
most ancient *superscription* of the Epistle is
in A B C simply: *to the Romans.* No more
appropriate soteriological letter could now be
sent "to the Romans" than this.] *To all the
beloved of God that are in Rome* would be a
less ambiguous order of the words. The
Epistle is not addressed to *all* that are in Rome,
but to all the *saints* there. Paul's earlier
epistles are addressed expressly to the *churches*
(1 Thess. 1: 1; 2 Thess. 1: 1: 1 Cor. 1: 1; 2 Cor. 1: 1; Gal. 1: 2.);
the later, to the *saints.* (Rom. 1: 7; Eph. 1: 1; Phil.
1: 1; Col. 1: 1.) "They were not called," says
Augustine, "in consequence of their being
holy; but they were made holy in consequence of their being called." [**Called to be
saints.** The words *called* (κλητοί) and *church*
(ἐκκλησία) are etymologically related, and both
signify, those who are, by God's grace, *called
out* from the world or mass of mankind to
become saints, sanctified in Christ Jesus, or
specially consecrated to his service. Those
who are professedly devoted to God are in the
New Testament called saints, whether inwardly sanctified by the Holy Spirit or not.
For different meanings of the word *saint*, see
Ellicott's "Commentary on Ephesians," 1: 1.
Bishop Lightfoot (on "Philippians," p. 13)
gives rather a gloomy picture of the *un*-organ-
ized condition of the Roman saints. He speaks
of them as "a heterogeneous mass, with diverse
feelings and sympathies (?), with no well-de-
fined organization." Meyer affirms that "the
'beloved of God in Rome, etc.,' *are* the church,
and it is to the *churches* that Paul has written,
where he does not write to specified *persons.*"
The Epistle to the Philippians is addressed
likewise to "saints," yet these had their
"overseers and deacons." And we read of

saints: Grace to you, and peace, from God our Father and the Lord Jesus Christ.

saints: Grace to you and peace from God our Father and the Lord Jesus Christ.

churches in individual houses, not only in the letters to the Colossians and Philemon, but in that to the Corinthians.]

Grace to you and peace, the divine favor, and the happiness resulting from that favor. [So Ellicott: " *Charis* expresses God's (undeserved) love toward man; *eirēne*, the state of peace and blessedness which results from it." *Charis*, or grace, according to Prof. Cremer, has respect to *sin*, and "gives prominence to the freeness and unconditional-ness of God's love," thus differing from *eleos*, or mercy, which is a fellow-feeling with wretchedness and misery. "The *charis* of God . . . is extended to men as they are guilty, his *eleos* as they are miserable." (Trench; "New Testament Synonyms.") The prayer that grace and peace from heaven may rest on the Roman saints, coming as it does from the affectionate, sympathizing heart of Paul, certainly represents *more* than the "general epistolary *chairein*," the wish of joy or prosperity. Conybeare and Howson happily allude to "the combination of the Oriental *peace* (*shalom*) with the Greek *grace* or *joy* (the Latin *gaudere*) in the opening salu-tations of all St. Paul's epistles," as "pro-claiming . . . the perpetual union of the Jew, the Greek, and the Roman." With the nouns grace, peace, the verb *may be*, or, as in the Epistles of Peter and Jude, *be multiplied*, is to be understood.] This form of salutation is peculiar to the New Testament. It is found in all Paul's epistles, with the addition of "mercy" in 1 and 2 Timothy; and, accord-ing to many manuscripts, in Titus. The com-mon classical form (χαίρειν) translated "greet-ing," is used only three times in the New Testament, Acts 15: 23; 23; 26; James 1: 1, and in one of these instances, it is found in the letter of a Roman magistrate. In the other two instances, it may be regarded as a peculiarity of the style of James, as he seems to have presided at the conference in Jerusa-lem from which the apostolical circular, in Acts 15: 23–29, emanated.

[From God our Father and (*from* **) the Lord Jesus Christ.** Meyer says: "God is never called *our and* Christ's Father" to-gether (compare 2 Tim. 1: 2; Titus 1: 4); yet this was Erasmus's rendering. God is our

Father by virtue of the "adoption" we have received through and in Christ. (8: 15.) This whole formula: " *Grace* . . . *Christ*," is ex-actly reproduced in the Epistles to the Corin-thians, Ephesians, Philippians, and Philemon. In Galatians it is "God the Father and our Lord Jesus Christ," and the same in 2 Thessa-lonians, save that the 'our' is omitted. In the letters to Timothy we have "grace, *mercy*, peace, from God the Father and Christ Jesus our Lord." And similarly in Titus (Revised Version), save that *mercy* is omitted, and Jesus is called *our Saviour*. In Colossians it simply reads, "from God our Father," while in 1 Thessalonians, we have merely: "Grace to you and peace." Thus, according to the revi-sion text, in eleven out of thirteen of Paul's epistles, the names of God the Father, and of Christ, are associated equally together as the source of "grace, mercy, and peace" to peni-tent and believing sinners, and "this associa-tion," to use the words of Dr. Hodge, "of the Father and Christ as equally the object of prayer and the source of spiritual blessings, is a conclusive proof that Paul regarded Christ as truly God." Meyer, on the other hand, says that "the formal equalization of God and Christ cannot be so certainly used as a proof of the divine nature of Christ—which, however, is otherwise firmly enough main-tained by Paul—since the different *predicates* (Father and Lord) imply the different con-ceptions of the *principal* and *mediate* cause." But no *creature*, certainly, can be equally as-sociated with God in any real communication of grace and peace to sinners. Among the teachers, sages, and saints of earth who lived prior to the time of Christ, and whom some writers are inclined to place nearly or quite on a level with the Saviour, stand pre-emi-nently the names of the "divine" and "god-like" Socrates, Plato, and Seneca. But (and may the almost blasphemous supposition be pardoned), could either of their poor names, or the names of any of our modern philoso-phic or poetic sages, or of our literary demi-gods, be well substituted *here* for that of the Lord Jesus Christ?]

The *salutatory* portion of the Introduction to the Epistle ends here. It is remarkable for having so many doctrinal clauses, paren-

8 First, I thank my God through Jesus Christ for you all, that your faith is spoken of throughout the whole world.

8 First, I thank my God through Jesus Christ for you all, [1] that your faith is proclaimed throughout 9 the whole world. For God is my witness, whom I

1 Or, *because.*

thetically introduced. There is, however, something of a kindred character in the introductions to Galatians, Titus, and, still more noticeably, in the introduction to Hebrews. How full of Christ this introduction is! He is mentioned four times by name, besides two or three other distinct references, in these seven verses. [" We ask, as we read the sentence, whether any one has ever compressed more thoughts into fewer words, and whether any letter was ever written which swept so vast an horizon in its few opening lines?"— Farrar.]

(*b*) Conciliatory. (Ver. 8–15.)

8. First. This word naturally creates the expectation of a corresponding *second*, if not of a further numerical designation of particulars. But such further enumeration is not *necessarily* implied in it, and does not always follow. See similar instances in 3 : 2, where the same Greek word is translated, "chiefly"; Acts 1 : 1, where it is translated, "former"; 1 Cor. 11 : 18 ; 1 Tim. 2 : 1, translated " first of all." It is not necessary to assume, as Meyer does, that "something further was meant to be subjoined, but amidst the ideas that now crowd upon him, he abandons this design." Sometimes the word may denote merely that the particular mentioned is the *most important* of all, as in Matt. 6 : 33.[1] **I thank my God through Jesus Christ.** Paul generally begins his epistles with some expressions of thankfulness. 1 Cor. 1 : 4; Phil. 1 : 3; Col. 1 : 3; 1 Thess. 1 : 2; 2 Thess. 1 : 3 ; Philemon 4; compare Eph. 1 : 16. The letter to the Galatians forms a significant exception. Those to Timothy and Titus are exceptions also, for a different reason, probably because intimacy of friendship, and fullness of confidence made such a formal expression superfluous.[2] 'My God.' This appropriation of God, by faith, hope, and love, is one of the most sure characteristics, and one of the most blessed experiences, of the child of God. (Ps. 63 : 1.) The expression

occurs often in the Psalms, and in the epistles, but is found only once (except as used by the Saviour) in the gospels. (John 20 : 28.) Luther used to say that he thanked God for the little words in the Bible, such as *my*, *thy*, and *our*. [The apostle, it will be noticed, does not praise or thank his Roman brethren for their faith, but God is thanked for it, as being a divine gift; and, as Dr. Gifford (Bible, or "Speaker's Commentary") remarks, he seemingly "regards their faith as a gift to himself."] As all God's favors come to us through Christ, so all our responsive acknowledgments of gratitude should return to God through him. (Col. 3 ; 17 ; Eph. 5 : 20 ; Heb. 13 : 15.) No man cometh to the Father, even in thanksgiving, but by him. [" All our services need to be cleansed and hallowed by passing through the hands of our most holy and undefiled High Priest." (Barrow.) Meyer, (and, similarly, De Wette, Alford, and Philippi) regards Christ not only as the mediating presenter of the thanksgiving, but also as the mediating causal agent of the faith for which Paul gives thanks.] **For you all.** [The common text has, *in behalf of* (ὑπέρ), while the revisers read, *concerning* (περί) you all.] This is a high encomium ; but some reproofs and admonitions in later portions of the Epistle show that the word "all" must not be pressed with too strict an emphasis. **That your faith.** [Prof. Cremer says : " The New Testament conception of faith includes three main elements, mutually connected and requisite, though, according to circumstances, sometimes one, and sometimes another may be more prominent—namely, (1) a fully convinced *acknowledgment* of the revelation of grace ; (2) a self-surrendering *fellowship* (adhesion); (3) a fully-assured and unswerving *trust* (and with. this, at the same time, *hope*) in the God of salvation, or in Christ." See Ellicott on Gal. 1 : 23; Lightfoot on Gal., page 154, also notes on ver. 5. Faith, subjectively considered, "as the inward experi-

---

[1] Alford (and so Stuart) finds the contrasting thought in the thirteenth verse, whose δέ corresponds with our (πρῶτον μέν) : " Ye indeed are prospering in the faith, but (*de*) I still am anxious *further* to advance that

fruitfulness." Godet finds a virtual *secondly* in **ver.** 10, but this reference does not seem so natural.—(F.)

[2] Still, in 1 Tim. 1 : 12 ; 2 Tim. 1 : 3, he has thanks to give (χάριν ἔχω).—(F.)]

9 For God is my witness, whom I serve with my spirit in the gospel of his Son, that without ceasing I make mention of you always in my prayers;

serve in my spirit in the gospel of his Son, how un-

ence of belief, and trust in Christ'' (Boise), must ever have a doctrinal basis on which to rest.] **Spoken of throughout the whole world.** This was the ground of his thanksgiving. The verb here used is in several places translated "preached." (Acts 4: 2; 13: 5, 38; 17: 3, 13; Col. 1: 28.) It implies that their faith was *spoken of* frequently and emphatically as a remarkable thing, worthy to be *announced* everywhere. [In the Revised Version the verb is generally rendered *proclaim*. The faith in Christ was, of course, proclaimed by believers unto believers in the way of commendation. Unbelievers might say that this sect of which the Roman Christians formed a part, was "everywhere spoken against." For the "Judgments of early Pagan writers on Christianity," see notes on ver. 16.] 'Throughout the whole world.' While it cannot be denied that there is an element of hyperbole here (as in 10: 18; Col. 1: 6; 1 Thess. 1: 8), yet the expression shows how very widely the gospel had already been preached, less than thirty years after our Lord's ascension. The Roman Empire was commonly spoken of as the whole world—"orbis terrarum"—compare Luke 2: 1; and we know that the gospel had already been preached in most of its chief cities, as Jerusalem, Antioch, Smyrna, Ephesus, Thessalonica, Corinth, Athens, and Rome. Compare 15: 19. It is important to observe the all-wise providence of God, in this rapid and wide diffusion of the gospel during the apostolic age. Starting from Jerusalem, the centre of revealed religion, it had already reached Rome, the centre of the political world; from Jerusalem, the city of *dispersion*, to Rome, the city of *aggregation*.

9. For God is my witness. [This example of Paul shows that the name of God may be appealed to on solemn and proper occasions, but will not justify light and thoughtless swearing—the swearing of common conversation.] This solemn appeal to God is not uncommon in Paul's epistles. (2 Cor. 1: 23; 11: 31; Gal. 1: 20; Phil. 1: 8; 1 Thess. 2: 5. Like the formal oath, it partakes of the nature of worship. As he (by the use of 'for,' etc.) appeals to his prayers in proof of his thankfulness, so he appeals to God in proof of his prayers. No

one but God could know how unceasingly he prayed for them. The occasion fully justified this solemnity. It is important that those whom we wish to benefit should be fully persuaded of our interest in them, and our prayers for them. Paul here teaches us, by example, our duty to be thankful to God for the faith of distant heathen converts, and to pray for them. **Whom I serve.** [Compare Acts 27: 23, "Whose I am and whom I serve."] The word here translated 'serve' (λατρεύω, *latreuō*) imports a sacred religious service, in distinction from ordinary, regular serving, for which the Greek language has a more generic word. The generic word (δουλεύειν) is used in Matt. 6: 24; Luke 15: 29; Rom. 6: 6, and about twenty other places, while this word appropriated to religious service is used, besides this passage, in Matt. 4: 10; Luke 2: 37; Acts 26: 7, and about a score of other places. The clause, **with** (in) **my spirit** (compare 2 Tim. 1: 3) marks the living, inner sphere, and the following clause, **in the gospel of his Son,** the outward sphere of his sacred service. [Alford says: "The *serving God in his spirit* was a guarantee that the oath just taken was no mere form, but a solemn and earnest appeal of his spirit." And Umbreit, as quoted by Alford, remarks that the apostle, by the use of this verb (λατρεύω) "means that he is an intelligent, true priest of his God, not in the temple, but in his spirit, not at the altar, but at the gospel of his Son." There is another word (θρησκεία), found in Acts 26: 5; Col. 2: 18; James 1: 26, 27, which denotes an external, ceremonial religious service. Another term, (λειτουργία), whence comes our word *liturgy*, is used of public religious service, both of Jews and Christians (Heb. 10: 11; Acts 13: 2), and of other kinds of (public) service. (Rom. 15: 27, etc.) *Sebazomai* (σεβάζομαι), to worship, in ver. 25, denotes a devotional reverence. *Proskuneō* (προσκύνεω), to do homage, does not occur in this letter, but often in the gospels, Acts, and Revelation. *Latreuō*, literally, *to serve for hire*, and hence voluntarily, is thus an appropriate word to denote religious service. 'His Son' is commonly regarded either as genitive objective, gospel concerning his Son, or sub-

C

10 Making request, if by any means now at length I might have a prosperous journey by the will of God to come unto you.
11 For I long to see you, that I may impart unto you some spiritual gift, to the end ye may be established ;

ceasingly I make mention of you, always in my 10 prayers making request, if by any means now at length I may be prospered [1] by the will of God to 11 come unto you. For I long to see you, that I may

1 Gr. *in.*

---

jective, gospel made known by his Son. Perhaps we may name it the genitive of the contents or subject matter, denoting thus the gospel of which Christ is the subject and the substance.] The two words translated **that without ceasing** [so De Wette] might more exactly be rendered, 'how unceasingly.' They refer not merely to the fact, but to the degree, of his constancy in prayer for them. [For a like construction, see 2 Tim. 1: 3.] **I make mention of you always in my prayers.**—Paul affirms with equal emphasis in other epistles his constant prayers for the disciples to whom he wrote. (Eph. 1 : 16; Phil. 1 : 3, 4; Col. 1 : 3, 9; 1 Thess. 1 : 2.) [See also notes on 15 : 30. The word 'mention,' without the verb, signifies 'remembrance' (compare Phil. 1 : 3; 1 Thess. 3 : 6), and can, we think, be used in that signification here : for example, make remembrance of you, or call you to mind. The verb, though in the middle voice, is here simply active ; yet see Winer, 256. The Greek preposition (ἐπί) may here signify 'on occasion of,' hence 'at' or 'in' my prayers.] **10. Making request,** etc. In accordance with the order of the words in the original, and to avoid the tautology of 'unceasingly' and 'always' qualifying the same word, it would be well to join this latter adverb with 'making request.' The tenth verse then begins : 'Always in my prayers making request,' etc.[1]

If by any means now at length. The whole form of expression in this verse is very significant and characteristic, intimating his earnest desire to visit the Roman disciples, with the emphatic recognition of probable hindrances, suggested, or at least confirmed, by actual experience (compare ver. 13, also 15: 22), and ending by submitting the whole matter to the will of God. [Paul at this time was in fearful straits—so dark and uncertain was the prospect before him (Acts. 20 : 22 ; R m. 15, 30, 31) ;

and in God alone to whom he could make appeal and prayer was his help and hope.] This single verb translated **I might have a prosperous journey** has commonly the secondary and more general sense, "to be prospered," without any specific reference to the original idea of a journey. [Perhaps, forwarded, or *furthered*, may be the intermediate link between the literal and the tropical signification. The parting wish for the living and the dead among the Greeks is expressed by this word, meaning farewell.] So our words welfare and farewell, of similar etymology to the Greek word here used, have dropped the original idea of a journey, expressed by the syllable *fare*. Meyer translates the word here by an expression equivalent to "I shall have the good fortune." The reasons for preferring the more general secondary sense to the stricter etymological one are, that the apostle had not yet set out on his journey; and, which has the greater force, the fact that in the three other places in which the same word is used in the New Testament, the meaning seems to be simply "to be prospered," without any reference to a journey. (1 Cor. 16 ; 2 ; 3 John 2, twice.) [**By** (*in*) **the will of God to come unto you.** He bases his hoped-for prospering in his homeward journey *in* the will of God to whom, as Philippi remarks, "All the pious subordinate their wills" in all their proposed undertakings and in all their prayers. See 15 : 32 ; also Acts 18 : 21 ; 1 Cor. 4 : 19 ; 16 : 7 ; James 4 : 15. 'To come' depends on the verb prospered.]

11. He now gives the *reason* why he prayed for them so constantly.

For I long to see you. He did not merely desire or wish to see them : he *longed* for that privilege ; the word is emphatic. Compare 2 Cor. 9 : 14 ; Phil. 1 : 8 ; 2 : 26 ; 1 Thess. 3 : 6 : 2 Tim. 1 : 4. In the last two passages the Greek word is the same, though translated

---

[1]The word for prayers (προσευχή) is a sacred word, rare in profane authors, and according to Fritzsche, differs from (δέησις) *entreaty* arising from a sense of need, as *precatio* from *rogatio*. In other words, 'prayer' is

always addressed to God, 'entreaty' may be addressed to God or man. See Trench's "New Testament Synonyms," p. 189.—(F.)

12 That is, that I may be comforted together with you by the mutual faith both of you and me.

12 impart unto you some spiritual gift, to the end ye may be established; that is, that I with you may be comforted in you, each of us by the other's faith,

differently. The word 'see' is used here in a comprehensive sense, as often in our common speech, meaning to visit and converse with: indeed the word visit means primarily "to see." [Nearly a year before writing this letter, while laboring in Ephesus, Paul, after expressing his purpose to pass through Macedonia and Achaia to Jerusalem, then says: "After I have been there, I must also see Rome." (Acts 19 : 21.) The motive for his wishing to see the city of the Cæsars, the metropolis and mistress of the world, is indicated below. It was not to see its marble temples and palaces, its theatres, aqueducts, baths, and fountains, its columns and statues and triumphal arches, but to "preach the gospel," to advance the spiritual interests of his brethren, to strengthen them in the faith, and also—that he might have fruit among the Roman people as among other Gentiles—to win, if possible, the worshipers of Mars and Jupiter, of Bacchus and Venus, to the service of Christ.] **That I may impart unto you some spiritual gift.** Probably the reference is not to *miraculous* gifts in particular, but to spiritual benefit of whatever kind. His desire to see them was not for the gratification of curiosity, nor to receive attention, kindness, and honor from them, nor from any other selfish or secular motive; it was a benevolent desire; he wished to do them good spiritually. The three words 'some spiritual gift' are separated from each other in the original, in such a way as to make each more prominent, and to give a peculiar deli-

cacy and grace to the expression, which cannot be fully exhibited in English. His language does not imply that they were destitute of spiritual gifts, or particularly lacking in respect to them, but only that they had not all which it was possible and desirable for them to have; and there was, moreover, an indirect compliment to them in the implied assumption that nothing would be more grateful to them than an increase of spiritual gifts.[1] **To the end ye may be established.** Neither does this imply any special weakness or wavering on their part. All Christians need to be established—that is, to have their faith, hope and love, and all their graces confirmed and increased. Observe he does not say "that I may establish you," but 'that ye may be established.' There is no arrogant assumption, no appearance of desiring to make his own agency prominent.[2]

12. That is. [Compare 7: 18.] As if he wished to guard against any possible suspicion of assuming that the benefit was to be all on one side, he occupying the superior position of a giver, and they the humbler position of receivers, he adds 'that is,' or, *by this I mean to say*, **that I may be comforted.**[3] This verb is of very frequent occurrence in the New Testament; and is rendered most commonly, beseech, comfort, exhort. Neither of these English words fully expresses its meaning; but the word comfort, in its original, etymological sense (from the Latin "con" and "fortis") comes perhaps nearest to being

[1] From the supposed force of (μετά) in composition, Dr. Schaff renders the verb *share with you*. But this idea of mutual benefit is, we think, first introduced in the next verse. Had the verb been followed by the *genitive* of the thing, as is usual in the classics, the above rendering, perhaps, would be more plausible. But Winer, p. 198, says, in reference to this passage, and to 1 Thess. 2 : 8, that Paul could not have used the genitive after this verb, for "he did not purpose to communicate a portion of (from) a spiritual gift, or a portion of (from) the gospel." The verb is found elsewhere only in 12: 8; Luke 3: 11; Eph. 4: 28; 1 Thess. 2: 8. On πνευματικὸν (spiritual), as generally referring to the Holy Spirit, see Ellicott on Eph. 1: 3. The χάρισμα is distinguished from δῶρον as being a *gracious* gift. Any thing imparted by the Spirit through God's free grace, is a spiritual χάρισμα.—(F.)

[2] The construction here, εἰς, with the infinitive, ex-

pressive of purpose (similarly to τοῦ with the infinitive), is rather a favorite with Paul, occurring some seventeen times in this Epistle. See at ver. 20. His predilection for this is, according to Buttmann ("Grammar of the New Testament," pp. 236, 264, 266), similar to that of the Apostle John for ἵνα, *in order that*, the same occurring in his gospel nearly one hundred and fifty times, and in his epistles twenty-five times. The student will notice that the infinitive here, as generally throughout the New Testament, is *followed* by its subject.—(F.)

[3] The accusative-subject of the infinitive, μέ or ἐμέ (me), is here, according to a general rule, omitted, since the subject of the infinitive is the same as that of the leading verb. Notice also, as in ver. 22, and in many other places, how, in case of the suppressed accusative, the qualifying words are subjoined in the nominative. The verb is used only here as a compound.—(F.)

13 Now I would not have you ignorant, brethren, that oftentimes I purposed to come unto you, (but was

13 both yours and mine. And I would not have you ignorant, brethren, that oftentimes I purposed to come unto you (and was hindered hitherto), that I

equivalent. The corresponding abstract noun is translated by the words "exhortation," "consolation," "comfort"; and the corresponding personal noun (παράκλητος) when applied to the Holy Spirit, is translated "the Comforter" (John 14:16, 26; 15:26; 16:7), and once, when applied to Christ, "Advocate." (1 John 2:1.) The radical idea seems to be to comfort, or strengthen, by encouraging, as one is comforted and strengthened to meet difficulties and trials by having another *called to his side*, to cheer and help him. There is a peculiar delicate courtesy and condescension in the last two verses characteristic of Paul. He seems to wish to put himself on a level with those to whom he writes. [The infinitive here employed is by De Wette made to depend on the verb 'established.' Others regard it as parallel with to see (ἰδεῖν). This last is the view of Meyer, who says: "The delicate turn which he gives to the matter is this: '*to see you in order that I*,' etc., means nothing more than '*to be quickened along with you and among you.*'" The Bible Union renders this whole clause as follows: "That is, to be comforted together among you, by each other's faith, both yours and mine." The *mutual faith* is not faith in each other, but that faith which was common to both—faith *of you as well as of me*. "The arrangement of these words (the emphatic position of *you*—setting them before himself) bespeaks the delicacy and fine feeling of the apostle." (Philippi.) "There is a truth underlying the apostle's courtesy, which is not mere compliment. The most advanced Christian will receive something from the humblest." (Principal Sanday.)]

13. Now I would not have you ignorant. [The 'now' (δέ) is continuative and "slightly oppositive," not strongly so as in *but*. It naturally follows the thought that Paul had for many years so strongly desired to see the Roman Christians, and yet had stayed away all that time.] This expression [which generally introduces something new and important] is an illustration of that figure of speech (*meiōsis*), which is the opposite of

hyperbole, or exaggeration. Here *less* is said than is meant, and the phrase is equivalent to "I wish you to know." Often this is more forcible than the opposite figure. In that, reflection teaches us to *abate* something from the full meaning of the words; in this, reflection leads us to *add* something to the strict sense of the words. The effect of the expression here, as in 11:25; 1 Cor. 10:1; 12:1; 2 Cor. 1:8; 1 Thess. 4:13, is to lay an additional stress on the accompanying communication. **Brethren.** This is the first time that this word is found in the epistles. The most common designations of Christians in the New Testament are "disciples," "saints," "brethren"; but these different terms are found in very different *proportions* in different parts of the New Testament. The following table shows this very plainly:

	Gospels.	Acts.	Epistles.	
Disciples	230 times.	30 times.	0 times.	
Saints	0 (¹) "	4 (²) "	55 "	
Brethren	15 "	30 "	190 "	about.

This difference suggests several instructive reflections: one of these certainly is the importance attached in the Scriptures to the organization of the *church*. Of these three terms, "brethren" is the one that points most distinctly to the union of Christians in one family of God, one body of Christ, which is the church. (Eph. 2:19; 1 Tim. 3:15; Eph. 5:23; 5:30, Col. 1:24.) **Oftentimes I purposed to come unto you.** In 15:23 he tells them that he had cherished this purpose "for many years," [and in the same chapter he further makes known that he intended Spain, and not Rome, to be the Western terminus, and principal scene of his missionary labors]. The apostles were *sometimes* guided in their purposes and movements by immediate divine direction, as we learn from Acts 10:20; 16:6, 7; but not commonly: in ordinary cases, they formed their purposes, and laid their plans according to human sagacity, like other pious men, praying, of course, for divine guidance; and they were liable to be disappointed and hindered, just like other men. [Prof. Stuart thinks we may infer from this that "the apos-

¹ Matt. 27:52 is thought by some to refer to Old Testament saints.
² 9:13, 32, 41; 26:10.

let hitherto,) that I might have some fruit among you also, even as among other Gentiles.
14 I am debtor both to the Greeks, and to the Barbarians; both to the wise, and to the unwise.

might have some fruit in you also, even as in the 14 rest of the Gentiles. I am debtor both to Greeks and to Barbarians, both to the wise and to the foolish.

tles were (not) *uniformly* inspired in *all* which they purposed, said, or did."] **But was let hitherto.** What the nature of the letting, or hindrance, was we are not told. Very likely it was the more urgent call for his labors in nearer places, where Christ was less known, to which he alludes in 15: 20-23; or it may have been some express divine prohibition, as in 16: 7; or even some hindrance from an altogether *opposite* source, as in 1 Thess. 2: 18. **Hitherto.** The original word here used everywhere else in the New Testament refers to *place;* here, only to *time.* **That I might have some fruit.** [On the occasional use of the subjunctive (here, properly, *may* have) after a verb in the past tense, "to denote an action still *continuing,* either in itself, or in its results," see Winer, 287. This usage is quite frequent in this Epistle, the subjunctive taking the place of the classic optative, which mood has entirely disappeared from modern Greek. In ver. 11 we have the subjunctive after the present tense, the more usual, or, at least, the more natural, construction. The word 'some' (τινὰ) is here emphatic.[1] Most uncials locate it before the noun, which is not its usual order in the New Testament.] This 'fruit' may mean either the conversion of sinners, or the advancement of saints in holiness and Christian activity. The word is used in both applications. For the first, see John 4: 35, 36; 15: 16; for the second, Matt. 13: 23; Rom. 6: 22; Col. 1: 6. The latter sense is here preferred as being the more frequent, and agreeing better with ver. 11, 12. The last clause intimates that his hope of having some fruit at Rome was founded upon his experience elsewhere. [This clause is connected, in thought, with the one preceding the last. As previously, so here, the idea is implied that the benefit of Paul's labors among the

Romans was not to be wholly theirs. He desires 'fruit' as his "joy and rejoicing," and he modestly uses the word 'some.' In the New Testament, the word 'fruit' is generally used in a good sense. **Even as** (I *also* have fruit) **among other Gentiles.** Meyer says: "There was present to the apostle's mind the twofold conception, 'Among you also, as among,' and, 'Among you, as also among.'" The Roman Christians generally are here regarded as being formerly Gentiles, or heathen. This fact is clearly indicated in other passages of the Epistle, especially in the eleventh chapter.]

14. Paul considers himself a debtor to all classes of men[2] not on account of any favors which he had received from them; for he received little else than abuse and persecution; but in view of that law of Christian stewardship and responsibility by virtue of which every man—and pre-eminently every Christian—is bound to communicate to others every good thing which he possesses, in proportion to their need, and his own ability; and the greater his advantage over others, in respect to natural ability, and acquired knowledge, and providential favors, and gifts of grace, the greater his debt to them. Very few men, if any, owe their fellowmen as much as Paul did; and very few indeed, if any, feel the debt so profoundly, or discharge it so fully. If all who are more highly favored than their fellows had the spirit of Paul in this respect, we should not hear so much of the prejudice of the ignorant against the educated, nor would there be any manifestation of the *far more inexcusable* prejudice of the educated against the ignorant. Of the epithets which Paul applies to his creditors, the first two relate to national distinctions, the last two to personal distinctions.[3] He regarded himself as owing a debt to men of all

---

[1] See the different accent of τίνα in the "*what* fruit" of 6: 21.—(F.)

[2] τε καὶ, *not only* to the Greeks, *but also* to the barbarians, the last member being probably the more emphatic. See Prof. Thayer's "Lexicon."—(F.)

[3] At Corinth and Athens Paul would especially meet with the professedly "wise," but the "unwise" he would encounter everywhere. This last word (ἀνοήτοις) is

used in five other passages, Luke 24: 25; Gal. 3: 1, 3; 1 Tim. 6: 9; Titus 3: 3, and is in the Revised Version everywhere rendered *foolish.* This refers not so much to natural dullness of intellect as to an "insufficient application" of it. (Ellicott on Galatians 3: 1.) Of other kindred words, ἄφρων, "a strong term," seems to refer to senselessness, and ἀσύνετος to slowness of understanding. Compare Luke 12: 20; Mark 7: 18. Trench

15 So, as much as in me is, I am ready to preach the gospel to you that are at Rome also.

15 So, as much as in me is, I am ready to preach the 16 gospel to you also that are in Rome. For I am not

races, and of all degrees of culture. He who so regards himself has the highest qualification for doing good unto all men, as he has opportunity. (Gal. 6: 10.) [It was the apostle's wish, and it had been made his duty, to preach the gospel in Pagan Rome. Christ, the apostle's Lord and Master, had died for all; and to preach this gospel to Greeks and barbarians was the stewardship which was entrusted to him. It was for this he had been "set apart." From the Grecian standpoint, even the Romans would be styled "barbarians"—a term which properly embraced all non-Greek-speaking nations. But the Romans, in their pride, and with their general Grecian culture, regarded all nations as barbarous except the Greeks and themselves. Paul certainly would not class the Romans, to whom he was writing, with barbarians, much less, with the unwise. "He reckons as Greek those to whom he is writing in Greek." (Bengel.) The two words denote all Gentiles, all mankind indeed, with the exception of the Jews. In Jesus Christ there is neither Jew nor Greek, barbarian nor Scythian. (Col. 3: 11.)]¹

15. So, as much as in me is. [There are several different renderings of this clause but they do not materially affect the sense. "The on-my-part inclination" is preferred by Meyer; "So far as it concerns me there is an inclination," etc., is favored by De Wette. The *as-for-me* is "chosen out of a feeling of dependence on a higher will." (Meyer.)] **I**

am ready to preach the gospel to you that are at Rome also. 'So,'—that is, in accordance with this view of our indebtedness, 'As much as in me is, I am ready.' The expression indicates his modesty, perhaps with a thought of probable hindrance. The word 'ready' not merely denies any reluctance, but affirms a positive *forwardness*. The same word is translated "willing" in Matt. 26: 41, and "ready" in the corresponding passage of Mark (14: 38). The corresponding noun is translated "forwardness of mind," "readiness of mind," etc., in 2 Cor. 9: 2; Acts 17: 11; 2 Cor. 8: 11, 12, 19. 'To preach the gospel to you that are at Rome also.' The original is much briefer—"to preach the gospel" being expressed by a single word—literally, "evangelize." [This term² does not imply that Paul's preaching was to have reference solely to the unconverted, whether of Jews or Gentiles. The Roman *Christians* would need the gospel as it would be preached by the apostle. *To you* (the called saints) *that are in Rome also.* "Although you belong to the *wise*, this causes me no scruples as one who is *debtor to the wise.*" (Philippi.) As a debtor to the Gentiles, Paul would feel himself to be under special obligation to preach the gospel in Rome, the capital city of the Gentile world. Let us be thankful that some three years after this he was permitted to preach the gospel in Rome, though under different circumstances from those he expected. He went

remarks that "while the ασύνετος need not be more than intellectually deficient; in the ανόητος there is always a moral fault lying behind the intellectual." With Christ (and the same is true of Paul), "distinctions of race, intervals of ages, types of civilization, degrees of mental culture, are as nothing."— Liddon's "Bampton Lectures on our Lord's Divinity," p. 8.—(F.)

¹ Prof. Max Müller, in Lecture IV., p. 128, of his "Lectures on the Science of Language," thus remarks: "Not till that word 'barbarian' was struck out of the dictionary of mankind, and replaced by 'brother,' can we look even for the first beginnings of our science of language." This change was effected by Christianity. It was Christianity which first broke down the barriers between Jew and Gentile, between Greek and barbarian, between the white and the black. *Humanity* is a word which you look for in vain in Plato or Aristotle; the idea of mankind as one family, as the children of one God, is an idea of Christian growth; and the science of mankind, and of the languages of mankind is

a science which, without Christianity, would never have sprung into life. When people had been taught to look upon all men as brethren, then, and then only, did the variety of human speech present itself as a problem that called for a solution in the eyes of thoughtful observers; and I therefore date the real beginning of the science of language from the first day of Pentecost."—(F.)

² Ellicott says the verb evangelize "is used in the New Testament, both in the active (Rev. 10: 7), passive (Gal. 1: 11; Heb. 4: 6, and elsewhere), and middle. In the last form its constructions are singularly varied: it is used (a) absolutely, Rom. 15: 20; 1 Cor. 1: 17; (b) with a dative of person, Rom. 1: 15; (c) with an accusative of person, Acts 16: 10; 1 Peter 1: 12; (d) with an accusative of thing, Rom. 10: 15; Gal. 1: 23; (e) with an accusative of person and thing, Acts 13: 32; and lastly (f)—the most common construction—with a dative of person and accusative of thing, Luke 1: 19, and elsewhere."—(F.)

16 For I am not ashamed of the gospel of Christ: for it is the power of God unto salvation to every one that believeth; to the Jew first, and also to the Greek.

ashamed of the gospel: for it is the power of God unto salvation to every one that believeth; to the

there and preached there as Christ's ambassador, but "an ambassador in bonds." (Eph. 6: 20.) This, however, did not greatly hinder his evangelistic work in that place. "His bonds became manifest in Christ in the whole Pretorium," yea, even in the "household of Cæsar." (Phil. 1: 13; 4: 22.) To the Jews he testified the kingdom of God, and persuaded them concerning Jesus, both from the law of Moses and from the prophets, and for two whole years he, not now a servant only, but a chained prisoner of Christ Jesus, "received all that went in unto him, preaching the kingdom of God, etc., with all confidence."] So the apostle closes this second portion of his Introduction to the Epistle. It is eminently adapted to conciliate the good will of the Roman disciples, being replete with modesty, kindness, and proof of his unfeigned regard for them. The first clause of the succeeding verse may be regarded as the *hinge*, on which the discourse turns from what is introductory to the main subject of the Epistle, comprehensively expressed in the second clause.

PART II. DOCTRINAL. (Ch. 1: 16-11: 36.) [Of this section Dr. Shedd gives the following brief analysis: ' *Necessity* of gratuitous justification, 1-3: 20; *Nature* of gratuitous justification, 3: 21-4: 25; *Effects* of gratuitous justification, 5: 1-8: 39; *Application* of gratuitous justification, 9: 1-11: 36.' Dr. Gifford, in the "Bible Commentary," states it thus: "(*a*) The theme, 1: 16, 17; (*b*) The universal need of righteousness, 1: 18-3: 20; (*c*) The universality of righteousness by faith, 3: 21-5: 21; (*d*) The sanctification of the believer, 6: 1-8: 39; (*e*) The doctrine reconciled with Jewish unbelief, 9: 1-11: 36." Mr. Beet's synopsis is: "(1) All are guilty; (2) Justification and its results, 3: 21-5: 21; (3) The new life in Christ, 6: 1-8: 39; (4) Harmony of the Old and the New, 9: 1-11: 36."

De Wette furnishes this analysis: "Righteousness through faith, 1: 18-5: 21; Moral effects of justification, 6: 1-8: 39; Appendix: Lamentation, Explanation, and Consolation concerning the exclusion of a great part of the Jews from the Christian salvation, 9: 1-11: 36." Olshausen's analysis is as follows: "Sinfulness of the human race, 1: 18-3: 20; The new way of salvation by Christ, 3: 21-5: 11; The vicarious office of Christ, 5: 12-7: 6; Stages of the development of individuals and of the universe, 7: 7-8: 39; Relation of the Jews and Gentiles to the new way of salvation, 9: 1-11: 36.]

16. For I am not ashamed of the gospel of Christ: for, etc. The first 'for' introduces the reason why he had long desired to preach the gospel at Rome; the second 'for' introduces the reason why he was not ashamed of it. "I am not ashamed of the gospel of Christ." This affirmation was perhaps suggested by his mention of "*the wise*" in ver. 14, and by the peculiar position of the Romans, as citizens of the great capital which proudly styled itself "The Mistress of the World," very likely with a tacit remembrance, also, of the ill usage which he had received in other populous and highly civilized cities, as Corinth, Athens, Thessalonica, and Ephesus. The words 'of Christ' are wanting in the oldest MSS. [א A B C D* G]. [1] and are rejected by most critical editors. They are not necessary to the sense, as there is, properly speaking, no other gospel. (Gal. 1: 6, 7.) ["Not ashamed of the gospel." Mark the boldness of the apostle. "In truth," says Chalmers, "it is often a higher effort and evidence of intrepidity to front disgrace than it is to front danger. There is many a·man who would march up to the cannon's mouth for the honor of his country, yet would not face the laugh of his companions for the honor of his Saviour."

---

[1] The first four MSS. referred to (commonly called the Sinaitic, the Alexandrine, the Vatican, and the Codex of Ephraem), contain the Gospels and the Epistles—D, or Codex Bezae containing only the Gospels and the Acts. It should be remembered that D E F G and other MSS. of the Epistles are not the Gospel uncials, and are, most of them, considerably later. For a brief description of the oldest and most important MSS., see General Introduction, p. 36, seq, of the "Com-

mentary on Matthew." See, also, Dr. Mitchell's "Critical Handbook," p. 73; Dr. Schaff's "Companion of the Greek Testament," p. 103; G. E. Merrill's "Story of the Manuscripts"; Smith's "Bible Dictionary," Art. New Testament, by B. F. Westcott; Scrivener's "Introduction to the Criticism of the New Testament"; Warfield's "Textual Criticism of the New Testament," etc.—(F.)

We have in Paul's assertion, 'I am not ashamed,' a figure of speech by which less is said than is meant. Instead of not being ashamed of the gospel, he gloried in it, and in the suffering endured for its sake. (Col. 1: 24.) Most gladly, as he tells the Corinthians, would he spend and be spent for their souls (2 Cor. 12: 15), and to the Philippians he says: "If I am poured out (as a drink offering) upon the sacrifice and service of your faith, I joy and rejoice with you all." (Rev. Ver., 2: 17.) It *did* require great courage in Paul to preach the gospel of the cross to the then heathen world, even as it requires some courage in Christian ministers, and especially Christian missionaries, now. Paul knew from sad experience that the heathen priests and idol worshipers everywhere would oppose and ridicule the gospel of the crucified Galilean, would scout the idea of giving up their gods and their time-honored religion, their sacrifices, their festivals, and their pageantry, to become the followers of a Jew who had suffered an ignominious death, and the adherents of a new religion which had neither temples, nor altars, nor statues, nor showy ceremonials. The city where Paul wrote this letter abounded in "wise" men, or seekers after wisdom—men of culture and of "advanced thought," to whom the word of the cross which he preached was foolishness. (1 Cor. 1: 18.) Of the cultured Athenians, some mocked at Paul as being worse, we suppose, than a "babbler" when he began to speak to them of the risen Galilean. (Acts 17: 18, 32.) What cared they, to use Festus' language in part, about "one Jesus," a Jew who was put to death for his crimes, whom Paul affirmed to be alive? (Acts 25: 19.) To the Jew at Rome, as to the Jews everywhere, nothing was more abhorrent than the thought of a *crucified* Nazarene Messiah. And what could the religion of this Jesus, who was crucified as a malefactor with the consent of the Procurator Pilate, be to the Roman race generally, save what it was to Suetonius, Tacitus, and Pliny, a wretched, destructive, depraved, and immoderate superstition?[1] What sustained Paul in the preaching of

Christ crucified amid all these discouragements, we learn from the following clause.] **For it is the power of God unto salvation.** Christ himself is called the power of God in 1 Cor. 1: 24. Here 'the gospel' is so named, and in 1 Cor. 1: 18, "the preaching of the cross," which is only another name for the gospel. Efficient divine power resides in Christ; the gospel, or the preaching of the cross, is the medium through which he exerts his divine power, to the salvation of them that believe. [This is no new teaching of the apostle. In his first recorded sermon, preached at Antioch in Pisidia, on his first missionary journey, we hear him proclaiming remission of sins through Christ, and justification for all believers. (Acts 13: 38, 39.) Of course, in the apostle's view, this belief or faith—both words being etymologically related and denoting the same thing—is something more than mere intellectual belief. It is a confiding trust of the heart, and it works through love.] God's power is often *terrible* in nature and in providence, but in the gospel it is his *saving* power. What an encouragement this is to the weak human agents that proclaim this gospel! [Paul elsewhere (1 Cor. 15: 1, 2) speaks of "the gospel through which ye are saved," and James (1: 21) of the "implanted word which is able to save your souls." (Revised Version.) It is a salvation from sin, from the wrath of God, from death, and from perdition, partially realized in the present (Luke 19: 9), but fully completed only in the future. See 8: 24: 1 Thess. 5: 8; Heb. 1: 14; 2 Tim. 2: 10; 4: 18; 1 Peter 1: 5; 1 Cor. 15: 1, 2. And all this the gospel of Christ, which is the "mighty arm of God rescuing the world from perdition and bringing it salvation" (Godet), is able to secure. And it is this divine and saving gospel, and not worldly wisdom, philosophy, or science, which the ministers of Christ should preach without fear and without shame, even in this age of boasted culture and liberal thought, of skepticism and scoffing unbelief. Let no one be ashamed of that gospel which speaks to our guilty, polluted souls of God's pardoning love and of his

---

[1] Superstitio — "malefica," "exitabilis," "prava," 'inmodica" See references to early heathen testimony in "Biblical Repository" for January, 1838; "Christian Review" for January, 1859; "German Selections," p. 459; Dissertation III, of "Whiston's Appendix to Josephus"; Dr. Mitchell's "Handbook," p. 17: Farrar's "Life of Paul," Excursus XV; Gieseler's "Ecclesiastical History," 33; Rawlinson's "Historical Evidences," and all works which treat especially of the evidences of Christianity.—(F.)

17 For therein is the righteousness of God revealed | 17 Jew first, and also to the Greek. For therein is re-
                                                    | vealed a righteousness of God from faith unto faith:

sanctifying grace—the two greatest mercies a lost sinner can ask for or think of. To the natural man this gospel may seem a weak and foolish thing—the things of the Spirit being foolishness unto him. Yet it is the power and the wisdom of the Almighty and All-wise, the foolishness of whom, to use the sublime language of the apostle, is wiser than men, and the weakness of whom is stronger than men. (1 Cor. 1: 25.) Paul had experienced the saving power of this gospel, and this experience gave him a conviction of its reality, efficacy, and worth, which sustained him in preaching it even to a gainsaying world. *Christ* was to him peculiarly the power of God, for he had seen him and had received him, not as the lowly Nazarene in the days of his humiliation, but in his exaltation and glory, at the sight of which even Christ's bosom disciple, John, fell at his feet as dead. What we as Christians need, especially those of us who have been "separated unto the gospel of God," is to rely, not on our learning and culture, not on the rareness and richness of our style, or on our depth of thought— the excellency of our words, or of our wisdom, which we may well imagine to be foolishness with God—but on the omnipotence of our exalted Redeemer and on the divine power of gospel truth made efficacious by the Holy Spirit. Without the Spirit's aid to bless the truth and give it power, it were as much in vain for the minister of the gospel to preach to those who are dead in trespasses and in sins as for him to go into the burying ground and bid the sleeping dead rise from their graves. If we can testify to this divine power from our own experience, and if we can preach this truth in a plain, earnest, tender, sympathizing manner, we may hope, through God's blessing, to see the gospel's saving efficacy in the conversion of sinners.] There is a special propriety in Paul's emphasizing the *power* of the gospel in writing to the Romans, as there is in his emphasizing *wisdom* also in writing to the Greeks. (1 Cor. 1: 22-24.) Alford well remarks, that this clause

comprehends the *subject*, and might not inaptly form the *title* of the Epistle: 'The Gospel is the Power of God unto Salvation to Every One that Believeth.' [Philippi gives the theme of the Epistle in these words: The righteousness which avails before God comes to all men from faith only, and only this righteousness of faith has salvation or life for its result.] The universality implied in 'every one' in opposition to Jewish exclusiveness (1: 13-3: 20), the condition necessitated in the limiting clause, *that believeth* [in opposition to Jewish legalism] (3: 21-5: 11), and 'the power of God' acting 'unto salvation' (5: 12-8: 39), are the great subjects treated of in the first half of the Epistle. Observe how the *limitation* in respect to *character* is set over against the *universality* as to all *national* and *external* distinctions. So it is generally in the New Testament, and emphatically in that remarkable passage which has been called "the gospel in miniature." (John 3: 16.) **To the Jew first, and also to the Greek.**[1] 'To the Jew' first in order by divine appointment, and first in claim by divine promise ; but with no other precedence or pre-eminence. Compare 3: 1, 2, 9, and John 4: 22. 'The Greek' is here put comprehensively for the Gentile. Greek was the prevailing language of the Gentile world in those parts adjacent, and most familiar to the Jews. Indeed, the very word here used is translated "Gentile" in about one-third of the places where it occurs. See John 7: 35, twice; Rom. 2: 9, 10; 3: 9; 1 Cor. 10: 32; 12: 13. [A single Gentile must be denoted by the word "Greek," as the singular of "Gentiles" (ethnos) is not used of an individual. "Greeks" also might denote individual Gentiles, while "Gentiles" proper would be used of a class collectively.]

17. For therein is the righteousness of God revealed. [For similar phraseology, see Ps. 98: 2; in the Septuagint, Ps. 97: 2.] 'For' illustrates and confirms the statement of ver. 16. The gospel is the power of God unto salvation, *because* it reveals 'the right-eousness of God.' Hence the importance of

---

[1] These terms "embrace all nations, from the Jewish standpoint, as Greeks and Barbarians (ver. 14) do from the Grecian." (De Wette.) On the force of τε καὶ, see | ver. 14. Meyer says they "denote the equality of what is added."—(F.)

understanding aright what is meant by this expression; it is, more than any other single expression, the key to this Epistle, and, in fact, to the whole gospel as a saving power. What, then, are we to understand here by 'the righteousness of God'?[1] 1. It plainly does *not* denote the divine righteousness as a personal attribute of God, as it does in James 1: 20; Rom. 3: 5, 25, 26. It is not this which makes the gospel a *saving* divine power; nor is it this which is spoken of in Hab. 2: 4. It is not this to which the description in the context, and in other parts of this Epistle, is applicable. The righteousness here referred to is a *gift* from God to men. See 5: 17; Phil. 3: 9. It is conditioned on faith. [As here indicated, it flows *from* faith.] This condition is variously expressed.[2] It is evident that *men*, then, not God, are the subjects of whom this righteousness is predicated.

2. It plainly is *not* the moral rectitude in man which the law of God requires: for it is not *by* the law, Gal. 2: 21 (διά); 3: 21 (ἐκ), [or *in* the law, Phil. 3: 6] but without the law, Rom. 3: 21 (χωρίς); whereas the moral rectitude which God requires does consist precisely in conformity to his law; his law is the standard by which it is measured. Again, this righteousness is described as not being *our own*, but *broadly contrasted* with our own righteousness, which is by the law. (Rom. 9: 30-32; 10: 3, 5, 6; Gal. 2: 16; Phil. 3: 9.)

3. It is, then, the righteousness of *God*, as proceeding from him, and accepted by him (2: 13; 3: 20; Gal. 3: 11); and it is also no less truly the righteousness of the believing *man*, as provided for him, given to him, and conditioned on his faith. In short, it is very nearly

equivalent to *justification.* [Winer notices two interpretations of this phrase: that of Luther (which Philippi approves): the righteousness which avails before God (Rom. 2: 13; 3: 20; Gal. 3: 11), and "the righteousness which God imparts." He deems both appropriate in their right connections, but prefers the latter. Dr. Hodge says: "The gospel reveals a righteousness which God gives and which he approves." DeWette says: "God justifies for Christ's sake, on condition of faith in him as mediator; the result of his justification is righteousness from faith, and, because he imparts this freely, it is righteousness of God (genitive subjective) or, as in Phil. 3: 9, from God." Both nouns are without the article, yet the one is made sufficiently definite by the other. It is *God's* righteousness which is being revealed in and by the gospel. This righteousness, which comes from God through faith, and which is indeed a "gift" of God to us (5: 17), in virtue of which we, though guilty in ourselves, are justified by God and shall stand acquitted in the judgment as righteous, is opposed to a righteousness which is originated by ourselves, which is *our own*, which is derived not from faith and through grace, but "from works" and "from law." (Phil. 3: 9; Rom. 10: 3: 11: 6; Gal. 2: 16; 3: 21.) The righteousness, then, which God imparts and approves, consists chiefly in faith or trust in the Redeemer, and with this faith are joined both love and obedience; but our obedience and love and faith are all imperfect, and even faith itself can be counted as righteousness only "according to grace."][3]

4. This explanation of the expression is further confirmed by the usage of the verb

---

[1] The expression occurs twelve times in the New Testament (including several instances of "*his* righteousness," where the pronoun plainly refers to God): nine times in Paul's epistles (eight times in Romans, five times in chapter third)—namely, Matt. 6: 33; Rom. 1: 17; 3: 5, 21, 22, 25, 26; 10: 3, twice; 2 Cor. 5: 21; James 1: 20; 2 Peter 1: 1. ["*Righteousness* (δικαιοσύνη) occurs in the New Testament ninety-two times, and is always so rendered in the Common Version; δίκαιος eighty-one times, and is rendered *righteous* forty times, *just* thirty-five times. *right* five times, *meet* once; δικαίωμα occurs ten times, and is rendered *righteousness* four times, *justification* once, *judgment* once, and in the plural, *ordinances* three times, *judgments* once; δικαίωσις occurs twice, and is rendered *justification*." (Prof. Boise's "Notes on Romans.")]—(F.)

[2] It is expressed sometimes simply by the genitive case, as in 4: 11, 13; sometimes by various prepositions in the original, as ἐκ 9: 30: 10: 6; διά 3: 22; Phil. 3: 9; κατά Heb. 11: 7; ἐπί Phil 3: 9. It is well to mark with what fullness and emphasis this condition is expressed, particularly in 3: 22; Phil. 3: 9.—(F.)

[3] "The gospel makes known both the accomplished work of redemption itself and the means whereby man appropriates the redemption—namely, *faith in Christ* which, *imputed* to him as righteousness (4: 5), causes man to be regarded and treated by God out of grace and gratuitously (3: 24) as righteous, so that he, like one who has perfectly obeyed the law, is certain of the Messianic bliss destined for the righteous." (Meyer.)—(F.)

from faith to faith: as it is written, The just shall live by faith. | as it is written, But the righteous shall live from faith.

to justify, or make righteous, in such passages as 3: 26; 8: 33; Gal. 3: 11. ["The verb *to justify* (δικαιόω) occurs forty times in the New Testament, twenty-seven times in Paul's epistles. . . . It denotes an act of jurisdiction —the pronouncing of a sentence, not the infusion of a quality. . . . There is, to my knowledge, no passage in the New Testament, and only two or three in the Septuagint where this verb means to make just, or lead to righteousness." (Schaff.) "*Dikaioun*, even as used by Paul, denotes nothing else than the *judicial act* of God whereby man is pronounced free from guilt and punishment, and is thus recognized or represented as *dikaios*, righteous." (Cremer.) "*Dikaioun* is not only negative, to acquit, but also positive, to declare righteous, but never to make righteous." (DeWette.) It is to be noticed that 'to justify' implies something more than to pardon. A pardoned criminal is never said to be justified. Indeed, our earthly courts know nothing about justifying one who has been guilty. "Pardon and justification, therefore, are essentially different. The one is the remission of punishment, the other is a declaration that no ground for the infliction of punishment exists." (Hodge.)]

Compare, further, Schaff's elaborate and admirable note on 3: 24, in Lange's Commentary. Also the following from Meyer and De Wette. "Rightness with God—the relation of being right into which man is put by God (*i. e.*, by an act of God declaring him righteous)." (Meyer.) "Justification is properly after the old Protestant theologians to be taken in a forensic sense—that is, imputatively. . . . All interpretations which overlook the fact of imputation are erroneous." (DeWette.)

Therein is revealed. 'Therein'—that is, in the gospel. This righteousness was indeed *foreshadowed* in the Old Testament, but not *revealed*, unveiled, until gospel times. The present tense denotes a *continual* unfolding of this righteousness in the pages of the New Testament [or by the preaching of the apostles. (A. H.)] **From faith to faith.** There are many ingenious ways of explaining this phrase, such as faith in the Old Testament first, then in the New; from lower degrees of faith to higher, etc.; but they are all too

elaborate and over nice. [Meyer seems to favor the last view, and refers in support of it to 2 Cor. 2: 16. "from life unto life," etc. His statement is that "the revelation spoken of proceeds from faith, and is designed to produce faith." But the idea of an advance in faith seems somewhat irrelevant to the apostle's argument. The majority of commentators interpret it in the light of 3: 22, and regard this righteousness which comes from faith, as also a gift *to faith*, or to believers. "This righteousness proceeds from faith, and belongs to faith." (Ripley.) De Wette, Meyer and Alford *versus* Philippi and others, connect *from faith* with the verb *is revealed*, rather than with righteousness; yet see 10: 6, "the righteousness which is from faith"; also 3: 22; Phil. 3: 9, "the righteousness of God through faith," and "the righteousness from God upon faith." This view is given substantially in Godet's rendering: God's righteousness is revealed (as being) from faith.] It is better perhaps to regard the whole expression as simply intensive, without attempting too minute an analysis of it. It is all of faith, "from stem to stern" (prora et puppis), as *Bengel* says, in his own terse and pithy way. [According to Pauline usage, faith *per se* is not righteousness in us, for if so, our righteousness would be very imperfect; nor is it represented as meritorious. We are justified by grace through faith, but never is it said that we are justified on account of faith. We are justified gratuitously (3: 24), and our faith is reckoned for righteousness only in the way of grace. "It is the grace of God which leads him to justify any. Even faith in Christ has no virtue in itself. As an affection or act of the soul, it is inferior to love; and neither of them is half as steady or fervid as it ought to be. As strongly as possible, therefore, does Paul assert that justification is an act of free grace to the sinner on the part of God. Hence, faith does not justify as being in itself righteousness, obedience, a germ of righteousness, or an equivalent for obedience, but *as a total renunciation of all claim to personal righteousness and a sole reliance upon Christ* for acceptance with God. 'The glory of faith is that its utter emptiness opens to receive consummate good.' " Hovey's "Manual of Systematic

Theology," pp. 266, 268.] **As it is written, The just shall live by faith.** The quotation from Hab. 2: 4 is repeated in Gal. 3: 11 and Heb. 10: 38. By a slight transposition the passage might be made to read, *the just* (or justified) *by faith—shall live.* And this way of connecting the words might seem to give them additional pertinency in the present case; but when we examine the original passage, as it is found in the Old Testament, such an arrangement of the words, though adopted by Meyer and Winer, seems hardly consistent with the Hebrew text. [**As it is written.** Literally, *as it has been written* (and remains so). While there are no quotations from the Old Testament in First and Second Thessalonians, Philippians, Colossians (the letters to these churches being "intended in the main for Gentile Christians"— Farrar), they are very abundant in this Epistle, and are chiefly introduced (nineteen times) by the above formula. Farrar says: "There are about two hundred and seventy-eight quotations from the Old Testament in the New. Of these, fifty-three are identical in the Hebrew, Septuagint, and New Testament. In ten the Septuagint is correctly altered; in seventy-six it is altered incorrectly—*i. e.*, into greater divergence from the Hebrew; in thirty-seven it is accepted where it differs from the Hebrew; in ninety-nine all three differ, and there are three doubtful allusions." See also Dr. Schaff's "Companion to the Greek Testament," page 24. In Dr. S. Davidson's "Sacred Hermeneutics," two hundred and fifty-five quotations are given in Hebrew, in the Greek of the Septuagint and of the New Testament, and in English. Prof. Stuart reckons up five hundred and three quotations and allusions, and remarks that even this list "is far from comprehending all of this nature which the New Testament contains. The truth is, there is not a page, nor even a paragraph of any considerable length, belonging to the New Testament, which does not bear

the impress of the Old Testament upon it." Davidson finds fifty-one quotations in the Epistle to the Romans; Stuart gives fifty-eight quotations and allusions, while others put the number still higher. The largest number we have seen, if we mistake not, is given on pages 180 and 181 of Westcott and Hort's "Introduction to the New Testament in Greek." Paul, according to Dr. Schaff, "usually agrees with the Septuagint, except when he freely quotes from memory, or adapts the text to his argument."[1] Sometimes we have Moses saith, or Isaiah saith, or the Scripture saith, but never the especial gospel formula—"that it might be fulfilled." The New Testament writers and our divine Saviour himself found, it must be conceded, more of Christ and the gospel in the Old Testament than we should naturally have expected to find, and this shows us that the Old Testament was divinely designed to prefigure and illustrate the New. (See in "Christian Review," for April, 1856, an article by the writer, entitled, "Christ in the Old Testament.") "This retrospective use of the Old Testament," says Olshausen, "is rather to be derived from that Scriptural, fundamental view of it, which supposes that in it all the germs of the New Testament are already really contained, and that, therefore, the New Testament is only the fulfilling of the Old." Similarly, Ellicott: "This typical or allegorical interpretation is neither arbitrary nor of mere Rabbinical origin" [Rabbinisch-typischer Interpretationsweise.—Meyer], "but is to be referred to the inspiration of the Holy Spirit under which the apostle gives the literal meaning of the words their *fuller* and *deeper* application." The Hebrew of the passage quoted reads, "The just by his faithfulness shall live"; the Septuagint Version, "The just shall live by my faith"; while the author of the Epistle to the Hebrews has it, according to the Revised Version, "My righteous one shall live by faith."[2] As the faith of the righteous one

---

[1] See also "Quotations in the New Testament," by C. H. Toy, D. D., 1884, for an exhaustive catalogue of the citations and references in the New Testament.—A. H.

[2] Δίκαιος, just or righteous, "an adjective lying between the verb (δικαιόω, to justify) and the substantive (δικαιοσύνη, righteousness), and taking its color, more or less in different instances, from either. It is to be observed that we do not possess in English a family of

cognate, native words to express these Greek words, but are obliged to render the verb by the Latin derivative *justify*, while the kindred adjective and substantive are translated by the Saxon *righteous* and *righteousness*. A parallel difficulty arises in the case of the words πίστις and πιστεύω, rendered by the Latin *faith* and the Saxon *believe*."—" The Five Clergymen."—(F.)

18 For the wrath of God is revealed from heaven against all ungodliness and unrighteousness of men, who hold the truth in unrighteousness;

18 For [1]the wrath of God is revealed from heaven against all ungodliness and unrighteousness of men,

1 Or, *a wrath.*

---

in Habakkuk may be his trustworthiness, or "faith which may be relied on, not the faith which relies," so some (as Farrar) would regard this quotation as little more than an accommodation of the literal truth to the subject in hand. Yet there is, as Bishop Lightfoot remarks (on Gal. 3: 11, and page 155), "a close moral affinity between *trustworthiness* and *trustfulness*," or faith, the former at times approaching "near to the active sense; for constancy under temptation or danger, with an Israelite, could only spring from reliance on Jehovah." Delitzsch, as quoted by Philippi, affirms that "the apostle brings nothing to this passage that it does not contain. All that he does is to set its meaning —that the life of the righteous comes from faith—in the light of the New Testament." And Meyer says: "This faithfulness in the prophet's sense and the faith in the Christian sense have the same fundamental idea—*trustful self-surrender* to God." It was this passage of divine truth which brought light and peace to the mind of Luther, and gave him to the cause of the Reformation. In these last two verses we have a concise answer—which only the Holy Spirit could give—to that most momentous question: "How can man be just with God?"[1]]

18. For the wrath of God is revealed from heaven. [" An exordium terrible as lightning." (Melancthon.) Under the general division: "All are guilty," Mr. Beet gives the following sub-divisions: "For God is angry with all sin (1: 18-32); without respect of persons (2: 1-11); of this the giving of the law is no disproof (2: 12-24); nor is the rite of circumcision (2: 25-29); yet the Jews have real advantages (3: 1-9); but are condemned by their own law.

(3: 10-20.)"] The gospel way of justification by faith in Christ is man's only hope; 'for,' where there is no faith, there is no revelation of the righteousness of God, but a revelation of 'the wrath of God' instead. [According to Godet, the transition from ver. 17, indicated by *for* is this: "There is a revelation of righteousness by the gospel, because there is a revelation of wrath on the whole world." Similarly De Wette: "The righteousness of God (by which we are justified) presupposes God's wrath against sinners, or the unworthiness of men." The verb here, as in the preceding verse, is in the present tense, which denotes something constant or habitual, and is emphatic by position. "Generally," says Kühner, "both the first and last place in a sentence is considered emphatic, when words stand there which, according to the usual arrangement, would have a different position."] The same phrase, 'is revealed,' is used here as in the preceding verse: but whilst the *medium* of revelation in the preceding case is limited to the gospel by the expression, 'therein,' here there is a more *comprehensive* revelation, not only in the gospel, but also in man's moral nature, and in divine providence. [Compare ver. 24, seq.; also 2: 5.] In what sense is wrath ascribed to God? There is not in him any violent perturbation of feeling, such as usually accompanies wrath in man; but a real, unchangeable, intense displeasure against sin, having a necessary connection with his love, and his approval of righteousness. "If God is not angry with the ungodly and unrighteous, neither can he have any pleasure in the pious and the righteous; for in regard to things of an opposite nature, he must be affected by both or by

---

[1] " If we had retained our original righteousness, justice itself would have justified us; but, having sinned, the question, ' How shall man be justified with God?' is too difficult for created wisdom to solve. Whatever delight the Creator takes in honoring and rewarding righteousness, there is none left in this apostate world for him to honor or reward. ' All have sinned and come short of the glory of God.' If any child of Adam, therefore, be now accepted and rewarded as righteous, it must be on entirely different ground from that of his own righteousness. What ground this could be God

only knew." (A. Fuller.) This writer further notices how justification in the sight of God must differ from justification among men. Justification in human courts supposes a man to have been innocent rather than guilty, but justification by grace supposes the man to be guilty, and to have need of pardon. This pardon removes the curse, while justification confers the blessing of eternal life, and both are, through abounding grace in Jesus Christ, secured to those who in themselves are only deserving of death.—(F.)

neither." (Lactantius.) Compare Ps. 11: 5-7; 45: 6, 7. 'Is revealed from heaven.' It enters into men's minds as a persuasion which results, not from their own wills, but from a *divine* constitution of things. It is involuntary and ineffaceable. It is not the offspring of a distempered fancy, nor an invention of crafty priests or crafty kings, that they may excite men's fears, and so manage them the more easily for their own advantage: but it is revealed from heaven, from the abode of infinite wisdom and love. That is the place whence this stern doctrine of divine retribution originates. The wrath that condemns comes down from above upon men just as truly as the righteousness that justifies. [This *wrath*, according to Philippi, "denotes an inner determination of the divine nature itself, the inwardly energetic antagonism and repellant force of his holiness in relation to human sin, which divine affection, indeed, finds its expression in the infliction of punishment." Our merciful Saviour, who came from heaven, himself spoke of the wrath of God as abiding on the unbeliever. 'From heaven' is this wrath revealed, because there "the Lord hath prepared his throne," and thence "his judgments go forth as lightning." See "Bible Commentary." De Wette and Meyer suppose this revelation of wrath 'from heaven' consists in visible punishments and judgments inflicted on transgressors. Philippi, on the other hand, asserts that what is revealed by God or from heaven "always refers in the New Testament to an *extraordinary* revelation through miraculous acts, through the words of prophets and apostles, or inwardly through the Spirit of God." The verb in the present tense is, in his view, used for the future, and this revelation of wrath will take place in "the day of wrath and revelation of the righteous judgment of God." (2: 5.) Yet we must say that God's wrath, in some form or other, has always been manifested against all ungodliness and iniquity.] **Against all ungodliness and unrighteousness of men.** The order of the words is significant. Against 'ungodliness' first. The whole development of the argument in the remainder of this chapter emphasizes this order. It is, moreover, in accordance with the whole tenor of Scripture. Compare Matt. 6: 33; 22: 36-40. Note the comprehensiveness of the expression: against every kind and every degree, both of irreligion and immorality. How little do men in general regard the mere absence of a religious reverence for God as justly exposing them to his wrath! [By the use of the term 'men,' the correlative of 'God,' the apostle would indicate "the *audacity* of this God-opposing conduct." (Meyer.) How holy is our God, and how hateful to him is sin that man's ungodliness and unrighteousness, his "sins against the first and the second table" (Philippi), should call forth from him, whose name and nature is love, a revelation of his wrath and of his righteous judgment! We may remark that, in this chapter generally, special reference is had to the Gentiles, and not until the next chapter do the Jews come under consideration. Even the Gentiles repress the truth in unrighteousness and are conscious of deserving the wrath of God.] **Who hold the truth in unrighteousness.** The compound verb here used means not simply to hold, but to hold *fast*, as in Luke 8: 15 (translated *keep*); 1 Thess. 5: 21; Heb. 3: 6. 14; 10: 23, or to hold *back*, hold *down*, *repress*, as in Luke 4: 42 (translated *stayed*); Rom. 7: 6 (translated *held*); Philem. 13 (translated *retained*). This last sense is the only appropriate one here: men hold down, as in the Revised Version, repress religious truth by living 'in unrighteousness.' Their practical unrighteousness reacts upon the inward man, blinding the understanding, hardening the heart, stupefying the conscience. That this is the true meaning of the word, here translated *hold* is recognized by the best translators and commentators.[1] [Bengel: "Truth in the mind strives and urges, but man impedes it." The Bible Commentary observes here the contrast that the power unto salvation is for "every one that believeth"; the wrath is against them "that hold down the truth in unrighteousness."]

---

[1] Of the earlier English versions, Wickliffe, Tyndale, Cranmer, and the Genevan have *withhold*; the Rhemish has *detain*; Alford, *hold back*; the Vulgate and Beza, *detinent*; Diodati's Italian and DeLacy's French have *retain* (ritengono, retiennent); the Bible Society's French has *suppress* (suppriment); Luther's German has aufhalten [to *hinder*].

19 Because that which may be known of God is manifest in them ; for God hath shewed it unto them. 20 For the invisible things of him from the creation of the world are clearly seen, being understood by the

19 who ¹hinder the truth in unrighteousness; because that which may be known of God is manifest in 20 them; for God manifested it unto them. For the invisible things of him since the creation of the world are clearly seen, being perceived through the

1 Or, hold the truth.

19. Because. The connection of the thought is this: this charge which I bring against them is just; 'because' it is true; first, that they *have* the elementary knowledge of the truth (proved in ver. 19, 20), and, secondly, that they so *pervert* it (proved in ver. 21–23). The argument of ver. 18 to 20, though compressed, is very clear and conclusive. [Meyer and others see in this *because* the reason why God's wrath comes upon wicked men.] That which may be known of God—that is, whatever may be learned about God from nature and providence, apart from revelation. [According to Meyer, De Wette, and others, γνωστόν, which in the classics most frequently means *knowable*, does not occur in this sense in the New Testament, the LXX., or the Apocrypha, but signifies that which is actually known (γνωτόν). All that might be known of God was not manifest *in* the heathen ; but they did know, even apart from revelation, of a Creator, and of his everlasting power and divinity. (Acts 14 : 17; 17 : 27.) The heavens declared to them God's power and glory, but no inspired word revealed to them his will and grace. Godet, however, thinks the manifestation of that which is known is a "startling tautology." According to the teaching of this passage, it is plain that agnosticism cannot be justified even in the heathen.] **Is manifest in them.** Not merely *among* them, or *to* them, but *in* them—that is, in their hearts and consciences. This agrees with the following verse, and also with 2 : 15. **For God hath shewed it unto them.** It is manifest in them; for God manifested it to them. The Common Version fails to exhibit the intimate connection between the verb in this clause, and the adjective in the preceding clause. The indefinite past tense is preferable to the perfect here—'manifested,' to 'hath shewn,' or 'hath manifested.' God so framed the earth and man at the creation as to bear witness to himself. Compare Acts 14 : 17; 17 : 26, 27. ["He left not himself without witness." "By saying that *God manifested it,* he means that man was created to be a

spectator of this formed world, and that eyes were given him, that he might, by looking on so fair a picture, be led up to the Author himself." (Calvin.) If Paul, in this passage, had referred to an original revelation, as some have supposed, he would probably have used the word revealed.]

20. For the invisible things of him. [The adjective may mean *unseen,* or, *that which cannot be seen* (by the outward eye), *invisible.*] These invisible things are his unseen attributes and perfections [especially his everlasting power and divinity. With this passage, compare "Wisdom of Solomon," chap. 13.] **From the creation of the world.** 'From' is here to be understood in a *temporal* sense, equivalent to "ever since." To understand it as referring to the medium of that knowledge of God attributed to the heathen would be to make this and the following clause affirm the same thing, contrary to the very condensed style of the apostle in these verses. [Dr. Gifford, however, thinks the one clause may refer to the *source* of knowledge, the other to the *method* of its derivation.] **Are clearly seen**—literally, are looked down upon, looked at, observed, **being understood by the things that are made.** [Paul, as in the passages above cited, advanced similar ideas at Lystra and at Athens.] There is a verbal contradiction here, even more manifestly in the original [to see what is unseen, or invisible, a figure of speech called *oxymoron*] ; but it is easily explained. Invisible things cannot, of course, be clearly seen, in the literal sense of the words. But they are clearly seen by the exercise of the *mind* upon the things that are made, which is precisely what the apostle here affirms [in the use of the word *perceived*]. The things that are made strike the senses; the inference from them of a Divine Power strikes the considering mind. So Cicero says: Deum non vides —tamen agnoscis ex operibus ejus. "Tusc. Disp." 1 : 29. "Thou dost not see God: yet thou knowest him from his works." **Even**

things that are made, *even* his eternal power and God- | things that are made, *even* his everlasting power
head ; so that they are without excuse : | and divinity ; [1] that they may be without excuse:

1 Or, *so that they are.*

(literally, *both*) **his eternal power and** (eternal) **Godhead.** These are 'the invisible things of him.' His 'power' is the thought that first and most impressively strikes the considering mind on the contemplation of his works. [" Eternal, and Almighty, have always been recognized epithets of the Creator." (Alford.)] But, it may be asked, How can his 'eternal' power be inferred from the things that are made? They were not made from eternity. The apostle here assumes that the human mind is so constituted as to reject the idea that such power could ever have been *acquired*, such skill ever learned : he who has such power and skill must *always* have had it. [Possibly, too, their feeling of dependence, as well as the apparent dependence of all things begun, changing, and transient, may have led them to think of a Being independent, unchanging, eternal. Some, however, suppose that God, in addition to the light of nature, made to primeval man a special revelation of himself as Creator of all things. In some way or other, the Gentiles began with monotheism—they knew God (ver. 21), and in this matter they, though ignorant of our many natural sciences. and our modern scientific discoveries and inventions, differed widely from some of our "scientists," who, by means of the telescope and microscope, see everywhere, and in every thing throughout God's vast creation, so much of power, wisdom, order, beauty, adaptation, design, perfection—that they become "agnostics" who do not know much, or anything, about the being of an Almighty Creator, that Infinite Mind, which could alone plan and conserve such a universe as this. " Heathenism," says Meyer, "is not the primeval religion, from which man might gradually have risen to the knowledge of the true God ; but is, on the contrary, the result of a falling away from the known original revelation of the true God in his works."] Under the term, "Godhead" [properly, divinity (θειότης) not Godhead, or deity (θεότης), which dwells in Christ, see Col. 2: 9], the apostle comprehends whatever else of the divine perfections, besides eternal power, can be learned from the works of creation and

providence. The adjective "eternal" [not αἰώνιος, properly rendered, eternal; but ἀΐδιος, everlasting, from ἀεί, always, occurring also in Jude 6] is to be regarded as qualifying this word "Godhead," as well as the word "power" [the adjective not being repeated, since the nouns are of the same gender. For the same reason, the first noun only has the article. (Winer 527, 128.) (On τε—καὶ, see at ver. 14.)] **So that they are without excuse.** [The construction here, the preposition into, or unto (εἰς), with the infinitive and article, generally, if not universally, *telic*, denotes not a result (so that), but a purpose, *in order that*, and it is so regarded by Meyer (and Godet) in this place, his idea being that this seeing or perception of the divine attributes through his works, was so ordained, or purposely established, that sinning men should have no excuse. Lange regards this view as a predestinating men for guilt (not necessarily so, however), and with most commentators, sees here but a simple result. Yet what is Dr. Schaff's "(intended) result" but the divine purpose? The right view is very happily stated by Dr. Gifford: "God's *purpose* was to leave nothing undone on his part, the omission of which might give men an excuse for sin." A similar construction occurs in 1: 11 ; 3: 26 ; 4: 11 ; 16: 18; 6: 12 ; 7: 4, 5 ; 8: 29 ; 11: 11 ; 12: 2, 3 ; 15: 8, 13, 16. Meyer contends that all these infinitives have a telic force. Others deny this force of the preposition to or unto (εἰς) before an infinitive present. See Prof. Thayer's "Lexicon," p. 185.] Facts correspond with the apostle's statements throughout these verses. The heathen have more light than they are willing to improve. Their responsibility is measured by the light which they have *opportunity* to enjoy, and not by which they *choose* to appropriate. Many testimonies might easily be adduced, to prove that they have more light than they are willing to improve, and that they *know themselves* to be inexcusable. Take the following as a single specimen. Rev. A. W. Murray, after nearly forty years of extensive observation in the island world of Polynesia, says: "I have

21 Because that, when they knew God, they glorified *him* not as God, neither were thankful; but became vain in their imaginations, and their foolish heart was darkened.

21 because that, knowing God, they glorified him not as God, neither gave thanks; but became vain in their reasonings, and their senseless heart was

never found, in all my wanderings among savage tribes, any who had not some idea of a future life, and of beings superior to themselves, to whom they owed some sort of homage, and whom they feared, and sought in some way to propitiate. If the entire absence of all religious belief is to be found anywhere among the human family, I know of no place so likely as among the aborigines of Australia. There man has sunk about as low as he can sink; yet, among some of the tribes there is a distinct belief in a future life and a Supreme Being." One of the most forcible exhibitions of the inexcusableness of the heathen may be found in an excellent little tract, published many years ago by our veteran Burman missionary, Dr. Edward A. Stevens, entitled: "Are the Heathen in a Perishing Condition?" He shows that they themselves resent, as an insult to their understanding, the apology sometimes made for them, that the poor, simple creatures *know no better*. [On the fate of such heathen, see notes on 2: 12; 10: 14. We here would simply remark that if the heathen who have sinned though "without law," have no excuse, then they may be judged and condemned by our Lord and Saviour, and we must regard as false the dictum of the New Theology, or Progressive Orthodoxy, that all "those who are to stand before Christ as a Judge must first hear of him as a Saviour."] Note what an emphatic endorsement of the cosmological argument for the existence of God is contained in the above verses.

Observe, also, what a broad foundation is here laid for the science of Natural Theology —and that, too, in the midst of an argument evincing the value and necessity of a divine revelation. [Meyer notices "how completely in our passage the *transcendental* relation of God to the world—the negation of all identity of the two—lies at the foundation of the apostle's view. It does not exclude the *immanence* of God in the world, but it excludes all *pantheism*." Dr. Schaff says: "The book of nature is, as Basil calls it, a *paideuterion theognosias*, a school of the general knowledge of God; and there is no nation on earth which is entirely destitute of this knowledge."

Pitiably blind and ignorant must those persons be who can discern, in all this universe, no intelligent force, no sign of an Infinite Mind.]

21. The word **because** shows that this verse is designed to confirm and expand the thought expressed in the last clause of the preceding verse—to illustrate still further the inexcusableness of the heathen. **When they knew God** [literally, *having known God*] refers to ver. 19; it does not refer to that *saving* knowledge of God spoken of in such passages as Jer. 9: 24; John 17: 3, 25. **They glorified him not as God** ["according to the measure of his divine quality."--Meyer], **neither were thankful**—more literally, *neither gave thanks*. [Because of this the apostle asserts that they are without excuse, even while ignorant of the "historic Christ" or of God's amazing love in him.] The first clause relates to the adoration of the divine perfections in general; the second, to the acknowledgment of him as the Giver of every good. Bengel thus distinguishes them: "We ought to give thanks on account of his benefits; to glorify him, on account of his own perfections." They did neither. **But became vain in their imaginations.** [They turned their thoughts to that which is vain and empty, because in turning away from God they lost the highest object of their thought. See Weiss' "Biblical Theology of the New Testament," vol. I, p. 354.] The word translated 'became vain' is not used elsewhere in the New Testament [nor is it found in the Greek authors], but is used about half a dozen times in the Greek translation of the Old Testament, commonly called the Septuagint. In the language of the Old Testament, the word vanity is in many places nearly synonymous with falsehood, or sin in general, and especially idolatry. See Deut. 32: 21; 2 Kings 17: 15, 16. Compare also Acts 14: 15. The word here translated 'imaginations' (elsewhere 'thoughts,' 'reasonings') is generally in the New Testament used in an unfavorable sense. See Matt. 15: 19; Mark 7: 21; Luke 6: 8; 9: 46, 47. [Compare Rom. 14: 1; 1 Cor. 3: 20; 2 Cor. 10: 5; Phil. 2: 14; 1 Tim. 2: 8.] **And their foolish heart was darkened.** [The apostle in Eph. 4: 17-19 describes the Gentiles in much the

D

22 Professing themselves to be wise, they became fools.

23 And changed the glory of the uncorruptible God into an image made like to corruptible man, and to birds, and fourfooted beasts, and creeping things.

22 darkened. Professing themselves to be wise, they 23 became fools, and changed the glory of the incorruptible God for the likeness of an image of corruptible man, and of birds, and fourfooted beasts, and creeping things.

same language as he employs here, characterizing them as being vain, depraved, darkened, ignorant in their minds, and as hardened in their hearts, as being alienated from the life of God and past feeling, morally and spiritually dead. The term 'foolish,' as used here, is akin to *undiscerning;* implying a guilty misuse or non-use of the understanding. (See first note to ver. 14.) That their hearts had become thus wanting in understanding is implied in their *becoming vain* in their reasonings. Some of the thoughts, and even of the words which Paul uses in this description of the Gentiles, are found in the "Wisdom of Solomon," chapters 13 and 14.] The word 'heart,' in our common English speech, usually denotes the seat of the affections, in distinction from the intellect. But the use of the Greek word in the New Testament, and in the classical writers, and of the corresponding Hebrew word in the Old Testament, is not so limited, but includes the whole inner man, intellect as well as affections. See Matt. 13: 15; 15: 19; 2 Cor. 3: 15; 4: 6. Hence no particular stress is to be put on the word 'heart' in such passages as Ps. 14: 1; 53: 1; Rom. 10: 9, 10. So also the word usually translated "mind" sometimes includes the affections and desires, as in Eph. 2: 3. Thus the heathen, forsaking the truth, became vain in their imaginations, and forsaking the light, became darkened in their hearts. According to the Scripture [and to the teachings of history], the primeval religion was neither polytheism nor natureworship. If those who have only the light of nature are inexcusable for not glorifying God, nor being thankful, how much greater is the guilt of those who, with all the additional light of the gospel, still do not glorify him as God, and are not thankful for his manifold mercies.

22. Professing themselves to be wise, they became fools. Affirming that they were wise [while ignorant of the "ignorance that was in them"]. they became foolish. Their foolishness was only made more con-

spicuous by their pretensions to wisdom. This was eminently illustrated in the case of the so-called *sophists* among the Greeks, though it is hardly probable that the apostle had any specific reference to them. ["The foolishness of God is wiser than men," however much of wisdom they may arrogate to themselves. For a similar use of the word rendered 'professing,' see Acts 24: 9; 25: 19 (and Rev. 2: 2, according to our Textus Receptus). For the construction, see note on ver. 12. The description here given of the professedly wise is not wholly inapplicable to some of our modern scientists.]

23. The sense of this verse would be justly, though in the first part of the verse less literally, expressed by the following paraphrase: *and substituted for the glorious incorruptible God an image of the likeness of corruptible man,* etc. [Compare this language with Ps. 106: 20.] The Greeks and Romans worshiped for the most part representations of their false gods under the human form; but the Egyptians, and other still ruder nations, worshiped birds, as the ibis, or stork; four-footed beasts, as Apis, the sacred ox, the dog, and the cat; and even reptiles, or creeping things, as the crocodile, and the serpent. [The term *incorruptible,* as applied to God, occurs elsewhere only in 1 Tim. 1: 17, an important text in the history of the elder Edwards' religious experience. As to its distinction from the term immortal, see Trench's "Synonyms," p. 254. It is found elsewhere in 1 Cor. 9: 25; 15: 52; 1 Peter 1: 4, 23; 3: 4. The noun occurs in Rom. 2: 7; 1 Cor. 15: 42. 50, 53. 54; Eph. 6: 24; 2 Tim. 1: 10; Titus 2: 7. The heathen, instead of glorifying the Creator, worshiped him, if at all, as a created being—"for it is only such a being that can find its likeness in these images" (Weiss); thus degrading this incorruptible One "*in*[1] the likeness of an image (likeness consisting in an image) of corruptible man, and of birds, and of quadrupeds, and of reptiles." Meyer makes "birds," etc., in the same construction with *man—i. e.,* de-

[1] On the force of this *in*, as "to change something in gold," Winer thus remarks: "It is either an abbreviated expression, or 'gold is conceived of as that in which

the exchange is effected. The *in* of price is similar." This construction is commonly termed Hebraistic. Meyer, however, regards the *en* as instrumental.—(F.)

24 Wherefore God also gave them up to uncleanness, through the lusts of their own hearts, to dishonour their own bodies between themselves:

24 Wherefore God gave them up in the lusts of their hearts unto uncleanness, that their bodies should be
25 dishonoured among themselves: for that they ex-

pendent on *image.* The Egyptian worship of animals had at that time in part become domesticated in Rome, according to Tholuck and Lange.]

24. Here follows a description and enumeration of the vices which illustrate the 'unrighteousness' spoken of in ver. 18, as the preceding verses 21–23 illustrate the 'ungodliness' there mentioned. **Wherefore.** The apostle lays stress on the logical connection between their ungodliness and their unrighteousness—between their abandonment of God by idolatry, and God's abandonment of them to the unrestrained indulgence of unnatural lusts and every degrading vice and evil passion. The latter was the logical consequence, the actual result, and the just retribution of the former. Not content with the emphatic affirmation of this connection by the word 'wherefore' at the beginning of ver. 24, he reiterates it in ver. 26, "for this cause," and echoes it again in ver. 28, "and even as." He seems to wish to impress the thought deeply that the primal error, the first step in the downward course, was the abandonment of God as the sole object of worship; that the stream of vice has its source in ungodliness; that irreligion is the root of immorality. [See Müller's "Christian Doctrine of Sin," vol. I, p. 131; II, 470, Pulsford's Translation.] The converse would seem to follow—that there can be no true and complete morality which is not *rooted* in religion, in reverential regard for God. **God also gave them up to uncleanness.** That little word 'also' is not without significance; it seems to intimate that God's retributive abandonment of them corresponded, in proportion and progress, to their impious abandonment of him. [This, however, is omitted in the Revised Version.] He 'gave them up'; this expresses, on the one hand, something *more* than mere *permission,* and, on the other hand, something *less* than positive *impulse* toward any of these abominations. ["It is at least a judicial

abandonment" (Hodge), and is akin to what is implied in our Saviour's utterance, John 9: 39: "For judgment came I into this world that . . . they who (profess to) see might become blind."] The same idea is expressed elsewhere, both in the Old Testament and in the New. See Ps. 81: 12; Isa. 6: 10; Mark 4: 12; Acts 7: 42; Rom. 9: 18. All this takes place, at the same time, **through** (literally *in*) **the lusts of their own hearts.** [*Epithumia,* denoting, generally, evil desire (always so in the plural) is rendered *lust* in 6: 12; 7: 7; 13: 14, and concupiscence in 7: 8. The verb occurs in 7: 7; 13: 9, in connection with the tenth commandment.] This expression, *in the lusts,* not only specifies the department of their being *in* which this dishonor took place, but also intimates that they were perfectly voluntary; while God delivered them up to this uncleanness, they went into it in full accordance with the inclinations of their own hearts. [In Eph. 4: 19, we read that the Gentiles "*gave themselves up* to lasciviousness," and this twofold representation of divine and human agency is but a repetition of God's hardening Pharaoh's heart and of Pharaoh's hardening his own heart. "*He gives himself up,*" says Meyer, "while he *is given up* by God to that tragic *nexus* of moral destiny; and he becomes no machine of sin, but possesses at every moment the capacity of *repentance,* which the very reaction resulting from the feeling of the most terrible misery of sin—punished through sin—is designed to produce." In this penal retribution for man's apostasy, we see the beginnings of the manifestation of "God's wrath."] **To dishonour their own bodies between themselves.** This verse might be read more in accordance with the order of the words in the original Greek—"Wherefore God gave them up, in the lusts of their own hearts, to the uncleanness of their own bodies being dishonored among them." [1] The reading *them* is better sustained by the manuscripts than

---

[1] The form of the verb, being in the infinitive (either middle or passive) with τοῦ, usually denotes purpose (compare 7: 3; Acts 26: 18; 1 Cor. 10: 13; Heb. 10: 7), and this is expressed in the Revised Version, and is also favored, rightly, we think, by Philippi, Godet, and others. Yet this infinitive clause is by many (Tholuck Fritzsche, De Wette, Meyer) regarded as a noun in the genitive case of apposition, after the word uncleanness (Winer, 326; Buttmann, 268), the clause thus showing in what the uncleanness consisted.—(F.)

25 Who changed the truth of God into a lie, and worshipped and served the creature more than the Creator, who is blessed for ever. Amen.

changed the truth of God for a lie, and worshipped and served the creature rather than the Creator, who is blessed [1] for ever. Amen.

[1] Gr. *unto the ages.*

the reading *themselves;*[1] *among* is more exact than *between,* and the change in these two expressions favors the *passive* sense of the verb to dishonor, the form of which is ambiguous, admitting either the active or the passive sense, but with a presumption, apart from the above considerations, in favor of the latter. The expression "among them" is equivalent to "in their common intercourse." ["The most terrible misery of sin" is that sin leads to sin, and this too in the way of a descent from bad to worse. In the words of Schiller, quoted by Schaff—

This is the very curse of evil deed,
That of new evil it becomes the seed.[2]

And when one enters upon an evil course, he knows not to what depths of degradation he may be led. His language at first may be, " Is thy servant a dog that he should do this great thing?" and he ends with doing that which the very beasts would be ashamed to do. Thus, self-destroyed and lost in vileness, he may say with Mokanna, in the " Veiled Prophet of Khorassen":

Here, judge if hell, with all its power to damn,
Can add one curse to the foul thing I am.

And what a degradation is this, that those who were formed for God and who "knew God" and truth and duty, should, under this law of development, of moral seed-sowing and harvesting, be so far given over to diseased appetites or vile passions, that their noblest faculty, the sovereign power of will— that which they have " in superior distinction from the beast"—becomes subservient to their lusts and the means of sinking themselves lower than the brutes.]

25. Who changed the truth of God into

a lie. The word translated ' who' is not the simple relative pronoun, but a compound which [like the Latin, *quippe qui*] often intimates *a reason* for what precedes, "as being such who," or "because they were such as." [Buttmann, however, supposes that this form in the later language lost some of its original force.] 'Changed the truth of God into a lie'—equivalent to "exchanged the true God for a false," as in ver. 23. [Philo, speaking of the Israelites making the golden calf, says: "What a lie they subsituted for how great a reality!" "The truth of God," says Weiss, "stands for the true nature of God." The word "changed" here is stronger in form than the "changed" of ver. 23, and consequently has a stronger meaning, equivalent to *exchanged.* The preposition ' into,' accompanying the word lie, denotes "the element in which the change subsisted." (Alford.) See also on ver. 23.] **And worshipped and served.** The former verb [primarily meaning "to be afraid of," occurring only here, in form a passive deponent, and usually followed by the accusative] signifies inward reverence, and the latter outward acts of homage, as sacrifices, prayers, etc. [See notes on ver. 9, and compare Matt. 4 : 10 ; Luke 2 : 37.] **The creature** is put for created and material things in general. **More than the Creator** —beside, or in preference to, the Creator, implying exclusion ["*instead of* the Creator."— Winer], for the Creator allows no rival. **Who is blessed forever. Amen.**[3] This doxology forcibly indicates the apostle's pious horror at such a dishonor put upon God, and sets their sin in a stronger light. For similar examples of abrupt doxology in the midst of a sentence, see 2 Cor. 11: 31; Gal. 1: 5. It

[1] Our Textus Receptus has the reflexive, ἑαυτοῖς (themselves), the reading of D * * * E G K L. The older uncials ℵ A B C D * have αὐτοῖς, them. The Revisers have this latter form, yet render it as reflexive. The contracted form of the reflexive (ἑαυτοῖς) would be αὐτοῖς, but these contracted forms of the third person are supposed not to occur in the New Testament. See Buttmann, p. 111. Yet Westcott and Hort have this form, αὐτοῖς, in ver. 27. Meyer thinks the reflexive forms were frequently neglected by the copyists, and so would read the reflexive here, as in ver. 27.—(F.)

[2] Das eben ist der Fluch der bösen That

Das sie, fortzeugend, immer Böses muss gebären. (F.)

[3] "God *is* blessed unto the ages," even though men may dishonor and degrade him. Chrysostom says that it was not to avenge himself that God gave them up, for he suffered nothing—*i. e.,* he is forever blessed. Alford states that the verbal adjective here employed (εὐλογητός, blessed) is commonly used of God, but the participle (εὐλογημένος) oftener of man. See, however, εὐλογητός in Thayer's Lexicon, and notes on 9 : 5.—(F.)

26 For this cause God gave them up unto vile affections: for even their women did change the natural use into that which is against nature:
27 And likewise also the men, leaving the natural use of the woman, burned in their lust one toward another; men with men working that which is un-

26   For this cause God gave them up unto ¹vile passions: for their women changed the natural use into
27 that which is against nature: and likewise also the men, leaving the natural use of the woman, burned in their lust one toward another, men with men

¹ Gr. *passions of dishonour.*

gave a shock to the apostle's mind to think that men should be so infatuated as to turn away from the Creator to the creature, and led him to seek relief in a devout doxology. The idolatry of the heathen in our day ought to produce similar effects in the hearts of all Christians.

26. For this cause. So the apostle re-affirms what he had asserted in the beginning of ver. 24, the connection between their ungodly idolatries and their unnatural vices. Is it not a legitimate inference from what is here so emphatically insisted on, that as departure from God brought on all this degradation, so return to God is the only effectual cure? And is it not a fair application of this principle, that the elevation of the degraded communities and nations is to be expected and sought, not from commerce, civilization, secular education, or any other appliance of this nature, but chiefly from Christian missions—the faithful and persevering promulgation of the gospel among them? This, while it brings them back to God, will bring with it all other and secondary means of social, mental, moral, and material progress. **God gave them up unto vile affections.** Compare Eph. 4: 19. They are there said to "have *given themselves* over unto lasciviousness, to work all uncleanness with greediness." The same verb is used in both cases. God gave them up; they gave themselves up; there is no real contradiction: God gave them up, in the lusts of their own hearts, ver. 24: this last clause brings the two forms of statement into harmony. [On this verb, to *give up*, the same which occurs in ver. 24, Meyer thus remarks: "It expresses the *real active abandoning* on the part

of God," which, moreover, "is quite in keeping with the universal agency of God, in his physical and moral government of the world, without, however, making God appear as the author of sin, which, on the contrary, has its root in the *lusts of the heart*." This retributive abandoning is akin to the "judicial infatuation" implied in God's sending to those who received not the love of the truth "a working of delusion." (2 Thess. 2: 11, Rev. Ver.)] 'Vile affections,' disgraceful affections, or dishonorable passions, literally, "passions of dishonor." The word 'vile' here used in our common translation, is ambiguous. It has generally in the Scriptures, as almost always in our common speech at the present day, the sense of moral unworthiness. So also in 1 Sam. 3: 13. But in other places, it expresses only the want of value, which is the primitive sense of the word. So in 1 Sam. 15: 9. It is nearly akin to "humble" in 2 Sam. 6: 22, and in Phil. 3: 21, "our vile body"—literally, "the body of our humility," contrasted in the context with "the glorious body" which we are to receive at the coming of our Lord. **For even their women.** The prevalence of unnatural vice *even* among women, indicated, more forcibly than anything else, the depth of degradation and pollution into which mankind had sunk.¹

27. In this and the preceding verse, the apostle uses, instead of the words ordinarily translated "men" and "women," the words meaning "males" and "females," and so translated in Matt. 19: 4; Mark 10: 6, and Gal. 3: 28.² **Working that which is unseemly.** [More literally, *working out*, or *perpetrating* the (well-known) indecency.]

¹ Τε γάρ, *for indeed*, occurs again at 7: 7. If, however, τε is retained in the next verse, these correlatives equivalent to *both . . . and*, would signify that the females *as well as* the males were thus guilty. The word *use* (χρῆσιν) is to be supplied after the article τὴν in the last clause.—(F.)

² The first word for males is a later form for ἄρσενες, which occurs twice in this verse (below), and generally in the New Testament. Some important MSS. have here the older and more usual word, and there seems to

be no reason for using two different forms in the same verse. *Burned*, etc. The verb being a compound is equivalent to *burned out*, and since it is passive in form it may be passively rendered: *were fired* or *were inflamed*. The two classes of males are more particularly characterized in 1 Cor. 6: 9, as ἀρσενικοῖται and μαλακοί. Bengel says that "in stigmatizing sins we must often call a spade a spade." Yet no one can accuse the apostle of giving an unduly minute or indelicate description of the abominations of pagan sensuality.—(F.)

seemly, and receiving in themselves that recompense of their error which was meet.

working unseemliness, and receiving in themselves that recompense of their error which was due.

Receiving . . . that recompense of their error which was meet. If by their 'error' is meant their unnatural lusts, then the ' recompense' must be understood to mean the physical and moral consequences of such vices — bodily disease and pain, impotence and premature decay, mental imbecility, and corruption of the heart, conscience, and imagination—in a word, the defilement and debasement of the whole man. But if the 'error' means the forsaking of God, then the ' meet recompense' [1] will be those unnatural vices themselves, or, rather, their being abandoned of God to commit them. This last explanation accords best with the term *error*, which means literally, " wandering," and so is very suitable to express their wandering from God, while it seems too mild a term to be applied to their abominable and unnatural sensual lusts; and this explanation, too, is precisely in agreement with the entire context.

In proof of the *commonness* of these unnatural vices among the ancient heathen, Dr. Tholuck has accumulated abundant evidence out of their own testimonies. See " Biblical Repository," Vol. II, 1832, January number, pp. 80–123 ; April number, pp. 246–290 ; July number, pp. 441–494. Martial goes so far as to say, " No one is so tenderly modest as to fear being detected in their commission." [Dr. Döllinger, in his "Heidenthum and Judenthum," says (as quoted by Dr. Schaff in Lange) that "among the Greeks the vice of pederasty showed itself with all the symptoms of a great national disease, like a moral miasma. It revealed itself as a feeling which worked with more strength and energy than the love of woman among other peoples; it was more immoderate, more passionate in its outbreaks. It was characterized by frantic jealousy, unbounded devotion, sensual ardor, tender dalliance, nightly lingering before the door of the loved one—in fact, everything that belongs to the caricature of natural, sexual love. Even the sternest moralists were in the highest degree indulgent in their judgment of the practice—at times more than in-

dulgent; they treated it rather as a pleasant joke, and tolerated the companionship of the guilty. In the entire literature of the pre-Christian period, there is scarcely a writer to be found who declared himself decidedly against it. Rather was the whole society infected with it, and they breathed in the miasma with the air."] The apostle refers to the females first, probably as the most glaring proof of the general depravity, on the principle that "the corruption of the best things is the worst of all corruption" (*corruptio optimi pessima*). The degrading vices are still so common among the heathen, that modern missionaries have been accused by them of *forging* this account, and it has sometimes been found difficult to convince them that so accurate a picture of their morals was painted so long ago. Hence, we see why the apostle refers so particularly to practices so disgusting: they were very *common* among the heathen; they were intimately connected with the rites of idolatry, especially with the worship of Venus; and they were peculiarly illustrative of the depth of degradation into which the human race had plunged. Contrast this true picture with false representations often made of the comparative innocence and simplicity of the heathen. ["Those who know what Greek and Roman poets have written on the vices of their countrymen can best appreciate the grave and modest simplicity of the apostle's language." ("Bible Commentary.") But Paul needed not to read any Greek or Roman books, in order to know and to describe the unbridled licentiousness of his age. Farrar, on this point, thus remarks: "A Jew in a heathen city needed no books to reveal to him the 'depths of Satan.' In this respect, how startling a revelation to the modern world was the indisputable evidence of the ruins of Pompeii! Who would have expected to find the infamies of the Dead Sea cities paraded with such infinite shamelessness in every street of a little provincial town? What innocent snow could ever hide the guilty front of a life so unspeak-

---

1 Literally: "Receiving in themselves the recompense of their error which it was necessary " (to receive). " Ὀφείλει, *notat obligationem ; δεῖ, necessita-* *tem.*" See Trench on " New Testament Synonyms," p. 392. For the reflexive pronoun, in themselves, Westcott and Hort have the contracted form αὑτοῖς.—(F.)

| 28 And even as they did not like to retain God in *their* knowledge, God gave them over to a reprobate mind, to do those things which are not convenient; | 28   And even as they [1] refused to have God in *their* knowledge, God gave them up unto a reprobate mind, to do those things which are not fitting; |

1 Gr. *did not approve.*

ably abominable? Could anything short of the earthquake have engulphed it, or of the volcano have burned it up? And if Pompeii was like this, we may judge, from the works of Aristophanes and Athenæus, of Juvenal and Martial, of Petronius and Apuleius, of Strato and Meleager—which may be regarded as the 'pièces justificatives' of St. Paul's estimate of heathendom—what Tarsus and Ephesus, what Corinth and Miletus were likely to have been." Corinth, the city where Paul wrote this letter, had a reputation pre-eminent above all other cities for its unblushing licentiousness, and he had but to open his eyes to see it. "A thousand [female] Hierodouloi were consecrated to the service of impurity in the infamous temple of Aphrodite Pandemos." A "Corinthian girl" was but another name for harlot, and to "Corinthianize" meant to practice whoredom. (See Smith's "Greek and Roman Antiq.," Art. Hetæræ.) "In that age," says Meyer (Acts 15: 20.), "fornication was reckoned among the *adiaphora*, a thing morally indifferent." Paul, indeed, was writing to the Romans, but could the great city of Rome be much purer in its morals than the "little provincial town" near by?

It is true, as Dr. Schaff remarks, that "the history of Christian countries often presents a similar picture of moral corruption, with the exception of those unnatural vices described in ver. 26, 27, which have almost disappeared, or greatly diminished within the pale of civilization. . . . But there remains this radical difference: the heathen corruptions were produced and sanctioned by the heathen mythology and idolatry, while Christian nations are corrupt in spite of, and in direct opposition to, Christianity, which raises the highest standard of virtue, and acts continually on the world as a purifying and sanctifying power."]

28. A third recurrence to what has been so plainly said in ver. 24 and 26. **They did not like to retain God in their knowledge.** [The word for 'knowledge' is a compound, meaning "full knowledge," or "clear discernment." Meyer says their (simple) knowledge

of God derived from the revelation of nature (ver. 21.), ought to have been brought, by cultivation, to this full knowledge—a penetrating and living knowledge of God (Eph. 1: 17; 1 Cor. 13: 12.); but instead of this being the case, they had become "Gentiles who know not God."] We are here reminded again that they had voluntarily and wickedly quenched divine light which God had provided for them. (Ver. 18-21.) **God gave them over to a reprobate mind.** The retributive abandonment of them by God is here a third time noted. In ver. 24 and 26, it was to un cleanness or impurity, and to shameless passions; here it is to a reprobate mind. There is an etymological relation between this word *reprobate* and the verb 'did not like,' in the first clause of the verse, which does not at all appear in our translation. On the supposition that the apostle designed to have it noted, translators and commentators have made various ingenious endeavors to express it in English. *Alford's* expedient is perhaps as satisfactory and as little forced as any: "Because they *reprobated* the knowledge of God, God gave them over to a *reprobate* mind." [As Alford omits certain Greek words in his rendering, we give this quite literal translation which preserves the paronomasia, and pretty clearly expresses the sense: "As they did not *approve* to have God in full knowledge, God gave them up unto an *unapproved* mind"—that is, a mind rejected of him, like worthless coin that will not bear the test. The verb means to test, to prove, to approve. The adjective, occurring in seven other places, is, by the Revised Version, rendered *rejected* in 1 Cor. 9: 27; Heb. 6: 8, and *reprobate* in Titus 1: 16; 2 Tim. 3: 8; 2 Cor. 13: 5, 6, 7.] **To do those things which are not convenient.** [Another instance of the figure *meiosis*, where less is said than is meant. The verb in the present tense denotes an habitual doing.] The word 'convenient' here is equivalent to "becoming," not agreeable to the nature and duties of man. In the same sense, the same word [with a different prefix] is used in Eph. 5: 4; Philem. 8; Col. 3: 18 (translated "fit"). The sense in which we now commonly use

29 Being filled with all unrighteousness, fornication, wickedness, covetousness, maliciousness ; full of envy, murder, debate, deceit, malignity ; whisperers,
30 Backbiters, haters of God, despiteful, proud, boasters, inventors of evil things, disobedient to parents,

29 being filled with all unrighteousness, wickedness, covetousness, maliciousness ; full of envy, murder,
30 strife, deceit, malignity ; whisperers, backbiters, 1 hateful to God, insolent, haughty, boastful, invent-

---

1 Or, *haters of God.*

---

the word 'convenient' is expressed by an entirely different word, as in Mark 6: 21; 1 Cor. 16: 12.[1]

29-31. Being filled with all unrighteousness. [The participle 'filled' agrees with 'them' in ver. 28, the understood subject of the infinitive, 'to do.' Under the general head of 'unrighteousness,' Meyer places the vices of the following list as species.] A dark catalogue, and the darkest thing about it is its truthfulness. We will not dwell upon each separate charge in this divine indictment of sinful human nature, nor attempt by minute analysis to make out an orderly arrangement, which apparently was not aimed at by the writer. ["The accidental order of the arrangement intimates that all sins which can ever occur to one's mind are mutually related. It is, as it were, the opening of a sackful of sins, when it is all accident how the single grains fall out." (Philippi.)] Let some general criticisms suffice. The second, and last but one, in this list, 'fornication' and 'implacable,' are omitted in the best manuscripts. In several places, the precise *order* is uncertain, being different in different manuscripts. The change in ver. 29 of 'being filled' to 'full' seems to be made for the sake of variety, and not on account of any difference in the sense : as the former expression requires to be followed by "with," and the latter by "of" in English, so the corresponding Greek words require a change in the form of the words that follow. This prevents an unpleasant repetition of the same grammatical forms.[2] The words (ἀδικία and πονηρία) translated **unrighteousness** and **wickedness,** in ver. 29, differ in this respect, that the latter has a more active and energetic quality, which

would not be satisfied with depriving others of their due, but would delight in doing them as much harm as possible. A somewhat similar distinction seems to exist between the words translated **maliciousness** (κακία) and **malignity** (κακοηθεία) in the same verse; the former is simply "badness," while the latter carries with it the notion of an obstinate perversity in evil.[3] The word translated **debate** (ἔρις), in the same verse, is commonly translated 'strife' or 'contention ';' debate' only here and in 2 Cor. 12: 20. [On the word 'deceit' (δόλος, literally, a *bait*), Tholuck quotes Juvenal's "Quid Romæ faciam? Mentiri nescio"— "What can I do at Rome? I know not how to lie." The word **whisperers,** in contrast with (καταλάλους) *backbiters,* or, rather, open calumniators, denotes *secret* maligners or slanderers, or simply tale bearers. Some descendants of this tribe, and of other tribes mentioned, remain on earth until this day.] There has been much dispute about the sense of the compound word translated **haters of God** in ver. 30; the presumption, from its composition and accentuation, is strongly in favor of the *passive* sense, *hateful to God.* Alford says "it is *never* found in an *active* sense, but *always* in a *passive.*" Yet the active sense is here so much more appropriate to the context, the passive would put the word so out of due relation to the whole catalogue, that there is much reason for regarding our common translation as giving the correct sense; and indeed this active sense does not lack the authority of later Greek grammarians and commentators, as Suidas and Œcumenius of the tenth century. The three following words, translated **despiteful, proud, boasters,** are well dis-

---

1 On the distinction between (μὴ καθήκοντα, "the *genus* of that which is unseemly ") and (οὐκ ἀνῆκεν) (Eph. 5: 4), both of which may be rendered *not seemly,* see Meyer on this passage. In later Greek, however, the dependent negative (μὴ) seems at times to usurp the place of the direct negative (οὐ or οὐκ). This not liking to have God in one's knowledge has been not only the occasion of unseemly deeds in all ages, but is really the source of all the deistical infidel literature

which has been written against the Bible. "A bad life," as the infidel and profligate Earl of Rochester acknowledged when he came to himself, "is the only grand objection to this book."—(F.)

2 The word μεστούς, *full of, filled full,* is akin to our *stuffed,* as from a surfeit in eating.—(F.)

3 Aristotle defines it as "the disposition to take everything in the worst sense."

31 Without understanding, covenant-breakers, without natural affection, implacable, unmerciful:
32 Who, knowing the judgment of God, that they

31 ors of evil things, disobedient to parents, without understanding, covenant-breakers, without natural
32 affection, unmerciful: who, knowing the ordinance of God, that they who practise such things are

tinguished by Archbishop Trench in this triple paraphrase, "insolent and injurious in *acts*, proud in *thoughts*, boastful in *words*." Four of the above terms are the same that are used by Paul in 2 Tim. 3: 23, to describe the predicted corruption of the Church—namely, 'boasters,' 'proud,' 'disobedient to parents,' 'without natural affection.' A proof of this want of "natural affection" is found in the unnatural infanticide practiced to such an inconceivable extent by many ancient and modern pagan nations. Some pairs of words in the above list seem to be brought together through similarity of sound, as (φθόνον, φόνον, ἀσυνέτους, ἀσυνθέτους) envy, murder, senseless, faithless. For similar lists of vices, see 2 Cor. 12: 20; Gal. 5: 19; Eph. 5: 3; 1 Tim. 1: 9; 2 Tim. 3: 2. Some nine or ten of the sins enumerated here are expressly referred to in these lists. And all these vices and all the corruption indicated in these dark catalogues result, in the apostle's view, from dishonoring God, and from being unthankful for his mercies.] We add one more remark only, in regard to the division of the verses. It does not seem very happy, in several respects, particularly in disregarding the changes of syntax in the original. The word 'whisperers,' for instance, which is the first of a series of personal nouns, following a list of abstract terms, is very awkwardly separated from the word 'backbiters,' to which it has so close a relation, both in *form* and in *sense*. Ver. 29 should end with the word 'malignity,' and ver. 30 begin with the word 'backbiters.' The arrangement would also be more fully correspondent with the change of form in the original, if ver. 29 were divided into two, the first ending with 'maliciousness,' the last of the words that are construed with the participle followed by 'with,' and the second beginning with the adjective 'full.' [We may here properly ask if the apostle does not, in this description of the Gentile world, himself slander the Gentiles? Did every Greek and Roman man and woman with whom he met bear such a character as he here depicts? Would he deny to each and all of them any and every good trait? Could he deny some-

thing akin to "natural affection" even to the Maltese "barbarians" who showed to him and to his shipwrecked companions "no common kindness"? We think not. In the next chapter, ver. 14, 26, he implies that some Gentiles, at least, might "do by nature the things of the law." He evidently speaks of Gentiles as a class, and he no more slanders them than does the brother of the Gallio who befriended him, the moralist Seneca, the tutor of Nero, when he says: "All is full of crime and vice; there is more committed than can be healed by punishment. A monstrous prize contest of wickedness is going on. The desire to sin increases, and shame decreases day by day. . . . Vice is no longer practiced secretly, but in open view. Vileness gains in every street and in every breast to such an extent that innocence has become not only rare, but has ceased to exist." Paul's description, moreover, is written from that divine standpoint which sees adultery in a look and murder in a thought, and which looks on the secret intents and desires of the hearts. Written history, full of crimes as it is, is a spotless sheet compared with the unwritten history of the thoughts and inclinations of men's hearts.]

32. Who knowing the judgment of God. The same compound relative which begins ver. 25 begins this also: *they, being such as know the judgment of God.* 'The judgment of God' is here equivalent to "the righteous sentence of God." "His judgments" may mean either the judgments which he executes with his hand, or the judgments which he declares with his mouth. The former sense is much the most common in our ordinary speech; the latter is quite as common in the Scriptures, much more so in the Book of Psalms, and pre-eminently in Psalm 119. Here too the sense is nearer the latter than the former —that is, it means the judgments which he *forms* as to human conduct, though we cannot properly say in this instance the judgments of his mouth, because the persons here referred to are not supposed to know his revealed law. They know the judgment of God therefore by the law written in their own con-

which commit such things are worthy of death, not only do the same, but have pleasure in them that do them.

worthy of death, not only do the same, but also consent with them that practise them.

sciences. (2: 14, 15.) [The participle being a compound means that they fully knew, were perfectly aware of, the judgment of God. Degraded and sunk in vice as they were, their consciences were not so hardened and dead but that they clearly recognized the voice of duty and acknowledged the demerit of transgression—"their conscience bearing witness therewith, their thoughts one with another accusing or else excusing." The barbarians of Melita had clear ideas of justice and of the ill desert of wrong doing. (Acts 28: 4.)] **That they which commit such things.** [Alford finds in this clause God's righteous sentence.] The word here translated 'commit' is the same as that translated 'do' at the end of the verse. The word translated 'do' in the previous clause is a different word. Both are very common in this Epistle, and in the New Testament generally. It will help to put the English reader more nearly on a level with the intelligent reader of the original, if we distinguish between these words by translating the former *practice* and the latter *do.* This verse will then read, "Who knowing the judgment of God, that they which practice such things are worthy of death, not only do the same, but have pleasure in those who practice them." [The verb whence our "practice" is derived (πράσσω) seems to denote a habit and facility of doing, while the verb "to do" (ποιέω) refers rather to single acts performed often, with some degree of effort or difficulty.[1]] We shall adhere to this distinction wherever these words occur in this Epistle. It is to be regretted that the translators of the Common Version did not adopt this rule; but they tell us in their preface that they studiously avoided this "servile uniformity," as they style it. In doing so, they often mislead the English reader, and render a concordance of the English Bible of much less value than it would have been had they adhered more strictly to this wholesome rule of uniformity in rendering the same Greek word into English. **Are worthy of death.** It is well to note the use of the word 'death' in this first instance of its occurrence in this Epistle. It defines itself here as being that of

which transgressors of God's law are worthy —in other words, as synonymous with the desert and penalty of sin. Compare 5: 12–17, and particularly 6: 23. [As the poets of Pagan antiquity dwelt much upon the punishments inflicted in *hades*, the invisible world, so death to these heathen minds is supposed by most to have reference to the punishment of sin beyond the grave. "Death, in the sense of punishment in the other world." (Boise.) Any infliction of physical death is, of course, out of the question. Query: If the modern heathen, like the ancient, are "worthy of death," can it be supposed that God is under obligation to provide for them a future probation?] **Not only do the same, but have pleasure in them that do** (*practice*) **them.** [In the Roman Presbyter Clement's first letter to the Corinthians (ch. 16), written in the last part of the first century, we find a virtual quotation from these last four verses. Clement's reference to the "blessed Paul the apostle," his writings, his sufferings, and his preaching, "both in the east and in the west" —"even to the limit of the west"—is a very important proof of the genuineness of Paul's epistles.] 'Have pleasure in'—that is, *approve* The same word is rendered "allow" in Luke 11: 48, and "consent unto" in Acts 8: 1 and 22: 20. [In this last reference Paul charges himself with this aggravated degree of guilt in consenting to the murder of Stephen.] The form of expression in the last two clauses of this verse, *not only—but also* (the "also" is in the original, though it does not appear in the English) implies that the approval of such acts in others argues a greater degree of depravity than the doing of them ourselves. Men may *do* such things, under stress of temptation, without *approving* them. But when they *deliberately* and without being under temptation approve of them in others, this indicates a more profound moral corruption. Our judgment of other men's actions is usually more unbiased, and therefore more indicative of settled moral character than our judgment of our own. [It would seem as if a man *might* be wicked enough in himself, and be satisfied with his own wickedness, without

[1] See more fully under ποιέω, in Thayer's "Lexicon."--(F.)

CHAPTER II.

THEREFORE thou art inexcusable, O man, whoso-ever thou art that judgest: for wherein thou judgest another, thou condemnest thyself; for thou that judg-est doest the same things.

1 Wherefore thou art without excuse, O man, who-soever thou art that judgest: for wherein thou judg-est [1] another, thou condemnest thyself; for thou that 2 judgest dost practise the same things. [2] And we

1 Gr. the other......2 Many ancient authorities read For.

seeking to injure others or enticing them to commit sin, or rejoicing in the sins which they have committed. The apostle, in this passage and elsewhere, seems to indicate that there is a progress in wickedness as well as a growth in grace; that this progress is ever downward, and that it has in itself no re-straining power. Sin does not cure itself.]

Ch. 2: The apostle now proceeds to show that the Jews are under the same condemna-tion as the Gentiles; but he introduces this unwelcome topic skillfully, using general terms at first, without expressly naming the Jews. Some commentators refer the first half of this chapter to the Gentiles, either to their philosophers, their magistrates, or the better sort of people among them, in distinction from the baser multitude described in the previous chapter. But the context, and espe-cially in ver. 4, 5, 11, is decidedly in favor of referring it to the Jews.

[Godet thus introduces the thought of this chapter: "In the midst of this flood of pollu-tions and iniquities which Gentile society pre-sents to view, the apostle sees one who, like a judge from the height of his tribunal, sends a stern look over the corrupt mass, condemning the evil which reigns in it, and applauding the wrath of God which punishes it. It is this new personage whom he apostrophizes in the following word."]

1. Therefore (διό, literally, *on which ac-count, wherefore*) refers to the previous verse. They who *approve* such things are worthy of death; but the Jews might say: "We disap-prove and denounce these sins of the Gen-tiles." 'Therefore,' the apostle might retort, you are surely **inexcusable** for committing the same. [Meyer makes this 'therefore' take a retrospective glance over the whole of the last chapter after ver. 17, with a particu-lar reference to the 'inexcusable' of ver. 20, and gives the idea in these words: "Before the mirror of this Gentile life of sin all excuse vanishes from thee, O man, who judgest, for

this mirror reflects thine own conduct, which thou thyself therefore condemnest by thy judgment. A deeply tragic *de te narratur*, into which the proud Jewish consciousness sees itself all of a sudden transferred."] The word here translated 'inexcusable' is pre-cisely the same as that translated "without excuse" in 1: 20. Both should be translated alike. In the Bible Union Version both are translated "without excuse"; this is an im-provement upon the Common Version, but 'inexcusable' would be better still as being nearer to the original in form, and just as near, at least, in sense. **O man, whosoever thou art that judgest.** [This 'O man' is made to bear the name Jew in ver. 17. Butt-mann remarks ("Grammar," p. 140) that the interjection does not occur so often in the New Testament with the vocative as it does in classic Greek, and that it "generally has an emphatic character, and so contains rather an exclamation than a simple address."] Using the second person singular here instead of the third plural, as in the previous chapter, Paul seems to imagine one of his own countrymen present and condemning the sins of the Gen-tiles. This gives great vivacity to his dis-course. Yet he purposely uses the indefinite expression, 'whosoever thou art,' not ready yet to call out the Jew by name. [Bishop Wordsworth says, Paul uses 'man' instead of Jew, because "the proposition is one of uni-versal application, and because he would ap-proach the Jew with gentleness, and not exasperate him by any abrupt denunciation." "Whosoever thou art, even if thou art a Jew." (Fritzsche.)] **For where-in thou judgest another.** ['Wherein,' "in the matter in which." (Alford.)] *The other* would be more literal than 'another'—that is, the other party, hinting at the Jewish habit of separating themselves in thought from the Gentiles, almost as if they belonged to a different species. **For thou that judg-est doest the same things.** [Paul here suddenly brings home to the Jew Nathan's accusation to David: "Thou art the man."

2 But we are sure that the judgment of God is according to truth against them which commit such things.
3 And thinkest thou this, O man, that judgest them which do such things, and doest the same, that thou shalt escape the judgment of God?

know that the judgment of God is according to truth 3 against them that practise such things. And reckonest thou this, O man, who judgest them that practise such things, and doest the same, that thou shalt

'Thou that judgest' has a "reproachful emphasis." (Meyer.) The Jew, and especially the Pharisee, regarded the word "sinners" as but another name for Gentiles (Gal. 2:15), and characteristically judged them as being the abandoned of God. Philippi says that "this passion on the part of the Jews for condemning others gives the apostle an excellent vantage ground for the judgment he has to pass upon them."] *Practicest*, or *dost practice*, which last is more agreeable to the ear, would be preferable to 'doest,' according to the principle laid down in the notes on the last verse of Chapter I. The apostle asserts the fact that the Jews (while reprovingly judging the Gentiles for their misdeeds) practice 'the same things' (τα αὐτά), and leaves it to the conscience of the person addressed. That the Jewish nation was at this time very corrupt, and that many of the worst vices of the heathen were common among them, is manifest from the testimonies of Josephus and the Rabbins, as well as from the New Testament. They may have been comparatively free from idolatry in its most literal form; but they were just as truly transgressors of the moral law of God, and so virtually practiced the same things as the Gentiles. The principle of the apostle's argument commends itself to common sense; Cicero states it substantially in these words: "All things which you blame in another, you are bound to avoid yourself." ("Oration against Verres," 5.)

2. But we are sure—*we know*, that is, every one knows: our own nature assents to the proposition. ["Paul thus implies the tacit concurrence of the Jew in this sentence of condemnation." (Boise.)] The reading "for" in place of 'but' has the better support from the manuscripts. [Retaining the 'but' of our common and revised text, we should have this meaning: "you may judge falsely and hypocritically, 'but' the judgment of God is according to truth."] The

emphasis of the statement seems to belong to the latter clause of the verse—the judgment of God is against them that practice such things, and this judgment is according to the truth of the case, without any partiality; according to facts and character, without regard to the distinction between Jew and Gentile, or to any external difference. ["The judgment of God, unlike the inconsistent judgment of man in ver. 1, is directed according to truth against the doers of evil." ("Bible Commentary.") For "commit" read '*practice*' as in the Revised Version.]

3. And thinkest thou this, [*But thinkest thou*, etc.—i. e., though thou knowest that God's judgment is according to truth] **O man, that judgest them which do** (*practice*) **such things.** The question here, as often in Paul's epistles, and indeed in argumentative and rhetorical discourse generally, is equivalent to an emphatic *negative*. [The word translated do (πράσσω), which has already occurred thrice in this chapter, is rightly rendered *practice* in the Revised Version, and is thus distinguished from *doest* (ποιῶν) in the next clause.] **That thou shalt escape.** 'Thou' is emphatic: its very presence in the original shows this; for the forms of the verb, in Greek, as in many other languages, sufficiently determine the number and person, so that the pronoun is not needed, except when there is some reason for emphasizing it.[1] "If others cannot escape your judgment, do you think that you can escape God's?"—Calvin. [This utterance of the apostle sounds like the voice of one crying in the wilderness, calling to repentance those self-righteous ones who, while pronouncing a condemnatory judgment on others, felt themselves secure as being the children of Abraham, and therefore exempt from the judgment of God. "According to the Jewish conceit, only the *Gentiles* were to be judged, whereas all Israel were to share in the Messianic kingdom as its native children, Matt. 8: 12." (Meyer.)]

---

[1] Buttmann, in his "Grammar of the New Testament Greek," sees in the language of the New Testament a greater departure from classic usage than Winer was inclined to acknowledge, and thinks "the personal pronouns were frequently employed where no reason of importance is obvious," and refers to this passage as an example (with others), but, as it seems to us, without due reason.—(F.)

4 Or despisest thou the riches of his goodness and forbearance and longsuffering; not knowing that the goodness of God leadeth thee to repentance?

4 escape the judgment of God? Or despisest thou the riches of his goodness and forbearance and longsuffering, not knowing that the goodness of God leadeth 5 thee to repentance? but after thy hardness and im-

4. Or despisest thou, etc. The force of the disjunctive conjunction [here drawing attention to a new question][1] may perhaps be explained in this way: Do you imagine, without any pretense of reason, that you shall escape God's judgment? *or*, ["in case thou hast not this conceit" (Meyer)], do you base your hope of escape from future retribution on the forbearance of God hitherto? If so, that is a flagrant abuse of that forbearance, which is in effect *despising* it, under pretense of *honoring* it.[2] **The riches of his goodness,** etc. 'Riches,' as synonymous with abundance and greatness, is a very common expression with the apostle. (9: 23; 11: 33; Eph. 1: 7; 2; 4, 7; 3: 16; Col. 1: 27.) 'His goodness,' his kindness expressed in bestowing favors and withholding punishment.[3] **Forbearance and long suffering.** [Paul speaks of the "wrath of God," but these words show us that he is "slow to wrath." By the repetition of the connective 'and,' as also by the repeated use of the article (equivalent in the last two instances to the pronoun *his*), the apostle seems desirous to dwell upon and to emphasize the merciful attributes of God. Most expositors regard the forbearance and the long-suffering as explanatory of the goodness, as if it read: 'Even of his forbearance and his long-suffering'; but it seems most natural to regard them as having the same regimen as goodness—*i. e.*, in the genitive case, after riches.] The former word expresses his slowness to inflict punishment; the latter, his slowness to take offense. The former, as the actual result, proceeds from the latter, as the abiding inward cause. The former, moreover, seems to hint—so, perhaps, does the latter, though somewhat less obviously, at the *limit*, which may not be passed. God holds back his vengeance for a while; he suffers *long*, but not forever. They who think they may continue to live in sin with impunity, because they have been so long unpunished, may

fancy that they are *magnifying* God's goodness; but in reality they are *vilifying* it, abusing his forbearance, despising his long suffering, by their contemptuous unconcern as to the holy purpose of it. Compare 2 Peter 3: 9. [Trench, defining 'long-suffering' (μακροθυμία) and 'endurance' (ὑπομονή), says the former will be found to express patience in regard to persons, the latter in respect of things; and that of these two, "only 'long-suffering' is an attribute of God."] **Not knowing.** Not knowing to any practical purpose—a guilty ignorance. They *might* know it, and *ought* to know it. **Leadeth thee to repentance.** ["Objectively spoken." (De Wette.) God's forbearance and mercies despised lead to indifference in a life of sin and to a treasuring up of wrath rather than to repentance. Paul in his preaching inculcated "repentance toward God," as well as "faith toward our Lord Jesus Christ." (Acts 20: 21; also 17: 30; 26: 20.) Yet in the epistles he uses the noun only here and in 2 Cor. 7: 9, 10; 2 Tim. 2: 25, and the verb "repent" only once, 2 Cor. 12: 21—faith, rather than repentance, being the predominant word in the epistles. Ellicott, however, remarks that he partially replaces these words by reconcile, reconciliation, etc.] The form of the verb does not necessarily express the full accomplishment of the result, but the *design* and *tendency*, a *leading* toward this result, which is often *felt*, where it is not *yielded* to, but even *consciously resisted*. ["God's leading is as real as man's resistance to being led." (Gifford.)] This would be better expressed in our language, with equal fidelity to the original, by the form, "is leading thee." [Paul teaches that God in his benignity wishes none to be lost, but would have all men to be saved, to come to repentance, and to the acknowledging of the truth. Compare 1 Tim. 2: 4. Yet men living under the full blaze of gospel light reject the

---

[1] Some make the question end with *repentance*, others with *God* in the next verse, while Alford thinks "the enquiry loses itself in the digressive clauses following, and nowhere comes pointedly to an end."—(F.)

[2] This as a verb of *feeling* (hence, caring for, contemning, admiring) is usually followed by the genitive, the

object being "conceived as operating upon the feeling subject—consequently, as the point *from* which the feeling proceeds."—Winer, 204.—(F.)

[3] Trench call this χρηστότης (goodness or benignity) a "beautiful word," and it occurs in the New Testament only in the writings of Paul.—(F.)

5 But, after thy hardness and impenitent heart, treasurest up unto thyself wrath against the day of wrath and revelation of the righteous judgment of God;

penitent heart treasurest up for thyself wrath in the day of wrath and revelation of the righteous judg-
6 ment of God; who will render to every man accord-

truth, and choose not to repent nor to be saved.]

5. But, after thy hardness—that is, according to thy hardness, agreeable to its nature, and proportioned to its degree. "When thou are neither softened by kindness, nor subdued by fear, what can be harder than thou art?" (Theophylact.) **And impenitent heart.** This word *impenitent* is found only here. [What sinners should especially dread in their deferring of repentance is the hardening process of sin, by which repentance becomes at last an impossibility. Fritzsche and Philippi understand the word 'impenitent' to mean in this place not only unrepentant, but incapable of repentance. The epithet is placed before the noun to give it a slight emphasis. (Winer, p. 524.)] **Treasurest up unto thyself wrath.** The expression to 'treasure up' is generally applied to something good and valuable, or at least so regarded; but is sometimes used of evil things, both in the New Testament and in other writings. The noun is so used in Luke 6 : 45. 'Treasurest up' here is *heapest up*, the idea of abundance, not that of quality, being predominant. [This treasuring up of wrath contrasts sadly with the riches of God's goodness; but according to Paul's representation it is the sinner (and not God) who is heaping up for himself this fearful treasure. "What thou layest up, a little every day, thou wilt find a mass hereafter." (Augustine.)] **Against the day of wrath**—literally, *in the day of wrath*, to be signally manifested, to break out, in the day of wrath. [In reference to this "day," compare ver. 16. It stands without the article, but is sufficiently defined by the nouns in the genitive which follow it. The omission of the article is sometimes owing to the use of a preposition (Winer, 126), and sometimes the article is omitted on the common principle of "correlation," by which "if the governing noun is without the article, the governed will be equally so" (Ellicott), and *vice versa*. Compare 2 Cor. 6 : 2; Eph. 4 : 30; Phil. 1 : 6. Some few man-

uscripts, versions, and Fathers have an *and* after revelation.] **And revelation of the righteous judgment of God.** 'Righteous judgment' is expressed here by a single compound word, not elsewhere found.[1] The day referred to will be a day of completed redemption to the godly; a day of wrath to the ungodly. See how closely these two opposite contemporaneous results are brought together in 2 Thess. 1 : 6–10. God's abused goodness is thus made the occasion of just the opposite results to those which it was intended to produce. [This "day of revelation" (ἀποκάλυψις) has probable reference to the revelation of our Lord Jesus Christ from heaven. See 1 Cor. 1 : 7; 2 Thess. 1 : 7; 1 Peter 1 : 7, 13; 4 : 13. In other epistles the apostle speaks of the "future appearing" (ἐπιφάνεια) or "manifestation" of Christ (see 2 Thess. 2 : 8; 1 Tim. 6 : 14; 2 Tim. 1 : 10; 4 : 1, 8; Titus 2 : 13); or of his "coming" or "presence" (παρουσία). See 1 Cor. 15 : 23; 1 Thess. 2 : 19; 3 : 13; 4 : 15; 5 : 23; 2 Thess. 2 : 1, 8; see also Matt. 24 : 3, 27, 37, 39; James 5 : 7, 8; 2 Peter 1 : 16; 3 : 4, 12; 1 John 2 : 28.[2] But in this Epistle he does not expressly mention the coming or day of the Lord, though in 13 : 12 he affirms that "the day is at hand." Olshausen supposes that at the date of this Epistle Paul had changed his views as to the near coming of Christ, and that he no longer expected to live until his Lord's return. But in nearly all his later letters there is expressed more or less of this expectation. "Our Lord cometh" (μαρὰν ἀθά). Even in 2 Timothy, when the time of his departure *had* come, he speaks, as with his dying breath, of the day and the appearing of the Lord, of being preserved unto his heavenly kingdom, and he classes himself with those who have loved and who still love his appearing. 2 Tim. 1 : 12; 4 : 1, 8, 18; compare 1 Tim. 6 : 14. Surely in this representation we can find no evidence of mistaken or changed views. And in his earlier epistles, though he says, as in 1 Thess. 4 : 15, "We which are alive and remain unto the coming of the Lord," yet in 1 Corinthians, which was written but a

---

[1] For other newly-constructed words in the New Testament, see Winer, p. 25.—(F.)

[2] The word παρουσία occurs elsewhere in 1 Cor. 16 : 17; 2 Cor. 7 : 6, 7; 10 : 10; Phil. 1 : 26; 2 : 12; 2 Thess. 2 : 9.—(F.)

6 Who will render to every man according to his deeds: | 7 ing to his works: to them that by [1] patience in well-

1 Or, *steadfastness*.

short time previous to our Epistle, and in which he speaks repeatedly of the coming and the day of Christ, and affirms, "We all shall not sleep," etc., closing indeed with maran-atha; he nevertheless says: "God hath both raised up the Lord, and will also *raise up* us by his own power. 1 Cor. 16: 14; compare 2 Cor. 4: 14. Thus nothing decisive can be determined from the use of "us" and "we" in this connection. Whatever Paul may have thought of the day and revelation of Christ, he could say: "He which hath begun a good work in you will perform it until the day of Jesus Christ"; could speak of waiting for a Saviour; could say, "The Lord is at hand," and yet could talk of life's uncertainty and of his departure, as we do of ours, and of his hoping to attain unto the (blessed) resurrection from the dead. (Phil. 1: 6, 20-23; 3: 11, 20; 4: 5.) It is astonishing to see how ready some are to speak of the apostle's mistaken view of this subject, and of his finding out his mistake. Ellicott, on the phrase, 'day of Christ Jesus,' thus remarks: "That St. Paul in these words assumes the nearness of the coming of the Lord cannot be positively asserted. . . . It may be fairly said that he is here (Phil. 1: 6), using language which has not so much a mere historical as a general and *practical* reference; the day of Christ, whether far or near, is the decisive day to each individual; it is practically coincident with the day of his death, and becomes, when addressed to the individual, an exaltation and amplification of that term. Death, indeed, as has been well remarked by Bishop Reynolds, is dwelt upon but little in the New Testament; it is to the resurrection and to the day of Christ that the eyes of the believer are directed." See at 13: 12 for further remarks on this subject.]

6. Who will render to every man according to his deeds. [The same words are found in Prov. 24: 12. The compound verb here used means, *to give in full.*] Observe that the apostle is here expounding the *law*, not the *gospel*. Yet it is equally true, under the gospel, that God's judgment will be according to each man's deeds, though the saved will not be saved *by* [or on the ground of] their

works. (Matt. 16: 27; 25: 31-46; 2 Cor. 5: 10; Gal. 6; 7, 8; Eph. 6: 8; Rev. 2: 23; 22: 12.) The righteous will be rewarded according to their works, as justified and accepted servants of the Lord; the wicked will be punished according to their works, as impenitent transgressors of his holy law. "It is a weak inference," says Calvin, "to conclude anything to be *merit*, because it is rewarded." [De Wette says: "Paul speaks here not from a Christian but from a legal standpoint." Similarly Bengel, Tholuck, Hodge, and others. But if we look upon this rewarding of believers according to their works as being a reward of grace, we see no necessity for regarding this standard of God's judgment as determined from a legal standpoint. "In the reward there is a certain retrospect to the work done, but no proportion between them, except such as may have been established by the free appointment of the Giver, and the only claim which it justifies is upon his promise." (Trench on "the Parable of the Laborers in the Vineyard.") It is important to notice that Paul nowhere says we are saved and rewarded for the merit of our works, not even *propter fidem*, on account of, or on the ground of our faith. "Not from works of righteousness which we have done," and not "according to debt," are we saved and rewarded. Yet God is pleased *graciously* to reward the works of believers, works which are "the practical evidence and measure of their faith." "But this equivalent," says Dr. Weiss, "is not to be regarded in the rigid judicial sense as an external balancing of wages and service. . . . It is grace which presents the reward and enables one to attain it." The awards to the righteous and the wicked are not only different, but are given on different principles. The retributive reward of unbelievers will be not only according to their works, but because of, or on the ground of their works. It will be an award of debt, of wages *due* to sin. To the righteous the award of eternal life will be by gift of grace, yet according to their works of righteousness. And this eternal life will be to some more than it will be to others, even according to their works, and according to the measure of their

7 To them who by patient continuance in well doing seek for glory and honour and immortality, eternal life:

8 eternal life: but unto them that are factious, and

doing seek for glory and honour and incorruption,

---

capacities. If any think it selfish and mercenary for believers to look unto the future recompense of reward we would answer in the words of St. Bernard: " *True* love is not mercenary, although a reward follows it." Dr. Thomas Playfere, Professor of Divinity at Cambringe (1600), a strong Calvinist, thus speaks on this point: " If ye be loving children indeed, though there were no hell to fear, no heaven to hope for, no torments to dread, no rewards to expect, yet ye will obey your good Father and be the sorrowfullest creatures in the world if you have but once displeased him, only for the mere love ye bear towards him, and for the unspeakable love he hath showed towards you."] [1]

7. [To bring out the full force of the Greek (the μέν, in this verse, which corresponds with δέ, of ver. 8), we may render: **To them,** *on the one hand,* **who,** etc.]. **Patient continuance** [or, *stedfastness,* as in the margin of the Revised Version] is expressed in the Greek by one word, translated simply "patience" in about thirty places, "patient waiting" in 2 Thess. 3 : 5, and "enduring" in 2 Cor. 1 : 6. It differs from our word "patience," in having a more active, energetic sense, which is not badly paraphrased here by the expression "patient continuance," but might be more briefly rendered by the single word "constancy," here and in many other places. Here, "constancy in good works." Compare Luke 8 : 15. It is only another form of the same radical word, which is translated "to endure," in the expression, "he that endureth to the end," in Matt. 10 : 22, and in nearly a dozen other places. **Seek for glory and honour and immortality.** The word 'glory' first occurs here in this sense, as something which man is to seek as his chief and eternal good. It is defined by Webster ("Syntax and Synonyms of the New Testament," p. 205) as " the future state of acknowledged perfection

which God designs for man." In this comprehensive sense it seems to be used here, and in many other places of this Epistle, as in ver. 10 of this chapter, 3 : 23 ; 5 : 2 ; 8 : 18 ; 9 : 23. These three terms may be taken as a comprehensive description of the future salvation [two of these elements being in ver. 10, expressly combined in the "eternal life"], in these three aspects or elements of it, the 'glory' of perfected character [compare Matt. 13 : 43] ; the 'honour' connected with it, as the prize of victory (1 Cor. 9 : 25 ; Phil. 3 : 14 ; 2 Tim. 4 : 8 ; James 1 : 12 ; 1 Peter 5 : 4), the reigning with Christ (8 : 17 ; 2 Tim. 2 : 12) ; and its *imperishableness* (1 Cor. 15 : 52 ; 1 Peter 1 : 4 : Rev. 21 : 4). [This 'immortality,' or 'incorruption' rather (compare 2 Tim. 1 : 10 ; also 1 Cor. 15 : 42, 52, 53, 54), being one of glory and blessedness, is not antithetical to annihilation or non-existence, Besides, we have no occasion for seeking an endless existence, for this is ours as an inalienable possession. As Haley in his " Discrepancies of the Bible" remarks : " The Greek word used here is not 'immortality' (ἀθανασία), but 'incorruption' (ἀφθαρσία, translated 'sincerity' in Eph. 6 : 24), and points to that exemption from moral corruption which saints are seeking here and which they will fully attain in heaven." This word as we suppose denotes not being, but a state of being, an unending state of glory and honor, and *implies,* of course, an endless existence. The adjective from it is applied not only to risen saints, but to God, in Rom. 1 : 23 ; 1 Tim. 1 : 17.] The *seeking* here implies deliberate *choice* and active *effort.* **Eternal life.** This is what God will render (ver. 6) to those who earnestly seek it by, or, *in* 'constancy of well doing.' [The epithet "eternal," (αἰώνιος), occurring in the New Testament seventy-one times according to Bruder, is applied to "life" forty-four times. [2] It is somewhat singular that the Greek 'eternal' should be derived from

---

[1] So sang Francis Xavier—
  " O deus, ego amo Te,
    Nec amo Te, ut salves me,
    Aut quia non amantes Te
    Æterno punis igne."

  My God I love thee—not because
  I hope for heaven thereby,

  Nor because those who love thee not
    Must burn eternally.
  See further in No. 333 of the Baptist Hymnal.—(F.)

[2] Some make it, mistakenly we think, forty-six. In 1 Tim. 6 : 19, Westcott and Hort give as the most approved text ὄντως instead of αἰωνίος. It is connected with fire, judgment, destruction, six times ; with glory three times ; with inheritance twice ; and once each

8 But unto them that are contentious, and do not obey the truth, but obey unrighteousness, indignation and wrath,

9 obey not the truth, but obey unrighteousness, *shall be* wrath and indignation, tribulation and anguish,

a word meaning "age" (αἰων), the same as the Latin 'eternal' from *aetas* (*aevum*, αἰών) age, yet both the Greek and the Latin words (αἰώνιος and *æternus*) properly signify eternal, and the one no more signifies *age-lasting* than does the other. It is only when this word refers to "punishment" and "destruction" that men have a motive to give a qualitative character, or to make it mean, *lasting for an age*. This unending life (ζωή) is something more than existence, is more than outward earthly life or living (βίος): it is life in the highest sense, "the truly life." (1 Tim. 6 : 19.) This eternal life is elsewhere in the New Testament contrasted with judgment (John 5 : 24), with corruption (Gal. 6 : 8), with perishing (John 3 : 16; 10 : 28), with death (Rom. 6 : 23), with God's abiding wrath (John 3 : 36), and with eternal punishment. (Matt. 25 : 46.) Compare "eternal destruction" in 2 Thess. 1 : 9. It consists in knowing God and keeping his commands, in knowing his Son, believing in him, and receiving him. This life is in his Son, and if we have him, we have life. We have the beginning of it here along with our animal and earthly life, and it abides within us, and will never grow old. (John 6 : 47 ; 1 John 3 : 15.) It is the gift of God to his adopted children—their incorruptible, unfading inheritance. Who are we or what have we done that we should be heirs of such an inheritance?]

8. But unto them that are contentious. The word translated 'contentious' means rather, "self-seeking": instead of being derived, as our translators seem to have supposed, from the word commonly translated "strife," it comes rather from a word which means "a hired laborer," and suggests the idea of a mercenary spirit. The persons to whom this epithet is applied, instead of seeking "glory, honor, and immortality," seek their own sordid ends. [Such persons generally cause factions, intrigues, and the noun is taken by some in this sense. The literal rendering is : to those *from* faction— that is, those who belong to it, or, as Fritzsche says, those who are derived *from* it, who

"have it as a parent." The like construction is found in Acts 10: 45; Gal. 3: 7, those from circumcision, those from faith. See Winer, ¿ 51, d. Corresponding with this, we have elsewhere the phrase, 'sons or children of disobedience,' etc.; see Eph. 2: 2. The word for faction or partisanship occurs elsewhere only in 2 Cor. 12: 20; Gal. 5: 20: Phil. 1: 16; 2: 3; James 3: 14, 16; see Ellicott on Gal. 5: 20.] **And do not obey the truth.** Gospel truth is not merely to be believed, but to be obeyed: it is very practical, and a mere intellectual assent to it, without corresponding affections and actions, is of no value in the sight of God. And they who do not obey the truth will be sure to obey unrighteousness. There can be no neutrality here. [The word for 'obey not' denotes that this disobedience springs from unbelief. 'Truth' is in the dative of reference or of the more remote object; they were disobedient in respect to 'the truth.' The word translated "truth" (ἀλήθεια) by its etymology denotes that which is *unconcealed*, manifest, open, hence the converse of that which is merely apparent, or false and hypocritical. Truth involves righteousness, and is opposed to 'unrighteousness' (ἀδικία). Hence we have in the Scriptures righteousness of truth, and the deceit of unrighteousness. (Eph. 4 : 24 ; 2 Thess. 2 : 10.)]. **Indignation and wrath.** These words, so closely allied in meaning, are coupled together in two other places in Paul's epistles. (Eph. 4 : 31 ; Col. 3 : 8.) They often occur separately, and both are commonly translated 'wrath,' but each is *once* translated 'indignation,' one here, and the other in Rev. 14 : 10. The one here translated 'wrath' (ὀργή) seems to refer more to the inward feeling, the one translated 'indignation' (θυμός) to the outward manifestation ; one is the heat of the fire, the other the bursting forth of the flame; one of the old Greek grammarians says, that the first is lasting, the second transitory. Both are repeatedly used in the expression, "the wrath of God." [In the revised text the order of the two nouns is reversed, and the rendering is

with gospel, covenant, things unseen, new and abiding relation of Onesimus, Spirit, God, consolation, home in the heavens, Christ's kingdom, redemption, salvation,

purpose, sin, and with the word power in a doxolgy (See " Bible Commentary " on 2 Thessalonians, p. 748.)— (F.)

E

9 Tribulation and anguish, upon every soul of man that doeth evil; of the Jew first, and also of the Gentile;

upon every soul of man that worketh evil, of the 10 Jew first, and also of the Greek; but glory and

made to correspond.] There is an irregularity in the grammatical construction here. The words 'indignation and wrath' appear to be governed, like the words 'eternal life' in the preceding verse, by the verb 'will render.' In ver. 6 that undoubtedly expresses the true sense; but as the words 'indignation and wrath' are in the nominative case in the Greek, it is necessary to supply the verb in the passive form, "indignation and wrath shall *be rendered*." The words at the beginning of the next verse are also in the nominative case, and so equally require a change in the verb. [Perhaps the apostle avoided saying: *God* will render anguish, etc., in order to indicate that these punishments are not altogether direct and positive inflictions from the hand of God, but that they may come upon the sinner in accordance with the nature and laws of his own being, or in accordance with the "constitution and course of nature." Compare 9: 22, and Schaff's note in Lange, p. 98. The change of construction gives at least variety and vivacity to the style.]

9. **Tribulation and anguish** (shall be or shall come). These two words are joined together again in 8: 35, and 2 Cor. 6: 4. [See, also, Isa. 8: 22; 30: 6; LXX.][1] [Instead of these terms we might have expected "eternal destruction" (2 Thess. 1: 9) as the correlative of "eternal life." As the apostle makes the reward of the righteous—glory, honor, and life —to be eternal, so, if we keep his "eternal destruction" in view, we must regard this wrath and this tribulation as likewise eternal.

At least, no one can say that it would be un-Pauline to regard these as eternal. Some persons, I know, are trying to cherish an "eternal hope" for all the ungodly who are living and have ever lived on earth, and indeed, for all the rebel host throughout creation. They trustingly hope that there will be no everlasting schism in God's universe, but that as all began in unity, and harmony, so all will end in harmony and peace. A most pleasing anticipation surely, and it only needs some scriptural foundation to warrant it. The

great trouble which lies in the way of accepting restorationist and universalistic views is, that if we shorten or do away with the "eternal punishment," we must shorten or do away with the "eternal life."] **Upon every soul of man**—that is, upon every single man. The 'soul' is not to be emphasized here, as if it were intended to specify that part of our nature as the sphere of the 'tribulation and anguish'; but the expression stands for the whole man, as in 13: 1. [Winer, Meyer, and others, think some reference is had to the soul as that part of man which feels pain, thus making the phrase nearly equivalent to every soul of man, or, soul of every man. Mehring, as quoted by Philippi, observes that the justification of the phrase lies in the fact that the soul, as the sole subject of feeling, is the real man. The soul is the vital principle in man, "the sphere of the will and affections, and the true centre of the personality." As distinguished from the spirit, it has special reference to our animal and sensuous nature. See note on Luke 1: 46, 47.] **That doeth evil.** The word translated 'doeth' here is different from both the words distinguished in 1: 32, and 2: 1, and may be more exactly translated "worketh," as it is in the following verse. So it will be translated wherever we meet it throughout the Epistle. [Its meaning as a compound is probably a little stronger than the simple verb, work. Perhaps it is nearly equivalent to our work out, accomplish, or bring to pass. 'Evil,' literally "the evil;" so, "the good," in the next verse. The neuter adjective with the article is thus often used as an abstract noun.] In chapter 7 we shall find all three of these words, "do, practice, work," in intimate connection. **Of the Jew first, and also of the Gentile.** In 1: 16, it is the "blessing" which is to come to the Jew 'first'; so also in the next verse. Here it is the penal *retribution*. 'First' does not mean "especially" here; for although that would be in accordance with the just rule laid down by our Lord in Luke 12: 47, 48, it would not agree so well with the

---

[1] The latter, as the stronger term, is always put last. The former (θλῖψις) is pressure from *without*, the latter (στενοχωρία, literally, *straitness of room*, which allows no

way of turning or escaping) is pressure from *within*. Compare 2 Cor. 4: 8, θλιβόμενοι, *pressed* on every side, but not στενοχωρούμενοι. – (F.)

10 But glory, honour, and peace, to every man that workett good ; to the Jew first, and also to the Gentile: 11 For there is no respect of persons with God. 12 For as many as have sinned without law shall also

honour and peace to every man that worketh good, 11 to the Jew first. and also to the Greek: for there 12 is no respect of persons with God. For as many as [1] have sinned without law shall also perish with-

1 Gr. sinned.

frequent use of the expression without the word 'first.' The Jew as having precedence in privileges, naturally takes precedence in the order of judgment. He is always named first, except in Col. 3: 11. The word for 'Gentile' in this and in the following verse, is, by the Revised Version, literally rendered Greek.

10. But glory, honour, and peace [will be rendered]. Instead of "immortality" (incorruption) here, we have 'peace,' the other two words being the same as in ver. 7. These are what God "will render" (ver. 6) to these two classes of men respectively. In their fullness, they will be realized only in the future world, according to the intimation in ver. 16. But many beginnings and foretastes of them, in both cases, are experienced in the present life, particularly in the case of the threatened evils. Much tribulation and anguish herald the coming wrath; and if but little of the glory and honor appear here (1 John 3: 2), the peace, at least, though not perfect nor uninterrupted, is real, and beyond all price.

11. For there is no respect of persons with God. [This 'respect of persons' (προσω-πολημψία, or, in some critical editions, προσω-πολημψία) is a New Testament word, yet derived from Old Testament phraseology. See Lev. 19: 15; Deut. 10: 17; 2 Chron. 19: 7; Job 34: 19; Mal. 2: 9; also Luke 20: 21; Matt. 22: 16; Acts 10: 34; Gal. 2: 6. It occurs elsewhere, in Paul's writings, only in Eph. 6: 9; Col. 3: 25. Compare James 2: 1 (9). Similar phraseology and a like idea are found in Ecclesiasticus, or Wisdom of Sirach 35: 12, 13. (LXX 33: 14-16.) Compare Wisdom of Solomon 6: 7. Prof. Shedd remarks that there "can be no partiality in the exercise of *mercy*, because there cannot be an obligation or claim of any kind in this case. . . . But there may be partiality in the administration of *justice*."] This verse states the principle of *impartiality* on which God will deal with Jews and Gentiles, in accordance with the statements in ver. 9 and 10, and in opposition to the fond fancy of the Jews that they had as

Jews, irrespective of their personal characters, a sort of monopoly of the divine favor. The doctrine that God is no respecter of persons is not to be understood in such a way as to limit his *sovereignty*; he dealeth with his creatures according to his good pleasure, giving to some much greater favors than to others; but he shows no capricious partiality, always, in his final judgment, holding an even balance between responsibilities and privileges, without regard to merely factitious distinctions. So it is that the succeeding context teaches us to understand the often misunderstood and often abused principle so emphatically affirmed in this verse. Compare Acts 10: 34, 35. Men are justified by faith, not by works; they will be judged according to their works, without any partiality [judged "according to truth," ver. 2.]

12. For as many as have sinned. [Literally, *sinned*—"spoken from the standpoint of the time of the judgment." (Meyer.)] We have now an expansion and illustration of the principle laid down in the preceding verse. God is impartial, 'for' he will judge men according to the light which they enjoy [or might and should have possessed]. **Without law** here can only mean without the written law, the law of Moses. If any were absolutely without law, they would be absolutely without sin; "for where no law is, there is no transgression." (4: 15.) The expression 'without law' is used (adjectively) in the same sense in 1 Cor. 9: 21 (four times). The word **also** in the second clause shows the corresponding relation between the verbs 'have sinned' and **shall perish** [i. e., they shall 'also perish without law.' "Their punishment shall be assigned without reference to the written law." (Hodge.)] This perishing is the opposite of "salvation" (1: 16), of "shall live" (1: 17), of "eternal life" (2: 7), of "glory," etc. (2: 10.) Compare John 3; 15; 1 Cor. 1: 18. It is the natural, and just, and necessary consequence of unpardoned sin. [The perishing of men without law, signifies, according to Dr. Hodge, that "their punishment shall be assigned without reference to

perish without law; and as many as have sinned in the law shall be judged by the law;

out law: and as many as have sinned under law 13 shall be judged by law; for not the hearers of the

the law." The apostle in his writings recognizes two classes, the saved and the perishing or lost. But when he speaks of those who "are perishing," as in 1 Cor. 1: 18; 2 Cor. 2: 15: 4: 3; 2 Thess. 2: 10, he does not imply that their souls are gradually losing their being and sinking into non-existence. Even the "eternal destruction" of 2 Thess. 1: 9 is not annihilation, but is rather an abiding alienation from God, a banishment away from the presence of the Lord and from the glory of his power. "Alienation from God," says Calvin, "is eternal death." Haley says, that the "mortal soulists" or annihilationists would, from their favorite proof texts, "prove too much, and so prove nothing. For they would prove that the Messiah was annihilated at his crucifixion, that the righteous are annihilated at death, that after the Israelites had annihilated themselves, there was still 'help' for them with all manner of similar absurdities." Does our Saviour assert that a prophet could not be annihilated except at Jerusalem? Are we to infer that the lost coin had gone out of existence? or that the substance of the perished wine bottles had ceased to be? After the prodigal had returned, could the father truly say that he had been annihilated or had lost his conscious existence? Is found, moreover, the proper correlative of "annihilated"? Our Saviour says that he came to seek and to save, not that which could be called lost by way of anticipation, but that which was already lost. A sinner can become lost to himself, to society, to usefulness, happiness, peace, God, and heaven, and still retain a conscious existence. These are for him a sadder loss than annihilation. Paul asserts the fact that the Gentiles sinned against the light of nature and the law written in their hearts, sinned "without excuse," and are "worthy of death." Even if favored with God's revealed will, men often choose not to repent, but harden their hearts in iniquity and heap up for themselves a treasure of wrath which they must experience in the day of wrath. Had the apostle been an advanced thinker of the more liberal school, this of course would have been the proper place for him to hint at the probability of a future probation for the heathen, and for others who do not have a fair chance in this

life for a decisive probation—the probability or certainty that before any man shall meet Christ as a judge (see. ver. 16) he will first have heard of him as a Saviour. But all this he has strangely neglected to do. Meyer sees no mitigation in the punishment of these persons without law—that is, Gentile evil doers, so long as they must perish. Our passage is indeed an echo of the truth; "the soul that sinneth, it shall die," but surely condemnation will be proportioned to light resisted, and perishing may be to one more than it is to another. The teachings of the New Testament on the subject of retribution do not shock our ideas of strictest justice, but make responsibility and guilt proportionate to light and advantage, and plainly reveal the fact of different degrees of retributive punishment. (Matt. 10: 15; 11: 21-24; 12: 41, 42; Luke 12: 47, 48.) What can be more consonant with our ideas of right and justice than our Saviour's teachings in regard to the many stripes and the few? His rule of accountability is infinitely better than any suppositions of ours as to what constitutes a fair probation. Indeed, an exact decision touching this point lies utterly beyond our power. If any were disposed to do so, they could easily construct a plausible argument showing that none of us have a "fair chance" in this life when an eternity is at stake—placed here, as it were, but a moment, in a world of darkness and temptation, with our almost ungovernable appetites and passions clamoring ever for indulgence, and the penalties of future retribution so far out of our sight and beyond the possibility of adequate conception. Reasoning in this way, we can well nigh get rid of every rule of felt duty and every measure of felt responsibility, and instead of acting as though a fair moral probation were granted to any of us we should be led to adopt the Epicurean motto: "Let us eat and drink, for to-morrow we die." Certainly, then, a "greater condemnation," a "sorer punishment" will be theirs who sin under the law, and who will be judged by the law than will fall to those who sin without the law and will perish without the law. Would it not be best then to withhold light and knowledge from the comparatively ignorant heathen? Our answer, to say nothing of our

13 (For not the hearers of the law *are* just before God, but the doers of the law shall be justified.

law are [1]just before God, but the doers of the law 14 shall be [2]justified: (for when Gentiles who have not

1 Or, *righteous*......2 Or, *accounted righteous*.

Saviour's command, is this, that *we* may withhold these blessings from them when we would have *our* light and *our* advantages less than they are. See notes on 3: 2.] Those who **have sinned in the law**—that is, the Jews who have the law of Moses. [In the verb we have the Greek historical aorist: 'sinned.' The word 'law' is here without the article, it being to the Jew nearly equivalent to a proper name which "does not *require* the article," though as the established sign of definiteness it is often joined to such names. (Winer's "New Testament Grammar," p. 112.) In this Epistle 'law' (νόμος), occurs thirty-four times without the article and thirty-five with it; in Galatians, twenty times without it and ten times with it.] **Shall be judged by the law.** Thus God's judgment of both Gentiles and Jews will be impartial, according to the light which each has enjoyed. [Philippi remarks that the "Gentiles as sinners *perish*, Jews as sinners are judged," and by this judgment, which is here equivalent to condemnation, "perhaps an aggravation of punishment is indicated." The word law being in the last two instances destitute of the article, is hence regarded by some as not referring to "the law" of Moses, but to law in general. It is sometimes rendered *a* law, but even the Gentiles sinned against *a* law, that which was written in their hearts. To render a Greek noun that has no article by the indefinite article *a* (see Canterbury Revision) is often quite as misleading as to render it by the definite article, *the*. The word law often occurs in this Epistle without the article, and evidently denotes in general the revealed law of God, the law of Moses. So Ellicott, Alford, Winer, and others. Bishop Lightfoot, however, says: "The written law, the Old Testament, is always "the law" (ὁ νόμος). The same word "without the article is law considered as a principle, exemplified no doubt chiefly and signally in the Mosaic law, but very much wider than this in its application." See Appendix in the Introduction of "The Bible Commentary," where this matter is fully discussed.]

13. [The Common Version begins a parenthesis with this verse; the American Revised

Version, with the next verse; the Canterbury Revision omits the brackets altogether.] The **for** at the beginning of this verse assigns a reason for the latter half of ver. 12. The Jews have the written law, but the possession of it does not justify them; 'for,' etc. **The hearers of the law** are spoken of, rather than the *readers* of it, because in those ancient times, in the scarcity of books, the law became known to the people chiefly by the public hearing of it in the synagogues, rather than by the private reading of it at home. Compare Acts 15: 21. ["The substantive (hearers) brings out more forcibly than the participial form (those hearing) would have done the *characteristic* feature: those whose business is hearing." (Meyer.) Critical editors omit the article before 'law' here, and in the next sentence, while the governing nouns in both places have the article. Compare ver. 27. This shows that in the use of the article the principle of "correlation" referred to in ver. 6 does not always hold. **Are just before God**—accounted righteous in his sight or presence; "the idea of locality suggested by the preposition being still retained in that of judgment at a tribunal." (Ellicott.)] **Shall be justified.** This verb occurs here for the first time in this Epistle. Taken in connection with the preceding clause, 'are just before God,' it affords important help in explaining the sense of the word 'righteousness.' See notes on 1: 17. To 'be justified' is to be exempt from condemnation, and acquitted in the divine judgment, so as to stand in favor with God and to enjoy the security and the blessings resulting from that favor. [With the last part of this verse compare 10: 5; Deut. 27: 26; Lev. 18: 5. 'Justified,' as Dr. Gifford remarks, cannot here mean *pardoned*, since the doer of the law has nothing to be pardoned for; nor can it mean *made* just, for he is just already by the supposition. It is the exact contrary to being "condemned." As no one can be justified by doing the law, Prof. Turner would give to this justified the meaning of accepted. But these two ideas virtually imply each other, and the Greek language has specific terms to express the idea of acceptance. "There is no

14 For when the Gentiles, which have not the law, do by nature the things contained in the law, these, having not the law, are a law unto themselves:

15 the law do by nature the things of the law, these, not having the law, are a law unto themselves ; in that

conflict here with the doctrine of justification by faith. The apostle cites an axiom in ethics—namely, that perfect personal obedience will be recognized and rewarded by that impartial Judge who is no respecter of persons, and that nothing short of this will be. That any man will actually appear before this tribunal with such an obedience is neither affirmed nor denied in the mere statement of the principle. The solution of this question must be sought elsewhere in the Epistle." (Shedd.)]

14. For when the Gentiles. Here the 'for' assigns a reason for the latter part of ver. 13. [Philippi and Godet make the 'for' substantiate the first part of ver. 13, and suppose that Paul, as a proof that mere hearers of the law are not justified, adduces the fact that unbelieving Gentiles are hearers of a law. This sense is appropriate enough, but I do not see how it can be derived from the text. It certainly requires no such supposition as that made by the apostle: when Gentiles *do* by nature the things of the law.] It would be better to omit the definite article before the word 'Gentiles.' It is not expressed in the original, and the indefinite character of the supposition is better expressed without it: 'When any Gentiles, if any ever do, for they as a class certainly do not,' etc. [So Fritzsche, Meyer, and others. But De Wette and Philippi think the word is sufficiently definite in itself, and may, without the article, be referred to the entire Gentile world. See 3: 29; 11: 13; 15: 10, 12; 1 Cor. 1: 23. A noun also may dispense with the article when joined, as here and in 9: 30, by an article to a limiting attributive. (Winer, p. 139; Buttmann, 92.] **Do by nature**—that is, by natural instinct, judgment, and reason ["the moral prompting of conscience left to itself." (Meyer)], without any such formal standard of duty as the Jews have; corresponding to 'without law' in the preceding verse. **The things contained in the law**—that is, the things which the law prescribes; when they do the things commanded, without a definite knowledge of the commandment. [**These having not the law.** The pronoun 'these,' though referring to a neuter noun, Gentiles,

is by a *constructio ad sensum* put in the masculine; the word 'law,' though without the article in the Greek, evidently refers to the revealed will of God. The *possession* of this law is here emphatically denied. In the former clause, 'having not the law,' the emphasis rests more upon the substantive—that is, the possession of *the law* is denied. By the use of the subjective negative (μή), the absence of law on the part of the Gentiles is represented as a supposition, as something existing not so much in fact as in thought.] **Are a law unto themselves.** This expression is sufficiently explained by the following verse. [Since '*a* law' may be just or unjust, God's law or man's law, Alford would make even this 'law' definite, thus: 'are (so far) *the law* to themselves.' The connection and thought of this verse are quite variously explained. The apostle affirms that the Gentiles have, as Farrar states it, "a natural law written on their hearts, and sufficiently clear to secure, at the Day of Judgment, their acquittal or condemnation," and, what is somewhat surprising, he even supposes that they or some of them do by nature perform the things of the (written) law, and in ver. 26, 27, he goes so far as to say: "If the uncircumcision (the Gentiles) keep the ordinances of the law," and "if they fulfil the law." Now they have not the written law, and the apostle is far from supposing that they perform all the "works of the law," but he does seem to imply that some of them do perform *certain things* of the law—that is, avoid murder, adultery, etc.; and he brings forward this fact here, though in a delicate and somewhat secret way, as being condemnatory ("shall judge thee," ver. 27) of those persons, the Jews, "who with the letter (of the law) and circumcision are yet transgressors of the law." Meyer's view of this verse is that "Paul desires simply to establish the *regulative principle* of justification through law in the case of the Gentiles." Prof. Stuart says "that the apostle is only laying down or illustrating a principle here, not relating a historical fact. . . . The writer means to say neither more nor less, than that the Gentiles may have the same kind of claims to be actually justified

15 Which shew the work of the law written in their hearts, their conscience also bearing witness, and *their*

they shew the work of the law written in their hearts, their conscience bearing witness therewith,

before God as the Jews; but, as the sequel shows most fully, neither Jew nor Gentile has any claim at all to justification, since both have violated the law under which they have lived." "It is remarkable," says Dr. Gifford, "that St. Paul here uses the exact words of Aristotle, who says, concerning men of eminent virtue and wisdom: 'Against such there is no law, for themselves are a law.'" The first clause is found in Gal. 5: 23.]

15. We have at the beginning of this verse the same compound relative spoken of in 1 : 25, with the force of a *reason*. **Which shew—** "since they are such as show." [They 'shew' openly, by their action—doing the things of the law. (Ver. 14, so De Wette, Meyer, Philippi, etc.) Others: by the testimony of their conscience.] **The work of the law.** They show the operation of the law; they show that what the law does is done in them; the law distinguishes between what is right and what is wrong [it commands and forbids]; this work is shown to be done in them. *How* it is done is immediately explained. **Written in their hearts.** They have a moral nature (ver. 14), which necessitates the recognition of right and wrong in actions. [This injunctive and interdicting work of the law written in men's hearts is generally spoken of as the unwritten law of God, but is here named written, in allusion to the law which was written on tablets of stone. For a like figure, see 2 Cor. 3: 3. Philippi says: "The works of the law are written in their hearts in so far as they confess in their hearts an obligation to do them." Paul "obviously means by this term the voice of God in the conscience" (Olshausen), and for this reason, perhaps, a change is made from the plural (hearts) to the singular (conscience). Prof. Boise calls attention to the frequent use in the New Testament of the verbal adjective (here γραπτὸν, *written*) instead of the aorist or perfect passive participle.]

Their conscience also bearing witness. The force of the word 'also' here is not very apparent. It is an attempt to express in English what is expressed in Greek by a preposition [σύν, *with*] combined with the participle "bearing witness," giving it the force of "co-witnessing," and so seeming to imply some other testimony, with which that of conscience is co-ordinate and concurrent. What is that other testimony? The testimony of the *actual fact*, says Meyer—that is, the *work of the law* is *shown* to be *written in their hearts* by their *actually doing* the things contained in the law (ver. 14); and then the testimony of their conscience 'also' confirms the same fact, by the accusing or excusing verdict which they pass upon the actions of themselves and one another. This is very intelligible; and if it were certain (as Meyer affirms) that this prefix syllable requires some such definite witness to be predicated, apart from that of conscience, no better explanation need be sought. But is it so certain that this prefix to the participle requires us to seek some other definite witness than that of conscience? The simple verb "to witness," in Greek, is never used in connection with the word conscience. The only other place where the two occur together in the New Testament is 9: 1, and there, as here, the participle has the prefix preposition. Indeed, the same prefix (σύν) is also the first syllable of the Greek word for "conscience." And the corresponding syllable, *con*, begins the class of words, both in Latin and English, that express this inward witness of our nature, as "*conscience, consciousness.*" Is there not in these agreeing compounds, in different languages, an intimation that this common syllable expresses only the *union* and *harmony* of all the faculties of our deeper and better nature in this inward witness? If this is the true explanation, the word *also* should be omitted, both here and in 9 : 1.[1] **And their**

---

[1] On the force of this participle, Alford, similarly to De Wette, thus remarks: "Confirming by its testimony, the σύν signifying the agreement of the witness with the deed [*i. e.*, with their *doing* the things of the law], perhaps, also, the σύν may be partly induced by the σύν in συνειδήσεως, conscience, referring to the reflective process in which a man confers, so to speak, with himself." Volkmar, as quoted by Godet, says: "Their conscience bears testimony besides the moral act itself, which already demonstrated the presence of the divine law." Philippi supposes that what their (reflective) conscience bears witness *to* is, that the work of the law is written on their hearts, though he confesses that the conscience *antecedens* is this law in the heart.--(F.)

thoughts the mean while accusing or else excusing one another;)
16 In the day when God shall judge the secrets of men by Jesus Christ according to my gospel.

and [1]their [2]thoughts one with another accusing or
16 else excusing *them;*) in the day when God [3]shall judge the secrets of men, according to my gospel, by Jesus Christ.

1 Or, *their thoughts accusing or else excusing* them *one with another*......2 Or, *reasonings*......3 Or. *judgeth.*

thoughts the mean while accusing or else excusing one another. The single word translated 'in the mean while,' is usually translated "between," and is closely connected with the word translated 'one another.' This seems the true connection from the position of the words [see Matt. 18 : 15], although the 'one another' might be regularly enough governed by the participles 'accusing and excusing.' The word which we translate "between" (μεταξύ) seems, however, to require an object more than the participles do. It is invariably followed by an object which it governs (seven times), except when it is used as a *noun,* John 4 : 31 (*meanwhile*), or as an *adjective,* Acts 13 : 42 (*next*). According to this view of the connection, the last part of this verse might better be translated—*and their thoughts between* (or among) *one another accusing,* or *even excusing.* [Meyer and Lange regard the *one another* as referring not to thoughts but to the Gentiles—*i. e.,* their thoughts are busy in approving or condemning the actions of their fellow-men. It seems most natural to regard the reciprocal pronoun here as reflexive, referring to thoughts or judgments—the judging and the strife being internal—while the participles may be taken as used absolutely, without any object expressed. A passage parallel to this is found in Philo: "That conviction which is the innate inhabitant of every soul, like an accuser, censures, charges, and upbraids; and again, as a judge, teaches, admonishes, and exhorts to repentance." "This judical process," says Dr. Schaff, "which takes place here in every man's heart, is a forerunner of the great judgment at the end of the world." Did we but realize the terrible power of a thoroughly

enlightened and awakened conscience, conjoined with a restored and perfect memory, each one would be moved to say :

> That to sit alone with my conscience
> Will be judgment enough for me.[1]]

The word translated 'else' would be more exactly translated *even;* it seems designed to intimate, what is undoubtedly true in the case of the persons referred to, that the thoughts have more frequent occasion to *accuse* than to *excuse;* that the former is the *rule,* the latter the exception.

16. [**In the day.** The word 'day' is without the article, yet is virtually defined by the clause which follows. Westcott and Hort, however, prefix the relative pronoun : in *what* day. We notice also that they prefer the present tense of the verb, judge. Where various readings occur, these critics, as in the case before us, frequently adopt the marginal reading of the Revised Version, and make the Revisers' text their secondary reading.] Almost all commentators perceive a necessity for inclosing the two or three preceding verses in parentheses. For the accusing and excusing office of conscience does not date from the Day of Judgment, however it may be *intensified* then. But there is a difference of opinion as to the extent of the parenthetic portion, some including three verses (13-15), and others only two (14, 15). The former view seems preferable, for this ver. 16 does not connect immediately with ver. 13 so appropriately as with ver. 12. The statement in ver. 13 seems much too *limited,* while that of ver. 12 is much more comprehensive. [Some, as Lachmann and Meyer, inclosing ver. 14, 15, in parentheses, erroneously connect this judg-

---

1 The terrible state of a remorseful conscience is well depicted in the lines from Byron's "Giaour":

> The mind that broods o'er guilty woes
> Is like the scorpion girt by fire.
> So writhes the mind Remorse hath riven,
> Unfit for earth, undoomed for heaven,
> Darkness above, despair beneath,
> Around it flame, within it death.

And in the tragedy of "Manfred," the same poet says the not even

> The innate tortures of that deep despair
> Which is remorse without the fear of hell,
> But all in all sufficient in itself,
> Would make a hell of heaven—can exorcise
> From out the unbounded soul the quick sense
> Of its own sins, wrongs, sufferance, and revenge
> Upon itself; there is no further pang
> Can deal that justice on the self-condemned
> He deals on his own soul.—(F.)

17 Behold, thou art called a Jew, and restest in the | 17   But if thou bearest the name of a Jew, and restest
aw, and makest thy boast of God, |

ment day with the 'shall be justified' of ver.
13. But no doers of the law will as such 'be
justified' on that day. Winer says rightly,
as we think, that **shall judge** glances back at
'shall be judged,' of ver. 12. So De Wette
and others. Alford goes back to the passage
ending with ver. 10. Hofmann and Lange
make this judging, accusing, or excusing day
to be whenever Paul's gospel was preached to
them, and translate, "when God judges,"
etc., not 'shall judge.' But Meyer says:
"The expressions in ver. 16 are so entirely
those formally used to denote the last judgment . . . that nothing else could occur to
any reader than the conception of that judgment, which, moreover, has been present to the
mind since ver. 2, and from which even 'according to my gospel' does not draw away
the attention." Philippi connects this verse
with the preceding, and thus explains the connection. The witness of conscience, spoken
of in ver. 15, referred to moral conduct in the
present life. But as the apostle was describing it, the thought was borne vividly in upon
his mind in the way indicated, how this would
manifest itself most decisively in the general
judgment. On this account he passes on to
the latter without so much as indicating the
change in the course of thought by varying
the phraseology, as by: *and this especially.*]
The secrets of men. The secret actions,
thoughts, designs, and motives. (Eccles. 12: 14.)
Not only things concealed from others, but
things only partially known to ourselves, will
God bring into judgment. Compare 1 Cor.
4: 4, 5. [How fearful must this judgment be
to any man, however outwardly moral, if all
the hidden deeps of life and all the secret
purposes and desires of his heart shall be thus
brought to light, especially if this judging
shall be attended with exposure. Men in this
world generally dread exposure of their
crimes far more than they do the crimes themselves, and the avoidance of this exposure is a
frequent cause of suicide. But there will be
no such escape in the world to come.] **By
Jesus Christ.** [These words point decisively
to the final judgment.] That Jesus Christ is
the appointed Judge of men is very plainly,
repeatedly, and emphatically affirmed in the
Scriptures. See Matt. 25: 31-46; John 5: 22,

27; Acts 10: 42; 17: 31; 1 Cor. 4: 5; 2 Cor. 5:
10. **According to my gospel.** The reference ('my gospel') is not specifically to the
Gospel of Luke, as was supposed by several of
the ancient Fathers [Origen, Eusebius, Je-
rome], an early tradition having represented
this gospel as written under Paul's supervision, and especially sanctioned by his approval; but rather the gospel which he
preached, in common with the other apostles.
He uses a similar expression in 16: 25; 2 Tim.
2: 8. Compare also 1 Cor. 15: 1. [He who
was "separated unto the gospel of God" and
who speaks in 1 Tim. 1: 11 of the "gospel
which was committed to my trust," could
well say, 'my gospel.']

The doctrine of a future judgment is an
important part of the gospel, and as such is to
be preached faithfully, solemnly, and tenderly.
It is, moreover, a reasonable ground for enforcing the duty of repentance, and is so represented by this same apostle in Acts 17: 31,
and perhaps also in 2 Cor. 5: 11, though the
sense of the expression in this last passage—
"the terror of the Lord"—admits a different
interpretation. ["Thus in ver. 14-16, St.
Paul shows that the principle stated in ver.
13 is a fact universal, and that the formal
distinction between Gentile and Jew, ver. 12,
does not involve any essential difference between them in reference to the divine judgment." (Gifford.) No one, methinks, can fail
to perceive how irrefutably antagonistic all
this teaching of the apostle is to the notion of
a future probation for "some heathen."]

17-20. The apostle having made his gradual and cautious approach to the Jew, as the
hawk, after wheeling awhile above his victim,
suddenly pounces down upon him, now singles
him out by name. These four verses are too
closely connected in one description to be separated without disadvantage. The word translated **behold** is, in the best manuscripts and in
most critical editions, divided into two words
(εἰ δὲ), which would be translated "but if," or
"if now": the hypothetical sentences thus
introduced extend through these four verses.
Thou art called a Jew. ["Thou hast a
title (Jew) in addition to (ἐπί) that which
other men possess." (Wordsworth.) De
Wette and Meyer regard the verb as simply

18 And knowest *his* will, and approvest the things that are more excellent, being instructed out of the law ;

18 upon ¹ the law, and gloriest in God, and knowest ²his will, and ³approvest the things that are excel- 19 lent, being instructed out of the law, and art confi-

1 Or, *a law*......2 Or, *the Will*......3 Or, *dost distinguish the things that differ.*

meaning "named." See Gen. 4: 17, 25, 26; LXX. The word Jew, etymologically, means *praised*, from *Judah*, the tribe in which the national and theocratic hopes of the Hebrews were centred. The virtue attached to this name may be seen from Gal. 2 : 14, 15 ; Rev. 2: 9. Meyer says : " The 'but' (δὲ) and the emphatic 'thou' are to be explained from the conception of the *contrast*, which the conduct of the Jews showed, to the proposition that only the doers of the law shall be justified."] To bear the name of Jew was, in their estimation, a great honor. The following clauses explain, in great part, why it was so. **And restest in the law** [or, *upon law*]. The Jew rested in the law in a twofold sense : his mind rested in it as a sure and ultimate rule of righteousness, in contrast with the uncertain and conflicting speculations of heathen philosophers and moralists ; and his hope relied upon it [or upon his possession and knowledge of it] as the ground of his acceptance with God. In the former view he was right : in the latter he was wrong. **And makest thy boast of God.** Literally, '*boastest in God.*'¹ [It will be noticed that all the particulars here enumerated, in which the Jew prided himself, are in themselves right and good. It was well to bear the name of a Jew, to rest upon the law, to glory in God, to know his will, etc.] While all other nations worshiped them that "by nature are no gods" (Gal. 4 : 8), the Jew prided himself on having the knowledge of the one true God. **And knowest his will.** The pronoun 'his' is not distinctly expressed, and *knowest the will* is the literal translation [the article being sometimes used as virtually equivalent to the pronoun]. The omission of the pronoun causes no obscurity, but may rather be regarded as adding force, inasmuch as it assumes that all doubt as to whose will is meant is precluded by the nature of the case. **And approvest the things that are more excellent.** This expression might be translated : *and triest* [distinguishest, or, as margin,

by American Revisers, "dost distinguish"] *the things that differ* [with special reference to discriminating between right and wrong, truth and error], without doing any violence to either the verb or the participle (differing or excelling). [The Revised Version (English Revisers) has *provest the things that differ* in the margin, and a similar interpretation is adopted by De Wette, Philippi, Godet, Alford, Stuart, Shedd.] But the common translation [favored by Meyer, Jowett, Gifford, Turner, Noyes, Hodge, Boise] seems more suitable to the context, both here and in Phil. 1 : 10, where the same expression occurs, and agrees better with the ordinary uses of both the verb from which the participle is derived (διαφέρειν ; see Matt. 6 : 26, "are better " ; 10: 31, " are of more value " ; 12 : 12, "is better "), and of the corresponding adjective (διάφορος),² see Heb. 1 : 4; 8: 6). **Being instructed** [continuously] **out of the law.** This clause explains the preceding. It was not by their superior natural shrewdness, or their superior moral uprightness, that they approved of what was excellent; but because they had in the law a divine rule of judgment. The present tense of the participle here, 'being instructed,' seems designed to intimate, not that they had been instructed in youth, once for all, but that they were continually receiving instruction, through the weekly reading and expounding of the law in the synagogue. The word translated 'instructed ' is emphatic. It is the word from which our "catechise " is derived [and properly denotes *oral* instruction]. Observe its use in Luke 1: 4; Acts 18 : 25 : Gal. 6 : 6 (twice). [" We may hence infer," says the elder Jonathan Edwards, "that no degree of speculative knowledge of things of religion is any certain sign of saving grace," and that a man may have "more knowledge of this sort than hundreds of true saints of an ordinary education and most divines, yet all is no certain evidence of any degree of saving grace in the heart." He also

---

¹ On the ending of this verb, which is one of the original uncontracted forms of the second person singular, passive and middle, and which occurs also in ver. 23 ; 11 : 18, the reader is referred to Winer, p. 76.

In its common contracted form it would be written καυχᾷ.—(F.)

² The participle is used only in the two passages Rom. 2: 18 ; Phil. 1 : 10.

19 And art confident that thou thyself art a guide of the blind, a light of them which are in darkness,
20 An instructor of the foolish, a teacher of babes, which hast the form of knowledge and of the truth in the law.
21 Thou therefore which teachest another, teachest thou not thyself? thou that preachest a man should not steal, dost thou steal?

dent that thou thyself art a guide of the blind, a
20 light of them that are in darkness, ¹a corrector of the foolish, a teacher of babes, having in the law
21 the form of knowledge and of the truth; thou therefore that teachest another, teachest thou not thyself?

---

¹ Or, an instructor.

---

remarks that "the devil has undoubtedly a great degree of speculative knowledge in divinity, having been, as it were, educated in the best divinity school in the universe," and that "it is not to be supposed that any mortal man, whether godly or ungodly, has an equal degree of speculative knowledge with the devil." See his Sermon XXVIII on "True Grace."] **And art confident,** etc. [The word for 'and' is not "the more emphatic and closer connective (καί), but the adjunctive (τε), and indicates that what follows is dependent on or flows from what precedes." (Winer, 434.)] In ver. 17, 18, we have four or five particulars denoting the advantages which the Jew claimed for himself; and in ver. 19, 20, as many particulars denoting his superiority to the Gentile. ["And first he takes the poor Gentile by the hand, as one does a blind man, offering to guide him; then he opens his eyes, dissipating his darkness by the light of revelation; then he rears him as one would bring up a person yet without reason; finally, when through all this care he has come to the stage of a little child (νήπιος, who cannot speak, a term used by the Jews to designate proselytes), he initiates him into the full knowledge of the truth by becoming his teacher." (Godet.) In Matt. 15: 14, our Lord upbraids the Pharisees as being blind leaders of the blind.] Observe how the arrogance of the Jew is set forth in the form of expression, 'art confident that thou thyself,' etc. It is probable that these very titles were assumed by the Jewish Rabbis and Pharisees. Indeed, Grotius mentions a work by Maimonides, of which the Rabbinic title, translated into Greek, would correspond precisely with the words here rendered: **an instructor of the foolish. Which hast** [literally, *having*, agreeing with thyself] **the form of knowledge and of the truth in the law.** The

word here translated 'form' [μόρφωσιν] is used only in one other place in the New Testament. In 2 Tim. 3: 5, it is used to mark the form in distinction from the reality: "having a form of godliness, but denying the power thereof." Here, however, the word does not seem to be used in the same superficial sense [but rather marks the reality, the substance with the form, as does the word form (μορφή) in Phil. 2: 6, 7. Weiss, in his "Biblical Theology," vol. 1, p. 319, says that the Jews possessed a "*copied representation* of the truth in the Old Testament law."] It was an embodiment of true knowledge, a real rule of right, which the apostle did not intend to disparage. Is it a mere fancy that in these verses (17-20) the apostle uses a certain grandiloquence, not unsuitable to the arrogant pretensions which he is describing?¹ Having thus far shown how much the Jews made of the theory of religion, he now proceeds to show how little regard they paid to the practice of it. And he does this with great energy of expression, and in what seems to be a tone of indignant surprise.

21, 22. Thou therefore. ["At length the apostle turns to strike." (Jowett.)] The 'therefore' marks the turn of the sentence after the hypothetical clauses commencing with ver. 17. [The thought of these clauses and of this 'therefore.' etc., seems to be this: thou, being all this, or rather, professing all this, how is it, *then*, that your conduct is such as it is—that is, the reverse of all your professions? This contradiction between profession and practice on the part of the Jews corresponds to that of the Gentiles (1:22), of whom the apostle says: "Professing themselves to be wise, they became fools," and acted accordingly.] There is much force in these interrogative sentences. The first is of a general nature—**teachest thou not thyself?**

---

¹ In ver. 17 and 18 we have five particulars, expressing what the Jew claimed for himself; and in ver. 19 and 20 we have likewise five particulars, expressing his relation to the Gentiles and the pre-eminence over

them; and to make the correspondence between the two pairs of verses more complete and noticeable, the last of the five particulars is in each case expressed in the original Greek by a participle.

22 Thou that sayest a man should not commit adultery, dost thou commit adultery? thou that abhorrest idols, dost thou commit sacrilege?
23 Thou that makest thy boast of the law, through breaking the law dishonourest thou God?

thou that preachest a man should not steal, dost 22 thou steal? thou that sayest a man should not commit adultery, dost thou commit adultery? thou that 23 abhorrest idols, dost thou rob temples? thou who gloriest in ¹ the law, through thy transgression of

1 Or, a law.

This is followed by three specific questions— or charges, we might call them, in the form of questions—each weightier than the preceding. [*Theft, adultery, sacrilege.* "Thou sinnest most grievously against thy neighbor, thyself, God. Paul had shewn to the Gentiles that their sins were first against God, next against themselves, next against others. He now inverts the order, for sins against God are very openly practiced among the Gentiles, but not by the Jew." (Bengel.) The infinitive clauses—not to steal, not to commit adultery—depend upon the Greek participles, which have here the force of command. The participles and verbs are all in the present tense, denoting present and continuous action.] The first two are very plain; the third may require a few words of explanation. Although the Jews, in the earlier periods of their history, were often reproved for their participation in the idolatrous practices of the heathen around and among them, yet after their return from their captivity in Babylon they seem to have been characterized generally by their intense abhorrence of idols. [Hence the apostle does not say: "Dost thou worship idols?" We may remark that the word **abhorrest** indicates that the idols were regarded as abominable things, alike polluted and polluting.] Josephus relates a striking proof of this abhorrence. When they understood that Pilate had ordered the military standards, adorned with portraits of the emperors, to be brought to Jerusalem, multitudes of them rushed to his palace in Cæsarea, and, disregarding alike his commands and his threats, declared their readiness to die rather than suffer their city to be so desecrated. ("Antiq.," XVIII, 3, 1; "Wars," II, 9, 2, and 3.) **Dost thou commit sacrilege?** [This is the marginal reading of the Revised Version. Jowett, in order to bring out the implied opposition, renders thus: "Dost thou who abhorrest idols rob the idol temples?" And this contrast is favored by most exposi-

tors.] Two questions arise here. Were the Jews guilty of profaning the heathen temples? Would the apostle account it *sacrilege* if they did so? As to the first question, it seems not unlikely that, either in the wantonness of their fanaticism or in their greed for the costly offerings with which idol temples were often adorned, they sometimes did this. An express prohibition of the latter form of profanation of heathen temples, in Deut. 7 : 25, shows that they were at least in danger of doing this.¹ [See also Josephus' "Antiq.," IV, 8, 10. Some, appealing to Mal. 1 : 8-14; 3 : 8-10; "Antiq.," XVIII, 3, 5, suppose that the robbery of that which belonged to, or was due to, God's temple is alluded to; but this view does not harmonize with the context.] As to the second question, it does not seem altogether improbable, especially in view of the prohibition just referred to, that the apostle might apply the word *sacrilege* to such a robbery. The case would then be as if he had said: "You profess to abhor idols, but you have no objection to making gain by doing what exposes you to the charge (on the part of the heathen) of sacrilege." [We should not naturally have supposed that the Jews were specially guilty of the sins enumerated, yet there is considerable evidence to substantiate the apostle's charges. Compare Matt. 19 : 8; 23 : 13-25; James 4 : 4-13; 5 : 1-6. The Jews themselves confess to the commonness of adultery in those times, even to the doing away with the ordeal of jealousy. (Farrar.) We suppose their wickedness was greatly augmented in the years immediately subsequent, especially during the Roman war. Josephus certainly sets it forth in a fearful light. See his "Wars," V, 9, 4; 10, 5; 13, 6.]
23, 24. Thou that makest thy boast of the law (literally, *in* the law), **through breaking the law dishonourest thou God?** [Inconsistently with thy professions, thou dishonorest God by violating his law. Meyer does not read this verse as a question,

¹ Meyer thinks "it may justly be inferred from Acts 19 : 37 that robbery of temples actually occurred among the Jews."

² The verb καυχᾶσαι, (see ver. 17), is the original uncontracted form of second person singular, passive, indicative middle.—(F.)

24 For the name of God is blasphemed among the Gentiles through you, as it is written.
25 For circumcision verily profiteth, if thou keep the law: but if thou be a breaker of the law, thy circumcision is made uncircumcision.
26 Therefore, if the uncircumcision keep the right-

24 the law dishonourest thou God? For the name of God is blasphemed among the Gentiles because of
25 you, even as it is written. For circumcision indeed profiteth, if thou be a doer of the law: but if thou be a transgressor of the law, thy circumcision is
26 become uncircumcision. If therefore the uncircum-

but finds in it an answer to "the four questions of reproachful astonishment."] **For the name of God is blasphemed among the Gentiles through you** (*on account of you*). [Who can doubt that the name of God is now blasphemed in heathen lands because of the wickednsss of men who profess to be Christians?] **As it is written.** Paul, in the above quotation, has in mind either Isa. 52: 5, or Ezek. 36 : 22. According to the Greek translation of the Old Testament [which here adds *among the Gentiles* to the original Hebrew], the former reference seems most probable; according to the English, the latter. [It may be added that the meaning of the passage in Ezekiel is pertinent, while that of the passage in Isaiah is not so, according to a very probable interpretation of the original. For it is clearly the Jews who are rebuked in Ezekiel, while it is the Gentiles who seem to be rebuked in Isaiah. But the passage of Isaiah is obscure. See Alexander on the passage. (A. H.)] [Paul by the use of *for*, which is his own word, appropriates a passage of Scripture as his own. "Hence *as it is written* is placed at the *end*, as is never done in the case of express quotations of Scripture. The historical sense of the passage is not here regarded, since Paul has not quoted it as a fulfilled prophecy, though otherwise with propriety in the sense of 3 : 19." (Meyer.)]

25. [The conjunction **for** corroborates the foregoing reasoning—that is, *in the same way circumcision*, etc. (Alford.)] **Circumcision verily profiteth, if thou keep** (dost practice) **the law; but if thou be a breaker** (transgressor) **of the law, thy circumcision is made uncircumcision.**[1] The apostle now meets the false dependence of the Jew upon his circumcision. It was a saying of the Rabbins, "a circumcised man does not go to hell." ["All the circumcised have part

in the world to come." "But for circumcision, heaven and earth could not exist." "So great is circumcision, that thirteen covenants were made concerning it." The word 'circumcision' is now for the first time mentioned, and it must have been a grievous thing to a Jew to have it, under any circumstances, put on a level with 'uncircumcision' which, in the words of Tholuck, signifies "the state of exclusion from a near connection with God." Thus to slight circumcision, the ordinance of God, the sign of God's covenant people, what could this be to a Jew of that day, but a dethronement of Jehovah, a contemptuous repudiation of his revealed will. "Is it not," he might ask, "by this covenant of circumcision that we become or are recognized as God's peculiar people, his adopted children; and if you repudiate this covenant, do you not make us orphans indeed? An uncircumcised Gentile equal in God's sight to one of his chosen people! Perish the thought!" We need not wonder that, to the Jew, untaught by the Spirit in regard to Abraham's faith and the true circumcision, the gospel which Paul preached should be a stumbling block.] The apostle's argument is, "inasmuch as your vile conduct shocks even the Gentiles, your claim to God's favor on the ground of your circumcision is outlawed; *for* the benefit of tne *sign* of the covenant is conditioned on the *fulfillment* of the covenant on your part; and you have not fulfilled it." The latter part of the verse is the emphatic part, on which the argument hinges. The topic which the apostle here touches, he resumes, and treats more fully, in the fourth chapter, ver. 9-12.

26, 27. Therefore if the uncircumcision keep,[2] etc. The general sense of these verses is very plain; the sign is quite subordinate to the thing signified; compliance with

---

[1] Literally, *has become*, but the perfect tense after subjunctives with ἐάν, expressing objective possibility, is equivalent to a present. See 7 : 2, Winer, 293.—(F.)

[2] In the subjunctive with ἐάν there is an "assumption of *objective* possibility, where experience will decide whether or not it is real." (Winer, 291.) With this

construction there is always implied a *sed dubito*, I *doubt*. For the frequent classic usage, εἰ with the optative, the New Testament has for the most part substituted εἰ with the indicative, or ἐάν with the subjunctive. See Buttmann, pp. 220-224.—(F.)

eousness of the law, shall not his uncircumcision be counted for circumcision?

27 And shall not uncircumcision which is by nature,

cision keep the ordinances of the law, shall not his

27 uncircumcision be reckoned for circumcision? and shall not the uncircumcision which is by nature, if

the moral conditions of the covenant is the essential thing; without this, the rite that seals it has no value. [The word for **keep** is in the present tense, and properly means to *guard habitually*.] **The righteousness of the law** means here the righteous moral precepts of the law; the word is not the same that is so often used in this Epistle, but a concrete derivative from it, or rather from the primitive adjective "righteous," and is in the plural number *righteousnesses*. Ver. 25 and 26 may be thus briefly paraphrased: "If thou art a breaker of the law, circumcision is no profit; if thou art a keeper of the law, uncircumcision is no damage." This was a hard saying for the Jew. [And we cannot wonder if the Jew, unenlightened by the Spirit of God, and ignorant of the circumcision of the heart, should indignantly respond: "You make an impossible supposition. You speak of the 'uncircumcision'—*i. e.*, the uncircumcised or Gentiles—as keeping the righteous appointments or ordinances of the law. Why, the chiefest ordinance of the law is circumcision itself!"] In what sense they are supposed by the apostle to keep the requirements of the law, we shall notice presently. **Shall not his uncircumcision be counted for circumcision?** See Peter's statement in Acts 10: 35. [Olshausen supposes that in this phrase, 'counted,' or reckoned, 'for circumcision,' "there is evidently an allusion to the 'counted for righteousness' in 4: 3; that which they have not is imputed to them as if they had it." He further says: "The ground of this imputation is this, that though they have not indeed the sign, they have instead of it the germ of that reality which the sign represents, . . . and therefore they may not untruly be regarded as such as have the sign also." Ellicott remarks that "the verb [λογί-ζομαι, *to account or reckon*] is rather a favorite word with St. Paul, being used in his epistles twenty-nine times (excluding quotations), and twice only (Mark 11: 31 is very doubtful) in the rest of the New Testament." This verb, commonly regarded as "deponent," is yet frequently used, as here and in 4: 5, in a passive sense. Buttmann thinks this phraseology: to be reckoned *as* (εἰς) is "borrowed

from the language of the LXX and a departure from classic usage." The Hebrew has the same idiom: to be reckoned for or to be reckoned as. Compare in the Hebrew Job 41: 24 (23); Lam. 4: 2; Num. 18: 27; Isa. 40: 15, with the Septuagint renderings.] The word 'not' is wanting in the Greek at the beginning of ver. 27. It was inserted by the English translators in order to show that the interrogative form of ver. 26 is continued to the end of this verse—very properly inserted, if the question be really continued. But in the judgment of Meyer, Lange, Alford, and others, the interrogation should end with ver. 26, and this verse be understood affirmatively. It is not very easy, nor very important to decide, as the question relates only to the form of the sentence, and not to the substance of the thought. On the one hand, the omission of the negative in such a case is unusual, and this favors the view of Meyer; but, on the other hand, the conjunction "and" and the position (in the Greek) of the verb "judge" favor the continuation of the interrogative form. And to this last we incline, with Olshausen, Lachmann, Ewald, etc. In what sense the **uncircumcision which is by nature** ["he who remains in his natural state of uncircumcision" (Alford)] **shall judge** the circumcised transgressor, is explained by such passages as Matt. 12: 41, 42; Heb. 11: 7. [Thus, "not only shall the Gentile take the place of the Jew, but shall condemn him." (Jowett.) "Those whom thou judgest shall in turn judge thee at the day of judgment, ver. 16." (Bengel.) "We pity the Gentiles," says Doddridge, "and we have reason to do it, for they are lamentably blind and dissolute; but let us take heed lest those appearances of virtue which are to be found among some of them condemn us who, with the letter of the law and the gospel and with the solemn tokens of a covenant relation to God, transgress his precepts and violate our engagements to him, so turning the means of goodness and happiness into the occasion of more aggravated guilt and misery." Will not the virtues of many unconverted men and non-professing Christians, and of many Christians whom we call unevangelical, condemn

if it fulfil the law, judge thee, who by the letter and circumcision dost transgress the law?

28 For he is not a Jew, which is one outwardly; neither *is that* circumcision, which is outward in the flesh:

29 But he *is* a Jew, which is one inwardly; and circumcision *is that* of the heart, in the spirit, *and* not in the letter; whose praise *is* not of men, but of God.

it fulfil the law, judge thee, who with the letter and
28 circumcision art a transgressor of the law? For he is not a Jew, who is one outwardly; neither is that
29 circumcision, which is outward in the flesh: but he is a Jew, who is one inwardly; and circumcision is that of the heart, in the spirit, not in the letter; whose praise is not of men, but of God.

---

some of us who, as being dead to sin, self, and the world, have been buried with Christ by baptism into death? "The unbaptized believer shall condemn the baptized unbeliever." Outward baptism is profitable, and it is a duty, but avails nothing without true repentance, and faith in the Lord Jesus Christ. To regard, as many do, the external ordinance as regenerating and saving, is to look for salvation in "works of righteousness which we have done." Peter himself denies that *outward* baptism "saves."] **By the letter and circumcision.** If we substitute *through*[1] for 'by,' the meaning will be more readily explained. It was not *by means of* the letter and circumcision that the Jew transgressed the law; but these are regarded as obstacles, or restraints, *through* which, as through a *hedge* by which God had graciously surrounded him, he *broke*, in his obstinate propensity to sin. *With* the letter and circumcision, *in spite of* the letter and circumcision, he transgresses the law. "None need be anxious," says Calvin, "about the worshipers to whom Paul here alludes (in the former part of this verse), for it is impossible to find them." [The apostle, in ver. 14, makes a like supposition in regard to the Gentiles as here in regard to the "uncircumcision." Only here the thing supposed is for the time conceived to be a fact, otherwise the article (ἡ) after uncircumcision would at least not be wanting. So Alford: "*Fulfilling* (as it does, as we have supposed) *the law*." Of course, the natural uncircumcision who had not the law of Moses could not literally keep its ordinances, and it required some courage on the part of Paul to make this affirmation, or supposition, rather, in the presence, as it were, of an opposing "Jew." Their obedience to the law could manifestly be only virtual and relative. As Meyer says: This observance of the Mosaic legal precepts or ordinances, "in *point of fact*, takes place when the Gentile obeys the moral law of nature." Godet,

however, and Philippi, in part, hold that the "uncircumcision" who "fulfill the law" are converted, though uncircumcised, Gentile Christians. But there are no persons who absolutely fulfill the law, least of all the "uncircumcision *which is by nature*." Such uncircumcision as this, which, moreover, is destitute of the "letter" of the law, cannot refer to Christian believers, nor even to "those fearing God," the uncircumcised, yet, half-Judaized Gentiles, the proselytes of the gate. Acts 10 : 2, 22; 13 : 16, 26.]

28, 29. For he is not a Jew, etc. The expression here is very elliptical, but the sense is very plain. [Dr. Schaff thus fills out the ellipses, substantially in the manner of De Wette: for not the outward (Jew) is a (true) Jew, neither is the outward fleshly (circumcision) a (true) circumcision, but the inward Jew (is a Jew) and circumcision of the heart, etc. (is circumcision). Meyer gives the last part thus: "But he is a Jew, who is so in secret and circumcision of the heart (is) in the spirit, not in the letter." As *circumcision* is without the article, some give this rendering: "and there is a circumcision of the heart," etc. In this passage, however, the Common Version, as Dr. Schaff says, "can scarcely be improved." In Phil. 3 : 3 Paul says: We are the (true) circumcision who serve (or worship) by the Spirit of God, and glory in Christ Jesus, and have no confidence in the flesh. What a debt of gratitude we owe to Paul under God for a gospel of liberty!] The existence and importance of a spiritual element in the Old Testament Dispensation is strongly emphasized, first in a negative form (ver. 28), and secondly in a positive form (ver. 29). See similar contrasts between the spirit and the letter in 7 : 6 and 2 Cor. 3 : 6. **In the spirit.** Some understand by 'spirit' here the spirit of man; others, the Spirit of God. [Meyer, Philippi, Godet, Hodge: 'in' meaning *by the Holy Spirit*.] The passages above cited seem to favor the

---

[1] διά with the genitive properly means *through,* and here "denotes the attendant circumstances." (Boise.)—F.)

CHAPTER III.

WHAT advantage then hath the Jew? or what profit *is there* of circumcision?

2 Much every way: chiefly because that unto them were committed the oracles of God.

1 What advantage then hath the Jew? **or what is** 2 the profit of circumcision? Much every way: **first** of all, that they were intrusted with the oracles of

---

reference to 'spirit' in the *abstract*, as distinguished from *letter*, to the *idea*, as distinguished from the form. [*In spirit* here seems properly antithetical to *in flesh* of ver. 28.] Spiritual circumcision [or circumcision of the heart] is often referred to in the Old Testament. See Lev. 26: 41; Deut. 10: 16; 30: 6; Jer. 4: 4; 9: 26; Ezek. 44: 9. Compare Acts 7: 51; Phil. 3: 3; Col. 2: 11. **Whose praise,** etc. The relative pronoun is here of uncertain gender. It is probably masculine, referring to the word *Jew* [so most commentators]; but so far as the form is concerned, it might be neuter, referring to the whole preceding sentence. So Meyer understands it. But the word 'praise' favors the more limited and *personal* reference. [The Jew sought outward praise, the approval of men. (John 5: 44; 12: 43.) God, who seeth in secret, alone can clearly recognize the inward circumcision, and his praise, compared with that of man, is above all price. The word 'praise' may have some reference to the meaning of "Jew," the *praised* one. "The Jew who is one inwardly, he is the Jew who has praise—*i. e.*, this is true Judaism." (Bengel.) Godet refers to the "remarkable parallelism" existing between this whole passage and the declaration of Jesus, Matt. 8: 11, 12: "Many shall come from the east and the west . . . but the sons of the kingdom," etc.] This passage suggests a serious admonition to those who are only nominally Christians, but strangers to the spiritual life. If mere external conformity and use of ordinances did not suffice to constitute a true Israelite, how much less does mere profession—the strictest observance of ceremonial and the liveliest zeal for orthodoxy—suffice to constitute a true Christian. It is just the essential thing which they lack.

Ch. 3: [In Chapter I is demonstrated the sinfulness of the Gentiles, and in Chapter II the similarly sinful state of the Jews. This third chapter shows that alike to Gentiles and to Jews, both being under condemnation.

notwithstanding the external advantages of the latter, there is but one method of justification—namely, that which is through faith in Jesus Christ set forth as a sacrifice for sin. We may give as the more important theme of this chapter: The only possible justification for mankind, sinful and condemned, is by grace through faith in Christ Jesus.] The preceding views (chapter 2) would naturally meet with objections in the mind of the Jew. The sum of these objections is comprehended in the inquiries of the first verse. What advantage has the Jew above the Gentile? What profit is there in circumcision? The objections are such as a Jew would naturally raise; but they are to be conceived as raised by the apostle himself, and not as if in actual dialogue with a Jewish objector.

1. What advantage then. [Literally: "*What, then* (under this condition of things), *is the advantage of the Jew*"—namely, above that of the Gentile? Ellicott characterizes 'then' (or *therefore*, οὖν) as "collective and retrospective."][1] Here are two questions; but the difference is more in form than in substance. All would be expressed in this: "What advantage has the circumcised Jew above the uncircumcised Gentile?" What the apostle has been saying in chapter 2, especially in ver. 25-29, obviously suggests this inquiry. He seems to have placed Gentile and Jew substantially on the same level before God, a view very offensive to Jewish pride. "If true Judaism and true circumcision be merely spiritual, what is the profit of external Judaism and ceremonial circumcision?" (Alford.)

2. Much every way: chiefly, because that unto them were committed the oracles of God. We have here the apostle's answer to the objection raised by the inquiries of the first verse. In strictness of construction, the answer is adjusted to the *first* form of the question only, for the word 'much' agrees in gender with the word 'advantage' and not with the word 'profit,' and very properly, as

---

[1] Crosby—in his Greek Grammar, ? 328—derives οὖν, from ᵉον, a dialectic form of ὤν, the present participle of the verb *to be*. meaning: it being so.—{S.}

this is the main question. There were many advantages, the apostle answers, or, more exactly, there was *much advantage in every respect;* but the chief advantage of all was the possession of 'the oracles of God,' the written law. Some of the other advantages are enumerated in 2 : 17–20, and in 9 : 4, 5; but in both these enumerations 'the oracles of God' under the name of "the law" have a prominent place. Compare also Ps. 147 : 19, 20. Notice how emphatically the apostle here affirms the divine inspiration of the Old Testament. [The word 'chiefly' doubtless expresses the idea of the apostle, though his words, *first of all* (Revised Version), naturally indicate a *secondly,* which, however, as in 1 : 8, is omitted. The usual explanation of this omission is that the apostle loses the grammatical sequence of thought by dwelling so long on the first member (Buttmann, 365); but see notes on 1 : 8. Godet thinks the preceding words, 'every way,' suggest this idea: "I might mention many things under this head, but I shall confine myself to one, which is in the front rank;" and adds : "This form of expression, far from indicating that he purposes to mention others, shows, on the contrary, why he will not mention them. They all flow from that which he proceeds to indicate." Perhaps this asseveration of the apostle is slightly apologetic, as going to show that he does not disparage the written law of Jehovah.] The words 'unto them' are not found in the original; they *seem* to be necessary, only because the translators misunderstood the construction of the verb, which they rendered 'were committed.' The translation should be : "They *were entrusted with* the oracles of God." The verb is passive in form, and when it is derived from the active sense "to believe," as it is in 2 Thess. 1 : 10 and 1 Tim. 3 : 16, it is passive in sense; but in the more common case, in which it is derived from the active sense "to entrust" [something to some one], it is invariably followed by the accusative of the object entrusted. An examination of the original in the following passages, the only places besides the one under examination where the passive form is found, makes this conclusion very plain : 1 Cor. 9 : 17; Gal. 2 : 7; 1 Thess. 2 : 4; 1 Tim. 1 : 11; Titus 1 : 3.[1] All the older versions led the way in this misconstruction of the verb. 'The oracles (λόγια) of God.'[2] The same word is applied to the Old Testament Scriptures in Acts 7 : 38; Heb. 5 : 12: 1 Peter 4 : 11. It is a great 'advantage' to possess the Holy Scriptures. It was so to those who had only the Old Testament; how much more to those who have both the Old Testament and the New. Yet how many neglect to improve this chief advantage which they have over the heathen. The Lord has himself here decided the important question, whether or not it is a blessing for the heathen to have the Scriptures and the knowledge of the way of salvation. True, those who reject the offer of salvation, and prefer darkness rather than light, will meet a much severer doom than if they had remained in ignorance; and these are usually the majority. Still, the possession of the gospel, the having of the opportunity to be saved, is a priceless benefit. So God regards the matter, and he here shows that he so regards it. He virtually shows that he so regards it by commanding us to make known the gospel to every creature; but he expressly declares that he so judges by pronouncing the possession of the Scriptures the chief advantage of the Jew over the Gentile. This text ought to silence forever the objection to missionary enterprise, so often advanced, that we do but increase the final condemnation of the heathen, in the majority of cases, by sending them the gospel. Indeed, this way of reasoning, if it were fairly applied, would prove quite too much; it would arrest the progress of evangelization altogether, at home and abroad. It would forbid us to make known the gospel to our countrymen, our neighbors, our own children, even,

---

[1] See further in Winer, pp. 229, 260. Buttmann (pp. 152, 189) makes this to be akin to the so-called Greek accusative, or accusative of limitation. Compare Heb. 2 : 17 : "Faithful (as to, in) things pertaining to God."—(F.)

[2] The word, while embracing all the sacred writings of the Old Covenant, may have special reference in this place to the prophetic statements or promises concerning the Messiah which are found in the Old Testament. The form of the word is thought by Bengel and Philippi to be a diminutive, having thus a reference to oracular brevity. According to Meyer, λογίδια would be the diminutive form. "λόγιον is used both in classical and Hellenistic Greek, chiefly of utterances of the Deity."—Philippi.—(F.)

3 For what if some did not believe? shall their unbelief make the faith of God without effect?
4 God forbid: yea, let God be true, but every man a
liar; as it is written, That thou mightest be justified

3 God. For what if some were without faith? shall
their want of faith make of none effect the faithful-
4 ness of God? [1] God forbid: yea, let God be found
true, but every man a liar; as it is written.

1 Gr. *Be it not so:* and so elsewhere.

lest we should only aggravate their final condemnation.[1]

3. For what if some did not believe?
A second objection is here presented. The
resemblance of the three principal words in
this verse is partially lost in the translation.
Alford [following De Wette] preserves it in
this way : " For what if some were unfaithful
[to the covenant], shall their unfaithfulnes
nullify the faithfulness of God?" [Dr. Hodge
puts this language in the mouth of a Jew,
relying for security on his covenant relation
to Abraham : " ' What if we were unfaithful,'
says the Jew, 'does that invalidate the faithfulness of God? Has he not promised to be a
God to Abraham and his seed?'" But this
does not well suit the connection. The disobedience, or rather disbelief, doubtless has
reference to these inestimable 'oracles,' which,
as being God's word, will not fail of fulfillment. Meyer and Godet think Paul has here
in mind the disbelief of the Jews in the Messiahship of Jesus: others make their unbelief
relate to their pre-Christian history.] The
case is mildly stated in the first clause:
'What if *some* did not believe?' It might
have been put more strongly, as it is by Isaiah
(53:1), and by the author of the Epistle to the
Hebrews (3:16). I think this verse from Hebrews should be translated: " For *who* having
heard, did provoke? But did not all those
who came out of Egypt by Moses?"[2] But
we may suppose that Paul purposely avoided,
as a Jewish objector would be likely to do,
stating the case in its full severity. [Yet
" many are only some when they are not the
whole." Compare 11 : 17.] The substance of
the objection here brought forward is : " Will
God fail to fulfill his promises because men

fail to fulfill their engagements?" [Some
separate the first two words from the rest and
render them : " For what?" or, " What then?
If some did not believe," etc. There is a
difference of idea between unbelieving and
unfaithful or untrue. Meyer and Philippi
take the words here in the sense of belief or
unbelief, denying that the word for unbelief
ever signifies unfaithfulness in the New Testament. The sense of the passage would then
be: 'Shall their unbelief destroy the trustworthiness or truthfulness of God so that he
should not keep his promises?' This rendering seems to accord best with the Pauline
use of the word faith or belief. Others would
give this translation as most appropriate:
'Shall their unfaithfulness nullify the faithfulness of God?' and adduce in support of
their view such passages as 2 Tim. 2 : 13;
Luke 12 : 46; Rev. 21 : 8.]

4. God forbid. This expression, which
occurs thirteen times in Paul's epistles and
only once elsewhere in the New Testament
(Luke 20:16), does not contain the name of God
in the original, but means simply " Let it not
be" [or, as the apostle uses it, something like:
Perish the thought! Dr. Riggs, however,
in his "Suggested Modifications of the Revised Version," thinks the phrase "by no
means" would be an adequate rendering.]
It were better to adhere to the above stricter
translation, or to render it, as the revisers of
the Bible Union and some others [Noyes]
have done, "far be it." Here, too, our translators followed all their English predecessors.
[**Let God be** (regarded as) **true.** God is
'true' (ἀληθής = *verax*) because he cannot lie :
he is 'true' (ἀληθινός = *verus*) as opposed to
false Gods or idols. This 'true' (compare

[1] We can imagine that Paul, under circumstances
like those in which many of our modern missionaries
have been placed, would have felt it to be a part of his
apostolic or missionary duty to set up schools, instruct
the people, translate the Bible, superintend its printing,
distribution, etc., so that all the people might possess
and be able to read the inestimable ' oracles of God.' But
how different his situation from that of many of our
missionaries! He had no new language to learn, much
less had he any to create or put into written form.
With the knowledge of Hebrew and Greek, he could

preach understandingly in almost every part of the
then known world. The people to whom he preached
were not simple-minded or infantile in understanding,
but were the most highly educated and cultured.—(F.)

[2] We may here remark concerning this translation
that τίνες, if its second letter have the acute accent, is
an interrogative pronoun ; if it is otherwise accented,
or stands as an enclitic without any accent, it is the
simple indefinite pronoun, as above. Compare the
τινὶ of 1 : 13 with τίνα of 6 : 21.—(F.)

in thy sayings, and mightest overcome when thou art judged.
5 But if our unrighteousness commend the righteousness of God, what shall we say? *Is* God unrighteous who taketh vengeance? (I speak as a man.)
6 God forbid: for then how shall God judge the world?

That thou mightest be justified in thy words, And mightest prevail when thou comest into judgment.
5 But if our unrighteousness commendeth the righteousness of God, what shall we say? Is God unrighteous who visiteth with wrath? (I speak after
6 the manner of men.) God forbid: for then how
7 shall God judge the world? ¹But if the truth of

¹ Many ancient authorities read *for*.

"God who cannot lie," Titus 1: 2) favors the interpretation *truthful* or *trustworthy* of the last verse.] The apostle indignantly repels the supposition that God should be untrue; sooner let that be admitted which David said in his haste: "All men are liars." (Ps. 116 : 11.) [Though it is doubtful whether Paul had this Psalm expressly in mind, since he proceeds immediately to quote from another.] And he very appropriately quotes the words in which David confesses himself a sinner, and ascribes righteousness and truth to God. (Ps. 51 : 4.) **That thou mightest overcome when thou art judged.** [*In order that thou mayest*, etc.]¹ The language 'That thou mightest overcome,' etc., seems to be borrowed from legal matters—at least it is such as is commonly used in such cases. [The translation of Noyes is as follows: "That thou mayest be justified in thy words and mayest overcome when thou art arraigned." This is an exactly literal quotation from the LXX, which, as Meyer concedes, "does not yield any essential difference of sense from the idea of the original text." If the last verb should be rendered—as by Meyer, Ewald, Philippi, and the Revised Version—actively, "when thou judgest," it would correspond more nearly to the Hebrew original.]

5. A third objection, arising from the way in which the previous one was answered. [Especial reference seems here to be had to the latter part of the preceding verse, where it is implied that God can turn man's sinful act to his own glory, the exhibition of his righteousness.] So far from God's taking

advantage of man's unfaithfulness to fail in fulfilling his promises, his veracity appears the more conspicuous in contrast with man's unfaithfulness. Compare the terms 'unrighteousness' and 'righteousness' in this verse with the unfaithfulness and faithfulness [or unbelief and trustworthiness] of ver. 3. If, then [as is actually the case], our unrighteousness thus commends [or sets forth] by contrast the righteousness of God, shall we say that God is unrighteous in taking [more literally, *who brings upon* us] vengeance? that he cannot righteously punish the sin which gives occasion to the fuller exhibition of his righteousness?² **I speak as a man.** *I speak as men are wont to speak.* This clause seems to be inserted apologetically, as if there were a kind of irreverence in the very supposition of any possible unrighteouness in God. Yet men do very often ascribe unrighteousness to God on suppositions that are true; so the apostle may well say: 'I speak as a man.' [De Wette on this phrase says: "I speak as men speak who often inconsiderately judge of God." Bishop Lightfoot notices that this expression is found only in the group of epistles to which this belongs—to wit: Corinthians and Galatians.]

6. God forbid: for then how shall God judge the world?³ The certainty that God *will* judge the world is assumed, as something that the Jewish objector admitted, and so the apostle might legitimately argue that any supposition incompatible with that admitted truth is thereby proved to be false. ["Paul assumes that only the righteous One can judge

¹ Instead of the subjunctive after ὅπως, some MSS. (א A D) have the future indicative, which, like the use of ἄν after ὅπως, occurs but rarely in the New Testament. (Buttmann, 214, 234.)—(F.)

² 'What shall we say,' or infer, occurs seven times in this Epistle (4 : 1; 6 : 1; 7 : 7; 8 : 31; 9 : 14, 30), and is found in none other of Paul's letters. Except in 7 : 31; 9 : 30, it introduces a false conclusion. "The wrath" (as in Revised Version) is that retributive wrath of God already spoken of (1 : 18; 2 : 5, 8). "This question," says Meyer, "is so put that, as in ver. 3, a nega-

tive answer is expected." For the particle (μή), when used as the sign of a question, always supposes an answer in the negative. See 9 : 20; 11 : 1; Winer, p. 511. Some writers think there are occasional exceptions to this rule.—(F.)

³ The normal force of the word here rendered 'for then' may be seen by supplying an ellipsis, thus: Far be it, *since* (in that case) how shall God judge the world? Buttmann (233, yet see 359) renders it by "*for*," simply: "For how shall God judge the world" (if he be unrighteous)?—(F.)

7 For if the truth of God hath more abounded
through my lie unto his glory; why yet am I also
judged as a sinner?
8 And not *rather*, (as we be slanderously reported,

God through my lie abounded unto his glory, why
8 am I also still judged as a sinner? and why not (as
we are slanderously reported, and as some affirm that

the world." (Weiss.) Some, however, regard this as assuming the very thing to be proved, and affirm that it is no more certain that the Judge of the world must be just than that God is just. (Hodge.) But it is a very natural assumption, for, "Shall not the judge of all the earth do right?" It seems likewise to be taken for granted that in God's judgment of the world of sinners there must be the infliction of wrath. The conscience of the transgressor acknowledges his desert of wrath, and even the righteousness of the Heavenly Father in inflicting it. Right reason would concede at once that God, though our Heavenly Father, has a right to visit with wrath where it would be improper for an earthly parent to do so. On this point, some men in their reasonings have made a mistake. In remembering the "fatherhood of God," they have forgotten his rightful and infinite sovereignty. Even Farrar acknowledges that "We may not push the truths of the finite and the temporal into the regions of the infinite and eternal."] The supposition that he could not righteously punish the unrighteousness which commended his righteousness, would be incompatible with his being the Judge of the world, for *all* unrighteousness of man is, or may be, the occasion of showing God's righteousness more conspicuously, and so there would be nothing left for him to judge and punish. The argument from the greater to the less, from the general to the particular, here, is the same in principle as in Matt. 6 : 25, and in 1 Cor. 6 : 2. [Hodge speaks of it as a *reductio ad absurdum*.] "Intellectual difficulties in religion are best met by moral axioms. It may sound plausible to say : 'If man's sin contributes ultimately to God's justification, God cannot justly punish it;' but conscience, ever a safer guide than the intellect, echoes the language of revelation, which declares the coming judgment, and that judgment presupposes that sin can be, and will be, justly punished. The method of Scripture is to state each of two apparently conflicting principles (*e. g.*, God's grace and man's responsibility)

singly and separately, and leave conscience, rather than intellect, to reconcile and adjust them." (Dr. Vaughan.) The expression 'God forbid' is explained under ver. 4.

7. This verse seems to be substantially but a restatement of the objection in ver. 5, but in the statement the *form* is changed in several particulars. The identity of the objection for substance is confirmed by the same introductory phrase in both. **For if.**[1] The differences of *form* are : 1. In ver. 5, first clause, man's unrighteousness is the subject and God's righteousness the object (grammatically speaking) ; while, in ver. 7, God's truth ["in fulfilling his promises" (Boise)] is the subject and man's falsehood the object. 2. In ver. 5, first clause, the *generic* terms, righteousness and unrighteousness, are used ; in ver. 7, the more specific terms, truth and falsehood, are substituted, suggested, doubtless, by ver. 4. 3. In ver. 5, second clause, the question is : Can God justly punish man? In ver. 7, the question is : Can man be justly punished? And this reversing of the difficulty from the divine side, or standpoint, to the human is emphasized by the use of the personal pronoun, **I also.** [The full force of this last clause is something like this : "Why am *even* I who *in my lie* have contributed to God's glory, *still judged* of God as a sinner?" The sinner is ever desirous to justify himself, even though he has to charge God foolishly and wickedly in doing so. "If there is evil in the world, who is responsible for it but God himself? And if my sin is God's glory, why is he angry with me, and why should not I be rewarded rather than punished?" Of course, he is not sincere in this self-defense, for he knows that in his transgression he did not *intend* God's glory.]

8. The answer to this modified form of the third objection is made somewhat obscure by the elliptical character of the verse. Yet the difficulty pertains rather to the precise grammatical construction of the sentence than to the nature of the argument. The insertion of two little words will help to develop the sense:

---

1 "But," rather than 'for,' is the better sustained reading in ver. 7.—(F.) [It seems to me that, according to Tischendorf's eighth edition. 'for' is sustained

by quite as much evidence as "but." Yet the authority, as furnished by manuscripts, versions, and patristic citations, is pretty evenly balanced.—A. H.]

"And why not rather say," etc.? Why not speak out the full thought which lurks in this objection? [In reference to this construction, see Winer, p. 628. Instead of **let us do evil,** etc., introduced as a quotation, and dependent on **we say,** we should naturally have expected a question similar in form to the preceding, the two questions reading thus: Why yet am I also judged as a sinner? And why should not I do evil, etc.? If we supply the word *say,* as some do, the construction becomes quite regular, thus: And why not *say,* as some affirm that we say, 'let us do evil,' etc.? Observe the change from the singular —"I," of ver. 7—to the plural of this verse. The simple outline of the objector's thought seems to be this: "If my unbelief, unrighteousness, untruth, contribute to God's glory, 'why yet am I also judged as a sinner;' and why should I not persevere in doing (what is called) evil that God's glory may be further enhanced; and why should not I be rewarded rather than punished therefor?" **Whose damnation** (*judgment*) **is just** is Paul's only answer to those who hold such abominable doctrine. "Syllogistically stated," says Farrar, "the existence of evil might be held to *demonstrate* either the weakness or cruelty of God, but such syllogisms, without the faintest attempt to answer them, are flung aside as valueless and irrelevant by the faith and conscience of mankind. The mere *statement* of some objections is their most effective refutation. . . . However logically correct, they are so morally repulsive, so spiritually false, that silence is the only answer of which they are worthy." But is it not a little singular that "advanced" objectors of our time will hardly allow the existence of any "evils" in this universe until you suggest to them the existence of an Almighty and all-wise One, who is able to control these evils and to educe good out of them? Yet, apart from the idea of a gracious and all-wise Providence, our ills would be evils indeed and well-nigh unbearable. We need in this world the sustaining thought which alone supported the Saviour: "The cup which *my Father* hath given me, shall I not drink it?"] It is not very strange that those high views of the divine sovereignty, which Paul sets forth in this Epistle,

should be malignantly misrepresented, as he says they were, and as, in fact, they still are. But he puts the brand of his severest reprobation upon the Jesuitical principle: 'Let us do evil, that good may come.' They who profess such a pernicious doctrine, he says [not those who so slander us], are justly condemned, whose condemnation, judgment [perhaps referring to their being 'judged as sinners '], is just.

Notice the different ways in which these three objections are answered. The first (verses 1, 2) by a direct and specific assertion; the second (verses 3, 4) by an indignant repudiation of the objector's inference (a more specific reply being reserved to 9: 6-13); the third (verses 5-8) by showing that the principle of the objection is at variance with admitted truth, and shocking to the moral sense, and so refutes itself. The review of these verses suggests several reflections: 1. It is legitimate to argue from our intuitive moral perceptions. 2. The doctrine which never provokes from perverse men such objections as these must be different from the doctrine which Paul preached. 3. The habit of objecting against the principles of the divine government, and the doctrines of the divine word, is no new thing. Christians need not be surprised nor perplexed when they meet with such objections. Most of the objections are only old ones revived—the very same in substance that the first promulgators of Christianity had to encounter. If they could meet them calmly and confidently, how little ought they to disturb us! 4. The way in which the apostle meets these objections may afford us instruction. There are three fundamental truths against which objections and cavils, however plausible, are not entitled to any weight. These are, (*a*) God's truth and righteousness; come what will, these are never to be questioned. (*b*) The future judgment; this is one of the surest doctrines of revelation, and one which meets an answering echo in the conscience of man. (*c*) The essential quality of moral actions; any doctrine or sentiment that shocks our fundamental moral perceptions must be rejected at once as coming from the father of lies.[1] [It will doubtless be urged by the objectors to the

---

[1] The "Memoirs and Confessions of Reinhard" (born 1753, died 1812, court preacher at Dresden from 1792) records an interesting illustration of the efficacy of settled moral principles in giving the mind a firm

and as some affirm that we say,) Let us do evil, that good may come? whose damnation is just.

9 What then? are we better *than they*? No, in no

we say), Let us do evil, that good may come? whose condemnation is just.

9 What then? are we better than they? No, in no

doctrine of "eternal punishment," that it perfectly "shocks" their moral sense, and that, therefore, there can never be in this universe of a God of love anything so utterly shocking as an individual suffering consciously to all eternity, even though this suffering be mental and in consequence of personal transgressions. We freely confess that the idea of an eternity of suffering is shocking to our natural feelings, and so is the bodily and mental anguish which men suffer in this world. We could not for an instant endure the sight of the collective amount of suffering which exists every moment in the earth. "Syllogistically stated," as Farrar says, "the existence of evil might be held to *demonstrate* either the weakness or the cruelty of God," that is, when regard is had to but one set of facts. From one point of view, no man living can explain a solitary groan, a single tear, in all this universe of God. And in a universe of chance neither this nor anything else can be explained. Still, all reflecting persons, with scarcely an exception, unite in declaring that God is good, though it is through his arrangement of causes and means and under his permission, that all this earthly suffering takes place. Nor would they perhaps be shocked at the idea of God's permitting a man to live forever on the earth, sinning and suffering in the manner he does now. So also an apostle, while not ignorant certainly of the pain and wretchedness experienced in this world of sin and death—a world which our limited wisdom and goodness would not care to create nor will to exist —could yet unhesitatingly affirm that "God is love!" Truly there is, notwithstanding such an inconceivable amount of human misery, abundant evidence of the goodness of

God, and hence the idea of such a degree of suffering in this world of sin, where yet God's power and providence have absolute control, and can also educe good out of evil, does not "shock our fundamental moral conceptions." Why may we not, during the eternity that is before us, cherish these same views of the goodness of God, and of his moral government, even though sin should be allowed to exist forever and as "eternal sin" (Mark 3: 29, Revised Version) to be eternally punished? Certainly our merciful Saviour could not have spoken of "eternal punishment" in the way he did—in contrast with "eternal life"— unless those words of fearful import were true. But it is in view of such teachings as these that, as in the apostle's time so nowadays, men who do not realize that it is not for "such poor creatures as we" fully to understand all parts of an "infinite scheme" (Butler), are disposed to charge God with unrighteousness.]

Having answered these objections, the apostle now returns to the point where he left off at the end of chapter 2. The Jews have great privileges and outward advantages; but in regard to justification before God, they stand on the same footing with the Gentiles.

9. What then? What is the result of the foregoing discussion? **Are we better than they?** That is, "we Jews, than they Gentiles?" "He addresses the Jews in the third person, when he claims a pre-eminence for them (verse 1), but joins himself with them in the first person now, in denying their superior merit." (Calvin.) The verb translated, "are we better?" is variously explained. It does not occur elsewhere in the New Testament. Literally, it would be translated, *do we hold ourselves before?* Probably

anchor, when assailed by a tempest of doubts and questionings. He was professor of both philosophy and theology in the University of Wittemberg, and required to lecture in both sciences, at a time when his own views were very unsettled. The striking of the clock which called him to the lecture room often found him walking his chamber with tears, engaged in earnest prayer to God, that he would not suffer him to say anything detrimental to religion and morality. Of his state of mind at this time he thus writes: "Notwithstanding the uncertainty, however, in which all my knowledge, even that which I had considered as rest-

ing upon a solid basis, was about this time involved, two principles remained by me unshaken: *first*, never to permit myself to indulge in any explanation in philosophy which did violence to my moral feelings; and *second*, never to assert anything in theology which was at variance with the obvious declarations of the Bible." Letter 7, p. 49. This little book, consisting of letters to a friend, giving an account of his education, was translated by Oliver A. Taylor, Resident Licentiate at Andover, Mass., and published in Boston, in 1832. It is an admirable help to students in theology. I fear it is now out of print.

wise: for we have before proved both Jews and Gentiles, that they are all under sin;
10 As it is written, There is none righteous, no, not one:
11 There is none that understandeth, there is none that seeketh after God.
12 They are all gone out of the way, they are together become unprofitable; there is none that doeth good, no, not one.

wise: for we before laid to the charge both of
10 Jews and Greeks, that they are all under sin; as it is written,
There is none righteous, no, not one;
11 There is none that understandeth,
There is none that seeketh after God;
12 They have all turned aside, they are together become unprofitable;
There is none that doeth good, no, not so much as one:

the meaning is, "have we any excuse?"—anything to hold before ourselves as a pretext? [So Meyer. The 'what,' however, cannot be joined to the verb, as this would require *nothing* (οὐδέν), instead of *no*, for an answer. The Canterbury Revision has this rendering: "are we in worse case than they?" and in the margin: "do we have any advantage?" or, "do we excel?" Godet renders it: "are we sheltered?" Beet: "are we shielding ourselves?" The verb here "clearly cannot be passive," according to Winer, though elsewhere in this form it is generally so used. It occurs only here in the New Testament.] The words 'than they' are not in the original; and if we have rightly apprehended the meaning of the verb, they are not needed. **No, in no wise.** [Literally—*not entirely.* Instead of this order of words we should have expected the reverse, as in 1 Cor. 16: 12. For the position of the negative here, which some regard as misplaced, see Winer, 554. "The Jew would say: *altogether*, but Paul contradicts him." (Bengel.) Morison, as quoted by Godet, thinks it enough to make a pause after *not* in reading, thus: *no, absolutely,* or *no, certainly.* Winer also remarks that "a half comma [after *not*] would at once remove all ambiguity." He supposes that the meaning "was probably indicated by the mode of utterance." Buttmann (pp. 381, 121) thinks that, according to New Testament usage, the position of the negative with the word meaning *every* or *all* (πᾶς) is oftentimes a matter of indifference.] The apostle answers the question here in just the opposite way to his answer of the question in verse 1. *There*, it was a question of comparative privileges and opportunities, in which the Jew had great advantages over the Gentile; *here*, it is a question of comparative standing before God in respect to justification, and in this the Jew had no advantage at all. **For we have before proved both Jews and**

Gentiles. ['For' confirms the preceding negation. The word 'proved' seems to have the force of a legal indictment: we have previously accused or charged Jews as well as Greeks as being all under sin, and we regard the accusation as good as proved. By the use of 'we,' he perhaps associates Christian believers with himself in this judgment, though it may be simply the plural of authorship. As in 1: 6; 2: 9, 10, so here, the apostle mentions the Jew before the Greek.] He had proved this in respect to the Gentiles in 1: 18–32; and in respect to the Jews in chapter 2. **Under sin** signifies to be under its power, and consequently liable to its penalty.[1] This charge, which he has already proved by describing their character and actions in his own words, he now proceeds to confirm by citing the words of the Old Testament.

10-18. ["The passages quoted describe the moral corruption of the times of David and the prophets, but indirectly of all times, since human nature is essentially the same always and everywhere." (Schaff.) "That complaint (of David and Isaiah) describes men as God looking down from heaven finds them, not as his grace makes them." (Bengel.)] The words immediately following **as it is written,** to the end of ver. 10, seem to be an epitome, in the apostle's own words, of the substance of what follows. The remainder to the end of ver. 18 is quoted almost literally, according to the Septuagint, from various places in the Psalms, and the prophecies of Isaiah. [Ver. 10-12 from Ps. 14: 1-3; ver. 13 from Ps. 5: 9; 140: 3; ver. 14 from Ps. 10: 7; ver. 15-17 from Isa. 59: 7, 8; ver. 18 from Ps. 36: 1. **There is none that understandeth,** etc.—literally, *he that understandeth is not* (or, *does not exist*). **There is none that seeketh after God,** etc. **There is none righteous,** etc. In the same Psalm (14), from which apparently this is quoted, **we**

---

[1] See the expressions: under law, under a curse, under grace, etc. All these nouns are in the accusative case, the dative after ὑπό, which would here seem to be quite as appropriate, not occurring in the New Testament.—(F.)

13 Their throat *is* an open sepulchre; with their tongues they have used deceit; the poison of asps *is* under their lips:
14 Whose mouth *is* full of cursing and bitterness:
15 Their feet *are* swift to shed blood:
16 Destruction and misery *are* in their ways:
17 And the way of peace have they not known:
18 There is no fear of God before their eyes.
19 Now we know that what things soever the law

13 Their throat is an open sepulchre:
    With their tongues they have used deceit:
    The poison of asps is under their lips:
14 Whose mouth is full of cursing and bitterness:
15 Their feet are swift to shed blood;
16 Destruction and misery are in their ways:
17 And the way of peace have they not known:
18 There is no fear of God before their eyes.
19 Now we know that what things soever the law

read of the generation of the *righteous*, and of the poor whose refuge is Jehovah. Yet there is no real inconsistency in these diverse representations. "In the deep inner sense which St. Paul gives to the passage, 'the generation of the righteous' would be the first to acknowledge that they form no exception to the universal sinfulness asserted in the opening verses of the Psalm." ("Bible Commentary.")] **Their throat is an open** sepulchre. [This thirteenth verse agrees wholly with the Septuagint.] Some understand the first clause as referring to the *insatiable destructiveness* of the *grave ;* ["It is death to some one whenever they open their mouths." (Grimm)]; others as representing the *nauseous* and *poisonous odor* that issues from a newly-opened sepulchre. The latter reference agrees better with the participle *opened*, and gives a sense more distinct from what follows in ver. 15-17. Calumny is a pestiferous vice. [Meyer finds the comparison in the point that "when the godless have opened their throats for lying and corrupting discourse, it is just as if a grave stood opened (observe the perfect) to which the corpse ought to be consigned for decay and destruction. So certainly and unavoidably corrupting is their discourse." It requires, as it would seem, more than one verse to describe the sins of throat, tongue, lips, and mouth. How much misery they bring to the world when they are under the dominion of sin! A hasty word ; how easily it is spoken even by a Christian believer! Yet how it grieves the Holy Spirit, and how it grieves his own spirit, and perchance the spirit of a fellow mortal, a fellow Christian.

Oh! many a shaft at random sent,
Finds mark the archer little meant.]

With their tongues they have used deceit. [Habitually used it (imperfect tense) ; and we may still exclaim: O thou deceitful tongue!] **The poison of asps is under their lips.** [In the expression (Ps. 10: 7) "under his tongue is mischief" most inter-

preters, according to Hengstenberg, take the metaphor "from the poison of serpents which is concealed under the teeth [in upper lip], and from thence is pressed out as mentioned in Ps. 140: 3, 'Adder's poison is under their lips.'"] "Behind the cunning of falsehood there is deadly malice." (Lange.) **Their feet are swift to shed blood.** They commit murder on the slightest provocation. **Destruction** [literally, *a breaking together* or *crushing*] **and misery are in their ways.** They spread destruction and misery in their ways, wherever they go. **And the way of peace have they not known.** They know not [nor wish to know] how to live peacefully, [or walk in the way of peace, "the way that leads to peace." (Schaff.)] The way of peace is one of happiness and safety, free from the 'destruction and misery' of the sinner's 'ways.' **No fear of God.** This corresponds with the 'no seeking after God' in ver. 11. How refreshing by way of contrast to think of one saying: "Whom have I in heaven but thee, and there is none upon earth that I desire beside thee!" This dark catalogue of divine testimonies to human depravity is not without orderly arrangement. Ver. 10-12 emphatically affirm the *universality* of human sinfulness ; ver. 13, 14, relate to sins of the *tongue ;* ver. 15-17, to sins in action, especially sins of *violence ;* ver. 18 assigns the inward sinful cause of all these vicious habits. They are traceable to the absence of pious reverence for God. Notice how this agrees with the representation in 1: 24-31.

19. Now we know. It is self-evident to all, it agrees with common sense. [The verb is literally *have seen*, but, used as in the present tense, signifies to know.] **The law**—that is, the Jewish law, not in a restricted sense (for these quotations are not from the Pentateuch, but from the Psalms and prophets), but in a broad sense equivalent to the Old Testament Scriptures. In this broad sense 'the law' is often used. See John 10: 34; 12: 34; 15: 25; 1 Cor. 14: 21, etc. [It is generally supposed that the Scriptures took thus the

saith, it saith to them who are under the law: that every mouth may be stopped, and all the world may become guilty before God.

20 Therefore by the deeds of the law there shall no flesh be justified in his sight: for by the law *is* the knowledge of sin.

saith, it speaketh to them that are under the law; that every mouth may be stopped, and all the world

20 may be brought under the judgment of God: because [1]by [2]the works of the law shall no flesh be [3]justified in his sight: for [4]through the law *cometh* the knowledge of sin.

1 Gr. *out of.*......2 Or, *works of law*......3 Or, *accounted righteous*......4 Or, *through law.*

name *law* from this, their more important part. Besides, the entire Scriptures, as Hengstenberg remarks, have a normal, or regulative character. The reference to the law here is apparently for the purpose of showing to the Jews that they, as well as the Gentiles, are under sin. "How this solemnly emphatic 'whatsoever' heaps upon the Jews the divine sentence of 'guilty,' and cuts off from them every refuge, as if this or that declaration did not apply to, or concern them!" (Meyer.)] **It saith to them who are under the law.** *It speaks* would be more exact. The two verbs [λέγειν and λαλεῖν, see λαλιά, Matt. 26: 73], "to say" and "to speak," are generally distinguished in translation, and should be always. Whatever the law *says*, it is *speaking* [*utters* its voice] to them who are under the law; *they* are certainly and most directly addressed, though not always *exclusively*. *In the law* would be a more literal translation: *in* it as their sphere of life. [Compare 2: 12.] **That every mouth may be stopped.** Compare this clause with ver. 9. [For the figure of stopping one's mouth, here, literally: *that every mouth may be hedged*, see Job 5: 16; Ps. 107: 42.] The conclusion seems, to a superficial view, broader than the premises; for the *immediate* context relates to the *Jews* alone. But the argument holds good; for the case of the Gentiles, before shown to be guilty, is now taken in, agreeably to what is said in ver. 9; and so **all the world becomes guilty before God.**] *May become accountable to God.* (Gifford.) The word "guilty," or "subject to the judgment of God," as in the marginal reading of the Common Version, occurs only here. Sin and redemption alike put us all on a level before God.]

20. Therefore by deeds of the law there shall no flesh be justified in his sight. *Because* would be the more exact translation of the first word.[1] The apostle regards the more general conclusion arrived at here as necessitating what he had said in ver. 19

['that every mouth may be stopped,' etc.] not, as 'therefore' would imply, as a *conclusion* from that verse. Not by the deeds of the Jewish law, but *by works of law*, in the broadest sense—broad enough to cover the conclusion, **all the world.** For an explanation of the meaning of the verb, to be justified, see the notes on 1: 17. [Paul's language here is similar to that in Ps. 143: 2: "Enter not into judgment with thy servant, for in thy sight shall no *man* living be justified." The apostle adds, '*by the deeds of the law*,' and substitutes for *living* the word 'flesh,' as denoting men in their weakness and sin. The same assertion is found in Gal. 2: 16. On the import of the term 'justified,' Dr. Hodge thus remarks: "It would be utterly unmeaning to say that 'no flesh shall be *pardoned* by the works of the law,' or that 'no man shall be sanctified by the deeds of the law.'" The construction is Hebraistic, the literal rendering being, 'not shall be justified every flesh.' By this idiom, non-justification is predicated of every, or all flesh; or, as we should say, no flesh or no man will be justified. In our idiom, the idea implied would be that some flesh, or some men, would be justified by legal works. The 'deeds (or *works*) of the law,' have no reference to the ceremonial, as distinguished from the moral law; for the Scriptures make no sharp distinction of this kind—such distinction being what may be termed an "afterthought of theology." Besides, these *works* here are used in contrast, not with other works, but with *faith*. It refers rather to the moral law; for the apostle immediately adds that **by the law is the knowledge of sin.** And in 7: 7 he avers that he "had not known sin except through the law" (Revised Version); "had not known coveting, except the (moral) law—the tenth commandment—had said, Thou shalt not covet." But do these works of law embrace in this connection what are elsewhere styled good works, and excellent works

---

1 "διότι occurs twenty-two times in the New Testament, and is everywhere causal, unless we give it an illative meaning here."—Boise.—(F.)

(ἔργα ἀγαθά, καλά, 2: 7; 2 Cor. 9: 8; Eph. 2: 10; Col. 1: 10; Titus 2: 7, 14; 3: 8, 14), or "works of grace"? The law, indeed, does not produce these good works; but are they not such as the law requires? If 'works of law' are taken in this last sense, then it would follow that we cannot be justified even by, on account of, our good works. And this is the invariable teaching of the Scriptures. Nowhere is it said that we are justified and saved on the ground of works, or of faith even, but we are justified gratuitously, by grace, through faith, through Christ, and in his blood. A salvation which is gratuitous, and by grace is not a salvation on the ground of works, whether 'works of law,' or 'works' generally, or 'works of righteousness'; and so it excludes all "boasting." (3: 24, 27, 28; 11: 6; Eph. 2: 8, 9; 2 Tim. 1: 9; Titus 3: 5, 7.) The Christian's "good works" are poor and imperfect, his tears of penitence, even, leaving a stain. They will not stand the test of the judgment for a moment. They all need washing in atoning blood. We therefore adopt the view which Philippi, in a lengthy discussion, advocates, in the third (not the first or second) edition of his commentary, that works of law are all works required by God's law, and in harmony with it, which, whether they are merely outward works of the unregenerate, or truly good works of the regenerate, do not justify before God, because they are a *consequent* of justification, and not a constituent element of it, and because in no case are they a perfect fulfillment of the law. 'Shall be justified.' "The future here is *ethical*—that is, it indicates not so much mere futurity as moral possibility, and with *not* (οὐ), in *not any flesh*, something that neither can, nor will ever happen." (Ellicott on Gal. 2: 16.) Winer, on this clause, says: "This is a rule which *will hold true* in the world." Some, however, refer the future tense of the verb to "the judgment of the great day."] **For through law is knowledge of sin.** ["The law brings *only* the knowledge of sin" (De Wette), and of course its works cannot bring justification to the guilty. "Life and death proceed not from the same fountain." (Calvin.) The word for knowledge is a compound, and signifies full knowledge, clear discernment or realization. See 1: 28; 10: 2. Watts very truly says:

In vain we ask God's righteous law
To justify us now,
Since to convince and to condemn
Is all the law can do.

Further on we shall see that the law, by virtue of its condemnatory and prohibitory nature, occasions the calling forth of the passions of sin and the abounding of trespasses and thus the working out of wrath. (7: 5; 5: 20; 4: 15.)] This is a very comprehensive declaration. The very *idea* of sin comes from the previous idea of law, as a rule of action, of which sin is a violation; all true knowledge of the *nature* of sin comes through the *precept* of the law: all correct estimate of the *evil* of sin comes through the *penalty* of the law: all just sense of *personal* sinfulness comes through the application of the law.

In this passage, (ver. 9-20,) the apostle aims a death blow at all the self-righteousness and self-complacency of sinful men. He proves, by divine testimonies, the universal depravity of human nature. He shows the corruption of our nature, in its trunk and in its root. He proves the impossibility of justification by works. He virtually asserts that to be justified by our works is neither more nor less than to be justified by our sins: for all the acts of a man, prior to his being justified freely by grace through faith, are comprehended in these two classes—acts of disobedience to the law of God, and acts of imperfect obedience. The first are positive sins, the last are sins by defect—that is, they are sins by as much as they fall short of perfect obedience. By which set of performances, then, is he to be justified? Not certainly by his positive transgressions, for these are the very deeds for which he is justly condemned. Can he be justified any more by his imperfect obedience—that is, by his sins of defect? This would be to suppose them no longer sins. Nay, we may go further, and say this would be to suppose an actual *merit* in his lesser sins sufficient to atone for the *demerit* of his greater sins. To such absurdities does the idea of justification by works lead. The whole question is closed forever by this divine sentence—"cursed is *every* one that *continueth not* in *all things* which are written in the book of the law, to do them." (Gal. 3: 10.)

21. The apostle has hitherto been showing the *need* of that "righteousness of God,"

21 But now the righteousness of God without the law is manifested, being witnessed by the law and the prophets;

21 But now apart from the law a righteousness of God hath been manifested, being witnessed by the law

which was indispensable, and yet unattainable by the law. He now begins a new division of his subject, the object of which is to show how that indispensable righteousness *can* be attained. [Under the general head of justification and its results (3 : 21-5 : 21) Beet gives this analysis : "Justification through faith and through Christ (3 : 21-26) ; by which all boasting is shut out (3 : 27-30) ; but, as the case of Abraham proves, the law is established (3 : 31-4 : 17) ; description of Abraham's faith (4 : 18-25) ; we have now a well-grounded hope (5 : 1-11); and the curse of Adam is reversed (5 : 12-19); the law was given to prepare for this (5 : 20-21)." We have now come to a section which Farrar says contains the very quintessence of Pauline theology, "and is one of the fullest and weightiest passages in all his writings." Its very words seem freighted with thought of highest moment. In these modern times men may not feel much interest in a discussion about law, faith, justification, etc. ; but these with the apostle were matters of gospel or no gospel, of life or death, of salvation or perdition. What an almost infinite solemnity of meaning there is in his words addressed to the Galatians : "I do not set aside the grace of God : for if there be righteousness through law, then Christ died without cause"—*died for nothing.* (Gal. 2 : 21 ; Bible Union Version.) And with what yearnings of heart he regarded these same Galatians as they were severing themselves from Christ and falling away from his grace. With similar feelings, perhaps, he has now taken a survey of the Gentile and Jewish world and sees them all alienated from the life of God, all under the power of sin, all exposed to God's judgment. And now to the Gentiles who are yet not so far lost in sin but that they clearly recognize God's just sentence and their desert of death, and to the Jews who may perchance have been brought by the law to the full knowledge of their sins, Paul proceeds to make known a righteousness of God which will be theirs through faith, and a way of justification through the redemption of Christ which will secure to them the life eternal. But how can

we rightly understand or fitly explain those things into which angels desire to look ?]

But now the righteousness of God, etc. [Luther thus renders : " But now is revealed, without the assistance of the law, the righteousness which avails before God."] **Now** (νυνί) is used here, not probably as an adverb of time [as it would be in classic Greek], but rather in a logical way, "as the case now stands"—that is, the attainment of righteousness by law being plainly out of the question.[1] Yet it is also true in a *temporal* sense, since this new way of righteousness is now for the first time fully revealed, so that there is a *coincidence* of the two senses in which this adverb is used; but the sense above explained is the predominant one, that of time is subordinate. See a similar use of the adverb *now* in 7 : 17; 1 Cor. 15 : 20; Heb. 8 : 6, etc. **Without the law.** Apart from law [or, without its co-operation. (De Wette.) And, according to this author, the antithesis of this would be: "Through the facts of the new revelation" has God's righteousness been manifested.[2]] These words are made emphatic in the original by their occupying the first place in the sentence. Some regard them as qualifying the phrase, 'righteousness of God'; others as qualifying the verb, 'is manifested.' The sense is not materially different, but the position of the words in the original would rather suggest that they are not to be exclusively connected with either. This whole matter (the righteousness itself and its manifestation) is out of the sphere of law, utterly excludes all merit of works. The expression **is manifested,** or, more exactly, *has been manifested*—the present of completed action (Meyer)—rather than "is revealed" (1 : 17), is eminently suitable here. It is no *new* thing, so far as God is concerned, nor yet wholly new to man, as the following words imply, but newly 'manifested,' with an emphasis upon that word. ["Having previously been hidden in God's counsels, it has now been made manifest in historical reality, in the person of Jesus Christ. . . . The manifestation, in fact, is complete; the revelation in

---

[1] In this sense the Greek writers would use νῦν.—(F.)
[2] The word for *without* (χωρίς, akin to χώρα, place or

room) conveys more than ἄνευ, the idea of separateness. —(F.)

22 Even the righteousness of God *which is* by faith of Jesus Christ unto all and upon all them that believe; for there is no difference:

22 and the prophets; even the righteousness of God through faith [1] in Jesus Christ unto all [2] them that 23 believe; for there is no distinction; for all [3] have

1 Or, *of*......2 Some ancient authorities add *and upon all*......3 Gr. *sinned*.

the gospel still goes on." (Gifford.)] **Being witnessed by the law and the prophets.** By the law, as in Gen. 49:10; Deut. 18:15, etc. By the prophets, as in Isa. 53; Jer. 23:6, etc. [The phrase 'the law and the prophets' is of frequent occurrence (Matt. 5:17; 7:12; 22:40; Acts 28:23), and denotes in general the Old Testament Scriptures. The gospel of gratuitous justification is shown by this reference to the Old Testament to be not an invention of Paul.] The present participle indicates a continuous, permanent manifestation in the abiding Scriptures. Compare 1:2.

22. Even the righteousness of God, etc. [The word for 'even' (δε) has generally a slightly oppositive force, and here, perhaps, introduces a contrast to the law of the last verse. Thus, though this righteousness is witnessed by the law, it is not gained by means of the law or by means of works, *but* by means of faith of (*in*) Jesus Christ.] Observe with what painstaking fullness the apostle shows us that this righteousness of God is conditioned on faith. ["Faith is at once the soul's highest exercise of freedom, its lowliest 'confession of sin,' and the only homage it can render to God." (Gifford.)] He repeats the expression 'the righteousness of God' in order to bring in this explanation, **by faith,** or *through* faith, **of Jesus Christ,** and then subjoins: [Which is] **unto all them that believe.** [A still fuller form which the apostle sometimes uses (as in ver. 24: Eph. 2:8) would be: "The righteousness of God which is *by grace* through faith," etc., grace being the objective, instrumental cause of salvation, faith the subjective *medium* by which it is received—grace imparting, faith receiving. See Ellicott on Eph. 2:8. Since 'righteousness' has no article in the original, the feminine article after the word 'God' is naturally dispensed with. Its omission also

here and in similar cases gives a more complete unity to the conception. (Winer, 135.) On 'righteousness of God,' see comments on 1:17. The meaning of this 'righteousness' (δικαιοσύνη) is indicated by the "being justified freely by his grace," etc. (ver. 24.) "This righteousness," says Godet, "is granted to *faith*, not assuredly because of any merit inherent in it, for this would be to fall back on *works*—the very thing which the New Dispensation wishes to exclude—but because of the *object* of faith. Therefore it is that this object is expressly mentioned—Jesus Christ." "The person of Christ in its unity and totality ('Jesus Christ') is the proper redemptive object of faith." (Dorner.)] The difference between the expressions **unto all and upon all** is commonly thus explained: Offered 'unto all,' and actually available to, or resting **upon all them that believe.** According to this explanation, 'all them that believe' is to be connected with the latter preposition, 'upon,' only, and not with the former, 'unto.' This would be tolerably satisfactory if the reading of the original were certainly genuine; but though defended by Meyer, the words 'and upon all' are rejected, or marked as doubtful, by most recent critics.[1] This, of course, forestalls all need of the above explanation and leaves no place for it. **For there is no difference.** There is no distinction of Jew and Gentile, or of any other kind, among men, as to the *need* of justification or the *way* to be justified. Whatever difference there may be as to the degree of sinfulness and blameworthiness, all are under the same condemnation by the law, and shut up to the same only hope of justification by the gospel. The Pharisee and the publican, the openly vicious and the comparatively moral, are alike lost if they look to the law, and may be alike saved if they look to Christ in faith.

[1] The addition of the second clause is designated by Westcott and Hort as "Western and Syrian" (their "Syrian" being nearly equivalent to Constantinopolitan, or the text of Chrysostom, a native and, for several years, a preacher of Antioch, in Syria, and, to my mind, *one* very good authority), and is regarded by them as one of those "conflate" or combined and, hence, fuller readings which are characteristic of our Textus Receptus, and which are generally discarded in their edition of the Greek Testament, as also in the Revised Version. Meyer retains the second clause and would connect believing with each "all." Prof. Jowett says that, "Of the two prepositions, εἰς represents the more internal and spiritual relation of the gospel to the individual soul, as ἐπί, its outward connection, with mankind collectively."—(F.)

23 For all have sinned, and come short of the glory of God;
24 Being justified freely by his grace through the redemption that is in Christ Jesus:

24 sinned, and fall short of the glory of God; being justified freely by his grace through the redemption
25 that is in Christ Jesus: whom God set forth [1]to be

1 Or, to be *propitiatory.*

This is a hard saying to the self-righteous; but it is just as certainly true as that "there is none other name under heaven given among men whereby we must be saved." (Acts 4 : 12.) "If you do not regard yourself as wholly undone under the law, you will keep out from your mind the whole clearness and comfort of the gospel." (Chalmers.)

23. For all have sinned, and come short—or, *fall short* (Revised Version)—**of the glory of God.** There is a *seeming* inaccuracy here in the *tense* of the second verb. It *appears* to be in the *perfect* tense, like the first verb, but is really in the *present*. There is no reason for supposing that the translators intended to mislead the English reader; the translation is not incorrect, though almost invariably misunderstood. The misunderstanding would have been effectually prevented had they inserted the auxiliary *do* before the second verb: *All have sinned, and do come short of the glory of God* is the precise form in which the apostle states the case, at least so far as the tense of the second verb is concerned.[1] The verb 'sinned' would be quite as accurately rendered without the 'have,' as referring to an indefinite past act. According to the most common use of the Greek tense here employed, the sins of mankind are here represented as "gathered into one act, regarded as prior to the manifestation of the righteousness." (Webster.) The *sinning* is represented as a fact that occurred in past time, the *coming short of the glory of God* as the present and abiding consequence. [The historical aorist, 'sinned'—according to Bengel, Olshausen, Wordsworth, Shedd—refers, primarily at least, to the fall of our race in Adam, which is the prolific source of all depravity and all sin. See 5 : 12. Prof. Shedd says: "It is the one original sin of *apostasy*, more than any particular transgressions that flow from it, that puts the Jew and Gentile upon the same footing, so that there is 'no difference' between them."] What is meant

by coming short of the glory of God? Here we have a great variety of explanations, some of them depending upon the view taken of the sense of the verb, and some upon the meaning assigned to the phrase, 'the glory of God.' As to the meaning of the verb, we remark that it does not mean to lose something once possessed, but to *fail* of *gaining* something once attainable. This excludes such explanations as that of Olshausen, to lose "the image of God in which man was created." The most pertinent text, perhaps, to illustrate the meaning of the verb here, is Heb. 4 : 1. As to the sense of the expression, 'the glory of God,' see the notes on 2 : 7. [Most expositors, we think, regard this phrase as nearly equivalent to the praise of God, "the *glory* that cometh from the *only* God." (Revised Version. John 5 : 44; 12 : 43.) But Meyer says: "The glory of God cannot, in reality, be anything essentially different from the righteousness of God, and cannot be merely future."]

24. Being justified. ["Suddenly thus is opened a more pleasant scene." (Bengel.)] This participle must agree grammatically with 'all' of ver. 23. But are 'all' actually justified? No; the present participle here used does not imply that: it is the customary form of stating a general truth or principle without affirming the universality of the fact. It describes, with what follows, the only mode of justification in the case of all who are justified; the justification of men is going on in this way and in no other. The apostle is careful not to use the *perfect* participle, as Luke does in 18 : 14, or the indefinite past, as he himself does in 5 : 1 of this Epistle, where it would be more exactly translated: "Having been justified." Either of these forms would represent the justification as an accomplished fact, and it is justly so represented in both the passages referred to; but the present participle does not so represent it, and in the passage under consideration it could not be truly so repre-

1 This verb—signifying, literally, *to be behind,* hence, *to fall short,* to lack—is properly followed, as here, by the genitive, the "whence case," the genitive of pro-

ceeding from, of separation, and removal. The verb, being in the middle voice, is supposed by some to indicate a felt need. Compare Luke 15 : 14.—(F.)

sented. [Winer says: "The apostle conceived the connection thus—and come short of the glory of God, in that (since) they are justified freely, etc.; the latter is proof of the former." And Godet paraphrases as follows: "Being *consequently* justified, *as we have just declared* (ver. 21, 22), freely, etc."] Dr. Schaff has a full and admirable note on the meaning of the verb "to justify" in Lange's commentary on this verse. [On the verb *to justify*, see notes on 1 : 17; also Dr. Hovey's "Manual of Theology," p. 264, *seq.;* and his "God with Us," pp. 114. 252. To justify, as defined by Prof. Cremer, is: "By a judicial decision to free from guilt, . . . and to represent as righteous." Almost every word here used in connection with "justified" shows that this term does not mean made righteous or sanctified.] **Freely by his grace.** These two qualifying terms, though intimately related, are not identical. The first denotes the entire freeness of justification, "without money and without price"; the second, the divine benignity, which is the source of that free gift. Again, the second might be true without the first. It would be a favor, an act of grace, on God's part, to grant to men justification on some easy and indulgent terms, though not as an absolutely free gift. [See 5 : 17, gift of righteousness, and Eph. 2 : 8, the gift of God. If it is without cost to us, it was not so to the Giver. The word translated 'freely' (δωρεάν)— or, better, *gratuitously*—is found elsewhere in Matt. 10 : 8; John 15 : 25; 2 Cor. 11 : 7; Gal. 2 : 21; 2 Thess. 3 : 8; Rev. 21 : 6; 22 : 17. 'Grace' here "is emphasized precisely as *divine*, opposed to all human co-operation." (Meyer.) On the antithesis of grace to any reward of work or to debt, see 4 : 4; 11 : 6. Compare Titus 3 : 5. Some persons, chiefly of the hyper-Calvinistic Antinomian School, have held that Christ, by his redemption, has fully paid the debt of sinners, so that they, if belonging to the number of the elect, are freed from desert of punishment, and can demand deliverance from death as a right, thus making crimes transferable, like debts. But we, as lost sinners, must ever seek this deliverance as an act of grace, such deliverance being through Christ's redemption, rendered consistent with justice, but not required by it. (Fuller.)] **Through the redemption**

(ἀπολύτρωσις) **that is in Christ Jesus.** 'Redemption' [a word which supposes the truth of ver. 9, that we are "all under sin" or in bondage to sin] is deliverance effected by paying a ransom. Compare 1 Cor. 1 : 30. See also Eph. 1 : 7; Col. 1 : 14, in both which places redemption is defined as "the forgiveness of sins," and in the former with the addition, "through his blood." (In the latter passage this qualification is omitted in the best editions of the original text.) Compare also the word "ransom" (λύτρον) in Matt. 20 : 28; Mark 10 : 45; (ἀντίλυτρον) 1 Tim. 2 : 6; and the noun "redemption" (λύτρωσις) in Heb. 9 : 12; and the verb "to redeem" in Titus 2 : 14; 1 Peter 1 : 18. [See also such kindred words as bought, purchased, etc., 1 Cor. 6 : 20; 7 : 23; Gal. 3 : 13; Rev. 5 : 9; also Acts 20 : 28. The purchase price paid, we may say, to the holiness of the infinitely holy and righteous Lawgiver and Judge was the "precious blood" of Jesus. See ver. 25; Eph. 1 : 7; 1 Peter 1 : 18, 19; 2 : 24; Rev. 5 : 9. Compare Matt. 20 : 28; 1 Tim. 2 : 6. This 'redemption,' which is in or rests in Christ, is to be considered as the objective, and faith as the subjective, medium of justification. (Philippi.) The redemption is from the curse, from sin, from death, and from Satan. "Every mode of conception which refers redemption and forgiveness of sins, not to a real atonement through the death of Christ, but, subjectively, to the dying and reviving with him, guaranteed and produced by that death, ... is opposed to the New Testament, a mixing up of justification and sanctification." (Meyer.) "Here is a foundation for the satisfaction theory of Anselm, but not for its grossly anthropopathic execution." (De Wette.)] The two verses following explain *how* this redemption was effected. **25. Whom God hath set forth.** [Middle voice: *set forth for himself,* for the exhibition or demonstration of his righteousness. (Winer, p. 254.) Godet remarks that "it is God himself who, according to this passage, is to be regarded as the *author* of the whole work of redemption. The salvation of the world is not therefore wrested from him, as is sometimes represented by the mediation of Christ." Compare 1 John 4 : 10; 2 Cor. 5 : 18; John 3 : 16.] God set Christ forth, or exhibited him to men historically by his in-

through faith in his blood, to declare his righteousness | his righteousness, because of the passing over of the

carnation. Compare Gal. 4: 4.[1] God (the Father) set forth for himself and before the world or universe, Christ Jesus the crucified, slain as a sacrifice for sins. **To be a propitiation.** The word for propitiation [used in the Septuagint for the mercy-seat, or propitiatory cove-- for the ark of the covenant] (ἱλαστή-ριον) is in form a verbal adjective, signifying *propitiatory*, and implying some such word as *sacrifice*, or *offering*, understood, with which it agrees. In the only other two cases where the word 'propitiation' is used in our English Bible, 1 John 2: 2; 4: 10, the Greek word (ἱλασμός) is a noun from the same root as the verbal adjective used here; and in both the above passages it is applied to Christ. The only defensible translation of the word here is 'propitiation' or 'propitiatory sacrifice.' The representation of Christ as an expiatory sacrifice for sin pervades the New Testament. He is said to have "given himself as an offering and a sacrifice," Eph. 5: 2, compare Heb. 10: 12; he is "our Passover, sacrificed for us," 1 Cor. 5: 7; he is "Lamb of God," John 1: 29, 36; 1 Peter 1: 19; Rev. 5: 6-9. This last title of Lamb is given to him nearly thirty times in the book of Revelation alone. [The word propitiation' here denotes that which propitiates God or his justice. See Dr. Hovey's "Manual of Theology," 210, seq., also his "God with Us," 114, seq., 252, seq. Godet, speaking against the false idea that propitiation is intended to originate a sentiment which did not exist in God before, says: "What it produces is such a change in the relation between God and the creature, that God can henceforth display toward sinful man one of the elements of his nature rather than another." And he approvingly quotes Gess as saying: "Divine love manifests itself in the gift of the Son, that it may be able afterward to diffuse itself in the heart by the gift of the Spirit." In the love of God there is, as he says: "(1), The love which precedes the propitiation and which determines to effect it; and (2), Love such that it can display itself when once the propitiation is effected."] **Through faith in his blood.** The precise

connection of these two clauses with each other, and with the preceding context, especially with the words 'propitiation' and 'set forth,' has given rise to some discussion. According to the common punctuation of the English, the two expressions would seem to have the most direct and intimate connection with each other, 'in his blood' being the object on which faith is exercised. In that case, we must understand by his blood that expiation for sin which he effected by the shedding of his blood. In no other sense can 'faith in his blood' be an efficacious means of propitiation for sin. But the lack of any Scripture warrant for the expression 'faith in the blood of Christ' is a strong objection to insisting on so close a relation between these two clauses. It is better to connect the clause 'in his blood' with the verb 'set forth,' and the clause 'through faith' with the noun 'propitiation'—*whom God set forth in his blood, as a propitiation through faith* [so Meyer]; or, which is but slightly different without so distinctly separating the verb and the noun, 'propitiation,' to join these two clauses with both, making the 'blood'—that is, the sacrificial death of Christ—the ground of the propitiatory virtue of his redemptive work and faith, exercised by the sinner, the condition of its propitiatory efficacy. **To declare his righteousness,** etc. Here it is necessary to make more important changes than are often required in our English translation, so excellent as a whole. "To declare his righteousness," literally, 'for manifestation[2] of his righteousness,'—that is, his judicial righteousness, or justice, as explained in the last part of the next verse. [This retributive righteousness or justice of God (defined by the phrase in the next verse: that he might be righteous, or just) is of course different from that righteousness of God through faith which has been manifested without the law.

Ver. 21 speaks of the manifestation of God's justifying righteousness, this verse speaks of the exhibition of his judicial righteousness. The reason for this exhibition is given under two aspects, the first stated being, perhaps, the

---

[1] [This is true ; but there seems to be no reference to the incarnation in this verse. It is Christ Jesus whom God is here affirmed to have set forth as a propitiation in his blood, or death, and not the eternal Word whom he exhibited to men by means of the incarnation.—[A. H.]

[2] ἔνδειξιν, whence our *indication*, see Eph. 2: 7, for an equivalent phrase.—(F.)

for the remission of sins that are past, through the forbearance of God;
26 To declare, *I say*, at this time his righteousness:

26 sins done aforetime, in the forbearance of God; for the shewing, *I say*, of his righteousness at this

---

more subordinate one.] **For the remission.** The word (ἄφεσις) usually translated 'remission' (or, in several places, *forgiveness*,) occurs seventeen times in the New Testament, but it is not used in this place. Instead of the ordinary word (ἄφεσις), the apostle uses another word (πάρεσις) which is found nowhere else in the Greek Testament, and which bears the same relation to the usual word that our word prætermission, or passing over, bears to remission. We can hardly suppose that he would have used a different word only here, unless he had designed to express a different sense. **[Sins that are past,** or formerly committed —that is, prior to the atoning death of Christ.][1] **Through** (literally, *in*) **the forbearance of God.** This word 'forbearance' confirms the correction just made in the word 'remission.' To pass over sin is the work of 'forbearance'; to remit sin is the work of grace. We would translate and explain the latter part of this verse as follows: "For manifestation of his righteousness on account of (or in respect to) the passing over of past sins, in the forbearance of God." During the past ages, God had not executed the judgment upon the sins of men which his righteousness had threatened, and seemed to demand; but had in his forbearance passed over, and seemingly ignored them. This made necessary some manifestation of his righteousness in this respect. (How could he righteously so pass by the sins of men? The setting forth of Christ as a propitiatory sacrifice answers this.) [God might have exhibited his righteousness or justice by visiting upon sinners his deserved wrath, the penalty of death; but this through his love for man he did not do. Yet thereby his justice seemed to be set aside or impaired,

and hence he "spared not his own Son but gave him up for us all." Says Andrew Fuller: "If the question were, Why did God give his Son to die for sinners rather than leave them to perish in their sins? the answer would be, Because he loved them. But if the question be, Why did he give his Son to be an atonement for sinners rather than save them without one? the answer would be, Because he loved righteousness and hated iniquity." Similarly Julius Müller: "To maintain the authority of the divine government in view of innumerable sins left unpunished (πάρεσις), it was necessary that God in establishing a new kingdom of love and grace should manifest his justice in the expiatory death of its founder and king." It is almost needless to say that such an exhibition as this of God's justice (and of his mercy, too, in behalf of sinners), and such a setting forth of Christ as a propitiatory covering and sacrifice for the sins of men, which Meyer calls "the epoch and turning point in the world's history," will not be lost and will never be repeated. Calvary witnessed the finishing of man's redemption; and never again will Christ be called from heaven to make atonement for sin. Godet says: "The righteousness of God once revealed in the sacrifice of the cross, this demonstration *remains*. Whatever happens, nothing can again efface it from the history of the world, nor from the conscience of mankind. Henceforth no illusion is possible; all sin must be pardoned—or judged."[2]

26. To declare, etc.—[literally, *for the manifestation of*, as in the previous verse. Some (Alford, Schaff) think that Paul would by the use of the article in this and not in the former verse distinguish this 'manifestation'

---

[1] Prof. Stuart remarks that if Jesus died only as a martyr to the truth, and his death had no *vicarious* influence, it could not avail for the forgiveness of sins (or the prætermission of sins) committed in the early ages—(F.)

[2] In illustration of the gracious efficacy of this verse we adduce the religious experience of the poet Cowper. After walking up and down his room in an almost despairing state of mind he at length seated himself by a window and opened a Bible which happened to be there, if perchance he might find some consolation. "The passage which met my eye was the twenty-fifth

verse of the third chapter of Romans. On reading it I immediately received power to believe. The rays of the Sun of Righteousness fell on me in all their fullness; I saw the complete sufficiency of the expiation which Christ had wrought for my pardon and entire justification. In an instant I believed and received the peace of the gospel. . . . . If the arm of the Almighty had not supported me, I believe I should have been overwhelmed with gratitude and joy. My eyes filled with tears, transports choked my utterance. I could only look to heaven in silent fear, overflowing with love and wonder."—(F.)

that he might be just, and the justifier of him which believeth in Jesus. | present season: that he might himself be [1] just, and the [1] justifier of him that [2] hath faith [3] in Jesus

from the other as being "the fuller and ultimate object." Meyer thinks the former is here resumed and made prominent, in order to emphasize the historical element (in this present time) not previously mentioned, and to bring into full view the end that was designed by God ("that he might be just") in the propitiation. In Godet's view, the "manifestation" is repeated to show what is the object to be gained in the *future*.] What in the previous verse was expressed in a somewhat incidental way, and with reference rather to his righteousness in not immediately and fully punishing sin, now comes out more emphatically with reference to his righteousness in forgiving sin. Note how emphatically the apostle declares that the "righteousness" of God is manifested by the vicarious sacrifice of Christ—the very thing which men often object to, as unrighteous in God. **At this time.** These words are contrasted not so much with the phrase "in the forbearance of God," as if that expression referred specially to the time of God's forbearance, as with the phrase "the sins that are past." The passing over of transgressions in times past, and the remission of sins now, both require to be reconciled with the righteousness of God. "The time of Christ is a time of critical decision, when the prætermission, the passing over, of sins, is at an end, and men must either accept the full remission of sins, or expose themselves to the judgment of a righteous God." (Schaff.) Many passages might be referred to as illustrating the same idea. See, for example, Luke 2: 34, 35; Acts 17: 30, 31; Heb. 9 . 15. [**That**—*in order that,* indicates the purpose, the "intended result" (Meyer), of setting forth Christ as a propitiatory sacrifice through faith in his blood.] **Might be just, and the justifier.** *Just and justifying* is the more literal translation; just in justifying, that his justice might be exercised and manifested even in the act of forgiving and accepting the sinful as righteous on their believing in Jesus. This last clause of the verse explains especially the object of the *manifestation*, but also truly and comprehensively of all that precedes, from the beginning of ver. 25. "This is the keystone, the

final aim of the whole affirmation: that he might be just and justifying the believer." (Meyer.) [If God could be really just (Paul uses the word meaning *to be*, not the word meaning *to become*, nearly equivalent to be *manifested* or *regarded* as just, see ver. 4) and could justify and save sinners apart from the obedience and sacrifice of a substitute, how is it that his own Son, the Son of his love, in human flesh was made to bear our iniquities and was bruised for our offences? Just and justifying the ungodly! "We have here the greatest paradox of the gospel; for in the law, God is seen as just and condemning; in the gospel, he is seen as being just himself and justifying the sinner." (Bengel.) This "sinner," however, is a penitent believer, one—literally, that is *of faith of* (in) *Jesus.* The uncials F G of the ninth century omit the name Jesus, while other copies vary the reading. Meyer, judging it to be a repetition from ver. 22, thinks it should be omitted, "notwithstanding the preponderating testimony in its favor."] Compare this whole passage with the Socinian idea of atonement as operating only *manward.* [Bishop Butler, in cautious but weighty language, states that "the doctrine of the gospel appears to be, not only that he taught the efficacy of repentance, but rendered it of the efficacy which it is by what he did and suffered for us, that he obtained for us the benefit of having our repentance accepted unto eternal life ; not only that he revealed to sinners that they were in a capacity of salvation, and how they might obtain it, but, moreover, that he put them into this capacity of salvation by what he did and suffered for them." Dr. Hovey says: "This passage (Rom. 3 : 24-26) seems to have been written for the very purpose of rendering forever vain and futile any attempt to limit the efficacy of the Atonement to its moral influence over men." See his "God with Us," pp. 100–155.] This is a standard passage, on the doctrine of *atonement.* Olshausen calls this passage "the Acropolis of the Christian faith." "There is perhaps no single passage in the book of inspiration," says Chalmers, "which reveals in a way so formal and authoritative as the one before us the path of transition by which a

27 Where *is* boasting then? It is excluded. By what law? of works? Nay; but by the law of faith.
28 Therefore we conclude that a man is justified by faith without the deeds of the law.

27 Where then is the glorying? It is excluded. By what manner of law? of works? Nay: but by a law of faith. [1] We reckon therefore that a man is justi-

1 Many ancient authorities read *For we reckon.*

sinner passes from a state of wrath to a state of acceptance. There is no passage, to which if we would only bring the docility and compliance of childhood, that is more fitted to guide and to turn an inquiring sinner into the way of peace."

On the relation of this passage to what follows, to the end of chapter 4, Alford remarks: "Jewish boasting is altogether removed by this truth; not, however, by making void the law, not by degrading Abraham from his pre-eminence; but by establishing the law, and showing that Abraham was really justified by faith, and is the father of the faithful." He now goes on to show, in the following verse, that this way of gratuitous justification, while it lays the firm foundation for the highest assurance, is also adapted to beget the deepest humility. When the hope of salvation rests on works, it can have no rational assurance. The man that is at all conscious of his great sinfulness—in other words, the man that has any real knowledge of himself, must be often troubled with misgivings, and harassing doubts and fears, so long as his hope of acceptance with God depends in any degree upon his own performances. There is no room, in his creed, for an intelligent confidence of his final salvation. But when Christ's perfect work of propitiation, and not his own imperfect and inconstant works of obedience, is the sole foundation on which he rests, he has a hope which is an anchor of his soul, sure and steadfast; and his consciousness of his many sins, and of the imperfection of his best acts of obedience, does not form any bar to his joyful assurance of salvation. So admirably, in the gospel scheme, are humility and assurance reconciled and combined!

27. [**Where is** (in the Greek *the*, equivalent, perhaps, to *our*) **boasting then?** 'Then' signifies an inference or conclusion drawn from the preceding passage. Are the statements in that passage the invention of the author's genius, the mere figment of his brain? or are they plain, sober, infinitely important truths? and do they furnish to our minds a

solid foundation for safe inference? There is no middle view which we can take of this matter. The apostle's inference from the asserted truths is that all 'boasting' on the part of sinners **is excluded,** or, in the words of Theodoret: "it no longer has room."] The "*boasting*" of the Jews "was excluded" once and forever, when God set forth his Son as a propitiation. The verb here is in the indefinite past tense; but this is one of the cases where it may most suitably be represented in English by the perfect: *has been excluded.* The contrast in the following words: **By what law?** [literally: *through what kind of law?*] is not between the law and the gospel, as two dispensations; but the word 'law' seems to be used here in what is sometimes called a rhetorical sense, nearly equivalent to the word "principle," or "rule": by what principle? **Of works? nay, but by the law** (*principle*) **of faith.** The word 'law' seems to be used in the like sense in 7: 21, 23, 25; 8: 2, etc. [For a man to believe in Christ who died that sinners might, through faith in him, be justified and saved, is to confess himself guilty and lost, and that his hope is not in himself but in the mercy of God. By the gospel man is thus both exalted and abased—exalted as to his nature, but abased as a sinner. From Jew and Gentile alike all glorying is excluded. Each one is asked: who maketh thee to differ? Each believer is assured that even his salvation *through faith* is a gift of God, and is not of himself or of his works, lest he should glory. The gospel teaches no Parkerian doctrine of self-sufficiency, but that a Christian's sufficiency is from God, and that if he glories he must glory in the Lord. (1 Cor. 1: 29, 31; 2 Cor 3: 5; Eph. 2: 8, 9.)]

28. Therefore we conclude (in Revised Version, *reckon*). [The Revisers retain this 'therefore,' which here marks a second inference of the apostle.] Instead of 'therefore,' the reading *for* [adopted by Westcott and Hort] is preferable. *For we reckon* instead of being a conclusion from what goes before is rather a reason for what goes before [a con-

29 *Is he* the God of the Jews only? *is he* not also of the Gentiles? Yes, of the Gentiles also:
30 Seeing *it is* one God, which shall justify the circumcision by faith, and uncircumcision through faith.

fied by faith apart from 1 the works of the law
29 Or is God *the God* of Jews only? Is he not *the*
30 God of Gentiles also? Yea, of Gentiles also: if so be that God is one, and he shall justify the circumcision 2 by faith, and the uncircumcision 3 through faith.

---

1 Or, *works of law*......2 Gr. *out of*......3 Or, *through the faith.*

---

firmation of the statement that faith excludes boasting.] **Without the deeds of the law.** This does not mean that a man, without the deeds of the law, is justified by faith; but it means, as it reads, that a man is justified by faith, without the deeds of the law—that is, that the deeds of the law contribute nothing toward his justification. The statement, interpreted fairly by the common laws of language, is not liable to the construction that a man who is justified by faith is under no obligation to perform the deeds of the law; but it would perhaps gain some additional security against such a misconstruction by being translated, "for we reckon that a man is justified by faith, apart from ($\chi\omega\rho\acute{\iota}\varsigma$) works of law." The same truth is stated, with emphatic reiteration, in Gal. 2 : 16. [This *reckoning* here seems to denote a fixed and final decision. On the word 'man' Chrysostom thus remarks: "He says not 'Jew,' nor 'he that is under law'; but having enlarged the area of his argument and opened the doors of salvation to the world, he says, 'man,' using the name common to the nature." We scarcely need say that the faith of which Paul speaks so much as being essential to salvation was no "dead" faith, but operative, "working through love," and bringing forth all the fruits of righteousness. If we are justified by faith solely, we are not justified by a faith which is or remains solitary. Justification is apart from works, but faith is not. Were it otherwise, faith would be inoperative, dead—in fact, no faith at all. Paul's faith was a deeply seated, a deeply earnest, an intensely active and operative principle, moving his whole being toward Christ and Christian duty. With his whole heart, as we believe, he would have subscribed to the truth of F. W. Robertson's statement that "Faith alone justifies; but not the faith which is alone," adding simply this, that the faith last spoken of did not deserve the name of faith. The Confession of Faith adopted by our Puritan Fathers at a synod held at Cambridge, 1648,

declares that "Faith thus receiving and resting on Christ and his righteousness is the alone instrument of justification; yet it is not alone in the person justified, but is ever accompanied with all other saving graces, and is no dead faith, but worketh by love." According to Paul's doctrinal scheme, believers are created in Christ Jesus for good works, and are to be zealous of good works; and he exhorts them to be careful to maintain good works, and to be rich in good works. (Eph. 2 : 10; Titus 2 ; 14; 3 : 14; 1 Tim. 6 : 18.) Nor did the faith which Luther advocated ignore good works. He says: "It is as impossible to separate works from faith as to separate heat and light from fire." Yet much abuse was heaped upon him by his opponents for his translation of this verse: "So now we hold that a man is justified, without the works of the law, *only* through faith" (*allein durch den Glauben—sola fide*, whence comes the epithet, Solifidians). The meaning is in the text, but a translation did not require its express statement.]

29, 30. Is he the God of the Jews only? is he not also of the Gentiles? [This query is designed to confirm the principle, stated in the last verse, that no man is justified by works of the law. The Gentiles have no such law as the Jews, and if one is justified before God only by works of law, then is God the God of the Jews only. **Seeing it is one God,** or, as rendered in the Revised Version, "If so be that God is one." This supposes a unity of dispensation. See Ellicott on Gal. 2: 5. The words 'Jews' and 'Gentiles' are without the article in the original, since, as proper names, the Greek does not require it.] **The circumcision—and uncircumcision** —that is the Jews and the Gentiles. **Shall justify.** The future is used here, not with reference to the day of judgment, but by a common idiom of most languages, to express a permanent purpose, or habit. The difference between the expres sions **by faith** (or, more literally, *from faith*)

31 Do we then make void the law through faith? God forbid: yea, we establish the law.

31 Do we then make [1] the law of none effect [2] through faith? God forbid: nay, we establish the law.

[1] Or, law......[2] Or, through the faith.

and **through** (*the*) *faith*,[1] does not seem to have any doctrinal significance. In ver. 28, faith stands in the Greek text without any preposition, but in a form which indicates that it is the instrumental cause, the "*sine quâ non*," of justification—the three forms of expression are equivalent. [It is not unnatural for writers to vary the choice of nearly synonymous words merely for the sake of variety, and this appears to have been often the case with Paul. See Winer, ¿ 50. De Wette, however, makes the *from* denote the objective *ground*, and *through*, the subjective *medium*. In the one case justification is represented, as a result of faith, or resulting from faith, and in the other as resulting by means of faith— faith being thus represented as a source and as a means. (Winer, p. 411.) Some have conjectured that *from* more appropriately refers to the Jews, members of the Commonwealth of Israel, while *through* relates to the admission of Gentile strangers. Yet *from* is used of Gentiles. (9: 30; Gal. 3: 8.) Calvin finds in this interchange of prepositions a delicate irony: "If any one wishes to have a difference made between the Gentile and the Jew, let him take this—that the one obtains righteousness *by* faith, and the other *through* faith," which, in our opinion, would be something like a "quip, or merry turn," which Cowper said could not be found in Paul's writings.]

31. Do we then make void the law through faith? [This law, according to De Wette (and Meyer), is "the Mosaic law which demands works." The word "make void" (καταργέω, the root of which is a—ἔργος, *not working, inoperative*, hence, *powerless*) is a favorite with Paul, being used in his epistles twenty-five times, and found only twice elsewhere. See also comments on 6: 6. For some other specially Pauline words and phrases, see notes on Acts 20: 35. Paul's doctrine of a righteousness apart from law, a justification apart from works (see ver. 21, 28), would naturally give rise to the idea that he nullified the law through faith.] The statement **we establish the law** admits of two explanations. 1.

We establish or confirm the law by the foregoing doctrine of faith as the indispensable condition of justification, because this doctrine effectually secures the fulfillment of the law. This truth, constantly affirmed or assumed in the Scriptures, is formally and elaborately proved in chapters 6, 7 and 8 of this Epistle. 2. We establish, or confirm the law, by our doctrine of justification by faith, because this way of justification agrees with the teaching of the law—that is, of the Old Testament. ["The principle of justifying faith is pointed out in the law itself." (De Wette.) "Justification by the grace of God through faith is already taught in the law." (Meyer.)] This has already been intimated in ver. 21, " witnessed by the law and the prophets;" and this the apostle immediately proceeds to show, in the next chapter, from the instances of Abraham and David. We conclude, therefore, that this latter explanation, as being more in agreement with the context, is what the apostle means by **we establish the law.** [In illustration of the truth of the apostle's assertion, Bishop Wordsworth adduces the following considerations—namely, the doctrine of justification is grounded on the testimony of the law that all are under sin; the sacrifice of Christ on the cross was pre-announced by the passover and other sacrifices of the law; the law reveals God as a just Judge who needs an adequate propitiation for sin; the death of Christ is such a propitiation; Christ has by his perfect obedience to the law, both in doing and suffering, established its moral dignity, etc., etc. According to Godet, Paul has shown that the teaching opposite to his would overturn the law " by keeping up the vainglory of man which the law was meant to destroy, and by violating monotheism on which it is based." Calvin says: "Where there is a coming to Christ there is first found in him the perfect righteousness of the law, which becomes ours by imputation, and then there is sanctification, by which our hearts are prepared to keep the law, which, indeed, is imperfectly done—but there is an aiming at the work. Similar is

[1] The article before the second faith, Prof. Boise says, " seems to point to the fact that the word had just been mentioned, and that *the faith* was the same in each case."—(B?

CHAPTER IV.

WHAT shall we say then that Abraham our father,
as pertaining to the flesh, hath found?
2 For if Abraham were justified by works, he hath
whereof to glory; but not before God.

1   What then shall we say ¹ that Abraham, our fore-
2 father ² hath found according to the flesh? For if
Abraham was justified ³ by works, he hath whereof

---

1 Some ancient authorities read *of Abraham, our forefather according to the flesh ?* ......2, Or, *according to the flesh, hath found ?*
3 Gr. *out of.*

---

the case with ceremonies. . . . Viewed in themselves they are vain and shadowy images, and then only do they attain anything real and solid, when their end is regarded. In this, then, consists their chief confirmation when they have obtained their accomplishment in Christ.''] The expression **God forbid** is explained in the note on ver. 4.

Ch. 4: [Justification by faith through grace, illustrated by examples from the Old Testament Scriptures.]
1. What shall we say then. What, then, if such be the way of justification, shall we say of the righteous men who lived under the Old Testament Dispensation? What has our forefather Abraham gained by the fleshly rite if justification is by faith? [De Wette gives this paraphrase : What, now (if, as ye Jews suppose, all depends upon works of law), shall we say that Abraham has obtained (namely, for his justification) according to the flesh? The Jews evidently supposed that Abraham obtained from his works justification before God, and hence had cause for glorying before God and man. The apostle, in what follows, seems to concede that if Abraham obtained from his own labor aught for justification, he had in this some ground for glorying, but denies that the justification thus supposedly obtained furnished any ground of glorying before God, and thus, in effect, denies that he was justified by works. Dr. Hodge thinks this chapter would have opened differently if the establishing of the law consisted merely in showing that the Old Testament Scriptures, by the examples of Abraham and David, taught the faith method of justification, or justification by grace.] The words **as pertaining to the flesh** should probably be connected with the verb **hath found** rather than with the words **our father** (or, *our forefather*, as it is in the most ancient manuscripts). These words, 'as pertaining to the flesh,' would seem superfluous and unmeaning when connected [as in the Canterbury Re-

vision] with Abraham, but have a very pertinent sense as connected with the verb. 'Hath found' is the more literal, but *hath gained* expresses the idea more clearly, and is justified by the use of the same verb in Heb. 9 : 12, where it is translated "obtained." [The meaning of the Greek expression translated 'as pertaining to the flesh' would be represented more exactly in this place by the phrase, "by way of the flesh," or, "in virtue of the flesh." Compare Matt. 19 : 3; 1 Cor. 3 : 10; 2 Thess. 1 : 12; 2 Tim. 1 : 9; Rom. 4 : 16. And 'the flesh' is here used as equivalent to the natural man, who works by and for himself, and as the antithesis of grace and the spirit of God. "What, then, shall we say that Abraham attained by virtue of the flesh?" (A. H.)] [Westcott and Hort, and the English Revisers in the margin, omit the verb 'hath found.' It should, without doubt, be retained, as the *for* of the next sentence seems to refer to it or to its answer.]
2. For if Abraham were justified by works, he hath whereof to glory. There is an appearance of inexactness, or want of perfect congruity, in the use of the *tenses* here, which does not belong to the original. 'If he *were* justified by works, he *would have* whereof to glory' (or ground of boasting), would be the more exact and regular construction; or, 'if he *was* justified by works, he *has* whereof to glory.' This last is, in fact, the precise form of the original sentence. [Prof. Stuart thinks the use of the present instead of the imperfect (εἶχε with ἄν) "shows a design on the part of the writer to say, not only that Abraham *would have had* ground of glorying, in case of perfect obedience, but that the same would have continued down to the then present time.''] We naturally expect here an answer to the question of the preceding verse, but the apostle seems to have regarded the true answer, "nothing at all" (so far as relates to justification), as so plain that it did not need to be stated. The 'for' assumes this answer : Abraham certainly gained no

3 For what saith the Scripture? Abraham believed God, and it was counted unto him for righteousness.

3 to glory: but not toward God. For what saith the scripture? And Abraham believed God, and it was

advantage in respect to his justification, by circumcision or any other work, 'for,' if he had, he would have ground of boasting before God, which he has not. [Godet thinks this verse gives the reason for putting the above question. The phrase 'by works' throws light on the phrase, 'pertaining to the flesh.' These 'works' pertain to the flesh, since they proceed not from the spirit or the spiritual element of faith. The reference to circumcision is excluded by the plural 'works.' (De Wette.)]

'Whereof to glory.' The noun so translated is only another form of the same word translated *boasting* in chapter 3 : 27. There the *act* of boasting is meant; here it is *matter* of boasting, or something to boast of. The apostle carefully observes the nice distinction between the two forms of the word. [The final clause **but not before God** is regarded by interpreters as one of special difficulty. It is understood by the Greek expositors—Chrysostom, Œcumenius, Theophylact, and Theodoret—as meaning that if Abraham had performed all the good works required by the law, he would have had ground for glorying in himself or in his own righteousness, but not in respect to God or what God had done for him. This interpretation is adopted by Meyer and Tholuck, but opposed by Philippi, on the ground that "this was precisely what the Jews maintained." But did the Jews maintain this? Did they not think themselves to be the favorites of heaven, and believe that God had given them the law by which they might work out their own salvation? Did they not think that they had ground for boasting in respect to God, even though they supposed themselves to be justified by works? Just this Paul denies. If Abraham was justified by works, he has ground for boasting in respect to himself, but not in respect to God. (A. H.)] [Meyer, as above intimated, follows the interpretation of the Greek expositors, thus: "Assuming that Abraham has been justified by works, he has cause for boasting—namely, that he has attained righteousness through his actions; but he has not this ground of boasting with respect to God (as if his justification were the *divine* act), since in the case supposed, it is not God to

whom he owes the justification, but, on the contrary, he has himself earned it." The Five Clergymen put a period after boasting, and give this rendering: 'But he hath none before God: for what saith the Scripture?']

3. For what saith the Scripture? [The interrogative form gives force and vigor to the passage cited. (10: 8; 11: 4.) The 'for' here confirms the last clause of ver. 2. That he has no ground to boast is certain; 'for' the Scripture says, etc. The passage here quoted is found in Gen. 15 : 6. The Scripture says that *faith*, and not works, was counted to Abraham for righteousness. This passage (found for substance in 1 Macc. 2 : 52) is cited almost verbatim from the Septuagint. See also Gal. 3: 6. In the Hebrew it reads: 'And he (Jehovah) counted it to him for righteousness.' Even in Abraham's believing God, as Meyer remarks, Paul has rightly discerned nothing substantially different from the Christian *faith*, since his faith had reference to the divine *promise*, and indeed, to *the* promise which he recognized as that which embraced in it the future Messiah. (John 8 ; 56.) "Faith," says Philippi, "does not justify man before God on account of its subjective character, a view which must be described as falling back to the legal standpoint, but it justifies man only on account of its object and import, which is no other than Christ, or God's forgiving grace in Christ. Even Abraham knew and in faith embraced the promise of this grace (see John 8: 56), and this faith was reckoned to him for righteousness." "It (faith) means believing, not, however, as a virtuous exercise of the mind, which God consented to accept instead of perfect obedience, but as having respect to the promised Messiah, and so to his righteousness as the ground of acceptance." (Andrew Fuller.)

"The meaning of the phrase: counted for righteousness, or to accept and treat as righteous, is here very plain. It signifies gratuitous or unmerited justification on the grounds already explained. By the apostle's own explanation in the context, this justification is one which is 'according to grace' (ver. 24) and 'apart from works.' (ver. 6). While faith, or belief, then, is absolutely necessary

4 Now to him that worketh is the reward not reckoned of grace, but of debt.
5 But to him that worketh not, but believeth on him that justifieth the ungodly, his faith is counted for righteousness.

4 reckoned unto him for righteousness. Now to him that worketh, the reward is not reckoned as of
5 grace, but as of debt. But to him that worketh not, but believeth on him that justifieth the ungodly, his

in order to prepare a man to become the proper subject of the gratuitous justification which the gospel proffers; while without faith he cannot be justified; yet faith is not in any *legal* sense the meritorious ground of justification, nor does the promise attached to it imply a reward of *merit*, but only of grace." (Prof. Stuart.)] Abraham showed his faith in God by leaving his own country at God's command; by believing God's promise, that he should have a numerous posterity, when the child of promise was not born, though he was about a hundred years old; and by giving that promised child as a sacrifice at the command of God. Compare Heb. 11: 8, 9, 12, 17-19. The apostle selects the second of the above instances for particular development in the context, (ver. 17-22); and, indeed, this was the exemplification of Abraham's faith specially referred to in the passage of Genesis, which he quotes. **It was counted unto him for righteousness:** 'it'—that is, his *believing* God, his faith. ["If the gospel of St. Matthew fitly opens the whole evangelical record by connecting it with the former Scriptures, so also for the same reason does this great Epistle open the doctrinal series: for what the one does in respect of fact the other does in respect of doctrine, justifying throughout the intimation with which it opens, that the gospel will here be treated as that 'which God had promised before by his prophets in the Holy Scriptures.' In the constant references and in the whole line of argument, we see the illustrious genealogy and lineal descent of the Christian doctrine of justification by faith, traced, like that of Jesus himself, from Abraham and David, and vindicated by the witness of the Law and the Prophets; so that we enter on the final exposition of the truth with a settled sense that in all the successive stages of its revelation the truth has still been one." (Bernard's "Progress of Doctrine in the New Testament," p. 167.) De Wette says: "When the apostle in this way unites the climax of religious development with the historical

point of beginning—for the developing series commenced with Abraham—he gives evidence of great historical insight."]

4. To confirm what he had already said in regard to Abraham's justification, he now shows that faith excludes works, as a ground of justification, inasmuch as they proceed from antagonistic principles, the former coming under the principle of *grace* [favor freely shown to the undeserving], and the latter under the principle of *merit*. It is no *favor* to give a man what he has *earned* or deserved. **Now to him that worketh** [Luther: "is occupied with works"]—that is, to him that earns wages by work. [The supposition here is that he does his work perfectly.] **Is the reward not reckoned of grace** (that is, *as a favor*) **but of** (or, *is paid as a*) **debt.** ['The reward'; as the noun has here the article, it is equivalent to the deserved reward. The word for debt is used by Paul only here. There is a sense in which it could be said that God would not owe us anything, even if we had done all "the things that were commanded." (Luke 17: 10.) It is because we are all undeserving, and can strictly claim nothing as a debt, that God in his sovereignty can justly give to the one hour laborer the same as to him who has borne the burden and heat of the day. (Matt. 20: 12.)[1] "The merit of a creature before the Creator is *pactional*. It is founded upon a promise or covenant, and not upon the original relation between the finite and the Infinite." (Shedd.)]

5. But to him that worketh not—that is, that does not earn anything by working [does not merit anything by full and perfect obedience, consequently, does not work for hire or reward. "By 'working not,' the apostle did not mean a wicked inaction, but a renunciation of works as the ground of acceptance with God." (A. Fuller.)[2] **The ungodly** [literally, 'the non-worshiper,' but used here in a more general sense], the natural state of all men, even Abraham not excepted. Compare 5: 6. It is utterly im-

---

[1] Trench remarks that this parable of the laborers in the vineyard "might justly be entitled: On the nature of rewards in the kingdom of God—the whole finding an instructive commentary in Rom. 4: 1-4."—(F.)

[2] The apostle, referring here to a *supposed* class, uses the subjective negative μή.

possible to *combine* faith and works, grace and merit, as joint and co-ordinate conditions of salvation. They will not amalgamate. Compare 11: 6. On the Romish (or any other) theory of justification by *inwrought* righteousness, there can be no intelligent ground of *assurance* of salvation for any man in this world. [On the word 'ungodly,' Meyer thus remarks: "It is not even to be weakened as equivalent to *unrighteous,* but has been purposely selected (compare 5: 6) in order to set forth the saving power of faith by as strong a contrast as possible to 'him that justifieth.'" The 'justifieth' explains the 'righteousness' which God imparts to the penitent believer. When God justifies an ungodly man, he does not justify his ungodly deeds, but he forgives him, being penitent, acquits him of deserved punishment, and restores him to favor. Though "justification respects a man as ungodly" (Edwards), yet it cannot be truly said that God justifies the ungodly man as such or remaining such, only so far as a penitent believer may in himself ever be regarded as sinful and deserving of condemnation. Jehovah will not justify the wicked (Ex. 23: 7)—that is, those who are determinedly such. Fuller says: "Saving faith, or faith that worketh by love, is necessary to justification, not as being the ground of our acceptance with God, not as a virtue of which justification is the reward, but as that without which we could not be united to a living Redeemer." And again: "Faith justifies not in respect of the act of believing, but of the righteousness on which it terminates." Prof. Stuart rightly enough remarks that "in all cases of *logizomai* (to reckon or impute) as applied to Abraham's faith, or that of others who follow his example, it is only *his* or *their* own faith which is counted for righteousness." But may we not find a gratuitous imputation in Abraham's case and in ours, in that a faith which viewed subjectively was not in the sight of God a perfect righteousness, was yet through grace and on account of the object of faith accepted for righteousness? Even the Christian's faith, which is in essence only the renunciation of all merit, and is but im-

perfect at best, is not in itself meritorious; and if this faith is reckoned for righteousness the objective ground of such gracious imputation is the righteousness of Christ. See Meyer's note on 4: 4, 5.[1]

"It is not in any wise on account of any excellency or value there is in faith that it appears in the sight of God a meet thing that he that believes should have this benefit of Christ assigned to him, but purely from the relation faith has to the person in whom this benefit is to be had, or as it unites to that Mediator in and by whom we are justified." (Edwards' "Justification by Faith Alone.") It is said that the parallel between Abraham and the Christian believer is not complete, *faith* being imputed to Abraham for righteousness; while Christ's righteousness—or, as Canon Evans of the "Bible Commentary" (1 Cor. 1: 30) would have it, the "righteousness of God the Father"—is imputed to the penitent sinner by faith. Again, if the righteousness of God is "*by* faith," then faith itself cannot be that righteousness. We answer that this faith, nevertheless, can through grace, and in view of Christ's merits, be reckoned for righteousness. And if faith in Christ as a condition (not the ground) of justification makes us righteous in God's sight, it is no contradiction to say that faith is reckoned to us for righteousness, and that this righteousness becomes ours through faith. Though "the Bible never says 'faith justifies'" (Schaff), yet we have the substantial equivalent of this, not only in the phrase, justified by faith, but in the expression, faith is reckoned for righteousness, which means that we are regarded and treated as righteous through faith in the Redeemer. See in 4: 5, 6, 9, 11, the frequent interchange of the expression, the imputation of faith for righteousness, and the imputation of righteousness to the believer. To reckon one's faith for righteousness is but another expression for imputing righteousness according to grace and without works (4: 5, 6, 16); and the imputing of Christ's righteousness to the believer simply denotes that "his perfect obedience is reckoned to our account, so that we have the benefit of it as though we performed it ourselves." (Edwards.) The faith which

---

[1] In Meyer's opinion, it is our subjective faith which is imputed for righteousness. yet "The merit of Christ always remains the meritorious cause to which we are indebted for the imputation of our faith."—(F.)

is reckoned for righteousness unites us to Christ, puts us, as it were, *in* Christ, God's well-beloved Son, so that God looks upon us, not as in our naked selves, but as in Christ, and thus regards us as sons and as righteous in and on account of Christ's righteousness. Philippi says: "The imputation of *faith* is of itself identical with the imputation of righteousness. With Paul faith is always in the act of justification, the opposite of works and the correlative notion to grace. (11:6.) Hence, with good reason, the evangelical church has explained the expression, 'faith is reckoned as righteousness'—seeing that this is done by grace for the sake of Christ's righteousness—as equivalent to the proposition: 'Christ's righteousness is reckoned to the believer as righteousness.' " Christ thus becomes the end or aim of the law for righteousness to the believer, and in him we become the righteousness of God. But the Scriptures do not in explicit phrase speak of imputing Christ's righteousness to the believer, and probably nearly all that is meant by this expression is that we, believing and trusting in him, are justified and saved through and on the ground of the merits of his righteousness. "Imputed righteousness is Christ's righteousness in the sense that it is the fruit and purchase of his work in the flesh." (Quotation in " Bible Commentary.") Of course, the righteousness of Christ cannot be actually communicated to us. It is, as Tuckney remarks, "proper to himself, and is as inseparable from him and as incommunicable to others as any other attribute of a thing or its essence itself." When Christ was made sin for us, he suffered for our transgressions, and was himself treated as a transgressor, but was not himself a sinner. He died the *just* for the unjust. " Debts are transferable, but crimes are not." (A. Fuller.) So by our union with Christ, and by virtue of his righteousness, we, though imperfect, are accepted as righteous. In Christ " we are 'made righteousness,' *as if* we had not sinned at all." (Charnock.) " The righteousness is still in

Christ, not in us, even when we are made partakers of the benefit of it." (Bunyan.) " Obedience itself may be and is imputed, while its effects only are imparted and consequently received." (A. Fuller.)[1] In regard to the question, whether the Scriptures impute that to a person which he himself does not possess, we will quote Prof. Cremer's remarks relating to the justification of Abraham. In the expression 'to impute for,' etc., as here used, "the actual fact," he says, "is not taken into account; the opposite rather is assumed, and according to this is the relationship or treatment regulated. That is transferred to the subject in question and imputed to him, which in and for itself does not belong to him; . . . . something is imputed to the person *per substitutionem*. The object in question supplies the place of that for which it answers; it is substituted for it. That this is the apostle's thought is clear from Rom. 4: 4, where the imputing of ver. 3 is distinctly described as imputing according to grace.[1] If this were not an imputing according to grace, a reckoning by substitution, the statement at the end should have been : His righteousness was imputed, etc. But faith is now put in the place of righteousness. Compare ver. 6, 'to whom God imputeth the righteousness without works,' which, according to ver. 8, denotes the forgiveness of sins. Thus this imputing by substitution, or according to grace, is a technical term for the justifying act of God." Similarly, Dr. Weiss: "God reserves it to himself to appoint a condition under which he justifies the sinner. This condition is faith. . . . Accordingly, the act of justification can also be described as that faith is reckoned by God as righteousness. This is a pure act of divine grace, for whatever faith may be, it is by no means righteousness in the original sense (in the sense of fulfilling the law), and God, accordingly, out of grace reckons something for righteousness which is not righteousness in itself, and on the ground of which he did not, therefore, need to justify."]

---

[1] See Andrew Fuller's " Three Conversations [between 'Peter, James, and John' (Booth, Fuller, and Ryland)] on Imputation, Substitution, and Particular Redemption."—(F.)

[2] As Prof. Shedd remarks· We never read of sin being imputed to men gratuitously, by way of favor, without works, or according to God's good pleasure. " The imputation of sin, both original and actual, is *according to debt only*." So eternal life is a free gift, but eternal death is " wages."—(F.)

6 Even as David also describeth the blessedness of the man, unto whom God imputeth righteousness without works,
7 *Saying*, Blessed *are* they whose iniquities are forgiven, and whose sins are covered.
8 Blessed *is* the man to whom the Lord will not impute sin.

6 faith is reckoned for righteousness. Even as David also pronounceth blessing upon the man, unto whom God reckoneth righteousness apart from works,
7 *Saying*,
    Blessed are they whose iniquities are forgiven,
    And whose sins are covered.
8 Blessed is the man to whom the Lord will not reckon sin.

6. Even as David also. The case of David, too, though not strictly co-ordinate with that of Abraham, as there is no mention made of faith, is pertinent in this respect, that David speaks of *free remission*, which is tantamount to justification; for there is no negative and neutral position midway between condemnation and justification. ["The appeal to David next after Abraham was peculiarly apposite, because Christ was and was called a Son of David, and to David next to Abraham the most definite promise of the Messiah had been given." (Philippi.)] **Describeth the blessedness of the man.** More literally, *speaks, or pronounces, the felicitation of the man.* ["Even as David also declareth the man blessed." ("The Five Clergymen.")] The verb here used hardly means to *describe:* it is the word commonly translated "to say," the same that is used in ver. 3: "what *saith* the Scripture." Neither is the noun used here the one properly equivalent to our word "blessedness"; instead of being derived directly from the adjective so often translated "blessed" or "happy," it is derived from it indirectly, through an intermediate verb, which means "to felicitate," or "pronounce happy." This is the verb which in Luke 1: 48 is translated "to call blessed," and in James 5: 11 "to count happy." These are the only places in the New Testament where it is used; and the noun here translated 'blessedness,' like the English word, is used in only one other place besides ver. 6 and 9 of this chapter—namely, in Gal. 4: 15. The meaning, then, is not to *describe* the blessedness, but to utter or pronounce the felicitation, or the happiness; and this is precisely what David does in the passage quoted. **Unto whom God imputeth righteousness without works.** This imputation of 'righteousness without works' [that is, without the merit of works], though not *expressed* in the passage quoted, is clearly *implied;* for free forgiveness, and non-imputation of sin, is gratuitous justification. [Paul has nowhere used the precise phrase: God imputes to us the righteousness of Christ apart from works, but it amounts to the same thing when he speaks of the righteousness of God which shall be ours through faith in Jesus Christ; when he asserts that we are justified gratuitously and by grace through the redemption which is in Christ Jesus; that "justification of life" is through the righteous act and obedience of the second Adam; that our faith in Christ, through which we are justified, is imputed to us for righteousness; that Christ is the end of the law for righteousness; that he is made unto us righteousness; and that we become the righteousness of God in him. See 1 Cor. 1: 30; 2 Cor. 5: 21. Meyer gives this as the equivalent of the last two references—namely, "by means of faith we, through the death of Christ, have been justified before God," and "In his atoning death our justification is grounded." This we may regard as imputed righteousness.]

7, 8. Blessed are they, etc. [More literally: *happy* (are they) **whose iniquities are** (were) **forgiven, and whose sins are** (were) **covered.**] The forgiveness is here represented as prior to and causative of the happiness experienced.[1] These expressions are found in Ps. 32: 1, 2. Our English translation of the Psalm agrees more exactly with the Hebrew than the version of the Seventy here [exactly] quoted does, in that it employs, like the Hebrew, three different words to express sin. In this triple felicitation, sin is viewed as a wrong against God (transgression) which needs to be *forgiven*,

---

[1] The Revised Version renders both verbs in the present tense, as though they were gnomic aorists. The intensive double negative, οὐ μή, is generally used, as here, with the subjunctive aorist, and regularly refers to the future, to what *in no wise* will or should take place. (Winer, p. 505.) The Greek subjunctive has in itself a look toward the future.—(F.)

9 *Cometh* this blessedness then upon the circumcision *only*, or upon the uncircumcision also? for we say that faith was reckoned to Abraham for righteousness.
10 How was it then reckoned? when he was in circumcision, or in uncircumcision? Not in circumcision, but in uncircumcision.
11 And he received the sign of circumcision, a seal

9 Is this blessing then pronounced upon the circumcision, or upon the uncircumcision also? for we say, To Abraham his faith was reckoned for righteousness.
10 How then was it reckoned? when he was in circumcision, or in uncircumcision? Not in circumcision, but in uncircumcision: and he received the sign of circumcision, a seal of the righteousness of

as a loathsome thing (sin) which needs to be *covered*,[1] and as a crime (iniquity) which needs to be *avenged* unless some satisfaction is rendered to justice; or, to express substantially the same distinctions more briefly, sin is represented as an offense against God's majesty, his purity, and his justice. This confirmation of the law through faith (3: 31), in ver. 1–8, derives peculiar force from the character of the two persons whom the apostle selects as illustrations. *Abraham* was the great progenitor of their race, whom they proudly called their father, and on whom their own Scriptures had bestowed the peculiar honor of being styled 'the friend of God.' (2 Chron. 20: 7; Isa. 41: 8.) Compare James 2: 23. *David* was their mighty king, the most distinguished ancestor and type of the Messiah, the man after God's own heart. (1 Sam. 13: 14.) Compare Acts 13: 22. If these two most renowned of their ancestors, who had so much to glory of, renounced all pretense of merit by works, and were justified before God solely by faith, what higher confirmation of the apostle's doctrine could be needed? Surely they could not claim to surpass these worthies in merit, nor hope to succeed where these had failed. [In these words of David we have, as Godet remarks, the negative side of justification, the evil which it removes; while in regard to Abraham it was only the positive side which was under treatment. the blessing it confers. Thus it is that the two passages complete one another.]

9. Cometh this blessedness (or, *felicitation*) **then,** etc. [An inference from ver. 3–9 in the form of an inquiry.] The apostle blends the two examples intimately together, and with good reasons, for Abraham was unquestionably included in the blessing pronounced by David, and David was no less unquestionably included among those justified by faith apart from works. Yet as the case of Abraham was best adapted to the apostle's purpose, partly on account of the form of

expression here again quoted, and partly on account of the *date* of his circumcision, he selects the example of Abraham for fuller development in what follows. It will be observed that the words 'cometh' and 'only' are supplied by the translators. The simple verb *is* might answer instead of the first [but the "is pronounced" of the Revised Version is still better; see ver. 6], and the second is clearly implied in the word 'also' after 'uncircumcision.' **For we say.** This expression implies an affirmative answer to the last clause of the question—"yes, upon the uncircumcision, also"—as is fully expressed in the similar case in 3 : 29. Thus the 'for' introduces the *proof* of that implied affirmative. [**We say that faith.** The article is connected with 'faith' in the Greek, and is here equivalent to *his* faith.]

10. How was it then reckoned? In what condition, then, was he when it was so reckoned, circumcised or uncircumcised? From Gen. 15 : 6; 16 : 1–4, 16, it appears that Abraham was said to have been justified by faith some months, at least, before the birth of Ishmael, and that he was eighty-six years old when Ishmael was born; and from Gen. 17 : 24, that he was ninety-nine years old when he was circumcised. His "faith was reckoned to him for righteousness," therefore at least thirteen or fourteen years ["perhaps as much as twenty-five" (Alford)] *before* he received the sign of circumcision. ["Circumcision was so little the ground of justification that it was rather the consequence of it." (De Wette.) "Abraham's righteousness through faith was attained when as yet there was no distinction between circumcised and uncircumcised, and to this mode of becoming just before God, independent of external conditions, Christianity, by its righteousness from faith, leads back again and continues it." (Meyer.)]

11. The sign of circumcision. This is what is called the genitive of apposition, when two words thus connected by 'of' relate to

[1] In the Old Testament God is often spoken of as *covering* sins, but this (quotation) is the only instance mentioned in the New Testament. Augustine says:

"If God covered sins he was unwilling to observe them, and if unwilling to observe he was unwilling to punish."—(F.)

of the righteousness of the faith which *he had yet* being | the faith which he had while he was in uncircumci-

the same thing: He received circumcision as a sign. See other examples of the same nature in 2 Cor. 1 : 22; 5 : 5; Eph. 6 : 14, etc. [Meyer thinks that with this sense the word 'sign' should have the article. His interpretation is: "A sign which took place through circumcision," the genitive defining the sign more precisely. Winer and De Wette regard it as simply genitive of apposition, like the phrase : Cities of Sodom and Gomorrah. (2 Peter 2 : 6.) On the absence of the article before the word 'sign,' see 2 : 6.] **A seal of the righteousness of the faith.** Setting the seal to a document is the final act of its confirmation. So circumcision is represented as a token or seal of God's covenant with Abraham. (Gen. 17 : 11.) [The word seal in connection with circumcision is used by Paul alone, and only in this place. In Genesis, circumcision is called the token of the covenant between God and Abraham. Regarded as a "seal," it seems designed to certify the reality and worth of Abraham's faith-righteousness. It has nothing to do directly with attesting or confirming the righteousness of the faith of any other individual. If every circumcised Jew who has lived from the days of Abraham until the present time were destitute of the righteousness of faith, still the sign they bore in their flesh would be a "seal of the righteousness of the faith which Abraham had while he was in uncircumcision." Dr. Hodge says that "all the Jews were professors of the true religion, and constituted the visible church, in which, by divine appointment, their children were included. This is the broad and enduring basis of infant church membership." We grant that this argument from circumcision will ever be the principal one for infant baptism. But how silent the apostle is as to the virtual transference of this chief rite of Judaism into the pale of Christianity! Was it because of the severity of his contest with Jewish legalism, which specially centred itself around this rite? Yet how easily he might have allayed—certainly to a great extent—the animosities and prejudices of these zealots for circumcision had he at once and plainly assured them that infant baptism, by divine appointment, was to take the place of circumcision. Let us consider,

for a moment, how in this country infant baptism (of females as well as males) would be paralleled with Jewish circumcision. First, and most essential of all, we must have an eminently pious forefather—a righteous, national founder. We have a Washington, who was, at least, remarkable for his unselfishness and his integrity, willing to become an humble, private citizen after winning the laurels of a great conqueror, which would seemingly entitle him to become the nation's perpetual dictator. God, for his great integrity, makes a special covenant with him and with his people, assuring him that he should be the father of a mighty nation, and that He would be in a special manner a God to him and to them forever. In token of this covenant, he bids Washington baptize himself, and all the children he might have, and all his slaves, and also gives command that henceforth every infant born in the nation should be baptized on the eighth day after its birth, and that every immigrant who wished to become an American citizen should also be baptized; and, finally, that every unbaptized person throughout the land in all coming generations should be cut off from his (or her) people. This would be circumcision-baptism, and our duty as parents in this matter would be very plain. In this kind of baptism we have a "seal" (an invisible one, however) of the rightness of the integrity of Washington before he was baptized, and every citizen of this country, though he be a traitor at heart, yet bears this (invisible) seal of the uprightness of Washington. But is such a national church (?) as this the model for a church of Christ? See further on this subject, chapter 26 of the writer's "Studies on Baptism;" also Dr. Arnold's excellent remarks in Appendix A of this volume.] **Which he had yet being uncircumcised.** The pronoun 'which' here (standing for the equally ambiguous Greek article) may refer to either of the words 'faith' or 'righteousness.' The former reference is the more natural, and seems to be confirmed by the intimate connection between faith and uncircumcision in the following clause, and also in the next verse. But if the pronoun (or, in Greek, the article) be referred to the word

uncircumcised: that he might be the father of all them that believe, though they be not circumcised; that righteousness might be imputed unto them also:

12 And the father of circumcision to them who are not of the circumcision only, but who also walk in the steps of that faith of our father Abraham, which *he had* being *yet* uncircumcised.

sion: that he might be the father of all them that believe, though they be in uncircumcision, that right-

12 eousness might be reckoned unto them; and the father of circumcision to them who not only are of the circumcision, but who also walk in the steps of that faith of our father Abraham which he had in

13 uncircumcision. For not [1] through the law was the

1 Or, *through law.*

'righteousness,' which *Alford* prefers, as more relevant to the apostle's argument, then the article before the word 'faith' should be canceled, and we should read: *A seal of the righteousness of faith* [equivalent here to *faith righteousness*] *which he had yet being uncircumcised.* The former construction (defended by De Wette and Meyer) is, however, preferred. **That he might be the father,** etc. [*In order that he might be,* etc. The present infinitive, in order to be, or, to his being, is best rendered by the auxiliary 'might,' though the present, 'may be' would well express its force. Prof. Boise remarks that the placing the subject directly after the infinitive instead of before it is especially frequent in the New Testament. Œcumenius observes that "as those in uncircumcision have not Abraham for their father, for the sole reason that he believed in an uncircumcised state, unless they are also imitators of his faith, so neither without this condition shall they of the circumcision have him for their father from the mere circumstance of his having been circumcised."] The fact that Abraham was declared to be justified by faith before he was circumcised gives believing Gentiles an equal title with believing Jews to be called his children, and to inherit, as his spiritual heirs, justification by faith. [The full force of the original is: Abraham received this sign and seal, *in order that* (by divine arrangement and purpose) he might be the father of all who believe through (in a state of) uncircumcision. Compare 2 : 27. The final 'that' is probably to be connected with believing, thus: Of all them who are believing, . . . in order that righteousness might be reckoned unto them. The *spiritual* fatherhood of Abraham is referred to by John the Baptist and by Christ himself. (Matt. 3 : 9; Luke 3 : 8; John 8 : 39.) The whole life of this "father of believers," says Tholuck, "displayed an extraordinary strength of faith. . . . On account of this persevering faith, he is highly extolled

even among the Jews (1 Macc. 2 : 52), 'Philo *de Abrahamo.*' "]

12. And (*that he might be,* is to be supplied from ver. 11) **the father of circumcision** (not to *all the circumcised,* but only) **to them who are not of the circumcision only, but who also walk in the steps of that faith ol our father Abraham, which he had being yet uncircumcised.** All seems plain here; but there is a grammatical difficulty in the original, arising from the article preceding the participle in the clause translated, 'but who also walk,' etc. We should be obliged, in strict accuracy, to translate as follows: to them who are not of the circumcision only, but also *to them* who walk, etc. Some meet this difficulty by saying that Paul wrote inaccurately here through negligence, others by supposing that the text has been corrupted in transcribing, of which there is no documentary evidence. We leave the difficulty with only this remark, that there is no reasonable doubt that our English translation expresses with substantial accuracy, the apostle's thought.[1] [Godet thinks to avoid the difficulty by rendering the first article (τοῖς) as a pronoun, and the second as a definite article—thus: those who are not only of the circumcision, but who *are also,* at the same time *the* (individuals)· or the walkers, etc. The application of the term *walking* to moral conduct is quite a peculiarity with Paul. See notes on 6 : 4. 'Steps' is in the dative of *norm,* or rule. (Buttmann: manner.) Literally, it reads: *those walking in* (or by) *the footsteps of the in-uncircumcision-faith of our father Abraham.* "Hence," says Godet, "it follows that it is not, properly speaking, for the Gentile believers to enter by the gate of the Jews, but for Jewish believers to enter by the gate of the Gentiles." "If these apostolic propositions," says Dr. J. B. Thomas, in his "Mould of Doctrines," p. 82, "be not seen at once clearly to obliterate the foundations of the national, the hereditary, and the sacramental theories of the church, it

[1] See Appendix A.

13 For the promise, that he should be the heir of the world, *was* not to Abraham, or to his seed, through the law, but through the righteousness of faith.

14 For if they which are of the law *be* heirs, faith is made void, and the promise made of none effect.

15 Because the law worketh wrath: for where no law is, *there is* no transgression.

promise to Abraham or to his seed, that he should be heir of the world, but through the righteous-
14 ness of faith. For if they who are of the law be heirs, faith is made void, and the promise is made
15 of none effect; for the law worketh wrath; but

would be vain to seek further to elaborate or emphasize them."]

13. If those who believe are Abraham's seed, then his promised inheritance is theirs. **The promise, that he should be the heir of the world.** We do not read any explicit promise of this sort, as given either to Abraham or to his seed. For 'the heir of the world' is too broad an expression to be limited to the land of Canaan; and, besides this, the land of Canaan was never promised to believing *Gentiles*, who are here plainly reckoned as the seed of Abraham. How, then, are Abraham and his seed the promised heirs of the world? It was promised to Abraham, that his seed should be as the stars of heaven (Gen. 15: 5); that he should be a father of many nations (Gen. 17 : 5); that in him and in his seed all nations should be blessed (Gen. 12 : 3; 18: 18); believers in Christ are his seed (Rom. 4: 11; Gal. 3 : 29); and they shall possess all nations, and shall inherit the world (Dan. 7 : 27; Matt. 5 : 5; 1 Cor. 3 : 22); again, Christ is preeminently the seed of Abraham (Gal. 3 : 16); he shall possess all the world (Ps. 2: 7, 8; Dan. 7 : 14; Rev. 11 : 15). The promise will be verified, therefore, both figuratively and explicitly, in the dominion of all nations given to believers; and literally and explicitly in the dominion of the world given to Christ. The expression 'heir of the world' derives peculiar emphasis from the fact that among the Hebrews things received by inheritance were alone inalienable; hence the frequency with which any firm and perpetual possession is called an inheritance. [The promise —namely, that Abraham should be heir of the world was not **through the law**—that is, it came not through the medium of the law, nor did it rest on the law as its ground. But the promise, like the inheritance, was a gift of grace (Gal. 3 : 18), and it was made to Abraham **through** (the medium of) **the righteousness of faith.** The declaration of

Abraham's righteousness through faith is recorded in Gen. 15: 6, but the promise in substance was made to him previously, and was renewed after this time. He had the righteousness of faith before its declaration was made.[1] Philippi thinks that by the use of present tense the inheritance of the world is represented as a present possession to Abraham.]

14. He here makes the supposition which was denied in ver. 13, and shows that its consequence would be of such a nature as to confirm that denial. **If they which** (who) **are of the law.** [On the force of this *of*, see 2: 8.] If they who rely upon their works are heirs, the covenant of faith **is made void,** is broken; faith *has been emptied* of its significance, and the promise has been virtually abolished. If the heirship is by merit, it can dispense with faith and promise. The apostle uses here very fit and forcible words. [How the promise is made of none effect is told, as De Wette and others think, in the next verse—to wit, "the law which produces wrath excludes grace, and therewith the promise." "With the word *promise* the apostle always associates the notion of the spontaneous, *unconditioned* promise of grace." (Philippi.) The inheritance through promise was bestowed graciously, as a free gift. (Gal. 3 : 18.) If inheritance is by the law, then, as Godet says, "it is all over at a stroke both with faith and with the promise; with faith, that is to say, with the hope of that final heritage, since the realization of that expectation would be bound to a condition which sinful man could not execute, the fulfillment of the law, and since faith would thus be deprived of its object; and next, with the promise itself; for. an impossible condition being attached to it, it would thereby be paralyzed in its effects."]

15. Because the law worketh wrath. The propriety of the reasoning—'because,' or

---

[1] The neuter article which heads the clause, 'that he should be the heir,' does not properly belong to the clause as a whole, as in 8 : 26, but to the infinitive (com-

pare ver. 16, 18), thus giving the verb greater prominence. The clause stands in apposition with *promise.* —(F.)

16 Therefore *it is* of faith, that *it might be* by grace; to the end the promise might be sure to all the seed; not to that only which is of the law, but to that also which is of the faith of Abraham; who is the father of us all,

16 For this cause *it is* of faith, that *it may be* according to grace; to the end that the promise may be sure to all the seed; not to that only which is of the law, but to that also which is of the faith of Abraham,

rather *for*—is seen in the natural antithesis between *promise* and *law;* the one founded on grace, and the other on justice, the one giving freely, and the other exacting sternly; so that they mutually exclude each other as grounds of inheritance. 'The law worketh wrath.' [Of course, then, it cannot confer the inheritance of promise. The law worketh out wrath through its transgression, and hence this wrath is not that of man against God, but that of God visited upon man on account of his transgressions.]¹ **For where no law is.** [*But,* instead of 'for,' is the reading adopted by Lachmann, Tischendorf, and Tregelles, according to preponderating evidence. The verse will then read: "But where there is no law, neither is there transgression." —A. H.] **There is no transgression.** ["Namely, which excites the wrath of God, the Lawgiver." (Meyer.)] We need not say, with Beza, "the reading *ought* to be, 'where law is, there transgression is'"; but we *may* say that this negative axiom implies, in this connection, the corresponding positive. If there *were* no law, there *could* be no transgression; but there is transgression, as all men know, and so the law may be said to work wrath, which is inseparably linked to transgression. [Elsewhere the apostle describes how sin as a principle (ἀνομία) is augmented into "transgression" by the law, which is the "power of sin." The wrath of God, as stated in 1: 18, seq., is due to the offenses even of the Gentiles who have not the law, but much more heavily must it rest upon those who transgress God's revealed will. "Thus," says Philippi, "the divine wrath and the punishment (κόλασις) annexed thereto, has its differences of degree."]

16. Therefore of faith. ['Therefore' (διὰ τοῦτο), *on account of.* This usually has reference to something preceding, here to ver. 14, 15, because not from *law,* therefore from *grace.* Alford, however, seems to refer it to a reason which follows.] What is the subject here? What is by faith? The *inheritance*

seems to be the most natural subject. **That it might** [through the divine purpose] **be by grace**—which it could not be if of works. ['Grace' here denies the meritoriousness, not only of works, but of faith. If believing in Christ, or faith in Christ, is in any sense a work or exercise of the human mind and heart, it is here denied to be the meritorious cause, or ground, of our justification. "Faith," says Calvin, "we compare to a vessel; for, unless we come empty with the mouth of our soul open to implore the grace of Christ, we cannot receive Christ. Whence it may be inferred that we do not detract from Christ the power of justifying, when we teach that faith receives him before it receives his righteousness. Nevertheless, I cannot admit . . . that faith is Christ; as though an earthen vessel were a treasure because gold is concealed in it. For faith, although intrinsically it is of no dignity or value, justifies us by an application of Christ just as a vessel full of money constitutes a man rich."] **To the end the promise might be sure to all the seed.** [The apostle here indicates the purpose of divine *grace.* In Paul's view, as Olshausen remarks, "Everything which depends upon the decision, faithfulness, and constancy of such an irresolute and wavering being as man is extremely uncertain. . . . The blessedness of the man is certain, only because God has promised it and firmly intends it, and he only who believes in this decided will of God has this salvation also wrought in him."] The emphatic words here are 'sure,' in contrast with made void of ver. 14, and 'all,' as explained in the following words: not only to Jews, but also to Gentiles, not only to the seed in the natural sense, but also to the seed in the spiritual sense. [Abraham is therefore the spiritual father of all who are spiritually circumcised, of all who are Jews inwardly—that is, of all true believers. (2: 29; Phil. 3: 3.) Christ is the true seed of Abraham to whom the promises were made, the seed through whom all nations of the earth should be

---

¹ ἔχθρα, enmity (against God), is ascribed by Paul to guilty men, but never ὀργή, wrath (towards God). This, however, is often predicated of God in his relation toward man. See 1: 18; 2: 5, 8; 3: 5; 5: 9; 9: 22; Eph. 2: 3; 5: 6· Col. 3: 6; 1 Thess. 1: 10; 2: 16; 5: 9, etc.— (F.)

17 (As it is written, I have made thee a father of many nations,) before him whom he believed, *even* God, who quickeneth the dead, and calleth those things which be not as though they were:
18 Who against hope believed in hope, that he might

17 who is the father of us all (as it is written, A fathe: of many nations have I made thee) before him whom he believed, *even* God, who quickeneth the dead, and calleth the things that are not, as though they 18 were. Who in hope believed against hope, to the

blessed, and we, by believing in Christ, and by virtue of a living fellowship with him, thus become sons of Abraham and heirs according to promise.]

17. (As it is written, I have made thee a father of many nations.[1] This parenthesis confirms the last clause of ver. 16 by quoting Gen. 17: 5 [exactly after the LXX], and so quoting it as to imply not only a comparison, or analogy, between the natural posterity, composed of many nations, and the spiritual posterity, composed of all believers; but so as to imply that the prophecy was directly applicable to the latter. 'I have made thee' [or, *have appointed thee*]. He was already, in God's sight, a 'father of many nations,' though not, in point of fact, until long after. **Before him whom he believed.** This clause is to be connected directly with the closing words of ver. 16, 'who is the father of us all.' ["A vivid realization," says Meyer, "of the believing patriarch as if he were standing there as father of us all before the face of God." Some, as Bengel, Philippi, Godet, think this *before*, etc., should be connected with a verb in the past tense, and not with 'is father,' etc., which refers to the time of Paul's writing. Philippi supplies: and as such he was appointed, or, and thus he stood there, etc., deriving these phrases from the preceding verb: 'I have made.' Our Common and Revised Versions regard the relative as in the genitive by attraction to the case of its antecedent, but this attraction in the New Testament occurs only with verbs that govern the accusative, and to believe (πιστεύω) is not followed by the accusative of person. Hence Winer, Meyer, Philippi resolve this phrase thus: before God (before) whom, in whose sight, he believed. "In this verb the faith of Abraham is again made prominent, in order to intimate afresh how this alone mediated the true spiritual and universal fatherhood of Abraham." (Philippi.)] **Who quick-**

eneth the dead. In allusion to the advanced age of Abraham and Sarah. Compare ver. 19 [and still primarily referring, we think, to the literal dead, as a "standing characteristic of the divine omnipotence." Compare Deut. 32: 39; 1 Sam. 2: 6; Wisd. of Sol. 16: 13; John 5: 21; 2 Cor. 1: 9; 1 Tim. 6: 13, etc. Meyer: "'Who quickeneth the dead and calleth the non-existent as though it were,' and certainly, therefore, can quicken the decayed powers of procreation and dispose of generations not yet in existence."] **And calleth those things which be not as though they were.** That is, Isaac, and Abraham's posterity in general. [Meyer translates and comments thus: "'who utters his disposing decree over that which does not exist, equally as over the existing.' What a lofty expression of all-commanding power! And how thoroughly in harmony with the then position of Abraham! For, as he stood before God and believed (Gen. 15: 6), God had just shown him the stars of heaven with the promise: 'so shall thy seed be.' So that God hereby issued his potent summons (so shall it be) to something that was not (the seed of Abraham) as though it had been." Alford makes this calling to mean speaking of. (9: 7.) Philippi, like Meyer, regards it as equivalent to issuing commands.][2] The remainder of the chapter is devoted to an encomium on Abraham, the father and pattern of believers.

18. Who against hope [where there was nothing to hope for (De Wette)] **believed in hope** [*on* the ground of *hope*]. Who hopefully believed in God, contrary to all human hope. Pious trust in God shines brightest when all human hope is quenched. [Chrysostom: "Past hope of man, in hope of God." Bengel: "He believed in the hope of the promise against the hope of reason." Meyer: "Abraham's faith was opposed to hope in its *objective* reference, and yet not despairing, but rather based on hope in its *subjective* reference—a significant oxymoron."] **That**

---

[1] The Greek has ὅτι as a part of the quotation. As a causal conjunction it might be rendered, *for* I have made thee, etc.—(F.)

[2] De Wette and others, taking ὡς in the sense of εἰς,

refer it to God's creative power. The force of the subjective negative μὴ is thus expressed by Godet: "He calls as being in existence what he knows himself to be non-existent."—(F.)

become the father of many nations, according to that which was spoken, So shall thy seed be.

19 And being not weak in faith, he considered not his own body now dead, when he was about a hundred years old, neither yet the deadness of Sarah's womb:

end that he might become a father of many nations, according to that which had been spoken, So shall 19 thy seed be. And without being weakened in faith he considered his own body [1] now as good as dead (he being about a hundred years old), and the deadness

---

1 Many ancient authorities omit *now.*

---

he might become the father of many nations. [The Greek word for *father* has here no article, and the Revised Version is therefore correct, 'a father.'] These words, alike in the original and in the English, admit of two interpretations. They may mean (*a*), he believed that he should become, which makes his becoming the father of many nations the direct object of his faith, the thing which he believed; or they may mean (*b*), he believed, in order that he might become, his believing was a necessary condition of his becoming. This last sense of the words is preferred, as being the more natural construction of the expression in the original text. The first view, however, is advocated by Stuart, and several able German commentators [among whom we may mention De Wette]. It is not to be understood, however, that Abraham believed *because he knew* that his believing was an indispensable condition of his becoming the father of many nations: in order that, always implies an *intelligent design* on the part of the *Divine Disposer* [see on 3: 4, and Winer p. 458], but does not necessarily imply a *conscious purpose* on the part of the *human actor;* and this distinction is of great importance to the right understanding of many clauses which are introduced by the formula, "in order that," or some equivalent expression. In reference to the ambiguity here, so exactly the same in the original Greek and in the English translation, it is not out of place to remark, that it is a rare excellence in a translation when it can successfully transfer a doubtful meaning from one language to another. This remark applies, of course, only to passages where, in the judgment of competent scholars, there is a *real uncertainty* in the meaning of the original. In every other case, an ambiguity in a translation is a serious defect. The last clause of Heb. 5: 7 presents another instance of a happy transference of an ambiguity from the Greek to the English, although there is perhaps less real doubt as to the true meaning of the original there than there is here. **So shall thy seed be**—that is, as the context in

Gen. 15: 5 more fully expresses, as numerous, or rather innumerable, as the stars of heaven. "And he brought him forth abroad, and said, Look now toward heaven, and tell (that is, count) the stars if thou be able to number them; and he said unto him: So shall thy seed be." [Paul, according to Calvin, "designedly adduced this quotation incomplete, in order to stimulate us to read the Scriptures."]

19. Being not weak in faith. [The force of the clause may be expressed thus: *because* he was not weak, etc.] By a figure of speech, which is the opposite of hyperbole or "exaggeration," the apostle here says *less* than he might truly have said. He might truly have said, "being exceedingly strong," instead of saying, "being not weak." But this way of speaking which he here uses is often more forcible than the opposite figure, as this excites the imagination to *fill out* the contracted idea, while the opposite figure tempts the critical faculty to *abate* something from the magnified expression. It would be well for enthusiastic speakers and writers to bear this principle in mind. That Abraham's faith, instead of being *weak*, was remarkably *strong*, is shown by the fact that **he considered not his own body now dead,** but believed God's promise, in spite of that consideration—that is, though he was well aware of the natural obstacle, in the bodily condition of both himself and his wife, he did not *regard* that circumstance as any valid objection to the fulfillment of God's promise, that he should have a numerous offspring. **When he was about a hundred years old.** [Bengel remarks that after Shem we read of no one one hundred years old who begat children. (Gen. 11.) He also says that Abraham's renewed bodily vigor remained even with his marriage with Keturah.] It appears from Gen. 18: 1, that Abraham was ninety-nine years old when the Lord renewed to him, for the last time before its fulfillment, the promise of a son by Sarah, who was then ninety years old (ver. 17), and from ver. 21 it would seem that Isaac was born just a year from that

H

20 He staggered not at the promise of God through unbelief; but was strong in faith, giving glory to God; 21 And being fully persuaded, that what he had promised, he was able also to perform.

20 of Sarah's womb: yea, looking unto the promise of God, he wavered not through unbelief, but waxed 21 strong through faith, giving glory to God, and being fully assured that, what he had promised, he was

time. So far as the record goes, it would appear that Abraham was just a hundred years old, and Sarah ninety-one, when Isaac was born. But Paul did not think necessary to be more exact, and so he says "about an hundred years old." Besides, he is not speaking of the precise time of Isaac's birth, but of the age of Abraham when he showed his strong faith by believing God's promise that a son should be born of Sarah a year from that time. [It should be remarked still further, that according to the highest critical authorities, the word *not* should be omitted after the word *considered.*[1] Thus: *And being not weak in faith, he considered his own body now dead, when he was about an hundred years old, and the deadness of Sarah's womb.* (Ver. 20·) *But staggered not,* etc. He took into earnest consideration the natural impossibility of offspring in such a case, but his faith in the promise of God was not thereby shaken. Some editors omit the word *now* before *dead*, and the sense is not injured by the omission; moreover, the insertion of it can be more readily explained than its omission, if it was a part of the original text.—A. H.]

20. He staggered not [literally—*was not divided.* The verb is passive in form, but may be used as in the middle voice.] He wavered not at the promise [or, *with respect to the* promise;—the Revisers' rendering does not here closely follow their text] through unbelief—that is, wavered not as he would have done if he had been weak in faith; **but was strong in faith** [literally, *made strong*, or *was instrengthened.* Paul himself was thus "instrengthened" at many times, and in his last hours especially, by the presence of his Saviour. (2 Tim. 4: 17.)] **Giving glory to God.** He gave glory to God, by confiding so implicitly in his truth and almighty power. But the expression naturally suggests the thought of some *oral expression* of adoration and thankfulness, some devout doxology.

There is no *record* of any such act; but it seems highly probable that the patriarch would not fail, on such an occasion, to give verbal utterance to his devout and grateful emotions.

21. And being fully persuaded. [This and the preceding participle are in the past tense, their action being contemporaneous with the verb was strengthened.] The participle translated *being fully persuaded* [from a verb meaning to bring full measure] is very emphatic. It is from the same verb that is translated in the same way in 14: 5. What an inestimable advantage it would be, not only to every Christian, but to every man enlightened by divine revelation, if he was *fully persuaded* that what God has promised he is able and determined also to perform! And how unreasonable and sinful it is to entertain any doubt or misgiving about the fulfillment of anything which God has promised, however difficult or impossible it may seem to our human conceptions! [The verb *promised*, etymologically signifying *to proclaim* (in the way of promise), is here in the perfect passive form with middle signification. The proper rendering of this clause, 'what he *hath* promised he *is* able also to do,' makes this declaration applicable for all time. Pareus says: "Doubt has two arguments: *Will* God do this, and *can* God do this? Faith has likewise two arguments: God *will* do this because he has promised, and he *can* do it because he is omnipotent." Concerning the faith of Abraham in his many trials and in his great trial, see Heb. 11: 8, 17. Have not we the same reason for confiding fully in God's promises as our spiritual father Abraham had? And cannot we yield the same implicit trust? *We* love to be trusted, to have our word believed. May we not reverently say that God loves to be trusted and believed? Certainly we honor him when we confide in his word, his power, and his grace.]

---

[1] The *not* is wanting in ℵ A B C and some cursives and early versions, but is retained as a part of the genuine text by such critics as Fritzsche, De Wette, and Meyer. The latter says: "This omission . . . manifestly arose from incorrectly having regard here to Gen. 17." Philippi, Lange, Alford, also favor the

retention of the negative. Buttmann, on the other hand, discards the *not*, and supplies in thought a μέν (indeed) to the verb, 'considered,' to which the following δε ('but staggered not,' etc.) is made to correspond. —(F.)

22 And therefore it was imputed to him for righteousness.
23 Now it was not written for his sake alone, that it
was imputed to him;
24 But for us also, to whom it shall be imputed, if we
believe on him that raised up Jesus our Lord from the
dead;
25 Who was delivered for our offences, and was raised
again for our justification.

22 able also to perform. Wherefore also it was reck-
23 oned unto him for righteousness. Now it was not
written for his sake alone, that it was reckoned unto
24 him, but for our sake also, unto whom it shall be
reckoned, who believe on him that raised Jesus
25 our Lord from the dead, who was delivered up for
our trespasses, and was raised for our justification.

---

22. And therefore [literally, 'wherefore also']—that is, because his faith in God was so complete and admirable [amid the strongest temptations to disbelieve]. The apostle now repeats the expression: **It** [that is, his believing] **was imputed unto him,** with a view of making the application to believers as the spiritual posterity of Abraham. [**For righteousness.** This *for*, as Meyer says, does not denote that faith has justification merely "in its train," or that its leads finally into righteousness, but the meaning of the expression is that faith is accounted, immediately and directly, *as* righteousness.]

23, 24. Now it was not written. We have here one of those instances of the niceties of Greek syntax, which cannot easily be fully exhibited in a translation. The formula "as it is written" occurs very often in the New Testament, in introducing passages from the Old. In such cases the verb is in the *perfect* tense, while here it is in what is called the aorist. The perfect always has a reference to the present time, describing the action as past indeed, but also as abiding in its permanent consequences; while the aorist simply describes the action as finished in some past time. The difference may be sufficiently represented in English by the expressions: "It *stands* written,"[1] and "it *was* written." Hence the propriety of the use of the perfect in the ordinary cases of quotation from the Old Testament, where the Scripture quoted is conceived of as a permanent record, without any particular reference to the time or act of writing it; and hence, also, the propriety of the aorist tense in this instance, where the *act* of writing is emphasized. This distinction is dwelt upon particularly here, because this aorist form is very rare in cases where the *inspired* writings are referred to. The only other instances in mind are 15:4 and 1 Cor. 10:11, in both which places, as here, the

object is to fix the attention on the act of writing. The unparalleled fullness and nicety of the Greek language in expressing grammatical relations, of which the passage under consideration is an instance, is one of many reasons why the Christian teacher should, when practicable, make himself familiarly acquainted with the original language in which the New Testament is written. **For his sake alone.** Not merely for the purpose of a historical affirmation and appreciation of Abraham's faith. **But for us also, to whom it shall be imputed.** [The *shall* is a separate verb in the original, and denotes something more than mere futurity, even the certainty and continuous accomplishment of the divine purpose.[2]] Such passages as this furnish a warrant for a sober and cautious generalization from the historical narratives of the Old Testament. See, as above, 15:4, and 1 Cor. 10:11; also 1 Cor. 9:10. **If we believe on him that raised up Jesus our Lord from the dead.** God is here represented as the object of *our* faith, in order to make the parallel with Abraham more complete. (Ver. 17.) ["We who believe on the same God on whom Abraham believed, but who appears to us in a peculiar relation as finisher of the work of redemption." (Tholuck.) This raising of Jesus from the dead seems here to be purposely referred to as being a specially great and gracious exercise of Omnipotence (we may well trust such a Being, and because of its importance as an essential element in man's full redemption.]

25. [Gifford: "The apostle thus returns to the main point of his subject (3:24), 'bringing in the cross into the midst.' (Chrysostom)." Hodge: "This verse is a comprehensive statement of the gospel." **Delivered**—*given up* to death. Compare 8:32; Eph. 5:2, 25; Isa. 53:12. See the touching particularity of the apostle's language in Gal. 2:20, where he

---

[1] Luther has used precisely this expression in his German translation, "es stehet geschrieben," "it *stands* written."

[2] The word λογίζομαι—to count, reckon, or impute—is used here for the seventh time in this chapter.—[F.]

says of Christ: "Who loved *me* and gave himself for *me*." If Christ died for all, why may not *every* reader of these lines adopt this same language?] The preposition [διά, which with the accusative "denotes either the moving or the final cause." (Boise.)] is the same in both clauses, in the Greek as well as in the English. Yet, while the same preposition is *suitable* for both clauses, it is evident that the relation of his being delivered up, to our offenses is not precisely the same as the relation of his being raised again, to our justification. He was delivered up, *because we had offended;* he was raised again, *that we might be* justified; he was delivered, *on account of* our offenses; he was raised again, *in order to* our justification. [As we are said to be justified on the ground of Christ's obedience and in his blood, so some, as Bishop Horsley in former times, and Godet in our own, have given the preposition the same meaning in both places; thus Godet: "In the same way as Jesus died for our offenses [committed]—that is, our (merited) condemnation, he was raised because of our (accomplished) justification. Our sin had killed him, our justification [accomplished] raised him again." He interprets 1 Cor. 15: 17, "If Jesus be not risen ye are yet in your sins" in a similar manner: "So long as (your) security is in prison, (your) debt is not paid; the immediate *effect* of payment would be his liberation." But would not his non-resurrection show that he died as one of us sinners, and that man therefore has no Saviour? Meyer's view is as follows: "The resurrection of the sacrificed One was required to produce in man *the faith* through which alone the objective fact of the atoning offering of Jesus could have the effect of justifying *subjectively*, because Christ is the propitiation (ἱλαστήριον) through faith." Alford's view is quite similar. Ellicott, on the "power of Christ's resurrection," says: "The resurrection of Christ has at least four spiritual efficacies—namely: (*a*) as quickening our souls, Eph. 2: 5; (*b*) as confirming the hope of our resurrection, Rom, 8: 1; (*c*) as assuring us of our *present* justification, Rom. 4: 24, 25 (*d*) as securing our final justification, our triumph over death, and participation in his

glory, 2 Cor. 4: 10, seq. Col. 3: 4."] This noun *justification* ["The establishment of a man as just by acquittal from guilt." (Cremer.)] is used only three times in our English New Testament—here, and in the 16th and 18th verse of the following chapter.[1] ["When the prison door," says Chalmers, "is opened to a criminal, and that by the very authority which lodged him there, it evinces that the debt of his transgression has been rendered, and that he now stands acquitted of all its penalties. It was not for his own, but for our offenses, that Jesus was delivered unto the death, and that his body was consigned to the imprisonment of the grave. And when an angel descended from heaven and rolled back the great stone from the door of the sepulchre, this speaks that the justice of God is satisfied, that the ransom of our iniquities has been paid, that Christ has rendered a full discharge of all that debt for which he undertook as the great surety between God and the sinners who believe in him " Dr. Schaff says: "Without the resurrection, the death of Christ would be of no avail, and his grave would be the grave of all our hopes, as the apostle clearly says. (1 Cor. 15: 17.) A gospel of a *dead* Saviour would be a miserable failure and delusion. . . . It is by the fact of the resurrection that Christ's death was shown to be the death of the innocent and righteous One for foreign guilt, and that it was accepted by God as a full satisfaction for the sins of the world." Dr. Weiss says: "For Paul the special significance of the resurrection must be this, that it proves that the death of Christ was not the death of the sinner. . . . Accordingly, the assurance that God cannot condemn us is owing primarily, it is true, to the death of Christ, but still more to his resurrection and exaltation to God's right hand, inasmuch as these first prove that his death was the death of the Mediator of salvation, who has redeemed us from condemnation. . . . The objective atonement was accomplished by means of the death of Christ, but the appropriation of it in justification is only possible if we believe in the saving significance of his death, and we can attain to faith in that only if it is sealed by means of the resurrection."]

---

[1] It corresponds exactly with the Greek word δικαίωσις, of which it is a translation, here and in 5: 18, the only two places where that word is found; not quite so exactly with the Greek word δικαίωμα, for which it stands in 5: 16, which is elsewhere translated " righteousness."

CHAPTER V.

THEREFORE being justified by faith, we have peace with God through our Lord Jesus Christ:

1 Being therefore justified [1] by faith, [2] we have peace 2 with God through our Lord Jesus Christ; through

1 Gr. *out of.* . . . .2 Many ancient authorities read *let us have.*

Observe, that the way of justification before God was substantially the same *before* Christ, as it is now, the same for Abraham and David, as it is for us.

The apostle here introduces what he follows in the next four chapters (5-8), "*death,* as connected with *sin,* and *life,* as connected with *righteousness.*" (Alford.) [Others, as Godet, Gifford, Turner, think that the subject of sanctification is not introduced until the sixth chapter.]

Ch. 5: In this chapter the apostle treats of the happy results of the gospel way of justification, both to the individual believer (ver. 1-11), and to the race at large. (Ver. 12-21.) [Perhaps as a general title to the chapter we might have something like this: Justification through Christ contrasted with condemnation through Adam. The more special subject of the first eleven verses is the certainty of final salvation for justified believers. (Godet.)]

1. Therefore. The last half of this verse is an inference from the preceding section. (3:21.) **Being justified by faith;** or, more exactly, *having been justified by faith,* for it is important to make the distinction here between the *past* participle, which represents justification as a *completed act,* and the *present* participle used in 3: 24, which represents justification as in process, conditioned on hypothetical faith. This difference, which is declared by the tense of the original participle, is also confirmed by the concluding part of the verse. Observe how closely 'having been justified' follows 'justification' in 4:25. This is liable to be overlooked on account of the division of the chapters. [For 'justified by faith,' Noyes has "accepted as righteous through faith." That our faith, subjectively considered, is not the ground or meritorious cause of our justification is affirmed in the "Formula Concordiæ": "Faith does not justify because it is so good a work or so distinguished a virtue, but because, in the promise of the gospel, it apprehends and embraces the merit of Christ."] **We have peace with God through our Lord Jesus Christ.** The

'peace with God' here spoken of is not to be confounded with "the peace of God" mentioned in Phil. 4:7; Col. 3:15. [In this last place the Revision has "peace of *Christ.*"] This peace with God [literally, *in relation to God*] is the new and friendly relation which has taken the place of the former estrangement, and enmity, and exposure to wrath, [a relation of peace with God, which has been mediated 'through our Lord Jesus Christ.'] That 'peace of God' is an *inward feeling.* To some extent they mutually imply each other. The new relation is the ground and source of the new feeling, without which the feeling, if in any sense possible, would be only a delusion. [This 'peace of God,' as Calvin remarks, "the Pharisee has not, who swells with false confidence in his own works; nor the stupid sinner who is not disquieted, being inebriated with the sweetness of his vices; for though neither of these seems to have a manifest disquietude as he has who is smitten with a consciousness of sin, yet, as they really do not approach the tribunal of God, they have no reconciliation with him."] There is an important and somewhat difficult question here in regard to the true reading of the original. Instead of 'we have,' some manuscripts [א * A B * C D K L] read *let us have.* [This subjunctive form 'let,' etc., is the rendering of the Canterbury Revision, and so of the verb rejoice in ver. 2, 3, though the latter verb, either indicative or subjunctive in form, cannot as subjunctive be well associated with the direct negative (*οὐ*). If the subjunctive here could be taken in a concessive sense—"we may have peace," etc.—it would give a very appropriate meaning; but such a use of the Greek subjunctive, Dr. Schaff says, is "somewhat doubtful." Alford adopts the hortatory rendering: 'Let us have peace,' and says: "This is the only admissible sense of the first person subjunctive in an affirmative sentence like the present." Yet he doubts whether this was the original reading.] The difference between the two forms of the Greek verb is only in a single letter; there was probably no difference in the common pro-

2 By whom also we have access by faith into this grace wherein we stand, and rejoice in hope of the glory of God.
3 And not only *so*, but we glory in tribulations also; knowing that tribulation worketh patience;

whom also we have had our access [1] by faith into this grace wherein we stand; and [2] we [3] rejoice in
3 hope of the glory of God. And not only so, but

1 Some ancient authorities omit *by faith*......2 Or, *let us rejoice*......3 Gr. *glory*.

nunciation of the two forms, and there is abundant evidence in the manuscripts that the two letters were often interchanged. The external evidence—from extant manuscripts, translations, and patristic citations—is strongly in favor of the latter form, 'let us have,' the five oldest manuscripts agreeing in presenting that form. On the other hand, the simple indicative form, 'we have,' is what seems most suitable in the connection of thought. In such a case, the latter argument, which belongs to what is called *internal* evidence, must be *very strong indeed* to outweigh a decided preponderance of *external* evidence in the opposite scale. Meyer [and so De Wette] thinks that in the present case the internal evidence must prevail over the external, and therefore reads, with the common English Version, 'we have peace with God.' We feel constrained, however, in spite of this high authority, and in spite of the confessed logical difficulty, to yield to the force of external testimony, and read, "let us have peace with God." [If logical coherence and clearness must in this case yield to external evidence, we may conceive of the apostle as saying: Since we have been justified by faith, let us *have*, let us *possess*, peace with God. At the time when we first trusted in Christ, we 'received the reconciliation.' (Ver. 11.) Let us *have* this relation of peace as a priceless treasure, and glory in all that it offers us. (A. H.)] This peace with God is the *first* of the blessings which the justified believer enjoys.

2. By whom also we have access. [Literally, *have had introduction*, etc., this past tense showing that the introduction, "not our coming, but Christ's bringing," is prior to *peace with God*. (Gifford.)] We have through Christ obtained the introduction [see Eph. 2:18; 3:12; compare 1 Peter 3:18] into this grace (of justification), and

having been so introduced, we abide and stand fast in it; and looking forward from this firm standing ground, we rejoice (or *make our boast*) in the expectation of something better still, even the glorious state of perfection which God has in store for us. (See notes on 2:7.) **[We rejoice.** That is, boast or glory "in a new and true manner. Compare 3:27." (Bengel.) Our glorying rests *upon* hope as its foundation. Some expositors, by making *into* (εἰς) mean *in*, would read, 'through faith in this grace,' and thus refer the 'access' of this verse (compare Eph. 3:12, where this word is used independently) to our *approach* through Christ to the Father (Eph. 2:18); but this, as De Wette says, is "wholly inadmissible," and in part (faith in this grace) is here "wholly senseless." The verb *stand* is perfect in form but present in meaning.] This joy in the hope of future glory [see 8:18; 2 Cor. 4:17; Col. 1:27; 1 Thess. 2:12; Titus 2:13] is the *second* blessing of the individual believer, and is intimately connected with that assured position in which he stands as fully forgiven and perfectly justified.

3, 4. And not only so. [Tholuck ("Studien und Kritiken," Vol. VIII, pp. 390, 391) finds in Paul's style of thinking and writing an image of the tide where one wave overtops another; the frequently recurring *not only so* (οὐ μόνον δέ) is the beat or swelling of the wave. See ver. 11; 8:23; 9:10. Prof. Stuart thinks the repetition of the phrase here corresponds with our first, second, third, in English.] A *third* blessed prerogative of the justified believer is that afflictions are made subservient to the confirmation of his hope. We not only rejoice in hope of future good, but we also rejoice or make our boast[1] in present troubles; not merely *in the midst* of them, and *in spite* of them, but actually *in* them, or *on account* of them, as the context implies; and this is in accordance both with Scripture precept and

1 The Canterbury Revision has here, as in the preceding verse, *let us rejoice*, a rendering which our American Revisers have properly discarded. This verb, meaning to exult or triumph, is in the Common Version oftener rendered by the word *glory* than by

any other, and is usually so rendered in the Revised Version. This Pauline word, as we may call it, occurs some thirty-six times in his epistles and only twice elsewhere—to wit, in James 1:9; 4:16.—(F.)

4 And patience, experience; and experience, hope:
5 And hope maketh not ashamed; because the love
of God is shed abroad in our hearts by the Holy
Ghost which is given unto us.

[1] we also [2] rejoice in our tribulations: knowing that
4 tribulation worketh [3] patience; and [3] patience, pro-
5 bation; and probation, hope: and hope putteth not
to shame; because the love of God hath been shed
abroad in our hearts through the Holy Spirit which

1 Or, *let us also rejoice* ......2 Gr. *glory* ......3 Or, *stedfastness*.

with recorded Christian experience. See Matt. 5 : 10-12; James 1 : 2-4; 1 Peter 4 : 13, 14; 2 Cor. 12 : 9, 10. [One thing which enabled the apostle to glory in his tribulations (literally, *the tribulations*) was the consciousness that he was suffering for Christ. We all have a sufficiency of trials and afflictions, but we fail to rejoice in them, or to be supported under them, as we should be, through the suspicion that they may have been sent to us, not for our love to Christ, but on account of our unfaithfulness or misdeeds.] **Knowing that.** Because we know that. **Tribulation worketh [out] patience.** *Endurance*, as less *passive* than patience, would better express the apostle's thought. See notes on 2 : 7. [The word literally means a remaining under, a bearing up under, the position of one who does not fretfully strive to throw off a burden, but, as Trench says, "under a great siege of trials bears up and does not lose heart or courage."] 'Tribulation' commonly works impatience in unbelievers, and sometimes in believers also. But in such cases, God's usual method is to add affliction to affliction, until the impatient soul is subdued under their weight and learns to be calmly submissive. Here the constancy and firmness of the believer under afflictions is assumed. We have in this statement, therefore, a good practical *test* by which to try our state. **And patience, experience.** *Endurance works* [first, a proving or testing, then] *approval*. The word here translated *experience* [used only by Paul] is the same that is translated 'proof' in 2 Cor. 2 : 9; 13 : 3; Phil. 2 : 22. [In this last text, "Ye know the proof" of Timothy, Ellicott regards this "proof" as equivalent to "tried character." James 1 : 12 is closely related to our passage both in thoughts and words: "Blessed is the man who *endureth* temptation (affliction), for when he is *tried*, he shall receive the crown of life," the object of his *hope*.] **And experience, hope.** When we have *endured* trouble, and the endurance has resulted favorably, it is inevitable that this proving of ourselves should strengthen and

brighten our hope. The hope that is born of faith takes on a new and more robust character when it has been confirmed by the experience of trial well endured.

Now, the apostle goes on to show the *certainty* of this hope as a *fourth* particular in the blessed results of this way of salvation to the individual believer. **5. And hope maketh not ashamed.** [Literally, *the hope*, which some regard as equivalent to *this* hope, but so the apostle did not write it. Abstract nouns in Greek, more frequently than in English, take the article, so that we cannot be sure of its having here any special emphasis. Yet it may refer to the hope just mentioned.] And our hope shames (us) not, by disappointing and mocking us ["the hope will be reality" (Bengel); "its issue in salvation most certain." (Calvin.)], **because the love of God (to us) is shed abroad in our hearts.** [Paul, in after years, in this very city of Rome to which he is now writing, had this same hope which maketh not ashamed even in the prospect of martyrdom, or, at least, in a state of uncertainty whether life or death lay before him. See Phil. 1 : 20. If we have the sense of God's love shed abroad in our hearts by the indwelling Holy Spirit, our Christian hope will never shame us; on the contrary, it will afford us the highest confidence and greatest glorying. A sense of God's love will also create in our hearts a love to God in return. (1 John 4 : 19.)] The expression 'the love of God' may mean either God's love to us or our love to God. There is nothing in the form of expression in either the Greek or the English to show which of the two meanings it has in any particular passage. It is certainly used in both senses in the Scriptures. It clearly means God's love to us in 8 : 39; 2 Cor. 13 : 14; and it just as clearly means our love to God in Luke 11 : 42; John 5 : 42: 1 John 3 : 17; 5 : 3. Hence its meaning must be determined in each case by the connected words and the course of thought. In this case, the connection seems to require us to understand by it God's love

6 For when we were yet without strength, in due time Christ died for the ungodly.

6 was given unto us. For while we were yet weak, in 7 due season Christ died for the ungodly. For scarce-

toward us, though some commentators, ancient as well as modern, have taken it in the other sense. But the expresssion 'shed abroad in our hearts,' or, as it might be quite literally rendered, *poured forth* [or, *poured out*], as well as the general course of thought, points rather to God's love toward us. [Compare ver. 8, and see Winer, p. 185. Prof. Cremer remarks that "in the Pauline writings the relation of men to God is only once expressed by the substantive *love* (ἀγάπη)—viz., 2 Thess. 3:5," and that in other instances where *love* is followed by the genitive it expresses the love of God or of Christ to us. He says: "It is contrary alike to Christian experience and to St. Paul's chain of thought, here and elsewhere, to make the certainty of Christian hope rest upon *love to* God existing in the heart." His definition of the word for love (ἀγάπη), a word not found in the profane writers nor in Philo or Josephus—"a word born within the bosom of revealed religion" (Trench)—is this: "It denotes the love which chooses its object with decision of will, so that it becomes self-denying or compassionate devotion to and for the same." "Classical Greek," he says, "knows nothing of the use of this word (ἀγαπᾶν) to designate compassionating love or the love that freely chooses its object." Another verb (φιλεῖν) denotes the love of natural inclination, affection, friendship (Latin, *amare*), while this verb corresponds to the Latin word *diligere*.] The verb 'is shed abroad,' or 'is poured forth,' implies an *abundant* communication or expansion of God's love in our hearts. The same verb is used in Acts 2:17, 18; 10:45; Titus 3:6, to express the plenteous *effusion* of the Holy Spirit. ["The love of God did not descend upon us as dew in drops, but as a stream has it poured forth itself into our hearts." (Philippi.) The heart, says Ellicott, "is properly the imaginary seat of the soul, and thence the seat and centre of the moral life viewed on the side of the affections." What greater blessing can we desire than that the indwelling Holy Spirit may continually and in rich abundance shed abroad in our hearts God's love and love to God in return? "Like an overflowing stream in a thirsty land, so is the rich flood of divine love poured out and shed

abroad in the heart." (Gifford.)] **By the Holy Ghost.** The Holy Spirit is here represented as displaying, expanding to the view of the soul God's love. This agrees with our Lord's words in John 16:14. It has been a subject of much critical discussion whether it is proper to speak of the Holy Spirit as acting upon the truth or only upon the mind and heart of man. Apart from all metaphysical niceties, this passage, and the one referred to above, seem to show that it is allowable to speak of the Spirit as acting upon the truth. [Is it said in either of these passages that the Holy Spirit acts *upon* the truth? Is anything more affirmed in John 16:14 than this, that the Holy Spirit would reveal Christ by means of the truth to the disciples? And is not that working *with the truth* rather than acting *upon the truth?* So, too, the words of Paul may imply that the Holy Spirit *makes use of truth* in pouring forth the love of God in believing hearts, inasmuch as we cannot see how he could otherwise reveal that love to their hearts; but does this imply any action of the Spirit on the truth itself? May not his action be altogether on the heart, either directly or by means of the truth? We are unable to see anything favorable to the view expressed by Dr. Arnold in either of these passages. (A. H.)] **Which is given** (more strictly, *was given*) **unto us.** *When* was this giving of the Spirit unto us? On the day of Pentecost, say various commentators But to refer it to the time of each individual's regeneration seems more suitable, especially as it is *Paul* who says this, for *he* certainly did not receive the gift on the day of Pentecost. [According to Paul's teaching, the Holy Spirit is not only given to us at particular times, but dwells within us, in our hearts, as an abiding, presence, so that our bodies are his temples. "Know ye not that your body is a temple of the-in-you Holy Spirit?" 1 Cor. 6:19; compare Gal. 4:6; 1 Cor. 3:16; 2 Cor. 1:22; 6:16. Meyer remarks that the divine love shed abroad by the Spirit in believing hearts "is to them, like the Spirit himself, the earnest of the hoped-for glory." See 2 Cor. 1:22; 5:5."]

6. The **for,** with which this verse is introduced, indicates that what follows is a signal

proof of that love of God to us which is shed
abroad in our hearts by the Spirit. **When
we were yet without strength.** When we
were impotent, powerless for good. [Dr. Gifford supposes a contrast here to the believer's
present state, as strong in hope, etc.] The
term 'without strength' is explained by the
stronger terms 'ungodly' and 'sinners.'
(Ver. 8.) [We are weak to do right, but strong
to do wrong; strong to sin, but weak to resist.
The special helplessness referred to here is
man's inability to redeem himself or put himself into a salvable state. He can make no
atonement for his sin nor deliver himself from
its power. "This inability to help ourselves
is a fact," says Prof. Boise, "which the philo-
sophical and religious systems of Asia and
Greece had failed to recognize or suitably to
emphasize." The text of the Revision has
two 'yets,' which occasion some difficulty,
though the sense of the passage is entirely
clear. Some render the first (ἔτι) *besides* or
moreover (like ἔτι δε; see Heb. 11 : 36). Others
think the repetition was for the sake of emphasis, and should be but once rendered.
Meyer rejects the latter *yet* (ἔτι) as ungenu-
ine.] The adjective here translated 'without
strength' is the same which is translated
'sick' in Matt. 25 : 39, 43, 44; Luke 10 : 9;
Acts 5 : 15, 16. Holiness is the healthy, strong
condition of the human soul. **In due time
Christ died.** There was a *due time*, a suitable *season*, for Christ to die. There was a
long, providential *preparation*, a remarkable
concurrence of many conditions, before "the
fulness of time" for God to "send forth his
Son" had come. What man could do to help
himself—by experience of the evil of sin, by
civil laws and religious rites, by philosophy,
by the help of divine laws and typical sacrifices—must first be shown. And then a select
nation must be prepared by centuries of discipline to comprehend the new doctrines;
time must be allowed for the human race to
grow out of the fabulous into the historic age,
so that the proofs of the *facts* connected with
the advent of the Son of God could be adequately established; a *language*, more copious
and precise than any earlier one, must be developed; a *government*, wider and stronger
than the world had before seen, must be con-

solidated, to favor unwittingly, even while it
wickedly opposed, the dissemination of the
gospel; and then, when all this protracted,
complex, wonderful preparation was completed, *in due time Christ died for the ungodly.*
[Philippi regards this 'due time' (κατὰ καιρὸν)
as meaning "at the appointed time." Of
course, the two views really imply each other.
Meyer remarks—with, perhaps, too great restriction of view—that the death of Jesus for
the ungodly took place at the proper season,
because, had it not taken place then, they
would, instead of the divine grace, have experienced the final righteous outbreak of divine
wrath, seeing that the time of the "passing
over" (3:25) and of the "forbearance" of God
had come to an end. Compare the idea of
the "fulness of the times" in Eph. 1 : 10;
Gal. 4 : 4. Dr. Schaff, speaking of the fitness
of time, race, country, as concerns the world's
Saviour, says: "We cannot conceive of his
advent at the time of Noah or Abraham, or in
China, or among the savage tribes of America.
History is a unit, and a gradual unfolding of
a divine plan of infinite wisdom. Christ is
the turning-point and centre of history, the
end of the old and the beginning of the new
humanity; a truth which is confessed, wit-
tingly or unwittingly, by every date from
A. D. throughout the civilized world." **For
the ungodly.** The word 'ungodly' is without the article in the original, as referring,
not to a class, but to all mankind.] It was
for the benefit of the ungodly, that he might
open for them a way out of their ungodliness
into the favor of God. [The 'for' in this
clause, like our English for, may signify 'instead of,' or 'for the benefit of,' but usually
has the latter signification. It seemingly expresses, more fully than 'instead of' (ἀντὶ), the
love and compassion of Christ. Dr. Gifford,
in the "Bible (Speaker's) Commentary," says:
"It would be enough to say that Christ
died 'in our stead' (ἀντὶ), if his death had
been unconscious, unwilling, or accidental."
"Strictly speaking," says Ellicott, "*for* (ὑπὲρ),
in its ethical sense, retains some trace of its
local meaning, 'bending *over* to protect,' and
thus points more immediately to the action
than to the object or circumstance from which
the action is supposed to spring."[1] Philippi

---

[1] "The latter relation," says Ellicott, "is more correctly defined by περὶ [*concerning, for*]. περὶ will thus
be more naturally used with the thing, 'sins,' ὑπὲρ with
the person, 'sinners,' and this, with a few exceptions

7 For scarcely for a righteous man will die: yet peradventure for a good man some would even dare to die.

ly for a righteous man will one die: for peradventure for the good man some one would even dare to

remarks that "one may die for and yet not instead of another, as the death that I submit to on another's behalf . . . does not always assume that he must have died if I had not died. Still, this will usually be the case, and with respect to Christ it *was* the case, his death being, as we know, from other sources, a vicarious, sacrificial death. Compare on 3 : 24. The phrases 'Christ died for us,' 'gave himself up for us; (Rom. 8 : 32; 14 : 15; 1 Cor. 1 : 13; 2 Cor. 5 : 14; Eph. 5 : 2; 1 Thess. 5 : 10; 1 Tim. 2 : 6; Titus 2 : 14), therefore, express the compassionate love of Christ's vicarious, sacrificial death, so that in the *for* the *instead of* is assumed or rather included. Compare Steiger on 1 Peter 3 : 18." Prof. Cremer says: "We must particularly keep in view the representation of death as a punitive sentence when mention is made of the death of Christ." And after referring to the Pauline expressions, dying to and with, he adds: "Bearing all this in mind, it is also clear how the matter stands with reference to Christ's dying for the ungodly, which, if it does not actually express the substitutionary import of Christ's death (compare διὰ, 1 Cor. 8 : 11), has meaning only upon the principle of this substitutionary import." Meyer states that Paul "has certainly regarded the death of Jesus as an act furnishing the *satisfactio vicaria*, as is clear from the fact that this bloody death was accounted by him as an expiatory sacrifice (3 : 25; Eph. 5 : 2; compare ἀντίλυτρον in 1 Tim. 2 : 6), but in no passage has he expressed the substitutionary relation by the usual preposition" (ἀντὶ). Our Saviour himself expresses this most clearly in Matt. 20 : 28; Mark 10 : 45, where he speaks of giving

his life a ransom *for* (ἀντὶ) many. 'Christ died for the ungodly,' not only for the weak, but for the wicked. The fact that the death of Christ for sins and in behalf of sinners is made so prominent in the New Testament Scriptures shows that he came into the world, not so much to be a teacher of men, or an example for men, as to become a propitiatory sacrifice for their sins. Not but that Jesus may be denominated the "Great Teacher," since he laid down certain great principles to guide men's thoughts and lives; yet he did not enter into the *minutiæ* of Christian instruction so fully as did the Apostle Paul.]

7. **For.** If we supply some such thought as this (which very naturally suggests itself), 'this was wonderful love indeed,' the 'for' will have its explanation. **Scarcely.** This infrequent word expresses the great *difficulty* of the case, as we might say, 'it would be *very hard* to find a man who would do this.' The only other place where it has the same English translation is the remarkable passage in 1 Peter 4 : 18 (which, by the way, is quoted verbatim from the Greek of the LXX in Prov. 11 : 31). But the same Greek word is found in Acts 14 : 18, there translated *scarce*, and also three times in Acts 27 : In ver. 7 (translated *scarce*), in ver. 8 (translated *hardly*), and in ver. 16, where the last clause may be rendered, "we could scarcely become masters of the boat." **For a righteous man will one die.** 'A righteous man' is contrasted with 'the ungodly' of the preceding verse. Hardly on behalf of a just man will any one die.[1] **Yet peradventure for a good**

(for example, 1 Cor. 15 : 3; Heb. 5 : 3), appears to be the usage of the New Testament." [In Heb. 5 : 3, the Revision text has not ὑπὲρ but περὶ ἁμαρτιῶν. Among other exceptions he might have referred to Gal. 1 : 4; Heb. 5 : 1; 7 : 27; 10 : 12.] He further says that ὑπὲρ in its ethical sense has principally and primarily the meaning *in behalf of*, or *for the good of*, especially in doctrinal passages where the atoning death of Christ is alluded to—for example, Gal. 3 : 13 (compare Philem. 13), where it may admit the second meaning (*instead of*) united with the first, though never *exclusively*. See his commentary on Gal. 1 : 4; 3 : 13; also Winer, p. 383, where he says "ὑπὲρ is nearly equivalent to ἀντὶ, instead of."—(F.)

[1] Buttmann (p. 218) thinks that Greek writers would probably have used, instead of this future, the optative mood with ἄν: 'Scarcely *would* any one die.' But this mood in the later Greek fell gradually into disuse, and modern Greek has given it up entirely. In the New Testament, as a dependent mood, it is almost completely ignored, as it occurs but a few times, and only in the writings of Luke. In Paul's writings the subjunctive is always used, even after the so-called historical tenses, the imperfect, aorist, and pluperfect. Winer thinks this latter mood was at times purposely employed to "denote an action still *continuing*, either in itself or in its results, or one frequently recurring;" and Buttmann says it is "especially suited to the expression of a purpose striving to become actual."—(F.)

8. But God commendeth his love toward us, in that, while we were yet sinners, Christ died for us. | 8 die. But God commendeth his own love toward us, in that, while we were yet sinners, Christ died for

man some would even dare to die. The little word (γὰρ) translated 'yet' is the same which is translated 'for' in the beginning of the verse and in hundreds of other places in the New Testament. The most satisfactory explanation of its being used here is to regard the passage as elliptical, some such expression as this being supplied in thought, "but I do not insist upon this," and then the 'for' in place of 'yet' will be suitable. [Concerning the three *fors* in this and the preceding verse, Winer thus remarks: "The first *for* simply refers to the fact which attested the love of God (ver. 5, Christ's dying for the ungodly); the second explains, *a contrario*, how death (of the innocent) for the guilty evinces transcendent love; the third substantiates the remark, 'scarcely for a righteous man,' etc.] In behalf of the *good* man perhaps some one even ventures to die. The verb translated 'would dare' is in the *indicative* mood, and is properly translated *dares* or *ventures*. Observe the distinction between 'a righteous man' and 'a good man.' 'A righteous man' is *just* to others; 'a good man' is *beneficent* to others. That this sense of the word good *belongs* to the Greek adjective here used is confirmed by Matt. 20 : 15, where it plainly has that sense, and also by the article, which emphasizes the distinction between a righteous man and a good man, and, finally, by the nature of the case; for it is much less difficult to believe that some one would be willing to die for the *beneficent* man, to whom he was bound by the tie of *gratitude* for some great favor, than that he would die for a *just* man, who had merely rendered to him his due. [There being nothing in the original corresponding to the word *man*, 'the good' has been by some taken absolutely for that which is good, as by Godet, and in the margin of the Canterbury Revision, while Julius Müller refers it to God who alone is good. The contrasted words 'ungodly,' 'sinners,' etc., show that just and good refer to persons, while no one certainly would die for an abstraction. Meyer, strange to say, allows no essential difference of idea in these two words. Instead of righteous, the Syriac, singularly enough, reads unrighteous, which reading, in Fritzsche's opinion, makes very good sense—

a sense, we should say, which hardly required expressing. Wordsworth, in illustration of one's willingness to die for a benefactor or for the sake of friendship, refers to the story of Orestes and Pylades, Alcestis and Admetus.] For **some,** we should here read 'some one,' for the pronoun is in the *singular* number; whereas 'some,' without the 'one,' when used of persons is properly plural.

8. [The word 'God' is wanting in the important Vatican MS. B, and in other copies its position varies, for which reasons it is rejected by Alford, though the word 'he,' supplied by Alford, is made to refer to God. There seems to be, however, no sufficient grounds to doubt its genuineness.] **Commendeth.** Makes manifest, and magnifies, as in 3 : 15. [This verb, primarily, means to set or place together; hence in later use it becomes nearly equivalent to prove, establish, or evince. Besides the places referred to, it occurs elsewhere in this Epistle only in 16 : 1, where it means to bring together (as friends), hence to commend. The present tense is used here to denote an always existing, ever-present truth.] **His love.** *His own love,* so the original reads, to distinguish it emphatically from the *human* love referred to in the previous verse [perhaps, also, to contrast it with our want of love and goodness. See 1 John 4 : 10: "Herein is love, not that we loved God, but that he loved us.] **Yet,** in contrast with the *now* of the next verse. **Sinners,** corresponding with 'ungodly' and 'without strength' (ver. 6), and contrasted with 'righteous' and 'good.' (Ver. 7.) "God showed *his own* love, in that Christ died for us; therefore he loved Christ as himself." (Bengel.) Or, therefore Christ is God; both inferences are equally valid. [If we compare this verse with 3 : 25, we see that the propitiatory offering of Christ was the means of exhibiting God's righteousness, and, at the same time, was also an expression of God's love. Paul does not here represent God the Father as all justice and Christ as all love, but shows us rather that God's love for sinful men was the same as Christ's. Godet observes that "this parallel has no meaning except as the sacrifice of Christ is to God the sacrifice of himself." Christ has "died for us sinners," and therefore we may be saved from

9 Much more then, being now justified by his blood, we shall be saved from wrath through him.
10 For if, when we were enemies, we were reconciled to God by the death of his Son; much more, being reconciled, we shall be saved by his life.

9 us. Much more then, being now justified [1] by his blood, shall we be saved from the wrath *of God*
10 through him. For if, while we were enemies, we were reconciled to God through the death of his Son, much more, being reconciled, shall we be

1 Gr. *in.*

wrath through him, and in none other is there salvation. (Acts 4 : 12.) Abundant provision is thus made for our salvation, yet we may die of starvation though food is heaped up all around us.]
9. Much more then. If he died for us while we were yet sinners, much more then will he save us now that we have been made righteous through his death. If he made so great a sacrifice to begin a work, much more will he add that completion, without which this costly beginning will be of no effect. **Justified by** [literally, *having been justified in*] **his blood** is a very strong expression. It certainly cannot import less than that his *vicarious death* was *indispensable* to our justification. **Saved from the wrath.** Literally, saved from *the wrath*, which was our confessed desert and our otherwise inevitable doom. [Christ's precious blood—in other words, his atoning death or "his accomplished and offered sacrifice" (Cremer)—is here represented as the source or ground of the sinner's justification. Meyer remarks that "faith as the recipient (ληπτικόν) of justification is understood as a matter of course (ver. 1), but is not mentioned here, because only what has been accomplished by *God* through *Christ* is taken into consideration."]
10. For if. ['For' assigns a special reason for the certainty of our salvation.] **When we were enemies.** [Prof. Boise remarks that the word for public enemies (πολέμιοι) "so common in classic Greek is not found in the New Testament."] In what sense is the word 'enemies' to be taken here? In the *active* sense, those who are opposed to God? or in the *passive* sense, those to whom God is opposed? The former is unquestionably the sense in which the word occurs most frequently in the Scriptures. But it certainly occurs also in the latter sense. Perhaps 11: 28, and 2 Thess. 3 : 15, are the clearest instances. Here the *passive* sense, obnoxious to the divine displeasure, is required ; for two reasons: 1. Because it is God's righteous opposition to us, rather than our unrighteous opposition to him, which is directly removed *by*

the blood of his Son; and, 2. Because it is the forensic, or judicial relation to God, not the moral — justification, not sanctification — of which the apostle is here treating. The best critical expositors are agreed in ascribing this sense to the word. Let the names of *De Wette, Alford, Meyer, Schaff,* suffice. [We add the names of Tholuck, Fritzsche, Philippi, Weiss, Gifford, and Godet. The latter says : " The enmity must above all belong to him to whom wrath is attributed ; and the blood of Christ, through which we have been justified, did not flow in the first place to work a change in our dispositions Godward, but to bring about a change in God's conduct toward us. Otherwise this bloody death would have to be called a demonstration of love and not of righteousness." On this subject of the influence of the atonement Godward, see Dr. Hovey's "God with Us," pp. 100–155, "Manual of Theology," 207, seq.] **Reconciled to God by the death of his Son** [or, *reconciled with God*—that is, restored to his favor]. While *reconciliation*, much more than *enmity*, may as a general rule be assumed to be *mutual*, the *prominent* idea here undoubtedly is, not the giving up of our hostility to God, but the restoration of his favor to us. This follows from what was said on the previous clause. [Dr. Hovey thus paraphrases this verse: "For if, when we were the objects of God's wrath (like rebels whom the king counts as enemies), we were put in a condition to receive his favor, by the death of his Son, how much more, having been put in that condition, shall we be saved in his life." See also Weiss' "Biblical Theology," Vol. I, p. 428.] **Much more.** ["An argument *a fortiori.* If the greater benefit has been bestowed, the less will not be withheld. If Christ has died for his enemies, he will surely save his friends." (Hodge.) " When one has done *the most* for his *enemies*, he does not refuse *the least* to his *friends.*" (Godet.) How much God has done for his enemies may be gathered from the words: 'death of his Son.'] **Being reconciled** (more exactly, *having been reconciled*), **we shall be saved by his life.** It is now

11 And not only *so*, but we also joy in God through our Lord Jesus Christ, by whom we have now received the atonement.

11 saved [1] by his life; and not only so, [2] but we also rejoice in God through our Lord Jesus Christ, through whom we have now received the reconciliation.

1 Gr. *in*.   2 Gr. *but also glorying*.

assumed, that the subjective reconciliation, the removal of our opposition to God, has also taken place; but no stress is laid on that assumption. 'By his life'—literally, *in his life* [in vital union with his life (Schaff); in the fact that he lives and intercedes. (Boise.) "Justification," says Godet, "rests only on faith in the *death* of Christ. Sanctification flows from the *life* of Christ by the work of the Holy Spirit." Compare John 14: 19, "Because I live ye shall live also." Prof. Stuart remarks that this passage (ver. 6-10) "seems to be more direct, in respect to the perseverance of the saints, than almost any other passage in the Scriptures"]. The close relation in which he placed himself to us, by dying for our sins, carries with it our being associated with him in his resurrection life. This topic is treated more fully in the next chapter.

We may regard *the whole work* of Christ as a Saviour, *for* us and *in* us, beginning with his vicarious propitiation for our sins, proceeding with our justification, and culminating in our salvation, as virtually comprehended in our *reconciliation*, with this distinction between the expressions *we were reconciled* and *having been reconciled*, in ver. 10, that whereas in the former expression the first step in the process, propitiation, is most prominent, in the latter expression, by a very natural progress in the thought, the *second* step, justification, is most prominent.

Recurring now to ver. 5, which was introduced by the remark that the apostle is now to set forth, as a *fourth* prerogative of the justified believer, the *certainty* of his hope, we have this course of thought in the development of that subject. God has already shown the fullness of his love to us by giving his Spirit (ver. 5), by giving his Son to die for us while we were yet sinners (ver. 6-8), and by having thus begun the work of our salvation when we were enemies, he has given the surest pledge that he will complete it now that we are reconciled to him. (Ver. 9, 10.) And now to sum up all in a *fifth* blessing, we boast

ourselves in God, having received, through Christ, this wonderful reconciliation with him.

11. It is very plain that the apostle would have us regard what he speaks of in this verse as distinct from, and added to, all the foregoing. The introductory words—**and not only so, but we also**—manifestly imply this. [1] [**But we also joy in God.** Literally, *but also glorying*. With this participle most commentators supply the present tense of the verb to be. The words imply not only that we are saved; but that we have a joyous consciousness of our salvation. See Winer, p. 351.] And indeed this boasting in a God reconciled to us is something more than peace with God (ver. 5); something more than boasting in the hope of future glory (ver. 2); something more than boasting in tribulations (ver. 3, 4); something different from the assured certainty of our Christian hope. (Ver. 5-10.) It is a higher experience than any of these, even that of which the Psalmist speaks, in Ps. 34: 2; 44: 8. **Have now received the atonement.** The word 'atonement' is used nowhere else in our New Testament. The Greek word (καταλλαγὴ), to which it here corresponds, is, however, used in two other places, in 11: 15 and in 2 Cor. 4: 18, 19, in which it is more suitably translated *reconciling* or *reconciliation*. We say this last is the more *suitable* translation, inasmuch as the word *atonement* has acquired in theological language a fixed, technical sense, which does not correspond with the sense of the Greek word here used. [Paul in 3: 25 spoke of Christ, set forth in his blood, as our propitiation, and he often uses the word for *redemption* (ἀπολύτρωσις); but the most proper word for *atonement* (ἱλασμός) is employed not by him but by the disciple of love. See 1 John 2: 2; 4: 10. Compare, also, the corresponding verb (ἱλάσκομαι) in Heb. 2: 17.] The noun here used is closely connected both in form and meaning with the verb translated *reconciled* in ver. 10. [The fact that we *receive* rather than make or give reconciliation shows the reconcilement to be in God's mind or disposition rather than in ours.

1 The δέ and ἀλλὰ, corresponding to the German *aber* and *sondern*, may thus be rendered: *Not only so, however, but also*, etc.

At least, its primary reference is to the new relation which God sustains to us. Prof. Cremer, after referring to some doubtful passages, says: "But Rom. 5 : 11 is decidedly opposed to the supposition that either a change of feeling on the part of man, brought about by the divine redemption, is referred to, or an alteration in his relation to God to be accomplished by man himself. It is God who forms the relation between himself and humanity anew; the part of humanity is to accept this reinstatement. . . . God establishes a relationship of peace between him and us by doing away with that which made him our *adversary* (ἀντίδικος), which directed his anger against us. . . . Thus reconciliation denotes the New Testament divine and saving act of redemption (ἀπολύτρωσις), in so far as God himself, by his taking upon himself and providing an atonement, establishes that relationship of peace with mankind which the demands of his justice had hitherto prevented." So De Wette: "We must think of this reconciliation as the removal of the wrath of God, ver. 9." And in this view nearly all commentators of note coincide "Nor is it any contradiction that while God's anger rested on mankind, his love instituted a scheme of reconciliation, because the enmity falls only on *sin;* the love, on the other hand, regards sinners." (Philippi.) "Since this enmity of God is only directed against man as a sinner, it naturally does not exclude grace which seeks to remove the cause of this enmity and thereby to render reconciliation possible." (Weiss, I, 429.) The verb used here (καταλλάσσω) occurs six times. (5 : 10 ; 1 Cor. 7 : 11 ; 2 Cor. 5 : 18, 19, 20.) Another related word (διαλλάσσω) is found once (Matt. 5 : 24), "first be reconciled to thy brother." In this case it is the injured or offended brother of thine who is really to become reconciled, and this example, with that of 1 Sam. 29 : 4 in the Septuagint (see Josephus' "Antiquities," V, 2, 8), shows us that in the expression 'we were reconciled to (or with) God,' God may be regarded as the party who was at enmity, whose wrath, through the expiation of Christ, has been removed, so that we may be received

into his favor. And this view is still further confirmed by the general representation of Scripture, that our reconciliation and justification are effected by the sufferings, the death, the blood of Christ, as a sacrifice for the sins of the world. Still, the "Christian reconciliation," as Trench remarks in his "Synonyms of the New Testament," "has two sides," the second and subordinate one being our reconciliation toward God, "the daily deposition, under the operation of the Holy Spirit, of the enmity of the old man toward God. 2 Cor. 5 : 20 ; compare 1 Cor. 7 : 11. All attempts to make this secondary to be indeed the primary meaning and intention of the word, rest not on an unprejudiced exegesis, but on a foregone determination to get rid of the reality of God's anger against the sinner." Accordingly, our hymn revisers, who have substituted "To God I'm reconciled" for "My God is reconciled," have made a "secondary meaning of the word" to usurp the place of the primary. For Scripture teaches us that God when he reconciled all things to himself through Jesus Christ, through the expiation he made for our sins on the cross, by virtue of which expiation the guilty who deserve to die may be justified and thus saved from deserved wrath (ver. 9), set up a relationship of peace not before existing (Cremer) ; and that Christ, by his propitiation and by his perfect obedience rendered to the will of God, has effected conditions of peace between God and the sinner, whereby he now comes and "preaches peace" to a guilty world. "Reconciliation," says Meyer, "has taken place *objectively* through the death of Christ, but is realized *subjectively* only when men *become believers,* whereby the reconciliation becomes appropriated to them." Compare 2 Cor. 5 : 18–20 ; Col. 1 : 20–22 ; Eph. 2 : 16, 17 ; 1 John 4 : 10. In the examples from Ephesians and Colossians another word (ἀποκαταλλάσσω) is used. Both sides of the Christian reconciliation are, we suppose, presented to view in 2 Cor. 5 : 18–20 ; Col. 1 : 20–22.][1]

The apostle has now completed his account of the *individual* blessings secured to the believer by the gospel way of justification ; and

[1] On the connection of ἱλάσκομαι (to make or be propitious) with reconciliation on the part of God, see Cremer's "Biblico-Theological Lexicon," Article καταλλάσσω ; on the deep meaning of ἱλασμός (propitiation or atonement), see Trench's "Synonyms," p. 292 ; and on this general subject, Dr. Hovey's "God with Us," pp. 114, 255.

12 Wherefore, as by one man sin entered into the world, and death by sin; and so death passed upon all men, for that all have sinned:

12   Therefore, as through one man sin entered into the world, and death through sin; and so death

from this point to the end of the chapter he treats of the way in which the human race is affected by this newly revealed method of justification. This is one of the most important, and one of the most difficult sections of the epistle. [The subject of which this section treats is *in itself* one of utmost difficulty, having to do with the "stubborn, terrible fact of the universal dominion of sin and death over the entire race." (Schaff.) Alford gives to this section (ver. 12-19) the following title: "The bringing in of reconciliation and life by Christ in its analogy to the bringing in of sin and death by Adam." Godet very happily introduces the topic which follows in these words: "After thus expounding in a first section (1: 18-3: 20) *universal condemnation*, in a second section (3: 21-5: 11) *universal justification*, there remains nothing more for the apostle to do than to compare these two vast dispensations by bringing together their two points of departure. Such is the subject of the third section which closes this fundamental part." Dr. Schaff gives very full notes on these verses in his edition of Lange's "Commentary," also a special section entitled: "Historical Statements on the Different Theories of Original Sin and Imputation."[1] We may here observe that to Paul alone of all New Testament writers, was it given to set forth the doctrine of our race connection with Adam's transgression, a doctrine nevertheless quite plainly intimated in the Old Testament. Yet "like a skillful physician the apostle goes not only to the root and fountainhead of the evil, but also to the root and fountainhead of the cure." (Dr. Schaff.)]

12. Wherefore (or, more properly, *therefore*) connects what follows as a conclusion from ver. 11, especially with the last clause, which may be regarded as a summary of the preceding verses of this chapter. [Since reconciliation contains an allusion to wrath, and so to condemnation as well as justification, the connection may be thus conceived, as by Godet: "Since, condemned as we all were, we

have found reconciliation in Christ, there is therefore between our relation to him and our relation to the head of natural humanity the following resemblance."] Reconciliation through Christ is now to be presented in a more general aspect, as affecting the destiny of the whole race, and in a new form, as illustrated by a comparison between Adam and Christ, or, more precisely, between the consequences of their relation to each. **As by one man sin entered into the world.** ['As.' This seems to begin a comparison, but we find no corresponding so in what follows. A simple and direct apodosis of the comparison would probably have run thus: *So* also by one man righteousness entered into the world and through righteousness life likewise entered. Tholuck, Philippi, Meyer find the second member of the comparison virtually in ver. 14, which speaks of Christ as the antitype of Adam. Most expositors find it included in ver. 18, where the whole subject is resumed and completed. As the word *as* does not always require a *so* (compare Matt. 25: 14), some regard this *as* as introducing the second member of the comparison in some such improbable way as this: "Therefore stands Christ in a similar relation to mankind *as* Adam through whom sin and death entered into the world" (DeWette), or, "therefore we received and appropriated the reconciliation through Christ in the same manner as by one man," etc. (Lange and, similarly, Alford.) See Dr. Arnold's remarks further on.] The occasion on which this comparison is introduced accounts for the mention of Adam only, without any allusion to Eve. The design of the apostle is "to compare the One man who, as the bringer of salvation, has become the beginner of the new humanity with the one man who, as beginner of the old humanity, became so destructive, in which collective reference the woman recedes into the background." (Meyer.) Three reasons for the omission of Eve's name are given by Bengel: 1. Adam had received the commandment

[1] These terms are, we believe, now commonly distinguished from each other—or at least may be properly distinguished—in this way: imputed sin has reference to the condemnation and death of our race as grounded in, and directly occasioned by, the sin of Adam, while original sin has reference to the natural proclivity of the human heart to evil.—(F.)

(apparently before the creation of Eve, Gen. 2 : 16, 17). 2. He was the head, not only of his race, but also of Eve. 3. If Adam had not obeyed his wife, only one would have sinned. (Sin would have ended where it began, with Eve.) [Dr. Shedd, however, would include both Adam and Eve under the general term man (ἄνθρωπος), as in Gen. 5 : 2, "God called *their* name Adam," or man. Fritzsche adopts the first of Bengel's reasons, and thus finds an excuse for Eve but none for Adam, making her offense relate rather to the matter of time and his to the matter of guilt. In this going back to Adam, our Epistle, as many expositors have noticed, is strikingly distinguished from the Epistle to the Galatians. "In the latter," as Godet says, "where Paul is attacking Judeo-Christianity, his argument starts from the theocratic history, from Abraham. In the former, which expounds the relation of the gospel to human nature, Jewish and Gentile, the argument starts from general history, from Adam, the father of all mankind. From the very beginning of the Epistle the standpoint is universal."] The New Testament plainly confirms the account in Genesis, by recognizing Eve as the first transgressor, in the only two passages where she is named— 2 Cor. 11 : 3; 1 Tim. 2 : 13. Adam is mentioned in the following places: Luke 3 : 38; Rom. 5 : 14, twice; 1 Cor. 15 : 22, 45; 1 Tim, 2 : 13, 14; Jude 14. **Sin,** not merely in the sense of actual transgression, but sin as a ruling power or principle. Throughout the whole section 'sin' is carefully distinguished from both "transgression" (ver. 14) and "offence." (Ver. 15, 16, 17, 20.) It is *personified* and represented as an active power. Neither of the other two words above named could be so represented with equal propriety. **Entered into the world**—that is, into this *human* world [the world of humanity, which by Paul was regarded as then existing]. The account of its entrance into this world shows plainly that it had entered into the *universe* before. **And death by sin.** [Literally, *and through sin*, *death* likewise entered. In Meyer's opinion, "that Adam was *created* immortal our passage does not affirm, and 1 Cor. 15 : 47 contains the opposite." He further says: "If Adam had not sinned, . . . he would have *become*

immortal through eating of the tree of life in Paradise. As he has sinned, however, the consequence thereof necessarily was 'death,' not only for himself, seeing that he had to leave Paradise, but for all his posterity likewise. From this consequence, which the sin of Adam had for *all*, it results . . . that the fall of Adam was the collective fall of the entire race, in so far as in fact all forfeited Paradise and herewith incurred death." Paul in this section seeks not so much the origin of sin as that of death. (Godet.) ˙Hence, one chief thing which we look for in this discussion is an explanation of the fact of death.] ' By sin '—that is, 'through sin,' as the means, and on account of sin, as its appointed penalty. What are we to understand by 'death' in this passage? *Primarily*, it means physical death, the separation of the soul from the body. Whatever else it *may* include, it *must* include this, otherwise there would be no propriety in using the word, and we may be sure the word would not have been used had the plain, literal sense of the word *formed no part* of its meaning here. And this is confirmed by ver. 14. But certainly *something more* than physical death is included in the word in this connection. In Gen. 2 : 17, we read that God said to Adam, "in the day that thou eatest thereof thou shalt surely die." Adam did not suffer physical death on the very day of his transgression. But he did suffer spiritual death, for sin is the separation of the soul from God, the fountain of life. And this spiritual death, unless some remedial agency comes in, naturally leads to, and culminates in, eternal death. See how sin and death are habitually connected in the Scriptures. (Gen. 2 : 17; Ezek. 18 : 4; Rom. 6 : 16, 21, 23; 7 : 10, 11; 8 : 13.) The death of the body is the palpable, representative test fact around which our reasonings naturally gather.[1] ["In order," says Prof. Cremer, "to the clear perception and understanding of . . . the New Testament use of this word (death), we must hold fast and abide by the fact that death, as the punishment pronounced by God upon sin, has a *punitive* significance. . . . Death, therefore, is a very comprehensive term, denoting all the punitive consequences of sin. . . . Hence we find that, according to the context, the

---

[1] See Appendix B.

reference is either (*a*) to death as the objective sentence and punishment appointed for man, or (*b*) to death as the state in which man is as condemned through sin." We suppose its chief reference here is to physical death, the death which reigned from Adam to Moses. (Ver. 14.) See 1 Cor. 15 : 21. Meyer and Godet refer to this solely. The sin of Eden as causative of our fall and death is referred to in the Apocrypha (2 Esdras 7 : 48): "O thou Adam, what hast thou done? for though it was thou that sinned, thou art not fallen alone, but we all that come of thee;" also Ecclus. 25 : 24: "Of the woman came the beginning of sin, and through her we all die;" and compare Wisd. 2 : 24. De Wette says: "No exegete can doubt that Paul teaches the extension both of sin and death from Adam to mankind."] **And so death passed upon all men.** 'And so'—that is, in agreement with, and by reason of, this connection between sin and death. 'Passed upon all men.' We have the same *verb* here which in the first clause is translated entered, but with a different preposition. The more exact representation of the original would be given by translating the two clauses thus: "Sin *came into* the world;" "death *came through*" to all men. The representation would thus be made perfectly correspondent to the original, if what we call the *pre*-positions could really be *pre*-posed or *pre*-fixed, as they are in the Greek, instead of being *post*-posed, as the idiom of our language requires them to be. We cannot say, as the Greeks did, "sin into-came the world," and death "through-came to all men." [This declaration, 'and so death passed through unto all men,' supposes the fact stated in the next clause, 'that all sinned' —that is, either collectively in Adam or as individuals or both. Pfleiderer, as quoted by Weiss, ' maintains that there is a double reason assigned for death passing unto all; namely, the sin of Adam and the sin of all, and that this is explicable only on the assumption that the sin of Adam was as such already the sin of all.' If we explain this passage by the nearly parallel statement of ver. 15, "the many died," etc., it would appear that death was made to extend to all men, not primarily

and solely by reason of their individual offenses, but by "the trespass of the one." Even Prof. Stuart acknowledges that the 'and so' of this clause intimates that "both the sins of men and their condemnation stand connected in some way or other with the first offense by Adam." De Wette remarks that this passing through of death upon all men differs from its entering into the world "as going from house to house differs from entering into a town."][1] **For that all have sinned.** The original expression which our translators rendered 'for that' has been variously understood—"in whom," or "in which man" ["*in whom* all have sinned"], say Origen, Augustine, Beza, Vulgate, Wycliffe; "on the supposition that," "in as far as," says Rothe [so Julius Müller]; but our translators were doubtless correct in saying 'for that' [which is nearly equivalent to 'because'; compare 2 Cor. 5 : 4]. We may *expand* this a little by saying "upon the occasion that," which would be a very close adherence to the original, and which would be equivalent to the still more expanded form, "on the ground of the fact that" *all sinned*. The most exact parallel in form, sense, and translation is 2 Cor. 5 : 14. Life was suspended on a certain condition—obedience; death was suspended on a certain condition—disobedience. All disobeyed, in consequence of which death, the original penalty of disobedience, came through to all men. 'All sinned' is more exact than 'all have sinned.' The verb here is in the same tense as the two preceding verbs, and there is no more reason why this should be translated 'have sinned' than why they should be translated 'has entered' and 'has passed.' But how are we to understand the expression 'all sinned'? Four different answers to this question may be briefly noticed:

1. All have actually and personally sinned:
2. All have become corrupt and sinful:
3. All did actually sin in Adam:
4. All virtually sinned in Adam, as the head of the human race, and the introducer of sin, which passes through to all.

1. The first view [advocated by Tholuck, De Wette, Fritzsche, Reuss, Lange, Barnes,

---

1 "εἰς with persons is not simply equivalent to πρός (to), but involves the idea of mingling with and association." (Ellicott.)—(F.)

Stuart, Ripley,] is inconsistent with the proper force of the *tense* of the verb, which properly signifies, not *do sin*, nor *have* sinned, nor *are accustomed* to sin ; but simply *sinned :* their sin is regarded as one act in some definite past time. [The connection of the "all sinned" in 3: 23, whether it exclude all reference to the primal sin or not, is wholly different from the "sinned" in this passage.] This first view is also inconsistent with the design of the passage, which is to show that Adam's sin, and not our own apart from his, is the cause of death. It is inconsistent with ver. 13, 14, which are intended to *prove* what is here asserted : but they do not prove that all have actually sinned, but rather the reverse. It is inconsistent with the analogy between Adam and Christ. There would not be, according to this view, that resemblance between the way in which we become sinners through Adam, and the way in which we become righteous through Christ, which is affirmed in ver. 19. [Dr. Hodge says : "It would make the apostle teach that as all men die because they personally sin, so all men live because they are personally and inherently righteous. This is contrary, not only to this whole passage, but to all Paul's teaching, and to the whole gospel." We think the stanza of Spengler, quoted by Müller in his "Christian Doctrine of Sin," to be doctrinally far more Pauline :

> As now we all by foreign guilt
>   In Adam are reviled,
> Therefore we all by foreign grace
>   In Christ are reconciled.]

It is inconsistent with the facts of the case. It is not true that all die because all have actually and personally sinned. Death is more extensive than personal transgression. This Paul himself declares in ver. 14. Infants die, though they have not personally sinned.

2. The second view [advocated by Melancthon, Calvin, Prof. Turner] is also inconsistent with the meaning of the word, and with the nature of the comparison. The verb does not mean to become corrupt and sinful, but simply to sin. [Alford blends the first and second view together, making the sin to be "both original and actual : in the *seed*, as planted in the nature by the sin of our forefather, and in the *fruit*, as developed by each

conscious responsible individual in his own practice."]

3. The third view [Haldane's, Edwards', Shedd's,] is regarded as simply inconceivable. The appeal to Heb. 7 : 9, 10, does not avail to make it conceivable, for the writer there takes pains to apprise us that he is not using language in a *literal* sense : "As I may so say" is a not uncommon phrase in the classics, in introducing a highly figurative expression, but is found nowhere else in the New Testament.

4. We are therefore shut up to this fourth sense of the expression, that all virtually sinned in the sin of Adam, who was the source, and then indeed, with Eve, *was the whole* of the human race. This interpretation is demanded by the *context :* by ver. 13 and 14, which contain the *proof* of what is here asserted ; by ver. 15–19, which assume this meaning as proved ; and by ver. 18, 19, which complete the comparison between Adam and Christ in accordance with this view. [Ver. 12 may be properly explained by the plainer and fuller assertions of ver. 15–19, since these assertions rest on this verse as a foundation. Notice the 'for if' in ver. 15, 17, 'so then' in ver. 18, 'for as' in ver. 19.] And it is confirmed, finally, by such passages as 1 Cor. 15: 22, and 2 Cor. 5: 14, which should be translated, "having judged this, that one died for all, therefore they all died." [Some interpret the phrase, 'for that all sinned,' as meaning that they sinned putatively or representatively ; "in other words, they were regarded and treated as sinners on account of Adam's sin." (Hodge.) To this view it is commonly objected that we did not elect Adam to be our agent or representative (yet God might have appointed him as such), and it does not appear that he consciously acted as such. Dr. Schaff says that Prof. Hodge "by rejecting the realistic theory of a participation of Adam's posterity in his fall, loses the basis for a just imputation, and resolves it into a legal fiction." Only a sinful and guilty being can be the subject of the displeasure of a holy and righteous God. "We do not object." he says, "to the doctrine of imputation in itself, but simply to that form of it which ignores or denies the *vital* nature of our connection with Adam and with Christ, as plainly taught in this whole section. Adam is our natural repre-

sentative, *de facto* as well as *de jure.* He is the root of humanity and his fall affected the stock and every branch, by the inherent law of organic life union. . . . . The human race is not a sand heap, but an organic unity ; and only on the ground of such a vital unity, as distinct from a mechanical or merely federal unity, can we understand and defend the doctrine of original sin, the imputation of Adam's sin, and of Christ's righteousness." The elder Edwards, who could not think of any condemnation without personal ill-desert, carried the notion of our personal identity with Adam so far as to say that his sin was "truly and properly " ours, and therefore God imputes it to us. If, however, we as individuals actually sinned in Adam, there would be no need of imputing *his* sin to us, since we should have sin of our own to answer for. Dr. Schaff, it will be seen, adopts the realistic Augustinian imputation theory which finds perhaps its truest expression in the familiar couplet of the old New England Primer:

> In Adam's fall,
> We sinned all.

And this, indeed, is the view of many of the more distinguished modern commentators, as Olshausen, Meyer, Philippi, Godet, Bishop Wordsworth, the "Speaker's Commentary," Ellicott's " New Testament Commentary," etc. This view well accords with the tenses of the verbs : "All sinned," and " death passed through upon all men "—that is, at a definite time in the past, and, as we think, harmonizes with the drift of the apostle's argument, and best explains the universal natural depravity of mankind.[1] But how can Dr. Schaff, with others holding similar views, say that this verb to sin "means real, actual sinning," and yet add that "all men sinned in Adam, *not indeed personally by conscious, actual transgressions, but virtually or potentially*"? Volumes, perhaps, have been written on these two words: *all sinned* (πάντες ἥμαρτον),[2] especially on *how* this 'all sinned' is connected with the phrase '*the one that sinned*' (ἑνὸς ἁμαρτήσαντος), and volumes more we fear will have to be written before that definition will be found which will to all persons and in all respects be satisfactory. The truth is, as Prof. Boise remarks, the *how* of this matter "is not discussed by the apostle." One thing, however, seems to be certain, namely, that the

[1] Prof. Stuart does not see anything which specially needs to be accounted for in the fact that all the descendants of Adam sin since *he* himself sinned who was created upright. He says, for substance, that as, according to Edwards, our race had a more favorable probation in Adam than we should have *in propria persona,* and yet he fell, it is therefore nothing wonderful that all his descendants fall, even though created upright and pure. But this, I think, does not follow. A strong man has an advantage in his strength, yet we conceive it possible that he might fall where a weaker man might stand. That a strong man fell simply shows that all others may fall, but does not prove that they certainly will. Edwards says that " an effect's happening once will not prove any fixed propensity or permanent influence." On the other hand, "a stated effect requires a stated cause," and in support of this postulate he adduces this illustration among others: "If such a case should happen that a person through the deceitful persuasions of a pretended friend, once takes an unwholesome and poisonous draught of a liquor he had no inclination to before; but after he has once taken of it, he be observed to act as one that has an insatiable, incurable thirst after more of the same"— so that he does and will indulge incessantly in the practice of drinking — "could it be said with good reason that a fixed propensity can no more be argued from his consequent common practice than from his first draught?" And he thinks it would be " weak

arguing " in an objector to say, " Do *you* tell me how it came to pass that he was guilty of that sin the first time, without a fixed inclination, and I will tell you how he is guilty of it so generally without a fixed inclination." One thing is certain, that theologians of every age and of every school, save the Pelagian and Socinian, have traced man's innate depravity to the sin of our first parents. " Whosoever," says Augustine, " contends that human nature in any age does not need the second Adam as a physician on the ground that it has not been vitiated in the first Adam, does not fall into an error which may be held without injury to the rule of faith, but by that very rule by which we are constituted Christians is convicted of being an enemy to the grace of God."—(F.)

[2] The " Five Clergymen " render this verb: *were sinners,* since this phrase " covers every sort of sin." Prof. J. R. Boise, in his notes on Romans, seems inclined to regard all the verbs of this verse as in the gnomic or iterative aorist, expressing as in the present tense a general truth or what is habitual. But the account here given of Adam, of his offense, and of its chiefest consequence, is manifestly historic, and it involves here a manifest incongruity to say: Through Adam sin *enters* into the world, etc. Besides, the use of this aorist in the New Testament is quite uncertain, and though affirmed by Buttmann, p. 201, is altogether denied by Winer, p. 277.—(F.)

apostle's argument requires us to keep two personages especially in view, who did not stand alone or act as private persons, but, as Melancthon states it, " merited " for others, yet "contrary things," and that as justification and salvation are conferred upon us on the ground of the obedience and righteousness of the second Adam, so condemnation and death have been visited upon us, upon our whole race, on the ground of the transgression of the first Adam. The apostle does not assert that Adam's transgression is the *sole* cause of the sinner's condemnation, nor does he ignore individual sins. He affirms that before the law was given "sin was in the world," and he speaks of our "many offences," and in a previous chapter declares that "they who sinned without law shall perish without law." Yet he does teach that the sin of Adam is the *primal* and *direct* cause of human depravity, sin, and death, and that in this respect he is a type of the last Adam from whom come directly our justification, life, and peace. " By one man (see especially in ver. 15, 17, the simple dative of means) sin entered and death by sin." "The judgment came of one unto condemnation." "Through one trespass it came unto all men to condemnation," which is here the same as saying that all men *were* condemned through the one trespass of Adam. Compare ver. 16, "the judgment was from one [*one offense*], unto condemnation." If we deny that this "one offence" is to us the ground of condemnation, we must also deny that Christ's righteousness is the ground of our justification. To assert that individual sins are the sole cause of man's condemnation and death would completely nullify the apostle's argument, and would be as false to Scripture as it to fact. Of what actual sins are irresponsible persons, infants, and children unborn, personally guilty that they should suffer the penalty of death? Their only sin for which they die—for there is no death without sin—is the imputed sin of Adam, unless it be, as some suppose (Origen, in olden times, Julius Müller, President Beecher), their individual sin in a previous state. That the apostle should ignore the fact that this very large part of our race suffer death is an impossibility, for he asserts that death through sin has passed through upon all men, and he expressly traces the death of all to the sin of

all, and hence this large class of dying persons must be put among the "all" who sinned. Nor will it do to interpret 'for that' as meaning *in so far as*, unless it be to express perhaps " different degrees of guilt and death" (Lange), because there must be a sin of all which is the cause of death to all. The apostle's argument, then, and we deem it irrefutable, is manifestly this: that there is a resemblance between the headship of Adam and of Christ, and that as by the trespass or transgression of Adam all men, even apart from their individual sins, are condemned and visited with death, so by the obedience of Christ, the second Adam, all who receive his grace are freely justified and crowned with everlasting blessedness apart from any inherent goodness or merit of their own. In the light of this argument, the phrase 'for that all sinned' must be interpreted. In 2 Cor. 5: 14, an "analogous though not parallel passage" (Godet), Paul asserts that because " one (Christ) died in behalf of all (or, instead of all) therefore all died." In like manner it may at least be said that as Adam sinned for all, to the disadvantage and condemnation of all, so they " all sinned." " The death of Christ was legally and effectively our death, and the sin of Adam was legally and effectively our sin." (Hodge.) "The apostle therefore represents the sin of mankind as objectively wrapped up in Adam, precisely as he contemplates the righteousness of mankind as objectively wrapped up in Christ." (Philippi.) Forbes wishes to find in this phrase an impartation as well as an imputation of sin, and this perhaps can be done. There is undeniably a sense in which we as a race *fell* in Adam (do we not rightly speak of our "fallen race"?), and there is a sense in which we as a race *sinned* in and through Adam, and so were put in the category of sinners. And this, we think, is the meaning of ver. 19, where Paul asserts that *through the disobedience of one man*, in which we all shared as a race, *the many*— that is, the whole race of mankind *were constituted*, set down in the place of, *sinners*, and are consequently treated as sinners. Olshausen, speaking of our being constituted sinners through Adam's offense, says: "Not the personal transgressions of individual men, but the disobedience of Adam was alone the foundation of all being sinners, and just so the reverse"—that is, in régard to our justification, solely through the obedience of Christ. He then adds: "No expression can be imagined by which Paul could have more distinctly defined ver. 12 and 15, and protected his meaning from erroneous conceptions; if, notwithstanding, he has not succeeded in preventing them, the cause of the failure can only at last be found in the heart's resistance to this doctrine, bringing, as it does, to nothing all man's self-sufficiency, a resistance which even unconsciously asserts itself while interpreting such passages."]

We must always bear in mind that death means more than the mere separation of soul and body, but that all which it means is so connected with this literal sense, that this last may be taken as a *representative fact:* where this is found, the rest will follow, without some extraordinary and superhuman intervention. Natural death is a part of the penalty; and so far the penalty goes into actual effect.

"The death of the soul," says Augustine, "takes place when God leaves it, as the death of the body takes place when the soul leaves it: it is then the death of both, that is, of the *whole man,* when a soul forsaken of God forsakes the body." ("De Civitate Dei," xiii, c. 1.) "Mors igitur animæ fit, cum eam deserit Deus: sicut corporis, cum id deserit anima. Ergo utriusque rei, id est, totius hominis mors est, cum anima a Deo deserta deserit corpus."

Bengel calls attention to the *arrangement* of the four clauses in this verse:

> Sin entered into the world,
> And death through sin;
> Death passed through to all men,
> For that all sinned;

and adds this remark: "Sin precedes death; but the *universality* of death is known before the universality of sin: and the clauses are conformed to this order."

There is still one more point to be considered in this verse, before we pass to the next. Looking at the verse as a whole, it is evidently grammatically incomplete. Three ways are proposed of supplying what is necessary to its completeness.

(*a*) To supply at the beginning, or, rather, after 'wherefore' (*therefore*) "it was"—[that is, our justification was by one man, *as* through

one man came our sin and condemnation], thus making all that follows the second member of the comparison, technically called the *apodosis,* instead of the first, the *protasis.* Alford takes this view, and refers to Matt. 25: 14, for a similar use of the word translated *as,* without any preceding *protasis.* [The *therefore,* at the beginning of our passage, indicating a new starting point, forbids such a close grammatical connection with the preceding passage.]

(*b*) Others regard this as the *protasis,* and find the *apodosis* in a later clause of the same verse, some in the clause immediately following, *so* being supplied, *and* being changed to *also: as by one man sin entered into the world, so also death by sin;* and some in the next clause, *and so* being changed to *so also.*

(*c*) Others find the *apodosis* in a subsequent verse; some in the expression, *who is the figure of him that was to come* in ver. 14; and some in the latter half of ver. 18, *even so,* etc.

All these except the last would be grammatically irregular, the last under (*b*) pre-eminently so. We prefer the last under (*c*). Had the comparison been completed, in regular form with its proper connection [Winer, 569] and without any parenthesis or digression, we suppose ver. 12 would have read on this wise: *therefore, as by one man sin entered,* etc., *even so by one man righteousness entered into the world, and life by righteousness.* And this is virtually the way in which it is completed in ver. 18, the terms being somewhat changed, to accord with the interposed verses. To this view the principal objections are, that the matter contained in ver. 13-17 is too long and too important to be treated as a parenthesis: and also that ver. 18 seems to be a *recapitulation* rather than a *resumption.* Neither of these objections seems insuperable: in fact, the last seems of very little weight; for it would be quite natural, in *recapitulating* to *resume* the regular grammatical or rhetorical form of the sentence. It is confessedly a case of peculiar difficulty; but this way of making out the connection seems to us to be encumbered with less serious difficulties than any other.

13, 14. It is generally agreed that these verses are designed to prove [or explain] the statement of ver. 12, that death passed upon all men on account of sin. What is the nature

13 (For until the law sin was in the world : but sin is not imputed when there is no law.

13 passed unto all men, for that all sinned:—for until the law sin was in the world: but sin is not imputed 14 when there is no law. Nevertheless death reigned

of the proof? The infliction of penal evils implies the violation of law. The violation of the law of Moses will not account for the universality of death, for men died before that law was given. The violation of the law of nature will not account for the universality of death, for those die who have never violated that law. Death is more extensive than the violation of the law of Moses; it is more extensive than the·violation of the law of nature. It is co-extensive with our connection with Adam. Here is a universal effect. Here are three causes proposed to account for that effect: Two of these causes are less extensive than the effect, the third is precisely co-extensive with the effect, and the effect is precisely what was foretold as the sure consequence of that particular cause. It follows, therefore, that men are subject to death on account of the sin of Adam. **For until the law.** For prior to the law, and up to the time of the law. [This is further explained by the phrase—from Adam to Moses. The word law in the original has no article, yet it must have special reference to *the* law. The Jews knew only of one law, that of Moses, and hence "law" to them was the same as "the law." So "world" in the following clause is destitute of the article, it being noticed by Winer under the general head of "words which denote objects, of which there is but one in existence, and which, therefore, approximate closely to proper names." Especially are such words found without the article "when, in connection with prepositions, etc., they form phrases of frequent occurrence."] **Sin was in the world.** [Continuously. The imperfect tense is used to express simultaneity, duration, non-completion. (Ellicott.)] There was sin in the world. This is proved by the fact that death, the consequence of sin, was all this time in the world. **But sin is not imputed when there is no law.** Sin is not reckoned as sin when there is no law. [It is not reckoned for punishment, or is not punished as transgression. (Meyer.)] The word translated *imputed* here is different in form (though the difference is not radical, both being derived from the same root) from that which is

usually so translated. The same form is not found elsewhere, except in Philem. (Ver. 18.) Some have inferred from this that the word here used means, is not *fully* or *strictly* reckoned, in the absence of express law. But this requires that the word *law* should be restricted to *express* or *written* law, a restriction not called for, and, in our view, not consistent with a right view of the apostle's argument. ["Not put into the account for punishment" is Dr. Shedd's view. But surely the apostle has repeatedly and plainly asserted that the wrath of God will be visited upon the Gentiles, who have not the law, but who yet are fully aware that for their sins they are deserving of death. Paul in the last chapter (ver. 15) affirmed that "where there is no law neither is there transgression." And his meaning in our passage must be that sin, in the absence of God's revealed will, is not reckoned or punished as transgression. It may be, as the Apostle John calls it, 'lawlessness' (ἀνομία), but not 'a transgression of law' (παράβασις νόμου). Yet death reigned from Adam to Moses, and if death was visited upon the people who lived during that time solely on account of their individual offenses, then their sin certainly was imputed to them. To get rid of this contradiction, Tholuck, Müller, Stuart, and others say that sin is not imputed *by men* where there is no law, and the idea then would be—though men in a state of nature, and in the absence of law, "make but little account of sin" (Stuart), yet in God's sight they do sin, and their sin, as such, is visited with death. But against this man-imputation view of sin, I would observe (*a*) that in the Scriptures, generally, God, and not man, is the one who imputes or does not impute sin; (*b*) that even Pagans, without any revelation, have recognized themselves as sinners (compare 1 : 32; 2 : 15), and the Jews, as we know, regarded the heathen Gentiles as pre-eminent sinners; and (*c*) that sinning men "make but little account" of sin whether committed before or after Moses, whether without law or with law. A better interpretation. and one quite as helpful to *their* view, would be something like this: Since prior to the time of Moses sin was in the world and

14 Nevertheless death reigned from Adam to Moses, even over them that had not sinned after the similitude of Adam's transgression, who is the figure of him that was to come.

from Adam unto Moses, even over them that had not sinned after the likeness of Adam's transgres-15 sion, who is a figure of him that was to come. But

death reigned during all that period, therefore though men were then destitute of the revealed will or law of God they yet sinned against *some* law, the law written in their hearts, for sin is not imputed and visited with death in the absence of *all* law. This view, which is adopted for substance by many interpreters, has some truth in it, but it makes a distinction, not apparent in the text, between the *law* (νόμον) of one line and the equipollent *law* of the line following. Both mean the same thing and are to be treated alike; and hence we are not to supply and emphasize an adjective, as we did above, before the second law. Not even the word *no*, which is inserted in our versions, is found in the original text. Supplying, as we may, the article to each *law*, we have this literal rendering: *For until the law sin was in the world, but sin is not taken into account, there not being the law,* or, *where the law is not;* and this manifestly correct rendering is wholly antagonistic to the above view. This view, moreover, neglects the strong adversative force of the Greek conjunction (ἀλλά, *but,* or, *nevertheless,* death reigned, etc.), and does not accord with the drift, as we apprehend it, of the apostle's argument.] **Nevertheless death reigned from Adam to Moses.** 'Nevertheless'—that is, although sin is not imputed when there is no law, yet the fact was that 'death reigned,' was not only in the world, but exercised a dominion which none could resist, and from which none were exempt. [Nevertheless or *but* "introduces an apparently contradictory phenomenon, confronting the *sin is not imputed, etc.;* one, however, which just proves that men have died, not through their own special sin, but through the sin of Adam, which was put to their account." (Meyer.) Death reigned in the world during a period when there was no law, which expressly threatened death as the penalty of transgression.] 'From Adam to Moses,' corresponding to the expression at the beginning of the verse—*until the law*—from Adam, the first transgressor, to Moses, the first lawgiver. **Even over them that had not sinned after the similitude of Adam's transgression.** Does this mean

"even over those who did not commit actual transgression, as Adam did?" or, "even over those who did not violate an express precept, as Adam did?" If the latter, it was equally true of *all* those who lived between Adam and Moses; if the former, it was true only of a *part,* a *certain class,* of those who lived between Adam and Moses—that is, of those who died in infancy. [Meyer, Lange, and Hodge think that two classes are here indicated, though the former two find here no reference made to infants. But most commentators recognize but one class and find no intended reference to infants. "Children are included, but not specially intended." (Schaff.)] Now the form of the expression intimates that the words following 'even' designate a certain *part* of those who lived between Adam and Moses, over whom it might less have been expected that death would reign, than over the rest. What class could this be except those *infants* over whom death reigned? But it may be objected that if infants are intended, there is no reason for the limitation 'from Adam to Moses,' inasmuch as death's reign over infants was in nowise affected by the giving of the law. We answer, that limitation was not made in direct connection with the reference to infants. It was the writer's *immediate* purpose to show that death was not the consequence of the violation of the law of Moses. The proof of this was, that death reigned before the law of Moses was given, and having made that necessary limitation here—when he adds, incidentally, 'even over them,' etc.—he did not think it necessary expressly to *remove* that limitation; it was no longer *necessary,* to be sure. The statement was equally true of infants without that limitation; but the argument is not vitiated by allowing that no longer necessary limitation to remain. Besides, as Meyer has observed, the word 'even' necessarily assumes a class of sinners before Moses, whose sin *was* after the similitude of Adam's transgression," and this ex cludes the idea that the distinction emphasized by *even* is between those who had violated a specific command and those who had not. Moreover, this distinction is much less important than that between those who have committed actual sin and those who have not, and therefore it is highly improbable that the former distinction would be emphasized and the latter altogether ignored. Finally, it seems to us simply incredible that in such a discussion as this so prominent and significant a factor as the death of infants should be unnoticed. Our principal reason for laying so much stress on this particular question is that the reference to infants is denied by so many commentators of note. [Notwithstanding Dr. Arnold's exceedingly able argument in defense of a reference to infants in this verse (see Appendix B), we are still inclined to hesitate, and, on the whole, are disposed to adopt Meyer's interpretation of these difficult verses. (13, 14.) His view, with which that of Philippi and Godet is substantially accordant, is: "If the death of men after Adam had been caused by their own sin, then in the case of all those who died during the period from Adam till the law, the sin which they committed must have been already reckoned to them as transgression of the law, just as Adam's sin was the transgression of the positive divine command, and as such brought upon him death. But this is inconceivable, because the law was not then in existence." It was, therefore, on account of the Adamic transgression that death reigned from Adam to Moses, not only over those individuals, like Noah, to whom special commands were given, but even over those who sinned only against the law written in their hearts—that is, those who did not sin after the likeness of Adam's transgression. Philippi, Gifford, Turner, Godet differ from Meyer's interpretation chiefly in this, that they think the apostle here refers only to one class, the whole human species living and dying between Adam and Moses. Edwards, Hodge, Shedd, and some other imputationists, with Dr. Arnold, make this latter clause refer to infants; but this seems untenable for several reasons: (a) We naturally infer that those who did not sin after the likeness of Adam's transgression did *actually* sin some other way. (b) If infants literally sinned in Adam, then we should naturally suppose that their transgression was just like Adam's. And this is what Prof. Shedd, by an almost unexampled subtlety of hypercriticism, deduces from this clause. These persons, he says, did not commit a sin resembling or

similar to Adam's, therefore they committed the same identical sin! (c) There is no special reason for referring to infants who lived in the period from Adam to Moses, since these were no more ignorant of law or innocent of personal transgression than those living at any other period of the world. (d) If the apostle had wished to single out or except a certain class (infants), he would naturally have specified them by name, which he could easily have done, and would not naturally have adopted a seemingly very blind method of doing so. (e) Not only is this class not mentioned by name, but no clear intimation is given that this class is specially had in view. (f) There is no *certainty* that the apostle intended to distinguish two classes of persons (as adults and infants) existing in the period between Adam and Moses over whom death reigned. (g) Had he wished thus sharply to distinguish them, he probably would have said something like this: Nevertheless, death reigned from Adam to Moses, not only over adult persons who sinned merely against the light of nature, but even over infants and unborn children who never had done anything either good or bad. (h) The sinning or not sinning in the likeness of Adam's transgression can more easily be predicated of such adult persons than it can of irresponsible infants. Yet we do not think that this large class of mankind are ignored in the apostle's argument. They are, in our view, embraced in the propositions—"*death* passed through upon *all* men," and "for that all sinned." As dying ones they cannot here be left out of consideration, for, as Meyer states it, "the question here is the connection between the *sin* of all and the *dying* of all."] **Who is the figure of him that was to come.** [Literally, *a type of the coming one*, spoken from a pre-Christian point of view. Fritzsche, De Wette, Alford, make this refer to Christ's final coming.] 'That was to come,' or, *the one about to be*—that is, the Messiah. In this brief clause, the analogy between Adam and Christ, which is the key of this whole section (ver. 12-21), is first explicitly stated. [Meyer's interpretation of ver. 13, 14 is in substance nearly as follows: Since in the absence of law there is no imputation of personal transgression, therefore the death which befel' those who did not, as Adam, sin against a

15 But not as the offence, so also *is* the free gift: for if through the offence of one many be dead, much more the grace of God, and the gift by grace, *which is* by one man, Jesus Christ, hath abounded unto many.

not as the trespass, so also *is* the free gift. For if by the trespass of the one the many died, much more did the grace of God, and the gift by the grace of the one man, Jesus Christ, abound unto the many.

positive law could not be derived from their individual sin committed before the law was given. Consequently, death in their case was caused, not by individual sins, but by the sin of Adam, who in this respect is a type of Christ; for as the sin of Adam, and not their self-originated sin, brought death to all, so the obedience of Christ, and not their own virtue, brought life to all. This view does not necessarily imply that sinners of the class referred to were not also condemned and punished for their own individual sins. Thus Bengel says: "It is not denied that death is the wages of any sin whatever, but it is proved that the first cause of death was the first sin."]

The following verses specify the *differences*, rather than the *resemblances*, between the objects compared. The resemblance implied in this word ' figure' (literally, *type*) may be summarily stated in the following formula, which, however, necessarily involves the most important points of difference: As Adam, the first man, communicated a degenerate human nature to all his natural offspring, so Christ, the new man, communicates a regenerate divine nature (2 Peter 1:4) to all his spiritual offspring. This statement is still further expanded by Carpzov, so as to embrace the substance of what is contained in ver. 12–19, thus:

1. The first Adam is the one man, the head and corrupter of the human race. (Ver. 12.) So Christ, the last Adam (1 Cor. 15: 45), he too is the one man, but God-man, the restorer of the human race. (Ver. 15, 17.)

2. The first Adam brought in sin, guilt, death. (Ver. 12, 18.) The last Adam procures the grace of God, righteousness, life. (Ver. 15-18.)

3. The one, by his transgression, brought guilt upon all men. (Ver. 15, 18, 19.) The other by his righteousness, brings back reconciliation to all who by faith lay hold on his merit. (Ver. 17.)

4. The first Adam sinned unto condemnation. (Ver. 16.) The last Adam, by his righteousness, brings us blessing unto life eternal.[1] (Ver. 18.)

[Though our heritage from Adam is one of woe, yet we have this to be thankful for, that through the first Adam we have the Second. "O felix culpa quæ talem et tantum meruit habere Redemptorem." "O fortunate offense which deserved to have such and so great a Redeemer." "I willingly consent," says Chalmers, "to have the guilt of Adam charged upon me, if, along with it, the overpassing righteousness of Christ shall be reckoned to me." (Ver. 15.) The connection of thought here is this: Adam, as a type, indeed resembles Christ, *but* there is this difference, etc. The design of the apostle leads him, as has been intimated, to emphasize the differences rather than the resemblances between the type and the antitype. Prof. Boise remarks that the logical order of a sentence would be *so as*, but Paul pursues the chronological order, mentioning the fall first; compare ver. 16.] **But not as the offence, so also is the free gift.** [Better: *the gift of grace.*] That is, not in all respects. What follows in this verse explains this. There was a similar relation of cause and consequence in the two cases; but both were of an opposite nature. 'The offence'—that is, the act of transgression, which brought in death—the *fall*, as the same word is translated in 11: 11, 12. [It is derived from a verb which means, to fall aside.] It is commonly translated *trespass* (wherever that English word occurs as a noun), sometimes *sin* (Eph. 1: 7; 2: 5: Col. 2: 13), once, *fault* (Gal. 6: 1); *offense* only in the last verse of the preceding chapter, and in ver. 15 (*twice*), 16, 17, 18, 20 of this. 'The free gift.' This word is not the direct antithesis to *offense* or *fall;* but having in mind chiefly the *consequence* of the *offense*

---

[1] 1. Primus Adamus est ille εἰς ἄνθρωπος, ille *unus*, generis caput humani et depravator. (Ver. 12.) Ita Christus ὁ ἔσχατος Ἀδάμ (1 Cor. 15 : 45), et ipse est unus ille, sed Θεάνθρωπος, generis humani instaurator. (Ver. 15, 17.)

2. Prior Adamus peccatum, reatum, mortem infert. (Ver. 12, 18.) Posterior gratiam Dei, justitiam, vitam comparat. (Ver. 15, 18.)

3. Ille, per unum delictum, reatum inducit ad omnes homines. (Ver. 15, 18. 19.) Hic, per unam justitiam, reconciliationem recuperat omnium hominum, ejus meritum fide complectentium. (Ver. 17.)

4. Adamus primus peccat ad condemnationem. (Ver. 16.) Adamus novissimus sua nos justitia felicitat ad vitam eternam. (Ver. 18.)

—namely, condemnation, the apostle uses the word which comprehensively expresses the proper antithesis to that consequence, and which is explained by the terms, *grace* and *gift*, with their adjuncts, in this and the two following verses. **For if through the offence of [*the*] one many be dead.** *The many died,* rather than 'many be dead,' is the exact translation of the original. The meaning of not a few passages is obscured, or altered, by the frequent mistranslation of the verb *to die.* See 2 Cor. 5: 14, where the verb translated "were dead" is precisely identical with that translated "died" in the same verse, except the difference of one letter, to mark the change from the singular number to the plural.[1] See also Gal. 2: 21. It is an entirely different expression in the original (νεκρός), which is correctly translated, *to be dead,* in such passages as Luke 15: 24, 32; Rom. 7: 8; 8: 10; Eph. 2: 1, 5; Col. 2: 13; James 2: 17; Rev. 1: 18; 2: 8; 3: 1. ["The death of the many is described here as the direct consequence of the trespass of the one." (Philippi.) Prof. Stuart also concedes that "Adam did by his offense cause death to come on all without exception," that "all have been introduced to sin and death by Adam," and that "the disobedience of Adam was a cause or ground why all men became sinners and therefore come into a state of condemnation." *The many* (used here in contrast with *the one*)—that is, all mankind died by means of Adam's offense, and they died at the same time that death passed through unto all men, and that was the time of Adam's transgression, in which all mankind were involved. We became in Adam a fallen, sinful, dying race. "The question," says Olshausen, "how in Adam all who were not yet in existence could sin with him [or how all could die in him] has difficulty in it only so long as the isolation of individuals is maintained."] **Much more.** [The presupposition on which this conclusion rests is that God would rather allow his goodness to prevail, than his severity. (Meyer.)]

This phrase is to be understood here in a logical, rather than in a quantitative sense—*with much more reason*, rather than in a *much greater degree.* The difference indicated in the first clause of this verse seems to be rather one of kind than of degree (Alford takes the contrary view); yet the idea of *degree* cannot be altogether excluded from the 'much more' in any of these three verses (15, 16, 17). It seems, however, more prominent in the next verse than in this. Here we regard the contrast as chiefly between the *kind*, or *nature*, of the consequences of the acts of the type (ver. 14) and of the antitype: on the one hand, *death*, on the other, a gracious and abounding *gift.* ["The word abound is doubtless an echo of Paul's own blessed experience." (Meyer.) A simple antithesis of the first clause would be, as Philippi observes: much more by the gracious gift of the One shall the many live. But Paul wishes to expand and emphasize the idea of the 'gift' (χάρισμα) and of its *abounding* through Jesus Christ. The grace abounding, says Dr. Gifford, "did not restore in the same form that which had been lost in Adam, but bestowed far more in new and better gifts."] The English reader might be in doubt, whether the relative 'which' refers to the word 'gift,' or to the word 'grace': the question would be only a grammatical one, the sense being substantially the same; but it is perfectly clear in the original, that the reference is to the latter word; and the clause might be translated, both more literally and less ambiguously, *the gift by* (or *in*) *the grace of the one man.* [Bengel calls the two articles which stand after 'grace,' nervosissimi, "most forcible." Their force perhaps can be fully expressed thus: by the grace (namely) by that of the one man, etc. De Wette, Fritzsche, and Meyer, *versus* Lange, Philippi, Godet, connect this clause, not with the noun gift, but with the verb abound, which seems to us incorrect. The points of contrast in this verse are—the trespass of the one (Adam) with its result, death, as our

---

1 "If one died for all then they all died"—that is, they died in Christ's dying. The same principle holds substantially true of the sinning and dying of the first Adam. These acts on the part of Adam were virtually the acts of the race. Dr. Gifford (in the Bible Commentary) says: "The apostle's whole reasoning rests ◄n these two principles: (1) Sin is the cause of death:

(2) By virtue of the unity of mankind, sin and death are both transmitted from one to all. Thus the sin of the many and the death of the many are included in the sin of the one and the death of the one, and there at their common source the connection between sin and death is fixed once for all."—(F.)

16 And not as *it was* by one that sinned, *so is* the gift: for the judgment *was* by one to condemnation, but the free gift *is* of many offences unto justification.
17 For if by one man's offence death reigned by one;

16 And not as through one that sinned, *so is* the gift: for the judgment *came* of one unto condemnation, but the free gift *came* of many trespasses unto ¹justification.
17 For if, by the trespass of the one, death reigned through the one; much more shall they that re_

1 Gr. *an act of righteousness.*

heritage of woe on the one hand, and on the other, the grace of God and the gift of righteousness (ver. 17) abounding to us through the grace of the one man Jesus Christ, who loved us and gave himself to be the propitiation for our sins.]

Now follows mention of a difference in *degree:* the evil consequences of *one trespass* come upon us from Adam; but the evil consequences of *many trespasses* are taken away by Christ.

16. And not as it was by one that sinned. [The codices D E F G and the Vulgate read 'one sin' instead of 'one that sinned,' which Meyer rejects as a "gloss." De Wette and Alford fill out the sentence thus: "not as that which originated, or took place, through one," etc. Meyer does not supply anything.] The preposition 'by,' occurring twice in this verse, represents two different prepositions in the Greek, the second of which [ἐκ, denoting source 'out of' which something issues] is the same that is translated 'of' in the last clause. Hence the more exact representation of the original would be: "And not as it was through one that sinned, so is the gift: for the judgment was from (or, *of*) one to condemnation, but the free gift is from (or, *of*) many offences unto justification." [Dr. Hodge says that "Judgment unto condemnation is a sentence of condemnation, and the free gift unto justification is gratuitous justification." Godet prefers, instead of 'many offences,' the rendering: 'offences of many,' but in this I think he stands alone.] After the second 'one' the word offense should be supplied. This is plain from the way in which the sentence is completed. [De Wette, Meyer, Philippi, Godet, Alford, looking backward to 'one that sinned,' rather than forward, would supply, properly we think, the word man or sinner after the second 'one.' Indeed, Philippi and others regard all the ones in this whole section as masculine, even those in ver. 18. The word rendered "justification" (δικαίωμα) differs from the word occurring in ver. 18; 4: 25, which has this special meaning. It properly

denotes a righteous or justifying act or a justifying sentence, "a justifying judgment." (Weiss.) It occurs elsewhere in ver. 18; 1: 32; 2: 26; 8: 4; Heb. 9: 1; Rev 15: 4; 19: 8; Luke 1: 6. Here it is the antithesis of condemnation, and in ver. 18 of trespass. Aristotle defines it as the amendment or reparation of an unjust act. Dr. Schaff makes it mean in both these verses, "*the righteous deed —* that is, the perfect obedience of Christ." Meyer and Godet regard it as a *sentence of justification* in both places. De Wette and Philippi and our Revised Version give it different senses in the two passages. This condemnation and justification, as we see from ver. 18, embraces "all men." The *second* difference here indicated between the influence of Adam and of Christ is that of condemnation and justification. (De Wette.)]

How clearly the one sin of Adam, rather than the many sins that originated from it, is here made the ground of condemnation. The whole contrast turns upon that point.

The next verse brings to view a third difference, both of kind and degree: we had no voluntary part in the sin of Adam; but voluntarily receive the grace of Christ: we might well expect, therefore, that the good which comes to us from the latter should outweigh the evil which comes to us from the former.

17. For if by one man's offence death reigned by one. [Each of the ones in this verse should have the article as in the Revised Version.] There is nothing in the first clause of this verse which needs explanation or comment. It simply reaffirms the causal connection between the sin of the first man and the reign of death over all men. The **abundance of grace** corresponds with the 'grace of God' that 'abounded' [and 'the gift of righteousness' with the 'gift by (Christ's) grace'] of ver. 15. Compare also John 10: 10. [This verse contrasts chiefly the reigning of death through Adam and the reigning of life through Christ. Godet thus gives the scope of the argument here presented: "For this terrible reign of

much more they which receive abundance of grace and of the gift of righteousness shall reign in life by one, Jesus Christ.)

ceive the abundance of grace and [1] of the gift of righteousness reign in life through the one, *even* Jesus

1 Some ancient authorities omit *of the gift.*

death, established on the weak foundation of a single sin and a single sinner, may serve as a *measure* to establish the greater certainty of the reign of life which will come to light among the justified by the freely accepted gift of God." On the verb 'reigned' Bengel thus remarks: "The word in the preterite looks back from the economy of grace to that of sin, as presently 'shall reign,' in the future, looks forward from the economy of sin to that of grace and eternal life; so ver. 19." Calvin in noticing the difference of these two reigns says: "The benefit of Christ does not come to all men, while Adam has involved his whole race in condemnation; and the reason of this is indeed evident; for as the curse we derive from Adam is conveyed to us by nature, it is no wonder that it includes the whole mass; but that we may come into participation of the grace of Christ, we must be ingrafted in him by faith. Hence, in order to partake of the miserable inheritance of sin it is enough for thee to be a man, for it dwells in flesh and blood; but in order to enjoy the righteousness of Christ it is necessary for thee to be a believer, for a participation of him is attained only by faith." Of all the fallen children of Adam, it is only **they which receive** the **abundance of grace** that **shall reign in life.**] The principal question in regard to the complex sentence which forms the latter part of this verse is, which are the emphatic clauses? Is the emphasis on 'they which receive,' or on 'shall reign,' or on 'in life'? There is no apparent reason for special emphasis upon the word 'life': it is required as the antithesis of the word 'death' in the first clause. Nor can 'shall reign' well be made more emphatic in the latter part of the verse, than 'reigned' was in the former part. But 'they which receive' introduces a new element. The position of the word in the Greek indicates emphasis: 'they which receive' is expressed by the article and the present participle, equivalent, as nearly as the idioms of the two languages admit, to 'those receiving' [the participle denoting a continued process. (Alford.)]; while the words 'abundance of grace and of the gift of right-

eousness,' being placed between the article and the participle, in a manner peculiar to the Greek language, the result, apparently designed, is to bring the participle as near as possible to the words, 'shall reign in life.' Again, the use of the *present* participle, instead of the past 'they who receive,' instead of 'they who received,' or 'who have received,' by making the participle more nearly equivalent to a *substantive,* as if he had said, *the receivers of,* etc. And finally, the fact that the construction of the sentence is changed, seemingly in order to bring the participle into this prominence confirms our view of its emphatic character: for the comparison which began with 'by one man's offence death reigned' would naturally and regularly have ended 'by one man's grace and righteousness life shall reign,' or in some similar way, if the apostle had not had a special reason for making the *personal receivers reign in life,* instead of saying *life shall reign.* [De Wette remarks that this form of expression was chosen to make prominent "the idea of free personality." On the distinction between life (ζωή), whose proper antithesis is death, and the life which we live (βίος)—that is, its means or manner, see Trench's "Synonyms," p. 91. Meyer says the words Jesus Christ "are added as if in triumph, in contradistinction to the unnamed but well-known *one* who occasioned the reign of death. Finally, we should not fail to notice how in this passage the glance proceeds from the state of grace (receiving), backward to the state of wrath (reigned), and forward to the state of glory (shall reign)." Philippi says: "As to this reigning of believers in eternal life, which is an inheriting, a being glorified, a reigning *with Christ,* compare 8: 17; 1 Cor. 4: 8; 6: 2, 3; 2 Tim. 2: 12; Rev. 20: 4; 22: 5. . . . . Christ atoned for *many* sins, and not merely abolished death, but planted life in its stead." "Far more," says Chrysostom, "than what we owed was paid by Christ, as much more as the immeasurable ocean exceeds a drop. Doubt not, therefore, O man, when beholding such a treasure of blessings, nor ask how the old spark of death and of sin has been extin-

18 Therefore, as by the offence of one *judgment came* upon all men to condemnation; even so by the righteousness of one *the free gift came* upon all men unto justification of life.

18 Christ. So then as through one trespass *the judgment came* unto all men to condemnation; even so through one act of righteousness *the free gift came* 19 unto all men to justification of life. For as through

guished, seeing that such a sea of the gift of grace has been poured upon it."]

The precise relation of these three verses to each other is, however, a question of no little difficulty, in regard to which the ablest commentators are by no means agreed. Alford makes ver. 15 point out a difference of *degree,* fixing the stress upon 'much more,' taken *quantitively;* ver. 16, a difference in *kind,* emphasizing the words *condemnation* and *righteousness;* and ver. 17, a second difference in kind between 'death' and 'life.' Lange says ver. 16 compares *things,* ver. 17, *persons.* Again, some regard ver. 17 as a mere amplification of ver. 15, the words 'offence,' 'gift,' and 'grace' being prominent in both. [The word 'gift' is wanting in B 49, but this is not sufficient to cast any serious doubt on its genuineness. Note how this righteousness of God through faith, whereby we receive the divine acquittal, is called a 'gift.' Compare Phil. 3 : 9, the righteousness *from* God upon faith.]

The two following verses are a condensed summary of the results of the parallel between Adam and Christ; but here, again, we meet with different explanations of the relation of the two to each other.

18. Therefore. [*Accordingly then,* or, *so then* (hinc igitur), a frequent expression with the apostle, and placed first in the sentence contrary to classical usage. Some critics state that the first word (ἄρα) refers rather to the internal cause, the second (οὖν) more to the external.[1] The *ones* of this verse, though commonly regarded as masculine, are properly neuter, and are rightly rendered in the Revised Version.] Here we have, according to the view presented at the close of the comments on ver. 12, the second member of the comparison begun in that verse. The substance of the first member is repeated, in the changed terms demanded by the inter-

vening statements, and then the regular formula, **even so,** introduces what virtually completes the comparison there begun, the precise terms being changed to conform to the restatement of the first member of the comparison in this verse. The elliptical form in which the last part of each member is stated requires the supply of some such nominatives as **judgment came** and **the free gift came.** These particular expressions are borrowed from ver. 16. [De Wette and Meyer simply supply: It happened or came.] There is a twofold ambiguity in the expression translated **by the offence of one, by the righteousness of one;** the more simple and natural translation would be—*by one offence, by one righteousness.* The latter translation is recommended by its greater simplicity and by the absence of the article in Greek,[2] and is liable to no objection sufficient to counterbalance these arguments. [The *condemnation* is to "death," with whatever this may include. The righteousness (δικαίωμα) here, in contrast with the trespass or fall of Adam, is supposed to differ in meaning from its use in ver. 16, where it is opposed to condemnation. It probably is here equivalent to the one obedient, righteous act of Christ (in death). Meyer and Godet, however, give it the same meaning in both places—a justifying sentence or judgment on the part of God on the ground of Christ's sacrificial death. We think it snould be referred to Christ who stands over against the one that sinned, and should be explained by the exactly paralled "*obedience* of the One" in the following verse. It seems to denote the ground of the believer's justification so far as this depends on the active obedience of Christ.] The difficulty arising from the second 'all men,' seeming to make the justification as *universal* as the condemnation, is met by recalling the 'they which receive,' etc., of ver. 17. The only reason why

[1] Or, as Prof. Boise puts it: ἄρα, a conclusion from what precedes; οὖν, a resumption of the sentence which was begun in ver. 12. We may here observe that ἄρα, with a different accent, is used as an interrogative particle.—(F.)

[2] Wherever in this section the word *one* occurs, with-

out any accompanying word to define it, if it refers to a *person,* it is preceded by the article (ver. 15, 17 thrice, 19); in ver. 12, 16, the place of the article is supplied by the word *man* in the first and by the words *that sinned* in the second.

19. For as by one man's disobedience many were | the one man's disobedience the many were made

the former is not as universal as the latter is because some do not receive it. Compare notes on 3 : 24. **Unto justification of life.** Justification leading to and resulting in eternal life. [As the apostle seems to say that 'the many' and 'the all' who are condemned in Adam are the same 'many' and the same 'all' who are justified and saved in Christ, we are sometimes asked why "all" does not mean "all" in the one case as well as in the other? The answer generally given is that the apostle here represents the *objective sufficiency* of the atonement, and that it did not belong to the scope of the passage to dwell on its subjective efficacy. "His only object," says Meyer, "was to set forth the all-embracing, blessed objective consequence of the one justication (δικαίωμα) in contrast to the all-destructive, objective consequence of the one trespass. Hence, just as little can anything be deduced from our passage as from 11 : 32 in favor of a final restoration." Yet the apostle does limit the many and the all who are through Christ's grace justified unto eternal life to those who "*receive* the abundance of grace and of the gift of righteousness."[1] By the apostle's scheme of doctrine all men, as a matter of fact, are divided into two classes, the one class under the headship of Adam and the other under the headship of Christ, and by the same scheme is everywhere supposed that as all those who are reckoned in the first Adam do actually pattern after him, the sinning one, so all those who are enrolled in Christ and are justified in him do actually pattern after the righteous One. If, now, it can be shown that the many and the all who are by nature and of necessity in the line of the first Adam, where is condemnation, sin, and death, do actually betake themselves to Christ and transfer themselves through divine grace to the line of the second Adam, do actually repent of their "many trespasses" and experience God's pardoning love, do actually

receive of the fullness of Christ's grace and righteousness, and do actually pattern after the Great Exemplar, then, and not otherwise, will the salvation of all men be clearly proved. Besides, the apostle elsewhere speaks of the resurrection of the unjust as well as of the just, of those who perish as well as of those who are saved, and of those "whose end is perdition" and "who shall suffer punishment, even eternal destruction from the presence of the Lord and from the glory of his power." A few words in regard to the future condition of those dying in infancy. We scarcely need an apostle to tell us that a condemnation and death has been visited upon them on account of sin not their own; hence on account of Adam's transgression. A part of this penalty they, in common with us all, must suffer. The great trouble respecting their case has reference to the evil that is in their hearts— their native depravity, their "original sin." With the elder Hodge, "we believe that the grace which is in Christ Jesus secures the salvation of all who have no personal sins to answer for." And the ground of our belief is the assurance that Christ who died for our fallen race, who is a propitiation for the sins of the whole world, who died for all, and who tasted death for every one, has not *necessarily* died in vain for any one of Adam's descendants. To suppose that our dying infants can have no Saviour, and no participancy in his salvation, but are *necessarily* debarred from the benefits of Christ's death, is to antagonize and overthrow the glorious gospel of the blessed God.[2] Of one thing we are absolutely certain, that our offspring, early called from earth, have no deeds done in the body to answer for, and hence will not be condemned for actual sin in the "judgment of the great day." For further discussion of these topics, see Dr. Arnold's remarks in Appendix B.]

19. For as by [the] one man's disobedience [the] many were made sinners.

---

[1] Prof. Boise, making the statements of ver. 18 assume the form of general truths, gives this comment: "The judgment enters into the midst of all men, leading them with certainty into condemnation, if no deliverer, no Saviour appears. The free gift enters into the midst of all men, leading them into justification of life, if they receive the abundance of the grace and of the

gift of righteousness. Alas, that so many forget or reject this condition!"—(F.)

[2] Hence we deem the couplet (of Robert Robinson?) to be dogmatically correct as relating to infants:

They die for Adam sinned,
They live for Jesus died.—(F.)

made sinners, so by the obedience of one shall many be made righteous." | sinners, even so through the obedience of the one

---

Much depends in this verse on the right understanding of the verb translated 'were made' and 'shall be made.' Dr. Hodge makes the remarkable statement that this verb "never in the New Testament means to make, in the sense of effecting or causing a person or thing to be in its character or nature other than it was before." It is a sufficient refutation of this statement to refer to a few places out of the more than a score in which it is used. (Matt. 24 : 45, 47; 25 : 21, 23; Acts 7 : 10, 27, 35; Heb. 7 : 28; 2 Peter 1 : 8.) Several of the earlier translators put 'became' instead of 'were made,' but 'shall be made' in the latter place where it occurs. *To constitute, to appoint,* are the most common meanings of the verb. On the twofold use of the word 'many' (properly 'the many,' for it has the article in both places), Alford has this criticism : "In order to make the comparison more strict, the *all* who have been made sinners are weakened to the indefinite *the many,* and *many* [Alford refers to such passages as Matt. 26 : 28; Mark 10 : 45] who shall be made righteous are enlarged to the indefinite *the many.* Thus a *common term* of *quantity* is found for both, the one extending to its largest numerical interpretation, the other restricted to its smallest." This criticism is very objectionable. It does not agree with the twofold *all* of the preceding verse. It makes an incoherent use of the article. It is too great a *refinement* of criticism to attribute to Paul. And the last statement, restricting *the many* that shall be made righteous to its *smallest* numerical interpretation, is rebuked by Rev. 7 : 9 and a multitude of similar passages. Much better is Dr. J. Brown's comment on these verses : "In fine, on the one hand, there is a multitude of men of every description, condemned and dying, entirely on account of the one fault of the one man Adam; and, on the other, a multitude of men of every description, justified and living, entirely on account of the one man Jesus Christ." [May not Alford's 'the one' mean '*the latter*'?] What is the relation of ver. 18 and 19 to each other? Is it that ver. 18 mainly compares *things* and ver. 19 mainly compares *persons?* Is it that ver. 18 shows how men are *regarded* by God on account of their respective con-

nections with Adam and Christ, and ver. 19 shows how they are *treated* by him on account of those respective connections? Or is it rather that ver. 18 is to be interpreted from a *forensic* point of view and ver. 19 from a *moral* point of view? In other words, does ver. 18 relate to *justification* and ver. 19 to *sanctification?* A comparison of the terms of the two verses seems favorable to this last view. On the one hand, we have 'offence' and 'condemnation,' 'righteousness' and 'justification,' abstract and legal terms; on the other, 'disobedience' and 'obedience,' 'made sinners' and 'made righteous,' moral and practical terms. It might, perhaps, be added that the future tense of the verb, 'shall be made' righteous, agrees well with this interpretation, as sending the thoughts forward to the future perfected righteousness of the saints; but it must in fairness be owned that the use of the future—'shall reign in life,' in ver. 17—weakens the force of that consideration. The fact that the proposed interpretation of ver. 19 introduces the subject of sanctification in chapter 5, whereas it is generally held that it does not come in until the beginning of chapter 6, is of little weight; for the difference is only of two verses, and the division of the chapters has no such authority that we may not disregard or change it whenever there is good reason, as there sometimes unquestionably is, for doing so. [Prof. Cremer says: "This verb denotes an actual appointment or setting down in a definite place. . . . The choice of the expression in Rom. 5 : 19 rather arose partly from its not being simply the moral quality that is referred to, but, above all, the thence resulting situation of those who are sinners (compare ver 18, which serves as a foundation for ver. 19), partly from regard to the influence exercised from another quarter, especially to the idea of justification," etc. "As our union with Adam," says Dr. Gifford, "made us all participators in the effects of his transgression, and thereby constituted us sinners, so union with Christ, who is our righteousness, is that which constitutes us essentially and formally [not inherently] righteous." The ideas of inherent sin and inherent righteousness belong, he says, to the following chapter. Both Philippi and Meyer interpret the verb as meaning—to set down as, or, put in the category of. "The many," says Meyer," "were put actually in the category of sinners, because, namely, they sinned in and with the fall of Adam. Thus through the disobedience of the one man, because all had part in it, has the position of all become that of sinners. The consequence of this—that they were subjected to punishment, were treated as sinners, and the like— is not here expressly included, but after the foregoing is obvious of itself." Further on he says: "*Shall be placed in the category of the righteous.* . . . Thus the obedience of the One has caused that at the judgment the many shall by God's sentence enter into the category of the righteous, as the disobedience of the one had caused the many to enter the opposite. In both cases the meritorious cause is the objective act of the two heads of the race (the sin of Adam—the death of Christ), to whom belong the many on both sides; while the subjective, mediating cause is the individual relation to those acts (communion in Adam's fall—faith)." Lange calls this "Augustinian dogmatics." Meyer would seem to be wrong in one thing, for believers are put in the category of the righteous long before they reach the judgment. They are constituted or established as righteous as soon as faith in Christ is imputed to them for righteousness. In Dr. Schaff's view, "the many were made sinners either by virtual participation in the fall of Adam or by actual practice, by repeating, as it were, the fall of Adam in their sinful conduct. Both interpretations are perfectly grammatical and do not exclude each other." Dr. Hodge discards this "idea of a mysterious identity of Adam and his race," yet seems to acknowledge it in part when he says "that in virtue of the union, representative *and natural*, between Adam and his posterity, his sin is the ground of their condemnation—that is, of their subjection to penal evils." In his view, we are "constituted sinners in a legal or forensic sense;" in other words, we are "regarded and treated" as sinners because of the sin of Adam, our appointed head and representative, the sin of Adam being thus "the judicial ground of the condemnation of his race." An imputation of this kind, which consists in putative sinning, Dr. Schaff calls

a "legal fiction." Alford thinks the kind of sin spoken of in this passage is "both original and actual," and furthermore says: "In Christ and united to him a man is *made righteous*, not by a fiction or *imputation only* of Christ's righteousness, but by a real and living spiritual union with a righteous Head as a righteous member." Prof. Stuart's view is that "men through the disobedience of Adam did become or were constituted *actual* sinners." Similarly to De Wette, he holds the sin and the righteousness, of this passage to be wholly personal, a view which makes condemnation and death to be solely the result of individual transgression. But this sentiment is no less contradictory to the truth of facts than it is antagonistic to some of the apostle's statements and to his general argument. In the phrase 'shall be made righteous,' "the future of the verb is used as in 3 : 20, because justification is to be conceived as an act not yet come to an end, but continuing in the future." (Philippi.) The 'for' with which this verse begins shows that this verse is explanatory and corroborative of the preceding, while the 'as' (ὥσπερ, not ὡς as in the last verse) not only resumes the comparison but indicates it in a more precise manner —for *just as*, etc. We therefore conceive that the verses are altogether too closely united to allow the expression of such different views (the forensic and the ethical) as Dr. Arnold and many others here find. "The word *righteous*," says Gōdet, "is applied as the sense of this whole part requires to *imputed* righteousness." Prof. Cremer, as we have seen, explains *constituted righteous* by the 'justification' (δικαίωσις) of the preceding verse. He also says that "'to justify' (δικαιοῦν), as used by Paul, denotes nothing else than the *judicial act* of God whereby man is pronounced free from guilt and punishment and is thus recognized or represented as righteous." In 2 : 13, the words "righteous before God" are paralled with the verb "shall be justified." So this clause, "shall be set down as righteous," "cannot mean that by the obedience of one the many shall be made holy." (Hodge.) In regard to the *obedience* of Christ, some, like Meyer, refer it to the death of Christ, which was pre-eminently his obedience to the will of the Father (Phil. 2 : 8; Heb. 5 : 8), while others refer it to his "collective life obedience," not

20 Moreover the law entered, that the offence might abound. But where sin abounded, grace did much more abound:

20 shall the many be made righteous. And [1] the law came in beside, that the trespass might abound; but where sin abounded, grace did abound more exceed-

1 Or, law.

excluding, of course, his obedience unto death. The emphasis which the Scriptures place on the *obedience* of Christ to the will of God plainly shows us that the atonement of Christ had primarily a Godward efficacy. How thankful we may well be that the Saviour's obedience was so different from that of any who thereby have been constituted righteous! Had he lived, though but for one moment, so imperfect, so unholy, as we are, our salvation must have been impossible, for we never could have heard of that obedience and that righteousness which shall justify many.]

20. [·· The apostle briefly notices what the Mosaic law has contributed to this condition " (De Wette), or, "What position does the law occupy in the religious history of mankind." (Boise.)] **Moreover.** Besides the fact of many being made sinners, and as a transition point to the result of many being made righteous. **The law**—that is, the law of Moses. [Here, as in ver. 13, the word law is without the article, and yet must have the specific reference indicated. Prof. Cremer says: "The article is usually wanting in places where stress is not laid upon its historical impress or outward form, but upon the conception itself; not upon *the law* which God gave, but upon *law as given by God*, and as therefore the only one that is or can be. So especially in passages where law (νόμος) is used alternately with and without the article." As a word of definite import it can, like a proper name, dispense with the article.] **Entered.** Literally, *came in besides.* The verb is the same as that translated *entered* in ver. 12, with an additional preposition prefixed, signifying *beside.* The two things mentioned in ver. 19 do not form a complete account of God's dealings with men; the law came in besides. [According to Meyer: the law came in alongside of the sin which had already entered.] It is true, that the law had been mentioned before, in ver. 13: but it is left out of view from that point, and is referred to again now, in a new connection, and for a new purpose. **That the offence might abound.** [*In order that the trespass* (of Adam?) *might be multiplied;* or, as Dr. Gif-

ford puts it, in order " that sin which already existed, however dormant or unrecognized, might take the definite form of active trespass or transgression of a known law."] It is sometimes needful to stimulate or develop the disease to a certain degree, in order to prepare for the more effectual application of the remedy. Compare 7: 8, and notes. [The law not only brings sin to consciousness but calls forth evil desire and occasions transgression. See 4: 15. "Without the law," says De Wette, "there is no Christ. If now the manifestation of Christ was without doubt a worthy purpose of God, need we refuse to recognize even in the activity of the law a divine purpose?" Calvin says: "It was needful that men's ruin should be more fully discovered to them, in order that a passage might be opened for the favor of God. They were, indeed, shipwrecked before the law was given; as, however, they seemed to themselves to swim while in their destruction, they were thrust down into the deep that their deliverance might appear more evident whence they emerge beyond all human expectation."

And therefore Law was given them to evince
Their natural pravity, by stirring up
Sin against Law to fight; that when they see
Law can discover sin, but not remove,
Save by those shadowy expiations weak,
The blood of bulls and goats, they may conclude
Some blood more precious must be paid for man.
—(Milton.)]

But where sin abounded, grace did much more abound. [De Wette here assigns to 'where' (οὖ) the very rare meaning of *when.*] 'But' this (namely, the making of the offense to abound) was not God's *ultimate* end in bringing in the law; for 'where sin abounded, grace did much more abound.' The word 'offence' is dropped, and the word 'sin' put in its place, as being a more generic term, and a more suitable antithesis to 'grace.' The word translated 'abound' in the last part of the verse is not the same as that so translated in the former part, 'that the offence might abound.' Both words are commonly translated as here, though the one used in the last part of the verse much more frequently

K

21 That as sin hath reigned unto death, even so might grace reign through righteousness unto eternal life by Jesus Christ our Lord.

21 ingly: that, as sin reigned in death, even so might grace reign through righteousness unto eternal life through Jesus Christ our Lord.

than the other. It is difficult to make a distinction between these two words throughout in translation. The Greek language is so copious in nice distinctions of words, that it is impossible to use a different and equally suitable English equivalent—copious as our own tongue is—for every different Greek word. [Philippi makes the latter verb, in its simple form, stronger in meaning than the former, its *more* (περισσόν) denoting absolute abundance, while the *more* (πλέον) of the former verb denotes only comparative abundance.] In the case of the two words here represented by *abound*, the one used in the former part of the verse might be translated *multiply*, or *increase*. Both these words are regularly used as the equivalents of Greek verbs different from those here used, and from each other. So difficult—nay, so impracticable—is it, to conform invariably and uniformly, to one of the soundest and most important rules of faithful translation. 'Did much more abound.' [This superabounding of grace has, of course, no reference to the *number* of individuals saved. All have sinned and no more than all can by grace be saved. On this superabounding grace to be experienced by penitent believers, Chalmers says: "It is likely enough that the apostle may have had in his mind the state of the redeemed when they are made to reign in life by Jesus Christ—as contrasted with what the state of man would have been had Adam persisted in innocency."] This 'much more' is expressed by prefixing a preposition to the verb 'abound'—*grace did superabound*. On this expression Bengel has one of his pithy epigrammatic notes: "He who conquers the conqueror of another is a third, superior to either: Sin conquered man; grace conquered sin: therefore grace is the supreme power."[1]

21. That [*in order that*] *even as* **sin hath reigned**—better, *sin reigned*—because the standing point of the sentence is the perfected reign of grace and righteousness hereafter. [Observe how sin is personified and represented as reigning like a king. How mighty has been its reign and how fearful the results!]

Unto death—literally, *in death*; death was the central act in which sin reigned, the arena of its triumph. ["Reigned in virtue of death." (Meyer.)] It is one of the commonest defects of our English Bible that it does not distinguish accurately enough between the Greek prepositions corresponding with *in* and *unto*. This fault is remedied in most of the newer revisions, as that of Dr. Noyes, and of the Bible Union, [and of the more recent Canterbury Revision]. **Even so might grace reign**—so also grace may reign. [Sin has reigned, death has reigned, grace will reign.] **Through righteousness**—by means of righteousness—that is, the righteousness of Christ, as in the preceding verses: not *in* righteousness, as it might have been, if the reference had been mainly to our being made personally righteous. **Unto eternal life.** [Dr. Hodge, in his comments on the closing part of this chapter, thus remarks: "That the benefits of redemption shall far outweigh the evils of the fall, is here clearly asserted." And one point given by him as confirmatory of this view is, that "The number of the saved will doubtless greatly exceed the number of the lost. Since the half of mankind die in infancy, and, according to the Protestant doctrine, are heirs of salvation, and since in the future state of the church the knowledge of the Lord is to cover the earth, we have reason to believe that the lost will bear to the saved no greater proportion than the inmates of a prison do to the mass of the community."] **Through our Lord Jesus Christ.** "The last word in this section is Jesus Christ our Lord, the one glorious solution of the Adamic fall and the dark problem of sin. Adam disappears, and Christ alone remains master of the field of battle, having slain the tyrants, Sin and Death." (Schaff.) "Who can rise from the perusal and contemplation of this wondrous passage, full of such profound views and pregnant meanings, with all its variously complicated yet beautifully discriminated relations and interlacements of members and thoughts, without an overpowering admiration and irresistible conviction of the *super-*

[1] "Victi victorem vincens, tertius utroque melior est. Hominem vicit peccatum; peccatum vicit gratia: ergo gratiae vis maxima."

CHAPTER VI.

W HAT shall we say then? Shall we continue in sin, that grace may abound?
2 God forbid. How shall we, that are dead to sin, live any longer therein?

1   What shall we say then? Shall·we continue in sin,
2 that grace may abound? God forbid. We who died,

human wisdom that must have dictated even its minutest detail!" (Forbes.)[1]

Ch. 6 : THE GOSPEL ADEQUATE TO PROCURE THE SANCTIFICATION OF MAN.

[With the last chapter, Paul, as is thought by many, completes his strictly doctrinal statement, and now for a time devotes his attention in main part to drawing inferences, making explanations, answering objections, and the like. The apostle, however, has much new and important doctrinal matter yet to be presented. He now proceeds to consider the "moral effects of justification" (De Wette), and in this chapter shows that justification by faith is incompatible with living in sin.] This and the two following chapters treat specially of sanctification, and show that the way of justification by free grace through faith, instead of affording license to sin, is more favorable to holiness than any system of justification by works could possibly be. In the first verse, the objection, that if grace abounds in consequence of sin, we may sin, in order that grace may abound, is stated in the form of a question; in the second verse, the question is answered in the negative, the validity of the question is denied; the remainder of the chapter is occupied in explaining the grounds of that denial, under these two heads: 1. The justified believer, agreeably to the very import of his baptism, is brought into such a connection and conformity with Christ, as dying and rising to a new life, that he cannot

continue in the old life of sin. (Ver. 3-14.) 2. The very fact that he is not under the law, but under grace, forbids that sin should have dominion over him, for his relation to the law and to grace is like that of a servant to his master ; before justification he is a servant of sin, under an influence which secures his obedience to evil ; after justification he is a servant of righteousness, under an influence which secures his obedience to good. (Ver. 14-23.)

1. What shall we say then? The form of expression, *what then shall we say ?* is used by Paul to introduce some objection or difficulty, as at 3 : 5 and 4 : 1. The difficulty here is suggested by what he had said in the last two verses of the preceding chapter, especially in the last clause of ver. 20. That clause might seem to imply that license to sin was afforded by the apostle's doctrine of a free forgiveness and justification, or, at least, that the motives to a holy life were somewhat weakened. It is the object of this chapter and the two following to show that, in fact, just the reverse of this is true. **Shall we continue** (or, *may we persist*) **in sin?** The verb is in the subjunctive, not in the indicative future, according to the best manuscripts, in what the Greek grammarians call the *deliberative* subjunctive, answering to the potential in English.[2]

2. God forbid—*let it not be*, or, *far be it*—used of what is contrary to reverence or precluded by some acknowledged fact or truth. See note on 3 : 4. Both are true here;

---

[1] General note in regard to the use of the word *life* (ζωή) in the New Testament. This word ζωή is used in the New Testament 135 times. (By John 66 times ; by Paul 38 times ; 14 times in the Epistle to the Romans.) It has the adjective αἰώνιος, eternal, connected with it 46 times (23 times by John ; 12 times by Paul.) [Or 44. See notes on αἰώνιος, eternal, on 2 : 7,9. 'Αΐδιος 1 : 20, and αἰώνων (of the ages), Eph. 3 : 11 ; 1 Tim: 1 : 17, are likewise rendered eternal, but these are not used in connection with ζωή. According to the Common Version the phrase, eternal life, occurs ten times in Paul's epistles. The reading, however, in 1 Tim. 6 : 19 is doubtful. The phrase is also found in one of Paul's discourses. Acts 13.] It refers clearly to natural life only not more than half a score of times. (Luke 1 : 75 [omitted in the

Revision] ; 16 ; 25 ; Acts 8 : 33 ; 17 : 25 ; Rom. 8 : 38 ; 1 Cor. 15 : 19 ; Phil. 1 : 20 ; 1 Tim. 4 : 8 ; James 4 : 14.) In three or four places its use is general or uncertain. (Luke 12 : 15, Rom. 6 : 4 ; 11 : 15.) We see therefore that the word relates to eternal life in about 123 out of 135 times, or in *ten* cases out of *eleven*.

[2] Prof. Boise remarks that the first person plural subjunctive is much more frequently hortatory (let us) than deliberative. In the *third* person the indicative future of questions is more frequent than the subjunctive. (Winer, 285.) This *continuing* is in a certain state or course, Ellicott says, "is a tropical use of the verb peculiar to St. Paul. The preposition ἐπι [in composition] appears to denote *rest* at a place and hints at a more protracted stay." (Col. 1 : 23 ; Phil. 1 : 24.)—(F.)

3 Know ye not, that so many of us as were baptized into Jesus Christ were baptized into his death?

3 to sin, how shall we any longer live therein? Or are ye ignorant that all we who were baptized into
4 Christ Jesus were baptized into his death? We were

the precluding fact is immediately specified. **How shall we, that are dead to sin?** *How shall we, being such as died to sin?* Here we have again the compound relative, with its suggestion of a reason noticed at 1 : 25. *Died* instead of 'are dead.' See on 5 : 15. [Possibly the tense of the verb has special reference to the time of baptism when in and by that ordinance a solemn profession of deadness to sin and to the world was made. In that act the world lost sight of us and we lost sight of the world. Godet, speaking of the "mirage of *absolute* deliverance," says that "if ever a believer could enter into the sphere of absolute holiness, a new fall, like that of Adam, would be needed to remove him from it;" and that this "death to sin is not an absolute cessation of sin at any moment whatever, but an absolute breaking of the will with it, a state no doubt, but a state of the *will*, which continues only so long as it keeps itself under the control of faith in Christ's death for sin." Our *death to sin* is very different from a *death of sin.* Still, we may well be thankful that there is a divine power that can help our feeble and uncertain wills. Alas for us were it otherwise!] **Live any longer therein?** Still live in it? [Would that all Christians who by and in their baptism professed deadness to sin might ever keep this verse in their minds, yea, bind it as a phylactery to their hearts and strive to carry out its teaching into consistent, daily practice! "Lavish and liberal," says Chalmers, "as the gospel is of its forgiveness of the past, it has no toleration either for the purpose or for the practices of sin in the future."] Mac-Knight says here, and on ver. 10, 11, "died *by* sin," and he adds this comment: "The common translation, how shall we that are dead to sin live any longer therein? is absurd,

for a person's living in sin who is dead to it is evidently a contradiction in terms." What he complains of as the *fault* of the expression is just its excellence. The apostle *wished* to show that it was a contradiction in terms. But the dying to sin is *figurative*, the living in sin *literal*, but both equally *real.* If a commentator has not some other qualifications besides a critical knowledge of *grammar* and *logic*, these qualifications will be a hindrance to him in interpreting such passages as "to know the love of Christ which passeth knowledge," "less than the least of all saints"— literally, "leaster than all saints." [Compare Milton's "And in the lowest deep a lower deep."] Even Dr. Campbell, with all his learning and good sense, could dilute "Lord, I believe; help thou mine unbelief," into "Lord, I believe; supply thou the defects of my faith!" Where was the cunning rhetorician?

3. Know ye not (*are ye ignorant* would be more literal), **that so many of us as were baptized into Jesus Christ?** This is a very literal translation of the apostle's words, and yet it seems to suggest something which those words do not—namely, that only a *part* of those addressed "were baptized into Jesus Christ." To avoid this misunderstanding, the words might be translated—not less *faithfully*, if somewhat less literally—*all we who were baptized into Jesus Christ.* ["By baptism *into Christ* we are initiated into a participation of Christ." (Calvin.) See similar examples in 1 Cor. 1 : 13; 10 : 2. "Baptism contains an avowal of our belonging to him [Christ] as our Master, of our union with him as our Head." (Ripley.)[1] "It is of course obvious that the idea of the baptism of children was wholly foreign to this view of the apostle." (Meyer.) "If St. Paul's language

---

[1] "Βαπτίζειν εἰς (literally, to baptize into) *never* means anything else than to *baptize in reference to, in respect to,* and the more special definitions of its import are furnished simply by the context. On *into Christ Jesus;* compare Acts 2 : 38; 8 : 16; 19 : 5. Undoubtedly the name 'Jesus' was *named* in baptizing. But the conception of becoming immersed *into* Christ is to be set aside and is not to be supported by the figurative expression in Gal. 3 : 27. The mystic character of our passage is not produced by so vague a sensuous con-

ception, which, moreover, has all the passages against it in which βαπτίζειν is coupled with *name* (Matt. 28 : 19; Acts 2 : 38; 10 : 48; 19 : 5; 1 Cor. 1 : 13), but is based on the ethical consciousness of that intimate appertaining to Christ into which baptism translates its recipients." (Meyer.) As *unto* seems to express this *belonging to* better than *into*, we should prefer to use the former word before what have been sometimes termed the *ideal elements* of baptism.—(F.)

4 Therefore we are buried with him by baptism into death: that like as Christ was raised up from the dead by the glory of the Father, even so we also should walk in newness of life.

buried therefore with him through baptism into death: that like as Christ was raised from the dead through the glory of the Father, so we also might
5 walk in newness of life. For if we have become

seems exaggerated, it is because we who were baptized as unconscious infants can hardly realize what baptism was to the adult believer in the apostolic age." ("Speaker's Commentary.")] We were baptized into union, participation, conformity with Christ, and that in respect to his death. "The rite of immersion in the baptismal water, and egress from it, was used as a symbol of breaking off all connection with the previous vicious life and giving ourselves to a new and purer one." (Bloomfield.)

4. Therefore. [Because we are dead, have been put to death through the body of Christ. (7:4.) Our burial by baptism has reference to a death already experienced. Baptism, as Godet remarks, is thus not a figure of *dying*, but a consequence, an external proof of death.] The word 'therefore' assumes that the question of the preceding verse admits of but one answer: "Yes, we know this;" or, rather, to suit the more exact form of the original question, as above suggested, "No, we are not ignorant of this": you admit, *then*, that we **are buried with him by baptism into death.** The verb, as in the previous verse, is in the past tense, and ought to be translated —*we were buried with him:* this makes the reference to the act and the time of baptism more prominent, than the present, 'are buried': besides, the present is hardly appropriate to describe a *transient act*, like baptism. 'By baptism into death': by means of our baptism into his death. Compare Col. 2: 12. [Meyer says: "In *reality* this burial with Christ is not a moral fact *distinct* from the having died with him . . . . but it sets forth the fullness and completeness of the relation, of which the recipient, in accordance with the *form* of baptism, so far as the latter takes place through sinking down and rising up (κατάδυσις and ἀνάδυσις), becomes conscious *successively*. The recipient—thus Paul figuratively represented the process—is conscious, (*a*) in the baptism *generally*: now am I entering into fellowship with the *death* of

Christ; (*b*) in the *immersion in particular:* now am I becoming *buried* with Christ; (*c*) and then in the emergence: now I *rise* to the new life with Christ. Compare on Col. 2: 12."

Lange speaks of being "buried in death," but the phrase in ver. 3, "*baptized* into death," shows that *into death* must here be connected with *baptism*. The absence of the article after baptism gives more unity to the conception, making the baptism into death as a single idea. "Buried into death," says De Wette, "if not nonsense is a pleonasm." We are not buried in order to die, we are buried with Christ by or in baptism because we are dead, and baptism (immersion) represents not only our death but burial. The death unto which we are baptized is left indefinite in this verse (the article also being probably generic), so that it "might be applied at once to his (Christ's) death and ours included in his." (Godet.) Meyer also says: "It is not specially the death of Christ which is again meant, as if 'his' were again annexed, but the description is generalized in a way that could not be misunderstood. Whosoever, namely, has been baptized unto the death of *Christ*, has in fact thereby received baptism *unto death*; that is, such a baptism that, taken away by it from his previous vital activity, he has become one belonging to death, one who has fallen under its sway."][1] **That like as Christ was raised up from the dead**—*in order that, as Christ was raised from the dead.* **By the glory of the Father** —glory and power (compare 1 Cor. 6: 14) are cognate ideas, as referred to God; see Col. 1: 11, "according to his glorious power." **Even so we also should walk in newness of life.** [On the use of the subjunctive (literally: in order that we *may* walk—that is, continuously) after a verb in the past tense (were buried), see note to 5: 7. The word 'walk,' as used of moral conduct, occurs some thirty-three times in Paul's epistles.] 'Should walk in newness of life': that is, in a new

---

[1] Βάπτισμα. The termination (μα) in Greek nouns, generally denotes effect or state rather than act. But this rule is not invariable (see, for example, γέννημα in the Lexicons), and the frequency of this termination is a peculiarity of the later Greek. There are two forms of this word in Latin (baptisma and baptismus), but they are used indiscriminately. Evidently a baptizing into death supposes some action.—(F.)

state, of which the characteristic is life. ["Not the life that is lived day by day (βίος), but the life which liveth in us (ζωή)." ("Bible Commentary.") See Col. 3: 3, 4. "Ye *died* and your *life* . . . *Christ* our life." Had the apostle said "in a new life," the idea of newness would have been less prominent. Compare 2 Cor. 5: 17. De Wette says, "The truth of the figure rests upon the fact that the resurrection of Jesus, as every resurrection, is not simply something physical, but also moral." "When you hear mention made of a *new life*," says Chrysostom, "be sure that implies a great change and diversity. For myself, I forthwith burst into tears and groans when I reflect what strictness Paul demands of us, and to what indolence we have given ourselves up, relapsing after baptism into our previous old age, returning to Egypt and hankering after the garlic, though we have tasted the manna."] There are two Greek adjectives which are alike translated *new* in our English Testament, but there is a very plain distinction between them. The most convenient passage to illustrate that distinction is the one in which our Lord speaks of the *new* wine, and the *new* bottles and the *old.* (Matt. 9 : 17 ; Mark 2 : 22 ; Luke 5 : 37, 38, 39.) The adjective *new* (νέος) applied to the wine means 'recently made, *new* as to age.' The adjective *new* (καινός) applied to the bottles means '*new* as to *quality*, unused, unworn.' No matter how long ago the bottles were *made*, if they have not been *used*, if they have not lost their *elasticity* by having wine fermented in them, they are still "new bottles." Now the word 'newness' in the passage before us is derived from the *latter* of these two adjectives ; so that the term 'newness of life,' does not refer to the *recent beginning* of the life (however truly it might be called *new* on that account), but to the changed *quality* or *character* of the life : it is a new *kind* of life that they are to *walk* in who have been 'baptized into Jesus Christ.' [This walking 'in newness of life' is used here as the antithesis of *were buried* and the correlative of *was raised.* The idea of a rising or being raised in baptism which is implied very plainly here and in the next verse, is, in Col. 2: 12, explicitly stated : we were buried with Christ in the (our) baptism and we were raised with Christ in the baptism. The Greek for baptism (βάπτισμα) does not, in

itself, any more than *immersion*, denote or absolutely require an emergence, yet both allow of it (in the same manner as *burial* allows of a *resurrection*), and the baptismal or immersion *ordinance* requires it, as otherwise we could not thereafter be taught to observe all the Saviour's commands, nor could we henceforth in this world "walk in newness of life."]

Note the teaching of this passage as to the *meaning* as well as the *act* of baptism. It implies in all cases a *saving union* with Christ [representing and] obliging to a new and holy life. [It is maintained by some that as no mention is made of the element water in these verses, therefore the baptism into Christ and the burial with Christ is wholly internal and spiritual and has no reference to the outward act. But granting the first part of this inference to be true, the second does not follow, for the spiritual may derive its imagery from the outward and literal. We maintain, however, the literalness of the baptism and the burial (by immersion), not of course excluding from them a spiritual import. In the first place, the phrases into repentance, into name, into Christ, into his death, do not represent proper baptismal elements. To sprinkle or to immerse a person or a people into a person or into a name is an incongruous figure, an impossible transaction. To be baptized unto a person or unto his name denotes an intimate appertaining to, a belonging to, that person as his disciples or followers. The wide distinction which some make between baptizing into a person and into his name is not warranted in the Scriptures. They both denote substantially the same thing—as, "baptized unto Moses," "baptized in (*into*) the name of Paul" (thereby becoming followers of Moses or followers of Paul), and as Christian writers generally regard this latter baptism (into a name) as external, so they may and should regard the former as external. Moreover, as John's baptism "unto repentance" was compatible with an outward ordinance, an immersion in water, so a baptism into Christ and into his death need not preclude such an ordinance. When we read in our religious journals that such and such persons were baptized into such a church or into its fellowship, does any one suppose the "church" or the "fellowship" to be a proper baptismal element or

5 For if we have been planted together in the like- | ¹united with *him* by the likeness of his death, we

1 Or, *united with the likeness* . . . *with the likeness.*

that it precludes a baptism into water? But if baptism into the name of Christ and into Christ is external, then the burial effected by that baptism is likewise external. Confirmatory of this view is the remarkable fact that the Scriptures *never speak of a burial with Christ save in connection with baptism.* When the apostle addressed all who in Rome had given themselves up to Christ by and in baptism, the Christians there could not have naturally thought of anything else save their outward baptism in water into or unto the name of the Lord Jesus. Furthermore, to suppose that their baptism here referred to was wholly internal and spiritual is to suppose that *all* the baptized believers in Rome were spiritually conformed to Christ and wholly dead to sin, a circumstance which probably was not true, and which, if true, neither Paul nor any being on earth could "know." By their baptism they became *professedly* and *engagedly* dead to sin, and hence Paul subsequently counsels them not to "obey the lusts" of their mortal bodies, but to "*reckon* themselves dead indeed to sin," and to "yield themselves to God *as if* alive from the dead." In like manner he writes to the Colossians who had been buried with Christ in the baptism (Col. 2 : 12, Revised Version): "If then ye were raised together with Christ, seek the things that are above." If their baptism was inward and spiritual, how is it that they were *not* "dead with Christ from the rudiments of the world" but were still "subject to [carnal] ordinances?" Had "all" the Corinthian Christians been spiritually and really baptized "into one body," their carnal "strifes" and "divisions" would not have been so flagrant and abundant. And had the Galatian Christians been spiritually baptized "into Christ," they would "all" indeed have been "one" in Christ Jesus, and we never should have heard of their removal to "another gospel." Yet all these baptisms

have been claimed as internal and spiritual. Of course, no outward rite could prove absolute deadness to sin, nor was such a proof necessary for the apostle's argument. It was enough for him to assure his Roman brethren that the initial, solemn baptismal rite, to which they had publicly submitted, imported deadness to sin, and that hence they could not consistently "continue in sin." Nor is burial in baptism proved to be spiritual from the assertion in Col. 2 : 12, "ye were raised *through the faith*," since if the literal rising were to "newness of life," it may well be said to be effected through faith in the power of God. The objection that the pagan Romans did not then bury but burnt their dead (how was it with the people of Colossæ?) does not deserve a moment's consideration. Christ our blessed Lord "was buried" (so Paul affirms in 1 Cor. 15 : 4, though some writers, who hold this baptism to be a spiritual sprinkling, deny his literal burial), and he was also raised, and we, by our baptismal or immersion rite, are conjoined with him both in an outward and in a spiritual manner in the *likeness* of his death and in the *likeness* of his resurrection.¹ This immersion-burial theory is no modern (Baptist) fancy, but was held by the whole Christian Church in early times, and since then by Luther, Zwingle, Beza, Bullinger, Tyndale, Cranmer, the authors of the "Assembly's Notations" (most of whom were members of the Westminster Assembly), by Adam Clarke and MacKnight, and even by Baxter, and Wesley, and Doddridge. For further views on this subject, see Dr. Arnold's remarks in Appendix C, also the writer's "Studies on Baptism."]

5. For if. These little words imply that what follows in this verse is but the legitimate *consequence* of what is stated in the first clause of the preceding verse, or, to vary the *form* of the connection, that which is affirmed in the second clause as the definite *design* of the

---

¹ It will be noticed that the words 'death' and 'dead' are here used in contrast with the idea of resurrection, and so are closely connected with the idea of burial. Thus Tertullian says: " By an image we *die* in baptism, but we truly *rise* in the flesh, as did also Christ." This *resurgimus*, or rising, is antithetic to the idea of a burial implied in his *morimur in baptismate.* Hence he calls baptism a *symbolum mortis*, a likeness of death. We doubt whether he would find an image of death in sprinkling. Had the apostle said, buried with Christ in the sprinkling, would not every one have felt an incongruity in the figure?—(F.)

ness of his death, we shall be also *in the likeness of his resurrection:*
6 Knowing this, that our old man is crucified with

6 shall be also *by the likeness* of his resurrection; knowing this, that our old man was crucified with *him,*

proposition affirmed in the first clause is in this verse affirmed as the *sure result* of the truth of that proposition. **We have been planted together.** The single word which is translated 'planted together' is a difficult word to translate into English. It is used nowhere else in the New Testament. It implies a vital, organic union, such as was fabled to exist in the case of the Centaur, which was, according to that fable, a union of the two natures of the man and the horse. *Grown together* would be as nearly a literal translation as can well be given. The translation 'planted together' no doubt originated in a mistaken view of the etymology of the word, and is particularly incongruous with the last part of the verse. To be 'planted together' in the likeness of his 'resurrection' would, indeed, be a very inapt figure of speech. "If we have become united," as the Bible Union Revision has it, is too vague and weak. *If we have become vitally conjoined* expresses the true idea, but is something of a paraphrase; **in the likeness of his death,** as our baptism imports, the resemblance will not end here, **but** [the strong adversative, ἀλλὰ] **we shall be also** —that is, *vitally conjoined* (with the likeness) of his resurrection, [The Revised Version inserts the word 'him' after 'united with,' and this, perhaps, gives the correct idea (Godet), though De Wette, Meyer, Alford, Philippi, and many others are opposed to the insertion. To be vitally conjoined to Christ in the likeness of his resurrection is equivalent to walking in "newness of life." (**Ver. 4.**) The future tense, *shall be* conjoined, denotes that which will always take place. Dr. Noyes gives this *ad sensum* rendering: "For if we have been made completely like him in his death, we shall be made like him in his resurrection also."] The words bracketed (italicised in the Common Version) are required to complete the sense.[1] See similar elliptical constructions in Matt. 5:20; John 5:36; Heb. 12:24. [It has been objected to the immersion-burial theory that it makes two ordinances represent mainly the same thing—namely, the death of Christ, omitting

all reference to the work of the Spirit. But this is quite a mistake. The theory in question makes the baptismal rite to symbolize not only the death or burial of Christ, but his resurrection; not only our dying with him, but our rising with him henceforth to walk in newness of life. If, now, our immersion in water may denote, much better than a slight sprinkling, an entire cleansing from sin and a rising to a new life, it certainly may well symbolize the "washing of regeneration and the renewing of the Holy Spirit."]

6. What in the preceding verses is presented as a matter of *doctrine* is here presented as a matter of *experience.* **Knowing this**—because we know this, because we shall remember and feel this. **That our old man is crucified with him.** 'Our old man': the adjective *old* [παλαιὸς, Latin *vetus,* not ἀρχαῖος, ancient, *priscus*] is the same that is used in reference to the wine bottles in our Lord's figure: see note on *newness of life,* ver. 4. It relates to *character,* not to *age.* When age is referred to, a different Greek adjective (πρεσβύτης) is used, as in Luke 1: 18; Titus 2: 2; Philem. 9. [Paul here first makes mention of 'the old man' (opposed to the "new man." (Eph. 4: 24; Col. 3: 10); or, in one view, to the "inward man" (7: 22; Eph. 3: 16)), by which he means, as Meyer says, "our personality in its entire sinful condition before regeneration." (John 3: 3.) Compare Eph. 4: 22; Col. 3: 9. The idea is Christian and not Jewish.] 'Is crucified with him': rather, 'was,' since the verb is in the *past* tense. [Meyer thinks the verb, *was crucified,* refers to the time "when we were baptized, and thereby transplanted into the fellowship of death." Lange calls this "rather a superficial view," and thinks our crucifixion took place potentially when Christ for us was nailed to the cross. Compare 7: 4. But though the apostle does not affirm that "we" were crucified in the baptism, yet we see not why the death represented by that baptism may not be termed a crucifixion of the old man and an abolishing or bringing to nought of the body of sin. 'Crucified': "How inter-

[1] So Meyer *versus* De Wette and others, who make the adjective here, though compounded with σύν, directly

govern the genitive. Compare 8: 29; Buttmann, p. 169. —(F.)

him, that the body of sin might be destroyed, that henceforth we should not serve sin.
7 For he that is dead is freed from sin.

that the body of sin might be done away, that so we 7 should no longer be in bondage to sin; for he that 8 hath died is [1]justified from sin. But if we died with

---

1 Or, *released.*

---

esting and impressive it is to regard the Christian as, in respect to his former inclination, undergoing a death, a crucifixion in company with his Lord!" (Ripley.) "The image of the Christian, as one with Christ, is still carried on. Man falls asunder into two parts, corresponding to the two divisions of Christ's life, and leaves one of those parts hanging upon the cross." (Jowett.) Compare Gal. 2: 20. "I have been crucified with Christ."] **That the body of sin.** The body which belongs to and serves sin: compare ver. 12, 13; 7: 23, 24; 8: 13; or, perhaps, sin personified, as having a body. See Col. 2: 11. [Sin uses and even rules the body, but the principle of "sin lies not in the body or flesh even, but in the will." (De Wette.) Of course, the body is not to be rendered inactive (ἀργός), only so far as the service of sin is concerned. Philippi, Hodge, Stuart, suppose sin to be here personified. The metaphor in *crucified* is more perfectly carried out by using the term *body.* (Boise.)] **Might be destroyed.** The verb translated 'might be destroyed' is one very frequently used by Paul, and variously translated in different places. It is the same which is translated *make without effect,* and *make of none effect,* in 3: 3 (see notes), and 4: 14, *destroy,* in 1 Cor. 6: 13; 15: 26; 2 Thess. 2: 8; Heb. 2: 14; and *abolish,* in 2 Cor. 3: 13; Eph. 2: 15: 2 Tim. 1: 10. It is used between twenty-five and thirty times, but only *once* out of Paul's epistles (Luke 13: 7, translated, *cumbereth*), unless Heb. 2: 14 be a second exception. **That henceforth we should not serve sin.** *That we should no longer serve sin:* that the body should no longer be the slave, under the dominion of sin.[1]

As Christ's death on account of sin was never to be repeated (ver. 7-10), so the believer

should regard his own separation from sin as *final.* (Ver. 11-14.)

7. For he that is dead is freed from sin. A literal translation of this verse would be, '*he that died has been justified from sin*'; see note on 5: 15. [Godet says: "is of right freed from sin." The more exact idea of the apostle, we think, is this; that one who has died with Christ and put off the body of sin, has been freed from sin's *condemning* power.] The verb which we translate '*has been justified*' is used about forty times in the New Testament (thirteen times in this Epistle) and is uniformly translated *to justify* in every other place.[2] Christ may properly be said to have been *justified from sin* when, after having died on account of sin, he was raised to the right hand of God, "separated (so should the translation be) from sinners, and made higher than the heavens." (Heb. 7: 26.) Compare also John 16: 8, 10. [The suggestion of Dr. Arnold that this verse relates to Christ has much in its favor, but as it is adopted by very few if any other commentators, it seems proper to mention two or three current interpretations. 1. It is supposed to be a general and popular statement, to the effect that, when a man is dead, he is no longer held to the law which he previously broke—a kind of legal maxim ; 'having died he has been justified (*acquitted*) from sin.' And this legal maxim is used to illustrate the state of one who, at regeneration, died to the law and its penalty, and entered into a new life. 2. 'He that is dead is freed from sin,' because by death he is freed from the body which is the seat of sin. This, according to Philippi and Schaff, is Meyer's view and must be rejected, because it "rests upon an anthropology as unbiblical as it is un-Pauline." 3. 'He that is dead to sin is freed from the slavery of sin.' "It

---

[1] The infinitive sentence, 'that we should not serve sin,' may, in Winer's opinion, be regarded as a noun in the genitive, dependent on the verb, *might be destroyed,* as being a verb which denotes separation. Buttmann makes its verbal nature and force more prominent. and regards it as an independent telic clause as if it began with ἵνα or ὅπως. "The application here made of the special kind of death suffered by our

Saviour to the spiritual death of the old man is the more emphatic inasmuch us the former is peculiarly accompanied with pain, and resembles the way in which the love of sin is actually extinguished in the Christian." (Tholuck.)—(F.)

[2] Rev. 22: 11 is not regarded as an exception, because this verb is not regarded as the true reading in that place.

8 Now if we be dead with Christ, we believe that we shall also live with him:
9 Knowing that Christ being raised from the dead dieth no more; death hath no more dominion over him.
10 For in that he died, he died unto sin once: but in that he liveth, he liveth unto God.

Christ, we believe that we shall also live with him; 9 knowing that Christ being raised from the dead dieth no more; death no more hath dominion over him. 10 For [1] the death that he died, he died unto sin [2] once:

1 Or, in that......2 Gr. once for all.

follows naturally from what precedes that here is meant the inner, spiritual death, carried into effect in believing fellowship with Christ's death, by which, as by death in general, all former relations and connections are dissolved, and therefore the connection with sin, which thus loses its old authority and power over man. But if man is absolved from sin, he ought not again to hold converse with it" (Philippi, and similarly Bengel, Olshausen, De Wette, Tholuck, and others). But the verb used signifies "has been *justified* or *acquitted*, not *has been freed*—that is, set free from the *penalty* rather than the power of sin. 4. 'He that is dead *with Christ*'—that is, brought in connection with his atoning death, 'is freed from guilt and punishment of sin by justification.' (So Scott, Mac Knight, Hodge.) This seems to be the best view, if the verse does not refer to Christ. (A. H.)]

8. Now if we be dead (or, *died*) **with Christ** (compare 2 Cor. 5: 14, Revised Version, "one died for all, therefore all died"). [This dying with Christ (to sin, compare ver. 10, 11) serves to explain the preceding verse: 'he that hath died is justified from sin' (Revised Version)—that is, sin cannot be his condemnation.] **We believe that we shall also live with him.**[1] [Compare 2 Tim. 2: 11.] This is not merely an exhortation—'we ought,' not merely a prediction—'we shall,' but a matter of experience—'we *believe* that we shall' participate in his new and deathless life, as we have participated in his death. This involves, of course, an ultimate participation in his heavenly life in glory, [a being

forever with the Lord, which seems to be Paul's idea of heaven. (1 Thess. 4 : 17.)] But we are not to infer, from the future tense, 'shall live with him,' that this glorified life is principally intended; for the future tense is to be understood, as in ver. 5, of the new Christian life on earth, as explained in ver. 6, 11-13, [or as Meyer terms it, "the ethical participation in the new everlasting life of Christ."]

9. Knowing (*because we know*) **that Christ being** (*having been*) **raised from the dead dieth no more.** He died, not that he might remain dead, but that he might be forever *superior* to death.[2] And so we, who died to sin once for all, must not again come under its dominion. **Death hath no more dominion over him.** It seemed to have a transient dominion over him, but *really* it never had. (John 10 : 17, 18; 2 : 19 : Matt. 26 : 53 ; Acts 2 : 24.) [In the last clause, 'him,' in the genitive, is governed by the verb, on the principle that verbs of ruling take the genitive as the case of dependence. The verb, derived from a noun, could be resolved thus: death *is lord* of him no longer. Compare 7: 1 ; 14: 9.]

10. For in that he died. There is a peculiar and unusual ellipsis in the Greek of this verse. Literally translated it would read—*what he died* and *what he liveth.*[3] Our translators, to make it more intelligible, inserted the preposition *in* and changed the relative into the demonstrative. In a similar case—I think the only similar one (Gal. 2 : 20)—they supplied the ellipsis in a different way, by inserting a noun corresponding to the verb

[1] Σύν (with), as distinguished from μετά, indicates a more intimate union, coherence rather than co-existence. (Winer, 391.) " Σύν with dative, *in company with ;* μετά with genitive, *participating with.*" (Boise.) —(F.)

[2] Paul elsewhere speaks of Christ as "the first born from the dead," the "first fruits of them that slept." Col. 1: 18; 1 Cor. 15: 20. Ellicott on the former passage says : " Others had been translated or had risen to die again. He had risen with glorified humanity to die no more : hence he is not called simply 'the first

that rose,' but with a note of generation, "first born from the dead." Query : Will any one dare to affirm that Christ was unconscious while he "slept" in the tomb, and that during all that time the world had virtually no Saviour ? Manifestly, his sleeping in death was compatible with the enjoyment of the Paradise of bliss. (Luke 23 : 43.)—(F.)

[3] This would be called the cognate accusative, Instead of this we may, as Prof. Boise remarks, regard the relative as in the accusative of specification, equivalent *as to what, as to the fact that.*—(F.)

---

11 Likewise reckon ye also yourselves to be dead indeed unto sin, but alive unto God through Jesus Christ our Lord.

but [1] the life that he liveth, he liveth unto God.
11 Even so reckon ye also yourselves to be dead unto sin, but alive unto God in Christ Jesus.

---

1 Or, *in that.*

---

in place of the relative—"*the life* which I now live" (for what I now live). Conforming the passage now before us with the one in Galatians, which seems to us the better way of supplying the ellipsis, we should read —*for the death that he died,* **he died unto sin once;** *but the life that he liveth,* **he liveth unto God.** The 'for' gives the *proof* of the preceding: Christ dieth no more; death hath no more dominion over him; 'for' he died to sin *once for all,* and lives unto God and with God among the immortals where they die no more. (Luke 20 : 36; Rev. 21 : 4.) 'He died unto sin'—that is, he had no more to do with it, either as tempting and persecuting him, or as annoying and grieving him by its hateful presence. Both the expressions 'he died unto sin,' 'he liveth unto God' seem to be used on account of the analogy; they are strictly applicable to us, only in a qualified sense to Christ. ["It may in a certain degree be affirmed that upon this earth our Saviour lived both to us and to his God, inasmuch as it was for our sakes that he lived in a certain connection with evil, sin, death, and Satan. This connection is now dissolved, and God is the only scope of his life." (Justinianus, as quoted by *Tholuck.*) Olshausen observes on this passage that "Christ died once for sin— that is, to extirpate it; and lives eternally for God—that is, to further righteousness." Philippi and Godet would make our Lord's dying to sin refer to his expiating and destroying it by his death. Meyer says: "He died *to its power,*" and in a similar way we are to deem ourselves dead to it. (Ver. 11.)] 'Once.' It is important to notice the import of the word; it means here *once for all.* It is opposed, not only to any *actual* repetition of his bloody sacrifice on the cross, but also to any *virtual* repetition of it in the *mass,* which professes, though an *unbloody* sacrifice, to have a like propitiatory efficacy. The same adverb is used in Heb. 10 : 10, where it is

translated "once for all." This expression is, however, liable to be misunderstood, as if *for all* meant *for all persons,* in distinction from the limitation of the design of his death to *some persons;* whereas it means for *all time,* in distinction from any *repetition* of his death. And *once* has the same meaning in Heb. 7 : 27; 9 : 12, where, as in the verse under consideration, the explanatory *for all* was not added by the translators. The original expression is precisely the same in all these four places. [It may be well for the reader to compare Jude (ver. 3) with the passages cited by Dr. Arnold, for "the faith which was once delivered to the saints" really means "the faith which was delivered *once for all* to the saints," and this description of "the faith" appears to forbid the hope of any further revelation of Christian truth. See note on this passage. (A. H.)]

11. Likewise. *So also*—that is, conformably to Christ — **reckon ye** (imperative) **yourselves to be dead indeed unto sin** (immovable by it, insensible to it),[1] **but alive** (or, *living,* full of energy and power) **unto God through** (rather, *in*) **Jesus Christ our Lord**—that is, by virtue of your *union* with him [or, as Winer has it, "in soul-nourishing fellowship with Christ." Meyer joins the words in Christ Jesus to both clauses, *dead* and *living,* De Wette only to the latter. The most important MSS. omit the words 'to be' and 'our Lord.'] Not his mediatorship, but his headship, is the prominent thought here.[2] [In regard to this mystical union of believers with and in Christ, the Apostles John and Paul are both at one. According to their teachings, "*believers are in Christ,* so as to be partakers in all that he does, and has, and is. They died with him, and rose with him, and live with him, and in him are seated in heavenly places. When the eye of God looks on them, they are found in Christ, and there is no condemnation to those that are in him,

---

1 Chalmers gives even to these phrases a "forensic meaning." Only as we are *in* Christ, and clothed with his righteousness and filled with his Spirit, can we truly reckon ourselves dead to sin and alive to God. How forceful the figure—*dead* to sin! We have all seen

how insensible is the dead body to all that is going on around it. It is moved by no tears or wailings of grief, no voice of affection, no music of earth, no thunders of the sky. It is *dead* to the world.—(F.)

2 See Appendix C.

12 Let not sin therefore reign in your mortal body, that ye should obey it in the lusts thereof.
13 Neither yield ye your members *as* instruments of unrighteousness unto sin: but yield yourselves unto

12 Let not sin therefore reign in your mortal body, 13 that ye should obey the lusts thereof: neither present your members unto sin *as* [1] instruments of unrighteousness; but present yourselves unto God, as alive

1 Or, *weapons.*

and they are righteous in his righteousness and loved with the love which rests on him, and are sons of God in his sonship and heirs with him of his inheritance, and are soon to be glorified with him in his glory." (Bernard's "Progress of Doctrine," p. 181.)[1] Paul's watchwords are "through Christ," "in Christ," "for Christ," "with Christ."]
"We should die as truly *to* sin as he died *for* sin, and live as truly *unto* God as he lives *with* God." (Adam Clarke.) Compare Gal. 2:19; 1 Peter 2:24.

12. Let not sin therefore reign [continue to reign, the verb being in the present tense]. Observe how sin is *personified* here as *reigning* and *being obeyed.* This shows that it is regarded as a *principle,* and not merely as an *act,* for an *act,* whether external or internal, whether mechanical or mental, could not consistently be so personified. 'Sin,' as the word is used here and in the following chapter, has been well defined as "a want of conformity to the law of God, whether in act, habit, or state." (Inconvenientia cum lege divina aut actus, aut habitus, aut status.) 'Let not sin therefore reign,' since it has been deposed. ["He does not say, let not the flesh live, neither act, but let not sin *reign.* . . . And surely it would be absurd for those who are bound for the kingdom of heaven to take sin for a queen and to choose to be her captives when called to reign along with Christ." (Chrysostom.)] **In your mortal body.** Why does he add 'mortal' here? To keep in view the connection between sin and death, partly, perhaps, as an enforcement of the exhortation, because the remembrance of the deadly consequence of sin would be a powerful dissuasive from it, but principally on

account of the antithesis, the life with Christ, which is exempt from death. [This mortal body, or body of sin and death, itself made mortal by reason of sin (called in Col. 2:11 and elsewhere "body of the sins of flesh"), being "organized flesh" (Cremer), is related to sin by the flesh composing it and by the soul inhabiting it, and is consequently subject to death as the penalty of sin. Yet even this body may be made a temple of the indwelling Holy Spirit. (1 Cor. 6:19.) Tholuck observes that the adjective mortal "is doubtless added —as Chrysostom, Grotius, and others remark —to encourage the Christian, by pointing his thoughts to that never-ending glory into which this frail tabernacle shall one day be transformed."] **That ye should obey it in the lusts thereof.** [This is the reading of ℵ A B C * and early versions, while D E F G read *it* alone.] The last word ('thereof') refers to the body. A large part of sin consists in, or arises from, yielding to the desires and appetites of the body. "The bodily appetites are the *fuel;* sin is the fire." (Bengel.) [The gratifying of our sensual appetites and desires yields a certain sort of pleasure, but sin's pleasures are full often followed by tears, and

> Sin's froth that foams for an hour,
> Leaves dregs that are tasted for years.]

13. Neither yield ye your members.[2] [The Revisers, by connecting 'sin' with 'members,' vary the order of the original but give clearness to its meaning.] 'Nor render your members unto sin' (as a soldier renders his service to his commander or a subject to his sovereign) **as instruments** (literally, *weapons*) **of unrighteousness** (for the promotion of unrighteousness); **but yield yourselves**

---

[1] Bernard thus beautifully describes the progress of doctrine on this one line from the gospels to the epistles: "In the Gospels we have stood like men who watch the rising of some great edifice, and who grow familiar with the outline and details of its exterior aspect. In the preaching of the Acts, we have seen the doors thrown open and joined the men who flock into it as their refuge and their home. In the Epistles we are actually within it, sheltered by its roof, encompassed

by its walls; we pass, as it were, from chamber to chamber, beholding the extent of its internal arrangements and the abundance of all things provided for our use. We are here ' *in* Christ Jesus' " (p. 182).—(F.)

[2] On the use of the negative μή with imperatives rather than οὐ, see Winer, ¿ 55. And as to the usage of correlative particles, observe how μηδὲ here follows μή as οὐδὲ follows οὐ in 2:28.—(F.)

God, as those that are alive from the dead, and your
members *as* instruments of righteousness unto God.
    14 For sin shall not have dominion over you: for ye
are not under the law, but under grace.
    15 What then? shall we sin, because we are not
under the law, but under grace? God forbid.

from the dead, and your members *as* [1] instruments
14 of righteousness unto God. For sin shall not have
dominion over you: for ye are not under law, but
under grace.
15   What then? shall we sin, because we are not under
16 law, but under grace? God forbid. Know ye not, that

1 Or, *weapons*.

to God, as those that are alive from the
dead, and your members as instruments
of righteousness unto God. Compare 12:1.
[The reflexive pronoun translated 'yourselves'
is properly in the third person, but is here and
elsewhere used for the second. 'Alive from
the dead.' Meyer regards these dead as those
who died with Christ to sin. Prof. Cremer
also explains the term as used here by a reference to ver. 8, 10, 11, and thinks that the
Greek word for 'dead' (νεκρός) is never to be
understood of "spiritual death," but that it
signifies rather "the state of those whose life
is appointed to death as the punishment of
sin." In his view, "dead (in) trespasses and
sins" would mean—doomed to death by reason of trespasses, dead *through* your trespasses,
as in the Revised Version, Eph. 2:1; Col.
2:13. Philippi and Godet, with most commentators, think of these 'dead' as the dead
in sin. There certainly does not appear to
be any proper *resurrection* change in passing
from a death *to* sin to a living unto God, since
these are virtually identical. The "Bible
Commentary" gives the force of the present
and aorist tenses thus: "Do not go on putting
your members at sin's disposal, but once for
all present (12:1) yourselves both body and
soul unto God."[1] The word rendered 'instruments' (favored by De Wette) always means
weapons in the New Testament. (Meyer.)
They are, properly, military weapons of the
heavier sort. Boise: "Present your members
as *heavy armor* of righteousness to God."
    The apostle depicts life as a contest and fight
whether for sin or righteousness. "St. Paul,"
says Bishop Wordsworth, "loves military
metaphors." 'Righteousness' (δικαιοσύνη) regarded as "conformity to the standard" is
here very properly opposed to 'sin' (ἁμαρτία),
which is a missing of the mark. (Cremer.) A
failing to hit the mark. (Thayer.)]

14. This verse seems to be of the nature of
an *assurance* [in which there lies a *very sweet
consolation* (Melanchthon)], confirming (for)
the possibility of the surrender to God commanded above. At the same time it serves as
a *transition* to the new phase of the argument,
presented in the verses that follow. See analysis at the beginning of the chapter. [Have
dominion. Death no longer lords it over
Christ, and sin shall no longer lord it over
you. It shall not be your master, for ye are
not in bondage to the law, which is the power
of sin, but ye are subject to grace, are under
the control of grace. "Grace not only washes
away sins, but keeps us from sinning."]
    15. What then shall we say? (compare
ver. 1) or 'what then' is the inference? *May we
sin*, subjunctive aorist [denoting some special
act of sin rather than a habit of sinning], not
future indicative, is the true reading. See on
ver. 1. How does this verse differ from ver. 1?
There it is May we persist in sin, in order
that grace may abound? Here it is May we
feel at liberty to sin, because we are not under
the law, but under grace? The first is a
question of positive and permanent action.
The second is an appeal to the Christian's
moral sense. The answer to both is the same:
let it not be. The inference is indignantly repudiated. ["We are not only not to 'continue in
sin,' but every single act of sin is to be avoided."
(Boise.) The grace of our God must not
be turned into lasciviousness. "We were
freed from the law not that we might hand
over the sovereignty to the flesh, but that we
might henceforth live unto God and fulfill his
will, only no longer on the ground of the
outer requirement of the law, but at the inner
instigation of the Spirit. Materially nothing
else is to be aimed at by means of the latter
than the former; for the love which the Spirit
works is the fulfilling of the law." (Weiss on

1 Winer (p. 313) says: "The present imperative denotes an action already begun and to be continued, or
one that is permanent and frequently recurring," while
the aorist imperative "denotes an action that is either
transient and instantaneous or to be undertaken but

once. . . . The aorist imperative is in general more
forcible and stringent than the present." Grammarians tell us that the aorist, though a past tense, rarely
denotes past time except in the indicative and participle.—(F.)

16 Know ye not, that to whom ye yield yourselves servants to obey, his servants ye are to whom ye obey: whether of sin unto death, or of obedience unto righteousness?

17 But God be thanked, that ye were the servants of sin, but ye have obeyed from the heart that form of doctrine which was delivered you.

to whom ye present yourselves as [1] servants unto obedience, his [1] servants ye are whom ye obey; whether of sin unto death, or of obedience unto righteousness?

17 But thanks be to God, [2] that, whereas ye were [1] servants of sin ye became obedient from the heart to that [3] form of teaching whereunto ye were delivered.

1 Gr. bondservants......2 Or, that ye were . . . but ye became......3 Or, pattern.

Paul's doctrine of "Freedom from the Law.")] "With the ungodly, not to be under the law means, not to be afraid to do whatever we please, and to be under grace means to be safe from damnation." (Beza.)

16. Know ye not. This is an appeal to common sense, [and hence the question requires no expressed answer. In negative interrogative sentences with not (οὐ), an affirmative answer is presumed.] Ye are the servants either of God or of sin; there is no third supposition. The yielding of ourselves servants for obedience to any one implies the serving—the being in reality the servants of—such person. The former is the practical fact; the latter is the inevitable conclusion. **Whether** (servants) **of sin unto death, or of obedience** (to God) **unto righteousness.** The slave of one man cannot be obedient to another man. The slave *must* serve his own master.[1] The preposition 'unto'—here, 'unto death'; 'unto righteousness,' marks result of service without implying intention or aim. Life, instead of 'righteousness,' would be the more exact antithesis to 'death': but righteousness best suits the apostle's course of thought here: *Tholuck* cites parallel passages from *Socrates* and *Seneca.* ['Death' (θάνατος), the opposite of righteousness (which has "eternal life" for its result), does not denote annihilation, nor does it here refer exclusively or mainly to physical death, this being not in all cases the result of individual sin. According to De Wette, it is, generally, the misery of sin, or more specifically, estrangement from the true life. In the light of ver. 21, 23, it must, we think, be regarded as the opposite of life eternal. Meyer *versus* De Wette, Philippi, Lange, Godet, and others, does not regard this 'righteousness' as moral righteousness (as in ver. 13), but, in the light of a final result and in antithesis to *death*, as the sentence of justification which will be awarded in the judgment. Some, as Alford, take 'righteousness,' and so 'death,' in its most general sense.]

17. Here the dilemma stated above is solved for them by an appeal to fact. And this is done in the form of a thanksgiving to God. We are not to understand the thanksgiving, however, as having reference only, or principally to the first clause, **ye were the servants of sin,** or even *equally* to both clauses: but the thanksgiving has *emphatic* reference to the second clause, which, however, presupposes the first, and could not have existed without it. 'Ye were,' is emphatic, the emphasis falling on the tense of the verb, [which implies that the bondage is a thing of the past; compare *Ilium fuit.*] The sense of the verse would be substantially preserved, if the first clause were expressed hypothetically, *though ye were,* or participially, *having been.* [This is substantially the view of Winer (p. 630) in opposition to Fritzsche, Meyer, Philippi, and others, who lay stress on the past tense of the verb (compare 1 Cor. 6: 11; Eph. 5: 8) in the manner indicated above.[2] A similar phraseology, connected, as here, with thanksgiving to God, is found in our Lord's words in Matt. 11: 25.] **Ye have obeyed,** etc. This sentence loses not a little of its significance from a change in our Common Version of the grammatical relations of the words. The latter verb as well as the former is in the second person. *Ye have obeyed from the heart that form* [probably the anti-Judaistic *type*] *of teaching into which ye were delivered.*[3] 'Ye were delivered,' by your own

---

1 "Ye cannot serve God *and* Mammon." Philippi, defining the force of τοί in ἤτοι says: "ἤτοι . . . ἤ, either *only*, this or that, tertium non datur." This particle is found only here in the New Testament.—(F.)

2 A μέν after the verb 'were,' in contrast with the following δέ (but), might here have naturally been expected, but is probably dispensed with because of the stress mentioned.—(F.)

3 On the grammatical construction of this sentence, see Winer, pp. 164, 261. The verb obey, which is usually followed by the dative, here has the accusative, owing, perhaps, to the attraction of the antecedent (itself in the relative clause) to the case of the relative, which is the reverse of the usual rule. In the LXX, however, this verb sometimes takes the simple accusative.—(F.)

18 Being then made free from sin, ye became the servants of righteousness.

19 I speak after the manner of men because of the infirmity of your flesh: for as ye have yielded your members servants to uncleanness and to iniquity unto

18 ered; and being made free from sin, ye became [1] serv-
19 ants of righteousness. I speak after the manner of men because of the infirmity of your flesh: for as ye presented your members as servants to uncleanness and to iniquity unto iniquity, even so now present

1 Gr. bondservants.

free act, and with gladness of *heart*, as plastic material, to be shaped and moulded by this doctrine. [With this *type* of doctrine (which Dr. J. B. Thomas in his "Mould of Doctrine" refers especially to baptism) compare the *form* of knowledge, 2: 20. If Paul could say: "thanks be to God," because the Roman Christians had received and obeyed the right form of gospel teaching, surely the type of teaching which we receive and obey or which religious teachers impart to others cannot be a matter of indifference. In studying or teaching God's word, how appropriate the prayer that we may be saved from all fatal or hurtful error, and be guided into all necessary truth! And in view of the darkness in us and around us, and of our dependence on divine illumination, no words of supplication can be more relevant than those of Young and of Milton:

> Teach my best reason, reason.

> What in me is dark,
> Illumine; what is low, raise and support.]

18. Being then made free from sin, etc. [Better: *but having been freed from sin, ye were made servants to righteousness.* There is no middle ground. The passive forms of participle and verb indicate divine agency or co-operation, and so in ver. 22.] Ye were freed from the service of sin, that ye might enter a new and better service—the service of righteousness. Yet this is truly a service as well as the other: *ye were enslaved,* or, *ye became enslaved,* to righteousness, the verb might be rendered. [Free, yet slaves: for a similar paradox, see 1 Cor. 7: 22. "If human action," says Prof. Cremer, "in sin (ἁμαρτία) misses its divine standard or goal, we can un-

derstand why 'conformity to the standard' (δικαιοσύνη) appears, especially in the Epistle to the Romans, as its opposite."]

19. After the manner of men. I speak in accordance with the human, fleshly nature and relationship of men—according to "what or how man or human nature is, what is peculiar to it." (Cremer.) Compare 3: 5. There is a difference of opinion in regard to the first part of this verse. Those who refer it to the words immediately *preceding*, regard it as a sort of *apology* for the expression, 'ye were enslaved to righteousness.' As if he had said, "the servant of righteousness is no *slave;* God's service is our only true freedom (Ps. 116: 16; 119: 45; Matt. 11: 30; John 8: 32, 34, 36; 1 John 5: 3); but I use this word to set the contrast more plainly before you. Both are equally a *service,* so far as *certainty of obedience* is concerned, though in other respects they differ widely: and I use this word also in condescension to the weakness of your flesh; for because of that weakness it *seems,* and in part *is,* a bondage." Others refer these words to what *follows,* and see in them a sort of apology for, or protest against, the low view of their obligations which he presents, in only requiring them to be *as* faithful in the service of righteousness as they had before been in the service of sin, whereas they ought to aim at a great deal more than this.[1] The former explanation is preferable; and it is a serious objection to the latter, that it assumes a false meaning in the words *as* and *even so,* which do not imply *equality of degree,* but only *similarity of fact.* **For as ye have yielded your members servants to uncleanness** (sins against your own persons), **and to iniquity**

[1] If we were anywhere nearly as active and persevering in the service of God as we were in the service of sin, we should expect with more confidence than we can now, the plaudit: "Well done, good and faithful servants." Instead of calling ourselves even "unprofitable servants," doing our whole duty to God, it sometimes seems that we should hardly be called servants at all. And what shall we say of those whose only striving is to resist the light and influence of the gospel in their service of sin? who make it their life's business,

seemingly, to find some excuse for their rejection of Christ and his service? Let them be assured that there is no good reason why they should not love and serve the Saviour, and that if they will strive but half as hard to be saved as to be lost, they will make their salvation sure. In regard to this "weakness of the flesh," some refer it to intellectual weakness (De Wette, Meyer, Philippi), others to moral weakness (Godet), or weakness of spiritual apprehension (D. Brown).—(F.)

iniquity; even so now yield your members servants to righteousness unto holiness.

20 For when ye were the servants of sin, ye were free from righteousness.

21 What fruit had ye then in those things whereof ye are now ashamed? for the end of those things is death.

your members *as* servants to righteousness unto 20 sanctification. For when ye were [1]servants of sin, 21 ye were free in regard of righteousness. What fruit then had ye at that time in the things whereof ye are now ashamed? for the end of those things is

1 Gr. *bondservants.*

(sins against God and your neighbor) **unto iniquity** (from one iniquity unto another), **even so now yield** [*at once* and *completely,* imperative aorist] **your members servants to righteousness unto holiness.** [The word rendered *iniquity,* is properly lawlessness, that "state of *moral license* which either knows not, or regards not, law, and in which the essence of sin abides." (1 John 3:4.) (Ellicott.) ' *Unto holiness*' denoting result. This word, (ἁγιασμός, not ἁγιωσύνη as in 1:4, also 2 Cor. 7:1; 1 Thess. 3:13), is in the Revised Version everywhere rendered "sanctification," while Meyer asserts that in the New Testament, "it is always holiness, not sanctification."][1] The word twice translated 'servants' (or, *slaves*) has an *adjective* form, being in the neuter gender, and agreeing in both cases with the word 'members.' Everywhere else it is a noun.

20. For introduces the *motive* for complying with the closing exhortation of the preceding verse. **When ye were the servants of sin.** In your former unconverted state. This is a true characterization of all the unregenerate: in various *forms* and in various *degrees,* they are all mastered by sin. **Ye were free from righteousness.** ["Miserable freedom!"] Ye were free in respect to righteousness: in point of *right,* bound to be righteous; but in point of *fact,* independent of its demands, and devoted to the service of the opposite master—sin.[2] 'Ye were free from

righteousness' does not mean, ye were without any righteousness—wholly sinful; but, ye felt no *obligation* to be righteous, ye enjoyed your liberty in sin, without restraint. Whether or not there is any real benefit, or satisfying enjoyment in that freedom, we learn from the next verse.

21. What fruit had ye then. [Tholuck gives the connection of this verse with the preceding as follows: "While engaged in the service of sin, you possessed, it is true, the advantage of standing entirely out of all subjection to righteousness, but let us look to what is to be the final result." The verb is in the imperfect tense: what fruit were ye having.][3] 'Then' is not an adverb of time here, but of reasoning; as when we say, "Well, then," in introducing some question. [The text, however, has another word (τότε) meaning then, or, at that time—namely, when ye were the servants of sin.] 'Fruit'—that is, benefit, advantageous result, or, result in general, whether good or bad. As this verse is commonly pointed, the question seems not to be answered; yet the last clause of the verse assumes that an unfavorable answer has been given, and assigns a reason for that answer. If we *divide* the first half of the verse, making the question end with the word, 'then,' and regarding the next clause as the answer, we shall get a different but very appropriate and forcible sense, thus: *what fruit then had ye at that time?* (fruit) **whereof ye are now**

1 Bengel arranges by degrees, thus: ἁγιασμός, ἁγιωσύνη, ἁγιότης, "sanctification," "sanctity," "holiness." The last two are predicated especially of Deity, the first cannot be, as it, by usage, implies the taint and stain of sin. Holiness in man is properly the result of a sanctifying process, or of sanctification, taken in its usual active sense. Our *complete* sanctification is holiness. The word ἁγιασμός (exclusively a Biblical term) occurs eight times in Paul's epistles, Rom. 6:19, 22; 1 Cor. 1:30; 1 Thess. 4:3, 4, 7; 2 Thess. 2:13; 1 Tim. 2:15; also in Heb. 12:14; 1 Peter 1:2. Prof. Cremer notes three places where the word is used in a *passive* signification, meaning holiness—to wit, Rom. 6:19, 22; 1 Cor. 1:30: ἁγιότης (holiness) occurs only in Heb. 12:

10. "Holiness is the moral quality to be acquired, but 'sanctification' (ἁγιασμός) includes the sanctifying act or process, as well as its result." "Bible Commentary."—(F.)

2 Ἐλεύθερος, from ἐλευθερῶ, i. q., ἔρχομαι, literally means, "free to go." The dative, which in classic Greek never follows the adjective 'free,' denotes, according to Cremer, the "moral relation of subjective surrender," similarly as in the expression, 'servants to uncleanness,' etc., in the last verse. It may be called the dative of respect or reference.—(F.)

3 Notice difference of accent between this τίνα (*what* fruit) and the τινὰ (*some* fruit) of 1:13.—(F.)

22 But now being made free from sin, and become servants to God, ye have your fruit unto holiness, and the end everlasting life.

22 death. But now being made free from sin, and become servants to God, ye have your fruit unto sancti-
23 fication, and the end eternal life. For the wages of

ashamed. For the end of those things is death.[1] The reasons in favor of this method of dividing and punctuating the verse are : that it supplies the answer to the question, which the last clause of the verse seems to require; that it does not require to be supplemented by the words 'in those things,' in the first clause of the verse, to which there is nothing answering in the Greek ; that it furnishes, without these supplemental words, a suitable antecedent (in the plural relative) to the *those things* of the last clause ; that it better agrees with the sense of the preposition, with the relative, *of which,* or *for which,* rendered 'whereof' in Common Version ; that it gives to the words, '*whereof ye are now ashamed,*' which otherwise seem but an incidental observation, not particularly relevant, a special pertinence and force; in fine, that it makes the relation of the three clauses more plain and pertinent: the first asks a question, the second answers it, the third gives a reason for the answer. But Meyer[2] objects, that this view is opposed to "the antithesis in ver. 22, where the *having* of fruit, and not its *quality,* is opposed to the preceding": but is not the *quality* expressed in the words, *unto holiness,* and do not these form a very suitable antithesis to fruit '*of which ye are ashamed*'? Again he objects, that the relative '*which*' is *plural,* whereas the word '*fruit*' is *singular :* but this can hardly be regarded as a serious objection, inasmuch as the word '*fruit*' is a noun of *multitude :* again

he objects, that the word '*fruit*' [in Paul's writings] has always a *good* sense, and that Paul negatives the evil sense, in Eph. 5: 11, by calling "the works of darkness *unfruitful* ": but for proof that the word may be used in an *evil* sense, see Matt. 7: 17–19; 12· 33 ; Rom. 7: 5. There are sufficiently respectable authorities, ancient and modern, on both sides : with Meyer and the Common [also the Revised] Version agree Chrysostom, Beza, Calvin, Grotius, Wetstein, Bengel, Fritzsche, Winer [Hodge, Stuart, Shedd, Westcott and Hort, etc.] But in favor of the other view, are Theodoret, Erasmus, Melanchthon, Tholuck, De Wette, Olshausen, [Philippi, Godet,] Ewald, Tischendorf, etc., etc.

22. But now. The 'now' is rather *logical* than *temporal,* yet in this case both senses coincide. [This phrase (νυνὶ δέ), expressive of strong contrast, occurs eighteen times in Paul's epistles. In the classics it is always used in a temporal sense.] **Being** (or, *having been*) **made free from sin ;** not having been made sinless, but having been emancipated from the bondage of sin.[3] **Become servants of God** (or, *having been enslaved to God;* compare ver. 18), or, 'having bound yourselves to the service of God.' **Ye have your fruit unto holiness** (or, *sanctification*), in contrast to ver. 21, with emphasis upon *have* and *holiness.* [Ye (no longer fruitless) "have your fruit in the direction of holiness." (Godet.) Less literally, Noyes: "Ye have holiness as

---

[1] We do not, then, as some vainly imagine, receive the full punishment of sin as we go along. "Destruction" lies at the *end* of the broad road. "The *end* of those things is death." "The end of whom is perdition." The death which sin deserves and incurs is an essential unity, manifesting itself, however, in diverse forms. It is death to the body ; death to holiness and true happiness ; death to eternal life in Christ. It is death physical, spiritual, eternal, the counterpart of the eternal life. De Wette says · "It is certain that here and in ver. 16. the idea of mere physical death does not suffice." On the bringing forth of fruit unto death, see ver. 5 of the next chapter.—(F.)

[2] Meyer's own explanation of the passage is this: *What fruit, now, had ye then of things over which ye are now ashamed*—that is, ye had then *no* fruit, no moral gain, etc., and the proof thereof is : for the final result of those things is death. What leads at last to death could bring you no moral gain.—(F.)

[3] Freed both from its curse and from its reigning power. When it is said of Christians that they are free from sin, and that they "cannot sin," we must regard such expressions as relating to the general character of the actions of the regenerate. Bengel, after Gataker, compares the regenerate to the magnetic needle—*quæ polum petit; facile dimovetur, sed semper polum repetit.* "The needle seeks the pole, is easily turned away, but always seeks it again." "The apostle does not expect from the Christian at once the total eradication of every sinful propensity in the heart, although that certainly is the ultimate end at which he aims, but for the present, that the ungodly inclinations shall merely not be lords of his inward life." (Tholuck.) Yet what Christian would not rejoice to be in such subjection to God and righteousness that he shall have no unholy desires; yea, that he shall attain to the non posse peccare—that is, "find it impossible to sin." Compare 1 John 3 : 9.—(F.)

23 For the wages of sin *is* death; but the gift of God *is* eternal life through Jesus Christ our Lord.

sin is death; but the free gift of God is eternal life in Christ Jesus our Lord.

CHAPTER VII.

K NOW ye not, brethren, (for I speak to them that know the law,) how that the law hath dominion over a man as long as he liveth?

1   Or are ye ignorant, brethren (for I speak to men that know [1] the law), how that the law hath do-

1 Or, *law.*

---

the fruit."] It is a great blessing, not a hard yoke, to have a holy character. **And the end** [ye have as the end] **everlasting life.** The present fruit, *holiness;* the future consummation, *life eternal.* [We have in this verse, remarkable for its depth and comprehensiveness, a miniature sketch of the entire history of a redeemed man, beginning, impliedly, with his bondage to sin while in a state of nature, and ending with the award of the life eternal. What great and blessed things are here spoken of, too great for our finite comprehension, and for us lost sinners almost too good to be true! We can only say: Blessed deliverance! blessed service! blessed fruit! blessed reward!]

23. For. This verse confirms the preceding, and all the more forcibly on account of the preliminary reference to the evil from which we are delivered. **The wages of sin.** Compare ver. 16, where sin is represented as a ruler or master, employing servants and paying them wages. The word translated 'wages' [1] was used to designate the pay of a soldier as our word *rations* is. It is used in this restricted sense in Luke 3 : 14. In 1 Cor. 9 : 7 it is translated *charges.* In 2 Cor. 11 : 8 it is in the singular number. These four places are the only ones where it is used in the New Testament. **Is death.** Not merely physical death, but the opposite of *life eternal.* [Godet says: "This term (death), according to the apostle, does not seem to denote the annihilation of the sinner. To pay any one is not to put him out of existence. It is rather to make him feel the painful consequence of his sin—to make him reap in the form of corruption what he has sowed in the form of sin."] **But the** (gracious) **gift of God.** The penalty of sin is called *wages,* earned,

and well deserved; but the fruit of righteousness is not a deserved reward, but the free gift of God's sovereign grace. **Is eternal life.** Not merely unending existence, but the highest form of life, consummate bliss, without alloy and without end. **Through Jesus Christ our Lord.** Literally, *in* Christ Jesus our Lord. The apostle says: "Your life is hid with Christ in God. When Christ, *who is* our life, shall appear, then shall ye also appear with him in glory." (Col. 3 : 3, 4.) We have not *this* precious treasure in earthen vessels (2 Cor. 4 : 7), where it would be very insecure, but in his almighty hand, where it is safe forever more. ["The doctrine of sanctification in this chapter, and that of justification in chapter 5, both end in the same triumphant conclusion." ("Bible Commentary.")]

Ch. 7: [Freedom from condemnation and the law of sin and death to be found only in Christ, to whom, as if by marriage, we are united (7: 1-8: 1).[2] Many give as the purport of ver. 14-25, "the utter insufficiency of the law to produce sanctification," or "the law powerless to enable the regenerate man to overcome sin." According to Philippi, Paul has pictured in 7: 14-8: 11, "two aspects of the life of the regenerate man." Olshausen, with a different view of this chapter, sees in ver. 7-24, "the development of the individual until his experience of redemption."] The relation of the believer to the law is now represented under a new figure—that of marriage. This is, in fact, a further illustration of the proposition laid down in 6: 14.

1. Know ye not, brethren? [Literally: *Or are ye ignorant, brethren?* The 'or' naturally relates to what immediately pre-

---

1 'Οψώνια, *vile verbum.* (Erasmus.)—(F.)

[2] It may be said that we, if regenerate, are already in Christ, and consequently should find this freedom from condemnation in ourselves. Yet nothing hinders the regenerate man from considering himself, apart from what he is in Christ. So Hofmann and Delitzsch.

Philippi calls this "an empty abstraction." Yet nothing is more common than for the Christian to think and to tell, in the way of contrast, what he is and deserves in himself, and what he is and hopes for "in Christ." —(F.)

2 For the woman which hath a husband is bound by the law to *her* husband as long as he liveth; but if the

minion over a man for so long a time as he liveth? 2 For the woman that hath a husband is bound by law to the husband while he liveth; but if the hus-

cedes; yet most expositors refer it back to 6: 14, " Ye are not under law but under grace." Do ye not know that ye are freed from subjection to the law, as a source and rule of justification, 'or are ye ignorant,' etc.? Meyer, however, refers the 'or' to the last-named affirmation — that concerning God's gift — " which affirmation could not be *truth*, if the Christian were not free from the law, and did not belong to the risen Christ instead."] The word 'brethren' is used here, not in the *national*, but in the Christian sense, as in 1: 13. We are not to regard Paul as addressing here the Jewish Christians in particular, but all the beloved of God in Rome (1: 7), whether Jews or Gentiles. **For I speak to them that know the law.** This is not to be understood *partitively*, as if he meant to say, 'I address myself now to those of you who are versed in the law'; but he addresses himself to them *collectively*. [" I am speaking to men acquainted with the law." (Alford.)] Not only were Jewish Christians and the Gentile proselytes acquainted with the law of Moses, but the Romans generally were a civilized people, and eminently a people who under. stood laws. **How that the law hath dominion over a man as long as he liveth?** [On the genitive case following the verb, 'have dominion,' see notes on 6: 9. As the subject of 'liveth' is not expressed. some supply 'law' rather than 'he,' thus: so long as the law is in force. But this does not accord so well with ver. 4. The last verb is an irregular contract, either indicative or subjunctive in form, but indicative in meaning. (Boise.) Philippi, somewhat strangely, interprets this 'liveth' ethically, "as long as a man lives his old natural life of sin."] The apostle's subsequent argument relates only to the *Mosaic* law; but the affirmation here made is equally true in general.

2. For the woman which hath a husband [literally, *the woman subject to a husband*]. This example seems to be chosen, among many others in which death dissolves a legal obligation, for the purpose of representing the union between Christ and the believer under the figure of the closest and tenderest of all human relations — that of

husband and wife. This comparison is repeatedly used, both in the Old Testament and in the New. (Isa. 54: 5; 62: 5; Jer. 3: 14; 31: 32; Hosea 2: 19; John 3: 29; 2 Cor. 11: 2; Rev. 19: 7; 21: 9; 22: 17.) [Paul here chooses the example of the *wife*, because Christ is to be the second husband. (Godet.)] A peculiarity of the illustration in the present case, which has caused needless perplexity to some, is the fact that, in the matter designed to be illustrated here, the party which *dies*, and not the *survivor*, is the one released from the bond. [The proper antithesis would be: the husband being dead, the wife is free to marry another, so the law being dead ye are free to be married to Christ. But Paul, wishing perhaps to avoid the phrase, *the law being dead*, which would be so offensive to Jewish ears, says: " *Ye* were rendered dead to the law," which of course implies that the law has for such persons become dead. Meyer says: "The semblance of inappropriateness vanishes on considering 'ye also' of ver. 4, from which it is plain that Paul in his illustration follows the view that the death of the husband implies in a metaphorical sense (by virtue of the union of the two spouses in one person), *the death of the woman also* as respected her married relation, and consequently her release from the law, in so far as it had bound her as a married wife to her husband."] The apostle, in using this illustration, would fix our attention to the one point, that death dissolves obligation in both cases. He does not undertake to point out either agreement or disagreement, in other respects. **Is bound** [or, as Winer puts it: *accordingly belongs*] **by the law to her husband as long as he liveth.** [The right of procuring divorce belonged to the husband (Deut. 24: 1, seq.), which implies "the law" that the woman was bound to her husband during his life.] Some have supposed that the apostle takes the illustration from the case of the wife, rather than of the husband, because it was then so *easy* and so *common*, both among Jews and Gentiles, for the husband to get release before death. It was a sure sign of moral degeneracy, and a fruitful cause of increasing it: how much more is it both, when, as in so many modern and so-called *Christian* communities, it is

husband be dead, she is loosed from the law of *her*
husband.

3 So then if, while *her* husband liveth, she be married
to another man, she shall be called an adulteress: but
if her husband be dead, she is free from that law; so
that she is no adulteress, though she be married to
another man.

4 Wherefore, my brethren, ye also are become dead
to the law by the body of Christ; that ye should be

band die, she is discharged from the law of the
3 husband. So then if, while the husband liveth, she
be joined to another man, she shall be called an
adulteress: but if the husband die, she is free from
the law, so that she is no adulteress, though she be
4 joined to another man. Wherefore, my brethren,
ye also were made dead to the law through the body

almost equally common, and equally easy for
either party to obtain a legal release for causes
comparatively trivial. **But if the husband
be dead** [or, better, *may have died*], **she is
loosed**—that is, has been set free and remains
so (perfect tense),[1] **from the law of her** (literally, *the*) **husband**—the law which defines
her relation to her husband. [Philippi says:
"We should have expected, *the law of her
husband is annulled* (3:31) *and she is free.*
But in energetic phraseology the notion of
abrogation is transferred to the person," and
we have this pregnant construction: she is
annulled (and made free) from the law.
"The apostle thus gives expression to the
thought lying at the basis of his argument,
that with the decease of the husband the wife
also has ceased to exist as respects her legal
connection with him. She is still existent,
but no longer bound to the law [which determines the relation of the wife to the hus-
band] to which she died with the death of the
husband."]

3. **So then,** or, *accordingly therefore:* the
coupling of these two logical particles is a
peculiarity of Paul's style, occurring twelve
times in his epistles [see 5: 18, note]. **If,
while her husband liveth, she be married
to another man** (more literally: *she become*
(wife) *to another husband*), **she shall be called
an adulteress.** [The verb here is in the
future of established rule. It primarily meant
to transact business, then to give response or
decision. In later usage it signified to do
business under a certain name or title, hence
to be named or called. Godet remarks that
"a large number of our family names are
names of some trade."] **But if her husband be dead** (better: *if the husband have
died*), **she is free from that law; so that
she is no adulteress, though she be
married to another man.** The last clause
may be rendered more literally, thus: (for)
having become (wife) *to another husband.*

[Meyer translates the last clause but one, "in
order that she be not an adulteress," adding
this explanation—"that is the *purpose,* involved in the divine legal ordinance, of her
freedom from the law." The form of expression is certainly favorable to this idea of
purpose, if it is not positively decisive. On
the infinitive clause in the genitive, indicating
purpose, see Winer, 324, 325. As a genitive
assigning cause or reason, it depends on the
statement, 'she is free,' etc.]

4. **Wherefore,** or, *so that.* [*So then,* or
accordingly, as in Lange. Beginning a
new clause with a finite verb, the conjunction (ὥστε) has the sense of *wherefore,
therefore.* (Winer, 301.) See also Buttmann,
243. The word seems to denote an actual
or natural sequence of fact more than a
mere logical inference.] We have here an
inference both from the general principle
(ver. 1) and from the particular illustration.
(Ver. 2, 3.) **My brethren, ye also,** as well as
in the case used for illustration, **are become
dead to the law**—rather, *were put to death
in respect to the law.* [And are thus "quite
like this wife who is dead (as a wife) through
her husband's death, and who thus has the
right to marry again. . . . As the new husband is a dead and risen Christ, the wife must
necessarily be represented as dead (through
the death of her first husband, the law) that
she may be in a position to be united to Christ
as one risen again. It is a marriage, as it
were, beyond the tomb." (Godet.)] The
verb is in the past tense and passive voice.
It is the same verb that is translated "to put
to death" in Matt. 26:59; 27:1; Mark 14:55;
1 Peter 3:18; and "kill" in Rom. 8:36; 2
Cor. 6:9. Perhaps the apostle preferred this
stronger expression (θανατόω) instead of the
common one (ἀποθνήσκω) "to die" (Rom. 6:8, etc.),
as conveying a more distinct allusion to the
violent death of Christ. He might have said,
'the law is dead to you,' but this, besides

---

[1] On the force of the perfect tense as denoting the present when it follows the subjunctive of objective
possibility, see 2: 25, and Winer, 293.—(F.)

married to another, *even* to him who is raised from the dead, that we should bring forth fruit unto God.

5 For when we were in the flesh, the motions of sins,

of Christ; that ye should be joined to another, *even* to him who was raised from the dead, that we might

5 bring forth fruit unto God. For when we were in the flesh, the [1] sinful passions, which were through

---

1 Gr. *passions of sins.*

---

being more offensive to the Jews, would not have agreed so well with the representation in the previous chapter. There we are said *to die* to sin. The argument here may be presented in a sort of tabular form, thus:

Death dissolves legal obligation:
Death has dissolved the legal obligation between husband and wife;
Therefore the wife is at liberty to be married to another.
Death has dissolved the legal obligation between the law and us;
Therefore we are at liberty to form another union.
There the survivor is released; here the one that dies.

By (or *through*) **the body of Christ**—that is, by the crucifixion of Christ's body. [Compare Col. 1 : 22; Heb. 10 : 5, 10; 1 Peter 2 : 24; also 2 Cor. 5 : 14. "If one died for all, then all died." Here and in the previous chapter the mystical union of the believer with Christ is everywhere brought to view or presupposed. We are crucified with Christ, we die with Christ, we are buried with Christ, we rise with Christ, we live and reign with Christ, etc.] **That ye should be married to another.** Not incorrect as to sense, though a more exact rendering would be: *That ye might become* (wife) *to another*, **to him who is raised from the dead.** [Compare Gal. 2 : 19: "Through the law I died to the law, that I might live unto God."] **That we should** (or *might*) **bring forth fruit unto God.** The *kind* of fruit which we are to bring forth is specified in Gal. 5 : 22, 23. [The idea of fruit-bearing may here have some reference to the marriage relation. Yet the figure of bringing forth fruit is used, independently of such relation, quite commonly in the Scriptures. The final aim of our having been made dead to the law, and of our becoming wedded to Christ, is that we may live with and for the risen Saviour a new and holy fruit-bearing life.] Observe the change from the *second* person in the first two verbs to the *first* person in the last. "As the argument advances, the language of the apostle becomes *communicative*, so that he includes

himself with his readers." (Meyer.) Compare 8 : 15.

5. For when we were in the flesh. [We should naturally have expected here, 'when we were under the law.' But the expression 'in the flesh' supposes the legal state prior to death with Christ.] This verse shows the need there was of a radical change, and confirms the last clause of the preceding verse. When we were in our carnal, unregenerate state (8 : 8, 9), which was, as the next verse intimates, a state of subjection to external rites and carnal commandments. (Gal. 4 : 9; Heb. 9 : 10.) "To be in the flesh is to be endowed only with the gifts of nature, while the peculiar grace is wanting, which God condescends to bestow on his own elect." (Calvin.) [The word translated 'flesh' [1] is of frequent occurrence in Paul's writings, and is found twenty-four times in this Epistle. It naturally denotes that which is weak and perishable, but is often used in the ethical sense of unclean, sinful. In 8 : 3 it is called the "flesh of sin," not because it is the source of sin or because it is essentially sinful, but because it has, in a special manner, been taken possession of and controlled by sin. Prof. Cremer says it signifies "the sinful condition of human nature in and according to its bodily manifestation." A glance at Gal. 5 : 19, "works of the flesh," shows that envying, enmity, wrath, are as much the fruit of the flesh, according to Paul's use of this term, as are the sensual acts of fornication, uncleanness, etc. According to 2 Cor. 10 : 2, 3, we may walk in the flesh, and yet not according to the flesh. As Christians, we must war with the flesh as long as we live, but not war according to the flesh.]

Observe the distinct notation of time, 'when we were.' **The motions of sins.** Literally, 'the passions of sins,' not merely sinful passions, but passions which are the occasions of, the excitements to, actual sins. [Alford has "strivings" of sins, "incitements" to sins; the Bible Union Version, "emotions of sins." The word ($\pi\alpha\theta\eta\mu\alpha\tau\alpha$) is usually rendered sufferings or afflictions. Gal. 5 : 24, in our Common

---

[1] $\Sigma\acute{\alpha}\rho\xi$, in distinction from $\kappa\rho\acute{\epsilon}\alpha\varsigma$, denotes living flesh and includes the idea of organism.—(F.)

which were by the law, did work in our members to bring forth fruit unto death.
6 But now we are delivered from the law, that being

the law, wrought in our members to bring forth 6 fruit unto death. But now we have been discharged from the law, having died to that wherein we were

Version, reads: "Have crucified the flesh with the affections and lusts;" in the Revised Version, "passions and lusts." It is a stronger word than desire, coveting, or lust (ἐπιθυμία), yet both may be regarded as sinful and both lead to sins. Thus the law not only produces a knowledge of sins, but is, in one sense, causative of sins. Adam Clarke, however, says that "the law is only the means of disclosing our sinful propensity, not of producing it. As a bright beam of the sun introduced into a room shows millions of motes in all directions—but these were not introduced by the light, but were there before . . . so the evil propensity was in the heart before, but there was not light sufficient to discover it." Paul, however, goes further than this, and makes the law, by its prohibitory, restraining power, the innocent means of exciting to activity the dormant sinful passions. See ver. 8.] **Which were by the law.** Which emotions were by means of the law, were provoked by the law's prohibition. "The strength of sin is the law." (1 Cor. 15 : 56.) [See ver. 8; also 5 : 20, "that the trespass might abound." The law has been represented as a *Zügel*, a *Spiegel*, and a *Riegel*, or a bridle, a mirror, and a bar. We naturally resist restraint. *Nitimur in vetitum semper, cupimusque negata:* "We always strive after that which is forbidden, and desire that which is denied." The reason why transgressors are not more conscious of their transgressions, and why their enmity against God is not often felt and shown, is that God leaves them, in a measure, to their own chosen ways, and does not exercise his full restrictive power. If God, to use the thought of another, should stretch a chain across the road to hinder the progress of one violating the Sabbath, the man would soon become conscious of wrathful feelings against his Maker.] **Did work in our members**—that is, wrought, or were active, in our members [thus making these members weapons of iniquity. 6 : 13; compare Col. 3 : 5]. The verb so translated, though

passive in form (or rather middle in the New Testament), is always active in sense. (Gal. 5 : 6; James 5 : 16.) [It has, according to Ellicott, "a persistent and effective character." The middle form of this verb is, in Paul's writings, always used of non-personal action. (Winer, 258.)] **To bring forth fruit unto death.** That we should bring forth fruit, or, to the bringing forth of fruit. 'Unto death' does not mean unto death as the final result, however true that sense might be; but death is personified as the antithesis to God at the end of ver. 4. That was fruit for *God*—God's fruit; this is fruit for *death*—death's fruit. [How vain, then, to look to the law for life or help when it only threatens with a curse, and, apart from Christ's grace, works only for and unto death. "That man that overtook you," said Christian, "was Moses. He spareth none, neither knoweth he how to show mercy to those that transgress the law." ("Pilgrim's Progress.")]

6. **But now,** in distinction from the 'when' at the beginning of ver. 5. **We are** (*have been*) **delivered from the law.** [That the law here referred to is the moral and not the ceremonial law is evident from the use of this word in the next verse, and in others which follow. We have been discharged from the law, not as as rule of duty, but as a ground or direct means of justification. "By the revelation and gift of grace, man's relation to the law as a criminal is done away." (Cremer.) "We are freed from the law when God emancipates us from its rigid exactions and curse, and endues us with his Spirit, through whom we walk in his ways." (Calvin.)] The indefinite past tense of the Greek here requires the perfect in English, as in 11 : 30, 31, and often—always indeed—where it has connected with it an adverb of present time.[1] **That being dead wherein we were held.** The participle translated 'being dead' is, according to the correct text, in the plural number, agreeing with 'we,' and not in the singular, agreeing

---

[1] We have this verb in ver. 3, and often elsewhere. See notes on 3 : 31; 6 : 6. Ellicott, on Col. 1 : 21, remarks that "in this union of the emphatic particle of absolutely present time with the aorist, the aorist is not

equivalent to a present or perfect, but marks with the proper force of the tense that the action followed a given event and is now done with." Still, we can do no better than to render it as perfect.—(F.)

dead wherein we were held; that we should serve in newness of spirit, and not *in* the oldness of the letter. 7 What shall we say then? *Is* the law sin? God forbid. Nay, I had not known sin, but by the law: for I had not known lust, except the law had said, Thou shalt not covet.

holden; so that we serve in newness of the spirit, and not in oldness of the letter. 7 What shall we say then? Is the law sin? God forbid. Howbeit, I had not known sin, except through [1] the law: for I had not known [2] coveting, except the 8 law had said, Thou shalt not [2] covet: but sin, finding

1 Or, *law*......2 Or, *lust*.

with 'that'—to wit, the law; and the true sense is, *we having died to that in which we were held*—namely, the law. The difference between the two forms of the word in Greek is only a difference of a single vowel, *e* (ε) instead of *o* (ο). This change is required alike by external and internal evidence. The plural form is required by the consistency of the representation. See ver. 4, and 6 : 2, 8, 11. [The verb 'held' (or, *held down*) occurs in 1 : 18.] **That we should serve.** 'So that we serve,' not 'should' serve. The inference is stated as a matter of fact, not merely as an obligation. **In newness of spirit, and not in the oldness of the letter.** [Luther: "In the new nature of the Spirit, and not in the old nature of the letter." Compare the like form of expression in 6 : 4.][1] In the new life of the Spirit, and not in the old life of the letter; in a new and hearty spiritual obedience, and not in the old and servile literal conformity. ["The Spirit—that is, the Holy Spirit of God, who originates and penetrates the Christian life—the first mention of the Spirit so much spoken of in chapter 8." (Alford.) So De Wette, Meyer, Philippi, Godet, Hodge, Riddle. As a proper name, it stands without the article. "The letter," says De Wette, "is the Mosaic law, after which, as an outward norm, the moral life of the Jews should be regulated." Compare 2 Cor. 3 : 6, 7: "The ministration of death in letters, written and engraven in stones;" "the letter killeth." Calvin says: "Before our will is formed according to the will of God by the Holy Spirit, we have in the law nothing but the outward letter, which, indeed, bridles our external actions, but does not in the least restrain the fury of our lusts. And he (Paul)

ascribes 'newness' to the Spirit because it succeeds the old man, as the letter is called 'old' because it perishes through the Spirit." For a like use of the word 'newness,' see 6 : 4.] That the new and hearty spiritual service was a service of God, and the old and literal service a service of sin, was so self-evident that no further definition was needed. When the life of a professed Christian contradicts this representation, it is no longer the Christian life.

The effect of the law is to make sin known (ver. 7) and to excite it to greater activity (ver. 8-11), so that, while the law is good (ver. 12), it becomes the occasion of manifesting more fully the exceeding sinfulness of sin. (Ver. 13.)

7. What shall we say then? Compare 4 : 1; 6 : 1. **Is the law sin?** A question suggested by ver. 5: "The motions of sins which were by the law." As the subject is abstract, an abstract predicate was suitable. He might have said: Is the law sinful? but that would have been less forcible. [This question relates to the law as being itself sinful rather than as being simply causative of sin.] **God forbid.** *No;* the law is not sin; that is not what I meant to say; but I did not know sin, etc.[2] **Except the law.** I did not understand the essential nature and comprehensiveness of sin [its power and enormity] except by the law. **Nay** (*for indeed*, τε γὰρ), **I had not known lust**—*coveteousness* (as sin)—**except the law had said, Thou shalt not covet.**[3] [Note the use of the prohibitory future, 'Thou shalt not covet,' instead of the imperative. This legal (Old Testament) idiom "views the command as already obeyed in the future, and is, therefore, more commanding in tone than the imperative." (Philippi.)]

---

[1] The negative μή rather than οὐ is used in telic sentences, and with the infinitive after ὥστε, denoting consequence, though this consequence be a matter of fact. It is admitted here because the contrasted noun is negatived and not the verb. (Buttmann, 349.)—(F.)

[2] With ἄν the rendering would be: I should not have known (such a thing as) sin. Here the apostle represents it more as an actual occurrence.—(F.)

[3] The word ᾔδειν, though pluperfect in form, is used for the imperfect, and its literal rendering here would be: *I was not knowing*, or, supplying ἄν, *I should not have known*. On the frequent omission of ἄν in the apodosis in later Greek, especially with the imperfect tense, see Winer, 305.—(F.)

8 But sin, taking occasion by the commandment, wrought in me all manner of concupiscence. For without the law sin *was* dead.

occasion, wrought in me through the commandment all manner of [1]coveting: for apart from [1]the law sin

1 Or, *lust*......2 Or, *law*.

'Lust,' or *coveteousness* [with the article, "the desire after whatever is forbidden" (Meyer)], here includes all unlawful desire, whatever be the object. "I should not have recognized such desire as sin if the law had not forbidden it." ["What the law forbids us to covet (Exod. 20 : 17 ; Deut. 5 : 21) was no concern of the apostle here, looking to the universality of his representation." (Meyer.) Two different verbs, meaning *know*, are used in this verse (to wit, γινώσκω and οἶδα). The former denotes, generally, a more intimate knowledge, a fuller understanding, than the latter, which means rather to know *about* something, to be aware of some fact. "*Ginosko* (the former), while it includes *oida* (the latter), contains also much more; piercing through circumstantial knowledge, it reaches to the discernment of the inner nature, of character. of moral qualities, habits, temper, affections. It signifies appreciation or experimental acquaintance, whether good or bad, such as exists between intimate friends or inveterate foes." ("Bible Commentary.") According to Prof. Cremer, the former implies an active "*personal* relation between the person knowing and the object known," whereas in the use of the latter the object of knowledge "has simply come within the sphere of perception, within the knower's circle of vision." The former (γινώσκω), therefore, is naturally used of Christian knowledge, the saving knowledge of God, of Christ, of truth and salvation. Though Paul here uses the pronoun, 'I,' he at the same time speaks representatively for others.] Observe how jealously the apostle guards against any disparagement of the law, both here and in ver. 12, 13.

8. But sin. The 'but' is explained by the emphatic negation in the preceding verse: No, indeed, the law is not sin ; but (it is true) that 'sin,' **taking occasion** [start, or impulse, hence "more than mere opportunity" (Alford)]—that is, finding the wherewith to attack me. [Sin is here, as in ver. 11, personified as an enemy.] It will be observed that the punctuation is changed in this verse, and the phrase 'by the commandment' is separated from 'taking occasion' [with which

Olshausen and Philippi would connect it] and joined with the following clause. There are two reasons for this change [favored by De Wette, Meyer Godet, and most expositors]: In the first place, the preposition *by* (διά) is not the one which would be used after 'taking occasion,' if those two clauses had been intended to be so connected, but the preposition *from* (ἐκ) would have been used; in the second place, the last clause of ver. 11, 'and *by it* slew me,' shows the true connection of 'by the commandment' with the following verb. [See also ver. 13.] **Wrought in me all manner of concupiscence ;** rather, *coveting* (Revised Version)—that is, of unlawful desire. [This word (ἐπιθυμία) is once used by our Saviour of holy desire. (Luke 22 : 15.) See also Gal. 5 : 17 : "The Spirit *lusteth* against the flesh."] Our common translation, by using such different words—*lust, covet, concupiscence*—in these two verses, loses much of the force of the apostle's language. The Bible Union Revision [as also the Canterbury Revision] avoids this fault. **For without** (or, *apart from*) **the law sin was dead**—that is, inoperative, inactive, comparatively. *Is*, rather than 'was,' should be supplied here; the affirmation is a general maxim. [This death of sin must be regarded as relative and not as absolute. In this death-state "sin cannot mature in its root; it cannot come to *transgression*." (Lange.) "The inward discord is not yet awakened." (De Wette.) "As a rapidly-flowing stream rolls calmly on so long as no object checks it, but foams and roars so soon as any hindrance stops it, just as calmly does the sinful element hold its course through the man so long as he does not stem it, but if he would realize the divine commandment, he begins to feel the force of the element of whose dominion he had as yet no suspicion." (Olshausen.) The law, coming home to the conscience in all its spirituality and power, and making known the guilt and condemnation attendant on its willful violation, may well be called "the *strength* of sin." (1 Cor. 15 : 56.) Meyer regards 'without the law' as utter absence, or utter ignorance, of the law, but this meaning ill accords with

9 For I was alive without the law once: but when | 9 *is* dead. And I was alive apart from [1] the law once:
the commandment came, sin revived, and I died. | but when the commandment came, sin revived, and

1 Or, *law.*

the next verse.] What can the word 'sin' denote, at the beginning and end of this verse but the *principle* of sin, depravity, indwelling sin?

9. For. The Greek particle at the beginning of this verse would be better translated, *now;* 'for,' of the Common Version, is too strong, 'and,' of the Bible Union Revision, is too weak. *Now* **I was alive** (or, *was living;* note the force of the imperfect tense) **without the law once**—better, *apart from the law formerly.* The law was to me (though a familiar object from my youth) an external, distant, object; it had not come home to me [in all its breadth and spirituality and *condemning* power]. When was this *formerly?* Not in some imaginary period of primeval or youthful innocence and piety (Origen, Augustine, Meyer, De Wette, Godet, and others), but, as explained below, before 'the commandment came' to the heart and conscience "with a convincing power and light." 'I was living' expresses activity, in contrast with 'dead,' at the end of the preceding verse. It expresses also the enjoyment of life, comparative peace, hopefulness, and security—security in its more appropriate sense, freedom from *care,* not from danger. [Melanchthon speaks of three states: of security, of being under the law, and of regeneration; and thinks the first state was the one here described by Paul. Philippi would place Paul's Pharisaic period in the second status, or would in a measure combine the first two together. This life-state apart from the law has no reference to childhood. It can better be predicated of the self-righteous, who are living at ease, whose consciences are at rest, and who are satisfied with themselves—like the young ruler, for example, who said: "All these things have I observed from my youth up; what lack I yet?" Saul the Pharisee, too, was thus alive when he could say of himself, in accordance with ordinary human judgment: "Touching the righteousness which is in the law, found blameless." See Phil. 3: 6, Revised Version.] **But when the commandment came**—to me personally, as a living power. (Heb. 4: 12.) **Sin revived, and I died.** [Not simply revived as from a state of dormancy, but sprang into life

as from a state of death. Stuart renders: "gathered new life"; Meyer: "came to life again" (resumed its proper living nature), which, in his view, is its sole meaning throughout the New Testament.] Before, *I* was alive, and *sin* was, to appearance, dead. Now the case is reversed: *Sin came to life, but I died.* Sin sprang into life and activity, aroused by the prohibitory commandment. But I died; I lost that comfortable, hopeful, self-complacency, which was my life before. If 'I was living' means "I was enjoying a sort of peace, security, and hopefulness," then 'I died' must mean "I fell into trouble, alarm, and despondency." "The death of sin is a man's life, and the life of sin his death." (Calvin.) How little men know of the sin that is in them, till the commandment comes! Preaching should be adapted to bring the commandment *home* to the unconverted. ['I died,' according to Prof. Turner, "expresses a consciousness of being condemned, and in a state of moral and penal death."] Meyer regards this dying as the incurring of eternal death. Hence in his view, the person who was alive without the law had not incurred this death. Prof. Stuart thinks the phrase 'I was alive' denotes that the subject was comparatively inactive in sin, or was not desperate in sin, and explains it by the Saviour's words: "If I had not come and spoken to them, they had not had sin." So, in his view, 'I died' signifies that the man came "under the active and predominating power and penalty of sin." To the common interpretation, "I once deemed myself spiritually alive, but when I came under conviction by the law, a sense of sin revived and I was brought to deem myself spiritually dead," he makes this objection, that this bringing a sinner under real and true conviction as to his desperate spiritual condition, would be to him the means of life, rather than of death, as is stated in the next verse. To affirm that the law "ruins sinners by bringing them under a sense of their guilt and condemnation," would, he says, be "a singular conclusion." But the apostle, in this representation, would seem to regard the law as the only Saviour, the only source of life and help and hope. And o'

10 And the commandment, which *was ordained* to life, I found *to be* unto death.
11 For sin, taking occasion by the commandment, deceived me, and by it slew *me.*
12 Wherefore the law *is* holy, and the commandment holy, and just, and good.

10 I died ; and the commandment, which *was* unto life, 11 this I found *to be* unto death: for sin, finding occasion, through the commandment beguiled me, and 12 through it slew me. So that the law is holy, and the commandment holy, and righteous, and good.

this supposition to be "slain by the law" (see ver. 11), to come to a vivid consciousness of condemnation, of desert of eternal death, and of the inability of the law to effect his deliverance, would be to him death indeed, were there no Christ by whom he could be made alive. And now that a Saviour is provided, and the gospel's offers made known, does not the convicted, burdened, lost sinner, who in his darkness and guilt cannot find the way of life, and who cries out in anguish for days or weeks or months, it may be, "What shall I do to be saved?" experience something of the misery of the lost, something of the pains of eternal death?]

10. And so, not something new and additional, but the same truth stated with change of grammatical subject: **The commandment, which was ordained to life** (better, *for* life—that is, meant for life, and tending to life), **I found to be unto death ;** or, 'this was found to be to me for death.' This is the literal translation of Paul's language. See the proof that the commandment was meant for life in Lev. 18: 5; Deut. 5: 33. [The Common Version omits the emphatic *this* (αὔτη, not ἡ αὐτή, *the same*) very *commandment was found,* or proved by personal experience, to be *for death.* The very disappointment which the earnest soul of Paul felt, when he found the law in which he trusted for life was only the means of death, must have been to him as death itself.]

11. The **for** explains how that came to pass which the preceding verse affirms. **For sin, taking** [*having taken*] **occasion.** On the punctuation of this verse, and the connection of the clauses, see note on ver. 8. **By the commandment, deceived me, and by it** (or *that*) **slew me.** ["Slain by the law." Compare 2 Cor. 3: 6. "The letter killeth." Every one made alive by Christ must first be slain by the law—must lie at the Saviour's feet as dead. When the commandment came home to the apostle's heart and conscience in all its obligatory and condemnatory power, sin gathered new life; it revived and he died. So whenever this law work takes place in

the sinner's soul, the Spirit discovers to him the plague, the desperate depravity of his heart, his carnal hopes are slain, and his mind is filled with darkness, anguish, and despair. In such a state as this he suffers, as we may suppose, the very torments of hell.] Compare 'I died.' (Ver. 9.) There seems to be an allusion here to the fall of our first parents: indeed, the verb translated 'deceived' is precisely the same as is found in the Greek translation of Gen. 3: 13, where the English reads 'beguiled.' Compare 2 Cor. 11: 3 ; 1 Tim. 2: 14. There, as here, there was both a deceiving and a slaying ; and both by means of (or through the intervention of) the commandment. Sin used the commandment to make that appear desirable to me which was really pernicious. [This would be the natural result of a *prohibitory* commandment, especially since "we always strive for the forbidden, and desire that which is denied."] Sin is always a deceiver. (Heb. 3: 13.) It always promises more pleasure and advantage than it gives. (Gen. 3: 5, 6.) And the commandment which forbids it becomes the occasion of increasing the deception; because it makes the seeming good greater beforehand by the prohibition, and the real evil greater afterward by the penalty.

12. Wherefore—better, *so that,* since it was not the law that was the efficient cause of sin, but my own perversely sinful disposition, taking occasion from the law ; **the law is holy, and the commandment holy**—in its source and nature, **and just,** in its precepts and penalty, **and good,** in its design. Observe how conclusively the question of ver. 7 is answered : the law, so far from being *sin* is wholly and emphatically the opposite. [The antithetic *but* (δέ) corresponding to the 'indeed' (μέν), is unexpressed, but is virtually contained in the next verse : The law 'indeed' is good (morally excellent, or perhaps beneficial, compare the 'righteous' and 'good' of 5: 7), *but* sin misuses it in working out death to me by that (law) which is good. (Winer, 575.) The commandment here characterized doubtless has special reference to that mentioned in

13 Was then that which is good made death unto me? God forbid. But sin, that it might appear sin, working death in me by that which is good; that sin by the commandment might become exceeding sinful.

13 Did then that which is good become death unto me? God forbid. But sin, that it might be shewn to be sin, by working death to me through that which is good;—that through the commandment 14 sin might become exceeding sinful. For we know

ver. 7, 'Thou shalt not covet.' "Were the law unjust in its requirements or its penalties, it were no merit in Jesus that he died to honor it, and to deliver us from its curse. Nor were it any mercy in God to grant us pardon for its transgression. As it is, we must subscribe to the justice of God in our condemnation." (Fuller.) Chalmers, speaking of the goodness of the law, not as a means of justification, but as a rule of moral conduct, says: "You may not be able to purchase the king's favor with gold; but he may grant you his favor, and, when he requires your appearance before him, it is still in gold he may require you to be invested. And thus of the law. It is not by your own righteous conformity thereto that you purchase God's favor, for this has been already purchased by the pure gold of the Saviour's righteousness, and is presented to all who believe on him. But still it is with your own personal righteousness that you must be gilded and adorned. It is not the price wherewith you have bought heaven, but it is the attire in which you must enter it."]

13. Was then that which is good made death unto me? The Revised Version is more exact: *"Did then that which is good become death unto me"?* [1] 'Death,' the abstract, as 'sin.' (Ver. 7.) Here, as there, the effect for the cause: is the law the cause of sin? has that which is good become to me the cause of death? that is, the efficient, responsible cause. **God forbid!** *far be it!* **But sin** has become to me the cause of death: in order **that it might appear sin,** in order that it might be seen in its true malignity. [He does not say: that it might *be* sin, since sin had a prior existence.] The word 'appear' is here emphatic. This manifestation of the evil nature and bitter consequence of sin, in turning that which is good into an occasion of death [the very worst of perversions], **working death in** (*to*) **me by that which is good**—was definitely ordained by God ('in order that'), as a necessary preparation for redemption. **That** (*in order that*), a still further and more ultimate divine purpose, **sin by** (*means of*) **the com-**

mandment might become exceeding sinful. The word translated 'exceeding'—that is, 'in overmeasure' [compare 1 Cor. 12: 31; 2 Cor. 1: 8; 4: 17; Gal. 1: 13], is the word *hyperbole*, the technical rhetorical term for exaggeration in speech. It might well be rendered *beyond measure.* 'Exceeding' sinful may have been strong enough at the time our own translators used it; but it has been so toned down by frequent use, that it seems too tame now. The word translated 'sinful' is usually a noun, and as such is translated *sinner* more than forty times; but here, and in three other places (Matt. 8: 38; Luke 5: 8; 24: 7), it is used as an adjective. Theophylact, one of the Greek commentators, uses this illustration: "Just as a disorder, when it has become worse, may be said to display, by means of the healing art, its malignity, as not being removed even by that."

With ver. 14 begins a section, in respect to which there has been a radical difference of opinion among the ablest commentators, from very ancient times. Does it describe the experience of a regenerate or of an unregenerate man? There is no question that the preceding section (ver. 7-13), applies to the unregenerate. And very many able commentators, both among the ancients and among the moderns, maintain that it is an unregenerate experience still which is described to the end of the chapter. It will suffice to mention the names of Theodoret, Julius Müller, Neander, Tholuck, Ewald, and Meyer. [We may add the names of Bengel, Hahn, Hengstenberg, Nitzsch, Rückert, De Wette, Stier, Kahnis, Godet, Olshausen, Wordsworth, Turner, Riddle, Schaff, Stuart. Olshausen and Turner would make ver. 25 begin a new experience and new chapter. Many of the writers named suppose that Paul's description has reference to the unregenerate, not as in a state of security, but as an awakened sinner. The "Bible Commentary" says: *inter regenerandum*, during the process of regeneration. Of the writers above named, Meyer is perhaps the most determined opponent of the view maintained

---

[1] Instead of the perfect tense, the oldest MSS. ℵ A B C D E give the verb in the aorist, ἐγένετο.—(F.)

14 For we know that the law is spiritual: but I am
carnal, sold under sin.

that the law is spiritual: but I am carnal, sold under

in this commentary.] On the other hand, it has seemed to many scholars, that the change of *tense* in the verbs, from the past to the present, in ver. 14 and onward, indicates a different date and phase of religious experience from the preceding, and that what is said from this point is rightly interpreted as the experience of a regenerate man. This view is defended by Jerome, Augustine (both of whom, however, originally held the opposite view), Melanchthon, Calvin, Beza, Krummacher, Delitzsch, Luthardt, and others. [Among these "others," we may mention the names of Luther, Chalmers, Brown, Haldane, Forbes, Philippi, Umbreit, Hofmann, Thomasius, Alford (substantially), Hodge, Shedd, Barnes, Boise. According to Augustine's statement, his change of views was owing to the writings of "Hilary, Gregory, Ambrose, and other holy and known doctors of the church," and thus was not due simply to his "warm dispute" with Pelagius. And Prof. Stuart's statement that "Augustine was the first who suggests the idea that this passage must be applied to Christian experience" would appear to be incorrect.] This view is adopted by the writer of these notes. For a fuller discussion of this difficult question, see Appendix D.

It should be here remembered, however, that those who adopt this view do not by any means regard these verses as designed to describe the normal experience of the Christian life,[1] but only that phase of it which comes to view, when the regenerate man allows himself to regard mainly his relations to the moral law, instead of looking to Christ as his surety and his righteousness. They believe that, as it was the design of the previous section (ver. 7-13) to show how powerless the law is to convert a sinner, so it is the design of this section (ver. 14-25) to show that the law is equally powerless to enable the regenerate man to overcome sin.

[The apostle in this section (ver. 14-25) represents the Christian as looking on and in himself, and comparing his thoughts and deeds with those which the perfect law of God requires. Hence the most advanced Christian, tried by this perfect standard, will be, and will feel himself to be, condemned and lost. His language will be : "With my mind I myself do indeed serve the law of God, but with the flesh the law of sin, and only in Christ Jesus is there freedom from condemnation." See ver. 25, and 8 : 1. From this point of view we may say, not only that "the law is powerless to enable the regenerate man to overcome sin," but that grace will not so sanctify our natures that we shall not need to be sheltered in Christ, in order to be justified and saved. Through Jesus Christ, who is "the Lord, our righteousness," do we give thanks to God for our deliverance both from condemnation and from the reigning power of sin. Philippi says that in the two passages (7 : 14-25 ; 8 : 1-11) "are pictured the two aspects ever appearing in mutual connection, of one and the same spiritual *status*, so that the regenerate man, according as his glance is directed to the one or the other aspect, is able to affirm both of himself at every moment; as well what is said in 7 : 23 as what is said in 8 : 2. Hence also ever rises from his heart with equal truth the twofold cry, as well : 'Oh, wretched man,' as 'I thank God.' "]

14. For we know. The 'for' is explanatory of the relative positions of sin and the law [and introduces, virtually, a proof of the intrinsic excellence of the law as drawn from Christian experience. None but the regenerate have this kind and degree of knowledge]. 'We know,' it is with us an understood and acknowledged principle, as in 2 : 2 ; 3 : 19. **That the law is spiritual,** as being from God, who is spirit, and as requiring of men spiritual purity. [It being spiritual in its nature also concerns itself not merely with outward acts, but with "the thoughts and intents of the heart." Its language is : Thou shalt not *covet*, shalt not indulge in "inordinate desires and sinful affections." "Civil

---

[1] Yet Philippi says that even the "normal condition" will allow the carnal principle to break out in word and deed, and come to open manifestation, though these will only be moments of ignorance, feebleness, and rashness, to which the innermost will of man refuses

its assent, with which he stands in no alliance, and to which he does not yield an unregretted and undisputed dominion. In this connection, compare Eph. 4: 22 ; Col. 3 : 5 ; Heb. 12 : 1.—(F.)

law judges but the act. . . . Only the revealed Nomos, just because it is *spiritual*,
judges even the evil desire and inclination
itself." (Philippi.)] **But I am carnal.**
There are two Greek adjectives, both derived
from the Greek noun, meaning *flesh* (σάρξ),
and differing in form only by a single letter
and the position of the accent, yet differing
widely in sense; one is *sarkinos* (σάρκινος), the
other *sarkikos* (σαρκικός). The first means,
properly, "consisting of the *material*, sarx,"
fleshy [or "fleshen," as Farrar has it] (Latin,
carneus, from carne, flesh); the second means
"partaking of the *quality*, sarx," fleshy
(Latin, carnalis). The first is, without dispute, the word used in 2 Cor. 3 : 3, "not in
tables of stone, but in *fleshy* tables of the
heart." The second is no less certainly the
word used in Rom. 15 : 27; 1 Cor. 9 : 11. It is
not strange that words so nearly alike in form
should sometimes be confounded with each
other in manuscripts. Out of about a dozen
places where one or the other occurs, there
are five places where the readings of different
manuscripts are divided between the two, and
there is only the one place, already cited
(2 Cor. 3 : 3), where *all* the manuscripts unite on
the former of the two words. In the passage
now before us, while the text used by our
translators had the *latter* of these words, the
best critical editions, following the oldest
manuscripts [א A B C D E F G], now have the
former. And the same is true of 1 Cor. 3 : 1
and Heb. 7 : 16. Meyer [and so Alford] regards the word sarkinos as the stronger of the
two [but Trench and Farrar the weaker]
in this connection, and derives from it, as
such, a special argument against the application of it to the regenerate. [He says: "This
is the Pauline expression of 'that which is
born of the flesh is flesh.'" (John 3 : 6.) He also
maintains, as a very strong argument in favor
of his view, that the work of the Spirit, so
often referred to in the next chapter, is not
mentioned in this entire section (only in ver.
6), and the flesh is here represented, not as
warring against the Spirit, as is the case with
the regenerate (Gal. 5 : 17), but only against the
person's own weak mind or inner man. There
would be much force in this argument if
the person in question was represented as a
psychical or natural man, for such have not
the Spirit and cannot receive the things of

the Spirit. But the inner man here spoken
of has rather the character of the new man
than of the old or natural man. Does not this
person, in his mind or inner man, discern
and approve (see 1 : 28; 2 : 18; 14 : 22) what is
the good and acceptable and perfect will of
God? But this is precisely the characteristic
of the *renewed* mind. (12 : 2.) "To suppose
that the unrenewed in mind can have the
gracious purpose, will, and feelings mentioned
in this passage, is to suppose that something
besides flesh is born of the flesh." (Philippi.)
If hatred of sin, delighting in God, and the
fixed will to do right are to be looked upon
as fruits of the flesh (Gal. 5 : 20) and not of the
Spirit, we must utterly despair of understanding the Pauline theology.] But it is just this
form of the word (σάρκινος), according to the
best authorities, which is applied in 1 Cor. 3 : 1
to those whom Paul there addresses as *brethren*, and expressly recognizes as being *in
Christ*, though but babes in him. [Thus a
Christian may, in one sense, be carnal or
rather fleshen, but not carnally minded. Compare also Heb. 7 : 16, where the commandment
is called fleshen and is not degraded by the
word (σαρκικός) *carnal*.] **Sold under sin.**
[Literally, *having been sold* to sin, and remaining still under bondage to it or under
its power. From ver. 22-25, we learn that
this man, along with the enforced, unwilling
service which he in his lower nature renders
to sin, also serves with his mind the law of
God; yea, even delights in that law and
wishes to do only that which is good. He
detests any service to sin, and exclaims: "It
is no longer I that do it." Blessed, methinks,
is any person who can truly say this, even
though he himself may cry out at times: "O
wretched man that I am!"] This expression,
'sold under sin,' is the most difficult one in
this whole passage to reconcile with the application of it to the regenerate. Feeling the
full force of the objection, I yet cannot regard
it as sufficient to negative the force of all the
considerations in favor of applying this part
of the passage to the regenerate. These considerations are presented more fully in the
Appendix already referred to. [In order to
interpret rightly the above expression, we
must know to whom it relates. We might
conceive of some deeply-dyed transgressor,
awakened. like Judas to a regretful conscious-

ness of his damning iniquity, heaping upon himself "sins infinite upon infinite, infinite upon infinite;" but these words were, as a matter of fact, the confession of the elder Edwards, the holiest man, perhaps, of modern Christendom. And in this style of self-reproach and abasement the saints of God have ever been wont to express their sense of shortcomings and unworthiness. Delitzsch remarks that the spiritually-minded man feels most acutely and profoundly that he has still in himself a carnal nature, and cannot ransom himself entirely from the power of sin, and by the very fact of his accusing himself in daily repentance as *fleshen*, he shows himself to be, as to the fundamental tendency of his personality, *spiritual*. Prof. Stuart maintains that the phraseology of this chapter can, with perhaps some slight modification, be applied either to the regenerate or unregenerate, and he would modify those expressions which seemingly imply the existence of grace in the heart. We maintain, with Dr. Arnold (see Appendix referred to), that if any of these expressions of the apostle are to be modified, it should be those which charge himself with sin. We also maintain that many of these expressions, even when modified, cannot be applied to an unregenerate person without antagonizing and overthrowing all of Paul's teaching in regard to man's lost and guilty state by nature. We think that Paul himself has sufficiently modified his own statements when he distinguishes his *fleshen self* (me—that is, my flesh), which hinders him from doing what he would and forces him to do what he hates, and which is under bondage to sin, from his proper self, his mind, his inner man, which hates sin, and has delight in God and serves his law. We hold that the whole bent of his mind is toward God, and that, instead of succumbing to sin "in every instance of contest," as Prof. Stuart maintains, his real self, his mind or inner man, never in any instance yields to sin. Any such yielding must be predicated of his fleshen self, or his complex self. "It is no longer I that do it." Is such a dividing up of the human or Christian self a contradiction and a riddle? What is man in his "best state" but a contradiction and a riddle? I wonder how any Christian, conversant with his own heart, can question the applicability to himself of the

apostle's description of the "remainders" of the sinful principle or habit in our fleshen natures. "There have been endless discussions," says Farrar, "as to whether Paul is speaking of himself or of others; whether he has in view the regenerate or the unregenerate man. Let even good men look into their own hearts and answer." De Wette, on ver. 25, says: That "in the man who is born again no serving the law of sin through the flesh can find place." I grant that the real "I myself" of the Christian cannot be said to serve the law of sin—certainly not as a full description of his heart and life. But if the regenerate have not a fleshen self, which does in a measure, or does at times, serve the law of sin, we must think there is not a single regenerate man on earth. But let us see what is *not* ascribed to the person here represented. He is not described as being a psychical or natural man, who has not the Spirit and receives not the things of the Spirit of God. (Jude 19; 1 Cor. 2:14.) He is not said to live or walk according to the flesh, or to fulfill the lust of the flesh. His mind is not vain, defiled, reprobate (Eph. 4:17; Titus 1:15; Rom. 1:28); a mind of the flesh (Col. 2:18); a carnal mind which is enmity against God. (Rom. 8:7.) Instead of hating God, he hates only sin, and his will is to serve God. "The real *ego* of the man is presented before us, on the one hand, entirely separate from sin and opposed to it, and, on the other, harmoniously united and bound up with the spiritual law of God. But manifestly only the ruling, not the inferior, part of man's nature can be described as the real ego." (Philippi.) Of course, we do not read that he is in a state of condemnation, and that the wrath of God is abiding on him. Let us also look at the next chapter, where the man (now certainly the regenerated Paul) has been released, as is commonly supposed, from his former miserable dualism, has obtained deliverance from the law of sin and of death, and has experienced "sanctification." But we find even here that his deliverance is still incomplete, that his groaning is not wholly a thing of the past. The flesh still presents its claims (ver. 12); he is compassed with infirmity (ver. 26); has not fully realized the great salvation, is saved in hope (ver. 24); the body is not fully redeemed from the bondage of sin, and, though he has the first fruits of the Spirit, the groaning within him-self continues (ver. 23); yea, a groaning at times too deep and great for utterance in words. (Ver. 26.) It is marvelous how this eighth chapter is contrasted by some persons with the seventh, as exhibiting a perfectly sancti-fied believer. Elsewhere, Paul speaks of the Christian life as an agonistic strife, a warfare, and we have every reason to suppose that he had the same contest with flesh and sin that we have. He could say to the Galatians (5:17), from his own experience, that the flesh lusteth against the Spirit, and the Spirit against the flesh, and that these are contrary the one to the other, thus hindering him from doing the things that he would. A short time before writing this letter to the Romans, he tells his Corinthian brethren of his groaning, in common with other Christians, under the weight of the fleshly tabernacle (2 Cor. 5:4), and in 1 Cor. 9:27, we see him both as a combatant and a herald in the Christian race, buffeting or bruising his own body, beating it black and blue, and bringing it into subjection. We suppose that Paul, with all his trials within and without, was in general a joyful Christian, trusting wholly in Christ, walking in the Spirit, and yielding but rarely, if ever, to the inordinate demands of the lower nature. Yet any hindrance which the law in his mem-bers interposed to his desired obedience to the law of the Spirit would be deemed by him a heavy bondage. And may we not suppose that there were times in his religious experi-ence, as in ours, of special temptation and depression, when his heart became, as it were, a battle ground where Christ and Satan strove for the mastery. Our Saviour, we know, was led from the joys of his baptism to the sore temptation of the desert. Thus in this world seasons of unusual mental or spiritual eleva-tion are often followed by a corresponding depression. And we have sometimes imag-ined that Paul, soon after his conversion and baptism, was led or driven by the Spirit into the wilderness of Arabia, and that there he sat literally at the foot of Sinai and listened with anguish of soul to its condemning thun-der; that there, in good measure, took place the great revulsion of his views and feelings in regard to the law and its chiefest ordi-nances; that there he learned fully to un-Jew himself, as it were, so that we never think of

him as being a Jew; and that there, in fine, he learned that only "in Christ" is there justification, redemption, and eternal life for a lost sinner. Certain it is that many Chris-tians virtually pass a considerable part of their lives near this awful burning mount, with one eye, indeed, directed to Calvary, a look which saves them from despair. "Every Christian," says Delitzsch, "is compelled to confirm what the apostle here says from his own personal experience." And Dr. Schaff, who regards this passage as descriptive of a state of awakening, says: "Thus much, how-ever, must be conceded to the Augustinian view that this contest is repeated in a modified form in the regenerate. So long as they are in the flesh, the old life of Adam rules beside the new life in Christ. Temptations from the world, assaults of Satan, disturb; not unfre-quently sin overcomes, and the believer, feel-ing deeply and painfully his own helplessness, turns in penitence to Christ's grace, to be the victor at last."

There are certain special objections of con-siderable apparent force which are urged against the view we have taken. Those men-tioned by Godet are in substance chiefly as follows: that in this chapter there is no marked and obvious point of transition, indi-cating the profound change from the Phari-saic state to the state of grace, no such sharp contrast in the description of these two states as there is in the delineation of chapter 7 and that of chapter 8, but all proceeds, as it were, on the same level, and the difference between Pharisee and Christian is much less marked than that between Christian and Christian; that Paul in ver. 14-25 has avoided all mention of the Spirit's aid, and made use only of terms denoting the natural faculties of the human soul, as mind, etc.; and in general that our view finds in the gospel a more burdensome law than that of Sinai itself. Still, if the statements advanced in this commentary here and elsewhere can be substantiated, these objections will go for nothing or be so ex-plained as to lose their importance. As some of these objections will be noticed further on, we will here simply say, 1. That the gospel furnishes no exemption from a persistent, bitter contest and struggle against Satan, self, and the world: and that the most devoted Christian, if he knows his own heart, will

15 For that which I do, I allow not: for what I would, that do I not; but what I hate, that do I.

16 If then I do that which I would not, I consent unto the law that *it is* good.

17 Now then it is no more I that do it, but sin that dwelleth in me.

15 sin. For that which I [1]do I know not: for not what I would, that do I practise; but what I hate, 16 that I do. But if what I would not, that I do, I 17 consent unto the law that it is good. So now it is no more I that [1]do it, but sin which dwelleth in me.

1 Gr. *work.*

confess perpetual shortcomings in thought, word, and life, as also frequent failures and defeats: 2. That there is, as we have seen, no such sharp contrast in the description of man's present spiritual state in chapters 7 and 8, as is sometimes supposed: 3. That if it was Paul's design to show that by the law of works, whether legal or gracious, no flesh could be justified and saved, then there would naturally be a certain uniformity of thought and style in the discussion of the theme: And 4. That we can find quite plainly indicated in this chapter the end of the legal and the beginning of the gracious state, it being a well understood matter that when the sinner is slain by the law and is left at Christ's feet as dead (ver. 11-13), he is made alive by the Lord and Giver of life.]

15. The struggle here begins between the two dispositions within, not merely with the law without. [How great is the evil of sin which has wrought such deep-seated schism and discord in the soul, and which leads even the regenerate and redeemed man within himself to groan and sigh, and even to exclaim at times: "O wretched man that I am!" And how blinded are they who do not feel this desperate depravity of their hearts!] **For** introduces the proof of the last clause, 'sold under sin.' **That which I do, I allow not.** *Know* is better than 'allow,' not only as being more literal, but because the not allowing what is performed is implied in the next clauses, and still further, because 'I know not' expresses just that perturbed state of mind which seems designed to be expressed, as we sometimes say, "I do not know how I came to do it." ["The regenerate man sins not consciously and willingly. . . . His better *ego* knows nothing of this act of his sinful nature. From this it certainly *follows*, of course, that this higher self does not acknowledge and approve such an act." (Philippi.)] The second **for** introduces the explanation of the way in which that which is affirmed in the preceding clause came to pass. **For what I would, that do I not; but what I hate,**

that I do. The Greek might be rendered thus: *For not what I wish, that do I practise; but what I hate, this I do.* [The negative (οὐ), placed at the beginning partly perhaps for the sake of emphasis, properly negatives, as in ver. 19, not the nearer but the remoter verb, thus: 'for what I would, that do I not.' What he, the better self, wills and hates is specified below as *good* and *evil.* The verb to will or wish (θέλω) is here regarded by Godet, Alford, and others, as simply expressive of desire, or what one would like. It is doubtless sometimes used with this sense. Ellicott says: "The distinction that *boulomai* (βούλομαι) is confined to the inclination, *ethelo* (ἐθέλω or θέλω) to that kind of wish in which there lies a *purpose* or *design* does not seem generally applicable to the New Testament (see Matt. 1: 19), and probably not always in classical Greek." The *will,* however, is here as energetic as the *hate,* and is a result of the divine inworking. See Phil. 2: 13. Compare what is said on 9: 19, respecting the use of these verbs.]

16. If then I do that which I would not, I consent unto the law that it is good. This may be translated: *But if what I do not wish this I do, I agree with the law that it is good.* The law and my wish tend the same way. [*Good—kalos* (καλός)—morally beautiful and excellent. Prof. Cremer says: "It is related to *agathos* (ἀγαθός), *good,* as the appearance to the essence. . . . It is not merely what is morally good and right, but also what recommends itself by its outward appearance."] "The assent of a man, given to the law against himself, is an illustrious trait of true religion, a powerful testimony for God." (Bengel.)

17. Now and **no more** denote a logical, not a chronological sequence. Compare ver. 20, and 11: 6. *Now then it is no longer I that perform it.* See Revised Version. [A very few expositors take one or both the adverbs in a temporal sense, pointing back to a time in which it was otherwise with the speaker. So Hofmann: but now no longer do I perform

18 For I know that in me (that is, in my flesh,) dwelleth no good thing: for to will is present with me; but *how* to perform that which is good I find not.

18 For I know that in me, that is, in my flesh, dwelleth no good thing: for to will is present with me,

it, etc., which is the literal rendering. The *I*, expressed in the Greek, is strongly emphatic.] The *I* here is equivalent to *the inward man* of ver. 22. The apostle does not mean to deny responsibility: but his language, in both this and the preceding verse, implies that his personality as a whole does not consent to sin. God has planted the passions in our nature; but he has also given us *the inward man* to control them. ["He can pay no higher tribute to the dignity of the Christian's position than when he says: It is not *I* that sin." (Philippi.) With this, the true and real *I*, he proceeds at once to contrast the lower and fleshen "me" in which sin dwells and in which good does not dwell. Yet in the spirit of true Christian penitence and humility he does not care, when speaking of his sin, to say that this "me" in which sin has its home is only "my flesh." He makes this express distinction only when, as in the next verse, he would not ignore the grace of God which was in him.] **But sin that dwelleth in me** [whence the phrase "indwelling sin." Indeed, the uncials ℵ B have the compound participle, indwelling]. "Sin has taken up its abode in me as an unlawful settler." (Olshausen.) This is not said as an exculpation; but to exhibit the power of indwelling sin. It is not only consistent with acknowledgment of responsibility, but is always united with self-condemnation and penitence. [Dr. Hodge remarks that "this doctrine of sin as indwelling is irreconcilable with the assumption that sin consists exclusively in acts of the will, or even, in the widest sense of the term, in voluntary action. An indweling act is a solecism. Sin in this, as in so many other places of Scripture, is presented as an abiding state of the mind, a disposition, or principle, manifesting itself in acts." Thomas Scott says, that this "energetic language" of the apostle "seems to have resulted from the extraordinary degree of St. Paul's sanctification, and the depth of his self-abasement and hatred of sin; and the reason of our not readily understanding him seems to be, because we are so far beneath

him in holiness, humility, acquaintance with the spirituality of God's law, and the evil of our own hearts."]

18. For I know [from personal experience] introduces the explanation of the clause last preceding, 'sin that dwelleth in me.' **That in me dwelleth**—better, *that there dwells not in me:* the *me* is here explained to mean the lower carnal self, **that is, in my flesh.** [This fleshen self supposes here the existence of the correlative pneumatic ego, a spiritual self.] Perhaps this explanation is added because of the opposite use of *I,* in the preceding verse, for the better self. Be that as it may, the very limitation of the denial of anything good, argues that the writer does not intend to represent himself as wholly unregenerate. And this is confirmed by the following clause, which is given, with its negative counterpart appended, as the proof from experience, of the absence of anything good in the lower nature. [On Paul's use of the term *flesh,* see notes on 2: 5. "Doubtless," says Tholuck, "the corporeal system is the organ through which many sins are executed, and doubtless also it too often prevails over the spiritual interests to the prejudice of the individual. Still we must take into consideration that *per se* that system cannot be evil: moreover, that it does not necessarily occasion inordinate desires, some discord in the spiritual part always needing to precede, before such a preponderance of the bodily appetites can take place. Not the flesh, but the mind of the flesh is evil." Still he acknowledges that flesh, according to the *usus loquendi* of the New Testament, denotes, in contrast with spirit, "human nature as weak and impotent to good." Dr. Weiss regards it (as used in the specially doctrinal epistles) as the "expression for the natural human being in its specific distinction from God" ("Bib. Theol.", Vol. I., p. 343), but we think, with Neander, that in the Pauline system it generally denotes human nature in its state of estrangement from the divine life.][1] **For to will** [the good] **is present with me,** or *to me* [it is

---

[1] Dr. Weiss thinks the meaning of (σάρξ) *sarx* is somewhat changed in the later epistles (*e. g.*, those of the imprisonment), where it specially denotes "human nature untouched by grace in general, and in this sense it is the seat of sin." A subject, certainly, may be differently or more fully developed in one epistle than

19 For the good that I would, I do not: but the evil which I would not, that I do.

20 Now if I do that I would not, it is no more I that do it, but sin that dwelleth in me.

19 but to ¹do that which is good *is* not. For the good which I would I do not: but the evil which I would 20 not, that I practise. But if what I would not, that I do, it is no more I that ¹do it, but sin which dwell-

1 Gr. *work.*

at hand, lies in my power (De Wette)]; **but how to perform that which is good I find not.** The verb 'I find' is wanting in the oldest manuscripts [א A B C]. The abrupt negative "not" or *no*, without any verb, is peculiarly appropriate and forcible. [This reading is adopted by the principal editors, Lachmann, Tischendorf, Tregelles, Westcott and Hort, but is not favored by Fritzsche, De Wette, Meyer.]

19. For introduces the proof of the preceding negation. **The good that I would, I do not:** and the alternative follows: **but the evil which I would not, that I do.** With more literal exactness this verse may be rendered thus: *For the good which I will, I do not; but the evil which I do not will, this I practise.* [This does not imply that the person described never does anything that is good, but—as we are all obliged to confess in prayer and song of ourselves—that sin is mixed with all he does. We may remark that even Pagans recognized in themselves a higher and a lower nature, and the contrariety of the two; and though their "better self" had little of that love of God and his law, or of that hatred of sin and self-loathing on account of sin, which were felt by the "inner man," as described by the apostle, yet they expressed this dualism and self-contradiction of their natures in terms very similar to those used by the apostle. The following passages are most frequently quoted by commentators. "For clearly I have two souls," in Zenophon's "Cyrop.," VI. 1. "For when the sinner wills not to sin but to do right, it is evident that what he wills he does not, and what he does not will he does." (Epictetus, 'Encheirid.," II. 26.)

> Aliudque cupido, Mens aliud suadet:
> Video meliora proboque, deteriora sequor.

"Desire persuades one way, the mind another; I see and approve the better, I follow the worse." (Ovid's "Metamorph.," VII., 16–

18.) The last part of this quotation has been versified as follows:

> I see the right and I approve it too,
> I hate the wrong and yet the wrong pursue.

On the doing of evil by a regenerate man Philippi thus remarks: "Even when the life of the regenerate man is holy and governed by the Spirit, the uninterrupted, persistent (or, the repressed and intermittent) sinful emotions of the heart may very well be described as a doing of evil that is not desired. To this is to be added that these very emotions never remain absolutely within, but, even apart from the manifold sins of ignorance, weakness, and unwatchfulness, in which they manifest themselves, leave their hindering or polluting influence on the best acts of the regenerated one, and thus envelop even his brightest experiences, as it were, with a veil of earthliness."]

20. He comes back now to the conclusion affirmed in ver. 17, having traced the process of proof step by step. **Now if,** etc. Translate: *If, now, what I do not will, this I do, it is no longer I that perform it:* the performance is no longer the act of my true self, but of *sin that dwelleth in me.* It is the sin principle in me, rather than my inward man, my real self, that performs the evil. Such a statement as this, separated from its connection, is easily perverted to an Antinomian and profane use. But to separate it from its connection is to pervert it. In its connection it is no immoral apology for sin, but a humiliating confession of sin. [Only he who has striven with all his powers, as if for and with his life, against sin (Heb. 12:4), and still finds its remainders within him, can truly say: It is no longer I that perform it.]

In the next three verses we have a summary of the results of ver. 14–20.

21. I find then a law (literally, *the law*), meaning this rule or principle; for the sense of the word *law* here and in ver. 23, 25, last

in another, but to suppose that Paul's views on this or any other subject had materially changed, is virtually to deny that he was a divinely inspired teacher. And **Dr. Weiss'** method of examining separately the writings

of a certain class or period, while useful in many respects, tends nevertheless to ignore the comprehensive character and unity of divine revelation.—(F.)

21 I find then a law, that, when I would do good, evil is present with me.
22 For I delight in the law of God after the inward man:
23 But I see another law in my members, warring against the law of my mind, and bringing me into captivity to the law of sin which is in my members.

21 eth in me. I find then ¹the law, that, to me who
22 would do good, evil is present. For I delight ²in
23 the law of God after the inward man: but I see a different law in my members, warring against the law of my mind, and bringing me into captivity
24 ³under the law of sin which is in my members. (

1 Or, *in regard of the law*......2 Gr. *with*.... .3 Gr. *in.* Many ancient authorities read *to.*

clause, see note on 3 : 27. **That, when I would do good**—literally, *that to me wishing to do the good, the evil is present to me.* [Interpreters differ greatly in their explanations of this verse. Meyer thinks "the law" here is the law of Moses, and this view seems to be hinted at in the marginal translation of the Revised Version. He would also connect the law with the participle *willing :* To me willing the law in order to do good. This interpretation has been called "forced" and "harsh." Others have made the law the object of the verb *to do,* and have put "the good" in apposition with the law. Many commentators have this literal rendering: "I find, therefore, for me who am desirous of doing the good, the rule that evil lies by me," and make this rule equivalent to the other or different law in the members. (ver. 23.) The verb whence comes the participle *wishing* (θέλω) commonly denotes in the classics *to will,* but in the New Testament often has the meaning of to wish or to desire. See note on ver. 15. In Phil. 2 : 13, Paul ascribes the will or desire (to do good) to God's efficient working. The reader will observe that throughout this passage there is no willing of what is evil.]

In the next two verses the apostle presents again the inward conflict in both its elements, but with a stronger statement of the better side than in ver. 16, and a weaker statement of the worse side than in ver. 14.

22. I delight in [literally, *rejoice with*] **the law of God** is stronger than *I consent to the law that it is good.* (ver. 16.) [Does not the Psalmist speak of the *blessedness* of the man "whose delight is in the law of the Lord"? The two parts of this verse show that mind and heart are both on the side of God.] *The inward man* corresponds to the *I* of ver. 17, 20, but is more emphatic. Both parts of this verse, as compared with the preceding (ver. 16-21), indicate a moral progress. [The following is the substance of Prof. Cremer's remarks on the "inner man" (see 2 Cor. 4 : 16; Eph. 3 : 16; and compare 1 Peter

3 : 3, 4): "The inner man denotes not in general the inner distinctive character of the man, but the inner spiritual and divine nature of the man in its antagonism to the flesh. It embraces that which, according to various aspects, is designated by the words mind, spirit, heart, in such wise, however, that reference to the spirit predominates. . . . As it is the inner man which experiences [daily] renewal (2 Cor. 4 : 16), strengthening by the Spirit (Eph. 3 : 16; compare Luke 1 : 80), and to which belongs the approval of a life devoted to God (Rom. 7 : 22), we are warranted in regarding it as synonym for *pneuma,* spirit, as used in Matt. 5 : 3; Rom. 8 : 10, and, indeed, in such a manner that inner man denotes the spirit as reflected in the mind or self-consciousness. This accordingly decides the question whether the expression applies to the regenerate or the unregenerate man. In the sense in which both possess the spirit, the inner man may be applied to both. By means of this expression, this spirit is defined as the proper true man, after deducting that which is visible to the fleshly eye." Paul thus speaks thrice of the inner man, and in every instance it is the regenerate man. The daily renovation of the inward man is but the contrast of the decaying of the fleshly tabernacle, and Paul could just as well pray that the new man might be strengthened with power as that the inward man might be. According to Philippi, Paul "chose this expression, inner man, rather than new or spiritual man, because he wished just to show that sin is a foreign power to the believer, bringing him into bondage against his will. This he does by showing how his real ego, the innermost ground and core of his desire and being, is free from sin. Thus there was here no occasion whatever for describing this innermost ground and core as expressly spiritual. Rather, on the contrary, since in the apostle's teaching it is self-evident . . . that only that which is created in man through the Sprit can be in sympathy with the spiritual law, the only thing of impor-

24 O wretched man that I am! who shall deliver me from the body of this death?

wretched man that I am! who shall deliver me out of ¹the body of this death? ²I thank God through

1 Or, *this body of death*......2 Many ancient authorities read *But thanks be to God.*

ance was to describe this desire of the spirit in man as his real ego, his real inward man."]

23. But I see [observe as a spectator] **another** (that is, a *different*) **law**—not merely another numerically, but a *different* generically—**in my members,** having its seat in the body, not in the inward man, **warring against the law of my mind,** which is in full sympathy with the law of God (ver. 22), **and bringing me into captivity to** (or *under*) **the law of sin which is in my members.** [The apostle here mentions four laws, but they are not all essentially different, the law in the members being equivalent to the law of sin, etc. The mind (or νοῦς), whose law harmonizes with that of God, denotes in the New Testament especially the organ of moral thinking and knowing, the moral reason, and is nearly equivalent to the reflective or moral consciousness. (Cremer.) In this chapter it is used antithetically to flesh, and is equivalent to the inner man. The apostle does not here affirm that his real self is taken captive to the law of sin. On the contrary, his mind serves the law of God. "In the redeemed man," says Philippi, "sin has withdrawn from the centre of personality to the circumference of elementary nature." "It is no more I that do it," etc. The *taken captive* is, literally, "taken by the spear"—that is, with force and against one's will. "*In* the law" is the reading of ℵ B D F K and several cursives.]

24. [**Wretched,** the adjective, is found elsewhere in Rev. 3 : 17, the noun in Rom. 3 : 16; James 5 : 1, and the verb in James 4 : 9.] This lamentation, **wretched man that I am!** [he does not here choose to call himself *guilty*] is not inconsistent with the idea of moral progress affirmed above. He is now looking back over the whole struggle; the nearer one comes to freedom, the more galling is the sense of remaining bondage. **Who shall** (*will*) **deliver me?** etc. [In all languages a question is often used to denote a wish. Winer—wrongly in part, we think—here regards it as denoting "perplexity and conscious helplessness."] This question is an expression of intense *desire*, but not of despair, for the answer is near at hand. [It is not the prayer of an

awakened sinner, appealing to God's mercy for a new heart, pardon of sin, and deliverance from eternal death. Paul well knew who was his Deliverer, and he feels no need of mentioning his name. "The cry is uttered," as De Wette observes, "in full consciousness of the deliverance which Christ has effected, and as leading to the expression of thanks which follow." (Alford.) "He asks not by whom he was to be delivered, as one in doubt, like unbelievers who understand not that there is but one real Deliverer, but it is the voice of one panting, and almost fainting, because he does not receive immediate help, as he longs for." (Calvin.) In Meyer's opinion, "such sighing is merely the operation of the so-called *gratia præveniens.*"] Grammatically, 'this' might agree with 'body,' but to connect it with 'death' is preferable. [So Winer: "As the apostle had already said much of death (ver. 10, seq.), he might naturally refer to it as *this death.*] This is not an expression of positive desire to die. If the word 'body' is to be referred at all to the human body in a literal sense, it is only as the usurped seat of sin. Some have supposed a reference in this expression to the custom of chaining a criminal to a dead body, and so leaving him to drag out a miserable, lingering existence in this loathsome companionship; a very certain and cruel custom [see Virgil's "Æneid," VIII, 485, seq.]; a very forcible figure of speech, but a very doubtful interpretation. [**Body of death,** which is subject to and belongs to death. (Gifford.) "The body by which I am enslaved to this deadly power of sin." With the apostle any bondage to the flesh was so far forth a bondage to the law of sin and death. Meyer gives this interpretation: "Who shall deliver me out of bondage under the law of sin into moral freedom, in which my body shall no longer serve as the seat of this shameful death? Hodge regards 'body' here as equivalent to a weight or burden. In the Wisdom of Solomon (9 : 15) we read that "the corruptible body presseth down the soul and the earthly tabernacle weigheth down the much musing mind."]

25 I thank God through Jesus Christ our Lord. So then with the mind I myself serve the law of God; but with the flesh the law of sin.

Jesus Christ our Lord. So then I of myself with the mind, indeed, serve the law of God; but with the flesh the law of sin.

25. I thank God [or, *thanks be to God,* the MSS. here varying in their testimony. The uncials D E have—*the grace of God* (will deliver, etc.), which in this connection is very tame]. **Through Jesus Christ our Lord.** An indirect, but substantial and emphatic answer to the question, or rather *wail*, of the preceding verse. [In the fullness of his deep emotion he does not explicitly state for what he gives thanks. But any one can understand that it is the longed-for deliverance from condemnation (8:1), and from the reigning power of sin and death. Meyer says: "There is not a change of person but of scene." But in his view the person of the last verse was unredeemed and out of Christ; and yet, now the same man is in Christ; and yet, again, he is simply the man himself and out of Christ. Olshausen, Lange, Hofmann, Wordsworth, find in this verse the beginning of a gracious experience.] He has found the longed-for Deliverer in Christ, but he addresses his thanksgiving to God, as the primal source of the mercy that provided the Deliverer. Compare 1 Cor. 15:57; Eph. 5:20; Col. 3:17. [Not only is thanksgiving offered in the name of Christ, but it is implied that the deliverance has been obtained through him (so Godet; see Noyes' translation, and De Wette on 1:8), and therefore the apostle would not hesitate to say: Jesus Christ is my Deliverer from this body of sin and death.] **So then** implies a summing up of the contents of ver. 14–24. **I myself.** [I Paul, "for my own person." (Meyer.) Some prefer: "I, in my real self," which makes good sense, only we have to suppose, as I think we may, that this full subject is not to be repeated in the next clause.] **With the mind serve the law of God, but with the flesh the law of sin.** [Nothing can be more self-evident than that the latter half of this verse presents, in the words of Prof. Stuart, "a summary of the whole preceding representation." To this statement Prof. Turner—who, with Stuart, regards the preceding representation as that of an unregenerate man—demurs, and says, that to make the phrase 'serve the law of God' "denote nothing more than the full acquiescence of the mind as under the influ-

ence of reason and conscience, is harsh. To serve is to obey, to do the commands of, and will not bear such a modified signification." This is strong confirmation of the correctness of our interpretation.] The apostle closes this remarkable account of the conflict of good and evil in human nature with an emphatic profession of the willingness of the spirit to serve the law of God, and a confession of the weakness of the flesh. (Matt. 26:4.) [Something more, we think, is expressed here than the "willingness of the spirit to serve the law of God." It is affirmed that the real self, the proper man, does actually serve the law of God (which is more than any unregenerate man ever did), and this is sufficient to show that the regenerate man is not here represented as having "nothing but an impotent and fruitless will to do what is good, along with a constant performing of what is evil." That a declaration of a present twofold service on the part of the apostle—that of the law of God with his mind and that of the law of sin with his flesh—should follow the thanksgiving for deliverance is especially a puzzle to those who maintain the view which is opposed to our own. Some would enclose the first clause of the verse in parenthesis and regard the space it occupies as a blank. By some it is looked upon as a gloss, taken in from the margin, and misplaced at that. And some have gone so far as to suppose a transposition of the two main parts of the verse. Others (Alford, Olshausen, Lange, Turner) find here a thoroughly new religious experience, and would connect this verse with the next chapter. Touching the division of chapters, we agree with Philippi, who thinks "the seventh chapter would conclude better with 8:11." Certainly the "I myself" is Paul the speaker, and the tense of the verb denotes his present experience and condition. The "I *of* myself," found in the American Revised Version, is by Forbes deemed "perhaps admissible in this sense only: 'I in myself, notwithstanding whatever progress in righteousness the Spirit of Christ may have wrought in me or will work in this life, am still most imperfect; with my mind, indeed, I serve the law of God, but with my flesh the

CHAPTER VIII.

THERE is therefore now no condemnation to them
which are in Christ Jesus, who walk not after the
flesh, but after the Spirit.

1   There is therefore now no condemnation to them
2   that are in Christ Jesus. For the law of the Spirit

law of sin, and tried by the law could not
be justified, but would come under condemnation, if viewed *in myself* and not in Christ
Jesus.' " "So vast a difference is there be-
twixt a Christian taken *in himself* and *in
Christ.*" (Leighton.) Meyer contends that
the view we have advocated would logically
require a transposition of the last clauses,
thus: "So, then, I myself with the flesh do,
indeed, serve the law of sin, but with the
mind the law of God." But against this, we
may say, that the design of Paul in this chapter leads him to emphasize the power of the
law of sin in our fleshen selves—to show, in
other words, that "the best obedience of our
hands" fails to fulfill the law's demands, and
that the holiness of the regenerate, being thus
imperfect, cannot free him from condemnation. We may properly notice that, as in ver.
23, where Paul speaks of becoming captive to
the law of sin, he limits this law, as he does
not elsewhere, to that which exists in his
members; so here, where he speaks of serving
the law of sin, he limits this service, as he
does not elsewhere (see 6: 6, 20, etc.), to the
flesh alone. We remark still further, that
this unwilling service of the law of sin with
the flesh, merely, is a vastly different thing
from a man's walking willingly and willfully,
and with his entire being, "after the flesh."]

Ch. 8: ["The chapter beginning with **no
condemnation** and ending with **no separation.**" We may give as its purport: the
present and future blessedness of the justified
in Christ in its especial connection with the
work of the Spirit, or, in general terms: "the
happy condition of the man in Christ"
(Meyer), or "the security of believers."
(Hodge.) De Wette gives the following as
the general analysis of this chapter: "(*a*) Ver.
1-4. Free from condemnation is the redeemed
man who lives in the Spirit. (*b*) Ver. 5-17.
This spiritual life leads him to the life of
blessedness, to adoption as God's child, and
to participancy in the glory of Christ. (*c*)
Ver. 18-30. This future glory of Christians is
assured by a universal longing, by a hope

verified in steadfastness and prayer, and by a
firm trust. (*d*) Ver. 31-39. Thus the Christian has nothing more to fear, but everything
to hope for; he cannot be separated from the
love of God in Christ." Olshausen makes 7:
25-8: 17 treat of the experience of redemption until the perfection of the individual life;
and 8: 18-39, of the perfection of the whole
creation with the children of God. Godet
gives as the theme of this chapter: The work
of the Holy Spirit in the justified believer—
(*a*) The victory of the Holy Spirit over sin
and death, 1-11; (*b*) Freed from sin and
death, the Christian becomes son and heir,
12-17; (*c*) Completion of the plan of salvation, notwithstanding the miseries of our
present condition, 18-30; (*d*) Hymn of the
assurance of salvation, 31-39. Meyer says it
is only with the beginning of this chapter
that "the *new* scene opens of which the cry
of thanksgiving (7: 25) was only a previous
glimpse, broken off again by the 'so then I
myself.'" *Per contra:* "The apostle now
presents to us the life of the regenerate man
under its other aspect." (Philippi.) These
two aspects of the Christian's experience correspond, in a manner, to the two states of the
unregenerate above depicted—namely, that
of carnal security and that of conviction of
sin.]

Grace accomplishes what the law could not
accomplish, agreeably to 6: 14; 7: 6 and 8:
1-17. (*a*) Grace furnishes not only a justifying righteousness (ver. 1); but also a regenerating and sanctifying power (ver. 2); (*b*) the
way in which this is done is briefly explained.
(Ver. 3, 4.)

1. Therefore now marks an inference from
7: 25, first clause. [So Fritzsche, Philippi. Alford and Lange connect this freedom from
condemnation with the serving the law of God
with the mind and delighting in that law,
since a person thus serving is supposed to be
"in Christ Jesus." Meyer connects this verse
with the immediately preceding, 'I myself,'
regarded as unregenerate and out of Christ,
in contrast with the renewed now found in
Christ. But the holiest believer on earth, if

viewed apart from Christ, could not escape condemnation or stand in the judgment for a moment. Nothing, we think, will so much surprise us when ushered into the light of eternity, compared with which the blaze of the midday sun is well nigh perfect darkness, as the sight and sense of our imperfections and sins. Bengel, Godet, and Stuart go back as far as to 7 : 6 for the connection. Haldane and Hodge regard this inference as the legitimate conclusion of all that Paul had previously established. The 'therefore now' of this verse decidedly favors the view we have taken of chapter 7. It shows that the idea of condemnation in ourselves and of justification in Christ alone has not been absent from the apostle's mind; and hence we may regard this verse as a key to the right interpretation of the preceding chapter, from which in fact it should not have been separated.] 'Now' is temporal and emphatic; 'now' that a deliverance has been effected, 7 : 24, 25, first clause. [Philippi, regarding 'now' as logical, finds this idea: "now from this it follows that on those who are in Christ Jesus no condemnation falls, for in him they have freedom from sin and death."] **No condemnation**—that is, no sentence of condemnation, as in 5 : 16, 18. **To them which are in Christ Jesus.** [Condemnation rests upon the sinner everywhere else than ' in Christ.' In him who bore our curse we find a shelter where no bolt of wrath can fall on our guilty heads. "The man," says Olshausen, "is not free from condemnation on account of his subjective condition, but for the sake of the objective work of Christ which he lays hold of in faith." In the lack of complete holiness we shall need for our justification to be "found in Christ," and to have a personal interest in his all-perfect righteousness. If the whole of this chapter were like two or three verses at the beginning taken by themselves, we then might imagine that "the redeemed man is *entirely* freed from the law of sin." (Meyer.) But this is far from being the case, and this complete deliverance from bondage by the teaching of

this very chapter, will not be effected until the future redemption and glorification of these our bodies of sin and death. Much of chapter 8, as a certain writer remarks, has regard to the conflict with sin and infirmity.] That vital spiritual union with Christ which results from a living faith in him, and which secures our justification and salvation is variously expressed; sometimes as here we are said to be 'in Christ,' sometimes Christ is said to be in us (Col. 1 ; 27), sometimes we are said to have put on Christ. (Gal. 3 : 27.) These and other similar expressions (John 15 : 5; Eph. 3 : 17, etc.) all point to the one blessed reality of a true union between Christ and his people. [Compare Rom. 6 : 11 ; 16 : 7 ; 1 Cor. 1 : 30; 15 : 18; Gal. 3 : 28; Eph. 2 : 13; Phil. 3 : 9; Col. 2 : 6, etc.[1] "The churches are in Christ, the persons are in Christ. They are found in Christ and preserved in Christ. They are saved and sanctified in Christ, are rooted, built up, and made perfect in Christ. Their ways are ways that be in Christ, their conversation is a good conversation in Christ, their faith, hope, love, joy, their whole life is in Christ. . . . . Finally, this character of existence is not changed by that which changes all besides. Those who have entered on it depart, but they die in the Lord, they sleep in Jesus, they are the dead in Christ; and when he shall appear, they will appear; and when he comes, God shall bring them with him, and they shall reign in life by one Jesus Christ." (Bernard's "Progress of Christian Doctrine.")] The remaining clauses of this verse, as read in our Common Version—"who walk not after the flesh, but after the Spirit"—are not supported by the oldest and best manuscripts [א B C D* F G.], and are justly omitted by Alford, Noyes, the Bible Union, and most critical editors of the Greek text. They were doubtless copied by some ancient scribe, with good intention, but not with good judgment, from ver. 4. where they are unquestionably genuine. Here they are introduced prematurely. [For other instances in this Epistle where the "oldest and best manuscripts"

---

[1] The phrase: " in Christ " is almost exclusively Pauline, it being found elsewhere only in 1 Peter 5 : 14; 3 : 16. John, however, often uses equivalent terms. The expression " in the Lord," occurring over forty times, is found outside of Paul's writings only in Rev. 14 : 13. Prof Cremer gives some fifty examples of " in Christ " where "a peculiar union of the Christian *subject* with the Lord is treated of," and fifteen other instances " in which the blessings of redemption, God's saving purpose, etc., are represented *objectively* as all included in Christ "—Christ being "in the fullest sense the *sphere* in which both the subject and object exist."—(F.)

2 For the law of the Spirit of life in Christ Jesus hath made me free from the law of sin and death.

of life in Christ Jesus made me free from the law of sin and death. For what the law could not do, 3

give a briefer reading, see 3: 22; 6: 11; 9: 28; 10: 15; 11: 6; 13: 9; 14: 6, 21; 15: 24. The Revisers, in common with all the more recent critical editors, have, in general, regarded the briefer readings as the original and genuine ones, and so have given their preference to the oldest MSS., though few in number (especially to א B., that is, the Sinaitic and the Vatican), rather than to the later and more numerous MSS. which support our Textus Receptus.]

2. For introduces the *reason* why there is no condemnation. **The law** in its broad rhetorical sense, as in 3: 27: 7: 23, etc. [Dr. Hodge makes this 'law of the Spirit,' etc., equivalent to the *gospel* which frees us from the law and from condemnation. And he gives the following as the meaning of this verse in connection with the preceding: "There is no condemnation to those who are in Christ, because they have been freed in him by the gospel of the life-giving Spirit, from that law which, although good in itself, is, through our corruption, the source of sin and death." Prof. Turner, while adopting a different view, yet says that "The whole clause may denote the gospel as a spiritual and life-communicating system." Still this does not seem to be the most natural interpretation of these words, 'the law of the Spirit of life,' and yet if we make this verse refer only to inward sanctification, we simply assert by means of the 'for' which assigns a reason for the affirmation of the verse preceding, that our freedom from condemnation, or our justification, depends upon our subjective righteousness, a view which clearly antagonizes the whole scheme of the gospel of grace. In this dilemma, Prof. Riddle would give to the 'no condemnation' a wider reference, 'having indeed a reference to the justifying act already past, but meaning rather, the continuance in a state of justification, culminating in final acquittal and glory." Hence he adopts in the main Calvin's interpretation of this verse: "The power of the life-giving Spirit delivered me in Christ Jesus (in virtue of union to him the fulfiller of the law and the deliverer from the law) from the law of sin and death." The connection of this verse with the immediately preceding and succeed-

ing shows conclusively that the idea of a justifying righteousness is still in the apostle's thought, but that in this idea that of a sanctifying righteousness is included. In consonance with this view, Dr. Hodge well remarks that "Justification is not on account of, or on the ground of, sanctification, but it is in order to it; and therefore the two are inseparable. The justified are always sanctified. And, therefore, so far as the meaning is concerned, there is no objection to saying, that the condemnation of sin of which the apostle here speaks [next verse], includes the idea of its extirpation or destruction as a necessary consequence." **Of the Spirit of life**—not the Holy Spirit; for the word *law* would not be so suitable, if that were the sense; but the principle, or power, of spiritual life—the counterpart of "the law of *sin* and *death*," both abstract terms, and therefore furnishing an additional reason why the antithetical 'spirit of life' should not be explained as referring to the personal Spirit. [Many commentators, however, as Tholuck, Gifford, De Wette, Meyer, Philippi, Godet, Lange, Alford, do adopt this reference, regarding the Spirit as the Lord and giver of life. Compare 2 Cor. 3: 6. The Spirit quickeneth or maketh alive. Taking the word in this sense we make this law, rule, or governing power within us to be the fruit of the Spirit. "The Spirit of life is that by which the spiritual life is effected in believers," (Tholuck), "the active and animating principle of Christian life." (Ellicott.)] **In Christ Jesus.** Christ Jesus is the Lord and Giver of spiritual life: it resides in him, and is dispensed by him. (John 1: 4.) [Most expositors, we think, connect the words *in Christ Jesus* with the verb. See Winer (p. 137), De Wette, Philippi. In Christ Jesus we are freed from condemnation. In Christ Jesus we are freed by the Spirit of life from the law, the reigning power, of sin and of death.] **Hath made me free.** [Compare 6: 20–22]: the indefinite past would be more appropriate, *freed me*, referring to the time of conversion. ["Here Paul speaks of himself for the last time as representing all believers." (Philippi.)] **From the law of sin and death**—[that is, from their condemning and controlling power. The dying re-

3 For what the law could not do, in that it was weak through the flesh, God sending his own Son in the likeness of sinful flesh, and for sin, condemned sin in the flesh:

[1] in that it was weak through the flesh, God, sending his own Son in the likeness of [2] sinful flesh [3] and 4 for sin, condemned sin in the flesh: that the [4] or-

1 Or, wherein......2 Gr. flesh of sin......3 Or, and as an offering for sin......4 Or, requirement.

mainders of sin were still left to molest and weary him. (Shedd.) Some commentators regard the freeing here spoken of as being a deliverance from condemnation rather than from the dominion of sin and death. In support of this view they adduce the connection of this verse with the preceding and following, the use of the past tense of the verb, and the consonance of this idea with the apostle's general and leading train of thought. We should wish to blend the two views together. And we think there is no insuperable difficulty in supposing that the apostle's teaching in these first four verses is this, that by virtue of our Lord's condemning sin in the flesh, and through the power of the Spirit of life, we are freed in Christ Jesus, both from condemnation and from the reigning power of sin. And truly such a declaration as this, which speaks to our sin-burdened souls of deliverance from condemnation and from the dominion of sin, may well be deemed by us as a gospel above all price.] The 'law' is not that of Moses which would not be so described; but, as above, the power or dominion of sin and death. Compare 7: 23, 25. [Sin and death, closely connected as cause and effect. The nouns being of dissimilar gender, each has the article.]

3. For—explanatory of ver. 2, showing the *method* of that liberation. **What the law could not do**—literally, *the impossibility of the law*, or the thing impossible to the law.[1] What this impossible thing of the law was is explained by what follows; but he first shows why this yet unexplained thing was impossible to the law; **in that** [because] **it** (the law) **was weak through the flesh.** The flesh was the medium through which the law wrought, and having to act through this medium, it proved too weak [to conquer sin or free from condemnation. It was weak and continued so: imperfect tense. "Paul clearly affirms," says Calvin, "that our sins were expiated by the death of Christ, because it

was impossible for the law to confer righteousness upon us." On this weakness of the law, which is but the weakness of our flesh, our helplessness under the bondage and curse of sin, see Gal. 3: 21; Heb. 7: 18.] By 'the flesh' we are to understand human nature in its unregenerate state, as in 7: 5, 18. **God** (did, by) **sending his own Son.** ["Just as by 'his own' (compare ver. 32), the filial relation of Christ is described as a metaphysical one, so by 'sending,' etc., Christ's personality is described as a pre-existent one. Compare Gal. 4: 4; John 10: 36; 17: 3, etc." (Philippi.) "The pre-existence and metaphysical sonship of Christ are implied." (Meyer.)] The next two clauses explain the *how* of this sending, **in the likeness of sinful flesh;** the proximate *why* of it, **and for sin;** and the last clause the *ultimate purpose* of it—to do that important thing which the law could not do, which now at last is plainly deduced to be this, **condemned sin in the flesh.** Observe that God sent his own Son 'in the likeness of sinful flesh'—[literally, 'flesh of sin'] not *in* sinful flesh, but in the *likeness* of it. Christ was sent into the world in the outward appearance of a sinful man, subject to all the conditions of sinful humanity, except sin itself. (Heb. 4: 15.) [Christ came "in the flesh," not, as Marcion held, in the likeness of it. We bear "the flesh of sin," Christ bore only its likeness, which likeness implies his sinlessness. "He had a nature like to that of sinful men, but himself had not a sinful nature." (De Wette.) Tertullian says: "In putting on our flesh he made it his own; in making it his own, he made it sinless." His fleshly or human nature so far resembled ours that he could be and was "tempted in all points like as we are, yet without sin." So the Divine One was made or appeared "in the likeness of men." (Phil. 2: 7.) Meyer finds in these verses (2, 3) a decisive negative answer to the question whether the Son of God would have appeared as man had man not become

---

[1] This may be regarded as in the accusative, either absolute (Olshausen), or after a verb (did) understood, but more probably it is in the nominative absolute, in apposition with the principal sentence following. So Buttmann, Winer, De Wette, Meyer, Philippi, Godet —(F.)

4 That the righteousness of the law might be fulfilled
in us, who walk not after the flesh, but after the Spirit.

dinance of the law might be fulfilled in us, who
5 walk not after the flesh, but after the spirit. For

sinful.] **And for sin**—it was 'sin' that made
his coming *necessary.* ⌜'Sin' was the special
name of the sin-offering in the Old Testament,
and many (Calvin, Hodge, and others) give
it this sense here. (See marginal reference to
the Revised Version; the Canterbury Revision transposes text and margin.) But the
expression : 'for—that is, concerning sin,'
seems to have a more general reference—
namely, that the sending of the Son of God
into this world had respect to sin—that is, to
its condemnation and extirpation.] The ultimate object of God's sending his Son is now
expressed in the words 'condemned sin in
the flesh'—what is the meaning of this, and
how did he do it? He condemned sin by
breaking its power, by robbing it of its dominion, which is a very *practical* condemnation
of it; and he did this ' in the flesh,' in that
very human nature in which sin had always
before so easily triumphed : the sphere of its
many and long-repeated victories was now at
last made the sphere of its signal and decisive
defeat: yes, *decisive* defeat ; for not for himself alone did Christ condemn sin ; but his
victory over it insured, as the next verse goes
on to state, the final victory over it on the
part of all his people. In fine, this important
verse may be paraphrased as follows : "For
God, by sending his own Son into the world,
in the likeness of sinful flesh (but not in the
reality, so far as *sin* is concerned), and for sin
(the existence of sin being the *occasion* for
sending him), did what it was impossible for
the law to do—namely, broke the power of sin,
and so convicted and condemned it as a usurper
and a tyrant, and did this in the very nature
through whose weakness that usurpation and
and tyranny had been so long maintained."
[Similarly the "Bible Commentary" : "He
'condemned sin in the flesh' as having no rightful place or power there, condemned it as an

enemy to be by his help conquered and cast
out.'' De Wette says : "Thus instead of sin's
bringing condemnation to us as hitherto, it is
itself now condemned and has lost its power.''
"God accomplished the judgment of condemnation pronounced against sin, and he
did this in sin's appropriate sphere, viz., in
the flesh.'' (Cremer.) The law could condemn sin in one sense, but could not put sin
to death, nor save the guilty. "Christ's holy
life was a living condemnation of sin'' (Godet),
but his expiatory death, wherein he bore our
sins, and curse, was its principal and final condemnation.[1] Milton very happily versifies
the Pauline theology on this point in Paradise Lost, XII., 388, where he speaks of Christ's
joining "Manhood to Godhead,'' and of his
"coming in the flesh,

> To a reproachful life and cursed death.'']

4. That—in order that, the purpose for
which God 'condemned sin in the flesh'—
the righteousness of the law—the righteous requirement of the law—**might be fulfilled in us**—really, now; perfectly, by-and-
by. [The word 'righteousness' (δικαίωμα) occurs here for the last time in this Epistle.
Compare 1 : 32; 2 : 26; 5 : 16, 18. Most modern
commentators think this term, in order to
suit the context, must be here referred solely
to the work of sanctification. But the righteous demand of the law requires, not only
perfect obedience, but punishment for transgression. See 1 : 32. As in 5 : 16 'righteousness' (δικαίωμα) is opposed to condemnation,
so there is a similar antithesis here. Compare
the verb 'condemned' with its related 'condemnation' in ver. 1. That the apostle here
has reference to justification as well as to
moral renewal is also evident from the passive
form of the verb and from the preposition :
'might be fulfilled in us;' not that we might

---

[1] Prof. Shedd thus makes *condemned* equivalent to
"vicariously punished "—God thus condemning sin in
the body or person of Christ. Many refer this condemnation of sin to the removal of sinfulness rather
than to the expiation of guilt, because Paul does not
say : in *his* flesh, and because he here treats of sanctification rather than of justification. Yet Paul never
in his scheme of doctrine widely separates a sanctifying from a justifying righteousness. And, again : in

what way can sin be extirpated other than by the
death of Christ and by the intercession of a crucified
and risen Saviour? "God by the death of his Son, so
condemned sin, as by this very (expiatory) condemnation to destroy it." (Philippi.) Of course, this view
does not set aside the fact that the incarnation itself of
the spotless Son of God was a virtual condemnati⌐n of
sin in the flesh.—(F.)

5 For they that are after the flesh do mind the things of the flesh: but they that are after the Spirit, the things of the Spirit.

they that are after the flesh do mind the things of the flesh; but they that are after the Spirit the

fulfill, or even that it might be fulfilled *by us*. To suppose that any man, though renewed in mind, can perfectly obey all the demands of the law so as thereby to free himself thenceforth from condemnation and secure acquittal at the judgment, is to make nonsense of much which the apostle thus far has written. "The interpretation which makes the apostle say that we are delivered from the law by the work of Christ, in order that the complete obedience which the law demands might be rendered by us, supposes what all Scripture and experience contradicts." (Hodge.) "Only because we are justified in Christ does the sin perpetually cleaving to us no longer come into account. Only thus can the holy acts, which are the fruits of God's Spirit in those who are righteous in Christ, be called a fulfilling of the law." (Philippi.) "Christ is the end of the law for righteousness to every one that believeth." The Christian, indeed, must have personal and real righteousness, in order to be accepted of God in the judgment, or to fulfill his high calling here. We were freed from the law and have become united to Christ, not that we may indulge in sin,—God forbid!—but that we may bring forth fruit unto God. (7:4.) Yet while we strive with all possible earnestness for a sanctified life, we would not dare to present such a life as the ground of our justification.] **Who walk** [being such persons as walk, etc., the article with the participle defining a class] **not after the flesh, but after the Spirit,** whose conduct and course of life are regulated, not according to the promptings of the natural man, but according to the dictates of the Holy Spirit. "When the soul is wedded to the Spirit, the flesh follows, like the handmaid who follows the wedded mistress to her husband's home, being thenceforward no longer the servant of the soul, but of the Spirit." (Tertullian.) [See Gal. 5:16, 18, where Spirit, also without the article, denotes the Holy Spirit.[1] Dr. Hodge remarks that this "second

clause of the verse is specially pertinent if the first treats of justification, [showing that] the benefits of Christ's death are experienced only by those who walk not after the flesh. . . . In the other view of the passage, the latter clause is altogether unnecessary. Why should Paul say that Christ died in order that they should be holy who are holy?"]

Introduction to Ver. 5-17.—Justification is, indeed, necessary to the existence of sanctification, but sanctification is equally necessary to the evidence of justification. [A gospel which should speak of a justification that favored indulgence in sin would be at once despoiled of all glory. They who are justified in Christ are also renewed in heart, and would not desire to live in sin, even if they could be permitted to do so.] The justified will certainly walk in newness of life:

(*a*) Because their inward moral disposition is thoroughly changed. (Ver. 5-8.)

5. The **for** is explanatory of the last clause of ver. 4 [showing that and why there is no agreement between the two methods of walking there spoken of]. **They that are after the flesh.** Compare John 3:6. [Such are wholly fleshen (σάρκινοι), even their minds are of flesh, possessed and ruled by the flesh. (Col. 2:18.)] **Do mind the things of the flesh.** They think of, care for, strive after [Wicliff: "savor"], 'the things of the flesh'— that is, its objects of desire. **But they that are after the Spirit** (do mind) **the things of the Spirit.** Their aims and objects of desire are spiritual. [The Canterbury Revision refers the word 'Spirit'—occurring in this verse, in ver. 6, 13, and the first in ver. 9 —to the human spirit. It is sometimes difficult to determine whether, in certain cases, this word denotes the human spirit or the divine, especially as in regenerate persons the human is supposed to be acted upon by, or even conjoined with, the divine. The spirit of man, the highest part of his nature, is defined by Cremer as "the divine life principle," or "the principle of the God-related life," and

---

[1] In a telic clause or verse like this, introduced by 'that' = in order that (ἵνα), nothing is stated to have actually occurred, and hence the subjective negative μὴ is used rather than οὐ. The same is true in imperative and subjunctive clauses. μὴ, however, is regularly used with articled participles which refer to a supposed genus or class, as in 4:5; 14:22.—(x.:

6 For to be carnally minded *is* death; but to be spiritually minded *is* life and peace.
7 Because the carnal mind *is* enmity against God: for it is not subject to the law of God, neither indeed can be.

6 things of the Spirit. For the mind of the flesh is death; but the mind of the Spirit is life and peace:
7 because the mind of the flesh is enmity against God; for it is not subject to the law of God, neither indeed

by Ellicott as "the seat of the inworking powers of grace." Prof. Riddle, in Lange's "Bible Work," also speaks of it as "the point of contact with divine influences." As connected with man's body and soul, the psychical or natural man, it needs cleansing and sanctification—in other words, needs to be divinely spiritualized. In ver. 10, the spirit, as opposed to 'body,' seems to denote "our spirit." (Ver. 16.) In other instances it may be indeed regarded as the human spirit, yet as renewed and pervaded by the Holy Spirit. Meyer, however, contends that "it never means, not even in contrast to flesh, the 'renewed spiritual nature' (Philippi), but the sanctifying divine principle itself objectively and distinct from the human spirit." Yet in ver. 10 he makes 'spirit,' in contrast with 'body,' refer to the human spirit.]

6. The spiritual man cannot mind the things of the flesh, **for to be carnally minded,** to have the thoughts, cares, and aims occupied with the things of the flesh, **is death**—is spiritual death, and tends to, and ends in, eternal death. ["The minding of the flesh" (nearly equivalent to purpose of the flesh) in the marginal reference of our Common Version very well expresses the sense of the original. Rev. J. Owen, in Calvin's "Commentary," says that "mindedness," the abstract of minding, would be more correct. Some commentators use the expression—*striving* of the flesh. On pages 232, seq., of Lange's "Commentary on Romans" will be found an excursus on the Biblical terms—body, flesh, soul, and spirit.] **But to be spiritually minded** [properly, *the mind of the Spirit*, the *animus* or disposition which the Spirit gives]. To be spiritually minded is to have the thoughts, cares, and aims occupied with the things of the Spirit, with the truths and hopes that he inspires, the blessings that he confers, the dispositions that he produces. **Is life and peace.** Peace is added to strengthen the argument. Says John Howe: "Life and peace in conjunction, not raging life, not stupid peace, but a placid, peaceful life, and a vital, vigorous rest and peace. It is not the life of a fury, nor the peace of a

stone; it is a life that hath peace in it, and peace that hath life in it." Observe how life and death are defined in this verse: Life, according to this apostolical definition, is something more than mere animated existence; death is something more than the separation of soul and body, something different from the mere negation of conscious existence, or annihilation. The Scriptures cannot be rightly interpreted if these apostolic definitions of life and death are ignored. [There is, indeed, a blissful peace in spiritual mindedness, but the ground of any true and abiding peace must be found outside of ourselves, not in any inward perfection, but in a consciousness of our good estate in Christ. In Christ alone can our souls find their only true resting place. "Our heart is restless till it rests in thee." (Augustine.) Only as we are justified by faith can we be freed from condemnation; only as we are justified by faith can we have peace with God or in our own souls. De Wette says it is "wholly false" to mix up in this passage the doctrine of justification, even when freedom from condemnation is spoken of. If so, then farewell to peace. "How," asks Olshausen, "can an exposition of the Christian religious development be possible unless the doctrines of satisfaction and justification form the turning points in it?"]

The next verse is an illustration and confirmation of the first part of ver. 6.

7. Because the carnal mind. This shows the reason why 'the carnal mind'—the mind of the flesh—is death, because it is **enmity against God** [who is the Giver of life]. This is a very strong statement; it arraigns as at enmity with God every unregenerate man and woman. For this carnal mind, as the connection plainly shows, is predicated of all who have not been born of the Spirit, and not merely of those who are grosser sinners, exceptionally sensual and polluted. Compare ver. 9. The apostle immediately brings forward a plain, practical proof of this grave charge. **For it is not subject to the law of God.** It does not submit itself to that divine rule of life which is the practical ex-

8 So then they that are in the flesh cannot please God.
9 But ye are not in the flesh, but in the Spirit, if so be that the Spirit of God dwell in you. Now if any man have not the Spirit of Christ, he is none of his.

8 can it be: and they that are in the flesh cannot
9 please God. But ye are not in the flesh, but in the Spirit, if so be that the Spirit of God dwelleth in you. But if any man hath not the Spirit of Christ,

pression of friendship with God. **Neither indeed can be** [without directly contradicting its nature]. "In just so far as it (the carnal mind) exists, it evidently does not submit itself to the law of God; and in so far as it has passed away and departed from a man, it does not at all exist, so that even thus it is not subject." (Œcumenius.) If one should object that the argument proves too much,— for even the regenerate, spiritual man does not always and perfectly obey the law of God,—the answer is, that this is accounted for only by the truth of the proposition. The reason why the new man's obedience is not uniform and perfect, is the fact that [while sin does not *reign* in his mortal body, yet] the remains of the old nature still cling to him; so that the objection, in fact, confirms the proposition. "How can snow be warmed?" asks Augustine. "By making it cease to be snow," he replies. [Compare Paul's description here of those persons whose being and walk are conformed to the flesh, whose very minds are of flesh, and which, as being wholly carnal, are at enmity with God and will not submit to his law, with the description which he gives in the last part of chapter 7 of that one (himself), who though with his *flesh* serving the law of sin, yet with his mind serves the law of God and delights in that law after the inward man. Cannot any one see the vast difference? Meyer, indeed, says that "*After conversion the flesh with its striving is ethically dead,*" and he refers to 6 : 6, seq.; also to Gal. 5 : 24: "They that are Christ's have crucified the flesh with its passions and lusts." This verse has sometimes caused us to tremble, yet our hope has strengthened itself in this thought—namely, that the crucifixion of the flesh may denote a *lingering* death.]

8. So then should rather be translated *and ;* it (δὲ) is continuative [and "slightly oppositive "] rather than *conclusive.*[1] By the phrase **they that are in the flesh** we are

to understand not they that are in the body, but they that are carnally minded (ver. 6, 7), and that walk after the flesh. (Ver. 4.) [In the flesh denotes "the ethical life-element in which they subsist, and which is the opposite of being in the Spirit, and in Christ." (Meyer.)] They **cannot please God ;** since their disposition, their *mind* is enmity toward him, their persons cannot be pleasing to him. [Augustine condensed : Not they who are in the body, but they who trust in the flesh and follow the lusts of the flesh, cannot please God. What! did not the holy patriarchs, prophets, martyrs, please him ? They carried the flesh, but were not carried by it. Not they who live in this world, but they who live a life of carnal pleasure in this world, they cannot please God.]

(*b*) The Spirit of God dwells in and actuates them. (Ver. 9-13.)

9. But ye [ye on the other hand. (Meyer.)] **are not in the flesh**—that is, not carnally minded; **but in the Spirit**—that is, spiritually minded; **if so be that the Spirit of God dwell in you** [has in you a permanent home]. The indwelling of the Spirit of God is what makes the difference between the carnally minded and the spiritually minded. See 1 Cor. 3: 16; 6: 19; 2 Tim. 1: 14.] [Meyer refers the first "Spirit" to the Holy Spirit, not, with Philippi, to a "spiritual nature." The 'if so be,' *if indeed*, does not imply any real doubt, yet, according to Meyer, "it conveys an indirect incitement to self-examination." 'Dwell' in you must not be diluted to dwelleth among you. See 1 Cor. 6: 19; Gal. 4: 6. But can there be in the regenerate indwelling sin and the indwelling Spirit? Most certainly. Yet the Spirit inhabits, rules, and fills the inner or real man, while sin dwells rather in the fleshen self. And thus it is that the "flesh lusteth against the Spirit and the Spirit against the flesh, that ye may not do the things that ye

---

[1] This little particle (δὲ) occurs six times in this and the three following verses. Its exact force, according to Ellicott, " is never *simply* connective, and it never loses all shades of its true oppositive character." It often " implies a further consideration of the subject under

another aspect." In translating it we have to choose between such words as but, moreover, now, and, etc. In this verse, Paul, by means of δὲ "passes from 'enmity toward God' to the other aspect of the matter. 'cannot please God.'" (Winer.)—(F.)

10 And if Christ *be* in you, the body *is* dead because of sin; but the spirit *is* life because of righteousness.

10 he is none of his. And if Christ is in you, the body is dead because of sin; but the spirit is life because

would." Rev. Ver. Gal. 5: 17; comp. Rom. 7: 19, "the good which I would I do not."] **Now if any man** (*one*) **have not.** [On the use of the direct negative after the conditional 'if,' (the 'not' qualifying simply the verb 'have'), see Winer 477, Buttmann 345, 347; compare also 11: 21.] **The Spirit of Christ** here is the same as the Spirit of God in the preceding clause. The two expressions are equivalent and interchangeable. Compare [Acts 16: 7, in Revised Version] Gal. 4: 6; Phil. 1: 19; 1 Peter 1: 11. [To have in us the Spirit which belongs to Christ, and which he can impart, as with his breath (John 20: 22), is the same as to have Christ himself. (Ver. 10; Eph. 3: 17.) Paul here speaks of the Spirit of *Christ* because he would make prominent the *Christian* characteristics of believers. "The Spirit of God, the Spirit of Christ, an illustrious testimony concerning the Holy Trinity." (Bengel.)] This passage is sometimes used in the sense—'if any man have not a Christlike spirit, he is none of his'—a sound, Scriptural sentiment; for the object of the Spirit of Christ dwelling in us is to make our spirits like to Christ's; but it is the personal Spirit of Christ that is here meant, and not a disposition like Christ's. **He**—rather, *This man.* There is an emphasis in the pronoun used here not adequately represented by the unemphatic 'he.' **Is none of his**—that is, he does not belong to Christ, and will not be owned by him at last.

The illustration of the *second* part of ver. 6 is now taken up, in contrast to the foregoing.

10. And if Christ be in you is the same as 'if the Spirit of God dwells in you.' ["The indwelling of Christ . . . is the result of the working of the Holy Spirit on the one side and the subjective reception of man (through faith, Eph. 3: 17) on the other." (Ellicott.)] **The body is dead** — surely doomed to die—**because** (*on account*) **of sin.** See ch. 5: 12. **But the spirit is life**—has life [wrapped up in itself], and shall have eternal life, **because** (*on account*) **of righteousness** — that righteousness which is already implanted, and which will be perfected. ['Dead' (νεκρός) is often used, says Prof. Cremer, "to denote the state of men still living, and we may understand it of the state of

those whose life is appointed to death as the punishment of sin." The death referred to in this verse is physical—the death of the body, not a death *to* sin, nor a rendering inactive of the "body of sin," as in 6: 6. Prof. Stuart regards it as the mortifying of our carnal passions, the crucifixion of the flesh. But is *sin* the ground or cause of this death, as *righteousness* is the cause or ground of life? The Revisers failed to bring out the strong contrast here implied by "indeed" (μεν) and "but" (δε). It is true, the apostle would say, that the body is dead, is subject to death, must die by reason of sin, but the spirit is life, etc. Even the believer's body partakes of death, is already in a death condition, is a "living corpse," on account of his own sin and on account of his race connection with Adam. In Adam all died and all die. And as the primal ground of bodily death is Adam's sin, so the primal ground of our Spirit's eternal life of blessedness is Christ's righteousness, and not our own. (Godet.) "The eternal life is based on the justification that has taken place for Christ's sake, and is appropriated by faith. . . . The moral righteousness of life, because never perfect, can never be the ground of 'the life.'" (Meyer.) "The *ground* of life is, and remains alone, the righteousness imputed to faith, from which issues the righteousness of life, or spiritual disposition by which faith is attested and maintained. . . . To refer righteousness in this verse to the righteousness of faith is not inconsistent with referring 'spirit' to the human spirit become *pneumatic.* For the first thing the human spirit does when renewed by the Spirit of God, is by faith to lay hold on the righteousness of Christ and the eternal life which that righteousness secures." (Philippi.)] The words 'body' and 'spirit' here are to be understood, literally, of the human body and human spirit: for (*a*) the change from the word 'flesh' (ver. 5-9) to the word 'body,' is presumptive evidence of the literal sense; (*b*) the expressions, 'on account of sin' and 'on account of righteousness,' require this sense—not (dead) "to sin," or 'in respect to sin,' as in 6: 2, 11; (*c*) the following verse decisively confirms this sense, so far as the word 'body' is concerned, and

11 But if the Spirit of him that raised up Jesus from the dead dwell in you, he that raised up Christ from the dead shall also quicken your mortal bodies by his Spirit that dwelleth in you.

11 of righteousness. But if the Spirit of him that raised up Jesus from the dead dwelleth in you, he that raised up Christ Jesus from the dead shall quicken also your mortal bodies [1] through his Spirit that dwelleth in you.

1 Many ancient authorities read *because of*.

indirectly confirms the same in respect to the antithetical term 'spirit.' [It was Andrew Fuller's dying request that Dr. Ryland should preach his funeral sermon from this text.]

11. ["According to ver 10, there was still left one power of death, that over the body. Paul now disposes of this also." (Meyer.) "According to the present verse, death is to be vanquished by a gradual process, and finally to be swallowed up in life." (Philippi.) "The divine life becomes through the Holy Spirit not only a *quality* of the human spirit: it becomes its *nature* in such wise that it can diffuse itself through the whole person, from the spirit to the soul and body." (Godet.) To the natural eye and sense, the grave is a dark-looking place, and would seem to be the sad end of our being; and with such natural views and feelings, we are tempted to say: For what nothingness hast thou created all the sons of men. (Ps. 89: 47.) But the apostle never appears to have had a doubt—certainly he has never expressed a doubt—respecting our survival of the tomb. He discusses at large in one of his epistles the nature of the resurrection body, but never the question: "Does death end all?"] **But if the Spirit of him that raised up** [literally, *awakened*] **Jesus from the dead dwell in you.** We have here the previous supposition, with an important addition, 'of him that raised up Jesus from the dead'—an addition which is of vital importance in the apostle's argument, as if he had said, 'this Spirit is powerful over death, and makes you partakers of Christ's resurrection; you have in you the same power which caused Christ to rise.' ['Raised up Jesus' . . . 'raised up Christ.' "The name Jesus refers to himself, the name Christ to us." (Bengel.) Hofmann remarks that the personal resurrection of Jesus merely assures us that God *can* raise us, but his resurrection, regarded as that of the Christ, assures us that

he *will do* so actually. Godet notices the appropriateness of the term awakening (as if from sleep) applied to Christ, and the term quickening, used of our mortal bodies, decayed and dissolved in dust. According to Alford, Paul does not say shall *raise* our mortal bodies, "because it is not merely the resurrection of the body which is in the apostle's view." Prof. Stuart regards this quickening of the body as wholly spiritual, making the body "a willing instrument of righteousness." And the principal reason for his view is that the bodies of the wicked, as well as the righteous, will be raised up at the last day. This is true; but the wicked will not attain unto the blessed resurrection of the just, their bodies will not be like the spiritual, heavenly bodies of the glorified, and will not be conformed to the body of Christ's glory. Certainly the resurrection of the body must be here the chief reference. And when this quickening takes place, the body will no more be called dead, or even mortal, since it will be no more a body of sin. The apostle's language supposes that all those whom he addresses would die before the personal coming of Christ, and therefore he did not regard this coming as something to happen within the lifetime of that generation. Compare 14: 8.] **By his Spirit that dwelleth in you;** or, according to a different reading of the original text, *on account of his Spirit which dwells in you.* The two readings of the Greek text stand nearly on an equality in respect to the support which they have from ancient manuscripts, quotations, and versions. The reading *on account of his Spirit* seems to me to have strong *internal* evidence in its favor: 1, as being the more difficult reading, according to the well-known rule of *Bengel* [1]; 2, on account of the emphatic way in which the indwelling of the Spirit is expressed (τὸ ἐνοικοῦν, in place of οἰκεῖ, ver. 9, 11); 3, as yielding a very pertinent and striking sense,

---

1 We have often thought of this "rule" when correcting proof sheets, for printers, at least, are very apt to make more difficult readings. But, of course, critical editors do not accept this rule without many qualifications.

12 Therefore, brethren, we are debtors, not to the flesh, to live after the flesh.
13 For if ye live after the flesh, ye shall die: but if ye through the Spirit do mortify the deeds of the body, ye shall live.

12 So then, brethren, we are debtors, not to the flesh,
13 to live after the flesh: for if ye live after the flesh, ye must die; but if by the Spirit ye put to death

for it suggests this important and interesting thought—that it would be derogatory to the dignity of the Divine Spirit, that the bodies which have been honored as the habitations of that Divine Guest should be suffered to become the irreclaimable victims of corruption. ["Such a body God will treat as he has treated that of his own Son." (Godet.)] Finally, this reading is adopted, in their critical editions and translations, by such scholars as Mill, Bengel, Alford, Meyer, Noyes, and the Bible Union Revisers. [The reading of our Common and of the Revised Version is supported by some of the oldest Uncial manuscripts ℵ A C, and is favored by Lachmann, Tischendorf (8), Westcott and Hort, De Wette. This reading was opposed by the Macedonian heretics, who denied the personality and divinity of the Holy Spirit.] Webster gives the following paraphrase of ver. 10, 11: "But if Christ is in you, while the body is dead (inevitably subject to death) owing to sin, the spirit is life (a living principle of action) owing to righteousness; if, however, the Spirit of him who raised up Jesus from the dead dwell in you, he who raised up Christ from the dead shall also make alive (shall renovate) your mortal bodies, owing to his Spirit, which dwelleth in you."

12. Therefore (inference from the preceding verse) **brethren, we are debtors** (a positive assertion, defined afterward only on its *negative* side) **not to the flesh, to live after the flesh**—*in order* that we should live after the flesh, *if* such a relation existed. [So De Wette, Meyer, Philippi, and others. But Winer (p. 326) would treat this infinitive clause in the genitive as he does that in 1: 24 —making it depend on the word 'debtors,' in conformity to the regular phrase, to be a debtor of any one (or thing)].[1] The corresponding positive side of the assertion, as deduced from ver. 11, would be, "we are debtors to the Spirit, to live after the Spirit"; and so, for substance, the relation is completed in the last clause of ver. 13. [The flesh

has done us no service that we who belong to Christ should live for it, or according to its dictates. It is the Spirit of life which is the source of our present spiritual life, without whose influence also we have no spiritual activity, peace, or joy, and it is the ground of our resurrection life. We should, therefore, live to the Spirit, and our lives should be controlled by the Spirit. The flesh, says Meyer, "has not deserved well of us!"] Chrysostom's comment on this verse is as follows: "We are debtors to the flesh in many respects, but not in this. We owe it nourishment, care, rest, healing when sick, and ten thousand other services. In order, therefore, that you may not suppose, when he says, 'we are not debtors to the flesh,' that he means by this to abolish or forbid such services, he explains himself, saying, 'to live after the flesh'—that is, we must not make the flesh the controller of our lives."

13. For if ye live after the flesh, ye shall (*will*) **die.** If, to repeat Chrysostom's phrase, ye make the flesh the controller of your lives, ye will die—that will be the suitable and certain end of your course. The death here referred to is what Œcumenius calls "the undying death in hell." This sense is confirmed by the antithetic **ye shall live** of the following clause. [The 'shall' here is a separate verb, denoting that which is about to be and necessarily will be. The inevitable result of carnal living is death in its comprehensive sense. We must undergo *physical* death even if we do not live after the flesh. Meyer refers it only to eternal death, "the deathless death in Gehenna." According to Philippi, "death, as the consequence of sin, denotes the *undivided* idea of divine penal judgment, consisting in every kind of physical and spiritual misery. . . . Here, above all, is meant spiritual and present, yet withal the bodily and the future death." We do not see in this declaration of the apostle, as Philippi does, "a *dictum probans* for the possibility of apostasy, the so-called *amis-*

[1] But Buttmann (p. 267) says: "The infinitive with τοῦ retains its entire verbal nature and force, so that

it depends merely outwardly upon a substantive in the leading clause." (F.)]

14 For as many as are led by the Spirit of God, they are the sons of God. | 14 the [1] deeds of the body, ye shall live. For as many as are led by the Spirit of God, these are sons of

---

1 Gr. *doings.*

sibilitas gratiæ."] **But if ye through the Spirit** [not in the human spirit (Philippi), but by] the Holy Spirit, **do mortify,** *put to death* [more literally, *are putting to death ;* compare Col. 3 : 5 ; Gal. 5 : 24], **the deeds of the body,** the practices of the body, **ye shall live** [in the full and highest sense], not 'ye will live,' as a natural consequence, as in the former case, 'ye will die,' but 'ye shall live,' as an assured gift from God, promised by his apostle. This distinction between the two futures is warranted by the difference of form in the original.[1]

A third reason why the justified will certainly walk in newness of life is now added :

(c) They are children of God, not only by a formal adoption on his part, but also by a filial spirit on theirs. (Ver. 14-17.)

14. For introduces the ground of the assurance contained in 'ye shall live.' For a *test,* by which we may know whether or not we **are led by the Spirit of God,** see Gal. 5 : 22, 23. [To be 'led by the Spirit of God,' though in the passive voice, "is not to be understood of the influence of a foreign power, giving as it were its impulse from without, but it is to be considered as the element of life, as deciding the tone of character and being, so that the Spirit of God generates also, where he works, a higher heavenly consciousness, a man of God, a son of God." (Olshausen.) In view of Scripture representation, here and elsewhere, no one of us can think too highly of our dependence on the Holy Spirit for our present and eternal salvation. And how blessed are they who are led not by worldly principle, not by personal ambition, not by carnal desire, not by self-will, or by what is self-pleasing even, but by the unerring Spirit.

It may be noted that in Gal. 5 : 18 we have this same construction, to be led by the Spirit, yet 'Spirit' (πνεῦμα) there is wholly undefined and is even destitute of the article. Both there and here the Spirit is in the dative case of agency after a passive verb.] **They are the sons of God**—these, and only these. The expression 'sons of God' includes these three ideas : 1. Likeness to God. 2. Objects of God's fatherly love. 3. Heirs of God's inheritance. The expressions 'sons of God' and "children of God," though so nearly related as to be in some connections interchangeable (Rom. 8 : 14, 16, 19, 21), are not to be regarded as identical. According to Olshausen, the word *son* (υἱός) expresses more definitely than the word *child* "the developed consciousness" of adoption. Alford says that the word *son* "implies a more mature and conscious member of God's family." It may be added, that while the word *children* emphasizes the natural and legal relations of *origin* and *heirship,* the word sons emphasizes the moral and spiritual relations of *likeness* and reciprocal *affection.* [The word for child (τέκνον), in some instances, seems to be used as a term of special endearment. Paul speaks of *children* of God in ver. 16, 21; 9 : 8; Phil. 2 : 15. John uses this expression invariably, while the Synoptic Gospels have only "Son of God." Christ is always called "Son," never, "child" of God.] But however the precise difference may be defined, the words should be distinguished in *translation.* This is not uniformly done in our common English Version. The word which properly means *sons* is translated *children* in at least *six* instances (Matt. 5 : 9, 45 ; Luke 20 : 36, twice ; Rom. 9 : 26 ; Gal. 3 : 26) ; while the word which properly means *children* is translated

---

[1] The "practices" of the body are here, as in Col. 3 : 9, regarded as evil. Indeed, the πράξεις of the New Testament, like our practices, generally have an evil signification, a striking comment on our wontedness to do evil. This word in the plural is used by Paul only in these two places. Some MSS., D E F G, have flesh here instead of body, which would seem to be a correction, as sin is not so often predicated of the body as of the flesh. The flesh, however, in its widest signification, makes use of the body as the instrument of sin, and so

it becomes a body of sin and death. "The body, as the external basis of human nature which has become sinful, the organized σάρξ, is consequently subject to death as the penalty of sin, and draws down the soul with it into the same doom unless the two be separated by the renewal of the spirit, the divine principle of the soul, in which case the body itself shall be finally exempted from the penalty and made a spiritual body." (Cremer.) —(F.)

15 Foi ye have not received the spirit of bondage again to fear; but ye have received the Spirit of adoption, whereby we cry, Abba, Father.

15 God. For ye received not the spirit of bondage again unto fear; but ye received the spirit of adoption, whereby we cry, Abba, Father. The Spirit

sons a score of times or more,[1] and in one place is translated *daughters*. (1 Peter 3: 6.)

15. An appeal to their conscious experience. **For ye have not received**—that is, when ye became Christians—**the spirit of bondage,** [a slavish spirit. Compare Gal. 6: 1; 1 Cor. 4: 21, "a spirit of love and meekness"—that is, a spirit whose characteristic was love and meekness. In opposition to Meyer and Godet, most expositors take this spirit of bondage in a wholly subjective sense. Ellicott gives this rule: "Where the Spirit is mentioned in connection with giving, it is better to refer it directly to the personal Holy Spirit. . . Where, however, as in 1 Cor. 4: 21; Gal. 6: 1, the connection is different, the spirit may be referred *immediately* to the human spirit, though even then *ultimately* to the Holy Spirit as the inworking power." Meyer, on the other hand, says: "This mysticism is not in harmony with the New Testament, which always distinguishes clearly and specifically between the Holy Spirit and the human spirit as in ver. 16."] Meyer thus renders this verse: "For ye received not (when the Holy Spirit was communicated to you) a spirit such as is the regulating power in the state of slavery . . . but a spirit which in the state of adoption is the ruling principle." The word 'again,' does not imply that they had ever before 'received' a spirit of bondage, but only that they had formerly been in bondage: the word 'again' is connected with 'bondage' only, not with 'received'; **to fear**—in order that ye should be afraid. These last two words, 'to fear,' are not to be intimately connected with 'bondage,' as if 'fear' were the hard master that held them in bondage; but fear is represented as the result of their bondage. [Meyer, and so De Wette, Philippi, and Godet, connects 'again' with 'fear,' thus: "in order that ye should once more (as under the law working wrath) be afraid." "The spirit of bondage (leading) back into fear." ("Five Clergymen".)] **But ye have received the Spirit of adoption**—the spirit that characterizes dutiful children, a spirit of filial confidence, in contrast with the former spirit of bondage. (Gal. 4: 4-6.) **Whereby we cry.** [In which, or whom (compare Eph. 6: 18), we cry aloud with boldness and confidence. Paul wishes to join himself with this cry. According to Gal. 4: 6, it is the Spirit of Christ in our hearts which cries 'Abba, Father,' and so we may from this point of view regard the spirit of adoption as something objective and as correspondent to this Spirit of Christ. Godet says: "It is impossible not to see in the Spirit of adoption the Spirit of God himself." Many commentators take the Spirit (πνεῦμα) of this verse as referring to God's Spirit, who works not bondage but adoption—thus putting these two nouns in the genitive of the *effect*.] **Abba, Father.** 'Abba' [from which our *abbot* is derived] is the later Hebrew word for 'Father.' The word is used only three times in the New Testament, twice by Paul, here, and in Gal. 4: 6, and once by our Lord, as recorded by Mark 14: 36. There is a peculiar significance in thus uniting the Old Testament name appropriated to express the divine Fatherhood of God toward his people (Isa. 63: 16; Jer. 3: 19; 31: 9; Hosea 11: 1), with the New Testament name, in which, through the adoption in Christ, the relationship is fully realized. (John 1: 12.) [The nominative is often used by the Greeks for the vocative in address, but the use of the article with such nominative is rather a peculiarity of the New Testament. The repetition of the words may be regarded as the outburst of that filial affection which one who was by nature a child of wrath may naturally feel toward the great Creator who has graciously adopted him as his child. The word 'adoption' in the New Testament (ver. 15, 23; 9: 4; Gal. 4: 5; Eph. 1: 5) denotes the receiving into the relationship of children, and never the simple relation of sonship. Prof. Cremer, however, thinks the idea of "the relationship of children, based upon adoption, . . . is perhaps to be admitted" here. There is at least this difference between adoption and sonship, the former implies the latter, but the latter does not necessarily imply the former.

---

[1] Matt. 9: 2; 21: 28, *twice*; Mark 2: 5; 13: 12 (translated *children* in same verse); Luke 2: 48; 15: 31; 16: 25; John 1: 12; 1 Cor. 4: 14, 17; Phil. 2: 15, 22; 1 Tim. 1: 2, 18; 2 Tim. 1: 2; 2: 1; Titus 1: 4; Philem. 10; 1 John 3: 1, 2 = 21 times.

16 The Spirit itself beareth witness with our spirit, that we are the children of God.

himself beareth witness with our spirit, that we are

This 'adoption' supposes that by nature we are not God's own children and we cannot be regarded as true sons, nor can we truly say 'Our Father,' or 'Abba, Father,' until by adoption God shall look upon us as being in Christ, his own well-beloved Son.]

16. [The absence of any connecting particle serves to indicate the commencement of a new subject. (Buttmann, 403; see 9 : 1; 10 : 1; 13 : 1.)] **The Spirit itself**—that is, the Holy Spirit. [Some have rendered this *the same Spirit*, but this would require a different form in the original. The word for Spirit being neuter, the pronoun is likewise neuter, while the Canterbury Revision renders it as masculine, and our American Revised Version, inconsistently, both masculine and neuter. See ver. 16, 26. We cannot properly attribute sex to the Deity, but we naturally prefer when speaking of God, who yet is Spirit, a masculine pronoun as more clearly indicative of personality. The Bible Union Version renders literally—the Spirit itself. The New Testament uses both it and he of the Holy Spirit, the latter, we think, only when a masculine noun referring to the Spirit immediately precedes or follows.] **Beareth witness with our spirit** (compare Rom. 5 : 5; 2 Cor. 1 : 22; 5 : 5; Eph. 1 : 13, 14; 4 : 30; 1 John 3 : 24; 4 : 13), **that we are the children of God.**[1] *The Spirit itself co-witnesseth with our spirit that we are children of God* would be a very literal translation of this verse. ["The word *children* emphasizes the heartiness of the filial feeling." (Lange.) Meyer says: "Paul distinguishes from the subjective self-consciousness, *I* am the child of God, the therewith accordant testimony of the objective Holy Spirit, *thou* art the child of God! The latter is the *yea* to the former, and thus it comes that we cry the Abba in the Spirit. Our older theologians (see especially Calovius) have rightly used our passage as a proof of the assurance of grace. . . . At the same time, it is also a clear proof against all pantheistic confusion of the divine and human spirit and consciousness, and no less against the assertion that Paul ascribes to

man, not a human spirit, but only the divine Spirit become subjective." De Wette (and Alford, who oftentimes closely follows De Wette), disregarding the preposition in composition, renders the verb, "bears witness to our spirit." The Spirit of God dwelling in the hearts of his adopted sons may very properly be said to co-witness *with* their spirits that they are God's children. On the witnessing and sealing work of the Spirit, see 2 Cor. 1 : 22; Eph. 1 : 13; 4 : 30; 1 John 3 : 24; 4 : 13; 5 : 7-11.] This co-witness of the Spirit of God with our spirit, whereby we are assured that we are children of God, is a very important and blessed reality. At the same time, it must be confessed that unless care is used to surround it with scriptural safeguards of interpretation, it is very liable to be abused, to the encouragement of pretensions that are presumptuous and self-deceptive. The Spirit of God in the inspired word plainly witnesses or testifies what are the characteristic affections, dispositions, and habits of the children of God. See Gal. 5 : 22, 23, and other kindred passages. Our human spirit witnesses or testifies in our consciousness, through faithful self-examination, what our own affections, dispositions, and habits are. When the testimonies or witnesses of these two spirits, the divine and the human, are placed alongside of each other, there will be manifest agreement or manifest disagreement. If the former, it may truly be said that the Spirit of God co-witnesseth with our spirit that we are children of God. The joint witness of these two is a *rational*, and no less an *evangelical*, ground of Christian assurance. I do not venture to say that this is the whole account of the matter, but I think it is an intelligible account, and, as far as it goes, a true and safe account of a matter, in regard to which misunderstanding is very common, and sometimes very mischievous. [To avoid self-deception, and to be saved from fanaticism, we should always test the supposed witnessing of the Spirit in our hearts by its witnessing "in the inspired word."]

17. Heirship [already hinted at in 4 : 13, 14]

---

[1] Nouns in Greek following the predicate verb, to be, are frequently without the article; but here the word meaning children (τέκνα) does not require the articl either in Greek or English.—(F.)

17 And if children, then heirs; heirs of God, and joint heirs with Christ; if so be that we suffer with *him*, that we may be also glorified together.
18 For I reckon that the sufferings of this present time *are* not worthy *to be compared* with the glory which shall be revealed in us.

17 children of God: and if children, then heirs; heirs of God, and joint-heirs with Christ; if so be that we suffer with *him*, that we may be also glorified with *him*.
18 For I reckon that the sufferings of this present time are not worthy to be compared with the glory

follows necessarily from childship. **And if** [we are] **children,** [we are] **then heirs.** 'Children' is naturally said here rather than sons, because the word is taken up from the preceding verse. Perhaps, also, this word may be preferred in both these verses as being more *comprehensive,* including both sexes equally. Besides, it is the more appropriate word in this connection, as being more distinctly the ground of heirship, which is descent, not moral likeness or filial feeling. It ought to be noted, however, that the word *son* is used in a similar connection, in Gal. 4 : 7. **Heirs of God.** Compare 1 Cor. 3 : 21-23. Truth, holiness, and bliss are infinite in God, and the same blessed trio, though finite, are ultimately full in his children. How much of outward dignity may be included in this heirship, who can tell? especially when it is added, **and joint heirs with** [literally, *of*] **Christ.** Compare John 17 : 22; Col. 3 : 4; Rev. 3 : 21. [Some suppose that the apostle in this representation has in his mind the Roman law of inheritance, which differed from the Jewish. According to the latter, the eldest son received a double share, while adopted children[1] were excluded from heirship, and even one's own daughters, unless there were no sons, the daughters receiving only a marriage portion. Under the Roman law, sons and daughters and adopted children shared alike. We, through the grace of God and by virtue of our adoption, share the same as our "elder brother" who is "heir of all things" (Heb. 1 : 2), while in ourselves we deserve only wrath. Children of human parentage are not always heirs in this world, nor do they always inherit great possessions. But the case is different with the children of God. The idea of being a son and heir of God and joint heir with Christ beggars all description, and we may well say, "Who can tell?" We often speak or read of wealthy persons as dying rich. But he alone can be said to die rich who, though poor in this world's goods, is yet rich in faith and heir of God's everlasting kingdom.] The sufferings which be-

lievers undergo in this life are not inconsistent with their being fully justified and accepted of God. (17-30.) For—(*a*) They suffer with Christ that they may be glorified with him. (Ver. 17, last two clauses.) **If so be that we suffer with him, that we may be also glorified together.** (Phil. 3 : 10, 11; 2 Tim. 2 : 11, 12.) [The particle—usually meaning that, or, in order that (ἵνα)—here expresses *necessary* result. (Winer.) It is only through a fellowship or participation in Christ's sufferings that we can have participancy in his resurrection and glory. We desire the glory, but naturally dread the sufferings. "If," says Philippi, "God has promised to the doing and suffering of his children,—not, indeed, heaven itself, but a special reward *in* heaven,—this is not a reward duly earned and merited from a righteous Judge, but unmerited reward from a gracious Father's goodness."] (*b*) There is an immeasurable disproportion between the present suffering and the future glory.

18. For I reckon. I myself have embraced this course, being convinced that, etc. [This reckoning "really contains both *I know* and am persuaded." (Meyer.) "The word implies a careful estimate, no hasty, superficial reckoning." (Boise.) "I have added up the items of suffering on the one side of the account and the grace and glory on the other, and, having made the calculation, I now strike the balance and declare the result. On St. Paul's peculiar qualification for making this estimate [as to the future glory], see on 2 Cor. 12 : 4." (Wordsworth.) On the apostle's acquaintance, previous to the writing of this letter, with the sufferings of this present time, see 2 Cor. 11 : 23-33. Yet he deems these sufferings, when contrasted with an eternal weight of glory, to be but a light and momentary affliction. (2 Cor. 4 : 17.)] **That the sufferings of this present time** [point of time] **are not worthy to be compared with the glory which shall be revealed in us** [which shall come upon us (εἰς ἡμᾶς) from without. (Meyer.) "The glory not merely

---

[1] It is doubtful, however, whether the Jews were acquainted with any proper adoption. Save in Paul's writings (8 : 15; 9 : 4; Gal. 4 : 5; Eph. 1 : 5), there is no υἱοθεσία, adoption, in all the Holy Scriptures.—(F.)

19 For the earnest expectation of the creature waiteth for the manifestation of the sons of God.

19 which shall be revealed to us-ward. For the earnest
expectation of the creation waiteth for the revealing

appearing to us, passing before our eyes, but
entering into us, so that we share it, are transformed into the same glory." (Boise.) Prof.
Boise, we may add, generally seeks to make
this preposition express some degree of within-
ness]. This 'glory' is the future state of acknowledged perfection which God designs for
men, as in 2 : 7 [compare 1 Peter 5 : 4]. 'Shall
be revealed' [not immediately, but in the
future] in contrast with this present time.
[This contrast of future glory with present
sufferings is strongly expressed by the emphatic position of the word translated 'which
shall be revealed' at the beginning of the
clause.] See the same thought, expressed
with even greater emphasis, in 2 Cor. 4 : 17.
The like thought is beautifully expanded by
Bernard, as quoted by Tholuck, "Commentary
on Romans," Vol. II., p. 85, Clark's English
edition : "Non sunt condignæ passiones hujus
temporis ad præteritam culpam, quæ remitti-
tur, ad præsentem consolationis gratiam, quæ
immittitur, ad futuram gloriam quæ promit-
titur." "The sufferings of the present time
are not worthy to be compared with the past
guilt which is *r*emitted, with the present grace
of consolation which is *im*mitted, with the
future glory which is *pr*omitted." Let the
barbarous literalness of the English be pardoned. It is necessary, in order to show the
peculiarity of the Latin.

The greatness of that future glory is seen,
(*a*) in the longing desire for its coming which
pervades all nature (ver. 19-22) ; (*b*) in the similar desire of believers, notwithstanding the
happiness which they enjoy in the present
foretastes of that glory. (ver. 23-25.)

19. For introduces the proof of the transcendent nature of this glory, [or as De Wette
and Meyer think, of the "*certainty*" of that
future manifestation." The present unsatisfied
longing of the whole creation supposes a better
state in which this longing will be satisfied.]
The earnest expectation — the word so
translated is a very expressive one, used only
here and in Phil. 1 : 20. It is borrowed from
that upward and forward movement of the

head which is the natural attitude of eager
expectancy. [Godet defines it as "a waiting
with the head raised and the eye fixed on
that point of the horizon from which the expected object is to come." See also Ellicott
on Phil. 1 : 20. According to De Wette and
Meyer, it is a *waiting* expectation rather than
an anxious one.] **Of the creature**—or, better, as translated in ver. 22, *of the creation*.
This word is very variously explained. We
simply remark here, that we understand by
it all animate and inanimate nature, as distinguished from mankind, referring to Appendix E, for the vindication of this sense of
the word. [This interpretation is adopted by
most commentators,[1] and yet we feel a difficulty in thus excluding mankind from the
groaning creation. We know that the ground
was cursed for man's sake, and though we
call this earth beautiful and fair, it is yet sin-
cursed.

> Some flowrets of Eden (we) still inherit,
> But the trail of the serpent is over them all.

We may suppose that this world was made a
world of death, and that animals from the
very first—ages though it be before man was
created—were endowed with decaying mortal
bodies, on account of sinning and dying man.
It may be deemed fitting that a world inhabited by sinful mortals should partake of
unrest, decay, dissolution. We may deem
that earthquakes, tornadoes, thunder-tem-
pests, and other like fearful and destructive
natural phenomena belong properly to a
world or world-system of disharmony and
sin. We are told indeed that lightning, for
example, purifies the air and is therefore a
blessing. Yes; but we are glad to think that
the air of heaven will need no purifying.
We also may hold it fitting that this material
creation, this earth, steeped as it has been
with man's pollution, tears, and blood, should
be burned up, renovated, and made a "new
earth." But how can *man* be excluded from
the "whole creation"? As Forbes says:
"Omit man—the animating centre of the

[1] Substantially by De Wette, Meyer, Philippi, Godet,
Alford, Hodge, Boise, and others. Some, as Dr. Ripley,
think especially of **sentient irrational creation**, or

animals ; Augustine and Turretine of men not yet believers, while some, as Chrysostom, Calvin, and Fritzsche, think only of inanimate creation.—(F.)

whole—and with what propriety could we speak of the creation or creature being made subject *willingly* or '*not willingly* to vanity'? *hoping* for deliverance? *waiting* 'for the manifestation of the sons of God?'" That we now sin willingly and willfully is no proof that the subjection of our race to vanity, decay, and death was of our choice. And cannot an 'earnest expectation' be better predicated even of wicked men, in their present state of disquietude and wretchedness, groaning under the burden of sin and longing in their inmost souls for something better,[1] than of the brute and material creation? Besides, does not the apostle's statement suppose that the creation eventually is to share, not only in some general deliverance at the revelation of the sons of God, but is to share the same deliverance which these experience, and is to be introduced even "into the liberty of the glory of the children of God"? The apostle elsewhere says that the fullness of the Gentiles should be brought in and all Israel should be saved, and hence he can assert, generally, that the creation (of mankind) shall be freed from the bondage of corruption, and shall enjoy the liberty of the glory of God's children. Dr. Gifford, who defines the word translated 'creature' as "the irrational creation, animate and inanimate," yet says that "Mankind, therefore, so far as they fulfill their proper destiny, in accordance with the great promise, 'in thy seed shall all the nations of the earth be blessed,' are all included among 'the sons of God.'" And the phrase "*ourselves also, which have the first fruits of the Spirit*" (ver. 23), naturally implies a contrast, not so much with material creation, stone and earth, or with brute creation, as with human kind who even in their rebellion against God do bitterly experience the unrest and misery of sin, as also the vanity of all earthly things. "The creation was made subject to vanity," and the heart language of every worldling since the days of fallen Adam is "vanity of vanities! all is vanity." "The whole creation" in Mark 16: 15 (compare Col. 1: 23 and Ellicott thereon) to whom the gospel should be preached, is mankind in general, and so if the whole creation here refers to mankind generally this does not hinder the distinguishing a part (those who have the first fruits of the Spirit) from the whole. "Where is the impropiety," asks Forbes, "in drawing a distinction between creation (including all mankind) as a whole, and those who, from their privileges and hopes, might be supposed exempted from the sufferings and distress common to all others?" Prof. Stuart on ver. 22, 23, says: "Not only have mankind in all ages down to the present hour been in a frail and suffering state, but even we," etc. "The whole human race has sighed and sorrowed together, until the present time. . . . But suppose now that the *natural* world is here represented as sighing and sorrowing . . . because it waited for its renovation, . . . was this a thing so *familiar* to all that the apostle could appeal to it by saying: *we know*"? Prof. Stuart thus refers "the creation" to mankind generally, as also Prof. Turner, and in this interpretation they essentially follow Augustine, J. Lightfoot, Turretin, etc. Some few (as Albert Barnes) refer it to Christians collectively. Olshausen, on the other hand, holds that the apostle extends his look over the *whole creation* inclusive of man, or at least of mankind out of Christianity. This also seems to be the view of Lange, Forbes, and Schaff. The latter says: "The whole creation rational as well as irrational, not yet redeemed, but needing and capable of redemption, here opposed to the new creation in Christ and in the regenerate. The children of God appear, on the one side, as the first fruits of the new creation, and the remaining creatures on the other, as consciously or unconsciously longing after the same redemption and renewal. This explanation seems to be the most correct one. It most satisfactorily accounts for the expressions: expectation, waiting, groaning, not willingly, and, the whole creation." While favorably inclined to this view, we must yet think that the apostle has the creature man chiefly in mind, otherwise he could not speak as he has without qualification of creation's sharing in the future glory of God's children.] **Waiteth for the manifestation** [in glory—literally, *the apocalypse*] **of the sons of God.** 'Awaits the

[1] Even a heathen Cicero could exclaim: "Oh, glorious day! when I shall depart to that divine company and assemblage of spirits, and quit this troubled and polluted scene." (De Senectute, ch. xxiii.)–·(F.)

20 For the creature was made subject to vanity, not willingly, but by reason of him who hath subjected *the same* in hope;

20 of the sons of God. For the creation was subjected to vanity, not of its own will, but by reason of him 21 who subjected it, [1] in hope that the creation itself

1 Or, *in hope; because the creation, etc.*

revelation' (the same verb and the same noun are used in 1 Cor. 1 : 7 of the manifestation, or revelation—there translated coming—of our Lord Jesus Christ. Compare 1 John 3 : 2.) [The verb [1] denotes the receiving of something out of the hands of one who extends it toward us from afar. (Godet.) Respecting this manifestation of the sons of God with Christ in glory, see Col. 3 : 4.]

20, 21. The ground of this longing. **For the creature was made subject to vanity** —that is, to instability, liability to change and decay. [Meyer says this 'vanity,' nothingness, "indicates here the empty—(that is, as having lost its primitive purport, which it had by creation) *quality of being*, to which 'the creation' (all nature) was changed from its original perfection. . . . The reference [as by De Wette] to an original 'vanity' introduced even by the act of creation is historically inappropriate (Gen. 1 : 31), and contrary to 'not willingly,' etc., which supposes a previous state *not* subject to vanity." According to Forbes, the expression : 'made subject to vanity,' " would seem specially to point to the doom pronounced on *man :* 'Dust thou art and unto dust shalt thou return,' and which is embodied in the very name of its first victim *(Abel = vanity)*." Professors Stuart and Turner refer this vanity to the frail, decaying, dying state of man. The apostle speaks of it further on as "the bondage of corruption." The noun occurs elsewhere in Eph. 4 : 17; 2 Peter 2 : 18. Trench remarks that this word is altogether strange to profane Greek (though the adjective form is used), and that the "heathen world was itself too deeply and hopelessly sunken in 'vanity' to be fully alive to the fact that it was sunken in it at all." If this 'vanity' be referred to the irrational creation, then we say with M. Reuss, " Everywhere our eyes meet images of death

and decay; the scourge of barrenness, the fury of the elements, the destructive instincts of beasts, the very laws which govern vegetation, everything gives nature a sombre hue."]

Not willingly—all these three expressions, ' was made subject' (passive), 'vanity' (not sin), 'not willingly' (without any fault [choice?] on its own part), confirm our interpretation of the word 'creation'; for they are not such expressions as would naturally be predicated of a free, intelligent, responsible, moral being, whose misery was the result of his own guilty choice of evil in preference to good. ' Was made subject to vanity.' When? At the fall of man. (Gen. 3 : 17, 18.) **But by reason of him**—but on account of him; the antithesis of 'not willingly'—**who hath subjected the same**—that is, God : the subject is assumed as well known; if it were any other than God, some explanation would be needed. [Yet some, as Chrysostom, Tholuck, suppose Adam is here referred to, while Hammond suggests the name of Satan, the prince of this world, and Godet hesitates between these two interpretations.[2]] **In**—[literally : *upon*] **hope**—it was not to a hopeless, unlimited doom, that the creation was made subject: the explanation immediately follows. [' Was subjected to vanity' . . . 'upon (or, in) hope.' "Surely this expression must compel us to see that *man* is he whom the apostle hitherto, down to ver. 22, has principally in his mind. . . . *Man in general*, we say ; for what else prepared the innumerable multitudes of the heathen, converted by the preaching of the apostles, to listen to the gospel, but the sickening experience they had had of the vanity to which they were left, and the bitter fruits they had reaped from sin? Shut out here, as the prevalent interpretation does, the Gentiles and the great body of the unconverted,[3] and what a strange

[1] Ἀπεκδέχεται, compounded of the verb δέχομαι, *to receive*, and two prepositions—ἀπὸ *from*, ἐκ, *out of.*

[2] Winer refers this subjection to the " will and command of God "—(διὰ with the accusative)—yet is of opinion that Paul intentionally avoided using διὰ with the genitive (equivalent to *God subjected it*), as " Adam's

sin was the proper and direct cause of the ' vanity.' " —(F.)

[3] The groaning of the " unconverted " and their sighing, involuntary and unconscious though it be, for something better, is well expressed by the misanthropic Byron (" Childe Harold's Pilgrimage," IV., CXXVI.):

21 Because the creature itself also shall be delivered from the bondage of corruption into the glorious liberty of the children of God.

22 For we know that the whole creation groaneth and travaileth in pain together until now.

also shall be delivered from the bondage of corruption into the liberty of the glory of the children of God. For we know that the whole creation groaneth

23 and travaileth in pain [1] together until now. And

---

1 Or, *with us*.

---

omission is attributed to St. Paul! . . . The *natural, material* world is brought into marked prominence, but the world of perishing *men* is left out!'' (Forbes)] **Because** [in the Revised Version, *that*, expressing not the reason of the hope but its substance] **the creature itself also**—this expression (especially the words *itself* and *also*) intimates a descending from the more to the less noble, which accords with what follows—**shall be delivered from the bondage of corruption** (and admitted) **into the glorious liberty of the children of God.** [" The *freedom* [from decay and death] is described as consisting in, belonging to, being one component part of, the glorified state of the children of God." (Alford.) So *corruption* is in the genitive of apposition, indicating that the bondage consists in corruption. It is obvious to remark that general expressions relating to the restoration or future glorification of the creation or of all things (2 Cor. 5 : 19 ; Eph. 1 : 10 ; Col. 1 : 20), are sometimes to be limited, as is evident from such passages as Matt. 17 : 11, "Elijah indeed cometh, and shall restore all things." Revised Version.] There seems to be here a pregnant intimation, that the inanimate and irrational creation is to participate, in some unexplained way, and in such degree as its nature allows, in the future glory of God's redeemed people. We shall find this intimation confirmed in the following verse. [In accordance with this view is the remark of Bengel: " Misfortunes have accrued to the creature from sin ; reparation will accrue to the creature from the glory of the sons of God." In Godet's view the inanimate and irrational creation will participate not in the glory, but only in the liberty of the glory of God's children. But as their bondage was corruption, so the freedom into which they will be introduced will consist in their participation in the glory of

the children of God. Whatever this creation is, it will be glorified in the same manner as the children of God will be glorified, and this supposes that the creation chiefly referred to, or "mankind in general," will yet become children and heirs of God. Even Meyer concedes that the creation will participate in a glory like that of God's children.]

22. For introduces the proof of what is affirmed in ver. 21. 'For' the groaning and travailing in which all nature unites cannot be without a meaning and an aim. It presupposes and heralds a coming deliverance, and so **we know that** such a deliverance is predestined. [So Meyer, while, in De Wette's view, Paul would prove the affirmation of ver. 19, 20 by appealing to a generally conceded truth.] **The whole creation groaneth and travaileth in pain together.** All the parts of this complex creation *unite* (this is the meaning of 'together') in this sad utterance. A bold and impressive figure of speech. That last verb, 'travaileth,' suggests, as do other prophetic Scriptures, the birth [with its attendant suffering] of a *new creation*. See Isa. 65 : 17 ; 66 : 22 ; Matt. 19 : 28 ; Acts 3 : 21 ; 2 Peter 3 : 13 ; Rev. 21 : 1, 5. **Until now.** This expression strengthens our interpretation, for it would not be appropriate if referred to the sufferings of Christians ; it points *too far back* to a state of things that has *long* existed. [The connection of earth's sorrows and of earth's redemption with 'the whole creation,' if taken in a literal sense, lies beyond our present comprehension. In our finiteness, who can understand and explain the universe? Compared with this illimitable universe, this world is less than a speck of dust, and we that creep upon earth's surface are as nothing. It seems to us almost like vanity, and like acting the part of the fly in the stage coach, to suppose that our little selves are of much

---

Our life is a false nature—'tis not in
The harmony of things—this hard decree,
This uneradicable taint of sin,
This boundless Upas, this all-blasting tree,
Whose root is earth, whose leaves and branches be

The skies which rain their plagues on man like dew,
Disease, death, bondage, all the woes we see,
And worse, the woes we see not, which throb through
The immedicable soul, with heart-aches ever new.
—(F.)

23 And not only *they*, but ourselves also, which have *the* firstfruits of the Spirit, even we ourselves groan within ourselves, waiting for the adoption, *to wit*, the redemption of our body.

not only so, but ourselves also, who have the first-fruits of the Spirit, even we ourselves groan within ourselves, waiting for *our* adoption, *to wit*, the re-

consequence in the universe, or that the universe is so much affected by our misdeeds and sufferings, and by what our Saviour has done and will do for us in the matter of our redemption. What is man that the infinite Creator and the whole creation should be mindful of him or interested in him? Yet the Scriptures lead us to believe that the interest of creation is centred around, and that, to some extent, its welfare is dependent upon, the one great event for the created universe; namely, the redemption of this earth by the Lord of Glory, together with the eternal glorification of the redeemed. See especially Col. 1 : 20; Eph. 1 : 10.[1] In Chalmers' "Astronomical Discourses," our readers will find much interesting speculation on a supposed connection of earth's redemption with the interests of the universe. See also Andrew Fuller's "The Gospel its own Witness," Part II., Chapter V.]

23. And not only they, but ourselves also, which have, etc. (literally, *having*)— that is, not only does the whole creation groan and travail together. It will be observed that the word 'they' is not in the original. ["The text here (ver. 23) is in inextricable confusion, but the sense very little affected." (Alford.) Some readings seem to make a distinction between those having the Spirit and 'ourselves.' According to Meyer, "The participle *having*, without the article, is fatal to every reference to subjects of two sorts."] 'But ourselves also,'—that is, Christians,—**which have the firstfruits of the Spirit.** 'First-fruits,' in distinction from subsequent gifts of the Spirit to later Christians, because it was a special privilege of the *earliest* Christians to receive that Spirit first. But this does not imply anything in the *quality* of the gift superior to that communication of the Spirit which all Christians shared in common.

[Some—as Bengel, Winer, Godet—regard the Spirit as in the genitive of apposition (as in the phrase: earnest of the Spirit), making the Spirit equivalent to the first fruits of God's gracious gifts. Usage, however, seems to require the genitive partitive, "as is involved in the very meaning of first fruits. Compare 16 : 5; 1 Cor. 15 : 20; 16 : 15; James 1 : 18." (Meyer.) But we need not suppose, as Dr. Arnold and many others—Olshausen, Meyer, Gifford, Turner—have done, that the apostle has reference here to the reception of the Spirit by the "*earliest* Christians," but may rather regard—with Tholuck, Philippi, and others—this first fruits (ἀπαρχή) of the Spirit as the *first part* of a subsequent "full harvest of spiritual blessings." The gift of the Spirit is here regarded as an earnest or pledge of the fullness of the Spirit's blessings which is yet to be imparted. Compare Eph. 1 : 14; 2 Cor. 1 : 22.] **Groan within ourselves.** Not groaning before men, but in the recesses of our own hearts, known only to God. ["The reader will not fail to recognize in this passage the very lamentation that is uttered elsewhere: 'O wretched man that I am! who shall deliver me from the body of this death?'" (Chalmers.) Compare the groaning utterances of 2 Cor. 5 : 2, 4, penned but a short time before writing this Epistle. In the reflexive pronoun rendered 'ourselves,' the third person plural is used for the first. This interchange of the third person for the first and second persons plural is a somewhat frequent usage in the New Testament, and is found in Greek authors. (Winer, 150.)] **Waiting for** ["expecting in full" (Boise)] **the adoption**[2] [in its full manifestation], **to wit, the redemption of our body.** The emancipation [not from our body, but] of our body from the defects and disadvantages of its earthly condition ["from sufferings and sins,

---

[1] Ellicott, on Col. 1 : 20, thus remarks: "*How* the reconciliation of Christ affects the spiritual world, . . . we know not and dare not speculate. This, however, we may fearlessly assert,—that the efficacy of the sacrifice of the Eternal Son is infinite and limitless, that it extends to all things in earth and heaven, and that it is the blessed medium by which, between God and his

creatures, whether angelical, human, animate, or inanimate, peace is wrought."—(F.)

[2] D F G omit the word 'adoption,' which, perhaps, was regarded as already possessed, and hence was inappropriate here. The article is probably omitted on account of its "connection with an apposition" (Winer., or "on account of its preceding its verb for emphasis' sake." (Alford.)—(F.)

24 For we are saved by hope: but hope that is seen is not hope: for what a man seeth, why doth he yet hope for?
25 But if we hope for that we see not, *then* do we with patience wait for *it*.

24 demption of our body. For [1] in hope were we saved: but hope that is seen is not hope: [2] for who [3] hopeth
25 for that which he seeth? But if we hope for that which we see not, *then* do we with [4] patience wait for it.

1 Or, *by*......2 Many ancient authorities read *for what a man seeth, why doth he yet hope for ?*......3 Some ancient authorities read *awaiteth*......4 Or, *stedfastness.*

from Satan and from death"] at the resurrection, and its transformation into the likeness of Christ's glorious body, will be the crowning act of our redemption and the crowning proof of our adoption. (1 Cor. 15:26, 54.) ["Beloved, now are we children of God (that is, have received the adoption), and it is not yet made manifest what we shall be. We know, that if he shall be manifested we shall be like him" (1 John 3:2, Revised Version), and the bodies of our humiliation shall be fashioned anew so as to be conformed to the body of his glory. (Phil. 3:21.) The Scriptures regard it as no light matter that our bodies have been made instruments of sin and have been subjected to disease, decay, death, and corruption. Some persons speak lightly of death, but the Scriptures never do this, neither can we when we feel at all the solemnity of so great and so untried a change, coming home to us personally and taking us, as it were, all to pieces; when, moreover, we realize how deep and universal is the dread of death or "dread of something after death," or when we think of the physical pains and mental agonies, the sad changes and disappointments, the tie sunderings and the tears, which are the accompaniments of death. To the true believer, death has, indeed, lost its chiefest sting, and it will be to him a gain. Still, death is sent upon all men as a punishment for sin, and is in itself a fearful and dreaded enemy. And there is enough of the bitterness of death remaining even to the Christian, for it still to be regarded as an enemy. And so, in one sense, the poet's words are true:

> Not all the preaching since Adam
> Has made Death other than Death.

How glorious will it be when we shall have passed safely beyond its power; yea, when Death itself, the last enemy, shall be brought to nought, and our bodies shall be fully and forever redeemed from the bondage of Satan and from the effects of sin!]

24. For we are saved by hope. 'For' points to the ground of their awaiting the adoption—namely, that its full consummation

is yet in the future, and therefore an object of expectation: For in hope we were made partakers of salvation [and "by hope the Christian can even now regard himself as saved." (Weiss.)] The verb is in the *past* tense. "Hope is, in fact, faith in its prospective attitude." (Tholuck.) (Heb. 11:1.) [The Canterbury Revision retains the *by* of our Common Version. "The dative, not of the means, but of the manner." (Bengel.) That is, we were saved, not by hope, but in hope. "In general," says Meyer, "Paul specifically distinguishes faith and hope, while he always bases salvation only on faith."] **But hope that is seen** [that is, whose object is before our eyes and within our grasp] **is not hope. For what a man seeth, why doth he yet hope for?** The nature of hope involves our patiently waiting for the good hoped for. "*With* vision, hope is needless." (Bengel.) The little word translated 'yet' (literally: and, also, even), when connected—as here—with an interrogative, conveys a sense of the utter superfluity of the thing. [The Revisers' text, it will be seen, reads somewhat differently.]

25. But if we hope for that we see not. [The verb 'see not,' as also 'seeth' in the preceding verse, is made emphatic in the original by its position at the head of the clause.] **Then do we with patience wait for it.** 'Patience,' or endurance, is the state in which and through which this waiting takes place. [The verb 'wait' refers back to the participle 'waiting' in ver. 23.] The preposition translated 'with' is more usually and more exactly translated *through*; the conception seems to be of a local character, in accordance with the most literal primitive sense of the word through, the time of waiting being regarded as an intervening space between the first expectation and the full fruition of the object hoped for. Compare note on 2:27. [See also Heb. 12:1: Let us through patience run the race set before us. Winer makes these expressions refer to "the state of mind in which one does something," thus retaining some

26 Likewise the Spirit also helpeth our infirmities: for we know not what we should pray for as we ought:

26   And in like manner the Spirit also helpeth our infirmity: for we know not how to pray as we

idea of instrumentality. The present tense of these verbs denotes that which is continued or habitual,—we hope, or are hoping; we wait for it, or "we continue expecting it in full." (Boise.)]

(c) Suitable spiritual supports are afforded them while these sufferings continue. (Ver. 26, 27.)

26. "The progress of thought is simple. If we hope for that we see not, then the matter stands with us (1) on the footing that we with patience wait, but likewise (2) on the footing that the Spirit helps us. The *likewise* introduces *a symmetrical corresponding relation*, which is *added*, on the *divine* side, *to our waiting*." (Meyer.) ["As the apostle had passed from the groaning of universal nature to that of the children of God, he now rises from the latter to that of the Holy Spirit himself." (Godet.)] **Likewise the** (Holy) **Spirit also helpeth our infirmities** (joins his activity with our weakness) in waiting for final redemption. The absence of adequate power in ourselves for this patient waiting is plainly implied.[1] Alford: "The Spirit helps our weakness,—helps us who are weak." The singular, infirmity, is doubtless the correct reading, being supported by the uncials ℵ A B C D. **For we know not** [literally, *for the what we should pray as it is proper, we know not*. The neuter article at the head of this clause gives it a "substantival character," and renders it more prominent. (Winer, 109.) On the use of the interrogative subjunctive, see Winer, 299.] 'For' assigns the reason why the Spirit intercedes. **As we ought.** "According to the present and ever-varying needs" would be a good paraphrase for the brief but comprehensive Greek phrase. Illustrations of the truth of the proposition here stated are abundant. For example: Abraham interceding for Sodom (Gen. 18 : 23-33); Moses for permission to enter Canaan (Deut.

3 : 23-27); Paul for the removal of the thorn in the flesh (2 Cor. 12 : 8, 9); Augustine's mother, that her son might not go to Rome (yet his going there led to his going to Milan, where he was converted). It was a saying of Pythagoras, that "men ought not to pray for themselves on account of their not knowing what is expedient for them." [The soul of our Redeemer, as we read in John 12 : 27, was once troubled or perplexed in regard to the definite object which should be prayed for. Yet whatever his desired petition might have been, he was always enabled to add: "Father, glorify thy name," and "Not my will but thine be done." Should not every right prayer be accompanied by these words? Certainly the Spirit 'helpeth' our infirmity, and though it is not here supposed that he gives us words to speak, yet it is possible that he may at times "indite" our petitions and give us assurance that they will be fully answered. Yet I think that these cases are of rare occurrence, and that the Christian is seldom assured by the Spirit that the bringing to pass of his will would be best for him or for others, or would be the most for God's glory, and that his prayers will thus be answered to the letter. We know of no test that will enable us uniformly to distinguish between the Spirit's assurance and mere self-assurance. We do know that many most devoted Christians have been deceived on this point. They have firmly believed, they have had full assurance, yet God has not answered their prayers in the way and form desired. How much better to leave the answer of our petitions with God, who, knowing what is best, will do for us what is best! Indeed, it would seem to be supremely selfish for the believer to desire that his will should always be regarded in heaven, or to feel that his prayers (save as he says, "Thy will be done") must always be answered to the very letter.][2]

---

[1] "The verb," says Godet, "is one of those admirable words easily formed by the Greek language: λαμβάνεσθαι (middle), to take a burden on oneself: σύν, *with* some one; ἀντί, *in his place*. So: To share a burden with one with the view of easing him. Compare Luke 10:40. . . . The Spirit supports us in the hour when we are ready to faint."—(F.)

[2] Never were more or (perhaps) truer prayers offered up throughout Christendom for the life of any man

than for that of the late President Garfield. But prayer did not save him. And yet many Christians were fully persuaded that in answer to so much earnest praying his life would be spared, and some went so far as to assert that his recovery might properly be regarded as a fair prayer test in contrast to that suggested by Prof. Tyndall. But did not such persons take too much for granted; namely, that his recovery from the assassin's shot would be for his own highest good, for the greatest

but the Spirit itself maketh intercession for us with groanings which cannot be uttered.

27 And he that searcheth the hearts knoweth what is the mind of the Spirit, because he maketh intercession for the saints according to *the will of* God.

ought; but the Spirit itself maketh intercession for

27 *us* with groanings which cannot be uttered; and he that searcheth the hearts knoweth what is the mind of the Spirit, [1] because he maketh intercession

28 for the saints according to *the will of* God. And we

1 Or, *that.*

But the Spirit itself. Plainly the Holy Spirit, and so confirmatory of the same application of the same phrase in ver. 16. **Maketh intercession for us** [another compound of three words][1] **with groanings which cannot be uttered.** The words 'for us' have not sufficient manuscript support. These *unuttered groanings,*[2] though traceable to the Holy Spirit, take place *within our hearts,* agreeably to ver. 23 ('groan within ourselves'). Compare "joy unspeakable" in 1 Peter 1 : 8, where the opposite emotion is characterized by an adjective, differing very slightly in the original from the one used here. Bengel remarks: "On both sides believers have those who groan with them and make common cause with them; below them the whole creation (ver. 22), above them the Spirit." Wickliffe's version of this passage is a quaint specimen of the English of his day: "The Spirit axeth for us with sorwinge, that moun not be telde out." [The Spirit as another "Helper" or "Advocate"—Common and also Revised Version, "Comforter"—(John 14 : 16) intercedes with God for us, and "uses the human organ for his sighing, as he likewise does elsewhere for his speaking. Matt. 10 : 20; see also on Gal. 4 : 6." (Meyer.) "The Holy Spirit . . . himself pleads in our prayers, raising us to higher and holier desires than we can express in words, which can only find utterance in sighings and aspirations." (Alford.) Olshausen, Lange, Stuart, Hodge, and others, take this intercessory groaning, in the manner of Augustine, in a subjective sense, regarding it as *our* groaning incited by the Holy Spirit.

Many, however, refer this groaning to the intercession of the objective Holy Spirit dwelling in us. This interceding of the Spirit of God in us, with groanings for God's help in our behalf, is something we cannot comprehend, but in one point of view it seems akin to the suffering and intercession of our divine Lord, if not in us, yet in the flesh, "for us men and for our salvation." Philippi says: "To suppose a sighing of the Spirit himself without mediation of man's spirit, is alike without meaning and Biblical analogy. . . . In the intimate marriage of God's Spirit with man's spirit, an incarnation of the former, as it were, takes place. The distinction between the intercession of the Spirit and the intercession of Christ is chiefly to be found in this,—that Christ intercedes without us, in and by himself, but the Spirit in and by us; Christ by the prevalence of his own merit, the Spirit on the ground of the merit of Christ."]

27. And (*now*) **he that searcheth the hearts**—this is an Old Testament description of God (1 Sam. 16 : 7; 1 Kings 8 : 39; Ps. 7 : 9; Prov. 15 : 11; Jer. 11 : 20; 17 : 9, 10), and specially appropriate here, because it is in the heart that the 'unuttered groanings' take place. Compare Gal. 4 : 6. **Knoweth what is the mind of the Spirit**—that is, of the Holy Spirit, as is required alike by the connection and by the usage in ver. 6, 7. **Because he maketh intercession, etc.** [Philippi gives this paraphrase: "As the Searcher of hearts, God knows what is the mind of the Spirit; and he knows it also because the Spirit intercedes for the saints in a way *agreeable to God;*" simi-

good of the nation, and for the special glory of God? And did not some in their prayers fail to add: "Nevertheless, not my will but thine be done"? But did all those prayers wholly fail of an answer? We think not. The particular blessings (as we deemed them) which were asked for were denied, but equivalent blessings were doubtless sent, or will be sent, in their stead, just as in the case of Paul's prayer for the removal of the thorn in his flesh. See 2 Cor. 12 : 7-9, and compare Rom. 1 : 10; 15 : 31, 32; see also notes on 15 : 32. Quite apt are the words of Shakespeare on this point:

　　We, ignorant of ourselves,
Beg often our own harms, which the wise Powers

Deny us for our good. So find we profit
　　By losing of our prayers.
　　　　—"Ant. and Cleop.," Act II., Scene I.--(F.)

1 The compounds of ὑπέρ—over, in behalf of, beyond (Latin: super)—are nearly all found in Paul's epistles. See ver. 37.—(F.)

2 ἀλαλήτος is by most commentators rendered *inexpressible*—that is, "groans which cannot be expressed in words." (Noyes.)—(F.)

3 φρόνημα (the result of thinking), thought, purpose, meaning, occurs four times and only in this Epistle.— (F.)

28 And we know that all things work together for good to them that love God, to them who are the called according to *his* purpose.

know that to them that love God [1] all things work together for good, *even* to them that are called according to *his* purpose. For whom he foreknew,

---

1 Some ancient authorities read *God worketh all things with them for good.*

---

larly De Wette and Alford.] **According to the will of God**—literally, *according to God.* The idea is fully and correctly expressed in our version, though the words, 'the will,' do not stand in the original. [Winer objects to the expression interceding 'according to *the will* of God,' because "of the Spirit no different intercession can be thought of." Hence he interprets the phrase (κατὰ θεὸν) 'toward God,' 'before God.' But this seems somewhat strained, and to make the apostle here simply to affirm that the Searcher of hearts knows that the Spirit intercedes before him for saints is, in the words of Dr. Hodge, "making the verse say comparatively little."] **For** (the) **saints**—that is, *for holy persons*, instead of 'for us' as in ver. 26 [Common Version].

28. And [or, *moreover*] **we know**—not merely by divine promise, but by present consciousness: **to them that love God**—this is no unusual way of designating true Christians. (1 Cor. 2: 9; 8: 3; James 1: 12.) The emphatic position of these words, in the original Greek, intimates that this assurance is the *peculiar privilege* of those that possess this character.[1] **That** [a new motive for 'patience,' ver. 25] **all things work together for good** —'all things,' with special reference to sufferings, afflictions, persecutions, calamities, etc., 'work together,' are conspiring harmoniously; [Westcott and Hort adopt here the reading of A B given in the margin of the Revised Version, "God worketh all things with them for good"; and Pauline usage would certainly favor the use here of a personal subject; see Buttmann, 193.] 'For good'—to a good result; for a benevolent and happy end: our

sanctification and perfection.[2] [Compare 1 Cor. 3: 21, 22. How great the consolation to feel that our sorest afflictions can be put among the 'all things' which will contribute to our good. Indeed, so comprehensive is this unlimited 'all things' that some include in it all that transpires under the universal government and providence of God, and Augustine went so far as to make the sins of believers conducive to their welfare—making them "more humble and docile"; but this consideration is evidently foreign to the apostle's line of thought. Still there is this truth in Augustine's view—namely, that the sorrows which our sins have brought upon us can be sanctified for our good. Only as we love God and have been called according to his purpose, can we truly say:

> Blessed be God for all,
> For all things here below;
> For every loss and every cross
> To my advantage grow.]

To them who are the called according to his purpose. ["Who called us with a holy calling, not a cording to our works"— actual or foreseen, not primarily by our own act and will—"but according to his own *purpose* and gràce which was given us in Christ Jesus before times eternal." (2 Tim. 1: 9, Rev. Ver.) The word 'purpose' (πρόθεσις) save in one instance (2 Tim. 3: 10) is in Paul's writings always used of God's "eternal purpose." Compare 9: 11; Eph. 1: (9), 11; 3: 11. This calling of God, connected as it is with his immutable purpose, "the purpose of the ages" (see Eph. 3: 11, Revised Version, margin), and "according to

---

1 "Ἀγαπᾶν denotes love as a direction of the will, *diligere.* . . . φιλεῖν (denoting the love of affection, friendship) is never used of the love of men toward God (but see 1 Cor. 16: 22). Love to God or our neighbor as a *command* is unheard of in the profane writers; this love again is always expressed by ἀγαπᾶν." [And Prof. Jowett says: "No Greek or Roman ever had the consciousness of love toward his god."] "'Ἀγαπᾶν and never φιλεῖν is used of love toward our enemies. . . . The range of φιλεῖν is wider than that of ἀγαπᾶν, but ἀγαπᾶν stands all the higher above φιλεῖν on account of its moral import." "'Ἀγάπη, a word formed perhaps by the LXX. as a companion to ἀγαπᾶν, and wholly un-

known in the classics, became in New Testament language the distinctive designation of holy and divine love, while the Greeks knew only ἔρως, φιλία, and στοργή." (Cremer.) See also notes on 5: 5. Ἀγαπᾶν occurs some 142 times in the New Testament, φιλεῖν 25 times.—(F.)

2 It was an ingenious and exhaustive textual division of his subject which a certain preacher made in discoursing from this text on "The Providence of God." It is 1. Universal—"all things." 2. Operative—"work." 3. Harmonious — "together." 4. Benevolent — "for good." 5. Special—"to them that love God."

29 For whom he did foreknow, he also did predestinate *to be* conformed to the image of his Son, that he
might be the firstborn among many brethren.

he also foreordained *to be* conformed to the image
of his Son, that he might be the firstborn among

election " (Rom. 9: 11) which was "before the
foundation of the world " (Eph. 1: 4), even "the
purpose of him who worketh all things after
the counsel of his own will " (Eph. 1: 11), cannot
of course be made in vain. To what or for
what great things we are called of God may be
seen in 1 Cor. 1: 9; 1 Thess. 2: 12; 2 Thess.
2: 14; 1 Tim. 6: 12; 1 Peter 5: 10. Obviously
those who love God have in their heavenly
calling additional evidence that all things
will contribute to their good.] Thus another
characteristic of true Christians is added: not
only do they love God; they are also 'called
according to his purpose': the former is the
effect and proof of the latter. It is quite in
accordance with the style of Scripture and of
common life to put that first which is tangible,
practical, phenomenal, and then that which is
back of it, and the *cause* of it, and so *logically*
precedent. See 10: 9; 2 Thess. 2: 13, etc.
[" As this purpose antedates creation, it must
be from and in himself alone, for, 'with
whom took he counsel?' Before the creation
it must obviously have been for the Creator
alone to determine what orders of being to
create, and what individuals, with what capacities to endue each, in what relations and circumstances to place him, and what issues to
bring about in regard to him. The objects to
be subserved by the existence of each and to
be effected by the divine administration
toward him, depended on God's sovereign
pleasure." (Ripley.)]

29. For—this verse and the following emphatically confirm ver. 28, showing that the
divine 'purpose,' advancing by regular steps
to its fulfillment, leads 'the called' surely to
glory: **whom he did foreknow, he also
did predestinate** (or, *foreordained*). [The
word 'predestinate' is derived from the Vulgate *prædestinavit*, through the Bishop's Bible
and Rheims Version. The phrase "*before
ordeyned*" occurs in Wickliffe's Version.]
Foreknowledge and foreordination must, according to the structure of the context, be
regarded as successive steps in the carrying
out of the eternal 'purpose.' We may conceive of God as exercising his omniscience in
surveying men, and selecting, on principles
and for reasons known only to himself, but

dictated by his consummate wisdom and goodness, whom he would ordain to eternal life.
And so the foreknowledge may be conceived
of as distinct from the foreordination, and
logically antecedent to it. [The word foreknow—containing "the idea of decision as
well as foreknowledge" (Boise,—occurs five
times in the New Testament. In two places
(Acts 26: 5; 2 Peter 3: 17), it signifies previous
knowledge on the part of men. In the other
instances, here, and 11: 2, and 1 Peter 1: 20,
it denotes the foreknowledge which existed in
God "before the foundation of the world "
(compare Rev. 17: 8), and which, as here
represented, was the ground of his predestination. The noun, foreknowledge, occurs but
twice (Acts 2: 23; 1 Peter 1: 2), and is associated with
the determinate counsel and election of God.
The divine foreknowledge, as many think,
denotes not simply prescience, but an approbation or choice from beforehand. "To foreknow," says Cremer, "is 'to unite oneself
before with some one,' compare Rom. 11: 2.
'God has not cast away his people with whom
he had joined himself'—that is, before this
union was historically realized." On our passage he says: "The context suggests the union
of the divine foreknowledge with the divine
purpose. As this latter word denotes God's saving decree preceding and forming the foundation of its temporal realization, so to foreknow
denotes the divine knowing as already present
in the divine decree before its manifestation
in history, . . . so that to foreknow corresponds with the choosing before the foundation
of the world, which in Eph. 1: 4 precedes [?]
the foreordination just as foreknow does here.
Foreknowing, however, essentially includes
a self-determining on God's part to this fellowship (whom God had beforehand entered into
fellowship with), whereas the choosing merely
expresses a determining directed to the objects
of the fellowship." Meyer and others ignore
any approving beforehand or any appropriating cognizance in the signification of this
word, and make it mean simply to know beforehand; "He foreknew them; namely, as those
who should one day, in the way of the divine
plan of salvation, be conformed to the image
of his Son," or as Godet (with a less degree

of Paulinism) has it: "whom God knew beforehand as certain to believe." The mere logical faculty would be well content with this affirmation, that God foreknew those whom he had purposed to save. "It is evident on the one hand," says Dr. Hodge, "that foreknowledge (πρόγνωσις) expresses something more than the prescience of which all men and all events are the objects, and, on the other, something different from the predestination expressed by the following word. . . . The foreknowledge, therefore, expresses the act of cognition or recognition, the fixing, so to speak, the mind upon, which involves the idea of selection." And this selection or choice is based not on any foreseen meritorious act of those chosen, but on the good pleasure and purpose of the chooser. "Far be it from us," says Augustine, "to ascribe the choice to the clay instead of the potter." Our Lord may say to all his disciples: "Ye did not choose me, but I chose you," (John 15: 16, Revised Version), and Paul's query: "Who maketh thee to differ?" can only be answered in one way. That this election or choice does not depend on God's foreknowledge of our faith or goodness is also evident from the declaration of the same apostle, that we were chosen in Christ "before the foundation of the world *that we should be holy.*" See Eph. 1: 4. "The divine foreknowledge," says Dr. Weiss, "is certainly not a foreknowledge of faith which he himself produces, but of a receptivity by which he alone can and will work faith." This writer does not state how this "receptivity" was foreknown. In the passage before us foreknowledge precedes the divine predestination, and so, in the phrase: "elect according to the foreknowledge of God" (1 Peter 1: 2), the foreknowledge seems to precede the election. Yet many theologians make God's foreknowledge to depend upon his decree. "If God foresees events, he must have predetermined them." (Hale.) "God could not foreknow that things would be, unless he had decreed they should be." (Edwards.) "The foundation of the foreknowledge of an event as certainly future is God's decree that made it future." (A. A. Hodge.) Omniscience certainly cannot foreknow a thing which is contingent, which may be or may not be. There must be an absolute certainty as to the existence of any future event,

though this sure event may be and is coupled with free, voluntary, responsible, action. We may purpose and determine to build a house at such a time and place, but we cannot foreknow the existence of that house, unless its existence is certain, and we in some way are made sure of its certainty. God's foreknowledge is of course different from ours. With him there is properly no lapse of time, no succession, no before or after; his knowledge is present, immediate, complete, yet it cannot dispense with this certainty. And in reference to human events happening in time we must speak as the Scriptures do, of God's *fore*knowing. But his foreknowledge and his predetermination are in fact co-ordinate and eternal. He cannot decree anything without knowing about that thing, and he cannot foreknow anything without decreeing it. Foreknowledge and foreordination involve each other. Foreknowledge in itself may not *cause* the certainty of future events, but it is a *proof* that those events must be certain. Prof. Stuart says that divine *foreknowledge* necessitates "the conclusion that *certainty* must exist, by the divine purpose and counsel, in regard to the called—a certainty not merely that they will be saved provided they believe and obey and persevere in so doing, but a certainty that 'the called according to his purpose' will be brought to believe, obey, and persevere, and will therefore obtain salvation; for such is the manifest tenor of the whole passage."] But this foreknowing must not be explained as merely the foreknowledge of their future repentance and faith; for this would make their repentance and faith the *cause*, and not, as they truly are, the *consequence*, of their foreordination. See 1 Cor. 4: 7. [The verb foreordained (προορίζω), nearly equivalent, etymologically, to our predetermine, is found six times in the New Testament (Acts 4: 28; Rom. 8: 29, 30; 1 Cor. 2: 7; Eph. 1: 5, 11), and in every instance is rendered *foreordained* in the Revised Version. As used by Paul, it denotes the divine predestination of individual believers to adoption as sons, to conformity with Christ, and to eternal glory. And according to apostolic teaching this predetermining of individuals to salvation took place "before the ages" and "before the foundation of the world" (compare 1 Cor. 2: 7; Eph. 1: 4, Rev. 17: 8), and is based simply on the eter-

nal purpose of God and the good pleasure of
his will. In Acts 4 : 28 we are taught that
the evil deeds of Christ's murderers were
connected with the divine predetermination.
But in all of Paul's writings, while he ascribes
the highest sovereignty to God, and affirms
that the potter has power over the clay from
the same lump to make vessels unto honor
and vessels unto dishonor, and that God hath
mercy on whom he will and whom he will he
hardeneth, he yet very carefully abstains
from saying that God himself has fitted any
vessel of wrath unto destruction, or that he
has predestinated any, according to his good
pleasure, unto perdition. The divine decrees
are, indeed, a "subject of itself rather intri-
cate" (Calvin), and are a stumbling-block
and an offense to many. Still, to our *logical*
understanding no conclusion seems more
legitimate and true than this, that God "according to the counsel of his will . . . hath
foreordained whatsoever comes to pass."[1] For
this is but saying that the divine and almighty
Architect, when he purposed creation, had
a full and perfect plan of all things, and that
the existing state of things fully accords with
his original plan. We pray, indeed, "Thy
will be done on earth," implying that it is not
done at present (compare 1 Tim. 2 : 4; 2 Peter
3 : 9); and yet we must at the same time acknowledge that God's eternal purpose can in
no instance fail of accomplishment, and that
even now his determinate counsel, his formed
purpose or decretive will, is done on earth,
otherwise we make him an ignorant or dis-

appointed weakling like ourselves.[2] It may
seem to us that predestination on the part of
God is inconsistent with human freedom, yet
both are reconcilable because both are true,
though it is impossible for us, with our present
limitations and in our present state of darkness and obscurity, fully to show their com-
patibility. We should, therefore, deny neither,
but firmly and boldly maintain both, even as
Peter and the other apostles do in Acts 2 : 23;
4 : 27, 28; compare 3 : 17, 18. "Him being
delivered up by the determinate counsel and
foreknowledge of God, ye by the hand of
lawless men did crucify and slay." (Acts 2 : 23,
Revised Version.) "Both Herod and Pontius Pilate
with the Gentiles and the peoples of Israel,
were gathered together, to do whatsoever thy
hand and thy counsel foreordained to come
to pass." (Acts 4 : 27, 28, Revised Version.) Compare
Matt. 18 : 7. We may properly add that some,
as Godet and Philippi, are of the opinion that
had Paul sought to resolve "the speculative
question between God's eternal plan and the
freedom of human determinations," he would
have done so "by means of the fact affirmed
by him of *divine foreknowledge.*" These
writers consequently hold to a predestination
which is not absolute, but which is based on
foreknowledge of faith. And Godet goes so far
as to imply that this foreseen faith which furnishes the ground for a predestination to glory
(he ignores any predestination *to faith*) must
not be a divine creation, but of human origi-
nation. But to our mind little aid comes from
any view we can take of foreknowledge, since

[1] We may even say, in general terms, that God's sovereign, eternal, purpose covers the actions and the
destiny of wicked and lost men. Thus Olshausen,
while discarding the idea of God's willing evil as evil,
or his working evil in the hearts of men, or his predestinating the evil to evil, yet affirms it to be "impossible to exclude evil, viewed as a phenomenon, from
the divine operations." All theists must admit that
evil takes place under God's *permissive* decree, or, at
least, that he permits evil to exist, and some such view
as this seems most accordant with the spirit and general tenor of the Scriptures; compare 9: 22, "endured
with much long suffering." Yet the Supralapsarian
predestinationist denies that this view has any great
advantage over his own, since any one is naturally held
responsible for permitting an evil if he could have prevented it. Nor can the permission theory dispute the
fact that the Omniscient God created those who he
foreknew would certainly be lost. In Calvin's view,
God predestinated all mankind in the person of Adam

to corruption, which involved them in condemnation
and eternal death, and he frankly confesses this to be
a *decretum horribile*—an awful decree—(the word *horribile* being used by Calvin, not in our sense of horrible,
but as something fearful or terrible, just as Luther, in
his baptismal prayer, speaks of God's "*horrible* judgment" in his destroying the wicked world with the
flood). Furthermore, from a Sublapsarian point of
view, he held that God by an absolute decree of *grace*
elected some from this *massa perditionis* to eternal life
and reprobated (with less exercise of power) others to
eternal damnation. Augustine, we believe, never advocated a predestination to eternal death, and most theologians have been content to say that God passed by or
left the vessels of wrath to bear the just consequences
of their sins.—(F.)

[2] On the secret and revealed or disposing and precep-
tive will of God, see Edwards' "Works," Vol. II., pp
161–164, 513–516, 546.—(F.)

we can think of nothing which God could foreknow save only that which he had determined to create. The view that God's "*foreseeing is seeing*—knowing what shall be is knowing what to him already is" (Godet)— is, perhaps, as satisfactory to our minds as any. Our own view, however, mainly accords with the following remarks of Alford: "It may suffice to say that, on the one hand, Scripture bears constant testimony to the fact that all believers are chosen and called by God, their whole spiritual life—in its origin, progress, and completion—being *from him;* while, on the other hand, its testimony is no less precise that he willeth all to be saved, and that none shall perish except by *willful rejection* of the truth. So that, on the one side, GOD'S SOVEREIGNTY, on the other, MAN'S FREE WILL, is plainly declared to us. *To receive, believe, and act on both these is our duty and our wisdom.* They belong, as truths, no less to *natural* than to revealed religion, and every one who believes in a God must acknowledge both. But all attempts to *bridge over the gulf between the two are futile* in the present imperfect condition of man." The following is the view of Prof. Riddle: "That the word means foreordained, predestinated, is certain; that it is here applied to individuals is obvious; that it implies a pre-terrestrial act of the Divine Mind is in accordance with the current of thought in the chapter, the Scriptural conception of God's purpose, and the use of the word in other passages. It is only one side of the truth, indeed, but the other side is not more firmly established by ignoring this. The only reconciliation of the difficulty is in practical Christian experience, and Paul is addressing himself to this throughout." Some deny that Paul in this discussion teaches the dogma of a *decretum absolutum,* which determined from all eternity that only a certain number shall certainly be saved, since his design in this passage is simply to show that all who are called according to God's purpose will never be separated from his love, and that as God is for them, all things, even afflictions and tribulations, will be made to contribute to their good. This is, indeed, his design, but his argumentation implies this at least,—that all who are justified and saved in Christ are called according to God's purpose, and were foreknown from eternity as his, and

were predestinated to be conformed to the image of his Son. And no one can suppose the apostle to have held that any of the incorrigibly impenitent were thus foreknown or predestinated or called. Yet all men are sincerely invited by the gospel message; all, we may believe, are to some extent moved by the Spirit; and hence all who refuse to obey are "without excuse."] **To be conformed to the image of his Son.** [Compare 2 Cor. 3 : 18. The adjective (σύμμορφος) 'conformed' occurs elsewhere only in Phil. 3 : 21, where it is followed, not as here by the genitive, but by the dative, and the reference is to the body of Christ's glory. In Phil. 3 : 10, a related verb speaks of conformity to Christ's death. In our passage, the conformity of the predestinate to the great Exemplar is both physical and spiritual. The divine predestination has always a gracious purpose. We are elect unto obedience; we were chosen that we should be holy. (1 Peter 1 : 2; Eph. 1 : 4.) Only the obedient and the holy can have any assurance of their heavenly calling. Have we not reason to fear that many professing Christians—so faint is their resemblance to Christ here—will never bear the glorious image of the Son of God?] The verb 'to be' is omitted in the Greek, perhaps on account of its being required in the next clause. The conformity here mentioned is to be perfected at the coming of Christ, according to 1 John 3 : 2. The word 'image' is not superfluous; Christ is the model, the pattern of glorified humanity. **That he might be the firstborn** [*in order that,* denoting the final aim, as regards Christ, of the predestinating] **among many brethren**—that is, that many might be conformed to his image, and so by grace be made worthy to be called his brethren. ["The object of the Christian scheme is that Christ may not stand alone in the isolated glory of his pre-existence, but that he may be surrounded by a numerous brotherhood fashioned after his likeness as he is in the likeness of God." (Principal Sanday, in Ellicott's "New Testament Commentary.") The term 'firstborn' denotes both priority and pre-eminence. It is this passage which authorizes us to speak of Christ as our Elder Brother.]

30. Moreover, whom he did predestinate, them he also called. [Some regard the verb 'called,' as also other verbs which

O

30 Moreover, whom he did predestinate, them he also
called: and whom he called, them he also justified:
and whom he justified, them he also glorified.
31 What shall we then say to these things? If God
be for us, who *can be* against us?

30 many brethren: and whom he foreordained, them
he also called: and whom he called, them he also
justified: and whom he justified, them he also glorified.
31 What then shall we say to these things? If God
32 *is* for us, who *is* against us? He that spared not his

follow, especially the last in the verse, as the past tense used for the present, and expressive of what is customary. A better view is that everthing connected with this divine economy of saving grace is so certain that, though future, it may be regarded as good as accomplished.] The calling here, as generally in the epistles, is not a mere outward invitation, or offer of salvation, but an inward calling, made effectual by the Holy Spirit. **And whom he called, them he also justified.** This shows conclusively by what kind of a calling it was. ["Though by choosing his people the Lord has adopted them as his children, yet we see that they enter not on so great a blessing till they are called." (Calvin.) "Effectual calling," says Edwards, "is the proper execution of election." Godet supposes that all men who hear the gospel have "an outward call by the word and an inward call by grace," and that "all are alike seriously called. Only it happens that some consent to yield to the call and others refuse." We imagine that this *happening* has something to do with the divine purpose. If all depended upon the human will, it might happen that none of the invited ones would be found among the heavenly guests.] **And whom he justified** [in a forensic sense opposed to condemned], **them he also glorified.** ["Whom God predestinated *before* the world, he called *from* the world, justified *in* the world, and will glorify *after* the world." Godet says that had Paul designed "to explain the order of salvation in all its elements, divine *and human,* he would have put *faith* between

calling and justification, and *holiness* between justification and glorification."] This last step in the process, though referring to what is yet future, is expressed, like the preceding steps, in the past tense, to show that these processes are all linked together in an indissoluble chain, so that where one is found the rest are sure to be found also; and the consummation is as sure as if it was already a matter of history.[1]

Conclusion as to the certainty of the salvation of Christians, ver. 31-39: Their salvation is certain (ver. 31), because God has given his Son (ver. 32, 33), and the Son of God has died and risen from the dead (ver. 34), and therefore they can never be separated from the love of either by any vicissitudes of the present life (ver. 36, 37), or by any other agencies or events whatsoever. (Ver. 38, 39.)

31. What shall we then say to these things? What, indeed, *can* the hesitating or discouraged soul find to say in view of such an array of the merciful acts of God's love [his predestinating, calling, justifying, glorifying purpose] as the apostle here presents? What but this: **If God be (*is*) for us, who can be (*is*) against us?** ["The inspired faith of the apostle, leaving all earthly things far down below his feet, reflects itself in the sublimity of the language." (Philippi.) "'What shall we then say' is used here," says Tholuck, "contrary to the apostle's custom, in a conclusion which has *not* a doubtful character." Ver. 30 of the next chapter also introduces a correct conclusion. Compare, on the other hand, 3:5; 4:1; 6:1; 7:7; 9:14.]

[1] This golden chain, to which no links are wanting, reaches from eternity to eternity—"from everlasting in predestination to everlasting in beatification." (St. Bernard.) On the connection of these links, Archbishop Leighton (on Peter) appropriately remarks that "Effectual calling is inseparably tied to this eternal foreknowledge or election on the one side and to salvation on the other. These two links of the chain are up in heaven in God's own hand, but this middle one is let down to earth into the hearts of his children, and they laying hold on it have sure hold on the other two, for no power can sever them." "Before the divine

intuition," says Tholuck, "which is independent of time, fallen humanity appears from all eternity, not only as redeemed, but likewise as enjoying the fruits of redemption and as exalted to glory." "No one," says Chalmers, "can read in the book of God's decrees that he has been predestined unto glory, but all may read in the book of his declarations what be the marks of those who travel thitherward. These he can compare with the book of his own character and experience, and he can count upon his own special destination to an eternity of bliss only in as far, and in no farther than, as he is sanctified."—(F.)

32 He that spared not his own Son, but delivered him up for us all, how shall he not with him also freely give us all things.

33 Who shall lay any thing to the charge of God's elect? *It is* God that justifieth.

34 Who *is* he that condemneth? *It is* Christ that died, yea rather, that is risen again, who is even at the right hand of God, who also maketh intercession for us.

own Son, but delivered him up for us all, how shall he not also with him freely give us all things?

33 Who shall lay anything to the charge of God's 34 elect? ¹ It is God that justifieth; who is he that condemneth? ² It is Christ Jesus that died, yea rather, that was raised from the dead, who is at the right hand of God, who also maketh intercession

1 Or, *Shall God that justifieth ?* ......2 Or, *Shall Christ Jesus that died, . . . us ?*

32. He that [(ὅς γε) he *who indeed*—that is, inasmuch as he, or being such an one as he] **spared not his own Son.** ['Spared' is an expressive word, denoting God's great sacrifice in giving up his only begotten Son— "the Son of his love." Compare in LXX., Gen. 22: 12. "God, so to speak, did violence to his paternal love." (Bengel.)¹] He surely, seeing he did not even spare his own Son (compare ver. 3, also John 3: 16; 5: 18), **but delivered him up**—(that is, to death) (compare 4: 25; Matt. 10 : 21)—**for us all** (the extent of this expression, so far as this particular passage is concerned, is defined by the *us* of the next clause), **how shall he not with him also freely give us all things?** —that is, all things pertaining to life and godliness. (2 Peter 1: 3.) "For to give us all things with him is less than to deliver up him to death for our sake." (Ambrosiaster.) [An argument from the greater to the less. God's eternal purpose to save, and the giving up to death of his own Son to effect that salvation, is a sufficient proof that he is "for us" and that he will withhold "no good thing."]

33. Who shall lay any thing, etc. Who shall bring an accusation against God's elect? [This verb, to accuse, is elsewhere followed by the simple dative.² The elect or chosen ones of God, some of whom certainly must be found in our Christian churches, have plenty of accusers in this world. Indeed, many of the so-called "world's people" live on the faults, real or imagined, of God's professed children—a most miserable diet!—and

some of them by their talk and action would seem to think that if they could take an imperfect minister and a few delinquent church members with them to the bar of God it would go all right with them in the judgment. No doubt God's true people are faulty enough. Indeed, their own hearts and consciences are their swiftest and loudest accusers. But if God will justify the sincerely penitent believer as being found in Christ, all accusations of the ungodly will be in vain, availing nothing either against the believer or for themselves at the bar of judgment where each one shall give account of himself alone. See 14: 12.] The impossibility of any charge against God's elect that should hinder his purpose to give them all things, is implied in the question ; and is indirectly asserted in the next clause: for the Judge himself, before whom the accusation would have to be presented, has already pronounced them acquitted. God is the one who justifies. [Compare this and the following verse with Isa. 50: 7-9.]

34. Who is he that condemneth? [or, *shall condemn*, according to Westcott and Hort and the Canterbury Revision. Prof. Cremer makes this 'condemneth' to mean not only to pronounce condemnation, but to execute it as a judge.] The first clause in this verse seems naturally to connect itself with the last clause of the preceding: but at this point there is a transition from God to Christ. As it is impossible that any accusation should frustrate the divine purpose to save them on God's part, so it is equally impossible on Christ's part. **It is Christ that**

---

1 " There is," says Chalmers, " an academic theology which would divest God of all sensibility, which would make of him a being devoid of all emotion and all tenderness, which concedes to him power and wisdom and a sort of cold and clear and faultless morality, but which would denude him of all those fond and fatherly regards that so endear an earthly parent to the children who have sprung from him. . . . I fear that such representations as these have done mischief in Christianity."—(F.)

2 Winer says that the use of prepositions with cases instead of cases alone, is a "general characteristic of (antique) simplicity," and especially accords with the "graphic and explicit phraseology of Orientals." Accordingly, " we find that in the New Testament, agreeably to the Eastern idiom and sometimes in direct imitation of it, prepositions are frequently employed where in classic Greek the simple cases would have sufficed even in prose."—(F.)

35 Who shall separate us from the love of Christ?
shall tribulation, or distress, or persecution, or famine,
or nakedness, or peril, or sword?

35 for us. Who shall separate us from the love [1] of
Christ? shall tribulation, or anguish, or persecution,

1 Some ancient authorities read *of God*.

---

died, etc. *Christ Jesus* (for that seems to be
the correct reading) *is he who died, yea, rather
that rose* ['*was raised*'; the Revisers' text has
from the dead (ἐκ νεκρῶν), the reading of ℵ A C].
Who is even at the right hand of God—
[literally: "*in* the right hand " (place), the
place of power and honor, the throne of deity.
Compare Eph. 1: 20; Rev. 3: 21: 22: 1],
(the word 'even' here is of doubtful genuineness). **Who also maketh intercession** (*intercedes*) **for us.** [The same verb occurs at
ver. 27; 11: 2 (at 8: 26 in a compounded
form), also Acts 25: 24; Heb. 7: 25. The
apostle has previously affirmed that Christ
was delivered up for our offenses and was
raised for our justification. And now, while
virtually everywhere present by his Spirit, he
is yet exalted at God's right hand in heaven
itself, there as our Paraclete to intercede for
us—the exaltation showing his ability, and
the intercession showing his willingness to
save. (Bengel.) As De Wette says: "All
the points of Christ's redemptive work from
his death to his still enduring intercession are
adduced in one series as grounds for refuting
the above question." Well may the apostle
ask: "Who shall separate us from the love
of Christ"?] De Wette, Alford, and other
critical editors, make each clause in ver. 33,
34, interrogative [as in the margin of the
Revised Version and in accordance with the
structure of ver. 35]. But it is better to regard
only the *first* clause in each verse as interrogative, and the succeeding clauses as indirect answers to the interrogatories [as is
done in Dr. Noyes' translation and in our
Common Version. This punctuation is also
adopted by Fritzsche, Philippi, Lange, Godet,
Hodge, Stuart, and others]. The structure of
ver. 34, particularly, is such as hardly to
admit of its being divided into four or five
separate questions, or regarded, after the first
clause, as one compound interrogatory. [The
text of the Revised Version, and of the Bible

Union gives still another mode of pointing,
which is substantially that of Meyer and
Gifford, only they would somewhat closely
join the beginning of ver. 35 with ver. 34,
thus: "Christ is he that died, . . . who shall
separate us from the love of Christ?"]

The particular mode in which Christ intercedes for us at the right hand of God, whether
directly and orally, or only by his presence
there, is nowhere explained. [Meyer says
this intercession must be conceived as vocal
and oral "because it is made by the glorified
God-man." This intercession, he further remarks, "is the continuous *bringing to bear* of
his work of atonement completed by his
'propitiation' on the part of Christ in his
glory with the Father; which we are to conceive of as real and—in virtue of the glorified
corporeity of the exalted Christ, as also in
virtue of the subordination in which he, even
as occupant of the same throne, stands to
the Father—as a *request* properly so-called
through which the 'continuus quasi vigor'
(Gerhard) of redemption takes place. Compare John 14: 16." Whatever the necessity
of this intercession, it is not to be found in
the fact that God the Father is all justice
and the Son all love, for the love of God
and of Christ for sinners is here represented
as the same. Still as God manifests his
mercy only in and through the incarnate
Redeemer, so he, apart from Christ, may be
regarded as the impersonation of justice, yea
as "a consuming fire." Justice demands the
sinner's death and even the penitent believer
is by this intercession shown to be both weak
and unworthy, and in himself deserving of
condemnation.]

**35. Who shall separate us from the
love of Christ?** [Meyer finds a virtual
answer to this question in the preceding statement: Christ is he that has died, etc., he will
never cease to love.] We might expect the
neuter, *what*, rather than 'who,' here; since

---

1 Mr. Spurgeon on one occasion, as reported to the
writer by a friend who was present, adduced a very
touching illustration of Christ's love and his readiness
to receive the coming sinner. While quoting a hymn
he **stopped** short at the lines wherein Christ was en-

treated to open his arms, etc., and said, suiting his
gestures to the words: "This is all a mistake. The
Saviour's arms are open; they were always open; *they
were nailed wide open on the cross.*"—(F.)

36 As it is written, For thy sake we are killed all the day long; we are accounted as sheep for the slaughter.
37 Nay, in all these things we are more than conquerors through him that loved us.
38 For I am persuaded, that neither death, nor life,

36 or famine, or nakedness, or peril, or sword? Even as it is written,
For thy sake we are killed all the day long;
We were accounted as sheep for the slaughter.
37 Nay, in all these things we are more than conquerors
38 through him that loved us. For I am persuaded, that

---

the enumeration that follows is not of *persons*, but of *states* and *things:* but no one of the things enumerated is of the neuter gender in the Greek language; a circumstance which materially weakens the force of Calvin's otherwise appropriate comment: "the masculine pronoun 'who' has a secret, emphatic sense. We can engage in combat with as many champions as there are different kinds of temptations." [The form of this pronoun is the same for both genders.]

What are we to understand by 'the love of Christ' here? Is it our love to Christ? or is it Christ's love to us? The nature of the things mentioned, as having apparently a tendency to lead us to forsake Christ, rather than to lead Christ to forsake us, might seem to favor the former view: but the demands of the argument, the language of ver. 38, 39, and especially the last clause of ver. 37, are decisive in favor of the latter sense. [Hence in all the trials and afflictions which can be laid upon Christ's chosen ones, they may yet be assured of his unceasing love. Not till Christ forgets the garden and the cross will he forget to love those for whom he died and whom he has redeemed. And nothing can happen to us in this universe of God which will prevent us from sharing in the love of him who with the gift of his own Son will freely give us all things besides. Barnes regards the genitive as objective, our love for Christ; and so do Lange and Forbes in part. Calvin, Rückert, De Wette, make the love of Christ to mean our sense of his love, but this is not expressed in the text.] Observe how climacteric the enumeration is, ending with **sword** as the instrument and emblem of the death penalty ["the instrument of St. Paul's own future martyrdom." (Wordsworth.) On the words, **tribulation** and **distress,** see notes on 2: 9.]

But these trials are nothing new; they are only what befell God's saints of old. (Heb. 11: 36-38.)

36. As it is written. (Ps. 44: 22.) **For thy sake we are killed** (or, *put to death*) **all the day long** [continuously, as indicated by the present tense and the specification of time: *all the day through*]. We are daily and hourly exposing ourselves to death. [De Wette: "many of us fall each day as an offering of our faith."] This citation is specially pertinent as following the word 'sword,' the *extreme* peril, with which the preceding list closes. **We are** [literally: *were*] **accounted** (*reckoned*) **as sheep for the slaughter,** [literally: *sheep of slaughter*]. Stuart: "slaughter-sheep." "There is," says Perowne, "this remarkable difference between the tone of the Psalmist and the tone of the apostle. The former cannot understand the chastening, and complains that God's heavy hand has been laid without cause upon his people; the latter can rejoice in persecution also, and exclaim: 'Nay, in all these things we are more than conquerors.'"]

37. Nay, in all these things. But [as opposed to a suppressed negative answer] 'in all these things' (enumerated in ver. 35). **We are more than conquerors.** *We are over victorious*, or, as Luther says, "we far overcome."[1] **Through him** [Christ, as in ver. 35; compare Rev. 1: 5] **that loved us.** It is he that helps us and enables us to gain this more than victory. [Our Almighty Saviour's power and love will make even our adversaries to fight on our side.]

38, 39. For I am persuaded. 'I have adopted and still retain the conviction;' to analyze, and express the full sense of, the perfect tense of the original verb. He now takes up and amplifies the 'more than conquerors.' **That neither death, nor life,**[2]—

---

[1] Ellicott remarks that "the apostle seems to have had a marked predilection" for compounds with ὑπέρ (over, beyond). Compare 5: 20; 2 Cor. 7: 4; 11: 5; Phil. 2. 9: 2 Thess. 1: 3; 1 Tim. 1: 14. "It is noticeable that ὑπέρ occurs nearly thrice as many times in St. Paul's epistles and the Epistle to the Hebrews, as in the

rest of the New Testament, and that, with a few exceptions (Mark 7: 37; Luke 6: 38, etc.), the compounds of ὑπέρ are all found in St. Paul's epistles." A few of the less important uncials, D E F G, here read διά with the accusative: *On account of* him who loved us.—(F.)

[2] οὔτε, οὔτε (neither, nor), unlike οὐδέ, οὐδέ (see 9: 16;

nor angels, nor principalities, nor powers, nor things present, nor things to come,

39 Nor height, nor depth, nor any other creature, shall be able to separate us from the love of God, which is in Christ Jesus our Lord.

neither death, nor life, nor angels, nor principalities, nor things present, nor things to come, nor powers,

39 nor height, nor depth, r.or any other [1] creature, shall be able to separate us from the love of God, which is in Christ Jesus our Lord.

[1] Or. *creation.*

the two most general states in which men can possibly be. Death is put first, perhaps on account of ver. 36. The order is reversed in 1 Cor. 3 : 22. **Nor angels, nor principalities.** By angels must be understood good angels, because the word is never used of evil angels without some explanatory addition. See Matt. 25 : 41 ; 2 Cor. 12 : 7 ; 2 Peter 2 : 4 ; Jude 6. [Some think that 1 Cor. 6 : 3 ; Heb. 2 : 16, are exceptions.] That an attempt on the part of good angels to separate Christians from the love of God, though not possible to be *believed* is allowable to be *conceived*, in a hypothetical way is proved by Gal. 1 : 8. There are some other passages of Scripture which show that some things which can never occur as facts may lawfully be stated as suppositions, and even argued from as such. (Heb. 6 : 4-6.) The 'principalities' here mentioned are doubtless some orders of celestial beings. The same might be said of the word 'powers,' if this were its proper place ; but there is convincing evidence that its true position is after the two following clauses, between 'things to come' and 'height,' and therefore it is doubtful whether it refers to *personal* powers or to powerful influences or tendencies. "We may observe here," says Calvin, "how vile all things ought to appear in our sight when compared to the glory of God, since we are allowed to abase even angels for the purpose of asserting his truth." **Nor things present** [perfect participle from ἐνίσ-τημι], **nor things to come.** Compare 1 Cor. 3 : 22. **Nor powers.** Besides the very strongly preponderating testimony of manuscripts, translations, and citations in favor of the position of the word 'powers' after 'things to come,' the structure of the whole passage is an incidental corroboration. We have first two pairs,—'death' and 'life,' 'angels' and 'principalities ; ' and then two triplets,— 'thing present,' 'things to come,' and 'powers ; ' 'height,' 'depth,' and 'any other creature ; ' and in each of the last two clauses the

antithetical pair is followed by a third particular of a more general character,—'powers,' 'any other creature.' **Nor height, nor depth.** Nothing above us, nothing below us. Many ingenious and elaborate conceits of learned commentators in interpreting these words might be cited, such as "heights of bliss and depths of misery," "heights of presumptuous speculation and depths of sin," "high hopes of honor and profound fears of disgrace," etc., etc. ; but the natural simplicity of such an enthusiastic utterance as this is incompatible with such artificial methods. **Nor any other creature,** or, *created thing.* A broad expression, comprehending whatever is not included in the preceding enumeration. [It would seem that the above enumeration of visible and invisible beings and powers throughout the universe, including all changes of time and all distances of space, might embrace all things which the mind could conceive of as being able to separate us from God's love ; but lest anything might supposedly be omitted from this category, the apostle adds this all-comprehensive statement—'nor any other creature,' not anything else, differing (ἑτέρα) from these, which has been (or which may be) created. "Well may we inquire : Who shall unclasp those everlasting arms that are about us ? Or : What shall cause us to despond or faint ?" (N. Colver, "Lectures on Romans.") "Yet it should be remembered that sin can do what all the tribulations of earth cannot ; it can separate us from God." (Philippi.) "God having once determined the reception of true Christians into his kingdom, all that *he* brings upon them, even tribulation itself, can be no hindrance in the way of that, provided only the Christian does not injure himself." (Tholuck.)] **Shall be able to separate us from the love of God, which is in Christ Jesus our Lord.** [Hence the safety of Christ's sheep though in the midst of wolves. Compare John 10 : 28, 29.] "The love of Christ is

1 Thess. 2 : 3), may be used, as here, without any antecedent simple negative. The same is true of μήτε, μήτε as compared with μήδε. See 6 : 12 ; 14 : 21. Godet re-

marks that "the adversaries who rise before the apostle's view seem to advance in pairs."—(F.)

nothing else than the love of God himself, which has its seat in Christ. God is the originating fountain, Christ the constant organ and mediating channel of one and the same love." (Meyer.) In ver. 31–33 God is the subject; at ver. 34 the subject is changed to Christ. And now in ver. 39 it is again the love of God, but "the love of God in Christ Jesus our Lord." This transition from God to Christ and back again, so common in the Scriptures, is among the strongest proofs of the absolute Deity of our Lord Jesus Christ.

On this whole passage Erasmus exclaims: "What did Cicero ever say more eloquent than this?" [On the way and order of salvation thus far marked out by the apostle, Godet, in his chapter of "Conclusions," thus remarks: "The first gift of grace which the gospel offers to man is, according to Paul, the gift of his justification, without any other condition than that which every one may fulfill at once—faith. This first act done, man is free from his guilt in relation to his God; no cloud any longer troubles his relation to him; peace takes the place of the inward unrest; and in this state of inward tranquillity there may be sown *the fruit of righteousness*—sanctification. The reconciled man becomes open to the communication of the Divine Spirit. As naturally as this guest must withdraw from a condemned heart, so necessarily does he come to dwell in the man whom nothing any longer separates from God, and he realizes within him Christ's life and death in the measure in which this life and death have been apprehended by his faith. Finally, to him who walks in this way, there opens up in the distance a new gift, the renewing of his body and the inheritance of glory, through his complete transformation into the likeness of the glorified Christ. What clearer, what simpler, what at once more really divine and human, than this order of salvation traced by the apostle! And what a seal has not the experience of ages impressed on this exposition contained in the first eight chapters of our Epistle! Let not him who desires to see such a work accomplished within himself, or who proposes to carry it out in others,—emancipation from guilt and victory over sin,—take to the task in any other way, if he would not miserably fail!"]

Ch. 9: [The principal aim of this chapter is to show that God makes no account of human claims founded on a merely carnal descent from Abraham. According to Philippi, it shows that out of the elect nation there is an election of grace, and that "not the natural but the spiritual seed of Abraham is destined to inherit the promise." Tholuck says: "We have to specify as the doctrinal import of 9: 1–29: God has the right to admit into the Messianic kingdom without regard to human claims; of 9: 30–10: 21: if Israel was not admitted, the fault lies in its unwillingness to submit to the way marked out by God; of chapter 11: the hardness which God in consequence of this brought upon Israel turns, however, to good, in that it helped on the admission of the Gentiles; and in the end the mass of the Jews shall obtain admission into God's kingdom." See also the general analysis of this and the two following chapters at 1: 15.]

The discussion which occupies this chapter and the two following was made necessary especially on account of the views of two classes of persons: 1. The unbelieving Jews, who regarded Paul as an enemy to the nation, and a traitor to the religion of his forefathers: 2. The believing Jews, who could not easily reconcile the unbelief and rejection of their countrymen with the promises of the Old Testament. Compare 3: 3. [In this section (altogether too important to be termed, as by De Wette, an "Appendix") wherein the apostle considers the hardening and falling away of the Jews, and God's choice of the Gentiles, giving them thus, in the words of Schaff, "an outline of a philosophy of church history," he expounds at some length the doctrines of the divine sovereignty and of election. Hence this discussion, which contains some things hard to be understood and harder to be received, "seems," as Olshausen remarks, "like the sixth chapter of St. John, calculated for the express purpose of sifting the Church of Christ." Philippi, in explaining the reason for this discussion, says: "Salvation was originally designed for every one that believeth, 'the Jew first.' But the result hitherto seemed to stand in express contrast with this design, and so far from corroborating *the Jew first*, rather gave the impression that God had broken the promise given to his

CHAPTER IX.

I SAY the truth in Christ, I lie not, my conscience also bearing me witness in the Holy Ghost,

1 I say the truth in Christ, I lie not, my conscience
2 bearing witness with me in the Holy Spirit, that I

covenant people and rejected his chosen nation of Israel." According to Godet, Paul's purpose was to solve "the greatest enigma of history: the *rejection* of the *elect* people."[1]

1. I say the truth in Christ. [Buttmann remarks that the absence of a connective particle, as at the beginning of this verse, serves to indicate the commencement of a new subject. See also 10: 1; 13: 1. Meyer says that the sorrow of which the apostle proceeds to speak "might be deemed incredible after the joyous triumph which had just been exhibited. Hence the extremely urgent asseveration with which he begins: 'Truth I speak in Christ, I lie not.'"] This double sanction of the truth which he was about to utter, first positively and then negatively, implies not only his own full assurance of its truth, but his persuasion of the importance of the like assurance on the part of his readers, with a suggestion of the possible lack of such assurance on their part. The tone of triumphant joy with which the preceding chapter closes, though in no wise inconsistent with the very opposite emotion which he is about to express, yet by the contrast greatly adds to the significance of his emphatic and twofold asseveration. And the solemnity of this asseveration is confirmed, on the positive side, by the addition, 'in Christ,' and on the negative, by the addition, **my conscience also bearing me witness—** [giving testimony with me—with my feelings

of assurance, or with my declaration] **in the Holy Ghost.** As if he had said, "I make no hasty or extravagant assertion: I speak the sober truth, as a Christian, and my conscience, enlightened by the Holy Spirit, bears me witness." So much pains does the apostle take to assure those to whom he has been obliged to declare unwelcome truths, of his tender regard for them. [The phrase, 'in Christ,' expresses "entire intimacy of most real fellowship,"—defining here, according to Ellicott, "the element or sphere *in which* the declaration is made." So Winer, p. 390, "*speak the truth in Christ* (as one living in Christ)." Compare 2 Cor. 2: 17; Eph. 4: 17; 1 Thess. 4: 1, etc. "By thus sinking his own personality, the solemnity of the apostle's declaration is greatly enhanced." See Ellicott on Eph. 4: 17. Some regard the phrase in the light of an oath, but this would require the preposition commonly used in such cases (πρός) with the genitive, unless a verb or adjective were expressed. On the co-witnessing of the apostle's conscience 'in the Holy Spirit,' Meyer thus remarks: "Paul knows that the witness of his conscience is not outside the Spirit that fills him, but *in* that Spirit." "The distinction between his own declaration and that of his conscience means that he has proved his feelings in regard to his people by the light of conscience and of the Spirit of God." (Lange.)]

[1] The apostle need not, in solving this "enigma," have occupied so many pages, nor brought forward so prominently the sovereign power and elective purpose of God had he believed in the semi-omnipotence and arbitrariness of man's free will. It was indeed strange that the Jews generally should have rejected the Messiah Jesus, who was himself a Jew according to the flesh, and that the Gentiles should so readily have received a salvation which was "from the Jews." But all the apostle needed to say, on the above supposition, was that, through the self-determining, indomitable power of the will, the Jews for various reasons, and yet against all reason, obstinately refused to receive the Son of David as their king, and what would be the final result of this rejection, neither he nor indeed the (so-called) Omniscient One himself, was at all able to tell. This, of course, would be placing man first and God last, or rather leaving him and his plan and pur-

pose (or indeed, any plan and purpose) in man's history out of view. What some men mean by the will's free self-determination, or the power of contrary choice, would render any "philosophy of history" impossible. While, however, we hold that man's will cannot create motives *ad libitum*, or act against all motives, we do believe that it can color motives and give them force and value. Yea, that motives are rather internal than external to the mind, and that they have too often been regarded as outward mechanical forces, acting upon the will as though it were a merely passive agent. It seems to us that in Edwards' "Dissertation on the Freedom of the Will," motive is, at times, too much regarded as something objective to, and separate from the will, or the soul willing. The will is an active agent, giving force and color to motives, and choosing from among motives, and is not determined or moved, like the hands of a clock, simply by external forces.—(F.)

2 That I have great heaviness and continual sorrow in my heart.
3 For I could wish that myself were accursed from Christ for my brethren, my kinsmen according to the flesh:

have great sorrow and unceasing pain in my heart.
3 For I could [1] wish that I myself were anathema from Christ for my brethren's sake, my kinsmen

1 Or, *pray.*

2. That I have great heaviness and continual sorrow. Of these two words translated 'heaviness' and 'sorrow,' the former is the word usually rendered sorrow (eleven times), while the latter is a stronger term, which occurs only here and in 1 Tim. 6: 10, and is translated "anguish" by Alford, Noyes, and the Bible Union. It was not enough to say that he had 'sorrow,' pain (λύπη), but he must add, 'anguish' (ὀδύνη); nor was that enough, but he must say great sorrow and continual anguish. And then he must add what is much more wonderful still. [According to Paul's teachings, Christians should always be joyful and rejoicing, and the apostle himself was doubtless, not a jovial, but a joyful and happy Christian—rejoicing in the Lord greatly and always. But we see that the happiness he felt in Christ's service was compatible with unceasing heart anguish for the conversion of his fellowmen. Yea, the more fully he experienced the blessedness of his heavenly calling in Christ Jesus, the deeper, it would seem, was his sorrow over the unbelief and impenitence of his countrymen. Yet, notwithstanding all his heart anguish for souls, we cannot suppose that he ever for an instant felt that he had greater love for sinners, or was more anxious for their conversion, than God himself who, in one sense, had power to convert the whole race of Israel in a moment. Nay, his soul would have shuddered at the blasphemous thought, even while he might be unable to explain God's forbearing to work this change in the hearts of men. For he knew the love of God to our lost race, in that he "spared not his own Son"; he knew that the love of Christ for perishing sinners surpassed all human knowledge; and, however great the mystery, he yet knew that the anxiety of his own heart was caused by the Spirit of God in him, making intercession for Israel with groanings too great for utterance in words. *We* sometimes have great sorrow of heart on account of disappointments, losses, afflictions, death, or calamities worse than death, but very few Christians, we fear, have any such anguish as the apostle felt for the conversion of sinners. Compare 2 Cor. 12: 15.]

3. Accursed from Christ—literally, *anathema from Christ*, implying separation from Christ as a Saviour, and involving the alternative of perdition. [For the use of the term 'anathema,' see Lev. 27: 28, 29, in the LXX., and compare Acts 23: 14; 1 Cor. 12: 3; 16: 22; Gal. 1: 8, 9.] But *did* Paul really wish this? He does not say so. He says, 'I could wish': I could, if it were *lawful;* I could, if it were *possible;* I could, if the realization of such a wish could procure the salvation of my countrymen.[1] No one is competent to interpret, or even to understand, this expression of Paul, except in so far as he is capable of entering by sympathy into Paul's inmost experience, his ardent patriotism, his fervent desire for the salvation of men. To bring to the explanation of such an utterance as this a calm, critical disposition, with whatever amount of exegetical learning, is to bring an utter disqualification to apprehend its true meaning. Tholuck was aware of this, when he said, "The objections against this expression all arise from a cool way of contemplating it, which altogether forgets what a loving heart, in the fervor of its passion, is capable of uttering." Bengel was aware of this, when he wrote, "if the soul be not far advanced, it is incapable of comprehending this, even as a little child is incapable of comprehending the courage of warlike heroes." Michaelis was unable to comprehend this, and so he calls it

[1] The literal rendering of this verb in the imperfect indicative is: 'I was wishing, or praying'—that is, if the thing wished for were possible. The act is represented as unfinished, an obstacle intervening. (Alford.) Hence the verb (ηὐχόμην) is here quasi-optative and signifies: 'I could wish,' etc. But this is to be distinguished from ηὐχόμην with ἄν. for this would probably mean: *I could wish* (but I will not). In Acts 26: 29 we have this verb in the optative mood with αν, meaning: *I could wish*—that is, if the wish were allowable (Buttmann, 217), or, if I obeyed the impulse of my own heart, though it may be unavailing. (Hackett.) See Winer, 303, 283, and for examples similar to the above, Acts 25: 22; Gal. 4: 20.—(F.)

4 Who are Israelites; to whom *pertaineth* the adoption, and the glory, and the covenants, and the giving of the law, and the service *of God*, and the promises;

4 according to the flesh: who are Israelites; whose is the adoption, and the glory, and the covenants, and the giving of the law, and the service *of God*,

"a fanatic prayer." We must notice the emphasis with which he specifies himself here —an emphasis not adequately represented in the Common Version: **I myself** in contrast with **my brethren** [themselves under a curse], **my kinsmen according to the flesh**[1]—and with this additional thought, '*even I myself*, whom you suppose to be so ill affected toward you' [or, *I myself*, to whom the love and presence of Christ would be a heaven forever.][2] Then he proceeds to mention other reasons, besides their natural kinship, for his glowing affection for them — namely, their peculiar national privileges and historic glories.

[The above prayer of the apostle is kindred in spirit to that of Moses, when he said: "*but* if not, blot me, I pray thee, out of thy book." (Exod. 32: 32.) In this prayer a Hopkins could find a text for "disinterested benevolence," and would infer that if a religious person "could know that God designed, for his own glory and the general good, to cast him into endless destruction, this would not make him cease to approve of his character. He would continue to be a friend of God and to be pleased with his moral perfections." See quotation and comments in Lange. In our view a "friend of God" could not suffer the "eternal destruction," which will be the final doom of those who know not God and obey not the gospel of our Lord Jesus. (2 Thess. 1: 8, 9, Revised Version.) Even if it were possible that the apostle could be accursed and separated from the enjoyment of Christ forever, though his loss and suffering on this account would be unspeakably great, we do not suppose that he would have exactly all the feelings and suffer precisely all the misery of the lost, who willfully and through enmity reject Christ. Only One could be made a curse for us, and we cannot believe that he, our blessed Saviour, could have actually experienced all the emotions and all the sufferings of the ungodly in the world of woe. Who can suppose that either our Lord, or his chiefest apostle, in consenting to become anathema for sinners,

was chargeable with the greatest of all absurdities "a holy willingness to be unholy"? The love which could lead Paul to wish under a certain supposition to be devoted to destruction or everlasting severance from Christ *for* (not necessarily, *in place of*) his Jewish kinsmen, flowed only from his love to Jesus, and would of itself, as Prof. Riddle remarks, "change hell to heaven." Olshausen, we observe, takes the preposition (ὑπέρ, *for*, *to the advantage of*) in the sense of, *instead of* (ἀντί), and, though in his views inclined somewhat to restorationism, yet remarks: "The whole passage loses its meaning and its deep earnestness if we suppose that Paul was really aware that every single individual of the Jewish nation, indeed all mankind, would in the end be blessed. These words, therefore, indirectly contain a strong proof of his conviction that there is a state of eternal damnation, as 2 Thess. 1: 8, 9, expressly declares."]

4. Who is here the compound relative. See 1: 25. **Israelites.** This was their most sacred and honorable name. The name Israel was given to Jacob by God himself on a memorable occasion. (Gen. 32: 28.) And the name derived from it, which he prayed to have named upon the two sons of Joseph (Gen. 48: 16), was the most distinguished of the titles by which his posterity were designated. See John 1: 47; Rom. 11: 1; 2 Cor. 11: 22. Next, after this heaven-bestowed name, the apostle mentions six of their peculiar and sacred distinctions as a people. **To whom pertaineth**—or, more briefly and literally, *whose* (*are*)—**the adoption**—that is, in a national sense, in distinction from all other peoples (Exod. 4: 22, 23; Deut. 14: 1; 32: 6; Isa. 1: 2; Jer. 31: 9); a great privilege, but not to be compared to the *personal* adoption, the prerogative of believers in Christ. **And the glory.** This probably refers to the bright cloud which, as a symbol of Jehovah's presence, went before them when they went up out of Egypt (Exod. 13: 21), abode upon Mount Sinai (Exod. 24: 16), and afterward rested on the tabernacle (Exod. 40: 34, 35) [and at times on the mercy seat

---

[1] " Christ was made a *curse* for us because we were his *kinsmen* " (Bengel.)—(F.)

[2] " Subject of the infinitive, *I myself*, same as that of

the finite verb: hence in the nominative " (Boise) rather than in the accusative.—(F.)

5 Whose *are* the fathers, and of whom as concerning the flesh Christ *came,* who is over all, God blessed forever. Amen.

5 and the promises; whose are the fathers, and of whom is Christ as concerning the flesh, [1] who is over 6 all, God blessed [2] for ever. Amen. But *it is* not as

---

1 Or, *flesh: he who is over all, God, be blessed for ever* . . . . . . 2 Gr. *unto the ages.*

---

of the ark (Lev. 16:2)]. This is what the Rabbins call the Shekinah, a word derived from the Hebrew verb which means *to settle down* or *rest upon,* as the cloud did upon the tabernacle. **And the covenants** [called in Eph. 2:12, *the covenants of promise*]. The plural form of this word, which is unusual, probably refers to the various *renewals* of the gracious engagement which God made first with Abraham (Gen. 15:18; 17:2, 4, 7-10), and afterward renewed to Isaac (Gen. 26:24), to Jacob (Gen. 28:13, 15), and to the whole people (Exod. 24:7, 8). [The codices B D E F G, with the Vulgate and several Fathers, read—*the covenant,* which, however, is adopted by no critical editors save Lachmann.] **And the giving of the law.** This refers to the transactions at Mount Sinai, recorded with such particularity in Exodus, chapters 19-23. [Some—as De Wette, Fritzsche, and others—make this law-giving equivalent to the law itself or its contents. But the giving of the law was to the Jews a greater honor than its mere possession, since it might have been received by them from other nations.] **And the service of God.** The words 'of God' are not in the original, but the word translated 'service' is sufficiently definite of itself, referring always to *religious* service, and including here the entire system of national worship as prescribed by the Lord and performed in the tabernacle and in the temple. [Compare Heb. 9:1. The "Five Clergymen" render it: Service of the sanctuary.] **And the promises.** [See 15:8.] No doubt the Messianic 'promises,' or those which relate to Christ and his kingdom, are especially meant." ["'Promises' (ἐπαγγελίαι) is intentionally put at the end, in order that now,—after mention of the *fathers* to whom, in the first instance, the promises were given, —the *Promised One himself* may follow." (Meyer.)]

5. The fathers. This term is especially

applied to Abraham, Isaac, and Jacob (Exod. 3:13, 15; 4:5; Acts 3:13; 7:32), but is not to be limited to them exclusively any more than the term patriarch (Acts 2:29; 7:8, 9.) **Of whom**—that is, of the Jews. The word 'whom' refers, not to the word 'fathers,' but back to the general subject of the preceding description, the same as the word 'who' at the beginning of ver. 4. **As concerning the flesh Christ came.** As to his human nature, which plainly implies that he had also a higher nature, how much higher the apostle immediately tells us in the most decisive terms! **Who is over all, God blessed for ever.** [Or, 'Who is God over all.' This last rendering is equally admissible as the other, and is preferred by Meyer[1]—that is, in case the sentence must be referred to Christ. Some, however, who hold that Christ is Lord of all, and that God, without the article (θεός), may be applied to him, as here and in John 1:1, as well as in John 1:18, according to some of the oldest and best manuscripts, yet hesitate to say that he is 'God over all.' But 'God' (θεός), though without the article, is often used in the New Testament to denote the Supreme Deity, and certainly the religion of the Bible knows no secondary, minor God. Hence, if Christ be God at all, he must be 'God over all.' "The absence of the article," says Philippi, "proves nothing, its use being here impossible, because God (θεός) is predicate, and the design is simply to affirm the *deity* of Christ (θεόν εἶναι). No doubt we might say, our God, Jesus Christ [using the article], but not, Christ is (ὁ θεός) the God, because he, whose Godhead is meant to be asserted, cannot be described as 'the God' already known."] This emphatic assertion of the supreme deity of our Lord seems too plain to admit of controversy. The only way in which its force can with any plausibility be evaded is by placing a period immediately before this clause, thus separating it

---

[1] This distinguished commentator, whose "grammatical accuracy and logical keenness" Biblical scholars will ever delight to acknowledge, and into whose exegetical labors they will not fail to enter, held that Christ, in accordance with Scripture teaching, had an eternal preexistent and God-equal being and nature; that in him

dwells the divine essence undivided and in its whole fullness, yet that *absolute* deity belongs only to the Father. Hence he believed in a subordination Trinity. But would it not appear from this representation as though some one had contradicted himself?—(F.)

from the name of Christ and making it a simple doxology to God the Father—"blessed forever be God, who is over all." The clauses are divided in this way by Lachmann, Tischendorf, and Meyer;[1] not, however, with the view of weakening the proof of Christ's divine nature, but on the ground that Paul never expressly applies the name God to Christ. But conceding for the moment the truth of that assertion, why should not Paul make such direct application of the term *in one case only*, as Meyer admits that John has done in the first verse of his Gospel? But we do not admit that this is the only instance in which Paul applies the term 'God' to Christ. On the contrary, we maintain that he calls Christ 'God' expressly in Titus 1 : 3 and 2 : 13, and by fair implication also in Phil. 2 : 6 and Col. 2 : 9. In fact, the whole tenor of the passage, interpreted as a doxology to Christ as God, agrees with Paul's way of introducing abrupt doxologies. See Rom. 1 : 25; 2 Cor. 11 : 31; 2 Tim. 4 : 18. Meyer admits that this last is an undoubted instance **of a** doxology to Christ. We adhere to the simplest and most natural punctuation and explanation of the verse, therefore, and regard it as a direct affirmation of the Godhead of Christ, parallel with John 1 : 1 and 20 : 28. The still more artificial punctuation, advocated by Erasmus and followed by Locke and Clarke, which places a period after the word 'all,' seems hardly to require any further notice. [The neuter article ($\tau\acute{o}$) before 'according to the flesh' ($\kappa\alpha\tau\grave{\alpha}\ \sigma\acute{\alpha}\rho\kappa\alpha$) puts the phrase in the accusative case, akin, perhaps, to the accusative of limitation or closer specification. (Buttmann, 152; Winer, 230.) See also 12 : 18. Alford sees in its use here an implication that

Christ was not *entirely* sprung from the Jews, but that he had a higher nature. Meyer also says that "such prepositional definitions with the accusative of the article certainly denote a complete contrast, which is either expressly stated, as in 12 : 5, or may be self-evident from the context, as 1 : 15; 12 : 18." If the whole clause after the word 'flesh' is a doxology to God the Father, the masculine article ($\acute{o}$) belongs to 'God' ($\theta\acute{e}os$). Compare 1 Cor. 3 : 7. And a literal translation of the whole would be: "The existing over-all God (be) blessed unto the ages!" "The existing" ($\acute{o}\ \check{\omega}\nu$), if it be referred to Christ, leaves 'God' ($\theta\acute{e}os$) without the article, and is equivalent to 'who is' ($\acute{o}s\ \check{e}\sigma\tau\iota$), or, according to Bishop Wordsworth, "who is existing." These same words are translated 'which is,' or, 'who is,' in John 1 : 18; 3 : 13; 2 Cor. 11 : 31; and 'who was' in John 12 : 17. Indeed, in 2 Cor. 11 : 31 we have not only the same construction, but, for the most part, the very words of our clause, and the passage is rendered: "God the Father . . . who is blessed unto the ages!" (Revised Version, margin.) So that both here and in Rom. 1 : 25, the only two places besides our passage where Paul uses the phrase "blessed unto the ages!" the reference is to a preceding subject. Since, therefore, there is no transition particle (like $\delta\acute{e}$ in 1 Tim. 1 : 17) to indicate a change of subject in our passage, and since the participle, 'being' or 'existing' ($\check{\omega}\nu$), appears somewhat superfluous and awkward if a doxology to God be supposed here, we naturally and necessarily, grammar and usage being taken into account, refer the whole clause to the preceding subject—Christ.[2] It is objected that elsewhere in the genuinely apostolical writings we do not find

---

[1] See foot-note, page 219.

[2] In the Appendix to the "Introduction of the Greek New Testament," by Westcott and Hort, the former remarks that "the juxtaposition of $\acute{o}\ X\rho\iota\sigma\tau\acute{o}s$ and $\acute{o}\ \check{\omega}\nu$ seems to make a change of subject improbable." Dr. Weiss, in his "Biblical Theology of the New Testament," Vol. I., p. 393, says that "the explanation which is most natural, and most in conformity with the language and the context, is that which makes it refer to Christ, and not to God." But Alford, with much more boldness, affirms that the rendering given by our Common and Revised Versions is "not only that most agreeable to the usage of the apostle, *but the only one admissible by the rules of grammar and arrangement.*" Another reason for referring this clause to Christ is

that, if this be a doxology to God the Father, the word 'blessed' ($\epsilon\mathring{v}\lambda o\gamma\eta\tau\acute{o}s$ or $\epsilon\mathring{v}\lambda o\gamma\eta\mu\acute{e}\nu os$), where no copula is expressed (compare 3 Kings 10 : 9; 2 Chron. 9 : 8; Job 1 : 21; Ps. 112 : 2, Septuagint Version, where the copula is used), should, by the invariable usage of the LXX. and of the New Testament, occupy the first place. See with $\epsilon\mathring{v}\lambda o\gamma\eta\tau\acute{o}s$, Luke 1 : 68; 2 Cor. 1 : 3; Eph. 1 : 3; 1 Peter 1 : 3; and with $\epsilon\mathring{v}\lambda o\gamma\eta\mu\acute{e}\nu os$, Matt. 21 : 9; 23 : 39; Mark 11 : 9; Luke 13 : 35; 19 : 38, etc. Liddon, in his Bampton Lectures, a most excellent treatise on "Our Lord's Supreme Divinity," says: "There are about forty places in the Old Testament, and five in the New, in which the formula of doxology occurs, and in every case the arrangement is the same: *Blessed be the God,* etc.—in other words, the predicate 'blessed' always

any doxology to Christ in the usual form. Both De Wette and Meyer concede that 2 Tim. 4 : 18 has such a doxology, "but this," says Meyer, "is just one of the traces of post-apostolical composition." And so the doxologies to Christ found in Heb. 13 : 21; 2 Peter 3 : 18; Rev. 1 : 6; 5 : 12, etc., rest under the same ban of discredit. Meyer also denies that the doxologies in Rom. 16 : 27; 1 Peter 4 : 11, refer to Christ; but denial is not always proof. Even if it be conceded that formal doxologies to Christ are wanting in Paul's epistles, no one, we suppose, would account for this want on the ground that the apostle could not conscientiously ascribe praise and glory and blessing to his adorable Redeemer. Besides, as Dr. Gifford in the "Bible Commentary" remarks, Meyer's objection is "wide of the mark," inasmuch as the clause before us, if applied to Christ, "is not a doxology at all," but is a simple assertion respecting the subject of the sentence in a manner wholly similar to 1 : 25; 2 Cor. 11 : 31, the only two places besides this in Paul's writings where the expression 'blessed unto the ages' (Revised Version, margin) is found. Were it a doubtful matter, also, whether Paul has elsewhere given the name of God to the Lord and Saviour of the New Testament, yet, as Philippi remarks, "he describes him indirectly as God, and therefore in any case thought of him as God, even if he did not call him so directly. For to whom belong divine attributes—like eternity (Col. 1 : 15, 17); omnipresence (Eph. 1 : 23; 4 : 10); and grace (Rom. 1 : 7; 1 Cor. 1 : 3, etc.); divine works, like the creation and preservation of the world (Col. 1 : 16, 17); and the dispensing of judgment (2 Cor. 5 : 10; 2 Thess. 1 : 7-10); and divine worship (Rom. 10 : 13; Phil. 2 : 10, 11)—is himself God." On the question whether the naming of Christ as God would not be inconsistent with Pauline usage, Prof. Cremer observes in substance

that the transition from the Son of God to God is a very easy one (John 10 : 23-38), and that Paul, who never speaks of Christ as the Son of man, should call him man (1 Tim. 2 : 5; Rom. 5 : 15, etc.), might likewise appear to be an inconsistency. But as "the man, Christ Jesus," is inferred from "the Son of man," so with equal justice we might infer the "God, Christ," from the "Son of God." Paul, in common with the earliest Christian disciples, worshiped Christ as divine, as One equal with God, in whom dwelt all the fullness of deity, or the divine essence, bodily, and was accustomed to direct prayer and supplication to him as One able to forgive and save. See Acts 22 : 16, 19; 2 Cor. 12 : 8, 9. Compare Rom. 10 : 12; Acts 2 : 21; 7 : 59; 9 : 14, 21; 1 Cor. 1 : 2; 2 Tim. 2 : 22. (See further at 10 : 12.) In the light, therefore, of Scripture teaching, we need not hesitate to affirm that Christ is both Lord of all and God over all, and is blessed forevermore. Meyer concedes that the language of our text, as far as the construction of words is concerned, may be applied to Christ, and it is a noteworthy fact that all the Fathers of the early Church—Irenæus, Tertullian, Origen, Cyprian, Hippolytus, Athanasius,[1] Basil, Gregory of Nyssa, Ambrose, Epiphanius, Chrysostom, Theodore of Mopsuestia, Cyril of Alexandria, Theodoret, Theophylact, Jerome, Augustine, Œcumenius, etc.—did apply it to Christ. Of the modern Germans who advocate the same view, Meyer mentions "Michaelis, Koppe, Tholuck, Flatt, Klee, Usteri, Benecke, Olshausen, Nielsen, Reithmayer, Maier, Beck, Philippi, Bisping, Gess, Krummacher, Jatho, Hahn, Thomasius, Ebrard, Ritschl, Hofmann, Weiss, Delitzsch, and others." Fritzsche, Winer, Ewald, and many others take the opposite view.

Two other principal points in favor of the

precedes the subject." Ps. 68 : 19 (Septuagint Version, 67 : 19) seems to be an exception. Yet the text here is probably corrupt, there being nothing in the Hebrew to correspond with the first "blessed." Perhaps the copula "is," rather than the imperative, should be understood here. Farrar and others, however, think it likely that Paul may have had the doxology of this Psalm in mind, and they find in this additional evidence that in our passage he calls Christ blessed, since in Eph. 4 : 8 he quotes the immediately preceding verse and applies it directly to Christ. It is, indeed, objected that εὐλογητός is nowhere else applied to Christ, but

only εὐλογημένος, as in Matt. 21 : 9; 23 : 39, and parallel passages, quoted above. But there is no essential difference in the meaning of the words, and in the Old Testament (LXX) we find εὐλογημένος as applied to God (1 Chron. 16 : 36; 2 Chron. 9 : 8; Ezek. 3 : 12), and εὐλογητός applied to man (versus Ellicott on Eph. 1 : 3; see Deut. 7 : 14; Ruth 2 : 20; 1 Sam. 15 : 13), and all these examples have the same Hebrew word in the original.—(F.)

[1] Meyer is mistaken, we think, when he says: "In the Arian controversies our passage was not made use of," for Athanasius, the so-called "father of orthodoxy," did thus use it.—(F.)

"ecclesiastical interpretation" of this passage remain to be noticed. I. A doxology to God the Father is here wholly inappropriate. Paul, indeed, mentions several blessings enjoyed by the Jews, yet he does not expressly specify them as gifts from God, and it was the thought of their being neglected or abused which now filled his soul with anguish. Who would expect from the apostle, in such a state of mind as this, an outburst of gratitude to God in view of his abused mercies? The proper place for a heartfelt doxology is just where Paul puts it—namely, at the end of the eleventh chapter, where he leaves the elder brother, the self-righteous Jewish legalist, and the younger brother, the Gentile prodigal, both lovingly reunited in their heavenly Father's house. On the other hand, an ascription of praise to Christ is here especially suitable, in view of his being set at nought by the Jews, and is exactly in the line of Paul's method, as indicated in 1 : 25, where, in contrast with the dishonor heaped upon God by the Gentiles, the affirmation is made that he 'is blessed for ever.' Dorner, in defense of this, "the most probable exposition," says: "A doxology to God would not fit in with the anguish at Israel's rejection, to which Paul gives utterance in ver. 1-5; on the other hand, the words, referred to Christ, whom Israel rejected in spite of his dignity, give a reason for this anguish. The continuation also of the sentence (ver. 6) with the conjunction (δέ) does not suit a doxology to God, but to Christ." ("System of Christian Doctrine," Vol. III., p. 175.) II. We should naturally expect, as an antithesis to 'as to the flesh' (κατὰ σάρκα), some reference (as in 1 : 3, 4, and elsewhere in the Scriptures) to the higher nature of Christ;[1] while, on the contrary, a doxology to God, besides being particularly unsuited to the context, would, as De Wette acknowledges, put Christ almost wholly into the shade. Indeed,

we may say with Philippi that the phrase 'according to the flesh' (κατὰ σάρκα) is introduced merely for the sake of the following contrast: 'Who is God over all.'[2] De Wette, who rejects the usual interpretation, thus sums up his views of this passage: "I especially hesitate at this, that [by viewing the whole clause as a doxology to God] not only nothing follows which, serving as a counterpoise to 'according to the flesh' (κατὰ σάρκα), sets forth Christ in his higher nature, but, as if to place him directly in the shade, God is designated as the One who is over all, without any special reason for such designation." After mentioning Erasmus' proposal to put a period after 'all,' as in Codex 71, he adds: "We have here, to be sure, the desired contrast, since Christ would be described as One who is over all (namely, the patriarchs), yet for the following doxology to God there certainly appears to be but very little reason; the absence of the article before the word God is surprising, and one would expect more justly than before that blessed (εὐλογητός) should precede. . . . Since no explanation *wholly* satisfies, another reading were desirable." But as concerns this passage there is no variation in the manuscripts, and we are satisfied with the reading as it is.]

The apostle now proceeds to vindicate God's truth and justice in the rejection of the Jews.

6. The first clause is elliptical: the complete expression of the verse would be: 'the case is not as though the word of God—(that is, the promise of special blessing to Abraham and his seed, of which the chief part was salvation through the Messiah), hath taken no effect, or in other words, failed of its fulfillment.' [Others fill out the ellipsis thus: (I say) not such a thing as that the word of God has come to nought. The verb strictly means *to fall from*, hence to fall down or through—that is, fail of accomplishment.] It seemed

---

[1] It has been objected that as it is we have no direct contrast to 'according to the flesh' (κατὰ σάρκα), but that a proper antithesis would require *according to the Spirit* (κατὰ πνεῦμα), as in 1 : 4, or, *according to his Godhead* (κατὰ θεότητα; compare Col. 2 : 9)—the whole reading something like this: "Of whom is Christ as respects the flesh, but who as respects his spiritual and higher nature, or his essential deity, is God over all." But the contrast here employed is just as expressive and appropriate as a direct and formal antithesis would have been.—(F.)

[2] This author has quite a full exposition of the text, and a defense of the ecclesiastical doctrine based, in some measure, upon it. For a brief summary of the "Scriptural Evidence of the Deity of Christ," see an article by the writer in the "Bibliotheca Sacra" for July, 1860. Since that paper was written, new manuscripts have been discovered, and it must now be conceded that *early* textual authority establishes the reading *who* instead of *God* in 1 Tim. 3 : 16. Philippi, however, still favors the reading of the Common Version.—(F.)

6 Not as though the word of God hath taken none effect. For they *are* not all Israel, which are of Israel: 7 Neither, because they are the seed of Abraham, *are they* all children: but, In Isaac shall thy seed be called. 8 That is, They which are the children of the flesh, these *are* not the children of God; but the children of the promise are counted for the seed.

7 though the word of God hath come to nought. For they are not all Israel that are of Israel: neither, because they are Abraham's seed, are they all children: but, In Isaac shall thy seed be called. That is, it is not the children of the flesh that are children of God; but the children of the promise are reck-

---

to the Jews generally that the word of God had come to nought, because they had not received the blessings which they understood to be promised: but the apostle shows them that they had misunderstood the promise, that it was not made to all the posterity of Abraham, but only to a selected portion of them, whom God owned as children of Abraham in a spiritual sense, [those, in other words, who are Jews "inwardly" (2: 29), who are the Israel of God (Gal. 6: 16), rather than Israel after the flesh. Dr. Weiss supposes the promise was given to the *nation* of the Jews, and not to all the individuals composing it. We see here that carnal descent, though from seed of divine promise, does of itself avail nothing]. **For they are not all Israel**—that is, true Israelites in God's esteem—**which are of Israel**—that is, who are the natural posterity of Jacob.

7. Neither, because they are the seed of Abraham. [Notice how '*neither*' (οὐδέ) is preceded by the direct simple negative (οὐ). Beginning with the previous sentence, we may give this literal rendering of the whole passage: "For not all who are of Israel (are) these Israel, neither, because they are Abraham's seed (are) all children " (of Abraham) —that is, in a true, spiritual sense. The pride and boast of the Jews was: "We have Abraham to our father." (Matt. 3: 9; Luke 3: 8; John 8: 39.)] 'The seed of Abraham' in this verse corresponds with 'of Israel,' of the preceding verse ["Israel after the flesh" (1 Cor. 10: 18)], and both are to be understood, literally, of the natural posterity of Abraham and Jacob, or Israel; and so, on the other hand, the term 'children' in this verse corresponds with 'Israel' of the preceding; and both are to be understood, figuratively, of the spiritual posterity of Abraham—that is, of those "who walk in the steps of the *faith* of our father Abraham." See Rom. 4: 12; Gal. 3: 9, 29; and John 8: 37, 39. [By these expressions the apostle indicates the possibility of a rejection of a part of the Jews, that people who felt themselves to be "the children of

the kingdom."] The quotation in the last clause of this verse—**but, In Isaac shall thy seed be called** ["a seed shall be called for thee"]—is taken quite literally from Gen. 21: 12 [without the formula of quotation, as being a well-known saying], and decisively confirms the previous assertion, that God never meant to be understood as promising the covenant blessings to all Abraham's posterity, but only to those in the line of Isaac [the child by virtue of promise], thus excluding, not only Ishmael and his posterity, as in the context of the passage just referred to, but equally the six sons of Keturah afterward born to him, and their descendants. (Gen. 25: 1, 2.) ["The seed subsisting in Isaac shall be called thy seed." (De Wette.) "Thy offspring shall be reckoned from Isaac." (Noyes.) Meyer and Philippi give this as the apostle's meaning: "The person of Isaac shall be regarded as the true seed or real descendant." "In thus adducing the case of Isaac and Ishmael the apostle certainly did not decide on the eternal state of either of them; yet the subject which he thus illustrated—namely, a remnant of believers among an unbelieving nation—must refer not to outward advantages and disadvantages, but to eternal salvation or damnation." (Scott.)]

8. That is, [which signifies. **They which are the children of the flesh,** etc. This sentence, literally translated, reads thus: "Not the children of the flesh (are) these the children of God." In other words, the children of the flesh are not thereby the children of God, even though they may have Abraham for their father]. Ishmael was the child of Abraham in a natural and usual way; Isaac in an unusual way, by virtue of an extraordinary promise of God. See Gal. 4: 23. The first was a child of the flesh; the second was a child of promise. And, as owing his birth to a special divine interposition, Isaac was a fit representative and type of all the children of God. See John 1: 12, 13. [**Children of the promise**—that is, "begotten by virtue of the divine promise" (Meyer), not

9 For this *is* the word of promise, At this time will I come, and Sarah shall have a son.

10 And not only *this;* but when Rebecca also had conceived by one, *even* by our father Isaac,

11 (For *the children* being not yet born, neither having done any good or evil, that the purpose of God according to election might stand, not of works, but of him that calleth;)

9 oned for a seed. For this is a word of promise. According to this season will I come, and Sarah

10 shall have a son. And not only so; but Rebecca also having conceived by one, *even* by our father

11 Isaac—for *the children* being not yet born, neither having done anything good or bad, that the purpose of God according to election might stand, not of

as Noyes has it: "children to whom the promise is made." "The children of the promise" are "those whom God gives to Abraham by spiritual generation. . . . They who interpret 'the children of promise' to mean those who by faith embrace the promise, say indeed what is fact, but do not speak with suitable precision, for the apostle in this place does not distinguish the children of Abraham from others by their faith as known, but he discourses concerning the primary cause—that is, the fountain of their faith itself, namely, the eternal purpose of gratuitous election." (Beza.)] **Are counted for the seed :** are esteemed by God as the seed of Abraham in the highest and truest sense. Compare notes on 3 : 1–6.

9. For this is the word of promise [or, ' *The word of promise is this* '] would be a very literal translation of the first clause of this verse. [Alford : " For this word was (one) of promise."] It is a specific proof of the last clause of the preceding verse. The quotation which follows expresses the sense of Gen. 18 : 10, 14. **At this time** means 'at this season, next year;' [in the Hebrew : *According to the living time*—that is, " *at the reviving season,* when this season revives, returns again, after passing away with the departing year." (Conant.) Gesenius makes this reviving time to be the coming spring. The clause: **And Sarah shall have a son**—*To Sarah shall be a son*—retains the form of the Hebrew, from which the Septuagint in Gen. 18: 10 varies].

10. And not only this. [We now advance from a word of divine promise to a word of divine appointment. (Meyer.)] It will be observed that the word 'this' is supplied by the translators. The expression in the original is elliptical, and the grammatical construction irregular, the name Rebecca being in the nominative without any verb ; and the sentence being resumed in ver. 12, after the parenthesis of ver. 11. in the altered form, *it was said to her.* [Many regard this nominative as absolute, and see in the sentence an *anacoluthon,* a changed

and unfinished construction. Noyes, Godet, and the Bible Union, seem to avoid this by translating : ' but when Rebecca also had conceived.' It would seem to be an " energetic breviloquence," as though Paul would say : ' not only is such the case with regard to Sarah, but there is Rebecca also.'] The ellipsis may be supplied thus : 'and not only was there a divine word of sovereign discrimination to Abraham, between his two sons, and in effect to Sarah likewise (see Gen. 18: 13–15), but Rebecca also had a similar divine message.' [So in substance, Winer, De Wette, Meyer. Philippi opposes this on the ground that the promise of ver. 9 was not given to Sarah, but to Abraham, and also that the saying of God in ver. 12 was to Rebecca no word of *promise.*] **But when Rebecca also had conceived** (twin sons) **by one, even by our father Isaac.** The phrase 'by one' seems to be suggested by the difference between this case and the former. In *that* case, there were two mothers, one a bond woman, and the other a free ; but in *this* case, there was but one mother, and but one father, which makes the sovereign limitation of the chosen posterity of Abraham to one of the twin sons the more significant, and this example therefore stronger than the former.

11. This verse completely overthrows the doctrine of the pre-existence of souls: the children **being not yet born,** and, of course, **neither having done any good or evil.** [Instead of ' evil ' (κακόν) the Revised text has *bad* (φαῦλον, found in א A B), which properly signifies *light* or *worthless, good-for-nothing,* hence, with a moral reference, *bad* or *ill,* (compare this with our word "naughty"), and means a little less than *wicked.* They were not guilty of personal, voluntary transgressions, yet, as belonging to Adam's fallen race, they both had natures inclined to sin. "As regards original sin, both children were alike, and as regards actual sin, neither had any." (Augustine.) Neither birth nor works gave them any claim.] **The purpose of God according to election,** or, 'the elective purpose of God,' is a very definite and strong expression. **Might stand** [properly, *may stand*, denoting permanence] ; this word is the opposite of that which in ver. 6 is translated 'hath taken none effect.' [This sentence in construction and thought would properly follow the first phrase of the next verse.] **Not of works** [properly defines 'purpose.' Some make it dependent on 'may stand.' The positive negative (οὐκ) is here used, since it is not immediately connected with 'that' (ἵνα) or the verb]. **But of him that calleth.** The absolute sovereignty of the divine election in the bestowment of spiritual blessings, irrespective of human works, performed or foreseen, could hardly be affirmed in stronger terms. ["The thought of an unconditional election of grace is here distinctly expressed, and the idea that 'not of works' excludes indeed all present merit, but not the future which God has foreseen, is wholly vain." (De Wette.) Besides, the works of Jacob, if foreseen, could not have furnished ground for his election, for his works were very nearly as ill as Esau's. Nor were the descendants of Jacob chosen to be God's peculiar people because of their worthiness, as Moses frequently reminded them. See Deut. 9 : 5. The purpose of God to bless Jacob was not, then, based on the merit of foreseen good works, or on the ground of any human claim, but was made according to God's free, yet not arbitrary, choice. "The purpose," says Philippi, "is described as made according to election, or determined by election, linked to election, in opposition to an indiscriminate, universal saving decree, having reference to the whole human race, or to a definite class of men." Similarly Meyer: "The purpose would have been no purpose *according to election*, if God had resolved to bless all without exception." The apostle, moreover, while denying that God's elective purpose is based on foreseen works, does not affirm that it depends on foreseen faith. Instead of saying "not from works but from faith," or on account of faith, he simply adds: *but from him that calleth.* And in 2 Tim. 1 : 9, Revised Version, he tells us that God's saving call is "not according to our works, but according to his own purpose and grace, which was given us in Christ Jesus before times eternal." Compare Eph. 1 : 11; 3 : 11.

Godet affirms that faith "cannot be a merit, since faith consists precisely in renouncing all merit," and hence that faith foreseen, unlike works foreseen, though a moral condition of election, would impose no obligation on God. To this, we reply, that if God's elective purpose from eternity is made to depend upon the foreseen faith of individuals, then God, even though no obligation be imposed on him, is yet no longer a sovereign disposer of grace, nor does he take the initiative in one's salvation. A faith which conditions a person's election, especially if not based on grace, should be begotten by that person; and if faith is originated by man, little is left for election or predestination to do. But Holy Scripture, instead of asserting that God's purpose according to election is grounded on any man's work or faith, explicitly declares that faith and repentance and obedience and salvation are the *result* of God's elective purpose. See 8 : 29; Eph. 2 : 8, 10; Phil. 2 : 13; 2 Thess. 2 : 13; 2 Tim. 2 : 25; 1 Peter 1 : 2, etc. Truly, as Augustine says: "God does not choose us because we believe, but *that* we may believe." Even the Arminian Remonstrants, in the third and fourth "points" of their controversy with Calvinism, affirm, "that true faith cannot proceed from the exercise of our natural faculties and powers, or from the force and operation of free will, since man, in consequence of his natural corruption, is incapable of thinking or doing any good thing;" and, "that this divine grace or energy of the Holy Ghost, which heals the disorders of a corrupt nature, *begins*, advances, and brings to perfection everything that can be called good in man, and that, consequently, all good works, without exception, are to be attributed to God alone and to the operation of his grace." It would do no harm if some of the diluted Calvinism of our day was tinctured with a little more of such Arminianism as this. Such views as these are antagonistic to the doctrine that God's elective purpose to save is conditioned on man's foreseen faith. Albert Barnes says, that the purpose of God "is not a purpose formed *because* he sees anything in the individuals as a ground for his choice, but for some reason which he has not explained and which in the Scripture is simply called *purpose* and *good pleasure.*" Such evidently was the apostle's view of God's purpose according to

12 It was said unto her, The elder shall serve the younger.

12 works, but of him that calleth, it was said unto her,

---

election; otherwise it would not have called forth what Calvin terms the "impure barkings" of those who, on account of such election, charged God with injustice. See ver. 14. Augustine, in controversy with the Pelagian idea, that God elects men because of their foreseen goodness, says: "Who but must wonder that this most ingenious sense should escape the apostle? For after proposing what was calculated to excite astonishment respecting those children unborn, he started to himself, by way of objection, the following question: 'What then, is there unrighteousness with God?' It was the place for him to answer, that God foresaw the merits of each of them. Yet he says nothing of this, but resorts to the decrees and mercy of God.'"

It is to be noticed, however, that in all Paul's writings there is no plainly specified election or predestination to eternal death. Calvin, who approached, perhaps, too near the precipice, concerning which Augustine said "Beware!" inferred the verity of an "eternal reprobation," and the mere logical faculty may, from one point of view, deem this inference to be unavoidable. But from the apostle's most explicit utterances, we learn that those whom God wills to blind and harden are incorrigible sinners, that those to whom he *willeth* to show *mercy* are, of course, lost and guilty, and that his election is *of grace*, and has reference, therefore, to the undeserving. The elect bear the name "vessels of *mercy*," which shows that they, like the vessels of wrath, are taken from a common " mass of perdition"; and if the former are saved, it is because of *gratuitous* election; if the latter are reprobated, it is because of their sins. All are alike undeserving, and hence God can, without partiality, have mercy on whom he will, can reject or pass by whom he will, and it is ours only to say: "Even so, Father, for so it seemed good in thy sight." For some further views on this general subject, see remarks on 8 : 29. To the question whether God's elective purpose regarding Jacob and Esau had reference to their temporal condition or to their eternal state, we should answer that, according to the apostle's representation, it had primary reference to their temporal state, and not so much to them as individuals as to their descendants. Paul certainly does not affirm in the next verse that Jacob was elected to eternal salvation and that Esau was reprobated to eternal death, but **the elder shall serve the younger.** Yet even the elder did not *personally* serve the younger, but, on the contrary, we read that Jacob, in consequence of his supplantings, was obliged to humble himself to the earth as a servant before his brother, and to say : "My lord, Esau!" The one, however, was elected to peculiar external advantages and to theocratic gracious privileges, to the use and enjoyment of which the other was not chosen, while still the other was not left entirely destitute of divine favor and blessing. Isaac was elected to a pre-eminence over Ishmael, and Jacob to a pre-eminence over Esau, yet, as Philippi observes, "even Ishmael is not left without promise (Gen. 16 : 10; 17 : 20), and is preserved by divine providence. (Gen. 21 : 17, seq.) Esau also receives his blessing (Gen. 27 : 39, seq.), while the life of Isaac and Jacob is fertile in peculiar trials and sorrows. And the posterity of Ishmael and Esau are, finally, in admission into the Messianic kingdom in accordance with the universal prophetic promises, to obtain a share in the loftiest prerogative of the chosen people." Yet in our view God's elective purpose, as set forth in the Scriptures, *does not* generally have reference to peoples and to their enjoyment of external privileges. That Paul in this Epistle makes divine election to be individual, gracious, and saving, is most clearly manifest. See ver. 23; 8 : 29; 11 : 5. And the apostle could well show this while explaining the temporary rejection of God's people, Israel, and without digressing to write a set treatise on election and reprobation. Thus, from the example of Jacob and Esau, Prof. Stuart derives this lesson: "If God did, according to election, make such distinctions among the legitimate and proper children of Isaac, the 'son of promise,' then the same God may choose, call, justify, and glorify those who are 'called' in respect to the heavenly inheritance. If it is not unjust or improper in one case to distribute favors 'according to his purpose,' then it is not in another." Dr. Shedd gives his views on these points as follows: "The theocratic election

13 As it is written, Jacob have I loved, but Esau have I hated.

14 What shall we say then? *Is there* unrighteousness with God? God forbid.

15 For he saith to Moses, I will have mercy on whom I will have mercy, and I will have compassion on whom I will have compassion.

13 The elder shall serve the younger. Even as it is written, Jacob I loved, but Esau I hated.

14 What shall we say, then? Is there unrighteous-
15 ness with God? God forbid. For he saith to Moses, I will have mercy on whom I have mercy, and I will have compassion on whom I have com-

---

of Isaac and Jacob illustrates the spiritual election of individuals; and the theocratic reprobation of Ishmael and Esau illustrates the spiritual reprobation of individuals. . . . The question arises whether the theocratic corresponded with the individual election and reprobation in the cases of Jacob and Esau themselves. The fact that each was a typical personage favors the affirmative, because the symbolical is most naturally homogeneous with that which it symbolizes. It would be unnatural to set forth a spiritually elect person as the type of the reprobated class, and *vice versa.* And the history of Esau shows that his sinful self-will was not overcome by the electing compassion of God. Esau renounced the religion of Abraham, Isaac, and Jacob, in which he had been educated, and to which he might still have adhered, even though he had, by the divine will, lost his primogeniture, and lapsed into idolatry with his descendants. He falls, therefore, into the same class with the apostate Jews, and though 'of Israel' was yet not Israel." (Ver. 6.) But we do not feel called upon to settle the eternal state of these individuals.]

13. The passage here cited [in confirmation of the preceding] is written in Mal. 1 : 2, 3. We must beware of weakening too much the expression **Esau have I hated,** since the descendants of Esau, to whom the language is particularly applied by Malachi, are described as "the people against whom the Lord hath indignation for ever." (Ver. 4.) [We read in the Wisdom of Solomon (11 : 24) : "Thou lovest all things and abhorrest nothing which thou hast made, for never wouldst thou have made anything, if thou hadst hated it." Certainly the "philanthropy" of God (Titus 3 : 4) would not allow him to hate absolutely and in a human manner any human being, even though sinful. We may suppose that he loved Esau personally with the love of compassion, while he could not have loved Jacob with entire complacency. Those who think that "hate" in Scripture usage sometimes means to love less, refer to such passages as

Gen. 29 : 30, 31; Luke 14 : 26, compared with Matt. 10 : 37, etc., where a less degree of love, compared with a greater, is termed hatred. The expression is anthropopathic, and refers not so much to the emotion as to the effect. (Philippi.) In Sirach 33 : 11, 12, we find a like declaration of the unequal distribution of God's gifts among men. Of course, any withholding of divine favors might seem an act of hatred. It often is an act of judgment against sinners. Haldane affirms that Esau, even before his birth, deserved God's hatred, because he sinned in Adam; but surely his Adamic transgression was not greater than that of Jacob.]

To this doctrine, that God chooses one and rejects another at his mere good pleasure, there are two objections urged: I. That it is unjust. (Ver. 14.) Answer 1. God *claims* this prerogative. (Ver. 15, 16.) Answer 2. He *exercises* it. (Ver. 17, 18.) II. That it destroys human responsibility. (Ver. 19.) Answer 1. The objection is irreverent. (Ver. 20, 21.) Answer 2. God only treats the rejected as they deserve, and the accepted better than they deserve (ver. 22-24); and neither of these is unjust.

14. Paul here states, in the form of a question, an objection which he sees likely to arise in the reader's mind from what has just been said (ver. 11-13); and before giving any specific answer to that objection, indignantly repels, as he does elsewhere (3 : 4, 5; Gal. 3 : 21), any aspersion upon the character of God. *Let it not be!* [The negative particle (μή) in this question supposes a negative answer.]

15. For he saith to Moses. The 'for' here assigns the reason why the apostle so emphatically repudiates any possible ascription of unrighteousness to God; 'for' he explicitly announces to Moses, as an axiom which he would have all men understand, that he is sovereign and self-moved in the distribution of his favors; that his mercy is pure mercy, and his compassion pure compassion, and that he owes no apology to any man for the manner in which he exercises his benevolence. **I will have mercy on whom**

---

16 So then *it is* not of him that willeth, nor of him that runneth, but of God that sheweth mercy.
17 For the Scripture saith unto Pharaoh, Even for

16 passion. So then it is not of him that willeth, nor of him that runneth, but of God that hath mercy.
17 For the scripture saith unto Pharaoh, For this very

I will have mercy, etc. The citation is from Exod. 33 : 19 [closely following the Septuagint, even to the rendering of the tenses. (The Hebrew is: *I have mercy on whom I will have mercy.* The Revised Version gives the Septuagint rendering.) This utterance of Jehovah to Moses is "to be understood in a causal sense as expressing the reason why Moses' request was granted—namely, that it was an act of unconditional grace and compassion on the part of God, to which no man, not even Moses, could lay any just claim." (Keil and Delitzsch.) "If to Moses God's favor was absolutely free and unmerited, how much more to others!" ("Bible Commentary.")] The two verbs here used have the same general sense, but the latter is the stronger expression [denoting a greater degree of pity, equivalent to "bewailing sympathy." (Meyer.)][1] The twofold expression is very emphatic, and intimates that God would have men understand, once for all, that he is not to be challenged to give an account of his reasons for showing favor to some men and not to others. ["No man may deal with God as if he were his creditor." (Bengel.)] It would be well for cavilers to remember this. The manner in which the apostle meets the objection here admonishes us that the surest way to determine what God's character allows him to do is to consult the Scriptures which are his word. ["Paul considers it enough to check vile barkings by the testimonies of Scripture." (Calvin.)]

16. So then it is not [in the power] **of him that willeth.** [Noyes: "It dependeth not on him that willeth."] What is the unexpressed subject of this sentence? That which is implied in the preceding verses, the mercy and compassion of God, or, more exactly, the obtaining of those divine favors and blessings which proceed from his mercy and compassion. Are we to conclude, then, that the willing and the running avail nothing? No, certainly not, for this would be to contradict the gracious promises of our Lord.

(Matt. 7 : 7, 8; John 5 : 40; Rev. 22 : 17, etc.) The apostolic exhortation is: "So run that ye may obtain." (1 Cor. 9 : 24, 26.) [See also Phil. 3 : 14; 2 Tim. 4 : 7.] But the meaning is, that the will and the power to run so as to obtain are themselves from God (Phil. 2 : 13), so that, in the ultimate analysis of the matter, it all depends upon God who showeth mercy. His gracious and sovereign will is before and behind, and beneath all human willing and running. ["The human striving is, indeed, necessary, but it ever remains dependent." (De Wette.) To will and to run in our own strength is vain, nor can any human willing or working lay God under obligations or furnish a ground of justification. "The mercy of God," says Dr. Ripley, "is not a result of a person's own will or desire for it, as the originating or procuring cause. . . . The apostle here denies the meritorious character of such desires and efforts, as if they would constitute a claim for the blessings. Not to man's desert, but to God's will and unmerited mercy, must blessings be traced." The Jews both willed and ran earnestly and sought eagerly after a law of righteousness, but "they stumbled." It is singular that some, like Chrysostom, put the utterance of this verse into the mouth of an opponent instead of regarding it as the apostle's own inference.] To suppose any special reference to Abraham's willing in favor of Ishmael, or Isaac's in favor of Esau, or to Esau's running to hunt venison for his father, as if these historic facts had suggested the form of the expression, is to narrow and limit the words unduly. They undoubtedly are borrowed from the Grecian games, to which Paul so often refers in his epistles. (1 Cor. 9 : 24-26; Gal. 2 : 2; 5 : 7; Phil. 2 : 16.) ["Observe that in the exercise of this sovereign choice God is here spoken of as *having mercy.*" (Boise.)]

17. For the Scripture saith unto Pharaoh. ['For' denotes a consequence *e contrario*, drawn from the preceding statement.] 'The Scripture' is here identified with its divine author, as in Gal. 3 : 8, 22; 4 : 30. The

---

[1] Compare λυπή and ὀδυνή **ṁ** ver. 2 for a corresponding advance of emphasis. The particle *an* (ἄν) belongs to the relative rather than to the verb (Buttmann, 217), making it equivalent to "whomsoever," and thereby indicating the freedom of the divine choice. This particle is, as here, commonly used in the New Testament with the subjunctive.—(F.)

this same purpose have I raised thee up, that I might shew my power in thee, and that my name might be declared thoughout all the earth.

purpose did I raise thee up, that I might shew in thee my power, and that my name might be pub-18 lished abroad in all the earth. So then he hath

quotation is from Exod. 9: 16. [The article with Pharaoh denotes the dative case and probably was not meant to particularize "the Pharaoh who lived in the time of Moses." (Bengel.) Compare *the Moses* in ver. 15. The Greek has a word (ὅτι), before the quotation, which is not translated. It is here, as frequently, merely the sign of quotation. It is worthy of remark that Pharaoh was not thus spoken to till after he or his land had been visited with six plagues.] The words **Have I raised thee up** are not to be understood specifically, of raising up to the throne, much less of raising up from sickness, as in James 5 : 15 (where only the context gives the verb this peculiar sense) ; but in a general sense. 'I have given thee thy place in history,' as the verb is used in Matt. 11 : 11; 24: 11; John 7 : 52, etc. This general sense alone suits the context, and the apostle's argument. [This verb is used about seventy times in the Septuagint. "In none of these cases does it mean to create, to produce, to raise up, in the sense of bringing into being." (Stuart.) Hence Beza's rendering: *feci ut existeres*, "I have caused thee to exist," would seem to be inadmissible. The Hebrew verb, "I caused thee to stand," is rather loosely rendered in the Septuagint, "on account of this thou wast preserved." Yet this in sense is akin to Isaac Leeser's version: "I allowed thee to remain," and to Dr. Gifford's in the "Bible Commentary," "I spared and upheld thee." These renderings convey the idea that the *continuing* of Pharaoh's life of rebellion was the means of magnifying the name and power of Jehovah. Meyer gives this paraphrase: "Thy whole historical appearance has been brought about by me, in order that," etc. De Wette's rendering, favored by Prof. Stuart, "I have incited thee to resistance," seems to be an addition to the text.] This is an illustration on the darker side ; and it is a vindication of

God's justice, on the assumed axiom that what he declares his purpose to do and actually does is right. There can be no higher proof that a thing is righteous than that *God does it*. **That I might shew my power in thee**—that is, by thy signal overthrow at the Red Sea.[1] **And that my name might be declared throughout all the earth.** The word translated 'declared' is an emphatic word, implying a thorough publication of God's righteous severity in Pharaoh's destruction. We have a record in Josh. 2: 9–11 of the effect which the report of God's judgment on Pharaoh had on the inhabitants of Jericho. [Compare also Exod. 15: 14, seq.] Meyer and Tholuck cite Greek and Roman authors of later times who refer to these things ; the dispersion of the Jews scattered the famous tidings far and wide among the nations ; the Koran helped to spread the story wherever it went ; and the Scriptures are fast publishing it literally 'throughout all the earth.' So it is that God's 'name,' his power and justice in the overthrow of the proud and hardened oppressor of his people, is gradually and at last universally made known throughout the whole world. ["God might have caused Pharaoh to be born in a cabin, where his proud obstinacy would have been displayed with no less self-will, but without any notable historical consequence. On the other hand, he might have placed on the throne of Egypt at that time a weak, easy-going man, who would have yielded at the first shock. What would have happened? Pharaoh in his obscure position would not have been less arrogant and perverse, but Israel would have gone forth from Egypt without *eclat*. No plagues one upon another, no Red Sea miraculously crossed, no Egyptian army destroyed; nothing of all that made so deep a furrow in the Israelitish conscience, and which remained for the elect people the immovable founda-

---

[1] The verb 'shew forth' occurs eleven times in the New Testament, but only in Paul's writings and in the Epistle to the Hebrews. It is in the middle voice (with transitive signification) and probably has a slight subjective reference. Thus: show forth *for myself*, or, *on my account*. Hence the pronoun 'my' is not redundant. The apostle substitutes for the *strength* (ἰσχυν) of the LXX. the more general term *power* (δύναμιν), also ὅπως —*that, to the end that*—for ἱνα—*that*, the latter commonly referring to the more direct, the former to the more remote or secondary purpose. The two verbs in the subjunctive, by which mood continuance of action or result is noted, might be rendered by the auxiliary *may*.—(F.)

18 Therefore hath he mercy on whom he will *have mercy*, and whom he will he hardeneth.

mercy on whom he will, and whom he will he hardeneth.

---

tion of their relation to Jehovah. And thereafter also no influence produced on the surrounding nations. The entire history would have taken another direction." (Godet.)]

18. Therefore hath he mercy on whom he will have mercy. [The ' whom ' (ὅν) of this clause, or the one on ' whom ' God wills to show 'mercy,' is not what the anti-supralapsarians call a "nonentity," nor is he a pure and innocent being, but an actually existing guilty and undeserving transgressor; otherwise God could show him no *mercy*. And it is precisely the same class of persons whom God, for reasons sufficient to himself, willeth to harden. The last clause of the verse : **And whom he will he hardeneth**—may well be read by sinful men with "bated breath," and feelings of awe.] In the account of God's dealings with Pharaoh in Exodus, we have these three modes of expression— "the Lord hardened Pharaoh's heart" : Exod. 4: 21 ; 7 : 3; 9 : 12; 10: 1, 20, 27 ; 11 : 10; 14: 4, 8; "Pharaoh hardened his heart" : Exod. 8: 15, 32 (in Heb. 8: 11, 28); 9 : 34; " Pharaoh's heart was hardened " [remained hardened]: Exod. 7: 13, 14, 22; 8: 19 [in Heb. 8: 15] ; 9 : 7, 35. No doubt all these three expressions refer to the same fact, but it does not follow that they all have the same meaning, nor are we at liberty to weaken the force of the first, and most frequent, by substituting for it, 'the Lord suffered Pharaoh to harden his heart.' The language itself, and the way in which Paul uses the illustration, imply something more than a mere passive *permission* on the part of God. The one point which must be guarded is, that God never *solicits* men to evil, and then punishes them for yielding to the solicitation. James 1 : 13 decisively negatives that idea. We will not undertake to explain precisely how God rightfully may, and sometimes actually does harden a man's heart (for the case of Pharaoh can hardly be considered a *solitary one*); but we will rather rest content with enforcing the Psalmist's solemn admonition, "Stand in awe and sin not." (4: 4.) [The first two examples

and the last but one of the first series of texts cited above are prophecies : ' will harden.' Omitting the two former, we may notice that it is said of Pharaoh seven times either that he hardened his heart, or that his heart remained hard, before it is affirmed, in 9 : 12, that Jehovah hardened him. " And even after that," as Godet says, as if a remnant of liberty still remained to him, it is said for a last time that " he hardened himself" (9 : 34), or " remained hardened." (9 : 35.) This is an instance of a man's giving himself up, and of God's giving him up, "to work iniquity." " When God hardens a man," says Charnock, " he only leaves him to his stony heart." Tholuck observes that—" In the case before us the divine agency must be limited to the fact that God brought about those circumstances which make a heart disposed to evil still harder. That God did thus to Pharaoh is shown by history. That such is the only sense in which it is said that God hardened Pharaoh is evinced by the fact of its being declared in the context *that Pharaoh hardened himself.*" Compare with this the exhortation of Ps. 95: 8; Heb. 3 : 8, 15, " harden not your hearts." The Scriptures which speak of God's hardening the heart of Pharaoh, at the same time blame him for his pride and self-will (Exod. 9 : 17; 10: 3, 4), while Pharaoh on his part makes frequent confession of sin. (Exod. 9 : 27; 10 : 16, 17.) We must hold to the truth of the apostle's statement, even though we think, with Philippi and Godet, that a different view would have been presented had Paul not been combating Pharisaic pretension and arrogance. Alford says: " Whatever difficulty there lies in this assertion that God hardeneth whom he will, lies also in the daily course of his providence, in which we see this hardening process going on in the case of the prosperous ungodly man." The conjecture of some that 'hardeneth' here means to treat harshly, in supposed accordance with Job 39 : 16, where the ostrich is spoken of as hardening her young, is scarcely worthy of notice.] [1]

---

[1] We are sorry to see that the *vom Strausse* (of the ostrich) of Philippi's commentary on this passage, is, probably from mere inadvertence, converted into a proper name in the generally excellent translation of this excellent work.—(F.)

19 Thou wilt say then unto me, Why doth he yet find fault? For who hath resisted his will?

19   Thou wilt say then unto me, Why doth he still

19. [Thou wilt say then unto me—not: *what shall we say then?* The sharp answer which follows shows that the apostle has as his opponent, not a modest inquirer, but an insolent antagonist. So Philippi, who thinks that Paul has an arrogant Jew before him in the whole of the present exposition.] **Why doth he yet find fault?** ['Yet'—that is, after he has hardened me, or "after he has taken away freedom and accountability through his purpose to harden." (De Wette.) How can he blame me for disobedience? "Why am I still judged as a sinner?" Meyer, seemingly against the context, regards the question as tragic rather than impious, "the expression of human weakness in presence of the divine decree of hardening." Who is able to resist the fixed purpose of the Almighty? Compare Acts 11: 17.] **Who hath resisted** (or, *resists*, the perfect being used as present) **his will?** If it is God's will to harden a man, since his will cannot be successfully resisted, how can he *blame* hardened sinners? This is a common objection to the view of God's sovereignty which Paul has presented. It is important and instructive to note how he meets this cavil.

[This verse shows us that other minds than ours have been troubled with the unfathomable mysteries of God's creation and moral government. Paul himself stood face to face

with all the deep, dark problems of the universe, and we do not suppose that even his mind was so far supernaturally enlightened as to be able to solve them. His language in 1 Cor. 13: 12 (Revised Version) is: "Now we see in a mirror, darkly" (margin, "Greek, in a riddle"); and we may well believe that the universe had for him its insoluble enigmas. In a coming chapter we shall see how he speaks of the "unsearchable judgments" and the "untraceable ways" of God. The verse before us presents a problem of exceeding difficulty.[1] We are held blamable for disobedience to God, and yet how is it possible for a weak and dependent creature to resist and thwart the will of the Omnipotent? Yet we do in this world resist and disobey his law, or revealed will, continually, otherwise all men would at once come to repentance (2 eter 3:9) and to a full knowledge of the truth (1 Tim. 2: 4), and we should not have been taught to pray: "Thy will ($\theta\acute{\epsilon}\lambda\eta\mu\alpha$) be done on earth as in heaven." A different word, however, is used for 'will' in our passage— (namely, $\beta o\acute{\nu}\lambda\eta\mu\alpha$) which here seems to denote his determinate, predetermining, immutable counsel (or $\beta o\nu\lambda\acute{\eta}$; see Acts 2: 23; 4: 28; Heb. 6: 17), which cannot be thwarted or withstood; and how can a frail creature of earth resist "the counsel of his will"? (Βουλὴν τοῦ θελήματος αὐτοῦ, Eph. 1: 11.[2]) Hence from

---

[1] "The great and perhaps ever insoluble problem still remains—namely, the ability of a created being to act contrary to the will of God—how God came to create a being with power to withstand him, the Almighty one." (Olshausen.) But if we cannot withstand or transgress, but do perfectly fulfill his decretive will, his eternal purpose, how can we be held blamable for transgression? We have here for certain a "plausible and formidable objection" (Hodge), and the apostle seeks rather to strike the objector dumb by rebuking his irreverent spirit, than to solve fully the speculative difficulty. We can see that there is in the objection a spirit of *disobedience* and rebellion, we can feel that there is some perversion or insufficient statement of the truth, but the logical faculty finds it a hard task to clear the question of all difficulty. "This is indeed," says Dr. Schaff, "one of the greatest and most difficult problems, which can never be fully solved from the standpoint of earthly knowledge. Only after the accomplished victory over evil, can the deep, dark enigma of evil, which forms the main difficulty of the problem, be solved."—(F.)

[2] A similar thought is expressed in 2 Chron. 20: 6; Job 9: 19 (LXX.); Wisdom of Solomon 12: 12. Θέλω and βούλομαι are both employed by way of contrast in Matt. 1: 19, the former, according to classic usage, generally denoting a volition; the latter, an inclination or propensity of the mind. [Here the reverse seems to me to be the fact. (A. H.)] Βούλομαι, to have in thought, to intend, is never used of brutes, while in Homer it is always used when speaking of the gods, since their wish is equivalent to effect. (Robinson, Liddell and Scott.) We may say that it is God's present βούλημα (using the term in the weaker sense of *desire*) that none should perish, but that all men should come to repentance (2 Peter 3: 9), and that it is his θέλημα, or will, that all men should be saved and come to a full knowledge of the truth. (1 Tim. 2: 4.) Yet this his desire and will surely do not come to pass in this world; but we can hardly say that either of these is his established, immutable counsel or purpose; otherwise this universal repentance and attainment of the truth would have already taken place. Prof. Turner seems inclined to think that even God's purpose may

20 Nay but, O man, who art thou that repliest against God? Shall the thing formed say to him that formed *it*, Why hast thou made me thus?
21 Hath not the potter power over the clay, of the

20 find fault? For who withstandeth his will? Nay but, O man, who art thou that repliest against God? Shall the thing formed say to him that formed it, 21 Why didst thou make me thus? Or hath not the

this view of the matter, the rebellious sinner is tempted to reply against God with very great freedom of language, and to say: "I am not to blame for resisting God's eternal purpose concerning me, since such resistance on my part is an impossibility;" or, "I do not resist God, for in hardening myself I have done nothing but obey him." Objections similar to the above are noticed by James (1:13) and by the Son of Sirach (Eccles. 15: 11, 12), and are rebutted by a direct denial. While therefore we cannot entirely remove the speculative difficulty attending this subject, we can tell the sinner that he is not sincere in making this objection; that he is offering it as a mere make-shift; that he knows God does not make him sin; that he is opposed to God and does disobey and resist God's will; and that he does this of his free choice; that he does not intend to obey, but he intends evil and makes this wickedness himself; that his alleged obedience is all a farce, and cannot be deemed by himself genuine, hearty, or meritorious. God by his providence may indeed give shape to the evil, and by his infinite power and wisdom cause it to promote his glory, and yet may rightfully punish the sinner for his intended transgression.]

20. Nay but, O man, etc. When the objector becomes too bold and irreverent, Paul rebukes his impiety before making any other reply to his objection. It does not become the creature to dispute with the Creator or to call him to account. [Nor will Jehovah upon compulsion give any account of his matters. Instead of the 'nay but,' we might properly read—*yea rather* (Luke 11:28), or, *indeed*, with a slight touch of irony. Through the inversion of words in the interrogative clause, a frequent usage in the New Testament, the 'thou' is rendered emphatic. The 'O man' is inserted to denote his inferiority and impotence as

contrasted with the Almighty. It has been said that this replying against God by so weak a creature as man shows that he has a free will, or, at least, that he can use his tongue very freely. If the sinner is rebellious against God and chooses to use his freedom, he can find much wherewith to reply against God. He would bring God down below the level of his creatures and make him *responsible*, as it were, for all that is ill in the universe. 'Nay but, O man,' thou art too weak and ignorant and insignificant to put on such airs of superiority and to contend so haughtily with God. **Shall the thing formed say,** etc. The Greek particle (μὴ) supposes a negative answer. The application of the term 'thing formed' (πλάσμα) to man is warranted by Gen. 2:7; Ps. 103:14—Septuagint Version (102:14), 'he knoweth our frame' (πλάσμα)—and 1 Tim. 2:13. In the Wisdom of Solomon (7:1), Adam is called the '*protoplast*.' The query seems to have reference, not to an original creation (as of clay with its properties), but to the making or fashioning of that which already exists. Dr. Hodge says: "It is to be borne in mind that Paul does not here speak of the right of God over his creatures as creatures, but as sinful creatures, as he himself clearly intimates in the next verse. It is the cavil of a sinful creature against his Creator that he is answering." Hence the question, as Dr. Shedd remarks, "is not, Why hast thou made me a sinner? but, Why hast thou left me in sin?" So if we apply this language to the Jewish people whom God formed into a nation, their query would be: "Why hast thou withheld thy mercy from thy people Israel, and why dost thou show thy favor to the Gentiles? Why hast thou rejected or passed by thy covenant people and adopted the uncircumcised heathen?"]

21. Hath not the potter power over the

fail of accomplishment. If this be so, then the eternal blessedness of the saints is not secure, and heaven itself may be lost out of God's universe. Dr. Shedd says: "The distinction between the will of desire and the will of decree is illustrated in the human sphere by the difference between inclination and volition. A man frequently opposes the inclination of his will by a volition of his will. He decides to do what he is dis-

inclined to do." In a similar way some speak of a principal or antecedent will and a consequent will. The "Bible Commentary" says: "When ἐθέλω (or θέλω) and βούλομαι are *distinguished*, the former means the simple, spontaneous will, the latter the conscious and deliberate purpose." See further on θέλω and βούλομαι, notes to 7:15, also a long discussion under θέλω in Thayer's Lexicon.—(F.)

same lump to make one vessel unto honour, and another unto dishonour?

potter a right over the clay, from the same lump to make one part a vessel unto honour, and another

clay, etc. ['Or' should precede 'hath,' as in the Revised Version. "It introduces a fresh ground of rebuke." (Alford.) 'Over the clay' (πηλοῦ) is here separated from its governing substantive, 'power,' owing, perhaps, to the joining together of words of similar or related import.] This figure is found repeatedly in the prophets. See Isa. 29:16; 45:9; 64:8; Jer. 18:6 [also Job 10:8, 9; Wisd. of Sol. 15:7; Ecclus. 33:13 (36:13, LXX.); 38:29, 30]. The comparison must not be pressed too far. It is just as impossible for man to have just cause to complain against God as it is for the clay to have cause to complain against the potter, but not for the same reason. In the case of the clay and the potter, the fault-finding is forbidden by the nature of the clay; in the case of man and his Maker, it is forbidden by the character of the Maker. The nature of the substance wrought upon forbids complaint in the former case; the character of the Being who works and none can hinder forbids it in the latter case. The authority of the worker is just as absolute in the one case as in the other; but, on the other hand, it is just as certain—nay, even more certain—that God will not treat creatures made in his own image as insensate clay, as that the potter will not treat the clay as if it were rational and moral and capable of knowing when it was ill-used. Having thus boldly rebuked the irreverence of the objector, Paul takes up the case more calmly and vindicates the justice of God's dealing with men. [As "the potter does not make the clay but digs it" (Bengel), so the reference here is not to an original creation of the clay. The lump with which the potter has to do is the clay with its natural properties, moistened and prepared for moulding. So the lump of humanity is humanity with its natural proneness to evil. "The words 'I will have mercy on whom I have mercy' imply that all deserved wrath, so that the lump of clay in the hands of the potter must refer to men already existing in God's foreknowledge as fallen creatures." (Scott.)[1] The potter has "authority"

or "right" (ἐξουσία) over the clay—not merely physical strength (ἰσχύς or δύναμις)—to make of one part a vessel unto honor (for honorable use) and of another a vessel unto dishonor. Compare 2 Tim. 2:20. None of these vessels are worthless, but all have some use, otherwise the apostle would not in this connection introduce the words 'unto' (εἰς), 'willing' (θελῶν), and 'that' (ἵνα). The clay in its inferiority cannot question the potter, but we may say that no potter has a right to spend his time and energies in making useless vessels, and no wise potter will make vessels merely for the sake of destroying them. But he may make from the same lump some vessels for honorable and some for ignoble use. These vessels are not necessarily identical with the vessels of mercy and of wrath named below. "The work of the skillful potter," says Godet, "is not the emblem of an arbitrary use of strength, but, on the contrary, of a deliberate and intelligent employment of the matter at his disposal." If we apply this figure of the clay to fallen humanity, then the lump may represent both Jews and Gentiles (ver. 24), and the apostle teaches us that the Jews could not demand of God that they should be made vessels unto honor and the Gentiles should be made vessels unto dishonor. Of the lump even of Jewish humanity God may make vessels unto dishonor. In determining which vessels to make, he does not act arbitrarily or without reason, for his attributes always act in harmony, and his power is ever the servant of his goodness, justice, and wisdom. Paul certainly would not regard it as a complete description of man to say that he is a lump of clay; but when one makes high pretensions, puts on airs, talks of merit, and lays claims, then the apostle would take down his pride and feeling of self-sufficiency by assuring him that he is but clay in the hands of the potter. Let us be thankful that God can take us from the lump and mass of perdition and mould us into vessels of glory. We are not a mere clod of inert and senseless clay; but it would be well for us to resign ourselves submissively

[1] 'The same lump.' Notice the position of the article. If it came after αὐτοῦ, the phrase would mean *the lump itself.* On the "one part" and "another" (of the Revised Version), see Winer. p. 105.

22 *What* if God, willing to shew *his* wrath, and to make his power known, endured with much longsuffering the vessels of wrath fitted to destruction:
23 And that he might make known the riches of his glory on the vessels of mercy, which he had afore prepared unto glory,

22 unto dishonour? What if God, [1] willing to shew his wrath, and to make his power known, endured with much longsuffering vessels of wrath fitted unto 23 destruction; [2] and that he might make known the riches of his glory upon vessels of mercy, which he

1 Or, *although willing*......2 Some ancient authorities omit *and*.

into the hands of God, as clay in the hands of a potter, that he may mould us (how easily!) into vessels of honor.]

22, 23. [**What** (or, *but*) **if,** etc., seems to introduce the answer to the objector's question. De Wette thinks that Paul in these verses had special reference to the Egyptians and the Israelites in Egypt. But, as Godet says, Paul has done with Pharaoh long ago. Philippi, however, supposes at least a *side glance* at Pharaoh.] There is some difficulty in the construction here, arising partly from its irregularity, and partly from the brevity and incompleteness of the expression. The following paraphrase may help to the right understanding of the sense: 'What ground of objection is there, or what fault can be found with the divine procedure [what adverse reply shall we make to God? (ver. 20)], if God, while purposing (θελῶν, wishing) to show his just severity and Almighty power upon those who deserved his displeasure, and were altogether fitted for perdition, yet endured them with much long-suffering before he inflicted punishment upon them; and, on the other hand, purposed to show [what if God willed to make known?] his rich and glorious mercy to those who were to be partakers of his compassion, and whom he had already prepared for salvation?' Surely there is nothing to complain of in all this. [While the margin of the American Revised Version—with Meyer, Philippi, Godet, and others—supplies an *although* before the participle 'willing', thus giving emphasis to the long-suffering, De Wette prefixes *since* or *because*, and says that God bore with Pharaoh, and did not at once annihilate him, in order the more to show his wrath and his power in him. Some (Meyer, Philippi, Godet) regard this as a strange kind of *long-suffering*, the design of which, accord-

ing to Weiss, was "to lead them to repentance." Yet the words referring to Pharaoh, 'for this very purpose have I raised thee up,' "make it certain that when St. Paul writes, 'God, willing to show,' he means, *because he willed*." ("Bible Commentary.") And certainly sinners can abuse God's long-suffering to the enhancing of their condemnation. Winer, De Wette, and Meyer regard the phrase **that he might make known** as directly dependent on the verb **endured,** giving this idea: "He endured these vessels of wrath, not only (or, as Meyer would have it, notwithstanding his desire) to show his wrath and make his power known, but also (by delaying punishment) to make known the riches of his glory," etc. Others—like Philippi, Godet, Stuart—would supply another *if willing* (εἰ θέλων) at the beginning of ver. 23, and regard 'that he might make known' as equivalent to and co-ordinate with the infinitive 'to make known' (γνωρίσαι) of the preceding verse. The former give this rendering: "What if God, willing to make known the riches of his glory (called us)," for which parenthetic clause Paul substitutes 'whom he hath called.' Prof. Stuart would supply: Had mercy on us, or, made known his rich grace toward us, etc.][r]

Observe that he speaks of the vessels of wrath as **fitted to destruction,** and of the vessels of mercy **which he had afore prepared unto glory.** God's agency in the case of these last is direct, positive, effective. And who these are he tells us in the next verse. [De Wette, Meyer, Philippi, Alford, Stuart, think this fitting for destruction is effected, according to the apostle's representation, by the agency of God. But Paul certainly avoids making such express representation, and we therefore may refrain from so doing. Dr.

---

[1] Our own preference also would be to supply some form of θέλω, but as *although willing* would in this case be inadmissible, we must so regard it in the former. Tὸ δυνατὸν (*power*) corresponds with δύναμιν, ver. 17. See ἀδύνατον, 8:3. The word 'vessels' in both verses is destitute of the article, but it may be inserted in the

translation, especially in the latter instance. The relative 'which' in our Common Version (properly *whom*), though referring to a neuter noun, 'vessels,' is here masculine, either by a *constructio ad sensum*, or, more probably by attraction to the following ἡμᾶς, us.—(F.)

24 Even us, whom he hath called, not of the Jews only, but also of the Gentiles?
25 As he saith also in Osee, I will call them my people, which were not my people; and her beloved, which was not beloved.

24 afore prepared unto glory, *even* us, whom he also called, not from the Jews only, but also from the
25 Gentiles? As he saith also in Hosea,
I will call that my people which was not my people; And her beloved, who was not beloved.

Gifford says that "both factors, God's probationary judgments and man's perverse will, conduce to the result, and it is the result only that is here expressed." Still, had this been spoken of as a divine result, we could only say, that as God hardened Pharaoh when he hardened himself, so he fits men for perdition when they are fitting themselves for it. The Gentiles, as we learn in 1 : 24, 26, 28, gave themselves up to iniquity, and God gave them up to a reprobate mind. That sinners do fit themselves as vessels destined for wrath is most plainly affirmed in the Scriptures. See 2 : 4; 1 Thess. 2 : 16, seq. And certainly God would not efficiently, and could not of his "good pleasure," prepare the vessels of wrath which are so displeasing to him. As Olshausen says: "The bearing *with much long-suffering* will not accord with the prominence thus given to the divine activity. There is something not only discordant but absolutely contradictory in the idea that God endures with much long-suffering what he has himself prepared." Four striking differences of representation are thus noticed by Godet: "I. The preposition πρό (beforehand) is wanting in the participle (fitted). Compare ver. 22. II. There the passive form instead of the active used here. (Ver. 23.) III. Here the aorist referring to the eternal act, as in 8 : 29, instead of the perfect (ver. 22), which denotes the present fact. IV. Here the verb *prepare*, which indicates the beginning of the development, instead of that of ver. 22, which indicates result. These four differences are not accidental, and leave no doubt as to the apostle's view." To take *fitted* here in the sense of *fit* is unwarrantable. We remark, that as these vessels of mercy are actually existing sinners who, though penitent, have by their sins made themselves objects of divine pity and have received divine *grace*, and as the vessels of wrath are actually existing sinners who, by their persistent wickedness, have made themselves objects of the divine displeasure (to whom, however, God does not wish to show the *riches* of his wrath), so the apostle has not here spoken of God's original creating act or purpose in either case.]

24. Even us, whom he hath called, etc. [See Eph. 2 : 10.] See also the analysis at the close of ver. 13. Two things are made plain in the preceding passage: 1. That the election here spoken of is to *eternal life*, and not merely to outward privileges. 2. That it is *sovereign* and *absolute*, and not based on the ground of foreseen choice or merit on the part of man. ['The vessels of mercy' (election) spoken of in the last verse are here explained as meaning 'us whom he hath called.' Instead of *which*, referring to its antecedent, *vessels*, we have the masculine pronoun 'whom,' agreeing, by attraction, with 'us' (ἡμᾶς) in the subordinate clause. According to the teaching of 8 : 29, 30, the called ones here are those, not only from the Jews, but also from the Gentiles, whom God foreknew and predestined to be his. As we understand these three last verses, the reasoning of the apostle is virtually this: What if God has willed to pass by the great mass of unbelieving and rebellious Jews and to call his elect ones principally from the Gentiles, who shall find fault with God for so doing? Calvin well remarks that "the grace of God is not so confined to the Jewish people that it cannot flow forth to other nations and to the whole world, nor is it so obligated to the Jews that it must reach all the sons of Abraham according to the flesh without exception." These elect Gentiles are Christ's "other sheep" which are not of the Jewish fold (John 10 : 16), and that God should call them to be his people, and should gather them within the Messianic fold, is, as the apostle goes on to show, but a fulfillment of the Old Testament prophecies.]

The remainder of this chapter is taken up with confirming the foregoing doctrine by testimonies from the prophets.

25, 26. As he saith also in Osee, etc. Both the quotations are from Hosea, the first from 2 : 23, the second from 1 : 10 [in the Hebrew, 2 : 25]. They were originally said of the apostate [and heathenized] tribes of Israel, but are applicable to the Gentiles as well. [The first quotation varies somewhat both from the Hebrew and the Septuagint. The negatived substantives **not my people** and

26 And it shall come to pass, *that* in the place where it was said unto them, Ye *are* not my people; there shall they be called the children of the living God.

27 Esaias also crieth concerning Israel, Though the number of the children of Israel be as the sand of the sea, a remnant shall be saved:

28 For he will finish the work, and cut *it* short in righteousness: because a short work will the Lord make upon the earth.

29 And as Esaias said before, Except the Lord of

26 And it shall be, *that* in the place where it was said unto them, Ye are not my people, There shall they be called sons of the living God.

27 And Isaiah crieth concerning Israel, If the number of the children of Israel be as the sand of the sea,

28 it is the remnant that shall be saved: for the Lord will execute *his* word upon the earth, finishing it

29 and cutting it short. And, as Isaiah hath said before,

---

not beloved are, in the original, represented to be the names of two of Hosea's children, which names were given them to symbolize the rejection of the house of Israel. "I will no more have mercy upon the house of Israel, . . . but I will have mercy upon the house of Judah." Yet God's mercy was not to be withheld forever. "For in the place," etc. The same passage is cited in 1 Peter 2 : 10.] The use of the feminine pronoun in the last part of ver. 25 is explained by the figurative representation, so common in the prophets, of the Jewish people as the spouse of God, and their forsaking of him as conjugal infidelity. **The place where it was said unto them, Ye are not my people** probably refers, not to any specific place, as Palestine, but, in general, wheresoever their apostasy from God has been known and spoken of, there shall also their recovery be known and spoken of.
27, 28. The two preceding verses, from Hosea's prophecies, show that those were to be included among the people of God who had heretofore been regarded as *aliens;* the two verses now before us show, from the prophecies of Isaiah, that the Jews, as such, were not to be included among his people in the coming time. Thus ver. 25, 26 are a commentary on the last clause of ver. 24, 'but also of the Gentiles,' and ver. 27, 28 on the clause immediately preceding, 'not of the Jews only.' [**Esaias also.** Meyer, regarding the word (δὲ) translated 'also' as antithetic, says it "leads over to *another* prophet," and paraphrases thus: " But *Isaiah*, what do we hear from him? We hear the cry respecting Israel," etc., instead of Hosea, speaking of the Gentiles.] **Crieth concerning Israel.** This verb indicates a loud and impassioned utterance. Compare John 1 : 15; 7 : 28, 37; 12 : 44; Acts 23 : 6; 24 : 21 [ὑπέρ in the sense of περί, *concerning*]. **A remnant** [ὑπόλειμμα in the Revised text, ὑπόλιμμα in Westcott and Hort] —that is, *only* a remnant shall be saved [in the Hebrew *shall return*, as from exile], the

mass of the people being rejected. The Rabbins have this saying: "Of six hundred thousand persons but two came to Canaan; so shall it be in the days of the Messiah." The quotation is from Isa. 10 : 22, 23 [and is slightly abbreviated from the LXX., which varies considerably from the original Hebrew. Meyer says: "The Seventy did not understand these words and translated them incorrectly," yet that Paul "felt no scruple in abiding by their translation, with a few unimportant deviations, since the sense is not less suitable than that of the original." The language of Isaiah is commonly supposed to have reference to a political deliverance of a remnant of Israel, which by Paul is regarded as a symbol of moral deliverance, the salvation of an elect seed. Compare 11 : 5. The fate of Sodom and Gomorrah has reference to something worse than a mere temporal and political overthrow]. The passage may be rendered: *For he is finishing and abridging the word in* [punitive] *righteousness, because an abridged word* [a word of swift judgment] *will the Lord make on the earth.* But there is a briefer reading of the original, which is adopted by Lachmann, Tischendorf, Westcott and Hort, and the Revisers, according to which the translation would be: *The Lord will perform his word upon the earth, finishing it and cutting it short.* The idea is, that the Lord will execute speedy and summary judgment, according to his word.
29. Esaias said before—that is, in a preceding part of his prophecies; so the word seems to be used in Gal. 1 : 9. [Tholuck, De Wette, Meyer, Philippi, and Godet prefer 'foretold' (compare 2 Peter 3 : 2), since mere priority of place in writing is an unimportant matter.] These words here cited are found in chapter 1 : 9 [and are cited verbatim from the LXX.]. **The Lord of Sabaoth.** The word 'Sabaoth' [one of the few words which Paul, following the Seventy, left untranslated; see "maranatha," 1 Cor. 16 : 22] means ' hosts '

Sabaoth had left us a seed, we had been as Sodoma, and been made like unto Gomorrah.

30 What shall we say then? That the Gentiles, which followed not after righteousness, have attained to righteousness, even the righteousness which is of faith.

31 But Israel, which followed after the law of righteousness, hath not attained to the law of righteousness.

Except the Lord of Sabaoth had left us a seed,
We had become as Sodom, and had been made like unto Gomorrah.

30 What shall we say then? That the Gentiles, who followed not after righteousness, attained to righteousness, even the righteousness which is of faith:

31 but Israel, following after a law of righteousness,

---

or 'armies.' It is used only here and in James 5 : 4 in the New Testament; but the expressions "God of hosts" and "Lord of hosts," where the same Hebrew word is used, are frequent in the Old Testament, and represent God as a great king, having mighty armies under his command. **We had been as Sodoma.** "Unless the Lord had left us a remnant, as a seed, to preserve us alive, we should have been utterly destroyed, like the cities of the plain." [On this verse Scott makes the following "practical observations": "Even among the vast number of professing Christians it is to be feared that but a remnant will be saved." Does the parable of the virgins make it probable that only one-half of Christ's disciples will be found truly "wise"? Would it be surprising that out of every twelve gospel ministers one should be finally lost? "Many will say to me in that day," etc. See Matt. 7 : 22. The fate and destiny of nations, as well as individuals, is in the hands of God, and we may well fear that he has not done dealing in righteousness with us as a people. Let us hope and pray that the Lord will leave to us also a seed of true believers to preserve our land from becoming as Sodom and Gomorrah.]

The apostle now proceeds to state the conclusion to which his argument has thus far brought him. [He now also proceeds to express fully what he has hitherto referred to cursorily—namely, the reception of the Gentiles and the exclusion of the Jews.]

30. That the Gentiles, etc. Some regard this as a question, thus: "What shall we say to the fact that," or, "shall we say that," etc. It seems properly to be an answer to **what shall we say then?** ['Gentiles' is without the article, signifying, according to Meyer (*versus* De Wette), not a class, but some of a class.] **Which followed** [*were following*] **not after righteousness.** Who were not, as the Jews were, definitely seeking righteousness by their own legal works. **Have attained,** etc.—not being hindered, as the

Jews were, by trusting to a false theory, have believed in Christ, and so obtained the righteousness of faith. [Some regard 'righteousness' here, and in some other places, as equivalent to justification. It amounts, indeed, nearly to the same thing, and yet the word used (δικαιοσύνη) does not properly signify justification. As Dr. Hodge says: "It means *righteousness*, the possession of which secures justification. Justification is a declarative act of God; righteousness is the ground on which that declaration is made." The figure used in this verse is that of the race course. Compare 'follow after' (διώκω) and 'apprehend' (καταλαμβάνω) in Phil. 3: 12. The former verb means to pursue, and when with hostile intent, to persecute. **Have attained to** (*laid hold on*) **righteousness** (not that of works), but **even the righteousness which is of** (proceeds from) **faith**—without protracted and painful endeavor, like the man who found a treasure in the field when he was not seeking it. (Godet.) Such righteousness as this, thus far in the world's history, has been laid hold on only by individual believers, not by nations as a whole.]

31. But Israel, which followed (literally, *following*) **after,** etc. **The** (*a*) **law of righteousness** — not here the righteousness of the law, but a law imparting righteousness, a justifying law. [The second 'righteousness' (in our Common Version) is wanting in nearly all the older manuscripts, and is omitted in the Revised Version, but seems quite necessary. The apostle frankly concedes that the Jews eagerly sought after a justifying righteousness, and this testimony is abundantly confirmed by the writings of the New Testament, of Josephus, of the Targums, etc. Indeed, Paul himself knew something about this earnest pursuit, from personal experience. The verb 'attain,' primarily meant, to come first or before another, to anticipate; see 1 Thess. 4: 15. This verse serves as a comment on ver. 16: "Not of him that runneth."] They who had not been seeking righteousness

32 Wherefore? Because *they sought it* not by faith, but as it were by the works of the law. For they stumbled at that stumblingstone ;
33 As it is written, Behold, I lay in Zion a stumblingstone and rock of offence: and whosoever believeth on him shall not be ashamed.

32 did not arrive at *that* law. Wherefore? [1] Because *they sought it* not by faith, but as it were by works.
33 They stumbled at the stone of stumbling ; even as it is written,
Behold, I lay in Zion a stone of stumbling and a rock of offence:
And he that believeth on [2] him shall not be put to shame.

1 Or, *Because*, doing it *not by faith, but as it were by works, they stumbled*......2 Or, *it*.

found it; and they who were seeking failed to find. An anomaly which calls for explanation : the explanation is at hand.

32. Wherefore? Why was this failure of the Jews? For what reason did they fail to attain what they sought? ["The Five Clergymen" give this rendering : *Wherefore? Because* (following after it) *not by faith, but as by the works of the law, they stumbled,* etc. See margin of the Revised Version.] It was because they sought it not by faith, but as if it were attainable by the works of the law. ['By faith' denotes the objective standard, as from works, the purely imaginary. (Winer.) The Revision omits the word 'law,' which is wanting in ℵ * A B F G, the Vulgate and several Fathers.] The verb 'sought' which is not in the original, is rightly supplied from ver. 31, where, however, it is translated 'followed after.' **For** [wanting in ℵ * A B D * F G] **they stumbled at that stumblingstone,** of which the prophet Isaiah speaks. [The 'stumbling' keeps up the figure of the race. Why does not Paul say : They stumbled at or because of God's eternal decree? Instead of this, he here seems to forget all that he has just said about predestination and hardening, and now speaks only of human activity and blameworthiness, doing this, too, as though he were not flatly contradicting himself! [1] Alford spoke truly when he said : "We shall find free will asserted strongly enough for all edifying purposes by this apostle when the time comes." Our natural preference, of course, would be to have the two views combined and reconciled. They are at least closely united in Acts 13 : 46-48, a passage which states the results of Paul's first recorded sermon : "Seeing ye judge yourselves unworthy of eternal

life . . . . and as many as were ordained to eternal life believed." This does not read as though foreordination and liberty of choice were, as has been thousands of times declared, incompatible and contradictory.]

The last clause of this verse might well have been joined to the following.

33. As it is written, etc. The apostle here joins two passages. (Isa. 28 : 16; 8 : 14.) Christ was laid in Zion for "a precious corner stone, a sure foundation," according to the former of these two passages ; but he becomes, according to the latter, **a stumblingstone and rock of offence** to those who reject him in their unbelief. [The apostle does not in this verse follow the Seventy. "Instead of giving to the stone the laudatory epithets applied in Isa. 28 : 16, he gives, out of Isa. 8 : 14, the well-known adjuncts of 'stumbling' and 'offence' and then returns to 28 : 16." (Davidson.) Paul wishes to tell here what Christ is to unbelievers. Compare Luke 20 : 17, 18. Both passages are quoted in 1 Peter 2 : 6, seq.) The 'offence,' is properly the trapstick which holds the bait, and which, when touched, springs the trap : hence a snare laid for an enemy, and, with a moral reference, any cause of falling. The 'every one' (πᾶς) is omitted from the Revision text, but all manuscripts give it in 10 : 11. The preposition (ἐπί) with 'believe' denotes reliance *on*. See notes on 3 : 25. The Hebrew for 'shall be ashamed' is to 'flee away,' as in terror. Paul here follows the Seventy.]

This last section (ver. 30-33) teaches us that the attempt, through a false theory, to make ourselves righteous in a way of our own, may be a greater hindrance to our salvation, than open wickedness and vice ; and herein it agrees with our Lord's saying in Matt. 21 : 31.

1 "Paul would have agreed better with himself if he had been a pupil of Aristotle instead of Gamaliel." (Fritzsche.) But truth demanded the presentation of both views, whether he could reconcile them or not. Had he merely presented one side and brought to view

only the "moral self-determination and spontaneity" of man, a creature in a universe created and governed by the eternal, Almighty, and Omniscient One, who could have held that to be a correct representation? —(F.)

CHAPTER X.

BRETHREN, my heart's desire and prayer to God for Israel is, that they might be saved.

2 For I bear them record that they have a zeal of God, but not according to knowledge.

1 Brethren, my heart's [1] desire and my supplication.

2 to God is for them, that they may be saved. For I bear them witness that they have a zeal for God, but

---

1 Gr. *good pleasure.*

Ch. 10 : ["Israel's Guilt" (Olshausen), or, more fully: The rejection of the Jews is owing to their unbelief.]

The subject introduced in the last four verses of the preceding chapter—namely, the failure of the Jews to attain to righteousness, and the reason of that failure, is continued in this chapter, after the apostle has expressed his earnest desire for their salvation, and his appreciation of their religious zeal, as he had previously expressed his appreciation of their distinguished privileges. (**9:** 4, 5.)

1. Brethren. This word might be regarded as addressed, in a national sense, to the unbelieving Jews, and so regarded, it would agree with many precedents in the use of the word by Paul (Acts 13: 26, 38; 22: 1; 23: 1, 6; 28: 17; Rom. 9: 3), and would be an example of his kind feelings toward them; but in this connection, as a direct address, it is more suitably referred to those Christian readers to whom the Epistle is addressed. Still, its occurrence here, where it is not called for to complete the sense, is naturally explained by the strong emotion which the subject referred to always excited in the mind of the apostle, and of which we have a signal example in the beginning of the previous chapter. The word translated *desire* is an emphatic word, expressive of earnest, benevolent desire, and is usually translated "good will," or "good pleasure." (Luke 2: 14; Eph. 1: 5, 9; Phil. 1: 15; 2: 13; 2 Thess. 1: 11.)[1] [**And prayer to God**—literally, *And the prayer to God.* The article before prayer is equivalent to the personal pronoun *my*. The word for prayer (δέησις) has the force of entreaty arising from a sense of want. Like our *petition*, it may be addressed to men, while the more usual word for prayer (προσευχή) has a sacred character, and "is always prayer to God." (Trench.)] **For Israel.** *For them* seems to be the true reading. The persons referred to had been so recently mentioned, and were so prominent in the apostle's mind, that the

pronoun was sufficiently plain. **That they might be saved**—literally, *for salvation*, the pronoun "their" being understood. [The apostle obviously felt the salvation of men to be an infinitely important matter, or he would not have sought for it with that intensity of desire, amounting even to an unceasing anguish of heart, which led him, to whom Christ was more than all the universe besides, to wish that he might be "anathema" from his Saviour, provided this could but secure their salvation. But we somewhat demur at Bengel's observation that "Paul would not thus have prayed had they been absolutely reprobated." For Paul has reference here to whole peoples, and has nothing to do with the fate of particular individuals. The reprobation of these does not argue the rejection of the nation. Besides, as Dr. Shedd remarks: "The Christian, in his ignorance of the divine purpose, must pray for all, in order to pray for any." Must we not think the apostle's interest in the spiritual welfare of the Jews was something wonderful and Christ-like, considering all the trouble and harm he had experienced from their opposition, their plots, and their lying in wait?]

2. For introduces the reason why he thus sympathizes with their efforts, though misdirected. **They have a zeal of God.** In such connections as this, 'of' is used where we should say *for*, as "zealous of the law" (Acts 21: 20), "zealous of the traditions of my fathers" (Gal. 1: 14), "the zeal of thine house" (John 2: 17). The Jews, as a people, were zealous religionists, **but not according to knowledge.** They had zeal enough, if it had been rightly informed and directed, to secure their salvation. [Their zeal was not such as results from full knowledge. "When Paul says, 'I bear them witness,' he seems to be alluding to his conduct of other days, and to say: I know something of it—of that zeal!" (Godet.) This, their zeal for God and his

---

1 The μὲν, untranslated, has no corresponding δὲ (but), yet this is virtually contained in ver. 3. My | heart's good will, etc., is for one thing, while they have been seeking another. —(F.)

3 For they, being ignorant of God's righteousness, and going about to establish their own righteousness, have not submitted themselves unto the righteousness of God.
4 For Christ is the end of the law for righteousness to every one that believeth.

3 not according to knowledge. For being ignorant of God's righteousness, and seeking to establish their own, they did not subject themselves to the right-
4 eousness of God. For Christ is the end of the law unto righteousness to every one that believeth.

law, is amply witnessed by Philo and Josephus. See Tholuck's "Commentary." So our Saviour, in Matt. 23: 15, speaks of their zeal in making proselytes. The Pharisees were the orthodox Jews of their day, and had a reputation for pre-eminent sanctity. And probably no word our Lord ever spoke was so astounding as that utterance of his in Matt. 5: 20: "Except your righteousness shall exceed the righteousness of the scribes and Pharisees!" Flacius, as quoted in Bengel, says: "The Jews had, and have, a zeal without knowledge; we, on the contrary, alas! have knowledge without zeal." [1] Religious indifference is always inexcusable, but religious zeal, when ill-informed and misdirected, may be just as disastrous in its results, so false and dangerous is the maxim that "it matters little what a man's belief is, if he is only sincere." The apostle immediately proceeds to point out what their mistake was; and it was no uncommon one.

3. [For they being ignorant. 'For' shows their lack of clear apprehension. Alford's rendering, *not recognizing*, implies that they were not absolutely lacking of information.] The expressions **God's righteousness** and 'the righteousness of God' mean God's way of making sinful men righteous, and accepting them as such according to the fuller explanation of this term given in the notes on 1: 17. [So Winer: "The righteousness of God denotes righteousness which God imparts; compare Phil. 3: 9, 'The righteousness from God.'"] **Going about.** This is an old English expression which means, simply, "seeking," or "endeavoring." The Greek verb, which means to seek, is repeatedly translated as above. (John 7: 19, 20; Acts 21: 31.) **Their own righteousness.** A righteousness devised and wrought by themselves, the fruit of their own works. Compare Phil. 3: 9. **Have not submitted themselves unto the righteousness of God.** This 'righteousness of God' is not only something offered to us as a free gift, but also something required of us as a divine obligation. Not to submit to it, not

to comply with God's ordinance, by a personal and practical acceptance of it, which always involves the discarding of our own righteousness, is not only an inexcusable mistake, but a fatal sin. [The Greek means, "Did not submit, or subject, themselves." Alford, however, renders it, "were not subjected." It is used in the same sense in 8: 20. To submit to God's righteousness supposes some self-denial on the part of those who would set up their own righteousness, some humbling of natural pride and feeling of self-sufficiency; supposes, consequently, a deep sense of one's need, ill desert, and lost condition. But to receive Christ, the end of the law for righteousness, is the only way in which the righteous requirement of the law can be fulfilled in us. Yet thousands on thousands of zealous religionists are at this very moment seeking, making it, as it were, their occupation to establish their own righteousness, which is but self-righteousness, and altogether imperfect; and, as a ground of justification, utterly worthless in the sight of God. Paul shows us here, and throughout this chapter, that the casting away of the Jews was owing to their own fault, their unbelief. They did not submit to the righteousness of God; they did not obey the gospel (ver. 16); they thrust from themselves the word of God, and judged themselves unworthy of eternal life. Having done this, they are given up of God to hardness of heart. But the next chapter shows us that the casting away, or rejection, of the Jewish people was to be but temporary, while, at the same time, God would overrule it to a blessed result, the opening of the door of faith to the Gentiles.]

4. Christ is the end of the law—is the object at which the law aimed. The law, if obeyed, would result in our becoming righteous before God, enjoying his favor, and securing eternal happiness. This is its end and aim. But having been once disobeyed, it becomes forever incapable of bringing us to this end. But Christ comes in and infallibly secures these results for all who believe in him. He is, therefore, to all such, 'the end

---

[1] The word ζῆλον is a *media vox*, a word used in both a good and a bad sense. Compare 13: 13.—(F.)

5 For Moses describeth the righteousness which is
of the law, That the man which doeth those things
shall live by them.
6 But the righteousness which is of faith speaketh

5 For Moses writeth that the man that doeth the
righteousness which is of the law shall live thereby.
6 But the righteousness which is of faith saith thus,

of the law for righteousness.' The proof of this immediately follows. [" The righteousness at which the law aims is accomplished in Christ." (Farrar.) This interpretation, favored by Alford and Stuart, certainly seems the most natural, and accords with the use of the word in "the end of the commandment," in 1 Tim. 1: 5. Yet most modern interpreters use this word in the sense of ending, or termination. The validity of the law has come to an end in Christ as it respects righteousness. **For righteousness** — either for the securing of righteousness, or, more generally, as it relates to righteousness.]

5. For Moses describeth, etc. See Lev. 18: 5. Paul could quote no higher human authority as to the true end of the law than that of Moses, through whom the law was given. [The 'for' introduces the proof of the impossibility of securing eternal life by one's own righteousness, or the righteousness of the law. The Greek text literally reads thus: "Moses writeth (concerning) the righteousness of the law" (compare John 1: 45)—literally, "Concerning whom Moses wrote," etc. **That the man which doeth those things shall live by them.** The Revisers' text (that the man who has done the righteousness which is of the law) adopts a different collocation of the words, and, instead of ' by (in) them,' has 'in it,' or ' thereby,' referring to righteousness. These words are again quoted in part in Gal. 3 · 12, "The man that doeth them shall live in them." As Paul was unacquainted with the results of modern Biblical (destructive) criticism, he must be excused for ascribing to Moses the authorship of Leviticus.] 'The man which doeth those things'—that is, who obeys those "statutes" and "judgments" mentioned in the same verse in Leviticus—'shall live by them,' shall obtain the true life, the favor of God, and eternal happiness. This shows what is meant by 'the end of the law.' The man who obeys it, universally, perfectly, constantly, shall be saved, or, rather, shall be safe. But there is no such man (Eccl. 7: 20), and the man who comes short of this, in any particular, is justly condemned. (Gal. 3: 10.)

This fifth verse describes the nature of the righteousness of the law; the next four verses contrast with this the righteousness of faith, the sixth and seventh negatively, and the eighth and ninth positively.

6, 7. [But the righteousness which is of faith. Dr. Hodge defines this righteousness as that which is received by faith. He maintains that "the righteousness which consists in faith or which flows from faith is our own righteousness." But this is not necessarily the case, and in the apostle's teaching, as we have seen, faith is counted as righteousness.] **Speaketh on this wise.** The quotation is from Deut. 30: 11, 12, with a running commentary by the apostle, adapting it to the facts of the Christian Dispensation. [In the passage quoted, Moses primarily is speaking of the commandment, or law, of God, and it is not asserted that he is describing the righteousness of faith. But Paul, personifying this righteousness, puts the words of Moses into its mouth as being more appropriately uttered by it than by the law. And, as Godet remarks, "There was a piquancy in thus replying to Moses by Moses, and in showing that what the lawgiver had written was still more true of the gospel than of the law." Paul evidently here clothes his thought in Old Testament phraseology, which originally had reference to another subject, altering such phraseology and adapting it to the subject in hand. Observe, in proof of this, his frequent 'that is.' A notable instance of such appropriation and adaptation may be seen in ver. 18. The apostle does not say or imply that the original passage had "a fundamental Messianic reference" (Philippi) or that Moses uttered these words as a typical prophetic description of the righteousness of faith. Yet he might well regard these words as specially applicable to faith in him who is the end of the law, and to the commandment to believe in him. (Alford.)] The language of the righteousness of faith does not make salvation to depend upon our perfect compliance with a set of rules, many and various, through our whole lives; but its conditions are simple and few. We are not required to begin at the

on this wise, Say not in thine heart, Who shall ascend into heaven? (that is, to bring Christ down *from above:*) 7 Or, Who shall descend into the deep? (that is, to bring up Christ again from the dead.) 8 But what saith it? The word is nigh thee, *even* in thy mouth, and in thy heart: that is, the word of faith, which we preach; 9 That if thou shalt confess with thy mouth the Lord

Say not in thy heart, Who shall ascend into heaven? 7 (that is, to bring Christ down:) or, Who shall descend into the abyss? (that is, to bring Christ up 8 from the dead.) But what saith it? The word is nigh thee, in thy mouth, and in thy heart: that is, 9 the word of faith, which we preach: [1] because if thou shalt [2] confess with thy mouth Jesus *as* Lord,

---

1 Or, *that*......2 Some ancient authorities read *confess the word with thy mouth, that Jesus* is *Lord*.

---

beginning—to go up to heaven in search of a Saviour, to beg him to come down and help us; nor to begin in the middle—to go down to the grave, and induce him to finish his begun work, by rising from the dead; but the work is all wrought out for us, "ordered in all things and sure" (2 Sam. 23: 5), a complete and finished salvation, waiting only for the act of faith on our part to make it effectual. Unasked and unsought, a Saviour has come down from heaven, died for our sins, risen for our justification, ascended to heaven, where he ever lives to intercede for us. Now follows the positive part of this blessed contrast to the righteousness of the law. [We need not, as some have done, regard the question **Who shall ascend into heaven?** as the inquiry of unbelief, as if the incarnation of Christ had not taken place and was an impossibility. Paul would simply affirm that we need do no great or impossible thing, that a salvation is already provided and brought home to each individual, and that there is no need of waiting; a Saviour *has* come, *has* died, *has* arisen. Nor need we suppose that the query has reference to a doubt whether Christ is *now* seated at the right hand of God in heaven. For this view would ill harmonize with the question which follows, if interpreted on the same principle, **who shall descend into the deep?** The confession of ver. 9 in regard to the *resurrection* shows that no doubt is here expressed as to the fact of Christ's death or of his descent to hades. This last query in the original Hebrew and in the Septuagint reads thus: ' Who will go over the sea for us,' but Paul changed 'beyond the sea' into 'the deep,' in order to secure a more direct contrast to heaven, and to denote the place of the dead, whither Christ descended and whence he rose.]

8, 9. But what saith it? It saith: **The

word is nigh[1] **thee,** etc. Moses saw the true righteousness, not as a distant and difficult thing, far off in heaven, or in the abyss, or across the sea, but as a thing that was near and simple. And the prophets had many glimpses of it as something far simpler, and, at the same time, far more radical than ritual observances: witness Isa. 1: 11-20; 58: 3-9, and notably the words in which Micah records the answer of Balaam to the questions of Balak, King of Moab. (6: 5-8.) "If you should not wish to cross your threshold," says Chrysostom, "you have it in your power to be saved while sitting at home; for the means of salvation are in thy mouth and in thy heart"—in thy mouth to confess, and in thy heart to believe. [To the words, 'in thy mouth and in thy heart,' the Septuagint adds: 'and in thy hands.' "In these words, Moses had in a sense, without suspecting it, given the exact formula of the righteousness of faith." (Godet.) In this representation by the apostle we have, according to Philippi, "a holy and charming play of God's Spirit on the words of the Lord." **The word of faith—** the word which "forms the substratum and object of faith" (Alford), or the word concerning faith (Noyes), or, which points to faith. (Boise.) This word of faith which we (Christian ministers, or I, Paul,) proclaim may be regarded as the "word of God," or, as in the Revision text, the word of *Christ*.] **If thou shalt confess**[2] **with** (literally, *in*) **thy mouth the Lord Jesus.** [The Revised Version margin gives here a slightly different reading, which Westcott and Hort have inserted in their text. The *first* word of the verse (ὅτι) if rendered 'that,' would indicate that this verse forms the substance of what is preached; if rendered 'for' or 'because' (Meyer, Philippi), it shows that this verse was intended to justify the application of

---

1 The word ἐγγύς (nigh), properly an adverb, is here used, like some other adverbs, as a preposition, followed by σου (thee), what we may call the genitive of place; compare 13: 11.—(F.)

2 The aorist subjunctive, ' if thou shouldst confess,' is, in conditional sentences, nearly equivalent to the future.—(F.)

Jesus, and shalt believe in thine heart that God hath raised him from the dead, thou shalt be saved.

10 For with the heart man believeth unto righteousness; and with the mouth confession is made unto salvation.

11 For the Scripture saith, Whosoever believeth on him shall not be ashamed.

12 For there is no difference between the Jew and

and shalt believe in thy heart that God raised him 10 from the dead, thou shalt be saved: for with the heart man believeth unto righteousness; and with 11 the mouth confession is made unto salvation. For the scripture saith, Whosoever believeth on him 12 shall not be put to shame. For there is no distinction between Jew and Greek: for the same *Lord* is

the Mosaic declaration to the preaching of faith.] Confession of Christ as Lord with the mouth will, if sincere, infallibly be accompanied by the other required forms of confession; and so this specific form of confession stands here as an appropriate representative of the outward and practical confession of Christ in general, according to 1 Cor. 12 : 3; and such confession is a condition of salvation, according to our Lord's own words. (Matt. 10 : 32, etc.) So, also, a hearty belief of the resurrection of Christ is suitably put for all that it implies—his atoning death (1 Cor. 15 : 17, 18), his divine Sonship (Rom. 1 : 4; 1 John 4 : 15), and, in general, the truth of all his teachings, his works, and his claims, for his resurrection is the divine seal and attestation of all these. "The heart requires the help of the mouth," says Theophylact, "for then faith shows forth and many are benefited; but the mouth also needs the heart, for many confess Christ in hypocrisy." [No one but he who has felt himself to be a lost sinner, and has thus felt the need of an Almighty Saviour, can truly confess Jesus as Lord, for "no man can say, Jesus is Lord but in the Holy Spirit." (1 Cor. 12 : 3.) In the writings of the apostles, the term *Lord* generally "serves to characterize either his pre-mundane or post-mundane existence, and therefore points him out either as Son of God or the exalted Son of man." (Philippi.)] Confession with the mouth is here mentioned before belief in the heart, agreeably to the ordinary method in common conversation, and in Scripture, of putting in the foreground what is outward and phenomenal, and afterward what is abstract and inward, though logically precedent. (John 3 : 5; 1 Peter 1 : 2; 2 Peter 1 : 10.) But this very common and popular order of speaking gives place to the logical order in the next verse. [Perhaps, also, the mouth confession was mentioned first to correspond with the position of 'mouth' in the Mosaic dictum of ver. 8. This rhetorical order of the words mouth, heart, has been frequently adduced to illustrate the meaning of the phrase "born of water and the

Spirit." There is a sense, however, in which mouth comes before heart, but there is no sense in which water (regarded as the water of baptism) precedes the birth from the Spirit. **Thou shalt be saved.** The result of such confessing faith corresponds with 'shall live' of ver. 5.]

10. [**For** is confirmatory of the preceding statement. **Believeth unto righteousness.** To believe unto righteousness is a believing which obtains righteousness, and to this faith of the heart must be added the confession of the mouth, in order to a full salvation.] There is here a change of construction in the English of the two clauses, but in the Greek both verbs are impersonal, and a very literal translation would be: "For with the heart it is believed unto righteousness, and with the mouth it is confessed unto salvation;" or, less literally, but more in conformity with English idiom: "With the heart faith is exercised unto righteousness, and with the mouth confession is made unto salvation." The confession of Christ is indispensable, for without it the evidence of justifying faith in the heart is incomplete. This is confirmed by another Scriptural citation.

11. **The Scripture saith.** This passage—from Isaiah 28 : 16, quoted also before at 9 : 33—closely accords with the Septuagint Version. The Hebrew reads: "He that believeth shall not make haste." The meaning is the same—"shall have no cause of shame, or fear, or flight." [The apostle adds "every one" (πᾶς), "a monosyllable more precious than the whole world" (Bengel), which is found neither in the Hebrew nor the Septuagint; but this form is found in Joel 2 : 3 (3 : 5), and is quoted in ver. 13. The idea of universality is conveyed by the indefinite participle. On this Hebraistic idiom, *every one*, connected with a negatived verb, see 3 : 20.]

12, 13. **There is no difference**—as to faith being the condition of righteousness or justification—**between the Jew and the Greek.** There is no distinction between Jew and Gentile as to the way of justification.

the Greek : for the same Lord over all is rich unto all that call upon him.

13 For whosever shall call upon the name of the Lord shall be saved.

Lord of all, and is rich unto all that call upon him : for, Whosoever shall call upon the name of the

14 Lord shall be saved. How then shall they call on

For the same Lord over all is rich, etc. [This clause may be rendered : *For the same is Lord of* (or, *over*) *all* (men), *being rich unto all*, etc. Meyer gives it : "The Lord of all is one and the same." Alford prefers the usual rendering. Compare 1 Cor. 12 : 5, 6. Mark how often Paul here uses the confirmatory 'for'—five times in ver. 10-13.] This 'Lord over all' is the Lord Jesus Christ, as the context, both preceding (ver. 9) and following (ver. 14, 15), very plainly shows. [So Tholuck, Rückert, De Wette, Philippi, Fritzsche, Hofmann, and others.] But the Lord mentioned by the prophet Joel (2 : 32) is Jehovah (that is the word in the Hebrew). Thus it appears that Jesus Christ is "Lord over all" (compare Acts 10 : 36) [and "God over all;" see 9 : 5], and is identified with the Jehovah of the Old Testament. ["JEHOVAH, but used here of Christ beyond a doubt, as the next verse shows. There is hardly a stronger proof, or one more irrefragable by those who deny the Godhead of our blessed Lord, of the unhesitating application to him by the apostle of the name and attributes of Jehovah." (Alford.) For other examples where Jehovah and the Lord Christ are convertible terms, see next verse as compared with Joel 3 : 5; 14 : 10, 11, with Isa. 45 : 23 (compare 2 Cor. 5 : 10; Phil. 2 : 11) ; 1 Cor. 10 : 4, 9, with Exod. 17 : 2, 7; Eph. 4 : 8, with Ps. 68 : 18, etc. On the use of 'Lord' (κυριος) in the New Testament, Prof. Stuart, in "Biblical Repository," 1831, p. 770, states, as the result of his investigation, "that in nearly all (about two hundred and forty) of the two hundred and forty-six instances in which Lord (κυριος) is used by Paul to designate Christ or God, independently of quotations from the Old Testament, it is applied to Christ." (The Epistle to the Hebrews is here included among Paul's writings.) See also notes on Acts 7 : 59. Some men even now, with Origen of olden time, hesitate to address our Saviour, 'Lord over all,' in prayer; but once his disciples were known as "callers on the name of Christ,' and this, too, before the name "Christians" was given them. See examples quoted under 9 : 5, to which many others might be added. Meyer says : "The

calling upon Christ is not the worshiping absolutely." But this idea, as Philippi says, using one of Meyer's phrases, is "arbitrarily imported." Has Jehovah revoked his own word and given his glory to another? Or did these saints forget the divine command : "Thou shalt worship the Lord thy God and him only shalt thou serve?" How true is the saying of Athanasius, that "we need a Redeemer who is our Lord by nature, in order that we may not by redemption again become the slaves of an idol."] The Lord is **rich unto all that call upon him.** The Jew need not grudge the Gentile his share in the riches : there is enough for all. [" 'Rich' and liberal, whom no multitude of believers, however great, can exhaust, who never is compelled to retrench." (Bengel.) **Whosoever shall call.** Literally : *For every one whosoever may or shall call*, etc. **Name of the Lord** represents what is revealed respecting the character and office work of our Saviour. See Hackett's "Acts," 2 : 38. Mark how all-embracing is the offer and possibility of salvation !]

In the remaining part of this chapter the apostle shows that the rejection of the Jews was their own fault, the consequence of their inexcusable unbelief [for "Israel hath not wanted preachers of this doctrine of salvation." (Tholuck.)]

14, 15. These two verses are introductory to what follows, to the end of the chapter. They point out what preceding conditions are indispensable to that saving invocation of the name of the Lord spoken of in ver. 13, indispensable alike to Jews and Gentiles, and so they form a suitable connection between the verses that precede and those that follow. [Even if, as some suppose, these are the words of a Jewish objector, excusing his people by alleging that the gospel had not been preached to them, even from this point of view these verses are to be regarded as setting forth essential truths. "No invocation without faith, no faith without hearing, no hearing without preaching, no preaching without sending." (Godet.) It seems to be an unavoidable inference from these verses, and

14 How then shall they call on him in whom they have not believed? and how shall they believe in him of whom they have not heard? and how shall they hear without a preacher?

him in whom they have not believed? and how shall they believe in him whom they have not heard? 15 and how shall they hear without a preacher? and

others immediately preceding (9-13), that there is no salvation for the heathen apart from their hearing and believing in the gospel. The teaching of our Epistle, indeed, supposes that the heathen, even in the absence of the gospel, have a probation in this life, they being a law unto themselves. And Peter goes so far as to say (Acts 10:35) that "in every nation he that feareth God and worketh righteousness is acceptable to him." Yet this same apostle, in ver. 43 of the same chapter, plainly implies that this supposed righteous Gentile must believe in Christ, in order to receive remission of sins. If any heathen should fully and always obey the inner, unwritten law, he would be saved, we may trust, on the ground of his merits who died for all. If they fail—as, we suppose, all do—to live up to the measure of light and knowledge which they possess or could have gained, they will doubtless suffer "stripes," whether "few" or "many" we leave to the Judge of all the earth, who will do right. We believe there are different degrees of happiness even in the heavenly state, and there may be as many degrees of unhappiness or misery in the world of the lost as there are in this world of sin and suffering. One thing is certain, that the Scriptures are silent as the grave touching any second or future probation for mankind between death and the judgment.[1] On the contrary, they almost everywhere express or imply the very contrary of this. And to my mind the *great*

change of death supposes an equally great change in the relation which we, as accountable beings, sustain to God. Thus no warrant from Scripture or reason, or from our knowledge of heathenism in any age or country, will justify us in hoping that for many of the unevangelized heathen there will be a full salvation. Still, *if* God sees in any heathen the controlling power of a right faith and spirit, I know not why the redemption of Christ may not be as available for him as for those of like faith and spirit who lived before his coming.] **How then** (since calling on the name of the Lord is the means of salvation) **shall they** (or, *can they*) **call on him** [αὐτὸν, *him*, understood] **in whom they have not believed?** Belief must precede invocation. [If we believe in Christ as our Lord and Saviour, we cannot but invoke him in prayer, for no one can be a Saviour of sinners whom we cannot call upon to save. Even when we ask anything *in his name*, we are graciously assured from his own lips that *he* will do it. (John 14:13, 14.)] **And how shall they** (or, *can they*) **believe in him of whom they have not heard?** Hearing must precede belief. [In these sentences, the Greek particle might be rendered *but* instead of *and*. The Revised Version omits *of* before *whom*, and rightly so, if Christ may be regarded as speaking through his preachers.[2]] **And how shall they** (or, *can they*) **hear without a preacher?** A message must be proclaimed

[1] This assertion as a general proposition will hold strictly true, even though it be conceded that, as a wholly exceptional instance, Christ did in his disembodied state go to "Hades" (the invisible world), and did there make proclamation of some kind to the imprisoned spirits of those who in the time of Noah were disobedient. (1 Peter 3:19.) There are those who think that Peter's statement to this effect is plain and undeniable, but the passage, standing confessedly alone in the Scriptures, must at least be deemed too unique and uncertain to warrant the general inference which some would derive from it. No one can tell how or why these particular persons were singled out in Hades and preached to exclusively, or what this preaching or proclamation was, or what was its effect. Besides, it is maintained by some of our best Greek scholars that the aorist participle (disobedient), without the article, marks he date or occasion of the preaching, thus showing

that this proclamation was made to them when once they were disobedient upon the earth. See Dr. Hovey's "Biblical Eschatology," p. 99; also Dr. N. M. Williams' "Commentary on Peter." Evidently the spirits of men who were once so "disobedient" that the mercy of God could not suffer them to live, and whom he subsequently confined "in prison" for punishment, are not the kind for whose benefit the speculations of some theologians would provide a future probation. Our Saviour's own words, for certain, give no warrant for the belief that he descended into any Hades *prison*, but rather that he returned unto the Father who sent him—that he went to "Paradise." And the Scriptures, in general, plainly teach us that "after death" cometh, not probation, but 'judgment.'—(F.)

[2] On the use of the genitive and accusative (see Eph 4:21) after the verb to hear, see Winer, p. 179; Buttmann, 166.—(F.)

15 And how shall they preach, except they be sent? as it is written, How beautiful are the feet of them that preach the gospel of peace, and bring glad tidings of good things!
16 But they have not all obeyed the gospel. For Esaias saith, Lord, who hath believed our report?

how shall they preach, except they be sent? even as it is written, How beautiful are the feet of them that bring [1] glad tidings of good things!
16 But they did not all hearken to the [2] glad tidings. For Isaiah said, Lord, who hath believed our re-

1 Or, a gospel......2 Or, gospel.

in order to be heard. ["The gospel does not fall like rain from the clouds, but is brought by the hands of men wherever it is sent from above." (Calvin.) The word which is to be proclaimed is Christ's (ver. 17, Revised Version), and its preachers are sent by him.[1]] **And how shall they preach, except they be sent?** A message necessarily implies a messenger. If, then, God has ordained that men should be saved by believing on Christ, he must have intended that Christ should be made known to them as a Saviour; if he has ordained the end, he must have ordained the means. Two practical observations are in place here. The first is—that the confession of Christ (ver. 9, 10) and the calling upon his name (ver. 12, 13) must be a sincere, heart-prompted confession and calling, and not a merely lip-service; this is implied, of course, in all cases where the Scriptures make saving results to depend upon any such oral utterance or outward act. The second observation is—that though the questions in these two verses are applied, in the verses that follow, as the apostle's argument here requires, particularly to the Jews, they form, by legitimate generalization, a valid and forcible argument, at all times, for sending preachers of the gospel to the heathen, and to all who are in ignorance or in error. **As it is written, How beautiful are the feet,** etc. —that is, how welcome and pleasant is the coming of those who bring glad tidings! This quotation is from Isa. 52: 7 [and follows the Hebrew rather than the Septuagint. The latter, in fact, wholly mistakes the meaning, and renders: "I am present as an hour (of bloom or beauty) upon the mountains." On 'beautiful' (ὡραῖοι, from ὥρα, hour), Trench remarks that every living thing has its hour or period of grace and beauty when it is loveliest and best; hence this adjective came first to mean timely and then beautiful. The apostle omits "upon the mountains" as not appropriate to his purpose. Modern Greek,

it is said, retains this same figure of speech, and the wish that one may be well-footed is that he may be the bearer of good news]. The expression borrows its form, probably, from the case of the messengers who came to Zion across the intervening mountains, announcing the speedy return of the captives from Babylon. But the words had from the beginning a reference to the glad tidings of the Messianic salvation, as the connection in which the prophet Isaiah introduces them plainly shows, and as even the Rabbinical interpreters perceived; so that it is in their real sense, and not merely in the way of accommodation, that the apostle here quotes them. **Preach the gospel of peace.** This clause is omitted by Lachmann and Tischendorf [also by Westcott and Hort], as not being found in the best manuscripts of the New Testament, though undoubtedly genuine in Isaiah. The only doubt is, whether Paul quoted so fully from Isaiah's prophecy. [Meyer, De Wette, Philippi, Godet, regard the omission as an error of the copyists.]

16. But [though the glad tidings were thus, supposedly, proclaimed] **they have not all obeyed the gospel**—better, they did not hearken to the good news. This is what the apostle affirms in regard to the Jews in the time of Isaiah, in respect to the good news of the Messiah to come; and what he *hints*, and might truly affirm, in regard to the Jews in his own time, in respect to the good news of the Messiah already come. In both cases, but especially in the last, he might have truly said that nearly all, or the great majority disbelieved; but he contents himself with saying, in effect, not all believed, thus courteously softening an unwelcome truth, instead of pressing it to its utmost extent. In fact, the language which he quotes from Isa. 53: 1, implies that there were but few who believed the prophet's report of the good news. [Perhaps the 'all' spoken of here contains some

1 On the frequent use of χωρὶς (apart from, without) in the New Testament, and its distinction from ἄνευ, see Ellicott on Eph. 2: 12.—(F.)

17 So then faith *cometh* by hearing, and hearing by the word of God.
18 But I say, Have they not heard? Yes verily, their sound went into all the earth, and their words unto the ends of the world.

17 port? So belief *cometh* of hearing, and hearing by the word of Christ. But I say, Did they not hear? Yea, verily,
Their sound went out into all the earth,
And their words unto the ends of [1] the world.

1 Gr. *the inhabited earth.*

allusion to what the 'all' should have done according to ver. 11–13. (De Wette.) The word *Lord* is found in the LXX, but not in the Hebrew.[1]]

17. This verse is a conclusion from the preceding, confirming also what was said in ver. 14, 15. The word translated 'hearing' (ἀκοή) is the same which in the preceding verse is translated 'report.' It means in both cases, "that which is heard"; and when an inspired prophet or apostle is the speaker, that which is heard is the "word of God," agreeably to 1 Thess. 2: 13. [The text of Tischendorf (8), Westcott and Hort, and of the Revisers, reads, "the word of Christ." Mr. Beet, in order to preserve the spirit of the original, gives this rendering: "Who has believed what we have heard? Therefore, faith comes from something heard, and that which is heard comes through the word of Christ." The following, perhaps, gives the meaning quite as well: Who hath believed our preaching? Accordingly, faith (belief) comes from preaching, and preaching comes through the word of Christ; in other words, the proclaimed message is given by command of Christ (Meyer), or, more probably, is contained in the word of Christ. (Cremer.)]

18. Surely the Jews cannot excuse their unbelief on the ground that they have not heard the gospel, for it has been preached without any restriction to both Jews and Gentiles, and, in fact, so widely, that the voice of the preachers may well be said, according to the Psalmist's description of the silent testimony of God's works, to have "gone forth into all the earth,"[2] etc. This

seems, at first view, a bold hyperbole; but it is hardly more than what is elsewhere said in more literal language. See Col. 1: 6, 23. The restricted national dispensation had given place to the proclamation of a *universal* gospel for all nations, the boundaries of Judaism had been overleaped, the Saviour of *the world* had issued his proclamation to every creature (Mark 16: 15), in all nations (Matt. 28: 19), and his obedient servants had begun the work of preaching the word everywhere (Acts 8: 4; Rom. 15: 19), and that universal work so well begun, and, indeed, already so far advanced, is to go on without cessation until all the ends of the world shall remember and turn to the Lord. (s. 22: 27.) [Yet, no one, we think, can suppose that by the words, "their sound" (or line) the *Psalmist* meant the sound of the gospel from the lips of its preachers. Paul here "simply uses Scriptural language to express his own ideas, as is done involuntarily almost by every preacher in every sermon." (Hodge.) Alford, however, does not see here any mere accommodation of language, but thinks that as the psalm is "a comparison of the sun and glory of the heavens with the word of God," so Paul took this text *in its context,* and followed up the comparison of the psalm.]

19. Nor can the Jew excuse himself on the ground that the nation was taken by surprise, without any previous intimation of God's purpose to give the Messianic salvation to the Gentiles; for both Moses and Isaiah had distinctly declared this, and the latter had predicted the unbelief and disobedience of the people of Israel, and the Lord's reproval of

1 The student will notice that the first verb and the last noun of this verse are both derived from ἀκούω, to hear.—(F.)

2 Of the two negatives in the clause, 'did they not hear,' the latter, οὐκ, according to Winer, belongs to the verb of the sentence, and the former alone is interrogatory, as, did they fail to hear? The answer would then be: nay rather, assuredly not. In this case, the answer would negative the *not* hearing, as the answer in ver. 19 would negative the *not* knowing. Winer

remarks that in interrogative sentences with μή, "the speaker always has his eye on a negative answer." Buttmann, however (p. 248), supposes the negatives of our text require, like the Latin *nonne*, an affirmative answer. The statement of Winer's is probably correct. Yet, according to our idiom, or usage, the proper, or, at least, the natural answer to this query, did they not hear? would be (if we borrow the corrective idea of μενοῦνγε), "Yes, they did hear; and more than this was true in regard to this matter."—(F.)

19 But I say, Did not Israel know? First Moses saith, I will provoke you to jealousy by them that are no people, and by a foolish nation I will anger you.
20 But Esaias is very bold, and saith, I was found of them that sought me not; I was made manifest unto them that asked not after me.
21 But to Israel he saith, All day long I have stretched forth my hands unto a disobedient and gainsaying people.

19 But I say, Did Israel not know? First Moses saith.
I will provoke you to jealousy with that which is no nation,
With a nation void of understanding will I anger you.
20 And Isaiah is very bold, and saith,
I was found of them that sought me not ;
I became manifest unto them that asked not of me.
21 But as to Israel he saith, All the day long did I spread out my hands unto a disobedient and gainsaying people.

them for it. **Did not Israel know?**[1] [The emphasis on the word 'Israel' (in the Revised Text) indicates not a little surprise at their supposed ignorance. Meyer finds in this query "a further possible exculpation for the Jews."] **First Moses saith.** Moses was the first to say this, so early were they distinctly apprised of God's purpose. **I will provoke you to jealousy by them that are no people.** (Deut. 32: 21.) The connection in which this passage occurs is very significant: "As you have provoked me to anger by your idolatries, I will provoke you to jealousy by transferring your abused privileges to those who have heretofore not been acknowledged as my people"; **and by a foolish nation will I anger you.** "I will make you angry by preferring to you a nation whom you despise as foolish, in contrast with your boasted wisdom." Compare 2: 17-20. "All other nations were as inferior to the Jews in religious knowledge as all other nations were to the Greeks in human culture." (Vaughan, apud Webster, p. 243.)[2]

20. But Esaias is very bold and saith. This passage is found in Isaiah 65: 1, the clauses being transposed by the apostle. It

was a bold saying indeed, and especially so in view of what follows, in which the disobedient and contradictory spirit of the Jews is put in contrast to the more docile temper of the Gentiles.[3]

21. But to Israel—that is, with reference to Israel. The passage here quoted immediately follows that which is quoted in the preceding verse, and both are spoken by the Lord in reply to the prophet's intercession in behalf of the people in the preceding chapter. **All day long,** he says, with patient long suffering, **I have stretched forth my hands** (in remonstrance and invitation) **to a disobedient and gainsaying people.** Instead of 'disobedient and gainsaying,' the Hebrew has "rebellious people" ['gainsaying' being added by the LXX.]. 'Disobedient and gainsaying' is the apostolic equivalent of the prophet's word "rebellious." 'Disobedient' was not enough. In addition to their negative non-compliance with the Lord's commands, they are represented as contradicting him to his face, like one who says: "I will not," when commanded to do some particular thing. For that is the meaning of 'gainsaying'—saying again, or, against what is com-

---

[1] This question, with the negative, μή, is equivalent to: was Israel ignorant of this? and hence requires a negative answer. See note on the preceding verse.—(F.)

[2] Epi, with the dative, is here over, on account of, a no-nation, not against, as the "Five Clergymen" and Alford render it ; for in this sense the accusative would be more suitable. These negatived substantives occur only in Old Testament quotations. The Common Version preserves the distinction between people and nation which is found in the Hebrew, but which is neglected by the Seventy, and by Paul.—(F.)

[3] The δέ, above, marks the transition to another prophet. According to Winer, Meyer, and others, the prophet (in the name of God) not only speaks out boldly, but he makes bold and says, so that the idea of the first verb is not made subordinate. With the passive ('was found') we have quite frequently, especially in the perfect and aorist, the dative of agency, instead of the genitive with ὑπό. But Winer remarks that the

dative in such a case "denotes the person not by whom something has been done, but to whom what has been done belongs." Here the finding which belonged to them is equivalent to a finding by them. Thus, to become known to a person is to become known by him. Some manuscripts, however, have ἐν (in) before the dative. Trench, in his "Synonyms," states that ἐρωτάω, the Latin rogare, implies that the one asking stands on a footing of equality or familiarity with him from whom the boon is asked; while αἰτέω, the Latin peto, is the "constant word for the seeking of the inferior from the superior." This view is combated by Prof. Cremer and others. See, also, Thayer's "Lexicon," sub voce, and compare 1 John 5: 16, and the use of ἐπερωτάω above. According to Meyer, this passage historically refers to the Jews ; but Paul sees in them, since they had become idolatrous and heathenish, a typical representation of the Gentiles. Others think the primary reference is to the Gentiles.—(F.)

CHAPTER XI.

I SAY then, Hath God cast away his people? God
  forbid. For I also am an Israelite, of the seed of
Abraham, *of* the tribe of Benjamin.
2 God hath not cast away his people which he foreknew. Wot ye not what the Scriptures saith of Elias?

1 I say then, Did God cast off his people? God forbid. For I also am an Israelite, of the seed of Abra-
2 ham, of the tribe of Benjamin. God did not cast
   off his people whom he foreknew. Or know ye not

manded, answering back. [Godet finds an
illustration of this in the Book of Malachi:
"And ye say!" From the above representation, "it is clear," as the last-named
commentator says, "that the apostle in no
wise puts the rejection of Israel to the account
of an unconditional, divine decree, but that
he ascribes the cause of it to Israel themselves." And Bengel remarks that the doctrine of a double will of God, of good pleasure,
and of sealing, is here shown to be absurd.
The denial, however, of a revealed and secret
will on the part of God, in other words, what
God desires in itself considered, and what he
purposes to do on the whole (H. B. Smith), is
not unattended with difficulty. See Edwards'
"Freedom of the Will," Part IV., § IX.,
IV.; also Vol. II., pp. 161, 162, 513-516.
With reference to Israel as a whole, it must
be said that there was *a rejection*, or *casting away* (ἀποβολή, 11: 15) of them on the part
of God; but this verse shows why and in
what spirit it was done. God has no pleasure
in the death of the wicked, yet who will say
that the transgressor's death is wholly contrary to the determinate counsel of God, the
counsel of his will? What Christian believer
is willing to confess, with the ancient Pagan
Greeks, that some things happen not only
with the will of God, but against his will, or
fixed purpose?]

We may now thus sum up the contents of
the last part of this chapter. (Ver. 18-21.) After
having shown, in a *general* way, that because
faith cometh by hearing the divine word, it
was necessary that the gospel should be
preached to all (ver. 14-17), he shows, *specially*,
that the heavenly truths had been preached
both to all the Gentiles (ver. 18), and also to the
Jews (ver. 19), but with unequal success; for
many of the Gentiles have believed (ver. 20),
while the Jews, for the most part, remained
obdurate (ver. 21).

The way is now prepared for a more favorable view of the *ultimate* purpose of God in
regard to the Jewish people.

Ch. 11: [The temporary casting away of
the Jews, the source of highest good both to
the Gentiles and to the Jewish race.]

The apostle now turns to a more hopeful
aspect of the destiny of the Jewish nation;
their rejection is neither total (ver. 1-10) nor
final. (Ver. 11-36.) It is limited both as to *persons* and as to *time*.

**1. I say then, Hath God cast away his
people?** [A question of the apostle's origina-
tion. Compare the more frequent: "What
then shall we say?"] This form of expression, 'I say then,' introduces, interrogatively,
a false inference which might be drawn from
the closing verses of the previous chapter, but
introduces it only in order to refute it. It is
implicitly refuted, as Bengel well says, in the
very statement of it, for he still calls them his
people. But it is more explicitly refuted by
the fact immediately referred to, that the
apostle himself was [no mere proselyte to
Judaism, but] an Israelite, and a representative of many other believing Israelites. So
he rejects the false inference with emphatic
earnestness: **God forbid**—*let not such a thing
be.* **For I also am** not only **an Israelite**
(see note on 9:4), but **of the tribe of Benjamin,** one of the two royal tribes of Israel
(1 Sam. 10: 20, 21; Acts 12: 21), the tribe so closely associated with the tribe of Judah, and, after the
return from the exile, almost identified with
it. (Ezra 4: 1; 10: 9.) So the very man who has
been saying these seemingly hard things
against the Jews is himself a Hebrew of the
Hebrews (Phil. 3: 5), and thus a fit representative
of the saved remnant [himself a living proof
that God had not thrust away all Israel. If
the truth of the supposition were conceded,
then, as Alford says, "it would exclude from
God's kingdom the writer himself"].

2. The inference which he had refuted in
the first verse, by citing an example which
proved it false, he now directly denies, and
adds a new refutation of it. **Which he foreknew**—which he selected as the chosen nation.
[Prof. Cremer: "God has not cast away his

how he maketh intercession to God against Israel, saying,
3 Lord, they have killed thy prophets, and digged down thine altars; and I am left alone, and they seek my life.
4 But what saith the answer of God unto him? I have reserved to myself seven thousand men, who have not bowed the knee to *the image* of Baal.

what the scripture saith [1] of Elijah? how he pleadeth 3 with God against Israel, Lord, they have killed thy prophets, they have digged down thine altars: and 4 I am left alone, and they seek my life. But what saith the answer of God unto him? I have left for myself seven thousand men, who have not bowed

1 Or, *in*.

people with whom he had before joined himself—that is, before this union was historically realized." Such a supposition would contradict the "immutability of his counsel." Mark the use of the direct negative in a positive statement.] We must not limit the expression 'his people,' here, to the elect Christian people of God found among the Jews, for this would make the question of ver. 1 self-contradictory, and the negation of this verse a mere truism. **Wot** (or, *know*) **ye not** [introduces another proof that God had not wholly cast off his people] **what the Scripture saith of Elias?** A literal translation would be: Saith in Elias, in the story of Elias. Compare Mark 12 : 26. **He maketh intercession to God** (*pleads with God*) **against Israel.** This is the only passage in Scripture where the word intercession has an unfavorable meaning, or is coupled with the preposition 'against.' [Yet see Acts 25 : 24. The verb, primarily, means to meet with, and with this the idea of making request or supplication is closely related.] This plea or protest of Elijah is found in 1 Kings 19 : 14 [and is quoted somewhat freely from the Septuagint. (3 Kings 19 : 14.) The word **saying** which precedes **Lord** in our Common Version is found only in two MSS.

3. They have killed thy prophets, and digged down thine altars. The verbs are in a past, not in the perfect, tense: *They slew thy prophets*; they *utterly overthrew* (or, *razed to the ground*) thine altars. **I am** (or, *was*) **left alone,** etc. These altars were probably those on the high places]. These words were spoken in the times of Ahaz and Jezebel, when the prophet had fled into the wilderness to save his life, which Jezebel had sworn to take before another day should pass. (1 Kings 19 : 2.) [The Greek word for ' life '—corresponding to the word used in the Hebrew—sometimes, as here, refers to the life of the body (compare Matt. 6 : 25), but often has reference to that part of man which can live apart from the body (compare Matt. 10 : 28), and is in our versions more frequently trans-

lated *soul* than ' life.'] Elijah seems to have been literally ' left alone ' as a true prophet of the Lord, and in his dejection he may have fancied himself the only true servant of God in the land. But the case was far from being as bad as that.

4. The sad complaint of Elijah, ' I am left alone,' was very probably uttered under an exaggerated view of the prevalence of evil, as was that of the Hebrew Psalmist, when he said in his haste: "All men are liars" (Ps. 116 : 11) ; but the Lord both reproved and encouraged him by the manner in which he responded to this doleful complaint. **The answer of God unto him,** or the response from the divine oracle, as the word (found nowhere else in the New Testament, though the verb occurs several times ; see 7 : 3) might be freely paraphrased, was this : **I have reserved to myself**—that is, I have kept faithful to myself and free from the prevalent idolatry, not merely one solitary prophet, but **seven thousand men, who have not bowed the knee to the image of Baal.** [This citation follows the Hebrew far more closely than it does the LXX. ' To myself ' is an addition of the apostle.] It will be observed that the words 'the image of' are supplied by the translators ; the original has merely, ' who have not bowed the knee to Baal.' The reason why the translators thought it necessary to add these apparently superfluous words undoubtedly was, that they found in the original Greek the feminine article prefixed to the name Baal, and believing that Baal, the sun god of the Phœnicians, was always regarded as a male divinity, and finding the masculine article in the LXX. in the passage which is here quoted, [though in other places the feminine is used], they supposed that the word ' image,' or some similar noun of the feminine gender in Greek, must be understood. There is reason to believe, however, that this fabulous divinity was regarded by its worshipers as combining both genders, and therefore it is better to omit the words in italics, as has been done by most

5 Even so then at this present time also there is a remnant according to the election of grace.
6 And if by grace, then *is it* no more of works : otherwise grace is no more grace. But if *it be* of works, then is it no more grace : otherwise work is no more work.
7 What then ? Israel hath not obtained that which he seeketh for ; but the election hath obtained it, and the rest were blinded.

5 the knee to Baal. Even so then at this present time also there is a remnant according to the election of
6 grace. But if it is by grace, it is no more of works :
7 otherwise grace is no more grace. What then ? That which Israel seeketh for, that he obtained not ; but the election obtained it, and the rest were hardened :

recent revisers of the English Bible, and read simply : *Who bowed not the knee to Baal.* [The singular, 'knee,' denotes a collective number considered as a single conception. (Philippi.) The number 'seven thousand,' is, perhaps, not to be taken with strict literalness. Seven is commonly regarded as the covenant number, or the number of completeness.]

5. Even so then [in correspondence with this historical precedent. An "analogical inference"]. The cases compared were very similar. Instead of the rejection of all save one, as Elijah in the earlier case and Paul in the later, there were seven thousand in Elijah's time, and "many thousands" of Jews in Paul's time (Acts 21 : 20), who were faithful worshipers of God and believers in Christ ; yet in both cases these thousands were but **a remnant,** a small minority, in comparison with the great mass of idolaters and unbelievers, and it was only through the gracious divine election that this remnant was saved from the general corruption. [Paul's language here, literally rendered, is : *Thus, therefore, also in the now time there has become* (and still exists) *a remnant.* **According to the election of grace** means in virtue of, or, in consequence of, an election made through grace. In this elect remnant, gathered out from an elect nation, we have an election within an election, an election of individuals to eternal life, who belonged to a people whom God elected to the *privileges* of grace. The election spoken of here is regarded from a sublapsarian point of view—that is, it supposes the gratuitously elected persons were guilty and undeserving sinners.]

6. And if by grace, then is it no more of works : otherwise grace is no more grace. [The apostle must here rest his argument a moment to give again the distinguish-

ing characteristic of this all-important 'grace.' The verse may be thus paraphrased : But (or. *now*) if this remnant has been selected and reserved through grace, it is no longer on account of the merit of works, since otherwise[1] grace would cease to show itself as grace. A purely gratuitous election will not allow any merit of works to be mixed up with this grace.] The apostle, not satisfied with having attributed the existence of even a remnant from the general wreck 'to the election of grace,' reiterates the statement in a negative form, and amplifies it, because it was so important to convince the Jews, who were bent on seeking salvation by works, that there was no hope in that direction, and that grace and works, as grounds of salvation, were antagonistic in their very nature, so that there could be no compromise between them, or amalgam of the one with the other. To imagine any such combination would be to suppose one or the other to change its very nature. Yet this is just what many men are still trying to do, depending mainly upon their own works for acceptance with God, but, after all, acknowledging their need of divine mercy. The last half of this verse, **But if it be of works,** etc., is rejected as spurious by some editors, though found in the Vatican manuscript, one of the oldest and best, to say the least.[2] But the doubt is practically of little importance, since it is merely a question of the more or less expansion of what is clearly expressed in the former part of the verse.

7. What then shall we conclude ? [What is to be inferred from the two (or five) preceding verses? We infer the reason why Israel has failed to obtain righteousness : because they, unlike the elect remnant, sought to obtain it by means of works. The verb for seek is a compound, meaning to seek after, and thus, to seek for zealously. **Election** in this verse

[1] Present indicatives after ἐπεί (since) are usually rendered as subjunctives. (Winer, 283.)—(F.)
[2] Yet this manuscript (B), on which textual critics have so greatly depended, and which is characterized

by Westcott and Hort as "neutral," or unmixed and independent, furnishes here a curious reading by its substituting the word 'grace' for the last 'work.'—(F.)

8 (According as it is written, God hath given them the spirit of slumber, eyes that they should not see, and ears that they should not hear;) unto this day.
9 And David saith, Let their table be made a snare, and a trap, and a stumblingblock, and a recompense unto them :
10 Let their eyes be darkened, that they may not see, and bow down their back alway.

8 according as it is written, God gave them a spirit of stupor, eyes that they should not see, and ears that they should not hear, unto this very day. And David saith,
Let their table be made a snare, and a trap,
And a stumblingblock, and a recompense unto them :
10   Let their eyes be darkened, that they may not see,
And bow thou down their back alway.

---

is used for the *elect*.] Paul's conclusion is that 'Israel did not find that which he is seeking'—namely, righteousness (9: 31), or justification; **but the election hath obtained it, and the rest were blinded**—or, rather, *were hardened*.[1] The apostle seems here to be preparing the way for what he has to say of a more favorable nature respecting 'the rest.'

8. Two passages are here combined—namely, Isa. 29: 10; Deut. 29: 4 (3) (compare Isa. 6: 9, 10), and quoted freely from the LXX. **The spirit of slumber,** or of stupefaction, such as is produced by a heavy blow or an intoxicating draught. [**Eyes that they should not see.** Philippi has it : "eyes of not seeing, or blind eyes," an incorrect rendering; see ver. 10. The substance of this **v**erse is found in Matt. 13: 14; John 12: 40; Acts 28: 26. The words ' unto this day ' are a part of the quotation. They occur as Paul's words in 2 Cor. 3: 14, where he affirms that the minds of the children of Israel were blinded, and that a vail is on their hearts.]

9. And David saith. Another similar prediction of the divine judgment upon the Jews from Ps. 69: 22, undoubtedly having a typical reference to the Messiah. The quotation begins with the figure of sudden calamity overtaking those who are feasting [at the banqueting *table*] in fancied security, and then passes to that of animals caught in a snare or trap (literally, a chase), and ends, still figur-

atively, but with another change, by the representation of a people suffering, as a just recompense for their sins, a judicial blindness and abandonment to be oppressed and crushed by haughty victors. [While Paul affirms that 'David' saith,' Meyer and others deny that David is the author of the psalm. "If Meyer is correct in his opinion, then the word 'David' would be used as a title of the entire collection of the Psalms. . . . But it is by no means certain that he is correct in his opinion." (Boise.) Possibly some of the last verses may have been a later edition. "Of all the psalms, the sixty-ninth is most frequently quoted in the New Testament, along with Ps. 22, as a prediction of Christ's sufferings." (Philippi.) In this quotation, Paul "follows the LXX, with some variations." The word for trap, or chase, is introduced here from Ps. 35: 8 in the LXX. **Stumblingblock.** See note on 9: 33.[2] The Hebrew original, as now pointed, has no word for 'recompense,' and instead of " bow thou down their back always," has, as in our Common and Revised Versions: "and make their loins continually to shake." But what shall we say as to the propriety of Christians indulging in such imprecations as these? The editor of Calvin's "Commentary on Romans" says that "no one is allowed to curse individuals, except he be inspired so as to know who those are who are given up by God to final judgment, which

---

[1] There is a difference of only one letter in Greek between these two words, ἐπηρωθήσαν and ἐπωρώθησαν. The passive form of this verb, together with the following context (see, also, 9: 18), indicates that this ' hardening' took place through the agency of God ; so most expositors. Calvin, on this verse, rather contrary to his usual method, argues for the supralapsarian view of a reprobation by God before the foundation of the world, while acknowledging that the passages here cited by Paul are adverse to such a view. He says: "They reason absurdly who, whenever a word is said of the proximate causes, strive, by bringing forward these, to cover the first which is hid from our view, as though God had not, before the fall of Adam, freely determined to do what seemed good to him, with respect

to the whole human race." This inference of Calvin is a very natural—it may be an unavoidable—conclusion of the mere logical faculty, exercising itself simply on one line of facts ; but it is confessedly a going beyond the *reasoning* of the apostle here, and generally throughout this Epistle. The Scriptures, as a whole, plainly teach that God efficaciously blinds and hardens men only as a judicial penalty or punishment for their disobedience and unbelief.—(F.)

[2] The accusatives, with the preposition εἰς, are here equivalent to nominatives. This construction may be regarded as Hebraistic. So in the phrase, " counted (εἰς) for righteousness," faith is not regarded as something *resulting* in righteousness, but *as* righteousness itself.—(F.)

11 I say then, Have they stumbled that they should fall? God forbid: but *rather* through their fall salvation *is come* unto the Gentiles, for to provoke them to jealousy.

12 Now if the fall of them *be* the riches of the world, and the diminishing of them the riches of the Gentiles; how much more their fulness?

11   I say then, Did they stumble that they might fall? God forbid: but by their [1] fall salvation *is come* unto 12 the Gentiles, for to provoke them to jealousy. Now if their fall is the riches of the world, and their less the riches of the Gentiles; how much more their

1 Or, *trespass.*

may be supposed to have been the case with the Psalmist and with St. Paul." Paul, however, does not wish these imprecations, but only quotes them in evidence of God's rejection of the Jewish people. We should say, moreover, that Christians are to bless, except when *divinely commissioned* to curse.]

11. From this point begins the second portion of the chapter, showing that the rejection of the Jews is not *final*, but that God designs, by means of it, to facilitate the salvation of the Gentiles (ver 11-16), who are admonished not to glory over the Jews (17-22). **Have they stumbled,** etc.—better, *Did they stumble, in order that they should fall?* [that is, utterly and forever lie prostrate? The word trip might here be substituted for ' stumble.' The proper word for stumble occurs at 9: 32. 'That' (ἵνα) indicates the final purpose of the divine judicial government. (Lange.) The **God forbid** occurs here for the tenth and last time in this Epistle. In Galatians it occurs three times, in First Corinthians once.] The stumbling of the Jews was not to result in a final and fatal fall. Far from it; **but through their fall** (*offense,* as the same word is translated six times in chapter 5 of this Epistle) **salvation is come unto the Gentiles.**[1] The emphatic sense in which the verb ' fall ' is here used, makes it unsuitable that its corresponding noun (πτῶμα, or πτῶσις) should be used to express that stumbling which is contrasted with the 'fall.' The word here used is translated ' fall ' in our Common Version only in this and the following verse. It was not a complete and final ' fall ' on their part, because it was not a complete and final *casting away* on God's part. Besides facilitating the conversion of the Gentiles, it had the further

design and effect, through their conversion, **to provoke them** (that is, the Jews) **to jealousy** [in other words, " to make them jealous of the Gentiles as having obtained blessings which the Jews regarded as peculiarly theirs; and thus to excite in them a desire to obtain the same blessings for themselves." (Ripley.) Noyes has it: excite them to emulation.] Of the two results mentioned, the first was the more immediate; the second the ultimate. This latter result will doubtless be realized hereafter on a much larger scale than it yet has been. The unbelief of the Jews was a benefit to the Gentiles in several ways. It made it evident that God did the Jews no injustice in turning to offer to the Gentiles those blessings which the Jews had rejected. See Matt. 21: 43; Acts 13: 46. [" Lo we turn to the Gentiles," not only willingly, but of necessity. (Acts.18: 6; 28: 28.)] It left the apostles more free, and, at the same time, more willing to preach the gospel to the Gentiles. It deprived the Jews of the power to insist on bringing the Gentiles under the yoke of the Mosaic laws, as they would have done if they had been in the majority, and as some of them, though in the minority, attempted to do. (Acts 15: 1.)

12. Now if the fall of them be the riches of the world, etc. Meyer calls this " an argument from the happy effect of a worse cause to the still happier effect of a better cause." If their stumbling has been the means of enriching the Gentile world with the blessing of salvation, how much greater the blessing which will result from **their fulness,** their general recovery, or "their numerous entrance into God's kingdom."[2]

13, 14. These verses seem as if designed to

[1] The word for ' fall,' rendered *trespass* in the Revision, literally means a falling aside. Chrysostom remarks that " as Paul had greatly run the Jews down, and strung accusation upon accusation, bringing forward prophet after prophet, crying out against them,—Isaiah, Elijah, Moses, David, and Hosea,—and that not once or twice, but frequently; so now, lest he might plunge them in despair, and, on the other hand, that he might

not lift the believing Gentiles into arrogance, he again consoles the Jews, saying, that by their fall salvation is come to the Gentiles." In this conversion of the Gentiles we have an instance of the last becoming first.—(F.)

[2] The word πλήρωμα (fullness) is found eighteen times in the New Testament, and in some connections is a very important doctrinal term. See Col. 2: 9, etc. Elli-

13 For I speak to you Gentiles, inasmuch as I am the apostle of the Gentiles, I magnify mine office:
14 If by any means I may provoke to emulation *them which are* my flesh, and might save some of them.
15 For if the casting away of them *be* the reconciling of the world, what *shall* the receiving *of them be*, but life from the dead?

13 fulness? But I speak to you that are Gentiles. Inasmuch then as I am an apostle of Gentiles, I
14 glorify my ministry: if by any means I may provoke to jealousy *them that are* my flesh, and may
15 save some of them. For if the casting away of them *is* the reconciling of the world, what *shall* the receiv-
16 ing *of them be*, but life from the dead? And if the

forestall some such thought as this in the minds of his Gentile readers. In writing to us (for the most part) Gentiles—["observe," says Meyer, "that Paul does not write 'to the Gentiles which are among you'"; compare, also, ver. 14, *my* (not *our*) flesh]—why do you express so much interest in the Jews, and devote so large a space in your letter to their condition and prospects? To which his answer is: "I do not forget that I am the apostle of the Gentiles—indeed, I am honoring my office as such in this way of speaking. I cannot do you a greater service than by doing my utmost for the conversion of my own people; for, great as is the blessing which you obtain through their rejection, a much greater will result through their recovery." **Provoke to emulation.** Compare 'provoke to jealousy' (ver. 11 and 10: 19); the original word is the same in all three cases [1] **Might save some of them.** Their salvation is here attributed to the human agency through which it is brought about, as in 1 Tim. 4: 16; 1 Cor. 7: 16; 9: 22, without derogating in the least from what is so emphatically asserted elsewhere of the divine will as the only efficient cause of salvation. See John 1: 13, 14; Eph. 2: 8-10.[2]

15. The idea of ver. 12 is here repeated in still more forcible language. [**For** assigns a *motive* for ver. 13, 14. The word for **casting away** occurs elsewhere only in Acts 27: 22. Philippi understands it of the *loss* which God's kingdom has sustained in their case, and

which is to be made up by the fullness of the Gentiles. It seems, however, to denote rejection as being antithetical to reception. The thought thus would be: If the partial and temporary casting away of the Jews (their loss or diminution) is the means of the Gentile world's reconciliation with God—that is, their 'riches.' (Ver. 12.) On this reconcilation, see Eph. 2: 11-22. To this day the Jews are a scattered and despised—in fact, a God-rejected people. They have lost their pre-eminence as the people of God. And this accords with our Lord's prediction in Matt. 21: 43: "The kingdom of God shall be taken away from you." But there is to be a reception, a taking of them back again. And what will the ingathering of these stiff-necked and inveterate enemies of Christ within the Christian fold be to the world but life from the dead? The Jewish race has thus, as a "burning bush" which is never consumed, been "miraculously preserved for some important action in the concluding chapter of the history of Christianity." (Schaff.)] The expression **life from the dead** is taken, by most of the early interpreters (Origen, Chrysostom) and by many of the modern (De Wette, Meyer, etc.), in a *literal* sense, with the idea that the recovery of the Jews will be speedily followed by the general resurrection and the final judgment. But this would be a sense of the words 'life from the dead' which would not be in accordance with Scriptural usage, and would not be sanctioned by either the preceding or the fol-

cott says: "Lexically considered, it has three possible meanings—one active (a) *implendi actio*, fulfilling; and two passive (b) *id quod impletum est*, that which is filled, Eph. 1: 23, and the more common (c) *id quo res impletur*, that by which anything is filled, which, again, often passes into the neutral and derivative (d) *affluentia, abundantia* (or fullness), especially in connection with abstract genitives." Compare 15: 29; Gal. 4: 4; Eph. 3: 19.—(F.)

[1] It is in this clause that some find a suppressed δέ (but), corresponding to the μέν above. Inasmuch as, or, in so far as I indeed am the apostle of the Gentiles, I glorify my office (preaching zealously to the Gentiles), *but* in this I have the benefit of the Jews in view (I will thus render the Jews emulous). Yet this view does

not necessarily exclude the idea of the benefit which would ultimately inure to the Gentiles from the restoration of the Jews. Buttmann thinks the μέν in this connection is not corresponsive, but, blended with the οὖν, is a particle of transition.—(F.)

[2] In the particle, εἴπως (*if by any means*), which precedes the last two verbs, and which introduces the more remote result of his Gentile ministry, "the idea of an *attempt* is conveyed, which may or may not be successful." (Ellicott.) Buttmann thinks the clause is dependent on a verb like *see*, understood. On the use of the indicative future after *if* (generally rendered *may* or *might*), see Winer, 300. The *them*, in idea, refers to 'my flesh.'—(F.)

16 For if the firstfruit *be* holy, the lump *is* also *holy:* and if the root *be* holy, so *are* the branches.

17 And if some of the branches be broken off, and thou, being a wild olive tree, wert graffed in among them, and with them partakest of the root and fatness of the olive tree;

firstfruit is holy, so is the lump: and if the root is 17 holy, so are the branches. But if some of the branches were broken off, and thou, being a wild olive, wast grafted in among them, and didst become partaker with them [1] of the root of the fatness

---

1 Many ancient authorities read *of the root and of the fatness.*

---

lowing context. But the ultimate restoration of the Jews to the favor of God seems here to be implied, as it is more positively still a little further on. [It was Paul's modest hope to be the means of saving only 'some' Jews and Gentiles in his lifetime (ver. 14; 1 Cor. 9: 22), and we cannot suppose that he at this time expected to live to see the great mass of the Gentile and Jewish world converted to God, or that the blessed resurrection life, "setting in with the advent" (παρουσία) (Meyer), would happen in a few months or years. Why, on this supposition, as Godet asks, use the expression *life* instead of the usual "resurrection"? And why omit the article before the word 'life' and not say, as usual, *the* life, eternal life? The truth is, 'life' is often used in the sense of highest felicity or blessedness (1 Thess. 3: 8), and 'life from the dead' is often taken in a spiritual sense. (6: 13; Luke 15: 24, 32, etc.) Paul thus felt—and so may we feel—that the conversion of Israel to Christ would be a blessed resurrection life to the world. Compare Ezek. 37: 1-11.]

16. For if the firstfruit be holy, the lump is also holy: and if the root be holy, so are the branches. [The student will notice that in the Common Version the verbs 'be,' 'is' and 'are' have been supplied, because they are omitted in the Greek. This omission is quite frequent in Paul's writings.] Observe the propriety of the terms here and their correspondence. 'The firstfruit' refers [not to the Passover sheaf offering (or, *omer* offering), nor to the Pentecostal two wave loaves (Lev. 23: 10, 17), but as connected with the 'lump,' the mixed and kneaded dough] to the heave offering to the Lord, of a cake made from the first of the dough (Num. 15: 19-21), whereby the whole 'lump' was regarded as consecrated. 'The root' refers to the patriarchal progenitors of the race, to Abraham especially, in whom 'the branches'—that is, his natural posterity—were regarded as consecrated to

God. Compare ver. 28. That the holiness here attributed to the 'lump' and to the 'branches,' by virtue of their connection with the 'firstfruit' and the 'root' respectively, was not a *moral* holiness, such as accompanies salvation, is plain from abundant testimonies of Scripture, such as Matt. 3: 9; John 8: 33, 39; Rom. 2: 29; and from the context in this very chapter. In the carrying out of the second figure—the first, that of the dough, not being followed up at all—the unbelieving descendants of Abraham—that is, those of them who had persistently rejected Christ—are styled *branches broken off.* (Ver. 17, 19, 20.) And yet there is a fitness in referring to the holiness of 'the root' in introducing the assurance of the final restoration of Israel to God's favor through faith. Holiness is habitually attributed in the Scriptures to that which has been consecrated to God, though it may be some inanimate object, incapable of possessing any moral quality. So when God shall restore Israel to his favor through their individual repentance and faith, he will but reassert his claim to that which was all along his own, by the right of an ancient and solemn consecration.

17, 18. [And if—better, *but if.* If notwithstanding this consecration of Abraham's race to God, some of the branches were spiritually severed from the parent trunk.] **Some.** More than this was actually true. Most, not all, of the branches were broken off, but the apostle speaks in a way less offensive to the Jew and better adapted to check the Gentile's pride. **And thou.** Here the apostle addresses himself directly to the believing Gentile. Compare 3: 3. **A wild olive tree.** A whole is here put for a part, a tree for a shoot; or, perhaps the word should be regarded as an adjective rather than a noun, in which case the proper translation would be simply *wild olive.* **Wert graffed in among them**—among the branches not broken off.[1] **Par-**

---

1 Some Christian writers, by making the good olive tree, into which the believing Gentiles are grafted, synonymous with the Mosaic national theocracy (whose

constitution and character we considered in notes on 4: 11), have inferred that the so-called Jewish Church and the Christian Church are identical, and that the

18 Boast not against the branches. But if thou boast, thou bearest not the root, but the root thee.
19 Thou wilt say then, The branches were broken off, that I might be graffed in.
20 Well; because of unbelief they were broken off, and thou standest by faith. Be not highminded, but fear:

18 of the olive tree; glory not over the branches: but if thou gloriest, it is not thou that bearest the root,
19 but the root thee. Thou wilt say then, Branches
20 were broken off, that I might be grafted in. Well; by their unbelief they were broken off, and thou standest by thy faith. Be not highminded, but fear:

takest (better, *didst become partakers*) **of the root and fatness of the olive tree.** ["The 'root' is a figure of fellowship; the 'fatness,' of the blessing connected with it." (De Wette.) The fatness of the olive is a Scriptural symbol of the Holy Spirit's gracious influences. The Revised Version reads, "root of the fatness," which must refer to the richness of the root, or the root as "the source of fatness." (Alford.)] The natural process of grafting is designed not to make the graft partaker of the *nature* of the tree, but to make the *fruit* partaker of the nature of the graft. The apostle reverses this, not through ignorance, but in order to make the illustration suit the fact illustrated. And he might do this the more allowably, as he does not speak directly of *fruit*, but of life and growth, in which respects the tree *does* communicate to the graft, and not the graft to the tree. [Any grafting may be said to be "contrary to nature" (ver. 24), but with us it is contrary both to nature and to practice to graft a wild scion into a good stock. In the East, however, the scion of the oleaster, or wild olive, is, as we are told, sometimes grafted in the good olive, in order to invigorate the tree. Yet the purpose of Paul in the use of this figure does not necessarily infer any reference to this custom.

Indeed, such a reference would, as Alford says, "completely stultify the illustration," the point of which is the benefit received rather than conferred by the graft. **Boast not** (*thou*) **against the branches**—namely, those which were broken off.] After the clause **but if thou boast** we may easily fill out the ellipsis by supplying the word *remember*, or some similar word. [On the ending of the verb, see at 2:17. The pronoun with 'not' in the next sentence is highly emphatic: Not *thou* the root bearest.]

19. Thou wilt say then, in justification of thy boasting. [The Revised Version has simply 'branches;' taken indefinitely, 'some' branches, as in ver. 17. Nearly all the uncial MSS. omit the article.] In the last clause of this verse the pronoun **I** is emphatic, and betrays a disposition to boast.

20. Well [or, *very well.* Our simple word 'well' is far from being as emphatic as the original. (Boise.)] The fact is granted, and when the reason of it is considered, it suggests a new argument against boasting, a new admonition against highmindedness. This verse shows that the branches broken off represent only those who had actually disbelieved the gospel, and not those to whom it had not yet been fairly preached. Of these, there were

ordinances of Judaism are simply changed in form by their introduction into Christianity, but remain the same in substance, and are still to be administered in accordance with their primitive rule. We may grant, without hesitation, that the spiritual Israel and the Christian Israel are substantially the same, so that when Christ's "other sheep" are brought in from among the Gentiles (John 10:16) there will be but "one flock and one shepherd." But to infer from this that the ordinances of Christianity are similar in character and import to those of Judaism, and are to be similarly administered, is to put a strain upon the argument which it cannot bear. One may, perhaps, say, with Godet, that, in Paul's view, "the believers of Israel are the nucleus round which are grouped the converts from among the Gentiles;" yet it must not be forgotten that this "Israel" had first to be converted to Christ and the gospel. "Otherwise," as the same writer remarks, "the gospel would have been Judaized, believing Gentiles would have been required to become proselytes of

Israel, and this would have been an end of salvation for the world and of the world for salvation." In this sense, as Meyer says, "Israel does not take in the church but the church takes in Israel," and hence the apostle speaks of the *receiving* of the believing Jews virtually into the *Christian* fold. It was *the* effort of the apostle's life " to disentangle the cause of the gospel from that of Judaism," and in his zeal to effect this he showed, on one occasion, no more regard for the chiefest of the Mosaic ordinances than to cry out: "Beware of the concision." (Phil. 3:2.) Our Saviour, also, was too wise to endeavor to patch up with new cloth the old garment of the worn-out past or to put the new wine of the gospel into the old skin bottles of Judaism. Listen, also, to Peter's discourse on the day of Pentecost: "Repent, and be baptized every one of you in the name of Jesus Christ." Was not this a new voice to be heard in Israel? And did it not more than intimate a new economy in the kingdom of grace?—(F.)

21 For if God spared not the natural branches, *take heed* lest he also spare not thee.
22 Behold therefore the goodness and severity of God: on them which fell, severity; but toward thee, goodness, if thou continue in *his* goodness: otherwise thou also shalt be cut off.

21 for if God spared not the natural branches, neither
22 will he spare thee. Behold then the goodness and severity of God: toward them that fell, severity; but toward thee, God's goodness, if thou continue in his goodness: otherwise thou also shalt be cut off.

not a few who would yet believe and be numbered among the saved remnant. [The words for **unbelief** and **faith** are in the so-called instrumental dative, which is generally translated *by* or *through*. The word **standest** in our text is used antithetically to falling (14:4), though some refer it to the standing as of a branch upon the olive tree. Paul, it will be noticed, forgets here to say that these Jews were broken off from the stock of the spiritual Israel and cast away by reason of the absolute decree of Jehovah; but, on the contrary, he charges their rejection solely to their own fault—their want of faith. Nor did these Jews ever think of charging their want of faith to God's decree of reprobation. And yet this unbelief of theirs was connected with a divine purpose.] **Be not highminded, but fear.** The 'fear' which the Gentile believer is here admonished to cherish is opposed not so much to confidence, as to presumption and careless living. [The present imperative (as in the case of the last two verbs) denotes "an action already begun and to be continued, or one that is permanent and frequently recurring." (Winer.) For example: 'Be not highminded' (as thou now art). So in 12:20: "If thine enemy hunger, feed him" (constantly in such a case). "It is a characteristic," says Philippi, "of the difference between the ethics of the ancient world and of Christianity, that a Greek uses 'high-minded' in a good sense and 'humble-minded' in a bad sense."]

21. [**If,** here equivalent to *since*, hence the use of the direct negative in the original.] **Take heed.** These words are supplied by the translators, it being necessary to supply some such words to express the sense of the original completely, as in ver. 18, where, however, our translators have left the manifest ellipsis to be filled out by the reader, instead of doing the work for him, as they have done here. [**Lest**—omitted by the Revisers, is usually followed by the subjunctive, and serves here to soften what otherwise would

be a menace into a simple warning. *I fear*, or, *it is to be feared, lest he will not spare even thee.* (Winer, 474.) With the Revisers' text no words need be supplied.]

22. Behold therefore the goodness and severity of God.[1] Both 'goodness' and 'severity' on the part of God are seen in very close connection in his dealings with the Jews and the Gentiles, in the beginning of the gospel history. **On them which fell** from their high privileges through unbelief, as the branch falls to the ground when severed from the tree, **severity; but toward thee, goodness.** [According to the Revisers' text we should have this rendering: upon them that fell severity is shown, or, there is severity—the nominative form being used rather than the objective. The word for 'severity' means literally, *a cutting off*, and carries out the figure of the branches broken off and falling from the tree. It occurs nowhere else in the New Testament. The word 'goodness' (in the Revision: "toward thee, God's goodness") primarily denotes *usefulness, serviceableness*.] The Gentile believer is here directly addressed as in each of the five preceding verses. **If thou continue in** (literally, *abide upon*) **his goodness**—if thou continue in that state of faith into which his goodness has brought thee, and on thy continuance in which his favor depends. (Acts 13:43.) [**Otherwise thou also shalt be cut off.** 'Thou also,' thou Gentile as well as the Jew. "The future passive, 'thou shalt be cut off' (by striking or smiting) abruptly closes the sentence, like the stroke of the axe cutting down the proud branch." (Godet.) Some find in the latter part of this verse a proof text for the possibility of an individual's falling from grace. But the apostle here is speaking of the people collectively and not of particular individuals. And Dr. Hodge goes so far as to affirm that "there is nothing in this (hypothetical) language inconsistent with the doctrine of the final perseverance of believers, even supposing the passage to refer to individuals."] These last five verses

1 'Behold' (ἴδε), imperative second aorist of εἶδον, sometimes a mere exclamation (John 19: 14), here governs the accusative.—(F.)

R

23 And they also, if they abide not still in unbelief, shall be graffed in: for God is able to graff them in again.

24 For if thou wert cut out of the olive tree which is

23 And they also, if they continue not in their unbelief, shall be grafted in: for God is able to graft them in again. For if thou wast cut out of that which is

24

are marked by repeated and emphatic warnings to Gentile believers against falling from a state of favor with God, as the Jews had fallen, after the same example of unbelief. And the warning is equally appropriate, and equally needful, to believers at the present time.

23. And they also.[1] The restoration of the Jews is here represented hypothetically, as something which God is perfectly *able* to accomplish. If the cause of their rejection is removed, if they do not persist in their unbelief, the only hindrance to their restoration will be taken away. The association of willingness with power is intimated in such passages as Rom. 14: 4; 16: 25; 2 Cor. 9: 8; Eph. 3: 20; Heb. 7: 25; 11: 19; Jude 24. **[For God is able.** The position of the Greek adjective for 'able' at the beginning of the sentence gives it great stress. We cannot suppose that Paul here represents the power of God as waiting for unbelieving Jews to give up their unbelief, for on this supposition there would be, as De Wette states it, no need for the exercise of the divine omnipotence. This last-named commentator further says, that "the apostle here obscurely includes in the *grafting in*, also the removal of their unbelief and the awakening of faith, and these especially he looks for from above." Until this day, alas, the same thick veil of prejudice and unbelief lies on their hearts, and though God has destroyed their temple and their altars, has abolished their priesthood, and the law on which it and all the Levitical rites were founded, has blotted out

their tribal distinctions and scattered their people all over the earth, and though very many of them have now become advanced rationalists, denying the miracles and the historic verity of the Old Testament, they yet, as a general thing, cling to a few of the ancient ceremonials, and still keep up their wonted isolation from all the rest of mankind.[2] But God is able to graft them in. To the apostle, not only at the time of writing this Epistle, but especially in after years, in this very city of Rome, when he sought to persuade the Jews concerning Jesus from morning till evening, while some believed and others disbelieved, and they could come to no agreement among themselves, this must have been his sole encouraging and sustaining thought, 'God is able to graff them in.' God is already bringing the world together as neighbors and to a common brotherhood, and, by his power, the remnant of Israel will yet be brought to Christ, where there is neither Jew nor Greek, and so all Israel shall be saved.]

24. Paul now proceeds a step further, and argues from the nature of the case that there is a presumption in favor of God's doing that which he certainly has power to do in this matter! [The **for** introducing additional evidence for their future re-ingrafting.] And from this point to the end of ver. 32, he more distinctly affirms, by virtue of his prophetic gift, the divine purpose that Israel shall be restored. The course of thought in these verses is thus traced by Dr. Hackett. "Not only is God able and willing to receive the Jews again, if

[1] Καὶ, δὲ, the former connects, the latter slightly contrasts. Grafting them 'again' (unless we take πάλιν in the sense of *back*) supposes a prior grafting which in their case did not take place. The meaning is: "again to unite them to the stock—namely, by ingrafting." (Winer.)—(F.)

[2] If any Christian brother wishes to abjure Christianity and become a strict orthodox Jew, and thus virtually eschew his relation to a common humanity, it will be needful for him, among other things, to acquire a sufficient knowledge of Hebrew, in order that he may pronounce Israel's confession of faith and read the prayers, to submit to circumcision as performed by the "Mohel," to immerse himself in water, to adopt a new

name, to observe the Levitical dietary laws, to abstain from intermarriage with other creeds, to commence the Sabbath Friday afternoon, half an hour before sunset, and generally to attend to the observances of the synagogue, of Jewish festival days, Jewish marriage, Jewish burial, etc. Thus doing he will become a Jew, and we may say, a *Pharisee*, one *separated* not only from Christ, but virtually from the common brotherhood of man. The reformed Jews are disposed to loosen some of these obligations, while those of the radical reform party are ready to give up, not only this non-intermarriage, but even the Sabbath and circumcision, the two fundamental principles of Judaism—(F.)

wild by nature, and wert graffed contrary to nature into a good olive tree ; how much more shall these, which be the natural *branches*, be graffed into their own olive tree?

25 For I would not, brethren, that ye should be ignorant of this mystery, lest ye should be wise in your own conceits, that blindness in part is happened to Israel, until the fulness of the Gentiles be come in.

by nature a wild olive tree, and wast grafted contrary to nature into a good olive tree : how much more shall these, which are the natural *branches*, be grafted into their own olive tree?

25 For I would not, brethren, have you ignorant of this mystery, lest ye be wise in your own conceits, that a hardening in part hath befallen Israel, until

they will repent, but he distinctly announces his purpose to secure their repentance and consequent restoration to his favor : the *time* of this event being when many Gentiles shall have been converted (ver. 25) ; the *means* of it, the effect this will have to remind the Jews of their duty (ver. 31) ; and the *pledge* of it, the declarations of Scripture (ver. 26, 27), and the unalterable faithfulness of God to his purposes and promises." (Ver. 27, 29.) [The expression **contrary to nature** probably refers to the grafting process in general, considered as an artificial proceeding. If it meant, contrary to *thy* (wild) nature, the pronoun, or at least the article, would have been prefixed to 'nature.' **These, which be the natural branches** are represented as having been 'broken off,' yet it would be pressing the figure too far to suppose that, in the apostle's mind, such dissevered branches could be engrafted. The disbelieving Jews are here simply regarded as branches which originally and by nature belonged to the good and holy olive tree "whose root the patriarchs are" (Meyer), and hence this is **their own olive tree.**]

25, 26. [**For** introduces a corroboration that they shall be grafted in, which is derived from divine revelation. Compare with this Eph. 3 : 3-6.] **I would not, brethren, that ye should be ignorant of this mystery** is used to announce some important and authoritative declaration of divine truth (1 Cor. 10 : 1 ; 1 Thess. 4 : 13) ; or some facts in his own history not previously known to his readers. (1 : 13 ; 2 Cor. 1 : 8.) The word ' mystery ' is applied —1. To such matters of fact as are inaccessible to reason, and can only be known through divine revelation. (16 : 25 ; 1 Cor. 2 : 7-10 ; Eph. 1 : 9, 10 ; 3 : 4-6 ; 6 : 19 ; Col. 1 : 26, 27.) 2. To such matters as are patent facts, but the *process* of which cannot be entirely taken by the reason. (1 Cor. 13 : 2 ; 14 : 2 ; Eph. 5 : 32 ; 1 Tim. 3 : 9, 16.) 3. To matters which

are no mystery in themselves, but by their figurative import. (Matt. 12 : 11 ; Mark 4 : 11 ; Luke 8 : 10 ; 2 Thess. 2 : 7 ; Rev. 1 : 20 ; 17 : 5.) (Tholuck.) The first definition applies here. That peculiar character of the gospel which placed the Gentiles on the same level with the Jews was in direct opposition to the strongest expectations and prejudices of the Jewish people, and next to the offense of the cross was perhaps the strongest obstacle in the way of their embracing Christianity. Compare the parable of the prodigal son, Luke 15 : 25-30. "The calling of the Jews *was* a mystery, the conversion of the Jews *is* so still." (Bengel.) [The word ' mystery ' is in the accusative case after the verb 'to be ignorant of' (ἀγνοεῖν), nearly equivalent to *fail to perceive.* On this word ' mystery,' De Wette says : "The apostle here speaks as a prophet." A Scripture mystery or secret which cannot in general be understood without a revelation is not that of classical antiquity, a something mysterious in itself, comprehensible only to the initiated, and to be concealed from the profane (Meyer) ; nor is it on the other hand an altogether unintelligible, incomprehensible revealed truth or doctrine.] **Lest ye should be wise in your own conceits.** [Literally, *that ye may not be wise with yourselves.*[1]] Compare Prov. 26 : 12, 16. "Lest ye should take to yourselves credit for superior wisdom above the Jews, in that ye have acknowledged and accepted Jesus as the Son of God." **Blindness** (or rather, *hardness*) **in part**—this hardness extending only to a part of the nation through a *part* of their history—**is happened to Israel.** [The article is used with ' Israel ' to indicate the case. Calvin interprets ' in part ' of a partial hardening, but see ' some ' in ver. 17.] **The fulness of the Gentiles** can hardly mean less than the whole number of the Gentile nations. So the word ' fulness ' is used in ver. 12, of the Jews as interpreted

---

[1] The MSS. A B have *in* yourselves. Notice how the third person (themselves) is here used for the second. **Winer** interprets παρά with the dative : "*before* your-

selves (as judges), in your own estimation, in your own eyes."—(F.)

26 And so all Israel shall be saved: as it is written
There shall come out of Sion the Deliverer, and shall
turn away ungodliness from Jacob:
27 For this *is* my covenant unto them, when I shall
take away their sins.

26 the fulness of the Gentiles be come in : and so all
Israel shall be saved : even as it is written,
There shall come out of Zion the Deliverer ;
He shall turn away [1] ungodliness from Jacob:
27   And this is [2] my covenant unto them,
When I shall take away their sins.

1 Gr. *ungodlinesses*.......2 Gr. *the covenant from me.*

by ver. 26.[1] **Be come in**—that is, into the kingdom of God where the writer and his readers already were. **And so,** in the manner, order, and time indicated, **all Israel shall be saved**—that is, the literal Israel, in the collective sense of the word, all the posterity of Jacob. That the word is to be taken in this sense and not in the sense of the *spiritual* Israel, including the Gentiles, is fairly inferred from the sharp distinction between Jews and Gentiles observed throughout this whole section ; see 9 : 24, 30, 31 ; 10 : 12, 19-21; 11 : 11, 12, 13, and especially in the immediate context, ver. 17, 31. [In our view Paul teaches that when the great mass or multitude of the Gentiles shall have accepted a Jewish Saviour and a salvation which is from the Jews, and shall have entered into the Messianic kingdom, then the Jews themselves, 'provoked to emulation,' will be ashamed to hold out longer in their opposition and exclusiveness, and Israel as a whole, perhaps "the whole nation which shall then be in existence" (Prof. Turner), will accept of Jesus as their Messiah, and the unspeakably blessed influence of their reception within the Christian fold will extend all over the Gentile world. (ver. 12. 15.) [2] But there is no necessity for supposing that every single individual Jew then living will be converted to Christ. As Alford says : " 'All Israel shall be saved,' Israel as a nation, not individuals ; nor is there the slightest ground for the notion of the *universal restoration*" (ἀποκατάστασις) of *all* the Jews who ever lived—the outcast sons of the kingdom and Judas himself not excepted. We may also add that the apostle is wholly silent as to any restoration of the Jews to Palestine (maintained by Delitzsch, Ebrard, and many others), or as to any future personal reign of Christ on David's throne at Jerusalem. " Nowhere," says De Wette (1 Thess. 4 : 17) " is there in Paul's writings a clear trace of an earthly kingdom of Christ."]
As it is written in Isa. 59 : 20, 21. The passage is quoted neither literally nor fully. Our Old Testament has "to Zion" [the LXX., "on account of Zion"] instead of **out of Sion**,[3] and "unto them that turn from transgression in Jacob" instead of (the Septuagint rendering) **shall turn away ungodliness** (literally, *ungodlinesses*) **from Jacob.** In both cases the English of the Old Testament is closer to the Hebrew. [This verse brings the Jew to a truly joyful outlook after a long dark way of rejection and hardening.]
27. For this is my covenant unto them [literally, the *covenant* (proceeding) *from me*] **when I shall take away their sins.** The first clause is a continuation (not a completion) of the quotation begun in the preceding verse

[1] This is the view of commentators generally. But Philippi and a few others regard this πλήρωμα or fullness as a supplement from the Gentiles which shall fill up a deficiency in Israel arising from the unbelieving Jews ; just as if Paul had written : until Israel's πλήρωμα from the Gentiles have come in. But this seems rather far fetched and does not accord with the general usage of the word.—(F.)

[2] Many of the Reformers thought that the great body of the Jews—so stiff-necked and hard-hearted were they—would never be converted, not even when the fullness of the Gentiles had come in. Luther, in his conviction of their depravity, asserted that " a Jewish heart is as hard as stock, stone, iron, or devil, which can in no way be moved." And Calvin interpreted 'all Israel' to mean the spiritual Israel gathered from both Jews and Gentiles. Beza seems to have been more hopeful of their conversion. Bengel, Olshausen, and now Philippi (in his Appendix to the Third Edition)

regard 'all Israel' as the remnant according to the election of grace—in other words, the elect and believing Jews. But Meyer sees no 'mystery' in this view, and certainly it does not seem much for Paul to say that the elect Jews will be saved. See 2 Cor. 3 : 14-16, where Paul speaks of the vail lying on the Jewish heart, which, upon their turning to the Lord, shall be taken away.—(F.)

[3] " St. Paul probably had in his mind such passages as Ps. 14 : 7, where 'out of Zion' is found." (Olshausen.) Compare Ps. 53 : 6 ; 110 : 2 in LXX. "Zion is the centre and capital of the theocracy, but the Messiah must first take up his abode there before he can issue from it." (Sanday.) The Hebrew signifies *to Zion* or *for, with respect to, Zion*, and so "even Paul's translation, 'from Zion,' although it seems completely to reverse the sense, is not so wholly inconsistent with it as has sometimes been pretended." (J. A. Alexander.)—(F.)

28 As concerning the gospel, *they are* enemies for your sakes: but as touching the election, *they are* beloved for the fathers' sakes.
29 For the gifts and calling of God *are* without repentance.
30 For as ye in times past have not believed God, yet have uow obtained mercy through their unbelief:
31 Even so have these also now not believed, that through your mercy they also may obtain mercy.

28 As touching the gospel, they are enemies for your sake: but as touching the election, they are beloved
29 for the fathers' sake. For the gifts and the calling
30 of God are [1] without repentance. For as ye in time past were disobedient to God, but now have obtained
31 mercy by their disobedience, even so have these also now been disobedient, that by the mercy shewn to
32 you they also may now obtain mercy. For God hath

---

[1] Gr. *not repented of.*

[compare Jer. 31 : 31, seq. ; LXX. 38 : 31]; the second clause is from Isa. 27 : 9 [see Septuagint Version]. Putting both passages together, and adding what is omitted from the first, we have, as the fulfillment or consummation of God's covenant with Israel, conversion from ungodliness and remission of sin. [Meyer, Philippi, and De Wette likewise refer the 'this' to what follows. The latter thus explains the passage : "In this consists my covenant with them that I shall have taken away their sins."]

28. As concerning the gospel, they are enemies for your sakes. As rejecters of the gospel, they are displeasing to God and exposed to his just wrath ; his enemies, not in the active sense of being opposed to him, but in the passive sense of being those to whom he is opposed. That this is the true explanation of the word 'enemies' appears from the preceding context (ver. 7, 8, 15, 22), and still more from the contrasted word 'beloved' in this same verse. They were excluded from God's favor by the rejection of the gospel, in order that all its blessings might come to you Gentiles. [Hence they may be said to be God's enemies, or that God treated them as enemies, not only on account of their rejection of the gospel, but also because of, or for the sake of its acceptance by the Gentiles. Of course, God may justly hate the sinner as such, or his sinful character and life, while he loves "the man created in his image, and for whom his Son died." (Godet.)] **But as touching the election,** the choice of them by God as his own people, **beloved for the fathers' sakes.** Not for the *merits* of the

fathers [compare Deut. 9 : 5, seq.], but because of the 'covenant' made with Abraham, renewed to Isaac and Jacob, and destined to have at last, as above shown, a glorious consummation. [Meyer interprets *the election* here as meaning the elect remnant.]

29. For the gifts and calling of God [gracious gifts, in general; and God's calling of the Jews to be his people, and thus to a glorious destination, in particular. The 'for' introduces a confirmation of the latter half of the preceding verse.] **Without repentance** means, simply, "unrepented of" on his part. ["The word is emphatic by position, and denotes the unchangeableness of the divine purpose." (Shedd.) Obviously this same principle holds true of all God's special gifts of grace to individual believers.[1] "While the apostle at other times makes the participation in the Abrahamic promises dependent on faith, he here hopes everything from God's mercy, as in ver. 23, of his omnipotence." (De Wette.)]

30, 31. These verses end by showing how God's unrepented purpose of mercy toward the Jewish nation is ultimately to have its fulfillment; and therefore they are appropriately introduced by **for. As ye** (Gentiles) **in times past have not believed** (or, as in Revised Version, *were disobedient to*) **God, yet have now obtained mercy through their unbelief** (or, *disobedience*), **even so have these also now not believed** (*disobeyed*, or, *become disobedient*) in order that **through your mercy** (*the mercy which you have received*) **they also may obtain mercy.** Being at last moved to seek it by beholding the bless-

---

[1] On the 'calling' of God, especially as it relates to individuals, Trench ("Notes on the Parables") has the following: "*καλεῖν* (to call), like the Latin *vocare*, is the technical word for inviting to a feast. It is also the word which St. Paul uses to express the union of an outward word-bidding and an inward Spirit-drawing, whereby God seeks to bring men into his kingdom. The answering word in St. John is *ἐλκύειν*, to draw.

(John 6 : 44 ; 12 : 32.) This attraction or bidding—outward by the word, inward by the Spirit—is the 'holy calling (2 Tim. 1 : 9), 'calling of God' (Rom. 11 : 29), 'heavenly calling' (Heb. 3 : 1), 'high calling' (Phil. 3 : 14) ;—which last is not the calling *to* a height, but the calling *from* a height; not as we have it, the 'high calling,' but the 'calling *from on high*.'"—(F.)

32 For God hath concluded them all in unbelief, that he might have mercy upon all.
33 O the depth of the riches both of the wisdom and knowledge of God! how unsearchable *are* his judgments, and his ways past finding out!

shut up all unto disobedience, that he might have mercy upon all.
33 O the depth [1] of the riches [2] both of the wisdom and the knowledge of God! how unsearchable are
34 his judgments, and his ways past tracing out! For

1 Or, *of the riches and the wisdom. etc......* 2 Or, *both of wisdom, etc.*

---

ings which it brings to you, according to what is said in ver. 14.[1] There is an analogy between the past and present conduct of God toward the Gentiles, and his present and future conduct toward the Jews. The apostle contrasts the former state of the Gentiles (disobedience through unbelief) with their present state (gracious salvation through faith), and the present state of the Jews (disobedience through unbelief) with their future state (gracious salvation through faith.) He compares the past state of the Gentiles with the present state of the Jews, and the present state of the Gentiles with the future state of the Jews. (J. Brown.)

32. For God hath concluded—literally, *shut up* [together, as in a prison, compare Gal. 3 : 22, Revised Version, "The Scripture shut up all things under sin." Instead of **all** (men), the MSS. D E have here *all things*, a reading probably derived from the text in Galatians. **Upon all**—literally, *the all; the* article may refer to Jews and Gentiles collectively, of whom mention has been made.] "Note this prime saying, which condemns all the world and man's righteousness, and alone exalts God's mercy to be obtained through faith." (Luther.) All, whether Jews or Gentiles, are alike shut up in disobedience; all are alike dependent on God's mercy. God's gracious act is as universal in its design and adaptation as man's sin. Whether or not men will *accept* it, this is a question of *fact;* see 1 Tim. 2 : 4 ; 2 Peter 3 : 9 ; 1 John 2 : 2. [Paul, in Gal. 3 : 22, shows that those who are thus shut up unto disobedience and under sin, will never experience the benefit of God's mercy, and will, consequently, ever remain in prison and in bondage, unless they become believers in Christ. "This contingency (whether men will accept God's mercy or not) is not here in view, but simply God's act itself." (Alford.)

"The universal restoration (ἀποκατάστασις) is not to be based on our passage." (Meyer.) We are only taught that the time is coming on the earth when God's mercy shall reach all nations and classes of men, when Jew and Gentile, the elder and the younger brother, will once more be gathered together in their Father's house, and when mankind in general will receive the salvation of God. "The apostle had begun this vast exposition of salvation with the fact of universal condemnation; he closes it with that of universal mercy. What could remain to him thereafter but to strike the hymn of adoration and praise?" (Godet.)] In view of the unsearchable wisdom of God displayed in all his dealings with both Jew and Gentile, the apostle breaks out into an admiring apostrophe, and so closes the argumentative part of the Epistle.

33. O the depth of the riches! ["Inexhaustible fullness." Bengel remarks that "Paul, in chapter 9, had been sailing, as it were, on a strait; he is now on the ocean."] As the words **riches, wisdom,** and **knowledge** are all in the same case, we may regard them as all co-ordinate and alike dependent on the word **depth**—'depth' of riches, 'depth' of wisdom, etc.; or, as our translators have done, make only the first of the three, 'riches,' directly depend on the word 'depth,' and the other two dependent on 'riches.' The difference in sense is unimportant, but the latter way of connecting the words is preferable, since the word 'riches,' when applied in a figurative sense to God, seems rather to demand, and commonly to have some defining adjunct—as, riches of his goodness (2:4), of his glory (9:23; Eph. 3:16), of his grace (Eph. 1:7; 2:7), etc. The word translated **unsearchable** is used only here, though the same English word is used in Eph. 3: 8 to translate the word here rendered **past finding out.** The

---

[1] In the beginning of the verse, the καί (also) of our Common text denotes that the Gentiles, as well as the Jews, had their period of rebellion. It is, however, omitted by the Revisers. On the use of a particle denoting present time with the aorist or past tense (were now compassionated or shown mercy), see notes on 7 : 6.

'Their disobedience' served, of course, merely as an 'occasion' of the Gentiles obtaining mercy. The position of 'your mercy' before ἵνα (*in order that*) is somewhat singular, yet is probably for the sake of emphasis —(F.)

34 For who hath known the mind of the Lord? or who hath been his counsellor?
35 Or who hath first given to him, and it shall be recompensed unto him again?
36 For of him, and through him, and to him, *are* all things: to whom *be* glory for ever. Amen.

who hath known the mind of the Lord? or who
35 hath been his counsellor? or who hath first given to him, and it shall be recompensed unto him again?
36 For of him, and through him, and unto him, are all things. To him *be* the glory [1] for ever. Amen.

1 Gr. *unto the ages.*

original adjectives are in both cases eminently appropriate to the nouns which they qualify. His **judgments**—that is, his decrees or purposes [especially his "hardening judgments" (Philippi)] are 'unsearchable,' or inscrutable, and **his ways,** or methods of procedure, are 'past finding (or, *tracing*) out,' but infinitely easy for God to reveal them when he sees fit. [The judgments and the ways of God are indeed a "vasty deep," and even when revealed cannot be fully comprehended by our finite minds. But while they are declared to be thus unsearchable, it may be well to recollect that Paul speaks of other things which are likewise past our comprehension—namely, God's "unspeakable gift" of a Saviour, "the unsearchable riches of Christ," and "the peace of God which passeth all understanding." See 2 Cor. 9: 15; Eph. 3: 8; Phil. 4: 7.]

34. These questions are quoted from Isa. 40: 13, 14. Compare also 1 Cor. 2: 16 [where the former clause is again quoted. A similar thought is also expressed in Wisdom of Solomon 9 : 13]. The first question may have special reference to God's knowledge, and the second to his wisdom; and so this verse confirms so much of the preceding, the interrogations being equivalent, as often, to a strong affirmation that *no one* has known his mind or has become his counselor; hence the introductory **for.** ["Many talk," says Bengel, "as if they were not only the Lord's counselors, but also his inquisitors, his patrons, or his judges. Scripture everywhere rests in this—that the Lord hath willed, and said, and done. It does not unfold the reasons of things, general or special. Respecting things too high for our infant conceptions, it refers us to eternity. (1 Cor. 13 : 9, seq.)"]

35. This is a manifest reference to Job 41 : 11 ["according to the Hebrew (41:3), not according to the LXX., whose translation is quite erroneous" (Meyer)]. **Who hath first given to him?** Who hath anticipated him, been beforehand with him in giving, so as to be entitled to any recompense? So as to place him under any obligation? Thus these three questions (ver. 34, 35) fitly correspond to the three attributes mentioned in ver. 33: **Who hath been his counsellor?**—to *wisdom.* **Who hath known?**—to *knowledge.* **Who hath given?**—to *riches.* ["This verse specifies the *depth of the riches* of God." (Bengel.)]

36. For of him. [The thought is: No one has done or can do this, 'for,' etc.] All things are 'of him' (or, *from him*) in their origin; **through him,** as to their subsistence and disposal; and **to him** (or, *for him*) as their end. "God is the *basis* of all that exists; for from him all took its rise. God is the *means* of all that exists; for he directs all that exists to its destination. God is the *end* of all that exists; for in him alone all the creatures rest. It is from God that man derives his being; to God must he return if he would truly be; through God must he be led to God; and thus God's mercy is the beginning, the middle, and the end." (Tholuck.) [Compare Col. 1: 16, where Paul affirms that all things were created in Christ,—as the causal element of their existence (Ellicott),—all things were created through him, and all things were created for him. If the Son had not been God, such an interchange of important relations, as Ellicott well remarks, would never had seemed possible. In the doxology, we supply after **glory** some form of the verb to be. Perhaps the Greek form which is used in expressing a wish (here, *may there be*) is most appropriate in this connection.]

The close of this verse reminds us of a saying of the Emperor Marcus Antoninus; but how much more sublime as well as more true is the apostle's doxology than the Stoic's apostrophe to nature: "All is from thee; all is in thee; all is for thee." To God, and not to nature [and 'not unto us'], **be glory for ever,** *unto the ages.* **Amen.** Thus the apostle devoutly closes the chapter and the formal *argument* of this Epistle. [And what but the strongest mental powers, enlightened and sustained by the Holy Spirit, could have kept the apostle's thought throughout all these chapters and

CHAPTER XII.

I BESEECH you therefore, brethren, by the mercies of God, that ye present your bodies a living sacrifice,

1 I beseech you therefore, brethren, by the mercies of God, to present your bodies a living sacrifice, holy,

verses—without the least sign of breaking down, sinking, or weakening—up to the lofty "height of this great argument!"[1]]

III. PRACTICAL. (Ch. 12–15 : 13.)
Ch. 12: [*Exhortations touching the more private and general duties of Christians.* "The chapter stands unrivalled as a spontaneous sketch of the fairest graces which can adorn the Christian life." (Farrar.) The subject of the following chapters is the "*Life* of the justified believer.*" It was no come down for the apostle to break off from the high arguing of a didactic treatise, and to inculcate the common duties which flow from the Christian faith, and which become the Christian life.[2] The apostle, as Godet observes, commencing this section with Christian consecration, then speaks of the Christian life in its two spheres of activity, treating in this chapter of the *religious* sphere, and in the next, of the *civil* sphere. Renan supposes that this and the two following chapters, though written by Paul, did not originally form a part of the genuine Epistle to the Romans; but his arguments or fancies are well answered by Godet.]

It is customary with Paul to close his epistles with a series of practical exhortations, not always very closely connected with the preceding doctrinal discussion, but always

very pertinent to the circumstances of those to whom the epistle is addressed.

1. [**I beseech,** or, *exhort,* with the related idea of comforting or encouraging. Compare Eph. 4: 1; 1 Thess. 4: 1. "Moses commands, the apostle exhorts." (Bengel.) This word is used above fifty times in Paul's epistles.] The word **therefore** connects the exhortation to entire consecration to God with the preceding course of thought, not merely in the closing verses of the preceding chapter, nor even in that chapter as a whole, but in the entire doctrinal discussion of the foregoing chapters. **By** (*through*) **the mercies of God** —in view of, and as a consequence of those divine mercies which have been so fully set forth in the body of the Epistle. [The tender —literally, wailing—compassions of God are here presented as a motive (διά) to thankful obedience and entire consecration. Cannot the same appeal be made to our grateful feelings in view of God's compassionate mercies by us so constantly experienced? Note how Paul, after writing of God's "wrath," and of his "hardening" sinners, and giving them the spirit of stupor, can yet speak so freely and unhesitatingly of the *mercies* of God. Compare 2 Cor. 1: 3, where God is called "the Father of mercies."] **That ye present your bodies.** Your entire selves [present at once, and once for all (aorist tense), 'your bodies,' in this verse, 'your minds,' in the

---

[1] In connection with this chapter, we would call attention to the remarkable religious movement which is now going on among the Jews in South Russia, under the leadership of Joseph Rabinowitz, a lawyer by profession, but now a baptized Christian believer. After visiting Jerusalem, and witnessing the desolation of Zion and the sad state of his own people, the last chapter of the Hebrew Bible (2 Chron. 36 : 14–16) came forcibly to his mind, and he was led to ask: "Can there be no 'remedy'?" This remedy he soon found in the gospel of Jesus of Nazareth, the Son of God, and this gospel he is now proclaiming to his "kinsmen according to the flesh." He proposes to organize a new sect, to be called Israelites of the New Covenant, and many Jews have already expressed a desire to join this Christian brotherhood. In a recent communication, he says: "By the help of God I placed the blessing, the New Testament, in many Jewish houses, and thousands of Israelites trust for salvation in the blessed blood of the Lord

Jesus Christ, who was crucified outside the gate of Jerusalem, to make an end of sin and to bring in everlasting righteousness." We may remark that the Hebrew translation of the New Testament, by Delitzsch, is having a wonderful sale, and is exerting a remarkable influence among the Jews in Eastern Russia, and even in far-distant Siberia.—(F.)

[2] "No one felt more deeply than Paul that it requires great principles to secure our faithfulness in little duties, and that every duty, however apparently insignificant, acquires a real grandeur when it is regarded in the light of those principles from which it fulfillment springs." (Farrar.) "Holy George Herbert," speaking, in his "Elixir," of doing all unto God, and *for his sake,* says:

"A servant with this clause
    Makes drudgery divine;
Who sweeps a room as for thy laws
    Makes that and the action fine."—(F.)

holy, acceptable unto God, *which is* your reasonable service.
2 And be not conformed to this world: but be ye

¹ acceptable to God, *which is* your ²spiritual ³service
2 And be not fashioned according to this ⁴world: but

---

¹ Gr. *well-pleasing*......² Gr. *belonging to the reason*......3 Or, *worship*......4 Or, *age*.

---

next (Meyer)—thus, a whole burnt offering, to be wholly consumed for God on his altar. The term 'bodies' may be taken in a literal sense, since their presentation to God may be a service of the mind, a rational service. Some think the word was chosen as having reference to the metaphor of sacrifice, and to the body regarded as the seat of sin. Olshausen thinks the word 'bodies' is used here to indicate that sanctification should extend to the lowest power of human nature] **A living sacrifice**—not only in distinction from the sacrifice of *dead* bodies, which the law *forbade*, and of *slain* bodies, which the law *required*, but in the sense of a *perpetual* sacrifice to be continually renewed. **Holy.** The Levitical sacrifices were required to be without natural or physical blemish; here, of course, the reference is to moral purity.¹ **Acceptable unto God.** God requires of us now no sacrifice of slain beasts; but the unreserved consecration of our persons to him in holy living is acceptable, well pleasing to him. [This term is frequently used by Paul, and except in Titus 2: 9, always in relation to God or to Christ. Compare 1 Peter 2: 5, "spiritual sacrifices acceptable to God."] **Your reasonable service.** The consecration of our *bodies* to God is an act of our *minds;* it is a *rational* (λογικός), or spiritual service. It is to be performed in a way suitable to the nature of man as a rational being, suitable to the nature of God as a spiritual being.² The word here translated 'service,' always refers to sacred or religious, never to merely common or secular service. It corresponds to our word service when the adjective *divine* is prefixed to it.

2. And be not conformed to this world.

[This, and the following verb, should probably be put in the infinitive in the same regimen as 'present.' This verb occurs also in 1 Peter 1: 14. In the use of this verb, Dr. Schaff sees a special adaptation to the changing and transitory *fashion* of this world. Compare 1 Cor. 7: 31. "The fashion (σχῆμα) of this world passeth away." See, also, the rendering of the Revised Version, "be not fashioned."] By **this world** we understand the whole world of the ungodly as contrasted with the disciples of Christ. ['This world,' or age (αἰὼν), is commonly defined as the temporary order of things in which sin predominates, to which the "age to come," the kingdom of God, or the holy state of things founded by Christ, is the exact contrast. In accordance with Scripture teaching, *ages* have already transpired, and in view of what is past, Paul speaks of living in "the ends of the ages." (1 Cor. 10: 11.) But he also speaks of "ages which are coming" (Eph. 2: 7); and "such expressions," says Ellicott, "deserve especial notice, as they incidentally prove how very ill founded is the popular opinion adopted by Meyer and others, that St. Paul believed the Advent of the Lord to be close at hand."] We are to avoid worldly conformity, not by any *oddity* of dress or manners, but by an inward transformation resulting in a knowledge, approval, and practice of that which God wills. We have in this verse an evil to be avoided, a remedy to be applied, and the happy results of applying it. [Would that Christians and churches in this age of worldly conformity might heed this warning voice of the apostle, and thus be saved from an "evil" which, perhaps more than any other, is eating out their spiritual life and power, and which thus mars

---

¹ This term, ἅγιος, holy (occurring in the classics, while its many New Testament derivatives are unknown), "is the rarest of five synonyms,—ἱερός, ὅσιος, σεμνός, ἁγνός,—which the Greeks had to express the idea of holiness, so far, at least, as they knew such an idea. In Biblical Greek . . . it is the only word by which the *biblical* conception of holiness is expressed, . . . whereas the most frequently occurring word in classical Greek, ἱερός, is almost completely excluded from Scripture use." (Cremer.)—(F.)

² Compare 1 Peter 2: 2, where he speaks of λογικὸς,

rational, or spiritual milk, "milk which nourishes the soul." (Grimm.) Clement of Alexandria speaks of logical medicines (medicines for the mind), logical food, logical water, logical baptism. "λογικός, pertaining to, and approved by, the reason." (Boise.) Prof. Cremer thinks it implies reasonable meditation or reflection in contrast with outward, thoughtless ceremony. This 'rational worship' is grammatically in apposition to the sentence, 'present your bodies,' etc.—(F.)

transformed by the renewing of your mind, that ye may prove what is that good, and acceptable, and perfect will of God.

3 For I say, through the grace given unto me, to every man that is among you, not to think of *himself* more highly than he ought to think; but to think soberly, according as God hath dealt to every man the measure of faith.

be ye transformed by the renewing of your mind, that ye may prove what is [1] the good and [2] acceptable and perfect will of God.

3 For I say, through the grace that was given me, to every man that is among you, not to think of himself more highly than he ought to think; but so to think as to think soberly, according as God hath dealt to each man a measure of faith. For even as

---

---

their influence for good, making them to *appear* so unlike the followers of the meek and lowly Saviour. Would that Christian men might lay aside all pernicious habits and wordly ostentation, and that Christian women might hang a portion of their jewelry and needless ornament on the Saviour's rugged, bleeding cross. This "vain glory of life" is unbecoming to a Christian, is, in many respects, pernicious in its influence, and must be offensive in the sight of our Heavenly Father. The apostle, in his earnestness, could not be content with a merely negative command, and hence he adds, **be ye transformed** — literally, *metamorphosed*, a term used of Christ's transfiguration. See, also, 2 Cor. 3: 18.] This does not imply that the persons addressed were as yet unregenerate, but only that their inward renewal, which had been distinctly professed in their baptism, was to be progressive, and to manifest its reality and power by a growing conformity to the will of God. [This transformation, equivalent to Christ's being formed in us (Gal. 4: 19), he tells them is secured through the **renewing of your mind**, which, as impaired and darkened by sin, has become a reprobate (or "unapproved) mind" (1: 28), or, "mind of the flesh." (Col. 2: 18.) This renewing is effected by the Holy Spirit (Eph. 4: 23; Titus 3: 5); and here again we have divine activity and human dependence and co-operation brought to view. The three adjectives, the first of which alone has the article on account of the general unity of their meaning, are to be used substantively (as in the margin of the Revised Version) unless we would assert the truism that God is well pleased with his own will.]

3. After the exhortation to entire consecration to God, the apostle enjoins the cultivation of particular graces and the practice of particular duties, beginning with humility [as, perhaps, the most important]. **For serves

to confirm the general exhortation of ver. 2, by a special requirement. (Meyer.) **I say, through the grace given unto me,** as an apostle to exhort and guide the church. [I exhort you, not in my own name or by mine own authority (the apostle himself thus setting an example of humility), but in virtue of, or by means of, the grace which was bestowed upon me.] **To every man that is among you**—a strong statement of the individual application of the admonition. [This would have applied to Peter himself had he been in Rome, but had this been so, Paul would not have thus written, or indeed would not have written at all. (Lange.) It would do no harm, however, if the church dignitaries now at Rome should heed this message of the apostle.] **To think soberly.** There is danger of our being puffed up with pride on account of God's gifts, whether ordinary or extraordinary. [There is a play upon words here in the original, which is thus brought out by Alford: "Not to be high minded above what he ought to be minded, but to be so minded as to be sober minded." This last term is specially employed by the Greeks to denote self-regulation or self-control.[1]] **According as God hath dealt to every man the measure of faith.** God has distributed his gifts and graces in different measure, according to his own wisdom. It belongs to Christian wisdom and humility to estimate ourselves accordingly, neither disparaging his gifts and our consequent responsibilities, nor overestimating them in our self-conceit. ["The emphatic position of each one ('every man') (placed in the original before the *as*) gives prominence to the idea of diversity between one man and another." (1 Cor. 3: 5; 7: 17.) ("Biblical Commentary.") We may describe faith as being the subjective principle of Christian endeavor, as divine grace is the objective.

---

1 The word παρά translated *above*, "means *beside* the mark or aim, and consequently (as the context may determine) sometimes *above*, as here, and sometimes *below*, as 2 Cor. 11: 24." (Winer.) Δεῖ (*it is fit*) denotes

necessity, and, as used here, moral obligation; φρονεῖν, *to feel* or *regard in mind*, is often used by Paul, especially in his later letters. The same injunction is repeated substantially in ver. 16, 'mind not high things.'—(F.)

4 For as we have many members in one body, and all members have not the same office:
5 So we, *being* many, are one body in Christ, and every one members one of another.
6 Having then gifts differing according to the grace that is given to us, whether prophecy, *let us prophesy* according to the proportion of faith;

we have many members in one body, and all the
5 members have not the same office: so we, who are many, are one body in Christ, and severally members
6 bers one of another. And having gifts differing according to the grace that was given to us, whether prophecy, *let us prophesy* according to the proportion
7 of our faith; or ministry, *let us give ourselves to our*

This measure of faith which each one has is a gift of grace. (Ver. 6.)]

4, 5. [For "elucidates the fact that God apportions variously to various persons, because the Christian community is like a *body* with many members having various duties" (Alford), thus furnishing a motive for giving heed to the exhortation. If all the members of Christ's body have not the same function or office, yet each one, the obscurest as well as the most prominent, has a work to do, and the humblest member, if faithful even in little things, will in no wise lose his reward. **Members one of another.** We are such only as we are members of the body of Christ, he being "the common element in which the union consists." [1]] See the same figure of the Christian community as one body developed still more fully by the apostle in 1 Cor. 12 : 12–27 ; compare also Eph. 4 : 11–16. It is a beautiful spectacle when a Christian church sets itself earnestly to realize this apostolic idea. Many a church now reputed feeble, and regarding itself so, would be surprised to find how strong it is, if it should truly grasp and carry out this idea. [Of the aphorism : "Diversity without unity is disorder, unity without diversity is death," the former member is most certainly true. Could the members of our churches, while each should be doing his own special work, yet feel and act as a *band* of loving, sympathizing brethren, thinking less of ourselves and more of our fellow members (Phil. 2 : 3, 4), more of Christ and his suffering cause, and willing to sacrifice for the sake of that cause, not only of our wealth or of our poverty, but, perchance, a little of our self-importance, self-will, and obstinacy (wherein we have to strive so hard to be *conscientious*), there would be left, as a source of weakness and reproach, but little of variance, disharmony, and strife. The Church of Christ would be a mighty power if her enemies could say

now as they did in earliest times : "Behold how these Christians love one another !"]

6-8. Having then gifts differing according to the grace that is given to us, etc. This is a rich and beautiful passage, somewhat elliptical, requiring supplementary words of the translators, and irregular in its grammatical construction, yet not obscure. [A few expositors, without supplying different verbs, render somewhat as follows : *we* are one body, etc., while having differing gifts, (having) prophecy, (having) ministry, etc. But this rendering ignores the disjunctive particle at the beginning of ver. 6, and also the fact that many of the following terms, such as simplicity, diligence, cheerfulness, denote neither the measure in which the gracious gift is given, nor the sphere in which it *is* exercised, but the way and manner in which it *should be* exercised. (Philippi.) Godet supplies but one brief sentence at the beginning, as follows : 'Having then gifts' . . . *let us exercise them,* etc. **Whether prophecy**—not here the foretelling of future events, but "an immediate occasional inspiration, leading the recipient to deliver, as the mouth of God, the particular communication which he had received, whether designed for instruction, exhortation, or comfort." (Hodge.) The gift as thus defined would seem specially to belong to the age of the apostles. On the extraordinary gifts of that age, see 1 Cor. 12 : 4–10. **According to the proportion of faith ;** or, measure of (our) faith ; see ver. 3, and the Revised Version. 'Faith' here is rightly regarded as subjective, equivalent to personal confidence in God or trust in Christ ; not 'faith,' referring to doctrine. Thus there is no reference here to what is called the "analogy of faith," although Wordsworth, Philippi, and Hodge contend for this view.] For one to speak in the proportion of faith is to speak in his prophecy only what God reveals to his faith, without adding any of his

---

[1] On the force of the neuter article τό in the Revision text, see at 9: 5. The preposition κατά, which should properly be followed by the accusative, serves here merely as an adverb. For similar examples, see Matt.

14: 19; John 8: 9; Rev. 21: 21. The phrase regarded as a noun in the "accusative of specification" is thus rendered by Meyer : "But in what concerns the individual relation" (we are members one of another).—(F.)

7 Or ministry, *let us wait* on *our* ministering; or he that teacheth, on teaching;
8 Or he that exhorteth, on exhortation: he that giveth, *let him do it* with simplicity; he that ruleth, with diligence; he that sheweth mercy, with cheerfulness.
9 *Let* love be without dissimulation. Abhor that which is evil; cleave to that which is good.
10 *Be* kindly affectioned one to another with brotherly love; in honour preferring one another;

8 ministry; or he that teacheth, to his teaching; or he that exhorteth, to his exhorting: he that giveth, *let him do it* with [1] liberality; he that ruleth, with diligence; he that sheweth mercy, with cheerfulness.
9 Let love be without hypocrisy. Abhor that which is evil; cleave to that which is good. In love of the brethren be tenderly affectioned one to another; in
11 honour preferring one another; in diligence not

---

1 Gr. *singleness.*

---

own inferences or conjectures. The word for **ministering,** or, *serving,* is the same which gives name to the deacon's office in Phil. 1: 1; 1 Tim. 3: 8, 12; compare also 1 Cor. 12: 5; Eph. 4: 12; but is probably used here in a more comprehensive sense, to include various forms of service. [**Or he that teacheth,** etc. If Paul had not changed the construction he would have written, *or teaching; or exhortation; or giving,* etc. He, however, retains the word 'whether' as if the construction was unchanged. The original word for exhort (see ver. 1, where it is translated "beseech") "combines the ideas of exhorting, and comforting, and encouraging." (Grimm.) It differs from *teaching,* in that it is rather directed to the *feelings,* while the latter is directed more to the understanding of the hearers. (Ellicott.)] **He that giveth, let him do it with simplicity.** This latter word is the same which is translated *liberality* and *bountifulness* in 2 Cor. 8: 2; 9: 11. [This word, rendered by Prof. Boise, "frank liberality" (used here with reference not to official distribution, but to personal imparting or giving), is found only in Paul's writings (seven times), and, according to Ellicott, "marks that *openness* (ἁπλόω, to spread out so that there are no folds) and sincerity of heart which repudiates *duplicity* in thought or action." Alford prefers the idea of open-handedness or liberality; compare also the use of the adverb in connection with God's giving, James 1: 5. **He that ruleth**—he that presides over others in the church (compare governments, 1 Cor. 12: 28), and possibly in the household—let such a one rule **with diligence,** or zeal. Most expositors think church overseers are here referred to, though, as Alford says, they seem to be brought in rather "low down in the list." Godet thinks that church officers have been already referred to under the term ministry.] **With cheerfulness.** The word used

here (ἱλαρότητι) is a particularly significant one, which occurs nowhere else in the New Testament. It might be translated: *with hilarity.* The corresponding adjective is used only in 2 Cor. 9: 7, where we read that "God loveth a *cheerful* giver."

9-21. ["Exhortations for all without distinction, headed by *love!*" (Meyer.)] **Let love be** [the imperative, being understood] **without dissimulation,** or, *unfeigned,* as the same Greek adjective is translated in 2 Cor. 6: 6; 1 Tim. 1: 5; 2 Tim. 1: 5; 1 Peter 1: 22 ("without hypocrisy" in James 3: 17; compare 1 John 3: 18). It is the part of unfeigned love to others to hate the *evil* that mars the imperfect characters of those whom we nevertheless sincerely *love,* and to attach ourselves to, and encourage the *good* that there is in them. This is loving them wisely, "for their good, to edification." (Rom. 15: 2.) [The present participles indicate that we should *habitually* **abhor that which is evil** wherever or in whomsoever it exits, and **cleave** ('attach'— literally, "glue" ourselves) **to that which is good,** wherever manifested.[1] Here and in Luke 6: 45, the form of the article shows the noun to be neuter; but as used in the Scriptures with the article, it generally has reference to persons, and it is mainly for this reason that the Lord's prayer in the Revision is made to speak of "the evil *one.*"]

10. Be kindly affectioned one to another with brotherly love. The word translated 'kindly affectioned' has for its root a word appropriated to designate that *natural* affection which exists between blood relations, and is here fitly employed to express that spiritual relationship which binds together the children of the same Heavenly Father by a tie stronger than that of blood [and makes them brothers and sisters, one family in Christ. The word for 'brotherly love' (φιλαδελφία, occurring

---

1 Of the two words frequently rendered 'evil,' πονηρός, the one here employed, and κακός, Trench says: "In πονηρός the positive activity of evil comes far more

decidedly out than in κακός." A man may be κακός, evil or wicked in himself, but one who is πονηρός is an evil-worker, a corrupter of others.—(F.)

11 Not slothful in business; fervent in spirit; serving the Lord;
12 Rejoicing in hope; patient in tribulation; continuing instant in prayer;
13 Distributing to the necessity of saints; given to hospitality.

12 slothful; fervent in spirit; serving ¹ the Lord; rejoicing in hope; patient in tribulation; continuing
13 stedfastly in prayer; communicating to the necessities of the saints; ² given to hospitality. Bless them

---

1 Some ancient authorities read *the opportunity*......2 Gr. *pursuing*.

---

elsewhere in 1 Thess. 4 : 9; Heb. 13 : 1; 1 Peter 1 : 22; 2 Peter 1 : 7) is placed first in the Greek, as in the Revised Version, because of emphasis. The same is true of all the leading nouns which follow down to ver. 14, and most of them might well hold their prominent place in a translation. Many of these nouns are in the so-called dative of reference or respect.] **In honour preferring one another**—or, more exactly, "preceding one another," "going before one another in giving honor," and so setting an attractive example. Compare Phil. 2 : 3.

11. Not slothful in business. This clause is very commonly understood as enjoining diligence in secular affairs; but this is not in accordance with the usage of the original word, which is translated 'business' only in this passage, usually "diligence," as in ver. 8 of this chapter, and in 2 Cor. 8 : 7; Heb. 6 : 11; 2 Peter 1 : 5; Jude 3. *Not slack in diligence*, or, *not remiss in zeal*, would be a fitter translation. The exhortation [compare the similar one in Eccl. 9 : 10] is in harmony with the whole context, in which strictly *religious* duties are enjoined. The service of the Lord should be prosecuted with a sustained zeal and a spirit glowing with sacred fervor. [**Fervent in spirit**—*in spirit be fervent*, or, *boiling*. Compare Acts 18 : 25. This is the opposite of being sluggish in diligence.¹ **Serving the Lord.** Instead of this, Meyer and Lange, with the uncials D * F G, read: *Serving the time*. It would be equivalent to *taking the circumstances into consideration, regulating oneself by them*. (Cremer.) The principal letters in the words for *Lord* and *time* are the same, so that the words, if abbreviated, could be easily mistaken. The weight of manuscript authority and of internal probability is in favor of the usual reading. De Wette well says: "The Christian should improve the time and opportunity (τὸν καιρόν), but not serve it."]

12. Rejoicing in hope; patient in tribulation, etc. In the first clause, the adjunct expresses the *ground* of the rejoicing [thus, *in*

virtue of hope, be joyful]; in the second, the state in which the patience is to be exercised [*amid tribulation, be steadfast*]; and in the third, the *habit* to which the instancy or tireless perseverance is to be applied [*in prayer, earnestly persevering*]. In reference to this last, compare Acts 1 : 14; 2 : 42; 6 : 4; Col. 4 : 2.

13. Distributing to the necessity (*necessities*) **of saints; given to hospitality.** Both these kindred duties were made more obligatory by the circumstances of those primitive times when Christians were so often subject to spoliation of goods and to persecutions. How well the early disciples obeyed this first admonition we learn from Acts 4 : 34, 35; 11 : 27-30; Rom. 15 : 25-27; 2 Cor. 8 : 1-4; 9 : 1, 2. The nature of the duty enjoined in the second admonition is shown, by the term used, to be something very different from that sumptuous entertainment of one's personal friends which is now commonly called 'hospitality.' It is rather the manifestation of our loving care for the *stranger* guest. [Instead of ' communicating' to the necessities of the saints, as in the Revised Version, we prefer, with many others, to take the participle intransitively; thus: *Participating in, sharing*, their necessities—that is, making them to be as our own. A few manuscripts read *remembrances* instead of *necessities*, but this, according to Westcott and Hort, is "probably a clerical error, due to the hasty reading of an ill-written MS." 'Given to hospitality'—more literally, *pursuing* hospitality. The verb from which this participle is derived is commonly used in the sense of *persecute*, as in the next verse. Godet says the term *pursuing* "shows that we are not to confine ourselves to according hospitality when it is asked, but that we should even seek opportunities of exercising it." The duties of beneficence and of hospitality are often enjoined in the Scriptures. Compare 1 Tim. 3 : 2; 6 : 18; Titus 1 : 8; Heb. 13 : 12; 1 Peter 4 : 9. From saints and strangers Paul now comes to persecutors.]

---

¹ "How much was Paul himself in this matter, with all his fervor of spirit, a shining model" 1. Cor. 9 : 19, seq.; Phil. 4 : 12, 13; 1 Cor. 4 : 11, seq.; 8 : 13; Acts 20 : 35; 16 : 3." (Meyer.)—(F.)

14 Bless them which persecute you : bless, and curse not.
15 Rejoice with them that do rejoice, and weep with them that weep.
16 *Be* of the same mind one toward another. Mind not high things, but condescend to men of low estate. Be not wise in your own conceits.
17 Recompense to no man evil for evil. Provide things honest in the sight of all men.

15 that persecute you ; bless, and curse not. Rejoice with them that rejoice ; weep with them that weep.
16 Be of the same mind one toward another. Set not your mind on high things, but ¹condescend to ²things that are lowly. Be not wise in your own
17 conceits. Render to no man evil for evil. Take thought for things honourable in the sight of all

1 Gr. *be carried away with*......2 Or, *them.*

14. Bless them which persecute you. This seems to be a quotation from the Sermon on the Mount. (Matt. 5 : 44; Luke 6 : 28.) Paul doubtless had knowledge of this injunction of our Lord, though he may hardly yet have read it in the gospels of Matthew and Luke. [The Revisers omit the passage from Matthew's Gospel. 'Bless' (εὐλογεῖτε) in the classics means merely *to speak well of.* **And curse not.** Only those may curse whom God has commissioned to imprecate his judgment on transgressors. To love and pray for and forgive our enemies and persecutors, or those whom we deem to be such, is a hard task for imperfectly sanctified human nature. One thought, however, may help us thus to feel and act—the thought that, if Christ were as quick to take offense and as slow to forgive as we are, none of us could be saved. The present tense of these verbs denotes an ever present duty.]

15. Rejoice with them that do rejoice, and weep with them that weep. Chrysostom remarks on this verse that it requires a more generous spirit to obey the first admonition than the second, since nature inclines us to weep when we see others weeping; but in the opposite case *envy* is apt to arise and make it difficult for us sincerely to rejoice with them. [In the New Testament, as in classic Greek, the infinitive is sometimes used imperatively. (See Phil. 3 : 16.) Some, as Buttmann, would supply here a verb (δεῖ), meaning "it is necessary," or "I exhort" as in ver. 1. "The exhortation of this verse is most important in our intercourse with our fellow-men, and implies the fullest human sympathy. How needful to a pastor!" (Boise.)]

16. Be of the same mind one toward another. [After participles, imperatives, and infinitives, we now come back again to participles. The verb *be ye* is supposed to be understood. The meaning is (Be ye) thinking, having in mind, the same thing, etc.]

The word used here refers to the affections and feelings rather than to intellectual beliefs. **Mind not high things, but condescend to men of low estate.** The words rendered 'high things' and 'men of low estate' are both adjectives. The first is certainly neuter, and is therefore properly translated. The second is an ambiguous form, which may be either masculine or neuter. [It is by usage generally masculine, though many here regard it, from its antithesis to high things, as neuter.] But the participle connected with it, and translated 'condescend,' favors the masculine sense of the adjective. It suggests the idea of leaving the path we were intending to walk in, in order to go along with another [and is generally used in a bad sense. (Gal. 2 : 13; 2 Peter 3 : 17.) The word 'condescend' savors a little too much of pride. *Be companions with the lowly* would be a better rendering. The apostle would thus have no abominable caste distinctions among Christians. With the ancient Greeks humility was not a virtue, and the Greek word for humble or low (ταπεινός) was used in an ill sense. Plato says humble (ταπεινός) and servile, and even Philo, according to Prof. Cremer, uses this word in a bad sense. Yet we believe that a few Greeks sometimes employ this word as meaning lowly rather than low or mean. Humility in the Scriptures is opposed to all self-righteousness, and that man is humble who takes a low estimate of himself—"esteems himself small before God and men." **Be not wise in your own conceits**—literally, *do not become wise with yourselves,* in your own estimation merely; similar to 11 : 25; see also Prov. 3 : 7. The self-conceit which the apostle condemns is greatly opposed to Christian harmony and union.]

17. [Recompense to no man evil for evil.¹ 'Evil for evil.' While Ellicott (on 1 Thess. 5 : 15) justifies the "usual and correct

¹ The participles in these virtually imperative sentences require the negative form, μηδείς (no one) rather than οὐδείς.—(F.)

18 If it be possible, as much as lieth in you, live peaceably with all men.

19 Dearly beloved, avenge not yourselves, but *rather* give place unto wrath: for it is written, Vengeance *is* mine; I will repay, saith the Lord.

20 Therefore if thine enemy hunger, feed him; if he thirst, give him drink: for in so doing thou shalt heap coals of fire on his head.

18 men. If it be possible, as much as in you lieth, be at 19 peace with all men. Avenge not yourselves, beloved, but give place unto [1] the wrath *of God;* for it is written, Vengeance belongeth unto me; I will recom-20 pense, saith the Lord. But if thine enemy hunger, feed him; if he thirst, give him to drink: for in so

[1] Or, *wrath.*

statement that Christianity was the first definitely to forbid the returning evil for evil," he does not deny that "individual instances of the recognition of this precept may be found in heathenism." Certainly Socrates, in "Crito," speaks against the retaliation of injuries. **Provide things honest** (as Paul himself did in 2 Cor. 8: 21), *have a care for,* "have regard to" (Noyes); found elsewhere only in 2 Cor. 8: 21; 1 Tim. 5: 8. This is virtually a quotation fron Prov. 3: 4, Septuagint. If the members of our churches obeyed this instruction, "those that are without" would have to provide for their famishing souls some other kind of diet than "the faults of Christians."] The word 'honest,' in the Scriptures, always has the meaning of *honorable,* according to the sense of the Latin word from which it is derived. It is opposed to what is unbecoming, rather than to what is unjust and unfair.

18. Live peaceably with all men—that is, do not disturb others, and do not be disturbed by them. The first is wholly in our own power, the second is not; hence the qualification, **if it be possible, as much as lieth in you.** ["Even those who are most quiet and peaceable, yet if they serve God faithfully, are often made 'men of strife.' We can but 'follow peace'; have the making only of one side of the bargain, and, therefore, can but, 'as much as in us lies,' live peaceably." (Matthew Henry.)—A. H.]

19. Dearly beloved. "The more difficult the duty, the more affectionate the address." (Tholuck.) [**Avenge not yourselves.** As injury may be more than an ill or evil, so avenging oneself is more than repaying evil for evil.[2]] **Give place unto wrath.** Allow room for God's anger; do not interfere with the divine prerogative by taking vengeance into your own hands. Other interpretations

are advocated, but this best suits the last part of the verse, and best explains the use of the Greek article with the word wrath—[literally, unto *the wrath* (that is, of God), so most commentators. We think, however, that the force of the article cannot be pressed here. Compare with this Ecclus. 38: 12, "give place to the physician"; Luke 14: 9, "give this man place"; also Eph. 4: 27, "neither give place to the devil." According to the usage of Paul, the word *wrath* is generally applied to God. If the reference here be to men's wrath, then, in accordance with the idiom of the above passages, we should naturally expect the exhortation would be, give *no* place to wrath, which would indeed be equivalent to giving it a wide berth, or having nothing to do with it. Some, after the analogy of the Latin phrase of similar import, *dare iræ spatium,* would give to the word 'place' the idea of temporal space, thus counseling *delay* to the exercise of wrath; but this appears to us hardly admissible.] **For it is written,** in Deut. 32: 35. The same passage is quoted also in Heb. 10: 30. [The quotation follows the Hebrew more nearly than it does the LXX. The words **saith the Lord** are added by Paul for the sake of emphasis.] It has often been said that belief in a God who takes vengeance tends to make men revengeful. This passage teaches exactly the contrary. See, also, the next verse.

20. Therefore, if thine enemy hunger, feed him, etc. ['But if,' according to another reading. 'Feed him' (present tense)—literally, *by morsels* or, from hand, and continually, see 11: 20.] **For in so doing** (or, *by so doing*) you will make him very uncomfortable, until he finds relief by coming to a better mind, which he will be likely soon to do under such treatment. [The general idea, probably, is this: By showing this kindness you will

[1] The limitation (as to) *what is from you,* what in you lies, what depends upon you, is what might be termed the accusative of closer specification, or the accusative of synecdoche. See ver. 5; 15: 17; Heb. 2: 17; 5: 1. The idea of the apostle is: Be at peace with all men if

they will let you. The verb, be at peace, is found elsewhere in Mark 9: 50; 2 Cor. 13: 11; 2 Thess. 5: 13.—(F.)

[2] Note here how the reflexive pronoun (themselves) is used for the second person.—(F)

21 Be not overcome of evil, but overcome evil with good.

21 doing thou shalt heap coals of fire upon his head. Be not overcome of evil, but overcome evil with good.

CHAPTER XIII.

LET every soul be subject unto the higher powers. For there is no power but of God: the powers that be are ordained of God.

2 Whosoever therefore resisteth the power, resisteth the ordinance of God: and they that resist shall receive to themselves damnation.

1 Let every soul be in subjection to the higher powers: for there is no power but of God; and the 2 *powers* that be are ordained of God. Therefore he that resisteth the power, withstandeth the ordinance of God: and they that withstand shall receive to

most effectually subdue him. This whole verse seems to be a very Christian precept, yet it is taken, word for word, from the Old Testament. See Prov. 25: 21, 22, Septuagint. Wordsworth says "the Holy Spirit, by the hand of St. Paul, has indited here a chapter of Christian Proverbs."]

21. Be not overcome of (*by*) **evil, but overcome evil with good** — [literally, *in the good* — namely, which thou shalt show thy enemy.] A fit condensation and close of this subject. [Erasmus, speaking of this chapter, says: "No song can be sweeter."]

Ch. 13: *Political and Social Duties—Subjection to Those in Authority.* [The Jews, who in accordance with Deut. 17: 15 were to have "no stranger" set over them as king, were everywhere restive under Roman rule, and even in Rome were not wholly submissive to authority. A short time previous to Paul's writing this letter, Claudius, the emperor, as both Suetonius and Luke inform us, expelled the Jews from Rome on account of their constant tumults (*tumultuantes*). And these may have been Jewish Christians, since their leader or instigator bore the name of Chrestus, which, according to Tertullian, was the usual way of pronouncing Christus or Christ. But in this early period the Roman authorities would scarcely recognize the distinctions between Jews and Jewish Christians. Gentile Christians also may naturally have felt that it would not be an unrighteous thing to resist or even plot against such a wicked and idolatrous government as that of Rome. Hence it was in the interest of all parties that Paul counselled obedience to rulers. Yet the principle incul-

cated holds good everywhere, since Christians everywhere are citizens of an earthly kingdom as well as of a heavenly kingdom, and they have duties to perform to the one as well as to the other. And in the beginning of Christianity it was of the utmost importance that Christians should, if possible, win by their well doing the favor of the higher powers.]

1. The exhortation is emphatic, **every soul,** yet in distinction from **the higher powers. The powers that be,** not the powers that were before the last change; this simplifies the duty of allegiance. [In passing from the consideration of the duties of spiritual to those of civil life, the apostle would indicate that Church and State are not identical, but are distinct, yet not antagonistic, and by his use of the phrase 'every soul' (properly a Hebraism for every person) would show, according to Godet, that a duty is involved which is naturally incumbent on every human being, an obligation not specially of the spiritual life, but of the *psychical* life which is the common domain of mankind. **Be subject**—literally, *subject itself.* The Revisers' rendering, "be in subjection to," gives the force of the present tense. 'The higher powers,' authorities set over us. The word 'power' here denotes rightful authority, and this is from God as its source, and all established authorities, Rome's imperial throne included, have been appointed by God. Literally: *There exists not authority except by God.*[1] Critical editors omit 'powers' in the last clause, and give the word 'God' without the article. With this verse compare Titus 3: 1; 1 Peter 2: 13.]

2. Whosoever therefore resisteth the power. [The authority which is here supposed to be accordant with the standard of

---

[1] Observe that ἐστίν, being emphatic, is not made an enclitic, as in ver. 3, 4, but has its accent simply thrown back on the penult. The Revisers have *by* (ὑπό) in both places, yet render, as in our Common Version, '*of* God.' De Wette and Meyer prefer *from* (ἀπό) in the first clause. The fundamental signification of ἀπό,

according to Buttmann, is departure from the *exterior* of an object, while ὑπό in general designates the more remote *internal* causal relation. Hence, ἀπό commonly designates the more remote and general, while ὑπό and ἐκ the more immediate and special cause or origin.—(F.)

3 For rulers are not a terror to good works, but to the evil. Wilt thou then not be afraid of the power? do that which is good, and thou shalt have praise of the same:
4 For he is the minister of God to thee for good. But if thou do that which is evil, be afraid; for he beareth not the sword in vain: for he is the minister of God, a revenger to *execute* wrath upon him that doeth evil.

3 themselves judgment. For rulers are not a terror to the good work, but to the evil. And wouldest thou have no fear of the power? do that which is good,
4 and thou shalt have praise from the same: for [1] he is a minister of God to thee for good. But if thou do that which is evil, be afraid; for [1] he beareth not the sword in vain: for [1] he is a minister of God, an
5 avenger for wrath to him that doeth evil. Where-

[1] Or, *it.*

right. **And they that resist**—literally (Common Version), *have resisted.* Jowett thus brings out the adversative sense of the particle translated 'and': *but* (whatever they may think) they that oppose, etc.] What kind of 'damnation' (κρίμα, *judgment*) is here meant is explained by the next verse—punishment from God, through his minister, the magistrate.[1]

3. [For rulers are not a terror to the good work. So the Revised Version, which follows here the reading of ℵ B A D * F Y P. Paul could hardly have made this unqualified assertion of rulers had the infamous Nero then begun his persecutions. The apostle, however, has ideal rulers chiefly in mind. "He is speaking of what may fairly be expected to be the case." (Wordsworth.) **Wilt thou then not be afraid of the power** (or, *Dost thou wish not to fear the authority?*) **do that which is good** (present imperative—do it as a constant practice), **and thou shalt have praise of the same** (*from it,* or, *the authority*). As Paul does not here suppose rulers to be tyrants, so he does not teach us what they who live under an insupportable tyranny are to do. But we know that he would counsel us to obey God and the "higher law," rather than the civil power, which should bid us violate the divine law. And how, under the teaching of Paul, could rulers *blame* their subjects for insubordination, if they themselves are a terror to good work, and not to evil? Still, we agree, in the main, with Alford, when he says: "Even where law is hard and unreasonable, not disobedience, but legitimate protest, is the duty of the Christian." It is sometimes a duty to suffer wrongfully. (1 Peter 2:19; 1 Cor. 6:7.)] This is wholesome doctrine for subjects, and no less wholesome reading for rulers. The apostle's assertion is, in general, true as a matter of fact, even of corrupt and oppressive governments. The Roman government had actually been a protection to Paul himself on several occasions:

In the case of Gallio at Corinth (Acts 18: 12-17), the town clerk at Ephesus (19: 35-41), Claudius Lysias at Jerusalem (21: 31-35; 22: 24-29; 23: 17-30), Festus at Cæsarea (25: 1-12). [See Farrar's "Life of St. Paul," pp. 323, 503, 504. Godet says: "Never has any power whatever laid down as a principle the punishment of good and the reward of evil; for thereby it would be its own destroyer."]

4. For he (*it,* the authority) **is the minister of God.** [The word for minister (διάκονος, deacon) is thought to be derived from a verb meaning *to run*—hence, a messenger or servant. Would the apostle call the vile and carnal Nero "a minister, an officer of God, a representative of divine authority"? (Renan.) We think not, certainly not a worthy representative. And we think that no words could more effectually shake the throne of iniquity which Nero subsequently occupied than Paul's description of that authority which is God-ordained, which is his minister for good, and which is a terror, not to good work, but to evil. **He beareth**—or, weareth, denoting habitual practice. To bear, or wear rather, implies a constant repetition of the simple action of the verb. **The sword**—or, sabre, spoken of, was a bent one, in opposition to the straight sword. As individuals, we have not the power or right to inflict capital punishment; and it may be a question whether, in strictness of speech, we have power to confer it; but it belongs to the God-ordained authority which is over us. Paul, on one occasion, affirmed that "if he had committed anything worthy of death, he refused not to die" (at the hands of the civil magistracy). Calvin calls this a remarkable passage for proving the *jus gladii* (*the right of the sword*). **A revenger to execute wrath,** or, better, as in Revised Version, "An avenger for wrath, or punishment," **upon him that doeth** (or, *practices*) **the evil.** 'Avenger' occurs elsewhere only in 1 Thess. 4: 6. Godet thinks the 'wrath' is

[1] The reflexive 'themselves' is in the so-called *dativus incommodi*, or dative of disadvantage. Notice in these two verses the frequent use of τάσσω and its compounds.—(F.)

5 Wherefore *ye* must needs be subject, not only for wrath, but also for conscience' sake.

6 For, for this cause pay ye tribute also: for they are God's ministers, attending continually upon this very thing.

fore *ye* must needs be in subjection, not only because 6 of the wrath, but also for conscience sake. For, for this cause ye pay tribute also; for they are ministers of God's service, attending continually upon this

---

God's wrath, which the magistrate, the representative of God, is bound to execute upon evil doers.]

The last clause is the antithesis of the first. The duty of a good ruler equally includes both. The 'sword' is the symbol of the power of life and death.

5. Wherefore ye must needs be subject, etc.[1] Not only as a prudent policy, but also as a religious duty. [Not only on account of the magistrate's wrath, but on account of one's own conscience. (Meyer.) Compare 1 Peter 2 : 13: "Be subject . . . for the Lord's sake." "It is self-evident," says Philippi, "that a Christian is never at liberty actually to co-operate in wrong even on the demand of authority. (Acts 4 : 19; 5 : 29.) If he obeys authority for God's sake, he cannot obey it in opposition to God." Whether, if called to obey under such circumstances, a Christian should actively rebel, or cheerfully submit to wrong-suffering and quietly pay the penalty of disobedience, is a question on which judgment and conscience must decide. Philippi says: "Let him never actively rebel." Alford and Godet would not apparently counsel rebellion, but the former remarks that "even the parental power does not extend to things unlawful. If the civil power commands us to violate the law of God, we must obey God before man." And Godet says: "For the very reason that the State governs in God's name, when it comes to order something contrary to God's law, there is nothing else to be done than to make it feel the contradiction between its conduct and its commission." He further asserts "that the submission required by Paul . . . does not at all exclude protestation in word and even resistance in deed, provided that to this latter there be joined the calm acceptance of the punishment inflicted." In this our free country we may, both as citizens and as Christians, adopt the motto: "Resistance to tyrants is obedience to God," and also to law in its best and highest sense. "Whenever *man* commands us to do anything that *God* forbids, or *forbids* us to do anything that *God* commands, we cannot and must not obey; for in such cases

as these, in obeying man we should be disobeying God." (Wordsworth.) See Dr. Hovey's "Manual of Theology and Ethics," pp. 411, 415.]

It is to be noted, that the above precepts and principles were written to the disciples at Rome at a time when their rulers were notoriously corrupt and tyrannical, just after the reign of Tiberius, Caligula, and Claudius, and during the reign of the infamous Nero. While they certainly afford no express warrant for rebellion, even against the most cruel and unjust government, they are not to be quoted as an express sanction of "the right divine of kings to govern wrong." It is easy to see what evils would have resulted from any explicit sanction in the Scriptures of the right of revolution. The *letter* seems severe, and to allow no exception; just as in the case of parents and children (Col. 3 : 20), husbands and wives (Eph. 5 : 22, 24), masters and servants. (Col. 3 : 22.) In all these cases, the letter of Christianity is modified by the *spirit*, and the two combined admirably adjust the balance, making our divine religion alike *conservative* and *progressive*, alike the firmest supporter of order and the truest promoter of freedom. *Note:* That if rebellion or revolution is ever justifiable, it is plain that the subject, and not the ruler, must be the judge, in each particular case, both of its lawfulness and of its expediency.

6. The words **pay ye tribute** may be either in the indicative mood, affirming the fact, or in the imperative, enjoining the duty: and there is precisely the same ambiguity in the Greek as in the English: but it is better to regard the verb as indicative ['ye pay tribute'; so De Wette, Meyer, and others], thus making the familiar fact of paying taxes a confirmation of the necessity affirmed in the preceding verse ('for'), corroborated, moreover, ('for this cause') by the additional consideration that they give their whole time to this divinely sanctioned ministry of government—**attending continually** (see 12: 12) **upon this very thing.** ['This very thing' is not the collection of taxes, as Olshausen, Philippi, and Noyes

---

[1] Some MSS. (D E F G) omit the word necessity ('must needs be') and read the verb as imperative. In our present text the copula 'is' must be supplied: There is a necessity to submit one's self.—(F.)

7 Render therefore to all their dues: tribute to whom tribute *is due*; custom to whom custom; fear to whom fear; honour to whom honour.

8 Owe no man any thing, but to love one another: for he that loveth another hath fulfilled the law.

7 very thing. Render to all their dues: tribute to whom tribute *is due*; custom to whom custom; fea₁ to whom fear; honour to whom honour.

8 Owe no man any thing, save to love one another: for he that loveth 1 his neighbour hath fulfilled 2 the

1 Gr. *the other*......2 Or, *law*.

suppose, but the nobler and higher function of government, indicated in the preceding verses. It is from this point of view that rulers are said to be ministers of God in behalf of the people. Paul in 15: 16 calls himself a minister of Jesus Christ for the Gentiles. The word in the Greek denotes a public minister. It occurs elsewhere only in Phil. 2: 25; Heb. 1: 7; 8: 2.]

7. [**Therefore** is omitted in the oldest manuscripts. **Render,** pay fully, **to all** in authority **their dues: tribute to whom tribute is due.** Both nouns being in the accusative case, we must render literally thus: 'pay fully the tribute to him (claiming) the tribute.' Nothing was so grievous and offensive to the Jews as this paying of tribute to a foreign power. A "publican" or tax gatherer for Rome would be a despised and hated person apart from his extortions.] The distinction between 'tribute' and 'custom' is, that the former denotes taxes on persons and lands, and the latter taxes [customs, duties] on goods or merchandise. The word 'fear' may be referred more particularly to higher magistrates, and to those having more direct authority over us; and the word 'honour' to all who are invested with office. There is a sense in which *all* men are to be honored, as God's creatures, and our fellow creatures (1 Peter 2: 17); but, over and above this, magistrates are entitled to be honored for their office. This is to be rendered to them as their due. It is a sad and inexcusable disregard of this apostolic injunction, when persons make less conscience of defrauding the government than of defrauding a neighbor. Tertullian says ("Apologet.," XLII.), to the honor of the early Christians, that what the Romans lost by the Christians refusing to bestow gifts on their temples, they gained by their conscientious payment of taxes. [Even our Saviour, as a loyal citizen of a heavenly and of an earthly kingdom, not only paid the temple tax (so most think) which was demanded of him (Matt. 17: 27), but his counsel was: render in full to Cæsar the tribute and everything else which belongs to Cæsar. (Matt. 22:

17-21; Luke 20: 22, seq.) It is noticeable, however, that while Paul characterizes even the civil powers of heathendom as ordained of God, and urges upon Christians the performance of their duties to these powers, he yet counsels his fellow-disciples to settle their own disputes among themselves and not bring them before the heathen tribunals. (1 Cor. 6: 1-8.)] It is to be noted that no particular form of government is alluded to here. Nothing is said about the king: the terms are all general; the 'higher powers;' 'rulers;' 'God's ministers.' It is *government*, not any particular *form* of government, that the Scriptures represent as of divine authority. *Love to all men enjoined.* Ver. 8–10.

["From the duty of submission to the State, Paul passes to that of justice in private relations" (Godet), and he again introduces the subject of love, since love is an "indispensable auxiliary of justice."

8. Owe no man any thing, but to love one another. This may be literally rendered: *Owe to no one nothing, except the loving one another.* The two subjective negative terms in this clause, both producing in the original but a single strengthened negation, show the verb 'owe' to be in the imperative mood.[1]] Leave no debt undischarged, except "the undying debt of love" (Bengel), "which you must always owe, because this alone holds the debtor even after it has been discharged." (Augustine.) ["He loves not truly who loves for the purpose of ceasing from loving." (Philippi.) **He that loveth another.** (Revised Version, margin, *the other*.) The last word was chosen with reference to the preceding 'one another.' **Hath fulfilled,** "the perfect tense pointing to a completed and *permanent* act." (Ellicott.) **Law** is without the article in the original, yet that the Mosaic law is meant is evident from the following verse. Paul in Gal. 5: 14 says that "all the law (hath been and) is fulfilled in one word: Thou shalt love thy neighbour as thyself." See in Matt. 22: 39 what our Saviour says respecting this commandment to love our neighbor.] "The expression 'fulfilled' de-

1 "The article," Winer says, "is put before the infinitive (here before ἀγαπᾶν, *to love*), when it is desired to make it a substantive, and thus give it greater promi. nence."—(F.)

9 For this, Thou shalt not commit adultery, Thou shalt not kill, Thou shalt not steal, Thou shalt not bear false witness, Thou shalt not covet ; and if *there be* any other commandment, it is briefly comprehended in this saying, namely, Thou shalt love thy neighbour as thyself.

10 Love worketh no ill to his neighbour: therefore love *is* the fulfilling of the law.

11 And that, knowing the time, that now *it is* high time to awake out of sleep: for now *is* our salvation nearer than when we believed.

9 law. For this, Thou shalt not commit adultery, Thou shalt not kill, Thou shalt not steal, Thou shalt not covet, and if there be any other commandment, it is summed up in this word, namely, Thou shalt love 10 thy neighbour as thyself. Love worketh no ill to his neighbour: love therefore is the fulfilment of [1] the law.

11 And this, knowing the season, that now it is high time for you to awake out of sleep: for now is [2] salvation nearer to us than when we *first* believed.

1 Or, *law*.... .2 Or, *our salvation nearer than when, etc.*

notes more than a simple performance ; it adds a *completeness* to the performance." (Webster and Wilkinson.) [" In and with the loving there has taken place what the Mosaic law prescribes in respect of duties toward one's neighbor, inasmuch as he who loves does not commit adultery, does not kill, does not steal, does not covet," etc. (Meyer.)]

9. [**For this.** See 8: 26. The neuter article in Greek makes all the commands which follow as one substantive, which is properly in the same construction as 'any other commandment'—that is, subject of the verb 'is comprehended.' **Comprehended in this saying**—literally, *united in one head*, summed up in this word. See Eph. 1: 10. **Thou shalt love.** This command, quoted from Lev. 19: 18, is also virtually made into a substantive by the neuter article (ἐν τῷ, equivalent to **namely**), which, however, is wanting in some manuscripts. **As thyself.** This shows that there may be a love of self which is proper, and which is far removed from selfishness.[1]] The ninth commandment, 'Thou shalt not bear false witness,' is omitted in the best manuscripts. **If there be any other commandment** is as much as to say, "Whatsoever other (different) commandment there may be." [In the order of commandments here quoted, the *sixth* follows the *seventh*, but see the same order in Luke 18: 20 and in one manuscript copy of the Septuagint. Probably Paul (and so Philo) followed copies of the Seventy, which had this order.]

10. Love worketh no ill to his neighbour. [We have here a summation, in a negative form, of the preceding negative commands. The word for 'neighbour' (πλησίον) is properly an adverb, but is converted into a noun by the use of the article. If this law of Christian love should control the hearts and lives of men, what a blessed change would at once be produced in the state of society ! A carrying out of the golden rule to universal practice would be an infallible cure for all our labor troubles and social evils.] **Therefore love is the fulfilling of the law.** Love becomes the fulfilling of the law by abstaining from all that the law forbids. [The *good* which love would do for our fellow-men is understood as a matter of course. And where there is true love for men, there will necessarily be love to God, and an obeying of the commands of the First Table. But this love of which Paul speaks is an ideal love, and not that imperfect love which exists among men, and which can never be a ground of justification.]

General exhortation to a Christian life, enforced by the consideration that the day of trial is near its close.

11. And that—*And this*, let us do this, referring to ver. 8. **Knowing the time.** Let the knowledge and consideration of the time [special season, or opportunity] be an additional enforcement of the admonition to discharge all our obligations and to cultivate love. **It is high time to awake** [or, be aroused at once from sleep. Compare Matt. 25: 5. The Bible Union renders it passively : 'Already were awaked.' The word for 'high time' is simply 'hour,' and with this some connect the adverb 'already,' rather than with the verb.[2]] Time to arouse ourselves from torpor to a more active and watchful way of living—language which may have been suggested by our Lord's words in Matt. 24: 42; Mark 13: 33; Luke 21: 28–36. **For now is our salvation nearer than when we believed.** The reference is to the beginning of our faith (when we became believers), and to the end or consummation of our salvation. [Meyer, De Wette, and Philippi render: "now is salvation nearer to us."

1 On the use of the third person (ἑαυτόν), for the second (σεαυτόν, which some MSS. actually exhibit), compare 12: 19; John 12: 8; 18: 34. In Rom. 8: 23, the third person is used for the first.—(F.)

2 The uncials ℵ * A B C P have *you* instead of *us.*—(F.)

12 The night is far spent, the day is at hand: let us therefore cast off the works of darkness, and let us put on the armour of light.

12 The night is far spent, and the day is hand: let us therefore cast off the works of darkness, and let us

Compare 10: 18: "The word is nigh thee." But Alford, with an eye to Luke 21: 28, prefers the rendering of our Common Version. This salvation, according to Prof. Stuart, is "the spiritual salvation which believers were to experience when transferred to the world of everlasting life and glory."]

12. The night is far spent [has far advanced. The want of connection here "adds vivacity to the expression." (Boise.) The metaphor of night and day in the first part of the verse is carried over into the second. As when we wake from sleep we lay aside the garments of the night and put on the day dress, so we should put off the works belonging to darkness, and put on the weapons (A D E read 'works') appropriate to the day. In Eph. 6: 11, 13, we are exhorted to put on the panoply of God, the whole armor which God has provided for every part of the Christian's person, except his back; for, as Bunyan remarks: "The Christian has no armor for his back." The figure of putting on clothing, or *enduing* [1] one's self, is a favorite one with Paul, and the Christian life is by him very frequently represented as a warfare. Compare 2 Cor. 10: 4; Eph. 6: 11, seq.; 1 Thess. 5: 8, etc.]

Commentators differ very much in regard to what is meant by the *night* and the *day* in this verse. Some refer these words to the night of adversity and Jewish persecution, and the day of deliverance from this, consequent upon the destruction of Jerusalem, and the breaking up of Judaism as a political and persecuting power. But it does not appear that the condition of Christians in *Rome* was much affected by this event, nor does there seem to be any allusion to it in the context. Another view is, that the night designates the period before Christ's second coming, as a time of imperfection and calamity; and the day the time of deliverance, prosperity, and happiness, beginning with his second advent. This view is held chiefly by those who believe that Paul, and the apostles generally, expected that Christ would come again in their own lifetime, or, at least, within a very short time—a view which we regard as derogatory to their inspiration, inconsistent with his express teachings, and at variance with

other intimations of Scripture. See Matt. 25: 36; 2 Thess. 2: 1-8; 2 Tim. 4: 6-8; 2 Peter 1: 13-15. [This view is also that of Meyer, who holds 'the night' to be this age, the time before the *advent* (παρουσία), and 'the day' to be the coming age, soon to be ushered in and bringing salvation. De Wette thinks 'the day' corresponds to salvation, the period of purity, perfection, and blessedness, which is to be introduced by the coming of Christ, while 'the night' is "the imperfect, sinful condition of this earthly life." Similarly, Godet, Philippi, and most interpreters.] Others understand by 'the night' this mortal life, as being to each one a period of comparative ignorance and trouble, and by 'the day' the time of each Christian's deliverance from the body by death and entrance into the immortal life of knowledge, happiness, and holiness. But this view, though the language, taken by itself, might easily bear this sense, seems to disconnect this verse too much from the preceding, which seems to require a reference to some change in the state of things in this present life, of which they had more definite knowledge than they can be supposed to have had in regard to the time of their departure out of this world. [Yet Godet asks: "Is not death for the individual what the advent (παρουσία) is for the church as a whole—meeting with the Lord?" And Philippi remarks that, "as respects the individual, death is equivalent to his coming to salvation, the resurrection from the dead equivalent to salvation coming to him."] Another view, which I regard as less objectionable than either of the foregoing, and, on the whole, to be preferred, is that which refers 'the night' to the season of pagan ignorance, immorality, and wretchedness, in which the Romans had formerly been living; and 'the day' to the season of Christian knowledge, purity, and happiness, which had begun to dawn upon them, and which was destined to grow brighter and brighter. We must remember that they were living in the transition period, when the light of Christianity was struggling successfully with the darkness of pagan idolatry; and although the overthrow of Paganism, and the formal establishment of Christianity under

---

[1] The verb here used is ἐνδύω, *to put on.*—(F.)

Constantine, was yet nearly three centuries in the future, and was not, on other accounts, such an event as an inspired apostle, if he foresaw it, could contemplate with unmingled joy, yet the growing progress of Christianity and decline of Paganism, which at last made that formal change possible, was matter of encouragement and rejoicing to every Christian; and this moral revolution, as we learn from the writings of Tertullian and other early Christians, had made signal progress and greatly changed the moral condition of the Roman Empire long before the days of Constantine. As to the great event of our Lord's advent, it is certain—

1. That the apostles did not *know* when Christ would come the second time.

2. That his coming is always drawing *nearer*.

3. That it may be considered as *near* at any time, in comparison with the eternity preceding and the eternity following it.

[Most commentators hold this 'day' (of salvation), of which Paul here speaks, to be our Lord's personal second advent. Some charge the apostle with advancing mistaken views on this subject in nearly all his epistles. Olshausen supposes that at the date of this letter he had ceased to entertain such views. It seems to me a matter of certainty that, if he had been mistaken, he lived long enough to find out his mistake, and would have been honest enough to make open acknowledgment of the same. Yet this he never did, and it does not seem proper in us to be the first to charge him with error. Others think the apostle never had definite convictions as to this matter, and that, as the day and the hour had never been revealed to him, so, though he may have had some expectations of our Lord's speedy return, perchance during his own lifetime, yet he never fully and explicitly declared himself on this point. But I think his language touching this matter has a positiveness and explicitness which do not belong to mere conjecture, and that, if he erred at all, he erred greatly, and has expressly declared that to be a fact which events have proved to be utterly false. In our view, the Scriptures speak of several different comings or manifestations of Christ. The first, as we may name it, is his coming and manifestation to his disciples by the Paraclete, or Helper —that is, the Holy Spirit. (John 14 : 18, 21, 23, 28; 16: 16, 22.) The second is his coming to receive his disciples, "at the termination of their labors on earth" (Ripley), unto himself in his Father's house. (John 14 : 3.) The verb "come" is here in the present tense, denoting a continuous coming, as if to take individuals to himself. It was in this way that he received the spirit of the first Christian martyr, Stephen, and this is the only way in which he has come to his disciples, in order to take them to himself, from that day to this. If the departure of Christians from this life is to be with Christ, and if their being absent from the body is to be at home with the Lord, then surely they are not obliged to wait until Christ's final coming at the Judgment Day, and the bringing in of the blessed resurrection state, before he will receive them to himself! The third we may mention is the coming of the Son of man in his kingdom, or the coming of his kingdom, which indeed is the only advent of which our Saviour spoke. This coming is said to be on and in the clouds of heaven, with great power and glory, with attendant angels and with a great sound of a trumpet. And one purpose of this coming was to gather together his elect from the four winds, or in other words to effect the deliverance or "redemption" of his people. The time of this coming is fixed beyond dispute. If we believe the Saviour' words, we must believe that it happened before the generation in which he lived had passed away, and that "some" whom our Saviour addressed lived to see the Son of man coming in his kingdom. (Matt. 24 : 34; 16 : 28; 10 : 23; 26 : 64.) Whether this coming had reference solely to the destruction of Jerusalem and the abrogation of the Jewish economy, with the consequent setting up of the world-wide Messianic kingdom, or whether, including this, it also took in the events which transpired at and subsequent to the Day of Pentecost, we need not now endeavor to determine. We would only remark that the comings of Christ, now referred to, were impersonal, and that as the first mentioned was an actual experience of the apostle, so the remaining two might be looked for by him as being at any time literally near at hand. The apostle in 2 Thess. 2: 3–8 seems to speak of a *special* apostasy which should happen in the future, a revelation and coming of the lawless one, the man of sin, the son of perdition, commonly regarded as Anti-Christ, whom the Lord Jesus shall slay with the breath of his mouth and bring to nought by the manifestation of his coming. And as the occasion and purpose of this coming seem to be special and limited, so many (as Edwards, David Brown, and others) regard this as a special and impersonal coming of Christ, and hence different from his second *personal* advent, his final coming, which is to bring an end to this age and this Dispensation of Grace, to change the living, to raise the just and unjust dead, to judge the world of mankind, and to take all his ransomed ones "in clouds," "into the air," up to heaven, *to be with him forever.* The question now is, did Paul affirm or expect that this second personal coming of Christ would or might happen in his own lifetime? To this question we say, emphatically, No. When he says to the Corinthians, literally, We all shall not sleep, such scholars as Winer and Meyer do, indeed, suppose it necessarily equivalent to saying: "None of us who are now living are going to die; we shall all live to the time of the advent, and then shall be changed." There is, however, no necessity, even in the expression itself, for this interpretation. See Buttmann, p. 121. Besides, Paul elsewhere in his Epistles to the Corinthians speaks of himself and others as living and dying and being raised from the dead, just as we do of ourselves. See 1 Cor. 6: 14; 11: 30; 15: 31; 2 Cor. 4: 14; 1: 8, etc. De Wette well says in substance that an exegete may charge the apostle with a false prophecy, but not with one that contradicts himself. The expressions: "We who are alive and remain," "*We* shall all be changed," etc., therefore prove nothing on this point, or at least are more than counterbalanced by the many repeated affirmations and intimations that death would befall himself and his readers, and that their mortal bodies would be quickened (see 8: 11) and they be raised up with Jesus and through his power. Compare with notes on 2: 5. See how after a few verses more (14: 7, 8) he speaks to the Roman disciples of living *and dying*, as their common lot, in precisely the same manner as we do. Compare Phil. 1: 20; 2: 17; 2 Cor. 7: 3. We have also noticed some of the great events which, according to this apostle, are to occur before the "end": the bringing in of the fullness or the great mass of the Gentiles, the conversion of all Israel, the consequent general awakening of the Gentile world to a

new spiritual life—life from the dead—and then, perhaps, the "falling away," and the 'perilous times,' etc. Surely this apostle did not imagine that all this would happen in a few months or years. According to the theory which some advocate, we should suppose the "men of Galilee," or Christ's apostles and disciples, who stood looking up into heaven to catch a glimpse of their ascended Lord, were assured that *they* should see this Jesus coming in like manner as they beheld him going into heaven. (Acts I: 11.) But instead of this, one of these Galilean men, not many days afterward, declared that the heaven must receive (and retain) this Jesus "until the times of restoration of all things," until "primeval order, purity, and happiness" shall be re-established throughout the earth. Many expressions in Paul's last letter (2 Tim.), at the date of whose writing the time of the apostle's departure by a violent death had come, would, if found in his earlier epistles, be thought by some to indicate his expectation of living to see his Lord's return. We refer to such expressions as loving Christ's appearing, giving charge by his appearing and kingdom, being saved unto his heavenly kingdom, his giving to Paul the crown of righteousness at that day, and his guarding the apostle's deposit against that day, etc. Now the indefinite "day" of our verse, unlike "that day," of which he speaks to Timothy, is not connected with any appearing, advent, or revelation of our Lord. Throughout this Epistle the apostle is wholly silent in regard to these things, and we doubt whether the Roman Christians were so familiar with the idea of Christ's speedy coming in the flesh that they would readily connect this undefined day with that event. 'The day' of this chapter is connected by its context with the doing of one's duty as citizens and members of society, the duty of obeying magistrates, paying tribute, honoring and loving all men, walking becomingly in the world, and mortifying the deeds of the flesh. The saints in Rome *knew* that they, in common with mankind in general, were entering upon a bright "day of Christian knowledge, purity, and happiness." They also *knew* that life was but a vapor, and that the day of "their deliverance from this present evil world, and introduction into the purity and blessedness of heaven" (Hodge), was at hand, and that in this sense (which many sup-

13 Let us walk honestly, as in the day; not in rioting and drunkenness, not in chambering and wantonness, not in strife and envying:
14 But put ye on the Lord Jesus Christ, and make not provision for the flesh, to *fulfil* the lusts *thereof*.

13 put on the armour of light. Let us walk honestly, as in the day; not in revelling and drunkenness, not in chambering and wantonness, not in strife and jealousy. But put ye on the Lord Jesus Christ, and
14 make not provision for the flesh, to·*fulfil* the lusts *thereof*.

pose to be the right one) their salvation was nearer than when they first believed. There are those, however, who believe that the apostle and other New Testament writers, while laboring under no mistaken view, may at times have referred even to Christ's second personal coming as being near, since it was practically coincident with the day of death (Ellicott), since it was always near to their feelings and consciousness (Hackett), since it was, and is, near, as compared with ages past, and since it was, and is, the *next* great event and glorious consummation of God's eternal plan of redemption.]

13. Let us walk. [With ethical reference, nearly equivalent to *live*. This verb, like the two immediately preceding, is in the so-called hortatory subjunctive.] The word translated 'honestly' [from an adjective which means well formed, graceful, becoming], is the same that is translated "decently" in 1 Cor. 14: 40. It means 'becomingly,' in a manner suited to the purity and dignity of the Christian profession. [**As in the day**—in the full light of day, when one avoids unbecoming behavior. There is here a latent reference to a previous walking in darkness.] **Not in rioting and drunkenness,** etc. These words explain the works of darkness named in the preceding verse. Three classes of such works are mentioned—intemperance, impurity, and discord; and each is described by two words.[1] The word translated 'rioting' ('reveling,' see Gal. 5: 21, and 1 Peter 4: 3) refers to such disorderly carousing as characterized the festivals of Bacchus. [Godet says: "*The works of night* are enumerated in pairs: First, sensuality in the forms of eating and drinking; then impurity, those of brutal libertinism and wanton lightness; finally, the passions which break out either in personal disputes or party quarrels. This last term seems to me to express the meaning of the word (ζῆλος) in this passage better than the translation, *jealousy*, or envy." Meyer contends for *jealousy* as the proper meaning of this last term; Fritzsche and Philippi for wrath or anger. The first

four words (rendered by Prof. Boise, "carousals, intoxications, licentious acts, debaucheries") are in the plural number, which here "denotes the various expressions, evidences, outbreaks, concrete manifestations, generally, of the quality expressed by the singular." Other, and more extended lists of the works of darkness, or of the flesh, are given in Gal. 5: 19; 2 Cor. 12: 20, 21.]

14. But put ye on the Lord Jesus Christ. [The putting on, or clothing ourselves with, another person, "is a strong expression, denoting the complete assumption of the nature, etc., of another" (Ellicott); in other words, the most intimate spiritual union and appropriation, such as is indicated by our baptism into Christ. (Gal. 3: 27.) If in the sight of God we bear the name and person of Christ we are reckoned more in him than in ourselves. (Calvin.) This command of the apostle, to put on Christ, is addressed to those who had already clothed themselves with Christ in baptism.] "Christ put on man in nature and condition: man should put on Christ in disposition and character. He became partaker of our physical nature. We should become partakers of his moral nature. Christ put on man, that man might put on Christ." (J. Brown.) This is the robe, not of justification, but of sanctification or personal holiness.

"The robe of righteousness which Christ gives us is a *medicated* robe, which *cures* the sores which it *covers*, which heals while it hides." (Alexander de Stourdza.) This word, put on, is elsewhere used with reference to the moral disposition of our Lord, and the Christian virtues and graces. See Gal. 3: 27; Eph. 4: 24; Col. 3: 10, 12; 1 Peter 5: 5. **Make not provision for the flesh, to fulfil the lusts thereof.** Take not any forethought for the flesh (for corrupt human nature) to fulfill its lusts; [literally, *with reference to lusts*. Noyes gives this rendering: "Think not about satisfying the lusts of the flesh." 'Flesh' and 'lusts' are in the original made emphatic by position. The flesh here is not regarded as that which is wholly impure and which should be "cruci-

---

[1] All these words are in the dative of manner.—(F.)

CHAPTER XIV.

HIM that is weak in the faith receive ye, *but* not to doubtful disputations.

1 But him that is weak in faith receive ye, *yet* not to doubtful disputations.

fied " (Gal. 5: 24); and hence the apostle does not absolutely forbid all care for the flesh. We may provide for the flesh, but not for the exciting and gratifying of its lusts. We owe a duty to our bodies which, though the seat of unlawful desires, are yet consecrated to God as temples of his Spirit, and consequently we owe a duty to the flesh, the living material of which these bodies are composed.] This passage, beginning with ver. 11, was the means of awakening Augustine, and of his conversion from a dissolute to a holy life:

["I flung myself down, how, I know not, under a certain fig-tree, giving free course to my tears, and the streams of mine eyes gushed out, an acceptable sacrifice unto thee. . . . I sent up these sorrowful cries: 'How long, how long? To-morrow, and to-morrow? Why not now? Why is there not this hour an end to mine uncleanness?'

" I was saying these things and weeping in the most bitter contrition of my heart, when, lo, I heard the voice, as of a boy or girl, I know not which, coming from a neighboring house, chanting, and oft repeating, 'tolle, lege; tolle lege,' 'take up and read, take up and read.' Immediately my countenance was changed and I began most earnestly to consider whether it was usual for children in any kind of game to sing such words: nor could I remember ever to have heard the like. So restraining the torrent of my tears, I rose up, interpreting it no other way than as a command to me from heaven to open the book and to read the first chapter I should light upon. . . . . I grasped, opened (the volume of the apostles), and in silence read that paragraph on which my eyes first fell,—' Not in rioting and drunkenness, not in chambering and wantonness, not in strife and envying, but put ye on the Lord Jesus Christ and make not provision for the flesh, to fulfil the lusts thereof.' No further would I read, nor did I need; for instantly, as the sentence ended—by a light, as it were, of security infused into my heart—all the gloom of doubt vanished away." (Augustine's "Confessions," VIII. 12, 28, 29.)]

Ch. 14: *Duties toward Christian brethren, especially toward those who are weak and over-scrupulous.* ["Behavior as to things morally indifferent." (Olshausen.) "A practical application of the law of love." (Godet.)]

1. Him that is weak in the faith.[1] One who is weak in the faith is not so fully confirmed in the gospel doctrine [or, "in moral conviction and feeling" (De Wette)] as to be free from all Jewish scruples in regard to distinctions of days and meats. Aside from the Jewish rules in regard to the prohibition of certain kinds of animal food, some Jewish Christians had scruples about eating meat or drinking wine at all in foreign lands, fearing lest they should incur defilement by eating or drinking what had been offered to idols. So they practiced a conscientious asceticism. Compare Dan. 1:8. [Also 1 Cor. 8:7; 10: 25, seq.; Acts 15:29. Pharisaic scrupulosity in regard to defilement is noticed in Mark 7:4; Acts 10:28. The question of meats and drinks, and ceremonial defilement and observance of days, must often have agitated the early churches. Compare with passages already cited, Col. 2:16-23; 1 Tim. 4:3; Heb. 9:10; 13:9. These matters, and especially the question of the use or non-use of the Mosaic ordinances, shook the Apostolic Church to its very foundations, and never since has the stability of the Church of Christ been threatened by questions so difficult and momentous. Who can tell how much the Christian Church owes to the influence of the Apostle Paul in settling these important matters? Who can tell how changed the history of the church would have been if Saul of Tarsus had never been "separated unto the gospel of God"?] **Receive ye**—or, *take to your hearts in brotherly fellowship*—**but not to doubtful disputations,** not to discrimination of thoughts, or to dispute about his scruples ["not unto discussions of opinions." (Boise.) Note here that the imperative, as usual, is accompanied by the subjective negative in the original.] A different class of persons is here had in view from those Judaizers opposed in the Epistle to the Gala-

---

[1] A masculine noun or participle in the singular, with the article, often denotes a whole class. Possibly the participle here used does not denote so permanent a weakness as the adjective would have done. The transitional δέ (but), leading over from a general to a special case, is not noticed in our Common Version.—(F.)

2 For one believeth that he may eat all things: another, who is weak, eateth herbs.
3 Let not him that eateth despise him that eateth not; and let not him which eateth not judge him that eateth; for God hath received him.
4 Who art thou that judgest another man's servant? to his own master he standeth or falleth; yea, he shall be holden up: for God is able to make him stand.

2 ¹doubtful disputations. One man hath faith to eat
3 all things: but he that is weak eateth herbs. Let not him that eateth set at nought him that eateth not; and let not him that eateth not judge him that
4 eateth: for God hath received him. Who art thou that judgest the ²servant of another? to his own lord he standeth or falleth. Yea, he shall be made to stand; for the Lord hath power to make him stand.

1 Or, *for decisions of doubts*......2 Gr. *household-servant*.

tians, and also from the ascetics rebuked in Col. 2 : 20–23. [Compare 1 Tim. 4 : 3. It is "we who are strong" who ought to bear the infirmities of the weak (15:1), and refrain from disputatious criticisms of our weaker brethren. The word 'thoughts' is, at least with adjuncts, always used in an ill sense in the New Testament. See 1 : 21.]

2. For one [the 'strong'] **believeth that he may eat** (hath faith to eat) **all things** (even such things as are considered by some unclean): **another, who is weak,** etc.¹ This verse explains what is meant by 'weak in the faith' in ver. 1. One who is clear and settled in his persuasions has confidence to eat anything eatable, whether 'flesh' or anything 'not unclean of itself' that is set before him. Another, who is timid and scrupulous, confines himself to a vegetable diet. [It is stated in Josephus' "Life," § 3, that certain Jewish priests, imprisoned at Rome, not forgetful of piety toward God, "subsisted on figs and nuts." And Jewish Christians at Rome would naturally have like conscientious scruples in regard to eating anything which was "common or unclean," or, in fact, anything prepared by Gentile hands. Compare Dan. 1 : 8–16; Tobit 1 : 10–12. The apostle, who reckons himself among the 'strong,' treats these weaker, yet conscientious brethren, with great mildness, since they had not relaxed their hold on Christ, and hence proceeds next to "recommend mutual forbearance, on the principle that each one serves the Lord according to his own conviction." (De Wette.) Paul's counsel here by no means warrants a church to receive as a Christian brother and fellow-member one whose religious faith or practice is seriously defective.]

3. Let not him that eateth, etc. Note how well chosen the words are. The eater, in his own convictions, would be in danger of *despising* [literally, *setting at nought*] the ab-

stainer as weakminded; the abstainer, cautious and timid, would be in danger of condemning the eater as too bold.² Note, also, how the apostle incidentally sides with the eater in the last clause, for the pronoun 'him' grammatically refers to the eater, though applicable, so far as the truth is concerned, to the abstainer also. The same thing may be observed in the next verse, where the same pronoun has the same grammatical reference. **For God hath received him**—hath accepted and acknowledged him as his true servant.

4. Who art thou that judgest another man's servant? It is none of thy business to pass a condemnatory judgment on another's servant. [Away with such "presumptuous intermeddling!" The 'thou' by its position is very emphatic. This household servant (see margin of Revised Version) was, in many cases, regarded as a member of the family. The participle (one judging) stands here, as often in the New Testament, in place of a relative clause.] **To his own master**—that is, to Christ, as appears from ver. 7, 8. [This 'master' is the 'another' of the preceding sentence. To this master alone does it belong to acquit or condemn his servant. And how comforting is the thought, when we perchance hear of alleged inconsistencies or misconduct of a professed servant of Christ, and feel it impossible to know and rightly judge all the circumstances of the case, that we are not to be his judge, but that to his own Master he standeth or falleth.] **Standeth or falleth**—that is, stands in or falls from his position as an accepted Christian, without any *direct* reference to the final judgment. **God is able to make him stand.** Willingness seems to be *implied* in this affirmation of ability, as in 11 : 23. [The Revision text has here the adjective 'able' instead of the verb, and reads: The *Lord* is able, etc. He is able to support the (strong) believer whom the weak

¹ Instead of a corresponding *another* (ὃς δέ), as in ver. 5, we have here the article with the participle—literally, *he who is weak.*—(F.)

² The phrase, *the non-eating* one, refers to a *supposed* class; hence the negative μή.—(F.)

5 One man esteemeth one day above another: another esteemeth every day *alike*. Let every man be fully persuaded in his own mind.

5 One man esteemeth one day above another: another esteemeth every day *alike*. Let each man be fully

one judges. Perhaps, however, the judging is here, as a general term, predicated of the strong as well as the weak.] The apostle now passes to another point, on which the difference of the strong and weak required the application of the same principles of mutual forbearance and charity.

5. One man (the weak) **esteemeth one day above another,** etc.—[literally, *judgeth day beyond day*, not alternate days, as would be the meaning in the classics, but one day more holy than another, while **another esteemeth** (*judgeth*) **every day** (holy). On the use of the relative instead of the article, for 'one' and 'another,' see 9: 21.] The word **alike** is not expressed in the Greek, but this, or some similar expression, is needed in English to make the sense plain. One man regards the Jewish festival days as more sacred than other days; another man makes no such discrimination. Let every one act on this subject according to his own settled conviction. [From Paul's language here, and in Gal. 4: 10; Col. 2: 16, some, as Alford, have inferred that the apostle regarded all days as alike common, and that "Sabbatical obligation to keep any day, whether seventh or first, was not recognized in apostolic times." I conceive it, however, an impossibility that a converted, believing Jew, of that age, in the absence of any express, authoritative repealing act, could come to regard his historical sacred Sabbath, "the Sabbath of Jehovah," as a common day, and its observance as a matter of indifference. The weekly Sabbath of the Jews was distinguished from all other of their festival days in that its name was written by the finger of God in the fourth commandment, and we, as Christian believers, must at least recognize in that command some essential fundamental principle that is binding on us and on all God's rational creatures. The Sabbath was made for man and therefore for Christians, and we believe that for Christians there remain the ten commandments, and that for them there remains, in a literal sense, a *Sabbatismos*, the keeping of a Sabbath.[1] Ellicott says: "The assertion of Alford cannot be substantiated. The Sabbath of the Jews, as

---

[1] It is objected by some that we do not observe the command of God if we keep the first day of the week instead of the seventh. But the command says nothing about the seventh day *of the week*, much less does it enjoin on us the keeping of the seventh day of the week as the week is now reckoned. Little is said about the week during the long Patriarchal Dispensation of twenty-five hundred years, and nothing is said directly of the Sabbath till we reach the time of Moses. There is no certain evidence that among the ancient nations which adopted the weekly division of time, the days of the week everywhere corresponded to each other, nor is there any proof that the weeks and the Sabbaths have come down to us from man's creation in regular succession and order. No one can now tell for certain which is the exact memorial day of God's seventh day rest. The command is, Remember the day of rest to keep it holy, and we certainly remember it on the Lord's Day. We are next commanded to labor six days, and this we do, or should do, it being as much of a command as any other. And after six days of toil we are commanded to rest on the seventh, or keep it as "a Sabbath," and this command we obey to the letter. The mere calling of our Christian Sabbath or Sunday the *first* day of the week does not in the least militate against or affect the strictest, most literal observance of the fourth commandment. And we cannot conceive it to be a crime if the Sabbatarian, having observed as sacred the forenoon of his *Saturday* Sabbath on the east side of the day line in the Pacific Ocean, should just remove a hair's breadth and finish his Sabbath observance by keeping the afternoon of *Sunday*, the so-called first day of the week, on the west side of the line. But granting that the sacred day has been changed, have the great body of Christians thereby become violators of God's command? No one will claim that the Sabbath law, as given and enforced by Moses, is binding in its literal exactness. Even the strictest Sabbatarian obeys it, but in part and only so far as he thinks it accordant with the Christian system and spirit. The only question which on this subject divides Christian believers is, how much of the Sabbath law of the older dispensation shall we, under the teachings and example of Christ, transfer to the new? The Sabbath was made for man, for all men, at all times, and everywhere. Hence, there is something in the Sabbath commandment which has a perpetual and universal binding force, some essential principle which can and should, always and everywhere, by all classes of men, by travelers abroad as well as by dwellers at home, be carried out into practice. This fundamental and universal principle is that a seventh part of our time should be weekly and stately kept as specially sacred to Jehovah. We contend therefore that Christians who sacredly observe the first day of the week, the resurrection day of our Lord, as their Sabbath, and as the memorial day both of finished creation and finished redemption, are not chargeable with violating the fourth commandment, but that they do keep it, if not with the closest literalism, yet most certainly in spirit and substance.—(F.)

6 He that regardeth the day, regardeth *it* unto the Lord; and he that regardeth not the day, to the Lord he doth not regard *it*. He that eateth, eateth to the Lord, for he giveth God thanks; and he that eateth not, to the Lord he eateth not, and giveth God thanks.

7 For none of us liveth to himself, and no man dieth to himself.

8 For whether we live, we live unto the Lord; and whether we die, we die unto the Lord: whether we live therefore, or die, we are the Lord's.

6 assured in his own mind. He that regardeth the day, regardeth it unto the Lord: and he that eateth, eateth unto the Lord, for he giveth God thanks; and he that eateth not, unto the Lord he eateth not, and

7 giveth God thanks. For none of us liveth to himself,

8 and none dieth to himself. For whether we live, we live unto the Lord; or whether we die, we die unto the Lord: whether we live therefore, or die, we are

---

involving other than mere national reminiscences (with Deut. 5: 15 contrast Exod. 20: 11) was a *shadow* of the Lord's Day. That a weekly seventh part of our time should be specially given up to God rests on considerations as old as creation, and that that seventh portion of the week should be the *first* day rests on apostolical and perhaps inferentially (as the Lord's appearances on that day seem to show) divine usage and appointment."[1] The verb **fully persuaded** we have had in 4: 21. The apostle is here speaking of things in themselves morally indifferent. Though one of the 'strong,' he does not command the weaker brethren to eat all things, or to esteem all days alike, but he leaves these *adiaphora*, or things indifferent, to each man's judgment and conscience. Yet if a weak brother is convinced that he ought not to eat anything common or unclean, and is grieved and made to stumble at the conduct of the strong brother who deems nothing to be unclean in itself, then this strong one, as we shall see, is counselled to yield a point of indifference out of regard to the convictions of the weaker brother, that he may not for the mere matter of food destroy him for whom Christ died. See in 1 Cor. 6: 12; 9: 22; 10: 23, how Paul exemplified his own precept.]

6. The second clause of this verse--**he that regardeth not the day,** etc.—is undoubtedly spurious. It has very slender support from the manuscripts (none from the oldest), and however true that may be which it affirms, it ought not to be regarded as a genuine part of Paul's letter. [**He that eateth not** (that is, of certain kinds of food), **to the Lord he eateth not, and giveth God thanks** (that is, for those kinds of food which he does eat). It is "for the Lord that he refrains from the eating (of flesh), persuaded that this abstinence tends to serve the interest of Christ." (Meyer.)][2]

There is no reason to regard what is said in these two verses, the fifth and the sixth, as having any reference to the first day of the week. We know that the practice of the earlier Christians differed as to the observance of the festival days of the Jews. We have no evidence that any Christians, in the days of the apostles, neglected to observe the first day of the week as the festival of Christ's resurrection. The word Sabbath, in Col. 2: 16, and, in fact, wherever it is used in the New Testament, refers to the Jewish Sabbath, the seventh day of the week. The first day of the week is never called by that name. The latter part of this verse establishes the fact, attested also by other evidence, that the primitive Christians were accustomed to give thanks to God at their daily meals. [For Scripture examples, see Matt. 15: 36; 26: 26; Acts 27: 35; 1 Cor. 10: 30; 11: 24; 1 Tim. 4: 4. Paul, however, may not here refer exclusively to the giving of thanks at table.] It would be well if all Christians at the present day would observe this good custom, as well as follow the wise and conciliatory counsels of the apostle in regard to censuring one another for differences in things neither obligatory nor sinful. The apostle now proceeds to give good reasons why we should neither judge nor despise one another on account of such differences.

7, 8. These verses contain a reason why we should not, in judging the conduct of our fellow-disciples, follow our natural impulses, but practice self-control, and subordinate all our conduct to the will and glory of Christ, whose we are, whether living or dying. [**For none of us liveth to himself,** etc. This is true, indeed, of our human relationship. Every one, no matter how low his standing, or isolated in society, exerts some influence, and *must* exert some influence for good or evil over

---

[1] For passages where the "first day of the week" is expressly mentioned, see Matt. 28: 1; Mark 16: 29; Luke 24: 1; John 20: 19 (26); Acts 20: 7; 1 Cor. 16: 2. Some have supposed the Pentecostal outpouring of the Spirit occurred also on the first day of the week. See Lev. 23: 11, 15; also the Article Pentecost, note b, in Smith's "Bible Dictionary."—(F.)

[2] Note here the use in the original of the two different negatives (μὴ, οὐκ).—(F.)

9 For to this end Christ both died, and rose, and revived, that he might be Lord both of the dead and living.
10 But why dost thou judge thy brother? or why dost thou set at nought thy brother? for we shall all stand before the judgment seat of Christ.
11 For it is written, *As* I live, saith the Lord, every

9 the Lord's. For to this end Christ died, and lived *again*, that he might be Lord of both the dead and
10 the living. But thou, why dost thou judge thy brother? or thou again, why dost thou set at nought thy brother? for we shall all stand before the judg-
11 ment-seat of God. For it is written,

others. But the apostle here has especially our divine relationship in mind, and asserts that we are the Lord's, and are living, not for ourselves, but for his service and glory. Our whole earthly existence, our life and death even, is a service for our sole Lord and Master. "Neither life nor death can make us cease to be his." (Jowett.) And how comforting the thought that, while we cannot do many things, or any great things, for God, we can serve him in little things in all our daily acts, when we toil with our minds or toil with our hands, and earn our bread with the sweat of our brow— yea, "whether we eat or drink, or *whatever* we do," we can do all to the glory of God! If we live, or if we die, we belong to Christ, and serve him. The reader may perhaps recollect that the words of this last verse form the inscription on Meyer's tombstone.] Dr. Malan, in one of his excellent tracts, speaks of death as an *act* of the Christian, his last earthly act of obedience to his Divine Master. He does not have his spirit torn from him against his will and in spite of his resistance, but he *yields up* his spirit at the divine summons, as did Christ himself. (Luke 23:46.)[1]

9. For to this end Christ both died, etc. The words 'and rose' should be omitted, as not belonging to the original text, according to the testimony of the best manuscripts. They add nothing to what is expressed by the other words of the passage. [Omit, also, 'both,' and read: Christ died and revived, or became alive. "The aorist often denotes the entrance into a state or condition." (Boise.) **To this end** refers to the final clause of the verse. **The dead and living.** The order of these words, the reverse of the usual one, is made to correspond with the preceding verbs, died and lived. "Christ's dominion over the dead refutes the notion of the insensibility of the soul while the body is in the grave." (Bengel.)

God is not the God of the non-existent, nor of the unconscious dead, but of the *living*; for all *live* (not merely exist) unto him. (Luke 20:38.) And so the apostle says, "whether we wake or sleep," whether we live or die, "we should *live* together with (or united with) him." (1 Thess. 5:10.) Paul thus plainly teaches us that death places the Christian with Christ (compare 2 Cor. 5:8; Phil. 1:23); and so he may well call death a gain. (Phil. 1:21.) Yet the Christian may not experience the fullest blessedness until after the resurrrection and the judgment.]

10, 11. The main subject is now resumed from ver. 3, and two cogent reasons are given why we should not judge nor despise our brother: First, because he is our brother, and second, because God will judge him. [The Revised Version gives the force of the original, which shows that the questions are directed to different individuals—the first one to the weaker in faith, the second to the stronger. **We shall all stand.** Those who judge and set at nought, and those who are judged and are set at nought. "Note how decisive is the testimony of such passages against any limitation of the universality of the final judgment." (Meyer.)] **The judgment seat of Christ.** [This reading is defended by Tholuck, De Wette, and Philippi.] It should, however, be, *the judgment seat of God.* The reading of all the best manuscripts puts this matter beyond question. And it is just as unquestionable that in 2 Cor. 5:10, "we must all appear before the judgment seat of Christ," is the true and undisputed reading. (Compare Matt. 25:31.) These passages are not contradictory. They are both combined and reconciled in Rom. 2:16. [Christ, as the glorified Son of man, will sit in judgment as God's representative.]

11. For it is written in Isa. 45:23. This language, which is here represented as spoken by

---

[1] According to John 21:19, we can glorify God even by the manner or kind of our death. Several MSS. give the indicative, rather than the subjunctive, form after ἐάν (εἰ—ἀν), if, or, whether: but that mood, after this particle, is exceedingly rare. Prof. Boise, after calling attention to the oft-recurring τέ of ver. 8,

"uniting the clauses in closer logical connection," then says: "Our union with Christ in life and death, and his entire ownership, could hardly be expressed in stronger language. Note the emphatic repetition of the word Lord."—(F.)

knee shall bow to me, and every tongue shall confess to God.

12 So then every one of us shall give account of himself to God.

13 Let us not therefore judge one another any more: but judge this rather, that no man put a stumblingblock or an occasion to fall in *his* brother's way.

As I live, saith the Lord, to me every knee shall bow,
And every tongue shall ¹ confess to God.

12 So then each one of us shall give account of himself to God.

13 Let us not therefore judge one another any more: but judge ye this rather, that no man put a stumbling-block in his brother's way, or an occasion of

1 Or, *give praise.*

the Lord (Jehovah, in the Hebrew of Isaiah, see ver. 19, 21, 25), is plainly applied to Christ in Phil. 2: 10, 11, thus agreeing with 2 Cor. 5: 10, and also other passages of inspired Scripture, in representing Christ as the final Judge of men, and identifying him with the supreme Jehovah of the Old Testament. [The original of the quotation has: "I have sworn by myself," instead of, 'as I live,' "and, every tongue shall swear," instead of, 'shall confess.' Paul here varies both from the Hebrew and most copies of the LXX. The words "saith the Lord" are added by himself. With the use of that (ὅτι) after solemn asseverations, a verb like *aver* is understood. The verb 'confess' is used in James 5: 16 of confession of sins, but here it denotes to render praise, or to do homage, whether it comes from the heart or not. As is shown in the next verse, each one's giving an account of himself to God is a confession made to him. So in Phil. 2: 10, 11, we are taught that in the name of Jesus every knee shall bow and every tongue shall confess that Jesus Christ is Lord. Yet this does not prove the truth of universal salvation. All the enemies of Christ, his betrayers, his earthly judges,—Annas, Caiaphas, Pilate,— his murderers, will give account of themselves at Christ's judgment seat, and by this act alone they will confess that he is Lord, and will thus do homage in and to his name.]

12. So then every one of us shall give account of himself to God. The context, both preceding and succeeding, seems to require a distinct emphasis on the words 'of himself,' with an almost equal stress on the last words, 'to God.' [Looking at the verse itself 'every (or, each) one' (ἕκαστος) would be the emphatic word. But does not every one of these words have a fearful emphasis for us sinners? In this world we are sometimes lost in a crowd or overlooked, but nothing of this kind will happen there when each one of us will give account of himself. A very few manuscripts, including, however, the Vatican

B, omit the words 'then' and 'to God,' and have the verb in a compound form, but the Revisers abide by the well-established reading of the Common text.] Every man's account will be *personal*, between himself and God alone, as the Judge. And this consideration, in both its aspects, should rebuke and restrain our severe judgments of one another.

The apostle now proceeds to amplify his admonition of the strong [since these are not always so inwardly and strongly bound by their convictions as the weak], not to use their Christian liberty in such a way as to damage their weaker brethren.

13. Let us not therefore judge [present tense, continue in the habit of judging ; **but if** you must judge, **judge this rather**—that is, let this be your judgment. 'This' refers to the following clause: **that no man put a stumblingblock or an occasion to fall,** etc. Notice how the infinitive is made a substantive by its prefixed article, and compare 2 Cor. 2: 1.] The word 'judge' here, in the second instance, seems to be used nearly in the sense of *resolve.* The same Greek word is translated "determine" in Acts 3: 13; 20: 16; 25: 25, and three or four other places, and "decree" in 1 Cor. 7: 37. The two words translated 'stumblingblock' and 'occasion to fall' differ very little in sense. Each is more than once translated by the same words, 'stumblingblock,' 'offence,' and they are joined together in 9: 33; 1 Peter 2: 8, as well as in this passage. They are applied to any act or course of conduct which tends to provoke others to sin. [Some regard the former (stone or block of wood) as the larger obstacle against which one would be very likely to fall, and the latter (trap or trapstick) as a smaller and more hidden obstacle which *might* occasion his fall or hinder his progress. The word for trap (σκάνδαλον, see 9: 33; 11: 9; 16: 17) is found twenty-five times in the LXX. and fifteen times in the New Testament, but seldom occurs in Greek profane writers.]

14 I know, and am persuaded by the Lord Jesus, that *there is* nothing unclean of itself: but to him that esteemeth any thing to be unclean, to him *it is* unclean.
15 But if thy brother be grieved with *thy* meat, now walkest thou not charitably. Destroy not him with thy meat, for whom Christ died.
16 Let not then your good be evil spoken of:

14 falling. I know, and am persuaded in the Lord Jesus, that nothing is unclean of itself: save that to him who accounteth anything to be unclean, to him
15 it is unclean. For if because of meat thy brother is grieved, thou walkest no longer in love. Destroy not
16 with thy meat him for whom Christ died. Let not
17 then your good be evil spoken of: for the kingdom

14. I know, and am persuaded, has the appearance of an anti-climax, and would really be such were the latter verb separated from its accompanying words **by the Lord Jesus**—[literally, *in* the Lord Jesus, in conscious fellowship with him]. This adjunct imparts a sacredness to his persuasion which raises it above the simple 'I know.' **There is nothing unclean of itself.**[1] Is not this virtually an affirmation that the Mosaic prohibitions in regard to particular kinds of meats had no foundation or reason in the nature of the meats themselves? Compare Acts 10 : 28; 1 Tim. 4 : 3, 4. The apostle here declares his theoretical agreement with those who did not regard the Mosaic distinctions of meats as any longer binding; and this declaration adds emphasis to his injunctions to those whom he recognizes as having a right view of their liberty, not to use it in such a way as to give offence or to present temptation to their weaker brethren. For that which he and those whom he is admonishing knew to be in itself lawful for them would defile the conscience of the weaker brethren if they should eat the same meats without the same convictions. The principle is an important one. Men are not always doing right when they act according to their consciences, for conscience is not the *ultimate* standard of right, since it may be only partially enlightened. But men are always guilty when they act *contrary* to their consciences, when they do what they do not believe to be right. Paul was conscientious in persecuting Christians before his conversion (Acts 26 : 9), but this did not make his conduct right as he himself came fully to understand afterward. (1 Cor. 15 : 9.) There was nothing morally defiling in eating meats that had once been forbidden to

the Jews, *but* [εἰ μή forming an exception to the *nothing unclean*] they would defile the conscience of him who should eat them, believing them to be still forbidden.

15. But if thy brother be grieved. [Instead of 'but,' the Revised Version has *for*. For if on account of meat (or, food) 'thy brother be grieved.' The thought of this verse, with this rendering, seems closely connected with ver. 13.] 'Be grieved'—be not only displeased for the moment, but led by thy example to do that on account of which he will afterward be grieved with himself. **Walkest thou not charitably**—literally, *walkest not according to love*, actest in a way which due love to thy brother forbids. [Such love as this "worketh no ill to his neighbor." The apostle here sets forth a very high and heavenly morality.] **Destroy not him.** "Do not pursue a course which tends, by leading him into sin, to destroy his soul, and which will, at least, destroy his peace." Bengel's note on the last clause of this verse is very pertinent and forceful: "Do not make more account of his meat than Christ did of his life." [Similarly, Alford: "Ruining, . . . by a MEAL of thine, a brother for whom Christ died!" See 1 Cor. 8 : 11. Notwithstanding the conative force of the present tense (do not *attempt* to destroy), Paul would here seem to teach that a person may perish for whom Christ died. But this does not prove that any one whom he purposed to save will ever fatally apostatize and finally perish.]

16. Let not then your good be evil spoken of. Their liberty in regard to distinction of meats was a good thing, but there was need of caution in the use of it, lest it should become an occasion of division among

---

[1] Literally: *Common through itself.* Three important MSS. ℵ B C, have here the full form ἑαυτοῦ (of itself), while other MSS. have a shorter form. Alford prefers the contracted form of the reflexive, αὑτοῦ, while Meyer adopts the personal αὐτοῦ of the neuter gender. Some, regarding it as masculine, have referred this last form to Christ; through *him* there is no longer anything unclean. The older MSS. do not give the breathings, and most critical editors of the New Testament do not give any

contracted forms of the reflexive pronoun in the third person. Both of the above verbs, 'I know' and 'am persuaded,' are perfect in form. On 'I know' (οἶδα), see 7: 7. Philippi thinks that the apostle here specially exhorts the strong, because their numbers were probably preponderant in the Roman Church, and their influence over the weak was more to be feared than the influence of the latter on the former.—(F.)

17 For the kingdom of God is not meat and drink; but righteousness, and peace, and joy in the Holy Ghost.

18 For he that in these things serveth Christ *is* acceptable to God, and approved of men.

19 Let us therefore follow after the things which make for peace, and things wherewith one may edify another.

20 For meat destroy not the work of God. All things indeed *are* pure; but *it is* evil for that man who eateth with offence.

of God is not eating and drinking, but righteousness 18 and peace and joy in the Holy Spirit. For he that herein serveth Christ is well-pleasing to God, and 19 approved of men. So then [1] let us follow after things which make for peace, and things whereby we may 20 edify one another. Overthrow not for meat's sake the work of God. All things indeed are clean; howbeit it is evil for that man who eateth with offence.

[1] Many ancient authorities read *we follow*.

---

brethren, and so a reproach to the Church of Christ. It surely was not worth while to run so great a risk. ['Your good,' according to Meyer, is the kingdom of God; with Philippi, it is the gospel; with De Wette, it is your strong faith. Let not your strength of faith, by reason of strife and schism, be calumniously spoken of by the heathen or unbelievers. The uncials D E F G read—"*our* good."]

17. The kingdom of God is not meat and drink—or, true religion does not consist in such external observances as eating and drinking, but that kingdom is within you (Luke 18 : 21), and consists in **righteousness,** rectitude of character, inward **peace,** and **joy in the Holy Ghost** (or Spirit), the Holy Spirit being the source of true religious peace and joy. [If regard be had to our relation to God, then this 'kingdom of God' (here mentioned for the first time in this Epistle) would consist, as De Wette states it, in "righteousness in its full sense, including justification," as also in our peace toward God as well as in inward peace. In Meyer's view, this kingdom of God is not an earthly moral kingdom, but the future Messianic kingdom, to be ushered in at the second coming of Christ—a sadly distorted view of the reign of Christ in and among the children of men.]

18. For he that in these things serveth Christ. He who cultivates the three great Christian graces just mentioned will not only be **acceptable to** (or, *please*) **God** and secure his favor, but will also be **approved of men** [will be able to stand their *testing*], and be secure against having his good evil spoken of. (Ver. 16.) [Instead of 'these things,' most manuscripts have the reading of the Revised text, *this*, which, grammatically, refers to the 'Spirit,' or to the phrase 'joy in the Holy Ghost'; or possibly it might express, as Alford states it, "the aggregate of the three"—that is, righteousness, peace, and joy. But most ex-

positors, disregarding the preponderating evidence of the MSS., prefer the plural, *these*, referring to the three great moral elements just mentioned. These, if taken in their Scriptural sense, are to be viewed doctrinally as well as ethically, else we should be obliged to regard a just, peaceful, cheerful man as a true Christian. (Hodge.) The elements, the great gifts and graces which constitute the essence of God's kingdom, are not of earth or of self, but of God, and are, indeed, the fruits of the Spirit.]

19. Let us therefore follow after [let us eagerly *pursue* (the word for *persecute*) **the things which make for peace,** or, *things of peace*—that is, which belong to and tend to peace. With the second clause, some less important manuscripts supply the verb: Let us guard or keep]. To **edify** is, literally, to *build up.* Both the individual Christian and the church at large are represented as a building, and the improving and perfecting of character in either is called edifying or building up. This verse is a practical exhortation suggested by the two preceding verses.

20. For meat. On account of meat (or food). The Christian is called **the work of God**—sometimes simply (Eph. 2 : 10); sometimes under the figure of a field to be tilled; more frequently under the figure of a house or temple to be built. (1 Cor. 3 : 9; 6 : 19.) In harmony with this figure, the word here translated **destroy** (different from the word so translated in ver. 15) means to pull down or take to pieces, being the antithesis of edifying in ver. 19. [The singular number, 'destroy' thou 'not' (strive thou not to destroy, present tense), refers back to ver. 15, 16.] **All things indeed are pure.** All kinds of food are lawful to be eaten, being clean in themselves (see ver. 14, and compare 1 Tim. 4 : 3, 4), but it is wrong for him, or there is evil to him, who may eat in such a way as to give offense to his brother, or to cause him to do anything contrary to his

21 *It is* good neither to eath flesh, nor to drink wine, nor *any thing* whereby thy brother stumbleth, or is offended, or is made weak.
22 Hast thou faith? have *it* to thyself before God. Happy *is* he that condemneth not himself in that thing which he alloweth.
23 And he that doubteth is damned if he eat, because *he eateth* not of faith: for whatsoever *is* not of faith is sin.

21 It is good not to eat flesh, nor to drink wine, nor *to do*
22 *any thing* whereby thy brother stumbleth.[1] The faith which thou hast, have thou to thyself before God. Happy is he that judgeth not himself in that which
23 he [2] approveth. But he that doubteth is condemned if he eat, because *he eateth* not of faith; and whatsoever is not of faith is sin.[3]

conscience.[1] [The immediately preceding and succeeding verses have reference to the strong, and so here the man who eateth through offense (so as to be an occasion of stumbling) is the strong in faith. So De Wette, Alford. Others, less correctly, interpret it, in the light of ver. 14, of the weak brother who, in eating, offends his own conscience.]

21. It is good. In opposition to what is evil or wrong. (Ver. 20.) **Neither to eat flesh.** [The word here used for flesh denotes slain flesh, in contrast with the ordinary word for living flesh. On the order of the negatives, see at 8: 38. The two verbs after **stumbleth** are omitted in the Revision, but are found in B D F L, Vulgate, and should not be condemned. **Nor** (to do) **anything whereby,** etc. Compare 1 Cor. 8: 13. We have here a most important principle of action—to wit, a regard to our influence, which will often enable us to decide as to the right or wrong of things in themselves, possibly indifferent or innocent. So far as ourselves are concerned, we may safely and rightly indulge in certain practices or habits; but when we know or suspect that such indulgence is hurtful in its influence on others, it then becomes a sin against God and man. Under this rule of action we may determine the rightfulness or the moral impropriety of participating in the so-called "worldly" (perhaps in themselves often innocent) amusements of our times. There are certain habits indulged in by some Christians, even by some Christian ministers, which *we* cannot place among the things morally indifferent and

innocent. In all these matters, we do well "not to please ourselves," but to follow that truly Christ-like principle which Paul himself both inculcated and practiced. "Whether therefore ye eat or drink, or whatsoever ye do, do all to the glory of God."]

22. Hast thou faith—or, a full persuasion that there is no sin in eating certain meats which thy brother regards as forbidden? Keep that persuasion to thyself; let it be between thee and thy God; do not parade it before thy brother in such a way as to shock his weak prejudices and tempt him to sin; be content with the happiness of acting consistently with thy principles, and be not over anxious to make thy brother see and act as thou doest.[2]

23. And he that doubteth. [See 4: 20, the only place in the Epistle where this word occurs. The word in the last verse, translated *judgeth* (κρίνων) in the Revised Version, occurs twice in this, compounded with different prepositions. The last compounded form is in the perfect *has been* (and is) *condemned*, lies under condemnation.] He is condemned who eats what he doubts his right to eat, because of that doubt; **for** [rather, *but*, introducing an axiom. (Alford)], whatever a man does while doubting whether he has a right to do it, that is sin. This is the same principle which is expressed in ver. 14. The passage does not mean what Augustine inferred from it, that the best actions of unbelievers are only "shining sins." Yet there is an important moral principle here. In every moral act there are two important elements to be considered—the act itself, and

1 The word *but*, corresponding to the preceding μέν (*indeed*), is stronger than δέ, and makes this clause "more strongly prominent."—(F.)

2 The Revisers insert a *which* in the first clause, and give a slightly different rendering without altering the meaning. For the word 'thyself' they have σαυτὸν, the contracted form of σεαυτὸν. In the last sentence of the verse, μή, with the participle, *judging* (in Common Version, 'condemneth'), refers to a supposed genus. Happy is the strong one who judges not himself, or is

liable to no self-judgment (Meyer) in pursuing that course which he approves after examination and testing. An Apocryphal addition to Luke 6: 4 (found in MS. D), is adduced by Olshausen as "very highly instructive for the understanding of this passage." It is there told that Jesus saw a man working on the Sabbath, and said to him: "If thou knowest what thou doest, thou art blessed; but if thou knowest not, thou art accursed, and a transgressor of the law."—(F.)

T

CHAPTER XV.

WE then that are strong ought to bear the infirmities of the weak, and not to please ourselves.

1 Now we that are strong ought to bear the infirm-
2 ities of the weak, and not to please ourselves. Let

the state of the actor's conscience. In order that an act may be wholly right, it must be right in *both* these respects; but in order to be wrong, it need be faulty in only *one* of them. This principle is pithily expressed in the Latin maxim: "Bonum non oritur, nisi ex omnibus causis integris: malum ex quovis defectu"— "the *right* is produced only by the perfection of *all* its parts; the wrong by a defect in any single part." It would be easy to quote from uninspired, and even Pagan moralists, sentiments more or less parallel to this of Paul. Pliny says (Epistle 1:18): "Quod dubitas, ne feceris"—"what you are in doubt about you must not do." Cicero less tersely says: "Bene praecipiunt, qui vetant quicquam agere, quod dubitas an æquum sit an iniquum" ("De Officiis" 1 : 9)—"They teach well who forbid us to do anything about which we are not sure whether it is just or unjust." There is a Rabbinical maxim which coincides more closely still with the language of Paul: "Quicquid utrum licitum sit an illicitum tu nescis, id tibi illicitum est"—"Concerning whatever thing you do not know, whether it is lawful or unlawful, that thing is unlawful *for you*." That was an excellent resolution of Jonathan Edwards, expressed with the precision of a metaphysician, as well as formed with the piety of a saint: "Resolved never to do any action about the lawfulness of which I am so doubtful at the time that I resolve to inquire afterward, unless I am equally doubtful whether it is lawful to omit it." [The preceding note merits deep consideration; for the language of Paul in this verse has been often misunderstood—*first*, by assuming that "faith" here means "trust in Christ," and *secondly*, by assuming that whatsoever is "of faith" is holy, because whatsoever is "not of faith" is sinful. The word "faith" signifies in this place belief or conviction— namely, belief or conviction that a given act is lawful and right before God; and the teaching of the apostle, as explained above, is clearly this—that it is sinful for any Christian to perform an act which he does not fully believe to be right, but not that it is sinful for him to perform an act without trust in Christ (though this is doubtless true), and still

less, that every act which is performed with trust in Christ is, therefore, sinless. Trust in Christ does not render a man holy in heart and life; it is rather a confession that he is not holy. But the word 'faith,' as Dr. Arnold clearly shows, does not here mean trust in Christ.— (A. H.)]

[In some manuscripts, but not the most important, the final doxology (16: 25-27) occurs here after ver. 23. Some suppose that this verse ended a church section, or lesson for public reading, and the doxology was appended to form a suitable close. Certainly the doxology, "now to him that is of power to *stablish* you," comes in appropriately here, where the *weak in faith* are spoken of. But, as Westcott and Hort affirm, "the cause of its insertion here cannot be known with certainty." Only a very few skeptical writers have doubted the genuineness of the two chapters which follow.]

Ch. 15 : *Continuation of the subject of chapter 14 to ver. 13* ["Christ an example of bearing with the weak." (Olshausen.) Thence to ver. 33 are personal explanations, embracing an apology, ver. 14–21, and notice of journeys, ver. 22–33.]

1. We then that are strong ought to bear the infirmities of the weak. Observe that here, as in 14: 4, the apostle takes the part of the 'strong' as being theoretically right, and thus adds to the strength of his plea for the weak. The word translated 'infirmities' is not used elsewhere in the New Testament, but is derived from the word rendered 'weak,' as in 14: 4. [The verb 'ought' is strongly emphatic by position, standing at the opening of the sentence. The words for 'strong' and 'weak' correspond in form to our *able* and *unable*. We who are able to carry the infirmities of the weak (unable) ought so to do. We are not only to bear with their weaknesses, but to carry them as if our own—a requirement which necessitates the putting of ourselves in the place of the weak. The apostle also counselled the Galatian Christians, "Bear ye one another's burdens, and so fulfil the law of Christ." (Gal. 6 : 2.) No Christian can so dissociate himself from others that he can live for himself

2 Let every one of us please *his* neighbour for *his* good to edification.

3 For even Christ pleased not himself; but, as it is written, The reproaches of them that reproached thee fell on me.

4 For whatsoever things were written aforetime were written for our learning, that we through patience and comfort of the Scriptures might have hope.

each one of us please his neighbour for that which is

3 good, unto edifying. For Christ also pleased not himself; but, as it is written, The reproaches of them

4 that reproached thee fell upon me. For whatsoever things were written aforetime were written for our

---

alone. And in all our relations of responsibility, in all our life's plans, and in all our actions, the *ought* idea should, as in our text, have the foremost, the emphatic place.] **And not to please ourselves.** [This pleasing of one's self seems, it must be confessed, to be in general the guiding principle of human action. Observe the use of the dependent negative here in contrast with the use of the direct negative in the narrative sentence of ver. 3, 'pleased not himself.' Notice also the third person of the reflexive pronoun as here used for the first.] This clause points out the root of those rash judgments and alienations of feeling among brethren, which the apostle is earnestly endeavoring to forestall. It is the want of that self-denying love, of which our Lord himself was the bright example (ver. 3), and which Paul also exemplified in an eminent degree. (1 Cor. 8: 13; 9: 22; 10: 33.) We show our strength, not by despising, but by tolerating, the infirmities of the weak, and our knowledge and enlarged views by bearing with the ignorance and narrow prejudices of others. ["Both parties are to receive each other in brotherly love (15: 7), without the stronger subjecting the scruples of the weaker to his criticism. But the stronger has thus a special duty of love to discharge, for to him alone is the matter in dispute a matter of indifference." (Weiss.)]

2. Let every one of us please his neighbour for his good to edification. We have here an excellent rule of Christian charity, well guarded. The wish to please our neighbor is a praiseworthy feeling, but we are to indulge it according to these two rules, namely, in ways which are right in the sight of God, and which tend to our neighbor's 'edification' —his building up in righteousness and Christian character. ['Edification' is a species under the genus, *good*. (Bengel.) Of the two prepositions in the original, the former seems to denote the more immediate, the latter the more ultimate purpose or result of the action. See Ellicott on Eph. 4: 12. The word for 'neighbor' is an adverb, and properly means *the one (being) near*. Observe that there is a wrong

way of pleasing our neighbors as well as a right one. See Gal. 1: 10; 1 Thess. 2: 4. We must please him or strive to please him, only as it will be for his good, only, too, in obedience to the divine will.]

3. The exhortations in the two preceding verses are now enforced by the example of Christ. **For even Christ,** though so much above the strongest of us, **pleased not himself; but** [the reverse of this is true. This is the great constraining motive for like action in us. Observe here the use of the objective negative where a fact is stated. The word *Christ*, standing in such a connection as this, is generally used by Paul as a proper name and without the article. Yet again in ver. 7 it has the article, and so in 1 Cor. 1: 13; 10: 4; 11: 3, etc., in all which cases it is used in the nominative. **As it is written,** in Ps. 69: 9. Winer remarks that the apostle, instead of saying, but to please God, he submitted to the most cruel reproaches, changes the construction by proceeding with a quotation from the Old Testament. The quotation is verbatim from the LXX. 68: 9. **Those that reproached thee.** Owing to its connection with a verb in the past tense, the present participle, *those reproaching thee*, may be rendered as in the past tense 'Thee' here refers to God. Though Christ in one sense pleased not himself ("otherwise he would have abstained from taking these sufferings on himself; compare Heb. 12: 2, 3; Phil. 2: 6-8." Meyer), yet he was pleased to obey the will of God and to say, "Lo I come." (Heb. 10: 7; compare Matt. 20: 28; John 4: 34.)] For the benefit and salvation of men Christ willingly suffered reproach from the enemies of God. The Messianic character of the psalm quoted from is evident from John 2: 17; 15: 25; 19: 28; Acts 1: 20.

4. For whatsoever things. [Westcott and Hort read: "All things whatsoever." "The apostle both justifies the above citation and prepares the way for the subject to be next introduced." (Alford.) We see here the value which such inspired writers as Paul placed on *all* the Old Testament Scriptures.] **Were**

5 N w the God of patience and consolation grant you to be likeminded one toward another according to Christ Jesus:

6 That ye may with one mind *and* one mouth glorify God, even the Father of our Lord Jesus Christ.

7 Wherefore receive ye one another, as Christ also received us, to the glory of God.

learning, that through [1] patience and through comfort of the scriptures we might have hope. Now the God of [1] patience and of comfort grant you to be of the same mind one with another according to Christ

6 Jesus: that with one accord ye may with one mouth glorify the [2] God and Father of our Lord Jesus

7 Christ. Wherefore receive ye one another, even as

8 Christ also received [3] you, to the glory of God. For

1 Or, *stedfastness*......2 Or, *God and the Father*......3 Some ancient authorities read *us.*

written for our learning (or, *instruction*) **that we through patience and comfort of the Scriptures might have hope.** This was the general object of all, and more specifically, with reference to the present subject, to contribute to our patience and comfort. The Scriptures teach us 'patience' in bearing the infirmities of others, and give us 'comfort' under the slight inconvenience which it may cost us to bear them; and in general 'the Scriptures' are the source of 'patience and comfort' by their precepts, their examples, their promises, and by the 'hope' of eternal life. [The comfort of the Scriptures is thus allied, not with apathy, but with endurance. The connection of these two words in the following verse indicates a similar close connection here—that is, they are both to be connected with 'the Scriptures.' The genitive is that of source or authorship. The 'hope' which we may have is commonly regarded as the Christian's special hope, the hope of glory. (5: 12.) There are but two things we can carry away with us when we leave this world: the one is the hope we may have in Jesus of forgiveness and of the life eternal; the other is the heavy burden of unrepented and unforgiven sin.]

5, 6. The apostle, recognizing God as the source of **patience and consolation** (comfort), as 'the Scriptures' are the means, prays that he may grant them harmony of feeling **to be like minded** [to mind the same things, as in 12: 16] among themselves (which, rather than exact unanimity of opinion, is the meaning of 'like minded' here), **according to** (the will and example of) **Christ Jesus,** our perfect pattern; so that they, with one accord or unanimously, **with** (literally, *in*) **one mind and one mouth** (with one inward spirit and one outward utterance) may **glorify God, even the Father** (or, the God and Father) **of our Lord Jesus Christ.** A touching prayer, or, rather, devout wish, with which to seal and enforce the preceding admonitions. [How strongly the Saviour desired the oneness of his people may be seen in John 17 : 21. De

Wette and Meyer prefer the rendering, '*even* the Father,' which is found in our Common Version, though the rendering of the Revised Version, *the God and Father,* is theologically and grammatically admissible. See Eph. 1: 17, also Matt. 27: 46; John 20: 17.]

7. Wherefore, on which account—namely, that the wish just expressed may be accomplished. **Receive ye one another** [or, rather, *take to yourselves* (implying more active effort) as Christian brethren, see 14: 1] both Jewish and Gentile believers, both the strong in faith and the weak. **As Christ also received us** (or, *you*). ' As' may be equivalent to *since* here, and so be referred to the *fact* that Christ received us as a *reason* why we should receive one another [compare 14: 3, 'for God hath received him']; or it may refer to the *manner* in which Christ received us, as the *rule* to teach us *how* we should receive another. The word is commonly taken in the former sense in this passage; but the manner in which the word 'also' is connected with it—the two being, in fact, joined together, making one compound word in the Greek—would justify the translation, *even as Christ also received us,* which would seem rather to suggest the *way* of receiving, as well as the *reason* for it. We must receive those whom Christ receives, *because* he receives them, and *as* he receives them. We must not set any limits to our brotherly love, which Christ has not set; and and we must not make any conditions of church membership which he has not made; nor must we ignore, or neglect to insist upon any that he has made. **The glory of God** was his end in forming the rules of his kingdom; and the glorifying God, as in ver. 9, should be ours in putting those rules in practice. We may sum up all in these three fundamental principles:

1. Christ is the only King and Lawgiver in his church. 2. The Scriptures are the only binding rule of faith and practice for his people in religious matters. 3. God's glory should be the supreme end in all Christian action, whether private or ecclesiastical.

8 Now I say that Jesus Christ was a minister of the circumcision for the truth of God, to confirm the promises *made* unto the fathers:
9 And that the Gentiles might glorify God for *his* mercy; as it is written, For this cause I will confess to thee among the Gentiles, and sing unto thy name.
10 And again he saith, Rejoice, ye Gentiles, with his people.
11 And again, Praise the Lord, all ye Gentiles; and *laud* him, all ye people.

I say, that Christ hath been made a minister of the circumcision for the truth of God, that he might
9 confirm the promises *given* unto the fathers, and that the Gentiles might glorify God for his mercy; as it is written,
Therefore will I [1] give praise unto thee among the Gentiles,
And sing unto thy name.
10 And again he saith,
Rejoice, ye Gentiles, with his people.
11 And again,
Praise the Lord, all ye Gentiles;
And let all the peoples praise him.

1 Or, *confess.*

8, 9. By the quotations in the ninth and three following verses, the apostle proves that God's purpose from the beginning was to comprehend both Jews and Gentiles in the wide embrace of his mercy, through the Messiah; and so he adds confirmation to the force of his exhortation to them to receive one another, and to the assurance that their doing so will redound to the glory of God. [**Now I say.** Instead of this phrase, most MSS. read *for,* which denotes a reason for the exhortation just given. Meyer renders: "*I mean, namely,*" thus making what follows to be explanatory of the preceding.] **A minister of the circumcision.** The apostle shows his Jewish brethren that he was not unmindful of a certain *temporal* priority of claim on their part, to the blessings of the Messianic kingdom, according to such passages as Matt. 15 : 26; Luke 24 : 47; John 4 : 22. [The word minister, or servant (διάκονος), whence our *deacon*, occurs elsewhere in this Epistle. See 13 : 4 (twice) and 16 : 1. Our Saviour said that he came to *minister unto* (διακονῆσαι) by giving his life a ransom for many. (Matt. 20 : 28.) But his earthly service was mainly for the circumcision, the Jews, the lost sheep of the house of Israel. Possibly the apostle may have made this concession to the Jews in order to humble the pride of the 'strong' Gentile Christians. (De Wette.) **Was**—the verb in the original is in the perfect, meaning, literally, *has become*, and denotes a past event, but still continuing in its effects.] **For the truth of God**—that is, to establish it by fulfilling the Messianic prophecies or **promises made unto the fathers. And that the Gentiles might glorify God for his mercy** [as the Jews for his truthfulness, his fidelity to his promises. Noyes makes the verb 'glorify' dependent on 'I say,' and gives this rendering: "(I say) that the Gentiles glorified God for his mercy." More probably

this verb is co-ordinate with the verb **confirm,** and thus the glorifying God by the Gentiles is represented as "the remote design of Christ's becoming a minister of the circumcision." Meyer says: "The connection of the Jewish Christians with Christ appears as the fulfillment of their theocratic claim; but that of the Gentile Christians as the enjoyment of grace, a distinction so set forth . . . designedly and ingeniously, in order to suggest to the Gentile Christians greater esteem for their weaker Jewish brethren."] It is true that there were *promises* of salvation for the Gentiles in the Old Testament, and that some of these promises were addressed directly *to* the Gentiles, as was true of the implied promises in ver. 10, 11; yet, as the prophets spoke and wrote immediately and chiefly to and for the Jews, the truth of God could not be said to be pledged to the former as directly and fully as to the latter. There was a formal *covenant* in the latter case, which there was not in the former; and this distinction is often recognized in the Scriptures as it is here. The quotation in ver. 9 is from Ps. 18 : 49 [and, save the omission of the word Lord, exactly accords with the LXX.] The words are put into the mouth of the Psalmist; but David here speaks as a type of Christ. [Philippi supposes the person offering praise may be "any messenger of salvation to the Gentile world."]

10, 11, 12. And again he saith, or, *it saith*—that is, the Scripture [which is easily understood from the words 'it is written' in the preceding verse]. **Rejoice, ye Gentiles, with his people.** These words are from Deut. 32 : 43 [and exactly follow the LXX.]. In the original Hebrew, as the English intimates by italics, there is nothing (save in one MS., Codex 146) to answer to the preposition 'with.' Literally it reads: "Rejoice, ye Gentiles, his people." Rejoice, ye nations, for **you,**

12 And again, Esaias saith, There shall be a root of Jesse, and he that shall rise to reign over the Gentiles; in him shall the Gentiles trust.
13 Now the God of hope fill you with all joy and peace in believing, that ye may abound in hope, through the power of the Holy Ghost.
14 And I myself also am persuaded of you, my

12 And again, Isaiah saith,
  There shall be the root of Jesse,
  And he that ariseth to rule over the Gentiles;
  On him shall the Gentiles hope.
13 Now the God of hope fill you with all joy and peace in believing, that ye may abound in hope, in the power of the Holy Spirit.
14 And I myself also am persuaded of you, my brethren,

too, have become his people. **And again**—in still another place. This is from Ps. 117 : 1 [and nearly accords with the LXX., 116 : 1]. A double exhortation to praise the Lord, addressed first to all nations, and secondly, to all peoples (for this word is in the plural number as well as the other). The two verbs differ in the Hebrew, as well as in the English, like the two nouns; but in both cases and in both languages they are substantially synonymous, the duplication being for the sake of emphasis and the difference for the sake of variety. [The verbs, though the same in the Greek (save that the latter is a compound), are in different tenses, the present and the aorist (the latter in the Revision being in the third person imperative instead of the second), yet the distinction in the meaning of these tenses seems here to be disregarded.] **And again, Esaias saith.** This is from Isa. 11 : 10 [and accords mainly with the LXX., while it varies considerably from the Hebrew. Davidson says: "The apostle, as in many other places, gives the sense without the exact words"]. **A root of Jesse** means here *an offspring of Jesse*, or a root shoot, as David was, and through David the Messiah, who was to reign over Jews and Gentiles with a wider and more permanent reign than David's was; and **in him** [literally, *on whom*, as a foundation] **shall the Gentiles trust,** or *hope*, as it should be rendered here, to agree with the corresponding noun in the next verse. ["The Gentiles formerly had no hope. See Eph. 2 : 12." (Bengel.)] It should be noticed that in these confirmatory citations [adduced one after another as with deepest emotion] the apostle quotes from the law (ver. 10), *the prophets* (ver. 12), and the Psalms (ver. 9, 11), thus bringing into the service of his argument all the parts of the threefold division of the Old Testament common among the Jews, and recognized by our Lord in Luke 24 : 44. [Query: Is there for Christian teachers and preachers any better way of viewing and of using the Old Testament Scriptures than that which Christ and his apostles practiced? See ver. 4.]

13. Now the God of hope. [Now may the God who gives *the hope* of eternal glory, **fill you with all** (with highest, with all possible) **joy and peace in believing**—without which 'believing,' or faith, there could be no joy or peace, and without which joy and peace, faith would be fruitless (Meyer)—in order **that ye may abound in hope, through** (in virtue of) **the power of the Holy Ghost,** who dwelleth and worketh in you. What large provision God—the God of constancy, of consolation, and of hope—has made that we, in the midst of earthly cares and sorrows, and with all our inward trials, may yet have hope and peace and joy—have them, too, in their highest measure, and have them in us continually, even as a well of water springing up, overflowing, and refreshing the soul unto everlasting life! It is a characteristic of Paul that he insists so much upon the Christian's *abounding* in grace and in every good work, and nothing could be more characteristically Pauline than this entire passage. (Boise.)] This verse forms an appropriate and beautiful close to the practical and hortatory part of the Epistle. The devout wish which Paul expresses is rich in the blessings of religious experience. Notice in respect to these blessings the excellence of their nature, the fullness of their measure, and the divine perfection of their source. How extravagant this wish would be if addressed to any but regenerate persons! What do any others know of fullness of joy and peace in believing, and of the power of the Holy Ghost?

IV. PERSONAL. (Ch. 15 : 14–16 : 23.)

The fourth division of the Epistle we have named Personal, because in it the apostle indicates the motives and feelings that prompted him to write. (15 : 14-33.) In the first place, he excuses his boldness. (Ver. 14-16.)

14. And I myself. ["Notwithstanding my exhortations." (De Wette.) **Also am persuaded.** Compare 8 : 38; 14 : 14. The particle translated 'and' is transitional, "leading over to the concluding portion of the Epistle." (Meyer.)] This emphatic assertion of his own persuasion in regard to their Chris-

brethren, that ye also are full of goodness, filled with all knowledge, able also to admonish one another.

15 Nevertheless, brethren, I have written the more boldly unto you in some sort, as putting you in mind, because of the grace that is given to me of God,

16 That I should be the minister of Jesus Christ to the Gentiles, ministering the gospel of God, that the offering up of the Gentiles might be acceptable, being sanctified by the Holy Ghost.

that ye yourselves are full of goodness, filled with all
15 knowledge, able also to admonish one another. But I write the more boldly unto you in some measure, as putting you again in remembrance, because of the
16 grace that was given me of God, that I should be a minister of Christ Jesus unto the Gentiles, [1] ministering the gospel of God, that the offering up of the Gentiles might be made acceptable, being sanctified

---

1 Gr. *ministering in sacrifice.*

---

tian character may, perhaps, have tacit reference to the high reputation which they enjoyed in the general judgment of mankind. See 1 : 8. The expressions **full of goodness, filled with all knowledge,** are not to be taken in their *highest possible* sense, but in a sober sense, sincere, and without flattery, and so taken they are a strong commendation of the disciples at Rome. The apostle evidently regarded them, as a whole, as persons of great Christian excellence, and there is no reason why *we* should regard them otherwise. **Able also to admonish one another,** and therefore not standing in *special need* of admonition from me or from others. Observe the qualifications needed for mutual admonition—large attainments in goodness and knowledge. [It requires quite as much wisdom and grace to give admonition properly as to receive it.]

15. I have written [properly, *I wrote.* Some regard this as the "epistolary aorist," the past tense being used by the writer instead of the present, because to the receiver the time of writing would be as past. Others think the past tense was employed here, because the Epistle was regarded as brought to a conclusion. **The more boldly**—"than from your Christian attainment was necessary." (Winer.)] The expression **in some sort**— literally, *in part*—qualifies the words *have written the more boldly,* and intimates that the boldness with which he has written (notwithstanding his good opinion of them, *nevertheless*) was limited to certain *parts* of the Epistle; such, perhaps, as 6 : 12-19 ; 11 : 17-25 ; 13 : 14. **Putting you in mind,** recalling to your memory, not as if I was giving some ideas or instructions of which you were altogether ignorant. **Because of the grace**—my apostolic office was the ground and reason of my boldness. [In 12 : 3, we have: "through (by means of) the grace.]" We have here an admirable combination of humility, courtesy, and dignity. [The grace referred to was given to Paul from God, through the mediate agency of Christ. (1 : 5.)

By reason of this abundant grace conferred on the apostle, and from the fact that he spoke and wrote "by revelation of Jesus Christ" (16 : 25 ; Gal. 1 : 12 ; Eph. 3 : 2, 3), his Epistles are to be received as something higher than merely human compositions, even as a message from God, or 'gospel of God.' If our advanced thinkers have had more revealed to them from heaven, and if they have more of God-given grace than Paul had, his utterances may well be made to give place to their improved theologic formulas, or, nebulous platitudes.]

16. That I should be the minister of Jesus Christ to the Gentiles. This explains what he means by the grace given to him of God. It was the favor of being called to be the apostle of the Gentiles. He elsewhere speaks very emphatically of this calling as a signal favor from God. (Eph. 3 : 8.) The words translated *minister* and *ministering* (λειτουργόν and ἱερουργοῦντα), though not having the same etymological relation to each other which the English words have, are yet alike in this, that both are based on the figurative representation of a priestly service. [On the word *minister,* one who ministers or serves in a public capacity, see 13 : 6. The verb occurs in 15 : 27 ; Acts 13 : 2 ; Heb. 10 : 11. The word for 'ministering' occurs only here. This sacrifical service is not to make an offering of the gospel, but to do holy service in the gospel, by means of which the offering (of the Gentiles) is prepared. (Cremer.) What an honor God conferred on the persecuting Saul of Tarsus, that he should be appointed an apostle and a priest to the Gentile world to prepare and present them as an offering to the Lord Jesus Christ!] This is believed to be the only passage where a word implying a *priestly* character or action is used, even figuratively, in reference to an apostle. The New Testament carefully abstains from applying the word *priest* to an apostle or preacher of the gospel. Christ is the Priest of the New Dispensation ; he alone offers sacrifice in the strict sense of the word. (Heb. 8 : 3.) **The**

17 I have therefore whereof I may glory through Jesus Christ in those things which pertain to God.
18 For I will not dare to speak of any of those things which Christ hath not wrought by me, to make the Gentiles obedient, by word and deed,
19 Through mighty signs and wonders, by the power

17 by the Holy Spirit. I have therefore my glorying in Christ Jesus in things pertaining to God. For I will
18 not dare to speak of any [1] things save those which Christ wrought through me, for the obedience of the
19 Gentiles, by word and deed, in the power of signs and wonders, in the power of [2] the Holy Spirit; so

---

1 Gr. *of those things which Christ wrought not through me* .....2 Many ancient authorities read *the Spirit of God.* One reads *the Spirit*

---

offering up of the Gentiles. This is what is called by the grammarians the genitive of apposition. The Gentiles are the offering. [This 'offering up,' or, simply, offering (προσφορὰ), 'of the Gentiles,' properly denotes a bloodless sacrifice. Paul's priestly service in preaching to the Gentiles was in order that the offering of the Gentiles might be well-pleasing, being *sanctified in* the element of the Holy Spirit's influence. This last clause " forms an antithesis to the external consecration of the Old Testament sacrifices." (Philippi.) In 12: 1, all Christians are, as priests, exhorted to offer a sacrifice to God, even their own bodies.]

In ver. 17-22, the apostle declares the extent and result of his apostolic labors.

17. [Therefore draws an inference from ver. 15, 16, which speak of his divinely appointed ministry to the Gentiles, **I have whereof I may glory,** literally, *the* glorying, equivalent to *my* glorying, as in the Revised Version. Yet this glorying was not in himself, but in Christ Jesus.] His glorying was no selfish or vain boasting, but **in those things which pertain to God**—that is, in his office and ministry; and in the way in which, **through Jesus Christ,** he had fulfilled his apostolical commission he might well glory as he does in 1 Cor. 15: 10, being careful, however, to give all the credit to the grace of God.[1]

18. The apostle was very careful not to appropriate to himself the credit of what others had wrought. He preferred pioneer work (ver. 20, 21), that he might not build on another man's foundation, or seem to boast of things made ready to his hand by others. (2 Cor. 10: 12-17.) He intimates, in the passage last referred to, that some professed servants of Christ were not equally scrupulous in this regard. [There seem to be two principal views which have guided expositors in the interpretation of this passage. One is that Paul by emphasizing the personal pronoun (δἰ ἐμοῦ, or, through me) or

the verb 'wrought,' contrasts himself with others, and his actual labors with those which others had professedly performed, and that he wishes to take no credit for labors which he, with Christ's help, had not actually performed. Another and preferable view (which, in harmony with the preceding verses, emphasizes ' *Christ*' rather than ' *me*') is, that Paul contrasts himself with Christ, and that he will take no credit to his labors save only as they are wrought by Christ. So far as the words are concerned, they will allow still another thought (favored by Godet)—namely, that almost everything had been wrought by Christ through Paul for the conversion of the Gentiles; he could hardly mention anything which had not been done. The relative 'which' stands for *of those things which.*] **To make the Gentiles obedient**—[literally, *for the obedience of the Gentiles.*] This was his aim, and it was largely successful; but while their actual obedience, in every case, was not necessary to the peace of his conscience, it was necessary to the full joy of his heart. His duty might be fulfilled without this, but not his desire. **By word and deed.** These words are to be connected with the clause: 'which Christ hath not wrought,' etc. Christ wrought through the apostle, to the conversion of the Gentiles, by deeds as well as by words. From this point the sentence is completed as if it had been begun in an affirmative and not in a negative form. [The two negatives, occurring in two different clauses blended by attraction, are yet equivalent to an affirmative. (Winer, 498.)]

19. Through mighty signs and wonders. [Better, *in the power of signs and wonders.*] The miraculous signs and wonders which Christ wrought by Paul [and which may be placed under the category of 'deed'] not only served as a proof of his apostleship (2 Cor. 12: 12), but also tended effectually to make the Gentiles obedient. See Acts 13: 9-12. But

---

1 In the phrase: 'things which pertain to God' (for like phraseology, see Heb. 2: 17; 5: 1) we have what is sometimes termed the Greek accusative, or accusative of

synecdoche, called by Buttmann, p. 152, the accusative of limitation. See on 12: 18.—(F.)

of the Spirit of God ; so that from Jerusalem, and round about unto Illyricum, I have fully preached the gospel of Christ.

20 Yea, so have I strived to preach the gospel, not where Christ was named, lest I should build upon another man's foundation :

that from Jerusalem, and round about even unto Illyricum, I have [1] fully preached the gospel of Christ ; yea, [2] making it my aim so to preach the gospel, not where Christ was *already* named, that I

---

1 Gr. *fulfilled* ...... 2 Gr. *being ambitious.*

---

it was the power of the Spirit of God [or the Holy Spirit, as in the Revision] that wrought most effectually to this end. Indeed, without this, the 'mighty signs and wonders' would not have brought a single Gentile soul to the saving obedience of faith. [Of these two forms of miracles, "the 'sign' includes more an objective, the 'wonder' more a subjective reference." (Philippi) The latter word, derived from a verb signifying *to watch*, is primarily "a sign claiming the observation, the wonder of men." It is never found alone in the New Testament. In 2 Cor. 12 : 12, Paul speaks to these very Corinthians in whose city he is now writing of the signs, wonders, and powers performed through him among them as signs of his apostleship. See Acts 14 : 3 ; 15 : 12 ; 16 : 16, seq. ; 19 : 11 ; 20 : 10, where mention is made of miracles wrought by the hands of Paul.] **So that from Jerusalem, and round about** [literally, and *in a circuit round*, in the regions surrounding Jerusalem]. He takes Jerusalem and its environs as his starting point, as that was the place where the other apostles, according to the Lord's direction (Luke 24 : 47), began their work, and where he himself first joined their fellowship (Acts 9 : 26-28), although he had before this preached at Damascus (Acts 9 : 19-22), and probably also in Arabia. (Gal. 1 : 17.) **Unto Illyricum.** This was a district lying along the eastern coast of the Adriatic. We have no mention in the Acts of Paul's preaching in that country ; but we know, from Acts 20 : 1-3, that he traversed Macedonia, which was adjacent to Illyricum, a short time before he wrote this Epistle ; and he probably at that time crossed the boundary and preached in Illyricum. He mentions this as the western limit, at that time, of his evangelical labors. From Jerusalem, a curve northerly and westerly to Illyricum, would be a distance of not far from fourteen hundred miles in length. [" Upon the southeast *terminus a quo* follows the northwest *terminus ad quem.*" (Philippi.) In 2 Tim. 4 : 10 we read of Titus going to Dal-

matia, a part of the Roman province of Illyricum, where Paul himself had probably labored (Acts 20 : 2), and whither he himself may have sent Titus.] **I have fully preached** [literally, *fulfilled*, **the gospel of Christ,** in its spirit and purpose, by preaching. Meyer : Brought to fulfillment—that is, spread the gospel abroad everywhere. Compare Col. 1 : 25 ; Acts 12 : 25. The gospel of Christ had been proclaimed in the most important places throughout this extensive circuit. The word 'Christ' in Paul's writings generally takes the article when dependent as here upon a preceding word. Were the apostle again on earth, could he not find a 'place' (ver. 23) and a necessity, too, in this same vast region for once more preaching 'the gospel of Christ' in its native simplicity, purity, and power ? Were he permitted to do so, he would, methinks, tell these peoples, as he did the Galatians : " Ye observe days and months and times and years. I am afraid of you, lest I have bestowed upon you labor in vain." (Gal. 4 : 10, 11.) Little did he imagine that after the lapse of eighteen centuries a few Christian people from this then unknown Western world would go to labor in those same regions as missionaries of the cross of Christ.] **20. Yea, so**—that is, according to the rule mentioned in the remainder of the verse. **Have I strived**—literally, *making it a point of honor.*[1] The verb translated 'strived' is used in only two other places : 2 Cor. 5 : 9 (translated "labor"), and 1 Thess. 4 : 11 (translated "study"). Comparing the three passages, we are led to infer that the apostle's idea of true *honor* in Christian service was this, that he was *ambitious*, as we might, without much license, translate the word, to do the most unostentatious, the most needful, the most laborious, the most self-denying work for Christ. The church would have great peace, and the whole world would soon have the gospel, if all ministers of Christ had this spirit. **Not** [this introduces the negative specification of the *so*, as the following *but* (ver. 21) introduces

---

[1] Instead of this participle agreeing with με in ver. 19. several manuscripts have the finite verb, which, however, is commonly regarded as a correction.—*s*

21 But as it is written, To whom he was not spoken of, they shall see: and they that have not heard shall understand.
22 For which cause also I have been much hindered from coming to you.
23 But now having no more place in these parts, and having a great desire these many years to come unto you;
24 Whensoever I take my journey into Spain, I will come to you: for I trust to see you in my journey, and

might not build upon another man's foundation:
21 but, as it is written,
They shall see, to whom no tidings of him came,
And they who have not heard shall understand.
22 Wherefore also I was hindered these many times
23 from coming to you: but now, having no more any place in these regions, and having these many years
24 a longing to come unto you, whensoever I go unto Spain (for I hope to see you in my journey, and to

the positive. (De Wette.)] **where Christ was named,** or where the gospel had been already preached. He preferred to do strictly pioneer missionary work in regions destitute of the gospel, and where the necessity was the most urgent, rather than **build upon another man's foundation.** [Dr. Gifford remarks that " Paul's letters to the Colossians and Laodiceans (among whom he had not labored at the time of writing to them) are sufficient proof that in writing to the Church at Rome he was not transgressing his rule to avoid building on another man's foundation." It seems almost needless to say that the apostle, in avoiding a field thus partially cultivated, had no selfish or unworthy motive.]

21. Having in the latter part of the previous verse described negatively the rule by which he was governed in selecting the field of his evangelistic labors, Paul now describes it positively by a quotation from Isa. 52: 15, taken quite literally from the LXX. [**To whom he was not spoken of**—literally, *to whom it was not announced concerning him.* The last two words, rightly filling out the sense, are not in the original Hebrew, but in the LXX. **They shall understand.** The verb means to send together, here, "to bring the outward object into connection with the inward sense." (Liddell and Scott.)]

22. For which cause—that is, on account of the above rule of choosing my field of labor [or, as De Wette states it: "because I had enough to do from Jerusalem to Illyricum"]. **I have been much hindered,** or, *many times hindered.* Compare 1: 13. [Some MSS. here read "often," as in 1: 13. The rendering of the Vulgate, *plerumque, for the most part,* supposes that Paul had other hindrances. The imperfect tense of the verb denotes in itself a continuous hindrance. The verb, denoting separation, is naturally followed by the genitive (here the genitive infinitive) as the case of departure or separation. Farrar notices that several expressions in this chapter are closely

analogous to some in the first chapter.] **From coming to you,** to whom I knew the gospel had been successfully preached. [Yet the fact that the Roman Church was founded by others was not the hindrance referred to, for this still remained. What hindered the apostle was his abundant labors in founding churches in destitute places in the East.]

23. Having no more place in these parts—having fully preached the gospel in the regions east of this, I regard my apostolic work in these parts as finished. [The whole statement shows that the hindrances referred to were now removed. According to Meyer, one motive which induced Paul now to visit Rome and the West, was the nearness of the coming of the Lord, which the apostle expected to behold in the flesh, but which could not take place, as the apostle himself has taught us, till the fullness of the Gentiles was brought in, and all Israel were saved! Who can think it possible that the apostle had such great expectations?] **Having a great desire** (*a longing,* it might well be translated) **these many years to come unto you.** It was about four years since Paul had met at Corinth Aquila and Priscilla, then lately come from Rome (Acts 18: 1-3); and although what he had heard from them during the time of his intimate connection with them (Acts 18: 3), doubtless increased his interest in the church at Rome, and his great desire to visit them (Acts 19: 21), we need not suppose that this was the first knowledge he had received of them. Probably he would hardly have spoken of his desire to visit them, as one which he had cherished for *many years,* if it had not been of longer date than that.

24. [The most important MSS. omit **I will come to you,** and retain the **for;** and this reading, though somewhat difficult and broken, is adopted by Westcott and Hort, and by the Revisers. Godet and Meyer drop the 'for,' thus making it all smooth reading. **Whensoever** (*as soon as.* see 1 Cor. 11: 34; Phil. 2:

to be brought on my way thitherward by you, if first I
be somewhat filled with your *company.*
25 But now I go unto Jerusalem to minister unto the
saints.

be brought on my way thitherward by you, if first
in some measure I shall have been satisfied with
25 your company),—but now, *I say,* I go unto Jerusalem,
26 ministering unto the saints. For it hath been the

---

23) **I take my journey into Spain, I will
come to you.**] Whether the apostle ever
made this journey to Spain cannot be possibly
determined.[1] If he did, it must have been at
a later period than that at which the Acts of
the Apostles ends. There is much reason to
think that between the time of the imprisonment at Rome, mentioned in the last chapter
of Acts, and his martyrdom in that city, he
was liberated, traveled in the Eastern parts,
and wrote the First Epistle to Timothy, and
the Epistle to Titus, after these things; and
then was a second time imprisoned in Rome,
where he wrote his Second Epistle to Timothy
shortly before his martyrdom. This view is
ably presented and defended in an appendix
at the close of the second volume of the work
on the "Life and Epistles of Paul," by Conybeare and Howson. But if the certainty of
this release and second imprisonment could be
made out, it would not carry with it the certainty that the apostle made his intended visit
to Spain during that intervening period between his two imprisonments. The early tradition is too vague and scanty to be the basis
of an intelligent belief. Probably this part of
the apostle's plan of his own life and labors
was never realized. **And to be brought on
my way thitherward by you.** Probably
he was accustomed, in his missionary travels,
to be escorted on his way, for a greater or less
distance, by some of the brethren whom he
was leaving (see Acts 15: 3; 17: 14, 15; 20:
38; 21: 5, 16 [compare 1 Cor. 16: 6; 2 Cor.
1: 16]), and he was hoping to receive the same
courtesy from them on his way to Spain. **If
first I be somewhat filled with your company.** The word 'company' is not in the

original Greek, but it is well supplied by the
translators, being, in fact, implied, and requisite to complete the sense. [The last clause,
literally rendered, is: *If I may first in part
be made full of you*—satisfied with your company—"not so much as I might wish, but as
much as circumstances will permit." (Grotius.) The delicacy of the apostle in all this
representation is genuine and consummate.
Prof. Boise, in his notes on this passage, says:
"It is a common experience in this world that
we cannot see enough of those whom we love.
Yonder there will be no more parting!" Yet
very precious and blessed to us in our frequent
earthly farewells, is the sentiment once addressed to the venerable missionary, Dr. Wil-
liam G. Schauffler, by Maria Dorothea, the
Christian Archduchess of Austria, on occasion
of his leave-taking, that "Christians never
see each other for the last time."] Paul was
evidently looking forward to a short sojourn
with the Roman brethren which would partly
(somewhat) satisfy his wishes; but only in
part, on account of its shortness. How different was the fact from his expectation! He
dwelt *two whole years* among them bound
with a chain. (Acts 28: 20, 30.)

25. But now—before I can indulge my
cherished longing to visit you. [This is mentioned as a hindrance to any immediate visit.
These words, 'but now,' which seem to connect
back with going to Spain, etc., occur also in
the beginning of ver. 23.] **I go** (*am going*) **to
Jerusalem** [his fifth journey thither, see Acts
9: 26; 11: 30; 15: 4; 18: 21.] **To minister**
(literally, *ministering*, present participle; the
journey was a part of the ministering) **unto
the saints.** ["Only they would that we

---

[1] The most important evidence in favor of the apostle's
visit to Spain is the testimony of Clement, the third
bishop of Rome, supposed by many to be the Clement
mentioned in Phil. 4: 3. In his first letter to the Corinthians, Clement writes as follows: "Paul received the
prize of endurance, having borne chains seven times,
having been banished, stoned, and having become a
herald in the East and in the West, teaching the whole
world; and having come *to the limit of the West;*
and having witnessed (as a martyr) before rulers, he
was thus released from the world, and went unto the
holy place." It is commonly and truly supposed that
Clement, living at Rome, could not speak of that city

or region as "the limit of the West." Muratori's
"Fragment on the Canon," written about A. D. 170,
makes mention of the "journey of Paul, setting forth
from the city (of Rome?) for Spain." Jerome, who
spent his early years in Rome, speaks of Paul as having
been set free by Nero that he might preach the gospel
"also in the regions of the West." Chrysostom and
Theodoret assert that the apostle went to Spain after
his imprisonment at Rome, and Irenæus refers to
churches in Spain as being somewhat ancient in his
times. *Spania* is another form of *Hispania,* usually
called *Iberia.*—(F.)

26 For it hath pleased them of Macedonia and Achaia to make a certain contribution for the poor saints which are at Jerusalem.

27 It hath pleased them verily , and their debtors they are. For if the Gentiles have been made partakers of their spiritual things, their duty is also to minister unto them in carnal things.

28 When therefore I have performed this, and have sealed to them this fruit, I will come by you into Spain.

good pleasure of Macedonia and Achaia to make a certain contribution for the poor among the saints 27 that are at Jerusalem. Yea, it hath been their good pleasure; and their debtors they are. For if the Gentiles have been made partakers of their spiritual things, they owe it *to them* also to minister unto 28 them in carnal things. When therefore I have accomplished this, and have sealed to them this fruit,

should remember the poor, which very thing I was also zealous to do.'' (Gal. 2: 10.) Paul had once before, in company with Barnabas, carried relief unto the brethren that dwelt in Judea. (Acts 11: 30.)] In reference to this proposed journey and ministering, compare Acts 19: 21; 20: 22; 24: 17; 1 Cor. 16: 1; 2 Cor. 8: 1-6; 9: 1. Such coincidences as these, of which we have many striking instances in the New Testament, not only throw light on the date of the epistles, but being evidently unstudied, are among the strongest evidences of historic truth. See Paley's '' Horæ Paulinæ.''

26. [**For it hath pleased them,** etc.—literally, *for Macedonia and Achaia were pleased,* or, thought it good. Instead of Achaia, we have in Acts 20: 2, Hellas, the more usual classic term for Greece. In his letters to the Corinthians (1 Cor. 16: 1; 2 Cor. 9: 2, and in this place), Paul, as Bengel remarks, ''proposes the Galatians as as an example to the Corinthians, the Corinthians to the Macedonians, and the Corinthians and Macedonians to the Romans. Great is the power of examples.'' Some have surmised that Paul is here giving a gentle hint to the Romans that a contribution from them would be acceptable, but this is altogether improbable. The earnest yet most delicate manner which he uses when seeking a contribution may be seen in 2 Cor., chapters 8 and 9. Query: Was it one motive of the apostle, in dwelling so long on this subject in his letter to the Corinthians, to stop their dissensions and divisions by enlisting their thoughts and energies in this charitable work? The word for **contribution** properly means a sharing of, or participation in, anything. It is frequently rendered fellowship, and it is the word which stands for the ''communion'' (that is, a partaking) of the body and blood of Christ. (1 Cor. 10: 16.) Compare also 2 Cor. 13: 14: ''The communion of the Holy Ghost.'' A fellowship or sharing in the necessities of others naturally finds its outward expression in the taking up of a collection

for them or making a contribution. The verb meaning *to share in,* sometimes rendered to distribute or communicate, occurs in the next verse and in 12: 13. Paul speaks somewhat slightingly of the contribution as 'a certain,' because any amount of material gifts conferred would to him appear small in comparison with the spiritual blessings received.] **For the poor saints**—literally, *poor of the saints,* implying that they were not all poor, and also implying that the alleged community of goods in the church at Jerusalem, if any such thing, in the proper sense of the words, had ever existed there, had ceased to exist before this.

27. It hath pleased them verily [better, *for they were pleased to do so*]. They have done it voluntarily, yet they have done only their *duty,* for **their debtors they are.** Having received from the Jewish believers in Jerusalem such great spiritual blessings, they are under obligation to supply, according to their ability, the temporal necessities of their Jewish brethren. [The word for 'debtors' is derived from a verb meaning *ought, it is a duty.*[1] The apostle regards this ministering to the bodily necessities of the saints as a priestly service for Christ and as truly a religious service as the preaching of the gospel of God. See in ver. 16, and compare Acts 13: 2. This is but one text out of many which makes it the duty of those who are taught in the word to communicate unto him that teacheth in ''carnal things'' and in ''all good things.'' (Gal. 6: 6; 1 Cor. 9: 11, 13, 14; 1 Tim. 5: 17, 18.)]

28. When therefore I have performed this, and have sealed to them this fruit—have made this contribution ['this fruit' of the faith and love of the Gentiles (Alford)] securely theirs, by actually delivering it into their hands—**I will come by you** [*through you,* through your city. Compare 2 Cor. 1: 16. The verb is sometimes used in the sense of coming back]. I will visit you on my way to Spain. See notes on ver. 24. [''Would a

1 Verbs of sharing usually govern the genitive (see Heb. 2: 14), but the verb here signifying *to participate in* is followed by the dative, as in 12: 13.—(F.)

29 And I am sure that, when I come unto you, I shall come in the fulness of the blessing of the gospel of Christ.

30 Now I beseech you, brethren, for the Lord Jesus Christ's sake, and for the love of the Spirit, that ye strive together with me in *your* prayers to God for me;

31 That I may be delivered from them that do not believe in Judea; and that my service which *I have* for Jerusalem may be accepted of the saints;

32 That I may come unto you with joy by the will of God, and may with you be refreshed.

29 I will go on by you unto Spain. And I know that, when I come unto you, I shall come in the fulness of the blessing of Christ.

30 Now I beseech you, brethren, by our Lord Jesus Christ, and by the love of the Spirit, that ye strive together with me in your prayers to God for me;

31 that I may be delivered from them that are disobedient in Judæa, and *that* my ministration which *I have* for Jerusalem may be acceptable to the saints;

32 that I may come unto you in joy through the will of

forger, writing in the apostle's name in the second century, have made him pen a plan of the future so different from the way in which things really came to pass?" (Godet.)]

29. And I am sure that, when I come, etc. The apostle's assurance on this subject [his bringing with him such abundance of spiritual blessing from Christ] was founded, not only on his conscious desire and purpose to do them good, but also, doubtless, on the remembrance of his experience in other churches that he had visited. ["Not many men would venture to speak so emphatically, but Paul was always perfectly frank in expressing what he felt." (Boise.)] **Of the gospel.** These words should be omitted, as lacking in the best manuscripts. *In the fullness of the blessing of Christ* is the true reading. This result, which he refers to in other words in 1 : 11, 12, was doubtless realized when he did at last visit them, though his expectation may not have been realized in regard to his journey to Spain.

30. Now I beseech you, brethren, for the Lord Jesus Christ's sake [I exhort you *through the Lord Jesus Christ* (a tender appeal to the Christian's heart), **and for** (or, *by*) **the love of the Spirit** (that love which is poured forth in the hearts of believers by the Holy Spirit), **that ye strive together with me,**—strive earnestly, wrestle together (as in the games),—**in your prayers to God for me.** Bengel says that "Paul is the only apostle who asks the prayers of believers for himself." In nearly all his epistles (see 2 Cor. 1 : 11; Eph. 6 : 19; Phil. 1 : 19; Col. 4 : 3; 1 Thess. 5 : 25; 2 Thess. 3 : 1; Philem. 22)[1] he entreats the prayers and supplications of his brethren in his behalf. Surely he must have thought that the "supplication of a righteous man availeth much." And if such a man as

he—inspired of God, endowed to work miracles, strong in faith, and gifted with mental endowments of the highest order—felt the need of the prayers of his brethren, how much more deeply may we feel the need of striving together, with and for one another, in prayer to God! More especially should they who are 'separated unto the gospel of God' have the earnest and constant—yea, the *wrestling* prayers of God's people]. Paul's manner is peculiarly earnest and solemn here. He not only asks their prayers, but asks them to 'strive' in prayer, and this, not only 'for the Lord Jesus Christ's sake,' which is no unusual expression with him, but also 'for the love of the Spirit,' an unprecedented and remarkable phrase, meaning that love of which the Holy Spirit is the author. See Gal. 5 : 22; Col. 1 : 8. This peculiar earnestness and solemnity finds its explanation in the following verse.

31. That I may be delivered, etc. He knew how bitter was the hatred of the unbelieving Jews toward him since his conversion (Acts 22 : 22), and with what suspicion he was regarded by the believers in Jerusalem [the Jewish *saints*, "all zealots for the law"]; see Acts 20 : 22, 23; 21 : 10-14, 20, 21; so that, although he was going to the latter on an errand of beneficence, he had reason to fear that his **service . . . for Jerusalem** ["my ministration[2] which is for Jerusalem"] might not be accepted; and the result showed that his forebodings were not without reason. See Acts 21-23.

32. That I may come unto you with joy. This is the third object for which he asks them to strive in prayer for him. It was most intimately connected with the preceding two. If the first (first half of ver. 31) was not granted, he could not come unto them at all; if the second (last half of ver. 31) was not granted, he could not come *with joy.* He

---

[1] Those who hold to the Pauline authorship of the "Hebrews" would cite 13 : 18 of that epistle. In most of his letters he assures his readers of his supplications on their behalf. See Rom. 1 : 9; 2 Cor. 13 : 7-9; Eph. 1 : 16; Phil. 1 : 4, 9; Col. 1 : 3, 9; 1 Thess. 1 : 2 (3 : 10); 2 Thess. 1 : 11; 2 Tim. 1 : 3; Philem. 4, etc.—(F.)

[2] For 'ministration' certain MSS. have the explanatory, *gift-bringing.*—(F.)

33 Now the God of peace *be* with you all. Amen. | 33 God, and together with you find rest. Now the God of peace be with you all. Amen.

hoped to be **refreshed** [that he *might find rest for himself*, after his many toils and dangers] by his Christian intercourse with them. [In many respects the apostle's prayer and the prayers of his brethren for him were not literally answered. He was indeed' delivered' out of the hands of the Jews, but this deliverance was into two years' imprisonment in Cæsarea, to be followed by a wearisomely protracted sea-voyage, with its attendant shipwreck, and this again by a two years' imprisonment in bonds at Rome. Instead of this he hoped soon to visit Rome, to be prospered on his journey thither, to be filled and refreshed with their company for a brief period, and then to be sent forward by them to Spain as the chief seat and scene of his labors. He did indeed 'see Rome'; he did go there, we must suppose, 'in the fullness of the blessing of Christ,' and not wholly without 'joy.' He did, doubtless, impart to the believers there 'some spiritual gift,' and though an ambassador of Christ in chains, he yet had, as we have seen at 1: 15, large opportunities for preaching the gospel in the world's capital, and he doubtless reaped there 'some fruit,' even as he had done among the rest of the Gentiles. Still his prayers were not fully answered. What then? Did Paul accuse himself, or were there any in his day to accuse him of "want of faith" as the reason his prayers were not answered to the letter? Far enough from this. Paul indeed prayed that he might be 'prospered' in his journey toward Rome, and that he ' might come in joy '; but his true prayer was that he might be prospered *in the will of God* (1: 10), and that he might come *through the will of God* (or, as several MSS. read : through the will of Christ Jesus). But it was God's will that Paul should visit Rome as a prisoner in chains, and it was the will and counsel of his Lord and Saviour that he should suffer still other things "for his name's sake." (Acts 9: 16.) But did not Paul, after all, make a mistake when he compromised with those law-zealous saints in Jerusalem? We have sometimes thought that he did so. But who knows best? Suppose that Paul, after stopping a few days in Judæa, had set out for Rome, and that after a prosperous journey thither and a short period of rest in that place, he had gone to Spain, and that he

had always had his liberty, never seeing the inside of a prison's walls, would this have been best for the world and the Church of Christ? Should we not have sadly missed his prison experience? And what could we have done without those prison letters of his, some of them, it may be, written with his own chained right hand? Is not "Paul, a prisoner of Christ Jesus," vastly better for the world than Paul with any other epithet? Was not Bunyan in prison a thousand times better for the cause of Christ than a Bunyan at liberty? If these things are so, then we may say that the prayers of Paul, whose meat and drink it was to do and suffer for the cause and glory of his Saviour, and according to his will, were answered—not answered, indeed, according to the plan he had marked out, but in a way which divine wisdom saw best. And who can tell us any better way? But it may be asked, whether God may not by his Spirit instruct the believer's mind, lead him to see just what to pray for, and give him the faith which will receive the exact answer desired? Certainly, he may do so; and some of the promises made by Christ specially, perhaps, to his more immediate disciples, and certain passages in one or two of the epistles have a look in this direction. But we do not think that God does this now, save in exceptional cases, nor do we think that even in these cases he invariably permits the praying man to know beforehand that his prayer will be answered to the very letter. It seems to me that if such faith and knowledge were given to any man, they would have been given to the apostle Paul. But they were certainly withholden from him when he prayed for the removal of the "thorn in the flesh" (2 Cor. 12: 7), and for a speedy and prosperous journey to Rome and to Spain.]

33. Now the God of peace be with you all. [A prayer naturally called forth by the thought of this world's unrest. Thankful we may well be to the God of grace and peace that, amid earthly toils and troubles, we may have "the inward peace of conscience, the fraternal peace of friendship, the heavenly peace of glory." (Lyra.)] This appears to be the end of the Epistle. It would be a very appropriate ending, especially in view of the last three chapters. It is supposed by some that

CHAPTER XVI.

I COMMEND unto you Phebe our sister, which is a servant of the church which is at Cenchrea: 2 That ye receive her in the Lord, as becometh saints, and that ye assist her in whatsoever business she hath need of you: for she hath been a succourer of many, and of myself also.	1 I commend unto you Phebe our sister, who is a 2 ¹ servant of the church that is at Cenchreæ: that ye receive her in the Lord, worthily of the saints, and that ye assist her in whatsoever matter she may have need of you: for she herself also hath been a succourer of many, and of mine own self.

¹ Or, *deaconess.*

---

the apostle penned this benediction as the termination of his letter, but not finding an opportunity to send it to Rome as soon as he expected, afterward added the salutations and other contents of chapter 16. If this supposition were true, we might be well thankful for the wise providence that caused the detention.

Ch. 16: [*Commendation, Salutations, Warning, Salutations of his Companions, Doxology.*]

The personal salutations in this chapter are important:

1. As evidences of the truth of Christianity. The mention of so many names and circumstances excludes all idea of forgery or fiction. But if the writing is authentic, the facts must be true.

2. As showing the personal character of the apostle. He was altogether and intensely human and social in his affections and sympathies. On this account these personal notices are worthy of the pen of inspiration.

3. As showing how social affections are sanctified by religion.

4. As showing how prominent a part was taken by women in the early diffusing of Christianity. Of the twenty-eight persons here named, eight, at least, perhaps nine, were women. And besides these there were doubtless some other women included in the households and churches named. [The names of these women are Phebe, Priscilla, Mary, Junia (?), Tryphena, Tryphosa, Persis, and Julia. Paul also salutes the mother of Rufus and the sister of Nereus, without giving their names. It was no unimportant part which women performed in the early history of Christianity.]

1. I commend unto you Phebe, etc. [On the meaning of the verb *commend*, see notes on 5: 8. 'Phebe.' This is one of the

names of the goddess Diana. Some others mentioned below—Nereus, Hermes (Hermas), are named after heathen divinities.] **Which is a servant.** The original word is the same which is translated "deacon" in Phil. 1: 1; 1 Tim. 3: 8, 12. The word is used thirty times in the New Testament, and is translated "minister" or "servant," except in the three places above noted. She may have been one of those women set apart in the early church to perform certain needful services to their own sex. We know that such a class existed as early as the time of Trajan and Pliny, less than half a century after the date of this Epistle;¹ and many commentators think that 1 Tim. 3: 11 refers to this class of persons, and should be translated "the women" (that is, who perform to their own sex similar offices to those which the deacons perform for men), and not "their wives," the word "their" being supplied by the translators. This view is somewhat favored by the use of the participle in Greek, expressed in English by the relative clause 'which is,' before the word 'servant.' **Cenchrea** was the port of Corinth on the East, eight or nine miles from the city.

2. He exhorts them to receive her religiously (as one who is) **in the Lord, as becometh saints**—in the way in which you, as Christians, ought to receive a fellow-Christian. **And that ye (may) assist her.** She was deserving of this by many titles,—as a woman, as a Christian, and as a helper, or protectress of many,—and it was especially fit that Paul should ask this on her behalf, because he had himself received kindness at her hands. [**In whatsoever business she hath need of you.** Taking the antecedent, 'business,' out of the relative clause, we might have this construction: assist her in any business in which she may have need of you.

---

¹ Pliny the younger, when Governor of the Province of Bythinia (died about A. D. 117), wrote to the Emperor Trajan that he thought it necessary to torture two Christian women "quæ ministræ dicebantur," who were called deaconesses, that he might find out the truth in regard to this new "superstition," afterward termed by him "pravam et immodicam," depraved and extravagant.—(F.)

3 Greet Priscilla and Aquila, my helpers in Christ Jesus:
4 Who have for my life laid down their own necks: unto whom not only I give thanks, but also all the churches of the Gentiles.

3 Salute Prisca and Aquila my fellow-workers in
4 Christ Jesus, who for my life laid down their own necks; unto whom not only I give thanks, but also
5 all the churches of the Gentiles: and *salute* the

For she hath been, etc. The Common Version, by omitting *also* (καὶ), fails to bring out the full idea of the original. Paul would say: Do you assist her, 'for she' (or, *this one*), too (on her part), has assisted many.[1] This language not only favors the supposition that she was a deaconess, but seems to imply that she was a person of some property and social position. ["Phebe may have rendered service to St. Paul at Cenchrea on the occasion mentioned in Acts 18: 18. His vow seems to point to a deliverance from danger or sickness." ("Biblical Commentary.") This Christian woman also rendered a most important service to the Christian Church, in bearing (if the subscription to our Common Version is true) this Epistle, a precious treasure, safely to the saints that were in Rome.]

3, 4. [Priscilla is the diminutive of Prisca, and this latter is the better-attested form in the manuscripts. Aquila (the Greek form, Aquilas, would better distinguish his sex) and Priscilla were Roman names, it being "common for Jews to assume such names out of Palestine." (Hackett.) Other Latin names mentioned here are Amplias (Ampliatus), Urbanus, Junia, Rufus, and Julia. All the rest are names of Greek origin. Juvenal called Rome a "Greek city." The name of the wife, Priscilla, is generally mentioned first perhaps on account of her "preponderant Christian activity" (Meyer), or, "relative superiority." (Hackett.) None of the persons whose names now follow, save, perhaps, that of Rufus, are elsewhere mentioned in the New Testament.] These persons [having been expelled from Rome as Jews, under Claudius] were at Corinth with Paul (Acts 18: 2), afterward at Ephesus (Acts 18: 26), where they still were when Paul wrote his first letter to the Corinthians (1 Cor. 16: 19), now at Rome, and later, still again at Ephesus. [The objection

of Renan, that this is "too nomadic a life," is well answered by Bishop Lightfoot. See "Biblical Commentary," p. 28.] When, and where, and how they had risked their own lives to save his, we are not informed; but we have the proof that he was grateful for it, and so, with good reason, were **all the churches of the Gentiles.** [Who (since they, οἵτινες) **laid down their own necks**—not literally, but *as if* under the executioner's axe. This, probably, was at Ephesus, where the apostle fought with men as with wild beasts, and had the sentence of death within himself, and despaired even of life. Aquila was a fellow-worker with Paul in tent making; but both he and Priscilla were fellow-workers with him in Christ Jesus. "Labor for the gospel lives and moves 'in Christ' as its very element." (Meyer.) How much a devoted lay-brother, an earnest Christian sister in the church, can do, in sustaining and encouraging the gospel minister, and in helping on the cause of Christ! Virtually they are preachers of the gospel, though themselves never occupying the "sacred desk."]

5. It seems to have been no uncommon thing for brethren who had convenient dwellings for the purpose to open their houses for the assemblies of Christian worshipers; and such assemblies are repeatedly called "churches," though probably not fully in the technical sense of that word. In a large city like Rome, such a custom must have been an important convenience. See ver. 14, 15; Col. 4: 15; Philem. 2. [According to 1 Cor. 16: 19, these two disciples, prior to this, had opened their house in Ephesus for such assemblies. "It is probable," says Dr. Hodge, "that from his occupation as tent maker, he had better accommodations for the meetings of the church than most other Christians." Some regard "the church in

---

[1] The student will notice that in the παραστῆτε and προστάσις of the original, there is a slight paronomasia. Instead of the demonstrative αὕτη (*this* one) of our Textus Receptus, the Revisers have the intensive pronoun αὐτή, *she herself*, or, simply, *she*, as this pronoun is commonly supposed to have a weakened force in the New Testament, though Winer thinks "it never occurs with-

out a certain emphasis." These pronouns are to be distinguished from the contracted forms, αὐτῇ (for ἑαυτῇ), *to herself*, and αὐτή (for ἡ αὐτή), *the same.* But these, and like contract forms of pronouns, are not now supposed to occur, or, at least but rarely, in the New Testament.—(F.)

5 Likewise *greet* the church that is in their house. Salute my well beloved Epenetus, who is the first fruits of Achaia unto Christ.

6 Greet Mary, who bestowed much labour on us.

7 Salute Andronicus and Junia, my kinsmen, and my fellow prisoners, who are of note among the apostles, who also were in Christ before me.

8 Greet Amplias, my beloved in the Lord.

9 Salute Urbane, our helper in Christ, and Stachys my beloved.

church that is in their house. Salute Epænetus my beloved, who is the firstfruits of Asia unto Christ.

6 Salute Mary, who bestowed much labour on you.

7 Salute Andronicus and ¹Junias, my kinsmen, and my fellow-prisoners, who are of note among the apostles, who also have been in Christ before me. Salute

8 Ampliatus my beloved in the Lord. Salute Urbanus

9 our fellow-worker in Christ, and Stachys my beloved.

---

1 Or, *Junia.*

---

their house" as the Christian members of the family; but this seems improbable. Justin Martyr speaks of Christians assembling at his house, when he was at Rome, for purposes of instruction. See Alford.] Instead of **Achaia,** we should read "Asia," on the authority of the best manuscripts. [This 'Asia' is Proconsular, or lesser Asia, on the western coast of Asia Minor. In 1 Cor. 16: 15, it is stated that the house of Stephanas was the first fruits of Achaia; so that if Achaia was here the genuine reading, we might reasonably suppose that **Epenetus** belonged to this 'house,' or, at least, that he was one of the earliest converts in that country.]

6. Greet Mary, who. [The compound relative here has the force of: for she, or, since she. See notes on 1: 25, and for similar compounds in this chapter, see ver. 4, 7, 12.] Who this person was and where she **bestowed** her **much labour** or toil **on us**—that is, on Paul and his fellow-laborers (or, according to the more approved reading on "you"—that is, on the disciples at Rome), must remain unknown to us. The pronouns, 'you' and 'us' differ in Greek only by a single vowel, and the pronunciation of these two vowels was very similar (in the modern Greek, precisely identical); so that they would be very easily confounded with each other, especially in copying from dictation. The manuscripts show that these pronouns were often interchanged. [The name 'Mary' (Hebrew, *Miriam*) indicates her Jewish descent. No doubt 'us' instead of 'you' was the original reading, as "elsewhere the apostle always brings out prominently the relations of the persons saluted to his own labors." (Lange.) The aorist tense of the verb possibly indicates that she performed no long-continued but some special act of service. Paul mentions four females in this chapter who labored or *toiled* much in the Lord.]

7. Whether the nominative of *Iounian* is *Junias,* a man, or *Junia,* a woman, is uncer-

tain. If the latter, as Chrysostom thought, with whom some modern commentators agree, she was probably the wife, or perhaps the sister, of Andronicus. But the prevalent opinion is that the name is of the masculine gender. **My kinsmen**—not merely in the national, but in the more personal sense. [Six persons in this chapter are called by Paul, his kinsmen.] **My fellow prisoners**—where and when can only be conjectured. Clement of Rome says that Paul was *seven* times in prison; compare 2 Cor. 11: 23, "in prisons more abundantly." **Of note among the apostles.** Honorably known by the apostles, is all the expression necessarily involves; not that they themselves were reckoned as apostles. **Who also were in Christ before me** ["entered the fellowship of Christ." (Meyer.) Alford says: "In the use of the perfect there is a mixed construction—'who have been longer than me,' and, 'who *were* before me.'"] Paul was not the *first* among the kindred to which he belonged, to believe in Christ. It is generally thought that Paul's conversion took place about three or four years after the crucifixion of Christ. [Paul elsewhere confesses himself to be "the least of the apostles," and here he says he was not the first of his kindred to become a Christian. Possibly the two persons named were converted at the Pentecost and were the real founders of the Roman Church. A few manuscripts make the *who* (by the use of τοῖς) refer to the apostles, a mistaken reference.]

8, 9. Greet Amplias. This is an abbreviation for Ampliatus, which is the form as found in several of the oldest manuscripts. [In like manner, Lucas was contracted from Lucanus, Silas from Silvanus, etc.] **My beloved in the Lord**—whom I love as a Christian. **Urbane** is the name of a man and not of a woman, as the form of the name in English might seem to intimate. **Our helper in Christ.** This Urbanus or Urban, seems to have rendered some assistance to the Roman

10 Salute Appelles approved in Christ. Salute them which are of Aristobulus' *household.*
11 Salute Herodion my kinsman. Greet them that be of the *household* of Narcissus, which are in the Lord.

10 Salute Apelles the approved in Christ. Salute them who are of the *household* of Aristobulus. Salute
11 Herodion my kinsman. Salute them of the *household*

disciples as well as to Paul—*our* fellow worker. **And Stachys my beloved.** In this instance, he does not add : 'in the Lord,' as he does in most cases ; yet doubtless 'Stachys' was also a disciple and was loved, like the rest, with Christian affection. [Ampliatus, Urbanus, Stachys, Apelles, Tryphena, Tryphosa, Rufus, Hermes, Patrobas (or, *Patrobius*), Hermas, Philologus, Julia, Nereus, "are found in the sepulchral inscriptions on the Appian way, as the names of persons connected with ' Cæsar's household,' and contemporary with St. Paul." ("Biblical Commentary.") Some of these names were very common in that age and country, others were comparatively rare. " At all events," says Bishop Lightfoot, "this investigation (of names) will not have been useless, if it has shown that the names and allusions at the close of the Roman Epistle are in keeping with the circumstances of the metropolis in St. Paul's day ; for thus it will have supplied an answer to two forms of objection ; the one denying the genuineness of the last two chapters of this letter, and the other, allowing their genuineness, but detaching the salutations from the rest, and assigning them to another Epistle." Dr. Gifford in the " Biblical Commentary," supposes these salutations belonged to a *second* letter to the Romans. But this and other suppositions which have been made, create more difficulty than they remove. The constant intercourse between Rome and the East, and Paul's protracted labors in all the latter region—giving him large opportunities for becoming acquainted with brethren from Rome or brethren visiting Rome — furnish sufficient explanation of the many salutations which he sends to the Roman Church.]

10. Of all those named, from the fifth verse to the tenth inclusive, nothing is known except what is here recorded. **Apelles** must not be confounded, as he has been by some of the ancients and by Grotius among the moderns, with Apollos mentioned in Acts 18 : 24 ; 19 : 1, and in several other places. [When Horace ("Sat." 1, v., 100), speaking of some superstition, says : " The Jew Apella may believe this, not I," he seems to make this name stand for a

typal Jew.] **Approved in Christ**—a Christian, proved by trial. **Aristobulus' household** — them which belong to Aristobulus. The word household is not in the original. [Yet the original shows us that not all the dependents of Aristobulus were saluted, but only some of them—namely, those, as we must suppose, who were 'in Christ.' The same holds true of the household of Narcissus in the next verse as is there expressly stated.] Why is no salutation sent to Aristobulus himself? Because he was no Christian, answers Meyer, unless he had previously died, in which case he may have been a Christian. But why may he not have been a Christian still living, but known by Paul to have been at this time absent from Rome? There is room for a supposition, not less plausible than either of those named by Meyer, and much more interesting and not destitute of some historical support. Rev. John Williams (1811-1861), in his " Ecclesiastical Antiquities of Cymry," says : "Arwystli, a man of Italy," is mentioned in the " Welsh Genealogies of the Saints," as one of four Christian missionaries, who accompanied Bran, the first Welsh Christian (converted while a captive in Rome) on his return to his native country. This Arwystli is supposed to be the same person as Aristobulus, mentioned in Paul's Epistle to the Romans. The formation of the name from the Greek would be in perfect accordance with the analogy of the Welsh language. But what adds the greatest support to this hypothesis is the fact that in the Greek menology Aristobulus is said to have been ordained by Paul as a bishop for the Britons. In this case the Greeks and the Welsh are witnesses wholly independent of each other, so that collusion is out of the question. See " Bibliotheca Sacra," October, 1875, pp. 656, 657. [There was also an Aristobulus, grandson of Herod the Great, who lived at Rome and was an intimate friend of Claudius. Some have supposed that his household (slaves) may have been bequeathed by him to the emperor, and that these may have formed a part of ' Cæsar's household.' (Phil. 4. 22.)]

11. Of **Herodion** [a name formed from Herod, like Cæsarion from Cæsar], the **kins-**

12 Salute Tryphena and Tryphosa, who labour in the Lord. Salute the beloved Persis, which laboured much in the Lord.
13 Salute Rufus chosen in the Lord, and his mother and mine.
14 Salute Asyncritus, Phlegon, Hermas, Patrobas, Hermes, and the brethren which are with them.
15 Salute Philologus, and Julia, Nereus, and his sister, and Olympas, and all the saints which are with them.

12 of Narcissus, who are in the Lord. Salute Tryphæna and Tryphosa, who labour in the Lord. Salute Persis the beloved, who laboured much in the Lord.
13 Salute Rufus the chosen in the Lord, and his mother
14 and mine. Salute Asyncritus, Phlegon, Hermes, Patrobas, Hermas, and the brethren that are with
15 them. Salute Philologus and Julia, Nereus and his sister, and Olympas, and all the saints that are with them

man of Paul, we know nothing further. **Narcissus,** a freedman and favorite of Claudius, say Grotius, Michaelis, and Neander; but this Narcissus was executed in the beginning of Nero's reign—about A. D. 55. (Tacitus "Annal." 13:1.) But his family may have been designated, as they are here, after his death. It is more probable, however, that this was another Narcissus, a favorite of Nero, put to death afterward by Galba.

12. Tryphena and Tryphosa were probably sisters. Meyer conjectures that these and **the beloved Persis** were deaconesses. The first two are described as laboring in the Lord by a present participle [while their names denote those who live voluptuously]. The last is mentioned as having toiled much, by a verb in the past tense. Perhaps she was unable now to work, through illness or age. [The name 'Persis' was probably derived from the country of Persia, just as Lydia denotes a Lydian, etc. Commentators note the delicacy of the apostle in here employing 'the' and not *my* before 'beloved,' the 'my beloved' being seemly only when referring to men, as in ver. 5, 8, 9. The apostle's frequent commendation of females who abounded in their Christian labors, toiling not only much, but, as the verb implies, laboriously, makes it evident that he would not restrict them from the most abundant Christian activity.]

13. This **Rufus** may have been the one mentioned in Mark 15: 21; but the name was a common one. **Chosen** [literally, *elect*] **in the Lord.** As this might, in a general sense, be said of every Christian, the special application of it to Rufus implies peculiar excellence—a choice Christian. **And his mother and mine.** 'His,' naturally; 'mine,' by her motherly care and my filial respect and gratitude. If the suggestion above, in regard to 'Rufus,' is correct, his mother was the wife of that Simon who bore the Saviour's cross. We know nothing of the time or manner in which she had shown motherly kindness to the apostle; but there is a grateful emphasis

[the pronoun 'mine' being emphatic by form and position], and a graceful delicacy in the way in which he here acknowledges the obligation. [" Let us remark, in closing, the exquisite delicacy and courtesy which guide the apostle in those distinguishing epithets with which he accompanies the names of the servants or handmaids of Christ, whom he mentions. Each of those descriptive titles is, as it were, the rough draft of the *new name* which those persons shall bear in glory." (Godet.)]

14, 15. These ten persons [perhaps less noted than the preceding, since they have no honorary epithets] are grouped into two equal companies, other unnamed persons being added to each company and embraced in the common salutation—in the first case under the designation **brethren,** in the second case with the title **saints.** These were probably persons accustomed to meet with those named for religious worship. Compare ver. 5. The **Hermas** mentioned in ver. 14 was not, as Origen believed, the author of the book called the "Shepherd of Hermas," in the collection attributed to the "Apostolical Fathers"; for that book belongs to a later age, and was probably written by another Hermas, brother of Pius I., Bishop of Rome, about the year 150. [Winer thinks that Hermas is probably a contraction for Hermodoros, as Olympas for Olumpiodorus.] It is uncertain whether the *Ioulian* of ver. 15 was a man (Julias) or a woman (Julia). If the latter, she was probably the wife of Philologus, and this is rendered somewhat more probable by the mention of **Nereus, and his sister** immediately after. [This closes the apostle's personal greetings. That Peter's name does not appear in this long catalogue shows that he was not then in Rome, otherwise he would have been saluted first of all. It is pleasant to think, and it certainly is highly probable, that some of these beloved Roman saints, whose names have now passed under review, formed a part of the two bands who, some three years later, went out on the Appian way—the one thirty miles to the *Tres*

16 Salute one another with a holy kiss. The churches of Christ salute you.

17 Now I beseech you, brethren, mark them which cause divisions and offences contrary to the doctrine which ye have learned ; and avoid them.

16 them. Salute one another with a holy kiss. All the churches of Christ salute you.

17 Now I beseech you, brethren, mark them that are causing the divisions and occasions of stumbling, contrary to the ¹ doctrine which ye learned : and

1 Or, *teaching.*

Tabernœ, and the other forty miles to the *Appii Forum*, to meet this *their beloved* apostle, now coming to them as Christ's "ambassador in chains." No wonder that at such an exhibition of Christian sympathy and love the apostle "thanked God and took courage," and that here at length his soul was filled with "joy," and his tired spirit found "rest."]

16. [The greetings which Paul has to offer *from himself* being concluded, he now desires that his readers should exchange greetings with one another. (Meyer.)] The salutation with a kiss was a common custom, as it still is among many Oriental nations, with *men* as well as women, like hand-shaking with us. Compare Matt. 26 : 49 ; Mark 14 : 45 ; Luke 7 : 45 ; 15 : 20 ; Acts 20 : 37. See similar injunctions in 1 Cor. 16 : 20 ; 2 Cor. 13 : 12 ; 1 Thess. 5 : 26 ; 1 Peter 5 : 14. **With (in) a holy kiss.** [The preposition is commonly supposed to be used either of accompaniment or of instrument. It properly marks the kiss as that in which the salutation consisted.] It was an early custom, as we learn from Justin Martyr, Tertullian, and the so-called "Apostolical Constitutions," at the close of the prayer before the Lord's Supper, for the disciples to exchange this salutation [the *osculum pacis* of Tertullian] with one another, men with men, and women with women. As a general custom, it was probably early laid aside. Some small sections of the church still retain it. Paul calls it 'holy' because it was an expression of the holy Christian fellowship of love. **The churches of Christ salute you.** It was no secret that Paul wished and intended to visit Rome. See Acts 19 : 21. And perhaps it was widely known among the churches that he was writing to the disciples there about this time, in which case it would be natural for them to send their Christian greeting through him. [We may also say that Paul *knew*, by his intercourse with the churches, that they were minded to send their love to the brethren that were in Rome.] The word *all* is prefixed to 'the churches' by Tischendorf [Westcott and Hort, and the Revisers],

and this reading is well sustained. At the close of these salutations, the apostle inserts a solemn warning against those erroneous teachers who cause divisions. (Ver. 17-20.)

17. I beseech you. An expression denoting the importance of the admonition and Paul's earnestness in it. **Mark them which cause (*the*) divisions and offences**—or, *watch them closely.* [These may include both Judaizing teachers and Gentile converts, perhaps the latter especially, as being more naturally inclined to Epicurean sensualism, or serving their own belly. We think, with most expositors, that "Paul is *not* here speaking against such as already were actually making divisions in Rome." On the contrary, he commends in highest terms their faith and their obedience. Ver. 19 ; see 1 : 8. Paul, writing from Corinth, where the church had been so distracted by parties, might very naturally give such counsel to any church. '*The* divisions' refer to such as were well known to the readers—divisions "which at that time arose in so many quarters in Pauline churches and might readily threaten the Romans also." (Meyer.) At a later period, these divisions may have actually commenced at Rome. See Phil. 1 : 15-17 ; 3 : 18.] **Contrary to the doctrine which ye have learned.** [This "'doctrine' must have been what we call Pauline, the pure gospel doctrine of Christ."] Heresy and schism are closely connected. False doctrine cannot be preached among those knowing and loving the truth without causing divisions and offenses, and those who seek, from ambitious and selfish motives, to make divisions and "to draw away disciples after them," are wont to devise some new and false doctrine as a means of accomplishing their object. (Acts 20 : 30.) **Avoid them.** He does not say "confute them" [or, hold a public discussion with them (Boise)], but turn away from them. "Bow ye away from them," is Wicliffe's translation of the expression. Compare 2 Thess. 3 : 6 ; 1 Tim. 6 : 5 ; Titus 3 : 10. [Tischendorf, and Westcott and Hort have the present tense—turn ye ever away from them.]

18 For they that are such serve not our Lord Jesus Christ, but their own belly ; and by good words and fair speeches deceive the hearts of the simple.
19 For your obedience is come abroad unto all *men*. I am glad therefore on your behalf: but yet I would have you wise unto that which is good, and simple concerning evil.
20 And the God of peace shall bruise Satan under your feet shortly. The grace of our Lord Jesus Christ *be* with you. Amen.
21 Timotheus my workfellow, and Lucius, and Jason, and Sosipater, my kinsmen, salute you.

18 turn away from them. For they that are such serve not our Lord Christ, but their own belly ; and by their smooth and fair speech they beguile the hearts
19 of the innocents. For your obedince is come abroad unto all men. I rejoice therefore over you : but I would have you wise unto that which is good, and
20 simple unto that which is evil. And the God of peace shall bruise Satan under your feet shortly. The grace of our Lord Jesus Christ be with you.
21 Timothy my fellow-worker saluteth you ; and

18, 19. [**For they that are such**—literally, *for the such* persons.] These makers of divisions and offenses, however fair and fine their pretensions and speeches might be, were not sincerely serving Christ, but rather serving their own sensual and selfish ends. And the aim of all their kind and plausible words is only to deceive those innocent ones who, being without guile themselves, are slow to suspect it in others.[1] But I do not expect that *you* will be so easily deceived, **for your obedience** (to the gospel) **is come abroad unto all men.** Respecting you, *therefore*, I have confidence and joy. Now my wish concerning you is that you may be **wise unto** (*in reference to*) **that which is good, and simple concerning evil,** pure from all admixture with it. The word here translated 'simple' [that which is without foreign admixture, hence in a "true and natural condition" (Trench)] is the same which is translated harmless in Phil. 2 : 15 and in Matt. 10 : 16. ["Be wise as serpents and harmless as doves." It requires, methinks, great prudence and grace to blend this serpent-wisdom and dove-harmlessness together. Meyer sees in this verse "a delicate combination of *warning* with the expression of firm confidence."]

20. The God of peace ["the God of whom peace is a characterizing attribute" (Ellicott)], so named in contrast with the makers of divisions. **Shall bruise Satan,** whose servants and emissaries these authors of strifes and offenses are. [We are taught here and elsewhere in the Scriptures that it is not the Virgin Mary who shall bruise the serpent's head, as the Decree on the Immaculate Con-

ception (enacted December 8th, 1854) declares, but the 'God of peace,' or he who is the seed of the woman, the Son of Mary and the Son of God. A very few authorities have here the verb in the optative mood : *May* the God of peace crush Satan, etc.] **Under your feet shortly.** Your conflict shall not be long; your victory shall be speedy and complete. [This 'shortly,' according to Godet, denotes, not the nearness of the event, but the celerity or quickness with which it shall be accomplished.] There is an apparent allusion here to Gen. 3 : 15. Every triumph of the Christian or of the church over the disturbers of their peace is a part and proof of Christ's victory over Satan. The brief doxology which follows seems again to close the Epistle. But the apostle has still some salutations to add and a more formal doxology to follow. This apparently broken and renewed conclusion is a characteristic of this Epistle [as also of several other of his letters. See Phil. 4 : 20, seq. ; 2 Thess. 3 : 16, seq. ; 1 Tim. 6 : 16, seq. ; 2 Tim. 4 : 18, seq.]

21. Timothy's name is joined with Paul's in the superscription of five of his letters. See 2 Cor. 1 : 1 ; Phil. 1 : 1 ; Col. 1 : 1 ; 1 Thess. 1 : 1 ; 2 Thess. 1 : 1. [On Timothy's long and intimate acquaintance with Paul, see Farrar's "Life of St. Paul," page 260.] But he may not have been with the apostle when *this* Epistle was begun, or the apostle may have had some other good reason for not inserting his name at the beginning. [According to Meyer, "Paul deemed it suitable to appear with his Epistle before the Roman Church, to which he was still so strange, in all his unique and undivided apostolical authority." **Lucius**

---

[1] In the MSS. D E F G, the word rendered 'fair speeches' (most frequently translated *blessing*) is wanting, being omitted, according to Meyer, "through the homœoteleuton," or mistake arising from similar endings of connected words. The *for* in ver. 19 seems to assign a reason for the above exhortation, their obedience to the faith furnishing a ground of confidence that they will heed the exhortation. The *you* in the phrase,

the-of-you-obedience, is thought by some to be emphatic as contrasted with *the simple*. Buttmann (p. 117) says that this intermediate position of the pronoun is peculiar to the style of Paul. Its regular position would be before the article or after the substantive, save when some adjective or adverbial limitation stands between them.—(F.)

22 I Tertius, who wrote *this* epistle, salute you in the Lord.
23 Gaius mine host, and of the whole church, saluteth you. Erastus the chamberlain of the city saluteth you, and Quartus a brother.
24 The grace of our Lord Jesus Christ *be* with you all. Amen.

22 Lucius and Jason and Sosipater, my kinsmen. 1 Tertius, 1 who write the epistle, salute you in the
23 Lord. Gaius my host, and of the whole church, saluteth you. Erastus the treasurer of the city saluteth you, and Quartus the brother.2

---

1 Or, *who write the epistle in the Lord, salute you*......2 Some ancient authorities insert here ver. 24, *The grace of our Lord Jesus Christ be with you all. Amen,* and omit the like words in ver. 20.

---

is probably "Lucius of Cyrene," mentioned in Acts 13: 1; certainly not Luke the evangelist, whose name is spelt differently [Loukas, Lucas, or Lucanus], and who is never called Paul's kinsman. [**Jason,** a Græcised name for Jesus, "perhaps identical with Jason of Thessalonica." (Philippi.) See Acts 17: 5, seq.] **Sosipater** is probably the same who is mentioned as a Berean, his name being abbreviated to "Sopater," in Acts 20: 4.

22. I Tertius, who wrote this epistle, salute you in the Lord. The name, 'Tertius,' is a Roman name; and probably this man, who is not mentioned elsewhere, was a Roman. The apostle was accustomed to employ an amanuensis, writing only the closing salutation with his own hand. See 1 Cor. 16: 21; Col. 4: 18; 2 Thess. 3: 17. It was appropriate that a Roman scribe should be selected to write this epistle at Paul's dictation. That he should use the first person in sending his own salutation, if not quite regular, was quite natural. ["It would have been altogether unseemly for Paul to send the salutation from Tertius as from a third person, while the latter himself wrote it down." (Philippi.) Meyer supposes that the Roman Christians might be acquainted with Tertius, who was probably an Italian; but it seems to me that the amanuensis of such a letter to such a people, would naturally feel interested in them, even though not personally acquainted.]

23. Gaius (in Latin, Caius) is probably the same whom Paul baptized (1 Cor. 1: 14), and may be the same with the one mentioned in Acts 20: 4 (Gaius of Derbe); but the name is so common that we cannot be sure of the identity. See Acts 19: 29; 3 John 1. **Mine host.** His house was Paul's home while this Epistle was penned [as that of Aquila, and, perhaps, of Justus, had been on a previous occasion. (Acts 18: 1-7.) This word means *guest* as well as *host.*] **And of the whole church.** The most natural interpretation of these words

is, that the church was accustomed to hold its meetings in Gaius' house; or they may mean, as Meyer suggests, that in consequence of his having the apostle for a guest, his house was the frequent resort of the Corinthian disciples in general. **Erastus, the chamberlain of the city**—or the city treasurer (of the city of Corinth), commonly identified with the one mentioned in Acts 19: 22, and 2 Tim. 4: 20; but the person mentioned in these two places seems to have been one of Paul's traveling assistants, which could hardly be reconciled with his holding the office here ascribed to him. It is possible, to be sure, that he may have afterward laid down that office to join Paul in his evangelical journeys and labors, and be described here as having held it, or, perhaps, as still holding it at the time the Epistle was written; but the name was not so unusual as to require this somewhat forced supposition. At any rate, this case would be rather an exceptional one among the disciples, according to what the apostle writes to the Corinthians (1 Cor. 1: 26): ["Not many mighty." Bengel remarks that "the faith of a most influential man must have been a source of joy to the Romans."] **Quartus, a brother,** is described by no more particular designation; but whether personally known or not to the disciples in Rome, he wished to join with those mentioned above in sending to them his brotherly greeting. [Comparatively unknown and insignificant he may have been, yet his Christian faith, in connection with but a possibly accidental and momentary interview with the apostle, has gained for his name what many seek and will not secure—an earthly immortality. Dr. Hackett, however, thinks that his being entitled *the brother* (not 'a brother,' as in our Common Version) "implies that he was well known to the Roman Christians."]

V. Conclusion. (Ver. 24–27.)

(*a*) *Benediction.*

24. This verse is not found in the four oldest manuscripts, ℵ A B C. It is probably copied

25 Now to him that is of power to stablish you according to my gospel, and the preaching of Jesus Christ, according to the revelation of the mystery, which was kept secret since the world began,
26 But now is made manifest, and by the Scriptures of the prophets, according to the commandment of the everlasting God, made known to all nations for the obedience of faith:

25 ¹ Now to him that is able to stablish you according to my gospel and the preaching of Jesus Christ, according to the revelation of the mystery which
26 hath been kept in silence through times eternal, but now is manifested, and ² by the scriptures of the prophets, according to the commandment of the eternal God, is made known unto all the nations

---

1 Some ancient authorities omit ver. 25-27.   Compare the end of ch. xiv......2 Gr. *through.*

---

from ver. 20, and well omitted by critical editors generally. [It is defended, however, by Meyer and Fritzsche.]

(b) *Doxology.*

25-27. [With this doxology compare the benediction of Jude (ver. 24, 25), which strongly resembles this in some points. "As a final, complete conclusion, we have now this doxology, rich in contents, deep in feeling (perhaps added by the apostle's own hand), in which the leading ideas contained in the whole Epistle . . . now further receive, in the fullest unison of inspired piety, their concentrated outburst for the ultimate true consecration of the whole. . . . Hence, it can by no means appear strange that such a doxology has obtained the character of overflowing fullness from the whole recollection of what had been written." (Meyer.)¹] [**To him that is of power to stablish you.** The ability of God *to establish* them was a doctrine much insisted on in the apostle's manner of preaching the gospel, and (to define the same thing in other words) in his preaching of Christ. [Meyer remarks that the above description of God "corresponds to the entire scope of the Epistle." A chief design of Paul's intended visit to the Roman Christians, was that they might be "established." (1: 11.) **According to** (*in conformity with*) **my gospel,** which is nothing else than Christ's own **preaching** through me (DeWette, Meyer), or, that preaching of which Christ is the subject. (Philippi, Godet.) **According to the revelation.** 'Revelation' has no article, because the following noun has none, and is itself preceded by a

preposition. The word is put by Meyer in the same construction as 'gospel' and 'preaching' —that is, dependent on the verb 'stablish.' We prefer with Alford and Godet to connect it with the preceding substantives as being explanatory of them, so that the idea of the whole would be : this my gospel which is but the preaching of which Christ is the sum and substance, is in accordance with a revelation of a mystery or secret, kept in silence. **Since the world began,** or, as in the Revised Version, *through times eternal.* This mystery must embrace the whole matter of human redemption, which, of course, would include the bestowment of the blessings of the gospel on the Gentiles, as in Eph. 3: 6. If, as Godet remarks, Paul's preaching of Christ was 'according to the revelation,' then we have in this Epistle not simply a creation of his powerful understanding, deserving our admiration, but the thought of God, deserving and demanding our faith, Compare Gal. 1: 11, 12; Eph. 3: 2-4; 1 Thess. 4: 8. The *times eternal,* commonly explained by the phrases, "from the foundation of the world," or "from the ages and from the generations" (compare Col. 1: 26; Eph. 3: 9), have here substantially the same meaning as *from eternity.*² **But now,** in contrast with 'times eternal,' **is made manifest,** or *has been manifested.* **And by** (*by means of*) **the Scriptures of the prophets,** or the prophetic Scriptures. **According to** (in consequence of, or in accordance with) **the commandment of the everlasting God** (who alone, as Meyer says, "could dispose of times eternal and of the present"), has been

---

¹ The important MSS. א B C D * E, and most of the early versions, locate the doxology here, at the end of the Epistle; L, and nearly all the cursives, at the end of chapter 14; while A P, and some cursives, have it in both places. Commentators, almost without exception, defend the genuineness of its present position. See note, end of chapter 14.--(F.)

² We do not suppose that the phrase 'eternal times' in itself strictly denotes eternity, since the expression, *before* eternal times, occurs more than once in Paul's writings. (2 Tim. 1: 9; Titus 1: 2), and because the word

'times' of itself excludes the idea of absolute eternity. Yet Ellicott remarks that the phrase, *before* times eternal, seems obviously to mean "from all eternity"— "times, in a word, which reach from eternity." "Eternal times," says Wordsworth, "are times which extend back till there was no time." Gifford: "Times reaching back to eternity." Prof. Grimm: "Without beginning." From this point of view the expressions, *from times eternal* and *from eternity,* would be virtually equivalent.— (F.)

27 To God only wise, *be* glory through Jesus Christ for ever. Amen.

27 unto obedience [1] of faith; to the only wise God, through Jesus Christ, [2] to whom be the glory [3] for ever. Amen.

1 Or, *to the faith*......2 Some ancient authorities omit *to whom*......3 **Gr.** *unto the ages.*

made known to all nations (or Gentile peoples) for (*in order to produce*) the obedience of faith, or *obedience to the faith.* To God only (or, *absolutely*) wise ; so called because the Infinite Disposer of all things requires wisdom as well as power. Be glory through Jesus Christ for ever. The Revised Version translates : "To the only wise God, through Jesus Christ, to whom be glory for ever. Amen," and adds in the margin, "Some ancient authorities omit *to whom.*" The 'whom' properly refers to Christ, and to him glory should be given 'for ever,' or *unto the ages.* By putting a semicolon after Christ, the "Five Clergymen" in their Revision make the 'whom' to refer to God, but for this reference we properly need not *to whom*, but, as in Eph. 3: 20 21, *to him.* If the relative is retained and treated as a relative, there would seem to be need of a verb to be supplied to the clauses : 'to him who is able,' 'to God only wise.' In Acts 20 : 32, Olshausen and Godet find a fitting word in connection with precisely similar phraseology, to wit : "I commend you to God . . . who is able to build you up," etc. The only serious objection to this supply is that it robs this passage of its evidently doxological form and character, while the chief subject of this section confessedly is God rather than Christ. Philippi also refers the doxology to Christ, but in another manner. "The apostle," he says, "meant to utter a doxology to the power and wisdom of God the Father ; but inasmuch as this wisdom was manifested in *Jesus Christ*, and he was thus the medium by which the divine wisdom was

revealed, the apostle transfers the doxology to him, and thus in blessing the Mediator and Revealer of the divine wisdom, blesses indirectly this God of wisdom, himself manifested in Christ." This really seems to cover the whole intent of the apostle as manifested in this passage. Since, however, the passage is diversely interpreted even by so-called orthodox expositors, it seems to me that we do well not to rely upon this as an indisputable proof text. For similar doxologies to Christ, see references at 9: 15.] The 'mystery' of God's great plan for saving men of all nations, though implicitly intimated by the prophets, was so little understood by the Jews generally [a "vail" lying upon their hearts, so that they could not look steadfastly on the end of that which was being done away], and so entirely unknown to the Gentiles that it may well be said to have been kept secret since the world began, until by the commandment of the everlasting God it was made manifest by the preaching of the gospel, so explaining and supplementing the Scriptures of the prophets as to make it known to all nations for the obedience of faith. Thus the apostle interweaves into this more extended concluding doxology a compendium of the subject of the whole Epistle and of his design in writing it, and so brings his work to a fit close by ascribing to God only wise, glory through Jesus Christ. for ever. Amen. ["And," says Bengel, "let every believing reader say, Amen," to which we would add : Let God be praised for giving to the world "The Epistle of Paul to the Romans." [1]]

[1] Godet, in the conclusion of his "Commentary," notices in so happy a manner two characteristic points of this Epistle, that we cannot withhold his remarks from our readers. He says : "The first point is the penetrating logic, the sure sweep of vision, which the apostle shows in the discussion of the different subjects which he takes up. Not an exaggeration, not a digression. The hot conflict which he had been maintaining in the previous years with the partisans of the legal system might have predisposed him to go beyond the limit of truth on some points in estimating Judaism. The incline was slippery ; of this we may easily convince ourselves by seeing into what errors it carried the authors of the so-called Epistle of Barnabas and of the letter to

Diognetus, and finally Marcion. And yet these men had guides before them—Paul's writings and the Epistle to the Hebrews—which might have helped them to weigh their judgments. Paul had none but himself ; he was under the influence of the strong reaction against the law into which his sudden change had thrown him, and of the violent resentment which must have been produced in him by the injustice and hatred of his Judaizing adversaries. And yet he moves, without wavering for an instant, on the straight line of truth, exhibiting the divinity of the Ancient Dispensation, and at the same time its profound contrast to the New, so that the result of his exposition is a complete view both of the difference and of the harmony between the two economies of salvation. And the same is the case, as we have seen, in all the questions which he touches. In matters where we still detect our modern writers, even the most sagacious and Christian, flagrantly guilty of exaggeration to the right or to the left, we discover in the apostle's view a fullness of truth which constantly excludes error. The second feature which strikes us in his writing is the perfect calmness with which he seems to handle truth. He does not seek it: he has it. Compare the Epistle to the Romans with Pascal's 'Thoughts,' and the distance will be seen between the apostle and the thinker of genius. It is also evident that the apostle himself draws his life from the faith which he preaches. He has faith in his faith, as one cannot have in his thought, for the very simple reason that this faith is not his discovery, but the gift of God. . . .

"And let us not forget that the experience of ages has spoken. It has put its seal to the conviction, which the apostle bore within him, that in *his gospel* he was giving to the world, not his own thought, but that of God. For history shows that a truly powerful and healthy Christianity has never developed except on the way of salvation traced by St. Paul.

"The New Testament contains two writings which admirably complete one another—the Epistle to the Romans and the Fourth Gospel. The one [the Gospel] presents for our contemplation the object of faith in its grander and perfect beauty; the union of man with God realized in One, in order to be at length realized through him in all. The other initiates us into the means of apprehending the salvation thus realized in one for all, and of appropriating it—the act of faith. There, the ideal realized, shining as on a celestial summit; here, the arduous pathway by which sinful man may succeed in reaching it. Let the church constantly possess herself of the Christ of John by means of the faith of Paul, and she will be preserved, not from persecution, but from a more terrible enemy, death."—(F.)

APPENDIXES.

APPENDIX A, TO CHAPTER 4: 11, PAGE 109.

THIS passage is sometimes used as an argument for Infant Baptism; and the words "sign" and "seal" are applied to the ordinances of Baptism and the Lord's Supper, as if they were the proper *key words* with which to open the doctrine of the "Christian Sacraments," as they are often called. They are so used in that excellent little volume, "The Way of Life," written by Dr. Charles Hodge, and published by the American Sunday School Union. That the words "sign" and "seal," in this passage, were not designed, and are not happily adapted for such a use, may be very easily shown. In the first place, there is nothing in the connection to indicate that Paul had in his mind any thought of Baptism or the Lord's Supper when he wrote this passage. In the second place, what is here said of circumcision is true of that rite only in the case of Abraham, and not at all of his posterity. It was indeed *to him*, what it was not at all *to them personally, a seal of the righteousness of the faith which he had yet being uncircumcised*. Since, then, these words would be unsuitable and untrue as an account of circumcision when applied to the posterity of Abraham, how much more are they unsuitable and untrue as an account of baptism when applied to the children of Christian believers.

But still farther, while we do not allow that the argument from circumcision to baptism has any legitimate warrant from Scripture, it may not be amiss to show how easily, on the admission of a Scriptural analogy between the Jewish and the Christian rites, the argument might be turned in a different direction. Dr. Hodge has this remark in his commentary on Rom. 4: 11: "All the Jews were professors of the true religion, and constituted the visible church, in which, by divine appointment, their children were included. This is the broad and enduring basis of infant church-membership." Let us examine this "broad and enduring basis," in the light of the following brief catechism.

CIRCUMCISION AND BAPTISM.

Q. Did the covenant which God made with Abraham and with his seed include both temporal and spiritual blessings?

A. It did.

Q. What were the temporal blessings promised in that covenant?

A. That his seed should be multiplied exceedingly, that they should possess the land of Canaan, and that they should be peculiarly the objects of God's providential care and blessing. (Gen. 18: 1–8.)

Q. What are the spiritual blessings promised in that covenant?

A. Justification by faith, and the promise of the Holy Spirit, in which are summarily included all the blessings of salvation. (Rom. 4: 11; Gal. 3: 14.)

Q. To whom do the temporal blessings of the covenant belong?

A. To the natural seed of Abraham.

Q. To whom do the spiritual blessings of the covenant belong?

A. To the spiritual seed of Abraham.

Q. What rite did God appoint, as a token of participation in the temporal blessings of the covenant?

A. Circumcision.

Q. What rite has God appointed, as a token of participation in the spiritual blessings of the covenant?

A. Baptism.

Q. Who then ought to receive the rite of circumcision?

A. The natural seed of Abraham.

Q. Who then ought to receive the rite of baptism?

A. The spiritual seed of Abraham.

Q. Who are the spiritual seed of Abraham?

A. Believers in Jesus Christ. (Rom. 4: 11, 12, 16; Gal. 3: 7, 29.)

APPENDIX B, TO CHAPTER 5: 12–21, PAGE 128.

GENERAL AND CONNECTED VIEW OF ROMANS 5: 12–21.

The consideration of the blessings which we enjoy in consequence of being justified by faith naturally suggests the *opposite evils* under which we were before suffering ("reconciled," "reconciliation," ver. 10, 11); and especially the consideration that all these blessings come to us (as so repeatedly noted in the preceding verses, 1, 2, 6, 8, 9, 10, 11) through *one man*, forcibly suggests the thought of that *other one man*, through whom those evils came upon us. It is the design of the latter part of this chapter to illustrate the excellent benefits of justification by faith in Christ in the light of this comparison between our first parent, whose sin brought upon us misery and condemnation, and Christ, who confers upon us righteousness and life. In other words, the apostle here traces both *sin* and *salvation* to their *personal sources* and compares them in these sources.

12. The completely expressed sense here would be, "as by one man sin entered into the world, and death by sin, so also by one man came righteousness, and life by righteousness." And the sense is so completed in substance in ver. 18, but in a form of statement modified by what more immediately precedes. Under the word *death*, I understand the apostle to include here, not only the death of the body, but all the evils of that condition to which our bodies and souls are subjected or exposed, here and hereafter, by reason of sin—all the consequences, in this life and in the life to come, of the loss of the divine favor, and the withholding of the Divine Spirit; the opposite, in a word, of all that is included in the word *life* in ver. 17, 18, 21. Augustine says "the soul dies when God forsakes it, just as the body dies when the soul forsakes it; and it is death in both respects, or the death of the whole man, when a soul forsaken of God forsakes the body." The death of the body is the palpable, practical, representative, test fact, around which our reasonings naturally gather. Of the group of connected evils comprehended in the penalty of sin, natural death is the most *obvious*, the most readily and universally noticed. Hence it is eminently suitable to represent and give name to the whole. And in some parts of the apostle's argument, this concrete fact is no doubt the prominent element. In a similar way the word *life*—which in its literal and lowest sense of animated existence is the *substratum* on which all other good that can be enjoyed by men must rest—represents and gives name to the whole.

This death is said to have passed through to all men because all sinned. Death and sin are co-extensive: death is universal *because* sin is universal. Wherever the *effect* is seen there the *cause* is proved to exist. The least that ἐφ' ᾧ ("for that") can fairly mean is, "on the *assumed condition* that all sinned." This is equivalent to saying, "on the ground that all sinned." Calling it an assumption, or a presupposition, will not affect the logical *connection* so distinctly affirmed.

13, 14. These verses contain the *proof* of what is affirmed in ver. 12. Before the law of Moses was given, the same effects of sin were no less manifest than afterward. But sin is not imputed when there is no law. If men had been under *no law* during all this time, they would not have been treated as *transgressors*. But the well-known *fact* is, that men were just as much subject to death before Moses as afterward. And even those who had not *actually sinned* (or, sinned in the same manner) as Adam did were no less subject to it than others; that is to say, infants died, as well as adult sinners. Hence it is plain that these suffered the consequences of sin, neither on account of the violation of the law of Moses, nor on account of the violation of the law of nature. On account of what, then, did they suffer these consequences of sin? Answer: on account of the disobedience of that *one man*, by whom, according to ver. 12, sin came into the world, and passed through to all men. "Since sin came into the world as an abnormal ethical principle, death came into the world with it as an abnormal physiological principle. Therefore the propagation of the abnormal principle of death presupposes the propagation of the abnormal principle of sin, in the actual sinning of all." (Lange on "Romans," p. 180.) While God will judge men impartially, and "render to every man according to his works," yet in respect to certain general principles and conditions of our being, he deals with his creature *man* as a *race*, he regards *humanity* as a *unit*. Meyer justly remarks, that the view that the death of individuals is the result of their personal sins, would vitiate and even contradict the whole parallel between Adam and Christ. (Vol. I, p. 248.)

A different explanation may be given of the expression "even over those who had not sinned after the similitude of Adam's transgression"—namely, that it refers merely to those who had not violated an *express precept*, as Adam did. This explanation seems to me liable to the following objections:

1. The distinction seems too unimportant. The heathen, according to the apostle, sin against sufficient light to make them inexcusable. (Ch. 1: 20.)

2. The form of expression seems to discriminate between a *certain class* of those between Adam and Moses, and the rest: it seems to imply that death reigned over a *particular class*, over whom it had apparently less right to reign than over those generally who lived before Moses.

3. The explanation objected to makes Paul say *less* than the truth of the case required.

4. It makes him say less in his *proof*, in ver. 14, than he had said in his *proposition*, in ver. 12, and so makes his argument inconclusive; for infants are certainly included in the clause, "and so death passed through to all men."

5. It represents him as *passing over* in silence the *most difficult* feature in the case, and so renders his argument defective at the most important point. The case of those who die in infancy seems naturally to come up here, and to require notice. It seems scarcely *credible* that they should be entirely ignored in an argument of this nature. (See the distinction between children and adults distinctly recognized in 9: 11; also Jonah 4: 11; Deut. 1: 39; Isa. 7: 16.)

6. It seems to be introducing a superfluous distinction, of which no use is made in the apostle's argument.

7. It seems to be *raising* an objection, without answering it. For those who are represented, according to this interpretation, as *less guilty*, are represented as suffering the same consequence of sin as the more guilty, who *have* violated an express precept. Death reigns alike over all. This objection is valid, of course, only in so far as death is here understood in its more *limited* sense.

8. It requires a somewhat forced limitation of the expression, "sin is not imputed when there is no law" (ver. 13), and then seems to contradict this limitation in the next verse, by the statement that those to whom sin was not imputed (comparatively), because they have not the law (of Moses) suffered just the same consequences of sin as those did to whom sin was imputed (fully), because they had the law of Moses.

On the supposition that this clause refers to infants, it does not necessarily decide their *future* condition. The fact that they suffer the death of the body on account of sin no more necessitates the inference of their future condemnation, than the fact that believers in Christ suffer the same evil necessitates *their* final condemnation. The *whole race* suffers this consequence of sin. Infants suffer less in death than believers in Christ. Since they are not, in this respect, treated worse than believers in this world, we have no ground, so far as this argument is concerned, to conclude that they will be condemned in the world to come. Of course, death must be taken in its more limited sense in this part of the apostle's argument; for here he is reasoning from *known* and *obvious facts*—from such of the evils consequent upon sin as are observed and experienced in this world. Yet the other connected evils would naturally follow, unless arrested by some special divine arrangement. Whether there would have been any remedy provided against the future consequences of sin in the case of infants, if there had not been any provided for adults, is a question which we may prudently leave undecided.

In the close of ver. 14, the apostle tells us that Adam was a type of Christ. He was the head and representative of the race of human sinners, as Christ is the Head and Representative of the race of saints. These are the two groups into which the apostle divides mankind. It is important to keep this in mind in the interpretation of the following verses. The three following verses qualify this typical resemblance, or explain its negative side, by showing the points of difference.

It is not easy to discern the precise points of difference which the apostle intends to *emphasize* in these three verses. They all illustrate this general statement, that the stream of blessings which flows to the race from Christ as a source (more strictly to those of our race who receive the abundance of grace, etc.), surpasses the stream of ills which flows to us from Adam. We gain in Christ more than we lost in Adam. But what specific aspect of this general truth is expressed in each of these verses? A careful examination of the words and forms of expression in each verse may help us to decide this question.

In ver. 15, the emphasis seems to be placed on the positive blessings, over and above the mere deliverance from penalty, which we gain in Christ. The contrast seems to be chiefly expressed by the words "grace," "gift," and "abounded," in opposition to "died." The latter is much more than neutralized by the former. In ver. 16, the point of emphasis seems to be the *one* trespass of Adam and the *many* personal trespasses which are cancelled in Christ. While we suffer from our connection with Adam the penalty of *one* transgression, we obtain from our connection with Christ the forgiveness of *many* transgressions.

It is important to note here, that the apostle is careful to make a distinction between the consequences of our own actual voluntary sins, and the evil which comes upon us solely or inevitably on account of Adam's sin. He seems in this to intimate:

1. That the consequences of our own many voluntary transgressions are much more serious than any consequences in which Adam's one transgression alone would have involved us.

2. That nevertheless Adam's one transgression does bring evils upon us, irrespective of any personal transgressions of our own.

3. The noting of this distinction between the direct and the indirect effects of Adam's sin, or, in other words, between the effects which are independent of our own will and action, and those in which our own will and action are concurrent and intensifying causes, goes to confirm our interpretation of the second clause of ver. 14, and to justify the application of that clause to those who suffer only such effects of Adam's sin as ensue without any co-operation on the part of his descendants. And this allusion to the distinction between the evils brought upon us by Adam's sin and the just penalty of our own many voluntary transgressions naturally introduces and helps to explain the precise emphasis of ver. 17. For here the emphasis seems to lie in the words "who receive abundance of grace," etc.; and the specific contrast seems to be between the

voluntariness of those who enjoy the benefits of Christ's righteousness, and the *involuntariness* of our participation in the consequences of Adam's sin (involuntariness, so far as the direct and unavoidable consequences are concerned). In support of this view it may be said:

1. That the use of the *present* participle, instead of the *aorist*, favors this interpretation. For while the aorist, οἱ λαβόντες, would simply mean "they who received the abundance of grace," the present, οἱ λαμβάνοντες, is more nearly equivalent to "the receivers of the abundance of grace," it has more of a *substantive* character, and is more naturally suggestive of a class of persons who are distinguished by this peculiarity, that they are the *receivers*, the *accepters*, of an offered benefit.

2. The *collocation* of the words seems intended to make the participle emphatic: it is not οἱ λαμβάνοντες τὴν περισσείαν, etc.; but οἱ τὴν περισσείαν τῆς χάριτος καὶ τῆς δωρεᾶς τῆς δικαιοσύνης λαμβάνοντες, the participle (*receiving*) being reserved to an emphatic position near the following verb.

3. The change in the subject of the verb, from *things* to *persons*, from ζωή (life), the appropriate contrast to θάνατος (death) above, to οἱ λαμβάνοντες (those receiving). This change is the more noticeable from the fact that the same verb is used in the contrasted clauses, thus: as the antithesis of *death reigned* we have, not *life reigned*, but *those receiving*, etc., *shall reign in life*. Notice also the position of *in life* (immediately before the verb in the Greek), as if it occurred to the writer that *life* belonged to the verb by right of rhetorical propriety, but overruled by a higher consideration. As it might be anticipated from the benevolence of God that he would make the good overbalance the evil, so this just anticipation is neatly confirmed by the additional circumstance that our connection with the source of evil was involuntary, while our connection with the source of good is voluntary. If this is the true explanation of this verse, it shows very explicitly between *what parties* the comparison is made throughout this section—namely, those on the one hand who are connected with Adam by natural birth, that is, all mankind, and those on the other hand who are connected with Christ by spiritual birth, that is, all believers.

In ver. 18, the apostle returns to what he had begun to state, but left unfinished, at ver. 12. What he there began to state was, that as sin and death came into the world through one man, Adam, and passed through from him to all his natural descendants, so righteousness and life came by one man, Christ, and passed through to all his spiritual posterity. He now completes the statement by adding the omitted part in verses 18, 19, carrying out the full parallel between Adam and Christ, in ver. 18, so far as relates to death on the one hand and life on the other; and in ver. 19, so far as relates to sin on the one hand and righteousness on the other. There seem to have been two interruptions in the apostle's argument, the first including verses 13 and 14, where he turns somewhat aside from his main course of thought to prove the statement contained in the last part of ver. 12, "for that all sinned"; and the second including verses 15 to 17, in which he pauses to qualify and limit the last clause of ver. 14, "who is the figure of him that was to come."

The principal difficulty in this view lies in the second "all." We must either

1. Take the whole in an unlimited sense, and admit alike universal justification and universal salvation; or,

2. Qualify the expression "justification of life," and regard it as having some lower sense, not implying the actual salvation of the justified; or,

3. Limit the sense of the word "all," and regard it as not absolutely including all mankind.

I adopt the *last* view, for the following reasons:

1. It is more agreeable to Scriptural and general usage to limit this word, than to limit the descriptive phrase "justification of life."

2. Adam and Christ, throughout this passage, are represented each as the *head* of a *certain class:* but that class does not consist in each case entirely of the same individuals. Adam's

"all" is equivalent to all the children of men: Christ's "all" is equivalent to all the children of God: Adam's "all" includes all who are born of the flesh; Christ's "all" includes all who are born of the Spirit. Each imparts what belongs to himself to *all* that are his;—Adam, his sin and death; Christ, his righteousness and life.

3. In the previous verse, the blessings which flow from Christ are distinctly limited to those who voluntarily *receive* his abundant grace.

The "all" in the last case, then, are all who are actually connected with Christ by regen- eration and faith; and in fact, numerically, these constitute "a great multitude which no man can number, out of every nation and kindred and people and tongue, who" will "have washed their robes and made them white in the blood of the Lamb." (Rev. 7 : 9, 14.)

19. As ver. 18 completes the parallel begun in verse 12 between Adam and Christ so far as the opposites death and life are concerned, so this verse completes the parallel so far as the opposites sin and righteousness are concerned. The use of the same terms "the many" to designate the two parties is to be explained in the same manner as the use of "all men" in both cases in ver. 18.

But here the question arises whether sin and righteousness are to be understood in the legal and forensic sense, or in the moral and practical sense; or, which is substantially the same thing, whether this last verse has reference to justification or to sanctification. The com- mentators generally refer it to the former, adopting various methods of explaining the relation between this verse and the preceding. I prefer to regard it as referring to sanctification, taking the terms "sin" and "righteousness" in their ethical rather than in their judicial sense. The very terms themselves, as contrasted with those in ver. 18, seem to point very distinctly to this interpretation. In the former verse we have "offence" and "condemnation" on the one hand, and "righteousness" and "justification" on the other, three out of the four distinctively forensic terms, and the fourth readily admitting the forensic sense. In the latter verse the terms are, on the one hand, "disobedience" and "sinners," and on the other "obedience" and "righteous," all naturally having the ethical sense, though the last is often used also in the forensic sense. Besides, the verb καθίστημι, "I constitute," which is used in both members of the comparison, denotes the *actual fact*, and not the legal relation. The word naturally points to what men are actually constituted or made, not to what they are legally regarded as being. If it be objected that they are not actually made righteous at once, but gradually and progressively, while they are made sinners at once by their own first sin, if not by Adam's, we answer, that the apostle has carefully provided for this objection by putting the verb in the past tense in the one case, and in the future tense in the other. They "were constituted sinners," they "shall be consti- tuted righteous." Their perfect justification secures their ultimate perfect sanctification.

This explanation introduces the subject of sanctification a few verses earlier than the common analysis. It is generally regarded as introduced at the beginning of chapter 6. But our interpretation makes chapter 5 : 19 give at least an anticipatory *hint* of the coming topic.

20. But the two great antithetical facts heretofore spoken of do not express the whole truth in regard to the matter in hand. The law of Moses "came in besides" (παρεισῆλθεν)— besides the fact of many being made sinners, and as a transition point to the other result of many being made righteous. This third term in God's dealings with men was introduced in order that transgression might multiply. The law caused transgression to multiply, partly by enlarging the rule of duty (4: 15), and partly by provoking the propensity to sin (7: 8). But the *ultimate* end which God had in view in thus introducing the law was, not that sin might multiply, but that grace might *superabound* through this very increase of transgression.

21. In other words, and finally, that as sin reigned in death, so grace might reign, by means of righteousness, unto life eternal, through Jesus Christ our Lord.

One serious logical difficulty which some have felt in regard to this whole representation apart from the objections already noticed is, that according to the apostle's argument it would seem that believers ought to be delivered from natural death. To this it may be answered:

1. Christ himself had to undergo death. If the believer were exempted from it, he woul be less conformed to his pattern.

2. This world is the theatre in which Christ's redeeming work is *progressively* accomplished. Pardon and justification are instantaneous and complete; but sanctification is gradual and life-long. So death will ultimately be abolished by Christ. (1 Cor. 15: 26.)

3. The triumph of grace in the believer's experience is even more illustrious by giving him peace in death, and victory in yielding to it, than it would be in exempting him from it. Death is now become one of the "all things" that "work together for good" to the believer. Instead of being all his lifetime in bondage to the fear of death (Heb. 2: 15), he accepts death as one of the crosses which Christ's grace makes welcome, in one respect the most welcome of all, because the *last*. How much the religion of Christ would lose, if it were despoiled of the glory in which it shines around the bedside of the dying saint! Higher considerations, then, than any seeming demands of logical consistency stand opposed to the believer's exemption from the sentence of natural death. If Christ's conquest over death had abolished it once for all, that would have been *one* decisive victory. As the case now stands, Christ's victory over death is reproduced and multipled at every triumphant departure of a believing soul, and death is thus sentenced to the mortification of *innumerable* defeats, culminating at last in his utter overthrow and annihilation.

APPENDIX C, TO ROMANS 6: 1–14, PAGE 155.

The reference which the apostle makes to baptism in the first few verses of this chapter is in some parts rendered obscure by his brief and elliptical manner of expression. But the general object and the emphatic points of the comparison are sufficiently plain.

The things to be observed here, as the *hinges* of the apostle's argument, and the key to the explanations of the particular expressions are the following:

1. A death and a new life, in a *spiritual* sense—a dying to sin, and a living anew to God; compared to

2. A death and a new life in a *literal* sense—the death of Christ, and his post-resurrection life; and illustrated by

3. A death and a new life in a *symbolical* sense—the submersion and emersion of the Christian in baptism.

Or, to express the same thing in a slightly altered form:

1. The dying to sin, and the rising to a new and holy life, which is realized in the Chris-tian's *spiritual* experience, is compared to

2. The *literal* dying and rising again of Christ, and represented by

3. The *symbolical* burial and resurrection of baptism.

Christ died and lived again; he was buried and he arose from the tomb. He died to sin, inasmuch as his death terminated that connection with sin which he had voluntarily assumed, and which caused all the sufferings of his earthly life, and finally his death on the cross. He lives unto God, inasmuch as he has returned to dwell in the bosom of the Father, in the glory which he had with the Father before the world was.

Believers are conformed to and conjoined with (σύμφυτοι) Christ in his death to sin and new life to God, inasmuch as they too have *renounced* sin, and *separated* themselves from it, so that it has now no more to do with them, nor they with it (rightfully) than a dead body has with the affairs of living men. They are alive unto God, inasmuch as they have devoted their lives to him, and are walking with him in a new life of filial obedience, intercourse, and confidence.

v

This conformity of believers to Christ is set forth in their *baptism*, which in the outward act resembles and represents his burial and resurrection, and, in its spiritual import, typifies and declares their dying to sin and living anew to God.

This comparison forcibly illustrates the importance of Scriptural baptism, and the evil that results from any change, either in the *subjects* or in the *act*. When any but professed *believers in Christ* are the *subjects*, baptism ceases to have the *spiritual significance* which the Scriptures ascribe to it. When the act is anything else than *immersion*, it ceases to have the *symbolical fitness* which belongs to its proper form. And when it loses both these, how much of its validity or sacredness remains?

As to the form in which baptism was administered in apostolical times, and as a general rule for twelve or thirteen centuries, the testimony of the most learned commentators, church historians, and antiquarians is very uniform and emphatic. The few that we give below as a specimen are copied from a recent work, entitled "The Act of Baptism," by Henry S. Burrage, published by the American Baptist Publication Society.

"This passage (Rom 6 : 4) cannot be understood unless it be borne in mind that the primitive baptism was by immersion." (Conybeare and Howson, "Life and Epistles of St. Paul," vol. II., p. 169.)

"There seems to be no reason to doubt that both here (Col. 2 : 12) and in Rom. 6 : 4, there is an allusion to the *katadusis* and *anadusis* [the sinking down and rising up] in baptism." (Bishop Ellicott, "Com. on Colossians," p. 166.)

"Baptism is the grave of the old man and the birth of the new. As he sinks beneath the baptismal waters the believer buries there all his corrupt affections and past sins; as he emerges thence he rises regenerate, quickened to new hopes and a new life. . . . Thus baptism is an image of his participation both in the death and resurrection of Christ. . . . For this two-fold image as it presents itself to St. Paul, see especially Rom. 6 : 3, et. seq." (Canon Lightfoot, "On Colossians," ch. 2 : 12.)

"As to the outward mode of administration of the ordinance, immersion, and not sprinkling, was unquestionably the original normal form. This is shown by the very meaning of the Greek words baptizo, baptisma, baptismos, used to designate the rite." (Schaff, "History of the Apostolic Church," vol. II., p. 256.)

"Baptism, which was the sign of admission into the church, was administered by immersion." (Pressensé, "Early Years of Christianity," p. 374.)

"There can be no question that the original form of baptism, the very meaning of the word, was complete immersion in the deep baptismal waters, and that for at least four centuries any other form was either unknown or regarded, unless in the case of dangerous illness, as an exceptional, almost a monstrous case." (Stanley, "History of the Eastern Church," p. 117.)

"Baptism was originally administered by immersion." (Guericke, "Church History," vol. I., p. 100.)

"The ceremony of immersion (the oldest form of baptism) was performed in the name of the three Persons of the Trinity." (Waddington, "Church History," p. 27.)

"The Baptists are, in fact, from the Protestant standpoint, unassailable; since for their demand of baptism by submersion they have the clear Bible text, and the authority of the church and of her testimony is regarded by neither party." (Dr. Dollinger, "Kirche and Kirchen," p. 337.)

"The testimony (that immersion was the primitive act of baptism) is ample and decisive. No matter of church history is clearer. The evidence is all one way, and all church historians of any repute agree in accepting it. It is a point on which ancient, mediæval, and modern historians alike, Catholic and Protestant, Lutheran and Calvinistic, have no controversy. And the simple reason for this unanimity is that the statements of the early Fathers are so clear.

and the light shed upon these statements from the early customs of the church is so conclusive, that no historian who cares for his reputation would dare to deny it, and no historian who is worthy of the name would wish to." (L. L. Paine, D. D. (Congregationalist), Professor of Church History in the Theological Seminary at Bangor, Maine.—"Christian Mirror," Aug. 3, 1875.)

["All commentators of note (except Stuart and Hodge) expressly admit or take it for granted that in this verse. . . . the ancient prevailing mode of baptism by immersion and emersion is implied as giving additional force to the idea of the going down of the old, and the rising up of the new man." (Dr. Schaff, in Lange's "Commentary on Romans.")

Among these "commentators of note" who have thus expressed their opinion, we may mention, besides those already quoted, the names of Ruckert, Fritzsche, Tholuck, De Wette, Meyer, Ebrard, Lange, Chalmers, Webster and Wilkinson, Alford, Philippi, and Godet, the last three somewhat cautiously.]

Similar testimonies and admissions might easily be largely multiplied; but there is no need; these few among the more recent will suffice.

APPENDIX D, TO ROMANS 7:7–25, PAGE 172.

Few passages are more contested than this. The two principal points are:

1. Whether the experience described in verses 14–25 is that of a regenerate man, or of an unregenerate man. It is generally admitted that verses 7–13 describe the experience of an unregenerate man.

2. Whether the apostle is here describing his own experience, or only uses the first person by way of accommodation, and for greater vivacity of representation.

A. In respect to the first question, the history of the two interpretations is briefly as follows: The earlier interpreters, down to the time of Augustine, uniformly [generally] explained the whole section as descriptive of the experience of a man not yet regenerated. Augustine himself at first followed this interpretation, but he afterward adopted and advocated the view that verses 14–25 are to be regarded as the experience of a renewed man. The earlier interpretation was followed by all the Reformers who leaned to Arminian views of doctrine, and by a few who did not. (Erasmus, Faustus Socinus, Raphelius, Arminius, Episcopius, Limborch, Clericus, Turretin, Bucer.[1]) Among more recent interpreters, the same view has been maintained by A. H. Francke, Bengel, Gottfried Arnold, Zinzendorf, Reinhard, Storr and Flatt, Knapp, etc.; and in our own times by Stier, Tholuck, Ruckert, De Wette, Meyer, Lange, and Stuart. Some of these held the above view with some modification. Tholuck, for example, says that verses 14–25 describe the experience of a legalist, zealously concerned about his sanctification and partially influenced by the Spirit of God.

On the other hand, the later view of Augustine was followed by Anselm, Thomas Aquinas, and Cornelius a Lapide, among the scholastic divines; by Luther, Melancthon, Calvin, and Beza, among the Reformers; by Spener, Buddaeus, and Koppe, in later times; and it has been adopted in our own day by Philippi, Alford, Barnes, Hodge, Haldane, Forbes, Dr. John Brown, and others.

Besides these two radically different views, there are several interpreters of note who take an intermediate and somewhat complex view. Olshausen says Paul, in verses 14–24, "*immediately* describes the state of man *before* regeneration, since his purpose is to set forth coherently the whole course of development; in the consciousness, however, that phenomena entirely similar present themselves within the regenerate man, he makes the description applicable to the regenerate also. The opinion, therefore, on the *one* side, that the apostle *immediately* and

---

[1] The last two did not lean toward Arminian views.

directly intends the regenerate, and on the *other* the assertion, that in the regenerate man *nothing* answering to the picture in verses 14–24 can be found, are alike entirely erroneous.   The distinction between the conflict and the fall of the unregenerate, and the conflict and fall of the regenerate, remains, notwithstanding the subjective feeling of their near affinity, objectively so great (as at verses 24, 25 will be proved), that anxiety lest the view proposed should strip regeneration of its essential character must appear evidently unfounded."

Alford's theory seems still more artificial and complicated.   "From verses 7–13 inclusive," he says, "is *historical*, and the I (ἐγὼ) there is the *historical self* under the working of conviction of sin and showing the work of the law; in other words, *the carnal self in the transition state*, under the first motions toward God generated by the law, which the law could never have perfected.   Then at ver. 14 Paul, according to a habit very common with him, keeps hold of the carnal self, and still having it in view *transfers himself into his present position*, altering the past tense into the present, still, however, meaning by I (ἐγὼ) in ver. 14, ' my flesh.'   But having passed into the present tense, he immediately mingles with this mere action of the law upon the natural conscience the motions of the will toward God, which are in conflict with the motions toward sin in the members.   And hence arises an apparent verbal confusion."   On ver. 14, " Hitherto has been *historical;* now the apostle passes to the *present time*, keeping hold yet of the carnal I (ἐγὼ) of former days, whose remnants are still energizing in the new man."   Does not this last clause take away all necessity for his complex theory?

Peter tells us that there are some things in the epistles of Paul which are hard to be understood.   (2 Peter 3 : 16.)   This statement is certainly applicable to the seventh chapter of the Epistle to the Romans.   The principal difficulty in determining whether the section included between verses 14 and 24 is intended to describe the experience of a man before his conversion, or afterward, arises from the fact that some of the expressions used seem to rise above the experience of any unregenerate person, while other expressions seem to fall below the experience of the Christian.   The principal expressions of this nature on both sides are the following: ["I hate" evil (ver. 15)]; "I consent unto the law" (ver. 16); "to will is present with me" (ver. 18); "when I would do good" (ver. 21); ['I delight in the law of God" (ver. 22)]; "with the mind I myself serve the law of God" (ver. 25).   Can these expressions be referred to any but a regenerate man?   Again: "But I am carnal, sold under sin" (ver. 14); "what I hate, that do I" (ver. 15); "in me (that is, in my flesh) dwelleth no good thing" (ver. 18); "but how to perform that which is good I find not" (ver. 18); "the evil which I would not, that I do" (ver. 19); "evil is present with me" (ver. 21); "I see another law in my members . . . bringing me into captivity to the law of sin" (ver. 23); "but with the flesh the law of sin" (ver. 25).   Can these expressions be referred to one who is justified and regenerate?

These are the difficulties between which we have to choose.   My own opinion is that the language in these verses is intended to show how powerless the law is to enable even a regenerate and justified person to overcome sin.   I suppose the conflict here described is just what *would be* the experience of every Christian, if he should look only to his legal relations, what *is* in fact a common experience with Christians, in just so far as they do regard themselves in their relation to the law, apart from their relation to Christ.   It is some presumption in favor of this view that Christian readers have very generally thought that they found one aspect of their own experience described here.   The common Christian instinct, if we may be allowed the expression, speaks in favor of this interpretation.   We regard this, not as conclusive, but as a consideration of no little weight.

The change in the *tenses* of the verb, at and after ver. 14, so uniformly observed, points to a transition to a new form of religious experience, bearing such a relation to the writer's *present* feelings as the former verses did not.   Between verses 7 and 13 inclusive, there are thirteen instances of the use of the verb and participle in narration, all in the past tense.   Between verses 14 and 25 inclusive there are twenty-six instances of the use of the finite verb, and six of the participle, all in the present tense. This change of tenses, from the past to the present, so suddenly made and so uniformly preserved, is of great significance, and requires to be accounted for in our interpretation of the passage. Those who deny that the experience of the regenerate is described in these last verses are obliged to admit that the forms of expression used by the apostle are just such as he would naturally use to describe his *present* experience at the time of writing. But Tholuck says, in reply to this, that "what is said from ver. 14 onward, with respect to the contest with the law, is just what was already said in the previous context; nor, considering the lively manner of describing which St. Paul has, is the circumstance that thenceforward verbs present are used by any means extraordinary." (Vol. II., p. 21, Clark's "Theo.," Library Ed.) Is not this treating too lightly so important a change in the language of the apostle? Is it true that there is no difference in the two parts of the description? In the first part he says: "Sin wrought in me all manner of concupiscence" (ver. 8); "sin slew me" (ver. 11); it "wrought death in me" (ver. 13). Does not this go beyond the expressions, "I am carnal, sold under sin"? And what is there in the former verses in any degree answering to such expressions as these: "I consent unto the law; I delight in the law of God after the inward man"; "I would do good"; "I hate the evil that I do"; "I serve the law of God with the mind"? Prof. Kendrick says, in a note to Olshausen, Vol. IV., p. 19: "I think the ground of the apostle's change of tense lies in the *vividness of his conception*, which naturally leads him to realize and depict the scene as if now actually passing within him. Besides, the *point* at which he passes from the past to the present is where, having occasion to state a universal truth, 'the law is spiritual,' and hence to use the present tense he naturally employs the present in the answering clause." This does not seem to me a satisfactory account of so marked a syntactical change.

Again, Stuart objects, that "the person represented in these verses *succumbs to sin in every instance of contest*." ("Excursus" VII., p. 467.) "An incessant and irreconcilable opposition is represented (ver. 14) as existing between the law of God and the person here described." (Page 465.) I think this is saying too much. Would the apostle say, "It is no more I that do it, but sin that dwelleth in me"; "I delight in the law of God after the inner man"; would he think it necessary to make the explanation, "I know that in me, *that is in my flesh*, dwelleth no good thing"; could he say, "With my mind I serve the law of God," if he intended to describe an experience in which the victory is *always* on the side of sin? This last expression cannot be referred to a later stage of experience, on account of the clause which immediately follows— "but with the flesh the law of sin." Is not, in fact, the statement in ver. 25 the key to the interpretation of the passage? The law which the *mind* serves is what determines the *character* of the man; and so I think the apostle here affirms, that the *habitual service* of the mind was rendered to the law of God, while at the same time the remains of the sinful nature habitually interfered with the perfection of this service, and frequently drew him into acts that belonged rather to the service of sin. It seems to me that there is not only a difference between the two sections as a whole, but a perceptible progress of experience for the better in the latter sections. Thus the "I consent unto the law," of ver. 16, becomes "I delight in the law," in ver. 22. And the "I," the word which denotes the entire personality, is more decidedly and permanently on the side of good in the latter verses than in the former. Compare, for instance, the "I" of verses 21–23 with that of verses 14–16.

If now we are compelled, in order to avoid an irreconcilable contradiction, to understand some of the stronger terms which the apostle uses in a modified sense, in other words, to admit that there is something of allowable *hyperbole* in his language, which class of terms shall we feel most at liberty so to modify, those in which he describes the action of the higher principle, or those in which he describes the action of the lower? Which would he be most likely to set forth in the natural exaggeration of strongly excited feeling, the workings of good in himself, or the workings of evil? To my mind, the latter seems altogether the more probable. He felt sin to be a grief, a burden, and a thraldom; and its influence over him in any degree seemed to him an intolerable usurpation. It would then be natural for him to set forth with something of hyperbole the evil that remains in the regenerate, and unnatural for him to exaggerate in like manner the better motions and inclinations that are sometimes felt by the unregenerate. Whatever may be thought of the state of mind which the apostle intended to describe here, there can be no doubt as to the state of his own mind when he wrote the description. He was then a converted person, all his sympathies were on the better side, and he regarded sin as loathsome and hateful.

(b) The question whether or not Paul is here describing his own personal experience is less essential than the former to a right understanding of his language. Still it is worthy of some consideration.

Most of those who deny the reference to the regenerate in ver. 14–25, also deny that Paul means to describe his own experience in either the former (ver. 7–13), or the latter portion (ver. 14–25).

The apostle's abundant use of the first person in this section is certainly a very strong argument for believing that he wishes to be understood as describing his own case. He does indeed speak, in 1 Cor. 4: 6, of transferring to himself and Apollos in a figure, or by way of illustration, what was of more general application; and various other instances of this are cited by Tholuck, in support of the view that he does the same here. But these instances have little in common with the passage under consideration. They consist only of brief expressions, in which he puts himself for the moment in the place of another. (1 Cor. 6: 12; 10: 29, 30; 13: 11, 12; Gal. 2: 18.) To do this is quite common with most writers. But it is a very different thing to carry on such a representation through the greater part of a chapter. In truth the frequency and emphasis with which he uses the first person is quite remarkable. From verse 7 to 25, inclusive, he uses the verb in the first person singular no less than twenty-seven times, the oblique cases of the pronoun of the first person seventeen times, and the nominative case "ego" eight times, seven times with the verb and once with the pronoun ($a\dot{v}\tau os$) added. In these last cases the use is of course emphatic. Thus the pronoun of the first person is used twenty-four times in these nineteen verses, six or seven times with marked emphasis. I doubt whether another passage of equal extent can be found in the New Testament, where the personal pronoun of the first person singular is used so abundantly. There is throughout an appearance of *reality*, and not of *allegory*.

It is obvious to remark, that the view here taken goes to confirm our previous view of the application of ver. 14–25 to the regenerate. This confirmation is very strong, when viewed in connection with the change of tenses from ver. 14, onward.

But if we have reason to regard this whole passage as descriptive of the apostle's own experience, the question arises, at what period of his life was this experience realized? So far as it is the experience of an unregenerate person—that is, so far as it is recorded in ver. 7–13—we may suppose that its culminating epoch was during those three days of blindness and fasting, which followed the first appearance of the Lord to him, and preceded his baptism. It is very commonly assumed, that his radical conversion took place at the moment of that appearance; but the only evidence of this is the question which he asked, apparently expressive of a spirit of obedience, "What shall I do, Lord?" (Acts 22: 10.) (The words in 9: 6 are interpolated.) On the other hand, he seems to have remained at least three days without comfort, and so far as the record states without prayer. (Acts 9: 11.) [Dr. Arnold, it will be perceived, does not absolutely deny the fact of Paul's praying during this time, and we see not how he could possibly keep from prayer. And if he was not then filled with the Spirit, certainly the Spirit was operating in his mind and heart, giving him inward light, and instructing him in the great truths of that theology which he afterward preached. That he was at this time a praying man seems evident from our Lord's first words to Ananias concerning him before his outward eyes were opened: "Behold, he prayeth," and from the fact that Ananias on visiting him immediately addressed him as a Christian "brother."] It was not until the visit of Ananias that he recovered his sight, that he was filled with the Holy Ghost (ver. 17), that he was ready to be baptized. (Ver. 18.) He does not seem to have had any spiritual relief until then. Without supposing, then, that he had never experienced before any part of that which he describes so graphically in ver. 7–9, we can hardly find any other time in his life to which that strongly marked conflict can be so reasonably assigned. Certainly it was not until then that he could say, "I died." As to the second part of this experience, which we suppose to be described in verses 14–24, that may have continued through the whole of his Christian life, in proportion as he compared himself with the standard of legal requirement; but would be less and less real to him, as indeed it seems to be here represented, in proportion as his spirit was imbued more and more with the doctrine of grace. Those whom we must allow to be Christians do find, or think they find, much in their own experience which answers to what the apostle here says. They would find nothing of this kind, if they were *perfect* in faith, and love, and holiness. They would find nothing else but this, if they looked only toward the law and its requirements. In fact, their actual experience is made up of the alternation and mixture of the distressing sense of remaining and often prevailing sin, and the happy assurance of free pardon, full justification, and ultimate perfect sanctification in Christ.

We are not to suppose that the apostle's experience was of a wholly different type in this respect from that of truly regenerate persons in the present day and in every age. The different states of religious experience described in ch. 7: 14–25 and ch. 8: 1–4, are not to be regarded as altogether different historical stages in the apostle's religious life, so that ch. 7: 14–25 describes his whole experience at one time, and ch. 8: 1–4, his whole experience at another and later period of his Christian course; but the two descriptions are rather to be regarded as representing his experience in different *attitudes* of *mind*, which partly alternated with each other, and were partly commingled throughout his Christian life.

I cannot forbear to refer, as in the main agreeing with and confirming the interpretation of this difficult passage here given, to a very able and exhaustive article, by Rev. W. N. Clarke, in the "Baptist Quarterly," for October, 1875, pp. 385–411.

APPENDIX E, TO ROMANS 8: 19–23, PAGE 197.

The meaning of the word translated 'creature,' or 'creation' (κτίσις). This word occurs in the New Testament nineteen times: Mark 10: 6; 13: 19; 16: 15; Rom. 1: 20, 25; 8: 19, 20, 21, 22, 39; 2 Cor. 5: 17; Gal. 6: 15; Col. 1: 15, 23; Heb. 4: 13; 9: 11; 1 Peter 2: 13; 2 Peter 3: 4; Rev. 3: 14.

In our common English version it is translated "creature" eleven times, "creation" six times (Mark 6: 10; 13: 9; Rom. 1: 20; 8: 22; 2 Peter 3: 4; Rev. 3: 14), and once it is translated "building" (Heb. 9: 11), and once "ordinance" (1 Peter 2: 13). Four of these passages belong to the place under consideration, leaving fifteen others from which to determine its prevailing sense. It is used to express the act of creating only in Rom. 1: 20. Elsewhere it always stands for that which is created, either for the creation as a whole, or for some particular created thing, or for some class or classes of created things. Twice it is used with the adjective "new," to designate the 'new creation,' or the 'new creature.' (2 Cor. 5: 17; Gal. 6: 15.) In 1 Peter 2: 13, with the epithet 'human' it has the sense of human 'ordinance' or 'institution'; and in Mark 16 · 15 it can only refer to mankind. In the remaining ten instances it has the general sense of 'creation,' or that which is created, not necessarily including more than this world in the majority of cases. In Col. 1: 23 it is referred by Robinson and Tholuck to mankind; but the Greek preposition "in" (ἐν), and the explanatory adjunct "which is under heaven," seem rather to require that it be understood here in a *local* sense. " In all creation which is under heaven " is Alford's translation.

The sense is disputed in Col. 1: 15 and Rev. 3: 14, some understanding it in these two places to refer to the 'new creation'; but if we take the word "firstborn" in the first of these passages in the sense of 'heir' or 'inheritor' (a sense justified by the use of the word in Deut. 21: 16), and understand the word "beginning" in the second passage in the sense of 'first principle,' or 'primal source,' all doctrinal difficulty will be avoided, and the word (κτίσις) will have its usual sense in both these places.

The usual meaning of this word, then, in the New Testament clearly is the creation, not necessarily extending beyond this world, and not excluding mankind. It is not applied to human creatures exclusively, except in Mark 16: 15; nor does it appear that it is ever applied to Christians exclusively, without the addition of the epithet "new."

On the whole, then, the demands of the context in relation to this word seem to be best answered by defining it as including the inanimate and irrational creation, so far as relates to this world. This sense corresponds with the ordinary use of the word, except in excluding mankind—for which exclusion the passage itself furnishes the reason. But can the inanimate and irrational creation be said to groan and travail in pain, and to hope for deliverance in connection with the manifestation of the sons of God? Certainly not, if we insist on taking these expressions in a strictly literal sense. But if we compare this language with the representations of the Old Testament prophets, and of the Apocalypse, in regard to the renovation of the earth in connection with the consummation of the Messiah's kingdom, we shall find nothing but what is in keeping with those Scriptural representations. The earth was cursed on account of Adam's sin (Gen. 3: 17, 18); it is to be delivered from the curse in connection with man's deliverance from sin. So much of it as is capable of feeling actually suffers under the bondage of corruption (the liability to pain and death), and under the abuse and wrongs inflicted by wicked and cruel men. Since these evils are real and heavy, since they are undeserved, since they are of long continuance, and since God has promised deliverance from them, the brute creation may fitly be represented as groaning under these evils, and longing for the promised deliverance. And since inanimate nature is also under the curse on account of sin; since it also suffers abuse, perversion, and distortion in various ways from man's folly, improvidence, and wickedness; and since it is also to be delivered from these evils—it, too, may well be represented as sharing in the groaning and the travail, in the longing and the hope.

As to the certainty of this future deliverance, all our knowledge must be derived from divine revelation. The skeptical scientist may scoff at the idea of such a change in the natural world on moral grounds; but he will never be able to prove that the material and brute creation did not lose much by man's fall into sin, and will not gain much by man's recovery to holiness. The renovation of the physical world at the advent of the Messiah was a dogma of the Rabbins, as may be seen from the passages cited by Tholuck and other commentators. They found the germ of their doctrine on this subject in such passages as Isa. 9: 6–9; 65: 17–25; Ezek. 34: 25–27; Hosea 2: 18–23. We have corresponding intimations in the New Testament, for the most part brief and suggestive merely, as Matt. 19: 28; Acts 3: 21; 2 Peter 3: 13; but sometimes more explicit and circumstantial, though in highly figurative language, as in Rev. 21.